INTRODUCTION TO
THE ODYSSEY SURVEYS OF AMERICAN WRITING

The Odyssey Surveys of American Writing consist of four books which, taken in chronological order, present the best and most representative American writing from its beginning to the 1960's. The series has been planned by a general editor, who has established the time limits and appropriate authors for each of the four surveys, determined the kinds of editorial apparatus used, and set general policies for texts and footnotes. These editorial policies are designed to create a consistent approach throughout the series, to present authoritative texts, to give the minimum in annotation, to supply factual rather than interpretative editorial materials, and to present through introductions and occasional headnotes the historical context within which the works originally appeared.

Each of the surveys has been edited by an expert in the area covered by the volume. Thus each volume represents the judgment of a specialist editor about the age which it covers. Within the broad editorial policies of the entire series, the editors of individual surveys have been given complete freedom for selections, types of approach, historical statements, critical attitudes, and texts. The result is that each survey reflects the best informed current attitudes toward the period it covers, and that each survey is different in method and critical assumptions. The general editor has seen as his primary duty the organization of these necessarily varied points of view and methods of approach into four volumes which maintain their distinctiveness and at the same time reflect the unique assumptions and ideals of their particular ages.

C. HUGH HOLMAN

THE ODYSSEY SURVEYS OF AMERICAN WRITING

General Editor: C. Hugh Holman, *University of North Carolina*

COLONIAL AND FEDERALIST AMERICAN WRITING (1607-1830)
Edited by George F. Horner and Robert A. Bain
University of North Carolina

THE ROMANTIC MOVEMENT IN AMERICAN WRITING (1830-1865)
Edited by Richard Harter Fogle
Tulane University

THE REALISTIC MOVEMENT IN AMERICAN WRITING (1865-1900)
Edited by Bruce R. McElderry, Jr.
University of Southern California

TWENTIETH CENTURY AMERICAN WRITING (1900-1960's)
Edited by William T. Stafford
Purdue University

COLONIAL *and* FEDERALIST AMERICAN WRITING

GEORGE F. HORNER
ROBERT A. BAIN
University of North Carolina

THE ODYSSEY PRESS · INC · NEW YORK

ACKNOWLEDGMENTS

THE COLUMBIA UNIVERSITY PRESS. For pp. 521-523 and pp. 531-535 from Vol. II, *Samuel Johnson, His Career and Writings*, eds. Herbert and Carol Schneider, 4 Vols. (New York, The Columbia University Press, 1929.) Copyright 1929 by the Columbia University Press. Reprinted by permission of the Columbia University Press. • HARPER & ROW, PUBLISHERS. For pp. 641-650, Urian Oakes, "An Elegy Upon the Death of the Reverend Mr. Thomas Shepard" from Vol. II of *The Puritans*, 2 Vols., eds. Perry Miller and Thomas H. Johnson (New York, Harper Torchbook edition published 1963 by Harper & Row, Publishers). Copyright 1938 by Perry Miller and Thomas H. Johnson. Revised bibliographies, copyright 1963 by Perry Miller and Thomas H. Johnson. Reprinted by Harper & Row by arrangement with the American Book Co. Reprinted here by permission of Harper & Row, Publishers. Spelling in Oakes' "Elegy" has been modernized in this volume by permission of Harper & Row, Publishers. • HARVARD UNIVERSITY PRESS. For pp. 180-183, Michael Wigglesworth, "The Praise of Eloquence," from Samuel E. Morison, *Harvard College in the Seventeenth Century, Part I, 1650-1708* (Cambridge, Mass., The Harvard University Press, 1936). Copyright 1936 by the Harvard University Press. Reprinted by permission of the Harvard University Press. • KENNETH B. MURDOCK. For passages from *Selections from Cotton Mather*, ed. Kenneth B. Murdock (New York, Harcourt, Brace and Co., 1926). Copyright 1926 by Kenneth B. Murdock. Reprinted by permission of Kenneth B. Murdock. • THE NEW-YORK HISTORICAL LIBRARY. For facsimile copy of Phillis Wheatley, "Liberty and Peace." Reprinted by permission of the New-York Historical Library. • NORTH CAROLINA HISTORICAL COMMISSION. STATE OF NORTH CAROLINA, DEPARTMENT OF ARCHIVES AND HISTORY. For pp. 85, 87, 89, and 91, *William Byrd's Histories of the Dividing Line*, ed. William K. Boyd (Raleigh, N.C., The North Carolina Historical Commission, 1929). Copyright 1929 by the North Carolina Historical Commission. Reprinted by permission of the North Carolina Historical Commission, State of North Carolina, Department of Archives and History. • THE PRINCETON UNIVERSITY PRESS. For passages from "Preparatory Meditations," from "God's Determinations," and for "Upon a Spider Catching a Fly," "Huswifery," and "The Ebb and Flow," from "Miscellaneous Poems," in *The Poetical Works of Edward Taylor*, ed. Thomas H. Johnson (New York, Rockland Editions, 1939). Copyright 1939 by Rockland Editions, New York. Reprinted by permission of the Princeton University Press. • HOUGHTON MIFFLIN COMPANY. For Excerpts from *Benjamin Tompson His Poems*, ed. Howard Judson Hall. • UNIVERSITY OF NORTH CAROLINA PRESS. For pp. 58-65 and pp. 162-163 from Thomas Jefferson, *Notes on the State of Virginia*, ed. William Peden. (Published for the Institute of Early American History and Culture at Williamsburg, Va., by the University of North Carolina Press, Chapel Hill, N.C., 1955). Copyright 1955 by the University of North Carolina Press. Reprinted by permission of the University of North Carolina Press. • PETER SMITH, PUBLISHER. For pp. 15-19, pp. 41-44, and pp. 52-56 from *The Journal of Madam Knight*, ed. George Parker Winship (New York, Peter Smith, Publisher, 1935), a facsimile reprint of the 1920 edition. Copyright 1935 by Peter Smith, Publisher. Reprinted by permission of Peter Smith, Publisher. • THE VIRGINIA HISTORICAL SOCIETY AND THE UNIVERSITY OF VIRGINIA PRESS. For p. 3 and pp. 35-37 from *The Poems of Charles Hansford*, eds. James A. Servies and Carl R. Dolmetsch (Published for the Virginia Historical Society by the University of North Carolina Press, Chapel Hill, N.C., 1961). Copyright 1962 by the Virginia Historical Society and the University of Virginia Press. Reprinted by permission of the Virginia Historical Society and the University of Virginia Press. • MAUDE WOODFIN AND MARION TINLING. For pp. 276-282 from *Another Secret Diary of William Byrd of Westover, 1739-1741*, eds. Maude Woodfin and Marion Tinling (Richmond, Va., The Dietz Press, Inc., 1942). Copyright 1942 by Maude Woodfin and Marion Tinling. Reprinted by permission of the estate of Maude

PREFACE

Over two centuries of American writing are represented by the selections in this volume. In these two centuries, England, whose literature provided the forms for American writing, passed from the late Renaissance to Victorian times, and the varied modes, interests, and attitudes of England were reflected in the American colonies, altered somewhat by the unique circumstances of colonial and national life. Despite conditions adverse to literary effort during much of the period, a considerable amount of writing was produced in a variety of forms and with a variety of attitudes and interests. The selections offered here are intended to represent the popular forms, to suggest the prominent concerns, and to trace the origins of attitudes and myths that become part of the American inheritance.

Selecting texts, particularly those from the seventeenth and eighteenth centuries, poses editorial problems, for much of Colonial American writing remains unedited or comes from the hands of nineteenth century editors who labored without the advantages of modern editing techniques. Within these limitations, the editors have attempted to reproduce accurate and representative texts. The readings have been selected from standard editions whenever possible, or from early texts collated with later editions, or from original editions when no subsequent text exists.

The editors have tried to preserve the integrity of the texts used; however, some changes, largely orthographic, have been made in the belief that the peculiarities of seventeenth and eighteenth century spelling and typography often stand between the contemporary reader and the work.

Upon request of the copyright holders of the poetry of Edward Taylor, his work has been reproduced exactly as it appears in the edition used.

The editors wish to thank the staffs of both the University of North Carolina and the Duke University Libraries for their cooperation in allowing us access to material in their rare book collections. Special thanks must go to Bonnie Bain for the tedious work of typing copy from microfilm and to Professor C. Hugh Holman for his encouragement, but most of all for his patience.

G. F. H.
R. A. B.

CONTENTS

The Seventeenth Century

The Eighteenth Century

The Federal Period

Short Fiction 727

The Seventeenth Century

INTRODUCTION

The motives that peopled America varied from immigrant to immigrant and colony to colony—individual freedom, personal aggrandizement, commercial exploitation, establishment of the New Canaan, or simple adventure moved men to this virgin land. The ventures were frequently imperfectly conceived and inadequately equipped, and the coastal land filled up slowly. During the seventeenth century communities were sparsely settled and separated from each other by forest and wilderness. Contact between them was difficult and infrequent except where rivers and bays made it possible. Consequently each "plantation" exercised considerable practical autonomy and took its own direction, often to the discomfiture of the underwriters who for the most part remained in England. Schemes and plans devised in England when confronted with the actualities of the new land had to be modified on the scene if the colony were to succeed. Much of the writing that was produced in the early period of each colony has its origin in this situation and represents the effort to describe conditions, to explain and to defend the actions taken. In mid-century, England was preoccupied with affairs at home, the civil war and the Puritan Interregnum, and the colonists were left to their own resources. Having learned something of local autonomy in the interval, they met the renewed efforts of the crown to extend its authority after 1688 with apprehension and some opposition. Because of the disturbances in England and the real and fancied opportunities in America, enough Englishmen had crossed the Atlantic so that by the end of the century colonies from South Carolina northward were firmly established along the seaboard. Throughout the century life was predominantly rural and agricultural. Except in such growing commercial centers as Boston, Philadelphia, and, late in the century, New York, the population was scattered in small towns and on small farms. This fact more than anything else accounts for the paucity of schools, colleges, and printing establishments, the media for the dissemination of literate culture.

Yet a surprising amount of writing was produced by the colonists, though much of it is in forms which are not popularly thought of as literature. These forms were not strange to seventeenth-century England, which produced its own quantity of travel books, histories, exemplary biographies, books of piety and sermons, tracts for the times, and religious or meditative verse. Thus the writing from the colonies was the product of the compulsion to explain themselves, to promulgate their opinions, to record their achievements for the guidance of their heirs, and of the desire to emulate the popular taste in England. If dramas were not written in the colonies, it was partially because of the distrust of the genre and partially because the practical circumstances of life did not provide the audiences for them.

The reports and promotional tracts, the "pamphlets of news" which began as simple journals of experience, developed a fairly standard pattern: a summary of personal experience to establish the author's authority, a description of the lay of the land, its soil, fauna and flora, and inhabitants, red and white, and a discussion, sometimes critical, often hortatory, of the requirements and of the opportunities for advancement. In these are found the beginnings of the American Dream, the attitude of mind that sees this new land as a place of infinite opportunity uninhibited by the restraints of older societies, a land in which will emerge a social organization that is to become the hope of the world. The histories, written partially to preserve the record, tend to become accounts of the heroic triumph over adversity. In them originate many details of the American mythology. Prominent here and in the "pamphlets of news" is the developing conception of the Indian, seen as a curiosity, an enemy, a friend, a nuisance, and a natural nobleman. The biographies, affected by the seventeenth-century "character" essays, provide models for exemplary conduct. The sermons, chiefly Puritan, promulgate civil as well as religious doctrine, and have an elaborate form of their own. In these and in the works of piety are imbedded attitudes which later become such commonplaces of American popular thought as to go largely unrecognized. The Puritan concern with salvation generated not only an introspective habit but also a paradoxical mixture of joy and guilt that is part of the American heritage. The verse of the period is largely public in character, written to specific purposes or occasions; little is private and personal. The function or use dominates. The versifier speaks for the occasion, the doctrine, the party, the sect, or the people. His audience is God or the mass of men; he rarely speaks to himself, a beloved one, or a circle of intimates. If he did engage in such private communication, it went largely unpublished.

Through much of the century, colonial style followed the fashions of England. It was sometimes pretentious, often almost a party badge, and nearly always consciously adopted. In general, those of the dissenting sects tended to write in the "plain" style, ranging from an honest vernacular to an unadorned but educated prose. If allusion or quotation appeared, it appeared more as supporting evidence than as adornment. Those of Royalist or Episcopal leaning, the "blubber-lipped" to the Puritan, tended to write a more rhetorical prose, indulging in tropes, figures, and ornament to achieve a distinctive elegance, appropriate to their affiliation. The capacity of the individual author is not always equal to his intentions and produces in many an awkward pretentiousness easily detected.

The contributions of the century to American writing are less in form and manner than in ideas. To the modern reader it is the matter that is of greater interest, an interest not solely antiquarian. Here are the beginnings of many American attitudes: the sense of American destiny, the roots of individual freedom, the right to revolt, the dependence on self-reliance, the practice of self-examination, and the irreconcilable conflict between conformity and dissent.

REPORTS AND PROMOTIONS

John Smith

(1580-1631)

Captain John Smith, soldier of fortune, sometime Turkish slave, and gentleman adventurer, came to Virginia in 1607 as shareholder and one of the governing council of the settlement at Jamestown. Seriously injured in 1609, he returned to England. In 1613 he made a voyage of exploration along the New England coast, and a second voyage in 1615. From these experiences and wide reading he produced a series of books related to the new land: A True Relation (London, 1608), A Map of Virginia (London, 1612), A Description of New England (London, 1620), The General History of Virginia, New England, and the Summer Isles (London, 1624), An Accidence; or, The Pathway . . . for All

Young Seamen (London, 1626), The True Travels . . . of Captain John Smith (London, 1630), and Advertisements for the Unexperienced Planters of New England (London, 1631).

BIBLIOGRAPHY: Edward Arber, ed. Travels and Works of Captain John Smith, 2 Vols. (Birmingham, Eng., 1884). A. G. Bradley, ed. Travels and Works of Captain John Smith, 2 Vols. (Edinburgh, 1910). Howard M. Jones, "The Literature of Colonial Virginia in the Seventeenth Century," Memoirs of the Amer. Acad. of Arts and Sciences (Boston, 1946). Bradford Smith, Captain John Smith, His Life and Legend (Philadelphia, 1953).

From A True Relation

Captain Newport having set things in order, set sail for England the 22 of June [1607], leaving provision for 13. or 14 weeks.

The day before the Ship's departure, the King of Pamaunke sent the Indian that had met us before in our discovery, to assure us peace; our fort being then palisaded round, and all our men in good health and comfort, albeit, that through some discontented humors, it did not so long continue. For the President and Captain Gosnold, with the rest of the Council, being for the most part discontented with one another, in so much, that things were neither carried with that discretion nor any business effected in such good sort as wisdom would, nor our own good and safety required, whereby, and through the hard dealing of our President, the rest of the Council being diversly affected through his audacious command; and for Captain Martin, albeit very honest, and wishing the best good, yet so sick and weak; and myself so disgrac'd through others' malice: through which disorder God (being angry with us) plagued us with such famine and sickness, that the living were scarce able to bury the dead: our want of sufficient and good victuals, with continual watching, four or five each night at three Bulwarks, being the chief cause: only of Sturgeon we had great store, whereon our men would so greedily surfeit, as it cost many their lives: the Sack, Aquavitae, and other preservatives for our health, being kept only in the President's hands, for his own diet, and his few associates.

Shortly after Captain Gosnold fell sick, and within three weeks died. Captain Ratcliffe being then also very sick and weak, and myself having also tasted of the extremity thereof, but by God's assistance being well recovered. Kendall about this time, for divers reasons deposed from being of the Council: and shortly after it pleased God (in our extremity) to move the Indians to bring us Corn, ere it was half ripe, to refresh us, when we rather expected when they would destroy us.

About the tenth of September there was about 46. of our men dead, at which time Captain Wingfield having ordered the affairs in such sort that he was generally hated of all, in which respect with one consent he was deposed from his presidency, and Captain Ratcliffe according to his course was elected.

Our provision being now within twenty days spent, the Indians brought us great store both of Corn and bread ready made: and also there came such abundance of Fowls into the Rivers, as greatly refreshed our weak estates, whereupon many of our weak men were presently able to go abroad.

As yet we had no houses to cover us, our Tents were rotten, and our Cabins worse than nought: our best commodity was Iron which we made into little chisels.

The President's, and Captain Martin's sickness, constrained me to be Cape Merchant, and yet to spare no pains in making houses for the company; who notwithstanding our misery, little ceased their malice, grudging, and muttering. . . .

Time thus passing away, and having not above 14. days' victuals left, some motions were made about our President's and Captain Archer's going for England, to procure a supply: in which meantime we had reasonably fitted us with houses. And our President and Captain Martin being able to walk abroad, with much ado it was concluded, that the pinnace and barge should go towards Powhatan, to trade for corn.

Lots were cast who should go in her, the chance was mine. . . .

All things being now ready for my journey to Powhatan, for the performance thereof, I had 8. men and myself for the barge, as well for discovery as trading; and in the Pinnace, 5. Mariners, and 2. landmen to take in our ladings at convenient places. . . .

Arriving at Weramocomoco, their Emperor proudly lying upon a Bedstead a foot high, upon ten or twelve Mats, richly hung with many Chains of great Pearls about his neck, and covered with a great Covering of Rahaughcums. At his head sat a woman, at his feet another; on each side sitting upon a Mat upon the ground, were ranged his chief men on each side the fire, ten in a rank, and behind them as many young women, each with a great Chain of white Beads over their shoulders, their heads painted in red: and with such a grave and Majestical countenance, as drave me into admiration to see such state in a naked Savage.

He kindly welcomed me with good words, and great Platters of sundry Victuals, assuring me his friendship, and my liberty within four days. He much delighted in Opechan Comough's relation of what I had described to him, and oft examined me upon the same.

After good deliberation, he began to describe to me the Countries beyond the Falls, with many of the rest; confirming what not only Opechancanoves, and an Indian which had been prisoner to Powhatan had before told me: but some called it five days, some six, some eight, where the said water dashed amongst many stones and rocks, each storm; which caused ofttimes the head of the River to be brackish.

Anchanachuck he described to be the people that had slain my brother: whose death he would revenge. He described also upon the same Sea, a mighty Nation called Pocoughtronack, a fierce Nation that did eat men, and warred with the people of Moyaoncer and Pataromerke, Nations upon the top of the head of the Bay, under his territories: where the year before they had slain a hundred. He signified their crowns were shaven, long hair in the neck, tied on a knot, Swords like Poleaxes.

Beyond them, he described people with short Coats, and Sleeves to the Elbows, that passed that way in Ships like ours. Many Kingdoms he described to me, to the head of the Bay, which seemed to be a mighty River issuing from mighty Mountains betwixt the two Seas: The people clothed at Ocamahowan, he also confirmed; and the Southerly Countries also, as the rest that reported us to be within a day and a half of Mangoge, two days of Chawwonock, 6. from Roonock, to the south part of the back sea: He described a country called Anone, where they have abundance of Brass, and houses walled as ours.

I requited his discourse (seeing what pride he had in his great and spacious Dominions, seeing that all he knew were under his Territories) in describing to him, the territories of Europe, which was subject to our great King whose subject I was, the innumerable multitude of his ships, I gave him to understand the noise of Trumpets, and terrible manner of fighting that were under Captain Newport my father: whom I entitled the Meworames, which they call the King of all the waters. At his greatness, he admired: and not a little feared. He desired me to forsake Paspahegh, and to live with him upon his River, a Country called Capa Howasicke. He promised to give me Corn, Venison, or what I wanted to feed us: Hatchets and Copper we should make him, and none should disturb us. . . .

Powhatan understanding we detained certain Savages, sent his Daughter, a child ten years old: which, not only for feature, countenance, and proportion, much exceedeth any of the rest of his people: but for wit and spirit, is the only Nonpareil of his Country. This he sent by his most trusty messenger, called Rawhunt, as much exceeding in deformity of person; but of a subtle wit and crafty understanding.

He, with a long circumstance, told me, how well Powhatan loved and respected me; and in that I should not doubt any way of his kindness, he had sent his child, which he most esteemed, to see me; a Deer and bread besides, for a present: desiring me that the Boy might come again, which he loved exceedingly. His little Daughter he had taught this lesson also, not taking notice at all of the Indians that had been prisoners three days, till that morning that she saw their fathers and friends come quietly, and in good terms to entreat their liberty.

In the afternoon, they being gone, we guarded them as before to the Church; and after prayer, gave them to Pocahuntas, the King's Daughter, in regard of her father's kindness in sending her. After having well fed them, as all the time of their imprisonment, we gave them their bows, arrows, or what else they had; and with much content, sent them packing. Pocahuntas also we requited with such trifles as contented her, to tell that we had used the Paspaheyans very kindly in so releasing them.

1608

From A *Map of Virginia*

There is but one entrance by sea into this country, and that is at the mouth of a very goodly Bay, the wideness whereof is near 18. or 20. miles. The cape on the South side is called Cape Henry in honor of our most noble Prince. The show of the land there, is a white hilly sand like unto the Downs, and along the shores great plenty of Pines and Firs.

The north Cape is called Cape Charles in honor of the worthy Duke of York.

Within is a country that may have the prerogative over the most pleasant places of Europe, Asia, Africa, or America, for large and pleasant navigable rivers: heaven and earth never agreed better to frame a place for man's habitation being of our constitutions, were it fully manured and inhabited by industrious people. Here are mountains, hills, plains, valleys, rivers and brooks all running most pleasantly into a fair Bay compassed but for the mouth with fruitful and delightsome land. In the Bay and rivers are many Isles both great and small, some woody, some plain, most of them low and not inhabited. This Bay lieth North and South in which the water floweth near 200 miles and hath a channel for 140 miles, of depth betwixt 7 and 15 fathoms, holding in breadth for the most part 10 or 14 miles. From the head of the Bay at the north, the land is mountainous, and so in a manner from thence by a Southwest line; So that the more Southward, the farther off from the Bay are those mountains. From which, fall certain brooks, which after come to five principal navigable rivers. These run from the Northwest into the Southeast, and so into the west side of the Bay, where the fall of every River is within 20 or 15 miles one of another. . . .

The country is not mountainous nor yet low but such pleasant plain hills and fertile valleys, one prettily crossing another, and watered so conveniently with their sweet brooks and crystal springs, as if art itself had devised them.

By the rivers are many plain marshes containing some 20, some 100, some 200 Acres, some more, some less. Other plains there are few, but only where the Savages inhabit: but all overgrown with trees and weeds being a plain wilderness as God first made it. . . .

At the end of the Bay where it is 6 or 7 miles in breadth, there fall into it 4 small rivers, 3 of them issuing from diverse bogs environed with high mountains.

There is one that cometh due north, 3 or 4 days' journey from the head of the Bay, and falls from rocks and mountains. Upon this river inhabit a people called Sasquesahanock.

They are seated 2 days higher than was passage for the discoverers' Barge, which was hardly 2 tons, and had in it but 12 men to perform this discovery, wherein they lay above the space of 12 weeks upon those great waters in those unknown Countries, having nothing but a little meal or oatmeal and water to feed them; and scarce half sufficient of that for half that time, but that by the Savages and by the plenty of fish they found in all places, they made themselves provision as opportunity served; yet had they not a mariner or any that had skill to trim their sails, use their oars, or any business belonging to the Barge, but 2 or 3. The rest being Gentlemen or as ignorant in such toil and labor: yet necessity in a short time, by their Captain's diligence and example, taught them to become so perfect, that what they did by such small means, I leave to the censure of the Reader to judge by this discourse and the annexed Map.

But to proceed, 60 of those Sasquesahanocks came to the discoverers with skins, Bows, Arrows, Targets, Beads, Swords, and Tobacco pipes for presents. Such great and well proportioned men, are seldom seen, for they seemed like Giants to the English, yea and to the neighbors: yet seemed of an honest and simple disposition, and they were with much ado restrained from adoring the discoverers as Gods. Those are the most strange people of all those Countries, both in language and attire; for their language it may well beseem their proportions, sounding from them, as it were a great voice in a vault, or cave, as an Echo. Their attire is the skins of Bears and Wolves, some have Cassocks made of Bears' heads and skins that a man's neck goes through the skin's neck, and the ears of the bear fastened to his shoulders behind, the nose and teeth hanging down his breast, and at the end of the nose hung a Bear's Paw: the half sleeves coming to the elbows were the necks of Bears and the arms through the mouth, with paws hanging at their noses. One had the head of a Wolf hanging in a chain for a Jewel; his Tobacco pipe 3 quarters of a yard long, prettily carved with a Bird, a Bear, a Deer, or some such device at the great end, sufficient to beat out the brains of a man: with bows, and arrows, and clubs, suitable to their greatness and conditions.

These are scarce known to Powhatan. They can make near 600 able and mighty men, and are palisaded in their Towns to defend them from the Massawomekes their mortal enemies. 5 of their chief Werowances came aboard the discoverers, and crossed the Bay in their Barge. The picture of the greatest of them is signified in the Map. The calf of whose leg was 3 quarters of a yard about: and all the rest of his limbs so answerable to that proportion, that he seemed the goodliest man that ever we beheld. His hair, the one side was long, the other shorn close with a ridge over his crown like a cock's comb. His arrows were five quarters of a yard long, headed with flints or splinters of stones, in form like a heart, an inch broad, and an inch and a half or more long. These he wore in a wolf's skin at his back for his quiver, his bow in the one hand and his club in the other, as is described.

OF THE NATURAL INHABITANTS OF VIRGINIA

Each household knoweth their own lands and gardens, and most live of their own labors.

For their apparel, they are sometime covered with the skins of wild beasts, which in winter are dressed with the hair, but in summer without. The better sort use large mantles of deer skins not much differing in fashion from the Irish mantles. Some embroidered with white beads, some with copper, other painted after their manner. But the common sort have scarce to cover their nakedness but with grass, the leaves of trees, or such like. We have seen some use mantles made of Turkey feathers, so prettily wrought and woven with threads that nothing could be discerned but the feathers, that was exceeding warm and very handsome. But the women are always covered about their middles with a skin and are very shamefaced to be seen bare.

They adorn themselves most with copper beads and paintings. Their women some have their legs, hands, breasts and face cunningly embroidered with diverse works, as beasts, serpents, artificially wrought into their flesh with black spots. In each ear commonly they have 3 great holes, whereat they hang chains, bracelets, or copper. Some of their men wear in those holes, a small green and yellow colored snake, near half a yard in length, which crawling and lapping herself about his neck often times familiarly would kiss his lips. Others wear a dead Rat tied by the tail. Some on their heads wear the wing of a bird or some large feather, with a Rattle. Those Rattles are somewhat like the chape of a Rapier but less, which they take from the tail of a snake. Many have the whole skin of a hawk or some strange fowl, stuffed with the wings abroad. Others a broad piece of copper, and some the hand of their enemy dried. Their heads and shoulders are painted red with the root Pocone brayed to powder mixed with oil; this they hold in summer to preserve them from the heat, and in winter from the cold. . . .

Their buildings and habitations are for the most part by the rivers or not far distant from some fresh spring. Their houses are built like our Arbors of small young sprigs bowed and tied, and so close covered with mats or the barks of trees very handsomely, that notwithstanding either wind, rain or weather, they are as warm as stoves, but very smoky; yet at the top of the house there is a hole made for the smoke to go into right over the fire. . . .

The men bestow their times in fishing, hunting, wars, and such manlike exercises, scorning to be seen in any womanlike exercise; which is the cause that the women be very painful and the men often idle. The women and children do the rest of the work. They make mats, baskets, pots, mortars; pound their corn, make their bread, prepare their victuals, plant their corn, gather their corn, bear all kind of burdens, and such like. . . .

For fishing and hunting and wars they use much their bow and arrows. They bring their bows to the form of ours by the scraping of a shell. Their arrows are made, some of straight young sprigs, which they head with bone some 2 or 3 inches long. These they use to shoot at squirrels on trees. Another sort of arrows they use, made of reeds. These are pieced with wood, headed with splinters of crystal or some sharp stone, the spurs of a Turkey, or the bill of some bird. For his knife, he hath the splinter of a reed to cut his feathers in form. With this knife also, he will joint a Deer or any beast; shape his shoes, buskins, mantles, &c. To make the notch of his arrow he hath the tooth of a Beaver set in a stick, wherewith he grateth it by degrees. His arrowhead he quickly maketh with a little bone, which he ever weareth at his bracer, of any splint of a stone, or glass in the form of a heart; and these they glue to the end of their arrows. With the sinews of Deer, and the tops of Deers' horns boiled to a jelly, they make a glue that will not dissolve in cold water. . . .

In their hunting and fishing they take extreme pains; yet it being their ordinary exercise from their infancy, they esteem it a pleasure and are very proud to be expert therein. And by their continual ranging, and travel, they know all the advantages and places most frequented with

Deer, Beasts, Fish, Fowl, Roots, and Berries. At their huntings they leave their habitations, and reduce themselves into companies, as the Tartars do, and go to the most desert places with their families, where they spend their time in hunting and fowling. 1612

John Hammond
(fl. 1635)

Little is known of John Hammond, who migrated to Virginia sometime beteen years. From Virginia, he moved to Maryland, where he lived for two years before returning to England and publishing *Leah and Rachel; or, The* fore 1636 and resided there for eigh-

Two Fruitful Sisters, Virginia and Maryland (London, 1656).

BIBLIOGRAPHY: Reprinted in Peter Force, *Tracts and Other Papers,* III (Washington, D.C., 1844). C. C. Hall, ed. *Narratives of Early Maryland, 1633-1684* (New York, 1910).

From *Leah and Rachel*

I have undertaken in this Book to give the true state of those places, according to the condition they are now in; and to declare either to distressed or discontented, that they need not doubt because of any rumor detracting from their goodnesses, to remove and cast themselves and Fortunes upon those Countries, in which if I should deviate from the truth; I have at this present carping enemies in London enough, to contradict and cry down me and this, for Impostors. It is not long since I came from thence (God knows sore against my will) having lived there upward of one and twenty years; nor do I intend (by God's assistance) to be long out of it again: and therefore can by experience, not hearsay . . . but truly let ye know, what they are, and how the people there live. Which when impartially viewed, will undoubtedly clear up those Foggy Mists, that hath to their own ruin blinded and kept off many from going thither, whose miseries and misfortunes by staying in England are much to be lamented, and much to be pitied.

In respect these two Sister Countries (though distinct Governments) are much of one nature, both for produce and manner of living; I shall only at present, Treat of the elder Sister Virginia, and in speaking of that include both: And ere I leave off, shall in particular rehearse the unnatural usage Maryland the younger Sister, hath had, not by Virginia; but by those Vipers she hath received and harbored with much kindness and hospitality.

The Country is reported to be an unhealthy place, a nest of Rogues, whores, dissolute and rooking persons; a place of intolerable labor, bad usage and hard diet, &c.

To Answer these several calumnies, I shall first show what it was? next, what it is?

At the first settling and many years after, it deserved most of those aspersions (nor were they then aspersions but truths) it was not settled at the public charge; but when found out, challenged, and maintained by Adventurers, whose avarice and inhumanity, brought in these inconveniences, which to this day brands Virginia.

Then were Jails emptied, youth seduced, infamous women drilled in, the provisions all brought out of England, and that embezzled by the Trustees (for they durst neither hunt, fowl, nor Fish, for fear of the Indian, which they stood in awe of), their labor was almost perpetual, their allowance of victual small, few or no cattle, no use of horses nor oxen to draw or carry, (which labors men supplied themselves) all which caused a mortality; no civil courts of justice but under a Marshal law, no redress of grievances, complaints were repayed with stripes, moneys with scoffs, tortures made delights, and in a word all and the worst that tyranny could inflict or act, which when complained of in England: (but so were they kept under that it was long ere they would suffer complaints to come home) the bondage was taken off, the people set free, and had lands assigned to each of them to live of themselves, and enjoy the benefit of their own industry. . . .

They . . . began to bud forth, to spread further, to gather wealth, which they rather profusely spent (as gotten with ease) than providently husbanded, or aimed at any public good; or to make a Country for posterity; but from hand to mouth, and for a present being; neglecting discoveries, planting of Orchards, providing for the Winter preservation of their stocks, or thinking of anything staple or firm; and whilest Tobacco, the only Commodity they had to subsist on, bore a price, they wholly and eagerly followed that, neglecting their very planting of Corn, and much relied on England for the chiefest part of their provisions; so that being not always amply supplied, they were often in such want, that their case and condition being related in England, it hindered and kept off many from going thither, who rather cast their eyes on the Barren and freezing soil of New England, than to join with such an indigent and sottish people, as were reported to be in Virginia.

Yet was not Virginia all this while without divers honest and virtuous inhabitants, who observing the general neglect and licentiousnesses there, caused Assemblies to be call'd and Laws to be made tending to the glory of God, the severe suppression of vices, and the compelling them not to neglect (upon strict punishments) planting and tending such quantities of Corn, as would not only serve themselves, their Cattle and Hogs plentifully, but to be enabled to supply New England (then in want) with such proportions, as were extreme reliefs, to them in their necessities.

From this industry of theirs and great plenty of Corn, (the main staff of life) proceeded that great plenty of Cattle and Hogs, (now innumerable) and out of which not only New England hath been stocked and relieved, but all other parts of the Indies inhabited by Englishmen.

The inhabitants now finding the benefit of their industries, began to look with delight on their increasing stock: (as nothing more pleasurable than profit), to take pride in their plentifully furnished Tables, to grow not only civil, but great observers of the Sabbath, to stand upon their reputations, and to be ashamed of that notorious manner of life they had formerly lived and wallowed in.

They then began to provide and send home for Gospel Ministers, and largely contributed for their maintenance; But Virginia savoring not handsomely in England, very few of good conversation would adventure thither, (as thinking it a place wherein surely the fear of God was not), yet many came, such as wore Black Coats, and could babble in a Pulpit, roar in a Tavern, exact from their Parishioners and rather by their dissoluteness destroy than feed their Flocks.

Loath was the Country to be wholly without Teachers, and therefore rather retain these than to be destitute; yet still endeavors for better in their places, which were obtained, and these Wolves in sheep's clothing, by their Assemblies questioned, silenced, and some forced to depart the Country.

Then began the Gospel to flourish, civil, honorable, and men of great estates flocked in: famous buildings went forward, Orchards innumerable were planted and preserved; Tradesmen set on work and encouraged staple Commodities, as Silk, Flax, Potashes, &c. of which I shall speak further hereafter, attempted on, and with good success brought to perfection; so that this Country which had a mean beginning, many back friends, two ruinous and bloody Massacres, hath by God's grace outgrown all, and is become a place of pleasure and plenty. . . .

I affirm the Country to be wholesome, healthy and fruitful; and a model on which industry may as much improve itself in, as in any habitable part of the World; yet not such a Lubberland as the Fiction of the land of Ease is reported to be, nor such a Utopian as Sr. Thomas More hath related to be found out. . . .

Those Servants that will be industrious may in their time of service gain a competent estate before their Freedoms, which is usually done by many, and they gain esteem and assistance that appear so industrious: There is no Master almost but will allow his Servant a parcel of clear ground to plant some Tobacco in for himself, which he may husband at those many idle times he hath allowed him and not prejudice, but rejoice his Master to see it, which in time of Shipping he may lay out for commodities, and in Summer sell them again with advantage, and get a Sow-Pig or two, which anybody almost will give him, and his Master suffer him to keep them with his own, which will be no charge to his Master, and with one year's increase of them may purchase a Cow Calf or two, and by that time he is for himself; he may have Cattle, Hogs and Tobacco of his own, and come to live gallantly; but this must be gained (as I said) by Industry and affability, not by sloth nor churlish behavior. . . .

But if any go thither, not in a condition of a Servant, but pay his or her passage, which is some six pounds: Let them not doubt but it is money well laid out; yet however let them not fail, although they carry little else, to take a Bed along with them, and then few Houses but will give them entertainment, either out of courtesy, or on reasonable terms; and I think it better for any that goes over free, and but in a mean condition, to hire himself for reasonable wages of Tobacco and Provision, the first year, provided he happen in an honest house, and where the Mistress is noted for a good Housewife, of which there are very many (notwithstanding the cry to the contrary) for by that means he will live free of disbursement, have something to help him the next year, and be carefully looked to in his sickness (if he chance to fall sick) and let him so covenant that exceptions may be made, that he work not much in the hot weather, a course we always take with our new hands (as they call them) the first year they come in. . . .

And therefore those that shall blemish Virginia anymore, do but like the Dog bark against the Moon, until they be blind and weary; and Virginia is now in that secure growing condition, that like the Moon so barked at, she will pass on her course, maugre all detractors, and a few years will bring it to that glorious happiness, that many of her calumniators will intercede to procure admittance thither, when it will be hard to be attained to; . . .

And therefore I cannot but admire, and indeed much pity the dull stupidity of people necessitated in England, who rather than they will remove themselves, live here a base, slavish, penurious life; as if there were a necessity to live and to live so, choosing rather than they will forsake England to stuff New-Gate, Bridewell, and other Jails with their carcasses, nay cleave to Tyburne itself; and so bring confusion to their souls, horror and infamy to their kindred or posterity, others itch out their wearisome lives in reliance of other men's charities, an uncertain and unmanly expectation; some more abhorring such courses betake themselves to almost perpetual and restless toil and drudgeries out of which (whilst their strength lasteth) they (observing hard diets, early and late hours) make hard shift to subsist hand to mouth, until age or sickness takes them off from labor and directs them the way to beggary, and such indeed are to be pitied, relieved and provided for.

I have seriously considered when I have (passing the streets) heard the several Cries, and noting the commodities, and the worth of them they have carried and cried up and down; how possibly a livelihood could be exacted out of them, as to cry Matches, Small-coal, Blacking, Pen and Ink, Thread-laces, and a hundred more such kind of trifling merchandises; then looking on the nastiness of their linen habits and bodies: I conclude if gain sufficient could be raised out of them for substance; yet their manner of living was degenerate and base; and their condition to be far below the meanest servant in Virginia. . . .

The Country is not only plentiful but pleasant and profitable, pleasant in regard of the brightness of the weather, the many delightful rivers, on which the inhabitants are settled (every man almost living in sight of a lovely river) the abundance of game, the extraordinary good neighborhood ad loving conversation they have one with the other.   1656

George Alsop
(1638-?)

Of humble beginnings, George Alsop moved to Maryland in 1658 as an indentured servant, returned to England c. 1664, published *A Character of the Province of Maryland* (London, 1666), and disappeared from view.

BIBLIOGRAPHY: J. G. Shea, ed. *A Character of the Province of Maryland* (New York, 1869, reissued Baltimore, 1880). Also by N. D. Mereness (Baltimore, 1902). C. C. Hall, ed. *Narratives of Early Maryland, 1633-1684* (New York, 1910).

From *A Character of the Province of Maryland*

CHAPTER I

Of the situation and plenty of the Province of Maryland.

The Deer here neither in shape nor action differ from our Deer in England: The Park they traverse their ranging and unmeasured walks in, is bounded and impanell'd in with no other pales than the rough and billowed Ocean: They are also mighty numerous in the Woods, and are little or not at all affrighted at the face of a man, but (like the Does of Whetston's Park) though their hides are not altogether so gaudy to extract an admiration from the beholder, yet they will stand (almost) till they be scratcht.

As for the Wolves, Bears, and Panthers of this Country, they inhabit commonly in great multitudes up in the remotest parts of the Continent; yet at some certain time they come down near the Plantations, but do little hurt or injury worth noting, and that which they do is of so degenerate and low a nature, (as in reference to the fierceness and heroic vigor that dwell in the same kind of Beasts in other Countries), that they are hardly worth mentioning: For the highest of their designs and circumventing reaches is but cowardly and base, only to steal a poor Pig, or kill a lost and half starved Calf. The Effigies of a man terrifies them dreadfully, for they no sooner espy him but their hearts are at their mouths, and the spurs upon their heels, they (having no more manners than Beasts) gallop away, and never bid them farewell that are behind them. . . .

As for those Beasts that were carried over at the first seating of the Country, to stock and increase the situation, as Cows, Horses, Sheep and Hogs, they are generally tame, and used near home, especially the Cows, Sheep and Horses. The Hogs, whose increase is innumerable in the Woods, do disfrequent home more than the rest of Creatures that are look'd upon as tame, yet with little trouble and pains they are slain and made provision of. Now they that will with a right Historical Survey, view the Woods of Mary-Land in this particular, as in reference to Swine, must upon necessity judge this Land lineally descended from the Gadarean Territories. . . .

Fowls of all sorts and varieties dwell at their several times and seasons here in Mary-Land: The Turkey, the Woodcock, the Pheasant, the Partridge, the Pigeon, and others, especially the Turkey, whom I have seen in whole hundreds in flights in the Woods of Mary-Land, being an extraordinary fat Fowl, whose flesh is very pleasant and sweet. These Fowls that I have named are entailed from generation to generation to the Woods. The Swans, the Geese and Ducks (with other Waterfowl) derogate in this point of settled residence; for they arrive in millionous multitudes in Mary-Land about the middle of September, and take their winged farewell about the midst of March: But while they do remain, and beleaguer the borders of the shore with their winged Dragoons, several of them are summoned by a Writ of *Fieri facias*, to answer their presumptuous contempt upon a Spit. . . .

All sorts of Grain, as Wheat, Rye, Barley, Oats, Peas, besides several others that have their original and birth from the fertile womb of this Land (and no where else), they all grow, increase, and thrive here in Mary-Land, without the chargeable and laborious manuring of the Land with Dung; increasing in such a measure and plenty, by the natural richness of the Earth, with the common, beneficial and convenient showers of rain that usually wait upon the several Fields of Grain (by a natural instinct), so that Famine (the dreadful Ghost of penury and want) is never known with his pale visage to haunt the Dominions of Mary-Land.

CHAPTER II

Of the Government and Natural disposition of the People.

Mary-Land, not from the remoteness of her situation, but from the regularity of her well ordered Government, may (without sin, I think) be called Singular: . . .

He that desires to see the real Platform of a quiet and sober Government extant, Superiority with a meek and yet commanding power sitting at the Helm, steering the actions of State quietly, through the multitude and diversity of Opinionous waves that diversely meet, let him look on Mary-Land with eyes admiring, and he'll then judge her, The Miracle of this Age. . . .

Once every year within this Province is an Assembly called, and out of every respective County (by the consent of the people) there is chosen a number of men, and to them is deliver'd up the Grievances of the Country; and they maturely debate the matters, and according to their Consciences make Laws for the general good of the people; and where any former Law that was made, seems and is prejudicial to the good or quietness of the Land, it is repeal'd. These men that determine on these matters for the Republic, are called Burgesses, and they commonly sit in Junto about six weeks, being for the most part good ordinary Householders of the several Counties, which do more by a plain and honest Conscience, than by artificial Syllogisms drest up in gilded Orations.

Here Suits and Trials in Law seldom hold dispute two Terms or Courts, but according as the Equity of the Cause appears is brought to a period. The Temples and Gray's Inn are clear out of fashion here: Marriot would sooner get a paunch-devouring meal for nothing, than for his invading Counsel. Here if the Lawyer had nothing else to maintain him but his bawling, he might button up his Chops, and burn his Buckram Bag, or else hang it upon a pin until its Antiquity had eaten it up with dirt and dust: Then with a Spade, like his Grandsire Adam, turn up the face of the Creation, purchasing his bread by the sweat of his brows, that before was got by the motionated Waterworks of his jaws. . . . Here the Constable hath no need of a train of Holberteers, that carry more Armor about them, than heart to guard him: Nor is he ever troubled to leave his Feathered Nest to some friendly successor, while he is placing of his Lantern-horn Guard at the end of some suspicious Street, to catch some Nightwalker, or Bachelor of Lechery, that has taken his Degree three story high in a Bawdy-house. Here's no Newgates for pilfering Felons, nor Ludgates for Debtors, nor any Bridewells to lash the soul of Concupiscence into a chaste Repentance. For as there is none of these Prisons in Mary-Land, so the merits of the Country deserves none, but if any be foully vicious, he is so reserv'd in it, that he seldom or never becomes popular. Common Alehouses, (whose dwellings are the only Receptacles of debauchery and baseness, and those Schools that train up Youth, as well as Age, to ruin) in this Province there are none; neither hath Youth his swing or range in such a profuse and unbridled liberty as in other Countries; for from an ancient Custom at the primitive seating of the place, the Son works as well as the Servant (an excellent cure for untam'd Youth), so that before they eat their bread, they are commonly taught how to earn it; . . . These Christian Natives of the Land, especially those of the Masculine Sex, are generally conveniently confident, reservedly subtle, quick in apprehending, but slow in resolving; and where they spy profit sailing towards them with the wings of a prosperous gale, there they become much familiar. The Women differ something in this point, though not much: They are extreme bashful at the first view, but after a continuance of time hath brought them acquainted, there they become discreetly familiar, and are much more talkative than men. All Complimental Courtships, drest up in critical Rarities, are mere strangers to them, plain wit comes nearest their Genius; so that he that intends to Court a Mary-Land Girl, must have something more than the Tautologies of a long-winded speech to carry on his design, or else he may (for ought I know) fall under the contempt of her frown, and his own windy Oration.

CHAPTER III

The necessariness of Servitude proved, with the common usage of Servants in Mary-Land, together with their Privileges.

There is no truer Emblem of Confusion either in Monarchy or Domestic Governments, than when either the Subject, or the Servant, strives for the upper hand of his Prince, or Master, and to be equal with him, from whom he receives his present subsistence: Why then, if Servitude be so necessary that no place can be governed in order, nor people live without it, this may serve to tell those which prick up their ears and bray against it, That they are none but Asses, and deserve the Bridle of a strict commanding power to rein them in: For I'm certainly confident, that there are several Thousands in most Kingdoms of Christendom, that could not at all live and subsist, unless they had served some prefixed time, to learn either some Trade, Art, or Science, and by either of them to extract their present livelihood.

Then methinks this may stop the mouths of those that will undiscreetly compassionate them that dwell under necessary Servitudes; for let but Parents of an indifferent capacity in Estates, when their Children's age by computation speak them seventeen or eighteen years old, turn them loose to the wide world, without a seven years' working Apprenticeship (being just brought up to the bare formality of a little reading and writing) and you shall immediately see how weak and shiftless they'll be towards the maintaining and supporting of themselves; . . . And let this be spoke to the deserved praise of Mary-Land, That the four years I served there were not to me so slavish, as a two years' Servitude of a Handicraft Apprenticeship was here in London; *Volenti enim nil difficile:* Not that I write this to seduce or delude any, or to draw them from their native soil, but out of a love to my Countrymen, whom in the general I wish well to, and that the lowest of them may live in such a capacity of Estate, as that the bare interest of their Livelihoods might not altogether depend upon persons of the greatest extendments.

Now those whose abilities here in England are capable of maintaining themselves in any reasonable and handsome manner, they had best so to remain, lest the roughness of the Ocean, together with the staring visages of the wild Animals, which they may see after their arrival into the Country, may alter the natural dispositions of their bodies, that the staid and solid part that kept its motion by Doctor Trig's purgationary operation, may run beyond the bias of the wheel in a violent and laxative confusion. . . .

They whose abilities cannot extend to purchase their own transportation over into Mary-Land, (and surely he that cannot command so small a sum for so great a matter, his life must needs be mighty low and dejected) I say they may for the debarment of a four years' sordid liberty, go over into this Province and there live plentiously well. And what's a four years' Servitude to advantage a man all the remainder of his days, making his predecessors happy in his sufficient abilities, which he attained to partly by the restrainment of so small a time?

CHAPTER IV

Upon Traffic, and what Merchandising Commodities this Province affords, also how Tobacco is planted and made fit for Commerce.

But stop (good Muse) lest I should, like the Parson of Pancras, run so far from my Text in half an hour, that a two hours' trot back again would hardly fetch it up: I had best while I am alive in my Doctrine, to think again of Mary-Land, lest the business of other Countries take up so much room in my brain, that I forget and bury her in oblivion. . . .

Tobacco is the only solid Staple Commodity of this Province: The use of it was first found out by the Indians many Ages ago, and transferr'd into Christendom by that great Discoverer of America, Columbus. It's generally made by all the Inhabitants of this Province, and between the months of March and April they sow the seed (which is much smaller than Mustard seed) in small beds and patches digg'd up and made so by art, and about May the Plants commonly appear green in those beds: In June they are transplanted from their beds, and set in little hillocks in distant rows, dug up for the same purpose; some twice or thrice they are weeded, and succored from their illegitimate Leaves that would be peeping out from the body of the Stalk. They top the several Plants as they find occasion in their predominating rankness: About the middle of September they cut the Tobacco down, and carry it into houses, (made for that purpose) to bring it to its purity: And after it has attained, by a convenient attendance upon time, to its perfection, it is then tied up in bundles, and packt into Hogsheads, and then laid by for the Trade.

Between November and January there arrives in this Province Shipping to the number of twenty sail and upwards, all Merchantmen loaden with Commodities to Traffic and dispose of, trucking with the Planter for Silks, Hollands, Serges, and Broadcloths, with other necessary Goods, priz'd at such and such rates as shall be judg'd on is fair and legal, for Tobacco at so much the pound, and advantage on both sides considered; the Planter for his work, and the Merchant for adventuring himself and his Commodity into so far a Country: Thus is the Trade on both sides drove on with a fair and honest Decorum. . . .

Tobacco is the current Coin of Mary-Land, and will sooner purchase Commodities from the Merchant, than money. I must confess the New England men that trade into this Province, had rather have fat Pork for their Goods, than Tobacco or Furs, which I conceive is, because their bodies being fast bound up with the cords of restringent Zeal, they are fain to make use of the lineaments of this Non-Canaanite creature physically to loosen them; for a bit of a pound upon a twopenny Rye loaf, according to the original Receipt, will bring the costiv'st red-ear'd Zealot in some three hours' time to a fine stool, if methodically observed.

1666

William Wood

(1603-?)

William Wood came to New England in 1629, travelled widely in the area, went to England in 1633; there he published *New England's Prospects* (London, 1634), then returned to Massachusetts in 1635, and soon after disappeared from history.

BIBLIOGRAPHY: Charles Deane, ed. *New England's Prospects* (Boston, 1865). Also edited by H. W. Boynton (Boston, 1898).

From *New England's Prospects*

PART I   CHAPTER V

Of the Herbs, Fruits, Woods, Waters and Minerals.

. . . The next commodity the land affords, is good store of Woods, & that not only such as may be needful for fuel, but likewise for the building of Ships, and houses, & Mills, and all manner of waterwork about which Wood is needful. The Timber of the Country grows straight, and tall, some trees being twenty, some thirty foot high, before they spread forth their branches; generally the Trees be not very thick, though there be many that will serve for Millposts, some being three foot and a half over. And whereas it is generally conceived, that the woods grow so thick, that there is no more clear ground than is hewed out by labor of man; it is nothing so; in many places, divers Acres being clear, so that one may ride ahunting in most places of the land, if he will venture himself for being lost: there is no underwood saving in swamps, and low grounds that are wet, in which the English get Osiers, and Hazels, and such small wood as is for their use. . . .

Though many of these trees may seem to have epithets contrary to the nature of them as they grow in England, yet are they agreeable with the Trees of that Country. The chief and common Timber for ordinary use is Oak, and Walnut: Of Oaks there be three kinds, the red Oak, white, and black; as these are different in kind, so are they chosen for such uses as they are most fit for, one kind being more fit for clapboard, others for sawn board, some fitter for shipping, others for houses. These Trees afford much Mast for Hogs, especially every third year, bearing a bigger Acorn than our English Oak. The Walnut tree is something different from the English Walnut, being a great deal more tough, and more service-able, and altogether as heavy: and whereas our Guns that are stocked with English Walnut, are soon broken and cracked in frost, being a brit-tle Wood; we are driven to stock them new with the Country Walnut, which will endure all blows, and weather; lasting time out of mind. These trees bear a very good Nut, something smaller, but nothing infe-rior in sweetness and goodness to the English Nut, having no bitter pill. . . .

The Cedar tree is a tree of no great growth, not bearing above a foot and a half square at the most, neither is it very high. I suppose they be much inferior to the Cedars of Lebanon so much commended in holy writ. This wood is more desired for ornament than substance, being of color red and white like Yew, smelling as sweet as Juniper; it is common-ly used for sealing of houses, and making of Chests, boxes, and staves. The Fir and Pine be trees that grow in many places, shooting up exceed-ing high, especially the Pine: they do afford good masts, good board, Rosin and Turpentine. Out of these Pines is gotten the candlewood that is so much spoken of, which may serve for a shift amongst poor folks; but I cannot commend it for singular good, because it is something flut-tish, dropping a pitchy kind of substance where it stands. . . .

The Hornbound tree is a tough kind of Wood, that requires so much pains in riving as is almost incredible, being the best for to make bowls and dishes, not being subject to crack or leak. This tree growing with broad-spread Arms, the vines wind their curling branches about them; which vines afford great store of grapes, which are very big both for the grape and Cluster, sweet and good: These be of two sorts, red and white, there is likewise a smaller kind of grape, which groweth in the Islands which is sooner ripe and more delectable; so that there is no known reason why as good wine may not be made in those parts, as well as in Bordeaux in France; being under the same degree. It is great pity no man sets upon such a venture, whereby he might in small time enrich himself, and benefit the Country, I know nothing which doth hinder but want of skillful men to manage such an employment: For the country is hot enough, the ground good enough, and many convenient hills which lie toward the south Sun, as if they were there placed for the purpose. . . .

CHAPTER VII

Beasts living in the water.

. . . Fourthly, the Beaver, concerning whom if I should at large discourse, according to knowledge or information, I might make a Volume. The wisdom and understanding of this Beast, will almost conclude him a reasonable creature: His shape is thick and short, having likewise short legs, feet like a Mole before, and behind like a Goose, a broad tail in form like a shoe-sole, very tough and strong; his head is something like an Otter's head, saving that his teeth before, be placed like the teeth of a Rabbit, two above, and two beneath; sharp and broad, with which he cuts down Trees as thick as a man's thigh, afterwards dividing them into lengths, according to the use they are appointed for. If one Beaver be too weak to carry the log, then another helps him; if they two be too weak, then *Multorum manibus grande levatur onus;* four more adding their help, being placed three to three, which set their teeth in one another's tough tails, and laying the load on the two hindermost, they draw the log to the desired place. That this may not seem altogether incredible, remember that the like almost may be seen in our Ants, which will join sometimes seven or eight together in the carrying of a burden. These Creatures build themselves houses of wood and clay, close by the Pond's sides, and knowing the Seasons, build them answerable houses, having them three stories high, so that as land floods are raised by great Rains, as the waters arise, they mount higher in their houses; as they assuage, they descend lower again. These houses are so strong, that no creature saving an industrious man with his penetrating tools can prejudice them, their ingress and egress being under water. These make likewise very good Ponds, knowing whence a stream runs from between two rising Hills, they will there pitch down piles of Wood, placing smaller rubbish before it with clay and sods, not leaving, till by their Art and Industry they have made a firm and curious dam-head, which may draw admiration from wise understanding men. These creatures keep themselves to their own families, never parting so long as they are able to keep house together: And it is commonly said, if any Beaver accidentally light into a strange place, he is made a drudge so long as he lives there, to carry at the greater end of the log, unless he creep away by stealth. Their wisdom secures them from the English, who seldom, or never kills any of them, being not patient to lay a long siege, or to be so often deceived by their cunning evasions, so that all the Beaver which the English have, comes first from the Indians, whose time and experience fits them for that employment.

CHAPTER VIII

Of the Birds and Fowls both of Land and Water.

. . . Codfish in these seas are larger than in Newfoundland, six or seven making a quintal, whereas there they have fifteen to the same weight; and though this they seem a base and more contemptible commodity in the judgment of more neat adventurers, yet it hath been the enrichment of other nations, and is likely to prove no small commodity to the planters, and likewise to England if it were thoroughly undertaken. Salt may be had from the Salt Islands, and as is supposed may be made in the country. The chief fish for trade is Cod, but for the use of the country, there is all manner of fish as followeth. . . .

The Bass is one of the best fish in the country, and though men are soon wearied with other fish, yet are they never with Bass; it is a delicate, fine, fat, fast fish, having a bone in his head, which contains a saucerful of marrow sweet and good, pleasant to the palate, and wholesome to the stomach. When there be great store of them, we only eat the heads, and salt up the bodies for winter, which exceeds Ling or Haberdine. Of these fish some be three and some four foot long, some bigger, some lesser: at some tides a man may catch a dozen or twenty of these in three hours, the way to catch them is with hook and line: The Fisherman taking a great Cod-line, to which he fasteneth a piece of Lobster, and throws it into the sea, the fish biting at it he pulls her to him, and knocks her on the head with a stick. These are at one time (when Alewives pass up the Rivers) to be catched in Rivers, in Lobster time at the Rocks, in Mackerel time in the Bays, at Michelmas in the Seas. When they use to tide it in and out to the Rivers and Creeks, the English at the top of an high water do cross the Creeks, with long seines or Bass Nets, which stop in the fish; and the water ebbing from them they are left on the dry ground, sometimes two or three thousand at a set, which are salted up against winter, or distributed to such as have present occasion either to spend them in their houses, or use them for their ground. . . . Alewives be a kind of fish which is much like a Herring, which in the latter end of April come up to the fresh Rivers to spawn, in such multitudes as is almost incredible, pressing up in such shallow waters as will scarce permit them to swim, having likewise such longing desire after the fresh water ponds, that no beatings with poles, or forcive agitations by other devices, will cause them to return to the sea, till they have cast their Spawn.

Lobsters be in plenty in most places, very large ones, some being 20 pound in weight; these are taken at a low water amongst the rocks, they are very good fish, the small ones being the best, their plenty makes them little esteemed and seldom eaten. The Indians get many of them every day for to bait their hooks withal, and to eat when they can get no Bass: The Oysters be great ones in form of a shoehorn, some be a foot long, these breed on certain banks that are bare every spring tide. This fish without the shell is so big that it must admit of a division before you can well get it into your mouth. . . .

Mussels be in great plenty, left only for the Hogs, which if they were in England would be more esteemed of the poorer sort. Clams or Clamps is a shellfish not much unlike a cockle, it lieth under the sand, every six or seven of them having a round hole to take air and receive water at. When the tide ebbs and flows, a man running over these Clam banks will presently be made all wet, by their spouting of water out of those small holes: These fish be in great plenty in most places of the country, which is a great commodity for the feeding of Swine. . . .

CHAPTER XI

Of the evils, and such as are hurtful in the Plantation.

. . . Thus have you heard of the worst of the country: but some peradventure may say no, and reply that they have heard that the people have been often driven to great wants and extremities; To which I answer, it is true that some have lived for a certain time with a little bread, other without any, yet all this argues nothing against the country in itself, but condemns the folly and improvidence of such as would venture into so rude and unmanaged a country, without so much provisions as should have comfortably maintained them in health and strength till by their labors they had brought the land to yield his fruit. I have myself heard some say that they heard it was a rich land, a brave country, but when they came there they could see nothing but a few Canvas Booths & old houses, supposing at the first to have found walled towns, fortifications, and corn fields, as if towns could have built themselves, or corn fields have grown of themselves, without the husbandry of man. These men missing of their expectations, returned home and railed against the Country. . . .

And whereas many do disparage the land saying a man cannot live without labor, in that they more disparage and discredit themselves, in giving the world occasion to take notice of their dronish disposition, that would live of the sweat of another man's brows: surely they were much deceived, or else ill informed, that ventured thither in hope to live in plenty and idleness, both at a time: and it is as much pity as he that can work and will not, should eat, as it is pity that he that would work and cannot, should fast. I condemn not such therefore as are now there, and are not able to work; but I advise for the future those men that are of weak constitutions to keep at home, if their estates cannot maintain servants. For all New England must be workers in some kind. . . .

CHAPTER XII

What provision is to be made for a Journey at Sea,
and what to carry with us for our use on land.

. . . Thus having showed what commodities are most useful, it will not be amiss to show you what men be most fit for these plantations.

First, men of good working, and contriving heads, a well experienced commonwealth's man for the good of the body politic in matters of advice and counsel, a well skilled and industrious husbandman, for tillage and improvements of grounds; an ingenious Carpenter, a cunning Joiner, a handy Cooper, such a one as can make strong ware for the use of the country, and a good brickmaker, a Tiler and a Smith, a Leather dresser, a Gardener, and a Tailor: one that hath good skill in the trade of fishing, is of special use, and so is a good Fowler, if there be any that has skill in any of these trades, if he can transport himself, he needs not fear but he may improve his time and endeavors to his own benefit, and comfort; if any cannot transport himself, he may provide himself of an honest master, and so may do as well. There is as much freedom and liberty for servants as in England and more too; a wronged servant shall have right *volens nolens* from his injurious master, and a wronged master shall have right of his injurious servant, as well as here: Wherefore let no servant be discouraged from the voyage, that intends it. And now whereas it is generally reported, that servants and poor men grow rich, and the masters and Gentry grow poor; I must needs confess that the diligent hand makes rich, and that laboring men having good store of employments, and as good pay, live well, and contentedly; but I cannot perceive that those that set them awork are any way impoverished by them; peradventure they have less money by reason of them, but never the less riches; a man's work well done being more beneficial than his money, or other dead commodities, which otherwise would lie by him to no purpose. If any men be so improvident as to set men about building of Castles in the Air, or other unnecessary employments, they may grow poor; but such as employ laborers about planting of Corn, building of houses, fencing in of ground, fishing, and divers other necessary occasions, shall receive as much or more by poor men's labors, than those that live in England do from the industry of such as they hire.　　　　1634

Thomas Morton
(c. 1575-1647)

Thomas Morton, adventurer with some legal training, came to New England originally in 1622, appeared a second time with Captain Wollaston in 1625, and remained there when Wollaston took most of his planters to Virginia. He was arrested at Merry Mount in June 1628 and sent to England for punishment. He reappeared in New England in 1629, was arrested a second time and returned to England where he became one of the principal witnesses in the attack on the Massachusetts Bay Colony Charter in 1632. *The New English Canaan* was entered in the Stationers' Register in 1633, though the earliest known printing is the Amsterdam edition of 1637. Morton returned to New England in 1643, was arrested for the third time in 1644, imprisoned for a year, fined and released. He appears to have settled thereafter in Maine.

BIBLIOGRAPHY: Peter Force, *Tracts and Other Papers*, II (Washington, D.C., 1838). Charles F. Adams, Jr., ed. *The New English Canaan, Publ. of Prince Soc.*, XIV (Boston, 1883). Henry Beston, *A Book of Gallant Vagabonds* (New York, 1925).

From *The New English Canaan*

CHAPTER IV

Of a Parliament held at Wessaguscus, and the Acts.

Master Weston's Plantation being settled at Wessaguscus, his Servants, many of them lazy persons that would use no endeavor to take the benefit of the Country, some of them fell sick and died.

One amongst the rest, an able bodied man that ranged the woods to see what it would afford, lighted by accident on an Indian barn, and from thence did take a cap full of corn; the Savage owner of it, finding by the foot some English had been there, came to the Plantation, and made complaint after this manner.

The chief Commander of the Company on this occasion called a Parliament of all his people, but those that were sick and ill at ease. And wisely now they must consult upon this huge complaint, that a privy knife or string of beads would well enough have qualified; and Edward Johnson was a special judge of this business; the fact was there in repetition; construction made that it was felony, and by the Laws of England punished with death; and this in execution must be put for an example, and likewise to appease the Savage: when straightways one arose, moved as it were with some compassion, and said he could not well gainsay the former sentence, yet he had conceived within the compass of his brain an

Embryo that was of special consequence to be delivered and cherished; he said that it would most aptly serve to pacify the Savage's complaint, and save the life of one that might, (if need should be,) stand them in some good stead, being young and strong, fit for resistance against an enemy, which might come unexpected for anything they knew. The Oration made was liked of everyone, and he entreated to proceed to show the means how this may be performed: says he, you all agree that one must die, and one shall die; this young man's clothes we will take off, and put upon one that is old and impotent, a sickly person that cannot escape death, such is the disease on him confirmed that die he must; put the young man's clothes on this man, and let the sick person be hanged in the other's stead: Amen says one; and so says many more.

And this had like to have proved their final sentence, and, being there confirmed by Act of Parliament, to after ages for a President: But that one with a ravenous voice begun to croak and bellow for revenge; and put by that conclusive motion, alleging such deceits might be a means hereafter to exasperate the minds of the complaining Savages, and that by his death the Savages should see their zeal to Justice; and therefore he should die: this was concluded; yet nevertheless a scruple was made; now to countermand this act, did represent itself unto their minds, which was, how they should do to get the man's good will? this was indeed a special obstacle: for without that, they all agreed it would be dangerous for any man to attempt the execution of it, lest mischief should befall them every man; he was a person that in his wrath did seem to be a second Sampson, able to beat out their brains with the jawbone of an Ass: therefore they called the man, and by persuasion got him fast bound in jest; and then hanged him up hard by in good earnest, who with a weapon, and at liberty, would have put all those wise judges of this Parliament to a pitiful *non plus*, (as it hath been credibly reported,) and made the chief Judge of them all buckle to him.

CHAPTER XIV

Of the Revels of New Canaan.

The Inhabitants of Pasonagessit, (having translated the name of their habitation from that ancient Savage name to Merry Mount, and being resolved to have the new name confirmed for a memorial to after ages,) did devise amongst themselves to have it performed in a solemn manner, with Revels and merriment after the old English custom; they prepared to set up a Maypole upon the festival day of Philip and Jacob, and therefore brewed a barrel of excellent beer and provided a case of bottles, to be spent, with other good cheer, for all comers of that day. And because they would have it in a complete form, they had prepared a song fitting to the time and present occasion. And upon Mayday they brought the

Maypole to the place appointed, with drums, guns, pistols and other fitting instruments, for that purpose; and there erected it with the help of Savages, that came thither of purpose to see the manner of our Revels. A goodly pine tree of 80 foot long was reared up, with a pair of buck-horns nailed on somewhat near unto the top of it: where it stood, as a fair sea mark for directions how to find out the way to mine Host of Merry Mount.

And because it should more fully appear to what end it was placed there, they had a poem in readiness made, which was fixed to the May-pole, to show the new name confirmed upon that plantation; which, al-though it were made according to the occurrence of the time, it, being Enigmatically composed, puzzled the Separatists most pitifully to ex-pound it, which, (for the better information of the reader,) I have here inserted.

THE POEM

Rise Oedipus, and, if thou canst, unfold
What means Caribdis underneath the mould,
When Scilla solitary on the ground
(Sitting in form of Niobe,) was found,
Till Amphitrite's Darling did acquaint   5
Grim Neptune with the Tenor of her plaint,
And caused him send forth Triton with the sound
Of Trumpet loud, at which the Seas were found
So full of Protean forms that the bold shore
Presented Scilla a new paramour   10

The man who brought her over was named Sam-son Job.

So strong as Sampson and so patient
As Job himself, directed thus, by fate,
To comfort Scilla so unfortunate.
I do profess, by Cupid's beauteous mother,
Here's Scogan's choice for Scilla, and none other;   15
Though Scilla's sick with grief, because no sign
Can there be found of virtue masculine.
Esculapius come; I know right well
His labor's lost when you may ring her Knell.
The fatal sisters' doom none can withstand,   20
Nor Citharea's power, who points to land
With proclamation that the first of May
At Merry Mount shall be kept holiday.

The setting up of this Maypole was a lamentable spectacle to the pre-cise Separatists, that lived at New Plymouth. They termed it an Idol; yea, they called it the Calf of Horeb, and stood at defiance with the place, naming it Mount Dagon; threatening to make it a woeful mount and not a merry mount.

The Riddle, for want of Oedipus, they could not expound; only they made some explication of part of it, and said it was meant by Sampson Job, the carpenter of the ship that brought over a woman to her husband, that had been there long before and thrived so well that he sent for her and her children to come to him; where shortly after he died: having no reason, but because of the sound of those two words; when as, (the truth is,) the man they applied it to was altogether unknown to the Author.

There was likewise a merry song made, which, (to make their Revels more fashionable,) was sung with a Chorus, every man bearing his part; which they performed in a dance, hand in hand about the Maypole, while one of the Company sung and filled out the good liquor, like Ganymede and Jupiter.

THE SONG

Chor.

Drink and be merry, merry, merry boys;
Let all your delight be in the Hymen's joys;
Io to Hymen, now the day is come,
About the merry Maypole take a Room.
Make green garlands, bring bottles out 5
And fill sweet Nectar freely about.
Uncover thy head and fear no harm,
For here's good liquor to keep it warm.
Then drink and be merry, &c.
Io to Hymen, &c. 10
Nectar is a thing assigned
By the Deity's own mind
To cure the heart oppressed with grief,
And of good liquors is the chief.
Then drink, &c. 15
Io to Hymen, &c.
Give to the Melancholy man
A cup or two of 't now and then;
This physic will soon revive his blood,
And make him be of a merrier mood. 20
Then drink, &c.
Io to Hymen, &c.
Give to the Nymph that's free from scorn
No Irish stuff nor Scotch over worn.

Lasses in beaver coats come away,   25
Ye shall be welcome to us night and day.
To drink and be merry &c.
Io to Hymen, &c.

This harmless mirth made by young men, (that lived in hope to have
wives brought over to them, that would save them a labor to make a
voyage to fetch any over,) was much distasted of the precise Separatists,
that keep much ado about the tithe of Meat and Cumin, troubling their
brains more than reason would require about things that are indifferent:
and from that time sought occasion against my honest Host of Merry
Mount, to overthrow his undertakings and to destroy his plantation quite
and clean. . . .

CHAPTER XV

Of a great Monster supposed to be at Merry Mount; and
the preparation made to destroy it.

The Separatists, envying the prosperity and hope of the Plantation at
Merry Mount, (which they perceived began to come forward, and to be
in a good way for gain in the Beaver trade,) conspired together against
mine Host especially, (who was the owner of that Plantation,) and made
up a party against him; and mustered up what aid they could, accounting of him as of a great Monster.

Many threatening speeches were given out both against his person and
his Habitation, which they divulged should be consumed with fire: And
taking advantage of the time when his company, (which seemed little to
regard their threats,) were gone up into the Inlands to trade with the
Savages for Beaver, they set upon my honest Host at a place called Wessaguscus, where, by accident, they found him. The inhabitants there
were in good hope of the subversion of the plantation at Merry Mount,
(which they principally aimed at;) and the rather because mine host was
a man that endeavored to advance the dignity of the Church of England;
which they, (on the contrary part,) would labor to vilify with uncivil
terms: inveighing against the sacred Book of Common Prayer, and mine
host that used it in a laudable manner amongst his family, as a practice
of piety.

There he would be a means to bring sacks to their mill, (such is the
thirst after Beaver,) and helped the conspirators to surprise mine host,
(who was there all alone;) and they charged him, (because they would
seem to have some reasonable cause against him to set a gloss upon their
malice,) with criminal things; . . .

It appears they were like bears' whelps in former time, when mine host's plantation was of as much strength as theirs, but now, (theirs being stronger,) they, (like overgrown bears,) seemed monstrous. In brief, mine host must endure to be their prisoner until they could contrive it so that they might send him for England, (as they said,) there to suffer according to the merit of the fact which they intended to father upon him; supposing, (belike), it would prove a heinous crime. . . .

The Conspirators sported themselves at my honest host, that meant them no hurt, and were so jocund that they feasted their bodies, and fell to tippling as if they had obtained a great prize; like the Trojans when they had the custody of Hippeus' pinetree horse.

Mine host feigned grief, and could not be persuaded either to eat or drink; because he knew emptiness would be a means to make him as watchful as the Geese kept in the Roman Capital: whereon, the contrary part, the conspirators would be so drowsy that he might have an opportunity to give them a slip, instead of a tester.

Six persons of the conspiracy were set to watch him at Wessaguscus: But he kept waking; and in the dead of night, (one lying on the bed for further surety,) up gets mine Host and got to the second door that he was to pass, which, notwithstanding the lock, he got open, and shut it after him with such violence that it affrighted some of the conspirators. . . .

Their grand leader, Captain Shrimp, took on most furiously and tore his clothes for anger, to see the empty nest, and their bird gone.

The rest were eager to have torn their hair from their heads; but it was so short that it would give them no hold. Now Captain Shrimp thought in the loss of this prize, (which he accounted his Masterpiece,) all his honor would be lost forever.

In the meantime mine Host was got home to Merry Mount through the woods, eight miles round about the head of the river Monatoquit that parted the two Plantations, finding his way by the help of the lightning, (for it thundered as he went terribly;) and there he prepared powder, three pounds dried, for his present employment, and four good guns for him and the two assistants left at his house, with bullets of several sizes, three hundred or thereabouts, to be used if the conspirators should pursue him thither: and these two persons promised their aids in the quarrel, and confirmed that promise with health in good *rosa solis*.

Now Captain Shrimp, the first Captain in the Land, (as he supposed,) must do some new act to repair this loss, and, to vindicate his reputation, who had sustained blemish by this oversight, begins now to study, how to repair or survive his honor: in this manner, calling of Council, they conclude.

He takes eight persons more to him, and, (like the nine Worthies of New Canaan,) they embark with preparation against Merry Mount, where this Monster of a man, as their phrase was, had his den; the whole number, had the rest not been from home, being but seven, would have given Captain Shrimp, (a quondam Drummer,) such a welcome as would have made him wish for a Drum as big as Diogenes' tub, that he might have crept into it out of sight.

Now the nine Worthies are approached, and mine Host prepared: having intelligence by a Savage, that hastened in love from Wessaguscus to give him notice of their intent.

One of mine Host's men proved a craven: the other had proved his wits to purchase a little valor, before mine Host had observed his posture.

. . . The nine worthies coming before the Den of this supposed Monster, (this seven-headed hydra, as they termed him,) and began, like Don Quixote against the Windmill, to beat a parley, and to offer quarter, if mine Host would yield; for they resolved to send him to England; and bade him lay by his arms.

But he, (who was the Son of a Soldier,) having taken up arms in his just defense, replied that he would not lay by those arms, because they were so needful at Sea, if he should be sent over. Yet, to save the effusion of so much worthy blood, as would have issued out of the veins of these 9 worthies of New Canaan, if mine Host should have played upon them out at his portholes, (for they came within danger like a flock of wild geese, as if they had been tailed one to another, as colts to be sold at a fair,) mine Host was content to yield upon quarter; and did capitulate with them in what manner it should be for more certainty, because he knew what Captain Shrimp was.

He expressed that no violence should be offered to his person, none to his goods, nor any of his Household: but that he should have his arms, and what else was requisite for the voyage: which their Herald returns, it was agreed upon, and should be performed.

But mine Host no sooner had set open the door, and issued out, but instantly Captain Shrimp and the rest of the worthies stepped to him, laid hold of his arms, and had him down: and so eagerly was every man bent against him, (not regarding any agreement made with such a carnal man,) that they fell upon him as if they would have eaten him: some of them were so violent that they would have a slice with scabbard, and all for haste; until an old Soldier, (of the Queen's, as the Proverb is,) that was there by accident, clapt his gun under the weapons, and sharply rebuked these worthies for their unworthy practices. So the matter was taken into more deliberate consideration.

Captain Shrimp, and the rest of the nine worthies, made themselves, (by this outrageous riot,) Masters of mine Host of Merry Mount, and disposed of what he had at his plantation.

1637

HISTORY

John Smith

Captain John Smith's *The General History of Virginia, New England, and the Summer Isles* was published in London in 1624; his *Advertisements for the Unexperienced Planters of New England* appeared in 1631. See Headnote to *A True Relation.*

From *The General History of Virginia*

BOOK IV

[Observations by William Simmons]

Now we all found the loss of Captain Smith, yea his greatest maligners could now curse his loss: as for corn provision and contribution from the Savages, we had nothing but mortal wounds, with clubs and arrows; as for our Hogs, Hens, Goats, Sheep, Horse, or what lived, our commanders, officers and Savages daily consumed them, some small proportions sometimes we tasted, till all was devoured; then swords, arms, pieces, or any thing, we traded with the Savages, whose cruel fingers were so often imbrued in our bloods, that what by their cruelty, our Governors' indiscretion, and the loss of our ships, of five hundred within six months after Captain Smith's departure, there remained not past sixty men, women and children, most miserable and poor creatures; and those were preserved for the most part, by roots, herbs, acorns, walnuts, berries, now and then a little fish: they that had starch in these extremities, made no small use of it; yea, even the very skins of our horses.

Nay, so great was our famine, that a Savage we slew and buried, the poorer sort took him up again and eat him; and so did divers one another boiled and stewed with roots and herbs: And one amongst the rest did kill his wife, powdered her, and had eaten part of her before it was known; for which he was executed, as he well deserved: now whether she was better roasted, boiled or carbonado'd, I know not; but of such a dish as powdered wife I never heard of.

This was that time, which still to this day we called the starving time; it were too vile to say, and scarce to be believed, what we endured: but the occasion was our own, for want of providence, industry, and government, and not the barrenness and defect of the Country, as is generally supposed; for till then in three years, for the numbers were landed us, we had never from England provision sufficient for six months, though it seemed by the bills of loading sufficient was sent us, such a glutton is the Sea, and such good fellows the Mariners; we as little tasted of the great proportion sent us, as they of our want and miseries, yet notwithstanding they ever overswayed and ruled the business, though we endured all that is said, and chiefly lived on what this good Country naturally afforded. Yet had we been even in Paradise itself with these Governors, it would not have been much better with us; yet there was amongst us, who had they had the government as Captain Smith appointed, but that they could not maintain it, would surely have kept us from those extremities of miseries. This in ten days more, would have supplanted us all with death.

But God that would not this Country should be unplanted, sent Sir Thomas Gates, and Sir George Sommers with one hundred and fifty people most happily preserved by the Bermudas to preserve us: strange it is to say how miraculously they were preserved in a leaking ship, as at large you may read in the ensuing History of those Islands.

[On Pocahontas]

During this time, the Lady Rebecca, alias Pocahontas, daughter to Powhatan, by the diligent care of Master John Rolfe her husband and his friends, was taught to speak such English as might well be understood, well instructed in Christianity, and was become very formal and civil after our English manner; she had also by him a child which she loved most dearly, and the Treasurer and Company took order both for the maintenance of her and it, besides there were divers persons of great rank and quality had been very kind to her; and before she arrived at London, Captain Smith to deserve her former courtesies, made her qualities known to the Queen's most excellent Majesty and her Court, and writ a little book to this effect to the Queen: An abstract whereof followeth.

To the most high and virtuous Princess, Queen Anne of Great Britain.

Most admired Queen, The love I bear my God, my King and Country, hath so oft emboldened me in the worst of extreme dangers, that now honesty doth constrain me to presume thus far beyond myself, to present your Majesty this short discourse: if ingratitude be a deadly poison to all honest virtues, I must be guilty of that crime if I should omit any means to be thankful.

So it is,

That some ten years ago being in Virginia, and taken prisoner by the power of Powhatan their chief King, I received from this great Savage exceeding great courtesy, especially from his son Nantaquaus, the most manliest, comeliest, boldest spirit, I ever saw in a Savage, and his sister Pocahontas, the King's most dear and well-beloved daughter, being but a child of twelve or thirteen years of age whose compassionate pitiful heart, of my desperate estate, gave me much cause to respect her: I being the first Christian this proud King and his grim attendants ever saw: and thus enthralled in their barbarous power, I cannot say I felt the least occasion of want that was in the power of those my mortal foes to prevent, notwithstanding all their threats. After some six weeks' fatting amongst those Savage Courtiers, at the minute of my execution, she hazarded the beating out of her own brains to save mine; and not only that, but so prevailed with her father, that I was safely conducted to Jamestown: where I found about eight and thirty miserable poor and sick creatures, to keep possession of all those large territories of Virginia; such was the weakness of this poor Commonwealth, as had the Savages not fed us, we directly had starved. And this relief, most gracious Queen, was commonly brought us by this Lady Pocahontas.

Notwithstanding all these passages, when inconstant Fortune turned our peace to war, this tender Virgin would still not spare to dare to visit us, and by her our jars have been oft appeased, and our wants still supplied; were it the policy of her father thus to employ her, or the ordinance of God thus to make her his instrument, or her extraordinary affection to our Nation, I know not: but of this I am sure; when her father with the utmost of his policy and power, sought to surprise me, having but eighteen with me, the dark night could not affright her from coming through the irksome woods, and with watered eyes gave me intelligence, with her best advice to escape his fury; which had he known, he had surely slain her.

Jamestown with her wild train she as freely frequented, as her father's habitation; and during the time of two or three years she next under God, was still the instrument to preserve this Colony from death, famine and utter confusion; which if in those times, had once been dissolved, Virginia might have lain as it was at our first arrival to this day. . . .

About two years after she herself was taken prisoner, being so detained near two years longer, the Colony by that means was relieved, peace concluded; and at last rejecting her barbarous condition, was married to an English Gentleman, with whom at this present she is in England; the first Christian ever of that Nation, the first Virginian ever spake English, or had a child in marriage by an Englishman: a matter surely, if my meaning be truly considered and well understood, worthy a Prince's understanding.

Thus, most gracious Lady, I have related to your Majesty, what at your best leisure our approved Histories will account you at large, and done in the time of your Majesty's life; and however this might be presented you from a more worthy pen, it cannot from a more honest heart, as yet I never begged anything of the state, or any: and it is my want of ability and her exceeding desert; your birth, means and authority; her birth, virtue, want and simplicity, doth make me thus bold, humbly to beseech your Majesty to take this knowledge of her, though it be from one so unworthy to be the reporter, as myself, her husband's estate not being able to make her fit to attend your Majesty. The most and least I can do, is to tell you this, because none so oft hath tried it as myself, and the rather being of so great a spirit, however her stature: if she should not be well received, seeing this Kingdom may rightly have a Kingdom by her means; her present love to us and Christianity might turn to such scorn and fury, as to divert all this good to the worst of evil: whereas finding so great a Queen should do her some honor more than she can imagine, for being so kind to your servants and subjects, would so ravish her with content, as endear her dearest blood to effect that, your Majesty and all the King's honest subjects most earnestly desire.

And so I humbly kiss your gracious hands.

1624

From *Advertisements for the Unexperienced Planters*

CHAPTER XI

. . . But seeing history is the memory of time, the life of the dead, and the happiness of the living; because I have more plainly discovered, and described, and discoursed of those Countries than any as yet I know, I am the bolder to continue the story, and do all men right so near as I can in those new beginnings, which hereafter perhaps may be in better request than a forest of nine days' pamphlets.

In the year 1629 about March, six good ships are gone with 350. men, women, and children; people professing themselves of good rank, zeal, means and quality: also 150. head of cattle, as horse, mares, and neat beasts; 41 goats, some coneys, with all provision for household and apparel; six pieces of great Ordnance for a Fort, with Muskets, Pikes, Corselets, Drums and Colors, with all provisions necessary for the good of man.

They are seated about 42 degrees and 38 minutes, at a place called by the natives Naemkecke, by our Royal King Charles, Bastable; but now by the planters, Salem: where they arrived for most part exceeding well, their cattle and all things else prospering exceedingly, far beyond their expectation.

At this place they found some reasonable good provision and houses built by some few of Dorchester, with whom they are joined in society with two hundred men.

An hundred and fifty more they have sent to the Massachusetts, which they call Charlton, or Charlestown. . . .

CHAPTER XIII

It is true, that Master John Winthrop, their now Governor, a worthy Gentleman both in estate and esteem, went so well provided (for six or seven hundred people went with him) as could be devised; but at Sea, such an extraordinary storm encountered his Fleet, continuing ten days, that of two hundred Cattle which were so tossed and bruised, threescore and ten died, many of their people fell sick, and in this perplexed estate, after ten weeks, they arrived [in June-July 1630] in New England at several times: where they found threescore of their people dead, the rest sick, nothing done; but all complaining, and all things so contrary to their expectation, that now every monstrous humor began to show itself.

And to second this, near as many more came after them, but so ill provided, with such multitudes of women and children, as redoubled their necessities.

This small trial of their patience caused among them no small confusion, and put the Governor and his Council to their utmost wits. Some could not endure the name of a Bishop, others not the sight of a Cross nor Surplice, others by no means the Book of Common Prayer. This absolute crew, only of the Elect, holding all (but such as themselves) reprobates and castaways, now make more haste to return to Babel as they termed England, than stay to enjoy the land they called Canaan: somewhat they must say to excuse themselves.

Those he found Brownists, he let go for New Plymouth; who are now betwixt four or five hundred, and live well without want.

Some two hundred of the rest he was content to return for England, whose clamors are as variable as their humors and Auditors. Some say they could see no timber of two feet diameter, some the Country is all Woods; others they drunk all the Springs and Ponds dry, yet like to famish for want of fresh water; some of the danger of the rattlesnake; and that others sold their provisions at what rates they pleased to them that wanted, and so returned to England great gainers out of others' miseries: yet all that returned are not of those humors.

Notwithstanding all this, the noble Governor was no way disanimated, neither repents him of his enterprise for all those mistakes: but did order all things with that temperance and discretion, and so relieved those that wanted with his own provision, that there is six or seven hundred remained with him; and more than 1600. English in all the Country, with three or four hundred head of Cattle.

CHAPTER XIV

Now because I have spoke so much for the body, give me leave to say somewhat of the soul; and the rather because I have been demanded by so many, how we began to preach the Gospel in Virginia, and by what authority; what Churches we had, our order of service, and maintenance for our ministers; therefore I think it not amiss to satisfy their demands, it being the mother of all our Plantations, entreating pride to spare laughter, to understand her simple beginning and proceedings.

When I went first to Virginia, I well remember we did hang an awning (which is an old sail) to three or four trees to shadow us from the Sun, our walls were rails of wood, our seats unhewed trees till we cut planks, our Pulpit a bar of wood nailed to two neighboring trees. In foul weather we shifted into an old rotten tent; for we had few better, and this came by the way of adventure for new. This was our Church, till we built a homely thing like a barn, set upon Cratchets, covered with rafts, sedge, and earth; so was also the walls: the best of our houses were of the like curiosity; but the most part far much worse workmanship, that could neither well defend from wind nor rain.

Yet we had daily Common Prayer morning and evening, every Sunday two Sermons, and every three months the holy Communion, till our Minister died: but our Prayers daily, with an Homily on Sundays, we continued two or three years after, till more Preachers came: and surely God did most mercifully hear us, till the continual inundations of mistaking directions, factions, and numbers of unprovided Libertines near consumed us all, as the Israelites in the wilderness.

Notwithstanding, out of the relics of our miseries, time and experience had brought that Country to a great happiness; had they not so much doted on their Tobacco, on whose fumish foundation there is small stability: there being so many good commodities besides. Yet by it they have builded many pretty Villages, fair houses, and Chapels, which are grown good Benefices of 120. pounds a year, besides their own mundane industry. But Jamestown was 500. pounds a year, as they say, appointed by the Council here, allowed by the Council there, and confirmed by the Archbishop of Canterbury his Grace, Primate and Metropolitan of all England, An. 1605. to Master Richard Hacluit, Prebend of Westminister: who by his authority sent Master Robert Hunt, an honest, religious, and courageous Divine; during whose life our factions were oft qualified, our wants and greatest extremities so comforted, that they seemed easy in comparison of what we endured after his memorable death.

Now in New England they have all our examples to teach them how to beware, and choose men, we being most ignorant in all things, or little better; therefore presage not the event of all such actions by our defailments: For they write, they doubt not ere long to be able to defend themselves against any indifferent enemy; in the interim, they have Preachers erected among themselves, and God's true Religion (they say) taught amongst them, the Sabbath day observed, the common Prayer (as I understand) and Sermons performed, and diligent catechising, with strict and careful exercise, and commendable good orders to bring those people with whom they have to deal withal into a Christian conversation, to live well, to fear God, serve the King, and love the Country; which done, in time from both those Plantations may grow a good addition to the Church of England: . . .

But as yet it is not well understood of any authority they have sought for the government and tranquility of the Church, which doth cause those suspicions of factions in Religion; wherein although I be no Divine, yet I hope without offense I may speak my opinion as well in this, as I have done in the rest. . . .

Therefore I doubt not but you will seek to the prime authority of the Church of England, for such an orderly authority as in most men's opinions is fit for you both to entreat for and to have, which I think will not be denied; and you have good reason, seeing you have such liberty to transport so many of his Majesty's subjects, with all sorts of cattle, arms, and provision as you please, and can provide means to accomplish: nor can you have any certain relief, nor long subsist, without more supplies from England. Besides, this might prevent many inconveniences may ensue, and would clearly take away all those idle and malicious rumors, and occasion you many good and great friends and assistance you yet dream not of; for you know better than I can tell, that the maintainers of good Orders and Laws is the best preservation next God of a Kingdom: . . .   1631

William Bradford

(1590-1657)

A Yorkshireman of the yeoman class, William Bradford fled from England to Holland with John Robinson's Separatist group in 1609; there he worked as a weaver and read widely. A planner of the *Mayflower* expedition, Bradford was elected governor of the Plymouth Colony in 1621, and served for thirty years as its leader. His work, used in manuscript by seventeenth and eigh-teenth-century historians as a principal source for their studies, disappeared during the Revolutionary War, but was rediscovered in 1855 in England. The first edition of *Of Plymoth Plantation* appeared in *Coll. Mass. Hist. Soc.*, 4th Ser., III (1856).

BIBLIOGRAPHY: Bradford, "Letter-Book, 1624-1630," *Coll. Mass. Hist.*

Soc., 1st Ser., III (1794). "Letters of William Bradford," *ibid.*, 4th Ser., VI (1863). W. C. Ford, ed. *Of Plymoth Plantation*, 2 Vols. (Boston, 1912). Also edited with commentary by S. E. Mori- son (New York, 1952). *DAB*. A. H. Plumb, *William Bradford of Plymouth* (Boston, 1920). Bradford Smith, *Bradford of Plymouth* (Philadelphia, 1952).

From *Of Plymouth Plantation*

THE FIRST BOOK

CHAPTER I

But that I may come more near my intendment; when as by the travel and diligence of some godly and zealous preachers, and God's blessing on their labors, as in other places of the land, so in the North parts, many became enlightened by the word of God, and had their ignorance and sins discovered unto them, and began by his grace to reform their lives, and make conscience of their ways, the work of God was no sooner manifest in them, but presently they were both scoffed and scorned by the profane multitude, and the ministers urged with the yoke of subscription, or else must be silenced; and the poor people were so vexed with apparitors, and pursuants, and the commissary courts, as truly their affliction was not small; which, notwithstanding, they bore sundry years with much patience, till they were occasioned (by the continuance and increase of these troubles, and other means which the Lord raised up in those days) to see further into things by the light of the word of God. How not only these base and beggarly ceremonies were unlawful, but also that the lordly and tyrannous power of the prelates ought not to be submitted unto; which thus, contrary to the freedom of the gospel, would load and burden men's consciences, and by their compulsive power make a profane mixture of persons and things in the worship of God. . . .

So many therefore of these professors as saw the evil of these things, in these parts, and whose hearts the Lord had touched with heavenly zeal for his truth, they shook off this yoke of anti-Christian bondage, and as the Lord's free people, joined themselves (by a covenant of the Lord) into a church estate, in the fellowship of the gospel, to walk in all his ways, made known, or to be made known unto them, according to their best endeavors, whatsoever it should cost them, the Lord assisting them. And that it cost them something this ensuing history will declare. . . .

But after these things they could not long continue in any peaceable condition, but were hunted and persecuted on every side, so as their former afflictions were but as fleabitings in comparison of these which now came upon them. For some were taken and clapt up in prison, others had their houses beset and watcht night and day, and hardly escaped their hands; and the most were fain to flee and leave their houses and habitations, and the means of their livelihood. Yet these and many other sharper things which afterward befell them, were no other than they looked for, and therefore were the better prepared to bear them by the assistance of God's grace and spirit. Yet seeing themselves thus molested, and that there was no hope of their continuance there, by a joint consent they resolved to go into the Low Countries, where they heard was freedom of Religion for all men; ...

CHAPTER II

Being thus constrained to leave their native soil and country, their lands and livings, and all their friends and familiar acquaintance, it was much, and thought marvelous by many. But to go into a country they knew not (but by hearsay), where they must learn a new language, and get their livings they knew not how, it being a dear place, and subject to the miseries of war, it was by many thought an adventure almost desperate, a case intolerable, and a misery worse than death. Especially seeing they were not acquainted with trades nor traffic, (by which that country doth subsist,) but had only been used to a plain country life, and the innocent trade of husbandry. But these things did not dismay them (though they did sometimes trouble them) for their desires were set on the ways of God, and to enjoy his ordinances; but they rested on his providence, and knew whom they had believed. ...

CHAPTER IV

After they had lived in this city about some 11. or 12. years, (which is the more observable being the whole time of that famous truce between that state and the Spaniards,) and sundry of them were taken away by death, and many others began to be well stricken in years, the grave mistress Experience having taught them many things, those prudent governors with sundry of the sagest members began both deeply to apprehend their present dangers, and wisely to foresee the future, and think of timely remedy. In the agitation of their thoughts, and much discourse of things hereabout, at length they began to incline to this conclusion, of removal to some other place. Not out of any newfangledness, or other such like giddy humor, by which men are oftentimes transported to their great hurt and danger, but for sundry weighty and solid reasons; some of the chief of which I will here briefly touch. And first, they saw and found by experience the hardness of the place and country to be such, as few in comparison would come to them, and fewer that would bide it out, and continue with them. ... But though they loved their persons, approved their cause, and honored their sufferings, yet they left them as it were weeping, as Orpah did her mother-in-law Naomi, or as those Romans did Cato in Utica, who desired to be excused and borne with, though they could not all be Cato's. For many, though they desired to enjoy the ordinances of God in their purity, and the liberty of the gospel with them, yet, alas, they admitted of bondage, with danger of conscience, rather than to endure these hardships; yea, some preferred and chose the prisons in England, rather than this liberty in Holland, with these afflictions. . . .

They saw that though the people generally bore all these difficulties very cheerfully, and with a resolute courage, being in the best and strength of their years, yet old age began to steal on many of them, (and their great and continual labors, with other crosses and sorrows, hastened it before the time,) so as it was not only probably thought, but apparently seen, that within a few years more they would be in danger to scatter, by necessities pressing them, or sink under their burdens, or both. And therefore according to the divine proverb, that a wise man seeth the plague when it cometh, and hideth himself, Pro. 22. 3., so they like skillful and beaten soldiers were fearful either to be entrapped or surrounded by their enemies, so as they should neither be able to fight nor flee; and therefore thought it better to dislodge betimes to some place of better advantage and less danger, if any such could be found. Thirdly; as necessity was a taskmaster over them, so they were forced to be such, not only to their servants, but in a sort, to their dearest children; the which as it did not a little wound the tender hearts of many a loving father and mother, so it produced likewise sundry sad and sorrowful effects. . . . But that which was more lamentable, and of all sorrows most heavy to be borne, was that many of their children, by these occasions, and the great licentiousness of youth in that country, and the manifold temptations of the place, were drawn away by evil examples into extravagant and dangerous courses, getting the reins off their necks, and departing from their parents. . . . So that they saw their posterity would be in danger to degenerate and be corrupted.

Lastly, (and which was not least,) a great hope and inward zeal they had of laying some good foundation, or at least to make some way thereunto, for the propagating and advancing the gospel of the kingdom of Christ in those remote parts of the world; yea, though they should be but even as stepping-stones unto others for the performing of so great a work.

These, and some other like reasons, moved them to undertake this resolution of their removal; the which they afterward prosecuted with so great difficulty, as by the sequel will appear.

The place they had thoughts on was some of those vast and unpeopled countries of America, which are fruitful and fit for habitation, being devoid of all civil inhabitants, where there are only savage and brutish men, which range up and down, little otherwise than the wild beasts of the same. This proposition being made public and coming to the scanning of all, it raised many variable opinions amongst men, and caused many fears and doubts amongst themselves. Some, from their reasons and hopes conceived, labored to stir up and encourage the rest to undertake and prosecute the same; others, again, out of their fears, objected against it, and sought to divert from it, alleging many things, and those neither unreasonable nor unprobable; as that it was a great design, and subject to many unconceivable perils and dangers; as, besides the casualties of the seas (which none can be freed from) the length of the voyage was such, as the weak bodies of women and other persons worn out with age and travail (as many of them were) could never be able to endure. And yet if they should, the miseries of the land which they should be exposed unto, would be too hard to be borne; and likely, some or all of them together, to consume and utterly to ruinate them. . . . And also those which should escape or overcome these difficulties, should yet be in continual danger of the savage people, who are cruel, barbarous, and most treacherous, being most furious in their rage, and merciless where they overcome; not being content only to kill, and take away life, but delight to torment men in the most bloody manner that may be; flaying some alive with the shells of fishes, cutting off the members and joints of others by piecemeal, and broiling on the coals, eat the collops of their flesh in their sight whilst they live; with other cruelties horrible to be related. And surely it could not be thought but the very hearing of these things could not but move the very bowels of men to grate within them, and make the weak to quake and tremble. . . .

It was answered, that all great and honorable actions are accompanied with great difficulties, and must be both enterprised and overcome with answerable courages. It was granted the dangers were great, but not desperate; the difficulties were many, but not invincible. For though there were many of them likely, yet they were not certain; it might be sundry of the things feared might never befall; others by provident care and the use of good means, might in a great measure be prevented; and all of them, through the help of God, by fortitude and patience, might either be borne, or overcome. . . . After many other particular things answered and alleged on both sides, it was fully concluded by the major part, to put this design in execution, and to prosecute it by the best means they could.

CHAPTER V

But at length the conclusion was, to live as a distinct body by themselves, under the general Government of Virginia; and by their friends to sue to his majesty that he would be pleased to grant them freedom of Religion; and that this might be obtained, they were put in good hope by some great persons, of good rank and quality, that were made their friends. Whereupon 2. were chosen and sent into England (at the charge of the rest) to solicit this matter, who found the Virginia Company very desirous to have them go thither, and willing to grant them a patent, with as ample privileges as they had, or could grant to any, and to give them the best furtherance they could. And some of the chief of that company doubted not to obtain their suit of the king for liberty in Religion. . . . But it proved a harder piece of work than they took it for; for though many means were used to bring it about, yet it could not be effected; . . . Yet thus far they prevailed in sounding his majesty's mind, that he would connive at them, and not molest them, provided they carried themselves peaceably. But to allow or tolerate them by his public authority, under his seal, they found it would not be. And this was all the chief of the Virginia company or any other of their best friends could do in the case. Yet they persuaded them to go on, for they presumed they should not be troubled. . . .

CHAPTER IX

. . . But to omit other things, (that I may be brief,) after long beating at sea they fell with that land which is called Cape Cod; the which being made and certainly known to be it, they were not a little joyful. After some deliberation had amongst themselves and with the master of the ship, they tacked about and resolved to stand for the southward (the wind and weather being fair) to find some place about Hudson's river for their habitation. But after they had sailed that course about half the day they fell amongst dangerous shoals and roaring breakers, and they were so far entangled therewith as they conceived themselves in great danger; and the wind shrinking upon them withal, they resolved to bear up again for the Cape, and thought themselves happy to get out of those dangers before night overtook them, as by God's providence they did. And the next day they got into the Cape-harbor where they rid in safety. . . .

Being thus arrived in a good harbor and brought safe to land, they fell upon their knees and blessed the God of heaven, who had brought them over the vast and furious ocean, and delivered them from all the perils and miseries thereof, again to set their feet on the firm and stable earth, their proper element. And no marvel if they were thus joyful, seeing wise Seneca was so affected with sailing a few miles on the coast of his own Italy; as he affirmed, that he had rather remain twenty years on his way by land, than pass by sea to any place in a short time; so tedious and dreadful was the same unto him. . . .

From hence they departed, and coasted all along, but discerned no place likely for harbor; and therefore hasted to a place that their pilot, (one Mr. Coppin who had been in the country before) did assure them was a good harbor, which he had been in, and they might fetch it before night; of which they were glad, for it began to be foul weather. After some hours' sailing, it began to snow and rain, and about the middle of the afternoon, the wind increased, and the sea became very rough, and they broke their rudder, and it was as much as 2 men could do to steer her with a couple of oars. But their pilot bade them be of good cheer, for he saw the harbor; but the storm increasing, and night drawing on, they bore what sail they could to get in, while they could see. But herewith they broke their mast in 3 pieces, and their sail fell over board, in a very grown sea, so as they had like to have been cast away; yet by God's mercy they recovered themselves, and having the flood with them, struck into the harbor. But when it came to, the pilot was deceived in the place, and said, the Lord be merciful unto them, for his eyes never saw that place before; and he and the mastermate would have run her ashore, in a cove full of breakers, before the wind. But a lusty seaman which steered, bade those which rowed, if they were men, about with her, or else they were all cast away; the which they did with speed. So he bid them be of good cheer and row lustily, for there was a fair sound before them, and he doubted not but they should find one place or other where they might ride in safety. And though it was very dark, and rained sore, yet in the end they got under the lee of a small island, and remained there all that night in safety. But they knew not this to be an island till morning, but were divided in their minds; some would keep the boat for fear they might be amongst the Indians; others were so weak and cold, they could not endure, but got ashore, and with much ado got fire, (all things being so wet,) and the rest were glad to come to them; for after midnight the wind shifted to the northwest, and it froze hard. But though this had been a day and night of much trouble and danger unto them, yet God gave them a morning of comfort and refreshing (as usually he doth to his children), for the next day was a fair sunshining day, and they found themselves to be on an island secure from the Indians, where they might dry their stuff, fix their pieces, and rest themselves, and gave God thanks for his mercies, in their manifold deliverances. And this being the last day of the week, they prepared there to keep the Sabbath. On Monday they sounded the harbor, and found it fit for shipping; and marched into the land, and found diverse cornfields, and little running brooks, a place (as they supposed) fit for situation; at least it was the best they could find, and the season, and their present necessity, made them glad to accept of it. So they returned to their ship again with this news to the rest of their people which did much comfort their hearts.

On the 15 of December: they weighed anchor to go to the place they had discovered, and came within 2 leagues of it, but were fain to bear up again; but the 16 day the wind came fair, and they arrived safe in this harbor. And afterwards took better view of the place, and resolved where to pitch their dwelling; and the 25 day began to erect the first house for common use to receive them and their goods.

THE SECOND BOOK

The rest of this History (if God give me life, and opportunity) I shall, for brevity's sake, handle by way of annals, noting only the heads of principal things, and passages as they fell in order of time, and may seem to be profitable to know, or to make use of. And this may be as the 2 Book.

ANNO 1623

All this while no supply was heard of, neither knew they when they might expect any. So they began to think how they might raise as much corn as they could, and obtain a better crop than they had done, that they might not still thus languish in misery. At length, after much debate of things, the Governor (with the advice of the chiefest amongst them) gave way that they should set corn every man for his own particular, and in that regard trust to themselves; in all other things to go on in the general way as before. And so assigned to every family a parcel of land, according to the proportion of their number for that end, only for present use (but made no division for inheritance), and ranged all boys and youth under some family. This had very good success; for it made all hands very industrious, so as much more corn was planted than otherwise would have been by any means the Governor or any other could use, and saved him a great deal of trouble, and gave far better content. The women now went willingly into the field, and took their little ones with them to set corn, which before would allege weakness and inability; whom to have compelled would have been thought great tyranny and oppression.

The experience that was had in this common course and condition, tried sundry years, and that amongst godly and sober men, may well evince the vanity of that conceit of Plato's and other ancients, applauded by some of later times,—that the taking away of property, and bringing in community into a commonwealth, would make them happy and flourishing; as if they were wiser than God. For this community (so far as it was) was found to breed much confusion and discontent, and retard much employment that would have been to their benefit and comfort. For the young men that were most able and fit for labor and service did repine that they should spend their time and strength to work for other men's wives and children, without any recompense. The strong, or man of parts, had no more in division of victuals and clothes, than he that was weak and not able to do a quarter the other could; this was thought injustice. The aged and graver men to be ranked and equalized in labors, and victuals, clothes, &c., with the meaner and younger sort, thought it some indignity and disrespect unto them. And for men's wives to be commanded to do service for other men, as dressing their meat, washing their clothes, &c., they deemed it a kind of slavery, neither could many husbands well brook it. Upon the point all being to have alike, and all to do alike, they thought themselves in the like condition, and one as good as another; and so, if it did not cut off those relations that God hath set amongst men, yet it did at least much diminish and take of the mutual respects that should be preserved amongst them. And would have been worse if they had been men of another condition. Let none object this is men's corruption, and nothing to the course itself. In answer, seeing all men have this corruption in them, God in his wisdom saw another course fitter for them. . . .

ANNO 1628

About some 3 or 4 years before this time, there came over one Captain Wollaston, (a man of pretty parts,) and with him 3 or 4 more of some eminence, who brought with them a great many servants, with provisions and other implements for to begin a plantation; and pitched themselves in a place within the Massachusetts, which they called, after their Captain's name, Mount-Wollaston. Amongst whom was one Mr. Morton, who, it should seem, had some small adventure (of his own or other men's) amongst them; but had little respect amongst them, and was slighted by the meanest servants. Having continued there some time, and not finding things to answer their expectations, nor profit to arise as they looked for, Captain Wollaston takes a great part of the servants, and transports them to Virginia, where he puts them off at good rates, selling their time to other men; . . . And he, with the consent of the said Rasdall, appointed one Fitcher to be his Lieutenant, and govern the remains of the plantation, till he or Rasdall returned to take further order thereabout. But this Morton abovesaid, having more craft than honesty, (who has been a kind of pettifogger, of Furnefell's Inn,) in the others' absence, watches an opportunity, (commons being but hard amongst them,) and got some strong drink and other junkets, and made them a feast; and after they were merry, he began to tell them, he would give them good counsel. You see (saith he) that many of your fellows are carried to Virginia; and if you stay till this Rasdall return, you will also be carried away and sold for slaves with the rest. Therefore I would advise you to thrust out this Lieutenant Fitcher; and I, having a part in the plantation, will receive you as my partners and consociates; so may you be free from service, and we will converse, trade, plant, and live together as equals, and support and protect one another, or to like effect. This counsel was easily received; so they took opportunity, and thrust Lieutenant Fitcher out of doors, and would suffer him to come no more amongst them, . . . After this they fell to great licentiousness, and led a dissolute life, pouring out themselves into all profaneness. And Morton became lord of misrule, and maintained (as it were) a school of Atheism. . . . They also set up a Maypole, drinking and dancing about it many days together, inviting the Indian women, for their consorts, dancing and frisking together, (like so many fairies, or furies rather,) and worse practices. As if they had anew revived and celebrated the feasts of the Roman Goddess Flora, or the beastly practices of the mad Bacchanalians. Morton likewise (to show his poetry) composed sundry rimes and verses, some tending to lasciviousness, and others to the detraction and scandal of some persons, which he affixed to this idle or idol Maypole. They changed also the name of their place, and instead of calling it Mount Wollaston, they call it Merry Mount, as if this jollity would have lasted ever. But this continued not long, for after Morton was sent for England, (as follows to be declared,) shortly after came over that worthy gentleman, Mr. John Indecott, who brought over a patent under the broad seal, for the government of the Massachusetts, who visiting those parts caused that Maypole to be cut down, and rebuked them for their profaneness, and admonished them to look there should be better walking; so they now, or others, changed the name of their place again, and called it Mount-Dagon.

Now to maintain this riotous prodigality and profuse excess, Morton, thinking himself lawless, and hearing what gain the French and fishermen made by trading of pieces, powder, and shot to the Indians, he, as the head of this consortship, began the practice of the same in these parts; and first he taught them how to use them, to charge, and discharge, and what proportion of powder to give the piece, according to the size or bigness of the same; and what shot to use for fowl, and what for deer. And having thus instructed them, he employed some of them to hunt and fowl for him, so as they became far more active in that employment than any of the English, by reason of their swiftness of foot, and nimbleness of body, being also quick-sighted, and by continual exercise well knowing the haunts of all sorts of game. So as when they saw the execution that a piece would do, and the benefit that might come by the same, they became mad, as it were, after them, and would not stick to give any prize they could attain to for them; accounting their bows and arrows but baubles in comparison of them.

And here I may take occasion to bewail the mischief that this wicked man began in these parts, and which since base covetousness prevailing in men that should know better, has now at length got the upper hand, and made this thing common, notwithstanding any laws to the contrary; so as the Indians are full of pieces all over, both fouling pieces, muskets, pistols, &c. They have also their molds to make shot, of all sorts, as musket bullets, pistol bullets, swan and goose shot, and of smaller sorts; yea, some have seen them have their screw plates to make screw pins themselves, when they want them, with sundry other implements, wherewith they are ordinarily better fitted and furnished than the English themselves. Yea, it is well known that they will have powder and shot, when the English want it, nor cannot get it; . . . O the horribleness of this villainy! how many both Dutch and English have been lately slain by those Indians, thus furnished; and no remedy provided, nay, the evil more increased, and the blood of their brethren sold for gain, as is to be feared; and in what danger all these colonies are in is too well known. Oh! that princes and parliaments would take some timely order to prevent this mischief, and at length to suppress it, by some exemplary punishment upon some of these gainthirsty murderers, (for they deserve no better title,) before their colonies in these parts be overthrown by these barbarous savages, thus armed with their own weapons, by these evil instruments, and traitors to their neighbors and country. But I have forgot myself, and have been too long in this digression; but now to return. This Morton having thus taught them the use of pieces, he sold them all he could spare; and he and his consorts determined to send for many out of England, and had by some of the ships sent for above a score. The which being known, and his neighbors meeting the Indians in the woods armed with guns in this sort, it was a terror unto them, who lived straggingly, and were of no strength in any place. . . . Besides, they saw they should keep no servants, for Morton would entertain any, how vile soever, and all the scum of the country, or any discontents, would flock to him from all places, if this nest was not broken; . . .

So sundry of the chief of the straggling plantations, meeting together, agreed by mutual consent to solicit those of Plymouth (who were then of more strength than them all) to join with them, to prevent the further growth of this mischief, and suppress Morton and his consorts before they grew to further head and strength. . . . Those of Plymouth being thus sought to by their messengers and letters, and weighing both their reasons, and the common danger, were willing to afford them their help; though themselves had least cause of fear or hurt. So, to be short, they first resolved jointly to write to him, and in a friendly and neighborly way to admonish him to forbear these courses, and sent a messenger with their letters to bring his answer. But he was so high as he scorned all advice, and asked who had to do with him; he had and would trade pieces with the Indians in dispite of all, with many other scurrilous terms full of disdain. They sent to him a second time, and bade him be better advised, and more temperate in his terms, for the country could not bear the injury he did; it was against their common safety, and against the king's proclamation. He answered in high terms as before, and that the king's proclamation was no law; demanding what penalty was upon it. It was answered, more than he could bear, his majesty's displeasure. But insolently he persisted, and said the king was dead and his displeasure with him, and many the like things; and threatened withal that if any came to molest him, let them look to themselves, for he would prepare for them. Upon which they saw there was no way but to take him by force; and having so far proceeded, now to give over would make him far more haughty and insolent. So they mutually resolved to proceed, and obtained of the Governor of Plymouth to send Captain Standish, and some other aid with him, to take Morton by force. The which accordingly was done; but they found him to stand stiffly in his defense, having made fast his doors, armed his consorts, set diverse dishes of powder and bullets ready on the table; and if they had not been over armed with drink, more hurt might have been done. They summoned him to yield, but he kept his house, and they could get nothing but scoffs and scorns from him; but at length, fearing they would do some violence to the house, he and some of his crew came out, but not to yield, but to shoot; but they were so steeled with drink as their pieces were too heavy for them; himself with a carbine (overcharged and almost half filled with powder and shot, as was after found) had thought to have shot Captain Standish; but he stept to him, and put by his piece, and took him. Neither was there any hurt done to any of either side, save that one was so drunk that he ran his own nose upon the point of a sword that one held before him as he entered the house; but he lost but a little of his hot blood. Morton they brought away to Plymouth, where he was kept, till a ship went from the Isle of Shoals for England, with which he was sent to the Council of New England; and letters written to give them information of his course and carriage; and also one was sent at their common charge to inform their Honors more particularly, and to prosecute against him. . . . But I have been too long about so unworthy a person, and bad a cause.

1856

Edward Johnson
(1598-1672)

Born in Canterbury, England, and trained as a joiner, Edward Johnson made his first trip to New England in 1630-1631. After returning to England to get his wife and family, he settled in Charlestown, Mass., in 1636. One of the founders of Woburn, Mass., in 1640, Johnson held numerous offices in the Massachusetts government. *The Wonder-Working Providence of Scion's*

Saviour in New England (London, published 1653, dated 1654) was first issued as *A History of New-England, from the English planting in the Yeere 1628 untill the Yeere 1652.*

BIBLIOGRAPHY: *DAB.* J. F. Jameson, ed. *The Wonder-Working Providence* (New York, 1910), with notes.

From *The Wonder-Working Providence of Scion's Saviour*

CHAPTER VIII
Of the wonderful Preparation the Lord Christ by his Providence, wrought for his peoples' abode in this Western world.

Now let all men know the admirable Acts of Christ for his Churches, and chosen, are universally over the whole Earth at one and the same time, but sorry man cannot so discourse of them; And therefore let us leave our English Nation in way of preparation for this Voyage intended, and tell of the marvelous doings of Christ preparing for his peoples' arrival in the Western World, whereas the Indians report they beheld to their great wonderment that perspicuous bright blazing Comet (which was so famously noted in Europe) anon after Sunset it appeared as they say in the Southwest, about three hours continuing in their Horizon, for the space of thirty sleeps (for so they reckon their days) after which uncouth sight they expected some strange things to follow, and the rather, because not long before the whole Nation of the Mattachusets were so affrighted with a Ship that arrived in their Bay, having never seen any before, thus they report some persons among them discerning a great thing to move toward them upon the Waters, wondering what Creature it should be, they run with their light canoes, (which are a kind of Boats made of Birch Rinds, and sowed together with the roots of white Cedar Trees) from place to place, stirring up all their Countrymen to come forth, and behold this monstrous thing; at this sudden news the shores for many miles were filled with this naked Nation, gazing at this wonder, till some of the stoutest among them manned out these Canoes, being armed with Bow and Arrows, they approached within shot of the Ship, being becalmed, they let fly their long shafts at her, which being headed with bone some stuck fast, and others dropped into the water, they wondering it did not cry, but kept quietly on toward them, till all of a sudden the Master caused a piece of Ordnance to be fired, which stroke such fear into the poor Indians, that they hasted to shore, having their wonders exceedingly increased; but being gotten among their great multitude, they waited to see the sequel with much amazement, till the Seamen furling up their sails came to an Anchor, manned out their long boat, and went on shore, at whose approach, the Indians fled, although now they saw they were men, who made signs to stay their flight, that they may have Trade with them, and to that end they brought certain Copper Kettles; the Indians by degrees made their approach nearer and nearer till they came to them, when beholding their Vessels, which they had set forth before them, the Indians knocking them were much delighted with the sound, and much more astonished to see they would not break, being so thin, for attaining those Vessels they brought them much Beaver, fraughting them richly away according to their desires, this was the first working providence of Christ to stir up our English Nation, to plant these parts in hope of a rich Trade for Beaverskins, and this made some of our Countrymen make their abode in these parts, whom this Army of Christ at their coming over found as fit helps to further their design in planting the Churches of Christ; Who by a more admirable act of his Providence not long after prepared for his peoples' arrival as followeth.

The Summer after the blazing Star (whose motion in the Heavens was from East to West, pointing out to the sons of men the progress of the glorious Gospel of Christ, the glorious King of his Churches) even about the year 1618, a little before the removal of that Church of Christ from Holland to Plymouth in New England, as the ancient Indians report, there befell a great mortality among them, the greatest that ever the memory of Father to Son took notice of, chiefly desolating those places, where the English afterward planted the Country of Pockanoky, Agissawamg, it was almost wholly deserted, insomuch that the Neighbor Indians did abandon those places for fear of death, fleeing more West & by South, observing the East and by Northern parts were most smitten with this contagion, the Abarginny men consisting of Mattachusets, Wippanaps and Tarratines were greatly weakened, and more especially the three Kingdoms or Sagamore ships of the Mattachusets, who were before this mortality most populous, having under them seven Dukedoms or petty Sagamores, and the Nianticks and Narrowganssits, who before this came were but of little note, yet were they now not much increased by such as fled thither for fear of death, the Pecods (who retained the Name of a war-like people, till afterwards conquered by the English) were also smitten at this time. Their Disease being a sore Consumption, sweeping away whole Families, but chiefly young Men and Children, the very seeds of increase. Their Powwows, which are their Doctors, working partly by Charms, and partly by Medicine, were much amazed to see their Wigwams lie full of dead Corpses, and that now neither Squantam nor Abbamocho could help, which are their good and bad God, and also their Powwows themselves were oft smitten with death's stroke, howling and much lamentation was heard among the living, who being possest with great fear, ofttimes left their dead unburied, their manner being such, that they remove their habitations at death of any, this great mortality being an unwonted thing, feared them the more because naturally the Country is very healthy. But by this means Christ (whose great and glorious works the Earth throughout are altogether for the benefit of his Churches and chosen) not only made room for his people to plant; but also tamed the hard and cruel hearts of these barbarous Indians, insomuch that half a handful of his people landing not long after in Plymouth-Plantation, found little resistance, of whom the Author purposes not to speak particularly, being prevented by the honored Mr. Winslow, who was an eye-witness of the work: only thus much by the way, they were sent to keep possession for their Brethren and fellow Soldiers, who arrived eight years after them, as in process of this story will God-willing appear: and verily herein they quit themselves like men, or rather Christ for and by them, maintaining the place notwithstanding the multitude of difficulties they met withal at their first landing, being in doubtful suspense what entertainment these Barbarians would give them, having with prayer supplicated the Lord in the Name of Christ their King and guide in this their undertaking, they manned out a Boat to discover what store of the Inhabitants were there. Now these men, whose courage exceeded the number, being guided by the provident hand of the most high, landed in some several places; and by making fires gave signs of their approach, now the Indians, whose dwellings are most near the waterside, appeared with their Bows bent and Arrows on the string, let fly their long shafts among this little company, whom they might soon have enclosed, but the Lord otherwise disposed of it, for one Captain Miles Standish having his fowling-piece in a readiness, presented full at them, his shot being directed by the provident Hand of the most high God, struck the stoutest Sachem among them on the right Arm, it being bent over his shoulder to reach an Arrow forth his Quiver, as their manner is to draw them forth in fight, at this stroke they all fled with great swiftness through the Woods and Thickets, then the English, who more thirsted after their conversion than destruction, returned to their Boat without receiving any damage, and soon after arrived where they left their Brethren, to whom they declared the good hand of God toward them, with thankful acknowledgement of this great work of his in preserving them; Yet did they all remain full of encumbered thoughts, the Indians, of whose multitudes they had now some intelligence, together with experience of spirits, and also knew well without commerce with them they were not like long to subsist.

But he, whose work they went about, wrought so rare a Providence for them, which cannot but be admired of all that hear it. Thus it fell as they were discoursing in the Boat they had built for shelter, all of a sudden, an Indian came in among them, at whose speech they were all aghast, he speaking in the English Language, "Much welcome Englishmen," their wonder was the greater, because upon those Coasts they supposed no English had so much as set foot, and verily Christ had prepared him on purpose to give his people entertainment, the Indian having lived in England two year, or thereabout, after which he returned home, and at this time had wandered into those parts in company of other Indians, all this, and the condition of the near adjoining Indians, he soon discovered unto them, at which they were transported beyond themselves very much, what with joy and the mixture of their former fear and affection intervening with the other, surprised all their senses of a sudden, that long it was ere each party could take its proper place, yea, and beyond all this Christ Jesus, by the power of his blessed Spirit, did now work upon all their faculties both of Soul and Body, the great impression of his present Providence might not soon be washed off with the following encumbered cares of a Desert Wilderness; but to contract, they made use of the present opportunity, and by the instrumental means of this Indian, became acquainted and reconciled with most of the Neighboring Indians. And afterward planted a Church of Christ there, and set up civil Government, calling the Name of the place Plymouth: under this jurisdiction there are ten Churches at this very day, this being the first place any English resorted unto for the advancement of the Kingly Government of Christ in this Western World.

1654

William Hubbard

(1621-1704)

Preacher and historian, William Hubbard moved in 1635 from Essex County, England, to Ipswich, Massachusetts. Following his graduation from Harvard in 1642, he studied medicine, but spent most of his life as pastor of First Church at Ipswich. Besides sermons such as *The Happiness of a People* (Boston, 1676), Hubbard wrote *A Narrative of the Troubles with the Indians in New-England* (Boston, 1677) and *A General History of New-England from the Discovery to 1680*, first printed in *Coll. Mass. Hist. Soc.*, 2nd Ser., V-VI (1815).

BIBLIOGRAPHY: *DAB*. J. L. Sibley, *Biographical Sketches of Graduates of Harvard University*, I (1873). K. B. Murdock, "William Hubbard and the Providential Interpretation of History," *Proc. Amer. Antiq. Soc.*, LII (1943).

From *A Narrative of the Troubles with the Indians*

THE PEQUOD WAR

The report of the unheard of cruelties forementioned, which had been perpetrated by the Pequods filling the ears of the English throughout the country; it was agreed by the joint consent of the English throughout the three colonies to unite all their forces together for suppressing the common enemy, early in the spring, A.D. 1637, who were also moved thereunto by their own necessities as well as by the earnest request of their friends at Connecticut.

Those of Plymouth being written unto by the Governor of the Massachusetts, appeared very cordially willing thereunto, to which end they agreed to send fifty men at their own charge, with as much speed as the matter required, . . . but before they could be dispatched away the next spring, news was brought that the enemy was wholly routed, so as their journey was stopped, and their good will accepted for the deed; . . . And for the other two colonies, those of Connecticut being quickened on by the spur of necessity, and present sense of the insolence daily acted at their very doors, were soonest upon their march, and by the good hand of God upon them, they had given the main stroke before the friends of the Massachusetts could come up with them, . . .

The colony of the Massachusetts determined to send an hundred and sixty, of whom an hundred and twenty were ordered under the conduct of Capt. Patrick of Watertown, and Capt. Trask of Salem, Capt. Stoughton of Dorchester being to command in chief; with whom was sent that holy man of God, Mr. John Wilson, (pastor of the church of Boston) the char-iots and horsemen of our Israel, by whose faith and prayer, as sometimes was said of Luther, (in reference to Germany) the country was preserved, so as it was confidently believed that no enemy should break in upon a place whilst he survived, which as some have observed accordingly came to pass.

The matter requiring great expedition, and it being long before the whole company could be dispatched away, Capt. Patrick with forty men were sent beforehand, to be sure to meet with those of Connecticut in case they should be in action, before the rest of our forces could get into a readiness, which accordingly came to pass; for the main business in tak-ing the fort was over, even before the said Patrick could get thither.

The assaulting and surprising of this Indian fort being the most re-markable piece of service in that whole expedition; take it as it was de-livered in writing by that valiant, faithful and prudent commander, Capt. Mason, chief in the action, who lived long after to reap the fruit of his labor, and enjoy the benefit of that day's service, having an inheritance given him in that part of the country, as a just reward of his faithful ser-vice on that day as well as at other times.

"On Saturday, myself, with Capt. Underhill, and Lt. Sealy, with our guard marched to Canonicus by land, being about five miles distant, where we were kindly entertained after their manner: . . . our Sabbath being on the morrow, we adjourned our meeting until Monday, at which time there assembled Miantonimo with the chiefest of them about two hundred men; and being solemnly set for consultation after their manner, told them we were now going, God assisting, to revenge the wrong com-mitted and bloodshed by their and our enemies, upon our native country-men, not anyway desiring their aid, unless they would voluntarily send, which they did exceedingly approve of: Moreover we told them that the English and they had always been friends for ought we knew, and so were we with the Indians that had not wronged Englishmen, which they acknowledged, and so made a large description of the Pequod's country, and told us they would send men with us; so we resolved there to keep our rendezvous at Canonicus' plantation, on the morrow night, being Tuesday; but the wind being stiff, we could not land our men until five or six of the clock in the afternoon, at which time I landed on Narragan-set shore with thirty-two men, and so marched to the place of rendezvous formerly appointed: Capt. Underhill and my Lt. landed the rest, and came up to me that night . . . whereupon we were constrained to set for-ward towards the Pequods, with seventy-seven English, and about sixty river Indians, and as I suppose near two hundred Narragansets, and marched that night to the eastern Nianticks, where we kept our rendez-vous that night: the Sachem of the place adding about an hundred of his men unto us.

"We set forward and marched about ten miles, where making an alta (or halt) there we held a consultation with the Indians, who desired to know what we intended. We told them that we resolved to assault Sassacous's fort, at which they were all stricken and as it were amazed with fear, as they plainly confessed; . . .

"About two hours before day we marched toward the fort, being weary and much spent; many of us having slept none at all.

"And so we began to march towards the fort, the Lord being pleased wonderfully to assist and encourage us, after a tedious march of three or four miles: About break of day we came fair in view of the fort, standing on the top of an hill not steep; the Indians all falling back, were suddenly vanished out of sight, so we made an alta, and sent back for our guide who had promised to go with us to the fort, but his heart we saw much failed him; we asked him what they intended who promised to wing us, and to surround the fort; he told us they were much afraid; but he, seeing our resolution, went to them and prevailed with divers of them to come up to us; we told them their best course would be to flank the fort on both sides, and having no time longer to confer, we proceeded; Capt. Underhill to the western entrance with one division, myself to the eastern as silent as possibly we could; so it pleased God we came up within two rods of the Palisado, before we were discovered, at which time a dog began to bark, and an Indian cried out, but not being myself rightly informed by the Indian guide, of the right entrance, though there was a little postern door, which I had thought to have attempted to break down with my foot; but the Lord directed me otherwise for the better; for I then feared we could not there enter with our arms, which proved true. So I suddenly hasted to the Palisado, and putting in the muzzle of my piece, and discharged upon them, and so did the rest with all celerity; we then suddenly hastened on toward that side which stood toward the water; where I concluded was an entrance, and instantly fell upon it, being only barred with two forked boughs, or branches of some trees, and hastening over them, I drew one after me: my Lieutenant drawing the other outward. We suddenly fell upon the wigwams; the Indians cried out in a most hideous manner, some issuing out of the wigwams, shooting at us desperately, and so creeping under beds that they had. We had resolved awhile not to have burned it, but seeing we could not come at them, I resolved to set it on fire, after divers of them were slain, and some of our men sore wounded; so entering one of their wigwams, I took a fire brand (at which time an Indian drawing an arrow had killed him, but one Davis, his Sergeant cut the bowstring with his cutlass) and suddenly kindled a fire in the mats wherewith they were covered, and fell to a retreat and surrounded the fort; the fire increasing violently, insomuch as that they were constrained to climb to the top of the Palisado; from whence they were soon fetched down, I suppose to the number of an hundred and forty. . . . Many of them issuing forth were suddenly slain either by the English or Indians, who were in a ring without us; all being dispatched and ended in the space of an hour, having two of our men slain, and sixteen wounded. . . ."

This service being thus happily accomplished by these few hands that came from Connecticut; within a while after, the forces sent from the Massachusetts under the conduct of Capt. Stoughton as commander in chief, arrived there also, who found a great part of the work done to their hands, in the surprisal of the Pequods' fort as aforesaid, which was yet but the breaking of the nest, and unkennelling those savage wolves; for the body of them, with Sassacous the chief Sachem (whose very name was a terror to all the Narragansets) were dispersed abroad and scattered all over their country, yet so far were the rest dismayed, that they never durst make any assault upon the English, who in several parties were scattered about in pursuit of them.

It was not long after Capt. Stoughton's soldiers came up, before news was brought of a great number of the enemy, that were discovered by the side of a river up the country, being first trepanned by the Narragansets, under pretence of securing them, but were truly hemmed in by them, though at a distance, yet so as they could not, or durst not stir, from the place, by which means our forces of the Massachusetts made an easy conquest of some hundreds of them, who were there cooped up as in a pound; not daring to fight, nor able to fly away, and so were all taken without any opposition. The men among them to the number of 30, were turned presently into Charon's ferryboat, under the command of skipper Gallop, who dispatched them a little without the harbor; the females and children were disposed of according to the will of the conquerors, some being given to the Narragansets, and other Indians that assisted in the service.

The rest of the enemy being first fired out of their stronghold, were taken and destroyed, a great number of them being seized in the places where they intended to have hid themselves, the rest fled out of their own country over Connecticut river, up towards the Dutch plantation. . . . Sassacous suspecting (and not without just cause) what the matter was, made his escape from the rest, with 20 or 30 of his men to the Mohawks, by whom himself and they that were with him, were all murdered afterward, being hired thereunto by the Narragansets, as was confidently affirmed and believed.

Thus this treacherous and cruel villain with his companions, having against his faith and promise, as well as contrary to the laws of nature and nations, murdered several others, both of the Dutch and English nation, is in the same manner himself, against the laws of hospitality murdered by those to whom he fled for refuge. Vengeance is mine, saith the Lord, I will repay it. . . .

In July 1638, Uncas the Sachem of the Mohegins, having entertained some of the Pequods, came to the Governor at Boston with a present, and was much dejected because it was not first accepted: But afterwards the Governor and Council being satisfied about his innocence, they accepted it, whereupon he promised to the order of the English, both touching the Pequods he had received, and as concerning the differences betwixt the Narragansets and himself, and confirmed all with this compliment; this heart, said he, (laying his hand upon his heart) is not mine but yours, command me any difficult service and I will do it, I have no men but they are all yours, I will never believe any Indian against the English any more; and so he continued for ever after, as may be seen in the following transactions between the Indians and the English: whereupon he was dismissed with some small reward, and went home very joyful, carrying a letter of approbation for himself and his men, through the English plantations.

This was the issue of the Pequod war, which in the day of it here in New England was as formidable to the country in general as the present war with Philip; the experience of which, because it may administer much comfort and encouragement to the surviving generation as well as of praise and thanksgiving to Almighty God, from all those who have thus long quietly enjoyed the benefit and reaped the fruit of their labor and courage who engaged therein, the more pains hath been taken to search out the broken pieces of that story and thus put them together, before the memory thereof was buried in the ruins of time, and past the recovery and knowledge of the present age. . . .

KING PHILIP'S WAR

. . . But perceiving that little good was to be done upon the enemy in those parts, it was agreed that what corn was left at Deerfield, being threshed out as well as they could in those tumults (above 3000 bushels was supposed to be there standing in stack) should be brought to Hadley, and to wait further time to fight the enemy. It came to Capt. Lothrop's turn, or rather it was his choice with about 30 men to guard several carts laden with corn and other goods. The company under Capt. Mosely then quartering at Deerfield, intended that day to pursue after the enemy. But upon Sept. 18, that most fatal day, the saddest that ever befell New England, as the company under Capt. Lothrop were marching along with the carts, (it may be too securely) never apprehending danger so near, they were suddenly set upon, and almost all cut off, (90 killed, teamsters included) not above 7 or 8 escaping: Which great defeat came to pass by the unadvised proceedings of the Captain (who was himself slain in the first assault) although he wanted neither courage nor skill to lead his soldiers; but having taken up a wrong notion about the best way and manner of fighting with the Indians (which he was always wont to argue for) viz. that it were best to deal with the Indians in their own way, i.e. by skulking behind trees, and taking their aim at single persons, which is the usual manner of the Indians fighting one with another; but herein was his great mistake, in not considering the great disadvantage a smaller company would have in dealing that way with a greater multitude: For if five have to deal with one, they may surround him, and every one take his aim at him, while he can level at but one of his enemies at a time: Which gross mistake of his, was the ruin of a choice company of young men, the very flower of the county of Essex, all culled out of the towns belonging to that county, none of which were ashamed to speak with the enemy in the gate: their dear relations at home mourning for them, like Rachel for her children, and would not be comforted, not only because they were not, but because they were so miserably lost.

. . . For the Indians, notwithstanding their subtlety and cruelty, durst not look an Englishman in the face in the open field, nor were they ever yet known to kill any man with their guns, unless when they could lie in wait for him in ambush, or behind some shelter, taking aim undiscovered; so that it was judged by those that escaped, that there were 7 or 800 Indians at least that encountered that company of 80 English, yet if they had kept together in a body, and fought marching, they might have escaped the numbers of the enemy, with little loss in comparison of what they sustained. For the valiant and successful Capt. Mosely, and his Lt. coming (though too late) to their rescue, marched through and through that great body of Indians, and yet came off with little or no loss in comparison of the other. . . .

INDIAN STRATEGY

It is worth the noting, what faithfulness and courage some of the Christian Indians, with the said Captain Pierce, showed in the fight. One of them, whose name was Amos, after the Captain was shot in his leg or thigh, so as he was not able to stand any longer, would not leave him, but charging his gun several times, fired stoutly upon the enemy, till he saw that there was no possibility for him to do any further good to Capt. Pierce, nor yet to save himself, if he stayed any longer; therefore he used this policy, perceiving that the enemy had all blackened their faces, he also stooping down pulled out some blacking out of a pouch he carried with him, discolored his face therewith, and so making himself look as much like Hobamackco, as any of his enemies, he ran amongst them a little while, and was taken for one of them, as if he had been searching for the English, until he had an opportunity to escape away among the bushes; therein imitating the cuttle fish, which, when it is pursued, or in danger, casteth out of its body a thick humor, as black as ink, through which it passes away unseen by the pursuer.

It is reported of another of these Cape Indians, (friends to the English of Plymouth) that being pursued by one of the enemy, he betook himself to a great rock where he sheltered himself for a while; at last perceiving that his enemy lay ready with his gun on the other side to discharge upon him, as soon as he stirred away from the place where he stood: In the issue he thought of this politic stratagem to save himself, and destroy his enemy, (for as Solomon said of old, wisdom is better than weapons of war) he took a stick, and hung his hat upon it, and then by degrees gently lifted it up, till he thought it would be seen, and so become a fit mark for the other that watched to take aim at. The other taking it to be his head, fired a gun and shot through the hat; which our Christian Indian perceiving, boldly held up his head and discharged his own gun upon the real head, not the hat of his adversary, whereby he shot him dead upon the place, and so had liberty to march away with the spoils of his enemy.

UNCAS

And because in the present narrative there hath been frequent mention made of Uncas, the Mohegin Sachem, and of his faithfulness to the interest of the English, I add in this place, that it is suspected by them that knew him best, that in his heart he is no better affected to the English or their religion, than the rest of his countrymen, and that it hath been his own advantage that hath led him to be thus true to them who have upheld him as formerly against the Pequods, so of late against the Narragansets; yet hath he not long since been convinced of the truth of our religion, and vanity of his own, as himself hath solemnly confessed; which will evidently appear by the passage that follows, which I shall here represent just as it was from under the hand of that Reverend person it relates unto, namely, Mr. Fitch, pastor of the church at Norwich, near unto Uncas's place. There was a great drought the last summer; but as it seems, it was more extreme in those parts than with us about Massachusetts; and although probably the English might have prayed for rain themselves without any motion from the Indians, yet their address to the said Mr. Fitch on such an account, with the consequences thereof, is very remarkable, which take in his own words:

"Concerning the drought, &c. the true narrative of that providence is this: In August last such was the want of rain, that the Indian corn was not only dried and parched up, but the apple trees withered, the fruit and leaves fell off as in autumn, and some trees seeming to be dead with that drought; the Indians came into town and lamented their want of rain, and that their powwows could get none in their way of worship, desiring me that I would seek to God for rain: I appointed a fast day for the purpose; the day being come it proved clear without any clouds until sunsetting when we came from the meeting, and then some clouds arose; the next day remained cloudy; then Uncas with many Indians came to my house, Uncas lamented there was such a want of rain: I asked whether if God should send us rain he would not attribute it to their powwows; he answered no, for they had done their utmost and all in vain; I replied, if you will declare it before all these Indians you shall see what God will do for us, for although this year he hath shown his anger against the English and not only against the Indians, yet he hath begun to save us, and I have found by experience twice in the like case, when we sought by fasting and prayer he hath given us rain, and never denied us. Then Uncas made a great speech to the Indians (which were many) confessing that if God should then send rain, it could not be ascribed to their powwowing, but must be acknowledged to be an answer of our prayers. This day they spread more and more, and the next day there was such plenty of rain that our river rose more than two feet in height."

1677

BIOGRAPHY

Increase Mather
(1639-1723)

Author of more than a hundred works, Increase Mather, the youngest son of Richard Mather, received his A.B. at Harvard in 1656 and his M.A. at Trinity College, Dublin, in 1658. After preaching in England, he returned to New England in 1661, took a position in his father's church at Dorchester, and married Maria Cotton, daughter of John Cotton, in 1662. Mather moved to the Second Church, Boston, in 1664, and thereafter held numerous clerical and political offices, among them the presidency of Harvard. Among his works are *The Life and Death . . . of Mr. Richard Mather* (Cambridge, 1670), *Kometographia;* or, *A Discourse Concerning Comets* (Boston, 1683), *An Arrow Against Profane and Promiscuous Dancing* (Boston, 1684), and *An Essay for Recording Illustrious Providences* (Boston, 1684).

BIBLIOGRAPHY: T. J. Holmes, *Increase Mather: A Bibliography of His Works,* 2 Vols. (Cleveland, 1931). *The Mather Papers,* in *Coll. Mass. Hist. Soc.,* 4th Ser., VIII (1868). S. A. Green, ed. *Diary by Increase Mather* (Cambridge, 1900), covers 1674-1687. K. B. Murdock, *Increase Mather: The Foremost American Puritan* (Cambridge, 1925).

From *The Life and Death of Mr. Richard Mather*

There is in the Parish of Winwick in the County of Lancaster, a small Country Town or Village called Lowton: In which Village Richard Mather was born Anno 1596. His Parents Thomas and Margarite Mather were of Ancient Families in Lowton aforesaid, but by reason of some unhappy Mortgages they were reduced unto a low condition as to the World. Nevertheless, God so disposed their hearts, that they were willing to Educate this their Son in good Learning: Concerning which he (after that the Lord was pleased to bestow not only Learning but Grace upon him) hath sometimes expressed himself, saying, By what principles and motives my Parents were chiefly induced to keep me at School, I have not to say, nor do I certainly know: But this I must needs say, that this was the singular good Providence of God towards me, (who hath the hearts of all men in his hand) thus to incline the hearts of my Parents; for in this thing the Lord of Heaven showed me such favor, as had not been showed to many my Predecessors and Contemporaries in that place.

Now his Parents being strongly bent in spirit to have their Son a

Scholar, they sent him to Winwick School, which was about four miles distant from his Father's house. In the Winter season they boarded him at Winwick; but such was his desire after knowledge, that in the summer he traveled every day thither. Whil'st he was thus at School he met with no small discouragement, for that the Schoolmaster under whom he was, although he had an excellent faculty for teaching in Grammar-Learning, and many were trained up by him, so as to be sent unto Oxford and Cambridge, for Instruction in higher Studies; yet was he very severe and partial in his discipline. Junius was almost quite discouraged from his Studies, when being a School boy his Master would beat him eight times a day whether in fault or no fault: The like Magisterial harshness caused him of whom we write, earnestly to desire that his Father would take him from School, and dispose of him to some other Calling. Himself afterwards, when he had waded through these difficulties, would say, God intended better for me, than I would have chosen for myself; and therefore my Father, though in other things indulgent enough, yet in this would never condescend to my request, but by putting me in hope that by his speaking to the Master, things would be amended, would still overrule me to go on in my Studies; and good it was for me to be overruled by him, and his discretion, rather than to be left to my own affection and desire. But Oh that all Schoolmasters would learn Wisdom, Moderation and Equity towards their Scholars, and seek rather to win the hearts of Children by righteous, loving, and courteous usage, than to alienate their minds by partiality and undue severity, which had been my utter undoing, had not the good Providence of God, and the Wisdom and Authority of my Father prevented. . . .

Having been thus long kept at School, he was called to leave his Father's Family. The occasion whereof was this. At a place called Toxteth Park near Liverpool, there dwelt a wise and Religious People, who being desirous of the good of themselves and their Posterity, intended to erect a School amongst them, for the Education of their Children. It came into their minds to send unto the Schoolmaster of Winwick, to inquire whether he had any of his Scholars whom he would recommend unto them for such a service: who having received their desires, forthwith communicated the same to this his Scholar, and to his Father, to see if the Motion would stand with their acceptance. He was desirous rather to have gone to the University, but his Father closed with the Offer; whence it was in fine mutually embraced, so that he removed from his Father's house to Toxteth (Anno 1611.) there to teach School. Nor is it any disparagement to his Worth that he was once a Schoolmaster; for very eminent Divines have been so, as of our own Nation, Mr. Hieron, Mr. Whitaker, Mr. Vines, not to mention others, but rather an Eminency; the like seldom known, that one should be found fit to be a Schoolmaster at fifteen years of Age: Yet the Lord helped him in those his young years to carry it with such Wisdom and Love and Gravity amongst his Scholars as was to admiration, so as that he was by them both loved and feared, beyond what is usual, even where there are aged Masters.

His being thus employed was more ways than one advantageous to him: for by this means he became a more accurate Grammarian than Divines usually are. Being also diligent in his Studies whil'st he continued in this way of Employment, he became a Proficient in other Arts, as in Logic, Rhetoric, yea and in Theology. Moreover, it afterwards appeared to be of God, that he was Called to such a work in such a place, for there the effectual Conversion of his Soul unto the Lord, was wrought in his tender years, even afore his going to Oxford; whence he was preserved from those Corruptions which undid many of his Contemporaries, through the Temptation which in the University they met with. The means of his Conversion was partly by seeing a strange difference between himself and sundry in that godly Family, where Divine Providence had cast his Lot in Toxteth, viz. the Family of Mr. Edward Aspinwall, who was a Learned and Religious Gentleman. Now he observed that the way and walking of that holy man, was such as himself had not as yet been accustomed unto, which caused sad fears to arise in his Soul, lest haply he might not be in the way which leadeth unto Eternal Salvation. Also Mr. Harrison, then a famous Minister at Hyton, Preaching upon Joh. 3. 3. concerning the necessity of Regeneration, and at the same time reading a book of Mr. Perkins his, showing how far a Reprobate may go, God blessed these three things not only to Conviction, but to Conversion. This was Anno 1614. The pangs of the New Birth were exceedingly terrible to him, inasmuch as many times when they were at Meals in the Family where he sojourned, he would absent himself to retire under hedges and other secret places, there to lament his misery before God. But after some time, the Lord revived his broken heart, by sending the Holy Spirit in the Ministry of the Word to apply the Precious Promises of the Gospel to his Soul.

Being thus become a New Creature, he was the more eminently a Blessing in the Family, and in the Calling which the Lord had disposed of him in: And such notice was taken of him, as that even from places remote Children were sent unto him for Instruction and Education; and many were, by the Lord's blessing upon his Endeavors, fitted for, and sent unto the University. Some years having been past over in this way of Employ, he resolved (σὺν Θεῷ) to spend some time in one of the Universities, as apprehending that there, by converse with Learned men, and other Advantages not elsewhere to be had, he might gain more than by his private Studies in the Country. Accordingly he went to Oxford, and continued for some time there in Brazen Nose College. Being there, he was variously affected: for it was a joy to him to find many there who had been his quondam Scholars. It was also a joy to him that he had such leisure to follow his Studies, and by Disputations, Lectures, Books, Conferences with Learned men, &c. marvelous Advantages to obtain a

Treasure of Knowledge. But his heart being afore this touched with the fear of God, the great Superstition and Profaneness which he was forced there to behold, was no small grief unto him.

Soon after his coming to Oxford, he came into Acquaintance with the Learned Doctor Worall, who was helpful to him in directing him as to the course of his private Studies. Amongst other things, he advised to read the Works of Peter Ramus; which counsel he followed, and saw no cause to repent of his so doing. But before he had spent so much time in Oxford as he could have wished that he might have done; the People in Toxteth, whose Children had been taught by him, sent to him, desiring that he would return unto them to instruct not so much their Children as themselves, and that not in mere Human Literature, but in the things of God. This Call, after due Consideration, for weighty Reasons he accepted of. Being then returned to Toxteth, he Preached his first Sermon November 30, 1618. There was a very great Concourse of people to hear him, and his Labors were highly accepted of by the judicious: Such was the vastness of his Memory, as that the things which he had prepared and intended to deliver at once, contained no less than six long Sermons. . . .

After that he had thus painfully and faithfully spent fifteen years in the Work of the Ministry, he that holds the Stars in his right hand, had more work for him to do elsewhere; and therefore the rage of Satan and wrath of men must be suffered to break forth, until this choice Instrument had his mouth stopped in unrighteousness. The Lecture which he kept at Prescot caused him to be much taken notice of, and so was the more unto the Adversaries of the Truth an object of Envy. *Magnam famam & magnam quietem eodem tempore nemo potest acquirere.* Quint. Wherefore Complaints being made against him for Non-Conformity to the Ceremonies, he was by the Prelates Suspended. This was in August, Anno 1633. Under this Suspension he continued until November following: But then, by means of the Intercession of some Gentlemen in Lancashire, and by the influence of Simon Byby (a near Alliance of the Bishops) he was restored again to his Public Ministry. After his Restoration he more fully searched into, and also in his Ministry handled the Points of Church Discipline. And God gave him in those days not only to see, but also to instruct others in the Substance of the Congregational Way, which came to pass by his much reading of the holy Scriptures, and his being very conversant in the Writings of Cartwright, Parker, Baynes, and Ames. But this restored Liberty continued not long; for Anno 1634. Bishop Neal (he who was sometimes by King James pleasantly admonished of his Preaching Popery, because of his carriage he taught the people to pray for a blessing upon his dead Predecessor) being now become Archbishop of York, sent his Visitors into Lancashire; of whom Doctor Cousins (whose Cozening Devotions Mr. Pryn hath made notorious to the World) was one: These Visitors being come into the Country μετὰ πιλλῆς ψαντασίας kept their Courts at Wigan; where, amongst many other unrighteous proceedings, having Mr. Mather convened before them, they passed a sentence of Suspension against him, merely for his Non-Conformity to the Inventions of men in the Worship of God. It was marvelous to see how God was with him, causing a Spirit of Courage and of Glory to rest upon him, and filling him with wisdom when he stood before those Judges, who were not willing that he should speak for himself, or declare the Reasons which convinced his Conscience of the unlawfulness of that Conformity which they required. Concerning the Lord's presence with him at that time, himself doth in a Manuscript left in his Study thus express it: In the passages of that day, I have this to bless the Name of God for, that the terror of their threatening words, of their Pursuivants, and of the rest of their Pomp, did not so terrify my mind, but that I could stand before them without being daunted in the least measure, but answered for myself such words of truth and soberness as the Lord put into my mouth, not being afraid of their faces at all: which supporting and comforting presence of the Lord I count not much less mercy, than if I had been altogether preserved out of their hands.

Being thus silenced from Public Preaching the Word, means was again used by Mr. Mather's friends to obtain his Liberty; but all in vain. The Visitor asked how long he had been a Minister? Answer was made, That he had been in the Ministry fifteen years. And (said he) how often hath he worn the Surplice? Answer was returned, that he had never worn it. What (said the Visitor, swearing as he spake it) preach Fifteen years and never wear a Surplice? It had been better for him that he had gotten Seven Bastards. This was a Visitor's judgment. ἐδέν ὑγιὲς.

Wherefore the case being thus, he betook himself to a private life: and no hope being left of enjoying Liberty again in his Native Land; foreseeing also (*Sapiens Divinat*) the approaching Calamities of England, he meditated a Removal into New England. . . .

Being then fully satisfied concerning the clearness of his call for New England, after many Prayers, and extraordinary seekings unto God, he engaged upon the transportation of himself and Family thither. His parting with his People and other Friends in Lancashire, was like Paul's taking his leave of Ephesus, with much sorrow, many tears being shed by those who expected to see his face no more in this world. This Journey was begun in April 1635 when he traveled to Bristol in order to take Ship there. In this Journey he was forced (as sometime Brentius was) to change his outward Habit that he might travel incognito, because Pursuivants were designed to Apprehend him; but by this means he escaped them. From Bristol he set Sail for New England May 23, 1635. The Lord, after manifold Trials of Faith and Patience, brought him in safety to the desired Haven. It is seldom known, that a man designed in God's Eternal Counsel to special Service for his Name, doth not at one time or other experience Eminent Deliverances of Providence: So it was with this Servant of the Lord not once nor twice. Sundry eminent Salvations from deadly Dangers did the Lord vouchsafe unto him in his Childhood, which he would speak of in his old Age: but the most remarkable and memorable of all other, was that which happened to him on the mighty Waters, where he that sits upon the Floods, and stilleth the raging of the Sea when the Waves thereof roar, and whom the winds obey, showed himself wonderful in goodness; for when the Vessel was upon the Coasts of New England, there arose a fearful Storm (which the Americans are wont to call an Hurricane) by means whereof they were in no small danger; And had not the Lord strangely turned the Wind in an instant, they had all perished upon the Rocks which were just before, and within sight of them in the Ship. The Relation of this observable Providence we shall here set down in Mr. Mather's own words, left written by himself in his Journal from Lancashire to New England. Thus he writeth concerning it.

August 15, 1635. The Lord had not yet done with us, nor had He let us see all His Power and Goodness which he would have us take the knowledge of: And therefore about break of day, he sent a most terrible Storm of Rain and Easterly Wind, whereby we were in as much danger, as I think ever people were. When we came to Land, we found many mighty Trees rent in pieces in the midst of the Bole, and others turned up by the Roots, by the fierceness thereof. We lost in that Morning three Anchors and Cables, one having never been in the water before; two were broken by the violence of the Storm, and the third cut by the Seamen in extremity of distress, to save the ship and their and our Lives. And when our Cables and Anchors were all lost, we had no outward means of Deliverance but by hoisting Sail, if so be we might get to Sea, from amongst the Islands and Rocks where we had Anchored: But the Lord let us see that our Sails could not save us neither, no more than the Cables and Anchors; for by the force of the Wind and Storm the Sails were rent asunder, and split in pieces as if they had been but rotten Rags, so that of divers of them there was scarce left as much as an handbreadth, that was not rent in pieces, or blown away into the Sea: So that at that time all hope that we should be saved, in regard of any outward appearance, was utterly taken away; and the rather, because we seemed to drive with full force of Wind directly upon a mighty Rock standing out in sight above water, so that we did but continually wait when we should hear and feel the doleful crashing of the Ship upon the Rock. In this extremity and appearance of Death, as distress and distraction would suffer us, we cried to the Lord, and he was pleased to have compassion upon us: for by his overruling Providence, and his own immediate good hand, he guided the Ship past the Rock, assuaged the violence of the Sea and of the Wind. It was a day much to be remembered, because on that day the Lord granted us as wonderful a deliverance, as I think ever any people had felt. The Seamen confessed they never knew the like. The Lord so imprint the memory of it in our hearts, that we may be the better for it, and be careful to please him, and to walk uprightly before him as long as we live. And I hope we shall not forget the passages of that morning until our dying day. In all this grievous Storm my fear was the less, when I considered the clearness of my Calling from God this way. And in some measure (the Lord's holy Name be blessed for it) he gave us hearts contented and willing that he should do with us and ours what he pleased, and what might be most for the glory of his Name, and in that we rested ourselves. But when news was brought us into the Gunroom that the danger was past, Oh how our hearts did then relent, and melt within us! We burst out into tears of joy amongst ourselves in love unto our gracious God, and admiration of his kindness, in granting to his poor Servants such an Extraordinary and Miraculous Deliverance. His holy Name be blessed forever!

Thus far is Mr. Mather's Relation of this signal Providence, as left written with his own hand. And this is the more to be taken notice of, because the lives of several Choice Instruments of God's Glory, were then saved: For not only Mr. Mather himself, but two of his Sons, who are now faithful Ministers of God, were in that Vessel; and so likewise was that Worthy Minister of Christ Mr. Jonathan Mitchell, late Faithful and Famous Pastor of the Church of Cambridge in New England, he being then a Child of Eleven years of Age. Also this Deliverance is the more remarkable, in that several Vessels were cast away in that Storm. A Ship called the *Angel Gabriel*, which set out from Bristol with the Vessel wherein Mr. Mather was, being then at Anchor at Pemequid, was broken in pieces; and the very same strange and sudden turn of Wind which saved the Vessel wherein Mr. Mather was, ruined the other which came from England at the same time. Also there was then a Ship, going between Piscataqua and the Bay, which was cast away in this Storm, and all the people therein lost, except two that were spared to report the News. And amongst others in that Vessel which then perished, there was a precious Minister of the Gospel, viz. Mr. Avery, who with his Wife and five Children all perished. This Minister (though it be a Digression, yet the Story being so worthy of remembrance, let it here be recorded) every moment expecting that the next Wave would be a Wave of Death, lifted up his eyes to Heaven, saying, Lord, I cannot challenge a Promise of the preservation of my life, but according to thy Covenant I challenge Heaven: Which he had no sooner spoken, but a Wave immediately came and swept him away, and so wafted him to Heaven indeed. And by the way let it further be noted, That this which hath been mentioned is the only Vessel which miscarried with Passengers from Old England to New; so signally did the Lord in his Providence own the Plantation of New England. . . .

As he was a man faithful and fearing God above many, so the Lord showed great faithfulness unto him, both in making him serviceable unto the last, yea and continuing the vigor of his Spirit, and power of his Ministry. Few men, though young, are known to Preach with such vigor as he did but ten days before his death. Also the Lord was faithful and gracious to him in respect to his Children. It was a special token of Divine favor unto some of the Ancients, that their Sons after them succeeded in the Ministry; so was it with the Fathers of Gregory, Nazianzen, Gregory Nyssa, Basil, Hilary, &c. And the Lord cheered the heart of this his Servant in his old Age, by giving him to see most of his Sons employed in the Ministry many years before their precious Father's decease. He left four Sons in that Work; one of whom, viz. Mr. Eleazer Mather, late Pastor of the Church at Northampton, in New England, went to his rest about three Months after his Father, with him to sound forth the praises of God amongst the Spirits of just men made perfect. The other three are yet surviving, viz. Mr. Samuel Mather, Teacher of a Church in Dublin; Mr. Nathaniel Mather, late Minister of Barnstable in Devon, and since in Rotterdam in Holland; and Increase Mather of Boston in New England.

Concerning his Judgment. Touching matters of Faith and Doctrine, his large Catechism which contains the Sum of the Body of Divinity, doth sufficiently manifest his Orthodoxness to the World. Indeed he was a strenuous opposer of the Errors of the Times. Touching Worship and Discipline, he was for the true Congregational Way, in opposition to both the Extremes of Brownism on the one hand, and Presbyterianism on the other hand. As for Brownism, he was of the same apprehension with Mr. Dod and Mr. Cotton. That God is not wont to make choice of men infamous for gross Vices (as that Brown and Barrow were) to be the Discoverers of momentous Truths. And to manifest that he was far from the Error of that Way, he hath left a judicious Manuscript, proving that although Power, i.e. Privilege and Liberty doth belong to the Fraternity, yet that Rule is proper to the Presbytery of the Church. As for Presbyterianism, his Printed Books in Answer to Mr. Herle and Mr. Rutherford, show how far he was distant from that Persuasion. Also some years before his Death, he prepared for the Press an Elaborate Discourse, Entitled, *A Plea for the Churches of New England;* divided into Two Parts: the former being an Answer to Mr. Rathband's *Narration of Church-Courses in New England;* The other containing Positive Grounds from Scripture and Reason, for the Justification of the Way of the Churches in New England. Not many weeks before his death a Friend acquainting him, that some reported that he had declared himself to be a Presbyterian; He replied, You tell me a strange thing: I have written Books in Defense of the Congregational Way, as differing from the Presbyterian, and doth anyone say I declared myself for that Persuasion? It is nothing so. At the same time it being said to him, that he had the principal hand in the Platform of Discipline, and had he not changed his judgment from that? His Answer was, No, not in any one particular that I know of.

His way of Preaching was plain, aiming to shoot his Arrows not over his peoples' heads, but into their Hearts and Consciences. Whence he studiously avoided obscure phrases, Exotic Words, or an unnecessary citation of Latin Sentences, which some men addict themselves to the use of. Mr. Dod was wont to say, That so much Latin was so much flesh in a Sermon: So did this humble man look upon the affectation of such things in a Popular Auditory to savor of Carnal wisdom. The Lord gave him an excellent faculty in making abstruse things plain, that in handling the deepest Mysteries he would accommodate himself to Vulgar Capacities, that even the meanest might learn something. He knew how to express καινὰ κοινῶ καὶ κοινά καινῶς. He would often use that Saying, *Artis est celare Artem*. And much approved that of Austin; If (said he) I preach Learnedly, then only the Learned and not the Unlearned can understand and profit by me; but if I preach plainly, then Learned and Unlearned both can understand, so I may profit all. He was Mighty in the Scriptures; Whence Mr. Hooker would say of him, My brother Mather is a mighty man. Also his usual way of Delivery was very Powerful, Awakening, and Zealous; especially in his younger years, there being few men of so great strength of body as he, which together with his natural fervor of Spirit, being sanctified, made his Ministry the more powerful. And the Lord went forth with his Labors to the Conversion of many both in England and in New England. Yet though his way of Preaching was plain and zealous, it was moreover Substantial and very Judicious. Even in his beginning times, Mr. Gillebrand (a famous Minister in Lancashire; and the more famous, for that though he did exceedingly Stammer in his ordinary discourse, he would Pray and Preach as fluently as any man) once having heard him Preach, asked what his Name might be? And answer being made that his Name was Mather; Nay (said Mr. Gillebrand) call him Matter, for believe it this man hath Substance in him. Yea, such was his Solidity of Judgment, that some who were his Opposites, yet did therefore greatly respect and honor him. Doctor Parr (then Bishop in the Isle of Man) having heard Mr. Mather was Silenced, lamented it, saying, If Mather be Silenced I am sorry for it, for he was a solid man, and the Church of God hath then a great loss. . . .

Notwithstanding those rare Gifts and Graces wherewith the Lord had adorned him, he was exceeding low and little in his own eyes. Some have thought that his greatest error was, that he did not magnify his Office, as he might and sometimes should have done. If a man must err, it is good erring on that hand. Humble enough, and good enough, was the frequent Saying of a great Divine. And another observeth, That every man hath just as much and no more true worth in him, as he hath Humility. Austin being asked which was the most excellent grace, answered, Humility; and which was the next, answered, Humility; and which was the third, replied again, Humility. That indeed is Comprehensively All, being of great price in the sight of God: And if so, Mr. Mather was a man of much Real Worth.

1670

JOURNALS AND DIARIES

John Winthrop
(1588-1649)

Born in Suffolk, England, the son of a well-to-do landowner, John Winthrop attended Trinity College, Cambridge, for about two years, then returned home to help his father manage Groton Manor, the family estate. He later practiced law in London. Winthrop was a leader of the Massachusetts Bay settlers who arrived in the New World aboard the *Arbella* in 1630. He was either governor or deputy governor of the colony from his arrival until his death. *The Journal*, a history of Massachusetts Bay from 1630 to 1649, was first printed as *A Journal of the Transactions and Occurrences in the Settlement of Massachusetts*, 2 Vols. (Hartford, 1790). After discovery of another manuscript, Winthrop's work was published as *The*

History of New England from 1630 to 1649, 2 Vols. (Boston, 1825-1826), edited by James Savage.

BIBLIOGRAPHY: Savage revised his edition in 1853. J. K. Hosmer, ed. *Winthrop's Journal*, 2 Vols. (New York, 1908). Allyn B. Forbes, gen. ed. *Winthrop Papers*, 5 Vols. (New York, 1929-1947). R. C. Winthrop, *Life and Letters of John Winthrop*, 2 Vols. (Boston, 1864-1867, 2nd ed. 1869). S. E. Morison, *Builders of the Bay Colony* (Boston, 1930). E. S. Morgan, *The Puritan Dilemma; The Story of John Winthrop* (Boston, 1958). D. B. Rutman, *Winthrop's Boston; Portrait of a Puritan Town, 1630-1649* (Chapel Hill, N.C., 1965).

From *The Journal*

[*July 5, 1632*] At Watertown there was (in the view of divers witnesses) a great combat between a mouse and a snake; and, after a long fight, the mouse prevailed and killed the snake. The pastor of Boston, Mr. Wilson, a very sincere, holy man, hearing of it, gave this interpretation: That the snake was the devil; the mouse was a poor contemptible people, which God had brought hither, which should overcome Satan here, and dispossess him of his kingdom. Upon the same occasion, he told the governor, that, before he was resolved to come into this country, he dreamed he was here, and that he saw a church arise out of the earth, which grew up and became a marvelous goodly church.

[*Nov. 5, 1634*] At the court of assistants complaint was made by some of the country, (viz., Richard Brown of Watertown, in the name of the rest,) that the ensign at Salem was defaced, viz. one part of the red cross taken out. Upon this, an attachment was awarded against Richard Davenport, ensign-bearer, to appear at the next court to answer. Much matter was made of this, as fearing it would be taken as an act of rebellion, or of like high nature, in defacing the king's colors; though the truth were, it was done upon this opinion, that the red cross was given to the King of England by the pope, as an ensign of victory, and so a superstitious thing, and a relic of antichrist. What proceeding was hereupon, will appear after, at next court, in the first month; (for, by reason of the great snows and frosts, we used not to keep courts in the three winter months).

[*Jan. 19, 1635*] All the ministers, except Mr. Ward of Ipswich, met at Boston, being requested by the governor and assistants, to consider of these two cases: 1. What we ought to do, if a general governor should be sent out of England? 2. Whether it be lawful for us to carry the cross in our banners?—In the first case, they all agreed, that, if a general governor were sent, we ought not to accept him, but defend our lawful possessions, (if we were able;) otherwise to avoid or protract. For the matter of the cross, they were divided, and so deferred it to another meeting.

[*April 30, 1635*] The governor and assistants sent for Mr. Williams. The occasion was, for that he had taught publicly, that a magistrate ought not to tender an oath to an unregenerate man, for that we thereby have communion with a wicked man in the worship of God, and cause him to take the name of God in vain. He was heard before all the ministers, and very clearly confuted. Mr. Endecott was at first of the same opinion, but he gave place to the truth.

[*May 6, 1635*] A general court was held at Newtown, where John Haynes, Esq., was chosen governor, Richard Bellingham, Esq., deputy governor, and Mr. Hough and Mr. Dummer chosen assistants to the former; and Mr. Ludlow, the late deputy, left out of the magistracy. The reason was, partly, because the people would exercise their absolute power, etc., and partly upon some speeches of the deputy, who protested against the election of the governor as void, for that the deputies of the several towns had agreed upon the election before they came, etc. But this was generally discussed, and the election adjudged good.

Mr. Endecott was also left out, and called into question about the defacing the cross in the ensign; and a committee was chosen, viz., every town chose one, (which yet were voted by all the people,) and the magistrates chose four, who, taking the charge to consider of the offense, and the censure due to it, and to certify the court, after one or two hours' time, made report to the court, that they found his offense to be great, viz., rash and without discretion, taking upon him more authority than he had, and not seeking advice of the court, etc.; uncharitable, in that he, judging the cross, etc., to be a sin, did content himself to have reformed it at Salem, not taking care that others might be brought out of it also; laying a blemish also upon the rest of the magistrates, as if they would suffer idolatry, etc., and giving occasion to the state of England to think ill of us;—for which they adjudged him worthy admonition, and to be disabled for one year from bearing any public office; declining any heavier sentence, because they were persuaded he did it out of tenderness of conscience, and not of any evil intent.

[*Nov. 1639*] At a general court holden at Boston, great complaint was made of the oppression used in the country in sale of foreign commodities; and Mr. Robert Keayne, who kept a shop in Boston, was notoriously above others observed and complained of; and, being convented, he was charged with many particulars; in some, for taking above six-pence in the shilling profit; in some above eight-pence; and, in some small things, above two for one; and being hereof convict, (as appears by the records.) he was fined £200, which came thus to pass: The deputies considered, apart, of his fine, and set it at £200; the magistrates agreed but to £100. So, the court being divided, at length it was agreed, that his fine should be £200, but he should pay but £100, and the other should be respited to the further consideration of the next general court. By this means the magistrates and deputies were brought to an accord, which otherwise had not been likely, and so much trouble might have grown, and the offender escaped censure. For the cry of the country was so great against oppression, and some of the elders and magistrates had declared such detestation of the corrupt practice of this man (which was the more observable, because he was wealthy and sold dearer than most other tradesmen, and for that he was of ill report for the like covetous practice in England, that incensed the deputies very much against him). And sure the course was very evil, especial circumstances considered: 1. He being an ancient professor of the gospel: 2. A man of eminent parts: 3. Wealthy, and having but one child: 4. Having come over for conscience's sake, and for the advancement of the gospel here: 5. Having been formerly dealt with and admonished, both by private friends and also by some of the magistrates and elders, and having promised reformation; being a member of a church and commonwealth now in their infancy, and under the curious observation of all churches and civil states in the world. These added much aggravation to his sin in the judgment of all men of understanding. Yet most of the magistrates (though they discerned of the offense clothed with all these circumstances) would have been more moderate in their censure: 1. Because there was no law in force to limit or direct men in point of profit in their trade. 2. Because it is the common practice, in all countries, for men to make use of advantages for raising the prices of their commodities. 3. Because (though he were chiefly aimed at, yet) he was not alone in this fault. 4. Because all men through the country, in sale of cattle, corn, labor, etc., were guilty of the like excess in prices. 5. Because a certain rule could not be found out for an equal rate between buyer and seller, though much labor had been bestowed in it, and divers laws had been made, which, upon experience, were repealed, as being neither safe nor equal. Lastly, and especially, because the law of God appoints no other punishment but double restitution; and, in some cases, as where the offender freely confesseth, and brings his offering, only half added to the principal. After the court had censured him, the church of Boston called him also in question, where (as before he had done in the court) he did, with tears, acknowledge and bewail his covetous and corrupt heart, yet making some excuse for many of the particulars, which were charged upon him, as partly by pretense of ignorance of the true price of some wares, and chiefly by being misled by some false principles, . . .

The rules for trading were these:—

1. A man may not sell above the current price, i.e., such a price as is usual in the time and place, and as another (who knows the worth of the commodity) would give for it, if he had occasion to use it; as that is called current money, which every man will take, etc.

2. When a man loseth in his commodity for want of skill, etc., he must look at it as his own fault or cross, and therefore must not lay it upon another.

3. Where a man loseth by casualty of sea, or, etc., it is a loss cast upon himself by providence, and he may not ease himself of it by casting it upon another; for so a man should seem to provide against all providences, etc., that he should never lose; but where there is a scarcity of the commodity, there men may raise their price; for now it is a hand of God upon the commodity, and not the person.

4. A man may not ask any more for his commodity than his selling price, as Ephron to Abraham, the land is worth thus much.

The cause being debated by the church, some were earnest to have him excommunicated; but the most thought an admonition would be sufficient.

[*Dec. 1639*] At the general court, an order was made to abolish that vain custom of drinking one to another, and that upon these and other grounds:

1. It was a thing of no good use.

2. It was an inducement to drunkenness, and occasion of quarreling and bloodshed.

3. It occasioned much waste of wine and beer.

4. It was very troublesome to many, especially the masters and mistresses of the feast, who were forced thereby to drink more oft than they would, etc. Yet divers (even godly persons) were very loath to part with this idle ceremony, though (when disputation was tendered) they had no list, nor, indeed, could find any arguments, to maintain it. Such power hath custom, etc.

[*June 22, 1642*] At the same general court there fell out a great business upon a very small occasion. Anno 1636, there was a stray sow in Boston, which was brought to Captain Keayne: he had it cried divers times, and divers came to see it, but none made claim to it for near a year. He kept it in his yard with a sow of his own. Afterwards one Sherman's wife, having lost such a sow, laid claim to it, but came not to see it, till Captain Keayne had killed his own sow. After being showed the stray sow and finding it to have other marks than she had claimed her sow by, she gave out that he had killed her sow. The noise hereof being spread about the town, the matter was brought before the elders of the church as a case of offense; many witnesses were examined, and Captain Keayne was cleared. She not being satisfied with this, by the instigation of one George Story, a young merchant of London, who kept in her house, (her husband being then in England,) and had been brought before the governor upon complaint of Captain Keayne as living under suspicion, she brought the cause to the inferior court at Boston, where, upon a full hearing, Capt. Keayne was again cleared, and the jury gave him £3 for his cost, and he bringing his action against Story and her for reporting about that he had stolen her sow, recovered £20 damages of either of them. Story upon this searcheth town and country to find matter against Captain Keayne about this stray sow, and got one of his witnesses to come into Salem court and to confess there that he had forsworn himself; and upon this he petitions in Sherman's name, to this general court, to have the cause heard again, which was granted, and the best part of seven days were spent in examining of witnesses and debating of the cause; and yet it was not determined, for there being nine magistrates and thirty deputies, no sentence could by law pass without the greater number of both, which neither plaintiff nor defendant had, for there were for the plaintiff two magistrates and fifteen deputies, and for the defendant seven magistrates and eight deputies, the other seven deputies stood doubtful. Much contention and earnestness there was, which indeed did mostly arise from the difficulty of the case, in regard of cross witnesses, and some prejudices (as one professed) against the person, which blinded some men's judgments that they could not attend the true nature and course of the evidence. For all the plaintiff's witnesses amounted to no more but an evidence of probability, so as they might all swear true, and yet the sow in question might not be the plaintiff's. But the defendant's witnesses gave a certain evidence, upon their certain knowledge, and that upon certain grounds, (and these as many and more and of as good credit as the others,) so as if this testimony were true, it was not possible the sow should be the plaintiff's. . . . Further, if the case had been doubtful, yet the defendant's lawful possession ought to have been preferred to the plaintiff's doubtful title, for in equali jure melior est conditio possidentis. But the defendant being of ill report in the country for a hard dealer in his course of trading, and having been formerly censured in the court and in the church also, by admonition for such offenses, carried many weak minds strongly against him. And the truth is, he was very worthy of blame in that kind, as divers others in the country were also in those times, though they were not detected as he was; yet to give every man his due, he was very useful to the country both by his hospitality and otherwise. But one dead fly spoils much good ointment.

There was great expectation in the country, by occasion of Story's clamors against him, that the cause would have passed against the captain, but falling out otherwise, gave occasion to many to speak unreverently of the court, especially of the magistrates, and the report went, that their negative voice had hindered the course of justice, and that these magistrates must be put out, that the power of the negative voice might be taken away. Thereupon it was thought fit by the governor and other of the magistrates to publish a declaration of the true state of the cause, that truth might not be condemned unknown. This was framed before the court brake up; for prevention whereof, the governor tendered a declaration in nature of a pacification, whereby it might have appeared, that, howsoever the members of the court dissented in judgment, yet they were the same in affection, and had a charitable opinion of each other; but this was opposed by some of the plaintiff's part, so it was laid by. And because there was much laboring in the country upon a false supposition, that the magistrate's negative voice stopped the plaintiff in the case of the sow, one of the magistrates published a declaration of the necessity of upholding the same.

[*July* 3, *1645*] According to this agreement, (5) (*July*) 3, presently after the lecture the magistrates and deputies took their places in the meeting house, and the people being come together, and the deputy governor placing himself within the bar, as at the time of the hearing, etc., the governor read the sentence of the court, without speaking any more, for the deputies had (by importunity) obtained a promise of silence from the magistrates. Then was the deputy governor desired by the court to go up and take his place again upon the bench, which he did accordingly, and the court being about to arise, he desired leave for a little speech, which was to this effect.

I suppose something may be expected from me, upon this charge that is befallen me, which moves me to speak now to you; yet I intend not to intermeddle in the proceedings of the court, or with any of the persons concerned therein. Only I bless God, that I see an issue of this troublesome business. I also acknowledge the justice of the court, and, for mine own part, I am well satisfied, I was publicly charged, and I am publicly and legally acquitted, which is all I did expect or desire. And though this be sufficient for my justification before men, yet not so before the God, who hath seen so much amiss in my dispensations (and even in this affair) as calls me to be humble. For to be publicly and criminally charged in this court, is matter of humiliation, (and I desire to make a right use of it,) notwithstanding I be thus acquitted. If her father had spit in her face, (saith the Lord concerning Miriam,) should she not have been ashamed seven days? Shame had lien upon her, whatever the occasion had been. I am unwilling to stay you from your urgent affairs, yet give me leave (upon this special occasion) to speak a little more to this assembly. It may be of some good use, to inform and rectify the judgments of some of the people, and may prevent such distempers as have arisen amongst us. The great questions that have troubled the country, are about the authority of the magistrates and the liberty of the people. It is yourselves who have called us to this office, and being called by you, we have our authority from God, in way of an ordinance, such as hath the image of God eminently stamped upon it, the contempt and violation whereof hath been vindicated with examples of divine vengeance. I entreat you to consider, that when you choose magistrates, you take them from among yourselves, men subject to like passions as you are. Therefore when you see infirmities in us, you should reflect upon your own, and that would make you bear the more with us, and not be severe censurers of the failings of your magistrates, when you have continual experience of the like infirmities in yourselves and others. We account him a good servant, who breaks not his covenant. The covenant between you and us is the oath you have taken of us, which is to this purpose, that we shall govern you and judge your causes by the rules of God's laws and our own, according to our best skill. When you agree with a workman to build you a ship or house, etc., he undertakes as well for his skill as for his faithfulness, for it is his profession, and you pay him for both. But when you call one to be a magistrate, he doth not profess nor undertake to have sufficient skill for that office, nor can you furnish him with gifts, etc., therefore you must run the hazard of his skill and ability. But if he fail in faithfulness, which by his oath he is bound unto, that he must answer for. If it fall out that the case be clear to common apprehension, and the rule clear also, if he transgress here, the error is not in the skill, but in the evil of the will: it must be required of him. But if the case be doubtful, or the rule doubtful, to men of such understanding and parts as your magistrates are, if your magistrates should err here, yourselves must bear it.

For the other point concerning liberty, I observe a great mistake in the country about that. There is a twofold liberty, natural (I mean as our nature is now corrupt) and civil or federal. The first is common to man with beasts and other creatures. By this, man, as he stands in relation to man simply, hath liberty to do what he lists; it is a liberty to evil as well as to good. This liberty is incompatible and inconsistent with authority, and cannot endure the least restraint of the most just authority. The exercise and maintaining of this liberty makes men grow more evil, and in time to be worse than brute beasts: *omnes sumus licentia deteriores.* This is that great enemy of truth and peace, that wild beast, which all the ordinances of God are bent against, to restrain and subdue it. The other kind of liberty I call civil or federal, it may also be termed moral, in reference to the covenant between God and man, in the moral law, and the politic covenants and constitutions, amongst men themselves. This liberty is the proper end and object of authority, and cannot subsist without it; and it is a liberty to that only which is good, just, and honest. This liberty you are to stand for, with the hazard (not only of your goods, but) of your lives, if need be. Whatsoever crosseth this, is not authority, but a distemper thereof. This liberty is maintained and exercised in a way of subjection to authority; it is of the same kind of liberty wherewith Christ hath made us free. The woman's own choice makes such a man her husband; yet being so chosen, he is her lord, and she is to be subject to him, yet in a way of liberty, not of bondage; and a true wife accounts her subjection her honor and freedom, and would not think her condition safe and free, but in her subjection to her husband's authority. Such is the liberty of the church under the authority of Christ, her king and husband; his yoke is so easy and sweet to her as a bride's ornaments; and if through frowardness or wantonness, etc., she shake it off, at any time, she is at no rest in her spirit, until she take it up again; and whether her lord smiles upon her, and embraceth her in his arms, or whether he frowns, or rebukes, or smites her, she apprehends the sweetness of his love in all, and is refreshed, supported, and instructed by every such dispensation of his authority over her. On the other side, ye know who they are that complain of this yoke and say, let us break their bands, etc., we will not have this man to rule over us. Even so, brethren, it will be between you and your magistrates. If you stand for your natural corrupt liberties, and will do what is good in your own eyes, you will not endure the least weight of authority, but will murmur, and oppose, and be always striving to shake off that yoke; but if you will be satisfied to enjoy such civil and lawful liberties, such as Christ allows you, then will you quietly and cheerfully submit unto that authority which is set over you, in all the administrations of it, for your good. Wherein, if we fail at any time, we hope we shall be willing (by God's assistance) to harken to good advice from any of you, or in any other way of God; so shall your liberties be preserved, in upholding the honor and power of authority amongst you.

[*March, 1647*] Mention was made before of some beginning to instruct the Indians, etc. Mr. John Eliot, teacher of the church of Roxbury, found such encouragement, as he took great pains to get their language, and in a few months could speak of the things of God to their understanding; and God prospered his endeavors, so as he kept a constant lecture to them in two places, one week at the wigwam of one Wabon, a new sachem near Watertown mill, and the other the next week in the wigwam of Cutshamekin near Dorchester mill. And for the furtherance of the work of God, divers of the English resorted to his lecture, and the governor and other of the magistrates and elders sometimes; and the Indians began to repair thither from other parts. His manner of proceeding was thus; he would persuade one of the other elders or some magistrate to begin the exercise with prayer in English; then he took a text, and read it first in the Indian language, and after in English; then he preached to them in Indian about an hour; (but first I should have spoke of the catechizing their children, who were soon brought to answer him some short questions, whereupon he gave each of them an apple or a cake) then he demanded of some of the chiefs, if they understood him; if they answered, yea, then he asked of them if they had any questions to propound. And they had usually two or three or more questions, which he did resolve. At one time (when the governor was there and about two hundred people, Indian and English, in one wigwam of Cutshamekin's) an old man asked him, if God would receive such an old man as he was; to whom he answered by opening the parable of the workmen that were hired into the vineyard; and when he had opened it, he asked the old man, if he did believe it, who answered he did, and was ready to weep. A second question was, what was the reason, that when all Englishmen did know God, yet some of them were poor. His answer was, 1. that God knows it is better for his children to be good than to be rich; he knows withal, that if some of them had riches, they would abuse them, and wax proud and wanton, etc., therefore he gives them no more riches than may be needful for them, that they may be kept from pride, etc., to depend upon him, 2. he would hereby have men know, that he hath better blessings to bestow upon good men than riches, etc., and that their best portion is in heaven, etc. A third question was, if a man had two wives, (which was ordinary with them,) seeing he must put away one, which he should put away. To this it was answered, that by the law of God the first is the true wife, and the other is no wife; but if such a case fell out, they should then repair to the magistrates, and they would direct them what to do, for it might be, that the first wife might be an adulteress, etc., and then she was to be put away. When all their questions were resolved, he concluded with prayer in the Indian language.

The Indians were usually very attentive, and kept their children so quiet as caused no disturbance. Some of them began to be seriously affected, and to understand the things of God, and they were generally ready to reform whatsoever they were told to be against the word of God, as their sorcery, (which they call powwowing,) their whoredoms, etc., idleness, etc. The Indians grew very inquisitive after knowledge both in things divine and also human, so as one of them, meeting with an honest plain Englishman, would needs know of him, what were the first beginnings (which we call principles) of a commonwealth. The Englishman, being far short in the knowledge of such matters, yet ashamed that an Indian should find an Englishman ignorant of anything, bethought himself what answer to give him, at last resolved upon this, viz. that the first principle of a commonwealth was salt, for (saith he) by means of salt we can keep our flesh and fish, to have it ready when we need it, whereas you lose much for want of it, and are sometimes ready to starve. A second principle is iron, for thereby we fell trees, build houses, till our land, etc. A third is, ships, by which we carry forth such commodities as we have to spare, and fetch in such as we need, as cloth, wine, etc. Alas! (saith the Indian) then I fear, we shall never be a commonwealth, for we can neither make salt, nor iron, nor ships.   1790

Samuel Sewall

(1652-1730)

Samuel Sewall was born at Bishopstoke, England, and moved at the age of nine to Boston. Graduated from Harvard in 1671, he was appointed a tutor there in 1673, and served as manager of the colony's printing press from 1681 to 1684. Sewall held numerous judicial appointments, the most prominent being a judge at the Salem witch trials. He was the only one of the three judges to recant publicly his role in the Salem affair. Sewall wrote *The Selling of Joseph* (Boston, 1700), an early anti-slavery essay; however, he is best remembered for his *Diary*, a record of events from 1674 to 1729.

BIBLIOGRAPHY: *Diary of Samuel Sewall*, 3 Vols. in *Coll. Mass. Hist. Soc.*, 5th Ser., V-VII (1878-1882). Mark Van Doren, ed. *Samuel Sewall's Diary* (New York, 1927, 1963), abridged. *Letter-Book of Samuel Sewall*, 2 Vols. in *Coll. Mass. Hist. Soc.*, 6th Ser., I-II (1886-1888). N. H. Chamberlain, *Samuel Sewall and the World He Lived In* (Boston, 1897). Ola E. Winslow, *Samuel Sewall of Boston* (New York, 1964).

From *The Diary*

[Selected Entries]

Saturday Even. Aug. 12, 1676, just as prayer ended Tim. Dwight sank down in a Swoon, and for a good space was as if he perceived not what was done to him: after, kicked and sprawled, knocking his hands and feet upon the floor like a distracted man. Was carried pickpack to bed by John Alcock, there his clothes pulled off. In the night it seems he talked of ships, his master, father, and uncle Eliot. The Sabbath following Father went to him, spake to him to know what ailed him, asked if he would be prayed for, and for what he would desire his friends to pray. He answered, for more sight of sin, and God's healing grace. I asked him, being alone with him, whether his troubles were from some outward cause or spiritual. He answered, spiritual. I asked him why then he could not tell it his master, as well as any other, since it is the honor of any man to see sin and be sorry for it. He gave no answer, as I remember. Asked him if he would go to meeting. He said, 'twas in vain for him; his day was out. I asked, what day: he answered, of Grace. I told him 'twas sin for anyone to conclude themselves Reprobate, that this was all one. He said he would speak more, but could not. &c. Notwithstanding all this semblance (and much more than is written) of compunction for Sin, 'tis to be feared that his trouble arose from a maid whom he passionately loved: for that when Mr. Dwight and his master had agreed to let him go to her, he eftsoons grew well.

Feb. 23, 1677. Mr. Torrey spake with my Father at Mrs. Norton's, told him that he would fain have me preach, and not leave off my studies to follow Merchandise. Note. The evening before, Feb. 22, I resolved (if I could get an opportunity) to speak with Mr. Torrey, and ask his Counsel as to coming into Church, about my estate, and the temptations that made me to fear. But he went home when I was at the Warehouse about Wood that Tho. Elkins brought.

Thursday, Nov. 12. [1685] Mr. Moodey preaches from Isa. 57. 1. Mr. Cobbet's Funeral Sermon; said also of Mr. Chauncy that he was a Man of Singular Worth. Said but 2 of the First Generation left.

After, the Ministers of this Town Come to the Court and complain against a Dancing Master who seeks to set up here and hath mixt Dances, and his time of Meeting is Lecture-Day; and 'tis reported he should say that by one Play he could teach more Divinity than Mr. Willard or the Old Testament. Mr. Moodey said 'twas not a time for N. E. to dance. Mr. Mather struck at the Root, speaking against mixt Dances.

March 19. [1689] Saw Paul's, which is a great and excellent piece of work for the Arches and Pillars and Porches. The Stairs are five foot ½ long and four Inches deep, winding about a great hollow Pillar of about six foot Diameter. March 20. Went and saw Weavers' Hall and Goldsmiths' Hall. Went into Guild-Hall and saw the manner of choosing the Mayor. About 16 were put up, though I think but four were intended. Pilkington and Stamp had by much the most Hands, yet those for fatal Moor and Rayment would have a Poll, which the Court of Aldermen in their Scarlet Gowns ordered to be at four o'clock. They sat at the Hustings. Sheriffs in their Gold Chains managed the Election. Common Sergeant [counsel of the Mayor and Aldermen] made a speech. When the People cry'd, a Hall, a Hall, the Aldermen came up two by two, the Mace carried before them, came in at the door opposite to the Street door out of another apartment. I stood in the Clock-Gallery.

Sabbath, Jan. 12. [1690] Richard Dumer, a flourishing youth of 9 years old, dies of the Smallpox. I tell Sam. of it and what need he had to prepare for Death, and therefore to endeavor really to pray when he said over the Lord's Prayer: He seem'd not much to mind, eating an Apple; but when he came to say, Our father, he burst out into a bitter Cry, and when I askt what was the matter and he could speak, he burst out into a bitter Cry and said he was afraid he should die. I pray'd with him, and read Scriptures comforting against death, as, O death where is thy sting,

&c. All things yours. Life and Immortality brought to light by Christ, &c. 'Twas at noon.

April 11, 1692. Went to Salem, where, in the Meetinghouse, the persons accused of Witchcraft were examined; was a very great Assembly; 'twas awful to see how the afflicted persons were agitated. Mr. Noyes pray'd at the beginning, and Mr. Higginson concluded. Woe, Woe, Woe, Witchcraft.

[*Augt. 19, 1692*] This day George Burrough, John Willard, John Procter, Martha Carrier and George Jacobs were executed at Salem, a very great number of Spectators being present. Mr. Cotton Mather was there, Mr. Sims, Hale, Noyes, Chiever, &c. All of them said they were innocent, Carrier and all. Mr. Mather says they all died by a Righteous Sentence. Mr. Burrough by his Speech, Prayer, protestation of his Innocence, did much move unthinking persons, which occasions their speaking hardly concerning his being executed.

Augt. 25. Fast at the old First Church, respecting the Witchraft, Drought, &c.

Monday, Sept. 19, 1692. About noon, at Salem, Giles Corey was pressed to death for standing Mute; much pains was used with him two days, one after another, by the Court and Capt. Gardner of Nantucket who had been of his acquaintance: but all in vain.

Sept. 21. A petition is sent to Town in behalf of Dorcas Hoar, who now confesses: Accordingly an order is sent to the Sheriff to forbear her Execution, notwithstanding her being in the Warrant to die tomorrow. This is the first condemned person who has confess'd.

Nov. 6. Joseph threw a knob of Brass and hit his Sister Betty on the forehead so as to make it bleed and swell; upon which, and for his playing at Prayer time, and eating when Return Thanks, I whip'd him pretty smartly. When I first went in (call'd by his Grandmother) he sought to shadow and hide himself from me behind the head of the Cradle: which gave me the sorrowful remembrance of Adam's carriage.

Nov. 22, 1692. I prayed that God would pardon all my Sinful Wanderings, and direct me for the future. That God would bless the Assembly in their debates, and that would choose and assist our Judges, &c., and save New England as to Enemies and Witchcrafts, and vindicate the late Judges, consisting with his Justice and Holiness, &c., with Fasting.

[*Jan. 15, 1697*] Copy of the Bill I put up on the Fastday; giving it to Mr. Willard as he passed by, and standing up at the reading of it, and bowing when finished; in the Afternoon.

Samuel Sewall, sensible of the reiterated strokes of God upon himself and family; and being sensible, that as to the Guilt contracted upon the opening of the late Commission of Oyer and Terminer at Salem (to which the order for this Day relates) he is, upon many accounts, more concerned than any that he knows of, Desires to take the Blame and shame of it, Asking pardon of men, And especially desiring prayers that God, who has an Unlimited Authority, would pardon that sin and all other his sins; personal and Relative: And according to his infinite Benignity, and Sovereignty, Not Visit the sin of him, or of any other, upon himself or any of his, nor upon the Land: But that He would powerfully defend him against all Temptations to Sin, for the future; and vouchsafe him the efficacious, saving Conduct of his Word and Spirit.

Jan. 1, 1701. Just about Break-a-day Jacob Amsden and 3 other Trumpeters gave a Blast with the Trumpets on the common near Mr. Alford's. Then went to the Green Chamber, and sounded there till about sunrise. Bellman said these verses a little before Break-a-day, which I printed and gave them.

> Once more! our God vouchsafe to shine:
> Correct the Coldness of our Clime.
> Make haste with thy Impartial Light,
> And terminate this long dark night.
>
> Give the poor Indians Eyes to see
> The Light of Life: and set them free.
> So Men shall God in Christ adore,
> And worship Idols vain, no more.
>
> So Asia, and Africa,
> Europa, with America;
> All Four, in Consort join'd, shall Sing
> New Songs of Praise to Christ our King.

The Trumpeters cost me five pieces 8/8. Gave to the College Library Dr. Owen's two last Volumes on the Hebrews. Sent them by Amsden. When was about to part with Dr. Owen, I look'd, to read some difficult place; pitch'd on v. 11th of the 8th Chapter—Know the Lord—I read it over and over one time and another and could not be satisfied: At last this came in my mind Know the Lord, i.e. Know the Messiah, to whom the word Lord is very much appropriated &c. *vide locum.* Now my mind was at quiet, and all seem'd to run smooth. As I hope this is Truth, so I bless God for this New Year's Gift; which I also writ in a spare place, and gave it with the Book to the College.

Monday, June 2, 1701. Mr. Pemberton preaches the Artillery Sermon, from Luke. 3-14. Dine at Monk's. Because of the Rain and Mist, this day, the election is made upon the Townhouse, Sewall. Capt.; Tho. Hutchinson Lieut.; Tho. Savage jr., Ensign.; Tho. Fitch, 1 Sergt.: Oliver Noyes 2: Hab. Savage 3: Charles Chauncy 4. Call'd down the Council out of the Chamber, set their chairs below; Col. Pynchon gave the Staves and Ensign. I said was surpris'd to see they had mistaken a sorry pruning Hook for a Military Spear; but paid such a deference to the Company that would rather run the venture of exposing my own inability, than give any occasion to suspect I slighted their call. To Sergeant Fitch, Doubted not but if I could give anything tolerable words of command, he would mend them in a vigorous and speedy performance: was glad of so good a Hand to me and the Company (Mr. Noyes abroad in the Galley). To Hab. Savage. The savages are soldiers *ex Traduce;* in imitation of his honored father, Uncle, and Grandfather, hop'd for worthy performances from him. To Ch. Chauncy, Had such a honor for your Grandfather and father, that was glad was join'd with me in this Relation. Drew out before Mr. Ushers, gave 3 volleys. Drew into the Townhouse again; sent Sergeant Chauncy for Mr. Pemberton, who said he was glad to see the staff in my hand; pray'd with us. Had the company to my house, treated them with bread, Beer, wine Sillibub.—They order'd Capt. Checkly and me to Thank Mr. Pemberton for his Sermon, which we did on Tuesday, desiring a copy.

Oct. 20. Mr. Cotton Mather came to Mr. Wilkins's shop, and there talked very sharply against me as if I had used his father worse than a Negro; spake so loud that people in the street might hear him. Then went and told Sam, That one pleaded much for Negroes, and he had used his father worse than a Negro, and told him that was his Father. I had read in the morn Mr. Dod's saying; Sanctified Afflictions are good Promotions. I found it now a cordial. . . . Oct. 9 I sent Mr. Increase Mather a Haunch of very good Venison; I hope in that I did not treat him as a Negro.

Feb. 22. [1703] Mrs. Willard and several of her children had like to have been cast away coming from Cambridge by Water, wind was so very high; put ashore at last on Muddy River Marsh: Got to the Governor's by that time 'twas dark. This morning as I was praying alone, I was much affected to think how concern'd and inquisitive I was in my Journeying about my Way; whether I was in the right or no; and yet not so constantly and effectually inquisitive about my Way to Heaven, although I was equally hastening to my Journey's End; whether in the right or wrong way. May He who is the Way, the Truth, and the Life, bring me into and always keep me in the right Way!

July 6 [1715] . . . This day it is Fifty-four years Since I first was brought ashore to Boston near where Scarlet's wharf now is, July, 6, 1661, Lord's Day. The Lord help me to Redeem the Time which passes so swiftly. I was then a poor little Schoolboy of Nine years and 1/4 old. This day I have written a Letter to my Cousin Joseph Moodey, student in Harvard College, mending a Copy of his verses showed me by his Father.

July 26. [1715] Go to Cambridge with Mr. Lynde in Stedman's Calash. Mr. Brattle prays at opening the court. All the Justices there. Chief Justice dines not with us, by reason of the Sickness of Madam Brattle.

July 27. By candlelight Adjourn *sine Die.*

July 28. Mrs. Brattle dies at 2 p. m.

July 30. Mrs. Brattle Buried; Bearers: President, Mr. Angier; Gibbs, Wadsworth; Pemberton, Bradstreet. Fellows Flint, Holyoke, Robie had Scarves. After the women followed Lt. Gov. Usher, Sewall; Jos. Lynde,

Em. Hutchison; Tho. Oliver, Francis Foxcroft esqr. 'Twas Six o'clock when came out of the Burying place; so I came Straight home upon my Gray Horse; Saw a Rainbow in Charlestown Marketplace. Caus'd the Shops to be shut up, as I rode along. Got home very comfortably. *Laus Deo.* 'Twas a great Funeral, and would probably have been much greater, but for the Abundance of Rain which fell this day, and danger of more throughout the Afternoon.

Monday, Aug. 8. Set out at 11 at night on Horseback with Tho. Wallis to inspect the order of the Town.

Constable Eady, Mr. Allen, Salter, Herishor Simson, Howel, Mr. John Marion. Dissipated the players at Nine Pins at Mount-Whoredom.

Benjamin Davis, Chairmaker, and Jacob Hasy were two of them. Reproved Thomas Messenger for entertaining them.

As came home between 2 and three took up Peter Griffis the notorious Burglarer, and committed him to Prison. Generally, the Town was peaceable and in good order.

Friday, Oct. 18. [1717] My wife grows worse and exceedingly Restless. Pray'd God to look upon her. Ask'd not after my going to bed. Had the advice of Mr. Williams and Dr. Cutler.

7th day, Oct. 19. Call'd Dr. C. Mather to pray, which he did excellently in the Dining Room, having Suggested good Thoughts to my wife before he went down. After, Mr. Wadsworth pray'd in the Chamber when 'twas suppos'd my wife took little notice. About a quarter of an hour past four, my dear Wife expired in the Afternoon, whereby the Chamber was fill'd with a Flood of Tears. God is teaching me a new Lesson; to live a Widower's Life. Lord help me to Learn; and be a Sun and Shield, to me, now so much of my Comfort and Defense are taken away.

Oct. 20. I go to the public Worship forenoon and Afternoon. My Son has much ado to read the Note I put up, being overwhelm'd with tears.

Midweek, Oct. 23. My dear Wife is inter'd. Bearers: Lt. Gov. Dummer, Maj. Gen. Winthrop; Col. Elisha Hutchinson, Col. Townsend; Andrew Belcher esq. and Simeon Stoddard esq. I intended Col. Taylor for a Bearer, but he was from home. Had very Comfortable weather. Brother Gerrish pray'd with us when return'd from the Tomb: I went into it. Gov. had a Scarf and Ring, and the Bearers, Gov. Dudley, Brother Sewall, Hirst, Gerrish. Was very destitute for want of the help of Son Hirst, and cousin Jane Green. This was the first day of the Gen. Court. Gave the Deputies Books. Allen's Alarm. They sent Mr. Isa. Tay and Capt. Wadsworth to me to Thank me.

May 14. [1720] Plentiful refreshing Rain, Mr. Cooper and I dine at Mr. Stoddard's. This day I gave Mr. Cooper Pool's *Synopsis Criticorum;* to Mr. J. Sewall Pagnin's *Thesaurus;* to Mr. Prince, Calvin's *Opuscula:* to Mr. Colman, in one of his Fountains, a Twenty-shilling-Bill to buy Gloves. To the Governor, and as many as were in Council, Fountains.

Oct. 11. I writ a few Lines to Madam Winthrop to this purpose:

"Madam, These wait on you with Mr. Mayhew's Sermon, and Account of the state of the Indians on Martha's Vinyard. I thank you for your Unmerited Favors of yesterday; and hope to have the Happiness of Waiting on you tomorrow before Eight o'clock after Noon. I pray God to keep you, and give you a joyful entrance upon the Two Hundred and twentyninth year of Christopher Columbus his Discovery; and take Leave, who am, Madam, your humble Servant. S.S."

Oct. 12. At Madam Winthrop's Steps I took leave of Capt. Hill, &c.

Mrs. Anne Cotton came to door ('twas before 8) said Madam Winthrop was within, directed me into the little Room, where she was full of work behind a Stand; Mrs. Cotton came in and stood. Madam Winthrop pointed to her to set me a Chair. Madam Winthrop's Countenance was much changed from what 'twas on Monday, look'd dark and lowering. At last, the work, (black stuff or Silk) was taken away, I got my Chair in place, had some Converse, but very Cold and indifferent to what 'twas before. Ask'd her to acquit me of Rudeness if I drew off her Glove. Enquiring the reason, I told her 'twas great odds between handling a dead Goat, and a living Lady. Got it off. I told her I had one Petition to ask of her, that was, that she would take off the Negative she laid on me the third of October; She readily answer'd she could not, and enlarg'd upon it; She told me of it so soon as she could; could not leave her house, children, neighbors, business. I told her she might do some Good to help and support me. . . . She thank'd me for my Book, (Mr. Mayhew's Sermon), But said not a word of the Letter. When she insisted on the Negative, I pray'd there might be no more Thunder and Lightning, I should not sleep all night. I gave her Dr. Preston, *The Church's Marriage and the Church's Carriage,* which cost me 6s at the Sale. . . . Sarah fill'd a Glass of Wine, she drank to me, I to her, She sent Juno home with me with a good Lantern, I gave her 6d. and bid her thank her Mistress.

Monday, Nov. 7. . . . I went to Madam Winthrop; found her rocking her little Katee in the Cradle. I excus'd my Coming so late (near Eight). She set me an arm'd Chair and Cushion; and so the Cradle was between her arm'd Chair and mine. Gave her the remnant of my Almonds; She did not eat of them as before; but laid them away; I said I came to inquire whether she had alter'd her mind since Friday, or remained of the same mind still. She said, Thereabouts. I told her I loved her, and was so fond as to think that she loved me: She said had a great respect for me. I told her, I had made her an offer, without asking any advice; she had so many to advise with, that 'twas a hindrance. The Fire was come to one short Brand besides the Block, which Brand was set up in end; at last it fell to pieces, and no Recruit was made: She gave me a Glass of Wine. I think I repeated again that I would go home and bewail my Rashness in making more haste than good Speed. I would endeavor to contain myself, and not go on to solicit her to do that which she could not Consent to. Took leave of her. As came down the steps she bid me have a Care.

Treated me Courteously. Told her she had enter'd the 4th year of her Widowhood. I had given her the *News-Letter* before: I did not bid her draw off her Glove as sometime I had done. Her Dress was not so clean as sometime it had been. *Jehovah jireh!*

Midweek, Nov. 9. Dine at Brother Stoddard's: were so kind as to inquire of me if they should invite Madam Winthrop; I answer'd No.

Lords day, Dec. 17. [1727] I was surprised to hear Mr. Thacher of Milton, my old Friend, pray'd for as dangerously Sick. Next day. Dec. 18, 1727. I am inform'd by Mr. Gerrish, that my dear friend died last night; which I doubt bodes ill to Milton and the Province, his dying at this Time, though in the 77th year of his Age. *Deus avertat Omen!*

Friday, Dec. 22. The day after the Fast, was inter'd. Bearers: Rev. Mr. Nehemiah Walter, Mr. Joseph Baxter; Mr. John Swift, Mr. Sam. Hunt; Mr. Joseph Sewall, Mr. Thomas Prince. I was inclin'd before, and having a pair of Gloves sent me, I determined to go to the Funeral, if the Weather prov'd favorable, which it did, and I hired Blake's Coach with four Horses; my Son, Mr. Cooper and Mr. Prince went with me. Refresh'd there with Meat and Drink; got thither about half-an-hour past one. It was sad to see triumphed over my dear Friend! I rode in my Coach to the Burying place; not being able to get nearer by reason of the many Horses. From thence went directly up the Hill where the Smith's Shop, and so home very comfortably and easily, the ground being mollified. But when I came to my own Gate, going in, I fell down, a board slipping under my Left foot, my right Leg raised off the skin, and put me to a great deal of pain, especially when 'twas washed with Rum. It was good for me that I was thus Afflicted that my spirit might be brought into a frame more suitable to the Solemnity, which is apt to be too light; and by the loss of some of my Skin, and blood I might be awakened to prepare for my own Dissolution. . . . Mr. Millar, the Church of England Minister, was there. At this Funeral I heard of the death of my good old Tenant Capt. Nathan Niles, that very Friday morn. I have now been at the Interment of 4 of my Classmates. First, the Rev. Mr. William Adams at Dedham, Midweek, Augt. 19, 1685. Second, Mr. John Bowles, at Roxbury, March, 31, 1691. Was one of his Bearers. Third, Capt. Samuel Phips at Charlestown. He was laid in his Son-in-Law Lemon's Tomb. Had a good pair of Gloves, and a gold Ring. He was Clerk of the Court and Register many years. Clerk to his death, and his Son succeeded him. Was Precentor many years to the congregation. Inter'd Aug. 9, 1725. Fourth, the Rev. Mr. Thacher at Milton. Now I can go to no more Funerals of my Classmates; nor none be at mine; for the survivors, the Rev. Mr. Samuel Mather at Windsor, and the Rev. Mr. Taylor at Westfield, are one Hundred Miles off, and are entirely enfeebled. I humbly pray that Christ may be graciously present with us all Three both in Life, and in Death, and then we shall safely and Comfortably walk through the shady valley that leads to Glory.   1878-1882

WORKS OF PIETY AND DOCTRINE

John Cotton
(1584-1652)

Born in Derby, England, the son of a lawyer, John Cotton entered Trinity College, Cambridge, in 1597, was made a fellow of Emmanuel College in 1603, and was ordained to the ministry in 1610. To avoid a summons to appear before Archbishop Laud, Cotton and his family fled to Boston in 1633. From his arrival in Massachusetts Bay, he was one of the principal preachers and theologians of Puritanism. His essays written during the Cotton-Williams controversy include *A Letter . . . to Mr. Williams* (London, 1643) and *The Bloody Tenent, Washed and Made White in the Blood of the Lamb* (London, 1647). Among his other works are *The Way of Life* (London, 1641), *The Covenant of Grace* (London, 1655), and numerous explications of books of the Bible.

BIBLIOGRAPHY: J. H. Tuttle, "Writings of Rev. John Cotton," *Bibliographical Essays: A Tribute to Wilberforce Eames* (Cambridge, Mass., 1924), pp. 363-380. Lazar Ziff, *The Career of John Cotton* (Princeton, 1962). E. H. Emerson, *John Cotton* (New York, 1965).

From *A Brief Exposition Upon Ecclesiastes*

ECCLES. 12. PART OF V. 9. WITH 10

Yea he gave good heed, and sought out, and set in order many Proverbs.

10. *The Preacher sought to find out acceptable words; and that which was written was upright, even words of truth.*

Solomon in teaching the people, he sought out, and weighed, and set in order words of weight and delight, words of uprightness and truth.

Solomon, though a wise man, (none like him;) yea; though immediately inspired by the Holy Ghost; yet he set all his Logic awork in teachings and writings to the people. For whereas there be three acts or exercises of Logic, 1. Invention; 2. Judgment; 3. Method; and in these three the whole work of Logic is accomplished; Solomon set all these awork to find out a fit matter and words for the instruction of the people. *Investigavit,* he sought out, is the work of invention; *libravit, trutinavit,* he weighed (as in a balance) is the work of judgment. He set in order, is the work of method.

Words of weight: משלים Proverbs, that is, words of weight, of power, of authority, such as are apt to sink, not only (like David's stone into the forehead of Goliah) but into the heart of the stoutest.

Reason why so called, from their effect: First, as convincing and pressing down a proud spirit, 2 *Cor.* 10.4,5. Secondly, lifting up an humble spirit, *Isai.* 66.2. & 50.4. Thirdly, directing and ordering their own lives, and others, *Ps.* 119.125.

Words of delight, or acceptable words, not to the humors of the people, but first, to the good pleasure of God, *Gal.* 1.10. Secondly, to the estate of the people, *Gal.* 4.20.

Reason 1. As being most suitable to the image of God in his children. These words are as a seal, their hearts as wax; For all delight springeth from correspondency between the faculty and the object.

Reason 2. As making us men of delight, first to God; secondly, to our brethren, *Psalm* 16.3.

Words or writings of uprightness or righteousness.

Reason 1. As suitable to God's will, which is the rule of Right.

Reason 2. As aiming at right ends, the glory of God, the good of Churches, Commonwealths, Families, souls.

Reason 3. As making us upright.

Words of truth.

Reason 1. As proceeding from the Spirit of truth.

Reason 2. As speaking of all men's persons, estates; of God, his counsels and ways, as they be without error or guile.

Reason 3. As making us true.

Object. 1. But Penmen of Scripture speak from immediate revelation, 2 *Tim.* 3.16. 2 *Pet.* 1.21. Therefore not in a way of Logical discourse or study.

Answ. It followeth not; for God breatheth as well in meditation as in sudden raptures. *Jude* 3. 1 *Tim.* 4,13,15. 2 *Tim.* 2.15.

Object. 2. *Luke* 21,14,15.

Answ. It is a word of encouragement to Martyrs and Confessors that suffer in a good cause, to expect immediate assistance, where they cannot well forecast or premeditate to answer to sudden and unknown questions. Otherwise, if a man knew beforehand their Interrogatories, it were expedient to study how, and what to answer, *Prov.* 15.28.

Use 1. To reprove wearisomeness of the instructions taught in this book: When will our Teacher have done with this argument? that we might have none of Christ; but indeed a gracious heart seeth the more need of Christ in the vanity of the creature.

Use 2. To reprove the rejection of studied Sermons.

Use 3. To teach Preachers the Imitation of Solomon in studious Invention, Judgment, and order of words, first of power; secondly, of delight; thirdly, of uprightness; fourthly, of truth, *Jer.* 48.10. *Jude* 3. Talents should be employed to best advantage.

Use 4. Sermons may be elaborate without quotations.

Use 5. To exhort to the diligent reading and hearing of Scripture, even Solomon's books; they are studiously written: they are words of power, delight, uprightness, truth.

ECCLES. 12.11

11. *The words of the wise are as goads, and as nails fastened by the masters of assemblies, which are given from one shepherd.*

Use 1. See here what manner of persons the penmen of Scriptures and the Preachers of them be, to wit, 1. For their gifts, wise. 2. For their office, Masters of Assemblies. 3. For their calling, given by one Pastor, as in the former Doctrine.

Use 2. To teach the Masters of Assemblies, how the word should be handled wisely according to the sense of Scripture, and to the estate of the people. As Goads, 1. Sharply, piercingly, *Titus* 1.13. quickening a dull spirit, *Psal.* 119. 93. 2. Subduing and wounding an enemy, whether lust or gainsayer (as Shamgar's Goad, *Judg.* 3.31.) 2 *Cor.* 10.4,5. *Titus* 1.9. As Nails, 1. Driving at first the sharp but small end into the heart; things that may most easily sink and take place, and enter, *Heb.* 5.11,12,13. 2. Following the word with stronger matter which may hold the heart strongly and closely to God, to Brethren, and to Duty.

Implanted: this done by dispensing the word, 1. In faithful simplicity, *Jer.* 23.28,29. Humane wit and authorities added to it do but adulterate it, like as Paint doth marble, or as honey and wine in children's milk: as painted glass windows darken the light: as a bombasted sword hindreth cutting. 2. In manifestation of the spirit breathing and speaking in the Scripture, and breathing and speaking in the hearts, and words, and lives of Ministers. Hence power, 1 *Cor.* 2.2,3,4. 2 *Cor.* 13.3,4.

1654

From *The Way of Life*

SIN'S DEADLY WOUND
ACTS 2.37

Now when they heard this, they were pricked in their hearts.

Having spoken of the Prophesy of the pouring out of the Spirit in the days of the Gospel, we come now to speak of the accomplishment thereof, which though it finally intend the Calling of the Jews, yet it is accomplished in the Conversion of those by Peter's Sermon, expressed in the Text.

The whole Book of the Acts is a Story or a Register of the Acts of the Apostles, that is, of their Sermons, their doings, their works, whether their Institutions and Ordinances in establishing the Church, or their Miracles wrought to confirm them, or their Journeys, or their sufferings. Therefore if you would read with profit this Book of the Acts, you are to consider in every Chapter of them therein, what is recorded, such journeys and such Sermons, such Miracles, and such sufferings. These are of singular use of direction for the Church of God.

In this Chapter, there are two Acts described. First, their prophecying with new and strange Tongues, from ver. 2. to the end of the 13. amplified by many arguments, as also by a double effect it wrought in those that heard them. First, amazement in some, ver. 12. Secondly, others mocked and said, *These men are full of new Wine.*

The second Act was a Sermon of Peter's, upon that occasion, to repel and refute that calumniation of drunkenness, which they put upon the Apostles, described from ver. 14. to 36. In which Sermon the Apostle doth prove, that they did not this by the spirit of the Buttery, or Wine Cellar, but by the power of the Holy Ghost, by a new Spirit of God come upon them, according to what was prophesied in the Old Testament. Now this spirit thus poured out, the Apostles further amplifies and sets forth the giver of it, the Lord Jesus Christ, as delivered into their hands by the determinate Counsel of God, and by them wickedly crucified and slain, who yet notwithstanding sets forth the same Christ as rising from the dead, and ascending into Heaven, and having received the Spirit from the Father, he sheds it abroad to the edification of the Church; from whence (ver. 36.) he concludes. Let the whole house of Israel know assuredly, that this Jesus whom you have crucified, is the Lord Christ, that this is the Messiah, whom they have thus crucified. *Now when they heard this, they were pricked in their hearts.* And see then, this Sermon of Peter's is amplified by a threefold effect. First, the humiliation of the hearers, *They were pricked in their hearts,* ver. 37,38,39,40. Secondly, the Baptizing of 3000. souls, that were converted upon this occasion ver. 41. Thirdly, the Religious, charitable, comfortable fellowship of those Converts together, ver. 42. to 47.

We are now to speak of the first of these effects. And that is the humiliation of the hearers. They were pricked in their hearts; which words contain four parts.

1. The kind of spiritual affliction wherewith they were exercised; pricked at the heart.

2. The effect of this pricking wrought in them, a resignation of themselves to the Apostles' counsel and direction, and an humble and rever-

ent request of them to direct them what to do; Men and Brethren, a word they had not wont to express.

3. This humiliation is expressed by the cause of it; They hearing their particular sins charged upon their souls, hearing it was Christ they had crucified, then they were pricked in their hearts.

4. This humiliation is amplified by the subject persons; those that before were amazed, and mocked, are now pricked in their hearts.

Now of the first; The kind of spiritual affliction on these hearers were exercised with; pricked in their hearts.

Doctrine. *The very first work of living and saving grace, gives a deadly stroke to the life of sinful nature.*

A Note which I never handled heretofore, but you shall find it evident in the Text, and agreeable to the Principles of Christian Religion. In the Text, these men that were thus pricked in their hearts, had they received any saving grace before? No; Some of them were amazed: Now, amazed hearers, are ignorant hearers, for all amazement springs from ignorance; had they been the sheep of Christ, they would have known his voice, *Joh.* 10.27. They were also scornful proud hearers; scorning is a fruit of pride; but this was the time that God intended to show them mercy. Now then, what is the first grace that is wrought in them? After by hearing they understood, *They were pricked in their hearts;* not in their eyes only, to weep for their sins, nor in tongue only to cry out, but in their hearts; that is a mortal wound to Nature, the least prick of the heart, is the death of nature, be the piercing of it never so little, the sting of a Bee, or the prick of a Needle, the very life of nature runs out, and it cannot possibly be healed: you may prick a man in the tongue, in the eye, and save his life; but once prick the heart, & you give a deadly wound to nature; the vitals waste presently, much ado to sustain life for a moment. See then, this is the first work of saving and living grace, An heart once pricked can never be healed; and therefore you never read that God heals man's corrupt nature, He *heals not a stony heart, but takes it away, and gives a man a new heart, Ezek.* 36.26. Prick the heart, and it will never leave trickling and bleeding, till the whole life of nature be consumed. I will further open this point. First, let me show you what is meant by the heart. Secondly, what by pricking of the heart. Thirdly, the Reason, and then the Application.

1. By the heart you must not understand, that fleshly part of the body which is the seat of life, called *Primum vivens & ultimum moriens.* Godly sorrow doth not kill man's bodily life, it works not death, *2 Cor.* 7.10. But it is meant the will of a man, which lies in the heart, for as the understanding lies in the head or brain, so the will is seated in the heart: so as a good frame in the heart, and wisdom in the brain, makes a complete man.

Now this heart or will of a man, is that whereby we choose or refuse a thing, so the heart is taken, *Ezek.* 36.26. An heart of stone, is a stubborn and obstinate heart or will; an heart of flesh, is an heart that is tractable, and soon pierced; now then this was the piercing of the will of these hearers.

2. What is it to be pricked in the heart. First, the heart is said to be pricked, when it is afflicted with these two principal affections that are said to wound the heart, the one is sorrow and grief, and the other is care, 1 *Tim.* 6.10. Then is the heart pricked, when God afflicts it with sorrow and grief for sin; grief for sin, and care for reformation of it. They were pierced with many sorrows for piercing of Christ, and care to be delivered from that sin: there are other affections that usually follow these, as sometimes fear and trembling, *Ezra* 9.10. Sometimes shame, *Jer.* 31.19. Sometimes Indignation, 2 *Cor.* 7.11. But sorrow and care, these most pierce; but these affections never pierce the heart, till first hatred and loathing of sin be wrought in a man, *Rom.* 7.15. and this springs from a change wrought in the will, which makes us loath ourselves for our sins, *Job* 40.3,4 and 42.6. And when God gives his people new hearts, they shall loathe themselves, *Ezek.* 36.26,32. Here is first loathing of sin, and ourselves for sin; from whence springs hatred of sin, from thence, sorrow, grief, care, shame and indignation for sin.

Secondly, But piercing also implies something more, as to express it from what Surgeons are wont to say; They say, all piercing of a member, is piercing of the body that is compact together; *Dissolutio membri vitalis*, is *dissolutio compositi*, It is a *dissolution of the whole frame of nature.* If a vital member be wounded, it is not possible to heal it; it is *Dissolutio compositi.* They say true, that the heart and brain are the vessels of life, and as soon as one of these vessels are broken, the life of man runs out like water spilt upon the ground, the liveliest spirits soon evaporated, and the life and blood issues, and cannot possibly continue. And to this estate of a man doth the holy Ghost here allude; They were wounded in that part that was most vital, and by this means all that sinful life, that before was laid up in the stubborn will, begins to trickle down when the heart is prickt, sin is dropping and running out. But which is more, not only sinful lusts, but all affections to all outward comforts, they begin now to have no mind to any of them, till God gather up their spirits again; but for the present the world is crucified to him, *Gal.* 6.14. Wonder it is to see what little respect a pricked heart hath to the things of this life, as these Converts, ver. 42.44, they laid themselves level with their brethren, and now they are forever at a loss for the world, and all covetous inclinations to the world, they forever trickle down, that leak is never stopped any more.

3. Look as you see in pricking this bodily heart, a man is presently surprised with anguish and pain, and knows not what to do, so a man pricked in the will or heart knows not in the world which way to turn him; Sirs, *what must I do to be saved?* Acts 16.11. he saw now that there

was but a step between him and the nethermost hell, and therefore now, Sirs, what must I do?

Reas. 1. Taken from that fellowship that we are to have with Christ in his death, before we can have fellowship with him in his *Resurrection, Rom.* 6.3 to 11. The old man must be crucified, that henceforth we may not serve sin, but be free to righteousness; we must die to sin, and then to the world, *Gal.* 6.14.

Reas. 2. Taken from the good pleasure of God in our first conversion, to espouse and marry us unto his Son, which cannot be till our first husband be dead, *Rom.* 7.3, 4. Now because God intends a marriage Covenant betwixt Christ and our souls, in first conversion, he will therefore have sin first mortified in us, our first husband must lie a bleeding his last blood before we can be married to Christ.

Reas. 3. Taken from the sharp opposites which we in our first conversion have to deal withal. As first we have to deal with the Word of God, and that is sharper than a two-edge sword, *Heb.* 4.11. It is called goads and nails, *Eccles.* 12.11. Sharp and keen arrows, *Psal.* 45.5. Again, we have to deal with our sins, and that is a sting, 1 *Cor.* 15.56. And these inflame like venom. Another sharp opposite is the wrath of God, against which it is hard for a man to kick and spurn, *Acts* 9.5. this is a piercing sorrow, *Lam.* 3.65. Having thus to deal with these sharp opposites, we must needs be pricked and wounded.

Use 1. For trial of our estates, whether God hath wrought in us any first works of saving and living grace: Dost thou find thy will and inclination to die and decay in thee, so as that thou hast no desire or delight in sin? the liveliest spirit thou hast to this or that sin, is now evaporated and wasted, and thy heart is furnished with graces opposite to those sins; then I say, thy heart is pierced and wounded; thou now refusest, loathest, and hatest that sin upon which thy heart was most set, thou grievest for it, and takest care how to be shut of it, abstaineth from it, and art ashamed of it: If it be thus with thee, then surely God hath pierced thy heart, and thou art in an estate of salvation; otherwise let me say thus unto thee, A man may be pricked in the eye to weep for sin, in the tongue to cry out for sin, in the foot begin to amend his way, & yet not have his heart pricked, nor have any living or saving grace; a man may be fearful of sin, grow more careful of good duties, be more fruitful in good ways, and be not pricked in heart, but only in conscience or understanding; he may cry out of his sin as Judas did, *Mat.* 27.4. he thought but to have made a jest of betraying Christ, but when he saw it was the hour and power of darkness that Christ was taken and condemned, then was he pricked in conscience and cried out bitterly, and now would have no reward for his treason; he was pricked in his hands, feet, tongue, and eyes, and conscience; But was this any good evidence that he was pricked in his heart? No, for he goes on still to choose sin: had his will been pricked, he would never have hanged himself; in such a case a man may find a sin too sharp for him, and yet all be but anguishes of conscience, the heart still ready to choose another sin, but that is an ill sign; a man may sometimes be pricked in his shoulder, as Herod was, *Mar.* 6.20. reform many things, yet still cleave to an Harlot: John shall rather die, than the vital spirits of his sin shall perish. If this be thy case, then flatter not thyself, thou are yet in the gall of bitterness; Thou saist thou art heart-whole, thou thankest God, but the more is thy pity; if thou beest heart-whole after so much sickness, and crosses, and afflictions, and sins, This is a miserable wholeness. For had saving grace seized upon thy will, thy heart would have been pierced & broken; but if a man's heart come to look at all sin as bitter, he doth not balk any sin, his heart chooseth sin no more; if he see it is a sin, his heart recoils back again, and closeth not with it; if there be no sin, but thy heart runs from it, and thy affections are dying and decaying towards them all, then though it may be thou canst not weep so much as some men can do for the very prick of conscience, nor art so forward in some duties as some are, who are but very hypocrites, and cannot cry out so much as some can, yet if thy heart be dead to all sin, thou takest no pleasure in any, but they are as bitter to thee as gall and wormwood;—Then God hath shed abroad the first work of saving grace in thy heart, and it will continue last, and this is no small matter of consolation.

Use 2. A direction and advertisement to such as yet find their hearts whole and unbroken; Take heed how you content yourselves in such a condition. Consider what our Saviour said to Saul, *It is hard to kick against the pricks,* to dash the naked soul against the curse and wrath of God is an hard business, and so it is for these men, to persecute the Lord of life to the death; but many a man that goes on in sin, saith, he feels no such hard work in sin; but thou wilt feel at the last, that it hath been but dashing against pricks, and if not in this world, then with more horror in another; you little know what anguish of soul for sin means; Can you provoke God to anger and not yourselves to confusion?

Use 3. Of exhortation to every soul that is in any measure pierced in heart with sense of sin; Think not thyselves undone, judge righteous judgment, or if it be the case of any of thy friends, say not they are undone, he hath now no mind to the world; but not so, if with pricking of conscience, the heart be pricked too, then fear him not, God will gather up his spirit to his calling again: If therefore your hearts be broken, bless God on that behalf, it is the best news that ever came to you; When God comes to redeem a sinner from sin, and the punishment of it, he will not content himself with the conscience, or mouth, or eyes, but the chiefest part of the soul must lie at stake for it, before him, he will have sin bleed to death. When God had threatened Nineveh with destruction, it would not have prevailed with God to prevent the punishment, if all the Harlots of the Country had come and humbled themselves before him, but the

King must humble himself to the dust: The heart of a man is the principal faculty of the soul, it rules all, it sets hand and tongue, all within, and all without awork. Now because the will is principal in the soul, then if God mean we shall be saved, he will have the principal part of the soul to lie in the dust, the liveliest corruption must trickle down upon the ground; therefore be content to stoop to it, and be glad you may.

Use 4. To teach Ministers not to be afraid sometimes of driving nails to the head, not to the consciences, but to the hearts of sinners. There are a generation of Preachers that would now have no Law preached, but now only to draw men on to Christ, by the love of Christ. It is true, this we should labor to do, but how must we do it? Do you think God will marry us to Christ, before our first husband be dead? unless the sinful hearts of men be pricked, unless the proud, wanton, and stubborn heart be pierced and wounded to the death? Therefore there is no hope of salvation unless it be thus with you. Why, you say, But he did but here preach, and they hear the Gospel. It is true, I grant a man may preach the Gospel, and wound men's souls as much by the Law; but yet know this, he preached the Gospel legally, not the promises of the Gospel, but the duties of the Gospel, and their sins against the Gospel, convincing them that they had sinned against the Lord of Life, and Glory. This is preaching of the Gospel legally, and a special means to pierce the hearts of men.

Use 5. Of consolation to all those souls that have found their hearts pricked: Many a soul is troubled because it cannot weep for sin, but if you can but find your hearts broken and departing from sin, if your hearts sit loose from sin, and refuse all sin, one sin as well as another, if God give thee a heart to avoid sin, and to do that which is good in his sight, if the life of thy sin decays, then blessed art thou of the Lord, Christ hath set his stamp upon thee, and will challenge thee for his own.

Use 6. This may serve for an use of exhortation to every soul of us whose souls have been pierced and pricked, that you freely let them run and bleed still; never daub up the wound, let it forever be bleeding; pray not so much to God for the healing of your hearts, as entreat him to create a new heart in you, *Ezek.* 36.26. By no means restrain the issue of sin, but if your heart be once pierced, let it then forever bleed. So far as terrors may hinder the peace of your consciences, labor to heal that; But you that love the Lord hate evil, *Psal.* 97.10. Be sure you forever keep the heart open to any charitable employment, for the refreshment of your poor brethren, as these pierced hearts in the Text did, they distributed what they had according as every man had need, and they were then full of the holy Ghost, and did eat their bread, not with churlishness, but with gladness and singleness of heart. What would it profit a man to win the whole world, and to lose his own soul? Consider it therefore, so much as God hath pricked thy heart, so much it sits loose from the world; an heart once pierced would think it a base part to talk of charges when it comes to lay out its estate for his brethren's necessities; Therefore let your hearts forever run freely to all good offices in the behalf of your brethren.

1641

Thomas Shepard
(1605-1649)

Born at Towcester, England, Thomas Shepard was educated at Emmanuel College, Cambridge, where he received his B.A. in 1624, his M.A. in 1627, and was shortly thereafter ordained to the ministry. He moved to Boston in 1635; the following year he became pastor of the church at Newtown (Cambridge) and was a founder of Harvard College. *The Sincere Convert* (London, 1641), a popular collection of sermons, went through twenty-one editions between its publication and 1812.

BIBLIOGRAPHY: John Albro, ed. *The Works of Thomas Shepard*, 3 Vols. (Boston, 1853), biography in Vol. I. Nehemiah Adams, ed. *The Autobiography of Thomas Shepard* (Boston, 1832). S. E. Morison, *Builders of the Bay Colony* (Boston, 1930).

From *The Sincere Convert*

CHAPTER V

That those that are saved are very few; and that those that are saved, are saved with very much difficulty.

Strait is the gate, and narrow is the way that leadeth unto life, and few there be that find it, Mat. 7.14.

Here are two parts.

1. The paucity of them that shall be saved: few find the way thither.

2. The difficulty of being saved: Strait and narrow is the way and gate unto life.

Hence arise two Doctrines.

1. That the number of them that shall be saved is very small, *Luke.* 13. 24. the Devil hath his drove, and swarms to go to hell, as fast as Bees to their Hive; Christ hath his Flock, and that is but a little flock; hence God's children are called Jewels, *Mal.* 3. 17. which commonly are kept secret, in respect of the other lumber in the house; hence they are called Strangers and Pilgrims, which are very few in respect of the inhabitants of the country through which they pass: hence they are called sons of

God, 1 *John* 3.2. Of the blood Royal, which are few in respect of common subjects.

But see the truth of this point in these two things.

First, look to all ages and times of the world. Secondly, to all places and persons in the world, and we shall see few men were saved.

1. Look to all ages, and we shall find but a handful saved. As soon as ever the Lord began to keep house, and there were but two families in it, there was a bloody Cain living, and a good Abel slain. And as the world increased in number, so in wickedness, *Gen.* 6.12. it is said, All flesh had corrupted their ways, and amongst so many thousand men, not one righteous but Noah, and his family; and yet in the Ark there crept in a cursed Cham.

Afterwards as Abraham's posterity increased, so we see their sin abounded. When his posterity was in Egypt, where one would think, if ever men were good, now it would appear, being so heavily afflicted by Pharaoh, being by so many miracles miraculously delivered by the hand of Moses, yet most of these God was wroth with, *Heb.* 3.12. and only two of them, Caleb and Joshua went into Canaan, a type of heaven. Look into Solomon's time, what glorious times! what great profession was there then! Yet after his death, ten Tribes fell to the odious sin of Idolatry, following the command of Jeroboam their King. Look further into Isaiah's time, when there were multitudes of Sacrifices and prayers, *Isa.* 1.11, yet then there was but a remnant, nay, a very little remnant that should be saved. And look to the time of Christ's coming in the flesh, (for I pick out the best time of all) when one would think by such Sermons he preached, such miracles he wrought, such a life as he led, all the Jews would have entertained him, yet it is said, *He came unto his own, and they received him not.* So few, that Christ himself admires at one good Nathaniel, *behold an Israelite in whom there is no guile.* In the Apostles' time, many indeed were converted, but few comparatively, and amongst the best Churches many bad: as that at Philippi, *Phil.* 3. 18. Many had a name to live, but were dead, and few only kept their garments unspotted. And presently after the Apostles' time, *many grievous wolves came and devoured the sheep;* and so in succeeding ages, *Rev.* 12.9. *All the earth wondered at the whore in scarlet.*

And in Luther's time, when the light began to arise again, he saw so many carnal Gospelers, that he breaks out in one Sermon, into these speeches, *God grant I may never live to see those bloody days that are coming upon an ungodly world.* Latimer heard so much profaneness in his time, that he thought verily doomsday was just at hand. And have not our ears heard censuring those in the Palatinate, where (as 'tis reported) many have fallen from the glorious Gospel to Popery, as fast as leaves fall in Autumn? Who would have thought there had lurked such hearts under such a show of detesting Popery, as was among them before? And at Christ's coming, shall he find faith on the earth?

2. Let us look into all places and persons, and see how few shall be saved. The world is now split into four parts, Europe, Asia, Africa, and America; and the three biggest parts are drowned in a deluge of profaneness and superstition; they do not so much as profess Christ; you may see the sentence of death written on these men's foreheads. *Jer.* 10 *ult.* But let us look upon the best part of the world, and that is Europe, how few shall be saved there? First, the Grecian Church, howsoever now in these days, their good patriarch of Constantinople is about a general Reformation among them, and hath done much good; yet are they for the present, and have been for the most part of them, without the saving means of knowledge. They content themselves with their old superstitions, having little or no preaching at all. And for the other parts, as Italy, Spain, France, Germany, for the most part they are Popish; and see the end of these men, 2 *Thes* 2.9,10,11,12. And now amongst them that carry the badge of honesty, I will not speak what mine ears have heard, and my heart believes concerning other Churches: I will come into our own Church of England, which is the most flourishing Church in the world: never had Church such Preachers, such means; yet have we not some Chapels and Churches stand as dark lanterns without light, where people are led with blind, or idle, or licentious Ministers, and so both fall into the ditch?

Nay even amongst them that have the means of grace, but few shall be saved. It may be sometimes amongst ninety-nine in a parish, Christ sends a minister to call some one lost sheep among them, *Mat.* 13. Three grounds were bad where the seed was sown, and only one ground good. It's a strange speech of Chrysostom in his fourth Sermon to the people of Antioch, where he was much beloved and did much good: How many do you think (saith he) shall be saved in this city? It will be an hard speech to you, but I will speak it; though here be so many thousands of you, yet there cannot be found an hundred that shall be saved, and I doubt of them too; for what villainy is there among youth? what sloth in old men? and so he goes on. So say I, never tell me we are baptized, and are Christians, and trust to Christ; let us but separate the Goats from the sheep, and exclude none but such as the Scripture doth, and sets a cross upon their doors, with, Lord have mercy upon them, and we shall see only few in the City shall be saved.

1. Cast out all the profane people among us, as drunkards, swearers, whores, liars, which the Scripture brands for black sheep, and condemns them in an hundred places.

2. Set by all Civil men, that are but Wolves chained up, tame Devils, swine in a fair meadow, that pay all they owe, and do nobody any harm, yet do none any great good, that plead for themselves and say, Who can say black is mine eye? These are righteous men, whom Christ never came to call; For he came not to call the righteous, but sinners to repentance.

3. Cast by all Hypocrites, that like stage players, in the sight of others,

act the parts of Kings, and honest men; when look upon them in their tiring hours, they are but base varlets.

4. Formal Professors, and Carnal Gospelers, that have a thing like faith and like sorrow, and like true repentance, and like good desires, but yet they be but pictures, they deceive others and themselves too, *2 Tim.* 3.5.

Set by these four sorts, how few then are to be saved, even among them that are hatcht in the bosom of the Church?

First, here then is an Use of encouragement. Be not discouraged by the name of singularity. What? do you think yourself wiser than others? and shall none be saved but such as are so precise as Ministers prate? Are you wiser than others that you think none shall go to heaven but yourself? I tell you if you would be saved, you must be singular men, not out of faction, but out of conscience, *Acts* 24.16.

Secondly, here is matter of terror to all those that be of opinion, that few shall be saved; and therefore when they are convinced of the danger of sin by the Word, they fly to this shelter, If I be damned, it will be woe to many more beside me then; as though most should not be damned. Oh yes, the most of them that live in the Church shall perish: and this made an Hermit which Theodoret mentions, to live 15. years in a cell in a desolate wilderness, with nothing but bread and water, and yet doubted after all his sorrow, whether he should be saved or no. Oh! God's wrath is heavy, which thou shalt one day bear.

Thirdly, this ministereth exhortation to all confident people, that think they believe and say, they doubt not but to be saved, and hence do not much fear death. Oh! learn hence to suspect and fear your estates, and fear it so much, that thou canst not be quiet until thou hast got some assurance thou shalt be saved. When Christ told his Disciples that one of them should betray him, they all said, Master, Is it I? but if he had said, eleven of them should betray him, all except one, would they not all conclude, Surely it is I? If the Lord had said, only Few shall be damned, every man might fear, It may be it is I; but now he says most shall, every man may cry out and say, Surely it is I. No humble heart, but is driven to and fro with many stinging fears this way; yet there is a generation of presumptuous, brazen-fac'd, bold people, that confidently think of themselves, as the Jews of the Pharisees (being so holy and strict) that if God save but two in the world, they shall make one.

The child of God indeed is bold as a Lion; but he hath God's Spirit and promise, assuring him of his eternal welfare. But I speak of divers that have no sound ground to prove this point (which they pertinaciously defend) that they shall be saved. This confident humor rageth most of all in our old professors at large, who think, that's a jest indeed, that having been of a good belief so long, that they now should be so far behind hand, as to begin the work, and lay the foundation anew. And not only among these, but amongst divers sorts of people whom the Devil never troubles, because he is sure of them already, and therefore cries peace in their ears, whose consciences never trouble them, because that hath shut its eyes; and hence they sleep, and sleeping dream, that God is merciful unto them, and will be so; yet never see they are deceived, until they awake with the flames of hell about their ears; and the world troubles them not, they have their hearts' desire here, because they are friends to it, and so enemies to God. And Ministers never trouble them, for they have none such as are fit for that work near them; or if they have, they can sit and sleep in the Church, and choose whether they will believe him. And their friends never trouble them, because they are afraid to displease them. And God himself never troubles them, because that time is to come hereafter. This one truth well pondered and thought on, may damp thine heart, and make thy conscience fly in thy face, and say, Thou art the man; it may be there are better in hell than thyself that art so confident; and therefore tell me what hast thou to say for thyself, that thou shalt be saved? In what thing hast thou gone beyond them that think they are rich and want nothing, who yet are poor, blind, miserable, and naked?

Thou wilt say happily, first, I have left my sins I once lived in, and am now no drunkard, no swearer, no liar, &c.

I answer, thou mayest be washt from thy mire (the pollution of the world) and yet be a swine in God's account, 2 *Pet.* 2. 20. thou mayest live a blameless, innocent, honest, smooth life, and yet be a miserable creature still, *Phil.* 3.6.

But I pray, and that often.

This thou mayest do, and yet never be saved. *Isai.* 1. 11. To what purpose is your multitude of Sacrifices? Nay thou mayest pray with much affection, with a good heart, as thou thinkest, yet a thousand miles off from being saved, *Prov.* 1. 28.

But I fast sometimes, as well as pray.

So did the Scribes and Pharisees, even twice a week, which could not be public, but private fasts. And yet this righteousness could never save them.

But I hear the word of God, and like the best Preachers.

This thou mayest do too, and yet never be saved. Nay, thou mayest so hear, as to receive much joy and comfort in hearing, nay, to believe and catch hold on Christ, and so say and think he is thine, and yet not be saved: as the stony ground did, *Matth.* 13. who heard the word with joy, and for a season believed.

I read the Scriptures often.

This you may do too, and yet never be saved; as the Pharisees, who were so perfect in reading the Bible, that Christ needed but only say, It hath been said of old time, for they knew the text and place well enough without intimation.

But I am grieved and am sorrowful, and repent for my sins past.

Judas did thus, *Mat.* 27. 3. he repents himself with a legal repentance for fear of hell, and with a natural sorrow for dealing so unkindly with Christ, in betraying not only blood, but innocent blood. True humiliation is ever accompanied with hearty reformation.

Oh! but I love good men, and their company.

So did the five foolish Virgins love the company, and (at the time of extremity) the very oil and grace of the wise, yet they were locked out of the gates of mercy.

But God hath given me more knowledge than others, or than I myself had once.

This thou mayest have, and be able to teach others, and think so of thyself too, and yet never be saved.

But I keep the Lord's day strictly.

So did the Jews, whom yet Christ condemned, and were never saved. I have very many good desires and endeavors to get heaven.

These thou and thousands may have, and yet miss of heaven.

Many shall seek to enter in at that narrow gate, and not be able.

True, thou wilt say, many men do many duties, but without any life or zeal; I am zealous.

So thou mayest be, and yet never be saved, as Jehu; Paul was zealous when he was a Pharisee, and if he was so for a false Religion, and a bad cause, why much more mayest thou be for a good cause; so zealous as not only to cry out against profaneness in the wicked, but civil honesty of others, and hypocrisy of others, yea, even of the coldness of the best of God's people: thou mayest be the forehorse in the Team, and the Ringleader of good exercises amongst the best men, (as Joash a wicked King was the first that complained of the negligence of his best Officers in not repairing the Temple) and so stir them up unto it: nay, thou mayest be so forward, as to be persecuted, and not yield an inch, nor shrink in the wetting, but mayest manfully and courageously stand it out in time of persecution, as the thorny ground did: so zealous thou mayest be, as to like best of, and to flock most unto the most zealous Preachers, that search men's consciences best, as the whole country of Judea came flocking to John's Ministry, and delighted to hear him for a season; nay, thou mayest be zealous as to take sweet delight in doing of all these things, *Isa.* 58. 2, 3. *They delight in approaching near unto God,* yet come short of heaven.

But thou wilt say, True, many a man rides post, that breaks his neck at last: many a man is zealous, but his fire is soon quench'd, and his zeal is soon spent; they hold not out; whereas I am constant, and persevere in godly courses.

So did that young man, yet he was a graceless man, *Mat.* 19. 20. *All these things have I done from my youth:* what lack I yet?

It is true, hypocrites may persevere, but they know themselves to be naught all the while, and so deceive others: but I am persuaded that I am in God's favor, and in a safe and happy estate, since I do all with a good heart for God.

This thou mayest verily think of thyself, and yet be deceived, and damned, and go to the Devil at last. *There is a way* (saith Solomon) *that seemeth right to a man, but the end thereof is the way of death.* For he is an hypocrite not only that makes a seeming outward show of what he hath not, but also that hath a true show of what indeed there is not. The first sort of hypocrites deceive others only; the later having some inward, yet common work, deceive themselves too, *Jam.* 1. 26. *If any man seem to be religious* (so many are, and so deceive the world,) but it is added, *deceiving his own soul.* Nay, thou mayest go so fairly, and live so honestly, that all the best Christians about thee may think well of thee, and never suspect thee, and so mayest pass through the world, and die with a deluded comfort, that thou shalt go to heaven, and be canonized for a Saint in thy Funeral Sermon, and never know thou art counterfeit, till the Lord brings thee to thy strict and last examination, and so thou receivest that dreadful sentence, *Go ye cursed.* So it was with the five foolish Virgins that were never discovered by the wise, nor by themselves, until the gate of grace was shut upon them. If thou hast therefore no better evidences to show for thyself, that thine estate is good, than these, I'll not give a pin's point for all thy flattering false hopes of being saved: but it may be thou hast never yet come so far as to this pitch; and if not, Lord, what will become of thee? •Suspect thyself much, and when in this shipwreck of souls thou seest so many thousands sink, cry out, and conclude, It's a wonder of wonders, and a thousand and a thousand to one, if ever thou comest safe to shore.

Oh! strive then to be one of them that shall be saved, though it cost thee thy blood, and the loss of all that thou hast, labor to go beyond all those that go so far, and yet perish at the last. Do not say, that seeing so few shall be saved, therefore this discourageth me from seeking, because all my labor may be in vain. Consider that Christ here makes another and a better use of it, *Luk.* 3. 24. Seeing that *many shall seek and not enter, therefore* (saith he) *strive to enter in at the strait gate;* venture at least, and try what the Lord will do for thee.

Wherein doth the child of God, (and so how may I) go beyond these hypocrites that go so far?

In three things principally.

First, no unregenerate man, though he go never so far, let him do never so much, but he lives in some one sin or other, secret or open, little or great. Judas went far, but he was covetous. Herod went far, but he loved his Herodias. Every dog hath his kennel, every swine hath his swill, and every wicked man his lust; for no unregenerate man hath fruition of God to content him, and there is no man's heart but it must have some good to content it, which good is to be found only in the fountain of all good, and that is God; or in the cistern, and that is in the creatures:

hence a man having lost full content in God, he seeks for, and feeds upon contentment in the creature which he makes a God to him, and here lies his lust or sin, which he must need live in. Hence, ask those men that go very far, and take their penny for good silver, and commend themselves for their good desires: I say, ask them, if they have no sin; Yes, say they, who can live without sin? and so they give way to sin, and therefore live in sin; Nay, commonly, all the duties, prayers, care, and zeal of the best hypocrites are to hide a lust; as the whore in the Proverbs; that wipes her mouth, and goes to the Temple, and pays her vows; or to feed a lust, as Jehu his zeal against Baal, was to get a Kingdom. There remains a root of bitterness in the best hypocrites, which howsoever it be lopt off sometimes by sickness or horror of conscience, and a man hath purposes never to commit again, yet there it secretly lurks; and though it seemeth to be bound and conquered by the Word, or by Prayer, or by outward Crosses, or while the hand of God is upon a man, yet the inward strength and power of it remains still; and therefore when temptations, like strong Philistines, are upon this man again, he breaks all vows, promises, bonds of God, and will save the life of his sin.

Secondly, no unregenerate man or woman ever came to be poor in spirit, and so to be carried out of all duties unto Christ: if it were possible for them to forsake and break loose forever from all sin, yet here they stick as the Scribes and Pharisees, and so like zealous Paul before his conversion, they fasted and prayed, and kept the Sabbath, but they rested in their legal righteousness, and in the performance of these and the like duties. Take the best Hypocrite that hath the most strong persuasions of God's love to him, and ask him, why he hopes to be saved. He will answer, I pray, read, hear, love good men, cry out of the sins of the time. And tell him again, that a Hypocrite may climb these stairs and go as far; He will reply, true indeed, but they do not what they do with a sound heart, but to be seen of men. Mark now, how these men feel a good heart in themselves, and in all things they do, and therefore feel not a want of all good, which is poverty of spirit, and therefore here they fall short. Isai. 66. 2. there were divers Hypocrites forward for the worship of God in the Temple, but God loathes these, because not poor in spirit, to them only it is said the Lord will look. I have seen many professors very forward for all good duties, but as ignorant of Christ when they are sifted, as blocks. And if a man (as few do) know not Christ, he must rest in his duties, because he knows not Christ, to whom he must go and be carried if ever he be saved. I have heard of a man that being condemned to die, thought to escape the gallows, and to save himself from hanging by a certain gift he said he had of whistling; so men seek to save themselves by their gifts of knowledge, gifts of memory, gifts of prayer, and when they see they must die for their sins, this is the ruin of many a soul, that though he forsake Egypt and his sins, and fleshpots there, and will never be so as he hath been, yet he never cometh into Canaan, but loseth himself and his soul in a wilderness of many duties, and there perisheth.

Thirdly, if any unregenerate man come unto Christ, he never gets into Christ, that is, never takes his eternal rest and lodging in Jesus Christ only, *Heb.* 4. 4. Judas followed Christ for the Bag, he would have the Bag and Christ too. The young man came unto Christ to be his Disciple, but he would have Christ and the world too; they will not content themselves with Christ alone, nor with the world alone, but make their markets out of both, like whorish wives, that will please their husbands and others too. Men in distress of conscience, if they have comfort from Christ, they are contented; if they have salvation from hell by Christ, they are contented, but Christ himself contents them not. Thus far an hypocrite goes not. So much for the first Doctrine observed out of the Text. I come now to the second.

Doct. 2. That those that are saved, are saved with much difficulty: or it is a wonderful hard thing to be saved.

The gate is strait, and therefore a man must sweat and strive to enter; both the entrance is difficult, and the progress of salvation too. Jesus Christ is not got with a wet finger. It is not wishing and desiring to be saved, will bring men to heaven; hell's mouth is full of good wishes. It is not shedding a tear at a Sermon, or blubbering now and then in a corner, and saying over thy prayers, and crying God mercy for thy sins, will save thee. It is not *Lord have mercy upon us*, will do thee good. It is not coming constantly to Church; these are easy matters. But it is a tough work, a wonderful hard matter to be saved, 1 *Pet.* 4. 18. Hence the way to heaven is compared to a Race, where a man must put forth all his strength, and stretch every limb, and all to get forward. Hence a Christian's life is compared to wrestling, *Eph.* 6. 12. All the policy and power of hell buckle together against a Christian, therefore he must look to himself, or else he falls. Hence it is compared to fighting, 2 *Tim.* 4. 7. a man must fight against the Devil, the World, Himself; who shoot poisoned bullets in the soul, where a man must kill or be killed. God hath not lined the way to Christ with velvet, nor strewed it with rushes. He will never feed a slothful humor in man, who will be saved if Christ and Heaven would drop into their mouths, and if any would bear their charges thither: If Christ might be bought for a few cold wishes, and lazy desires, he would be of small reckoning amongst men, who would say, lightly come lightly go. Indeed Christ's yoke is easy in itself, and when a man is got into Christ, nothing is so sweet; but for a carnal dull heart, it is hard to draw in it; for,

There are 4. strait gates which every one must pass through before he can enter into heaven.

1. There is the strait gate of Humiliation: God saveth none, but first he humbleth them; now it is hard to pass through the gates and flames of hell; for a heart as stiff a stake, to bow; as hard as a stone, to bleed for the least prick, not to mourn for one sin, but all sins; and not for a fit,

but all a man's lifetime; Oh it is hard for a man to suffer himself to be loaden with sin, and prest to death for sin, so as never to love sin more, but to spit in the face of that which he once loved as dearly as his life. It is easy to drop a tear or two, and be Sermon-sick; but to have a heart rent for sin, and from sin, this is true humiliation, and this is hard.

2. The strait gate of Faith, *Eph.* 1. 19. It's an easy matter to presume, but hard to believe in Christ. It is easy for a man that was never humbled, to believe and say, 'Tis but believing: but it is a hard matter for a man humbled, when he sees all his sins in order before him, the Devil and Conscience roaring upon him, and crying out against him, and God frowning upon him, now to call God Father, is an hard work. Judas had rather be hang'd than believe. It is hard to see a Christ as a rock to stand upon, when we are overwhelmed with sorrow of heart for sin. It is hard to prize Christ above ten thousand worlds of pearl: 'tis hard to desire Christ, and nothing but Christ; hard to follow Christ all the day long, and never to be quiet till he is got in thine arms, and then with Simeon to say, Lord now lettest thou thy Servant depart in peace.

3. The strait gate of Repentance. It is an easy matter for a man to confess himself to be a sinner, and to cry God's forgiveness until next time: but to have a bitter sorrow and so to turn from all sin, and to return to God, and all the ways of God; which is true repentance indeed; this is hard.

4. The strait gate of opposition of Devils, the World, and a man's own Self, who knock a man down when he begins to look towards Christ and heaven.

Hence learn, that every easy way to heaven is a false way, although ministers should preach it out of their Pulpits, and Angels should publish it out of heaven.

Now there are nine easy ways to heaven, (as men think) all which lead to hell.

1. The common broad way, wherein a whole parish may all go a breadth in it; tell these people they shall be damned; their answer is, then woe to many more besides me.

2. The way of Civil education, whereby many wild natures are by little and little tamed, and like wolves are chained up easily while they are young.

3. Balam's way of good wishes, whereby many people will confess their ignorance, forgetfulness, and that they cannot make such shows as others do, but they thank God their hearts are as good, and God for his part accepts (say they) the will for the deed. And, My son give me thine heart; the heart is all in all, and so long they hope to do well enough. Poor deluded creatures thus think to break through armies of sins, Devils, temptations, and to break open the very gates of Heaven with a few good wishes; they think to come to their journey's end without legs, because their hearts are good to God.

4. The way of Formality, whereby men rest in the performances of most or of all external duties without inward life, *Mark*. 1. 14. Every man must have some Religion, some fig leaves to hide their nakedness. Now this Religion must be either true Religion, or the false one; if the true, he must either take up the power of it, but that he will not, because it is burdensome; or the form of it, and this being easy men embrace it as their God, and will rather lose their lives than their Religion thus taken up. This form of Religion is the easiest Religion in the world; partly, because it easeth men of trouble of conscience, quieting that: Thou hast sinned, saith conscience, and God is offended, take a book and pray, keep thy conscience better, and bring thy Bible with thee. Now conscience is silent, being charmed down with the form of Religion, as the Devil is driven away (as they say) with holy water; partly also because the form of religion credits a man, partly because it is easy in itself; it's of a light carriage, being but the shadow and picture of the substance of religion; as now, what an easy matter it is to come to Church? They hear (at least outwardly) very attentively an hour and more, and then to turn to a proof, and to turn down a leaf, here's the form. But now to spend Saturday night, and all the whole Sabbath day morning, in trimming the Lamp, and in getting oil in the heart to meet the Bridegroom the next day, and so meet him in the Word, and there to tremble at the voice of God, and suck the breast while it is open; and when the word is done, to go aside privately, and there to chew upon the word, there to lament with tears all the vain thoughts in duties, deadness in hearing, this is hard, because this is the power of godliness, and this men will not take up: so for private prayer, what an easy matter is it for a man to say over a few prayers out of some devout book, or to repeat some old prayer got by heart since a child, or to have two or three short-winded wishes for God's mercy in the morning and at night; this form is easy: but now to prepare the heart by serious meditation of God and man's self before he prays, then to come to God with a bleeding hunger-starved heart, not only with a desire, but with a warrant, I must have such or such a mercy, and there to wrestle with God, although it be an hour or two together for a blessing, this is too hard; men think none do thus, and therefore they will not.

Fifthly, the way of presumption, whereby men having seen their sins, catch hold easily upon God's mercy, and snatch comforts, before they are reached out unto them. There is no word of comfort in the book of God intended for such as regard iniquity in their hearts, though they do not act it in their lives. Their only comfort is, that the sentence of damnation is not yet executed upon them.

Sixthly, the way of sloth, whereby men lie still, and say God must do all; If the Lord would set up a Pulpit at the Alehouse door, it may be they would hear oftener. If God will always thunder, they will always pray; if strike them now and then with sickness, God shall be paid with good words and promises enow, that they will be better if they live; but as long as peace lasts, they will run to Hell as fast as they can; and if God will not catch them, they care not, they will not return.

Seventhly, the way of carelessness, when men feeling many difficulties, pass through some of them, but not all, and what they cannot get now, they feed themselves with a false hope they shall hereafter: they are content to be called Precisians, and fools, and crazy brains, but they want brokenness of heart, and they will pray (it may be) for it, and pass by that difficulty; but to keep the wound always open, this they will not do, to be always sighing for help, and never to give themselves rest till their hearts are humbled; that they will not; these have a name to live, yet are dead.

Eighthly, the way of moderation or honest discretion, *Rev.* 3. 16. which indeed is nothing but lukewarmness of the soul, and that is, when a man contrives and cuts out such a way to Heaven, as he may be hated of none, but please all, and so do anything for a quiet life, and so sleep in a whole skin. The Lord saith, *He that will live godly, must suffer persecution:* No, not so, Lord. Surely (think they) if men were discreet and wise, it would prevent a great deal of trouble and opposition in good courses; this man will commend those that are most zealous, if they were but wise; if he meet with a black-mouth'd swearer, he will not reprove him, lest he be displeased with him; if he meet with an honest man, he'll yield to all he saith, that so he may commend him; and when he meets them both together, they shall be both alike welcome, (whatever he thinks) to his house and table, because he would fain be at peace with all men.

Ninthly, and lastly, the way of Self-love, whereby a man fearing terribly he shall be damned, useth diligently all means whereby he shall be saved. Here is the strongest difficulty of all, to row against the stream, and to hate a man's self, and then to follow Christ fully.   1641

Roger Williams
(c. 1603-1683)

Roger Williams, the son of a London merchant, graduated from Pembroke College, Cambridge, in 1627. He was ordained to the ministry about 1629, moved to New England in 1631, and was chosen minister at Salem in 1634 in defiance of the General Court. Banished from Salem in 1635 for his "newe and dangerous opinions," he fled to Narragansett County, where he founded Providence in 1636. He helped secure charters for Providence in 1644 and again in 1663; from 1654 to 1657 he served as governor of the colony. Williams died in poverty following several years in the Indian trade. His works include *The Bloody Tenent of Persecution* (London, 1644), *The Bloody Tenent Yet More Bloody* (London, 1652), *A Key into the Lan-*

guage of America (London, 1643), and the "Letter to the Town of Providence," written in 1655.

BIBLIOGRAPHY: The Writings of Roger Williams, 6 Vols. (Providence, 1866-1874). The Complete Writings of Roger Williams, 7 Vols. (New York, 1963). Vol. 7 includes new material and an essay by Perry Miller. Samuel Brockunier, The Irrepressible Democrat: Roger Williams (New York, 1940). Perry Miller, Roger Williams, His Contribution to the American Tradition (Indianapolis, 1953). Ola E. Winslow, Master Roger Williams: A Biography (New York, 1957).

From The Bloody Tenent of Persecution for the Cause of Conscience

[PREFACE]

First, That the blood of so many hundred thousand souls of Protestants and Papists, spilt in the Wars of present and former Ages, for their respective Consciences, is not required nor accepted by Jesus Christ the Prince of Peace.

Secondly, Pregnant Scriptures and Arguments are throughout the Work proposed against the Doctrine of persecution for cause of Conscience.

Thirdly, Satisfactory Answers are given to Scriptures, and objections produced by Mr. Calvin, Beza, Mr. Cotton, and the Ministers of the New English Churches and others former and later, tending to prove the Doctrine of persecution for cause of Conscience.

Fourthly, the Doctrine of persecution for cause of Conscience, is proved guilty of all the blood of the Souls crying for vengeance under the Altar.

Fifthly, All Civil States with their Officers of justice in their respective constitutions and administrations are proved essentially Civil, and therefore not Judges, Governors or Defenders of the Spiritual or Christian State and Worship.

Sixthly, It is the will and command of God, that (since the coming of his Son the Lord Jesus) a permission of the most Paganish, Jewish, Turkish, or Antichristian consciences and worships, be granted to all men in all Nations and Countries: and that they are only to be fought against with that Sword which is only (in Soul matters) able to conquer, to wit, the Sword of God's Spirit, the Word of God.

Seventhly, The State of the Land of Israel, the Kings and people thereof in Peace & War, is proved figurative and ceremonial, and no pattern nor precedent for any Kingdom or civil state in the world to follow.

Eighthly, God requireth not an uniformity of Religion to be enacted and enforced in any civil state; which enforced uniformity (sooner or later) is the greatest occasion of civil War, ravishing of conscience, persecution of Christ Jesus in his servants, and of the hypocrisy and destruction of millions of souls.

Ninthly, In holding an enforced uniformity of Religion in a civil state, we must necessarily disclaim our desires and hopes of the Jews' conversion to Christ.

Tenthly, An enforced uniformity of Religion throughout a Nation or civil state, confounds the Civil and Religious, denies the principles of Christianity and civility, and that Jesus Christ is come in the Flesh.

Eleventhly, The permission of other consciences and worships than a state professeth, only can (according to God) procure a firm and lasting peace, (good assurance being taken according to the wisdom of the civil state for uniformity of civil obedience from all sorts.)

Twelfthly, lastly, true civility and Christianity may both flourish in a state or Kingdom, notwithstanding the permission of divers and contrary consciences, either of Jew or Gentile. . . .

The Answer of Mr. John Cotton of Boston in New England, To the aforesaid Arguments against Persecution for Cause of Conscience. Professedly maintaining Persecution for Cause of Conscience.

The Question which you put, is, Whether Persecution for cause of Conscience, be not against the Doctrine of Jesus Christ the King of Kings.

Now by Persecution for Cause of Conscience, I conceive you mean, either for professing some point of Doctrine which you believe in Conscience to be the Truth, or the practicing some Work which in Conscience you believe to be a Religious Duty.

Now in Points of Doctrine some are fundamental, without right belief whereof a Man cannot be saved: Others are circumstantial or less principal, wherein Men may differ in judgment, without prejudice of salvation on either part.

In like sort, in Points of Practice, some concern the weightier Duties of the Law, as, What God we worship, and with what kind of Worship; whether such, as if it be Right, fellowship with God is held; if Corrupt, fellowship with Him is lost.

Again, in Points of Doctrine and Worship less Principal: either they are held forth in a meek and peaceable way, though the Things be Erroneous or unlawful: Or they are held forth with such Arrogance and Impetuousness, as tendeth and reacheth (even of itself) to the disturbance of Civil Peace.

Finally, let me add this one distinction more: When we are persecuted for Conscience' sake, It is either for Conscience rightly informed, or for erroneous and blind Conscience.

These things premised, I would lay down mine Answer to the Question in certain Conclusions.

1. First, it is not lawful to persecute any for Conscience' sake Rightly informed; for in persecuting such, Christ himself is persecuted in them, *Acts* 9. 4.

2. Secondly, for an Erroneous and blind Conscience, (even in fundamental and weighty Points) It is not lawful to persecute any, till after
Admonition once or twice: and so the Apostle directeth, *Tit.* 3. 10. and
giveth the Reason, that in fundamental and principal points of Doctrine
or Worship, the Word of God in such things is so clear, that he cannot
but be convinced in Conscience of the dangerous Error of his way, after
once or twice Admonition, wisely and faithfully dispensed. And then if
any one persist, it is not out of Conscience, but against his Conscience, as
the Apostle saith, *vers.* 11. He is subverted and sinneth, being condemned of Himself, that is, of his own Conscience. So that if such a Man
after such Admonition shall still persist in the Error of his way, and be
therefore punished; He is not persecuted for Cause of Conscience, but for
sinning against his Own Conscience.

3. Thirdly, In things of lesser moment, whether Points of Doctrine or
Worship, If a man hold them forth in a Spirit of Christian Meekness and
Love (though with Zeal and Constancy) he is not to be persecuted, but
tolerated, till God may be pleased to manifest his Truth to him, *Phil.* 3.
17. *Rom.* 14. 1, 2, 3, 4.

But if a Man hold forth or profess any Error or false way, with a boisterous and arrogant spirit, to the disturbance of Civil peace, he may justly be punished according to the quality and measure of the disturbance
caused by him. . . .

A Reply to the aforesaid Answer of Mr. Cotton. In a Conference between Truth and Peace.

CHAPTER I

Truth. In what dark corner of the World (sweet Peace) are we two
met? How hath this present evil World banished Me from all the Coasts
& Quarters of it? and how hath the Righteous God in judgment taken
Thee from the Earth, *Rev.* 6. 4.

Peace. 'Tis lamentably true (blessed Truth) the foundations of the
World have long been out of course: the Gates of Earth and Hell have
conspired together to intercept our joyful meeting and our holy kisses:
With what a wearied, tired Wing have I flown over Nations, Kingdoms,
Cities, Towns, to find out precious Truth?

Truth. The like enquiries in my flights and travels have I made for
Peace, and still am told, she hath left the Earth, and fled to Heaven.

Peace. Dear Truth, What is the Earth but a dungeon of darkness,
where Truth is not?

Truth. And what's the Peace thereof but a fleeting dream, thine Ape
and Counterfeit?

Peace. O where's the Promise of the God of Heaven, that Righteousness and Peace shall kiss each other?

Truth. Patience (sweet Peace) these Heavens and Earth are growing
Old, and shall be changed like a Garment, *Psal.* 102. They shall melt

away, and be burnt up with all the Works that are therein; and the most high Eternal Creator, shall gloriously create New Heavens and New Earth, wherein dwells Righteousness, 2 *Pet.* 3. Our kisses then shall have their endless date of pure and sweetest joys? till then both Thou and I must hope, and wait, and bear the fury of the Dragon's wrath, whose monstrous Lies and Furies shall with himself be cast into the lake of Fire, the second death, *Revel.* 20.

Peace. Most precious Truth, thou knowest we are both pursued and laid for: Mine heart is full of sighs, mine eyes with tears: Where can I better vent my full oppressed bosom, than into thine, whose faithful lips may for these few hours revive my drooping wandering spirits, and here begin to wipe Tears from mine eyes, and the eyes of my dearest Children?

Truth. Sweet daughter of the God of Peace, begin; pour out thy sorrows, vent thy complaints: how joyful am I to improve these precious Minutes to revive our Hearts, both thine and mine, and the hearts of all that love the Truth and Peace, *Zach.* 8. . . .

CHAPTER II

. . . *Truth.* Sweet Peace, what hast thou there?

Peace. Arguments against persecution for cause of Conscience.

Truth. And what there?

Peace. An Answer to such Arguments, contrarily maintaining such persecution for cause of Conscience.

Truth. These Arguments against such persecution, and the Answer pleading for it, written (as Love hopes) from godly intentions, hearts, and hands, yet in a marvelous different style and manner. The Arguments against persecution in milk, the Answer for it (as I may say) in blood.

The Author of these Arguments (against persecution) (as I have been informed) being committed by some then in power, close prisoner to Newgate, for the witness of some truths of Jesus, and having not the use of Pen and Ink, wrote these Arguments in Milk, in sheets of Paper, brought to him by the Woman his Keeper, from a friend in London, as the stopples of his Milk bottle.

In such Paper written with Milk nothing will appear, but the way of reading it by fire being known to this friend who received the Papers, he transcribed and kept together the Papers, although the Author himself could not correct, nor view what himself had written.

It was in milk, tending to soul nourishment, even for Babes and Sucklings in Christ.

It was in milk, spiritually white, pure and innocent, like those white horses of the Word of truth and meekness, and the white Linen or Armor of righteousness, in the Army of Jesus. *Rev.* 6 & 19.

It was in milk, soft, meek, peaceable and gentle, tending both to the peace of souls, and the peace of States and Kingdoms.

Peace. The Answer (though I hope out of milky pure intentions) is returned in blood: bloody & slaughterous conclusions; bloody to the souls of all men, forc'd to the Religion and Worship which every civil State or Commonweal agrees on, and compels all subjects to in a dissembled uniformity.

Bloody to the bodies, first of the holy witnesses of Christ Jesus, who testify against such invented worships.

Secondly, of the Nations and Peoples slaughtering each other for their several respective Religions and Consciences.

CHAPTER III

Truth. In the Answer Mr. Cotton first lays down several distinctions and conclusions of his own, tending to prove persecution.

Secondly, Answers to the Scriptures, and Arguments proposed against persecution.

Peace. The first distinction is this: By persecution for cause of Conscience, "I conceive you mean either for professing some point of doctrine which you believe in conscience to be the truth, or for practicing some work which you believe in conscience to be a religious duty."

Truth. I acknowledge that to molest any person, Jew or Gentile, for either professing doctrine, or practicing worship merely religious or spiritual, it is to persecute him, and such a person (whatever his doctrine or practice be true or false) suffereth persecution for conscience.

But withal I desire it may be well observed, that this distinction is not full and complete: For beside this that a man may be persecuted because he holdeth or practiceth what he believes in conscience to be a Truth, (as Daniel did, for which he was cast into the Lions' den, *Dan.* 6.) and many thousands of Christians, because they durst not cease to preach and practice what they believed was by God commanded, as the Apostles answered (*Acts* 4. & 5.) I say besides this a man may also be persecuted, because he dares not be constrained to yield obedience to such doctrines and worships as are by men invented and appointed. So the three famous Jews were cast into the fiery furnace for refusing to fall down (in a nonconformity to the whole conforming world) before the golden Image, *Dan.* 3. 21. So thousands of Christ's witnesses (and of late in those bloody Marian days) have rather chose to yield their bodies to all sorts of torments, than to subscribe to doctrines, or practice worships, unto which the States and Times (as Nabuchadnezzar to his golden Image) have compelled and urged them.

A chaste wife will not only abhor to be restrained from her husband's bed, as adulterous and polluted, but also abhor (if not much more) to be constrained to the bed of a stranger. And what is abominable in corporal, is much more loathsome in spiritual whoredom and defilement.

The Spouse of Christ Jesus who could not find her soul's beloved in the ways of his worship and Ministry, (*Cant.* 1. 3. and 5. Chapters) abhorred to turn aside to other Flocks, Worships, &c. and to embrace the bosom of a false Christ, *Cant.* 1. 8.

CHAPTER VI

[*Truth*] . . . First, what is civil Peace, (wherein we shall vindicate thy name the better.)

Secondly, what it is to hold forth a Doctrine or Practice in this impetuousness or arrogance.

First, for civil peace, what is it but *pax civitatis*, the peace of the City, whether an English City, Scotch, or Irish City, or further abroad, French, Spanish, Turkish City, &c.

Thus it pleased the Father of Lights to define it, *Jerem.* 29. 7. Pray for the peace of the City; which peace of the City, or Citizens, so compacted in a civil way of union, may be entire, unbroken, safe, &c. notwithstanding so many thousands of God's people the Jews, were there in bondage, and would neither be constrained to the worship of the City Babel, nor restrained from so much of the worship of the true God, as they then could practice, as is plain in the practice of the 3 Worthies, Shadrach, Misach, and Abednego, as also of Daniel, *Dan.* 3. & *Dan.* 6. the peace of the City or Kingdom, being a far different Peace from the Peace of the Religion or Spiritual Worship, maintained & professed of the Citizens. This Peace of their Worship (which worship also in some Cities being various) being a false Peace, God's people were and ought to be Nonconformitants, not daring either to be restrained from the true, or constrained to false Worship, and yet without breach of the Civil or City peace, properly so called.

Peace. Hence it is that so many glorious and flourishing Cities of the World maintain their Civil peace, yea the very Americans & wildest Pagans keep the peace of their Towns or Cities; though neither in one nor the other can any man prove a true Church of God in those places, and consequently no spiritual and heavenly peace: The Peace spiritual (whether true or false) being of a higher and far different nature from the Peace of the place or people, being merely and essentially civil and humane.

Truth. O how lost are the sons of men in this point? To illustrate this: The Church or company of worshippers (whether true or false) is like unto a Body or College of Physicians in a City; like unto a Corporation, Society, or Company of East-India or Turkey-Merchants, or any other Society or Company in London: which Companies may hold their Courts, keep their Records, hold disputations; and in matters concerning their Society, may dissent, divide, break into Schisms and Factions, sue and implead each other at the Law, yea wholly break up and dissolve into pieces and nothing, and yet the peace of the City not be in the least measure impaired or disturbed; because the essence or being of the City, and so the well-being and peace thereof is essentially distinct from those particular Societies; the City-Courts, City-Laws, City-punishments distinct from theirs. The City was before them, and stands absolute and entire, when such a Corporation or Society is taken down. For instance further, The City or Civil state of Ephesus was essentially distinct from the worship of Diana in the City, or of the whole city. Again, the Church of Christ in Ephesus (which were God's people, converted and call'd out from the worship of that City unto Christianity or worship of God in Christ) was distinct from both.

CHAPTER XXXIII

Peace. Yea but it is said that the blind Pharisees misguiding the subjects of a Civil State, greatly sin against a Civil State, and therefore justly suffer civil punishment; for shall the Civil Magistrate take care of outsides only, to wit, of the bodies of men, and not of souls, in laboring to procure their everlasting welfare?

Truth. I answer, It is a truth, the mischief of a blind Pharisee's blind guidance is greater than if he acted Treasons, Murders, &c. and the loss of one soul by his seduction is a greater mischief than if he blew up Parliaments, and cuts the throats of Kings or Emperors, so precious is that invaluable Jewel of a Soul, above all the present lives and bodies of all the men in the world! and therefore a firm Justice calling for eye for eye, tooth for tooth, life for life; calls also soul for soul, which the blind-guiding seducing Pharisee shall surely pay in that dreadful Ditch, which the Lord Jesus speaks of, but this sentence against him the Lord Jesus only pronounceth in His Church, His spiritual judicature, and executes this sentence in part at present and hereafter to all eternity: Such a sentence no Civil Judge can pass, such a Death no Civil sword can inflict.

I answer secondly, Dead men cannot be infected, the civil state, the world, being in a natural state dead in sin (whatever be the State Religion unto which persons are forced) it is impossible it should be infected: Indeed the living, the believing, the Church and spiritual state, that and that only is capable of infection; for whose help we shall presently see what preservatives, and remedies the Lord Jesus hath appointed.

Moreover as we see in a common plague or infection the names are taken how many are to die, and not one more shall be struck, than the destroying Angel hath the names of. So here, whatever be the soul infection breathed out from the lying lips of a plague-sick Pharisee, yet the names are taken, not one elect or chosen of God shall perish, God's sheep are safe in His eternal hand and counsel, and he that knows his material, knows also his mystical stars, their numbers, and calls them every one by name, none fall into the Ditch on the blind Pharisee's back, but such as were ordained to that condemnation, both guide and followers, 1 *Pet.* 2. 8. *Jude* 4. The vessels of wrath shall break and split, and only they to the praise of God's eternal justice, *Rom.* 9.

CHAPTER LXXX

Peace. Yea but (say they) the godly will not persist in Heresy or turbulent Schism, when they are convinced in Conscience, &c.

Truth. Sweet Truth, if the Civil Court and Magistracy must judge (as before I have written) and those Civil Courts are as lawful, consisting of natural men as of godly persons, then what consequences necessarily will follow, I have before mentioned. And I add, according to this conclusion it must follow, that, if the most godly persons yield not to once or twice Admonition (as is maintained by the Answerer) they must necessarily be esteemed obstinate persons, for if they were godly (saith he) they would yield. Must it not then be said (as it was by one, passing sentence of Banishment upon some, whose godliness was acknowledged) that he that commanded the Judge not to respect the poor in the cause of judgment, commands him not to respect the holy or the godly person?

Hence I could name the place and time when a godly man, a most desirable person for his trade, &c. (yet something different in conscience) propounded his willingness and desire to come to dwell in a certain Town in New England; it was answered by the Chief of the place, This man differs from us, and we desire not to be troubled. So that in conclusion (for no other reason in the world) the poor man, though godly, useful and peaceable, could not be admitted to a Civil Being and Habitation on the Common Earth in that Wilderness amongst them.

The latter part of the Answer concerning the Heretic or obstinate person to be excommunicated, and the scandalous offender to be punished in the Commonweal, which neither of both come near our Question: I have spoken of I fear too largely already.

Peace. Mr. Cotton concludes with a confident persuasion of having removed the grounds of that great error, viz., that persons are not to be persecuted for cause of conscience.

Truth. And I believe (dear Peace) it shall appear to them that (with fear and trembling at the word of the Lord) examine these passages, that the charge of error reboundeth back, even such an error, as may well be called the bloody tenent, so directly contradicting the spirit and mind and practice of the Prince of Peace; so deeply guilty of the blood of souls compelled and forced to Hypocrisy in a spiritual and soul rape; so deeply guilty of the blood of the Souls under the Altar, persecuted in all ages for the cause of Conscience, and so destructive to the civil peace and welfare of all Kingdoms, Countries, and Commonwealths.   1644

To the Town of Providence

PROVIDENCE, January, 1655.

That ever I should speak or write a tittle, that tends to such an infinite liberty of conscience, is a mistake, and which I have ever disclaimed and abhorred. To prevent such mistakes, I shall at present only propose this case: There goes many a ship to sea, with many hundred souls in one ship, whose weal and woe is common, and is a true picture of a commonwealth, or a human combination or society. It hath fallen out sometimes, that both papists and protestants, Jews and Turks, may be embarked in one ship; upon which supposal I affirm, that all the liberty of conscience, that ever I pleaded for, turns upon these two hinges—that none of the papists, protestants, Jews, or Turks, be forced to come to the ship's prayers or worship, nor compelled from their own particular prayers or worship, if they practice any. I further add, that I never denied, that notwithstanding this liberty, the commander of this ship ought to command the ship's course, yea, and also command that justice, peace and sobriety, be kept and practiced, both among the seamen and all the passengers. If any of the seamen refuse to perform their services, or passengers to pay their freight; if any refuse to help, in person or purse, towards the common charges or defense; if any refuse to obey the common laws and orders of the ship, concerning their common peace or preservation; if any shall mutiny and rise up against their commanders and officers; if any should preach or write that there ought to be no commanders or officers, because all are equal in Christ, therefore no masters nor officers, no laws nor orders, nor corrections nor punishments;—I say, I never denied, but in such cases, whatever is pretended, the commander or commanders may judge, resist, compel and punish such transgressors, according to their deserts and merits. This if seriously and honestly minded, may, if it so please the Father of lights, let in some light to such as willingly shut not their eyes.

I remain studious of your common peace and liberty.

ROGER WILLIAMS

Nathaniel Ward
(c. 1578-1652)

Lawyer and clergyman, Nathaniel Ward was born at Haverhill, Essex, England, and received his B.A. in 1599 and his M.A. in 1603 from Emmanuel College, Cambridge. After travelling on the continent where he studied for the ministry, Ward returned to England in 1624, held several clerical positions, and moved to New England in 1634. He was minister at Ipswich (Aggawam) for only two years, but remained in Massachusetts until 1646. Ward was largely responsible for the *Body of Liberties* (1641), the legal code of Massachusetts Bay. *The Simple Cobbler of Aggawam in America*, written in 1645, was published in London in 1647 under the name of Theodore de la Guard.

BIBLIOGRAPHY: L. C. Wroth, ed. *The Simple Cobbler of Aggawam* (New York, 1937). J. W. Dean, *A Memoir of the Rev. Nathaniel Ward* (Albany, 1868). S. E. Morison, *The Builders of the Bay Colony* (Boston, 1930).

From *The Simple Cobbler of Aggawam*

Either I am in an Apoplexy, or that man is in a Lethargy, who doth not now sensibly feel God shaking the Heavens over his head, and the Earth under his feet: The Heavens so, as the Sun begins to turn into darkness, the Moon into blood, the Stars to fall down to the ground; So that little Light of Comfort or Counsel is left to the sons of men: The Earth so, as the foundations are failing, the righteous scarce know where to find rest, the Inhabitants stagger like drunken men; it is in a manner dissolved both in Religions and Relations: And no marvel; for, they have defiled it by transgressing the Laws, changing the Ordinances, and breaking the Everlasting Covenant. The Truths of God are the Pillars of the world, whereon States and Churches may stand quiet if they will; if they will not, He can easily shake them off into delusions, and distractions enough.

Satan is now in his passions, he feels his passion approaching; he loves to fish in roiled waters. Though that Dragon cannot sting the vitals of the Elect mortally, yet that Beelzebub can flyblow their Intellectuals miserably: The finer Religion grows, the finer he spins his Cobwebs, he will hold pace with Christ so long as his wits will serve him. He sees himself beaten out of gross Idolatries, Heresies, Ceremonies, where the Light breaks forth with power; he will therefore bestir him to prevaricate Evangelical Truths, and Ordinances, . . .

Nor shall he need to stretch his strength overmuch in this work: Too many men having not laid their foundation sure, nor ballasted their Spirits deep with humility and fear, are prest enough of themselves to evaporate their own apprehensions. Those that are acquainted with Story know, it hath ever been so in new Editions of Churches: Such as are least able, are most busy to pudder in the rubbish, and to raise dust in the eyes of more steady Repairers. Civil Commotions make room for uncivil practices: Religious mutations, for irreligious opinions: Change of Air, discovers corrupt bodies; Reformation of Religion, unsound minds. . . .

The next perplexed Question, with pious and ponderous men, will be: What should be done for the healing of these comfortless exulcerations. I am the unablest adviser of a thousand, the unworthiest of ten thousand; yet I hope I may presume to assert what follows without just offense.

First, such as have given or taken any unfriendly reports of us New-English, should do well to recollect themselves. We have been reputed a Colluvies of wild Opinionists, swarmed into a remote wilderness to find elbowroom for our fanatic Doctrines and practices: I trust our diligence past, and constant sedulity against such persons and courses, will plead better things for us. I dare take upon me, to be the Herald of New England so far, as to proclaim to the world, in the name of our Colony, that all Familists, Antinomians, Anabaptists, and other Enthusiasts, shall have free Liberty to keep away from us, and such as will come to be gone as fast as they can, the sooner the better.

Secondly, I dare aver, that God doth nowhere in his word tolerate Christian States, to give Tolerations to such adversaries of His Truth, if they have power in their hands to suppress them. . . .

If the devil might have his free option, I believe he would ask nothing else, but liberty to enfranchise all false Religions, and to embondage the true; nor should he need: It is much to be feared, that lax Tolerations upon State pretences and planting necessities, will be the next subtle Stratagem he will spread, to distate the Truth of God and supplant the peace of the Churches. . . .

My heart hath naturally detested four things: The standing of the Apocrypha in the Bible; Foreigners dwelling in my Country, to crowd our native Subjects into the corners of the Earth; Alchemized coins; Tolerations of divers Religions, or of one Religion in segregant shapes: He that willingly assents to the last, if he examines his heart by daylight, his conscience will tell him, he is either an Atheist, or an Heretic, or an Hypocrite, or at best a captive to some lust: Poly-piety is the greatest impiety in the world. . . .

He that is willing to tolerate any Religion, or discrepant way of Religion, besides his own, unless it be in matters merely indifferent, either doubts of his own, or is not sincere in it.

He that is willing to tolerate any unsound Opinion, that his own may also be tolerated, though never so sound, will for a need hang God's Bible at the Devil's girdle. . . .

Here I hold myself bound to set up a Beacon, to give warning of a new-sprung Sect of Phrantasticks, which would persuade themselves and others, that they have discovered the Nor-west passage to Heaven. These wits of the game, cry up and down in corners such bold ignotions of a new Gospel, new Christ, new Faith, and new gay-nothings, as trouble unsettled heads, querulous hearts, and not a little grieve the Spirit of God. I desire all good men may be saved from their Lunatic Creed, by Infidelity; and rather believe these torrid overtures will prove in time, nothing but horrid raptures down to the lowest hell, from which he that would be delivered, let him avoid these blasphemers, a late fry of croaking Frogs, not to be endured in a Religious State, no, if it were possible, not an hour. . . .

Lastly, I dare aver, that it ill becomes Christians anything well-shod with the preparation of the Gospel, to meditate flight from their dear Country upon these disturbances. Stand your ground ye Eleazars and

Shammahs, stir not a foot so long as you have half a foot of ground to stand upon: after one or two such Worthies, a great Victory may be regained, and flying Israel may return to a rich spoil. Englishmen, be advised to love England, with your hearts and to preserve it by your Prayers. I am bold to say that since the pure Primitive time, the Gospel never thrived so well in any soil on earth, as in the British; . . .

Ye say, why come not we over to help the Lord against the Mighty, in these Sacred battles?

I answer, many here are diligently observing the counsel of the same Prophet, 22. 10. *Weep not for him that is dead, neither bemoan him; but weep for him that is gone away and shall return no more to see his Native Country.* Divers make it an Article of our American Creed, which a celebrate Divine of England hath observed upon *Heb.* 11. 9. That no man ought to forsake his own country, but upon extraordinary cause, and when that cause ceaseth, he is bound in conscience to return if he can: . . .

Should I not keep promise in speaking a little to Women's fashions, they would take it unkindly: I was loath to pester better matter with such stuff; I rather thought it meet to let them stand by themselves, like the *Quae Genus* in the Grammar; being Deficients, or Redundants, not to be brought under any Rule: I shall therefore make bold for this once, to borrow a little of their loose tongued Liberty, and misspend a word or two upon their long-wasted, but short-skirted patience: a little use of my stirrup will do no harm.

It is known more than enough, that I am neither Niggard, nor Cynic, to the due bravery of the true Gentry: if any man mislikes a bully among drossock more than I, let him take her for his labor: I honor the woman that can honor herself with her attire: a good Text always deserves a fair Margent: I am not much offended if I see a trim, far trimmer than she that wears it: in a word, whatever Christianity or Civility will allow, I can afford with London measure: but when I hear a nugiperous Gentledame inquire what dress the Queen is in this week: what the nudiustertian fashion of the Court; I mean the very newest: with edge to be in it in all haste, whatever it be; I look at her as the very gizzard of a trifle, the product of a quarter of a cypher, the epitome of nothing, fitter to be kickt, if she were of a kickable substance, than either honor'd or humor'd.

To speak moderately, I truly confess, it is beyond the ken of my understanding to conceive, how these women should have any true grace, or valuable virtue, that have so little wit, as to disfigure themselves with such exotic garbs, as not only dismantles their native lovely lustre, but transclouts them into gant bar-geese, ill-shapen-shotten-shell-fish, Egyptian Hieroglyphics, or at the best into French flirts of the pastery, which a proper English woman should scorn with her heels: it is no marvel they wear drails on the hinder part of their heads, having nothing as it seems in the fore-part, but a few Squirrels' brains to help them frisk from [one] ill-favor'd fashion to another. . . .

The World is full of care, much like unto a bubble;
Women and care, and care and women, and women and care and trouble.

The Verses are even enough for such odd pegma's. I can make myself
sick at any time, with comparing the dazzling splendor wherewith our
Gentlewomen were embellished in some former habits, with the gut-
foundered goosedom, wherewith they are now surcingled and debauched.
We have about five or six of them in our Colony: if I see any of them accidentally, I cannot cleanse my fancy of them for a month after. I have
been a solitary widower almost most twelve years, purposed lately to
make a step over to my Native Country for a yoke-fellow: but when I
consider how women there have tripe-wifed themselves with their clad-
ments, I have no heart to the voyage, least their nauseous shapes and the
Sea, should work too sorely upon my stomach. . . .

If any man think I have spoken rather merrily than seriously he is
much mistaken, I have written what I write with all the indignation I
can, and no more than I ought. I confess I veer'd my tongue to this kind
of Language *de industria* though unwillingly, supposing those I speak to
are incapable of grave and rational arguments.

ERRATA AT NON CORRIGENDA

Now I come to rub over my work, I find five or six things like faults,
which would be mended or commended, I know not well which, nor
greatly care.

1. For *Levity,* read, *Lepidity,*—and that a very little, and that very
necessary, if not unavoidable. . . .

To speak to light heads with heavy words, were to break their necks:
to clothe Summer matter, with Winter Rug, would make the Reader
sweat. It is music to me, to hear every Ditty speak its spirit in its apt
tune: every breast, to sing its proper part, and every creature, to express
itself in its natural note: should I hear a Mouse roar like a Bear, a Cat
low like an Ox, or a Horse whistle like a Red-breast, it would scare—me.

The world's a well-strung fiddle, man's tongue the quill,
    That fills the world with fumble for want of skill,
When things and words in tune and tone do meet,
    The universal song goes smooth and sweet.

2. For *audacity,* read, *veracity,* or *Verum Gallice non libenter audis.*
Mart. Flattery never doth well, but when it is whispered through a pair
of lisping teeth; Truth best, when it is spoken out, through a pair of open
lips. Ye make such a noise there, with Drums and Trumpets, that if I
should not speak loud, ye could not hear me:

He that to tall men speaks, must lift up 's head,
    And when h' hath done, must set it where he did:
He that to proud men talks, must put on pride;
    And when h' hath done, 'tis good to lay 't aside.

3. For, *Yes, but you speak at three thousand miles distance, which every Coward dare do*, read, *if my heart deceives me not, I would speak thus, in the Presence Chamber or House of Commons;* . . .

> When Kings are lost, and Subjects cast away,
>   A faithful heart should speak what tongue can say:
> It skills not where this faithful heart doth dwell,
>   His faithful dealing should be taken well.

4. For, *affected terms*, read *I hope not*—If I affect terms, it is my feebleness; friends that know me, think I do not: I confess, I see I have here and there taken a few finish stitches, which may haply please a few Velvet ears; but I cannot now well pull them out, unless I should seam-rend all. . . .

I honor them with my heart, that can express more than ordinary matter in ordinary words: it is a pleasing eloquence; them more, that study wisely and soberly to enhance their native language; them most of all, that esteem the late significant speech, the third great blessing of the Land; . . . Affected terms are unaffecting things to solid hearers; yet I hold him prudent, that in these fastidious times, will help disedged appetites with convenient condiments, and bangled ears, with pretty quick plucks.

5. For, *You verse it simply, what need have we of your thin Poetry;* read, *I confess I wonder at it myself, that I should turn Poet:* I can impute it to nothing, but to the flatuousness of our diet: they are but sudden raptures soon up, soon down.

6. For *tediousness*, read, *I am sorry for it*—We have a strong weakness in N.E. that when we are speaking, we know not how to conclude: we make many ends, before we make an end: the fault is in the Climate; we cannot help it though we can, which is the Arch infirmity in all morality: . . .

For, *all my other faults, which may be more and greater than I see,* read, *I am heartily sorry for them, before I know them, lest I should forget it after;* and humbly crave pardon at adventure, having nothing that I can think of, to plead but this, . . .

> Poor Cobblers well may fault it now and then,
>   They're ever mending faults for other men.
> And if I work for nought, why is it said,
>   This bungling Cobbler would be soundly paid?

1647

Increase Mather

An Essay for the Recording of Il-
lustrious Providences was first pub-
lished in Boston in 1684. See Head-
note to Mather's *The Life and Death*
of Mr. Richard Mather.

From *An Essay for the Recording of Illustrious Providences*

CHAPTER V

Concerning Things Preternatural Which Have Happened In New England.

Inasmuch as things which are preternatural, and not accomplished without diabolical operation, do more rarely happen, it is pity but that they should be observed. Several accidents of that kind have happened in New England, which I shall here faithfully relate, so far as I have been able to come unto the knowledge of them. . . .

As there have been several persons vexed with evil spirits, so divers houses have been woefully haunted by them. In the year 1679, the house of William Morse, in Newberry in New England, was strangely disquieted by a demon. After those troubles began, he did, by the advice of friends, write down the particulars of those unusual accidents. And the account which he giveth thereof is as followeth:—

On December 3, in the night time, he and his wife heard a noise upon the roof of their house, as if sticks and stones had been thrown against it with great violence; whereupon he rose out of his bed, but could see nothing. Locking the doors fast, he returned to bed again. About midnight they heard an hog making a great noise in the house, so that the man rose again, and found a great hog in the house; the door being shut, but upon the opening of the door it ran out.

On December 8, in the morning, there were five great stones and bricks by an invisible hand thrown in at the west end of the house while the man's wife was making the bed; the bedstead was lifted up from the floor, and the bedstaff flung out of the window, and a cat was hurled at her; a long staff danced up and down the chimney; a burnt brick, and a piece of a weather-board, were thrown in at the window. . . .

At another time an iron crook that was hanged on a nail, violently flew up and down; also a chair flew about, and at last lighted on the table where victuals stood ready for them to eat, and was likely to spoil all, only by a nimble catching they saved some of their meal with the loss of the rest and the overturning of their table.

People were sometimes barricado'd out of doors, when as yet there was nobody to do it; and a chest was removed from place to place, no hand touching it. Their keys being tied together, one was taken from the rest, and the remaining two would fly about making a loud noise by knocking against each other. But the greatest part of this devil's feats were his mischievous ones, wherein indeed he was sometimes antic enough too, and therein the chief sufferers were, the man and his wife, and his grandson. The man especially had his share in these diabolical molestations. For one while they could not eat their suppers quietly, but had the ashes on the hearth before their eyes thrown into their victuals, yea, and upon their heads and clothes, insomuch that they were forced up into their chamber, and yet they had no rest there; for one of the man's shoes being left below, it was filled with ashes and coals, and thrown up after them. Their light was beaten out, and, they being laid in their bed with their little boy between them, a great stone (from the floor of the loft) weighing above three pounds was thrown upon the man's stomach, and he turning it down upon the floor, it was once more thrown upon him. A box and a board were likewise thrown upon them all; and a bag of hops was taken out of their chest, therewith they were beaten, till some of the hops were scattered on the floor, where the bag was then laid and left. . . .

On January 23 (in particular), the man had an iron pin twice thrown at him, and his inkhorn was taken away from him while he was writing; and when by all his seeking it he could not find it, at last he saw it drop out of the air, down by the fire. A piece of leather was twice thrown at him; and a shoe was laid upon his shoulder, which he catching at, was suddenly rapt from him. A handful of ashes was thrown at his face, and upon his clothes; and the shoe was then clapt upon his head, and upon it he clapt his hand, holding it so fast, that somewhat unseen pulled him with it backward on the floor. . . .

February 2. While he and his boy were eating of cheese, the pieces which he cut were wrested from them, but they were afterwards found upon the table, under an apron and a pair of breeches; and also from the fire arose little sticks and ashes, which flying upon the man and his boy, brought them into an uncomfortable pickle. But as for the boy, which the last passage spoke of, there remains much to be said concerning him and a principal sufferer in these afflictions: for on the 18th of December, he sitting by his grandfather, was hurried into great motions, and the man thereupon took him, and made him stand between his legs; but the chair danced up and down, and had like to have cast both man and boy into the fire; and the child was afterwards flung about in such a manner, as that they feared that his brains would have been beaten out; and in the evening he was tossed as afore, and the man tried the project of holding him, but ineffectually. The lad was soon put to bed, and they presently heard a huge noise, and demanded what was the matter? and he answered, that his bedstead leaped up and down; and they (i.e. the man

and his wife) went up, and at first found all quiet, but before they had
been there long, they saw the board by his bed trembling by him, and
the bedclothes flying off him; the latter they laid on immediately, but
they were no sooner on than off; so they took him out of his bed for
quietness.

December 29. The boy was violently thrown to and fro, only they carried him to the house of a doctor in the town, and there he was free from
disturbances; but returning home at night, his former trouble began, and
the man taking him by the hand, they were both of them almost tript
into the fire. They put him to bed and he was attended with the same
iterated loss of his clothes, shaking off his bedboard, and noises that he
had in his last conflict; they took him up, designing to sit by the fire, but
the doors clattered, and the chair was thrown at him; wherefore they carried him to the doctor's house, and so for that night all was well. . . .

All this while the devil did not use to appear in any visible shape, only
they would think they had hold of the hand that sometimes scratched
them; but it would give them the slip. And once the man was discern-
ably beaten by a fist, and an hand got hold of his wrist, which he saw
but could not catch; and the likeness of a blackamoor child did appear
from under the rug and blanket, where the man lay, and it would rise
up, fall down, nod, and slip under the clothes, when they endeavored to
clasp it, never speaking anything.

Neither were there many words spoken by Satan all this time; only
once, having put out their light, they heard a scraping on the boards, and
then a piping and drumming on them, which was followed with a voice,
singing, "Revenge! Revenge! Sweet is revenge!" And they being well
terrified with it, called upon God: the issue of which was, that suddenly,
with a mournful note, there were six times over uttered such expressions
as "Alas! me knock no more! me knock no more!" and now all ceased.

The man does, moreover, affirm that a seaman (being a mate of a ship)
coming often to visit him told him, that they wronged his wife who suspected her to be guilty of witchcraft; and that the boy (his grandchild)
was the cause of this trouble; and that if he would let him have the boy
one day, he would warrant him his house should be no more troubled as
it had been. To which motion he consented. The mate came the next day
betimes, and the boy was with him until night; since which time his
house, he saith, has not been molested with evil spirits.

Thus far is the relation concerning the demon at William Morse his
house in Newberry. The true reason of these strange disturbances is as
yet not certainly known: some (as has been hinted) did suspect Morse's
wife to be guilty of witchcraft. . . . Others were apt to think that a seaman, by some suspected to be a conjuror, set the devil on work thus to
disquiet Morse's family; or, it may be, some other thing, as yet kept hid
in the secrets of Providence, might be the true original of all this trouble.

CHAPTER VIII

Several Cases of Conscience Considered.

The preceding relations about witchcrafts and diabolical impostures give us too just occasion to make enquiry into some cases of conscience, respecting things of this nature. And in the first place the *quaere* may be:

Whether it is lawful to make use of any sort of herbs or plants to preserve from witchcrafts, or from the power of evil spirits? The answer unto which is: That it is in no wise lawful, but that all attempts of that nature are magical and diabolical, and therefore detestable superstition; . . .

There is another case of conscience which may here be enquired into, viz. "Whether it be lawful to bind persons suspected for witches, and so cast them into the water, in order to making a discovery of their innocency or guiltiness; so that if they keep above the water, they shall be deemed as confederate with the devil; but if they sink they are to be acquitted from the crime of witchcraft?" As for this way of purgation, it cannot be denied but that some learned men have indulged it. King James approveth of it in his *Discourse of Witchcraft*, b. iii, ch. 6, supposing that the water refuseth to receive witches into its bosom, because they have perfidiously violated their covenant with God, confirmed by water in baptism. Kornmannus and Scribonius do, upon the same ground, justify this way of trial. But a worthy casuist of our own giveth a judicious reply to this supposal, viz. that all water is not the water of baptism, but that only which is used in the very act of baptism. Moreover, according to this notion the *proba* would serve only for such persons as have been baptized. . . . Amongst English authors, Dr. Cotta hath endeavored to show the unlawfulness of using such a practice; also, Mr. Perkins is so far from approving by this probation by cold water, as that he rather inclines to think that the persons who put it in practice are themselves, after a sort, practicers of witchcraft. . . . And that it is utterly unlawful I am by the following reasons convinced:

1. This practice has no foundation in nature, nor in Scripture. If the water will bear none but witches, this must needs proceed either from some natural or some supernatural cause. No natural cause is, or can be, assigned why the bodies of such persons should swim rather than of any other. The bodies of witches have not lost their natural properties: they have weight in them as well as others. Moral changes and viciousness of mind make no alteration as to these natural proprieties which are inseparable from the body. . . . But if the experiment be supernatural, it must either be divine or diabolical. It is not divine, for the Scripture does nowhere appoint any such course to be taken to find out whether persons are in league with the devil or no. It remains, then, that the experiment is diabolical. If it be said that the devil has made a compact with wizards, that they shall not be drowned, and by that means that covenant

is discovered, the reply is, we may not in the least build upon the devil's word. By this objection, the matter is ultimately resolved into a diabolical faith. And shall that cast the scale when the lives of men are concerned? Suppose the devil saith, these persons are witches, must the judge, therefore, condemn them?

2. Experience hath proved this to be a fallacious way of trying witches, therefore it ought not to be practiced. Thereby guilty persons may happen to be acquitted, and the innocent to be condemned. . . . Malderus saith, it has been known that the very same persons being often brought to this probation by water, did at one time swim and another time sink; and this difference has sometimes happened according to the different persons making the experiment upon them; in which respect one might with greater reason conclude that the persons who used the experiment were witches, than that the persons tried were so.

3. This way of purgation is to be accounted of, like other provocations or appeals to the judgment of God, invented by men; such as campfight, explorations by hot water, &c. In former times it hath been customary (and I suppose 'tis so still among the Norwegians) that the suspected party was to put his hand into scalding water, and if he received no hurt thereby then was he reputed innocent; but if otherwise, judged as guilty. Also, the trial by fire ordeal has been used in our nation in times of darkness. . . . These bloody kind of experiments are now generally banished out of the world. It is pity the ordeal by cold water is not exploded with the other.

4. This vulgar probation (as it useth to be called) was first taken up in times of superstition, being (as before was hinted of other magical impostures) propagated from Pagans to Papists, who would (as may be gathered from Bernard's 66 *Serm. in Cantica*) sometimes bring those that were under suspicion for heresy unto their purgation in this way. We know that our ancestors, the old Pagan Saxons, had amongst them four sorts of ordeal (i.e., trial or judgment, as the Saxon word signifies), whereby, when sufficient proof was wanting, they sought (according as the prince of darkness had instructed them) to find out the truth concerning suspected persons, one of which ordeals was this, the persons surmised to be guilty, having cords tied under their arms, were thrown with it into some river, to see whether they would sink or swim: so that this probation was not originally confined to witches, but others supposed to be criminals were thus to be tried; but in some countries they thought meet thus to examine none but those who have been suspected for familiarity with the devil. That this custom was in its first rise superstitious, is evident from the ceremonies of old used about it. . . .

It was in my thoughts to have handled some other cases of the like nature with these insisted on; but upon further consideration, I suppose it less needful, the practices which have given occasion for them being so grossly superstitious, as that they are ashamed to show their heads openly. . . . These kind of practices appear at first blush to be diabolical, so that I shall not multiply words in evincing the evil of them. It is noted that the children of Israel did secretly those things that are not right against the Lord their God, 2 *Kings* xvii, 9. I am told that there are some who secretly practice such abominations as these last mentioned, unto whom the Lord in mercy give deep and unfeigned repentance and pardon or their grievous sin.

CHAPTER X

Of Remarkable Tempests, Etc. in New England.

Other remarkables, besides those already mentioned, have happened in this country, many of which I cannot insert, as not having received a full and clear account concerning them. Nevertheless, such particulars as I have by good and credible hands been informed of, I shall further add. . . .

Some remarkable land floods have likewise happened in New England. Nor is that which came to pass this present year to be here wholly passed over in silence. In the spring time, the great river at Connecticut useth to overflow, but this year it did so after Midsummer, and that twice; for, July 20, 1683, a considerable flood unexpectedly arose, which proved detrimental to many in that colony. But on August 13, a second and a more dreadful flood came: the waters were then observed to rise twenty-six foot above their usual boundaries: the grass in the meadows, also the English grain, was carried away before it; the Indian corn, by the long continuance of the waters, is spoiled, so that the four river towns, viz. Windsor, Hartford, Weathersfield, Middle-town, are extreme sufferers. They write from thence, that some who had hundreds of bushels of corn in the morning, at night had not one peck left for their families to live upon. There is an awful intimation of Divine displeasure remarkable in this matter, inasmuch as August 8, a day of public humiliation, with fasting and prayer, was attended in that colony, partly on the account of God's hand against them in the former flood, the next week after which the hand of God was stretched out over them again in the same way, after a more terrible manner than at first. It is also remarkable that so many places should suffer by inundations as this year it hath been; for at the very same time when the flood happened at Connecticut, there was an hurricane in Virginia, attended with a great exundation of the rivers there, so as that their tobacco and Indian corn is very much damnified. . . . Whether there might not be some such natural reason of the great flood in Connecticut at this time, the ingenious upon the place, who know best how things are there circumstanced, may consider. With us in Boston it was then at first an Euroclydon; but in the afternoon the wind became southerly, when it blew with the greatest fierceness. If it were so at Connecticut, it seems very probable that the fury of the wind gave a check to the free passage of the river, which caused the sudden overflowing of the waters.   1684

VERSE

The Bay Psalm Book

The Whole Book of Psalms Faithfully Translated into English Meter (Cambridge, Mass., 1640), commonly known as *The Bay Psalm Book,* was the first book written and published in North America. Translated by a committee of Puritan worthies—among them John Cotton, Richard Mather, Thomas Welde, John Eliot, and Richard Lyon—the *Bay Psalm Book* was printed on the Cambridge press of Stephen Day. At least two hands, those of John Cotton and Richard Mather, are evident in "The Preface." Authorship of the various psalms is almost impossible to assign; however, Cotton has been credited with composition of the Twenty-third Psalm.

BIBLIOGRAPHY: Wilberforce Eames, ed. *The Bay Psalm Book* (New York, 1903). Zoltan Haraszti, ed. *The Bay Psalm Book* (Chicago, 1956). Haraszti, *The Enigma of the Bay Psalm Book* (Chicago, 1956).

From *The Bay Psalm Book*

THE PREFACE

The singing of Psalms, though it breathe forth nothing but holy harmony, and melody: yet such is the subtlety of the enemy, and the enmity of our nature against the Lord, & his ways, that our hearts can find matter of discord in this harmony, and crotchets of division in this holy melody. For there have been three questions especially stirring concerning singing. First, what psalms are to be sung in churches? whether David's and other scripture psalms, or the psalms invented by the gifts of godly men in every age of the church. Secondly, if scripture psalms, whether in their own words, or in such meter as English poetry is wont to run in? Thirdly, by whom are they to be sung? whether by the whole churches together with their voices? or by one man singing alone and the rest joining in silence, & in the close saying amen.

Touching the first, certainly the singing of David's psalms was an acceptable worship of God, not only in his own, but in succeeding times. . . . So that if the singing David's psalms be a moral duty & therefore perpetual; then we under the New Testament are bound to sing them as well as they under the Old: and if we are expressly commanded to sing Psalms, Hymns, and spiritual songs, then either we must sing David's psalms, or else may affirm they are not spiritual songs: which being penned by an extraordinary gift of the Spirit, for the sake especially of God's spiritual Israel, not to be read and preached only (as other parts of holy writ) but to be sung also, they are therefore most spiritual, and still to be sung of all the Israel of God: . . .

As for the scruple that some take at the translation of the book of psalms into meter, because David's psalms were sung in his own words without meter: we answer—First. There are many verses together in several psalms of David which run in rhythms (as those that know the Hebrew and as Buxtorf shows *Thesau.* pa. 029) which shows at least the lawfulness of singing psalms in English rhythms.

Secondly. The psalms are penned in such verses as are suitable to the poetry of the Hebrew language, and not in the common style of such other books of the Old Testament as are not poetical; now no Protestant doubteth but that all the books of the scripture should by God's ordinance be extant in the mother tongue of each nation, that they may be understood of all, hence the psalms are to be translated into our English tongue; and if in our English tongue we are to sing them, then as all our English songs (according to the course of our English poetry) do run in meter, so ought David's psalms to be translated into meter, that so we may sing the Lord's songs, as in our English tongue so in such verses as are familiar to an English ear which are commonly metrical: and as it can be no just offense to any good conscience, to sing David's Hebrew songs in English words, so neither to sing his poetical verses in English poetical meter: men might as well stumble at singing the Hebrew psalms in our English tunes (and not in the Hebrew tunes) as at singing them in English meter, (which are our verses) and not in such verses as are generally used by David according to the poetry of the Hebrew language: but the truth is, as the Lord hath hid from us the Hebrew tunes, lest we should think ourselves bound to imitate them; so also the course and frame (for the most part) of their Hebrew poetry, that we might not think ourselves bound to imitate that, but that every nation without scruple might follow as the grave sort of tunes of their own country songs, so the graver sort of verses of their own country poetry.

Neither let any think, that for the meter's sake we have taken liberty or poetical license to depart from the true and proper sense of David's words in the Hebrew verses, no; but it hath been one part of our religious care and faithful endeavor, to keep close to the original text.

As for other objections taken from the difficulty of Ainsworth's tunes, and the corruptions in our common psalm books, we hope they are answered in this new edition of psalms which we here present to God and his Churches. For although we have cause to bless God in many respects for the religious endeavors of the translators of the psalms into meter usually annexed to our Bibles, yet it is not unknown to the godly learned that they have rather presented a paraphrase than the words of David translated according to the rule 2 *Chron.* 29. 30. and that their addition to the words, detractions from the words are not seldom and rare, but very frequent and many times needless, (which we suppose would not be approved of if the psalms were so translated into prose) and that their variations of the sense, and alterations of the sacred text too frequently, may justly minister matter of offense to them that are able to compare the translation with the text; of which failings, some judicious have oft complained, others have been grieved, whereupon it hath been generally desired, that as we do enjoy other, so (if it were the Lord's will) we might enjoy this ordinance also in its native purity: we have therefore done our endeavor to make a plain and familiar translation of the psalms and words of David into English meter, and have not so much as presumed to paraphrase to give the sense of his meaning in other words; we have therefore attended herein as our chief guide the original, shunning all additions, except such as even the best translators of them in prose supply, avoiding all material detractions from words or sense. The word ן which we translate *and* as it is redundant sometime in the Hebrew, so sometime (though not very often) it hath been left out and yet not then, if the sense were not fair without it.

As for our translations, we have with our English Bibles (to which next to the Original we have had respect) used the Idioms of our own tongue instead of Hebraisms, lest they might seem English barbarisms. Synonymies we use indifferently: as *folk* for *people,* and *Lord* for *Jehovah,* and sometime (though seldom) *God* for *Jehovah;* for which (as for some other interpretations of places cited in the New Testament) we have the scriptures' authority *Ps.* 14. with 53. *Heb.* 1. 6. with *Psalm* 97. 7. Where a phrase is doubtful we have followed that which (in our own apprehension) is most genuine & edifying:

Sometime we have contracted, sometime dilated the same Hebrew word, both for the sense and the verse's sake: which dilatation we conceive to be no paraphrastical addition no more than the contraction of a true and full translation to be any unfaithful detraction or diminution: as when we dilate *who healeth* and say *he it is who healeth;* so when we contract, *those that stand in awe of God* and say *God's fearers.*

Lastly. Because some Hebrew words have a more full and emphatical signification than any one English word can or doth sometime express, hence we have done that sometime which faithful translators may do, viz. not only to translate the word but the emphasis of it; as ל אֵ *mighty God,* for *God.* ךְ רַ בָּ *humbly bless* for *bless; rise to stand, Psalm* 1. for *stand, truth and faithfulness* for *truth.* Howbeit, for the verse's sake we do not always thus, yet we render the word truly though not fully; as when we sometimes say *rejoice* for *shout for joy.*

As for all other changes of numbers, tenses, and characters of speech, they are such as either the Hebrew will unforcedly bear, or our English forcibly calls for, or they no way change the sense; and such are printed usually in another character.

If therefore the verses are not always so smooth and elegant as some may desire or expect; let them consider that God's Altar needs not our polishings: *Ex. 20.* for we have respected rather a plain translation, than to smooth our verses with the sweetness of any paraphrase, and so have attended Conscience rather than Elegance, fidelity rather than poetry, in translating the Hebrew words into English language, and David's poetry into English meter; that so we may sing in Sion the Lord's songs of praise according to his own will; until he take us from hence, and wipe away all our tears, & bid us enter into our master's joy to sing eternal Hallelujahs.

PSALM 23

A PSALM OF DAVID

The Lord to me a shepherd is,
   want therefore shall not I.
2 He in the folds of tender grass,
   doth cause me down to lie:
To waters calm me gently leads
3   Restore my soul doth he:
   he doth in paths of righteousness:
   for his name's sake lead me.
4 Yea though in valley of death's shade
   I walk, none ill I'll fear:
   because thou art with me, thy rod,
   and staff my comfort are.
5 For me a table thou hast spread,
   in presence of my foes:
   thou dost anoint my head with oil.
   my cup it overflows.
6 Goodness & mercy surely shall
   all my days follow me:
   and in the Lord's house I shall dwell
   so long as days shall be.

PSALM 100

A PSALM OF PRAISE

Make ye a joyful sounding noise
　　unto Jehovah, all the earth:
2 Serve ye Jehovah with gladness:
　　before his presence come with mirth.
3 Know, that Jehovah he is God,
　　who hath us formed it is he,
　　& not ourselves: his own people
　　& sheep of his pasture are we.
4 Enter into his gates with praise,
　　into his Courts with thankfulness:
　　make ye confession unto him,
　　& his name reverently bless,
5 Because Jehovah he is good,
　　forevermore is his mercy:
　　& unto generations all
　　continue doth his verity.

ANOTHER OF THE SAME

Make ye a joyful noise unto
　　Jehovah all the earth:
2 Serve ye Jehovah with gladness:
　　before him come with mirth.
3 Know, that Jehovah he is God,
　　not we ourselves, but he
　　hath made us. His people, & sheep
　　of his pasture are we.
4 O enter ye into his gates
　　with praise, & thankfulness
　　into his Courts: confess to him,
　　& his Name do ye bless.
5 Because Jehovah he is good,
　　his bounteous mercy
　　is everlasting: & his truth
　　is to eternity.

1640

The Burwell Papers

The author of the Burwell Papers, an account of Nathaniel Bacon's Rebellion in Virginia in 1676, remains unknown, though it has been suggested that either John or Ann Cotton of Queen's Creek, Va., may have written the narrative. The manuscript, discovered shortly after the Revolutionary War in the papers of Capt. Nathaniel Burwell, was first published in the *Coll. Mass. Hist. Soc.*, 2nd Ser., I (1814) and in a corrected edition in the *Proc. Mass. Hist. Soc.* (1866-1867).

BIBLIOGRAPHY: Jay B. Hubbell, "John and Ann Cotton, of 'Queen's Creek,' Virginia," *Amer. Lit.*, X (1938), 179-201.

From *Burwell Papers*

Bacon having for some time, been besieged by sickness, and now not able to hold out any longer; all his strength, and provisions being spent, surrendered up that Fort he was no longer able to keep, into the hands of that grim and all-conquering Captain, Death; after that he had implor'd the assistance of the above mentioned Minister, for the well-making his Articles of Rendition. The only Religious duty (as they say) he was observ'd to perform during these Intrigues of affairs, in which he was so considerable an actor, and so much concern'd, that rather than he would decline the cause, he became so deeply engaged in, in the first rise thereof, though much urged by arguments of dehortations, by his nearest Relations and best friends, that he subjected himself to all those inconveniences that, singly, might bring a Man of a more Robust frame to his last home. After he was dead he was bemoaned in these following lines (drawn by the Man that waited upon his person, as it is said) and who attended his Corpse to their Burial place: But where deposited till the General day, not known, only to those who are resolutely silent in that particular. There was many copies of Verses made after his departure, calculated to the Latitude of their affections who composed them; as a relish taken from both appetites I have here sent you a couple.

Bacon's Epitaph, made by his Man.

Death why so cruell what no other way
To manifest thy spleen, but thus to slay
Our hopes of safety; liberty, our all
Which, through thy tyranny, with him must fall
To its late Chaos? Had thy rigid force
Been dealt by retail, and not thus in gross

5

Grief had been silent: Now we must complain
Since thou, in him, has more than thousand slain
Whose lives and safeties did so much depend
On him their life, with him their lives must end.   10
   If't be a sin to think Death brib'd can be
We must be guilty; say 'twas bribery
Guided the fatal shaft. Virginia's foes
To whom for secret crimes, just vengeance owes
Deserved plagues, dreading their just desert   15
Corrupted Death by Paracelsian art
Him to destroy; whose well tried courage such,
Their heartless hearts, nor arms, nor strength could touch.
   Who now must heal those wounds, or stop that blood
The Heathen made, and drew into a flood?   20
Who is't must plead our Cause? nor Trump nor Drum
Nor Deputations; these alas are dumb.
And Cannot speak. Our Arms (though ne'er so strong)
Will want the aid of his Commanding tongue,
Which Conquer'd more than Caesar: He o'erthrew   25
Only the outward frame; this Could subdue
The rugged works of nature. Souls replete
With dull Chill'd cold, he'd animate with heat
Drawn forth of reason's Lymbick. In a word
Mars and Minerva, both in him Concurred   30
For arts, for arms, whose pen and sword alike
As Cato's did, may admiration strike
Into his foes; while they confess with all
It was their guilt styl'd him a Criminal.
Only this difference doth from truth proceed   35
They in the guilt, he in the name must bleed
While none shall dare his Obsequies to sing
In deserved measures; until time shall bring
Truth Crown'd with freedom, and from danger free
To sound his praises to posterity.   40
   Here let him rest; while we this truth report
He's gone from hence unto a higher Court
To plead his Cause: where he by this doth know
Whether to Caesar he was friend, or foe.

Upon the Death of G. B.

Whether to Caesar he was Friend or Foe?
Pox take such Ignorance, do you not know?
Can he be Friend to Caesar, that shall bring
The Arms of Hell, to fight against the King?
(Treason, Rebellion) then what reason have   5

We for to wait upon him to his Grave,
There to express our passions? Wilt not be
Worse than his Crimes, to sing his Elegy
In well tun'd numbers; where each Ella bears
(To his Flagitious name) a flood of tears?   10
A name that hath more souls with sorrow fed,
Than wretched Niobe, single tears ere shed;
A name that fill'd all hearts, all ears, with pain,
Until blest fate proclaimed, Death had him slain.
Then how can it be counted for a sin   15
Though Death (nay though myself) had bribed been,
To guide the fatal shaft? we honor all
That lends a hand unto a Traitor's fall.
What though the well paid Rochit soundly ply
And box the Pulpit, into flattery;   20
Urging his Rhetoric, and strain'd eloquence,
T' adorn incoffin'd filth and excrements;
Though the Defunct (like ours) ne'er tried
A well intended deed until he died?
'Twill be nor sin, nor shame, for us, to say   25
A two-fold Passion checker-works this day
Of Joy and Sorrow; yet the last doth move
On feet impotent, wanting strength to prove
(Nor can the art of Logic yield relief)
How Joy should be surmounted, by our grief.   30
Yet that we Grieve it cannot be denied,
But 'tis because he was, not 'cause he died.
So wept the poor distressed, Ilium Dames
Hearing those nam'd, their City put in flames,
And Country ruin'd; If we thus lament   35
It is against our present Joy's consent.
For if the rule, in Physic, true doth prove,
Remove the cause, th' effects will after move,
We have outliv'd our sorrows; since we see
The Causes shifting, of our misery.   40
   Nor is't a single cause, that's slipt away,
That made us warble out, a well-a-day.
The Brains to plot, the hands to execute
Projected ills, Death Jointly did nonsuit
At his black Bar. And what no Bail could save   45
He hath committed Prisoner to the Grave;
From whence there's no reprieve. Death keep him close
We have too many Devils still go loose.

                         c. 1676, 1814

Anne Bradstreet
(c. 1612-1672)

Anne Dudley Bradstreet, the wife of Simon Bradstreet, migrated with her husband to New England in the Winthrop party of 1630. After residing briefly at Salem, Boston, Cambridge, and Ipswich, the Bradstreets settled permanently at North Andover some time before 1644. Mrs. Bradstreet's *The Tenth Muse Lately Sprung Up in America* was published in London in 1650. A second edition appeared as *Several Poems* (Boston, 1678), with later verse, notably "Contemplations."

BIBLIOGRAPHY: J. H. Ellis, ed. *The Works of Mrs. Anne Bradstreet in Prose and Verse* (Charlestown, Mass., 1867, Gloucester, Mass., 1962). Josephine K. Piercy, ed. *The Tenth Muse* (Gainesville, Fla., 1965), facsimile of 1650 edition. Helen Campbell, *Anne Bradstreet and Her Times* (Boston, 1891). Piercy, *Anne Bradstreet* (New York, 1965).

From *The Tenth Muse*

THE PROLOGUE

1.

To sing of Wars, of Captains, and of Kings,
Of Cities founded, Commonwealths begun,
For my mean pen are too superior things:
Or how they all, or each their dates have run
Let Poets and Historians set these forth,   5
My obscure Lines shall not so dim their worth.

2.

But when my wondering eyes and envious heart
Great Bartas' sugar'd lines, do but read o'er
Fool I do grudge the Muses did not part
'Twixt him and me that overfluent store;   10
A Bartas can, do what a Bartas will
But simple I according to my skill.

5.

I am obnoxious to each carping tongue
Who says my hand a needle better fits,
A Poet's pen all scorn I should thus wrong,   15
For such despite they cast on Female wits:
If what I do prove well, it won't advance,
They'll say it's stolen, or else it was by chance.

6.

But sure the Antique Greeks were far more mild
Else of our Sex, why feigned they those Nine   20
And poesy made, Calliope's own Child;
So 'mongst the rest they placed the Arts Divine,
But this weak knot, they will full soon untie,
The Greeks did nought, but play the fools & lie.

7.

Let Greeks be Greeks, and women what they are   25
Men have precedency and still excel,
It is but vain unjustly to wage war;
Men can do best, and women know it well
Preeminence in all and each is yours;
Yet grant some small acknowledgment of ours.   30

8.

And oh ye high flown quills that soar the Skies,
And ever with your prey still catch your praise,
If e'er you deign these lowly lines your eyes
Give Thyme or Parsley wreath, I ask no bays,
This mean and unrefined ure of mine   35
Will make you glistering gold, but more to shine.

1650

OF THE FOUR AGES OF MAN
Old Age

What you have been, ev'n such have I before:
And all you say, say I, and somewhat more.
Babe's innocence, youth's wildness I have seen,
And in perplexed middle Age have been:
Sickness, dangers, and anxieties have passed,   5
And on this stage am come to act my last. . . .
It's not my valor, honor, nor my gold,
My ruin'd house now falling can uphold.
It's not my learning Rhetoric wit so large,
Hath now the power, death's warfare to discharge.   10
It's not my goodly state, nor bed of down
That can refresh, or ease, if Conscience frown.
Nor from Alliance can I now have hope,
But what I have done well, that is my prop;
He that in youth is godly, wise and sage,   15
Provides a staff then to support his Age.
Mutations great, some joyful and some sad,

In this short pilgrimage I oft have had.
Sometimes the Heavens with plenty smil'd on me
Sometime again rain'd all Adversity.   20
Sometimes in honor, sometimes in disgrace,
Sometimes an Abject, then again in place.
Such private changes oft mine eyes have seen,
In various times of state I've also been.
I've seen a Kingdom flourish like a tree,   25
When it was rul'd by that Celestial she;
And like a Cedar, others so surmount:
That but for shrubs they did themselves account. . . .
I saw all peace at home, terror to foes,
But ah, I saw at last those eyes to close,   30
And then methought the day at noon grew dark
When it had lost that radiant Sun-like Spark:
In midst of griefs I saw our hopes revive,
(For 'twas our hopes then kept our hearts alive)
We chang'd our queen for king under whose rays   35
We joy'd in many blest and prosperous days.
I've seen a Prince, the glory of our land
In prime of youth seiz'd by heaven's angry hand,
Which fill'd our hearts with fears, with tears our eyes,
Wailing his fate, & our own destinies.   40
I've seen from Rome an execrable thing,
A Plot to blow up Nobles and their King,
But saw their horrid fact soon disappointed,
And Land & Nobles sav'd with their anointed.
I've Princes seen to live on others' lands;   45
A royal one by gifts from strangers' hands
Admired for their magnanimity,
Who lost a Princedom and a Monarchy.
I've seen unworthy men advanced high,
(And better ones suffer extremity)   50
But neither favor, riches, title, State,
Could length their days or once reverse their fate . . . .
I've seen and so have you, for 'tis but late,
The desolation of a goodly State,
Plotted and acted so that none can tell,   55
Who gave the counsel, but the Prince of hell,
Three hundred thousand slaughtered innocents, . . .
What are my thoughts, this is no time to say.
Men may more freely speak another day.
These are no old-wives' tales, but this is truth,   60
We old men love to tell what's done in youth.
But I return from whence I stept awry,

My memory is bad, my brain is dry:
Mine Almond tree, grey hairs, do flourish now,
And back once straight, apace begins to bow: 65
My grinders now are few, my sight doth fail,
My skin is wrinkled, and my cheeks are pale,
No more rejoice at music's pleasing noise,
But waking glad to hear the cock's shrill voice. . . .
My golden Bowl and silver Cord e'er long   70
Shall both be broke, by racking death so strong: . . .
Yea, knowing much, the pleasant'st life of all,
Hath yet among those sweets some bitter gall;
Though reading others' works doth much refresh,
Yet studying much brings weariness to th' flesh: 75
My studies, labors, readings all are done,
And my last period now ev'n almost run.
Corruption my Father I do call,
Mother and Sisters both, the worms that crawl
In my dark house, such kindred I have store,   80
Where I shall rest till heavens shall be no more,
And when this flesh shall rot and be consum'd,
This body by this Soul shall be assum'd:
And I shall see with these same very eyes,
My strong Redeemer coming in the Skies.   85
Triumph I shall o'er sin, o'er death, o'er Hell,
And in that hope I bid you all farewell.   1650

THE FOUR SEASONS OF THE YEAR

Spring

Another four I've left yet to bring on,
Of four times four the last *Quaternion,*
The Winter, Summer, Autumn & the Spring,
In season all these Seasons I shall bring:
Sweet Spring like man in his Minority   5
At present claim'd, and had priority.
With smiling face and garments somewhat green,
She trimm'd her locks, which late had frosted been,
Nor hot nor cold, she spake, but with a breath,
Fit to revive, the numbed earth from death.   10
Three months (quoth she) are 'lotted to my share
March, April, May of all the rest most fair.
Tenth of the first, Sol into Aries enters,
And bids defiance to all tedious winters,
Crosseth the Line, and equals night and day,   15
(Still adds to th' last till after pleasant May)

And now makes glad the darkened northern wights
Who for some months have seen but starry lights.
Now goes the Plowman to his merry toil,
He might unloose his winter locked soil: 20
The Seedsman too, doth lavish out his grain,
In hope the more he casts, the more to gain:
The Gardener now superfluous branches lops,
And poles erects for his young clambering hops.
Now digs then sows his herbs, his flowers & roots   25
And carefully manures his trees of fruits.
The Pleiades their influence now give,
And all that seem'd as dead afresh doth live.
The croaking frogs, whom nipping winter kill'd
Like birds now chirp, and hop about the field,   30
The Nightingale, the black-bird and the Thrush
Now tune their lays, on sprays of every bush.
The wanton frisking Kid, and soft-fleec'd Lambs
Do jump and play before their feeding Dams,
The tender tops of budding grass they crop,   35
They joy in what they have, but more in hope:
For though the frost hath lost his binding power,
Yet many a fleece of snow and stormy shower
Doth darken Sol's bright eye, makes us remember
The pinching North-west wind of cold December.   40
My second month is April, green and fair,
Of longer days, and a more temperate Air:
The Sun in Taurus keeps his residence,
And with his warmer beams glanceth from thence
This is the month whose fruitful showers produces   45
All set and sown for all delights and uses:
The Pear, the Plum, and Apple tree now flourish
The grass grows long the hungry beast to nourish.
The Primrose pale, and azure violet
Among the verduous grass hath nature set,   50
That when the Sun on's Love (the earth) doth shine
These might as lace set out her garment fine.
The fearful bird his little house now builds
In trees and walls, in Cities and in fields.
The outside strong, the inside warm and neat;   55
A natural Artificer complete.
The clucking hen her chirping chickens leads
With wings & beak defends them from the gledes.
My next and last is fruitful pleasant May,
Wherein the earth is clad in rich array,   60
The Sun now enters loving Gemini,

And heats us with the glances of his eye,
Our thicker raiment makes us lay aside
Lest by his fervor we be torrified.
All flowers the Sun now with his beams discloses,   65
Except the double pinks and matchless Roses.
Now swarms the busy, witty, honeybee,
Whose praise deserves a page from more than me.
The cleanly Houswife's Dairy's now in th' prime,
Her shelves and firkins fill'd for winter time.   70
The meads with Cowslips, Honeysuckles dight,
One hangs his head, the other stands upright:
But both rejoice at th' heaven's clear smiling face,
More at her showers, which water them a space.
For fruits my Season yields the early Cherry,   75
The hasty Peas, and wholesome cool Strawberry.
More solid fruits require a longer time,
Each Season hath his fruit, so hath each Clime:
Each man his own peculiar excellence,
But none in all that hath preeminence.   80
Sweet fragrant Spring, with thy short pittance fly
Let some describe thee better than can I.
Yet above all this privilege is thine,
Thy days still lengthen without least decline.   1650

LONGING FOR HEAVEN

As weary pilgrim, now at rest,
    Hugs with delight his silent nest
His wasted limbs, now lie full soft
    That merry steps, have trodden oft
Blesses himself, to think upon   5
    his dangers past, and travails done
The burning sun no more shall heat
    Nor stormy rains, on him shall beat.
The briars and thorns no more shall scratch
    nor hungry wolves at him shall catch   10
He erring paths no more shall tread
    nor wild fruits eat, instead of bread,
For waters cold he doth not long
    for thirst no more shall parch his tongue
No rugged stones his feet shall gall   15
    nor stumps nor rocks cause him to fall
All cares and fears, he bids farewell
    and means in safety now to dwell.
A pilgrim I, on earth, perplext

with sins with cares and sorrows vext 20
By age and pains brought to decay
  and my Clay house mouldering away
Oh how I long to be at rest
  and soar on high among the blest.
This body shall in silence sleep 25
  Mine eyes no more shall ever weep
No fainting fits shall me assail
  nor grinding pains my body frail
With cares and fears ne'er cumbered be
  Nor losses know, nor sorrows see 30
What tho my flesh shall there consume
  it is the bed Christ did perfume
And when a few years shall be gone
  this mortal shall be cloth'd upon
A Corrupt Carcass down it lies 35
  a glorious body it shall rise
In weakness and dishonor sown
  in power 'tis rais'd by Christ alone
Then soul and body shall unite
  and of their maker have the sight 40
Such lasting joys shall there behold
  as ear ne'er heard nor tongue e'er told
Lord make me ready for that day
  then Come dear bridegroom Come away.

1678

UPON MY SON SAMUEL HIS GOING FOR ENGLAND, NOVEMBER 6, 1657

Thou mighty God of Sea and Land,
I here resign into thy hand
The Son of Prayers, of vows, of tears,
The child I stay'd for many years.
Thou heard'st me then, and gav'st him me; 5
Hear me again, I give him Thee.
He's mine, but more, O Lord, thine own,
For sure thy Grace on him is shown.
No friend I have like Thee to trust,
For mortal helps are brittle Dust. 10
Preserve, O Lord, from storms and wrack,
Protect him there, and bring him back;
And if thou shalt spare me a space,
That I again may see his face,
Then shall I celebrate thy Praise, 15
And Bless thee for 't even all my Days.
If otherwise I go to Rest,

Thy Will be done, for that is best;
Persuade my heart I shall him see
For ever happefy'd with Thee.   20

                                              1678

TO MY DEAR AND LOVING HUSBAND

If ever two were one, then surely we.
If ever man were lov'd by wife, then thee;
If ever wife was happy in a man,
Compare with me ye women if you can.
I prize thy love more than whole Mines of gold,   5
Or all the riches that the East doth hold.
My love is such that Rivers cannot quench,
Nor ought but love from thee, give recompense.
Thy love is such I can no way repay,
The heavens reward thee manifold I pray.   10
Then while we live, in love let's so persevere,
That when we live no more, we may live ever.

                                              1678

CONTEMPLATIONS

21

Under the cooling shadow of a stately Elm
Close sat I by a goodly River's side,
Where gliding streams the Rocks did overwhelm;
A lonely place, with pleasures dignified.
I once that lov'd the shady woods so well,   5
Now thought the rivers did the trees excel,
And if the sun would ever shine, there would I dwell.

22

While on the stealing stream I fixed mine eye,
Which to the long'd for Ocean held its course,
I markt, nor crooks, nor rubs that there did lie   10
Could hinder ought, but still augment its force:
O happy Flood, quoth I, that holds thy race
Till thou arrive at thy beloved place,
Nor is it rocks or shoals that can obstruct thy pace.

23

Nor is't enough, that thou alone may'st slide,   15
But hundred brooks in thy clear waves do meet,
So hand in hand along with thee they glide
To Thetis' house, where all embrace and greet:

Thou Emblem true, of what I count the best,
O could I lead my Rivolets to rest,   20
So may we press to that vast mansion, ever blest.

27

O merry Bird (said I) that fears no snares,
That neither toils nor hoards up in thy barn,
Feels no sad thoughts, nor cruciating cares
To gain more good, or shun what might thee harm   25
Thy clothes ne'er wear, thy meat is everywhere,
Thy bed a bough, thy drink the water clear,
Reminds not what is past, nor what's to come dost fear.

28

The dawning morn with songs thou dost prevent,
Sets hundred notes unto thy feathered crew,   30
So each one tunes his pretty instrument,
And warbling out the old, begin anew,
And thus they pass their youth in summer season,
Then follow thee into a better Region,
Where winter's never felt by that sweet airy legion.   35

29

Man at the best a creature frail and vain,
In knowledge ignorant, in strength but weak,
Subject to sorrows, losses, sickness, pain,
Each storm his state, his mind, his body break,
From some of these he never finds cessation,   40
But day or night, within, without, vexation,
Troubles from foes, from friends, from dearest, near'st Relation
And yet this sinful creature, frail and vain,
This lump of wretchedness, of sin and sorrow,
This weather-beaten vessel wrackt with pain,   45
Joys not in hope of an eternal morrow;
Nor all his losses, crosses and vexation,
In weight, in frequency and long duration
Can make him deeply groan for that divine Translation.

                                                            1678

MEDITATIONS DIVINE AND MORAL

III

Youth is the time of getting, middle age of improving, and old age of
spending; a negligent youth is usually attended by an ignorant middle
age, and both by an empty old age. He that hath nothing to feed on but
vanity and lies must needs lie down in the Bed of sorrow.

IV

A ship that bears much sail, and little or no ballast, is easily overset; and that man, whose head hath great abilities, and his heart little or no grace, is in danger of foundering.

VI

The finest bread hath the least bran; the purest honey, the least wax; and the sincerest Christian, the least self-love.

VIII

Downy beds make drowsy persons, but hard lodging keeps the eyes open. A prosperous state makes a secure Christian, but adversity makes him Consider.

IX

Sweet words are like honey, a little may refresh, but too much gluts the stomach.

X

Diverse children have their different natures; some are like flesh which nothing but salt will keep from putrefaction; some again like tender fruits that are best preserved with sugar; those parents are wise that can fit their nurture according to their Nature.

XII

Authority without wisdom is like a heavy axe without an edge, fitter to bruise than polish.

XIII

The reason why Christians are so loth to exchange this world for a better, is because they have more sense than faith: they see what they enjoy, they do but hope for that which is to Come.

XIX

Corn, till it have past through the Mill and been ground to powder, is not fit for bread. God so deals with his servants: he grinds them with grief and pain till they turn to dust, and then are they fit manchet for his Mansion.

XXI

He that walks among briars and thorns will be very careful where he sets his foot. And he that passes through the wilderness of this world, had need ponder all his steps.

LV

We read of ten lepers that were Cleansed, but of one that returned thanks: we are more ready to receive mercies than we are to acknowledge them: men can use great importunity when they are in distresses, and show great ingratitude after their successes; but he that ordereth his conversation aright, will glorify him that heard him in the day of his trouble.

LVIII

Sin and shame ever go together. He that would be freed from the last, must be sure to shun the company of the first.

1678

John Norton
(1606-1663)

A leader among early New England ministers, John Norton was born in Hertfordshire, England, received his B.A. in 1624 and his M.A. in 1627 from Peterhouse College, Cambridge, and settled at Ipswich, Mass., in 1635. His prose writings include a biography of John Cotton (London, 1658), *The Orthodox Evangelist* (London, 1654), and *New England Rent at the Blas-* *phemies of the Present Generation* (Cambridge, Mass., 1659). His "A Funeral Elegy Upon . . . Mrs. Anne Bradstreet" appeared in the 1678 edition of her *Several Poems*.

BIBLIOGRAPHY: *DAB*. A. W. McClure, *The Lives of John Wilson, John Norton, and John Davenport* (Boston, 1846).

A Funeral Elegy

*Upon that Pattern and Patron of Virtue, the truly pious, peerless
& matchless Gentlewoman Mrs. Anne Bradstreet.*

> Ask not why hearts turn Magazines of passions,
> And why that grief is clad in sev'ral fashions;
> Why She on progress goes, and doth not borrow
> The smallest respite from th' extremes of sorrow,
> Her misery is got to such an height,   5
> As makes the earth groan to support its weight,
> Such storms of woe, so strongly have beset her,
> She hath no place for worse, nor hope for better;
> Her comfort is, if any for her be,

That none can show more cause of grief than she.   10
Ask not why some in mournful black are clad;
The Sun is set, there needs must be a shade.
Ask not why every face a sadness shrouds;
The setting Sun o'ercast us hath with Clouds.
Ask not why the great glory of the Sky   15
That gilds the stars with heavenly Alchemy,
Which all the world doth lighten with his rays,
The Perslan God, the Monarch of the days;
Ask not the reason of his ecstasy,
Paleness of late, in midnoon Majesty,   20
Why that the palefac'd Empress of the night
Disrob'd her brother of his glorious light.
Did not the language of the stars foretell
A mournful Scene when they with tears did swell?
Did not the glorious people of the Sky   25
Seem sensible of future misery?
Did not the lowering heavens seem to express
The world's great loss, and their unhappiness?
Behold how tears flow from the learned hill,
How the bereaved Nine do daily fill   30
The bosom of the fleeting Air with groans,
And woeful Accents, which witness their moans.
How do the Goddesses of verse, the learned choir
Lament their rival Quill, which all admire?
Could Maro's Muse but hear her lively strain,   35
He would condemn his works to fire again.
Methinks I hear the Patron of the Spring,
The unshorn Diety abruptly sing.
Some do for anguish weep, for anger I
That Ignorance should live, and Art should die.   40
Black, fatal, dismal, inauspicious day,
Unblest forever by Sol's precious Ray,
Be it the first of Miseries to all;
Or last of Life, defam'd for Funeral.
When this day yearly comes, let every one,   45
Cast in their urn, the black and dismal stone.
Succeeding years as they their circuit go,
Leap o'er this day, as a sad time of woe.
Farewell my Muse, since thou hast left thy shrine,
I am unblest in one, but blest in nine.   50
Fair Thespian Ladies, light your torches all,
Attend your glory to its Funeral,
To court her ashes with a learned tear,
A briny sacrifice, let not a smile appear.

Grave Matron, whoso seeks to blazon thee, 55
Needs not make use of wit's false Heraldry;
Whoso should give thee all thy worth would swell
So high, as 'twould turn the world infidel.
Had he great Maro's Muse, or Tully's tongue,
Or raping numbers like the Thracian Song, 60
In crowning of her merits he would be
Sumptuously poor, low in Hyperbole.
To write is easy; but to write on thee,
Truth would be thought to forfeit modesty.
He'll seem a Poet that shall speak but true; 65
Hyperbole's in others, are thy due.
Like a most servile flatterer he will show
Though he write truth, and make the subject, You.
Virtue ne'er dies, time will a Poet raise
Born under better Stars, shall sing thy praise. 70
Praise her who list, yet he shall be a debtor
For Art ne'er feign'd, nor Nature fram'd a better.
Her virtues were so great, that they do raise
A work to trouble fame, astonish praise.
When as her Name doth but salute the ear, 75
Men think that they perfections abstract hear.
Her breast was a brave Palace, a Broad-street,
Where all heroic ample thoughts did meet,
Where nature such a Tenement had ta'en,
That others' souls, to hers, dwelt in a lane. 80
Beneath her feet, pale envy bites her chain,
And poison Malice, whets her sting in vain.
Let every Laurel, every Myrtle bough
Be stript for leaves t' adorn and load her brow.
Victorious wreaths, which 'cause they never fade 85
Wise elder times for Kings and Poets made.
Let not her happy memory e'er lack
Its worth in Fame's eternal Almanac,
Which none shall read, but straight their loss deplore,
And blame their Fates they were not born before. 90
Do not old men rejoice their Fates did last,
And infants too, that theirs did make such haste,
In such a welcome time to bring them forth,
That they might be a witness to her worth.
Who undertakes this subject to commend 95
Shall nothing find so hard as how to end.

Finis & non.
Omnia Romanæ fileant Miracula Gentis. 1678

Urian Oakes

(c. 1631-1681)

Born in England, Urian Oakes moved with his parents to New England in 1640, received his B.A. from Harvard in 1649, was a fellow there, and returned to England to preach in 1653. Oakes became pastor of the church at Cambridge, Mass., in 1671, and after serving as acting president of Harvard for five years, was finally appointed president in 1680. His works include *New-England Pleaded With* (Boston, 1673), an essay condemning toleration, and *An Elegy upon the Death of the Reverend Mr. Thomas Shepard* (Cambridge, 1677).

BIBLIOGRAPHY: *DAB.* J. L. Sibley, *Biographical Sketches of Harvard Graduates,* I (1873), 173-185.

An Elegy Upon the Death of the Reverend Mr. Thomas Shepard

1

Oh! that I were a Poet now in grain!
How would I invocate the Muses all
To deign their presence, lend their flowing Vein,
And help to grace dear Shepard's Funeral!
    How would I paint our griefs, and succors borrow   5
    From Art and Fancy, to limn out our sorrow!

2

Now could I wish (if wishing would obtain)
The sprightliest Efforts of Poetic Rage,
To vent my Griefs, make others feel my pain,
For this loss of the Glory of our Age.   10
    Here is a subject for the loftiest Verse
    That ever waited on the bravest Hearse.

3

And could my Pen ingeniously distill
The purest Spirits of a sparkling wit
In rare conceits, the quintessence of skill   15
In Elegiac Strains; none like to it:
    I should think all too little to condole
    The fatal loss (to us) of such a Soul.

4

Could I take highest Flights of Fancy, soar
Aloft; If Wit's Monopoly were mine: 20

All would be much too low, too light, too poor,
To pay due tribute to this great Divine.
    Ah! Wit avails not, when th' Heart's like to break,
    Great griefs are Tongue-tied, when the lesser speak.

5

Away loose rein'd Careers of Poetry,   25
The celebrated Sisters may be gone;
We need no Mourning Women's Elegy,
No forc'd, affected, artificial Tone.
    Great and good Shepard's Dead! Ah! this alone
    Will set our eyes abroach, dissolve a stone.   30

6

Poetic Raptures are of no esteem,
Daring Hyperboles have here no place,
Luxuriant Wits on such a copious Theme,
Would shame themselves, and blush to show their face.
    Here's worth enough to overmatch the skill   35
    Of the most stately Poet Laureate's Quill.

7

Exuberant Fancies useless here I deem,
Transcendent virtue scorns feign'd Elegies:
He that gives Shepard half his due, may seem,
If Strangers hear it, to Hyperbolize.   40
    Let him that can, tell what his virtues were,
    And say, this Star mov'd in no common Sphere.

8

Here need no Spices, Odors, curious Arts,
No skill of Egypt, to embalm the Name
Of such a Worthy: let men speak their hearts,   45
They'll say, He merits an Immortal Fame.
    When Shepard is forgot, all must conclude,
    This is prodigious ingratitude.

9

But live he shall in many a grateful Breast,
Where he hath rear'd himself a Monument,   50
A Monument more stately than the best,
On which Immensest Treasures have been spent.
    Could you but into th' Hearts of thousands peep,
    There would you read his Name engraven deep.

10

Oh! that my head were Waters, and mine Eyes   55
A flowing Spring of Tears, still issuing forth
In streams of bitterness, to solemnize
The Obits of this Man of matchless worth!
   Next to the Tears our sins do need and crave,
   I would bestow my Tears on Shepard's Grave.   60

11

Not that he needs our Tears: for he hath dropt
His measure full; not one Tear more shall fall
Into God's Bottle from his eyes; Death stopt
That watercourse, his sorrows ending all.
   He Fears, he Cares, he Sighs, he Weeps no more: 65
   He's past all storms, Arriv'd at th' wished Shore.

12

Dear Shepard could we reach so high a strain
Of pure Seraphic love, as to divest
Ourselves, and love, of self-respects, thy gain
Would joy us, though it cross our interest.   70
   Then would we silence all complaints with this,
   Our Dearest Friend is doubtless gone to Bliss.

13

Ah! but the Lesson's hard, thus to deny
Our own dear selves, to part with such a Loan
Of Heaven (in time of such necessity)   75
And love thy comforts better than our own.
   Then let us moan our loss, adjourn our glee,
   Till we come thither to rejoice with thee.

14

As when some formidable Comets blaze,
As when Portentous Prodigies appear,   80
Poor Mortals with amazement stand and gaze,
With hearts affrighted, and with trembling fear:
   So are we all amazed at this blow,
   Sadly portending some approaching woe.

15

We shall not summon bold Astrologers,   85
To tell us what the Stars say in the case,
(Those Cousin-Germans to black Conjurers)

We have a sacred Oracle that says,
  When th' Righteous perish, men of mercy go,
  It is a sure presage of coming woe.   90

16

He was (ah woeful word! to say he was)
Our wrestling Israel, second unto none,
The man that stood i' th' gap, to keep the pass,
To stop the Troops of Judgments rushing on.
    This Man the honor had to hold the hand   95
    Of an incensed God against our Land.

17

When such a Pillar's fallen (Oh such an one!)
When such a glorious, shining Light's put out,
When Chariot and Horsemen thus are gone;
Well may we fear some Downfall, Darkness, Rout.   100
    When such a Bank's broke down, there's sad occasion
    To wail, and dread some grievous Inundation.

18

What! must we with our God, and Glory part?
Lord! Is thy Treaty with New England come
Thus to an end? And is War in thy Heart?   105
That this Ambassador is called home.
    So Earthly Gods (Kings) when they War intend,
    Call home their Ministers, and Treaties end.

19

Oh for the Raptures, Transports, Inspirations
Of Israel's Singers when his Jonathan's Fall   110
So tun'd his mourning Harp! what Lamentations
Then would I make for Shepard's Funeral
    How truly can I say, as well as He?
    My Dearest Brother I'm distress'd for thee.

20

How Lovely, Worthy, Peerless, in my view?   115
How Precious, Pleasant hast thou been to me?
How Learned, Prudent, Pious, Grave, and True?
And what a Faithful Friend? who like to thee?
    Mine Eye's desire is vanish'd: who can tell
    Where lives my dearest Shepard's Parallel?   120

21

'Tis strange to think: but we may well believe,
That not a few of different Persuasions
From this great Worthy, do now truly grieve
I' th' Mourning crowd, and join their Lamentations.
    Such Powers Magnetic had He to draw to Him   125
    The very Hearts, and Souls, of all that knew Him!

22

Art, Nature, Grace, in Him were all combin'd
To show the World a matchless Paragon:
In whom of Radiant Virtues no less shin'd,
Than a whole Constellation: but he's gone!   130
    He's gone alas! Down in the Dust must lie
    As much of this rare Person as could die.

23

If to have solid Judgment, Pregnant Parts,
A piercing Wit, and comprehensive Brain;
If to have gone the Round of all the Arts,   135
Immunity from Death's Arrest would gain,
    Shepard would have been Death-proof, and secure
    From that All conquering Hand, I'm very sure.

24

If Holy Life, and Deeds of Charity,
If Grace illustrious, and Virtue tried,   140
If modest Carriage, rare Humility,
Could have brib'd Death, good Shepard had not died.
    Oh! but inexorable Death attacks
    The best Men, and promiscuous havoc makes.

25

Come tell me, Critics, have you ever known   145
Such Zeal, so temper'd well with moderation?
Such Prudence, and such Innocence met in one?
Such Parts, so little Pride and Ostentation?
    Let Momus carp, and Envy do her worst,
    And swell with Spleen and Rancor till she burst.   150

26

To be descended well, doth that commend?
Can Sons their Fathers' Glory call their own?
Our Shepard justly might to this pretend,
(His Blessed Father was of high Renown,

Both Englands speak him great, admire his Name)   155
But his own personal worth's a better claim.

27

Great was the Father, once a glorious Light
Among us, Famous to an high Degree:
Great was this Son: indeed (to do him right)
As Great and Good (to say no more) as He.   160
   A double portion of his Father's Spirit
   Did this (his Eldest) Son, through Grace, inherit.

28

His Look commanded Reverence and Awe,
Though Mild and Amiable, not Austere:
Well Humor'd was He (as I ever saw)   165
And rul'd by Love and Wisdom, more than Fear.
   The Muses, and the Graces too, conspir'd
   To set forth this Rare Piece, to be admir'd.

29

He govern'd well the Tongue (that busy thing,
Unruly, Lawless and Pragmatical)   170
Gravely Reserv'd, in Speech not lavishing,
Neither too sparing, nor too liberal.
   His Words were few, well season'd, wisely weigh'd,
   And in his Tongue the Law of kindness sway'd.

30

Learned he was beyond the common Size,   175
Befriended much by Nature in his Wit,
And Temper, (Sweet, Sedate, Ingenious, Wise)
And (which crown'd all) he was Heaven's Favorite:
   On whom the God of all Grace did command,
   And shower down Blessings with a liberal hand.   180

31

Wise He, not wily, was; Grave, not Morose;
Not stiff, but steady; Serious, but not Sour;
Concern'd for all, as if he had no Foes;
(Strange if he had!) and would not waste an Hour.
   Thoughtful and Active for the common good: 185
   And yet his own place wisely understood.

32

Nothing could make him stray from Duty; Death
Was not so frightful to him, as Omission
Of Ministerial work; he fear'd no breath
Infectious, i' th' discharge of his Commission.   190
   Rather than run from's work, he chose to die,
   Boldly to run on Death, than duty fly.

33

(Cruel Disease! that didst (like Highwaymen)
Assault the honest Traveler in his way,
And rob dear Shepard of his life (Ah!) then,   195
When he was on the Road, where Duty lay.
   Forbear, bold Pen! 'twas God that took him thus,
   To give him great Reward, and punish us.)

34

Zealous in God's cause, but meek in his own;
Modest of Nature, bold as any Lion,   200
Where Conscience was concern'd: and there were none
More constant Mourners for afflicted Sion:
   So general was his care for th' Churches all,
   His Spirit seemed Apostolical.

35

Large was his Heart, to spend without regret,   205
Rejoicing to do good: not like those Moles
That root i' th' Earth, or roam abroad, to get
All for themselves (those sorry, narrow Souls!)
   But He, like th' Sun (i' th' Center, as some say)
   Diffus'd his Rays of Goodness every way.   210

36

He breath'd Love, and pursu'd Peace in his day,
As if his Soul were made of Harmony:
Scarce ever more of Goodness crowded lay
In such a piece of frail Mortality.
   Sure Father Wilson's genuine Son was he,   215
   New England's Paul had such a Timothy.

37

No slave to th' World's grand Idols; but he flew
At Fairer Quarries, without stooping down
To Sublunary prey: his great Soul knew

Ambition none, but of the Heavenly Crown.   220
   Now he hath won it, and shall wear't with Honor,
   Adoring Grace, and God in Christ, the Donor.

                        38

A Friend to Truth, a constant Foe to Error,
Powerful i' th' Pulpit, and sweet in converse,
To weak ones gentle, to th' Profane a Terror.   225
Who can his virtues, and good works rehearse?
   The Scripture-Bishop's Character read o'er,
   Say this was Shepard's: what need I say more?

                        39

I say no more: let them that can declare
His rich and rare endowments, paint this Sun,   230
With all its dazzling Rays: But I despair,
Hopeless by any hand to see it done.
   They that can Shepard's goodness well display,
   Must be as good as he: But who are they?

                        40

See where our Sister Charlestown sits and Moans!   235
Poor Widowed Charlestown! all in Dust, in Tears!
Mark how she wrings her hands! hear how she groans!
See how she weeps! what sorrow like to hers!
   Charlestown, that might for joy compare of late
   With all about her, now looks desolate.   240

                        41

As you have seen some Pale, Wan, Ghastly look,
When grisly Death, that will not be said nay,
Hath seiz'd all for itself, Possession took,
And turn'd the Soul out of its house of Clay:
   So Visag'd is poor Charlestown at this day;   245
   Shepard, her very Soul, is torn away.

                        42

Cambridge groans under this so heavy cross,
And Sympathizes with her Sister dear;
Renews her Griefs afresh for her old loss
Of her own Shepard, and drops many a Tear.   250
   Cambridge and Charlestown now joint Mourners are,
   And this tremendous loss between them share.

43

Must Learning's Friend (Ah! worth us all) go thus?
That Great Support to Harvard's Nursery!
Our Fellow (that no Fellow had with us)   255
Is gone to Heaven's great University.
    Ours now indeed's a lifeless Corporation,
    The Soul is fled, that gave it Animation!

44

Poor Harvard's Sons are in their Mourning Dress:
Their sure Friend's gone! their Hearts have put on
    Mourning;   260
Within their Walls are Sighs, Tears, Pensiveness;
Their new Foundations dread an overturning.
    Harvard! where's such a fast Friend left to thee!
    Unless thy great Friend, Leveret, it be.

45

We must not with our greatest Sovereign strive,   265
Who dare find fault with him that is most High?
That hath an absolute Prerogative,
And doth his pleasure: none may ask him, why?
    We're Clay lumps, Dust heaps, nothings in his sight:
    The Judge of all the Earth doth always right.   270

46

Ah! could not Prayers and Tears prevail with God!
Was there no warding off that dreadful Blow!
And was there no averting of that Rod!
Must Shepard die! and that good Angel go!
    Alas! Our heinous sins (more than our hates)   275
    It seems, were louder, and outcried our Prayers.

47

See what our sins have done! what Ruins wrought
And how they have pluck'd out our very eyes!
Our sins have slain our Shepard! we have bought,
And dearly paid for, our Enormities.   280
    Ah Cursed sins! that strike at God, and kill
    His Servants, and the Blood of Prophets spill.

48

As you would loathe the Sword that's warm and red,
As you would hate the hands that are embru'd

I' th' Heart's blood of your dearest Friends: so dread,   285
And hate your sins; Oh! let them be pursu'd:
 Revenges take on bloody sins: for there's
 No Refuge-City for these Murderers.

49

In vain we build the Prophets' Sepulchers,
In vain bedew their Tombs with Tears, when Dead;   290
In vain bewail the Deaths of Ministers,
Whilst Prophet-killing sins are harbored.
 Those that these Murderous Traitors favor, hide;
 Are with the blood of Prophets deeply dyed.

50

New England! know thy Heart-plague: feel this blow;   295
A blow that sorely wounds both Head and Heart,
A blow that reaches All, both high and low,
A blow that may be felt in every part.
 Mourn that this Great Man's fallen in Israel:
 Lest it be said, with him New England fell!   300

51

Farewell, Dear Shepard! Thou are gone before,
Made free of Heaven, where thou shalt sing loud Hymns
Of High triumphant Praises evermore,
In the sweet Choir of Saints and Seraphims.
 Lord! look on us here, clogg'd with sin and clay,   305
 And we, through Grace, shall be as happy as they.

52

My Dearest, Inmost, Bosom Friend, is Gone!
Gone is my sweet Companion, Soul's delight!
Now in an Huddling Crowd I'm all alone,
And almost could bid all the World Goodnight: 310
 Blest be my Rock! God lives: Oh let him be,
 As He is, so All in All to me.

The Bereaved, Sorrowful
URIAN OAKES
1677

Michael Wigglesworth

(1631-1705)

At the age of seven, Michael Wigglesworth migrated from his birthplace in Yorkshire, England, to Massachusetts Bay and finally to New Haven. After graduating from Harvard in 1651, he spent the remainder of his life as a physician and as pastor of the church at Malden, Mass. None of the 1800 copies of the first edition of *The Day of Doom; or, A Poetical Description of the Great and Last Judgment* (Cambridge, Mass., 1662) is known to exist, but the volume was a best-seller and was frequently reprinted. "The Praise of Eloquence," a college oration probably delivered late in 1650, was first printed in S. E. Morison, *Harvard College in the Seventeenth Century* (Cambridge, 1936).

BIBLIOGRAPHY: K. B. Murdock, ed. *The Day of Doom* (New York, 1929), with introd. E. S. Morgan, ed. "The Diary of Michael Wigglesworth," *Publ. Colonial Soc. Mass. (Transactions 1942-1946)*, XXXV (1951), 311-444. Richard Crowder, *No Featherbed to Heaven; A Biography of Michael Wigglesworth* (Mich. State U. Press, 1962).

From *The Praise of Eloquence*

How sweetly doth eloquence even enforce truth upon the understanding, and subtly convey knowledge into the mind be it never so dull of conceiving, and sluggish in yielding its assent. So that let a good Orator put forth the utmost of his skill, and you shall hear him so lay open and unfold, so evidence and demonstrate from point to point what he hath in hand, that he will make a very block understand his discourse. Let him be to give a description of something absent or unknown; how strangely doth he realize and make it present to his hearers' apprehensions, framing in their minds as exact an idea of that which they never saw, as they can possibly have of anything that they have been longest and best acquainted with. Or doth he take upon him to personate some others in word or deeds why he presents his hearers not with a lifeless picture, but with the living persons of those concerning whom he speaks. They see, they hear, they handle them, they walk, they talk with them, and what not? Or is he to speak about such things as are already known? Why should he here discourse after the vulgar manner, and deliver his mind as a cobbler would do: his hearers might then have some ground to say they knew as much as their orator could teach them. But by the power of eloquence old truth receives a new habit. Though its essence be the same yet its visage is so altered that it may currently pass and be accepted as a novelty. . . . So that Eloquence gives new luster and beauty, new strength, new vigor, new life unto truth; presenting it with such variety as refresheth, actuating it with such hidden powerful energy, that a few languid sparks are blown up to a shining flame.

And which is yet more: Eloquence doth not only revive the things known but secretly convey life into the hearers' understanding rousing it out of its former slumber, quickening it beyond its natural vigor, elevating it above its ordinary conception. There are not only objects set before it, but eyes (after a sort) given it to see these objects in such wise as it never saw. Yea it is strengthened as to apprehend that which is taught it, so of itself with enlargement to comprehend many things which are not made known unto it. Hence it comes to pass that after the hearing of a well-composed speech livelily expresst the understanding of the Auditor is so framed into the mold of Eloquence, that he could almost go away and compose the like himself either upon the same or another subject. And what's the reason of this? why his mind is transported with a kind of rapture, and inspired with a certain oratoric fury, as if the orator together with his words had breathed his soul and spirit into those that hear him.

These and the like effects hath Eloquence upon the understanding. But furthermore 'tis a fit bait to catch the will and affections. For hereby they are not only laid in wait for, but surprised: nor only surprised, but subdued; nor only subdued, but triumphed over. Yet Eloquence beguiles with such honesty, subdues with such mildness, triumphs with such sweetness: that here to be surprised is nothing dangerous, here to be subject is the best freedom, this kind of servitude is more desirable than liberty. For whereas our untractable nature refuseth to be drawn, and a stiff will scorns to be compell'd: yet by the power of well-composed speech nature is drawn against the stream with delight, and the will after a sort compelled with its own consent. Although for a time it struggle and make resistance, yet at length it suffers itself to be vanquisht, and takes a secret contentment in being overcome.

In like manner, for the affections. Look as a mighty river augmented with excessive rains or winter snows swelling above its wonted channel bears down banks and bridges, overflows fields and hedges, sweeps away all before it, that might obstruct its passage: so Eloquence overturns, overturns all things that stand in its way, and carries them down with the irresistible stream of its all controlling power. Wonderful it were to speak of the several discoveries of the power in several affections: wonderful but to think in general, how like a blustering tempest it one while drives before it the raging billows of this troubled Ocean: how other whiles (as though it had them in fetters it curbs and calms the fury at a word. And all this without offering violence to the parties so affected; nay with a secret pleasure and delight it stirs men up to the greatest displeasure and distaste. Doth it affect with grief? why to be so grieved is no grievance. Doth it kindle coals, nay flames of fiery indignation? Why those flames burn not, but rather cherish. Doth it draw tears from the eyes? Why even tears flow with pleasure. . . .

But I need instance no more. Some of you I hope will by this time assent unto what has been hitherto prov'd that Eloquence is of such useful concernment and powerful operation. But methinks I hear some still objecting. 'Tis very true Eloquence is a desirable thing, but what are we the better for knowing its worth unless we could hope ourselves to attain it? It is indeed a right excellent endowment but 'tis not every capacity, nay scarce one of a hundreth that can reach it. How many men of good parts do we find that yet excel not here? Cicero indeed, a man in whom vast understanding and natural fluent facility of speech conspire together; no marvel if he make judges weep and princes tremble. But to what purpose is it for a man of weak parts and mean abilities to labor after that which he is never like to compass? Had we not as good toss our caps against the wind as weary out ourselves in the pursuit of that which so few can reach to?

Ans. To these I would answer first, the reason why so few attain it is because there are few that indeed desire it. Hence they run not as if they meant to win, they pursue not as if they hop't to overtake. But secondly let me answer them with Turner's words upon this very argument *Negligentiam nostram arguit, qui cum non possumus. Quod debemus, optimus, nolumus quod possumus, benè.* We cannot do what we would therefore will not do what we may. This savors of a slothful system. Because we cannot keep pace with the horsemen, shall we refuse to accompany the footmen? Because we cannot run, shall we sit down and refuse to go? We cannot reach so far as ourselves desire and as some others it may be attain, shall we not therefore reach as far as our endeavors may carry us? Because we cannot be *Oratores optimi,* do we content ourselves to be *Oratores Pessimi?*

And as for those that have most excell'd in this kind, whence had they their excellency? They did not come declaiming into the world: they were not born with orations in their mouths: eloquence did not sit upon their lips whilest they lay in their cradles: neither did they suck it in from their mothers' breasts. But if you examine the matter you shall find that by incredible pains and daily exercise, they even turn'd the course of nature into another channel, and cut out a way for the gentle stream of Eloquence, where natural impediments seem'd altogether to deny it passage: thereby effecting as much as another could brag, *viam aut inveniam aut faciam:* . . .

Go too therefore my fellow students (for to you I address my speech, my superiors I attempt not to speak to, desiring rather to learn of them more of this nature, but) to you give me leave to say: Let no man hereafter tell me I despair of excelling in the oratorical faculty, therefore 'tis bootless to endeavor. . . . Would you then obtain this skill? Take De-

mosthenes his course; gird up your loins, put to your shoulders, and to it
again, and again, and again, let nothing discourage you. Know that to be
a dunce, to be a stammerer, unable to bring forth three or four sentences
hanging well together, this is an easy matter: but to become an able
speaker, *hic labor, hoc opus est.*   1650, 1936

From *The Day of Doom*

TO THE CHRISTIAN READER

Reader, I am a fool,
And have adventured
To play the fool this once for Christ,
The more his fame to spread.
If this my foolishness   5
Help thee to be more wise,
I have attained what I seek,
And what I only prize. . . .

For his dear sake have I
This service undertaken,   10
For I am bound to honor Him
Who hath not me forsaken.
I am a Debtor too,
Unto the sons of Men,
Whom, wanting other means, I would   15
Advantage with my Pen.

I would, but (ah!) my strength,
When tried, proves so small,
That to the ground without effect
My wishes often fall.   20
Weak heads, and hands, and states,
Great things cannot produce;
And therefore I this little Piece
Have publish'd for thine use.

Although the thing be small,   25
Yet my good will therein,
Is nothing less than if it had
A larger Volume been.
Accept it then in love,
And read it for thy good;   30
There's nothing in't can do thee hurt,
If rightly understood. . . .

Oh get a part in Christ,
And make the Judge thy Friend;
So shalt thou be assured of   35
A happy, glorious end.
Thus prays thy real Friend,
And Servant for Christ's sake,
Who, had he strength would not refuse
More pains for thee to take.   40

THE DAY OF DOOM

1

The security of
the World before
Christ's coming
to judgment.
Luke 12:19

Still was the night, serene and bright,
    when all Men sleeping lay;
Calm with the season, and carnal reason
    thought so 'twould last for aye.
"Soul, take thine ease, let sorrow cease;   5
    much good thou hast in store:"
This was their Song, their Cups among,
    the evening before.

2

Wallowing in all kind of Sin,
    vile Wretches lay secure;   10
The best of men had scarcely then
Mat. 25:5   their Lamps kept in good ure.
Virgins unwise, who through disguise
    amongst the best were number'd,
Had clos'd their eyes; yea, and the Wise   15
    through sloth and frailty slumber'd.

3

Like as of old, when men grow bold,
Mat. 24:37, 38   God's threatenings to contemn,
Who stopt their Ear, and would not hear,
    when Mercy warned them,   20
But took their course, without remorse,
    till God began to pour
Destruction the World upon
    in a tempestuous shower.

5

The suddenness,
Majesty, &
Terror of Christ's
appearing.
Mat. 25:6
2 Pet. 3:10

For at midnight brake forth a light,   25
   which turns the night to day,
And speedily an hideous cry
   did all the World dismay.
Sinners awake, their hearts do ache,
   trembling their loins surpriseth;   30
Amaz'd with fear, by what they hear,
   each one of them ariseth.

8

Ye sons of men that durst contemn
   the Threatenings of God's Word,
How cheer you now? your hearts, I trow,   35
   are thrill'd as with a sword.
Now Atheist blind, whose brutish mind
   a God could never see,
Dost thou perceive, dost now believe
   that Christ thy Judge shall be?   40

9

Stout Courages, (whose hardiness
   could Death and Hell outface,)
Are you as bold, now you behold
   your Judge draw near apace?
They cry, "No, no: Alas! and woe!   45
   our courage all is gone:
Our hardiness (fool hardiness)
   hath us undone, undone."

10

No heart so bold, but now grows cold,
   and almost dead with fear;   50
Rev. 6:15
No eye so dry, but now can cry,
   and pour out many a tear.
Earth's Potentates and pow'rful States,
   Captains and Men of Might,
Are quite abasht, their courage dasht,   55
   at this most dreadful sight.

11

Mean men lament, great men do rent
    their Robes, and tear their hair;
Mat. 24:30   They do not spare their flesh to tear
      through horrible despair.   60
All kindreds wail: all hearts do fail;
    horror the World doth fill
With weeping eyes and loud outcries,
    yet knows not how to kill.

14

The Judge draws nigh, exalted high   65
Mat. 25:31   upon a lofty Throne,
Amidst the throng of Angels strong,
    lo, Israel's Holy One!
The excellence of whose Presence
    and awful Majesty,   70
Amazeth Nature, and every Creature,
    doth more than terrify.

16

Whose Glory bright, whose wondrous Might,
    whose Power Imperial,
So far surpass whatever was   75
    in Realms Terrestrial,
That tongues of men (nor Angel's pen)
    cannot the same express,
And therefore I must pass it by,
    lest speaking should transgress.   80

17

1 Thes. 4:16
Resurrection of the Dead.
John 5:28, 29   Before his Throne a Trump is blown,
    proclaiming th' Day of Doom;
Forthwith he cries, "Ye Dead arise,
    and unto Judgment come."
No sooner said, but 'tis obey'd;   85
    Sepulchers open'd are:
Dead bodies all rise at his call,
    and's mighty Power declare.

19

The living
Changed.

The same translates from Mortal states
    to Immortality,   90
All that survive and be alive,
    i' th' twinkling of an eye;

Luk. 20:36
I Cor. 15:52

That so they may abide for aye,
    to endless weal or woe;
Both the Renate and Reprobate   95
    are made to die no more.

22

Who are
Christ's Sheep.
Mat. 5:10, 11

At Christ's right hand the Sheep do stand,
    his holy Martyrs, who
For his dear Name suffering shame,
    calamity and woe,   100
Like Champions stood and with their Blood
    their Testimony sealed;
Whose innocence without offence,
    to Christ their Judge appealed.

23

Heb. 12:5, 6, 7

Next unto whom there find a room   105
    all Christ's afflicted ones,
Who being chastised, neither despised
    nor sank amidst their groans;
Who by the Rod were turn'd to God,
    and loved him the more,   110
Not murmuring nor quarreling
    when they were chast'ned sore.

24

Luke 7:41, 47

Moreover, such as loved much,
    that had not such a trial,
As might constrain to so great pain,   115
    and such deep self-denial;
Yet ready were the Cross to bear,
    when Christ them call'd thereto,
And did rejoice to hear his voice,
    they're counted Sheep also.   120

25

Joh. 21:15
Mat. 19:14
Joh. 3:3

Christ's Flock of Lambs there also stands,
    whose Faith were weak, yet true;
All sound Believers (Gospel receivers)
    whose Grace was small, but grew:
And them among an Infant throng   125
    of Babes, for whom Christ died;
Whom for his own, by ways unknown
    to Men, he sanctified.

27

*The Goats
described or the
several sorts of
Reprobates on
the left hand.
Mat. 24:51*

At Christ's left hand the Goats do stand,
    all whining Hypocrites,   130
Who for self ends did seem Christ's friends,
    but foster'd guileful sprites;
Who Sheep resembled, but they dissembled,
    (their hearts were not sincere);
Who once did throng Christ's Lambs among,   135
    but now must not come near.

28

*Luk. 11:24, 26
Heb. 6:4, 5, 6
Heb. 10:29*

Apostates base and runaways,
    such as have Christ forsaken,
Of whom the Devil, with seven more evil,
    hath fresh possession taken;   140
Sinners ingrain, reserv'd to pain
    and torments most severe:
Because 'gainst light they sinn'd with spite,
    are also placed there.

29

There also stand a num'rous band,   145
    that no profession made

*Luk. 12:47
Prov. 1:24, 26
Joh. 3:19*

Of Godliness, nor to redress
    their ways at all essay'd;
Who better knew, but (sinful Crew)
    Gospel and Law despised;   150
Who all Christ's knocks withstood like blocks
    and would not be advised.

30

Moreover, there with them appear
    a number, numberless

Gal. 3:10
1 Cor. 6:9
Rev. 21:8

Of great and small, vile wretches all,   155
    that did God's Law transgress. . . .

34

Their place there find all Heathen blind,
    that Nature's light abused,

Rom. 2:13

Although they had no tidings glad,
    of Gospel grace refused.   160
There stand all Nations and Generations
    of Adam's Progeny,
Whom Christ redeem'd not, whom Christ esteem'd not,
    through Infidelity.

36

Fast by them stand at Christ's left hand   165
    the Lion fierce and fell,
The Dragon bold, that Serpent old,
    that hurried Souls to Hell.

1 Cor. 6:3

There also stand, under command,
    legions of Sprites unclean,   170
And hellish Fiends, that are no friends
    to God, nor unto Men.

38

All silence keep, both Goats and Sheep,
    before the Judge's Throne;

*The Saints
cleared &
justified.*

With mild aspect to his Elect   175
    then spake the Holy One:
"My Sheep draw near, your Sentence hear,
    which is to you no dread,
Who clearly now discern, and know
    your sins are pardoned.   180

39

2 Cor. 5:10
Eccles. 3:17
Joh. 3:18

" 'Twas meet that ye should judged be,
    that so the World may spy
No cause of grudge, when as I Judge
    and deal impartially.
Know therefore all both great and small,   185
    the ground and reason why
These Men do stand at my right hand
    and look so cheerfully.

40

Joh. 17:6
Eph. 1:4

"These Men be those my Father chose
   before the World's foundation,   190
And to me gave, that I should save
   from Death and Condemnation;
For whose dear sake I flesh did take,
   was of a Woman born,
And did inure my self t' endure,   195
   unjust reproach and scorn.

41

Rev. 1:5

"For them it was that I did pass
   through sorrows many a one:
That I drank up that bitter Cup,
   which made me sigh and groan.   200
The Cross his pain I did sustain;
   yea more, my Father's ire
I underwent, my Blood I spent
   to save them from Hell fire.

42

Eph. 2:1, 3

"Thus I esteem'd, thus I redeem'd   205
   all these from every Nation,
That they may be (as now you see)
   a chosen Generation.
What if erewhile they were as vile,
   and bad as any be,   210
And yet from all their guilt and thrall
   at once I set them free?

43

Mat. 20:13, 15
Rom. 9:20, 21

"My grace to one is wrong to none;
   none can Election claim;
Amongst all those their souls that lose,   215
   none can Rejection blame.
He that may choose, or else refuse,
   all men to save or spill,
May this Man choose, and that refuse,
   redeeming whom he will.   220

47

Isa. 53:11, 12
Rom. 8:16, 17,
33, 34
John 3:18

"Their debts are paid, their peace is made,
   their sins remitted are;
Therefore at once I do pronounce,
   and openly declare,

That Heav'n is theirs, that they be Heirs   225
  of Life and of Salvation;
Nor ever shall they come at all
  to Death or to Damnation."

50

That those whom they did wrong and slay,
  must now their judgment see!   230
Such whom they slighted and once despited,
  must now their Judges be!
Thus 'tis decreed, such is their meed,
1 Cor. 6:2   and guerdon glorious;
With Christ they sit, Judging is fit   235
  to plague the Impious.

67

Rom. 6:23   Earth's dwellers all, both great and small,
  have wrought iniquity,
And suffer must, for it is just,
  Eternal misery.   240
Amongst the many there come not any,
  before the Judge's face,
That able are themselves to clear,
  of all this cursed Race.

68

Nevertheless, they all express,   245
  (Christ granting liberty,)
What for their way they have to say,
  how they have liv'd, and why.
Hypocrites plead   They all draw near, and seek to clear
for themselves   themselves by making pleas; 250
There Hypocrites, false hearted wights,
  do make such pleas as these:

69

"Lord, in thy Name and by the same,
  we Devils dispossess'd;
Mat. 7:21, 22,   We rais'd the dead, and ministered   255
23   succor to the distress'd.
Our painful teaching, and powerful preaching
  by thine own wondrous might,
Did throughly win to God from sin
  many a wretched wight."   260

70

*The judge reply-
eth. Joh. 6:70*
1 Cor. 9:27

"All this," quoth he, "may granted be,
   and your case little better'd,
Who still remain under a chain
   and many irons fetter'd.
You that the dead have quickened,   265
   and rescu'd from the grave,
Yourselves were dead, yet never needed
   a Christ your souls to save.

71

"You that could preach, and others teach
   what way to life doth lead;   270

*Rom. 2:19:21,
22, 23*

Why were you slack to find that track,
   and in that way to tread? . . ."

92

*Civil honest men's
pleas.*
Luk. 18:11

Then were brought nigh a Company
   of Civil honest Men,
That lov'd true dealing and hated stealing,   275
   ne'er wrong'd their Brethren;
Who pleaded thus: "Thou knowest us
   that we were blameless livers; . . .

94

"We hated vice and set great price,
   by virtuous conversation;   280
And by the same we got a name,
   and no small commendation. . . ."

96

Then answered unto their dread,
   the Judge: "True Piety
God doth desire and eke require   285
   no less than honesty.
Justice demands at all your hands
   perfect Obedience;
If but in part you have come short,
   that is a just offense.   290

97

"On Earth below, where men did owe
   a thousand pounds and more,
Could twenty pence it recompense?

could that have clear'd the score?
Think you to buy Felicity   295
   with part of what's due debt?
Or for desert of one small part,
   the whole should off be set?

99

1 Sam. 16:7
2 Chron. 25:2

"God looks upon th' affection
   and temper of the heart;   300
Not only on the action,
   and the external part.
Whatever end vain men pretend,
   God knows the verity,
And by the end which they intend   305
   their words and deeds doth try.

100

Heb. 11:6

"Without true Faith, the Scripture saith,
   God cannot take delight
In any deed, that doth proceed
   from any sinful wight. . . .   310

104

Mat. 6:5

"Again you thought and mainly sought
   a name with men t' acquire;
Pride bare the Bell that made you swell,
   any your own selves admire.
Mean fruit it is, and vile, I wiss,   315
   that springs from such a root;
Virtue divine and genuine
   wonts not from pride to shoot."

107

Those that
pretend want of
opportunity
to repent.
Prov. 27:1
Jam. 4:13

A wondrous Crowd then 'gan aloud,
   thus for themselves to say,   320
"We did intend, Lord, to amend,
   and to reform our way.
Our true intent was to repent,
   and make our peace with thee;
But sudden death stopping our breath,   325
   left us no liberty."

109

Are confuted
and Convinced
Eccles. 12:1
Rev. 2:21

To whom the Judge: "Where you allege
    the shortness of the space,
That from your birth you liv'd on earth,
    to compass saving Grace;   330
It was Free Grace that any space
    was given you at all,
To turn from evil, defy the Devil,
    and upon God to call.

113

"Had your intent been to repent,   335
    and had you it desir'd,

Luk. 13:24, 25
Etc.
Phil. 2:12

There would have been endeavors seen
    before your time expir'd.
God makes no treasure, nor hath he pleasure,
    in idle purposes;   340
Such fair pretenses are foul offenses,
    and cloaks for wickedness."

114

Then were brought in and charg'd with sin,
    another Company,

Some plead
Examples of their
betters.
Mat. 18:7

Who by Petition obtain'd permission   345
    to make Apology:
They argued, "We were misled,
    as is well known to thee,
By their example that had more ample
    abilities than we."   350

116

The Judge replies: "I gave you eyes,
    and light to see your way,

Who are told that
Examples are
no Rules.
Psal. 19:8, 11
Exo. 23:2
Psal. 50:17, 18

Which had you lov'd and well improv'd
    you had not gone astray.
My Word was pure, the Rule was sure,   355
    why did you it forsake,
Or thereon trample, and men's example
    your Directory make?

117

"This you well knew: that God is true,
  and that most men are liars,   360
2 Tim. 3:5
In word professing holiness,
  in deed thereof deniers.
O simple fools! that having Rules,
  your lives to regulate,
Would then refuse, and rather choose   365
  vile men to imitate."

121

Some plead
the Scriptures'
darkness. And
difference amongst
Interpreters.
2 Pet. 3:16
"We had the Word," say some, "O Lord,
  but wiser men than we
Could never yet interpret it,
  but always disagree.   370
How could we fools be led by Rules,
  so far beyond our ken,
Which to explain did so much pain,
  and puzzle wisest men?"

122

"Was all my Word abstruse and hard?"   375
  the Judge then answered;
They are confuted.
Pro. 14:6
Isa. 35:8
Hos. 8:12
"It did contain much Truth so plain,
  you might have run and read,
But what was hard you never car'd
  to know nor studied,   380
And things that were most plain and clear
  you never practiced."

124

Others the fear of
Persecution.
Acts 28:22
Then came in view another Crew,
  and 'gan to make their pleas;
Amongst the rest, some of the best   385
  had such poor shifts as these:
"Thou know'st right well, who all canst tell
  we liv'd amongst thy foes,
Who the Renate did sorely hate,
  and goodness much oppose.   390

125

"We holiness durst not profess,
  fearing to be forlorn
John 12:42, 43
Of all our friends, and for amends
  to be the wicked's scorn.

We knew their anger would much endanger 395
   our lives, and our estates;
Therefore, for fear, we durst appear
   no better than our mates."

126

*They are
answered.
Luk. 12:4, 5
Isa. 51:12, 13*

To whom the Lord returns this word:
   "O wonderful deceits! 400
To cast off awe of God's strict Law,
   and fear men's wrath and threats;
To fear hell fire and God's fierce ire
   less than the rage of men,
As if God's wrath, could do less scath 405
   than wrath of brethren.

128

*Luk. 9:23, 24, 25
Chap. 16:25*

"To please your kin, men's love to win,
   to flow in wordly wealth,
To save your skin, these things have been
   more than Eternal health. 410
You had your choice, wherein rejoice,
   it was your portion,
For which you chose your Souls t' expose
   unto Perdition."

144

Then at the Bar arraigned are 415
   an impudenter sort,

*Some pretend they
were shut out from
Heaven by God's
Decree.
Rom. 9:18, 19*

Who to evade the guilt that's laid
   upon them, thus retort;
"How could we cease thus to transgress?
   how could we Hell avoid, 420
Whom God's Decree shut out from thee,
   and sign'd to be destroy'd?"

147

*Their pleas
taken off.
Luk. 13:27
2 Pet. 1:9, 10
compared with
Mat. 19:6*

Christ readily makes this Reply:
   "I damn you not because
You are rejected, or not elected;
   but you have broke my Laws. 425
It is but vain your wits to strain,
   the end and means to sever;
Men fondly seek to part or break
   what God hath link'd together. 430

148

Acts 3:19
& 16:31
1 Sam. 2:15
John 3:19
Joh. 5:40
2 Thes. 2:11, 12

"Whom God will save, such he will have,
  the means of life to use;
Whom he'll pass by, shall choose to die,
  and ways of life refuse.
He that foresees, and foredecrees,   435
  in wisdom order'd has,
That man's free will, electing ill,
  shall bring his Will to pass.

153

"You argue then: 'But abject men,
  whom God resolves to spill,   440
Cannot repent, nor their hearts rent;
  nor can they change their will.'
Nor for his *Can* is any man
  adjudged unto Hell:

John 3:19

But for his *Will* to do what's ill,   445
  and nilling to do well."

187

Mat. 22:12
Rom. 2:5, 6
Luk. 19:42

Their mouths are shut, each man is put
  to silence and to shame,
Nor have they aught within their thought,
  Christ's Justice for to blame.
The Judge is just, and plague them must,   450
  nor will he Mercy show
(For Mercy's day is past away)
  to any of this Crew.

189

O dismal day! whither shall they   455
  for help and succour flee?
To God above, with hopes to move
  their greatest Enemy:
His wrath is great, whose burning heat
  no floods of tears can slake: 460

Isa. 33:14
Psal. 11:6
Numb. 23:19

His Word stands fast, that they be cast
  into the burning Lake.

192

2 Pet. 3:10

And by and by the flaming Sky
  shall drop like molten Lead
About their ears, t' increase their fears,   465
  and aggravate their dread.

To Angels good that ever stood
    in their integrity,
Should they betake themselves, and make
    their suit incessantly?   470

193

Mat. 13:41,
42

They neither skill, nor do they will
    to work them any ease;
They will not mourn to see them burn,
    nor beg for their release.
To wicked men, their brethren   475
    in sin and wickedness,

Rev. 20:13,
15

Should they make moan? their case is one;
    they're in the same distress.

194

Ah, cold comfort, and mean support
    from such like Comforters!   480
Ah! little joy of Company,
    and fellow sufferers!

Luk. 16:28

Such shall increase their hearts' disease,
    and add unto their woe,
Because that they brought to decay   485
    themselves and many mo'.

196

Where tender love men's hearts did move
    unto a sympathy,
And bearing part of others' smart
    in their anxiety,   490

1 Cor. 6:2

Now such compassion is out of fashion,
    and wholly laid aside;
No friends so near, but Saints to hear
    their Sentence can abide.

197

One natural Brother beholds another   495
    in this astonied fit,

Compare
Prov. 1:26 with
1 Joh. 3:2 &
2 Cor. 5:16

Yet sorrows not thereat a jot,
    nor pities him a whit.
The godly Wife conceives no grief,
    nor can she shed a tear   500
For the sad state of her dear Mate,
    when she his doom doth hear.

199

The tender Mother will own no other
   of all her numerous brood,
But such as stand at Christ's right hand,   505
   acquitted through his Blood.

Luk. 16:25

The pious Father had now much rather
   his graceless Son should lie
In Hell with Devils, for all his evils,
   burning eternally,   510

200

Than God most High should injury

Psal. 58:10

   by sparing him sustain;
And doth rejoice to hear Christ's voice
   adjudging him to pain.
Thus having all, both great and small,   515
   convinc'd and silenced,
Christ did proceed their Doom to read,
   and thus it uttered:

201

The Judge pronounceth the Sentence of condemnation. Mat. 25:41

"Ye sinful wights, and cursed sprites,
   that work Iniquity,   520
Depart together from me forever
   to endless Misery;
Your portion take in yonder Lake,
   where Fire and Brimstone flameth;
Suffer the smart, which your desert   525
   as its due wages claimeth."

. . . .

1662

A SHORT DISCOURSE ON ETERNITY

1

What Mortal man can with his Span
   mete out Eternity?

Isa. 57:15
Mark. 3:29
Mat. 25:46

Or fathom it by depth of Wit,
   or strength of Memory?
The lofty Sky is not so high,   5
   Hell's depth to this is small;
The World so wide is but a stride,
   compared therewithal.

4

Tell every Star both near and far,
 in Heav'ns bright Canopy,   10
That doth appear throughout the year,
 of high or low degree:
Tell every Tree that thou canst see
 in this vast Wilderness,
Up in the Woods, down by the Floods,   15
 in thousand miles' Progress:

5

The sum is vast, yet not so vast
 but that thou may'st go on
To multiply the Leaves thereby,
 that hang those Trees upon: 20
Add thereunto the Drops that thou
 imaginest to be
In April Showers, that bring forth Flowers,
 and blossoms plenteously:

6

Number the Fowls and living Souls   25
 that through the Air do Fly,
The winged Hosts in all their Coasts
 beneath the Starry Sky:
Count all the Grass as thou dost pass
 through many a pasture land,   30
And dewy Drops that on the tops
 of Herbs and Plants do stand:

7

Number the Sand upon the Strand,
 and Atoms of the Air;
And do thy best on Man and Beast,   35
 to reckon every Hair:
2 Thes. 1:9
Rev. 14:11
Take all the Dust, if so thou lust,
 and add to thine Account:
Yet shall the Years of Sinners' tears,
 the Number far surmount.   40

8

Naught join'd to naught can ne'er make aught,
    nor Cyphers make a Sum;
Nor things Finite, to infinite
    by multiplying come:
A Cockleshell may serve as well   45
    to lade the Ocean dry,
As finite things and Reckonings
    to bound Eternity.

9

O happy they that live for aye,
1 Thes. 4:17   with Christ in Heav'n above!   50
Rom. 8:38, 39 Who know withal that nothing shall
    deprive them of his love.
Eternity, Eternity!
    Oh, were it not for thee,
The Saints in bliss and happiness   55
    could never happy be.

12

Lament and mourn you that must burn
Luk. 13:28   amidst those flaming Seas:
Mat. 25:41, 46 If once you come to such a doom,
Rev. 14:11   forever farewell ease.   60
O sad estate and desperate,
    that never can be mended,
Until God's Will shall change, or till
    Eternity be ended!

13

If anyone this Question   65
    shall unto me propound:
What! have the years of Sinners' tears
    no limits or no bound?
Mark. 9:43   It kills our heart to think to smart,
44   and pains that last forever;   70
And hear of fire that shall expire,
    or be extinguish'd never.

14

I'll Answer make (and let them take
  my words as I intend them;
For this is all the Cordial   75
  that here I have to lend them)
When Heav'n shall cease to flow with peace
  and all felicity,
Then Hell may cease to be the place
  of Woe and Misery.   80

15

When Heav'n is Hell, when Ill is Well,
  when Virtue turns to Vice,
When wrong is Right, when Dark is Light,
  when Naught is of great price:
Then may the years of Sinners' tears   85
  and sufferings expire,
And all the Hosts and damned Ghosts
  escape out of Hell fire.

1662

Benjamin Tompson
(1642-1714)

Born at Quincey (now Braintree), Mass., Benjamin Tompson was graduated from Harvard in 1662 and spent most of his life as a schoolmaster at Charlestown, Braintree, Boston, and Roxbury. Throughout his life, he also worked as a physician. Among his works are *New England's Crisis* (Boston, 1676), *New England's Tears for Her Present Miseries* (London, 1676), and several elegies.

BIBLIOGRAPHY: *DAB.* J. H. Hall, ed. *Benjamin Tompson . . . His Poems* (Boston, 1924).

From *New England's Crisis*

THE PROLOGUE

The times wherein old Pompion was a Saint,
When men far'd hardly yet without complaint
On vilest Cates; the dainty Indian Maize
Was eat with Clamshells out of wooden Trays

Under thatcht Huts without the cry of Rent,   5
And the best Sauce to every Dish, Content.
When Flesh was food, & hairy skins made coats,
And men as well as birds had chirping Notes.
When Simnels were accounted noble blood
Among the tribes of common herbage food.   10
Of Ceres' bounty form'd was many a knack
Enough to fill poor Robin's Almanac.
These golden times (too fortunate to hold)
Were quickly sinn'd away for love of gold.
'Twas then among the bushes, not the street   15
If one in place did an inferior meet,
Good morrow Brother, is there ought you want?
Take freely of me, what I have you ha'n't.
Plain Tom and Dick would pass as current now,
As ever since Your Servant Sir and bow.   20
Deep-skirted doublets, puritanic capes
Which now would render men like upright Apes,
Was comlier wear our wiser Fathers thought
Than the cast fashions from all Europe brought.
'Twas in those days an honest Grace would hold   25
Till an hot puddin grew at heart a cold.
And men had better stomachs to religion
Than I to capon, turkey-cock or pigeon.
When honest Sisters met to pray not prate
About their own and not their neighbors' state. . . .   30
'Twas long before spiders & worms had drawn
Their dungy webs or hid with cheating Lawn
New England's beauties, which still seem'd to me
Illustrious in their own simplicity.
'Twas ere the neighboring Virgin land had broke   35
The Hogsheads of her worse than hellish smoke.
'Twas ere the Island sent their Presents in,
Which but to use counted next to sin.
'Twas ere a Barge had made so rich a freight
As Chocolate, dust gold and bits of eight.   40
Ere wines from France and Moscovadoe too
Without the which the drink will scarcely do,
From western Isles, ere fruits and delicacies,
Did rot maids' teeth & spoil their handsome faces.
Or ere these times did chance the noise of war   45
Was from our towns and hearts removed far.
No Bugbear Comets in the crystal air
To drive our Christian Planters to despair.
No sooner pagan malice peeped forth

But Valor snib'd it; then were men of worth   50
Who by their prayers slew thousands Angel-like,
Their weapons are unseen with which they strike.
Then had the Churches rest, as yet the coals
Were covered up in most contentious souls.
Freeness in Judgment, union in affection,   55
Dear love, sound truth they were our grand protection;
These were the twins which in our Councils sate,
These gave prognostics of our future fate,
If these be longer liv'd our hopes increase,
These wars will usher in a longer peace: 60
But if New England's love die in its youth
The grave will open next for blessed Truth.
This Theme is out of date, the peaceful hours
When Castles needed not but pleasant bowers.
Not ink, but blood and tears now serve the turn   65
To draw the figure of New England's Urn.
New England's hour of passion is at hand,
No power except Divine can it withstand;
Scarce hath her glass of fifty years run out,
But her old prosperous Steeds turn heads about,   70
Tracking themselves back to their poor beginnings;
To fear and fare upon their fruits of sinnings:
So that the mirror of the Christian world
Lies burnt to heaps in part, her Streamers furl'd;
Grief reigns, joys flee and dismal fears surprise,   75
Not dastard spirits only but the wise. . . .
This is the Prologue to thy future woe,
The Epilogue no mortal yet can know.

NEW ENGLAND'S CRISIS

In seventy-five the Critic of our years
Commenc'd our war with Phillip and his peers.
Whither the sun in Leo had inspir'd
A fev'rish heat, and Pagan spirits fir'd?
Whither some Romish Agent hatcht the plot?   5
Or whither they themselves? appeareth not.
Whither our infant thrivings did invite?
Or whither to our lands pretended right?
Is hard to say; but Indian spirits need
No grounds but lust to make a Christian bleed.   10

And here methinks I see this greasy Lout
With all his pagan slaves coil'd round about,
Assuming all the majesty his throne

Of rotten stump, or of the rugged stone
Could yield; casting some bacon-rind-like looks,   15
Enough to fright a Student from his books,
Thus treat his peers, & next to them his Commons,
Kennel'd together all without a summons.
"My friends, our Fathers were not half so wise
As we ourselves who see with younger eyes.   20
They sell our land to English man who teach
Our nation all so fast to pray and preach:
Of all our country they enjoy the best,
And quickly they intend to have the rest.
This no wunnegin, so big matchit law,   25
Which our old fathers' fathers never saw.
These English make and we must keep them too,
Which is too hard for them or us to do,
We drink we so big whipt, but English they
Go sneep, no more, or else a little pay.   30
Me meddle Squaw me hang'd, our fathers kept
What Squaws they would whither they wakt or slept.
Now if you'll fight I'll get you English coats,
And wine to drink out of their Captains' throats.
The richest merchants' houses shall be ours,   35
We'll lie no more on mats or dwell in bowers,
We'll have their silken wives take they our Squaws,
They shall be whipt by virtue of our laws.
If ere we strike 'tis now before they swell
To greater swarms than we know how to quell.   40
This my resolve, let neighboring Sachems know,
And every one that hath club, gun or bow."
This was assented to, and for a close
He strokt his smutty beard and curst his foes.
This counsel lightning like their tribes invade,   45
And something like a muster's quickly made,
A ragged regiment, a naked swarm,
Whom hopes of booty doth with courage arm,
Set forthwith bloody hearts, the first they meet
Of men or beasts they butcher at their feet.   50
They round our skirts, they pare, they fleece, they kill,
And to our bordering towns do what they will.
Poor Hovels (better far than Caesar's court
In the experience of the meaner sort)
Receive from them their doom next execution,   55
By flames reduc'd to horror and confusion:
Here might be seen the smoking funeral piles
Of wildered towns pitcht distant many miles.

Here might be seen the infant from the breast
Snatcht by a pagan hand to lasting rest: 60
The mother Rachel-like shrieks out *my child,*
She wrings her hands and raves as she were wild.
The bruitish wolves suppress her anxious moan
By cruelties more deadly of her own.
Will she or nill the chastest turtle must   65
Taste of the pangs of their unbridled lust.
From farms to farms, from towns to towns they post,
They strip, they bind, they ravish, flay and roast. . . .
These tidings ebbing from the outward parts
Makes tradesmen cast aside their wonted Arts   70
And study arms: the craving merchants plot
Not to augment but keep what they have got.
And every soul which hath but common sense
Thinks it the time to make a just defense.
Alarums everywhere resound in streets,   75
From west sad tidings with the Eastern meets. . . .

Canonicus precincts there swarms unite,
Rather to keep a winter guard than fight.
A dern and dismal swamp some Scout had found
Whose bosom was a spot of rising ground   80
Hedg'd up with mighty oaks, maples and ashes,
Nurst up with springs, quick bogs & mirey plashes,
A place which nature coin'd on very nonce
For tigers not for men to be a sconce.
'Twas here these Monsters shapt and fac'd like men   85
Took up there Rendezvous and brumal den,
Deeming the depth of snow, hail, frost and ice
Would make our Infantry more tame and wise
Than by & by forsaking beds and loving wives,
Merely for Indian skins to hazard lives: 90
These hopes had something calm'd the boiling passion
Of this incorrigible warlike nation.
During this short Parenthesis of peace
Our forces found, but left him not at ease.
Here English valor most illustrious shone,   95
Finding their numbers ten times ten to one.
A shower of leaden hail our captains feel
Which made the bravest blades among us reel.
Like to some anthill newly spurn'd abroad,
Where each takes heels and bears away his load: 100
Instead of plate and jewels, Indian trays
With baskets up they snatch and run their ways.

Sundry the flames arrest and some the blade,
By bullets heaps on heaps of Indians laid.
The Flames like lightning in their narrow streets   105
Dart in the face of every one it meets.
Here might be heard an hideous Indian cry,
Of wounded ones who in the Wigwams fry.
Had we been Cannibals here might we feast
On brave Westphalia gammons ready drest.   110
The tawny hue is Ethiopic made
Of such on whom Vulcan his clutches laid.
Their fate was sudden, our advantage great
To give them once for all a grand defeat;
But tedious travel had so crampt our toes   115
It was too hard a task to chase the foes.
Distinctness in the numbers of the slain,
Or the account of Pagans which remain
Are both uncertain, losses of our own
Are too too sadly felt, too sadly known.   120
War digs a common grave for friends and foes,
Captains in with the common soldier throws. . . .

. . . the mounting clouds of smoke
From martyr'd towns the heav'ns for aid invoke:
Churches, barns, houses with most ponderous things   125
Made volatile fly o'er the land with wings.
Hundreds of cattle now they sacrifice
For airy spirits up to gormandize;
And to the Molech of their hellish guts,
Which craves the flesh in gross, their ale in butts. 130
Lancaster, Medfield, Mendon, wildered Groton,
With many Villages by me not thought on
Die in their youth by fire that useful foe,
Which this grand cheat the world will overflow.
The wandering Priest to every one he meets   135
Preaches his Church's funeral in the streets.
Sheep from their fold are frighted, Keepers too
Put to their trumps not knowing what to do.
This monster War hath hatcht a beauteous dove
In dogged hearts, of most unfeigned love,   140
Fraternal love the livery of a Saint
Being come in fashion though by sad constraint,
Which if it thrive and prosper with us long
Will make New England forty thousand strong.
    But off the Table hand, let this suffice   145
As the abridgment of our miseries.

If Mildew, Famine, Sword, and fired Towns,
If Slaughter, Captivating, Deaths and wounds,
If daily whippings once reform our ways,
These all will issue in our Father's Praise;   150
If otherwise, the sword must never rest
Till all New England's Glory it divest.

1676

NEW ENGLAND'S CRISIS

A SUPPLEMENT

What means this silence of Harvardine quills
While Mars triumphant thunders on our hills.
Have pagan priests their Eloquence confin'd
To no man's use but the mysterious mind?
Have Pawaws charm'd that art which was so rife   5
To crouch to every Don that lost his life?
But now whole towns and Churches fire and die
Without the pity of an Elegy.
Nay rather should my quills were they all swords
Wear to the hilts in some lamenting words.   10
I dare not style them poetry but truth,
The dwingling products of my crazy youth.
If these essays shall raise some quainter pens
'Twill to the Writer make a rich amends.

THE TOWN CALLED PROVIDENCE, ITS FATE

Why muse we thus to see the wheels run 'cross
Since Providence itself sustains a loss:
And yet should Providence forget to watch
I fear the enemy would all dispatch;
Celestial lights would soon forget their line,   5
The wandering planets would forget to shine,
The stars run all out of their common spheres,
And quickly fall together by the ears:
Kingdoms would jostles out their Kings and set
The poor Mechanic up whom next they met,   10
Or rather would whole kingdoms with the world
Into a Chaos their first egg be hurl'd.
There's none this Providence of the Most High
Who can survive and write its Elegy:
But of a solitary town I write,   15
A place of darkness yet receiving light

From pagan hands, a miscellaneous nest
Of error's Hectors, where they sought a rest
Out of the reach of Laws but not of God,
Since they have felt the smart of common rod.   20
'Twas much I thought they did escape so long,
Who Gospel truth so manifestly wrong:
For one Lot's sake perhaps, or else I think
Justice did at greatest offenders wink
But now the shot is paid, I hope the dross   25
Will be cashiered in this common loss.
Houses with substance feel uplifting wings,
The earth remains, the last of human things:
But know the dismal day draws near wherein
The fire shall earth itself dissolve and sin.   30

CHELMSFORD'S FATE

Ere famous Winthrop's bones are laid to rest
The pagans Chelmsford with sad flames arrest,
Making an artificial day of night
By that plantation's formidable light.
Here's midnight shrieks and Soul-amazing moans,   5
Enough to melt the very marble stones:
Fire-brands and bullets, darts and deaths and wounds
Confusive outcries everywhere resounds:
The natives shooting with the mixed cries,
With all the cruelties the foes devise   10
Might fill a volume, but I leave a space
For mercies still successive in their place
Not doubting but the foes have done their worst,
And shall by heaven suddenly be curst.

Let this dear Lord the sad Conclusion be   15
Of poor New England's dismal tragedy.
Let not the glory of thy former work
Blasphemed be by pagan Jew or Turk:
But in its funeral ashes write thy Name
So fair all Nations may expound the same: 20
Out of her ashes let a Phoenix rise
That may outshine the first and be more wise.
1676

ON A FORTIFICATION

At Boston begun by Women
Dux Femina Facti

A Grand attempt some Amazonian Dames
Contrive whereby to glorify their names,
A Ruff for Boston Neck of mud and turf,
Reaching from side to side from surf to surf,
Their nimble hands spin up like Christmas pies,   5
Their pastry by degrees on high doth rise.
The wheel at home counts it an holiday,
Since while the Mistress worketh it may play.
A tribe of female hands, but manly hearts
Forsake at home their pasty-crust and tarts   10
To knead the dirt, the samplers down they hurl,
Their undulating silks they closely furl.
The pick-axe one as a Commandress holds,
While t' other at her awkness gently scolds.
One puffs and sweats, the other mutters why   15
Can't you promove your work so fast as I?
Some dig, some delve, and others' hands do feel
The little wagons weight with single wheel.
And least some fainting fits the weak surprise,
They want no sack nor cakes, they are more wise.   20
These brave essays draw forth Male stronger hands
More like to Dawbers than to Martial bands:
These do the work, and sturdy bulwarks raise,
But the beginners well deserve the praise.

                    1676

From *New England's Tears*

M. J. ANTONOMIE's *The Grand Sachem's Death*

A Breathing time of silence had my Pen,
But finds a scribbling matter once again.
In Narragansett Land near Paquetuck,
The English with the Natives try a pluck:
Here in an Isthmus pitcht the foes their tents,   5
Here quartered their naked Regiments:
Some grope for Lobsters, some to clam banks run,
And some lie beautifying in the Sun:

Some sit in Council, others treating squaws;
Some grinding parcht Corn with the Querns their Jaws.   10
Some sing their Captains' dooms, others are lousing,
Some pawawing, some wenching, and some drowsing.
And herein Antonomie among the rest,
All up in Wampam Belts, most richly drest:
Sate as the Dagon of their motley crew,   15
Not thinking that his downfall would ensue:
Whose Pedigree should I presume to write,
To Hesiod's *Theognis* run I might.
Our Checker'd Bands of Whites and Tawnies join'd,
These in their close Retirements quickly find;   20
Down to the Earth our Martial gallants fall,
And like to insects on the Natives crawl.
Old Uncus' tribe who ever had been true,
Upon the moving Forest nimbly flew.
The English them as they are flying meet,   25
And multitudes they tumble at their feet.
Some captiv'd, others wounded, many slain,
Like Hydra's Heads, yet ne'er the less remain.
And here that Lucifer receives defeat,
Who scorns with any less than Princes treat.   30
What Necklace could New England better please,
Than Heads strung thick upon a thread of these,
Him they dispatch, and hundreds more are hurl'd,
Him to attend upon in th' other world:
Whose hunting bouts will heavily go on,   35
His Legs must stay until the Head come on.
That fancy which so stiffly they maintain,
That such on hunting go who hence are slain.
I hope ere long will quite convinced be,
By many Heads chopt off as fine as he: 40
His (a brave present) kist the grateful Hand,
Of Dons who in our Southern Tract command.

Least such Mœcænas's beyond Sea should,
Restrain their yearly showers of Goods and Gold,
Be pleas'd to know there is an hopeful race,   45
Who as you oft have been inform'd have grace.
These are confin'd under Christian Wings,
And hopes we have never to feel their stings.
A natural Prison wall'd with Sea and Isles,
From our Metropolis not many miles.   50

1676

UPON THE ELABORATE SURVEY OF NEW ENGLAND'S PASSIONS FROM
THE NATIVES BY THE IMPARTIAL PEN OF THAT WORTHY DIVINE
MR. WILLIAM HUBBARD

A Country's Thanks with Garlands ready lie
To wreathe the Brows of your Divinity
Renowned Sir: to write the Church's War
In ancient times fell to the Prophets' share;
New England's Chronicles are to be had   5
From Nathan's Pen, or Manuscript of Gád.
Purchase wrote much, Hacluyt traversed far,
Smith and Dutch John de Laet famous are,
Martyr, with learn'd Acosta thousands too,
Here's novelties and style which all outdo,   10
Wrote by exacter hand than ever took
Historian's Pen since Europe we foresook.
I took your Muse for old Columbus' Ghost,
Who scrapt acquaintance with this western Coast,
But in converse some pages I might find   15
Than all Columbus' Gems a brighter mind.
Former Adventures did at best beguile
About these Natives Rise (obscure as Nile)
Their grand Apostle writes of their return,
Williams their Language; Hubbard how they burn, 20
Rob, kill and Roast, lead Captive, flay, blaspheme;
Of English valor too he makes his Theme,
Whose tragical account may Christened be
New England's Travels through the bloody Sea.
Drake gat renown by creeping round the old;   25
To treat of this New World our Author's bold.
Names uncouth which ne'er Minshew could reduce
By's *Polyglotton* to the vulgar use.
Unheard of places like some New Atlantis,
Before in fancy only, now Newlandis: 30
New found and subtle Stratagems of War,
We can quaint Elton and brave Barriffe spare:
New Discipline and Charges of Command
Are cloth'd in Indian by this English hand.
Moxon who drew two Globes, or whosoe'er   35
Must make a third, or else the old ones tear,
To find a Room for thy new Map by which
Thy friends and Country all thou dost enrich.
    Gratitudinis ergo apposuit

INDIAN CAPTIVITY

Mary Rowlandson
(c. 1635-c. 1678)

The daughter of John White, who settled at Salem, Mass., in 1638, Mary White Rowlandson was the wife of the Rev. Joseph Rowlandson of Lancaster, Mass. The account of her eleven-week captivity by Indians, a book frequently reprinted in New England, was entitled *The Sovereignty and Goodness of God, Together With the Faithfulness of His Promises Displayed; Being a Narra-* tive of the Captivity and Restoration of Mrs. Mary Rowlandson (Cambridge, Mass., 1682).

BIBLIOGRAPHY: H. S. Nourse and J. E. Thayer, eds. *A Narrative of the Captivity* . . . (Lancaster, Mass., 1903). Also in C. H. Lincoln, ed. *Narratives of the Indian Wars, 1675-1699* (New York, 1913).

From *A Narrative of the Captivity of Mrs. Mary Rowlandson*

On the tenth of February 1675, Came the Indians with great numbers upon Lancaster: Their first coming was about Sunrising; hearing the noise of some Guns, we looked out; several Houses were burning, and the Smoke ascending to Heaven. There were five persons taken in one house, the Father, and the Mother and a sucking Child, they knockt on the head; the other two they took and carried away alive. There were two others, who being out of their Garrison upon some occasion, were set upon; one was knockt on the head, the other escaped: Another there was who running along was shot and wounded, and fell down; he begged of them his life, promising them Money (as they told me) but they would not hearken to him but knockt him in head, and stript him naked, and split open his Bowels. Another seeing many of the Indians about his Barn, ventured and went out, but was quickly shot down. There were three others belonging to the same Garrison who were killed; the Indians getting up upon the roof of the Barn, had advantage to shoot down upon them over their Fortification. Thus these murderous wretches went on, burning, and destroying before them.

At length they came and beset our own house, and quickly it was the dolefullest day that ever mine eyes saw. The House stood upon the edge of a hill; some of the Indians got behind the hill, others into the Barn, and others behind anything that could shelter them; from all which places they shot against the House, so that the Bullets seemed to fly like hail; and quickly they wounded one man among us, then another, and then a third, About two hours (according to my observation, in that amazing time) they had been about the house before they prevailed to fire it (which they did with Flax and Hemp, which they brought out of the Barn, and there being no defence about the House, only two Flankers at two opposite corners and one of them not finished) they fired it once and one ventured out and quenched it, but they quickly fired it again, and that took. Now is the dreadful hour come, that I have often heard of (in time of War, as it was the case of others) but now mine eyes see it. Some in our house were fighting for their lives, others wallowing in their blood, the House on fire over our heads, and the bloody Heathen ready to knock us on the head, if we stirred out: Now might we hear Mothers & Children crying out for themselves, and one another, Lord, What shall we do? Then I took my Children (and one of my sisters, hers) to go forth and leave the house: but as soon as we came to the door and appeared, the Indians shot so thick that the bullets rattled against the House, as if one had taken an handful of stones and threw them, so that we were fain to give back. We had six stout Dogs belonging to our Garrison, but none of them would stir, though another time, if any Indian had come to the door, they were ready to fly upon him and tear him down. The Lord hereby would make us the more to acknowledge his hand, and to see that our help is always in him. But out we must go, the fire increasing, and coming along behind us, roaring, and the Indians gaping before us with their Guns, Spears and Hatchets to devour us. No sooner were we out of the House, but my Brother-in-Law (being before wounded, in defending the house, in or near the throat) fell down dead, whereat the Indians scornfully shouted, and hallowed, and were presently upon him, stripping off his clothes, the bullets flying thick, one went through my side, and the same (as would seem) through the bowels and hand of my dear Child in my arms. One of my elder Sister's Children, named William, had then his Leg broken, which the Indians perceiving, they knockt him on head. Thus were we butchered by those merciless Heathen, standing amazed, with the blood running down to our heels. My eldest Sister being yet in the House, and seeing those woeful sights, the Infidels hauling Mothers one way, and Children another, and some wallowing in their blood: and her elder Son telling her that her Son William was dead, and myself was wounded, she said, And, Lord, let me die with them; which was no sooner said, but she was struck with a Bullet,

and fell down dead over the threshold. I hope she is reaping the fruit of
her good labors, being faithful to the service of God in her place. In her
younger years she lay under much trouble upon spiritual accounts, till it
pleased God to make that precious Scripture take hold of her heart, 2
Cor. 12. 9. *And he said unto me, my Grace is sufficient for thee.* More
than twenty years after I have heard her tell how sweet and comfortable
that place was to her. But to return: The Indians laid hold of us, pulling
me one way, and the Children another, and said, Come go along with us;
I told them they would kill me: they answered, If I were willing to go
along with them, they would not hurt me.

Oh the doleful sight that now was to behold at this House! *Come, behold the works of the Lord, what desolations he has made in the Earth.*
Of thirty-seven persons who were in this one House, none escaped either
present death, or a bitter captivity, save only one, who might say as he.
Job 1. 15, *And I only am escaped alone to tell the News.* There were
twelve killed, some shot, some stab'd with their Spears, some knock'd
down with their Hatchets. When we are in prosperity, Oh the little that
we think of such dreadful sights, and to see our dear Friends, and Relations lie bleeding out their heart-blood upon the ground. There was one
who was chopt into the head with a Hatchet, and stript naked, and yet
was crawling up and down. It is a solemn sight to see so many Christians
lying in their blood, some here, and some there, like a company of Sheep
torn by Wolves, All of them stript naked by a company of hell-hounds,
roaring, singing, ranting and insulting, as if they would have torn our
very hearts out; yet the Lord by his Almighty power preserved a number
of us from death, for there were twenty-four of us taken alive and carried
Captive.

I had often before this said, that if the Indians should come, I should
choose rather to be killed by them than taken alive but when it came to
the trial my mind changed; their glittering weapons so daunted my spirit,
that I chose rather to go along with those (as I may say) ravenous Beasts,
than that moment to end my days; and that I may the better declare
what happened to me during that grievous Captivity, I shall particularly
speak of the several Removes we had up and down the Wilderness.

The twentieth Remove

It was their usual manner to remove, when they had done any mischief, lest they should be found out: and so they did at this time. We
went about three or four miles, and there they built a great Wigwam, big
enough to hold an hundred Indians, which they did in preparation to a
great day of Dancing. They would say now amongst themselves, that the
Governor would be so angry for his loss at Sudbury, that he would send
no more about the Captives, which made me grieve and tremble. My Sister being not far from the place where we now were: and hearing that I

was here, desired her master to let her come and see me, and he was willing to it, and would go with her: but she being ready before him, told him she would go before, and was come within a Mile or two of the place; Then he overtook her, and began to rant as if he had been mad; and made her go back again in the Rain; so that I never saw her till I saw her in Charlestown. But the Lord requited many of their ill doings, for this Indian her Master, was hanged afterward at Boston. The Indians now began to come from all quarters, against their merry dancing day. Among some of them came one Goodwife Kettle: I told her my heart was so heavy that it was ready to break: so is mine too said she, but yet said, I hope we shall hear some good news shortly. I could hear how earnestly my Sister desired to see me, & I as earnestly desired to see her: and yet neither of us could get an opportunity. My Daughter was also now about a mile off, and I had not seen her in nine or ten weeks, as I had not seen my Sister since our first taking. I earnestly desired them to let me go and see them: yea, I entreated, begged, and persuaded them, but to let me see my Daughter; and yet so hard hearted were they, that they would not suffer it. They made use of their tyrannical power whilst they had it: but through the Lord's wonderful mercy, their time was now but short.

On a Sabbath day, the Sun being about an hour high in the afternoon; came Mr. John Hoar (the Council permitting him, and his own forward spirit inclining him) together with the two forementioned Indians, Tom and Peter, with their third Letter from the Council. When they came near, I was abroad: though I saw them not, they presently called me in, and bade me sit down and not stir. Then they catched up their Guns, and away they ran, as if an Enemy had been at hand; and the Guns went off apace. I manifested some great trouble, and they asked me what was the matter? I told them, I thought they had killed the Englishman (for they had in the meantime informed me that an Englishman was come) they said, No; They shot over his Horse and under, and before his Horse; and they pusht him this way and that way, at their pleasure: showing what they could do: Then they let them come to their Wigwams. I begged of them to let me see the Englishman, but they would not. But there was I fain to sit their pleasure. When they had talked their fill with him, they suffered me to go to him. We asked each other of our welfare, and how my Husband did, and all my Friends? He told me they were all well, and would be glad to see me. Amongst other things which my Husband sent me, there came a pound of Tobacco: which I sold for nine shillings in Money: for many of the Indians for want of Tobacco, smoked Hemlock, and Ground Ivy. It was a great mistake in any, who thought I sent for Tobacco: for through the favor of God, that desire was overcome. I now asked them, whither I should go home with Mr. Hoar? They answered No, one and another of them: and it being night, we lay down with that answer; in the morning, Mr. Hoar invited the Saggamores to Dinner; but when we went to get it ready, we found that they had stolen the greatest part of the Provision Mr. Hoar had brought, out of his Bags, in the night. And we may see the wonderful power of God, in that one passage, in that when there was such a great number of the Indians together, and so greedy of a little good food; and no English there, but Mr. Hoar and myself: that there they did not knock us in the head, and take what we had: there being not only some Provision, but also Trading cloth, a part of the twenty pounds agreed upon: But instead of doing us any mischief, they seemed to be ashamed of the fact, and said, it were some Matchit Indian that did it. Oh, that we could believe that there is no thing too hard for God! God showed his Power over the Heathen in this, as he did over the hungry Lions when Daniel was cast into the Den. Mr. Hoar called them betime to Dinner, but they ate very little, they being so busy in dressing themselves, and getting ready for their Dance: which was carried on by eight of them, four Men and four Squaws: My master and mistress being two. He was dressed in his Holland shirt, with great Laces sewed at the tail of it, he had his silver Buttons, his white Stockings, his Garters were hung round with Shillings, and he had Girdles of Wampom upon his head and shoulders. She had a Kersey Coat, and covered with Girdles of Wampom from the Loins upward: her arms from her elbows to her hands were covered with Bracelets; there were handfuls of Necklaces about her neck, and several sorts of Jewels in her ears. She had fine red Stockings, and white Shoes, her hair powdered and face painted Red, that was always before Black. And all the Dancers were after the same manner. There were two other singing and knocking on a Kettle for their music. They kept hopping up and down one after another, with a Kettle of water in the midst, standing warm upon some Embers, to drink of when they were dry. They held on till it was almost night, throwing out Wampom to the standers by. At night I asked them again, if I should go home? They all as one said No, except my Husband would come for me. When we were lain down, my Master went out of the Wigwam, and by and by sent in an Indian called James the Printer, who told Mr. Hoar, that my Master would let me go home tomorrow, if he would let him have one pint of Liquors. Then Mr. Hoar called his own Indians, Tom and Peter, and bid them go and see whither he would promise it before them three: and if he would, he should have it; which he did, and he had it. Then Philip smelling the business call'd me to him, and asked me what I would give him, to tell me some good news, and speak a good word for me. I told him, I could not tell what to give him, I would anything I had, and asked him what he would have? He said, two Coats and twenty shillings in Money, and half a bushel of seed Corn, and some Tobacco. I thanked him for his love: but I knew the good news as well as the crafty Fox. My Master after he had had his drink, quickly came ranting into the Wigwam again, and called for Mr. Hoar, drinking to him, and saying, He was a good man: and then again he would say, Hang him Rogue: Being almost drunk, he would drink to him, and yet presently say he should be hanged. Then he called for me, I trembled to hear him, yet I was fain to go to him, and he drank to me, showing no incivility. He was the first Indian I saw drunk all the while that I was amongst them. At last his Squaw ran out, and he after her, round the Wigwam, with his money jingling at his knees: But she escaped him: But having an old Squaw he ran to her: and so through the Lord's mercy, we were no more troubled that night. Yet I had not a comfortable night's rest: for I think I can say, I did not sleep for three nights together. The night before the Letter came from the Council, I could not rest, I was so full of fears and troubles, God many times leaving us most in the dark, when deliverance is nearest: yea, at this time I could not rest night nor day. The next night I was overjoyed, Mr. Hoar being come, and that with such good tidings. The third night I was even swallowed up with the thoughts of things, viz. that ever I should go home again; and that I must go, leaving my Children behind me in the Wilderness; so that sleep was now almost departed from mine eyes.

On Tuesday morning they called their General Court (as they call it) to consult and determine, whether I should go home or no: And they all as one man did seemingly consent to it, that I should go home; except Philip, who would not come among them. . . .

But to return again to my going home, where we may see a remarkable change of Providence: At first they were all against it, except my Husband would come for me; but afterwards they assented to it, and seemed much to rejoice in it; some askt me to send them some Bread, others some Tobacco, others shaking me by the hand, offering me a Hood and Scarf to ride in; not one moving hand or tongue against it. Thus hath the Lord answered my poor desire, and the many earnest requests of others put up unto God for me. In my travels an Indian came to me, and told me, if I were willing, he and his Squaw would run away, and go home along with me: I told him No: I was not willing to run away, but desired to wait God's time, that I might go home quietly, and without fear. And now God hath granted me my desire. O the wonderful power of God that I have seen, and the experience that I have had: I have been in the midst of those roaring Lions, and Savage Bears, that feared neither God, nor Man, nor the Devil, by night and day, alone and in company: sleeping all sorts together, and yet not one of them ever offered me the least abuse of unchastity to me, in word or action. Though some are ready to say, I speak it for my own credit; But I speak it in the presence of God, and to his Glory. God's Power is as great now, and as sufficient to save, as when he preserved Daniel in the Lions' Den; or the three Children in the fiery Furnace. I may well say as his *Psal. 107. 12, Oh give thanks unto the Lord for he is good, for his mercy endureth forever.* Let the Redeemed of the Lord say so, whom he hath redeemed from the hand of the Enemy, especially that I should come away in the midst of so many hundreds of Enemies quietly and peaceably, and not a

Dog moving his tongue. So I took my leave of them, and in coming along my heart melted into tears, more than all the while I was with them, and I was almost swallowed up with the thoughts that ever I should go home again. About the Sun going down, Mr. Hoar, and myself, and the two Indians came to Lancaster, and a solemn sight it was to me. There had I lived many comfortable years amongst my Relations and Neighbors, and now not one Christian to be seen, nor one house left standing. We went on to a Farm house that was yet standing, where we lay all night: and a comfortable lodging we had, though nothing but straw to lie on. The Lord preserved us in safety that night, and raised us up again in the morning, and carried us along, that before noon, we came to Concord. Now was I full of joy, and yet not without sorrow: joy to see such a lovely sight, so many Christians together, and some of them my Neighbors: There I met with my Brother, and my Brother-in-Law, who asked me, if I knew where his Wife was? Poor heart! he had helped to bury her, and knew it not; she being shot down by the house was partly burnt: so that those who were at Boston at the desolation of the Town, and came back afterward, and buried the dead, did not know her. Yet I was not without sorrow, to think how many were looking and longing, and my own Children amongst the rest, to enjoy that deliverance that I had now received, and I did not know whither ever I should see them again. Being recruited with food and raiment we went to Boston that day, where I met with my dear Husband, but the thoughts of our dear Children, one being dead, and the other we could not tell where, abated our comfort each to other. . . . About this time the Council had ordered a day of public Thanksgiving: though I thought I had still cause of mourning, and being unsettled in our minds, we thought we would ride toward the Eastward, to see if we could hear anything concerning our Children. And as we were riding along (God is the wise disposer of all things) between Ipswich and Rowly we met with Mr. William Hubbard, who told us that our Son Joseph was come into Major Waldren's, and another with him, which was my Sister's Son. I asked him how he knew it? He said, the Major himself told him so. So along we went till we came to Newbury; and their Minister being absent, they desired my Husband to Preach the Thanksgiving for them; but he was not willing to stay there that night, but would go over to Salisbury, to hear further, and come again in the morning; which he did, and Preached there that day. At night, when he had done, one came and told him that his Daughter was come in at Providence: Here was mercy on both hands: Now hath God fulfilled that precious Scripture which was such a comfort to me in my distressed condition. When my heart was ready to sink into the Earth (my Children being gone I could not tell whither) and my knees trembled under me, And I was walking through the valley of the shadow of Death: Then the Lord brought, and now has fulfilled that reviving word unto me: *Thus saith the Lord, Refrain thy voice from weeping, and thine eyes from tears, for thy Work shall be rewarded, saith the Lord, and they shall come again from the Land of the Enemy.* . . .

I have seen the extreme vanity of this World: One hour I have been in health, and wealth, wanting nothing: But the next hour in sickness and wounds, and death, having nothing but sorrow and affliction.

Before I knew what affliction meant, I was ready sometimes to wish for it. When I lived in prosperity; having the comforts of the World about me, my relations by me, my Heart cheerful: and taking little care for anything; and yet seeing many, whom I preferred before myself, under many trials and afflictions, in sickness, weakness, poverty, losses, crosses, and cares of the World, I should be sometimes jealous least I should have my portion in this life, and that Scripture would come to my mind, *Heb.* 12. 6. *For whom the Lord loveth he chasteneth, and scourgeth every Son whom he receiveth.* But now I see the Lord had his time to scourge and chasten me. The portion of some is to have their afflictions by drops, now one drop and then another; but the dregs of the Cup, the Wine of astonishment: like a sweeping rain that leaveth no food, did the Lord prepare to be my portion. Affliction I wanted, and affliction I had, full measure (I thought) pressed down and running over; yet I see, when God calls a Person to anything, and through never so many difficulties, yet he is fully able to carry them through and make them see, and say they have been gainers thereby. And I hope I can say in some measure, As David did, *It is good for me that I have been afflicted.* The Lord hath showed me the vanity of these outward things. That they are the Vanity of vanities, and vexation of spirit; that they are but a shadow, a blast, a bubble, and things of no continuance. That we must rely on God himself, and our whole dependence must be upon him. If trouble from smaller matters begin to arise in me, I have something at hand to check myself with, and say, why am I troubled? It was but the other day that if I had had the world, I would have given it for my freedom, or to have been a Servant to a Christian. I have learned to look beyond present and smaller troubles, and to be quieted under them, as Moses said, *Exod.* 14. 13. *Stand still and see the salvation of the Lord.*

1682

EDWARD TAYLOR

(c. 1645-1729)

CHRONOLOGY:

1642-1645? Born Leicestershire, England, probably at Sketchley; probably educated at nonconformist school.

1668 Arrived at Boston, July 5; enrolled as Harvard sophomore.

1671 A.B., Harvard. Took lifetime pastorate at Westfield, Mass. Not ordained until 1679.

1674 Married Elizabeth Fitch.

1678 Became freeman at Westfield.

1682-1725 Composition of *Sacramental Meditations* or *Preparatory Meditations*, a series of 217 poems written regularly "before My Approach to the Lord's Supper." Series I (1682-1693) and II (1693-1725).

1689 Wife Elizabeth died; wrote "A Funeral Poem."

1690 Probable completion of *God's Determinations Touching His Elect.*

1692 Married Ruth Wyllys.

1701-03 *Christographia* sermons.

1720 Received M.A. from Harvard.

1725-26 Taylor's health failed; preached final sermon in 1726.

1729 Died June 24; buried at Westfield.

1937 His poetry, first published.

BIBLIOGRAPHY:

T. H. Johnson, *The Poetical Works of Edward Taylor* (New York, 1939). Johnson, ed. "The Topical Verses of Edward Taylor," *Publ. Colonial Soc. of Mass.*, XXXIV (1943), 513-554. Donald Stanford, ed. *The Poems of Edward Taylor* (Yale, 1960), with Foreword by Louis Martz. "Diary of Edward Taylor," *Proc. Mass. Hist. Soc.*, XVIII (1880-81), 4-18, extracts. Norman Grabo, ed. *Christographia* (New Haven, 1962). Grabo, *Edward Taylor* (New York, 1961).

From *Gods Determinations*

THE PREFACE

Infinity, when all things it beheld
In Nothing, and of Nothing all did build,
Upon what Base was fixt the Lath, wherein
He turn'd this Globe, and riggalld it so trim?
Who blew the Bellows of his Furnace Vast?   5
Or held the Mould wherein the world was Cast?
Who laid its Corner Stone? Or whose Command?
Where stand the Pillars upon which it stands?
Who Lac'de and Fillitted the earth so fine,
With Rivers like green Ribbons Smaragdine?   10
Who made the Sea's its Selvedge, and it locks
Like a Quilt Ball within a Silver Box?
Who Spread its Canopy? Or Curtains Spun?

Who in this Bowling Alley bowld the Sun?
Who made it always when it rises set   15
To go at once both down, and up to get?
Who th'Curtain rods made for this Tapistry?
Who hung the twinckling Lanthorns in the Sky?
Who? who did this? or who is he? Why, know
Its Onely Might Almighty this did doe.   20
His hand hath made this noble worke which Stands
His Glorious Handywork not made by hands.
Who spake all things from nothing; and with ease
Can speake all things to nothing, if he please.
Whose Little finger at his pleasure Can   25
Out mete ten thousand worlds with halfe a Span:
Whose Might Almighty can by half a looks
Root up the rocks and rock the hills by th'roots.
Can take this mighty World up in his hande,
And shake it like a Squitchen or a Wand.   30
Whose single Frown will make the Heavens shake
Like as an aspen leafe the Winde makes quake.
Oh! what a might is this Whose single frown
Doth shake the world as it would shake it down?
Which All from Nothing fet, from Nothing, All: 35
Hath All on Nothing set, lets Nothing fall.
Gave All to nothing Man indeed, whereby
Through nothing man all might him Glorify.
In Nothing then imbosst the brightest Gem
More pretious than all pretiousness in them.   40
But Nothing man did throw down all by Sin:
And darkened that lightsom Gem in him.
   That now his Brightest Diamond is grown
   Darker by far than any Coalpit Stone. . . .

FIRST SATANS ASSAULT AGAINST THOSE THAT FIRST CAME UP TO MERCYS TERMS

Satan

Soon ripe, soon rot. Young Saint, Old Divell. Loe
Why to an Empty Whistle did you goe?
What Come Uncalld? And Run unsent for? Stay
Its Childrens Bread: Hands off: out, Dogs, away.

Soul

It's not an Empty Whistle: yet withall,
And if it be a Whistle, then a Call: 5
A Call to Childrens Bread, which take we may.
Thou onely art the Dog whipt hence away.

Satan

If I then you: for by Apostasy
You are the Imps of Death as much as I.   10
And Death doth reign o're you through Sin: you see,
As well as Sin doth reign to Death in mee.

Soul

It is deni'd: Gods Mercy taking place,
Prepared Grace for us, and us for Grace.
And Graces Coach in Grace hath fetcht us in,   15
Unto her Feast. We shall not dy in Sin.

Satan

If it be so, your sins are Crucifide:
Which if they be, they struggl'd when they di'de.
It is not so with you: you judge before
You felt them gird, you'de got them out of Doore.   20

Soul

Mercy the Quartermaster speedily,
Did stifle Sin, and still its hidious Cry,
Whose Knife at first stuck in its heart to th'head:
That sin, before it hard did sprunt, fell dead.

Satan

A mere Delusion! Nature shows that Life   25
Will strugle most upon the bloody Knife
And so will Sin. Nay Christ doth onely Call,
And offer ease to such as are in thrall.

Soul

He offer'd unto mee, and I receiv'd
Of what hee wrought, I am not yet bereav'd.   30
Though Justice set Amercement on mee
Mercy hath took it off, and set me free.

Satan

Is Mercy impudent? or Justice blinde?
I am to make distraint on thee Designd.
The North must wake before the South proves Kind.   35
The Law must breake before the Gospell binde.

Soul

But Giliads Balm, like Balsom heald my wound
Makes not the Patient sore, yet leaves him sound.

The Gospell did the Law prevent: my heart
Is therefore dresst from Sin: and did not smart.   40

Satan

A likely thing! Oh shame! presume on Grace!
Here's Sin in Grain: it hath a Double Face.
Come, Come with mee I'le shew your Outs, and Inns,
Your Inside, and your out: your Holy things.
   For these I will anatomize then see,   45
   Believe your very Eyes, believe not mee.

THE ACCUSATION OF THE INWARD MAN

You want Cleare Spectacles: your eyes are dim:
Turn inside out: and turn your Eyes within.
Your sins like motes in th'sun do swim: nay see
Your Mites are Molehills, Molehills Mountains bee.
Your Mountain Sins do magnitude transcend: 5
Whose number's numberless, and do want end.
The Understandings dark, and therefore Will
Account of Ill for Good, and Good for ill.
As to a Purblinde man men oft appeare
Like Walking Trees within the Hemisphere.   10
So in the judgment Carnall things Excell:
Pleasures and Profits beare away the Bell.
The Will is hereupon perverted so,
It laquyes after ill, doth good foregoe.
The Reasonable Soule doth much delight   15
A Pickpack t'ride o'th'Sensuall Appitite.
And hence the heart is hardened and toyes,
With Love, Delight, and Joy, yea Vanities.

Make but a thorow search, and you may spy
Your soul a trudging hard, though secretly   20
Upon the feet of your Affections mute.
And hankering after all forbidden fruite.
Ask but yourselfe in secret laying neer
Thy head thereto: 'twill Whisper in thine eare
That it is tickled much, though secretly.   25
And greatly itches after Vilany.
'Twill fleere thee in thy face, and though it say,
It must not tell, it scorns to tell thee nay.
But Slack the rains, and Come a Loophole lower:
You'l finde it was but Pen-coop't up before.   30
Nay, muster up your thoughts, and take the Pole

Of what walk in the Entry of your Soule
Which if you do, you certainly will finde
With Robbers, Cut-throats, Theives its mostly linde.
And hundred Roagues you'l finde, ly gaming there. 35
For one true man, that in that path appears.
Your True man too's oft footsore, sildom is,
Sound Winde, and Limb: and still to add to this,
He's but a Traviller within that Way:
Whereas the rest there pitch their Tents, and stay. 40
Nay, nay, what thoughts Unclean? Lacivious?
Blasphemous? Murderous? and Malicious?
Tyranick? Wrathfull? Atheistick rise
Of Evills New, and Old, of e'ry Sise?
These bed, and board here, make the heart a sty 45
Of all Abominable Brothlery.
       Then is it pure? is this the fruite of Grace?
       If so, how do yee: You and I Embrace.

THE SOUL ACCUSED IN ITS SERVING GOD

When thou dost go to serve thy God, behold
What greate Distractions do thy Soule infold?
How thy Religious Worship's much abusde?
And with Confusion greate thy Soul's amus'de?
What thoughts to God on Errand dost thou send 5
That have not Sin therein, or in the End? . . .
    What's thy Repentance? Can'st thou come and show
By those salt Rivers which do Ebb, and Flow
By th'motion of that Ocean Vast within,
Of pickled sorrow rising for thy Sin? 10
For Sin prooves very Costly unto all.
It Cost Saint Peter bitter tears, and Paul.
Thy joy is groundless, Faith is false, thy Hope
Presumption, and Desire is almost broke.
Zeale Wildfire is, thy Pray'res are sapless most, 15
Or like the Whistling of some Dead mans Ghost:
Thy Holy Conference is onely like
An Empty Voice that tooteth through a pipe.
Thy Soule doth peep out at thine Eares, and Eyes
To bless those bawbles that are earthly toyes. 20
But when Gods Words in at those Windows peepe
To kiss thy Soul, thy Soul lies dead asleep.
Examine but thy Conscience, her reply,
Will suite hereto: For Conscience dare notly.

When did thine Eyes run down for sin as sin,   25
That thus thy heart runs up with joy to sing?
    Thy sins do sculk under a flowrisht paint.
    Hence thou a Sinner art, or I a Saint.

Soul

Well, Satan, well: with thee I'le parle no more.
But do adjure thee hence: begone therefore.   30
If I as yet was thine, I thus do say
I from thy flag would quickly flag away.
    Begone therefore; to him I'le send a groane
    Against thee drawn, who makes my heart his Throne.

THE SOULS GROAN TO CHRIST FOR SUCCOUR

 Good Lord, behold this Dreadfull Enemy
    Who makes me tremble with his fierce assaults,
I dare not trust, yet feare to give the ly,
    For in my soul, my soul finds many faults.
    And though I justify myselfe to's face: 5
    I do Condemn myselfe before thy Grace.

He strives to mount my sins, and them advance
    Above thy Merits, Pardons, or Good Will
Thy Grace to lessen, and thy Wrath t'inhance
    As if thou couldst not pay the sinners bill.   10
    He Chiefly injures thy rich Grace, I finde
    Though I confess my heart to sin inclin'de.

Those Graces which thy Grace enwrought in mee,
    He makes as nothing but a pack of Sins.
He maketh Grace no grace, but Crueltie,   15
    Is Graces Honey Comb, a Comb of Stings?
    This makes me ready leave thy Grace and run.
    Which if I do, I finde I am undone.

I know he is thy Cur, therefore I bee
    Perplexed lest I from thy Pasture stray.   20
He bayghs, and barks so veh'mently at mee.
    Come rate this Cur, Lord, breake his teeth I pray.
    Remember me I humbly pray thee first.
    Then halter up this Cur that is so Curst.

CHRISTS REPLY

Peace, Peace, my Hony, do not Cry,
My Little Darling, wipe thine eye,
   Oh Cheer, Cheer up, come see.
Is anything too deare, my Dove,
Is anything too good, my Love   5
   To get or give for thee?

If in the severall thou art
This Yelper fierce will at thee bark:
   That thou art mine this shows.
As Spot barks back the sheep again   10
Before they to the Pound are ta'ne,
   So he and hence 'way goes.

But yet this Cur that bayghs so sore
Is broken tootht, and muzzled sure,
   Fear not, my Pritty Heart.   15
His barking is to make thee Cling
Close underneath thy Saviours Wing.
   Why did my sweeten start?

And if he run an inch too far,
I'le Check his Chain, and rate the Cur.   20
   My Chick, keep clost to mee.
The Poles shall sooner kiss, and greet
And Paralells shall sooner meet
   Than thou shalt harmed bee.

He seeks to aggrivate thy sin   25
And screw them to the highest pin,
   To make thy faith to quaile.
Yet mountain Sins like mites should show
And then these mites for naught should goe
   Could he but once prevaile.   30

I smote thy sins upon the Head.
They Dead'ned are, though not quite dead:
   And shall not rise again.
I'l put away the Guilt thereof,
And purge its Filthiness cleare off: 35
   My Blood doth out the stain.

And though thy judgment was remiss
Thy Headstrong Will too Wilfull is.
　　I will Renew the same.
And though thou do too frequently　　　　　　　40
Offend as heretofore hereby
　　I'l not severly blaim.

And though thy senses do inveagle
Thy Noble Soul to tend the Beagle,
　　That t'hunt her games forth go.　　　　　　45
I'le Lure her back to me, and Change
Those fond Affections that do range
　　As yelping beagles doe.

Although thy sins increase their race,
And though when thou hast sought for Grace,　　50
　　Thou fallst more than before
If thou by true Repentence Rise,
And Faith makes me thy Sacrifice,
　　I'l pardon all, though more.

· · · · ·

I dare the World therefore to show　　　　　　55
A God like me, to anger slow:
　　Whose wrath is full of Grace.
Doth hate all Sins both Greate, and small:
Yet when Repented, pardons all.
　　Frowns with a Smiling Face.　　　　　　　60

As for thy outward Postures each,
Thy Gestures, Actions, and thy Speech,
　　I Eye and Eying spare,
If thou repent. My Grace is more
Ten thousand times still tribled ore　　　　　　65
　　Than thou canst want, or ware.

· · · · ·

Though to thy Griefe, poor Heart, thou finde
In Pray're too oft a wandring minde,
　　In Sermons Spirits dull.
Though faith in firy furnace flags,　　　　　　70
And Zeale in Chilly Seasons lags.
　　Temptations powerfull.

These faults are his, and none of thine
So far as thou dost them decline.
  Come then receive my Grace.   75
And when he buffits thee therefore
If thou my aid, and Grace implore
  I'le shew a pleasant face.

But still look for Temptations Deep,
Whilst that thy Noble Sparke doth keep   80
  Within a Mudwald Cote.
These White Frosts and the Showers that fall
Are but to whiten thee withall.
  Not rot the Web they smote.

If in the fire where Gold is tride   85
Thy Soule is put, and purifide
  Wilt thou lament thy loss?
If silver-like this fire refine
Thy Soul and make it brighter shine:
  Wilt thou bewaile the Dross?   90

Oh! fight my Field: no Colours fear:
I'l be thy Front, I'l be thy reare.
  Fail not: my Battells fight.
Defy the Tempter, and his Mock.
Anchor thy heart on mee thy Rock.   95
  I do in thee Delight.

THE PREFACE

Soul

Long lookt for Sir! Happy, right Happy Saint.
I long to lay before you my Complaint:
And gain your Counsill: but you're strange: and I
Through backwardness lost opportunity.

Saint

How is't good Sir: methinks I finde there dart   5
Some pleasant Hopes of you within my heart.
What is your Rantery declinde, foregone?
Your looks are like the Earth you Tread upon.

Soul

Its true: I do, and well may look so, too
For worse than mee the world did never show.　　　10
My sins are dide in grain: all Grace I lack.
This doth my Soul on tenterhooks enwrack.
Wherefore I Counsill Crave touching my sin
My Want of Grace. Temptations too within.

SOME OF SATANS SOPHESTRY

The Tempter greatly seeks, though secretly,
　With an Ath'istick Hoodwinke man to blinde,
That so the Footsteps of the Deity
　Might stand no longer stampt upon his minde.
　Which when he can't blot out, by blinding quite,　　5
　He strives to turn him from the Purer Light.

With Wiles enough, he on his thoughts intrudes,
　That God's a Heape of Contradictions high,
But when these thoughts man from his thoughts excludes
　Thou knowst not then (saith he) this Mystery.　　10
　And when the first String breaks, he strives to bring
　Into sins brambles by the other string.

When God Calls out a Soule, he subtilly
　Saith God is kinde: you need not yet forsake
Your Sins: but if he doth, he doth reply,　　15
　Thou'st outstood Grace. Justice will vengeance take.
　He'l tell you you Presume on Grace, to fright
　You to despare, beholding Justice bright.

　　　　　.　.　.　.　.

While man thinks slightly, that he will repent,
　There's time enough (saith he), it's easly done.　　20
But when repent he doth, the time is spent,
　Saith he, it is too late to be begun.
　To keep man from't, it's easly done, saith he,
　To dant him in't, he saith, it Cannot bee.

So Faith is easy till the Soule resolves　　25
　To Live to Christ, and upon Christ rely.
Then Saving Faith he bold presumption Calls.
　Hast thou (saith he) in Christ propriety?
　The Faithfulls Faith, he stiles Presumption great,
　But the Presumptuous, theirs is Faith Compleat.　　30

Nay though the Faith be true he acts so sly,
    As to raise doubts: and then it must not do:
Unless Assurance do it Certify:
      Which if it do, it douts of it also.
      Faith is without Assurance shuffled out,   35
      And if Assurance be, that's still a Doubt.

        .   .   .   .

Should any Soule once an Assurance get,
    Into his hands, soon Satans Pick-Lock key
With Sinfull Wards Unlocks his Cabinet
      To Steal the Jewell in it thence away.   40
      The Soul thus pillag'de, droops unto the grave.
      It's greater grief to lose than not to have.

        .   .   .   .

Thus I might search, Poor Soul, the Magazeen
    Of Gospell Graces over: I might paint
Out Satan sculking each side each unseen   45
      To Hoodwinck Sinners, and to hopple Saints.
      For he to dim their Grace, and slick up sin
      Calls Brass bright Gold, bright Golde but brass or tin.

        .   .   .   .

When God awakes a Soule he'l seeke to thrust
    It on Despare for want of Grace or get   50
And puff't with Pride, or in Securety hush't
      Or Couzen it with Graces Counterfet.
      Which if he can't he'l Carp at Grace, and raile
      And say, this is not Grace, it thus doth faile.

And thus he strives with Spite, Spleen, bitter Gall   55
    That Sinners might Dishonour God Most high:
That Saints might never honour God at all.
      That those in Sin, Those not in Grace might dy.
      And that the Righteous, Gracious, Pious, Grave,
      Might have no Comfort of the Grace they have.   60

Lest you be foild herewith, watch well unto
    Your Soul, that thrice Ennobled noble Gem:
For Sins are flaws therein, and double woe
      Belongs thereto if it be found in them.
      Are Flaws in Venice Glasses bad? What in   65
      Bright Diamonds? What then in man is Sin?

THE GLORY OF AND GRACE IN THE CHURCH SET OUT

   Come now behold
  Within this Knot What Flowers do grow:
   Spanglde like gold:
  Whence Wreaths of all Perfumes do flow.
Most Curious Colours of all sorts you shall   5
With all Sweet Spirits sent. Yet thats not all.

   Oh! Look, and finde
  These Choicest Flowers most richly sweet
   Are Disciplinde
  With Artificiall Angells meet.   10
An heap of Pearls is precious: but they shall
When set by Art Excell: Yet that's not all.

   Christ's Spirit showers
  Down in his Word, and Sacraments
   Upon these Flowers   15
  The Clouds of Grace Divinc Contents.
Such things of Wealthy Blessings on them fall
As make them sweetly thrive: Yet that's not all.

   Yet still behold!
  All flourish not at once. We see   20
   While some Unfold
  Their blushing Leaves, some buds there bee.
Here's Faith, Hope, Charity in flower, which call
On yonders in the Bud. Yet that's not all.

   But as they stand   25
  Like Beauties reeching in perfume
   A Divine Hand
  Doth hand them up to Glories room:
Where Each in sweet'ned Songs all Praises shall
Sing all ore heaven for aye. And that's but all.   30

THE SOULS ADMIRATION HEREUPON

  What I such Praises sing! How can it bee?
    Shall I in Heaven sing?
  What I, that scarce durst hope to see
    Lord, such a thing?
   Though nothing is too hard for thee: 5
   One Hope hereof seems hard to mee.

What, Can I ever tune those Melodies
  Who have no tune at all?
Not knowing where to stop nor Rise,
  Nor when to Fall.   10
  To sing thy Praise I am unfit.
  I have not learn'd my Gam-Ut yet.

But should these Praises on string'd Instruments
  Be sweetly tun'de? I finde
I nonplust am: for no Consents   15
  I ever minde.
  My Tongue is neither Quill, nor Bow:
  Nor Can my Fingers Quavers show.

But was it otherwise I have no Kit:
  Which though I had, I could   20
Not tune the strings, which soon would slip
  Though others should.
  But should they not, I cannot play:
  But for an F should strike an A.

And should thy Praise upon Winde Instruments 25
  Sound all o're Heaven Shrill?
My Breath will hardly through such Vents
  A Whistle fill,
  Which though it should, its past my spell
  By Stops, and Falls to sound it Well. 30

How should I then, joyn in such Exercise?
  One sight of thee'l intice
Mine Eyes to heft: Whose Extasies
  Will stob my Voice.
  Hereby mine Eyes will bind my Tongue. 35
  Unless thou, Lord, do Cut the thong.

What Use of Uselesse mee, then there, poore snake?
  There Saints, and Angels sing,
Thy Praise in full Cariere, which make
  The Heavens to ring.
  Yet if thou wilt thou Can'st me raise 40
  With Angels bright to sing thy Praise.

THE JOY OF CHURCH FELLOWSHIP RIGHTLY ATTENDED

In Heaven soaring up, I dropt an Eare
  On Earth: and oh! sweet Melody:

And listening, found it was the Saints who were
    Encoacht for Heaven that sang for Joy.
    For in Christs Coach they sweetly sing;   5
    As they to Glory ride therein.

Oh! joyous hearts! Enfir'de with holy Flame!
    Is speech thus tassled with praise?
Will not your inward fire of Joy contain;
    That it in open flames doth blaze?   10
    For in Christ's Coach Saints sweetly sing,
    As they to Glory ride therein.

And if a string do slip, by Chance, they soon
    Do screw it up again: whereby
They set it in a more melodious Tune   15
    And a Diviner Harmony.
    For in Christs Coach they sweetly sing
    As they to Glory ride therein.

In all their Acts, publick, and private, nay
    And secret too, they praise impart.   20
But in their Acts Divine and Worship, they
    With Hymns do offer up their Heart.
    Thus in Christs Coach they sweetly sing
    As they to Glory ride therein.

Some few not in; and some whose Time, and Place   25
    Block up this Coaches way do goe
As Travellers afoot, and so do trace
    The Road that gives them right thereto
    While in this Coach these sweetly sing
    As they to Glory ride therein.   30

                 c. 1690, 1939

From *Preparatory Meditations*

THE EXPERIENCE

Oh! that I always breath'd in such an aire,
    As I suckt in, feeding on sweet Content!
Disht up unto my Soul ev'n in that pray're
    Pour'de out to God over last Sacrament.
    What Beam of Light wrapt up my sight to finde   5
    Me neerer God than ere Came in my minde?

Most strange it was! But yet more strange that shine
    Which filld my Soul then to the brim to spy
My Nature with thy Nature all Divine
    Together joyn'd in Him thats Thou, and I.   10
    Flesh of my Flesh, Bone of my Bone. There's run
    Thy Godhead, and my Manhood in thy Son.

Oh! that that Flame which thou didst on me Cast
    Might me enflame, and Lighten ery where.
Then Heaven to me would be less at last   15
    So much of heaven I should have while here.
    Oh! Sweet though Short! Ile not forget the same.
    My neerness, Lord, to thee did me Enflame.

I'le Claim my Right: Give place, ye Angells Bright.
    Ye further from the Godhead stande than I.   20
My Nature is your Lord; and doth Unite
    Better than Yours unto the Deity.
    Gods Throne is first and mine is next: to you
    Onely the place of Waiting-men is due.

Oh! that my Heart, thy Golden Harp might bee   25
    Well tun'd by Glorious Grace, that e'ry string
Screw'd to the highest pitch, might unto thee
    All Praises wrapt in sweetest Musick bring.
    I praise thee, Lord, and better praise thee would
    If what I had, my heart might ever hold.   30

        1939

ANOTHER MEDITATION AT THE SAME TIME

Am I thy Gold? Or Purse, Lord, for thy Wealth;
    Whether in mine, or mint refinde for thee?
Ime counted so, but count me o're thyselfe,
    Lest gold washt face, and brass in Heart I bee.
    I Feare my Touchstone touches when I try   5
    Mee, and my Counted Gold too overly.

Am I new minted by the Stamp indeed?
    Mine Eyes are dim; I cannot clearly see.
Be thou my Spectacles that I may read
    Thine Image, and Inscription stampt on mee.   10
    If thy bright Image do upon me stand
    I am a Golden Angell in thy hand.

Lord, make my Soule thy Plate: thine Image bright
    Within the Circle of the same enfoile.
And on its brims in golden Letters write   15
    Thy Superscription in an Holy style.
    Then I shall be thy Money, thou my Hord:
    Let me thy Angell bee, bee thou my Lord.

                    1939

MEDITATION. PS. 45.2. GRACE IN THY LIPS IS POURED OUT

Thy Humane Frame, my Glorious Lord, I spy,
    A Golden Still with Heavenly Choice drugs filld;
Thy Holy Love, the Glowing heate whereby,
    The Spirit of Grace is graciously distilld.
    Thy Mouth the Neck through which these spirits still.   5
    My Soul thy Violl make, and therewith fill.

Thy Speech the Liquour in thy Vessell stands,
    Well ting'd with Grace a blessed Tincture, Loe,
Thy Words distilld, Grace in thy Lips pourd, and,
    Give Graces Tinctur in them where they go.   10
    Thy words in graces tincture stilld, Lord, may
    The Tincture of thy Grace in me Convay.

That Golden Mint of Words, thy Mouth Divine,
    Doth tip these Words, which by my Fall were spoild;
And Dub with Gold dug out of Graces mine   15
    That they thine Image might have in them foild.
    Grace in thy Lips pourd out's as Liquid Gold.
    Thy Bottle make my Soule, Lord, it to hold.

                1683, 1937

MEDITATION. JOH. 6.51. I AM THE LIVING BREAD

I kening through Astronomy Divine
    The Worlds bright Battlement, wherein I spy
A Golden Path my Pensill cannot line,
    From that bright Throne unto my Threshold ly.
    And while my puzzled thoughts about it pore   5
    I finde the Bread of Life in't at my doore.

When that this Bird of Paradise put in
    This Wicker Cage (my Corps) to tweedle praise
Had peckt the Fruite forbad: and so did fling
    Away its Food; and lost its golden dayes;   10
    It fell into Celestiall Famine sore:
    And never could attain a morsell more.

Alas! alas! Poore Bird, what wilt thou doe?
    The Creatures field no food for Souls e're gave.
And if thou knock at Angells dores they show   15
    An Empty Barrell: they no soul bread have.
    Alas! Poore Bird, the Worlds White Loafe is done.
    And cannot yield thee here the smallest Crumb.

In this sad state, Gods Tender Bowells run
    Out streams of Grace: And he to end all strife   20
The Purest Wheate in Heaven, his deare-dear Son
    Grinds, and kneads up into this Bread of Life.
    Which Bread of Life from Heaven down came and stands
    Disht on thy Table up by Angells Hands.

Did God mould up this Bread in Heaven, and bake,   25
    Which from his Table came, and to thine goeth?
Doth he bespeake thee thus, This Soule Bread take.
    Come Eate thy fill of this thy Gods White Loafe?
    Its Food too fine for Angells, yet come, take
    And Eate thy fill. Its Heavens Sugar Cake.   30

What Grace is this knead in this Loafe? This thing
    Souls are but petty things it to admire.
Yee Angells, help: This fill would to the brim
    Heav'ns whelm'd-down Chrystall meele Bowle, yea and higher.
    This Bread of Life dropt in thy mouth, doth Cry.   35
    Eate, Eate me, Soul, and thou shalt never dy.
                                        1684, 1937

Miscellaneous Verses

UPON A SPIDER CATCHING A FLY

Thou sorrow, venom Elfe.
        Is this thy play,
To spin a web out of thyselfe
        To Catch a Fly?
            For Why?   5

I saw a pettish wasp
        Fall foule therein.
Whom yet thy Whorle pins did not clasp
        Lest he should fling
            His sting.   10

But as affraid, remote
 Didst stand hereat
And with thy little fingers stroke
 And gently tap
  His back.   15

Thus gently him didst treate
 Lest he should pet,
And in a froppish, waspish heate
 Should greatly fret
  Thy net.   20

Whereas the silly Fly,
 Caught by its leg
Thou by the throate tookst hastily
 And 'hinde the head
  Bite Dead.   25

This goes to pot, that not
 Nature doth call.
Strive not above what strength hath got
 Lest in the brawle
  Thou fall.   30

This Frey seems thus to us.
 Hells Spider gets
His intrails spun to whip Cords thus
 And wove to nets
  And sets.   35

To tangle Adams race
 In's stratigems
To their Destructions, spoil'd, made base
 By venom things
  Damn'd Sins.   40

But mighty, Gracious Lord
 Communicate
Thy Grace to breake the Cord, afford
 Us Glorys Gate
  And State.   45

We'l Nightingaile sing like
 When pearcht on high
In Glories Cage, thy glory, bright,
 And thankfully,
  For joy.   50

                          1939

UPON A WASP CHILD WITH COLD

The Bare that breaths the Northern blast
Did numb, Torpedo like, a Wasp
Whose stiffend limbs encrampt, lay bathing
In Sol's warm breath and shine as saving,
Which with her hands she chafes and stands   5
Rubbing her Legs, Shanks, Thighs, and hands.
Her pretty toes, and fingers ends
Nipt with this breath, she out extends
Unto the Sun, in greate desire
To warm her digits at that fire.   10
Doth hold her Temples in this state
Where pulse doth beate, and head doth ake.
Doth turn, and stretch her body small,
Doth Comb her velvet Capitall.
As if her little brain pan were   15
A Volume of Choice precepts cleare.
As if her sattin jacket hot
Contained Apothecaries Shop
Of Natures recepts, that prevails
To remedy all her sad ailes,   20
As if her velvet helmet high
Did turret rationality.
She fans her wing up to the Winde
As if her Pettycoate were lin'de,
With reasons fleece, and hoises sails   25
And hu'ming flies in thankfull gails
Unto her dun Curld palace Hall
Her warm thanks offering for all.

Lord cleare my misted sight that I
May hence view thy Divinity.   30
Some sparkes whereof thou up dost hasp
Within this little downy Wasp
In whose small Corporation wee
A school and a schoolmaster see
Where we may learn, and easily finde   35
A nimble Spirit bravely minde
Her worke in e'ry limb: and lace
It up neate with a vitall grace,
Acting each part though ne'er so small
Here of this Fustian animall.   40
Till I enravisht Climb into

The Godhead on this Lather doe.
Where all my pipes inspir'de upraise
An Heavenly musick furrd with praise.

1943

HUSWIFERY

Make me, O Lord, thy Spining Wheele compleate.
   Thy Holy Worde my Distaff make for mee.
Make mine Affections thy Swift Flyers neate
   And make my Soule thy holy Spoole to bee.
   My Conversation make to be thy Reele   5
   And reele the yarn thereon spun of thy Wheele.

Make me thy Loome then, knit therein this Twine:
   And make thy Holy Spirit, Lord, winde quills:
Then weave the Web thyselfe. The yarn is fine.
   Thine Ordinances make my Fulling Mills.   10
   Then dy the same in Heavenly Colours Choice,
All pinkt with Varnisht Flowers of Paradise.

Then cloath therewith mine Understanding, Will,
   Affections, Judgment, Conscience, Memory
My Words, and Actions, that their shine may fill   15
   My wayes with glory and thee glorify.
   Then mine apparell shall display before yee
That I am Cloathd in Holy robes for glory.

1937

THE EBB AND FLOW

When first thou on me Lord wrought'st thy Sweet Print,
   My heart was made thy tinder box.
   My 'ffections were thy tinder in't.
     Where fell thy Sparkes by drops.
Those holy Sparks of Heavenly Fire that came   5
Did ever catch and often out would flame.

But now my Heart is made thy Censar trim,
   Full of thy golden Altars fire,
   To offer up Sweet Incense in
     Unto thyselfe intire: 10
I finde my tinder scarce thy sparks can feel
That drop out from thy Holy flint and Steel.

Hence doubts out bud for feare thy fire in mee
   'S a mocking Ignis Fatuus
     Or lest thine Altars fire out bee,   15
       Its hid in ashes thus.
Yet when the bellows of thy Spirit blow
Away mine ashes, then thy fire doth glow.

                         1937

UPON THE SWEEPING FLOOD AUG: 13.14. 1683

Oh! that Id had a tear to've quencht that flame
   Which did dissolve the Heavens above
   Into those liquid drops that Came
     To drown our Carnall love.
Our cheeks were dry and eyes refusde to weep.   5
Tears bursting out ran down the skies darke Cheek.

Were th'Heavens sick? must wee their Doctors bee
   And physick them with pills, our sin?
   To make them purg and Vomit, see,
     And Excrements out fling?   10
We've griev'd them by such Physick that they shed
Their Excrements upon our lofty heads.

                         1943

COTTON MATHER

(1663-1728)

223

CHRONOLOGY:

Wrote 444 books, pamphlets, articles.

1663 Born Feb. 12, at Dorchester, Mass., the son of Increase and Maria (Cotton) Mather; early schooling at Boston Latin School and at home.

1675 Admitted to Harvard.

1678 Graduated from Harvard.

1680 Began to preach and to assist his father at Second Church, Boston.

1681 Received M.A. at Harvard.

1685 Ordained at Second Church, Boston; held office there for the rest of his life; served as his father's colleague.

1686 Married Abigail Phillips.

1689 Leader of open revolt against Gov. Edmund Andros; *Memorable Providences, Relating to Witchcrafts and Possessions* (Boston).

1690 Elected Harvard fellow; *The Way to Prosperity* (Boston).

1692 Salem witch trials; recommended milder punishment than death; power of Mathers began to wane.

1693 *Political Fables* circulated in manuscript, but unpublished until 1825; *The Wonders of the Invisible World* (Boston); investigation of bewitched girl; this account later included in Robert Calef's *More Wonders of the Invisible World* (London, 1700).

1699 *A Family Well-Ordered* (Boston).

1700 *Reasonable Religion* (Boston).

1701 *Some Few Remarks upon A Scandalous Book . . . By one Robert Calef* (Boston).

1702 Wife Abigail died; *Magnalia Christi Americana; or, The Ecclesiastical History of New England*, 2 Vols. (London).

1703 Appointed president of Harvard, but action later overruled; married Elizabeth Hubbard, a widow.

1706 *The Negro Christianized* (Boston).

1710 *Bonifacius* (Boston), or *Essays to Do Good*.

1713 Wife Elizabeth died; elected to Royal Society of England.

1716 Married Lydia George, a widow, who became mentally ill about 1717-1718; *Fair Dealing between Debtor and Creditor* (Boston).

1721 Elected president of Yale; *The Christian Philosopher* (London); *Some Account of . . . Inoculating . . . the Small Pox* (Boston), with Zabdiel Boylston; *The Accomplished Singer* (Boston).

1724 *Parentator* (Boston), a biography of his father.

1726 *Manuductio ad Ministerium* (Boston).

1728 Died February 13.

BIBLIOGRAPHY:

W. C. Ford, ed. *Diary of Cotton Mather*, in *Coll. Mass. Hist. Soc.*, 7th Ser., VII-VIII (1911-1912). Thomas Robbins, ed. *Magnalia Christi Americana*, 2 Vols. (Hartford, 1853-1855). K. B. Murdock, ed. *Selections from Cotton Mather* (New York, 1926). Barrett Wendell, *Cotton Mather: The Puritan Priest* (New York, 1891, also 1926). R. P. and Louise Boas, *Cotton Mather* (New York, 1928). O. T. Beall, Jr., and R. H. Shryock, *Cotton Mather, First Significant Figure in American Medicine* (Baltimore, 1954).

From *Political Fables*

THE NEW SETTLEMENT OF THE BIRDS IN NEW ENGLAND

The birds had maintained good order among themselves for several years, under the shelter of charters by Jupiter granted to several flocks among them: but heaven, to chastise many faults too observable in its birds, left them to be deprived of their ancient settlements. There were birds of all sorts in their several flocks; for some catched fish, some lived upon grains; the woodpeckers also made a great figure among them; some of them scraped for their living with their claws; and many supplied their nests, from beyond sea. Geese you may be sure there were good store, as there are everywhere. Moreover, when they had lost their charters, those poetical birds called harpies became really existent, and visited these flocks, not so much that they might build nests of their own, as plunder and pull down the nests of others.

2. There were many endeavors used by an eagle and a goldfinch, afterwards accompanied with two more,—no less deserving the love of all the flocks, than desirous to serve their interest,—that flew into Jupiter's palace, for the resettlement of good government among the birds. These endeavors did for awhile prosper no further than to stop the inroads of harpies or locusts; but at length Jupiter's court was willing that Jupiter's grace, which would have denied nothing for the advantage of them, whose wings had carried them a thousand leagues to serve his empire, should not be hindered from giving them a comfortable settlement, though not exactly in their old forms.

3. Upon this there grew a difference of opinion between some that were concerned for the welfare of the birds. Some were of opinion, that if Jupiter would not reinstate the birds in all their ancient circumstances, they had better accept of just nothing at all, but let all things be left for the harpies to commit as much rapine as they were doing when they were ejecting every poor bird out of his nest, that would not, at any excessive rate, produce a patent for it; and when Canary birds domineered over all the flocks. Others were of opinion, that the birds ought rather thankfully to accept the offers of Jupiter; and if anything were yet grievous, they might shortly see a fitter season to ask further favors, especially considering that Jupiter made them offer of such things as all the other American birds would part with more than half the feathers on their backs to purchase. He offered that the birds might be everlastingly confirmed in their titles to their nests and fields. He offered that not so much as a twig should be plucked from any tree the birds would roost upon, without their own consent. He offered that the birds might constantly make their own laws, and annually choose their own rulers. He offered that all strange birds might be made uncapable of a seat in their council. He offered that it should be made impossible for any to disturb

the birds in singing of their songs to the praise of their Maker, for which they had sought liberty in the wilderness. Finally, he offered that the kingfisher should have his commission to be their governor until they had settled what good orders among them they pleased; and that he should be more concerned than ever now to defend them from the French kites that were abroad. The kingfisher indeed was to have his negative upon the birds, but the birds were to have a negative too upon the kingfisher; and this was a privilege beyond what was enjoyed by the birds in any of the plantations, or even in Ireland itself.

4. The birds, not being agreed in their opinion, resolved that they would refer it to reasonable creatures to advise them upon this question—which of these was to be chosen; but when the reasonable creatures heard the question, they all declared none that had any reason could make any question of it.   c. 1693, 1825

From *Magnalia Christi Americana*

A GENERAL INTRODUCTION

1. I write the Wonders of the Christian Religion, flying from the deprivations of Europe, to the American Strand; and, assisted by the Holy Author of that Religion, I do with all conscience of Truth, required therein by Him, who is the Truth itself, report the wonderful displays of His infinite Power, Wisdom, Goodness, and Faithfulness, wherewith His Divine Providence hath irradiated an Indian Wilderness.

I relate the Considerable Matters, that produced and attended the First Settlement of Colonies, which have been renowned for the degree of Reformation, professed and attained by Evangelical Churches, erected in those ends of the earth; and a Field being thus prepared, I proceed unto a relation of the Considerable Matters which have been acted thereupon.

I first introduce the Actors, that have in a more exemplary manner served those Colonies; and give Remarkable Occurrences, in the exemplary Lives of many Magistrates, and of more Ministers, who so lived as to leave unto Posterity examples worthy of everlasting remembrance.

I add hereunto, the Notables of the only Protestant University that ever shone in that hemisphere of the New World; with particular instances of Criolians, in our Biography, provoking the whole world with virtuous objects of emulation.

I introduce then, the Actions of a more eminent importance, that have signalized those Colonies: whether the Establishments, directed by their Synods; with a rich variety of Synodical and Ecclesiastical Determinations; or, the Disturbances, with which they have been from all sorts of temptations and enemies tempestuated; and the Methods by which they have still weathered out each horrible tempest.

And into the midst of these Actions, I interpose an entire Book, wherein there is, with all possible veracity, a Collection made of Memorable Occurrences, and amazing Judgments and Mercies befalling many particular persons among the people of New England.

Let my readers expect all that I have promised them, in this Bill of Fare; and it may be they will find themselves entertained with yet many other passages, above and beyond their expectation, deserving likewise a room in History: in all which, there will be nothing but the Author's too mean way of preparing so great entertainments, to reproach the Invitation.

2. The reader will doubtless desire to know, what it was that

> *tot Volvere casus*
> *Insignes Pietate Viros, tot adire Labores,*
> *Impulerit.*

And our History shall, on many fit occasions which will be therein offered, endeavor, with all historical fidelity and simplicity, and with as little offense as may be, to satisfy him. The sum of the matter is, that from the very beginning of the Reformation in the English Nation, there hath always been a generation of Godly Men, desirous to pursue the Reformation of Religion, according to the Word of God, and the Example of the best Reformed Churches. . . . And there hath been another generation of men, who have still employed the power which they have generally still had in their hands, not only to stop the progress of the desired Reformation, but also, with innumerable vexations, to persecute those that most heartily wished well unto it. . . . Then 'twas that, as our great Owen hath expressed it, "Multitudes of pious, peaceable Protestants, were driven, by their severities, to leave their native country, and seek a refuge for their lives and liberties, with freedom for the worship of God, in a wilderness, in the ends of the earth."

3. It is the History of these Protestants that is here attempted: Protestants that highly honored and affected the Church of England, and humbly petition to be a part of it: but by the mistake of a few powerful brethren, driven to seek a place for the exercise of the Protestant Religion, according to the light of their consciences, in the deserts of America. And in this attempt I have proposed, not only to preserve and secure the interest of Religion in the Churches of that little country New England, so far as the Lord Jesus Christ may please to bless it for that end, but also to offer unto the Churches of the Reformation, abroad in the world, some small Memorials, that may be serviceable unto the designs of Reformation, whereto, I believe, they are quickly to be awakened. . . . It may be, 'tis not possible for me to do a greater service unto the Churches on the best Island of the universe, than to give a distinct relation of those great examples which have been occurring among Churches of exiles,

that were driven out of that Island, into an horrible wilderness, merely for their being well-willers unto the Reformation. . . .

5. Reader! I have done the part of an impartial historian, albeit not without all occasion perhaps, for the rule which a worthy writer, in his *Historica*, gives to every reader, *Historici legantur cum moderatione et venia, et cogitetur fieri non posse ut in omnibus circumstantiis sint lyncei.* Polybius complains of those historians, who always made either the Carthaginians brave, or the Romans base, or *e contra*, in all their actions, as their affection for their own party led them. I have endeavored, with all good conscience, to decline this writing merely for a party, or doing like the dealer in History, whom Lucian derides, for always calling the captain of his own party an Achilles, but of the adverse party a Thersites: nor have I added unto the just provocations for the complaint made by the Baron Maurier, that the greatest part of Histories are but so many panegyrics composed by interested hands, which elevate iniquity to the heavens, like Paterculus, and like Machiavel, who propose Tiberius Caesar, and Caesar Borgia, as examples fit for imitation, whereas true History would have exhibited them as horrid monsters—as very devils. 'Tis true, I am not of the opinion that one cannot merit the name of an impartial historian, except he write bare matters of fact without all reflection; for I can tell where to find this given as the definition of History, *Historia est rerum gestarum, cum laude aut vituperatione, narratio.* . . . I have not commended any person, but when I have really judged, not only that he deserved it, but also that it would be a benefit unto posterity to know wherein he deserved it: and my judgment of desert, hath not been biased by persons being of my own particular judgment, in matters of disputation, among the Churches of God. . . . Nor have I, on the other side, forebore to mention many censurable things, even in the best of my friends, when the things, in my opinion, were not good; or so bore away for Plancentia, in the course of our story, as to pass by Verona; but been mindful of the direction which Polybius gives to the historian: "It becomes him that writes an History, sometimes to extol enemies in his praises, when their praiseworthy actions bespeak it, and at the same time to reprove the best friends, when their deeds appear worthy of a reproof; in-as-much as History is good for nothing, if truth (which is the very eye of the animal) be not in it." Indeed, I have thought it my duty upon all accounts, (and if it have proceeded unto the degree of a fault, there is, it may be, something in my temper and nature that has betrayed me therein,) to be more sparing and easy, in thus mentioning of censurable things, than in my other liberty. . . . I have left unmentioned some censurable occurrences in the story of our Colonies, as things no less unuseful than improper to be raised out of the grave, wherein Oblivion hath now buried them; lest I should have incurred the *pasquil* bestowed upon Pope Urban, who, employing a committee to rip up the old errors

of his predecessors, one clapped a pair of spurs upon the heels of the statue of St. Peter; and a label from the statue of St. Paul opposite thereunto, upon the bridge, asked him, "Whither he was bound?" St. Peter answered, "I apprehend some danger in staying here; I fear they'll call me in question for denying my Master." And St. Paul replied, "Nay, then I had best be gone too, for they'll question me also for persecuting the Christians before my conversion." Briefly, my pen shall reproach none that can give a good word unto any good man that is not of their own faction, and shall fall out with none but those that can agree with no body else, except those of their own schism. . . .

All good men will not be satisfied with everything that is here set before them. In my own country, besides a considerable number of loose and vain inhabitants risen up, to whom the Congregational Church discipline, which cannot live well where the power of godliness dies, is become distasteful for the purity of it; there is also a number of eminently godly persons, who are for a larger way, and unto these my Church History will give distaste, by the things which it may happen to utter in favor of that Church discipline on some few occasions; and the discoveries which I may happen to make of my apprehensions, that Scripture, and reason, and antiquity is for it; and that it is not far from a glorious resurrection. But that, as the famous Mr. Baxter, after thirty or forty years' hard study, about the true instituted Church discipline, at last not only owned, but also invincibly proved, that it is the congregational; so, the further that the unprejudiced studies of learned men proceed in this matter, the more generally the Congregational Church discipline will be pronounced for. On the other side, there are some among us who very strictly profess the Congregational Church discipline, but at the same time they have an unhappy narrowness of soul, by which they confine their value and kindness too much unto their own party: and unto those my Church History will be offensive, because my regard unto our own declared principles does not hinder me from giving the right hand of fellowship unto the valuable servants of the Lord Jesus Christ, who find not our Church discipline as yet agreeable unto their present understandings and illuminations. If it be thus in my own country, it cannot be otherwise in that whereto I send this account of my own. Briefly, as it hath been said, that if all Episcopal men were like Archbishop Usher, and all Presbyterians like Stephen Marshal, and all Independents like Jeremiah Burroughs, the wounds of the Church would soon be healed; my essay to carry that spirit through this whole Church History, will bespeak wounds for it, from those that are of another spirit. And there will also be in every country those good men, who yet have not had the grace of Christ so far prevailing in them, as utterly to divest them of that piece of ill-nature which the Comedian resents, *In homine imperito, quo nil quicquam injustius, quia nisi quod ipse facit, nil recte factum putat.*

However, all these things, and an hundred more such things which I think of, are very small discouragements for such a service as I have here endeavored. I foresee a recompense which will abundantly swallow up all discouragements! It may be Strato the Philosopher counted himself well recompensed for his labors, when Ptolemy bestowed fourscore talents on him. It may be, Archimelus the poet counted himself well recompensed, when Hiero sent him a thousand bushels of wheat for one little epigram: and Saleius the poet might count himself well recompensed, when Vespasian sent him twelve thousand and five hundred philippics; and Oppian the poet might count himself well recompensed, when Caracalla sent him a piece of gold for every line that he had inscribed unto him. As I live in a country where such recompenses never were in fashion; it hath no preferments for me, and I shall count that I am well rewarded in it, if I can escape without being heavily reproached, censured and condemned, for what I have done: so I thank the Lord, I should exceedingly scorn all such mean considerations, I seek not out for benefactors, to whom these labors may be dedicated: there is ONE to whom all is due! from him I shall have a recompense: and what recompense? The recompense, whereof I do, with inexpressible joy, assure myself is this, That these my poor labors will certainly serve the Churches and interests of the Lord Jesus Christ. And I think I may say, that I ask to live no longer than I count a service unto the Lord Jesus Christ and his Churches, to be itself a glorious recompense for the doing of it.

FROM LIFE OF SIR WILLIAM PHIPS

Now, the arrival of Sir William Phips to the government of New England, was at a time when a governor would have had occasion for all the skill in sorcery that was ever necessary to a Jewish Counselor; a time when scores of poor people had newly fallen under a prodigious possession of devils, which it was then generally thought had been by witchcrafts introduced. It is to be confessed and bewailed, that many inhabitants of New England, and young people especially, had been led away with little sorceries, wherein they "did secretly those things that were not right against the Lord their God;" they would often cure hurts with spells, and practice detestable conjurations with sieves, and keys, and peas, and nails, and horseshoes, and other implements, to learn the things for which they had a forbidden and impious curiosity. Wretched books had stolen into the land, wherein fools were instructed how to become able fortune-tellers: among which, I wonder that a blacker brand is not set upon that fortune-telling wheel, which that sham-scribbler that goes under the letters of R.B. has promised in his "Delights for the Ingenious," as an honest and pleasant recreation: and by these books, the minds of many had been so poisoned, that they studied this finer witchcraft; until 'tis well if some of them were not betrayed into what is grosser, and more sensible and capital. Although these diabolical divinations are more ordinarily committed perhaps all over the whole world, than they are in the country of New England, yet, that being a country devoted unto the worship and service of the Lord Jesus Christ above the rest of the world, He signalized his vengeance against these wickednesses, with such extraordinary dispensations as have not been often seen in other places.

The devils which had been so played withal, and, it may be, by some few criminals more explicitly engaged and employed, now broke in upon the country, after as astonishing a manner as was ever heard of. Some scores of people, first about Salem, the center and first-born of all the towns in the colony, and afterwards in several other places, were arrested with many preternatural vexations upon their bodies, and a variety of cruel torments, which were evidently inflicted from the demons of the invisible world. The people that were infected and infested with such demons, in a few days' time arrived unto such a refining alteration upon their eyes, that they could see their tormentors: they saw a devil of a little stature, and of a tawny color, attended still with spectres that appeared in more humane circumstances. . . .

The afflicted wretches were horribly distorted and convulsed; they were pinched black and blue: pins would be run everywhere in their flesh; they would be scalded until they had blisters raised on them; and a thousand other things before hundreds of witnesses were done unto them, evidently preternatural: for if it were preternatural to keep a rigid fast for nine, yea, for fifteen days together; or if it were preternatural to have one's hands tied close together with a rope to be plainly seen, and then by unseen hands presently pulled up a great way from the earth before a crowd of people; such preternatural things were endured by them.

But of all the preternatural things which befell these people, there were none more unaccountable than those wherein the prestigious demons would ever now and then cover the most corporeal things in the world with a fascinating mist of invisibility.

Flashy people may burlesque these things, but when hundreds of the most sober people in a country where they have as much mother-wit certainly as the rest of mankind, know them to be true, nothing but the absurd and froward spirit of Sadducism can question them. I have not yet mentioned so much as one thing that will not be justified, if it be required by the oaths of more considerate persons than any that can ridicule these odd phenomena.

But the worst part of this astonishing tragedy is yet behind; wherein Sir William Phips, at last being dropt, as it were from the machine of heaven, was an instrument of easing the distresses of the land, now "so darkened by the wrath of the Lord of Hosts." There were very worthy men upon the spot where the assault from hell was first made, who apprehended themselves called from the God of heaven to sift the business unto the bottom of it; and, indeed, the continual impressions, which the outcries and the havocs of the afflicted people that lived nigh unto them caused on their minds, gave no little edge to this apprehension.

The persons were men eminent for wisdom and virtue, and they went about their enquiry into the matter, as driven unto it by a conscience of duty to God and the world. They did in the first place take it for granted that there are witches, or wicked children of men, who upon covenant-ing with, and commissioning of evil spirits, are attended by their ministry to accomplish the things desired of them: to satisfy them in which per-suasion, they had not only the assertions of the holy Scriptures—assertions which the witch-advocates cannot evade without shifts, too foolish for the prudent, or too profane for any honest man to use—and they had not only the well-attested relations of the gravest authors, from Bodin to Bovet, and from Binsfield to Brombal and Baxter—to deny all which, would be as reasonable as to turn the chronicles of all nations into romances of *Don Quixote* and the *Seven Champions;* but they had also an ocular demonstration in one who, a little before, had been executed for witch-craft, when Joseph Dudley, Esq. was the chief-judge. There was one whose magical images were found, and who, confessing her deeds, (when a jury of doctors returned her *compos mentis*) actually showed the whole court by what ceremonies used unto them she directed her familiar spirits how and where to cruciate the objects of her malice; and the experiment being made over and over again before the whole court, the effect fol-lowed exactly in the hurts done to the people at a distance from her. The existence of such witches was now taken for granted by those good men, wherein so far the generality of reasonable men have thought they ran well; and they soon received the confessions of some accused persons to confirm them in it: but then they took one thing more for granted, where-in 'tis now as generally thought they went out of the way. The afflicted people vehemently accused several persons in several places that the spectres which afflicted them, did exactly resemble them; until the im-portunity of the accusations did provoke the magistrates to examine them. When many of the accused came upon their examination, it was found that the demons then a thousand ways abusing of the poor afflict-ed people, had with a marvelous exactness represented them; . . .

Now, many good men took up an opinion, that the providence of God would not permit an innocent person to come under such a spectral rep-resentation; and that a concurrence of so many circumstances would prove an accused person to be in a confederacy with the demons thus afflicting of the neighbors; they judged that, except these things might amount unto a conviction, it would scarce be possible ever to convict a witch: and they had some philosophical schemes of witchcraft, and of the method and manner wherein magical poisons operate, which further sup-ported them in their opinion.

Sundry of the accused persons were brought unto their trial, while this opinion was yet prevailing in the minds of the judges and the juries, and perhaps the most of the people in the country, then mostly suffering; and though against some of them that were tried there came in so much other evidence of their diabolical compacts, that some of the most judicious, and yet vehement opposers of the notions then in vogue, publicly declared, "Had they themselves been on the bench, they could not have acquitted them;" nevertheless, divers were condemned, against whom the chief evidence was founded in the spectral exhibitions. . . .

On the other part, there were many persons of great judgment, piety and experience, who from the beginning were very much dissatisfied at these proceedings; they feared lest the devil would get so far into the faith of the people, that for the sake of many truths which they might find him telling of them, they would come at length to believe all his lies; whereupon what a desolation of names—yea, and of lives also—would ensue, a man might, without much witchcraft, be able to prognosticate; and they feared, lest in such an extraordinary descent of wicked spirits from their high places upon us, there might such principles be taken up, as, when put into practice, would unavoidably cause the righteous to perish with the wicked, and procure the blood-shed of persons like the Gibeonites, whom some learned men suppose to be under a false pretense of witchcraft, by Saul exterminated. . . .

In fine, the country was in a dreadful ferment, and wise men foresaw a long train of dismal and bloody consequences. Hereupon they first advised that the afflicted might be kept asunder in the closest privacy; and one particular person, (whom I have cause to know,) in pursuance of this advice, offered himself singly to provide accommodations for any six of them, that so the success of more than ordinary prayer with fasting might, with patience, be experienced, before any other courses were taken.

And Sir William Phips arriving to his government, after this ensnaring horrible storm was begun, did consult the neighboring ministers of the province, who made unto his Excellency and the council a return, . . .

The ministers of the province also being jealous lest this counsel should not be duly followed, requested the President of Harvard College to compose and publish (which he did) some cases of conscience referring to these difficulties: in which treatise he did, with demonstrations of incomparable reason and reading, evince it, that Satan may appear in the shape of an innocent and a virtuous person, to afflict those that suffer by the diabolical molestations: and that the ordeal of the sight, and the touch, is not a conviction of a covenant with the devil, but liable to great exceptions against the lawfulness, as well as the evidence of it: and that either a free and fair confession of the criminals, or the oath of two credible persons proving such things against the person accused, as none but such as have a familiarity with the devil can know, or do, is necessary to the proof of the crime. . . .

Now, upon a deliberate review of these things, his Excellency first reprieved, and then pardoned many of them that had been condemned; and there fell out several strange things that caused the spirit of the country to run as vehemently upon the acquitting of all the accused, as it by mistake ran at first upon the condemning of them. Some that had been zealously of the mind, that the devils could not in the shapes of good men afflict other men, were terribly confuted, by having their own shapes, and the shapes of their most intimate and valued friends, thus abused. And though more than twice twenty had made such voluntary, and harmonious, and uncontrollable confessions, that if they were all sham, there was therein the greatest violation made by the efficacy of the invisible world, upon the rules of understanding human affairs, that was ever seen since "God made man upon the earth," yet they did so recede from their confessions, that it was very clear, some of them had been hitherto, in a sort of a preternatural dream, wherein they had said of themselves, they knew not what themselves.

In fine, the last courts that sat upon this thorny business, finding that it was impossible to penetrate into the whole meaning of the things that had happened, and that so many unsearchable cheats were interwoven into the conclusion of a mysterious business, which perhaps had not crept thereinto at the beginning of it, they cleared the accused as fast as they tried them; and within a little while the afflicted were most of them delivered out of their troubles also; and the land had peace restored unto it, by the "God of peace, treading Satan under foot." . . .

Sir William Phips now beheld such demons hideously scattering fire about the country, in the exasperations which the minds of men were on these things rising unto; and therefore when he had well canvassed a cause, which perhaps might have puzzled the wisdom of the wisest men on earth to have managed, without any error in their administrations, he thought, if it would be any error at all, it would certainly be the safest for him to put a stop unto all future prosecutions, as far as it lay in him to do it.

He did so, and for it he had not only the printed acknowledgments of the New Englanders, who publicly thanked him, "As one of the tribe of Zebulun, raised up from among themselves, and spirited as well as commissioned to be the steersman of a vessel befogged in the *mare mortuum* of witchcraft, who now so happily steered her course, that she escaped shipwreck, and was safely again moored under the Cape of Good Hope; and cut asunder the Circean knot of enchantment, more difficult to be dissolved than the famous Gordian one of old."

But the Queen also did him the honor to write unto him those gracious letters, wherein her Majesty commended his conduct in these inexplicable matters.

FROM THE LIFE OF JOHN ELIOT

The titles of a Christian and of a minister have rendered our Eliot considerable; but there is one memorable title more, by which he has been signalized unto us. An honorable person did once in print put the name of an evangelist upon him; whereupon, in a letter of his to that person, afterwards printed, his expressions were, "There is a redundancy where you put the title of Evangelist upon me; I beseech you suppress all such things; let us do and speak and carry all things with humility; it is the Lord who hath done what is done; and it is most becoming the spirit of Jesus Christ to lift up him, and lay ourselves low; I wish that word could be obliterated." My reader sees what a caution Mr. Eliot long since entered against our giving him the title of an evangelist; but his death has now made it safe, and his life had long made it just, for us to acknowledge him with such a title. I know not whither that of an evangelist, or one separated for the employment of preaching the gospel in such places whereunto churches have hitherto been gathered, be not an office that should be continued in our days; but this I know, that our Eliot very notably did the service and business of such an officer. . . .

The natives of the country now possessed by the New Englanders had been forlorn and wretched heathen ever since their first herding here; and though we know not when or how those Indians first became inhabitants of this mighty continent, yet we may guess that probably the devil decoyed those miserable savages hither, in hopes that the gospel of the Lord Jesus Christ would never come here to destroy or disturb his absolute empire over them. But our Eliot was in such ill terms with the devil, as to alarm him with sounding the silver trumpets of Heaven in his territories, and make some noble and zealous attempts towards ousting him of ancient possessions here. There were, I think, twenty several nations (if I may call them so) of Indians upon that spot of ground which fell under the influence of our Three United Colonies; and our Eliot was willing to rescue as many of them as he could from that old usurping landlord of America, who is, "by the wrath of God, the prince of this world."

I cannot find that any besides the Holy Spirit of God first moved him to the blessed work of evangelizing these perishing Indians; it was that Holy Spirit which laid before his mind the idea of that which was on the seal of the Massachusetts colony: a poor Indian having a label going from his mouth, with a *Come Over and Help Us*. It was the spirit of our Lord Jesus Christ, which enkindled in him a pity for the dark souls of these natives, whom the "god of this world had blinded," through all the bypast ages. He was none of those that make "the salvation of the heathen" an article of their creed; but (setting aside the unrevealed and extraordinary steps which the "Holy One of Israel" may take out of his usual paths) he thought men to be lost if our gospel be hidden from them; and he was of the same opinion with one of the ancients, who said, "Some have endeavored to prove Plato a Christian till they prove themselves little better than heathens." It is indeed a principle in the Turkish Alcoran, that "let a man's religion be what it will, he shall be saved, if he conscientiously live up to the rules of it:" but our Eliot was no Mahometan. . . .

But when this charitable pity had once began to flame, there was a concurrence of many things to cast oil into it. All the good men in the country were glad of his engagement in such an undertaking; the ministers especially encouraged him, and those in the neighborhood kindly supplied his place, and performed his work in part for him at Roxbury, while he was abroad laboring among them that were without. Hereunto he was further awakened by those expressions in the royal charter, in the assurance and protection whereof this wilderness was first peopled; namely, "To win and incite the natives of that country to the knowledge and obedience of the only true God and Savior of mankind, and the Christian faith, in our royal intention, and the adventurer's free profession is the principal end of the plantation." And the remarkable zeal of the Romish missionaries, "compassing sea and land, that they might make proselytes," made his devout soul think of it with a further disdain, that we should come any whit behind in our care to evangelize the Indians whom we dwelt among. Lastly, when he had well begun this evangelical business, the good God, in an answer to his prayers, mercifully stirred up a liberal contribution among the godly people in England for the promoting of it; by means whereof a considerable estate and income was at length entrusted in the hands of an honorable corporation, by whom it is to this day very carefully employed in the Christian service which it was designed for. And then, in short, inasmuch as our Lord Jesus had bestowed on us, our Eliot was gratefully and generously desirous to obtain for him "the heathen for an inheritance, and the utmost parts of the earth for a possession."

The exemplary charity of this excellent person in this important affair, will not be seen in its due lusters, unless we make some reflections upon several circumstances which he beheld these forlorn Indians in. Know, then, that these doleful creatures are the veriest ruins of mankind which are to be found anywhere upon the face of the earth. No such estates are to be expected among them, as have been the baits which the pretended converters in other countries have snapped at. One might see among them what an hard master the devil is to the most devoted of his vassals! These abject creatures live in a country full of mines; we have already made entrance upon our iron; and in the very surface of the ground among us, it is thought there lies copper enough to supply all this world; besides other mines hereafter to be exposed; but our shiftless Indians were never owners of so much as a knife till we come among them; their name for an Englishman was a Knife-man; stone was instead of metal for their tools; and for their coins, they have only little beads with holes in them to string them upon a bracelet, whereof some are white; and of these there go six for a penny; some are black or blue; and of these, go three for a penny: this wampam, as they call it, is made of the shellfish which lies upon the seacoast continually.

They live in a country where we now have all the conveniences of human life: but as for them, their housing is nothing but a few mats tied about poles fastened in the earth, where a good fire is their bedclothes in the coldest seasons; their clothing is but skin of a beast, covering their hind parts, their foreparts having but a little apron, where nature calls for secrecy; their diet has not a greater dainty than their Nokehick—that is, a spoonful of their parched meal, with a spoonful of water, which will strengthen them to travel a day together; except we should mention the flesh of deers, bears, moose, raccoons, and the like, which they have when they can catch them; as also a little fish, which, if they would preserve, it was by drying, not by salting; for they had not a grain of salt in the world, I think, till we bestowed it on them. Their physic is, excepting a few odd specifics, which some of them encounter certain cases with, nothing hardly but an hothouse or a powaw; their hothouse is a little cave, about eight foot over, where, after they have terribly heated it, a crew of them go sit and sweat and smoke for an hour together, and then immediately run into some very cold adjacent brook, without the least mischief to them; it is this way they recover themselves from some diseases, particularly from the French; but in most of their dangerous distempers, it is a powaw that must be sent for; that is, a priest, who has more familiarity with Satan than his neighbors; this conjurer comes and roars, and howls, and uses magical ceremonies over the sick man, and will be well paid for it when he has done; if this don't effect the cure, the "man's time is come, and there's an end."

They live in a country full of the best ship-timber under heaven: but never saw a ship till some came from Europe hither; and then they were scared out of their wits to see the monster come sailing in, and spitting fire with a mighty noise out of her floating side; they cross the water in canoes, made sometimes of trees, which they burn and hew, till they have hollowed them; and sometimes of barks, which they stitch into a light sort of a vessel, to be easily carried over land; if they overset, it is but a little paddling like a dog, and they are soon where they were.

Their way of living is infinitely barbarous: the men are most abominably slothful; making their poor squaws, or wives, to plant and dress, and barn and beat their corn, and build their wigwams for them: which perhaps may be the reason of their extraordinary ease in childbirth. In the meantime, their chief employment, when they'll condescend unto any, is that of hunting; wherein they'll go out some scores, if not hundreds of them in a company, driving all before them. . . .

Their division of time is by sleeps, and moons, and winters; and, by lodging abroad, they have somewhat observed the motions of the stars; among which it has been surprising unto me to find that they have always called "Charles's Wain" by the name of Paukunnawaw, or the Bear, which is the name whereby Europeans also have distinguished it. Moreover, they have little, if any, traditions among them worthy of our notice; and reading and writing is altogether unknown to them, though there is a rock or two in the country that has unaccountable characters engraved upon it. All the religion they have amounts unto thus much: they believe that there are many gods, who made and own the several nations of the world; of which a certain great God in the south-west regions of heaven bears the greatest figure. They believe that every remarkable creature has a peculiar god within it or about it: there is with them a Sun God, a Moon God, and the like; and they cannot conceive but that the fire must be a kind of a god, inasmuch as a spark of it will soon produce very strange effects. They believe that when any good or ill happens to them, there is the favor or the anger of a god expressed in it; and hence, as in a time of calamity, they keep a dance, or a day of extravagant ridiculous devotions to their god; so in a time of prosperity they likewise have a feast, wherein they also make presents one unto another. Finally, they believe that their chief god (Kautantowit) made a man and a woman of a stone; which, upon dislike, he broke to pieces, and made another man and woman of a tree, which were the fountains of mankind; and that we all have in us immortal souls, which, if we were godly, shall go to a splendid entertainment with Kautantowit, but otherwise must wander about in restless horror forever. . . . This was the miserable people which our Eliot propounded unto himself to teach and save! And he had a double work incumbent on him; he was to make men of them, ere he could hope to see them saints; they must be civilized ere they could be Christianized; he could not, as Gregory once of our nation, see anything angelical to bespeak his labors for their eternal welfare: all among them was diabolical. To think on raising a number of these hideous creatures unto the elevations of our holy religion, must argue more than common or little sentiments in the undertaker; but the faith of an Eliot could encounter it! . . .

But I have not obtained the end of this history, nor may I let this history come to an end, until I do with some importunity bespeak the endeavors of good men everywhere to labor in that harvest which the blessed Eliot justly counted worthy of his utmost pains and cares. It was the confession of Themistocles, that the victory of Miltiades would not let him sleep in quietness; may those of our Eliot raise a like emulation in those that have now seen the life of this evangelical hero! One Robert Baily (a true son of Epiphanius) many years ago published a book, wherein several gross lies, by which the name of that John Cotton, who was known to be one of the holiest men then alive, was most injuriously made odious unto the churches abroad, were accompanied with some reflections upon poor New England, whereof this was one: "The way of their churches hath most exceedingly hindered the conversion of the poor pagans: of all that ever crossed the American seas, they are noted as most neglectful of the work of conversion." We have now seen those aspersions and calumnies abundantly wiped away. But let that which has been the vindication of New England, be also the emulation of the world; let not poor little New England be the only Protestant country that shall do any notable thing for "the propagation of the faith," unto those "dark corners of the earth which are full of cruel habitations." But the addresses of so mean a person as myself are like to prevail but little abroad with men of learning and figure in the world. However, I shall presume to utter my wishes in the sight of my readers; and it is possible that the great God, who "despises not the prayer of the poor," may, by the influences of his Holy Spirit upon the hearts of some whose eyes are upon these lines, give a blessed answer thereunto.

Wherefore, may the people of New England, who have seen so sensible a difference between the estates of those that sell drink and of those that preach truth unto the miserable savages among them, as that even this alone might inspire them, yet from a nobler consideration than that of their own outward prosperity thereby advanced, be encouraged still to prosecute, first the civilizing, and then the Christianizing of the barbarians in their neighborhood; and may the New Englanders be so far politic, as well as religious, as particularly to make a mission of the gospel unto the mighty nations of the Western Indians, whom the French have been of late so studiously, but so unsuccessfully tampering with; lest those horrid pagans, who lately (as it is credibly affirmed) had such a measure of devilism and insolence in them, as to shoot a volley of great and small shot against the heavens, in revenge upon "the man in the heavens," as they called our Lord, whom they counted the author of the heavy calamities which newly have distressed them; be found spared by our long-suffering Lord, (who then indeed presently tore the ground asunder, with immediate and horrible thunders from heaven round about them, but killed them not!) for a scourge to us, that have not used our advantages to make a virtuous people of them. If a King of the West Saxons long since ascribed all the disasters on any of their affairs to negligencies in this point, methinks the New Englanders may not count it unreasonable in this way to seek their own prosperity. Shall we do what we can that our Lord Jesus Christ may bestow upon America (which may more justly be called Columba) that salutation, "O my dove!"

1702

From *Bonifacius*

ON DOING GOOD TO OUR NEIGHBORS

This excellent zeal should be extended to the neighborhood. Neighbors! you stand related to each other; and you should contrive how others should have reason to rejoice in your neighborhood. "The righteous is more excellent than his neighbor;" but we shall scarcely allow him to be so, unless he be more excellent as a neighbor: he must excel in the duties of good neighborhood. Let that man be better than his neighbor, who labors most to be a better neighbor—to do most good to his neighbor. . . .

Neighbors! be concerned that the orphans and the widows may be well provided for. They meet with grievous difficulties, with unknown temptations. When their nearest relatives were living, they were perhaps, but meanly provided for: what then must be their present solitary condition? that condition should be well considered; and the result of the consideration should be, "I delivered the orphan who had no helper, and I caused the widow's heart to sing for joy."

By the same rule, all the afflicted in the neighborhood are to be considered. Would it be too much for you once in a week, at least, to think "What neighbor is reduced to pinching and painful poverty, or impoverished with heavy losses? What neighbor is languishing with sickness, especially with severe disease, and of long continuance? What neighbor is broken-hearted with the loss of a dear and desirable relative? What neighbor has a soul violently assaulted by the enemy of souls?" and then consider, "What can be done for such neighbors?"

In the first place, you will pity them. The evangelical precept is, "Have compassion one of another—be pitiful." It was of old and ever will be a just expectation, "to him that is afflicted, pity should be shown;" and let our pity to the distressed be expressed by our prayer for them. It would be a very lovely practice for you in the daily prayer of your closet every evening to think, "what miserable object have I seen today, for whom I may do well now to entreat the mercies of the Lord?" But this is not all; it is possible, nay probable, that you may do well to visit them; and when you visit them, comfort them; carry them some good word, which may raise gladness in a heart stooping with heaviness.

And, lastly: Render them all the assistance which their necessities may require. . . .

Would it be amiss for you, always to have lying by you, a list of the poor in your neighborhood, or of those whose calamities may call for the assistance of the neighborhood? Such a list would often furnish you with matter for useful conversation, when you are conversing with your friends, whom you may hereby "provoke to love and to good works."

I will go on to say, be glad of opportunities to do good in your neighborhood; yea, look out for them; lay hold on them with a rapturous assiduity. Be sorry for all the sad circumstances of your neighbor which render your exertions necessary; yet, be glad, if anyone tell you of them. Thank him who gives you the information, as having therein done you a very great kindness. Let him know that he could not, by any means, have obliged you more. Cheerfully embrace every opportunity of showing civility to your neighbors, whether by lending, by watching, or by any other method in your power. And let the pleasantness of your countenance prove that you do this willingly: ...

In promoting the good of the neighborhood, I wish above all, that you will consult their spiritual good. Be concerned lest "the deceitfulness of sin" should destroy any of your neighbors. If there be any idle people among them, take pains to cure them of their idleness: do not nourish and harden them in it, but find employment for them; set them to work, and keep them to work; and then be as bountiful to them as you please.

If any poor children in the neighborhood are totally destitute of education, do not suffer them to remain in that state. Let care be taken that they may be taught to read, to learn their catechism, and the truths and ways of their only Savior.

Once more. If any persons in the neighborhood are taking to bad courses, affectionately and faithfully admonish them: if any act as enemies to their own welfare, or that of their families, prudently dispense your admonitions to them: if there be any prayerless families, cease not to entreat and exhort them, till you have persuaded them to commence domestic worship. If there be any service of God or his people, to which anyone is backward, tenderly excite him to it. Whatever snare you perceive a neighbor exposed to, be so kind as to warn him against it. ...

That my proposal "to do good in the neighborhood, and as a neighbor," may be more fully formed and followed, I will conclude by reminding you that much self-denial will be requisite in the execution of it; you must be armed against all selfish intentions in these generous attempts. You must not employ your good actions as persons use water, which they pour into a pump, to draw up something for yourselves. Our Lord's direction is, "lend, hoping for nothing again," and do good to such as you are never likely to be the better for.

But then, there is something still higher to be required; that is, "do good to those neighbors who have done you harm;" so saith our Savior, "love your enemies; bless them that curse you; do good to them that hate you, and pray for them that despitefully use you, and persecute you." Yea, if an injury have been done you by anyone, consider it as a provocation to confer a benefit on him. This is noble! It will afford you much consolation. Some other method might make you even with your froward neighbors; but this will place you above them all. ...

But I must not stop here; something higher still is requisite. Do good to those neighbors who will speak evil of you for doing so: "Thus," saith our Savior, "ye shall be the children of the Highest, who is kind to the unthankful, and to the evil." You will constantly meet with monsters of ingratitude; and if you distinguish a person, by doing far more for him than for others, that very person perhaps will do you an injury. O the wisdom of Divine Providence, by which this is permitted, that you may learn to do good on a divine principle—good, merely for the sake of good! "Lord, increase our faith!"   1710

From *Manuductio ad Ministerium*

8. Poetry, whereof we have now even an Antediluvian Piece in our Hands, has from the Beginning been in such Request, that I must needs recommend unto you some Acquaintance with it. Though some have had a Soul so Unmusical, that they have decried all Verse, as being but a mere Playing and Fiddling upon Words; All Versifying, as if it were more Unnatural than if we should choose Dancing instead of Walking; and Rhyme, as if it were but a sort of Morisco Dancing with Bells: Yet I cannot wish you a Soul that shall be wholly Unpoetical. An Old Horace has left us an *Art of Poetry,* which you may do well to bestow a Perusal on. And besides your Lyric Hours, I wish you may so far understand an Epic Poem, that the Beauties of an Homer and a Virgil may be discerned with you. As to the Moral Part of Homer, 'tis true, and let me not be counted a Zoilus for saying so, that by first exhibiting their Gods as no better than Rogues, he set open the Floodgates for a prodigious Inundation of Wickedness to break in upon the Nations, and was one of the greatest Apostles the Devil ever had in the World. . . . But then, we are so much led into the Knowledge of Antiquities, by reading of this Poet, and into so many Parts of the Recondite Learning, that notwithstanding some little Nods in him, not a few Acute Pens besides the old Bishop of Thessalonica's, have got a Reputation by regaling us with Annotations upon him. Yea, Tho' One can't but smile at the Fancy of Croese, who tries with much Ostentation of Erudition, to show, That Homer has all along tendered us in a Disguise and Fable, the History of the Old Testament, yet many Illustrations of the sacred Scriptures, I find are to be fetched from him; who indeed had probably read what was Extant of them in his Days; Particularly, Our Eighteenth Psalm is what he has evidently imitated. Virgil too, who so much lived upon him, as well as after him, is unaccountably mad upon his Fate, which he makes to be he knows not what himself, but Superior to Gods as well as to Men, and through his whole Composures he so asserts the Doctrine of this Nonsensical Power, as is plainly inconsistent with all Virtue. . . . But then, This Poet also has abundance of Rare Antiquities for us: And such Things, as others besides a Servius, have imagined that they have instructed and obliged Mankind, by employing all their Days upon. Wherefore if his *Aeneas,* which tho' it were once near twenty times as big as he has left it, yet he has left it unfinished, may not appear so valuable to you, that you may think Twenty-Seven Verses of the Part that is the most finished in it, worth One and Twenty Hundred Pounds and odd Money, yet his *Georgics,* which he put his last Hand unto, will furnish you with many things far from Despicable. But after all, when I said, I was willing that the Beauties of these Two Poets, might become Visible to your Visive Faculty in Poetry, I did not mean, that you should Judge nothing to be

Admittable into an Epic Poem, which is not Authorized by their Example; but I perfectly concur with One who is inexpressibly more capable to be a Judge of such a Matter than I can be; That it is a false Critic who with a petulant Air, will insult Reason itself, if it presumes to oppose such Authority.

I proceed now to say, That if (under the Guidance of a *Vida*) you try your young Wings now and then to see what Flights you can make, at least for an Epigram, it may a little sharpen your Sense, and polish your Style, for more important Performances. . . . Nevertheless, I cannot but advise you, Withhold thy Throat from Thrist. Be not so set upon Poetry, as to be always poring on the Passionate and Measured Pages. Let not what should be Sauce rather than Food for you, Engross all your Application. Beware of a Boundless and Sickly Appetite, for the Reading of the Poems, which now the Rickety Nation swarms withal: And let not the Circean Cup intoxicate you. But especially preserve the Chastity of your Soul from the Dangers you may incur, by a Conversation with Muses that are no better than Harlots: Among which are others besides Ovid's Epistles, which for their Tendency to excite and foment Impure Flames, and cast Coals into your Bosom, deserve rather to be thrown into the Fire, than to be laid before the Eye which a Covenant should be made withal. Indeed, not merely for the Impurities which they convey, but also on some other Accounts, the Powers of Darkness have a Library among us, whereof the Poets have been the most Numerous as well as the most Venemous Authors. Most of the Modern Plays, as well as the Romances and Novels and Fictions, which are a sort of Poems, do belong to the Catalogue of this cursed Library. The Plays, I say, in which there are so many Passages, that have a Tendency to overthrow all Piety, that one whose Name is Bedford, has extracted near Seven Thousand Instances of them, from the Plays chiefly of but Five Years preceding. . . . As for those wretched Scribbles of Madmen, My Son, Touch them not, Taste them not, Handle them not: Thou wilt perish in the using of them. They are, The Dragons whose Contagious Breath Peoples the dark Retreats of Death. . . .

But there is, what I may rather call a Parentheses, than a Digression, which this may be not altogether an Improper Place for the introducing of.

There has been a deal of ado about a Style; So much, that I must offer you my Sentiments upon it. There is a Way of Writing, wherein the Author endeavors, that the Reader may have something to the Purpose in every Paragraph. There is not only a Vigor sensible in every Sentence, but the Paragraph is embellished with Profitable References, even to something beyond what is directly spoken. Formal and Painful Quotations are not studied; yet all that could be learnt from them is insinuated.

The Writer pretends not unto Reading, yet he could not have writ as he does if he had not Read very much in his Time; and his Composures are not only a Cloth of Gold, but also stuck with as many Jewels, as the Gown of a Russian Ambassador. This Way of Writing has been decried by many, and is at this Day more than ever so, for the same Reason, that in the old Story, the Grapes were decried, That they were not Ripe. A Lazy, Ignorant, Conceited Set of Authors, would persuade the whole Tribe, to lay aside that Way of Writing, for the same Reason that one would have persuaded his Brethren to part with the Encumbrance of their Bushy Tails. But, however Fashion and Humor may prevail, they must not think that the Club at their Coffeehouse is, All the World; but there will always be those, who will in this Case be governed by Indisputable Reason: And who will think that the real Excellency of a Book will never lie in saying of little; That the less one has for his Money in a Book, 'tis really the more Valuable for it; and that the less one is instructed in a Book, and the more of Superfluous Margin, and Superficial Harangue, and the less of Substantial Matter one has in it, the more 'tis to be accounted of. And if a more Massy Way of Writing be never so much disgusted at This Day, a Better Gust will come on, as will some other Thing, *quæ jam Cecidere*. In the meantime, Nothing appears to me more Impertinent and Ridiculous than the Modern Way, (I cannot say, Rule; for they have None!) of Criticizing. The Blades that set up for Critics, I know not who constituted or commission'd 'em!—they appear to me, for the most part as Contemptible, as they are a Supercilious Generation. For indeed no Two of them have the same Style; and they are as intolerably Cross-grain'd and severe in their Censures upon one another, as they are upon the rest of Mankind. But while each of them conceitedly enough, sets up for the Standard of Perfection, we are entirely at a Loss which Fire to follow. Nor can you easily find any one thing wherein they agree for their Style, except perhaps a perpetual Care to give us Jejune and Empty Pages, without such Touches of Erudition (to speak in the Style of an Ingenious Traveller) as may make the Discourses less Tedious, and more Enriching, to the Mind of him that peruses them. There is much Talk of a Florid Style, obtaining among the Pens, that are most in Vogue; but how often would it puzzle one, even with the best Glasses to find the Flowers! And if they were to be Chastised for it, it would be with much what as much of Justice, as Jerome was, for being a Ciceronian. After all, Every Man will have his own Style, which will distinguish him as much as his Gait: And if you can attain to that which I have newly described, but always writing so as to give an Easy Conveyance unto your Ideas, I would not have you by any Scourging be driven out of your Gait. . . .

However, since every Man will have his own Style, I would pray, that we may learn to treat one another with mutual Civilities and Condescensions, and handsomely indulge one another in this, as Gentlemen do in other Matters.

I wonder what ails People, that they can't let Cicero write in the Style of Cicero, and Seneca write in the (much other!) Style of Seneca; and own that Both may please in their several Ways. . . .

One Thing that I advise you to, is This. Keep your Quotidiana: I mean Have your Blank Books, in which Note with your Pen, for the most Part Every Day, (Let there be, *Nulla Dies sine Linea!*) Some Notable Thing, which in Reading you have newly met withal. By this Action you will fix the Valuable Notion in your Mind: And in a few Years, you will have a Treasure, from whence as a Scribe instructed for the Kingdom of Heaven, you may bring out Things New and Old, and have agreeable Grains of Salt for all your Discourses. You will not for this, Use the Unequal Way, of entering the Riches, of your Quotidiana, in Pages with the Titles of a Commonplace at the Tops of them, whereof some will be soon Crammed, and others remain Empty, perhaps all your Days: But, Enter the Things as they come, with only affixing the Number to them: And have, at the End of the Books an Alphabetical Index, of the Matter, with the Number at which it is to be met withal. Here you will anon have an inexhaustible Magazine; and if you live to Old Age, you will find, that, like Old Photius, you have prepared an Hive then to live upon. I will not say, you will be quickly as rich as Croesus; for poor Croesus will have no Riches comparable to what you will have in your Collections.

Another Thing that I advise you to, is This. Form a Sodality. What I mean, is, Prevail with a Fit Number, (Six or Seven may be a Competency, or Fewer, if you can't find so many,) of Sober, Ingenious, and Industrious Young Men, to Associate with you, and meet One Evening in a Week, for the spending of Two or Three Hours, in a Profitable Conversation. At this Interview, Let there be always a sort of Director, who shall propose this Question, (and see, that without needless Digressions and Excursions it be kept close unto,) What Remarkable and Memorable Matter has occurr'd in late Studies, that you thought now to be offered? Let the Question be Articulated, and more particularly and successively turn upon these articles. I. What in Philology? II. What in Philosophy? III. What in Geography, and the rest of the Mathematics? IV. What in History? V. What in Illustrations of the Sacred Scriptures; Or, Biblical Curiosities? Let each Person, in what Order they shall agree upon, give his Report as Concisely as may be. But it will not be expected, that each Person should be prepared, at every Time, with something on every Head: It is enough, that he bring in, for that Cell, which he happens to be best furnished for. All Altercations, and all Impertinencies, are to be forever banished from these Communications of the Sodality. But how much could I wish, that you could gain one Quarter of an Hour in the close of all, to relate, What rare Flight or fine Stroke of the Christian Ascetics, has been met withal; and what for the Animation of Practical Piety? Behold, a way to clench the Nails that have been struck into your Minds; and a Compendious and Charitable Course to come at the Wealth, which the Diligence of your Brethren has made them the Owners of; together with the generous Pleasure of making them the Partakers of yours.   1726

From *The Christian Philosopher*

THE INTRODUCTION

The Essays now before us will demonstrate, that Philosophy is no Enemy, but a mighty and wondrous Incentive to Religion; and they will exhibit that Philosophical Religion, which will carry with it a most sensible Character, and victorious Evidence of a reasonable Service. Glory to God in the Highest, and Good Will Towards Men, animated and exercised; and a Spirit of Devotion and of Charity inflamed, in such Methods as are offered in these Essays, cannot but be attended with more Benefits, than any Pen of ours can declare, or any Mind conceive.

In the Dispositions and Resolutions of Piety thus enkindled, a Man most effectually shows himself a Man, and with unutterable Satisfaction answers the grand End of his Being, which is, *To glorify God.* He discharges also the office of a Priest for the Creation, under the Influences of an admirable Savior, and therein asserts and assures his Title unto that Priesthood, which the Blessedness of the future State will very much consist in being advanced to. The whole World is indeed a Temple of God, built and filled by that Almighty Architect; and in this Temple, every such one, affecting himself with the Occasions for it, will speak of His Glory. He will also rise into that Superior Way of Thinking and of Living, which the Wisest of Men will choose to take; which the more Polite Part of Mankind, and the Honorable of the Earth, will esteem it no Dishonor for them to be acquainted with. Upon that Passage occurring in the best of Books, Ye Sons of the Mighty, ascribe unto the Lord Glory and Strength; it is a Gloss and an Hint of Munster, which carries with it a Cogency: *Nihil est tam sublime, tamque magnificum, quod non teneatur laudare et magnificare Deum Creatorem suum.* Behold, a Religion, which will be found without Controversy; a Religion, which will challenge all possible Regards from the High, as well as the Low, among the People; I will resume the Term, a Philosophical Religion: And yet how Evangelical!

In prosecuting this Intention, and in introducing almost every Article of it, the Reader will continually find some Author or other quoted. . . . But in these Quotations, there has been proposed, first, a due Gratitude unto those, who have been my Instructors; and indeed, something within me would have led me to it, if Pliny, who is one of them, had not given me a Rule; *Ingenuum est profiteri per quos profeceris.* It appears also but a piece of Justice, that the Names of those whom the Great God has distinguished, by employing them to make those Discoveries, which are here collected, should live and shine in every such Collection. Among these, let it be known, that there are especially Two, unto whom I have been more indebted, than unto many others; the Industrious Mr. Ray, and the Inquisitive Mr. Derham; *Fratrum dulce par.* upon whom, in divers Paragraphs of this Rhapsody, I have had very much of my Subsistence; (I hope without doing the part of a *Fidentinus* upon them) and I give thanks to Heaven for them.

'Tis true, some Scores of other Philosophers have been consulted on this Occasion; but an Industry so applied, has in it very little to bespeak any Praises for him that has used it: He earnestly renounces them, and solicits, that not only he, but the Greater Men, who have been his Teachers, may disappear before the Glorious God, whom these Essays are all written to represent as worthy to be praised, and by whose Grace we are what we are; nor have we anything but what we have received from Him. . . .

Most certainly there can be very little Pretence to an I, or Me, for what is done in these Essays. 'Tis done, and entirely, by the Help of God: This is all that can be pretended to.

There is very little, that may be said, really to be performed by the Hand that is now writing; but only the Devotionary Part of these Essays, though they are not altogether destitute of American Communications: And if the Virtuosos, and all the Genuine Philosophers of our Age, have approved the Design of the devout Ray and Derham, and others, in their Treatises; it cannot be distasteful unto them, to see what was more generally hinted at by those Excellent Persons, here more particularly carried on, and the more special Flights of the true Philosophical Religion exemplified. . . .

Let us conclude with a Remark of Minutius Fælix. "If so much Wisdom and Penetration be requisite to observe the wonderful Order and Design in the Structure of the World, how much more were necessary to form it!" If Men so much admire Philosophers, because they discover a small Part of the Wisdom that made all things; they must be stark blind, who do not admire that Wisdom itself!

ESSAY XXVI

Of the Vegetables

The Contrivance of our most Glorious Creator, in the Vegetables growing upon this Globe, cannot be wisely observed without Admiration and Astonishment.

We will single out some Remarkables, and glorify our God!

First, In what manner is Vegetation performed? And how is the Growth of Plants and the Increase of their Parts carried on? The excellent and ingenious Dr. John Woodward has, in the way of nice Experiment, brought this thing under a close Examination. It is evident that Water is necessary to Vegetation; there is a Water which ascends the Vessels of the Plants, much after the way of a Filtration; and the Plants take up a larger or lesser Quantity of this Fluid, according to their Dimensions. The much greater part of that fluid Mass which is conveyed to the Plants, does not abide there, but exhale through them up into the Atmosphere. Hence Countries that abound with bigger Plants are obnoxious to greater Damps, and Rains, and inconvenient Humidities. But there is also a terrestrial Matter which is mixed with this Water, and ascends up into the Plants with the Water: Something of this Matter will attend Water in all its motions, and stick by it after all its Percolations. Indeed the Quantity of this terrestrial Matter, which the Vapors carry up into the Atmosphere, is very fine, and not very much, but it is the truest and the best prepared vegetable Matter; for which cause it is that Rainwater is of such a singular Fertility. 'Tis true there is in Water a mineral Matter also, which is usually too scabrous, and ponderous, and inflexible, to enter the Pores of the Roots. Be the Earth ever so rich, 'tis observed little good will come of it, unless the Parts of it be loosened a little, and separated. And this probably is all the use of Nitre and other Salts to Plants, to loosen the Earth, and separate the Parts of it. It is this terrestrial Matter which fills the Plants; they are more or less nourished and augmented in proportion, as their Water conveys a greater or lesser quantity of proper terrestrial Matter to them. Nevertheless 'tis also probable that in this there is a variety; and all Plants are not formed and filled from the same sort of Corpuscles. Every Vegetable seems to require a peculiar and specific Matter for its Formation and Nourishment. If the Soil wherein a Seed is planted, have not all or most of the Ingredients necessary for the Vegetable to subsist upon, it will suffer accordingly. Thus Wheat sown upon a Tract of Land well furnish'd for the Supply of that Grain, will succeed very well, perhaps for divers Years, or, as the Husbandman expresses it, as long as the Ground is in heart; but anon it will produce no more of that Corn; it will of some other, perhaps of Barley: and when it will subsist this no more, still Oats will thrive there; and perhaps Peas after these. When the Ground has lain fallow some time, the Rain will pour down a fresh Stock upon it; and the care of the Tiller in manuring of it, lays upon it such things as are most impregnated with a Supply for Vegetation. It is observ'd that Spring water and Rainwater contain pretty near an equal charge of the vegetable Matter, but River water much more than either of them; and hence the Inundations of Rivers leave upon their Banks the fairest Crops in the World. It is now plain that Water is not the Matter that composes Vegetables, but the Agent that conveys that Matter to them, and introduces it into the several parts of them. Wherefore the plentiful provision of this Fluid supplied to all Parts of the Earth, is by our Woodward justly celebrated with a pious Acknowledgment of that natural Providence that superintends over the Globe which we inhabit. . . .

That I may a little contribute my two Mites to the illustration of the way wherein Vegetation is carried on, I will here communicate a couple of Experiments lately made in my Neighborhood.

My Neighbor planted a Row of Hills in his Field with our Indian Corn, but such a Grain as was color'd red and blue; the rest of the Field he planted with Corn of the most usual Color, which is yellow. To the most Windward side this Row infected four of the next neighboring Rows, and part of the fifth, and some of the sixth, to render them color'd like what grew on itself. But on the Leeward side no less than seven or eight Rows were so color'd, and some smaller impressions were made on those that were yet further distant.

The same Neighbor having his Garden often robb'd of the Squashes growing in it, planted some Gourds among them, which are to appearance very like them, and which he distinguish'd by certain adjacent marks, that he might not be himself imposed upon; by this means the Thieves 'tis true found a very bitter Sauce, but then all the Squashes were so infected and embitter'd, that he was not himself able to eat what the Thieves had left of them. . . .

How unaccountably is the Figure of Plants preserved? And how unaccountably their Growth determined? Our excellent Ray flies to an intelligent plastic Nature, which must understand and regulate the whole Economy.

Every particular part of the Plant has its astonishing Uses. The Roots give it a Stability, and fetch the Nourishment into it, which lies in the Earth ready for it. The Fibers contain and convey the Sap which carries up that Nourishment. The Plant has also larger Vessels, which entertain the proper and specific Juice of it; and others to carry the Air for its necessary respiration. The outer and inner Bark defend it from Annoyances, and contribute to its Augmentation. The Leaves embrace and preserve the Flower and Fruit as they come to their explication. . . .

How agreeable the Shade of Plants, let every Man say that sits under his own Vine, and under his own Fig tree!

How charming the Proportion and Pulchritude of the Leaves, the Flowers, the Fruits, he who confesses not, must be, as Dr. More says, one sunk into a forlorn pitch of Degeneracy, and stupid as a Beast.

Our Savior says of the Lilies (which some, not without reason, suppose to be Tulips) that Solomon in all his Glory was not arrayed like one of these. And it is observed by Spigelius, that the Art of the most skilful Painter cannot so mingle and temper his Colors, as exactly to imitate or counterfeit the native ones of the Flowers of Vegetables. . . .

The Anatomy of Plants, as it has been exhibited by the incomparable

Curiosity of Dr. Grew, what a vast Field of Wonders does it lead us into!

The most inimitable Structure of the Parts!

The particular Canals, and most adapted ones, for the conveyance of the lymphatic and essential Juices!

The Air Vessels in all their curious Coilings!

The Coverings which befriend them, a Work unspeakably more curious in reality than in appearance!

The strange Texture of the Leaves, the angular or circular, but always most orderly Position of their Fibers; the various Foldings, with a Duplicature, a Multiplicature, the Fore-row, the Back-row, the Tre-row; the noble Guard of the Films interposed!

The Flowers, their Gaiety and Fragrancy; the Perianthium or Empalement of them; their curious Foldings in the Calyx before their Expansion, with a close Couch or a concave Couch, a single Plait or a double Plait, or a Plait and Couch together, or a Row, or a Spire, or Plait and Spire together; and their luxuriant Colors after their Foliation, and the expanding of their Petala!

The Stamina, with their Apices; and the Stylus (called the Attire by Dr. Grew) which is found a sort of Male Sperm, to impregnate and fructify the Seed!

At last the whole Rudiments and Lineaments of the Parent Vegetable, surprisingly lock'd up in the little compass of the Fruit or Seed!

Gentlemen of Leisure, consult my illustrious Doctor, peruse his *Anatomy of Plants*, ponder his numberless Discoveries; but all the while consider that rare Person as inviting you to join with him in adoring the God of his Father, and the God who has done these excellent things, which ought to be known in all the Earth.   1721

The Eighteenth Century

INTRODUCTION

When in 1789 the present government of the United States was established, the colonies, which at the opening of the century consisted of a series of nearly isolated communities, now occupied a developed strip of land between the ocean and the Appalachian Mountains from Maine to Georgia. At the close of the French and Indian War in 1763, England had acquired all land east of the Mississippi river, but had closed the territory west of the mountains to settlers. As a result the land east of the mountains was filled by the descendants of earlier settlers and by an increasing flow of immigrants from Ireland and the continent of Europe, who brought with them non-English cultures and a disinterest in the fortunes of the English Crown. As the land filled, the formerly vague colonial boundaries had to be defined, a necessity which accounts for such ventures as that recorded by William Byrd in *The History of the Dividing Line*. Accompanying the rapid increase in population was an equally rapid growth in manufacturing and commerce, which in turn brought about the development of metropolitan centers, particularly the port cities of Boston, Newport, New York, Philadelphia, and Charlestown. The growth of population and its concentration in towns and cities was accompanied by a secularization of society and the development of new classes of citizens—tradesmen, merchants, artisans, and laborers—and by a rivalry between the urban and rural populace. Among the rapidly increasing trades was the trade of printing. Indeed, perhaps the two phenomena that had the greatest impact on the period and on literary production were the growth of cities and the expansion of printing.

Politically the period is marked by the settlers' increasing insistence on governing themselves. Colonial legislatures, preoccupied with their own internal affairs, learned, as had the British Parliament before them, to control the Royal or Proprietary Governors by control of the public purse. Having common enemies in the French and Indians, they learned also to cooperate. These legislatures levied taxes, raised troops, incurred debts, issued currency, instituted civil and criminal laws, and maintained agents to represent them before the Crown and Parliaments; in short, they excercised many of the rights of autonomous states and unwittingly prepared themselves for the independence to come. Economically, the period is marked by the expansion of commerce. To the earlier products, such as furs, tobacco, and marine stores, were added many manufactured goods—paper, hardware, leather goods, cloth, glass, household furnishings and rum. Some of these products like the Pennsylvania rifle, had an international market; most were sold in the colonies or the Bahamas and the Carribean islands. The effective marketing of these products introduced many new merchandising practices, shops, markets, and fairs, and the itinerant peddler was so prominent as to become a joke as early as the 1720's. In order to evade British efforts to restrain this trade, smuggling became a nearly honorable profession. To finance this trade, corporations, insurance companies, and banks were established and to facilitate it paper money was issued. Periodic recessions occurred which brought into being many of the now familiar devices to combat them—public works, the dole, price fixing, and the like. From all this activity, the "American" virtues emerged: industry, thrift, shrewdness, and a "rugged individualism" that bordered on lawlessness.

Despite the Enthusiasm of the 1740's, the influence of religion and the church declined. With the appearance of Whitefield and others in the 1740's, there was a rapid increase in the Methodist and Baptist sects, countered in part by an increase in the more liturgical Episcopal congregations. But the Enthusiasm of the 1740's was short-lived, although many of its practices, the camp meeting and the revival, persisted in the rural areas and on the frontier. In metropolitan centers, church membership was nominal for many citizens or nonexistent. Despite the efforts of town and city magistrates to preserve the Sabbath, many shops, markets, and taverns did business as usual, and many citizens engaged in festive rather than religious activities. Notable also, was the spread of Deism, which was avowed by many leading colonists in the last half of the century. Benjamin Franklin, whose attitude is representative of many, contributed to many Philadelphia churches but attended none with any regularity, and held that the best service man could render God was to deal fairly with his neighbors. There were individuals for whom religious practice was vital and a concern for the soul deep-felt, but for many, getting on in this world was more important than getting to heaven; indeed, success began to be equated with virtue, particularly when coupled with benevolence. The humanitarian impulses of the century are manifest in the many charitable organizations that came into being.

The growth of trade, industry, and urban centers brought a social structure different from that in the previous century. A pseudo-aristocracy based on wealth, family, and governmental position appeared in the cities and their environs, and a squirearchy based on land holdings showed itself in the Hudson River valley and in Virginia and South Carolina. For the members of those groups the austerities of colonial life disappeared; they built fine homes, furnished them well or even lavishly, wore clothes of the latest cut, kept carriages, servants and wine cellars, gave teas, dinners, and balls, and engaged in what a later age would call the conspicuous display of wealth. Many of these remained loyal to the Crown in Revolutionary times. In the cities a second group appeared, the small tradesmen and artisans, Franklin's "Leather Apron" men, and in the rural areas, a comparable group, the independent farmer. Self-taught, self-reliant, intent on achievement, and jealous of their personal independence, these formed a powerful and vocal group in the central and Northern colonies and supplied the chief support for the American Revolution. From this group the mutual improvement societies like Franklin's Junto drew their members, the more ambitious becoming the lawyers and doctors of the later years. A generally literate group, these professions produced much of the writing of the end of the period. The cities, also, developed a laboring-servant class which sporadically attempted organized action to improve its lot but without success. Society was fluid, however, and opportunity ever present. Benjamin Franklin is himself a prototype for the American rags-to-riches myth. Son of a small tradesman, he rapidly rose to affluence and influence; self-taught, he made significant contributions to scientific knowledge and won international renown; born to humble circumstances, he died one of the distinguished men of the century, here and abroad. Beyond the cities and the cultivated lands were the pioneer homesteads occupied by individuals little concerned with the political, economic, and social problems of either urban or farm areas. Because they were less educated, more simply mannered, and less sophisticated, the urban citizen derided them; terms like "bumpkin" and "lubberland" came into frequent use, and the pioneer idiom became a vehicle for humor.

Many individuals were constantly on the move in the pursuit of opportunity, from colony to colony, from farm to city, from city to the frontier. In the New England colonies the attraction of urban employment brought the abandoned farm into being. In Pennsylvania the insatiable desire of the German immigrant for tillable soil led him down the Shenandoah Valley into Western North Carolina. Merchants, peddlers, printers, opportunists in general moved up and down the seaboard, and the frontiersmen ranged over the Appalachian Mountains. As a consequence of this movement, roads were built, inns established, and the first guidebook, *The Vade Mecum of America*, appeared in 1732. To move trade goods, the Conestoga wagon was built, stagecoach lines were organized, and new occupations—stagecoach drivers, freight haulers, and drovers—came into being.

With increased wealth and the concentration of population, the colonies made great cultural advances. Formal education, largely privately supported, was increasingly available. Primary schools, some maintained out of public funds, were in many cities and towns, local academies were instituted, and collegiate instruction was expanded by the addition of such well-known institutions as Yale University, Princeton University, the University of Pennsylvania, the University of Columbia, Brown University, and Rutgers University. In all, some twenty-two present-day colleges and universities had their beginning in this period. Natural science, technical training, and the English language and literature were added to the curriculum, and professional instruction in law and medicine was begun. For the self-taught, some twenty public libraries were in operation by 1763, and booksellers and bookstores were present in every city. These imported and sold most of the significant titles published in England and on the continent during the period. Many private libraries were available to interested students. Such a library was James Logan's in Philadelphia, in which the younger Godfrey discovered Chaucer. As a consequence of formal and self-instruction, the level of literacy at the outbreak of the American Revolution was as high in the colonies as anywhere in the English speaking world.

The arts flourished. Pipe organs were imported by some churches; choirs were organized. The Moravian choir in Bethlehem and the Tunkard choir of the Ephrata Cloisters in Pennsylvania attracted visitors from overseas. Operas and symphony concerts were given in New York, Philadelphia, and Charlestown. Native composers were at work. In his day Francis Hopkinson was famous both as composer and poet. Theaters were erected in New York, Philadelphia, Williamsburg, and Charlestown; plays were written by native playwrights and were performed by traveling companies. Painters, sculptors, and engravers appeared, notably Smibert and Copley in Boston, and Benjamin West in Philadelphia. The latter was to succeed Sir Joshua Reynolds to the presidency of the Royal Academy. The first exhibition of American painting was held in New York in 1757. The club life, salons, and literary coteries, so prominent in eighteenth-century London, were imitated in the colonial cities. The cities themselves developed pride in their appearance. Philadelphia, the largest and most secular of the urban centers, had paved streets, street lights, parks, public buildings, fire companies, a library, a hospital, a college, a market, and an exchange. The general cultural advance in the period was considerable and nothing to be apologetic about.

A major contributor to this cultural advance was the spread of printing. When the century opened, printers had appeared in only three colonies; by the outbreak of the Revolution there was at least one press in every colony, and Boston and Philadelphia were prominent publishing centers, the former being surpassed in the British Empire only by London. With the printer came the newspaper and the magazine to provide an outlet for the productions of the literary coteries that grew up around them. By 1789, some 270 newspapers had been started, most to be short-lived, some to live until the Revolution put them out of business, and some to survive into modern times. The first newsheet, Benjamin Harris' *Public Occurrences,* appeared in Boston in 1690, but was immediately suppressed by the government. The first successful venture was John Campbell's *Boston News-Letter* of 1704, which under various hands continued until 1776. It was the newsheets that introduced and domesticated the *Spectator* essay in America, the first imitation appearing in James Franklin's *New-England Courant* in 1721. These newspapers contained usually an essay, a summary of the foreign and domestic news, notable addresses, proclamations and actions of the legislatures, shipping and market news, advertisements, and some poetry. Over a score of magazines were begun in the period, most short-lived. The first to appear was *The American Magazine,* edited by John Webbe and printed by Andrew Bradford in 1740, to be followed within a week by Benjamin Franklin's *General Magazine.* The magazine reflected the concerns of the period with economic and political affairs, with education, with religion and the spread of Deism, with science and medicine, and with the development of a native literature. The essay was the dominant form, but every magazine had a poetry section, and some short tales were printed. Subscribers were not numerous, distribution was expensive, and most magazines ended in financial failure. The newspapers and magazines stimulated local literary activity by providing a place for publication and, in turn, depended upon the local coteries for material. The forms for such writing were the prevailing literary forms and modes in England. Only the novel failed to have imitators on this side of the Atlantic in the period. The heated discussion prior to and during the Revolution tended to halt the adaptation of newer forms and to emphasize the satiric modes of the earlier eighteenth century. Not until the nation was established would the adaptation be continued. A word must be said for the lowly almanac. Over seventy series ran at one time or another in the period; some were as widely distributed as *Poor Richard.* By printing extracts from contemporary English literature, prose and verse, they assisted in the development of literary taste; through their advice on practiced methods in trade and agriculture, they contributed to the secularization of the age; and by their reiteration of the folk saw and wisdom, they dignified the pragmatic virtues of thrift, industry, and shrewdness. They reached a wider audience than any other periodical publication, and their influence on the popular mind was incalculable.

Histories, biographies, sermons, tracts, journals, diaries, and verse were still produced during this period, but with a difference in tone. Didactic intent is present, but it is less religious and moral and more social, political, and economic. History is more factual than exemplary, the lay-sermon and essay vie with the formal sermon, tracts are more concerned with public than church affairs, journals and diaries become records more of external acts than internal states, and verse tends to be more descriptive than introspective. The writer begins to have a concern for the effectiveness of his form equal to his concern with the propriety of his doctrine.

HISTORY

Robert Beverley

(c. 1673-1722)

The son of a wealthy Virginia family, Robert Beverley was educated in England, then returned home where he held numerous political offices. Returning to England in 1703, Beverley read the manuscript of John Oldmixon's *The British Empire in America*, found the volume full of inaccuracies, and wrote his *The History and Present State of Virginia* (London, 1705). His book was translated into French and published in Amsterdam in 1707, 1712, and 1718, and in Paris in 1707. A revised edition appeared in London in 1722. Beverley also wrote *An Abridgement of the Public Laws of Virginia* (London, 1722).

BIBLIOGRAPHY: Charles Campbell, ed. *The History and Present State of Virginia* (Richmond, Va., 1855) from 1722 text. Louis B. Wright, ed. *The History and Present State of Virginia* (Chapel Hill, N.C., 1947), from 1705 text. Wright, *The First Gentlemen of Virginia* (San Marino, Calif., 1940), Ch. X. Wright, "Beverley's *History* . . . (1705): A Neglected Classic," *Wm. and Mary Quart.*, Ser. 3, I (1944), 49-64.

From *The History and Present State of Virginia*

THE PREFACE

'Tis agreed, that Travellers are of all Men, the most suspected of Insincerity. This does not only hold, in their private Conversations; but likewise in the Grand Tours, and Travels, with which they pester the Public, and break the Bookseller. There are no Books, (the Legends of Saints always excepted,) so stuff'd with Poetical Stories, as Voyages; and the more distant the Countries lie, which they pretend to describe, the greater License those priviledg'd Authors take, in imposing upon the World. . . .

The English, it must be granted, invent more within the Compass of Probability, and are contented to be less Ornamental, while they are more Sincere.

I make no Question, but the following Account will come in for its Share of this Imputation. I shall be reputed as arrant a Traveller as the rest, and my Credit, (like that of Women,) will be condemn'd for the Sins of my Company. However, I entreat the gentle Reader to be so just, as not to convict me upon bare Suspicion; let the Evidence be plain, or at least amount to a violent Presumption, and then I don't fear being acquitted. If an honest Author might be believ'd in his own Case, I wou'd solemnly declare, that I have not knowingly asserted any untrue Thing in the whole Book. . . .

If I might be so happy, as to settle my Credit with the Reader, the next Favor I wou'd ask of him, shou'd be, not to Criticize too unmercifully upon my Style. I am an Indian, and don't pretend to be exact in my Language: But I hope the Plainness of my Dress, will give him the kinder Impressions of my Honesty, which is what I pretend to. Truth desires only to be understood, and never affects the Reputation of being finely equipp'd. It depends upon its own intrinsic Value, and, like Beauty, is rather conceal'd, than set off, by Ornament.

I wonder no Body has ever presented the World, with a tolerable Account of our Plantations. Nothing of that kind has yet appear'd, except some few General Descriptions, that have been calculated more for the Benefit of the Bookseller, than for the Information of Mankind. If I may judge of the rest, by what has been publish'd concerning Virginia, I will take the Liberty to say, that there's none of 'em either true, or so much as well invented. Such Accounts are as impertinent as ill Pictures, that resemble any Body, as much as the Persons they are drawn for. For my part, I have endeavor'd to hit the Likeness; though, perhaps, my Coloring may not have all the Life and Beauty I cou'd wish. . . . I have everywhere made it my chief Business, to avoid Partiality; and therefore have fairly expos'd the Inconveniencies, as well as proclaim'd the Excellencies of my Country.

BOOK I, CHAPTER I

. . . . .

26. Anno 1612, Two Ships more arriv'd with Supplies: And Capt. Argall, who commanded one of them, being sent in her to Patowmeck to buy Corn, he there met with Pocahontas, the Excellent Daughter of Powhatan; and having prevail'd with her to come Aboard to a Treat, he detain'd her Prisoner, and carried her to James-Town, designing to make Peace with her Father by her Release: But on the Contrary, that Prince resented the Affront very highly; and although he loved his Daughter with all imaginable Tenderness, yet he would not be brought to Terms by that unhandsome Treachery; till about Two Years after a Marriage being proposed between Mr. John Rolfe, an English Gentleman, and this Lady; which Powhatan taking to be a sincere Token of Friendship, he vouchsafed to consent to it, and to conclude a Peace.

Intermarriage had been indeed the Method proposed very often by the Indians in the Beginning, urging it frequently as a certain Rule, that the

English were not their Friends, if they refused it. And I can't but think it would have been happy for that Country, had they embraced this Proposal: For, the Jealousy of the Indians, which I take to be the Cause of most of the Rapings and Murders they committed, would by this Means have been altogether prevented, and consequently the Abundance of Blood that was shed on both sides would have been saved; the great Extremities they were so often reduced to, by which so many died, would not have happen'd; the Colony, instead of all these Losses of Men on both Sides, would have been increasing in Children to its Advantage; the Country would have escaped the Odium which undeservedly fell upon it, by the Errors and Convulsions in the first Management; and, in all Likelihood, many, if not most, of the Indians would have been converted to Christianity by this kind Method; the Country would have been full of People, by the Preservation of the many Christians and Indians that fell in the Wars between them. Besides, there would have been a Continuance of all those Nations of Indians that are now dwindled away to nothing by their frequent Removals, or are fled to other Parts; not to mention the Invitation that so much Success and Prosperity would have been for others to have gone over and settled there, instead of the Frights and Terrors that were produced by all those Misfortunes that happen'd.

27. Pocahontas being thus married in the Year 1613, a firm Peace was concluded with her Father, tho' he would not trust himself at her Wedding. Both the English and Indians thought themselves entirely secure and quiet. This brought in the Chickahomony Indians also, tho' not out of any Kindness or Respect to the English, but out of Fear of being, by their Assistance, brought under Powhatan's absolute Subjection, who used now and then to threaten and tyrannize over them.

28. Sir Thomas Dale returning for England Anno 1616. took with him Mr. Rolfe and his Wife Pocahontas, who upon the Marriage, was Christen'd, and call'd Rebecka. He left Capt. George Yardly Deputy-Governor during his Absence, the Country being then entirely at Peace; and arriv'd at Plymouth the 12th of June.

Capt. John Smith was at that Time in England, and hearing of the Arrival of Pocahontas at Portsmouth, used all the Means he could to express his Gratitude to her, as having formerly preserv'd his Life by the Hazard of her own: For, when by the Command of her Father, Capt. Smith's Head was upon the Block to have his Brains knock'd out, she saved his Head by laying hers close upon it. He was at that Time suddenly to embark for New England, and fearing he should fail before she got to London, he made an humble Petition to the Queen in her Behalf, . . .

30. This Account was presented to her Majesty, and graciously received: But before Captain Smith sail'd for New England, the Indian Princess arrived at London, and her Husband took Lodgings for her at Branford, to be a little out of the Smoke of the City, whither Capt.

Smith, with some of her Friends, went to see her, and congratulate her Arrival, letting her know the Address he had made to the Queen in her Favor.

Till this Lady arrived in England, she had all along been inform'd that Capt. Smith was dead, because he had been diverted from that Colony by making Settlements in the Second Plantation, now call'd New England: For which Reason, when she see him, she seem'd to think herself much affronted, for that they had dared to impose so gross an Untruth upon her, and at first Sight of him turn'd away. It cost him a great deal of Intreaty, and some Hours' Attendance, before she would do him the Honor to speak to him: But at last she was reconcil'd, and talk'd freely to him. She put him in mind of her former Kindnesses, and then upbraided him for his Forgetfulness of her, showing by her Reproaches, that even a State of Nature teaches to abhor Ingratitude.

She had in her Retinue a Great Man of her own Nation, whose Name was Uttamaccomack: This Man had Orders from Powhatan, to count the People in England, and give him an Account of their Number. Now the Indians having no Letters among them, he at his going ashore provided a Stick, in which he was to make a Notch for every Man he see: but this Accountant soon grew weary of that tedious Exercise, and threw his Stick away: And at his return, being asked by his King, How many People there were; He desired him to count the Stars in the Sky, the Leaves upon the Trees, and the Sand on the Seashore, for so many People (he said) were in England.

31. Pocahontas had many Honors done her by the Queen upon Account of Capt. Smith's Story; and being introduced by the Lady Delaware, she was frequently admitted to wait on her Majesty, and was publicly treated as a Prince's Daughter; she was carried to many Plays, Balls, and other public Entertainments, and very respectfully receiv'd by all the Ladies about the Court. Upon all which Occasions she behaved herself with so much Decency, and show'd so much Grandeur in her Deportment, that she made good the brightest Part of the Character Capt. Smith had given of her. In the meanwhile she gain'd the good Opinion of every Body, so much that the poor Gentleman her Husband had like to have been call'd to an Account for presuming to marry a Princess Royal without the King's Consent; because it had been suggested that he had taken Advantage of her being a Prisoner, and forc'd her to marry him. But upon a more perfect Representation of the Matter, his Majesty was pleased at last to declare himself satisfied.

Everybody paid this young Lady all imaginable Respect; and it is supposed, she would have sufficiently acknowledged those Favors, had she lived to return to her own Country, by bringing the Indians to have a kinder Disposition towards the English. But upon her Return she was unfortunately taken ill at Gravesend, and died in a few Days after, giving great Testimony all the Time she lay sick, of her being a very good Christian. She left Issue one Son, nam'd Thomas Rolfe, whose Posterity is at this Day in good Repute in Virginia.

32. Captain Yardly made but a very ill Governor, he let the Buildings and Forts go to Ruin; not regarding the Security of the People against the Indians, neglecting the Corn, and applying all Hands to plant Tobacco, which promised the most immediate Gain. In this Condition they were when Capt. Samuel Argall was sent thither Governor, Anno 1617. who found the Number of People reduc'd to something more than Four Hundred, of which not above Half were fit for Labor. In the meanwhile the Indians mixing among 'em, got Experience daily in Fire-Arms, and some of 'em were instructed therein by the English themselves, and employ'd to hunt and kill wild Fowl for them. So great was their Security upon this Marriage: But Governor Argall not liking those Methods, reguated them on his Arrival, and Capt. Yardly return'd to England.

BOOK II, CHAPTER 8

. . . I take this story of Smith's to be only an example of Huskanawing, which being a Ceremony then altogether unknown to him, he might easily mistake some of the circumstances of it.

The Solemnity of Huskanawing is commonly practis'd once every fourteen or sixteen years, or oftener, as their young men happen to grow up. It is an Institution or Discipline which all young men must pass, before they can be admitted to be of the number of the Great men, or Cockarouses of the Nation; whereas by Captain Smith's Relation, they were only set apart to supply the Priesthood. The whole Ceremony is performed after the following manner.

The choicest and briskest young men of the Town, and such only as have acquired some Treasure by their Travels and Hunting, are chosen out by the Rulers to be Huskanawed; and whoever refuses to undergo this Process, dare not remain among them. Several of those odd preparatory Fopperies are premis'd in the beginning, which have been before related; but the principal part of the business is to carry them into the Woods, and there keep them under confinement, and destitute of all Society, for several months; giving them no other sustenance, but the Infusion, or Decoction of some Poisonous Intoxicating Roots; by virtue of which Physic, and by the severity of the discipline, which they undergo, they become stark staring Mad: In which raving condition they are kept eighteen or twenty days. During these extremities, they are shut up, night and day, in a strong Inclosure made on purpose; one of which I saw, belonging to the Paumaunkie Indians, in the year 1694. It was in shape like a Sugarloaf, and every way open like a Lattice, for the Air to pass through. In this Cage thirteen young Men had been Huskanaw'd, and had not been a month set at liberty, when I saw it. Upon this occasion it is pretended, that these poor Creatures drink so much of that

Water of Lethe, that they perfectly lose the remembrance of all former things, even of their Parents, their Treasure, and their Language. When the Doctors find that they have drank sufficiently of the Wysoccan, (so they call this mad Potion) they gradually restore them to their Senses again, by lessening the Intoxication of their Diet; but before they are perfectly well, they bring them back into their Towns, while they are still wild and crazy, through the Violence of the Medicine. After this they are very fearful of discovering anything of their former remembrance; for if such a thing should happen to any of them, they must immediately be Huskanaw'd again; and the second time the usage is so severe, that seldom anyone escapes with Life. Thus they must pretend to have forgot the very use of their Tongues, so as not to be able to speak, nor understand anything that is spoken, till they learn it again. Now whether this be real or counterfeit, I don't know; but certain it is, that they will not for some time take notice of any body, nor any thing, with which they were before acquainted, being still under the guard of their Keepers, who constantly wait upon them every where, till they have learnt all things perfectly over again. Thus they unlive their former lives, and commence Men, by forgetting that they ever have been Boys. If under this Exercise any one should die, I suppose the Story of Okee, mention'd by Smith, is the Salvo for it: For (says he) Okee was to have such as were his by lot; and such were said to be Sacrificed.

Now this Conjecture is the more probable, because we know that Okee has not a share in every Huskanawing; for tho' two young men happen'd to come short home, in that of the Pamaunkie Indians, which was perform'd in the year 1694, yet the Appamattucks, formerly a great Nation, tho now an inconsiderable people, made an Huskanaw in the year 1690, and brought home the same number they carried out.

33. I can account no other way for the great pains and secrecy of the Keepers, during the whole process of this discipline, but by assuring you, that it is the most meritorious thing in the World, to discharge that trust well, in order to their preferment to the greatest posts in the Nation, which they claim as their undoubted right, in the next promotion. On the other hand, they are sure of a speedy Passport into the other World, if they should by their Levity or Neglect, show themselves in the least unfaithful.

Those which I ever observ'd to have been Huskanawed, were lively handsome well timber'd young men, from fifteen to twenty years of age or upward, and such as were generally reputed rich.

I confess, I judged it at first sight to be only an Invention of the Seniors, to engross the young men's Riches to themselves; for, after suffering this operation, they never pretended to call to mind any thing of their former property: But their Goods were either shared among the old men, or brought to some public use; and so those Younkers were oblig'd to begin the World again.

But the Indians detest this opinion, and pretend that this violent method of taking away the Memory, is to release the Youth from all their Childish impressions, and from that strong Partiality to persons and things, which is contracted before Reason comes to take place. They hope by this proceeding, to root out all the prepossessions and unreasonable prejudices which are fixt in the minds of Children. So that, when the Young men come to themselves again, their Reason may act freely, without being biass'd by the Cheats of Custom and Education. Thus also they become discharg'd from the remembrance of any ties by Blood, and are establisht in a state of equality and perfect freedom, to order their actions, and dispose of their persons, as they think fit, without any other Control, than that of the Law of Nature. By this means also they become qualified, when they have any Public Office, equally and impartially to administer Justice, without having respect either to Friend or Relation.

BOOK III, CHAPTER 19

. . . . .

79. That which makes this Country most unfortunate, is, that it must submit to receive its Character from the Mouths not only of unfit, but very unequal Judges; For, all its Reproaches happen after this manner.

Many of the Merchants and others that go thither from England, make no distinction between a cold, and a hot Country: but wisely go sweltering about in their thick Clothes all the Summer, because they used to do so in their Northern Climate; and then unfairly complain of the heat of the Country. They greedily Surfeit with their delicious Fruits, and are guilty of great Intemperance, through the exceeding Generosity of the Inhabitants; by which means they fall Sick, and then unjustly complain of the unhealthiness of the Country. In the next place, the Sailors for want of Towns there, are put to the hardship of rolling most of the Tobacco, a Mile or more, to the Waterside; this Splinters their Hands sometimes, and provokes 'em to curse the Country. Such Exercise, and a bright Sun, makes them hot, and then they imprudently fall to drinking cold Water, or perhaps New Cider, which in its Season, they find at every Planter's House; Or else they greedily devour all the green Fruit, and unripe Trash they can meet with, and so fall into Fluxes, Fevers, and the Bellyache; and then, to spare their own Indiscretion, they in their Tarpawlin Language, cry, God D—— the Country. This is the true State of the case, as to the Complaints of its being Sickly; For, by the most impartial Observation I can make, if People will be persuaded to be Temperate, and take due care of themselves, I believe it is as healthy a Country, as any under Heaven: but the extraordinary pleasantness of the Weather, and the goodness of the Fruit, lead People into many Temptations. The clearness and brightness of the Sky, add new vigor to their Spirits, and perfectly remove all Splenetic and sullen Thoughts. Here they enjoy all the benefits of a warm Sun, and by their shady Groves, are protected from its Inconvenience. Here all their Senses are entertain'd with an endless Succession of Native Pleasures. Their Eyes are ravished with the Beauties of naked Nature. Their Ears are Serenaded with the perpetual murmur of Brooks, and the thorough bass which the Wind plays, when it wantons through the Trees; the merry Birds too, join their pleasing Notes to this rural Consort, especially the Mock-birds, who love Society so well, that whenever they see Mankind, they will perch upon a Twig very near them, and sing the sweetest wild Airs in the World: But what is most remarkable in these Melodious Animals, they will frequently fly at small distances before a Traveller, warbling out their Notes several Miles on end, and by their Music, make a Man forget the Fatigues of his Journey. Their Taste is regaled with the most delicious Fruits, which without Art they have in great Variety and Perfection. And then their smell is refreshed with an eternal fragrancy of Flowers and Sweets, with which Nature perfumes and adorns the Woods almost the whole year round.

Have you pleasure in a Garden? All things thrive in it, most surprisingly; you can't walk by a Bed of Flowers, but besides the entertainment of their Beauty, your Eyes will be saluted with the charming colors of the Humming Bird, which revels among the Flowers, and licks off the Dew and Honey from their tender Leaves, on which it only feeds. Its size is not half so large as an English Wren, and its color is a glorious shining mixture of Scarlet, Green, and Gold. Colonel Byrd, in his Garden, which is the finest in that Country, has a Summer-House set round with the Indian Honey-Suckle, which all the Summer is continually full of sweet Flowers, in which these Birds delight exceedingly. Upon these Flowers, I have seen ten or a dozen of these Beautiful Creatures together, which sported about me so familiarly, that with their little Wings they often fann'd my Face.

80. On the other side, all the Annoyances and Inconveniences of the Country, may fairly be summed up, under these three Heads, Thunder, Heat, and troublesome Vermin.

I confess, in the hottest part of Summer, they have sometimes very loud and surprising Thunder, but rarely any Damage happens by it. On the contrary, it is of such advantage to the cooling and refining of the Air, that it is oftener wished for, than fear'd. But they have no Earthquakes, which the Caribbee Islands are so much troubled with.

Their Heat is very seldom troublesome, and then only by the accident of a perfect Calm, which happens perhaps two or three times in a year, and lasts but a few Hours at a time; and even that Inconvenience is made easy by cool Shades, by open Airy rooms, Summer-Houses, Arbors, and Grottos: But the Spring and Fall, afford as pleasant Weather, as Mahomet promis'd in his Paradise.

All the troublesome Vermin, that ever I heard any Body complain of, are either Frogs, Snakes, Musketa's, Chinches, Seedticks, or Redworms, by some call'd Potato lice. Of all which I shall give an account in their Order.

Some People have been so ill inform'd, as to say, that Virginia is full of Toads, though there never yet was seen one Toad in it. The Marshes, Fens, and Watery Grounds, are indeed full of harmless Frogs, which do no hurt, except by the noise of their croaking Notes: but in the upper parts of the Country, where the Land is high and dry, they are very scarce. In the Swamps and running Streams, they have Frogs of an incredible bigness, which are call'd Bullfrogs, from the roaring they make. Last year I found one of these near a Stream of fresh Water, of so prodigious a Magnitude, that when I extended its Legs, I found the distance betwixt them, to be seventeen Inches and an half. I am confident, six Frenchmen might have made a comfortable Meal of its Carcass.

BOOK III, CHAPTER XXI

. . . . .

95. The Inhabitants are very Courteous to Travelers, who need no other Recommendation, but the being Human Creatures. A Stranger has no more to do, but to inquire upon the Road, where any Gentleman, or good Housekeeper Lives, and there he may depend upon being received with Hospitality. This good Nature is so general among their People, that the Gentry when they go abroad, order their Principal Servant to entertain all Visitors, with every thing the Plantation affords. And the poor Planters, who have but one Bed, will very often sit up, or lie upon a Form or Couch all Night, to make room for a weary Traveler, to repose himself after his Journey.

If there happens to be a Churl, that either out of Covetousness, or Ill-nature, won't comply with this generous Custom, he has a mark of Infamy set upon him, and is abhorr'd by all. But I must confess, (and am heartily sorry for the occasion) that this good Neighborhood has of late been much depraved by the present Governor, who practices the detestable Politics of governing by Parties; by which, Feuds and Heart burnings have been kindled in the Minds of the People; and Friendship, Hospitality, and Good-Neighborhood, have been extremely discouraged.

1705

John Lawson

(?-1711)

John Lawson, probably of Yorkshire, England, left Charleston, S.C., in December of 1700 to explore the piedmont of North Carolina. After spending several years traveling in North Carolina, he returned to England in 1708 to publish *A New Voyage to Carolina*, first printed in John Stevens' *A New Collection of Voyages and Travels* (London, 1708). The book appeared separately as *A New Voyage to Carolina* (London, 1709), was reissued as *The History of Carolina* (London, 1714, 1718), and was translated into German (Hamburg, 1712, 1722). On another exploring expedition, Lawson was killed by Tuscaroras in 1711.

BIBLIOGRAPHY: *DAB*. Frances Latham Harriss, ed. *Lawson's History of North Carolina* (Richmond, Va., 1937, 1952). Other editions are Charlotte, N.C., 1903; Raleigh, N.C., 1860 and 1911.

From *The History of North Carolina*

CHAPTER I

. . . The Indians, I was now speaking of, were not content with the common Enemies that lessen and destroy their countrymen, but invented an infallible Stratagem to purge their tribe, and reduce their Multitude into far less numbers. Their Contrivance was thus, as a Trader amongst them informed me.

They seeing several Ships coming in, to bring the English Supplies from Old England, one chief part of their Cargo being for a Trade with the Indians, some of the Craftiest of them had observed, that the Ships came always in at one place, which made them very confident that Way was the exact road to England; and seeing so many ships come thence they believed it could not be far thither, esteeming the English that were among them no better than cheats, and thought if they could carry the Skins and Furs they got themselves to England, which was inhabited with a better sort of People than those amongst them, that they should purchase twenty times the Value of every Pelt they sold Abroad, in consideration of what rates they sold for at Home. The intended barter was very well approved of, and after a general Consultation of the ablest Heads amongst them, it was, *Nemine Contradicente,* agreed upon, immediately to make an addition of their fleet, by building more canoes, and those to be of the best sort, and biggest Size, as fit for their intended Discovery. Some Indians were employed about making the Canoes, others to hunting, everyone to the Post he was most fit for, all Endeavors intending towards an able Fleet and Cargo for Europe. The affair was carried on with a great deal of Secrecy and Expedition, so as in a Small Time they had gotten a Navy, Loading Provisions, and hands ready to set sail, leaving only the Old, Impotent and Minors at Home till their successful return. The Wind presenting, they set up their mat sails, and were scarce out of sight when there rose a tempest, which it's supposed carried one part of these Indian Merchants, by Way of the other World, whilst the others were taken up at Sea by an English Ship and sold for Slaves to the Islands. The remainder are better satisfied with their Imbecilities in such an undertaking, nothing affronting them more than to rehearse their Voyage to England. . . .

Many of the French follow a trade with the Indians, living very conveniently for that interest. There is about seventy Families seated on this River, who live as Decently and Happily, as any Planters in these Southward parts of America. The French being a temperate Industrious People, some of them bringing very little of Effects, yet by their endeavors and Mutual Assistance amongst themselves (which is highly to be Commended) have outstript our English, who brought with them larger Fortunes, tho' as it seems less endeavor to manage their Talent to the best Advantage. 'Tis admirable to see what time and Industry will (with God's Blessing) effect. Carolina affording many strange Revolutions in the Age of a Man, Daily Instances presenting themselves to our view, of so many, from Despicable beginnings, which in a short time arrive to very splendid Conditions. Here propriety hath a large Scope, there being no strict law to bind our privileges. A Quest after Game, being as freely and peremptorily enjoyed by the meanest Planter, as he that is in the Highest Dignity, or wealthiest in the Province. Deer and other game that are naturally wild, being not immur'd or preserv'd within boundaries to satisfy the appetite of the rich alone. A poor laborer, that is Master of his Gun, etc., hath as good a claim to have continu'd Courses of Delicacies crowded upon his Table, as he that is Master of a Greater Purse. . . .

The next day, we travel'd on our Way, and about Noon, came up with a settlement of Santee Indians, there being Plantations lying scattering here and there, for a great many miles. They came out to meet us, being acquainted with one of our Company, and made us very welcome with fat barbecu'd Venison, which the Woman of the Cabin took and tore in Pieces with her teeth, so put it into a mortar, beating it to Rags, afterwards stews it with Water, and other Ingredients, which makes a very savory Dish.

At these Cabins came to visit us the King of the Santee Nation. He brought with him their chief Doctor, or Physician, who was warmly and neatly clad with a Match-Coat, made of Turkey's Feathers, which makes a pretty Show, seeming as if it was a Garment of the deepest silk shag. These Indians have great skill in their medical matters, this doctor perfected his cures, by proper Vegetables, etc., of which they have plenty, and are well acquainted with their specific virtue. I have seen such admirable Cures, performed by these Savages, which would puzzle a great many graduate practitioners, to trace their Steps in healing, with the same expedition, Ease, and Success; using no racking instruments in their Surgery, nor nice Rules of Diet, and Physic, to certify the saying *"Qui medici vivit, miserere vivit."* In wounds which penetrate deep, and seem Mortal they order a spare Diet, with drinking Fountain Water. The Indians are an easy, credulous People, and most notoriously cheated by their priests and conjurers, both Trades meeting ever in one Person, and most commonly a spice of Quackship, added to the other two ingredients, which renders that cunning Knave the Imposter to be more rely'd upon; thence a fitter instrument to cheat these ignorant people. . . .

This day all of us had a mind to have rested, but the Indian was much against it, alleging that the place we lay in was not good to hunt in, telling us if we would go on, by Noon he would bring us to a more convenient place; so we moved on, and about twelve o'clock we came to the most amazing prospect I have ever seen in Carolina; we traveled by a Swamp side, which swamp I believe to be no less than 20 miles over, the other side being as far as I could well discern, there appearing great ridges of Mountains, bearing from us W. N. W. One Alp with a Top like a sugar loaf, advanced its head above all the rest very considerably; the day was very serene, which gave us the advantage of seeing a long way; These Mountains were clothed all over with Trees, which seemed to us to be very large Timbers.

At the sight of this fair Prospect we stayed all night; our Indian going about half an hour before us, had provided three fat turkeys ere we got up to him.

The Swamp I now spoke of is not a miry Bog, as others generally are, but you go down to it through a steep Bank, at the foot of which begins this Valley, where you may go dry for perhaps 200 yards, then you meet with a small Brook or Run of Water, about 2 or 3 foot deep, then dry Land for such another space, so another Brook, thus continuing. The land of this Percoarson, or Valley, being extraordinarily rich, and runs of water well stored with Fowl. It is the Head of one of the branches of Santee River; but a further discovery time would not permit; only one thing is very remarkable; there growing all over this Swamp a tall lofty Bay Tree, but is not the same as in England. These being in their verdure all the winter long; which appears here when you stand on the ridge, (where our path lay) as if it were one pleasant, green field, and as even as a Bowling-green to the Eye of the Beholder; being hemmed in on one side with these Ledges of vast High Mountains. . . .

The next day it proved a small drizzly Rain which is rare; there happening not the tenth part of Foggy Weather towards these Mountains, as visits those parts near the Seaboard. The Indian killed 15 Turkeys this day, there coming out of the Swamp about Sunrising flocks of these Fowl; containing several hundred in a gang, who feed upon the Acorns it being most Oak that grow in these Woods. There are but very few Pines in those Quarters. . . .

The Land we passed over this day was most of it good, and the worst passable. At night we killed a possum, being cloy'd with Turkeys, made a dish of that, which tasted much between young pork and veal, their Fat being as white as any I ever saw. . . .

The next morning Santee Jack told us, we should reach the Indian Settlement betimes that Day, about noon we passed by several fair Savannas, very rich and dry; seeing great copses of many Acres that bore nothing but Bushes about the Bigness of Box-trees; which (in the season) afford great quantities of small Blackberries, very pleasant Fruit and very much like our Blues or Huckleberries, that grow on Heaths in England. Hard by the Savannahs we found the Town, where we halted; . . .

The Town consists not of above a dozen Houses, they having other straggling Plantations up and down the Country, and are seated upon a small Branch of Santee River. Their Place hath curious dry Savannahs and Marshes adjoining to it, and would prove an exceedingly thriving Range for Cattle, and Hogs, provided the English were seated thereon. Besides the Land is good for Plantations. . . .

The Congerees are kind and affable to the English, the Queen being very kind, giving us what Rarities her Cabin afforded, as Loblolly made of Indian Corn and Dry'd Peaches. These Congerees have abundance of Storks and Cranes in their Savannas. They take them before they can fly, and breed them as tame and familiar as a Dunghill Fowl. They had a tame Crane at one of these Cabins, that was scarce less than six foot in height, his head being round, with a shining natural Crimson Hue, which they all have. These are a very Comely sort of Indians, there being a strange Difference in the Proportion and Beauty of these Heathens. Altho' their Tribes or Nations border one upon another, yet you may discern as great an Alteration in their features and Dispositions, as you can in their speech, which generally proves quite different from each other, tho' their Nations be not above twenty Miles in Distance. The Women here being as handsome as most I have met withal, being several fine figured Brounetto's amongst them. These lassies stick not upon hand long, for they marry when very young, as at 12 or 14 years of age. The English Traders are seldom without an Indian Female for his bedfellow, alleging these reasons as sufficient to allow of such familiarity. First, they being remote from any White People, that it preserves their friendship with the Heathens, they esteeming a white man's Child much above one of their own getting, the Indian Mistress ever securing her White friend provisions whilst he stays amongst them, and lastly the correspondence makes them learn the Indian tongue sooner, they being of the Frenchmen's opinion, how that an English Wife teaches her Husband more English in one night, than a Schoolmaster can in a week. . . .

Now, to return to our state House, whither we were entertained by the

Grandees; as soon as we came into it, they placed our Englishmen near the King; it being my fortune to sit next to him, having his Great General or War Captain on my other hand. The House is as Dark as a Dungeon and as hot as one of the Dutch Stoves in Holland. They had made a circular Fire of split canes in the middle of the House; It was one Man's employment to add more split Reeds to this at one end as it consumed at the other, there being a small Vacancy left to supply it with Fuel. They brought in great store of Loblolly, and other Medleys, made of Indian Grain, stewed Peaches, Bear Venison, etc., everyone bringing some offering to enlarge the banquet, according to his Degree and Quality. When all the Viands were brought in the first Figure began with kicking out the Dogs. . . .

After the dogs had fled the room, the Company was summoned by beat of Drum; the Music being made of dress'd deer's Skin, tied hot upon an earthen Porridge Pot. Presently came in five men dressed up in Feathers, their Faces being covered with Vizards made of Gourds, round their Ankles and Knees were hung bells of several sorts, having Wooden Falchions in their Hands (such as Stage Fencers commonly Use); in this dress they danced about an hour, showing many strange gestures, and brandishing their Wooden Weapons, as if they were going to fight each other; often walking very nimbly around the room without making the least noise with their bells (a thing I much admired at) again turning their bodies, arms and legs into such frightful postures, that you would have guessed they were quite raving mad: At last they cut two or three high capers and left the room. In their stead came in a parcel of women and girls, to the number of Thirty odd, everyone taking place according to her degree of stature, the tallest leading the dance, and the least of all being placed last; with these they made a circular Dance, like a ring, representing the Shape of the fire they danced about; Many of these had great Horse Belts about their legs, and small Hawks' Bells about their necks.

Next day having some occasion to write, the Indian King, who saw me, believed that he could write as well as I. Whereupon I wrote a word and gave it to him to copy, which he did with more exactness than any European could have done, that was illiterate. It was so well that he who could have read mine might have done the same by his. Afterwards he took great delight in making fish-hooks of his own invention which would have been a good Piece for an Antiquary to have puzzled his brains withal, in tracing out the Characters of all the oriental Tongues. He sent for several Indians to his Cabin to look at his handiwork and both he and they thought I could read his writing as well as I could my own. I had a Manual in my pocket that had King David's Picture in it, and in one of his Private retirements. The Indian asked me who that Indian represented? I told him that it was the Picture of a good King that lived according to the rules of Morality, doing all as he would be done by, ordering all his life to the service of the Creator of all things; and being now above us in Heaven with God Almighty, who had rewarded him with all the delightful pleasures imaginable in the other World, for his Obedience to him in this. I concluded with telling him that we received nothing here below, as Food, Raiment, etc., but what came from the Omnipotent Being. They listened to my Discourse with a profound Silence, assuring me that they believed what I said to be true. No man living will ever be able to make these Heathens sensible to the Happiness of a future state, except he now and then mentions some lively carnal Representation, which may quicken their apprehensions, and make them thirst after such a gainful exchange; for were the best lecture that ever was preached by man given to an ignorant sort of people, in a more learned style than their mean capacities are able to understand, the Intent would prove ineffectual, and the Hearers would be left in a greater Labyrinth than their Teacher found them in. But dispense the Precepts of our Faith according to the Pupil's capacity, and there is nothing in our Religion but what an indifferent reason is in some measure able to comprehend tho' a New England Minister blames the French Jesuits for this way of proceeding, as being quite contrary to the true Christian Practice, and affirms it to be no ready or true Method, to establish a lively representation of our Christian Belief amongst these Infidels.

CHAPTER II

. . .The Province of Carolina is separated from Virginia by a Due West Line, which begins at Currituck Inlet, in 36 degrees, 30 minutes, of Northern Latitude, and extends indefinitely to the Westward, and thence to the Southward, as far as 29 Degrees, which is a vast amount of Sea Coast. But having already treated as far as is necessary, concerning South Carolina, I shall confine myself in the ensuing Sheets, to give my reader a description of that part of the country only which lies between Currituck and Cape Fear River, and is almost 34 degrees North. And this is commonly called North Carolina.

This part of Carolina is faced with a chain of Sand Banks, which defends it from the violence and Insults of the Atlantic Ocean, by which barrier a vast Sound is hemmed in, which fronts the Mouths of the Navigable Pleasant Rivers of this Fertile Country, and into which they disgorge themselves. Thro' the same are inlets of several depths of Water. Some of these Channels admit only of Sloops, Brigantines, small Barks and Ketches; and such are Currituck, Roanoke, and the Sound above Hatteras; whilst others can receive Ships of Burden, as Ocracoke, Topsail Inlet, and Cape Fear, as appears by my chart.

The first discovery and settlement of this country was by the Procurement of Sir Walter Raleigh, in conjunction with some public spirited Gentlemen of that Age, under the Protection of Queen Elizabeth, for which reason it was then named Virginia, being begun on that part named Roanoke Island, where the ruins of a Fort are to be seen to this day, as well as some old English Coins which have been lately found; and a Brass Gun, one Powder Horn, and one small quarter-deck gun, made of Iron Staves, and hooped with the same metal; which method of making guns might very probably be made use of in those days; for the Convenience of Infant Colonies.

A farther confirmation of this we have from the Hatteras Indians, who either then lived on Roanoke Island, or much frequented it. These tell us that several of their ancestors were white People, and could talk in a Book, as we do; the truth of which is confirmed by grey Eyes being found frequently amongst these Indians, and no others. They value themselves extremely for their Affinity to the English, and are ready to do them all friendly offices. It is probable that this settlement miscarried for want of timely supplies from England, or thro' the treachery of the Natives, for we may reasonably suppose that the English were forced to co-habit with them for relief and conversation, and that in process of Time, they conformed themselves to the Manners of their Indian Relations. And thus we see how apt Human Nature is to degenerate.

I cannot forbear inserting here a pleasant story that passes for an un-contested Truth amongst the Inhabitants of this Place; which is that the Ship which brought the first Colonies, does often appear amongst them under sail, in a gallant Posture, which they call Sir Walter Raleigh's Ship; and the truth of this has been affirmed to me, by men of the best Credit in the Country.

A second settlement of this country was made about 50 years ago, in that part we now call Albemarle Country, and chiefly in Chowan Precinct, by several substantial planters, from Virginia and other Plantations, who finding mild winters and a fertile soil, beyond Expectation, producing everything that was planted to a prodigious increase; their Cattle, Horses, Sheep and Swine, breeding very fat, and passing the winter without any Assistance from the Planter; so that everything seemed to come by nature; the Husbandman living almost void of care, and free from those fatigues which are absolutely requisite in Winter-Countries; these encouragements induced them to stand their ground, altho' but a handful of people, seated at great distances from each other, and amidst a vast number of Indians from different Nations, who were then in Carolina. Nevertheless I say, the fame of this new discovered Summer-Country spread through the neighboring Colonies, and in a few years drew a considerable number of families thereto, who all found Land enough to settle themselves in, (had they been many thousand more) and that which was very good and commodiously seated, both for Profit and Pleasure. And indeed, most of the Plantations in Carolina, naturally enjoy a very noble prospect of large and spacious Rivers, pleasant Savannas, and fine Meadows, with their green liveries, interwoven with beautiful flowers of most glorious colors, which the several seasons afford, hedged in with famous groves of the ever famous Tulip tree, the stately Laurel, and Bays equalizing the Oak in bigness and growth; Myrtle, Woodbines, Jessamines, Honeysuckles, and several other fragrant Vines and Evergreens, whose aspiring branches shadow and interweave themselves with the loftiest timbers, yielding a pleasant Prospect, Shade and Smell, proper habitations for the sweet singing Birds, that melodiously entertain such as travel through the Woods of Carolina. . . .

As the Land is very fruitful, so are the Planters kind and hospitable to all that come and visit them; there being very few housekeepers, but what live nobly, and give away more provisions to Coasters and Guests who come to them, than they expend among their own families.

The Wheat of this place is very good, seldom yielding less than thirtyfold, provided the Land is good where it is sown; Not but that there has been sixty-six Increase for one measure sown in Piny-Land, which we account the meanest sort. And I have been informed by people of Credit, that Wheat which was planted in very rich Land, brought a hundred and odd Pecks for one. If our Planters, when they found such great increase, would be so curious as to make nice Observations of the Soil, and other remarkable Accidents, they would soon be acquainted with the nature of the earth and Climate, and be qualified to manage their Agriculture to more Certainty, and greater advantage; whereby they might arrive to the Crops and Harvests of Babylon, and those other fruitful countries so much talked of. For I must confess that I never saw one acre of Land Managed as it ought to be in Carolina, since I knew it; and were they as negligent in their Husbandry in Europe, as they are in Carolina, their Land would produce nothing but Weeds and Straw. . . .

The Indian corn or maize proves the most useful grain in the world; and had it not been for the fruitfulness of this species, it would have proved very difficult to have settled some of the Plantations in America. It is very nourishing whether in bread, sodden or otherwise, and those poor Christian servants in Virginia, Maryland and the other northerly Plantations, that have been forced to live wholly upon it, do manifestly prove, that it is the most nourishing grain, for a man to subsist on, without any other victuals. And this assertion is made good by the negro slaves, who in many places eat nothing except this Indian Corn and Salt. Pigs and Poultry fed with this grain prove the sweetest of all others. It refuses no ground except the barren sand, and when planted in good ground will repay the planter seven or eight hundred fold, besides the Stalks bruised and boiled, make very pleasant Beer, being sweet like the Sugar-Cane. . . .

As for those of our own country in Carolina, some of the Men are very Laborious, and make great Improvements in their way; but I dare hardly give 'em the character in General. The easy way of living in that Plentiful Country, makes a great many Planters very negligent, which, were they otherwise, the Colony might now have been in a far better condition than it is as to trade and other advantages which universal industry would have led them into.

The Women are the most Industrious Sex in that place, and by their good Housewifery, make a good deal of Cloth of their own cotton, Wool and Flax; some of them keeping their families (though large) very decently apparel'd, both with linens and Woolens, so that they have no occasion to run into the Merchant's debt, or lay their Money out on stores for clothing.

The Christian Natives of Carolina are a straight, clean-limbed People; the Children being seldom or never troubled with Rickets, or those other distempers that the Europeans are visited withal. 'Tis next to a Miracle to see one of them deformed in body. The vicinity of the Sun makes no impression on Men, who labor out of doors or use the Waters. As for those Women who do not expose themselves to the Weather, they are often very Fair, and generally as Well-Featured as you shall see anywhere, and have very brisk charming eyes, which sets them off to advantage. They marry very young, some at thirteen and fourteen; and she that stays until twenty is reckoned a Stale Maid; which is a very indifferent character in that warm country. The Women are very fruitful, most of the Houses being full of little ones. It has been observed that women long married, and without children in other places, have removed to Carolina and become Joyful Mothers. . . . The girls are not bred up to the wheel and Sewing only, but the dairy and affairs of the House they are very well acquainted withal; so that you shall see them whilst very young, manage their business with a great deal of Conduct and Alacrity. The children of both Sexes are very docile, and learn anything with a great deal of ease and Method, and those that have the advantage of education, write good hands and prove good accountants, which is most Coveted, and indeed most necessary in these Parts. The young men are commonly of a bashful sober behavior; few proving prodigals to consume what the industry of their parents has left them, but commonly improve it. . . .

And now, as to the other Advantages the Country Affords, we do not guess at them at present, because as I said before, the best part of this country is not inhabited by the English, from whence probably will hereafter spring productions that this age does not dream of, and of much more advantage to the inhabitants than any things we are yet acquainted withal. . . .   1708

Cadwallader Colden
(1688-1776)

The son of a Scots minister, Cadwallader Colden received his A.B. at Edinburgh in 1705, then studied medicine in London. From 1710 to 1718, he was a businessman and physician in Philadelphia; in 1718 he moved to New York where he held political appointments and served as Lieutenant Governor of the colony from 1761 until his death. Colden wrote several studies in philosophy, science, and medicine, but he is best known for *The History of the Five Indian Nations Depending on the Province of New York* (New York, 1727). In a revised edition (London, 1747), Colden added a second part which brought his history up to the Treaty of Ryswick of 1697. A "Continuation" or third part was printed in Vol. IX of *The Letters and Papers of Cadwallader Colden* in the *N.Y. Hist. Soc. Colls.*, LXVIII (1937).

BIBLIOGRAPHY: *The Letters and Papers of Cadwallader Colden, 1711–1775*, 9 Vols. in *N.Y. Hist. Soc. Colls.*, L–LVI (1917–1923) and LXVII–LXVIII (1937). *Colden Letter Books, 1760–1775* in *N.Y. Hist. Soc. Colls.*, IX–X (1876–1877). *The History of the Five Indian Nations* (Ithaca, N.Y., 1958), reprint of Parts I (1727) and II (1747). Also ed. by John G. Shea (New York, 1866). Alice M. Keys, *Cadwallader Colden: A Representative Eighteenth Century Official* (New York, 1906).

From *The History of the Five Indian Nations*

A SHORT VIEW OF THE FORM OF GOVERNMENT OF THE FIVE NATIONS

It is necessary to know something of the Form of Government of the People whose History one reads. A few words will serve to give the Reader a general Notion of that of the Five Nations, because it still remains under Original Simplicity, free from those complicated Contrivances which have become necessary to those Nations where Deceit and Cunning have increased as much as their Knowledge and Wisdom.

The Five Nations (as their Name denotes) consist of so many Tribes or Nations join'd together by a League or Confederacy, like the United Provinces, without any Superiority of any one over the other. This Union has continued so long that the Christians know nothing of the Original of it.

They are known to the English under the Names of Mohawks, Oneydoes, Onnondagas, Cayugas and Sennekas; but it is probable that this Union at first consisted only of three Nations, *viz.* the Mohawks, Onnondagas and Sennekas, and that the Oneydoes and Cayugas were afterwards adopted or received into this League; for the Oneydoes acknowledge the Mohawks to be their Fathers, as the Cayugas do the Sennekas to be theirs.

Each of the Nations are distinguished into 3 Tribes or Families, who distinguish themselves by three different sorts of Arms or Ensigns, viz. the Tortoise, the Bear & the Wolf. The Sachems of these Families, when they sign any Public Papers, put the Mark or Ensign of their Family to it.

Each Nation is an absolute Republic by itself, govern'd in all Public Affairs of War and Peace by the Sachems or Old Men, whose Authority and Power is gain'd by and consists wholly in the Opinion the rest of the Nation have of their Wisdom and Integrity. They never execute their Resolutions by Compulsion or Force upon any of their People. Honor and Esteem are their Principal Rewards, as Shame & being Despised are their Punishments. They have certain Customs which they observe in their Public Affairs with other Nations, and in their Private Affairs among themselves, which it is scandalous for any one not to observe, and draw after them public or private Resentment when they are broke.

Their Generals and Captains obtain their Authority likewise by the general Opinion of their Courage and Conduct, and lose it by a Failure in those Virtues.

Their Great Men, both Sachems and Captains, are generally poorer than the common People, for they affect to give away and distribute all the Presents or Plunder they get in their Treaties or War, so as to leave nothing to themselves. If they should once be suspected of Selfishness, they would grow mean in the opinion of their Countrymen, and would consequently lose their Authority.

Their Affairs of Great Consequence, which concern all the Nations, are Transacted in a General Meeting of the Sachems of every Nation. These Conventions are generally held at Onnondaga, which is nearly in the Center of all the Five Nations. But they have fixed upon Albany to be the Place for their Solemn Treaties with the English Colonies.

The Tuscaroras, since the War they had with the People of Carolina, fled to the Five Nations, and are now incorporated with them, so that they now properly consist of Six Nations (tho' they still retain the old Name among the English). The Tuscaroras, since they came under the Government of New York, behave themselves well, and remain peaceable and quiet. By which may be seen the advantage of using the Indians well; and, I believe, if they were still better used, (as there is room enough to do it) the Indians would be proportionably more Useful to us.

As I am fond to think, that the present state of the Indian Nations exactly shows the most Ancient and Original Condition of almost every Nation; so I believe, here we may with more certainty see the Original Form of all Government, than in the most curious Speculations of the Learned; and that the Patriarchal, and other Schemes in Politics are no better than Hypotheses in Philosophy, and as prejudicial to real Knowledge.

PART I, CHAPTER I

. . . Thus began a War and Hatred between the French and the Five Nations, which cost the French much Blood, and more than once had like to have occasioned the entire Destruction of their Colony. The War had driven the Adirondacks to Quebec, and the desire of Trading with the French, had drawn likewise all their Allies that way, who agreed with them jointly, to make War against the Five Nations, and to attack them in their own Country.

Mr. Champlain desiring to give his Allies Proof of his Love, and the Valor of the French Nation, put himself at the Head of a Body of Adirondacks, and passed with them into Corlars Lake, which from this time the French have called by Mr. Champlain's name.

They had not long been in the Lake before they discover'd a Body of the Five Nations going to War. As soon as they saw each other, Shouts and Cries began on both Sides. Mr. Champlain made his men keep their Canoes at some distance; The Five Nations in the meantime landed, and began to entrench themselves, by cutting down the Trees round them; The Adirondacks stopt their Canoes near the Enemy, & sent to offer them Battle, who answer'd, That they must stay till Morning, when both sides would have the Advantage of the Day Light: The night passed in Dancing and War Songs, mixed with a thousand Reproaches against each other. Mr. Champlain had put some French in each Canoe, and order'd them not to show themselves, that their appearance might be the greater surprise to the Enemy, in the time of the Battle. As soon as daylight appeared, the Adirondacks landed, in order of Battle, & the Five Nations to the Number of 200 Men marched out of their Entrenchments, and put themselves in order, with three Captains in the Front, having large Plumes of Feathers on their Heads, and then advanced with a grave Air and slow Pace. The Adirondacks gave a great Shout and open'd to the Right and Left, to give room for Mr. Champlain and the French to advance: This new Sight surprised the Enemy, and made them halt, to consider it, upon which the French firing, the three Captains were killed: This more surpris'd the Five Nations; for they knew that their Captains had a kind of Cuirass made of pieces of Wood join'd together, that was Proof against Arrows, and they could not perceive in what manner the Wound was given, by which they fell so suddenly. Then the Adirondacks gave a terrible Shout, and attacked the Enemy, who received them bravely, but a second Volley from the French, put them into such Confusion (having never before seen fire Arms) that they immediately fled. The Adirondacks took twelve Prisoners, and as the Custom of the Indians is, burnt one of them alive, with great Cruelty; His Torment had continued much longer than it did, if Mr. Champlain had not in Compassion & abhorrence of such Barbarity, Shot the poor Wretch thro' the Head.

The Adirondacks having their Numbers thus very much increased, and their fire Arms giving them new Confidence, proposed nothing less to themselves, than the entire Destruction of the Five Nations, by open Force; And upon this their Young Warriors became Fierce and Insolent, and could not be kept under any Discipline, Order or Subjection to their Chiefs or Captains, but upon all Occasions rashly attacked the Enemy, who were oblig'd to keep themselves upon the Defensive, and to make up what they wanted in Force, by Stratagems, and a skillful management of the War. The Young Men of the Five Nations soon perceived the Advantages they gain'd by this Conduct, and every day grew more submissive to their Captains, and diligent in executing any Enterprise, while the Adirondacks confiding in their Numbers and their fire Arms, thought of nothing but of Conquering by mere Force.

The Five Nations sent out small Parties only, who meeting with great Numbers of the Adirondacks, retired before them, with seeming Fear and Terror, while the Adirondacks pursued them with Fury, and without thought, till they were cunningly drawn into Ambuscades, where most of their men were kill'd or taken Prisoners, with little or no loss to the Five Nations.

By these means and their being frequently surprised by the Five Nations, while they remain'd confident in their Number, the Adirondacks wasted away, and their boldest Soldiers were almost entirely destroyed, while the Number of the Five Nations rather increased by the addition of the Prisoners which they took from the Shawanons.

It has been a constant Maxim with the Five Nations, to save the Children and Young Men of the People they Conquer, to adopt them into their own Nation, and to educate them as their own Children, without Distinction; These young People soon forget their own Country and Nation; and by this Policy the Five Nations make up the Losses which their Nation suffers by the People they lose in War. The wisest and best Soldiers of the Adirondacks when it was too late, discovered that they must imitate and learn the Art of War from those Enemies, that they at first Despised. Now five of their Chief Captains endeavor to perform by themselves singly, with Art and by Stratagem, what they could not perform by Force at the Head of their Armies; but they having no longer any hopes of Conquering their Enemies, their thoughts were only set on Revenge.

The Five Nations had taken one of the chief Captains of the Adirondacks, and had burnt him alive. This gave Piskaret, who was the chief Captain of the Adirondacks so deep a Resentment, that the Difficulty or Danger of the most desperate Attempt made no Impression upon his Spirit, where he had the hope of Revenge.

I shall give the Particulars of this from the French Accounts; for by it the nature of the Indians, and the manner of their making War, may be more easily understood.

Piskaret, with four other Captains, set out from Trois Rivieres in one

Canoe, each being provided with three Fuzees. In two days they reach'd Sorel River, where they perceiv'd five Canoes of the Five Nations with ten Men in each. At first those of the Five Nations believed that this Canoe was the van of some considerable Party, and therefore went from it with all the force of their Paddles. When they saw that after a considerable time, no others followed, they returned, and as soon as they came within call, they raised their War-Shout, which they call Sassakue, and bid Piskaret and his Fellows Surrender. He answered, That he was their Prisoner, and that he could no longer survive the Captain they had burnt; but that he might not be accused of surrendering Cowardly, he bid them advance to the middle of the River which they did, with surprising Swiftness. Piskaret had before hand loaded all his Arms with two Bullets each, which he join'd together with a small Wire ten Inches in length with design to tear the Canoes in pieces (which it could not fail to do, they being made only of Birch Bark) and gave his Companions Direction, each to choose a Canoe, and level his shot between Wind and Water.

As the Canoes approached, he made as if he had design'd to escape; and to prevent him, those of the Five Nations separated from each other with too much Precipitation, and Surrounded him. The Adirondacks, the better to amuse the Enemy, sung their Death Song, as ready to surrender themselves, when every one suddenly took his Piece and fired upon the Canoes, which they Reiterated three times, with the Arms that lay ready. Those of the Five Nations were extremely surpris'd; for Fire Arms were still terrible to them, and they tumbled out of their Canoes, which immediately sunk. The Adirondacks knock't them all on the head in the Water, except some of the chiefs that they made Prisoners, whose Fate was as cruel as that of the Adirondack Captain, who had been burnt alive.

Piskaret was so far from having his Revenge glutted with this Slaughter, and the cruel Torments with which he made his Prisoners die, that it seem'd rather to give a keener edge to it; for he soon after attempted another enterprise in which the boldest of his Countrymen durst not accompany him.

He was well acquainted with the Country of the Five Nations, he set out alone about the time that the Snow began to melt, with the precaution of putting the hinder part of his Snow Shoes forward, that if any should happen upon his footsteps, they might think that he was gone the contrary way; and for further security went along a Ridge, where the Snow was melted, and where his footsteps could not be discovered, but in a few places. When he found himself near one of the Villages of the Five Nations he hid himself in a hollow Tree: In the Night he found out a Place nearer at hand, and more proper to retire into, for the execution of any Enterprise. He found four Piles of Wood standing close together, which the Indians had provided against the Winter and their busy times, in the middle of which was a hollow place, in which he thought he could safely hide. The whole Village was fast asleep when he enter'd a Cabin, kill'd four Persons and took off their Scalps, being all that were in the House, and then return'd quietly into his Hole. In the Morning the whole Village was in an Alarm, as soon as the Murder was discovered, and the young Men made all possible haste to follow the Murderer. They discover'd Piskaret's footsteps, which appear'd to them to be the footsteps of some Person that fled; this encourag'd them in their Pursuit: Sometimes they lost the Track, and sometimes found it again, till at last they entirely lost it, where the Snow was melted, and they were forced to return, after much useless fatigue. Piskaret quiet in the midst of his Enemies waited with impatience for the Night. As soon as he saw that it was time to act (*viz.* in the first part of the night, when the Indians are observed to sleep very fast) he enter'd into another Cabin, where he kill'd every Person in it, & immediately retir'd into his Woodpile. In the morning there was a greater Outcry than before, nothing was seen but Wailing, Tears, and a general Consternation. Everyone runs in quest of the Murderer, but no Track to be seen besides the Track which they saw the day before. They search'd the Woods, Swamps and Clifts of the Rocks, but no Murderer to be found. They began to suspect Piskaret, whose Boldness and Cunning was too well known to them. They agreed that two men next night should watch in every Cabin. All day long he was contriving some new Stratagem, he bundles up his Scalps, and in the night he slips out of his lurking place, He approaches one of the Cabins as quietly as possible and peeps thro' a hole to see what could be done, there he perceived Guards on the Watch, he went to another, where he found the same care. When he discover'd that they were everywhere upon their Guard he resolved to strike his last blow, and opened a Door, where he found a Sentinel nodding with his Pipe in his mouth, Piskaret split his Skull with his Hatchet, but had not time to take his Scalp, for another man who watched at the other end of the Cabin, raised the cry, and Piskaret fled. The whole Village immediately was in an Uproar, while he got off as fast as he could; Many pursued him, but as he was so swift as to run down the Wild Cows and the Deer, the pursuit gave him no great uneasiness; When he perceived they came near him, he would Hello to them, to quicken their pace, then spring from them like a Buck. When he gain'd any distance he would loiter till they came near, then hello, and fly. Thus he continued all day, with design to tire them out, with the hopes of overtaking him.

As they pursued only a single Man, five or six only of the Nimblest young Men continued the Chase, till being tired they were forced to rest in the Night, which when Piskaret observed, he hid himself near them in a hollow Tree. They had not time to take Victuals with them, and being wearied & hungry, and not apprehending any Attack from a single Person that fled, they all soon fell asleep. Piskaret observ'd them, fell upon them, kill'd them all, and carried away their Scalps.[1]

These Stories may seem incredible to many, but will not appear to be Improbable to those who know how extremely Revengeful the Indians naturally are. That they every day undertake the greatest Fatigues, the longest Journeys, and the greatest Dangers, to gratify that Devouring Passion, which seems to gnaw their Souls, and gives them no ease till it is satisfied. All Barbarous Nations have been observed to be Revengeful and Cruel, the certain Consequences of an unbounded Revenge, as the Curbing of these Passions is the happy Effect of being Civilized.

CHAPTER III

. . . Before I proceed further it will be necessary to insert a Remarkable Speech made by the Onnondagas and Cayugas, to the two Governors, on the 2d day of August, [1684] *viz.*

"Brother Corlaer;[2]

"Your Sachem is a great Sachem, and We are but a small People. But when the English came first to Manhattan,[3] Aragiske,[4] and to Yakokranagary,[5] they were then but a Small People, and we Great. Then, because we found you a good People, we treated you civilly, and gave you Land. We hope therefore, now that you are Great and we Small, you will protect us from the French. If you do not, we shall lose all our Hunting, and our Beavers. The French will get all the Beaver. They are now angry with us, because we carry our Beaver to our Brethren.

"We have put our Lands and our Selves under the Protection of the great Duke of York, the Brother of your great Sachem, who is likewise a great Sachem.

"We have given the Susquehanna River, which We won with the Sword, to this Government, and we desire that it may be a Branch of the great Tree that grows in this Place, the top of which reaches the Sun, and its Branches shelter us from the French, and all other Nations. Our Fire burns in your Houses, and your Fire burns with us. We desire that it may always be so.

"We will not that any of the great Penn's People settle upon the Susquehanna River; for we have no other Land to leave to our Children.

[1] These are the Trophies of Victory which all the Indian Nations carry home with them, if they have time to flay the Scalp from the Skull of their Enemies, when they have killed them; and sometimes they are so cruel as to flay the Scalp off, without killing them, or otherwise wounding them, but leave them in this miserable Condition with their Skull bare. [The notes throughout this selection are Colden's.]

[2] Or Corlard, Schenectady. But the Five Nations generally call the Governor of New York by this Name, and they often likewise comprehend under it the People of this Province.

[3] New York.

[4] Virginia.

[5] Maryland.

"Our young People are Soldiers, and when they are disobliged they are like Wolves in the Woods, as you Sachem of Virginia very well know.

"We have put ourselves under the great Sachem Charles, that lives on the other side of the great Lake. We give you these two White drest Deer-Skins to be sent to the great Sachem, that he may write on them, and put a great Red Seal to them, to Confirm what We now do, and put the Susquehanna River above the Wasuhta[6] and all the rest of our Land under the great Duke of York, and give that Land to nobody else. Our Brethren, his People, have been like Fathers to our Wives and Children, and have given us Bread, when we were in need of it: We will not therefore join ourselves or our Lands to any other Government but this. We desire Corlaer, our Governor, may send over this Proposition to the great Sachem, Charles, who dwells on the other side the great Lake, with this Belt of Wampum, and this other smaller Belt to the Duke of York, his Brother; And we give you, Corlaer, this Beaver, to send over this Proposition.

"You great Man of Virginia, We let you know, that great Penn did speak to us here in Corlaer's House, by his Agents, and desired to buy the Susquehanna River of us, but we would not hearken to him; for we had fasten'd it to this Government. We desire of you therefore, that you would bear Witness of what we now do, and that we now Confirm what we have done before. Let your Friend, the great Sachem that lives on the other side of the great Lake, know this, that We being a Free People, tho' united to the English, may give our Lands, and be join'd to the Sachem we like best. We give this Beaver to Remember what we say."

1727

[6] The Falls.

PERIODICAL ESSAYS

The New-England Courant

On August 7, 1721, James Franklin (1697–1735) published in Boston the first number of *The New-England Courant*, the first American paper to imitate *The Spectator*. Besides publishing young Benjamin Franklin's "Do-Good Papers," *The Courant* printed original essays by numerous hands, among them a group known as the "Couranteers" or "The Hell-Fire Club." When James Franklin was forbidden to print a paper without official approval, he continued *The Courant* under the name of Benjamin Franklin. *The Courant* ceased publication late in 1726 or early in 1727.

BIBLIOGRAPHY: Elizabeth C. Cook, *Literary Influences in Colonial Newspapers, 1704–1750* (New York, 1912), pp. 8–30. W. C. Ford, "Franklin's New England Courant," *Proc. Mass. Hist. Soc.*, LVII (1923–24), 336–353. Harold L. Dean, "The New England Courant, 1721–26: A Chapter in the History of American Culture," Ph.D. Thesis (Brown University, 1942).

From *The New-England Courant*

ESSAYS AND LETTERS

August 7, 1721

It's an hard case, that a Man can't appear in Print nowadays, unless he'll undergo the Mortification of Answering to ten thousand senseless and Impertinent Questions like these, Pray Sir, from whence came you? And what Age may you be of, may I be so bold? Was you bred at College Sir? And can you (like some of them) square the Circle, and cypher as far as the Black Art? &c. Now, tho' I must confess it's something irksome to a Man in haste, thus to be stopp'd at his first setting-out, yet in Compliance to the Custom of the Country where I now set up for an Author, I'll immediately stop short, and give my gentle Reader some Account of my Person and my rare Endowments.

As for my Age, I'm some odd Years; and a few Days under twice twenty and three, therefore I hope no One will hereafter object against my soaring now and then with the grave Wits of the Age, since I have dropt my collar Feathers, and am pretty well fledg'd: but if they should tell me that I am not yet fit nor worthy to keep Company with such Illustrious Sages, for my Beard doesn't yet reach down to my Girdle, I shall make them no other Answer than this, *Barba non facit Philosophum.*

I make no Question my gentle Readers, but that you're very Impatient to see me entirely dissected, and to have a full View of my outward as well as inward Man, but as I stopt short now, merely to oblige you, so I shall stop as short here, and give no farther Account of myself until this Day fortnight, when you shall have a farther Account of this useful Design, and of my best Endowment of Body and Mind.

And to engage the World to converse farther with us, they'll find me in the good Company of a certain Set of Men, of whom I hope to give a very good Account,

> Who like faithful Shepherds take care of their Flocks,
> By teaching and practicing what's Orthodox,
> Pray hard against Sickness, yet preach up the POX!

N.B. This Paper will be published once a Fortnight, and out of mere Kindness to my Brother-Writers, I intend now and then to be (like them) very, very dull; for I have a strong Fancy, that unless I am sometimes flat and low, this Paper will not be very grateful to them.

abnormit sapiens.—Hor.

March 12, 1722

To the Author of the *New-England Courant*

Sir,

By the last Gazette I understand the Town is to be Favored with some Medical Cases, being the Author's proper Observations. That he may have a Precedent to go by, and be sufficiently furnished with hard Words, which altho' he himself does not understand, may be of use to amuse his Patients and Readers: Please to advise him to Hall's Coffee House, to a London Paper call'd *Pharmacopeia Circumforaneus;* Or, The Horse Doctor's Harangue to the credulous Mob: And for the benefit of the Public allow the following Sample of it, a place in your Paper.

Gentlemen, I Waltho Van Claturbank, Ulcocalculus, &c. out of mere Pity to myself, and languishing Mortals, &c. have been at last prevailed upon to oblige the World with this Notice.

My Medicines work either Hypnotically, Hydrotically, Cathartically, Poppismatically, Hydrogogically, Pneumatically, or Synechdochically.

By my Pulvis Vermifugus, I brought away Worms by Urine as long as the Maypole in the Strand, when it flourished in its primitive Prolixity, tho' I confess not altogether so thick.

Gentlemen, beware of Counterfeits, for there are such abroad. A certain outlandish Pretender to Physic, a young raw Fellow, lately recommended to the Mufti, gave him a Potion of Physic for a certain disorder in his Head, proceeding from a foul Stomach; it wrought so severely by throwing out a Deluge of Black Choler and nasty Stuff, that had it not been for the timely interposition of his Friends, he would have Spew'd up his Guts and burst his Gall Bladder. I advised him to have no more dealings with such Aesculapiedes's. Notwithstanding, he as I am told, has had a second Dose more Detersive and Inciding than the first; I wish the violent Operation and Straining may not occasion an Extravasation in his Brains, and oblige him to a confinement in the Infirmary in the Common. The Hades! the Hades! of Seven Hundred and Sixty who died of the natural Small Pox last September, October, and November, he killed near Seven Hundred, tho' perhaps it exceeds the number of his Patients. *Ubi duo Medici, ibi tres Athei*, that is, in broad English, Three halfs of our Practitioners are wicked Men.

I cur'd Prester John's Grandmother of a Stupendious Dolor about the *Os Sacrum*, so that the good old Lady really fear'd the perdition of Huckle Bone. I did it by fomenting her Posteriors with a Mummy of Nature call'd Pilgrim's Salve, mixt up with Spirit of Mugwort Tartaragraphated thro' an Alembic of Crystalline Transfluency.

So Ignorant and Addle-pated are the Empirics abroad, that when a Person is within Two or Three Hours of Death, they pretend to his Friends that he is upon the Recovery. Nay further, I can name a certain Virtuoso who from a Scotomia and Vertigo is dead, and has smell'd Cadaverous many Years; yet these foolish pretending Quacks tell us it is only a *Passio Hypocondrica*, and use his Corpse like a living Christian, first by gentle Administrations, then Inoculation and counter-Inoculation, Rubisicantia Vesicantia, &c. and last week from a strong Stimulatory Cathartic which has lodged sometime in his Bowels, he purged along with Excrement such a quantity of vicious matter, that all the Town were obliged to hold their Noses. O the Mania! O the Vesania of our Practitioners!

I cur'd an Alderman of Grand Cairo, who had been Sick Seven Years of the Plague, in 46 minutes. And by the like Empirical Remedies, I lately cured Duke Phalorix of a Dropsy of which he died.

I cur'd likewise the Duchess of Boromolpho of a Cramp in her Tongue; and the Count de Rodomontado corrupt with an Iliac Passion, contracted by eating buttered Parsnips.

In *Bostonopolis* I perform'd the *Transplantatio Variolarum* on *Effendi Blanco*, A Grecian, Great Counsellor of a Great Counsellor to one of the Bashas of Nov-Anglia on the Atlantic. I'll swear it secur'd him against ever having the Small Pox in the Common Way; and upon my Word and Honor, it cur'd him of a Pthifis of Consumption of which he died. *Ven-*

ienti occurrite morbo, Transplantation! Inoculation! Who is for Inoculation! Gentlemen, you see my Certificate for this Turkish Practice, attested by some of the Sons of Mahomet.

Quarenda pecunia primum est; be not Sick too late.

Oct. 8, 1722
Nuhaven, Sept. 20, 1722

Master Coranto,

Thare has bein a most grevous rout and hurle-burle amung us, ever sense the nine Ministurs are turn'd *Hi-Church-men:* Fokes sa, they have draun up a riting and sind it, wharin tha declar, that all owr Churches are no Churches, and owr Ministurs no Ministurs, and that tha have no more Athorriti to administur the Ordenances thun so mani Porturs or Plow-Joggurs: Sum of owr Pepel danse ater thare Pipe, and tel us that owr Ministurs formurli ware ordan'd by Midwives and Coblurs; but other sa that this is folce Doktrin, and belongs to the Church of Rume; and thare hes bin a strange Man amung us, sum sa he is a Jeshuet, othurs say he is Tore: For my Part I dont noe him; but I herd sum of my naburs sa tha fere him as bad as a Rattel-snak, and othurs admir him as much. He it is (Fokes sa) that hes converted owr Ministurs, by tauking with um, and lending um Boocks: And tis sed he tuk grate Panes with the Pepel to inliten um. Now tis buzd abute, that in ordur to Salvashun, we must beleve the unenteurrupted Sukseshun of Bishups from the Upostels, and the Heredere Endefezabel Rite of Prenses, and that Parlementare Rite is a mere Noshun; that all the Churches in the Wurld that ant govern'd by Bishups, are not part of the Cathalike Church, but are out of the ordnare Rode of Salvashun. For my Part, I wod fane noe whathar these are Docktrins of the Church of Ingland: Tha sa the Ministurs ar not abel to anser um, and so tha make this exkuse, becose tis the Istablisht Church; but I think it is hi time for um to rite abute this Mattur, when all the Pepel are runnin mad.

I am, Mustur Coranto,
Yors tel Deth,
JETHRO STANDFAST

March 11, 1723

To old JANUS the Couranteer

Sir,

The extraordinary Disturbance made at Mr. Gatchell's Dancing School in Hannover-Street, may be thought worth taking Notice of in Your

Paper. On Thursday the 28th of February, a Company of Young Lads, who were deny'd Admittance, after firing several Volleys of Oaths and Curses, threatening to kill Mr. Gatchell, and using abundance of obscene Discourse not fit to be mention'd, they fell upon the Glass Windows, shatter'd them all to Pieces, & broke one of the Iron Bars. On Monday Night last 10 of them were brought before a Justice of the Peace, who was oblig'd to remove from his House to the Town-House, by Reason of the great Concourse of People. The Lads owned they were there, but denied the Fact: However, several Witnesses being sworn against them, they were bound over to Answer it at the Sessions. 'Tis now grown too common for our Children and Youth to Swear and Curse in the Streets, and to abuse with foul Language, not only one another, but their Superiors; And this growing Wickedness is certainly in great Measure owing to the many Servants brought from other Countries, who seldom fail of ruining most of the Children in the Families where they live. But I leave others to propose a Method for preventing or punishing these Enormities and remain,

Sir,

Your Humble Servant, &c.

April 15, 1723

To old Master JANUS

Sir,

The extravagant Notions which some Men entertain from the Influence of Education and Custom, may be thought worth Notice in your paper, if we consider only, that the Sufferings of its late Publisher were owing in a great measure to his carrying it on in an unusual Method. Had he stayed till some Gentlemen of the best Reputation in our Country had run the venture of being witty, and wrote a competent Number of Joco-Serious Dialogues, he might have continu'd his Paper without incurring the charge of Shocking and Heaven-rending Blasphemy! I must ask Mr. Symmes's Pardon, if I improve his late Joco-Serious Discourse concerning Regular Singing, in Vindication of the *Courant:* And if I am as merry with the Anti-Couranteers as he is with the scrupulous Consciences of his Anti-Regular-Singers, I may yet hope to find Five able Hands in Town and Country, who will (at least) approve of the Substance and Design of the Letter.

And now, you Gentlemen, who are the avowed Enemies of the *Courant,* let me beseech you to beware of a certain Joco-Serious Dialogue, wrote by a Clergyman, (Heaven forgive him!) which inevitably tends to the Subversion of your Religion. Have you not often said, that the *Courant* offended GOD because it offended good People? And has not *he* (think you) offended many a weak Brother, almost as weak as yourselves, by declaring against the *good old Way* of Singing? Are not the Select-Men of Milton good Men, who have the Protestant Religion so much at heart as to forbid the teaching of Regular Singing in their Borders, lest it should infect the whole Town with Popery; and will not they (think you) be offended with this abominable Joco-Serious Confabulation? You make a grievous Complaint against the *Courant,* because (you say) it exposes the Failings of particular Persons. And does not Mr. Symmes (not to mention all his broad Hints) in Scorn call one of his Neighbors a good Man who is shy of his Bible, &c. Nay does he not say of one whom he calls a Reverend Brother, that whatever he is for a Christian, he is but a poor Tool of a Scholar, and ridicule him both in English and Latin? Fie upon him! Has he never heard of the Fate of Mr. Turner (a Gentleman of the Law) who was indicted by the Grand-jury of Plymouth County for profaning the Name of Justice O——s, or which he was oblig'd to stand at the Bar and plead Not Guilty before the whole Court? And does he not know, that a famous Country justice sent a Warrant after poor Jeremiah Levett of Rochester, because he (being of no good Name and Fame) did upon the 19th Day of March, 1717.18. give out and utter reviling and blasphemous Words against a Justice of the Peace? I can assure him this is true, for I have a Copy of the Warrant now in my Hands. And is it not a greater Crime to write Blasphemy against a Minister of the Gospel, than to give out and utter reviling and blasphemous Words against a Justice of the Peace? But further Gentlemen, I desire you to consider how intolerably he has abus'd your Ancestors, by saying some of your Fathers and Grandfathers could not read, and that they are gone to Heaven the wrong way. The Reverend Mr. Alsop indeed says, that some Men are sent to Heaven upon pain of Death; but shou'd you meet with such a Phrase in the *Courant,* wou'd you not presently affirm it to be against the Principles of Religion? I have but one thing more to observe to you, Gentlemen, and that is, that you bitterly inveigh against the *Courant* when you find things serious and comical inserted in the same Paper, tho' in different Pieces: But has not Mr. Symmes quoted Texts of Scripture in the same Page wherein he reproaches the Anti-Regular-Singers with their Ignorance of the Gunpowder-Plot? And has he not mixt the Faithful Servants of Jesus Christ, Learning and Wisdom and Piety, Family Religion, &c. in the same Page with Barns, Ploughs and Carts, and whole Barrels of Herring? Is he not very often witty and good humour'd at the proper Cost and Charge of Solomon, the Prophets and Apostles? &c. What else can you make of his saying, (p. 34.) "In plain English Neighbor, a broad Laugh, is all the Answer such whimsical Objections deserve: or rather, a hearty, Scowl or deep Sigh, to observe the doleful Effects of Man's Apostasy. To be oppress'd with such Objections would make a wise man mad, Eccl. 7.7.?"

Upon the whole, Friend Janus, we may conclude, that the Anti-Couranteers are a sort of Precisians, who mistaking Religion for the peculiar Whims of their own distemper'd Brain, are for cutting or stretching all Men to their own Standard of Thinking. I wish Mr. Symmes's Character may secure him from the Woes and Curses they are so free of dispensing among their dissenting Neighbors, who are so unfortunate as to discover a Cheerfulness becoming Christianity. Sir Thomas Pope Blount in his *Essays*, has said enough to convince us of the Unreasonableness of this sour Temper among Christians; and with his Words I shall conclude.

"Certainly (says he) of all Sorts of Men, none do more mistake the Divine Nature, and by consequence do greater mischief to Religion, than those who would persuade us, That to be truly Religious, is to renounce all the Pleasures of Human Life; As if Religion were a *Caput Mortuuri*, a heavy, dull, insipid thing; that has neither Heat, Life, nor motion in it: Or were intended for a Medusa's Head to transform Men into Monuments of Stone. Whereas (really) Religion is of an Active Principle, it not only elevates the Mind, and invigorates the Fancy; but it admits of Mirth, and pleasantness of Conversation, and indulges us in our Christian Liberties; and for this reason, says the Lord Bacon, *It is no less impious to shut where God Almighty has open'd, than to open where God Almighty has shut.* But, I say, if Men will suffer themselves to be thus impos'd upon, as to Believe, That Religion requires any such unnecessary Rigors and Austerities, all that can be said, is, The fault does not lie in Religion, but in their Understandings; Nor is this to paint Religion like herself, but rather like one of the Furies with nothing but Whips and Snakes about her. And so, they Worship God just as the Indians do the Devil, not as they love him, but because they are afraid of him. It is not therefore to be wonder'd, that since their Notions of God are such, their Way of Worship is agreeable thereunto; And hence it is, That these Men serve our God, just as some Idolaters Worship theirs; with painful Convulsions of Body, and unnatural Distortions of Face, and all the dismal solemnities of a gloomy Soul, and a dejected Countenance. Now these are the Men, who upon all Occasions are so apt to condemn their Brethren, and, as if they were of God's Cabinet Council, pretend to know the Final Decrees of the Almighty. But alas! who is sufficient for these Things? Certainly, no Man can render himself more foolishly ridiculous, than by meddling with these Secrets of Heaven."

I am, Sir, Your Humble Servant,
TIMOTHY WIGSTAFF

The South Carolina Gazette

With the financial support of Benjamin Franklin, Thomas Whitmarsh (d. 1733) established *The South Carolina Gazette* at Charleston on Jan. 8, 1732. When Whitmarsh died, Lewis Timothy (d. 1738), another of Franklin's printers, assumed editorship; following Timothy's death, his family continued the paper, which ceased publication in 1775. Only three of the anonymously written "Meddlers Club Papers" appeared in *The Gazette*, but the paper printed a considerable number of original essays.

BIBLIOGRAPHY: *The South Carolina Gazette, 1732–1775*, in *South Carolina Newspapers, 1732–1782*, Microfilm, Charleston Library Society (Charleston, S.C., 1956). Hennig Cohen, *The South Carolina Gazette, 1732–1775* (Columbia, S.C., 1953).

From *The South Carolina Gazette*

From THE MEDDLERS CLUB PAPERS

August 16, 1735

To Mr. Lewis Timothy.
Now we for want of Buss——ness come
To you to be thus troublesome,
To interrupt the better sort
Of Disputants, and not spoil sport.

Sir,

Among the innumerable and various Clubs, both in Europe and America, many of whom the famous *Spectator* and *Tatler* give an Account of, I know of none by the name of the *Meddlers Club:* This name I believe is new, and an Original; I am sure it is in this part of the World. It is not long since, that a parcel of young illiterate Fellows assembled together, and erected a Club of the name above mentioned, one of whom I have the happiness to be. We consist of six Persons only, and the rest have ordered me to write to you, and desire, if you have nothing else of greater moment, to insert this in your Gazette, we are constant Readers of your Papers, three of the Club taking them: And altho' the highest of our Wit does not come up to that of a Waterman's Boy, or a Pie-corner Bard, yet we have forsooth set up for Reformers, (that is of ourselves) or Meddlers of Nobody's business, or to speak plainer, of everybody's: For we have set that refin'd Maxim of Nobody's meaning everybody; tho' we shall in particular avoid all personal Reflections, and don't doubt but our Countrymen will be as well pleased to see the Attempts of Carolinians, tho' weak, as to see foreign Pieces of more refin'd Sense, since our Intentions are good, tho' our Capacities small.

You must know then that our Club is made up of the following persons,

Imprimis, The first in degree, called Jack, would be Taller: For tho' he is the least person among us, yet according to the old Proverb, *of little head great Wit,* we have, and I hope not unjustly, thought that a little Body must have most Sense. His Talent consists chiefly in contradicting others, and thinks he knows more than all the Club; for which reason I have plac'd him first.

Item, the second is Tom Snigger, his Talent lies most in telling Stories, and because nobody else will, laughs at them himself.

Item, The third is Dick Haughty; he thinks merit no where but in fine Clothes, but is otherwise a very agreeable person.

Item, The fourth is Will Generous; I can't describe his Talent any otherwise, only to let the World know, that he is not covetous, though a little conceited.

Item, The fifth is called Ralph Hippo; he was formerly Clerk to a Horse Doctor, from whom Ralph has gain'd so much Experience, that he is ever boasting, that he believes himself able to wash the fairest Woman's hands clean when they are dirty, if she would let him, tho' perhaps it might cost her Life.

Item, The Sixth and last is myself, whose name is Bob Careless, because I am the most careless Fellow breathing.

The rest of the Members have imposed this Task upon me, because it was in opposition to my Temper, and in all I have said you may see how carelessly I have display'd our several Talents: I hope some one of the others will write next and describe them better; for they say, if you will receive and print their Performances, you may depend upon hearing from us once a month without fail, especially if the Town receive them well, which they desire to see signified in your Paper.

With all these extraordinary Endowments we have, as I said before, set up ourselves for Meddlers, and tho' perhaps some of us may chance to get our Heads broke for it, yet if you'll assist, we doubt not, (after reforming ourselves a little) but we shall be able to divert nobody into a better Opinion of us; for we have resolved not to meddle with Church or State Affairs, but to learn Morality ourselves (which we want God knows), satirize our Friends, and speak well of our Enemies, not the Country's Enemies, but the private ones this Undertaking will bring upon us, for you know *all good Designs are attended with Envy.*

We derived our name from a *Medlar,* as some call it, which is never ripe till rotten, and I believe we shall be the same: Others call them Parsimons, i.e. Parsimony, which I interpret to be Coveteousness; but as we are of so small standing, we have not yet bought a Dictionary to explain such Words to us; however we will not be coveteous, tho' we are Meddlers. We took the hint of having Six from a learned Dispute between two Hackney-Wits about the Proverb, *that a half Loaf was better than no Bread,* the one affirming that Proverb to be of no sense, and the other that it was: The Moderator, who was a M.A., after hearing the reasons on both sides, allowed both Arguments to be equally good, like a Diagonal line drawn through a Quadrangle makes two equilateral Triangles. We are canvassing this sentence, and have form'd ourselves into two Triangles, but can't bring it to bear: If any of your Readers can assist us, we shall be oblig'd to them, otherwise I am afraid we must remain as great Blockheads on that Subject as we was before commenced Meddlers, and

Sir,

Your most humble Servants.

Sign'd by order of the Club,

Bob Careless

August 30, 1735

Ill Customs by Degrees to Habits rise,
Ill Habits soon become exalted Vice.

DRYDEN

Sir,

In the two last we have sufficiently shown our Design of Meddling, in this you have more of the Proceedings of our Club, and we intend to let no Vice escape our censure, whether 'tis heeded or not.—The Vice that was debated on this Evening, altho' 'tis plain to the whole Town, yet 'tis so little minded, or else so customary that 'tis unobserved to be one, is the Vice of the Bay.

—Says Dick Haughty, I can't help taking Notice of the great Concourse of People of both Sexes that assembles on the Bay almost every Evening: And I think as we are Meddlers that that is a Topic worthy our Observation; for in my Opinion, it is a Custom that will never resound to the Honor of Carolina, and tends to promote Vice and Irreligion in many Degrees. And tho' it may be objected that the Heat of the Climate will not permit them to walk in the Day, and it can't but conduce to their Health to walk and take the air; yet I think there are many more fitting places to walk on than the Bay: For have we not many fine Greens near the Town much better accommodated for Air, than a Place which continually has all the nauseous Smells of Tar, Pitch, Brimstone, &c. and what not, and where every Jack Tar has the Liberty to view & remark the most celebrated Beauties of Charles Town, and where besides (if any Air is) there's such a continual Dust, that I should think it were enough to deter any Lady from appearing, lest her Organs of perspiration should be stopt, and she be suffocated.

Your Observation is right, reply'd Will Generous, for I have heard that in Great Britain the Ladies and Gentlemen choose the Parks and such like Places to walk and take the Air in, but I never heard of any Place's making use of the Wharfs for such Purpose, except this, and in my humble Opinion I think the Greens a much better Place than the Bay.

Besides, says Ralph Hippo, Salt-Water Air does not agree with chaste and virtuous Minds, for 'tis notorious that Sea-faring Men are more venereal than others, and I believe it has the same effect on—

Hold, says Bob Careless. Did you never hear that the Ancients defined Venus to be Sea-born, and it plainly appears that their Definition was just, since the most of her Votaries in Charles Town make their Victories in the sight of the Sea, and her mischievous Son Cupid has shot more Darts on the Bay than in all Carolina; besides 'tis there that little Elf triumphs, and 'tis there he wounded me, and I have just reason to complain, since the Fair is inexorable and otherwise employ'd: for

> Cupid, I hear, has got two Darts,
> With which he pierces Lovers' hearts,
> The one of Gold which causes Love,
> The other Lead dire Hate does move.

and he has shot his Leaden one at her, and his Golden one at me—

I shall only add, says Tom Snigger, that I have heard it said, that most Women love Sea-faring Men better than Land Men, and who knows but most that appear there do it with a design to pick up a Sea spark, since they have all unanimously agreed that the Bay must be the happy Place of their Walks, and altho' Night has no Eyes, yet the Ladies' Eyes will give Light enough to distinguish who is a Seaman, and who is not.

It being my Turn next, I told them I concurred in all their Opinions, and would add something of my own, tho' I thought it dangerous to meddle with the Fair Sex, yet since it was the Will of the Club, I should think myself unworthy of the Honor of being a Meddler, if I did not my Endeavors as well as the rest, and I think as the Text says, that an ill Custom may soon breed an ill Habit, &c. For should one of those illustrious Fair Ones happen to be singled out by one who was no better than a common Jack Tar but should have borrowed some finer Clothes, and should pretend to be a Gentleman, and tho' of so short an Acquaintance as two or three Evenings, after promising the Fair One Marriage, should find her pliant, desire her to walk a little further in private, and there perform what I dare not name,

> The willing Fair she soon consents,
> Till marks appear, she then repents.

What a Scandal is here brought upon her Friends, if she has any! and a Disgrace to herself as long as she lives; and all this occasion'd by the Vice of the Bay. I would not have the Ladies cruel, but I would have them be cautious with whom they deal with, and not be too fond and obliging to Strangers, whilst our perhaps more deserving Carolinians lay ne-

glected. If the foregoing have any effects upon this Vice, we have our
End and Aim; if not, we have done our Duty as Meddlers, and so shall
rest contented on that head.—If you see fit to give this a Place in your
Gazette, you will oblige

Your Friends and humble Servants the Meddlers

Sign'd

JACK WOULD BE TALLER

A Reply to the Meddlers

September 6, 1735

Every Fool is Meddling

PROVERBS XX. VERSE 3.

To Mr. Lewis Timothy, Printer in Charles-Town.

SIR,

Observing for some time past, for want of something either foreign, or
some more sprightly Genius among ourselves to fill the first part of your
Papers, that you have been forced to complete your Sheet with anything
that comes to hand, I (who am your Subscriber and a Carolinian) thought
I might as well for once see something from myself in your Paper, at a
time when it has been lately fill'd with so unedifying and impertinent
Stuff, from a Club rightly by themselves termed Meddlers. A Name truly
worthy, and defined with the utmost Accuracy from the Word Parsimo-
nious, that from Parsimons, then with an *i.e.* (to let you know they
would understand Latin) Meddlers. A pretty beginning and no less ending without Connection, Sense or Harmony, saving the Name of the Club
agreeing with the particular Talents of its addled Clubsters. I am sorry
that they think so much of their own parts, that they would make the
World believe they were Carolinians, when their Performance is so void
of Sense, and their Design (if I may so call it) but sprung from the spurious Issue of a boozy bottle. We your Subscribers in this part had as lief
you would relate the celebrated History of *Jack the Giantkiller*, or *Tom
Thumb's Exploits*, which would bring to remembrance the Innocency of
our childish Years, when such Trifles were relished. I have not had my
second Paper, and am not sorry, since I find by the third a Continuation
of their first, but the third informs of their learned Debate they had of
the Vice of the Bay, where Tar, and Jack Tar is the most of the Subject, the offensiveness of Tar; a smell most People counts healthy, when
the inoffensiveness of common sweet Powder strikes them dead, if it
comes within a quarter of a Mile of their Wigs. I think the Ladies are
much obliged to the worthy Censors for cautioning them against Jack

Tars in Gentlemen's Coats; and with an Air of severity, desire they wou'd spend their evening walk on the Green, which I dare answer for them, they think much more proper for their Occasions than the Bay, the most frequented place in Town, thereby intimating their Desire to give a green Gown behind a Pine Bush, which wou'd be more pleasant than in a Cart. But not to be further tedious, as I expect to be answered by Bob the Careless Secretary, who never had care in his life but this once in characterizing himself in his true Colors that without studying he may easily guess, I say without further answering what they may say, I refer him to the above Motto which I think is *a propos* both to their Principles as the name of their Club. I conclude myself.

Diogenes Rusticus

The Virginia Gazette

William Parks (c. 1698–1750), a protege of Benjamin Franklin, published the first number of *The Virginia Gazette* on Aug. 6, 1736, at Williamsburg. After Parks' death, the paper continued under other editors until 1780. "The Monitor Essays," anonymous contributions probably written by students and faculty at William and Mary College, appeared in *The Gazette* in 1736–1737. Though the first five numbers of the paper are not extant, at least twenty-two "Monitor Essays" were written. While many of *The Gazette's* essays were reprinted from other papers, about half of the essays appearing before 1766 were original contributions.

BIBLIOGRAPHY: *The Virginia Gazette of Williamsburg, 1736 to 1780*, Microfilm, Institute of Early American History and Culture (Williamsburg, Va., 1950). William H. Castles, Jr., *The Virginia Gazette, 1736–1766: Its Editors, Editorial Policies, and Literary Content*, Ph.D. Thesis (University of Tenn., 1962), University Microfilms, Inc., Ann Arbor, Mich.

From *The Virginia Gazette*

From THE MONITOR ESSAYS

The MONITOR. No. 6

Sept. 10, 1736

Simia quam similis, turpissima bestia, nobis?
CIC., *de Nat. Deorum*

The other Night, as I was lolling in my Elbow-Chair, in my Study, I was contriving some Method to give our Fair Letitia Tattle a View of my long Nose; when, of a sudden, I was surpris'd with Three Taps at the Door of my outward Chamber. My Man Dominic going to the Door, which was only half shut, flew back again in a great Fright, and told me he was sure it was the Devil, for he never saw such a Figure before. Pray, Sir, said I, desire the civil Gentleman to walk in; and do you set Chairs.

At the first Interview, I was inclin'd to my Man's Opinion, that 'twas a Devil; but whether Male, or Female, was in Doubt.

The Figure was upwards of Six Feet, a swarthy Complexion, a large Bottle-Nose, that spread so far on each Cheek, that took a great deal off from the Length of the Face; the Eyes no bigger than Ferrets', and full as Red; the Mouth very large, and the Under-Lip hung over the Chin. The Dress was a Man's Hat; a Woman's short Cloak, that hung loose down to the Waist, which play'd to and fro', and gave Air to the Body (which was without Stays); from the Waist downwards, was a large Pair of Trousers fit for a Burgher-Master.

As soon as we were seated, Dominic trembling, got behind my Chair, and whisper'd me, the Candle burnt blue. I order'd him to withdraw, and shut the Door after him, which he was willing to comply with. After taking a thorough View, I desired to know in what Manner I was to address myself, Sir, or Madam? The Answer was, I am a Woman, Sir, and Mistress of a large Family; I find you are much surpris'd at my Dress, therefore I shall explain it, and proceed to my Business.

You are to know, Sir, I am a Woman of Fashion; I was born and bred in France, and the Dress you see me in, was French originally, but now modeliz'd.

In the Years 19 and 20, which were the Two Years, France, Holland, and England, were searching for the Philosopher's Stone, I was then at what we Women call, Years of Discretion; that is, to be capable of Distinguishing, to know what's Becoming, and what not. In the first Place we, One and All, agreed to shave—our Heads; and to supply this Defect (if any were so stupid as to think it one) a Peruke was propos'd, curl'd quite round, and very short, like unto that of a Shock Dog, which we call the *Tête de Mutton:* Upon this a Coif was sew'd; so that without any Trouble, we could dress, and undress the Head. This I left off upon my Arrival; and to supply the Place, betook me to the Man's Hat.

The next Thing to complete our French Dress, was the Robe *Volante*, what the Vulgar call'd a *Sac*. This was a loose Gown full of Pleats, and without any Girdle: In which Habit we frequently took the Air on Horseback. I must inform you, our Manner there was to ride on Stride; therefore to answer that Part of the Dress, you see me loose to the Waist. As to my Breeches, they are an Improvement upon the Fashion, and what our Sex, when accustom'd to, will not dislike to wear.

I told her, I thank'd her for her Relation, but that I was going to be busy, therefore desired her to be Brief: To which she reply'd, Sir, I'll take up as little of your Time as possible, and therefore shall come to the Point.

I am inform'd you are acquainted with the *Monitor;* and therefore what I have to propose, is to serve him: I love to do all the Good in my Power: I have Six Daughters (God bless them all!) and each of them capable of any Post he shall think proper to confer upon them.

Here I was more confounded than ever, and took the Woman to be mad; to which I reply'd, Madam, What Post are they desirous of? O! Sir, reply'd the Lady, they have different Talents. There's my Eldest Daughter Miss Leer, is as good a Girl at Attraction, as any in the Country; and will draw a Circle about her immediately where ever she goes.

Then my Second, Miss Sly; She has not one Bit of French in her, she's as Secret as Death.—Believe me, Sir, she was once in a Company of 12 Women for 6 Hours, and never opened her Lips. You may set her down for some important Occasion.

My Third Daughter, Miss Fidget; She's here and there and everywhere; she never misses a Tea-Table, if there be Ten within the Compass of her Visits in a Day. There she hears Slander, Back-biting, and Scandal; which may turn out to some Use.

As to my Fourth Daughter, Amoret; She's a fine Girl, that's the Truth on't: She's forever moist'ning her Lips with her Tongue, that gives them a pouting Ripeness that tempts all the young Fellows in the Town; then she's a Girl of a very inquisitive Temper; so she may be excellent in her Way.

My Fifth Daughter, Phillis; She's an unaccountable Girl. The first Week of every Moon, she's dying for Love of some Adonis, or other.—She's forever receiving or answering of Billet-doux, and Scraps of Poetry; which may not be amiss.

As to my youngest Daughter, Euphemia; She's courted by Sir Politic Would-be; he can inform her how Affairs stand in——(but no Matter) She's a Girl of a bright Genius, and very willing; therefore, I take her to be undeniable.

And now, Sir, I have given you an Account of my Family. I live a great Way off; and as this was my chief Errand, I hope you'll dispatch me to my Satisfaction. If you please to enjoin them or me to Secrecy, they're within Call.

To which I reply'd, since they were so desirous of Employment, I would engage them or the *Monitor;* but could not put them into immediate Service, 'til the *Monitor* had weigh'd the Matter, and considered their respective Qualifications: That if she pleas'd to send for them, I would talk to them: Upon which the good Lady, with the utmost Transport, seiz'd hold of a Pen, call'd for Half a Sheet of Paper, and dispatch'd her Messenger directly. I importun'd her, in the meantime, to refresh her self, and recruit her Spirits with a Glass of Wine, after her Fatigue; and in a short Space of Time, the Ladies appear'd. After a little Discourse,

they told me, if I distrusted their Honors, they were willing to be enjoin'd by Oath. Upon which I thought I could not administer any Oath
upon the Occasion, more binding than that of the Free Masons; and,
after fast'ning the Door, and going thro' some of the usual Forms, I tender'd it to them, which they took with great Solemnity.

N.B. Their different Employments will be settled as soon as possible.

Z

The MONITOR. No. 9

Oct. 15, 1736

Cautus enim metuit foveam Lupus, accipiterque
Suspectos laqueos, et opertum miluus hamum.
Oderunt peccare Boni Virtutis amore,
Tu nihil admittes in te formidine poenae;
Sit spes fallendi: Miscebis sacra profanis.

HOR., *Epist. xvi. Lib. I.*

Worshipful Sir,

I Beg Leave to know, if it be decent to laugh at a Humorous Scene,
without putting my Fan before my Face?

When I was last in Town, I had the Pleasure of being an humble
Spectator to see the *Beaux-Stratagem* perform'd; Where, I confess, I was
highly delighted with Love's Catechism. Miss Tancrede (who sat next to
me,) of a sudden, gave me a most terrible Hunch with her Elbow, and
told me, I was the most insufferable Coquette that liv'd; that she should
never be able to come in Company with me for so indecent an Action, as
to giggle at Archer's kissing of Cherry, without hiding my Face. I look
upon this to be as gross an Affront, as ever was offered to a Woman of
my Fashion: If your Worship thinks it worthy your Notice, 'twill be a
sufficient Satisfaction to your humble Servant,

ARABELLA SLY

There is nothing more commendable in the Fair Sex, than a free and
easy Behavior: A Woman of Sense may take all innocent Liberties, without deserving that malicious Title of a Coquette; and may observe a
proper Decorum, without coming under the Censure of a Prude.

Freedom in Conversation, when carried on with good Breeding, makes
every One amiable; it opens the Heart, and gives a Grace to the Action;
it often makes a Friend an Enemy, and a Relation of a Friend; and may
be justly deem'd one of the greatest of Blessings.

The Demeanor of a Coquette, has something Sprightly and Gay; and,
when she means to give no Offence (but on the contrary, to display her
Charms, and throw off her little Witticisms,) she hurts none but herself;

which, generally ends with the same Fate as that of a Moth: But a Prude is the most unsociable Creature living.

Honest Jack Pamflino informs me, That in the Year 1718, he made his Address to a Prude; that he observed a strict Decorum at his first Approach, and had the Honor to salute her Cheek: At his first Visit he remark'd her whole Time was employed to keep her Feet from peeping from under her Petticoat, and examining the Pins of her Neck-Handkerchief, lest one of them should be displac'd, and expose the Charms that lay under Cover. Her Fortune was great, and made him Cautious, and upon his Guard, lest any Expression (that might be thought obscene) should inadvertently drop from his Mouth in Conversation, and give Offence. He came away satisfy'd with his Conduct; and, in a short Time, paid his Devoirs to the Lady again: The Discourse running upon the News of the Town, he, unluckily, related a Fact of a certain Lady's losing her Garter in the Drawing-Room: upon which she flew out of Company in a great Passion, and was above a Fortnight before she would be reconcil'd to receive another Visit from him. After taking a great deal of Pains by Letter, to convince her how much he had been in the Wrong, and acknowledging his Fault, he was admitted again. He went on with great Success, for about a Month, and the Lady receiv'd his warm Address without so much *Fierte* and Bashfulness as before: This gave him Hopes that he had cur'd her of that Self-conceitedness, and Formality she had been brought up in. The Day of Marriage being fix'd, honest Jack thought himself sure of his Mistress; but, unfortunately, happen'd to praise the Fashion of the Ladies wearing their Stays low before; which exasperated the Virtuous Dame in such a Manner, that she declared, that the very Expression was indecent: This put her into another Frenzy, discarded her Lover, never to see him more.

In about Three Weeks after this Affair, she married an honest Country Gentleman, who unfortunately died a few Days after the Consummation of the Wedding.

The Lady, so disconsolate at the Loss of her Husband, was not to be comforted; her Affliction insupportable; and, had it not been for another Lover which she accepted of in Three Days after the Funeral, she was resolv'd, like the Ephesian Dame, to have been interr'd with her dear Husband.

'Tis strange! we do not give ourselves Leave to consult Nature a little more; we could never thus degenerate into the Stupidity of Brutes, nor become such refined Fools. But the Prejudice of Education is so prevalent, that few are able to walk by their own Light; which will be forever an Argument for the extravagant Singularities we are so liable to.

William Smith of New York

(1728-1793)

Jurist and historian, William Smith was born in New York City, was graduated from Yale in 1745, and was admitted to law practice in 1750. Smith and William Livingston were the principal contributors to *The Independent Reflector,* a weekly magazine published in New York from Nov. 1752 to Nov. 1753. Besides "Of the Use, Abuse, and Liberty of the Press," Smith wrote nine other essays and was co-author of at least four more; Livingston has been credited with authorship of twenty-two. A loyalist during the Revolution, Smith fled to England in 1783, then in 1786 moved to Canada. Among his other works is *The History of the Province of New York* (London, 1757; Albany, N.Y., 1814).

BIBLIOGRAPHY: William H. W. Sabine, ed. *Historical Memoirs . . . of William Smith,* 2 Vols. (New York, 1956). Dorothy R. Dillon, *The New York Triumvirate* (New York, 1949). '*The Independent Reflector,*' ed. Milton M. Klein (Cambridge, Mass., 1963).

From *The Independent Reflector*

NUMBER XL

Thursday, August 30, 1753

OF THE USE, ABUSE, AND LIBERTY OF THE PRESS

. . . Arts in my Train,
And azure-mantled Science, swift we spread
A Sounding Pinion.

THOM. LIB.

Whether the Art of Printing has been of greater Service or Detriment to the World, has frequently been made the Subject of fruitless Controversy. The best Things have been perverted to serve the vilest Purposes, their being therefore subject to Abuse, is an illogical Argument against their Utility. Before the Invention of the Press, the Progress of Knowledge was slow, because the Methods of diffusing it were laborious and expensive. The shortest Production was too costly to its Author; and unless the Writer had an opulent Fortune, or rich Patrons to pay off his Amanuenses, he was driven to the Necessity of retailing his Compositions. To arrive at Fame and literary Glory, was not in the Power of every great Genius; and doubtless Posterity has lost the Sentiments of many eminent Men, which might have been equally useful and important, with the Writings of those, who make the brightest Appearance in the Annals of Fame. It is otherwise since the Discovery of the Art of *Printing*. The most inferior Genius, however impoverished, can spread his Thoughts thro' a Kingdom. The Public has the Advantage of the Sentiments of all its Individuals. Thro' the Press, Writers of every Character and Genius, may promulge their Opinions; and all conspire to rear and support the Republic of Letters. The Patriot can by this Means, diffuse his salutary Principles thro' the Breasts of his Countrymen, interpose his friendly Advice unasked, warn them against approaching Danger, unite them against the Arm of despotic Power, and perhaps, at the Expense of but a few Sheets of Paper, save the State from impending Destruction. The Divine is not confined within the narrow Limits of his parochial Duties, but may preach in his Writings to the whole World. Like Powers in Mechanics, he does as it were, multiply himself: For at the Instant he Visits the Sick of his own Parish, he is perhaps consoling Hundreds against the Fears of Death, in foreign Nations and different Languages, and preaching to many Thousands at the same Time. And surely his Pleasure must equal his Labors, when he reflects, that his pastoral Care extends thro' the whole Christianiz'd World; that however thin and secluded his particular Parish may be, yet that several Nations are within the Sphere of his Influence; that he shall even live after his Death, and Thousands whom he never saw, be his Crown of rejoicing at the great Day of Judgment. Such also are the Advantages of Printing, to the Philosopher, the Moralist, the Lawyer, and Men of every other Profession and Character, whose Sentiments may be diffused with the greatest Ease and Dispatch, and comparatively speaking at a trifling Expense. In short, as the glorious Luminary of the Heavens, darts its Rays with incredible Velocity, to the most distant Confines of our System, so the Press, as from one common Center, diffuses the bright Beams of Knowledge, with prodigious Dispatch, thro' the vast Extent of the civilized World.

Secrecy, is another Advantage, which an Author had not before the Art of Printing was discovered. As long as Power may be perverted, from the original Design of its being lodged with the Magistrate, for protecting the Innocent and punishing the Guilty, so long it will be necessary to conceal the Author who remarks it, from the Malice of the Officer guilty of so pernicious a Perversion; and by Means of this Art he may write undiscovered, as it is impossible to detect him by the Types of the Press.

It must indeed be confessed, that this useful Discovery has, like many others, been prostituted to serve the basest Ends. This great Means of Knowledge, this grand Security of civil Liberty, has been the Tool of arbitrary Power, Popery, Bigotry, Superstition, Profaneness, and even of Ignorance itself. The Press groans under the Weight of the most horrid Impieties, the most ruinous and destructive Principles in Religion and Politics, the idlest Romances, the most contemptible Fustian, Slander and Impotence. But to shut up the Press because it has been abused, would be like burning our Bibles and proscribing Religion, because its Doctrines have been disobeyed and misrepresented; or like throwing off all Law and Restraint, and sinking into a State of Nature, because the over-grown Power of the civil Ruler, abusing his Trust, has sacrificed the Lives and Properties of his Subjects, to lawless and tyrannical Sway. The horrid Practices of Nero, would by no Means have been a sufficient Reason for the Destruction of the Roman Polity. Nor had it been less than Madness in the English Nation, to have dissolved the Bonds of our Constitution, and sunk into Anarchy and Confusion, even tho' Charles I and James II had provoked the just Resentment of an injured and oppressed People. Such a Condition would have been worse than that of Syracuse, under the most unlimited Despotism. The Truth is, the Tyrant should in such Case be deposed, but the State should survive him; and rather than live without Law, without Society, and the innumerable Blessings it includes, better would it be, to suffer with only a distant Hope of Redress, the ungoverned Sway of the most arbitrary Monarch the World ever saw.

The wide Influence of the Press is so dangerous to arbitrary Governments, that in some of them it is shut up, and in others greatly restrained. The Liberty of complaining, of carrying that Complaint to the Throne itself, and of breathing the Sighs of an afflicted, oppressed Nation, has too great a Tendency to produce a Revolution to be suffered in despotic Governments. No Press is tolerated in the Ottoman Empire. Power supported without Right, cannot bear, and therefore will not submit itself to a public Examination. Knowledge inspires a Love of Liberty,— and Liberty in the People, is incompatible with the Security of an arbitrary Legislator. To the same Causes are to be ascribed, the Restrictions on the Press in Roman Catholic Countries: Notwithstanding which, the Grand Seignior surpasses the Pope in Policy, which is not the only Proof of his Holiness's Fallibility. That Hierarchy which supports itself by keeping the People in Ignorance, and inhibiting its Devotees the Use of the Bible, oppugns its own Principles, by admitting the Use of the Press; which, as it affords the Opportunity of diffusing Knowledge and Truth thro' the World, must, by inevitable Consequence, equally spread abroad a Contempt of his Holiness, and the Worship, Discipline and Doctrines of his Church. Neither the Amours of Henry VIII which to asperse Protestantism, the Papists ascribe as its Origin, nor any other natural Cause, had so happy Tendency to destroy the Power of the See of Rome, as the Liberty of the Press. Popery and Slavery could not stand before true Religion and Liberty; and as the Press was the Instrument of both, the Rights of St. Peter's chair were no sooner publicly contested, than despised and diminished.—

No Nation in Europe, is more jealous of the Liberty of the Press than the English, nor is there a People, among whom it is so grossly abused. With us, the most unbounded Licentiousness prevails. We are so besotted with the Love of Liberty, that running into Extremes; we even tolerate those Things which naturally tend to its Subversion. And what is still more surprising, an Author justly chargeable with Principles destructive of our Constitution, with Doctrines the most abject and slavish, may proceed even with inveterate Malice, to vilify, burlesque and deny our greatest Immunities and Privileges, and shall yet be suffered to justify himself under the unrestrainable Rights of the Press. An Absurdity grossly stupid and mischievous. What! sap the Constitution, disturb the public Tranquility, and ruin the State, and yet plead a Right to such Liberty derived from the Law of that State! The Liberty of the Press, like Civil Liberty, is talked of by many, and understood but by few; the latter is taken by Multitudes, for an irrefrainable License of acting at Pleasure; an equal Unrestraint in Writing, is often argued from the former, but both are false and equally dangerous to our Constitution. Civil Liberty is built upon a Surrender of so much of our natural Liberty, as is necessary for the good Ends of Government; and the Liberty of the Press, is always to be restricted from becoming a Prejudice to the public Weal. The Design of entering into a State of Society, is to promote and secure the Happiness of its Individuals. Whatever tends to this End, is politically lawful, and no State can permit any Practice detrimental to the public Tranquility, but in direct Opposition to its fundamental Principles. Agreeable to this Doctrine I lay it down as a Rule, that when the Press is prejudicial to the public Weal, it is abused: and that the Prohibition of printing any Thing, not repugnant to the Prosperity of the State, is an unjustifiable and tyrannical Usurpation.

If, on the one Hand, we suppose any broader Foundation for the Liberty of the Press, it will become more destructive of public Peace, than if it were wholly shut up: And a Freedom of publishing what is not prejudicial to the general Good, must be allowed; because, what can do no Harm can be no Evil, and there can be no Punishment without a Transgression. Besides, a Promotion of the public Welfare, of which the Press is often an Instrument, should be so far from suffering Discouragements, that as it is a political Virtue, it merits rather the Rewards than the Frowns of the Magistrate. Thus the Press will have all that Liberty which is due to it, and never be checked, but where its being unrestricted will prove an Evil, and therefore only where it ought to be checked. Liberty and Science may then spread their Wings, and take the most unbounded Flights. But should Tyranny erect its formidable Head, and extend its Iron Scepter, the Nation may publish, and any private Person represent the general Calamity with Impunity. Does Corruption or Venality prevail, the Patriot is at Liberty to inveigh and suppress it. The boldest Criminal lies open to Censure and Satire, and any Man may expose and detect him. The Divine may put Vice at a Stand; every Attack upon the public Welfare may be reprehended, and every destructive Scheme baffled and exposed; for all Men are free in that Way, to defeat every Project that is detrimental to the Public. This Privilege is a great One, and we should all conspire to maintain it. This is the true Liberty of the Press, for which Englishmen ought to contend. Such a Liberty can never be dangerous, either to the Public, or their Ruler; but on the contrary may often be necessary. What a certain great Politician said of the Freedom of Speech, is so applicable to that of the Press, that I cannot omit its Insertion. "The more," says he, "Men express of their Hate and Resentment, perhaps the less they retain, and sometimes they vent the Whole that Way: But these Passions, where they are smothered, will be apt to fester, to grow venomous, and to discharge themselves by a more dangerous Organ than the Mouth, even by an armed and vindictive Hand. Less dangerous is a railing Mouth, than a Heart filled and inflamed with Bitterness and Curses; and more terrible to a Prince, ought to be the secret Execrations of his People, than their open Revilings, or, than even the Assaults of his Enemies."

All those who oppose the Freedom I have contended for,—a Liberty of promoting the common Good of Society, and of publishing any Thing else not repugnant thereto,—are Enemies to the Common Wealth; and many will fall under this Character, who are as ready to cry out for the Liberty of the Press as the warmest Patriot. Of this the various Orders that obtain amongst Men, furnish sufficient Examples: I shall instance but in two.

Never does a Writer of Genius and Spirit appear, unshackled with blind Prejudices and little Attachments to Party. A Writer who exposes the Roguery of Ecclesiastics, and displays the Beauty of genuine unadulterated Christianity, but he gives as it were Birth to a swarm of impotent Scribblers, who arrogate to themselves an Authority from God, to anathemize and deliver him over to the Devil; and the sooner to complete his Doom, will invoke the secular Arm for Assistance. Strange that they should have a Power from God to consign a Man over to eternal Torments, and yet be restrained by that very God, from illuminating his Understanding by Fire and Faggot, unless at the good Pleasure of the Magistrate! Such as these I call Enemies, both to the Press and the Public, tho' the former groans under the Burden of their Nonsense, Superstition and Bigotry.

The Press is forever in the Mouths of Printers, and one would imagine, that as they live by its Liberty, they would understand its true Limits, and endeavor to preserve its rightful Extent. But the Truth is, there is scarce one in Twenty of them, that knows the one or aims at the other.

A Printer ought not to publish everything that is offered him; but what is conducive of general Utility, he should not refuse, be the Author a Christian, Jew, Turk or Infidel. Such Refusal is an immediate Abridgment of the Freedom of the Press. When on the other Hand, he prostitutes his Art by the Publication of any Thing injurious to his Country, it is criminal,—It is high Treason against the State. The usual Alarm rung in such Cases, the common Cry of an Attack upon the LIBERTY OF THE PRESS, is groundless and trifling. The Press neither has, nor can have such a Liberty, and whenever it is assumed, the Printer should be punished. Private Interest indeed has, with many of them, such irresistible Charms, and the general Good is so feeble a Motive, that the only Liberty they know and wish for, is of publishing everything with Impunity for which they are paid. I could name a Printer, so attached to his private Interest, that for the sake of advancing it, set up a Press, deserted his Religion, made himself the Tool of a Party he despised, privately contemned and vilified his own Correspondents, published the most infamous Falsehoods against others, slandered half the People of his Country, promised afterwards to desist, broke that Promise, continued the Publication of his Lies, Forgeries and Misrepresentations; and to complete his Malignity, obstinately refused to print the Answers or Vindications of the Persons he had abused; and yet even this Wretch, had the Impudence to talk of the *Liberty of the Press*. God forbid! that every Printer should deserve so infamous a Character. There are among them, Men of Sense, Ingenuity, and rational Lovers of Liberty, for which the greater Part are less solicitous than the Generality of other Men, as a Confinement of the Press to its true Limits, is more frequently opposed to their private Advantage. It would be easy to enumerate a Variety of others, equally Pretenders to a Regard for the *Liberty of the Press,* and as evidently Enemies to the *Press* and the *Public:* But I shall reserve the farther Consideration of this Subject for a following Year, when the Conduct of Bigots and their Adherents, will, probably, supply me with some necessary Remarks.

William Smith of Philadelphia
(1727-1803)

Writer and teacher, William Smith was born in Aberdeen, Scotland, received his A.M. from the University of Aberdeen in 1741, and after spending several years in London, moved to New York in 1751. In 1754, Smith became a teacher at the College of Philadelphia and was made Provost in 1755. Among his students were Benjamin West, Francis Hopkinson, and Thomas Godfrey. In addition, Smith edited and wrote for *The American Magazine and Monthly Chronicle,* published from October 1757 through October 1858. To *The American Magazine,* Smith contributed "The Hermit Essays." Other works include *A General Idea of the College of Mirania* (New York, 1753), and *Discourses on Public Occasions* (Philadelphia, 1759). *The Works of William Smith,* 2 Vols. (Philadelphia, 1803), appeared shortly after his death.

BIBLIOGRAPHY: H. W. Smith, *Life and Correspondence of the Rev. William Smith,* 2 Vols. (Philadelphia, 1880). Charles J. Stillé, *A Memoir of the Rev. William Smith* (Philadelphia, 1869). A. F. Gegenheimer, *William Smith, Educator and Churchman* (Philadelphia, 1943).

From *The American Magazine and Monthly Chronicle*

THE HERMIT ESSAYS

The HERMIT, No. I.

To the Proprietors &c.

GENTLEMEN   October 1757

Sequester'd as I am from the world and most of its concerns, your plan for publishing an *American Magazine* has found its way to my retreat. As I have always been a friend to works of this nature, especially when their chief end is made to consist in advancing the interest of virtue and knowledge, I find myself strongly prompted, both by duty and inclination, to contribute my endeavors, and give all the assistance in my power, for promoting a design that appears so well calculated for the public good. It is, therefore, my purpose, to offer you my reflections, once a month, upon such subjects as correspond with the character which the good providence of heaven has called me to sustain; and these, you may easily guess, will be of the serious and moral kind.

But that your readers may be the better able to form a notion of the entertainment they are to expect from me, and to satisfy a curiosity natural enough to those who look for anything of importance from an author, the subject of this first paper shall be my own History; or, at least, so much of it as has a more immediate relation to the character I bear.

My parents were among the first of those, who left their native soil and dearest connections, with the laudable design of improving their fortunes, and seeking a settlement in this new world. Many were the dangers and difficulties which they encountered, both while they were at sea, and after their arrival here. My father, who was bred a gentleman and a scholar, and consequently unaccustomed to manual labor, was nevertheless obliged to put his hand to the plow, as there was at that time but little other means of getting a subsistence here. My mother, who was descended from a very good family in Yorkshire, and brought up in the most tender and delicate manner, was constrained to forget the softness of her education, and to bear a part, with her yoke-fellow, in most of the labors of his farm. Custom, however, which is justly called a second nature, made even their toils, at length, to become easy and agreeable.

Thus were they employed for several years, till the smiles of heaven upon their industry blessed them with a comfortable subsistence, and enabled them to pass the remainder of their days, without labor and without care. Happy were they in themselves, and happy in the friendship and good offices of all around them! One thought alone would sometimes give a damp to their domestic joys, and render them a little unsatisfied with all their worldly bliss. They had as yet never been favored with an offspring, and it grieved them to reflect, that the little fortune which they had collected, by the labor of their own hands, should become the inheritance of strangers. But their anxiety in this respect was at length removed. Scarce were they sat down to rest from their toils, and taste the sweets of their honest industry, before an indulgent providence was pleased to send me into the world, as the wished-for heir of their well earned patrimony.

My father, who was a man of singular piety, and looked upon my birth as the highest instance of the favor of heaven upon his old age, named me Theodore, (or the gift of God) and determined, from that moment, to devote me to the service of his maker, as the only acknowledgment he could offer for the repeated blessings showered upon him. For this purpose, he took upon himself the care of my education, as there was at that time no public American seminary erected near him, and he did not choose, for many reasons, to risk my going to any distant university. He was, indeed, in himself every way qualified for this task; and to him alone I am indebted, not only for my skill in languages and philosophy, but, what is of still higher and more lasting importance, for my knowledge of the principles of morality and sound religion. Unfortunately for me, the good man was called to a better state, before I was of full age; and consequently he failed in his expectation of seeing me fixed in the ministry during his own life.

It was, however, one of his last charges to me, that I should spare no pains to prepare myself for that sacred office; and therefore, he enjoined me that, as soon as I had seen his remains decently interred, and had placed my aged mother under the care of a relation, whom he had named for that purpose, I should take the tour of Europe, in order to join to the knowledge of books, what is commonly called, the knowledge of the great world. With this view, he recommended it to me to visit the most remarkable cities and universities, and to make my observations upon the different characters and manners of men, their state and condition with respect to learning and commerce, their modes of government, religion, customs, and the like. To qualify me for this, and keep me untainted from the vices of the world, during my peregrination in it, he gave me the most wholesome instructions for my conduct, a copy of which I shall insert in some of my succeeding Essays, for the common benefit of all young travelers, into whose hands they may fall; and happy will it be for them, if they make the same good use of his wise precepts, which, by the kind providence of heaven, I have been enabled to make. . . .

THEODORE, or, the HERMIT, No. III.

January 1758

Quintilio si quid recitares, corrige sodes
Hoc aiebit et hoc—

HOR. *Art Poet,*
Whate'er a candid critic spies amiss,
Correct he'll say my friend, this here and this.

Our last contained our discovery of the HERMIT'S habitation, the pious ecstacy in which we found him rapt, our mutual address and compliments; reserving for the present occasion an account of the advice he gave us, in the quality of proprietors of this magazine; which, after a short pause, he delivered as follows—

Gentlemen,

Your undertaking is laudable but arduous. You are not to consider yourselves as writing for the *few.* You are to instruct and entertain the *many;* which will deserve, nay demand, the utmost exertion of your faculties. Without doubt, you have duly weighed them, and found them not unequal to the task. Yet, give me leave to utter my sentiments with freedom. The fate of others, who have enterprised the same attempt, makes me anxious for yours. They failed in the execution; and had I no higher opinion of your merit than of theirs who have gone before you in works of the like kind in this country, the name of THEODORE should not have swelled the list of your correspondents. Interested, therefore, as I am in the success of your scheme, I may claim a right of pointing out to you some of the principal difficulties you have to encounter in your way.

First then, you can never be too curious in the choice of your subjects. There is no circumstance more closely connected with the success of writing than this. What you lay before the public should not only be important, but interesting. It should not only edify the Head, but affect the Heart. However learned and accurate you may show yourselves to be, the world will but little thank you for a dry, insipid, formal piece of Morality. This is a wide and noble field I grant, but then it is a beaten one; and nothing bribes the attention like Novelty and Variety.

The two main subjects, which have employed the pens of the wise in all ages, are RELIGION and GOVERNMENT; and in countries where there is no liberty to animadvert freely on these topics, there are none besides which merit the care of a good man. Yet to launch headlong into Religion is often to sound the trump of controversy, and dash against the rock of scandal; and, as to Politics, you'll find them a hedge of thorns and briars.

What then is to be done? To be general is to be dull and unaffecting, and to be particular is to be odious and offensive. A hard dilemma this for a writer! The best counsel I can administer in such a case, to avoid both inconveniences, is to watch conjunctures. These will always produce something that a sagacious observer may turn to his purpose. A topic that would scarce be listened to at one period of time, may become the sole object of attention at another. Alas! what are the affairs of this world, but continual flux and revolution? all is change and instability! Moment after moment sees innumerable beings exist and disappear. Events of the greatest import, the fate of kingdoms and of kings, the weal or woe of thousands, may hang on that mere instant of time, that vanished ere I spoke. What then is permanent and immutable? He, only He who made, sustains, regulates and pervades this universal frame—

O thou eternal self-existing, self-supported being; whose pure unsearchable essence excludes all shadow of variation; who art the same today, yesterday and forever! corroborate my soul with stability and perseverance. Abstract me from this world and all its tinsel vanities! Teach me to raise my hopes and affections to thee the sovereign good, that I may not be moved nor shaken by the events of this transitory scene, but look continually forward to that grand and awful period, when time and change and suffering shall be no more—

But, forgive me, gentlemen, these sudden ejaculations, which a view of the endless vicissitudes of this life naturally excited—I was recommending to you an attention to conjunctures and circumstances, to enable you at once to instruct and please your readers. By this means you will secure one great point, that of rousing the Attention, and will be at greater liberty to bestow your pains upon the other two, namely to please the Imagination and satisfy the Understanding; which three requisites constitute the whole merit and essence of literary composition. While you keep these ends in view, even your lighter and more humorous essays will have some useful Moral couched in them, agreeable to the fine precept of Horace—

Omne tulit punctum, qui miscuit utile dulci.

But though I have mentioned above the rocks and difficulties that beset religious and political subjects, yet, gentlemen, as you avow yourselves the friends of mankind, no circumstances ought to deter you from your duty in this respect. There are times and occasions, when to be silent on these topics would be criminal and base in the highest degree. There are times and occasions when you ought to lift up your voice like a trumpet, in the cause of your God and your Country; and call all the Man, all the Patriot and all the Christian forth.

In such a grand cause, much circumspection will be required, and there are innumerable ways by which it may be betrayed. Ignorance may be fatal to it. An overheated zeal or timid caution may equally hurt it. Power may control or seduce you; the fumes of popularity may intoxicate you or should your virtue be proof against these trials, yet conjunctures may happen, so critically circumstanced, as to puzzle the ablest head and soundest heart. Tyranny may sometimes wear the face of Justice; Licentiousness may assume the mask of freedom; Hypocrisy may put on the garb of religion; and the vilest designs that faction, discord or ambition ever planned, may veil themselves in the cloak of patriotism and public spirit!

How, then, gentlemen, must an honest writer, uninfluenced by party rage or any other motive but a genuine love of Truth and Liberty develop the cheat and show it in its proper colors to the world? I who employ my thoughts on far other subjects than the mysteries of state, or the subtleties of the human heart, am very unfit for such a task. Buried in this humble, silent and sequestered hut, I have industriously explored, and resolutely extinguished every spark of ambition in my own soul. Like one that has happily gained some port of safety, after being long tossed on the stormy ocean, I here ruminate on the past and look forward to the future, without busying myself in the affairs of men; being little more than a spectator in this world—

> I hear the tumult of the distant throng,
> As that of seas remote, or dying storms.
> Eager ambition's fiery chase I see;
> I see the circling hunt of noisy men
> Burst *Law's* enclosure, leap the bounds of *Right*,
> Pursuing and pursu'd, each others' prey,
> As wolves for rapine, as the fox for wiles.

But, gentlemen, tho' this be the present frame of my mind, and tho' my whole care be to hush each boisterous passion into repose, and maintain an intercourse with him whose eyes are too pure to behold iniquity; yet there was a time when my bosom, like yours, glowed with the concerns of this world. And ambition hath had its turn with me as well as with others. My pen and my tongue have heretofore been embarked in the cause of Liberty and Truth; and while I breathe, my heart shall own no subject preferable to these, excepting my great Creator's praise. In this view, then, I presume to point out to you the conduct you should pursue, for the detection of masked tyranny and sanctified imposture.

1. Consider the Religion of your country as that of the blessed Jesus, flowing uncorrupted from his sacred oracles; a religion whose essence is charity and its fruit good works and assurance forever!

2. Consider the Government of your country as a government of laws, founded on reciprocal obligations between the governors and governed; where your Liberty and your Life depend not on the arbitrary will of one man, nor of a set of men, but on the known and established rules of justice; even your Peers being your judges.

Possessed of this idea of British religion and British government, let no motive on earth ever induce you tamely to suffer them to be infringed. Cry aloud and spare not on every approach of danger, that may threaten their subversion. Arguments will scarcely be wanting if you are truly inflamed in such a cause, and whatever you may suffer in the prosecution of it, will redound to your glory either in this world or the next. It has, indeed, been the constant endeavor of all wicked men to stop the avenues of knowledge and tie up the mouths of those whom they judged capable of unmasking their iniquitous designs. For where truth can once be extinguished, Slavery will soon prevail. But the man who considers Liberty as his birthright, will never be a silent spectator of the approaching misery. He will think it his duty to show a manly and intrepid spirit on the occasion; and should bonds or imprisonment be his fate, yet even from the dark mansions of a Dungeon his tongue will sound forth lessons of wisdom, and his bosom beat for his country's good—

Here our venerable friend concluded; and the moon had now ascended half way up the Heavens, glimmering through the trees and impearling the surface of the waters. We courteously took our leave, and pursued our way to our respective homes in this city.

I. AND M.

TRACTS
FOR THE TIMES

Robert Calef
(1648-1719)

Probably born in England, Robert Calef was settled in Boston as a cloth merchant by 1688. In 1693, he charged Cotton Mather with trying to renew the witchcraft delusions. Calef had read the manuscript of "Another Brand Pluckt out of the Burning," Mather's account of his exorcising seventeen-year-old Margaret Rule, and insinuated that Mather's interest might have been other than official. After his arrest for libel, Calef incorporated Mather's account into a volume with his own comments and testimony of witnesses of the Salem witch trials. Calef finished the project in 1697, but was unable to find a printer. *More Wonders of the Invisible World* appeared in London in 1700.

BIBLIOGRAPHY: *DAB.* George L. Burr, *Narratives of the Witchcraft Cases, 1648–1706* (New York, 1914). Burr, *The Literature of Witchcraft* (New York, 1890).

From *More Wonders of the Invisible World*

POSTSCRIPT

. . . As to the supposed witchcrafts in New England, having already said so much thereof, there is the less remains to be added.

In the times of Sir Edmond Andros's government, Goody Glover, a despised, crazy, ill-conditioned old woman, an Irish Roman Catholic, was tried for afflicting Goodwin's children; by the account of which trial, taken in shorthand for the use of the jury, it may appear that the generality of her answers were nonsense, and her behavior like that of one distracted. Yet the doctors, finding her as she had been for many years, brought her in *compos mentis;* and setting aside her crazy answers to some ensnaring questions, the proof against her was wholly deficient. The jury brought her in guilty.

Mr. Cotton Mather was the most active and forward of any minister in the country in those matters, taking home one of the children, and managing such intrigues with that child, and printing such an account of the whole in his *Memorable Providences*, as conduced much to the kindling of those flames, that in Sir William's time threatened the destruction of this country.

King Saul in destroying the witches out of Israel is thought by many to have exceeded, and in his zeal to have slain the Gibeonites wrongfully under that notion; yet went after this to a witch to know his fortune. For his wrongfully destroying the Gibeonites (besides the judgments of God upon the land) his sons were hanged; and for his going to the witch, himself was cut off. Our Sir William Phips did not do this; but, as appears by this book, had first his fortune told him, (by such as the author counts no better) and though he put it off (to his pastor, who he knew approved not thereof) as if it were brought to him in writing, without his seeking, &c. yet by his bringing it so far, and safe keeping it so many years, it appears he made some account of it; for which he gave the writer, after he had found the wreck, as a reward, more than two hundred pounds. His telling his wife, that he should be a commander, should have a brick house in Greenlane, &c. might be in confidence of some such prediction; and that he could foretell to him that he should be governor of New England, was probably such an one, the scriptures not having revealed it. Such predictions would have been counted, at Salem, pregnant proofs of witchcraft, and much better than what were against several that suffered there. But Sir William, when the witchcrafts at Salem began (in his esteem) to look formidable, that he might act safely in this affair, asked the advice of the ministers in and near Boston. The whole of their advice and answer is printed in *Cases of Conscience*, the last pages. But lest the world should be ignorant who it was that drew the said advice, in this book of the life of Sir William Phips, are these words, *The ministers made to his excellency and the council a return, drawn up at their desire, by Mr. Mather the younger, as I have been informed.* Mr. C. M. therein intending to beguile the world, and make them think that another, and not himself, had taken that notice of his (supposed) good service done therein, which otherwise would have been ascribed to those ministers in general; though indeed the advice then given looks most like a thing of his composing, as carrying both fire to increase, and water to quench, the conflagration; particularly after the devil's testimony, by the supposed afflicted, had so prevailed, as to take away the life of one, and the liberty of an hundred, and the whole country set into a most dreadful consternation, then this advice is given, ushered in with thanks for what was already done, and in conclusion putting the government upon a speedy and vigorous prosecution, according to the laws of God, and the wholesome statutes of the English nation; so adding oil, rather than water, to the flame: for who so little acquainted with the proceedings of England, as not to know that they have taken some methods, with those here used, to discover who were witches? The rest of the advice, consisting of cautions and directions, is inserted in this book of the life of Sir William: so that if Sir William, looking upon the thanks for what was past, and exhortation to proceed, went on to take away the lives of nineteen more, this is according to the advice said to be given him by the ministers; and if the devil, after those executions, be affronted, by disbelieving his testimony, and by clearing and pardoning all the rest of the accused, yet this also is, according to that advice, but to cast the scale. The same that drew this advice saith, in *Wonders of the Invisible World, Enchantments Encountered,* that to have a hand in anything that may stifle or obstruct a regular detection of that witchcraft, is what we may well with a holy fear avoid: their majesties' good subjects must not every day be torn to pieces by horrid witchcraft, and those bloody felons be wholly left unprosecuted; the witchcraft is a business that will not be shammed. The pastor of that church, of which Sir William was a member, being of this principle, and thus declaring it, after the former advice, no wonder though it cast the scale against those cautions. It is rather a wonder that no more blood was shed; for if that advice of his pastor could still have prevailed with the governor, witchcraft had not been so shammed off as it was. Yet now, in this book of the life of Sir William, the pardoning the prisoners when condemned, and clearing the jails, is called a vanquishing the devil; adding this conquest to the rest of the noble achievements of Sir William, though performed not only without, but directly against, his pastor's advice. But this is not all; though this book pretends to raise a statue in honor of Sir William, yet it appears it was the least part of the design of the author to honor him, but it was rather to honor himself, and the ministers; it being so unjust to Sir William, as to give a full account of the cautions given him, but designedly hiding from the reader the encouragements and exhortations to proceed, that were laid before him, (under the name of the ministers' advice;) in effect telling the world that those executions at Salem were without and against the advice of the ministers, exprest in those cautions, purposely hiding their giving thanks for what was already done, and exhorting to proceed; thereby rendering Sir William of so sanguinary a complexion, that the ministers had such cause to fear his going on with the tragedy, though against their advice, that they desired the president to write his *Cases of Conscience,* &c. To plead misinformation will not salve here, however it may seem to palliate other things, but is a manifest, designed travesty, or misrepresentation, of the minister's advice to Sir William, a hiding the truth, and a wronging the dead, whom the author so much pretends to honor; for which the acknowledgments ought to be as universal as the offence. But though the ministers' advice, or rather Mr. Cotton Mather's, was perfectly ambidexter, giving as great or greater encouragement to proceed in those dark methods, than cautions against them; yet many eminent persons being accused, there was a necessity of a stop to be put to it. If it be true, what was said at the council board in answer to the commendations of Sir William for his stopping the proceedings about witchcraft, viz. that it was high time for him to stop it, his own lady being accused; if that assertion were a truth, then New England may seem to be more beholden to the accusers for accusing her, and thereby necessitating a stop, than to Sir William, or to the advice that was given him by his pastor.

Mr. Cotton Mather, having been very forward to write books of witchcraft, has not been so forward either to explain or to defend the doctrinal part thereof; and his belief (which he had a year's time to compose) he durst not venture, so as to be copied. Yet in this book of the life of Sir William he sufficiently testifies his retaining that heterodox belief, seeking by frightful stories of the sufferings of some, and the refined sight of others, &c. to obtrude upon the world, and confirm it in such a belief as hitherto he either cannot or will not defend, as if the blood already shed thereby were not sufficient.

Mr. I. Mather, in his *Cases of Conscience,* tells of a bewitched eye, and that such can see more than others. They were certainly bewitched eyes, that could see as well shut as open, and that could see what never was; that could see the prisoners upon the afflicted, harming them, when those whose eyes were not bewitched could have sworn that they did not stir from the bar. The accusers are said to have suffered much by biting, and the prints of just such a set of teeth, as those they accused had, would be seen on their flesh; but such as had not such bewitched eyes have seen the accusers bite themselves, and then complain of the accused. It has also been seen, when the accused, instead of having just such a set of teeth, has not had one in his head. They were such bewitched eyes, that could see the poisonous powder (brought by spectres) and that could see in the ashes the print of the brand, there invisibly heating to torment the pretended sufferers with, &c.

These, with the rest of such legends, have this direct tendency, viz. to tell the world that the devil is more ready to serve his votaries, by his doing for them things above or against the course of nature, showing himself to them and making explicit contracts with them, &c. than the Divine Being is to his faithful servants; and that as he is willing, so also able, to perform their desires. The way whereby these people are believed to arrive at a power to afflict their neighbors, is by a compact with the devil, and that they have a power to commission him to those evils. However irrational, or unscriptural, such assertions are, yet they seem a necessary part of the faith of such as maintain the belief of such a sort of witches.

As the scriptures know nothing of a covenanting or commissioning witch, so reason cannot conceive how mortals should by their wickedness arrive at a power to commission angels, fallen angels, against their innocent neighbors. But the scriptures are full in it, and the instances numerous, that the Almighty Divine Being has this prerogative, to make use of what instruments he pleaseth, in afflicting any, and consequently to commission devils: and though this word, commissioning, in the author's former books, might be thought to be by inadvertency, yet now, after he hath been cautioned of it, still to persist in it seems highly criminal; and therefore, in the name of God, I here charge such belief as guilty of sacrilege in the highest nature, and so much worse than stealing church .plate, &c. as it is a higher offence to steal any of the glorious attributes of the Almighty, to bestow them upon mortals, than it is to steal the utensils appropriated to his service. And whether to ascribe such power of commissioning devils to the worst of men, be not direct blasphemy, I leave to others better able to determine. Where the Pharisees were so wicked as to ascribe to Beelzebub the mighty works of Christ (whereby he did manifestly show forth his power and godhead) then it was that our Savior declared the sin against the Holy Ghost to be unpardonable.

When the righteous God is contending with apostate sinners for their departures from him, by his judgments, as plagues, earthquakes, storms and tempests, sicknesses and diseases, wars, loss of cattle, &c. then not only to ascribe this to the devil, but to charge one another with sending or commissioning those devils to do these things, is so abominable and so wicked, that it requires a better judgment than mine to give it its just denomination.

But that Christians, so called, should not only charge their fellow Christians therewith, but proceed to trials and executions; crediting that enemy to all goodness, and accuser of the brethren, rather than believe their neighbors in their own defense; this is so diabolical a wickedness, as cannot proceed but from a doctrine of devils; how far damnable it is, let others discuss. Though such things were acting in this country in Sir William's time, yet there is a discourse of a guardian angel, as then overseeing it: which notion, however, it may suit the faith of Ethnics, or the fancies of Trithemius, it is certain that the Omnipresent Being stands not in need, as earthy potentates do, of governing the world by viceregents. And if Sir William had such an invisible pattern to imitate, no wonder though some of his actions were unaccountable, especially those relating to witchcraft: for if there was in those actions an angel superintending, there is little reason to think it was Gabriel, or the spirit of Mercury; nor Hanael, the angel or spirit of Venus; nor yet Samuel, the angel or spirit of Mars; names feigned by the said Trithemius, &c. It may rather be thought to be Apollyon, or Abaddon.

Objection. But here it will be said, What, are there no witches? Does not the law of God command that they should be extirpated? Is the command vain and unintelligible?

Sol. For any to say that a witch is one that makes a compact with, and commissions devils, &c. is indeed to render the law of God vain and unintelligible, as having provided no way whereby they might be detected, and proved to be such; and how the Jews waded through this difficulty for so many ages, without the supplement of Mr. Perkins and Bernard thereto, would be very mysterious. But to him that can read the scriptures without prejudice from education, &c. it will manifestly appear that the scripture is full and intelligible, both as to the crime, and means to detect the culpable. He that shall hereafter see any person, who, to confirm people in a false belief about the power of witches and devils, pretending to a sign to confirm it; such as knocking off of invisible chains with the hand, driving away devils by brushing, striking with a sword or stick, to wound a person at a great distance, &c. may (according to that head of Mr. Gaule's, quoted by Mr. C. M. and so often herein before recited, and so well-proved by scripture) conclude that he has seen witchcraft performed.

If Balaam became a sorcerer by sacrificing and praying to the true God against his visible people, then he that shall pray that the afflicted (by their spectral sight) may accuse some other persons (whereby their reputations and lives may be endangered) such will justly deserve the name of a sorcerer. If any person pretends to know more than can be known by human means, and professeth at the same time that they have it from the black man, i.e. the devil, and shall from hence give testimony against the lives of others, they are manifestly such as have a familiar spirit; and if any, knowing them to have their information from the black man, shall be inquisitive of them for their testimony against others, they therein are dealing with such as have a familiar spirit.

And if these shall pretend to see the dead by their spectral sight, and others shall be inquisitive of them, and receive their answers what it is the dead say, and who it is they accuse, both the one and the other are by scripture guilty of necromancy.

These are all of them crimes as easily proved as any whatsoever, and that by such proof as the law of God requires, so that it is no unintelligible law.

But if the iniquity of the times be such that these criminals not only escape, being indemnified, but are encouraged in their wickedness, and made use of to take away the lives of others, this is worse than a making the law of God vain, it being a rendering of it dangerous, against the lives of innocents, and without all hopes of better, so long as these bloody principles remain.

As long as Christians do esteem the law of God to be imperfect, as not describing that crime that it requires to be punished by death:

As long as men suffer themselves to be poisoned in their education, and be grounded in a false belief by the books of the heathen:

As long as the devil shall be believed to have a natural power to act above and against the course of nature:

As long as the witches shall be believed to have a power to commission him:

As long as the devil's testimony, by the pretended afflicted, shall be received as more valid to condemn, than their plea of not guilty to acquit:

As long as the accused shall have their lives and liberties confirmed and restored to them upon their confessing themselves guilty:

As long as the accused shall be forced to undergo hardships and torments for their not confessing:

As long as teats for the devil to suck are searched for upon the bodies of the accused, as a token of guilt:

As long as the Lord's prayer shall be profaned, by being made a test, who are culpable:

As long as witchcraft, sorcery, familiar spirits, and necromancy, shall be improved to discover who are witches, &c.

So long it may be expected that innocents will suffer as witches:

So long God will be daily dishonored, and so long his judgments must be expected to be continued.   1700

Andrew Hamilton

(c. 1676-1741)

Andrew Hamilton apparently arrived in Virginia in the late 1600's, then settled in Maryland in 1708. After a trip to England in 1712-1713, he moved to Philadelphia, where he was appointed Attorney General of Pennsylvania in 1717 and served in the state Assembly from 1727 to 1739. In 1735, he went to New York City to defend John Peter Zenger (1697-1746), editor and printer of the *New-York Weekly Journal*, who had published articles critical of New York authorities and who had been arrested and charged with seditious libel. Unable to obtain council (his New York attorneys had been disbarred, Zenger and his friends sought Hamilton's aid. Hamilton's plea be-

fore the jury brought a verdict of "not guilty." Hamilton's account of his speech, edited by James Alexander, one of Zenger's disbarred lawyers, appeared as *A Brief Narrative of the Case and Trial of John Peter Zenger* (New York, 1736).

BIBLIOGRAPHY: Burton A. Konkle, *The Life of Andrew Hamilton, 1676-1741* (Philadelphia, 1941). Livingston Rutherford, *John Peter Zenger: His Press, His Trial . . .* (New York, 1904, 1941). *A Brief Narrative of the Case and Trial of John Peter Zenger*, ed. Stanley Katz (Cambridge, Mass., 1963). *The Trial of Peter Zenger*, ed. Vincent Buranelli (New York, 1957).

From *A Brief Narrative of the Case and Trial of John Peter Zenger*

Mr. Hamilton. If a Libel is understood in the large and unlimited Sense urged by Mr. Attorney, there is scarce a Writing I know that may not be called a Libel, or scarce any Person safe from being called to an Account as a Libeler: For Moses, meek as he was, libeled Cain; and who is it that has not libeled the Devil? For according to Mr. Attorney it is no Justification to say one has a bad Name. Echard has libeled our good King William; Burnet has libeled among many others King Charles and King James; and Rapin has libeled them all. How must a Man speak or write, or what must he hear, read or sing? Or when must he laugh, so as be secure from being taken up as a Libeler? I sincerely believe, that were some Persons to go thro' the Streets of New York nowadays, and read a Part of the Bible, if it was not known to be such, Mr. Attorney, with the help of his Innuendos, would easily turn it into a Libel. As for instance, Is. IX. 16. *The Leaders of the People cause them to err, and they that are led by them are destroyed.* But should Mr. Attorney go about to make this a Libel, he would read it thus; *The Leaders of the People* [innuendo, the Governor and Council of New York] *cause them* [innuendo, the People of this Province] *to err, and they* [the People of this Province meaning] *that are led by them* [the Governor and Council meaning] *are destroyed* [innuendo, are deceived into the Loss of their Liberty] which is the worst Kind of Destruction. Or if some Persons should publicly repeat, in a Manner not pleasing to his Betters, the 10th and 11th Verses of the LVI. Chap. of the same Book, there Mr. Attorney would have a large Field to display his Skill, in the artful Application of his Innuendos. The Words are, *His Watchmen are all blind, they are ignorant, &c. Yea, they are greedy dogs, that can never have enough.* But to make them a Libel, there is according to Mr. Attorney's Doctrine, no more wanting but the Aid of his Skill, in the right adapting his Innuendos. As for Instance; *His Watchmen* [innuendo, the Governor's Council and Assembly] *are blind, they are ignorant* [innuendo, will not see the dangerous Designs of His Excellency] *Yea, they* [the Governor and Council meaning] *are greedy Dogs, which can never have enough* [innuendo, enough of Riches and Power.] Such an Instance as this is seems only fit to be laugh'd at; but I may appeal to Mr. Attorney himself, whether these are not at least equally proper to be applied to His Excellency and His Ministers, as some of the Inferences and Innuendos in his Information against my Client. Then if Mr. Attorney is at Liberty to come into Court, and file an Information in the King's Name, without Leave, who is secure, whom he is pleased to prosecute as a Libeler? And as the Crown Law is contended for in bad Times, there is no Remedy for the greatest Oppression of this Sort, even tho the Party prosecuted is acquitted with Honor. And give me Leave to say, as great Men as any in Britain, have boldly asserted, That the Mode of Prosecuting by Information (when a Grand Jury will not find *Billa vera*) is a national Grievance, and greatly inconsistent with that Freedom, which the Subjects of England enjoy in most other Cases. But if we are so unhappy as not to be able to ward off this Stroke of Power directly, yet let us take Care not to be cheated out of our Liberties, by Forms and Appearances; let us always be sure that the Charge in the Information is made out clearly even beyond a Doubt; for tho Matters in the Information may be called Form upon Trial, yet they may be, and often have been found to be Matters of Substance upon giving Judgment.

Gentlemen; The Danger is great, in Proportion to the Mischief that may happen, through our too great Credulity. A proper Confidence in a Court, is commendable; but as the Verdict (what ever it is) will be yours, you ought to refer no Part of your Duty to the Discretion of other Persons. If you should be of the Opinion, that there is no Falsehood in Mr. Zenger's Papers, you will, nay (pardon me for the Expression) you ought to say so; because you don't know whether others (I mean the Court) may be of that Opinion. It is your Right to do so, and there is much depending upon your Resolution, as well as upon your Integrity.

The loss of liberty to a generous Mind, is worse than Death; and yet we know there have been those in all Ages, who for the sake of Preferment, or some imaginary Honor, have freely lent a helping Hand, to oppress, nay to destroy their Country. This brings to my Mind that saying of the immortal Brutus, when he look'd upon the Creatures of Caesar, who were very great Men, but by no Means good Men. "You Romans," said Brutus, "if yet I may call you so, consider what you are doing; remember that you are assisting Caesar to forge those very Chains, which one day he will make yourselves wear." This is what every Man (that values Freedom) ought to consider: He should act by Judgment and not by Affection or Self-Interest; for, where those prevail, No Ties of either Country or Kindred are regarded; as upon the other Hand, the Man, who loves his Country, prefers its Liberty to all other Considerations, well knowing that without Liberty, Life is a Misery.

A famous Instance of this you will find in the History of another brave Roman of the same Name, I mean Lucius Junius Brutus, whose story is well known and therefore I shall mention no more of it, than only to show the Value he put upon the Freedom of his Country. After this great Man, with his Fellow Citizens whom he had engag'd in the Cause, had banish'd Tarquin the Proud, the last King of Rome, from a Throne which he ascended by inhuman Murders and possess'd by the most dreadful Tyranny and Proscriptions, and had by this Means, amass'd incredible Riches, even sufficient to bribe to his Interest, many of the young Nobility of Rome, to assist him in recovering the Crown; but the Plot being discovered, the principal Conspirators were apprehended, among whom were two of the Sons of Junius Brutus. It was absolutely necessary that some should be made Examples of, to deter others from attempting the restoring of Tarquin and destroying the Liberty of Rome. And to effect this it was, that Lucius Junius Brutus, one of the Consuls of Rome, in the Presence of the Roman People, sat Judge and condemned his own Sons, as Traitors to their Country: And to give the last Proof of his exalted Virtue, and his Love of Liberty: He with a Firmness of Mind, (only becoming so great a Man) caus'd their Heads to be struck off in his own Presence; and when he observ'd that his rigid Virtue, occasion'd a sort of Horror among the People, it is observ'd he only said. "My Fellow-Citizens, do not think that this Proceeds from any Want of natural Affection: No, The Death of the Sons of Brutus can affect Brutus only; but the Loss of Liberty will affect my Country." Thus highly was Liberty esteem'd in those Days that a Father could sacrifice his Sons to save his Country, But why do I go to Heathen Rome, to bring Instances of the Love of Liberty, the best Blood in Britain has been shed in the Cause of Liberty; and the Freedom we enjoy at this Day, may be said to be (in a great Measure) owing to the glorious Stand the famous Hamden, and other of our Countrymen, made against the arbitrary Demands, and illegal Impositions, of the Times in which they lived; who rather than give up the Rights of Englishmen, and submit to pay an illegal Tax, of no more, I think, than 3 shillings, resolv'd to undergo, and for their Liberty of their Country did undergo the greatest Extremities, in that arbitrary and terrible Court of Star Chamber, to whose arbitrary Proceedings, (it being compos'd of the principal Men of the Realm, and calculated to support arbitrary Government) no Bounds or Limits could be set, nor could any other Hand remove the Evil but a Parliament.

Power may justly be compar'd to a great River, while kept within its due Bounds, is both Beautiful and Useful; but when it overflows, its Banks, it is then too impetuous to be stemm'd, it bears down all before it, and brings Destruction and Desolation wherever it comes. If then this is the Nature of Power, let us at least do our Duty, and like wise Men (who value Freedom) use our utmost Care to support Liberty, the only Bulwark against lawless Power, which in all Ages has sacrificed to its wild Lust and boundless Ambition, the Blood of the best Men that ever liv'd.

I hope to be pardon'd Sir for my Zeal upon this Occasion; it is an old and wise Caution. That when our Neighbor's House is on Fire, we ought to take Care of our own. For tho' Blessed be God, I live in a Government where Liberty is well understood, and freely enjoy'd: yet Experience has shown us all (I'm sure it has to me) that a bad Precedent in one Government, is soon set up for an Authority in another; and therefore I cannot but think it mine, and every Honest Man's Duty, that (while we pay all due Obedience to Men in Authority) we ought at the same Time to be upon our Guard against Power, wherever we apprehend that it may affect ourselves or our Fellow-Subjects.

I am truly very unequal to such an Undertaking on many Accounts.

And you see I labor under the Weight of many Years, and am born down with great Infirmities of Body; yet Old and Weak as I am, I should think it my Duty if required, to go to the utmost Part of the Land, where my Service cou'd be of any Use in assisting to quench the Flame of Prosecutions upon Informations, set on Foot by the Government, to deprive a People of the Right of Remonstrating, (and complaining too) of the arbitrary Attempts of Men in Power. Men who injure and oppress the People under their Administration provoke them to cry out and complain; and then make that very Complaint the Foundation for new Oppressions and Prosecutions. I wish I could say there were no Instances of this Kind. But to conclude; the Question before the Court and you Gentlemen of the Jury, is not of small nor private Concern, it is not the Cause of the poor Printer, nor of New York alone, which you are now trying: No! It may in its Consequence, affect every Freeman that lives under a British Government on the main of America. It is the best Cause. It is the Cause of Liberty; and I make no Doubt but your upright Conduct, this Day, will not only entitle you to the Love and Esteem of your Fellow-Citizens; but every Man who prefers Freedom to a Life of slavery will bless and honor You, as Men who have baffled the Attempt of Tyranny; and by an impartial and uncorrupt Verdict, have laid a noble Foundation for securing to ourselves, our Posterity, and our Neighbors, That, to which Nature and the Laws of our Country have given us a Right,—the Liberty—both of exposing and opposing arbitrary Power (in these Parts of the World, at least) by speaking and writing Truth.

Here Mr. Attorney observ'd, that Mr. Hamilton had gone very much out of the Way, and had made himself and the People very merry: But that he had been citing Cases, not at all to the Purpose; he said, there was no such Cause as Mr. Bushel's or Sir Edward Hale's before the Court; and he could not find out what the Court or Jury had to do with Dispensations, Riots or unlawful Assemblies: All that the Jury had to consider of was Mr. Zenger's Printing and Publishing two scandalous Libels, which very highly reflected on his Excellency and the principal Men concern'd in the Administration of this Government, which is confess'd. That is, the Printing and Publishing of the Journals set forth in the Information is confess'd. And concluded that as Mr. Hamilton had confess'd the Printing, and there could be no doubt but they were scandalous Papers, highly reflecting upon his Excellency, and the principal Magistrates in the Province. And therefore he made no Doubt but the Jury would find the Defendant Guilty, and would refer to the Court for their Direction.

Mr. Ch. Just. Gentlemen of the Jury. The great Pains Mr. Hamilton has taken, to show how little Regard Juries are to Pay to the Opinion of the Judges; and his insisting so much upon the Conduct of some Judges in Trials of this kind; is done no doubt, with a Design that you should take but very little Notice, of what I might say upon this Occasion. I shall therefore only observe to you that, as the Facts or Words in the Information are confessed: The only Thing that can come in Question before you is, whether the Words as set forth in the Information make a Libel. And that is a Matter of Law, no Doubt, and which you may leave to the Court. But I shall trouble you no further with anything more of my own, but read to you the Words of a learned and upright Judge in a case of the like Nature.

"To say that corrupt Officers are appointed to administer Affairs, is certainly a Reflection on the Government. If People should not be called to account for possessing the People with an ill Opinion of the Government, no Government can subsist, For it is very necessary for all Governments that the People should have a good Opinion of it. And nothing can be worse to any Government, than to endeavor to procure Animosities; as to the Management of it, this has been always look'd upon as a Crime, and no Government can be safe without it be punished.

"Now you are to consider, whether these Words I have read to you, do not tend to beget an ill opinion of the Administration of the Government? To tell us, that those that are employed know nothing of the Matter, and those that do know are not employed. Men are not adapted to Offices, but Offices, to Men, out of a particular Regard to their Interest, and not to their Fitness for the Places; this is the Purport of these Papers."

Mr. Hamilton. I humbly beg Your Honor's Pardon: I am very much misapprehended, if you suppose what I said was so designed.

Sir, you know; I made an Apology for the Freedom I found myself under a Necessity of using upon this Occasion. I said, there was Nothing personal designed; it arose from the Nature of our Defense.

The Jury withdrew and in a small Time returned and being asked by the Clerk whether they were agreed of their Verdict, and whether John Peter Zenger was guilty of Printing and Publishing the Libels in the Information mentioned? They answered by Thomas Hunt, their Foreman, Not Guilty, Upon which there were three Huzzas in the Hall, which was crowded with People and the next Day I was discharged from my Imprisonment.   1736

Samuel Johnson
(1696-1772)

Born at Guilford, Conn., and educated at Collegiate College (later Yale), Samuel Johnson was ordained minister of the Congregational Church at West Haven in 1720. In 1722, however, he sailed for England where he took orders in the English Church in 1723. The following year, he became minister of the Stratford, Conn., church, a post he held for 32 years. In 1754, Johnson was selected the first president of Kings College (Columbia University) and held this position until his retirement in 1763. Among his works are *An Introduction to the Study of Philosophy* (London, 1731, 1744), *Ethices Elementa* (Boston, 1746), and *Elementa Philosophica* (Philadelphia, 1752). *Raphael, or the Genius of the English America: A Rhapsody* was written after 1763 but was unpublished until 1929.

BIBLIOGRAPHY: Herbert and Carol Schneider, *Samuel Johnson; President of Kings College: His Career and Writings*, 4 Vols. (New York, 1929). I. W. Riley, *American Philosophy, the Early Schools* (New York, 1907). Adam L. Jones, *Early American Philosophers* (New York, 1958).

From Raphael, or The Genius of the English America: A Rhapsody

PART I

Aristocles to Crito

1. I should be wanting (dear Crito) in that friendship which has many years subsisted between us, if I should neglect to give you an account of a most important conversation which happened to me not long since. I was invited one evening by a pleasant setting sun and a serene fragrant air to take a walk in a delightful neighboring field, amidst a most beautiful grove of trees of various sorts, where Nature had plentifully poured out her verdure and bounty. It is under a gradually rising hill, at the foot of which runs rushing down among the rocks, and sometimes with sudden rapid falls, a most delicious rivulet of pure water; on the one hand, taking its rise from a thicket of trees, and on the other hand, losing itself in a gentle winding stream amidst grass and flowers of various hue, in a pleasant meadow below; beyond which, on one side, the sea at a distance, with two or three small islands, terminates the prospect, and on the other, a beautiful landscape of pleasant pastures, flocks, and herds, and a delightful country village with mighty hills and vales beyond them, of various heights and distances.

In this place I delight sometimes solitary, and sometimes in company with a philosophical friend to spend an hour or two of vacant time, and being at this time alone, I was deeply musing on the weakness of human nature, and the many empty debates in philosophy, religion and politics that obtain among the inhabitants of this our mansion, and considering how easily they might most of them be accommodated, did men but give themselves leave calmly to think and reflect and consider things as being what they really are, without suffering themselves to be imposed on by empty names and sounds, without prejudice and partiality and with that temper wherewith it becomes them to treat one another, and duly disengaged from every consideration besides the pure disinterested love of truth and right. This led me to think what a contemptible figure they must needs make in the eyes of those superior intelligences who are the immediate attendants of the Almighty, and are said to be by Him appointed the guardians of human affairs. Surely, thought I, if they know what passes among us, they must think as despicably of our low way of thinking, and of the trifling controversies that subsist among us, as we do of the low imaginations and little squabbles and debates that pass among children.

2. While I was thus entertaining my thoughts, I was surprised upon casting my eyes among the trees towards the top of the hill, with the sight of a seemingly extraordinary person coming towards me in the habit of the remotest antiquity, with a most venerable but pleasant and benign aspect, of a beautiful countenance and agreeable air, mixed with seriousness, sweetness, and benevolence. As he approached me I soon discovered in myself signs of awe and surprise because his habit and manner were such as bespoke him an appearance certainly very extraordinary, and as he came up, I addressed him with ceremonies of the profoundest respect and veneration; whereupon with an air of the greatest tenderness and compassion for my surprise, he spoke to me and said: Be not surprised, O Aristocles, or in the least concerned at my making this sudden and extraordinary appearance to you in this solitary place; for I am your friend and the friend of mankind, and am neither a stranger to your name nor condition in the world, nor to the affairs of the rest of your species, and come to you with no other views than those of benevolence towards you and that race of intelligent beings to which you belong, and to suggest to you several things in the course of a few hours' conversation which it may be of use to you and your country to consider in order to promote their good and happiness.

May I then, said I, presume upon your great benignity and condescension so far as to express my desire of knowing who it is I have the honor to speak to and that thus deigns to converse with me in this retired place? Be not, said he, in the least surprised if I let you know that I am indeed one of an order of intelligences superior to you, not clothed with flesh and blood, nor confined to the same laws and limitations of being and acting to which you are tied in this your state of probation. But know, however, that by how much greater the dignity is to which the rational nature is advanced in the intelligent and moral system, by so much the more it abounds in what you call humanity, candor, and benevolence; and therefore you are at liberty without reserve or distance and without fear or diffidence to ask me any questions you shall think proper, and to converse with me with the same openness, freedom and ease and with as little ceremony as you would with any of your friends or such as you have a respectful regard for among your own species; and for this present intercourse you may call me Raphael.

This, I said, is an instance of unspeakable goodness and condescension, and which I am not able to express sufficient thankfulness for; and I shall endeavor to use the liberty you have given me with that deference and veneration which is due to your superior nature and character. May I know then, continued I, the occasion of this your unexpected appearance and condescending intercourse with one of our inferior order of rational beings in this lower world?—In order to this, said he, you must know (what indeed you are not altogether ignorant of) that of us who are continually employed on the greatest and important behests of the most high God, father of spirits, the almighty creator and supreme king and lord of all things and his great Son and vice-regent, the visible creator, lord and governor of the whole natural and moral world, and whose business it is to minister to Him in the moral government of the whole rational creation, I say, of us some there are who are destined to inspect the affairs of particular kingdoms, countries, and provinces, and to promote the general good and welfare of the nations or people assigned to our charge; and the business allotted to me is to be the guardian or genius of New England. In this quality it is that I now appear to you with a design, as I said, to communicate a few things which, if duly attended to, may have some tendency to render you a flourishing and happy people. And the reason why I appear to you in this solitary retreat, is because I know you are extremely solicitous for the public good of mankind and your country, and at leisure to attend to what may be suggested to you on this subject, and would willingly communicate it to others. . . .

8. And in order to understand (said he) wherein public good consists, which implies the public weal and happiness of mankind and what force is connected with it or tends to it, I wish to divide it into two kinds: moral and political. I will begin with moral good, which is the foundation of it, and in order to which it is necessary I should begin with truth, with which they are both in the nature of things connected. For truth, as I have said, is nothing else but things considered as being what they really are, and he is said to know the truth that apprehends things as being what they are, their beings and relations, connections, and dependencies as they stand variously situated one to another. And things are said to be good as they answer their several ends according to their several situa-

tions and relations one to another, and as conspiring to the harmony, order, beauty and advantage of the whole, and particularly to the well-being and happiness of the rational nature. Now, therefore, if we would consider things as being what they really are, we must consider them as constituting one entire system, wherein everything is contrived and adjusted in such a manner by the great Creator and Lord of all, that there is a mutual connection, dependence and subordination of things in regard one to another and to the whole. And this universal system consists of two sorts of beings *toto coelo* different and distinct one from another, and yet in a most wonderful manner connected with one another so as to make one entire system of the universe composed of two great systems entirely different and heterogeneous. The system of intelligent and active beings is called the moral world. And the system of passive and inert sensible beings is called the natural world. The intelligent part of God's creation, for whose sake all other things were made, is his chief care, inasmuch as they bear his own image, being capable of conscious perception, activity and happiness, and consequently of moral government, for which reason they are called the moral world. He being himself absolutely self-sufficient and perfectly happy, his design in giving them being could be no other than the displaying and communication of his goodness to them in order to render them happy. They being by nature intelligent, free, self-determining agents, their perfection and happiness must consist in their own activity and freely exerting the powers He had given them according to the law of their nature, i.e., according to the truth of things and the just sense of their minds or the right dictates of their understandings. This, God knowing it to be our happiness, is for the same reason his will. And as this our intelligent free activity makes us naturally capable of moral government, it sets us in the relation of subjects to Him that made us, and whose property we are, and therefore He is to be considered as a moral Governor and Lord in regard to us to whom we are therefore accountable for our behavior and conduct. Those affections or actions which are suitable or correspondent to the truth of our intelligent nature as being what we are and so situated as we are, being those which constitute our happiness, are therefore to be considered as the laws of God in regard to us to which it is our bounden duty to yield obedience, whether they be discovered by our own reason or dictated by God himself, and in a free and voluntary conformity to these laws from a sense of duty to Him, consists moral good, and the contrary is moral evil. But besides these for answering certain ends of government, God has generally enacted arbitrary laws and constitutions as proper means of trial, for proof of our obedience, prescribing or forbidding such actions as have not antecedently any natural intrinsic good or evil in them; for it has generally been his method with his intelligent creatures to place them at first in a state and under circumstances of trial and probation, and ever to treat them according as they should conduct themselves; but at all times and under all circumstances the sole end of his dispensations towards them is his inducing and engaging them to a willing and cheerful obedience to those laws and rules in conformity to which their true perfection and happiness and his greatest glory consists.

The begetting in them pleasure or pain in consequence of such actions as tend to their weal or ruin, is the great means of God's maintaining this his moral government over them, and all things or actions are to be considered as natural good or evil in regard to them according as they procure pleasure or pain, so that the great end of natural good or pleasure is to promote or engage their moral good or virtue and obedience, and the sole end of natural evil or pain is to prevent or cure moral evil or vice and disobedience. All nature therefore, or the whole system of the natural world, was by the allwise and good God contrived, created and suited to the moral world, not only as the great object of and means to direct their activity for attaining pleasure and avoiding pain, but moreover chiefly and ultimately as a great means and engine for the promoting of moral good, i.e., for the securing and engaging them to virtue in obedience to Him, their great lord and moral governor; and is therefore to be considered by them as a sort of language whereby He, their maker and Lord, displays his wisdom, power and goodness and makes Himself and his will known to them and renders them happy or miserable according as they are obedient or disobedient to it. So that by this glorious show of nature, this wonderful, universal, stable language of God to his intelligent creatures, and the pleasures it begets in them, they are taught and obliged to acknowledge, love and adore Him their great creator and benefactor, and like Him be kind and just, true and faithful one to another; and by the pains it produces in them annexed to and in consequence of their contrary conduct, it is designed to show them the great evil and mischief of sin, and to reduce them back to their obedience; and thus far extends the religion of nature strictly so-called. But where this end cannot by this means be sufficiently attained (as in the case of your wayward and inconsiderate race it could not), God has discovered himself and his will in the method of revealed religion, providing another kind of language and means to the purpose of reducing them back and further obliging them to moral practice, and obedience, and moreover to secure to them pardon and acceptance in consequence thereof.

9. Now, from this general sketch of God's moral government of the world you plainly see that if you would consider things as being what they really are, you must consider not only the whole corporeal and sensible, but also the whole intelligent and rational creation, and particularly mankind as being a system wherein all the parts or individuals are so connected one with another as to constitute one great whole under the conduct and management of the one great creator, governor and disposer

of all things, and particularly the several members of the moral system, as being so related by the constitution and condition of their natures, not only to Him their common Father and Lord, but also to one another, as that they cannot act consistent with the truth of things, unless they conduct themselves, both towards Him their head and one another as members of that whole, according as suits their several relations and situations. In such a conduct therefore consists public good of the moral kind as being in the nature of things attended with universal harmony, order, tranquility and joy; and consequently each one's private good cannot be regularly and reasonably enjoyed, i.e., it cannot be really good, unless it be considered with subordination and enjoyed with resignation to the good of the whole. It is therefore upon the public good or the good of the whole that all the eternal rules of righteousness are founded, and according to the truth of things, as God will not break in upon the general laws of the corporeal nature or the sake of any particular conveniences, so neither may these general laws of the rational nature be transgressed by men or any other kind of intelligences, for the sake of any private good whatsoever, which, however, may be sufficiently enjoyed, and is then sincerely enjoyed when we indulge it consistent with and in subordination to that of the whole.

Since, therefore, the interest of virtue and righteousness is the interest and cause of God and what cannot but be dear to Him, it being his own image and likeness and necessary to the happiness of his creatures, it cannot be but that He must reward those that are obedient to his laws and punish those that are disobedient. But because motives from this your present state of probation will in many cases prove insufficient to secure the interest of virtue, it is necessary to take into the account the consideration of your future state of retribution; for that you shall live hereafter and be capable of endless happiness or misery he cannot doubt who considers that your souls are beings of an entirely different nature from your bodies and therefore can't be subject to any corporeal laws and affections, and who withal believes what all nature abundantly teaches, that there is a most wise, righteous and good God, who can't but delight in virtue and righteousness and therefore will make it happy, which, since in fact it is not, and indeed can't be here as things now stand, it must be provided for in a better state hereafter; so that no consistent notion can be formed of your present state, without considering it as only your first entrance into being and a state of childhood, discipline and probation with a view to your being treated hereafter according as you shall have conducted yourselves here.

And finally from what has been said it is apparent that moral obligation to virtue or moral good is the will of God, our creator, and governor, who being absolutely perfect and self-sufficient can have no other end in creating and governing the moral world than the good and happiness of it; and therefore all such affections and actions as, in the whole, are from the nature and truth of things, necessary to the happiness of the rational nature, are the laws of it, and the will of God concerning it; because in willing its happiness, He must will and require all such actions and forbearances, such a conduct and behavior, as is necessary from the constitution of it, to render it a regular, orderly and happy system. And therefore the virtue or moral good of every particular person in the whole moral system must consist in the designed and voluntary conformity of his will and behavior to this will of God our supreme King and moral Governor, i.e., in willing and promoting the general good and happiness of the whole as He does. And consequently, the criterion by which to determine particularly what the will of God is, or what his laws in the government of the moral world are, is the truth of things, i.e., things considered as being what they really are, as tending or not tending to make us, in the whole, ultimately happy, or (which is the same thing) the general good of the whole system, on which depends the weal and happiness of every particular person; which, what it is, and wherein it consists, may be discovered in a good measure and clearly demonstrated by the right use of our reason. The natural obligation to virtue is founded in the necessity that God and nature lays us under to desire and pursue our own happiness. In short, therefore, whatever can be discovered by the clear deductions of right reason to be for the good of the whole moral system as tending in the nature and truth of things to render the rational nature in the whole ultimately happy, that is right, and it is our duty to do it, and the contrary is wrong; that we are obliged to do and the contrary to avoid, as we desire and would expect to be happy, and as being the will and law of God, our great creator, lord and moral governor, whose will and the sole end of whose government and dispensations respecting us, his creatures and subjects, is that we should by this means be ultimately happy.

c. 1763, 1929

Thomas Paine

(1737-1809)

Born and educated in England, Thomas Paine worked as a staymaker, a seaman, an exciseman, and a teacher before arriving in America late in 1772 with a letter of introduction from Benjamin Franklin. From 1775 to 1777, he was editor of *The Pennsylvania Magazine;* in Jan. 1776, he published *Common Sense* (Philadelphia), which was reprinted throughout the colonies. The sixteen papers entitled *The Crisis* were printed as pamphlets between Dec. 19, 1776, and Dec. 9, 1783, and were signed "Common Sense." After 1787, Paine spent most of his time in England and France, where he was involved in the revolutionary struggles on the continent. Among his other works are *The Rights of Man* (London, 1791–1792), an answer to Edmund Burke's *Reflections on the French Revolution,* and *The Age of Reason* (London and Paris, 1794–1796). Paine died June 8, 1809, and was buried at New Rochelle, N.Y.

BIBLIOGRAPHY: *The Writings of Thomas Paine,* 4 Vols., ed. Moncure Conway (New York, 1894–1896). *Life and Writings of Thomas Paine,* 10 Vols., ed. Daniel E. Wheeler (New York, 1908). *The Complete Works of Thomas Paine,* 2 Vols., ed. Phillip S. Foner (New York, 1945). *Thomas Paine: Representative Selections,* ed. Harry H. Clark (New York, 1944). *The Selected Works of Thomas Paine,* ed. Howard Fast (New York, 1945). Moncure Conway, *The Life of Thomas Paine,* 2 Vols. (New York, 1892).

From *Common Sense*

THOUGHTS ON THE PRESENT STATE OF AMERICAN AFFAIRS

In the following pages I offer nothing more than simple facts, plain arguments, and common sense: and have no other preliminaries to settle with the reader, than that he will divest himself of prejudice and prepossession, and suffer his reason and his feelings to determine for themselves: that he will put on, or rather that he will not put off, the true character of a man, and generously enlarge his views beyond the present day.

Volumes have been written on the subject of the struggle between England and America. Men of all ranks have embarked in the controversy, from different motives, and with various designs; but all have been ineffectual, and the period of debate is closed. Arms as the last resource decide the contest; the appeal was the choice of the King, and the Continent has accepted the challenge. . . .

As much hath been said of the advantages of reconciliation, which, like an agreeable dream, hath passed away and left us as we were, it is but right that we should examine the contrary side of the argument, and inquire into some of the many material injuries which these Colonies sustain, and always will sustain, by being connected with and dependent on Great Britain. To examine that connection and dependence, on the principles of nature and common sense, to see what we have to trust to, if separated, and what we are to expect, if dependent.

I have heard it asserted by some, that as America has flourished under her former connection with Great Britain, the same connection is necessary towards her future happiness, and will always have the same effect. Nothing can be more fallacious than this kind of argument. We may as well assert that because a child has thrived upon milk, that it is never to have meat, or that the first twenty years of our lives is to become a precedent for the next twenty. But even this is admitting more than is true; for I answer roundly, that America would have flourished as much, and probably much more, had no European power taken any notice of her. The commerce by which she hath enriched herself are the necessaries of life, and will always have a market while eating is the custom of Europe.

But she has protected us, say some. That she hath engrossed us is true, and defended the Continent at our expense as well as her own, is admitted; and she would have defended Turkey from the same motive, viz. for the sake of trade and dominion.

Alas! we have been long led away by ancient prejudices and made large sacrifices to superstition. We have boasted the protection of Great Britain, without considering, that her motive was interest not attachment; and that she did not protect us from our enemies on our account; but from her enemies on her own account, from those who had no quarrel with us on any other account, and who will always be our enemies on the same account. Let Britain waive her pretensions to the Continent, or the Continent throw off the dependence, and we should be at peace with France and Spain, were they at war with Britain. The miseries of Hanover's last war ought to warn us against connections. . . .

But Britain is the parent country, say some. Then the more shame upon her conduct. Even brutes do not devour their young, nor savages make war upon their families; Wherefore, the assertion, if true, turns to her reproach; but it happens not to be true, or only partly so, and the phrase parent or mother country hath been jesuitically adopted by the King and his parasites, with a low papistical design of gaining an unfair bias on the credulous weakness of our minds. Europe, and not England, is the parent country of America. This new World hath been the asylum for the persecuted lovers of civil and religious liberty from every part of Europe. Hither have they fled, not from the tender embraces of the mother, but from the cruelty of the monster; and it is so far true of England, that the same tyranny which drove the first emigrants from home, pursues their descendants still.

In this extensive quarter of the globe, we forget the narrow limits of three hundred and sixty miles (the extent of England) and carry our friendship on a larger scale; we claim brotherhood with every European Christian, and triumph in the generosity of the sentiment. . . .

Much hath been said of the united strength of Britain and the Colonies, that in conjunction they might bid defiance to the world: But this is mere presumption; the fate of war is uncertain, neither do the expressions mean anything; for this continent would never suffer itself to be drained of inhabitants, to support the British arms in either Asia, Africa, or Europe.

Besides, what have we to do with setting the world at defiance? Our plan is commerce, and that, well attended to, will secure us the peace and friendship of all Europe; because it is the interest of all Europe to have America a free port. Her trade will always be a protection, and her barrenness of gold and silver secure her from invaders.

334 / Thomas Paine

I challenge the warmest advocate for reconciliation to show a single advantage that this continent can reap by being connected with Great Britain. I repeat the challenge; not a single advantage is derived. Our corn will fetch its price in any market in Europe, and our imported goods must be paid for by them where we will.

But the injuries and disadvantages which we sustain by that connection, are without number; and our duty to mankind at large, as well as to ourselves, instruct us to renounce the alliance: because, any submission to, or dependence on, Great Britain, tends directly to involve this Continent in European wars and quarrels, and set us at variance with nations who would otherwise seek our friendship, and against whom we have neither anger nor complaint. As Europe is our market for trade, we ought to form no partial connection with any part of it. It is the true interest of America to steer clear of European contentions, which she can never do, while, by her dependence on Britain, she is made the make-weight in the scale of British politics.

Europe is too thickly planted with Kingdoms to be long at peace, and whenever a war breaks out between England and any foreign power, the trade of America goes to ruin, because of her connection with Britain. The next war may not turn out like the last, and should it not, the advocates for reconciliation now will be wishing for separation then, because neutrality in that case would be a safer convoy than a man of war. Every thing that is right or reasonable pleads for separation. The blood of the slain, the weeping voice of nature cries, 'TIS TIME TO PART. Even the distance at which the Almighty hath placed England and America is a strong and natural proof that the authority of the one over the other, was never the design of Heaven. The time likewise at which the Continent was discovered, adds weight to the argument, and the manner in which it was peopled, increases the force of it. The Reformation was preceded by the discovery of America: As if the Almighty graciously meant to open a sanctuary to the persecuted in future years, when home should afford neither friendship nor safety. . . .

Though I would carefully avoid giving unnecessary offence, yet I am inclined to believe, that all those who espouse the doctrine of reconciliation, may be included within the following descriptions.

Interested men, who are not to be trusted, weak men who cannot see, prejudiced men who will not see, and a certain set of moderate men who think better of the European world than it deserves; and this last class, by an ill-judged deliberation, will be the cause of more calamities to this Continent than all the other three.

It is the good fortune of many to live distant from the scene of present sorrow; the evil is not sufficiently brought to their doors to make them feel the precariousness with which all American property is possessed. But let our imaginations transport us a few moments to Boston; that seat of wretchedness will teach us wisdom, and instruct us forever to renounce a power in whom we can have no trust. The inhabitants of that unfortunate city who but a few months ago were in ease and affluence, have now no other alternative than to stay and starve, or turn out to beg. Endangered by the fire of their friends if they continue within the city, and plundered by the soldiery if they leave it, in their present situation they are prisoners without the hope of redemption, and in a general attack for their relief they would be exposed to the fury of both armies.

Men of passive tempers look somewhat lightly over the offences of Great Britain, and, still hoping for the best, are apt to call out, *Come, come, we shall be friends again for all this.* But examine the passions and feelings of mankind: bring the doctrine of reconciliation to the touchstone of nature, and then tell me whether you can hereafter love, honor, and faithfully serve the power that hath carried fire and sword into your land? If you cannot do all these, then are you only deceiving yourselves, and by your delay bringing ruin upon posterity. Your future connection with Britain, whom you can neither love nor honor, will be forced and unnatural, and being formed only on the plan of present convenience, will in a little time fall into a relapse more wretched than the first. But if you say, you can still pass the violations over, then I ask, hath your house been burnt? Hath your property been destroyed before your face? Are your wife and children destitute of a bed to lie on, or bread to live on? Have you lost a parent or a child by their hands, and yourself the ruined and wretched survivor If you have not, then are you not a judge of those who have. But if you have, and can still shake hands with the murderers, then are you unworthy the name of husband, father, friend, or lover, and whatever may be your rank or title in life, you have the heart of a coward, and the spirit of a sycophant.

This is not inflaming or exaggerating matters, but trying them by those feelings and affections which nature justifies, and without which we should be incapable of discharging the social duties of life, or enjoying the felicities of it. I mean not to exhibit horror for the purpose of provoking revenge, but to awaken us from fatal and unmanly slumbers, that we may pursue determinately some fixed object. 'Tis not in the power of Britain or of Europe to conquer America, if she doth not conquer herself by delay and timidity. The present winter is worth an age if rightly employed, but if lost or neglected the whole Continent will partake of the misfortune; and there is no punishment which that man doth not deserve, be he who, or what, or where he will, that may be the means of sacrificing a season so precious and useful.

'Tis repugnant to reason, to the universal order of things, to all examples from former ages, to suppose that this Continent can long remain subject to any external power. . . .

As to government matters, 'tis not in the power of Britain to do this continent justice: the business of it will soon be too weighty and intricate to be managed with any tolerable degree of convenience, by a power so distant from us, and so very ignorant of us; for if they cannot conquer us, they cannot govern us. To be always running three or four thousand miles with a tale or a petition, waiting four or five months for an answer, which, when obtained, requires five or six more to explain it in, will in a few years be looked upon as folly and childishness. There was a time when it was proper, and there is a proper time for it to cease.

Small islands not capable of protecting themselves are the proper objects for government to take under their care; but there is something absurd, in supposing a Continent to be perpetually governed by an island. In no instance hath nature made the satellite larger than its primary planet; and as England and America, with respect to each other, reverse the common order of nature, it is evident that they belong to different systems. England to Europe: America to itself.

I am not induced by motives of pride, party, or resentment to espouse the doctrine of separation and independence; I am clearly, positively, and conscientiously persuaded that it is the true interest of this Continent to be so; that everything short of *that* is mere patchwork, that it can afford no lasting felicity,—that it is leaving the sword to our children, and shrinking back at a time when a little more, a little further, would have rendered this Continent the glory of the earth.

As Britain hath not manifested the least inclination towards a compromise, we may be assured that no terms can be obtained worthy the acceptance of the Continent, or any ways equal to the expense of blood and treasure we have been already put to. . . .

Ye that tell us of harmony and reconciliation, can ye restore to us the time that is past? Can ye give to prostitution its former innocence? neither can ye reconcile Britain and America. The last cord now is broken, the people of England are presenting addresses against us. There are injuries which nature cannot forgive; she would cease to be nature if she did. As well can the lover forgive the ravisher of his mistress, as the Continent forgive the murders of Britain. The Almighty hath implanted in us these unextinguishable feelings for good and wise purposes. They are the Guardians of his Image in our hearts. They distinguish us from the herd of common animals. The social compact would dissolve, and justice be extirpated from the earth, or have only a casual existence were we callous to the touches of affection. The robber and the murderer would often escape unpunished, did not the injuries which our tempers sustain, provoke us into justice.

O! ye that love mankind! Ye that dare oppose not only the tyranny but the tyrant, stand forth! Every spot of the old world is overrun with oppression. Freedom hath been hunted round the Globe. Asia and Africa have long expelled her. Europe regards her like a stranger, and England hath given her warning to depart. O! receive the fugitive, and prepare in time an asylum for mankind.   1776

From *The Crisis*

I

These are the times that try men's souls. The summer soldier and the sunshine patriot will, in this crisis, shrink from the service of their country; but he that stands it *now*, deserves the love and thanks of man and woman. Tyranny, like hell, is not easily conquered; yet we have this consolation with us, that the harder the conflict, the more glorious the triumph. What we obtain too cheap, we esteem too lightly: it is dearness only that gives everything its value. Heaven knows how to put a proper price upon its goods; and it would be strange indeed if so celestial an article as FREEDOM should not be highly rated. Britain, with an army to enforce her tyranny, has declared that she has a right (not only to TAX) but "to BIND us in ALL CASES WHATSOEVER," and if being bound in that manner, is not slavery, then is there not such a thing as slavery upon earth. Even the expression is impious; for so unlimited a power can belong only to God.

Whether the independence of the continent was declared too soon, or delayed too long, I will not now enter into as an argument; my own simple opinion is, that had it been eight months earlier, it would have been much better. We did not make a proper use of last winter, neither could we, while we were in a dependent state. However, the fault, if it were one, was all our own[1]; we have none to blame but ourselves. But no great deal is lost yet. All that Howe has been doing for this month past, is rather a ravage than a conquest, which the spirit of the Jerseys, a year ago, would have quickly repulsed, and which time and a little resolution will soon recover.

I have as little superstition in me as any man living, but my secret opinion has ever been, and still is, that God Almighty will not give up a people to military destruction, or leave them unsupportedly to perish, who have so earnestly and so repeatedly sought to avoid the calamities of war, by every decent method which wisdom could invent. Neither have I so much of the infidel in me, as to suppose that He has relinquished the government of the world, and given us up to the care of devils; and as I do not, I cannot see on what grounds the king of Britain can look up to heaven for help against us: a common murderer, a highwayman, or a house-breaker, has as good a pretense as he.

'Tis surprising to see how rapidly a panic will sometimes run through a country. All nations and ages have been subject to them: Britain has trembled like an ague at the report of a French fleet of flat bottomed boats; and in the fourteenth [fifteenth] century the whole English army,

[1] The present winter is worth an age, if rightly employed; but, if lost or neglected, the whole continent will partake of the evil; and there is no punishment that man does not deserve, be he who, or what, or where he will, that may be the means of sacrificing a season so precious and useful. [Paine's Note.]

after ravaging the kingdom of France, was driven back like men petrified with fear; and this brave exploit was performed by a few broken forces collected and headed by a woman, Joan of Arc. Would that heaven might inspire some Jersey maid to spirit up her countrymen, and save her fair fellow sufferers from ravage and ravishment! Yet panics, in some cases, have their uses; they produce as much good as hurt. Their duration is always short; the mind soon grows through them, and acquires a firmer habit than before. But their peculiar advantage is, that they are the touchstones of sincerity and hypocrisy, and bring things and men to light, which might otherwise have lain forever undiscovered. In fact, they have the same effect on secret traitors, which an imaginary apparition would have upon a private murderer. They sift out the hidden thoughts of man, and hold them up in public to the world. Many a disguised tory has lately shown his head, that shall penitentially solemnize with curses the day on which Howe arrived upon the Delaware. . . .

I shall not now attempt to give all the particulars of our retreat to the Delaware; suffice it for the present to say, that both officers and men, though greatly harassed and fatigued, frequently without rest, covering, or provision, the inevitable consequences of a long retreat, bore it with a manly and martial spirit. All their wishes centered in one, which was, that the country would turn out and help them to drive the enemy back. Voltaire has remarked that king William never appeared to full advantage but in difficulties and in action; the same remark may be made on General Washington, for the character fits him. There is a natural firmness in some minds which cannot be unlocked by trifles, but which, when unlocked, discovers a cabinet of fortitude; and I reckon it among those kind of public blessings, which we do not immediately see, that God hath blessed him with uninterrupted health, and given him a mind that can even flourish upon care.

I shall conclude this paper with some miscellaneous remarks on the state of our affairs; and shall begin with asking the following question, Why is it that the enemy have left the New-England provinces, and made these middle ones the seat of war? The answer is easy: New-England is not infested with tories, and we are. I have been tender in raising the cry against these men, and used numberless arguments to show them their danger, but it will not do to sacrifice a world either to their folly or their baseness. The period is now arrived, in which either they or we must change our sentiments, or one or both must fall. And what is a tory? Good God! what is he? I should not be afraid to go with a hundred whigs against a thousand tories, were they to attempt to get into arms. Every tory is a coward; for servile, slavish, self-interested fear is the foundation of toryism; and a man under such influence, though he may be cruel, never can be brave. . . .

I once felt all that kind of anger, which a man ought to feel, against the mean principles that are held by the tories: a noted one, who kept a tavern at Amboy, was standing at his door, with as pretty a child in his hand, about eight or nine years old, as I ever saw, and after speaking his mind as freely as he thought was prudent, finished with this unfatherly expression, "Well! give me peace in my day." Not a man lives on the continent but fully believes that a separation must some time or other finally take place, and a generous parent should have said, "If there must be trouble, let it be in my day, that my child may have peace"; and this single reflection, well applied, is sufficient to awaken every man to duty. Not a place upon earth might be so happy as America. Her situation is remote from all the wrangling world, and she has nothing to do but to trade with them. A man can distinguish himself between temper and principle, and I am as confident, as I am that God governs the world, that America will never be happy till she gets clear of foreign dominion. Wars, without ceasing, will break out till that period arrives, and the continent must in the end be conqueror; for though the flame of liberty may sometimes cease to shine, the coal can never expire. . . .

Quitting this class of men, I turn with the warm ardor of a friend to those who have nobly stood, and are yet determined to stand the matter out: I call not upon a few, but upon all: not on *this* state or *that* state, but on *every* state: up and help us; lay your shoulders to the wheel; better have too much force than too little, when so great an object is at stake. Let it be told to the future world, that in the depth of winter, when nothing but hope and virtue could survive, that the city and the country, alarmed at one common danger, came forth to meet and to repulse it. Say not that thousands are gone, turn out your tens of thousands; throw not the burden of the day upon Providence, but "show your faith by your works," that God may bless you. It matters not where you live, or what rank of life you hold, the evil or the blessing will reach you all. The far and the near, the home counties and the back, the rich and the poor, will suffer or rejoice alike. The heart that feels not now, is dead: the blood of his children will curse his cowardice, who shrinks back at a time when a little might have saved the whole, and made *them* happy. I love the man that can smile in trouble, that can gather strength from distress, and grow brave by reflection. 'Tis the business of little minds to shrink; but he whose heart is firm, and whose conscience approves his conduct, will pursue his principles unto death. . . .

I thank God, that I fear not. I see no real cause for fear. I know our situation well, and can see the way out of it. While our army was collected, Howe dared not risk a battle; and it is no credit to him that he decamped from the White Plains, and waited a mean opportunity to ravage the defenseless Jerseys; but it is great credit to us, that, with a handful of men, we sustained an orderly retreat for near an hundred miles, brought off our ammunition, all our field pieces, the greatest part of our stores, and had four rivers to pass. None can say that our retreat was precipitate, for we were near three weeks in performing it, that the country might have time to come in. Twice we marched back to meet the enemy, and remained out till dark. The sign of fear was not seen in our camp, and had not some of the cowardly and disaffected inhabitants spread false alarms through the country, the Jerseys had never been ravaged. Once more we are again collected and collecting; our new army at both ends of the continent is recruiting fast, and we shall be able to open the next campaign with sixty thousand men, well armed and clothed. This is our situation, and who will may know it. By perseverance and fortitude we have the prospect of a glorious issue; by cowardice and submission, the sad choice of a variety of evils—a ravaged country—a depopulated city—habitations without safety, and slavery without hope—our homes turned into barracks and bawdy-houses for Hessians, and a future race to provide for, whose fathers we shall doubt of. Look on this picture and weep over it! and if there yet remains one thoughtless wretch who believes it not, let him suffer it unlamented.

COMMON SENSE
1776

Thomas Jefferson
(1743-1826)

Statesman and President, diplomat and lawyer, writer and thinker, Thomas Jefferson was born in Albermarle County, Va., the son of a prosperous planter. He graduated from William and Mary College in 1762 and was admitted to law practice in 1767. Among the many offices he held were member of the Virginia House of Burgesses (1769–1774), member of Continental Congress (1775–1776), Governor of Virginia (1779–1781), a commissioner and U.S. Minister to France (1784–1789), Secretary of State (1790–1793), and President (1801–1809). From 1809 till his death, Jefferson lived at Monticello; one of his major contributions during this period was the founding of the University of Virginia (1819). Among Jefferson's writings are A Summary View of the Rights of British America (Williamsburg, Va., 1774), The Declaration of Independence (1776), and Notes on the State of Virginia (Paris,

1785). A French translation of Notes was published in 1787; another edition was printed by John Stockdale in London (1787), and the first American edition was published in Philadelphia in 1788.

BIBLIOGRAPHY: The Writings of Thomas Jefferson, 10 Vols., ed. Paul L. Ford (New York, 1892–1899). The Writings of Thomas Jefferson, 20 Vols., ed. A. A. Lipscomb and A. L. Bergh (Washington, 1903). In progress The Papers of Thomas Jefferson, 15 Vols., ed. Julian P. Boyd (Princeton, 1950–1958), of a projected 50 Vols. Adrienne Koch, The Philosophy of Thomas Jefferson (New York, 1943). Gilbert Chinard, Thomas Jefferson: The Apostle of Americanism (Boston, 1929). Other biographers include Claude G. Bowers, Marie Kimball, Dumas Malone, and Nathan Schachner.

From *Notes on the State of Virginia*

QUERY VI

PRODUCTIONS MINERAL, VEGETABLE AND ANIMAL

*A notice of the mines and other subterraneous riches; its trees,
plants, fruits, &c.*

. . . Hitherto I have considered this hypothesis as applied to brute animals only, and not in its extension to the man of America, whether aboriginal or transplanted. It is the opinion of Mons. de Buffon that the former furnishes no exception to it: "Although the savage of the new world is about the same height as man in our world, this does not suffice for him to constitute an exception to the general fact that all living nature has become smaller on that continent. The savage is feeble, and has small organs of generation; he has neither hair nor beard, and no ardor whatever for his female; although swifter than the European because he is better accustomed to running, he is, on the other hand, less strong in body; he is also less sensitive, and yet more timid and cowardly; he has no vivacity, no activity of mind; the activity of his body is less an exercise, a voluntary motion, than a necessary action caused by want; relieve him of hunger and thirst, and you deprive him of the active principle of all his movements; he will rest stupidly upon his legs or lying down entire days. There is no need for seeking further the cause of the isolated mode of life of these savages and their repugnance for society: the most precious spark of the fire of nature has been refused to them; they lack ardor for their females, and consequently have no love for their fellow men: not knowing this strongest and most tender of all affections, their other feelings are also cold and languid; they love their parents and children but little; the most intimate of all ties, the family connection, binds them therefore but loosely together; between family and family there is no tie at all; hence they have no communion, no commonwealth, no state of society. Physical love constitutes their only morality; their heart is icy, their society cold, and their rule harsh. They look upon their wives only as servants for all work, or as beasts of burden, which they load without consideration with the burden of their hunting, and which they compel without mercy, without gratitude, to perform tasks which are often beyond their strength. They have only few children, and they take little care of them. Everywhere the original defect appears: they are indifferent because they have little sexual capacity, and this indifference to the other sex is the fundamental defect which weakens their nature, prevents its development, and—destroying the very germs of life—uproots society at the same time. Man is here no exception to the general rule. Nature, by refusing him the power of love, has treated him worse and lowered him deeper than any animal." An afflicting picture indeed, which, for the honor of human nature, I am glad to believe has no original. Of the Indian of South America I know nothing; for I would not honor with the appellation of knowledge, what I derive from the fables published of them. These I believe to be just as true as the fables of Æsop. This belief is founded on what I have seen of man, white, red, and black, and what has been written of him by authors, enlightened themselves, and writing amidst an enlightened people. The Indian of North America being more within our reach, I can speak of him somewhat from my own knowledge, but more from the information of others better acquainted with him, and on whose truth and judgment I can rely. From these sources I am able to say, in contradiction to this representation, that he is neither more defective in ardor, nor more impotent with his female, than the white reduced to the same diet and exercise: that he is brave, when an enterprise depends on bravery; education with him making the point of honor consist in the destruction of an enemy by stratagem, and in the preservation of his own person free from injury; or perhaps this is nature; while it is education which teaches us to honor force more than finesse; that he will defend himself against an host of enemies, always choosing to be killed, rather than to surrender, though it be to the whites, who he knows will treat him well: that in other situations also he meets death with more deliberation, and endures tortures with a firmness unknown almost to religious enthusiasm with us: that he is affectionate to his children, careful of them, and indulgent in the extreme: that his affections comprehend his other connections, weakening, as with us, from circle to circle, as they recede from the center: that his friendships are strong and faithful to the uttermost extremity: that his sensibility is keen, even the warriors weeping most bitterly on the loss of their children, though in general they endeavor to appear superior to human events: that his vivacity and activity of mind is equal to ours in the same situation; hence his eagerness for hunting, and for games of chance. The women are submitted to unjust drudgery. This I believe is the case with every barbarous people. With such, force is law. The stronger sex therefore imposes on the weaker. It is civilization alone which replaces women in the enjoyment of their natural equality. That first teaches us to subdue the selfish passions, and to respect those rights in others which we value in ourselves. Were we in equal barbarism, our females would be equal drudges. The man with them is less strong than with us, but their woman stronger than ours; and both for the same obvious reason; because our man and their woman is habituated to labor, and formed by it. With both races the sex which is indulged with ease is least athletic. An Indian man is small in the hand and wrist for the same reason for which a sailor is large and strong in the arms and shoulders, and a porter in the legs and thighs.—They raise fewer children than we do. The causes of this are to be found, not in a difference of nature, but of circumstance. The women very frequently attending the men in their parties of war and of hunting, child-bearing becomes extremely inconvenient to them. It is said, therefore, that they have learnt the practice of procuring abortion by the use of some vegetable; and that it even extends to prevent conception for a considerable time after. During these parties they are exposed to numerous hazards, to excessive exertions, to the greatest extremities of hunger. Even at their homes the nation depends for food, through a certain part of every year, on the gleanings of the forest: that is, they experience a famine once in every year. With all animals, if the female be badly fed, or not fed at all, her young perish: and if both male and female be reduced to like want, generation becomes less active, less productive. To the obstacles then of want and hazard, which nature has opposed to the multiplication of wild animals, for the purpose of restraining their numbers within certain bounds, those of labor and of voluntary abortion are added with the Indian. No wonder then if they multiply less than we do. Where food is regularly supplied, a single farm will show more of cattle, than a whole country of forests can of buffaloes. The same Indian women, when married to white traders, who feed them and their children plentifully and regularly, who exempt them from excessive drudgery, who keep them stationary and unexposed to accident, produce and raise as many children as the white women. Instances are known, under these circumstances, of their rearing a dozen children. An inhuman practice once prevailed in this country of making slaves of the Indians. (This practice commenced with the Spaniards with the first discovery of America). It is a fact well known with us, that the Indian women so enslaved produced and raised as numerous families as either the whites or blacks among whom they lived.—It has been said, that Indians have less hair than the whites, except on the head. But this is a fact of which fair proof can scarcely be had. With them it is disgraceful to be hairy on the body. They say it likens them to hogs. They therefore pluck the hair as fast as it appears. But the traders who marry their women, and prevail on them to discontinue this practice, say, that nature is the same with them as with the whites. Nor, if the fact be true, is the consequence necessary which has been drawn from it. Negroes have notoriously less hair than the whites; yet they are more ardent. But if cold and moisture be the agents of nature for diminishing the races of animals, how comes she all at once to suspend their operation as to the physical man of the new world, whom the Count acknowledges to be "about the same size as the man of our hemisphere," and to let loose their influence on his moral faculties? How has this "combination of the elements and other physical causes, so contrary to the enlargement of animal nature in this new world, these obstacles to the development and formation of great germs," been arrested and suspended, so as to permit the human body to acquire its just dimensions, and by what inconceivable process has their action been directed on his mind alone? To judge of the truth of this, to form a just estimate of their genius and mental powers, more facts are wanting, and great allowance to be made for those circumstances of their situation which call for a display of particular talents only. This done, we shall probably find that they are formed in mind as well as in body, on the same module with the "Homo sapiens Europæus." The principles of their society forbidding all compulsion, they are to be led to duty and to enterprise by personal influence and persuasion. Hence eloquence in council, bravery and address in war, become the foundations of all consequence with them. To these acquirements all their faculties are directed. Of their bravery and address in war we have multiplied proofs, because we have been the subjects on which they were exercised. Of their eminence in oratory we have fewer examples, because it is displayed chiefly in their own councils. Some, however, we have of very superior luster. I may challenge the whole orations of Demosthenes and Cicero, and of any more eminent orator, if Europe has furnished more eminent, to produce a single passage, superior to the speech of Logan, a Mingo chief, to Lord Dunmore, when governor of this state. And, as a testimony of their talents in this line, I beg leave to introduce it, first stating the incidents necessary for understanding it. In the spring of the year 1774, a robbery was committed by some Indians on certain land-adventurers on the river Ohio. The whites in that quarter, according to their custom, undertook to punish this outrage in a summary way. Captain Michael Cresap, and a certain Daniel Great-house, leading on these parties, surprised, at different times, travelling and hunting parties of the Indians, having their women and children with them, and murdered many. Among these were unfortunately the family of Logan, a chief celebrated in peace and war, and long distinguished as the friend of the whites. This unworthy return provoked his vengeance. He accordingly signalized himself in the war which ensued. In the autumn of the same year a decisive battle was fought at the mouth of the Great Kanhaway, between the collected forces of the Shawanese, Mingoes, and Delawares, and a detachment of the Virginia militia. The Indians were defeated, and sued for peace. Logan however disdained to be seen among the suppliants. But, lest the sincerity of a treaty should be distrusted, from which so distinguished a chief absented himself, he sent by a messenger the following speech to be delivered to Lord Dunmore.

"I appeal to any white man to say, if ever he entered Logan's cabin hungry, and he gave him not meat; if ever he came cold and naked, and he clothed him not. During the course of the last long and bloody war, Logan remained idle in his cabin, an advocate for peace. Such was my love for the whites, that my countrymen pointed as they passed, and said, 'Logan is the friend of white men.' I had even thought to have lived with you, but for the injuries of one man. Col. Cresap, the last spring, in cold blood, and unprovoked, murdered all the relations of Logan, not sparing even my women and children. There runs not a drop of my blood in the veins of any living creature. This called on me for revenge. I have sought it: I have killed many: I have fully glutted my vengeance. For my country, I rejoice at the beams of peace. But do not harbor a thought that mine is the joy of fear. Logan never felt fear. He will not turn on his heel to save his life. Who is there to mourn for Logan?—Not one."

Before we condemn the Indians of this continent as wanting genius, we must consider that letters have not yet been introduced among them. Were we to compare them in their present state with the Europeans North of the Alps, when the Roman arms and arts first crossed those mountains, the comparison would be unequal, because, at that time, those parts of Europe were swarming with numbers; because numbers produce emulation, and multiply the chances of improvement, and one improvement begets another. Yet I may safely ask, How many good poets, how many able mathematicians, how many great inventors in arts or sciences, had Europe North of the Alps then produced? And it was sixteen centuries after this before a Newton could be formed. I do not mean to deny, that there are varieties in the race of man, distinguished by their powers both of body and mind. I believe there are, as I see to be the case in the races of other animals. I only mean to suggest a doubt, whether the bulk and faculties of animals depend on the side of the Atlantic on which their food happens to grow, or which furnishes the elements of which they are compounded? Whether nature has enlisted herself as a cis- or trans-atlantic partisan? I am induced to suspect, there has been more eloquence than sound reasoning displayed in support of this theory; that it is one of those cases where the judgment has been seduced by a glowing pen: and whilst I render every tribute of honor and esteem to the celebrated Zoologist, who has added, and is still adding, so many precious things to the treasures of science, I must doubt whether in this instance he has not cherished error also, by lending her for a moment his vivid imagination and bewitching language.

So far the Count de Buffon has carried this new theory of the tendency of nature to belittle her productions on this side of the Atlantic. Its application to the race of whites, transplanted from Europe, remained for the Abbé Raynal. "One must be astonished (he says) that America has not yet produced one good poet, one able mathematician, one man of genius in a single art or a single science." "America has not yet produced one good poet." When we shall have existed as a people as long as the Greeks did before they produced a Homer, the Romans a Virgil, the French a Racine and Voltaire, the English a Shakespeare and Milton, should this reproach be still true, we will enquire from what unfriendly causes it has proceeded, that the other countries of Europe and quarters of the earth shall not have inscribed any name in the roll of poets. But neither has America produced "one able mathematician, one man of genius in a single art or a single science." In war we have produced a Washington, whose memory will be adored while liberty shall have votaries, whose name will triumph over time, and will in future ages assume its just station among the most celebrated worthies of the world, when that wretched philosophy shall be forgotten which would have arranged him among the degeneracies of nature. In physics we have produced a Franklin, than whom no one of the present age has made more important discoveries, nor has enriched philosophy with more, or more ingenious solutions of the phenomena of nature. We have supposed Mr. Rittenhouse second to no astronomer living: that in genius he must be the first, because he is self-taught. As an artist he has exhibited as great a proof of mechanical genius as the world has ever produced. He has not indeed made a world; but he has by imitation approached nearer its Maker than any man who has lived from the creation to this day. As in philosophy and war, so in government, in oratory, in painting, in the plastic art, we might show that America, though but a child of yesterday, has already given hopeful proofs of genius, as well of the nobler kinds, which arouse the best feelings of man, which call him into action, which substantiate his freedom, and conduct him to happiness, as of the subordinate, which serve to amuse him only. We therefore suppose, that this reproach is as unjust as it is unkind; and that, of the geniuses which adorn the present age, America contributes its full share. For comparing it with those countries, where genius is most cultivated, where are the most excellent models for art, and scaffoldings for the attainment of science, as France and England for instance, we calculate thus. The United States contain three millions of inhabitants; France twenty millions; and the British islands ten. We produce a Washington, a Franklin, a Rittenhouse. France then should have half a dozen in each of these lines, and Great Britain half that number, equally eminent. It may be true, that France has: we are but just becoming acquainted with her, and our acquaintance so far gives us high ideas of the genius of her inhabitants. It would be injuring too many of them to name particularly a Voltaire, a Buffon, the constellation of Encyclopedists, the Abbé Raynal himself, &c. &c. We therefore have reason to believe she can produce her full quota of genius. The present war having so long cut off all communication with Great Britain, we are not able to make a fair estimate of the state of science in that country. The spirit in which she wages war is the only sample before our eyes, and that does not seem the legitimate offspring either of science or of civilization. The sun of her glory is fast descending to the horizon. Her philosophy has crossed the Channel, her freedom the Atlantic, and herself seems passing to that awful dissolution, whose issue is not given human foresight to scan. . . .

QUERY XVIII

MANNERS

The particular customs and manners that may happen to be received in that state?

It is difficult to determine on the standard by which the manners of a nation may be tried, whether *catholic,* or *particular.* It is more difficult for a native to bring to that standard the manners of his own nation, familiarized to him by habit. There must doubtless be an unhappy influence on the manners of our people produced by the existence of slavery among us. The whole commerce between master and slave is a perpetual exercise of the most boisterous passions, the most unremitting despotism on the one part, and degrading submissions on the other. Our children see this, and learn to imitate it; or man is an imitative animal. This quality is the germ of all education in him. From his cradle to his grave he is learning to do what he sees others do. If a parent could find no motive either in his philanthropy or his self-love, for restraining the intemperance of passion towards his slave, it should always be a sufficient one that his child is present. But generally it is not sufficient. The parent storms, the child looks on, catches the lineaments of wrath, puts on the same airs in the circle of smaller slaves, gives a loose to his worst of passions, and thus nursed, educated, and daily exercised in tyranny, cannot but be stamped by it with odious peculiarities. The man must be a prodigy who can retain his manners and morals undepraved by such circumstances. And with what execration should the statesman be loaded, who permitting one half the citizens thus to trample on the rights of the other, transforms those into despots, and these into enemies, destroys the morals of the one part, and the amor patriæ of the other. For if a slave can have a country in this world, it must be any other in preference to that in which he is born to live and labor for another: in which he must lock up the faculties of his nature, contribute as far as depends on his individual endeavors to the evanishment of the human race, or entail his own miserable condition on the endless generations proceeding from him. With the morals of the people, their industry also is destroyed. For in a warm climate, no man will labor for himself who can make another labor for him. This is so true, that of the proprietors of slaves a very small proportion indeed are ever seen to labor. And can the liberties of a nation be thought secure when we have removed their only firm basis, a conviction in the minds of the people that these liberties are of the gift of God? That they are not to be violated but with his wrath? Indeed I tremble for my country when I reflect that God is just: that his justice cannot sleep forever: that considering numbers, nature and natural means only, a revolution of the wheel of fortune, an exchange of situation, is among possible events: that it may become probable by supernatural interference! The Almighty has no attribute which can take side with us in such a contest.—But it is impossible to be temperate and to pursue this subject through the various considerations of policy, of morals, of history natural and civil. We must be contented to hope they will force their way into everyone's mind. I think a change already perceptible, since the origin of the present revolution. The spirit of the master is abating, that of the slave rising from the dust, his condition mollifying, the way I hope preparing, under the auspices of heaven, for a total emancipation, and that this is disposed, in the order of events, to be with the consent of the masters, rather than by their extirpation.   1785

The Federalist Papers

James Madison (1751–1836), Alexunder Hamilton (1757–1804), and John Jay (1745–1829) wrote the eighty-five *Federalist Papers* in support of the Constitution, seventy-seven of which originally appeared in three New York papers: the *Independent Journal,* the *Packet,* and the *Daily Advertiser.* Hamilton is credited with authorship of fifty-one essays, Madison with twenty-six, Jay with five, and Madison and Hamilton with joint authorship of three. When Hamilton gathered the papers for publication in two volumes in 1788, he added the last eight.

BIBLIOGRAPHY: *The Federalist Papers,* ed. Paul L. Ford (New York, 1898). Also edited with comments and introductions by Henry Cabot Lodge (New York, 1888); Benjamin F. Wright (Cambridge, Mass., 1961); Jacob E. Cooke (Middletown, Conn., 1961); Charles A. Beard (Garden City, N.Y., 1948); Max Beloff (Oxford, Eng., 1948); Gottfried Dietze (Baltimore, 1960). John S. Bassett, *Selections from The Federalist* (New York, 1921). Frederick Moestetler and David L. Wallace, *Inference and Disputed Authorship: The Federalist* (Reading, Mass., 1964).

From *The Federalist Papers*

From the New York Packet, Friday, November 23, 1787

THE FEDERALIST. NO. X
(MADISON)

To the People of the State of New York:

Among the numerous advantages promised by a well-constructed Union, none deserves to be more accurately developed than its tendency to break and control the violence of faction. The friend of popular governments never finds himself so much alarmed for their character and fate, as when he contemplates their propensity to this dangerous vice. He will not fail, therefore, to set a due value on any plan which, without violating the principles to which he is attached, provides a proper cure for it. The instability, injustice, and confusion introduced into the public councils, have, in truth, been the mortal diseases under which popular governments have everywhere perished; as they continue to be the favorite and fruitful topics from which the adversaries to liberty derive their most specious declamations. The valuable improvements made by the American constitutions on the popular models, both ancient and modern, cannot certainly be too much admired; but it would be an unwarrantable partiality, to contend that they have as effectually obviated the danger on this side, as was wished and expected. Complaints are everywhere heard from our most considerate and virtuous citizens, equally the friends of public and private faith, and of public and personal liberty, that our governments are too unstable, that the public good is disregarded in the conflicts of rival parties, and that measures are too often decided, not according to the rules of justice and the rights of the minor party, but by the superior force of an interested and overbearing majority. However anxiously we may wish that these complaints had no foundation, the evidence of known facts will not permit us to deny that they are in some degree true. It will be found, indeed, on a candid review of our situation, that some of the distresses under which we labor have been erroneously charged on the operation of our governments; but it will be found, at the same time, that other causes will not alone account for many of our heaviest misfortunes; and, particularly, for that prevailing and increasing distrust of public engagements, and alarm for private rights, which are echoed from one end of the continent to the other. These must be chiefly, if not wholly, effects of the unsteadiness and injustice with which a factious spirit has tainted our public administrations.

By a faction, I understand a number of citizens, whether amounting to a majority or minority of the whole, who are united and actuated by some common impulse of passion, or of interest, adverse to the rights of other citizens, or to the permanent and aggregate interests of the community.

There are two methods of curing the mischiefs of faction: the one, by removing its causes; the other, by controlling its effects.

There are again two methods of removing the causes of faction: the one, by detroying the liberty which is essential to its existence; the other, by giving to every citizen the same opinions, the same passions, and the same interests.

It could never be more truly said than of the first remedy, that it was worse than the disease. Liberty is to faction what air is to fire, an aliment without which it instantly expires. But it could not be less folly to abolish liberty, which is essential to political life, because it nourishes faction, than it would be to wish the annihilation of air, which is essential to animal life, because it imparts to fire its destructive agency.

The second expedient is as impracticable as the first would be unwise. As long as the reason of man continues fallible, and he is at liberty to exercise it, different opinions will be formed. As long as the connection subsists between his reason and his self-love, his opinions and his passions will have a reciprocal influence on each other; and the former will be objects to which the latter will attach themselves. The diversity in the faculties of men, from which the rights of property originate, is not less an insuperable obstacle to a uniformity of interests. The protection of these faculties is the first object of government. From the protection of different and unequal faculties of acquiring property, the possession of different degrees and kinds of property immediately results; and from the influence of these on the sentiments and views of the respective proprietors, ensues a division of the society into different interests and parties.

The latent causes of faction are thus sown in the nature of man; and we see them everywhere brought into different degrees of activity, according to the different circumstances of civil society. A zeal for different opinions concerning religion, concerning government, and many other points, as well of speculation as of practice; an attachment to different leaders ambitiously contending for preeminence and power; or to persons of other descriptions whose fortunes have been interesting to the human passions, have, in turn, divided mankind into parties, inflamed them with mutual animosity, and rendered them much more disposed to vex and oppress each other than to cooperate for their common good. So strong is this propensity of mankind to fall into mutual animosities, that where no substantial occasion presents itself, the most frivolous and fanciful distinctions have been sufficient to kindle their unfriendly passions and excite their most violent conflicts. But the most common and durable source of factions has been the various and unequal distribution of property. Those who hold and those who are without property have ever formed distinct interests in society. Those who are creditors, and those who are debtors, fall under a like discrimination. A landed interest, a manufacturing interest, a mercantile interest, a moneyed interest, with many lesser interests, grow up of necessity in civilized nations, and divide them into different classes, actuated by different sentiments and views. The regulation of these various and interfering interests forms the principal task of modern legislation, and involves the spirit of party and faction in the necessary and ordinary operations of the government.

No man is allowed to be a judge in his own cause, because his interest would certainly bias his judgment, and, not improbably, corrupt his integrity. With equal, nay with greater reason, a body of men are unfit to be both judges and parties at the same time; yet what are many of the most important acts of legislation, but so many judical determinations, not indeed concerning the rights of single persons, but concerning the rights of large bodies of citizens? And what are the different classes of legislators but advocates and parties to the causes which they determine?

Is a law proposed concerning private debts? It is a question to which the creditors are parties on one side and the debtors on the other. Justice ought to hold the balance between them. Yet the parties are, and must be, themselves the judges; and the most numerous party, or, in other words, the most powerful faction must be expected to prevail. Shall domestic manufactures be encouraged, and in what degree, by restrictions on foreign manufactures? are questions which would be differently decided by the landed and the manufacturing classes, and probably by neither with a sole regard to justice and the public good. The apportionment of taxes on the various descriptions of property is an act which seems to require the most exact impartiality; yet there is, perhaps, no legislative act in which greater opportunity and temptation are given to a predominant party to trample on the rules of justice. Every shilling with which they overburden the inferior number, is a shilling saved to their own pockets.

It is in vain to say that enlightened statesmen will be able to adjust these clashing interests, and render them all subservient to the public good. Enlightened statesmen will not always be at the helm. Nor, in many cases, can such an adjustment be made at all without taking into view indirect and remote considerations, which will rarely prevail over the immediate interest which one party may find in disregarding the rights of another or the good of the whole.

The inference to which we are brought is, that the *causes* of faction cannot be removed, and that relief is only to be sought in the means of controlling its *effects*.

If a faction consists of less than a majority, relief is supplied by the republican principle, which enables the majority to defeat its sinister views by regular vote. It may clog the administration, it may convulse the society; but it will be unable to execute and mask its violence under the forms of the Constitution. When a majority is included in a faction, the form of popular government, on the other hand, enables it to sacrifice to its ruling passion or interest both the public good and the rights of other citizens. To secure the public good and private rights against the danger of such a faction, and at the same time to preserve the spirit and the form of popular government, is then the great object to which our inquiries are directed. Let me add that it is the great desideratum by which this form of government can be rescued from the opprobrium under which it has so long labored, and be recommended to the esteem and adoption of mankind.

By what means is this object attainable? Evidently by one of two only. Either the existence of the same passion or interest in a majority at the same time must be prevented, or the majority, having such coexistent passion or interest, must be rendered, by their number and local situation, unable to concert and carry into effect schemes of oppression. If the impulse and the opportunity be suffered to coincide, we well know that neither moral nor religious motives can be relied on as an adequate control. They are not found to be such on the injustice and violence of individuals, and lose their efficacy in proportion to the number combined together, that is, in proportion as their efficacy becomes needful.

From this view of the subject it may be concluded that a pure democracy, by which I mean a society consisting of a small number of citizens, who assemble and administer the government in person, can admit of no cure for the mischiefs of faction. A common passion or interest will, in almost every case, be felt by a majority of the whole; a communication and concert result from the form of government itself; and there is nothing to check the inducements to sacrifice the weaker party or an obnoxious individual. Hence it is that such democracies have ever been spectacles of turbulence and contention; have ever been found incompatible with personal security or the rights of property; and have in general been as short in their lives as they have been violent in their deaths. Theoretic politicians, who have patronized this species of government, have erroneously supposed that by reducing mankind to a perfect equality in their political rights, they would, at the same time, be perfectly equalized and assimilated in their possessions, their opinions, and their passions.

A republic, by which I mean a government in which the scheme of representation takes place, opens a different prospect, and promises the cure for which we are seeking. Let us examine the points in which it varies from pure democracy, and we shall comprehend both the nature of the cure and the efficacy which it must derive from the Union.

The two great points of difference between a democracy and a republic are: first, the delegation of the government, in the latter, to a small number of citizens elected by the rest; secondly, the greater number of citizens, and greater sphere of country, over which the latter may be extended.

The effect of the first difference is, on the one hand, to refine and enlarge the public views, by passing them through the medium of a chosen body of citizens, whose wisdom may best discern the true interest of their country, and whose patriotism and love of justice will be least likely to sacrifice it to temporary or partial considerations. Under such a regulation, it may well happen that the public voice, pronounced by the representatives of the people, will be more consonant to the public good than if pronounced by the people themselves, convened for the purpose. On the other hand, the effect may be inverted. Men of factious tempers, of local prejudices, or of sinister designs, may, by intrigue, by corruption, or by other means, first obtain the suffrages, and then betray the interests, of the people. The question resulting is, whether small or extensive republics are more favorable to the election of proper guardians of the public weal; and it is clearly decided in favor of the latter by two obvious considerations:

In the first place, it is to be remarked that, however small the republic may be, the representatives must be raised to a certain number, in order to guard against the cabals of a few; and that, however large it may be, they must be limited to a certain number, in order to guard against the confusion of a multitude. Hence, the number of representatives in the two cases not being in proportion to that of the two constituents, and being proportionally greater in the small republic, it follows that, if the proportion of fit characters be not less in the large than in the small republic, the former will present a greater option, and consequently a greater probability of a fit choice.

In the next place, as each representative will be chosen by a greater number of citizens in the large than in the small republic, it will be more difficult for unworthy candidates to practice with success the vicious arts by which elections are too often carried; and the suffrages of the people being more free, will be more likely to center in men who possess the most attractive merit and the most diffusive and established characters.

It must be confessed that in this, as in most other cases, there is a mean, on both sides of which inconveniences will be found to lie. By enlarging too much the number of electors, you render the representative too little acquainted with all their local circumstances and lesser interests; as by reducing it too much, you render him unduly attached to these, and too little fit to comprehend and pursue great and national objects. The federal Constitution forms a happy combination in this respect; the great and aggregate interests being referred to the national, the local and particular to the State legislatures.

The other point of difference is, the greater number of citizens and extent of territory which may be brought within the compass of republican than of democratic government; and it is this circumstance principally which renders factious combinations less to be dreaded in the former than in the latter. The smaller the society, the fewer probably will be the distinct parties and interests composing it; the fewer the distinct parties and interests, the more frequently will a majority be found of the same party; and the smaller the number of individuals composing a majority, and the smaller the compass within which they are placed, the more easily will they concert and execute their plans of oppression. Extend the sphere, and you take in a greater variety of parties and interests; you make it less probable that a majority of the whole will have a common motive to invade the rights of other citizens; or if such a common motive exists, it will be more difficult for all who feel it to discover their own strength, and to act in unison with each other. Besides other impediments, it may be remarked that, where there is a consciousness of unjust or dishonorable purposes, communication is always checked by distrust in proportion to the number whose concurrence is necessary.

Hence, it clearly appears, that the same advantage which a republic has over a democracy, in controlling the effects of faction, is enjoyed by a large over a small republic,—is enjoyed by the Union over the States

composing it. Does the advantage consist in the substitution of representatives whose enlightened views and virtuous sentiments render them
superior to local prejudices and to schemes of injustice? It will not be denied that the representation of the Union will be most likely to possess
these requisite endowments. Does it consist in the greater security afforded by a greater variety of parties, against the event of any one party
being able to outnumber and oppress the rest? In an equal degree does
the increased variety of parties comprised within the Union, increase this
security. Does it, in fine, consist in the greater obstacles opposed to the
concert and accomplishment of the secret wishes of an unjust and interested majority? Here, again, the extent of the Union gives it the most
palpable advantage.

The influence of factious leaders may kindle a flame within their particular States, but will be unable to spread a general conflagration
through the other States. A religious sect may degenerate into a political
faction in a part of the Confederacy; but the variety of sects dispersed
over the entire face of it must secure the national councils against any
danger from that source. A rage for paper money, for an abolition of
debts, for an equal division of property, or for any other improper or
wicked project, will be less apt to pervade the whole body of the Union
than a particular member of it; in the same proportion as such a malady
is more likely to taint a particular county or district, than an entire State.

In the extent and proper structure of the Union, therefore, we behold
a republican remedy for the diseases most incident to republican government. And according to the degree of pleasure and pride we feel in being
republicans, ought to be our zeal in cherishing the spirit and supporting
the character of Federalists.

PUBLIUS
1787

ALMANACS

Nathaniel Ames

There are three Nathaniel Ameses, grandfather, father, and son. The first Nathaniel (1677–1736), taught his son the astronomy and mathematics necessary to the almanac maker; the second Nathaniel (1708–1764), physician, wit, and tavern-keeper in Dedham, Mass., father of the third Nathaniel and the better known Fisher Ames, began the almanac in 1726 and continued it to his death; the third Nathaniel (1741–1822), also a physician, continued it to 1775. The title of the first issue, *An Astronomical Diary or an Almanac For the Year of Our Lord Christ, 1726*, is varied with slight change through the years; The *Almanac* was first printed by Bartholomew Green in Boston, and later by other Boston printers.

BIBLIOGRAPHY: Sam Briggs, *The Essays, Humor, and Poems of Nathaniel Ames* (Cleveland, 1891). *DAB*.

From *The Almanac*

WIT AND WISDOM

Now what remains to comfort up our lives
Is cordial liquor and kind loving wives.

1729

When tender lambs with wolves delight to play,
Or from the west shall spring the break of day,
When rocks forget their ponderous weight and fly,
Like waving atoms in the Empty sky,
Then shall vain notions by traditions bred
Among the vulgar be abolished.

1730

'Tis cold my Friends: the dull and tedious nights
Old bachelors and widowers invites
To marry, now in haste.

1735

Three things breed jealousy: a mighty state,
a rich treasure, and a fair wife.

1735

"I give and I devise," old Euclio said
And sigh'd, "my lands and tenements to Ned."
"Your money, Sir?" "My money, sir! What all?
Why, if I must," then wept, "I give it all to Paul."

1740

Ladies of pleasure
Improve their leisure
In Drinking
Tea

1741

The days that's past were happy golden times
When men were sentenced only for their crimes,
For lying, stealing, whoring, swearing, drinking;
But men are damn'd at noon-day now for thinking.
At their tribunal they'll not deign to save
One soul that thinks not just as they would have.

1744

An honest man may take a knave's advice,
But idiots only will be a cozen'd twice.

1745

I should predict good weather this week, but
there's so many courts, the lawyers may raise
a storm.

1750

If you fall into misfortune, creep through
the bushes which have the least briars.

1758

Learning makes a good man better, but a
bad man worse.

1758

DREAMS

Dreams are but interludes which fancy makes;
When monarch Reason sleeps, this Mimic wakes,
Compounds a medley of disjointed things,
A mob of cobblers and a court of kings.
Light fumes are merry, grosser fumes are sad;   5
Both are the reasonable Soul run mad,
And many monstrous forms in sleep we see
That never were, nor are, nor e'er can be.
Sometimes forgotten things, long cast behind,
Rush forward in the brain, and come to mind;   10
The nurse's legends are for truths received,
And the man dreams but what the boy believed.

                    1755

INDUSTRY

Few people know it, yet, dear sir, 'tis true
Men should have somewhat evermore to do.
Hard labor's tedious, everyone must own,
But surely better such by far than none.
The perfect drone, the quite Impertinent,   5
Whose life at nothing aims, but—to be spent,
Such heaven visits for some mighty ill,
'Tis sure the hardest labor to sit still.
Hence, that unhappy tribe who naught pursue,
Who sin for want of something else to do.   10
Sir John is bless'd with riches, honor, love,
And to be bless'd, indeed, needs only move;
For want of this, with pain he lives away,
A lump of hardly animated clay,
Dull 'till his double bottle does him right,   15
He's easy, just at twelve o'clock at night.
Thus for one sparkling hour alone he's blest
While spleen and headache seize on all the rest.
What numbers sloth with gloomy humors fills,
Racking their brains with visionary ills!   20
Hence what loud outcries, and well-meaning rage,
What endless quarrels at the present age!
How many blame, how often may we hear,
"Such vice! Well, sure, the last day must be near!"
T'avoid such wild, imaginary pains,   25
The sad creation of distemper'd brains,
Dispatch, dear friend, move, labor, sweat, run, fly,
Do ought—but think the Day of Judgment nigh.

There are, who've lost all relish for delight,
With them no earthly thing is ever right. . . .   30
How many such, in indolence grown old
With vigor ne'er do anything but scold,
Whose spirits only from ill humor get,
Like wines that die, unless upon the fret.
Wearied of flouncing to himself alone,   35
Acerbus keeps a man to fret upon.
The fellow's nothing in the earth to do
But sit quiet and be scolded to. . . .
As for myself, whom poverty prevents
From being angry at so great expense,   40
Who, should I ever be inclin'd to rage,
For want of slaves, war with myself must wage.
Must rail, and hear, chastising be chastised,
Be both the tyrant and the tyrannized.
I choose to labor rather than to fret;   45
What's rage in some, in me goes off in sweat.
If times are ill, and things seem never worse,
Men, manners to reclaim—I take my horse.
One mile reforms them, or if aught remain
Unpurg'd—'Tis but to ride as far again.   50
Thus on myself in toils I spend my rage;
I pay the fine and that absolves the age.
Sometimes, still more, to interrupt my ease,
I take the pen and write such things as these,
Which though all other merit be denied,   55
Show my devotion still to be employed.
Add too, tho' writing be itself a curse,
Yet some distempers are a cure for worse.
And since midst indolence, spleen will prevail,
Since who do nothing else are sure to rail,   60
Man should be suffered thus to play the fool,
To keep from hurt, as children go to school.
You should not pine in spite of Nature—True;
Yet sure 'tis greater trouble if—you do.
And if 'tis laboring only, Men profess   65
Who writes the hardest, writes with most success.

                                   1757

TRAVELERS AND OBSERVERS

Sarah Kemble Knight

(1666-1727)

Teacher and diarist, Sarah Kemble Knight was the daughter of a Boston merchant and the wife of Captain Richard Knight, a widower whom she married in 1689. Madam Knight kept a writing school in Boston and was apparently employed as a recorder of public documents. After 1714, she lived in Connecticut. *The Journal of Madam Knight* recounts her journey on horseback from Boston to New York in 1704. The account was first edited by Theodore Dwight and published as *The Journals of Madam Knight and Rev. Mr. Buckingham* (New York, 1825). Four other editions of *The Journal* appeared before 1901.

BIBLIOGRAPHY: *DAB*. *The Journal*, in *Littell's Living Age* (June 26, 1858), ed. with notes by W. R. Deane. *The Journal of Madam Knight*, ed. George P. Winship (Boston, 1920), facsimile reissue, 1935.

From *Her Private Journal of a Journey from Boston to New York*

From hence we kept on, with more ease than before: the way being smooth and even, the night warm and serene, and the Tall and thick Trees at a distance, especially when the moon glar'd light through the branches fill'd my Imagination with the pleasant delusion of a Sumptuous city, fill'd with famous Buildings and churches, with their spiring steeples, Balconies, Galleries and I know not what: Grandeurs which I had heard of, and which the stories of foreign countries had given me the Idea of.

> Here stood a Lofty church—there is a steeple,
> And there the Grand Parade—O see the people!
> That Famous Castle there, were I but nigh,
> To see the moat and Bridge and walls so high—
> They're very fine! says my deluded eye.

Being thus agreeably entertain'd without a thought of anything but thoughts themselves, I on a sudden was Rous'd from these pleasing Imaginations, by the Post's sounding his horn, which assured me he was arrived at the Stage, where we were to Lodge: and that music was then most musical and agreeable to me.

Being come to Mr. Havens', I was very civilly Received, and courteously entertained, in a clean comfortable House; and the Good woman was very active in helping off my Riding clothes, and then ask't what I would eat. I told her I had some Chocolate, if she would prepare it; which with the help of some Milk, and a little clean brass Kettle, she soon effected to my satisfaction. I then betook me to my Apartment, which was a little Room parted from the Kitchen by a single board partition; where, after I had noted the Occurrences of the past day, I went to bed, which, tho' pretty hard, Yet neat and handsome. But I could get no sleep, because of the Clamor of some of the Town topers in next Room, Who were entered into a strong debate concerning the Signification of the name of their Country, (viz.) Narraganset. One said it was named so by the Indians, because there grew a Brier there, of a prodigious Height and bigness, . . . His Antagonist Replied no—It was from a Spring it had its name. . . . He utter'd with such a Roaring voice and Thundering blows with the fist of wickedness on the Table, that it pierced my very head. I heartily fretted, and wish't 'um tongue tied; but with as little success as a friend of mine once, who was (as she said) kept a whole night awake, on a Journey, by a country Lieut. and a Sergeant, Ensign and a Deacon, contriving how to bring a triangle into a Square. . . .

I set my Candle on a Chest by the bedside, and setting up, fell to my old way of composing my Resentments, in the following manner:

> I ask thy Aid, O Potent Rum!
> To Charm these wrangling Topers Dumb.
> Thou hast their Giddy Brains possest—
> The man confounded with the Beast—
> And I, poor I, can get no rest.
> Intoxicate them with thy fumes:
> O still their Tongues till morning comes!

And I know not but my wishes took effect; for the dispute soon ended with t'other Dram; and so Good night! . . .

Being at a merchant's house, in comes a tall country fellow, with his alforjas full of Tobacco; for they seldom Lose their Cud, but keep Chewing and Spitting as long as their eyes are open,—he advanc't to the middle of the Room, makes an Awkward Nod, and spitting a Large deal of Aromatic Tincture, he gave a scrape with his shovel-like shoe, leaving a small shovel full of dirt on the floor, made a full stop, Hugging his own pretty Body with his hands under his arms, Stood staring round him, like a Cat let out of a Basket. At last, like the creature Balaam Rode on, he opened his mouth and said: have You any Ribbonin' for Hatbands to sell I pray? The Questions and Answers about the pay being past, the Ribbon is brought and opened. Bumpkin Simpers, cries it's confounded Gay I vow; and beck'ning to the door, in comes Joan Tawdry, dropping about 50 curtsies, and stands by him: he shows her the Ribbon. Law You, says she, it's right Gent, do You, take it, 'tis dreadful pretty. Then she inquires, have You any hood silk I pray? which being brought and bought, Have You any thread silk to sew it with says she, which being accommodated with they Departed. They Generally stand after they come in a great while speechless, and sometimes don't say a word till they are askt what they want, which I Impute to the Awe they stand in of the merchants, who they are constantly almost Indebted to; and must take what they bring without Liberty to choose for themselves; but they serve them as well, making the merchants stay long enough for their pay.

We may Observe here the great necessity and benefit both of Education and Conversation; for these people have as Large a portion of mother wit, and sometimes a Larger, than those who have been brought up in Cities; But for want of improvements, Render themselves almost Ridiculous, as above. I should be glad if they would leave such follies, and am sure all that Love Clean Houses (at least) would be glad on't too.

They are generally very plain in their dress, throughout all the Colony, as I saw, and follow one another in their modes; that You may know where they belong, especially the women, meet them where you will. . . .

The City of New York is a pleasant, well compacted place, situated on a Commodious River which is a fine harbor for shipping. The Buildings Brick Generally, very stately and high, though not altogether like ours in Boston. The Bricks in some of the Houses are of divers Colors and laid in Checkers, being glazed look very agreeable. The inside of them are neat to admiration, the wooden work, for only the walls are plastered, and the Summers and Joists are planed and kept very white scour'd as so is all the partitions if made of Boards. The fireplaces have no Jambs (as ours have) But the Backs run flush with the walls, and the Hearth is of Tiles and is as far out into the Room at the Ends as before the fire, which is Generally Five foot in the Lower rooms, and the piece over where the mantle tree should be is made as ours with Joiners' work, and as I suppose is fasten'd to iron rods inside. The House where the Vendue was, had Chimney Corners like ours, and they and the hearths were laid with the finest tile that I ever see, and the staircases laid all with white tile which is ever clean, and so are the walls of the Kitchen which had a Brick floor. . . . They are not strict in keeping the Sabbath as in Boston and other places where I had been, But seem to deal with great exactness as far as I see or Deal with. They are sociable to one another and Courteous and Civil to strangers and fare well in their house. The English go very fashionable in their dress. But the Dutch, especially the middling sort, differ from our women, in their habit go loose, wear French muches which are like a Cap and a headband in one, leaving their ears bare, which are set out with Jewels of a large size and many in number. And their fingers hoop't with Rings, some with large stones in them of many Colors as were their pendants in their ears, which You should see very old women wear as well as Young.

They have Vendues very frequently and make their Earnings very well by them, for they treat with good Liquor Liberally, and the Customers Drink as Liberally and Generally pay for it as well, by paying for that which they Bid up Briskly for, after the sack has gone plentifully about, tho' sometimes good penny worths are got there. Their Diversions in the Winter is Riding Sleighs about three or four Miles out of Town, where they have Houses of entertainment at a place called the Bowery, and some go to friends' Houses who handsomely treat them. Mr. Burroughs carried his spouse and Daughter and myself out to one Madame Dowes, a Gentlewoman that lived at a farmhouse, who gave us a handsome Entertainment of five or six Dishes and choice Beer and metheglin, Cider, &c. all which she said was the produce of her farm. I believe we met 50 or 60 sleighs that day—they fly with great swiftness and some are so furious that they'll turn out of the path for none except a Loaden Cart. Nor do they spare for any diversion the place affords, and sociable to a degree, their Tables being as free to their Neighbors as to themselves.

1704, 1825

Alexander Hamilton
(1712-1756)

Born and educated in Edinburgh, Scotland, Alexander Hamilton moved to Annapolis, Md., in 1739 to practice medicine. Hamilton recorded his journey of 1624 miles to the northern colonies in *The Itinerarium*, written in 1744, but unpublished until 1907. Hamilton also wrote a history of the Tuesday Club, social club for Annapolis gentlemen.

BIBLIOGRAPHY: A. B. Hart, ed. *Hamilton's Itinerarium* (St. Louis, 1907). Carl Bridenbaugh, ed. *The Itinerarium of Dr. Alexander Hamilton, 1744* (Chapel Hill, N.C., 1948).

From *The Itinerarium*

Annapolis, Wednesday, May 30th.—I set out from Annapolis in Maryland, upon Wednesday the 30th of May at eleven o'clock in the morning; contrary winds and bad weather prevented my intended passage over Chesapeake Bay; so taking the Patapscoe road, I proposed going by the way of Bohemia to Newtown upon Chester, a very circumflex course, but as the journey was intended only for health and recreation, I was indifferent whether I took the nearest or the farthest route, having likewise a desire to see that part of the country. . . .

Friday, June 8th [Philadelphia].—I dined at a tavern with a very mixed company of different nations and religions. There were Scots, English, Dutch, Germans, and Irish; there were Roman Catholics, Churchmen, Presbyterians, Quakers, Newlightmen, Methodists, Seventhdaymen, Moravians, Anabaptists, and one Jew. The whole company consisted of twenty-five, planted round an oblong table, in a great hall well stocked with flies. . . . At six o'clock I went to the coffee-house and drank a dish of coffee with Mr. H——l.

After staying there an hour or two, I was introduced by Dr. Phineas Bond into the Governor's Club, a society of gentlemen that meet at a tavern every night, and converse on various subjects. The Governor gives them his presence once a week, which is generally upon Wednesday, so that I did not see him there. Our conversation was entertaining; the subject was the English poets and some of the foreign writers, particularly Cervantes, author of *Don Quixote,* whom we loaded with eulogiums due to his character.

At eleven o'clock I left this club and went to my lodging. . . .

The heat in this city is excessive, the sun's rays being reflected with such power from the brick houses, and from the street pavement, which is brick; the people commonly use awnings of painted cloth or duck over their shop doors and windows, and at sunset throw bucketsful of water upon the pavement, which gives a sensible cool. They are stocked with plenty of excellent water in this city, there being a pump at almost every fifty paces' distance.

There are a great number of balconies to their houses, where sometimes the men sit in a cool habit and smoke.

The market in this city is perhaps the largest in North America. It is kept twice a week, upon Wednesdays and Saturdays. The street where it stands, called Market Street, is large and spacious, composed of the best houses in the city.

They have but one public clock here, which strikes the hour, but has neither index nor dialplate. It is strange they should want such an ornament and conveniency in so large a place, but the chief part of the community consisting of Quakers they would seem to shun ornament in their public edifices as well as in their apparel or dress. . . .

I never was in a place so populous where the *gout* for public gay diversions prevailed so little. There is no such thing as assemblies of the gentry among them, either for dancing or music; these they have had an utter aversion to ever since Whitefield preached among them. Their chief employ, indeed, is traffic and mercantile business, which turns their thoughts from these levities. Some Virginia gentlemen that came here with the Commissioners of the Indian treaty were desirous of having a ball, but could find none of the female sex in a humor for it. Strange influence of religious enthusiasm upon human nature to excite an aversion at these innocent amusements for the most part so agreeable and entertaining to the young and gay. . . .

Sunday, June 10th.—I intended to have gone to church or meeting to edify by the Word, but was diverted from my good purpose by some polite company I fell into, who were all utter strangers to churches and meetings. But I understood that my negro Dromo very piously stepped into the Lutheran Church to be edified with a sermon preached in High Dutch, which, I believe, when dressed up in the fashion of a discourse, he understood every bit as well as English, and so might edify as much with the one as he could have done with the other. . . .

I must make a few remarks before I leave this place. The people in general are inquisitive concerning strangers. If they find one comes there upon the account of trade or traffic, they are fond of dealing with him and cheating him, if they can. If he comes for pleasure or curiosity, they take little or no notice of him, unless he be a person of more than ordinary rank; they they know as well as others how to fawn and cringe. . . .

They have in general a bad notion of the neighboring Province, Maryland, esteeming the people a set of cunning sharpers; but my notion of the affair is, that the Pennsylvanians are not a whit inferior to them in the science of chicane, only their method of tricking is different. A Pennsylvanian will tell a lie with a sanctified, solemn face; a Marylander perhaps will convey his fib in a volley of oaths; but the effect and point in view are the same, tho' the manner of operating be different. . . .

There is polite conversation here among the better sort, among whom there is no scarcity of men of learning and good sense. The ladies, for the most part, keep at home and seldom appear in the streets, never in public assemblies, except at the churches or meetings; therefore I cannot with certainty enlarge upon their charms, having had little or no opportunity to see them either congregated or separate, but to be sure the Philadelphia dames are as handsome as their neighbors.

Tuesday, June 26th [Albany].—The Patroon is a young man, of a good mien and presence. He is a bachelor, nor can his friends persuade him to marry. By paying too much homage to Bacchus, he has acquired a hypochondriac habit. He has a great number of tenants upon his manor, and he told me himself that he could muster 600 men fit to bear arms. Mr. M——s and I dined at his house, and were handsomely entertained with good viands and wine. After dinner he showed us his garden and parks, and Mr. M——s got into one of his long harangues of farming and improvement of ground.

At four o'clock M——s and I returned to town, where M——s having a general acquaintance he introduced me into about twenty or thirty houses, where I went thro' the farce of kissing most of the women, a manner of salutation which is expected (as M——s told me) from strangers coming there. I told him it was very well, if he led the way I should follow, which he did with clerical gravity. This might almost pass for a penance, for the generality of the women here, both old and young, are remarkably ugly. . . .

This city is enclosed by a rampart or wall of wooden palisadoes, about ten feet high and a foot thick, being the trunks of pine-trees rammed into the ground, pinned close together, and ending each in a point at top. Here they call them stoccadoes. At each 200 feet distance, round this wall is a block house, and from the north gate of the city runs a thick stone wall down into the river, 200 feet long, at each end of which is a block house. In these block houses about fifty of the city militia keep guard every night, and the word *all's well* walks constantly round all night long from sentry to sentry and round the fort. There are five or six gates to this city, the chief of which are the north and the south gates. In the city are about 4,000 inhabitants, mostly Dutch or of Dutch extract.

The Dutch here keep their houses very neat and clean, both without and within. Their chamber floors are generally laid with rough plank, which in time, by constant rubbing and scrubbing, becomes as smooth as if it had been planed. Their chambers and rooms are large and handsome. They have their beds generally in alcoves, so that you may go thro' all the rooms of a great house and see never a bed. They affect pictures much, particularly scripture history, with which they adorn their rooms. They set out their cabinets and *buffets* much with china. Their kitchens are likewise very clean, and there they hang earthen or delft plates and dishes all round the walls, in manner of pictures, having a hole drilled thro' the edge of the plate or dish, and a loop of ribbon put into it to hang it by; but notwithstanding all this nicety and cleanliness in their houses they are in their persons slovenly and dirty. They live here very frugally and plain, for the chief merit among them seems to be riches, which they spare no pains or trouble to acquire, but are a civil and hospitable people in their way, but at best rustic and unpolished. . . .

They live in their houses in Albany as if it were in prisons, all their doors and windows being perpetually shut. But the reason of this may be the little desire they have for conversation and society, their whole thoughts being turned upon profit and gain, which necessarily makes them live retired and frugal. At least this is the common character of the Dutch everywhere. But indeed the excessive cold winters here oblige

them in that season to keep all snug and close, and they have not summer sufficient to revive heat in their veins, so as to make them uneasy or
put it in their heads to air themselves. They are a healthy, long-lived
people, many in this city being in age near or above 100 years, and
eighty is a very common age. They are subject to rotten teeth and scor-
butic gums, which, I suppose, is caused by the cold air, and their constant diet of salt provisions in the winter; for in that season they are obliged to lay in, as for a sea voyage, there being no stirring out of doors
then for fear of never stirring again. As to religion they have little of it
among them, and of enthusiasm not a grain. The bulk of them, if anything, are of the Lutheran Church.

Their women in general, both old and young, are the hardest favored
ever I beheld. Their old women wear a comical headdress, large pendants, short petticoats, and they stare upon one like witches. . . .

Sunday, July 22d [Boston].—After breakfast I went with Mr. Hughes
to Hooper's meeting, where we heard a very good discourse, and saw a
genteel congregation. The ladies were most of them in high dress. This
meetinghouse is a handsome new wooden building, with a huge spire or
steeple at the north end of it. The pulpit is large and neat, with a large
sounding board, supported at each end with pilasters of the Doric order,
fluted, and behind it there is a high arched door, over which hangs a
green curtain. The pulpit cushion is of green velvet, and all the windows
in the meeting are mounted with green curtains.

After dismissing I went to Change, and returning from thence dined
with Mr. Lechmere. There was a lady at table of a very masculine make,
but dressed fine *à la mode.* She did not appear till dinner was almost
over, pretending she could not endure the smell of the victuals, and was
every now and then lugging out her sal volatile and Hungary water, but
this I observed was only a modish air, for she made a shift betwixt times
to swallow down as much beef and pudding as anybody at the table; in
short her teeth went as fast as her tongue, and the motion of both was
perpetual.

After dinner I went to the English chapel with Mr. Lechmere, and
heard a small organ played by an indifferent organist. A certain pedan-
tic Irishman preached to us, who had much of the brogue. He gave us
rather a philosophical lecture than a sermon, . . . but of all places the
pulpit is the most improper for the ostentatious of this sort; the language and phraseology of which sacred *rostrum* ought to be as plain to the
plowman as the scholar.

There sat some Indians in a pew near me who stank so that they had
almost made me turn up my dinner. They made a profound reverence to
the parson when he finished; the men bowed, and the squaws curtsied. . . .

Monday, July 23d.—This morning I walked abroad with Mr. Hughes,
and passed over the dam at the reservoir to the north end of the town. . . .
We next viewed the new Market house, an elegant building of brick,

with a cupola on the top, in length about 130 feet, in breadth betwixt 40 and 50. This was built at the proper expense of one Funell, a substantial merchant of this place, lately dead, and presented by him to the public. It is called by the name of Funell Hall, and stands near a little inlet of water, called the Town dock, over which, a little below the Market house, is a wooden drawbridge that turns upon hinges that small vessels may pass and lie above it. In low tides this inlet is a very stinking puddle. . . .

I went this night to visit Mr. Smibert, the limner, where I saw a collection of fine pictures, among the rest that part of Scipio's history in Spain where he delivers the lady to the prince to whom she had been betrothed. The passions are all well touched in the several faces. Scipio's face expresses a majestic generosity, that of the young prince gratitude and modest love; and some Roman soldiers, standing under a row of pillars apart, in seeming discourse, have admiration delineated in their faces. But what I admired most of the painter's fancy in this piece is an image or phantom of chastity behind the *solium* upon which Scipio sits, standing on tiptoe to crown him, and yet appears as if she could not reach his head, which expresses a good emblem of the virtue of this action. . . .

Friday, July 27th.—This day proving very rainy I was prevented in my intention to travel eastward. . . . At night I went to the Physical Club at the Sun Tavern, according to appointment, where we drank punch, smoked tobacco, and talked of sundry physical matters.

Douglass, the physician here, is a man of good learning, but mischievously given to criticism, and the most complete snarler ever I knew. He is loath to allow learning, merit, or a character to anybody. He is of the clinical class of physicians, and laughs at all theory and practice founded upon it, looking upon empiricism or bare experience as the only firm basis upon which practice ought to be founded. He has got here about him a set of disciples, who greedily draw in his doctrines, and being but half learned themselves have not wit enough to discover the foibles and mistakes of their preceptor. This man I esteem a notorious physical heretic, capable to corrupt and vitiate the practice of the place by spreading his erroneous doctrines among his shallow brethren. . . .

Thursday, August 16th.—The people here have lately been, and indeed are now in great confusion and much infested with enthusiasm from the preaching of some fanatics and Newlight teachers, but now this humor begins to lessen. The people are generally more captivated with speculative than with practical religion. It is not by half such a flagrant sin to cheat and cozen one's neighbor, as it is to ride about for pleasure on the sabbath day, or to neglect going to church and singing of psalms. The middling sort of people here are to a degree disingenuous and dissembling, which appears even in their common conversation, in which their indirect and dubious answers to the plainest and fairest questions show their suspicions of one another. The better sort are polite, mannerly, and hospitable to strangers,—such strangers I mean as come not to trade among them (for of them they are jealous). There is more hospitality and frankness shown here to strangers than either at York or at Philadelphia, and in the place there is an abundance of men of learning and parts so that one is at no loss for agreeable conversation, nor for any set of company he pleases. Assemblies of the gayer sort are frequent here, the gentlemen and ladies meeting almost every week at concerts of music and balls. I was present at two or three such, and saw as fine a ring of ladies, as good dancing, and heard music as elegant as I had been witness to anywhere. I must take notice that this place abounds with pretty women, who appear rather more abroad than they do at York, and dress elegantly. They are for the most part free and affable as well as pretty. I saw not one prude while I was here.

Sunday, August 26th [New London].—I went home at six o'clock, and Deacon Green's son came to see me. He entertained me with the history of the behavior of one Davenport, a fanatic preacher there, who told his flock in one of his enthusiastic rhapsodies, that in order to be saved they ought to burn all their idols. They began this conflagration with a pile of books in the public street, among which were Tillotson's *Sermons,* Beveridge's *Thoughts,* Drillincourt on *Death,* Sherlock, and many other excellent authors, and sang psalms and hymns over the pile while it was a-burning. They did not stop here, but the women made up a lofty pile of hoop petticoats, silk gowns, short cloaks, cambric caps, red-heeled shoes, fans, necklaces, gloves, and other such apparel, and, what was merry enough, Davenport's own idol, with which he topped the pile, was a pair of old wore-out plush breeches, but this bonfire was happily prevented by one more moderate than the rest, who found means to persuade them that making such a sacrifice was not necessary for their salvation, and so everyone carried off their idols again which was lucky for Davenport . . . , for the devil another pair of breeches had he but these same old plush ones which were going to be offered up as an expiatory sacrifice. Mr. Green took his leave of me at ten o'clock, and I went to bed.

Thursday, September 27th [Annapolis]. I arrived at Annapolis at two o'clock afternoon, and so ended my peregrinations.

In these my northern travels I compassed my design, in obtaining a better state of health, which was the purpose of my journey. I found but little difference in the manners and character of the people in the different Provinces I passed thro'; but as to constitutions and complexions, air and government, I found some variety. Their forms of government in the northern Provinces I look upon to be much better and happier than ours, which is a poor, sickly, convulsed State. Their air and living to the northward is likewise much preferable, and the people of a more gigantic size and make. . . .

In this itineration I completed, by land and water together, a course of 1624 miles. The northern parts I found in general much better settled than the southern. As to politeness and humanity they are much alike, except in the great towns, where the inhabitants are more civilized, especially at Boston.

1744, 1907

Michel-Guillaume Jean de Crèvecœur

(1735-1813)

Michel-Guillaume Jean de Crèvecœur was born in Caen, France, received part of his education in London, and from 1754 to 1759 served in Montcalm's army in New France, perhaps as a map-maker. After 1759, he explored New York, Pennsylvania, and perhaps as far south as the Carolinas, then settled on a farm in Orange County, N.Y., in 1769. Of Loyalist sympathies during the Revolution, he spent from 1780 to 1783 in England and France. He returned to New York City as French consul in 1783 to find that his wife had died and his three children were missing, though he later found two of them. In 1790 he sailed for France, where he spent the remainder of his life. *Letters from an American Farmer* (London, 1782) appeared over the name of "J. Hector St. John," and was published in Paris in 1783. Mathew Carey's press at Philadelphia printed an edition in 1793. Among his other works are *Voyage dans la Haute Pensylvanie et dans l'Etat de New-York*, 3 Vols. (Paris, 1801) and *Sketches of Eighteenth Century America*, eds. H. L. Bourdin, R. H. Gabriel, and S. T. Williams (New Haven, 1925), a group of essays discovered by Bourdin in 1922 and apparently intended as part of the 1782 *Letters*.

BIBLIOGRAPHY: Howard C. Rice, *Le Cultivateur Américain: Etude sur l'Œuvre de Saint John de Crèvecœur* (Paris, 1933). Julia P. Mitchell, *St. Jean de Crèvecœur* (New York, 1916). *Letters from an American Farmer*, eds. W. P. Trent and Ludwig Lewisohn (New York, 1925; first issued 1904). Also ed. Warren B. Blake (New York, 1962). *Eighteenth-Century Travels in Pennsylvania and New York*, trans. and ed. Percy G. Adams (Lexington, Ky., 1961). *Journey into Northern Pennsylvania and the State of New York*, trans. Clarissa S. Bostelmann (Ann Arbor, Mich., 1964).

From *Letters from an American Farmer*

I

. . . Our minister often comes to see me, though he lives upwards of twenty miles distant. I have shown him your letter, asked his advice, and solicited his assistance; he tells me, that he hath no time to spare, for that like the rest of us must till his farm, and is moreover to study what he is to say on the sabbath. My wife (and I never do anything without consulting her) laughs, and tells me that you cannot be in earnest. What! says she, James, wouldst thee pretend to send epistles to a great European man, who hath lived abundance of time in that big house called Cambridge; where, they say, that worldly learning is so abundant, that people gets it only by breathing the air of the place? Wouldst not thee be ashamed to write unto a man who has never in his life done a single day's work, no, not even felled a tree; who hath expended the Lord knows how many years in studying stars, geometry, stones, and flies, and in reading folio books? . . . Surely he means to jeer thee! I am sure he does, he cannot be in a real fair earnest. James, thee must read this letter over again, paragraph by paragraph, and warily observe whether thee can'st perceive some words of jesting; something that hath more than one meaning: and now I think on it, husband, I wish thee wouldst let me see his letter; . . . She then read it herself very attentively: our minister was present, we listened to, and weighed every syllable: we all unanimously concluded that you must have been in a sober earnest intention, as my wife calls it; and your request appeared to be candid and sincere. . . .

You say you want nothing of me but what lies within the reach of my experience and knowledge; this I understand very well; the difficulty is, how to collect, digest, and arrange what I know? Next you assert, that writing letters is nothing more than talking on paper; which, I must confess, appeared to me quite a new thought.—Well then, observed our minister, neighbor James, as you can talk well, I am sure you must write tolerably well also; imagine, then, that Mr. F. B. is still here, and simply write down what you would say to him. . . . Although he is a man of learning and taste, yet I am sure he will read your letters with pleasure: if they be not elegant, they will smell of the woods, and be a little wild; I know your turn, they will contain some matters which he never knew before. Some people are so fond of novelty, that they will overlook many errors of language for the sake of information. We are all apt to love and admire exotics, tho' they may be often inferior to what we possess; . . .

Don't you think, neighbor James, that the mind of a good and enlightened Englishman would be more improved in remarking throughout these provinces the causes which render so many people happy? In delineating the unnoticed means by which we daily increase the extent of our settlements? How we convert huge forests into pleasing fields, and exhibit through these thirteen provinces so singular a display of easy subsistence and political felicity. . . .

III

. . . What a train of pleasing ideas this fair spectacle must suggest; it is a prospect which must inspire a good citizen with the most heartfelt pleasure. The difficulty consists in the manner of viewing so extensive a scene. He is arrived on a new continent; a modern society offers itself to his contemplation, different from what he had hitherto seen. It is not composed, as in Europe, of great lords who possess everything, and of a herd of people who have nothing. . . . We are a people of cultivators, scattered over an immense territory, communicating with each other by means of good roads and navigable rivers, united by the silken bands of mild government, all respecting the laws, without dreading their power, because they are equitable. We are all animated with the spirit of an industry which is unfettered and unrestrained, because each person works for himself. If he travels through our rural districts he views not the hostile castle, and the haughty mansion, contrasted with the clay-built hut and miserable cabin, where cattle and men help to keep each other warm, and dwell in meanness, smoke, and indigence. A pleasing uniformity of decent competence appears throughout our habitations. The meanest of our log houses is a dry and comfortable habitation. Lawyer or merchant are the fairest titles our towns afford; that of a farmer is the only appellation of the rural inhabitants of our country. . . . Here man is free as he ought to be; nor is this pleasing equality so transitory as many others are. Many ages will not see the shores of our great lakes replenished with inland nations, nor the unknown bounds of North America entirely peopled.

In this great American asylum, the poor of Europe have by some means met together, and in consequence of various causes; to what purpose should they ask one another what countrymen they are? Alas, two thirds of them had no country. Can a wretch who wanders about, who works and starves, whose life is a continual scene of sore affliction or pinching penury; can that man call England or any other kingdom his country? A country that had no bread for him, whose fields procured him no harvest, who met with nothing but the frowns of the rich, the severity of the laws, with jails and punishments; who owned not a single foot of the extensive surface of this planet? No! urged by a variety of motives, here they came. Everything has tended to regenerate them; new laws, a new mode of living, a new social system; here they are become men. . . . What then is the American, this new man? He is either an European, or the descendant of an European, hence that strange mixture of blood, which you will find in no other country. I could point out to you a family whose grandfather was an Englishman, whose wife was Dutch, whose son married a French woman, and whose present four sons have now four wives of different nations. *He* is an American, who, leaving behind him all his ancient prejudices and manners, receives new ones from the new mode of life he has embraced, the new government he obeys, and the new rank he holds. He becomes an American by being received in the broad lap of our great *Alma Mater*. Here individuals of all nations are melted into a new race race of men, whose labors and posterity will one day cause great changes in the world. Americans are the western pilgrims, who are carrying along with them that great mass of arts, sciences, vigor, and industry which began long since in the east; they will finish the great circle. The Americans were once scattered all over Europe; here they are incorporated into one of the finest systems of population which has ever appeared, and which will hereafter become distinct by the power of the different climates they inhabit. The American ought therefore to love this country much better than that wherein either he or his forefathers were born. Here the rewards of his industry follow with equal steps the progress of his labor; his labor is founded on the basis of nature, *self-interest;* can it want a stronger allurement? Wives and children, who before in vain demanded of him a morsel of bread, now, fat and frolicsome, gladly help their father to clear those fields whence exuberant crops are to arise to feed and to clothe them all; without any part being claimed, either by a despotic prince, a rich abbot, or a mighty lord. Here religion demands but little of him; a small voluntary salary to the minister, and gratitude to God; can he refuse these? The American is a new man, who acts upon new principles; he must therefore entertain new ideas, and form new opinions. From involuntary idleness, servile dependence, penury, and useless labor, he has passed to toils of a very different nature, rewarded by ample subsistence.—This is an American. . . .

Men are like plants; the goodness and flavor of the fruit proceeds from the peculiar soil and exposition in which they grow. We are nothing but what we derive from the air we breathe, the climate we inhabit, the government we obey, the system of religion we profess, and the nature of our employment. . . . There is room for everybody in America; has he any particular talent, or industry? he exerts it in order to procure a livelihood, and it succeeds. Is he a merchant? the avenues of trade are infinite; is he eminent in any respect? he will be employed and respected. Does he love a country life? pleasant farms present themselves; he may purchase what he wants, and thereby become an American farmer. Is he a laborer, sober and industrious? he need not go many miles, nor receive many informations before he will be hired, well fed at the table of his employer, and paid four or five times more than he can get in Europe. Does he want uncultivated lands? thousands of acres present themselves, which he may purchase cheap. Whatever be his talents or inclinations, if they are moderate, he may satisfy them. I do not mean that everyone who comes will grow rich in a little time; no, but he may procure an easy, decent maintenance, by his industry. Instead of starving he will be fed, instead of being idle he will have employment; and these are riches enough for such men as come over here.

VI

The vessels most proper for whale fishing are brigs of about 150 tons burthen, particularly when they are intended for distant latitudes; they always man them with thirteen hands, in order that they may row two whaleboats; the crews of which must necessarily consist of six, four at the oars, one standing on the bows with the harpoon, and the other at the helm. It is also necessary that there should be two of these boats, that if one should be destroyed in attacking the whale, the other, which is never engaged at the same time, may be ready to save the hands. Five of the thirteen are always Indians; the last of the complement remains on board to steer the vessel during the action. They have no wages; each draws a certain established share in partnership with the proprietor of the vessel; by which economy they are all proportionately concerned in the success of the enterprise, and all equally alert and vigilant. None of these whale-men ever exceed the age of forty: they look on those who are past that period not to be possessed of all that vigor and agility which so adventur-ous a business requires. Indeed if you attentively consider the immense disporportion between the object assailed and the assailants; if you think on the diminutive size, and weakness of their frail vehicle; if you recol-lect the treachery of the element on which this scene is transacted; the sudden and unforeseen accidents of winds, etc., you will readily acknowl-edge that it must require the most consummate exertion of all the strength, agility, and judgment, of which the bodies and minds of men are capable, to undertake these adventurous encounters.

As soon as they arrive in those latitudes where they expect to meet with whales, a man is sent up to the mast head; if he sees one, he imme-diately cries out AWAITE PAWANA, *here is a whale;* they all remain still and silent until he repeats PAWANA, *a whale,* when in less than six minutes the two boats are launched, filled with every implement necessary for the attack. They row toward the whale with astonishing velocity; and as the Indians early became their fellow-laborers in this new warfare, you can easily conceive how the Nattick expressions became familiar on board the whaleboats. Formerly it often happened that whale vessels were manned with none but Indians and the master; recollect also that the Nantucket people understand the Nattick, and that there are always five of these people on board. There are various ways of approaching the whale, ac-cording to their peculiar species; and this previous knowledge is of the ut-most consequence. When these boats are arrived at a reasonable distance, one of them rests on its oars and stands off, as a witness of the approaching engagement; near the bows of the other the harpooner stands up, and on him principally depends the success of the enterprise. He wears a jacket closely buttoned, and round his head a handkerchief tightly bound: in his hands he holds the dreadful weapon, made of the best steel, marked some-times with the name of their town, and sometimes with that of their vessel; to the shaft of which the end of a cord of due length, coiled up with the utmost care in the middle of the boat, is firmly tied; the other end is fas-tened to the bottom of the boat. Thus prepared they row in profound si-lence, leaving the whole conduct of the enterprise to the harpooner and to the steersman, attentively following their directions. When the former judges himself to be near enough to the whale, that is, at the distance of about fifteen feet, he bids them stop; perhaps she has a calf, whose safety attracts all the attention of the dam, which is a favorable circumstance; perhaps she is of a dangerous species, and it is safest to retire, though their ardor will seldom permit them; perhaps she is asleep, in that case he balances high the harpoon, trying in this important moment to collect all the energy of which he is capable. He launches it forth—she is struck: from her first movements they judge of her temper, as well as of their future success. Sometimes in the immediate impulse of rage, she will attack the boat and demolish it with one stroke of her tail; in an instant the frail vehicle disappears and the assailants are immersed in the dreadful element. Were the whale armed with the jaws of a shark, and as voracious, they never would return home to amuse their listening wives with the interesting tale of the adventure. At other times she will dive and disappear from human sight; and everything must give way to her velocity, or else all is lost. Sometimes she will swim away as if untouched, and draw the cord with such swiftness that it will set the edge of the boat on fire by the friction. If she rises before she has run out the whole length, she is looked upon as a sure prey. The blood she has lost in her flight, weakens her so much, that if she sinks again, it is but for a short time; the boat follows her course with almost equal speed. She soon reappears; tired at last with convulsing the element; which she tinges with her blood, she dies, and floats on the surface. At other times it may happen that she is not dangerously wounded, though she carries the harpoon fast in her body; when she will alternately dive and rise, and swim on with unabated vigor. She then soon reaches beyond the length of the cord, and carries the boat along with amazing velocity: this sudden impediment sometimes will retard her speed, at other times it only serves to rouse her anger, and to accelerate her progress. The harpooner, with the axe in his hands, stands ready. When he observes that the bows of the boat are greatly pulled down by the diving whale, and that it begins to sink deep and to take much water, he brings the axe almost in contact with the cord; he pauses, still flattering himself that she will relax; but the moment grows critical, unavoidable danger approaches: sometimes men more intent on gain, than on the preservation of their lives, will run great risks; and it is wonderful how far these people have carried their daring courage at this awful moment! But it is vain to hope, their lives must be saved, the cord is cut, the boat rises again. If after thus getting loose, she reappears, they will attack and wound her a second time. She soon dies, and when dead she is towed alongside of their vessel, where she is fastened.

The next operation is to cut with axes and spades, every part of her body which yields oil; the kettles are set a boiling, they fill their barrels as fast as it is made; but as this operation is much slower than that of *cutting up,* they fill the hold of their ship with those fragments, lest a storm should arise and oblige them to abandon their prize. It is astonishing what a quantity of oil some of these fish will yield, and what profit it affords to those who are fortunate enough to overtake them.

1782

John Woolman

(1720-1772)

John Woolman, a Quaker leader and an early advocate of the abolition of slavery, was born on a farm near Burlington, N.J., and in 1740 moved to Mount Holly, N.J., as a tailor's apprentice. At the age of twenty-three, Woolman committed his life to the Quaker ministry and devoted the rest of his years to traveling and preaching. After his first trip south to Virginia and the Carolinas in 1746, he turned his attention to the slavery problem. Woolman died of smallpox at York, England, while he was ministering to the poor. Among the separate works published during his lifetime are *Some Considerations on the Keeping of Negroes* (Philadelphia, 1762) and *Considerations on the True Harmony of Mankind* (Philadelphia,

1770). *The Works of John Woolman* (Philadelphia, 1774) has been reprinted frequently, and *The Journal* (Part I of the 1774 *Works*) has gone through more than forty editions.

BIBLIOGRAPHY: *The Journal and Essays of John Woolman,* ed. Amelia M. Gummere (New York, 1922) with biography. *The Journal and Other Writings,* ed. Vida D. Scudder (London, 1910). *The Journal,* ed. Janet Whitney (Chicago, 1950). *The Journal . . . and A Plea for the Poor,* ed. Frederick B. Tolles (New York, 1961), based on J. G. Whittier text of 1871. Janet Whitney, *John Woolman: American Quaker* (Boston, 1942). Reginald Reynolds, *The Wisdom of John Woolman* (London, 1948).

From *The Journal*

CHAPTER ONE

I have often felt a Motion of Love to leave some Hints in Writing of my Experience of the Goodness of God; and now, in the thirty-sixth Year of my Age, I begin this Work.

I was born in Northampton, in Burlington County, West-Jersey, in the Year 1720; and before I was seven Years old I began to be acquainted with the Operations of divine Love. Through the Care of my Parents, I was taught to read nearly as soon as I was capable of it; and, as I went from School one seventh Day, I remember, while my Companions went to play by the Way, I went forward out of Sight, and, sitting down, I read the 22d Chapter of the Revelations: "He showed me a pure River of Water of Life, clear as Crystal, proceeding out of the Throne of God and of the Lamb, etc." and, in reading it, my Mind was drawn to seek after that pure Habitation, which, I then believed, God had prepared for his Servants. The Place where I sat, and the Sweetness that attended my Mind, remain fresh in my Memory. . . .

A Thing remarkable in my Childhood was, that once, going to a Neighbor's House, I saw, on the Way, a Robin sitting on her Nest, and as I came near she went off, but, having young ones, flew about, and with many Cries expressed her Concern for them; I stood and threw stones at her, till, one striking her, she fell down dead: At first I was pleased with the Exploit, but after a few Minutes was seized with Horror, as having, in a sportive Way, killed an innocent Creature while she was careful for her Young: I beheld her lying dead, and thought these young ones, for which she was so careful, must now perish for want of their Dam to nourish them; and, after some painful Considerations on the Subject, I climbed up the Tree, took all the young Birds, and killed them; supposing that better than to leave them to pine away and die miserably: And believed, in this Case, that Scripture-proverb was fulfilled, "The tender Mercies of the Wicked are cruel." I then went on my Errand, but, for some Hours, could think of little else but the Cruelties I had committed, and was much troubled.

Having attained the Age of sixteen Years, I began to love wanton Company; and though I was preserved from profane Language, or scandalous Conduct, still I perceived a Plant in me which produced much wild Grapes; yet my merciful Father forsook me not utterly, but, at Times, through his Grace, I was brought seriously to consider my Ways; and the Sight of my Backslidings affected me with Sorrow; but, for want of rightly attending to the Reproofs of Instruction, Vanity was added to Vanity, and Repentance to Repentance: Upon the whole, my Mind was more and more alienated from the Truth, and I hastened toward Destruction. While I meditate on the Gulf towards which I traveled, and reflect on my youthful Disobedience, for these Things I weep, mine Eyes run down with Water. . . .

Thus Time passed on: My Heart was replenished with Mirth and Wantonness, and pleasing Scenes of Vanity were presented to my Imagination, till I attained the Age of eighteen Years; near which Time I felt the Judgments of God, in my Soul, like a consuming Fire; and, looking over my past Life, the Prospect was moving.—I was often sad, and longed to be delivered from those Vanities; then again, my Heart was strongly inclined to them, and there was in me a sore Conflict: At Times I turned to Folly, and then again, Sorrow and Confusion took hold of me. In a while, I resolved totally to leave off some of my Vanities; but there was a secret Reserve, in my Heart, of the more refined Part of them, and I was not low enough to find true Peace. Thus, for some Months, I had great Troubles; there remaining in me an unsubjected Will, which rendered my Labors fruitless, till at length, through the merciful Continuance of heavenly Visitations, I was made to bow down in Spirit before the Lord. I remember one Evening I had spent some Time in reading a pious Author; and walking out alone, I humbly prayed to the Lord for his Help, that I might be delivered from all those Vanities which so ensnared me. Thus, being brought low, he helped me; and, as I learned to bear the Cross, I felt Refreshment to come from his Presence; but, not keeping in that Strength which gave Victory, I lost Ground again; the Sense of which greatly affected me; and I sought Deserts and lonely Places, and there, with Tears, did confess my Sins to God, and humbly craved Help of him. And I may say with Reverence, he was near to me in my Troubles, and in those Times of Humiliation opened my Ear to Discipline.

CHAPTER TWO

. . . From Virginia, we crossed over the River Patomac, at Hoe's Ferry, and made a general Visit to the Meetings of Friends on the Western Shore of Maryland; and were at their Quarterly-meeting. We had some hard Labor amongst them, endeavoring to discharge our Duty honestly as Way opened, in the Love of Truth: And thence taking sundry Meetings in our Way, we passed homeward; where, through the Favor of divine Providence we reached the sixteenth Day of the sixth Month, in the Year 1746; and I may say that, through the Assistance of the Holy Spirit, my Companion and I traveled in Harmony, and parted in the Nearness of true brotherly Love.

Two Things were remarkable to me in this Journey; first, in Regard to my Entertainment, when I ate, drank, and lodged at free-cost, with People who lived in Ease on the hard Labor of their Slaves, I felt uneasy; and, as my Mind was inward to the Lord, I found, from Place to Place, this Uneasiness return upon me, at Times, through the whole Visit. Where the Masters bore a good Share of the Burden, and lived frugally, so that their Servants were well provided for, and their Labor moderate, I felt more easy; but where they lived in a costly Way, and laid heavy Burdens on their Slaves, my Exercise was often great, and I frequently had Conversation with them, in private, concerning it. Secondly; this Trade of importing Slaves from their native Country being much encouraged amongst them, and the white People and their Children so generally living without much Labor, was frequently the Subject of my serious Thoughts: And I saw in these southern Provinces so may Vices and Corruptions, increased by this Trade and this Way of Life, that it appeared to me as a Gloom over the Land; and though now many willingly run into it, yet, in future, the Consequence will be grievous to Posterity: I express it as it hath appeared to me, not at once nor twice, but as a Matter fixed on my Mind. . . .

CHAPTER THREE

. . . Until this Year, 1756, I continued to retail Goods, besides following my Trade as a Tailor; about which Time, I grew uneasy on Account of my Business growing too cumbersome: I had begun with selling Trimmings for Garments, and from thence proceeded to sell Cloths and Linens; and, at length, having got a considerable Shop of Goods, my Trade increased every Year, and the Road to large Business appeared open; but I felt a Stop in my Mind.

Through the Mercies of the Almighty, I had, in a good degree, learned to be content with a plain Way of Living: I had but a small Family; and, on serious Consideration, I believed Truth did not require me to engage in much cumbering Affairs: It had been my general Practice to buy and sell Things really useful: Things that served chiefly to please the vain Mind in People, I was not easy to trade in; seldom did it; and, whenever I did, I found it weaken me as a Christian.

The Increase of Business became my Burden; for, though my natural Inclination was toward Merchandise, yet I believed Truth required me to live more free from outward Cumbers: and there was now a Strife in my Mind between the two; and in this Exercise my Prayers were put up to the Lord, who graciously heard me, and gave me a Heart resigned to his holy Will: Then I lessened my outward Business; and, as I had Opportunity, told my Customers of my Intention, that they might consider what Shop to turn to: And, in a while, wholly laid down Merchandise, following my Trade, as a Tailor, myself only, having no Apprentice. I also had a Nursery of Apple trees; in which I employed some of my Time in hoeing, grafting, trimming, and inoculating. In Merchandise it is the Custom, where I lived, to sell chiefly on Credit, and poor People often get in Debt; and when Payment is expected, not having wherewith to pay, their Creditors often sue for it at Law. Having often observed Occurrences of this Kind, I found it good for me to advise poor People to take such Goods as were most useful and not costly.

In the Time of Trading, I had an Opportunity of seeing, that the too liberal Use of spirituous Liquors, and the Custom of wearing too costly Apparel, led some People into great Inconveniences; and these two Things appear to be often connected; for, by not attending to that Use of Things which is consistent with universal Righteousness, there is an Increase of Labor which extends beyond what our heavenly Father intends for us: And by great Labor, and often by much Sweating, there is, even among such as are not Drunkards, a craving of some Liquors to revive the Spirits; that, partly by the luxurious Drinking of some, and partly by the Drinking of others (led to it through immoderate Labor), very great Quantities of Rum are every Year expended in our Colonies; the greater Part of which we should have no Need of, did we steadily attend to pure Wisdom. . . .

Though trading in Things useful is an honest Employ; yet, through the great Number of Superfluities which are bought and sold, and through the Corruption of the Times, they, who apply to merchandise for a Living have great Need to be well experienced in that Precept which the Prophet Jeremiah laid down for his Scribe: "Seekest thou great Things for thyself? seek them not."

CHAPTER FOUR

. . . At Monalen, a Friend gave me some Accounts of a religious Society among the Dutch, called Mennonists; and, amongst other Things, related a Passage in Substance as follows:—One of the Mennonists having Acquaintance with a Man of another Society at a considerable Distance, and being with his Wagon on Business near the House of his said Acquaintance, and Night coming on, he had Thoughts of putting up with him; but passing by his Fields, and observing the distressed Appearance of his Slaves, he kindled a Fire in the Woods hard by, and lay there that Night: His said Acquaintance hearing where he lodged, and afterward meeting the Mennonist, told him of it; adding, he should have been heartily welcome at his House; and, from their Acquaintance in former Time, wondered at his Conduct in that Case. The Mennonist replied, Ever since I lodged by thy Field, I have wanted an Opportunity to speak with thee: The Matter was; I intended to have come to thy House for Entertainment, but, seeing thy Slaves at their Work, and observing the Manner of their Dress, I had no liking to come to partake with thee: Then admonished him to use them with more Humanity; and added, As I lay by the Fire that Night, I thought that, as I was a Man of Substance, thou wouldst have received me freely; but, if I had been as poor as one of thy Slaves, and had no Power to help myself, I should have received from thy Hand no kinder Usage than they . . . .

CHAPTER EIGHT

. . . In my Youth I was used to hard Labor; and, though I was middling healthy, yet my Nature was not fitted to endure so much as many others: So that, being often weary, I was prepared to sympathize with those whose Circumstances in Life, as free Men, required constant Labor to answer the Demands of their Creditors, and with others under Oppression. In the Uneasiness of Body, which I have many Times felt by too much Labor, not as a forced but as a voluntary Oppression, I have often been excited to think on the original Cause of that Oppression, which is imposed on many in the World: And, the latter Part of the Time wherein I labored on our Plantation, my Heart, through the fresh Visitations of heavenly Love, being often tender, and my leisure Time frequently spent in reading the Life and Doctrines of our blessed Redeemer, the Account of the Sufferings of Martyrs, and the History of the first Rise of our Society, a Belief was gradually settled in my Mind, that if such, as had great Estates, generally lived in that Humility and Plainness which belongs to a Christian Life, and laid much easier Rents and Interests on their Lands and Monies, and thus led the Way to a right Use of Things, so great a Number of People might be employed in Things useful, that Labor, both for Men and other Creatures, would need to be no more than an agreeable Employ; and divers Branches of Business, which serve chiefly to please the natural Inclinations of our Minds, and which, at present, seem necessary to circulate that Wealth which some gather, might, in this Way of pure Wisdom, be discontinued. And, as I have thus considered these Things, a Query, at Times, hath arisen: Do I, in all my Proceedings, keep to that Use of Things which is agreeable to universal Righteousness? And then there hath some Degree of Sadness, at Times, come over me, for that I accustomed myself to some Things, which occasioned more Labor than I believe divine Wisdom intends for us. . . .

As he is the Perfection of Power, of Wisdom, and of Goodness, so, I believe, he hath provided, that so much Labor shall be necessary for Men's Support, in this World, as would, being rightly divided, be a suitable Employment of their Time; and that we cannot go into Superfluities, or grasp after Wealth in a Way contrary to his Wisdom, without having Connection with some Degree of Oppression, and with that Spirit which leads to Self-exaltation and Strife, and which frequently brings Calamities on Countries, by Parties contending about their Claims.

CHAPTER TEN

. . . As my lodging in the Steerage, now near a Week, hath afforded me sundry Opportunities of seeing, hearing, and feeling, with respect to the Life and Spirit of many poor Sailors, an inward Exercise of Soul hath attended me, in regard to placing our Children and Youth where they may be likely to be exampled and instructed in the pure Fear of the Lord; and I, being much amongst the Seamen, have, from a Motion of Love, sundry Times taken Opportunities, with one of them at a Time alone, and in a free Conversation labored to turn their Minds toward the Fear of the Lord: And this Day we had a Meeting in the Cabin, where my Heart was contrite under a Feeling of divine Love. . . .

Now, concerning Lads being trained up as Seamen; I believe a Communication from one Part of the World to some other Parts of it, by Sea, is, at Times, consistent with the Will of our heavenly Father; and to educate some Youth in the Practice of sailing, I believe, may be right: But how lamentable is the present Corruption of the World! how impure are the Channels through which Trade hath a Conveyance! how great is that Danger, to which poor Lads are now exposed, when placed on shipboard to learn the Art of sailing! . . .

Rising to work in the Night is not commonly pleasant in any case; but, in dark rainy Nights, it is very disagreeable, even though each Man were furnished with all Conveniences: But, if Men must go out at Midnight, to help manage the Ship in the Rain, and, having small Room to sleep and lay their Garments in, are often beset to furnish themselves for the Watch, their Garments or something relating to their Business being wanting and not easily found, when, from the Urgency occasioned by high Winds, they are hastened and called up suddenly, here is a Trial of Patience on the poor Sailors and the poor Lads their Companions.

If, after they have been on Deck several Hours in the Night, and come down into the Steerage soaking wet, and are so close stowed that proper Convenience for change of Garment is not easily come at, but for Want of proper Room, their wet Garments are thrown in Heaps, and sometimes, through much crowding, are trodden under Foot in going to their Lodgings and getting out of them, and they have great Difficulties, at Times, each one to find his own, here are Trials on the poor Sailors.

Now, as I have been with them in my Lodge, my Heart hath often yearned for them, and tender Desires have been raised in me, that all Owners and Masters of Vessels may dwell in the Love of God, and therein act uprightly; and, by seeking less for Gain, and looking carefully to their Ways, may earnestly labor to remove all Cause of Provocation from the poor Seamen, either to fret or use Excess of Strong drink; for, indeed, the poor Creatures, at Times, in the Wet and Cold, seem to apply to Strong drink to supply the Want of other Convenience.

Great Reformation in the World is wanting; and the Necessity of it, amongst these who do Business on great Waters, hath, at this Time, been abundantly opened before me.   1774

Timothy Dwight

(1752-1817)

Among the prose works of Timothy Dwight is his *Travels in New-England and New-York*, 4 vols. (Hartford, 1821–1822), a journal of his excursions, taken primarily for health reasons, during his presidency at Yale (1795–1817). Dwight took these trips during college holidays and reportedly walked some 2,000 miles and rode horseback some 3,000 more in his travels.

BIBLIOGRAPHY: See Headnote to Dwight's *Greenfield Hill.*

From *Travels in New-England and New-York*

BOOK I, LETTER IV

The thunder-storms of this country, generally so styled because a considerable number of them are actually storms, are in most cases equally beneficial and delightful. An immense grandeur invests them during the time of their approach. They are so frequent in ordinary seasons as to furnish an ample supply of rain for the demands of vegetation. The wind which brings them, and which blows one or two days after they have passed over, is remarkably pure, refreshing, and healthy. The earth, particularly in the months of May and June, the richest season of vegetation, is beautiful beyond description. The verdure glows with new life—the flowers exult with additional beauty and fragrance—

> "The birds their notes renew; and bleating herds
> Attest their joy, that hill and valley rings."

The sun, in the meantime, beams through the purified atmosphere with a peculiar splendor. One, and often two rainbows are finely painted on the reverse of the departing storm. The clouds in the western regions, wrought into the boldest figures, and tinged in different places with all the elegant hues of the prismatic image, present to the eye mountains with summits of gold, and precipices of fire.

LETTER XXIV

The legislature of each town is, like that of Athens, composed of the inhabitants, personally present; a majority of whom decides every question. The proceedings of this legislature are all controlled by exact rules, and are under the direction of the proper officers. The confusion incident to popular meetings, and so often disgraceful to those of Athens and Rome, is effectually prevented. . . .

By these local legislatures a multitude of important concerns are managed, too numerous and unwieldy to be adjusted by the legislature of the state, and far better known by those, who actually superintend them, than by any other persons. They have a deep interest in these concerns, and therefore will not neglect them; understand them perfectly, and will therefore regulate them wisely; are always present, and therefore can meet and act on every emergency.

In these little schools men commence their apprenticeship to public life, and learn to do public business. Here the young speaker makes his first essays; and here his talents are displayed, marked, and acknowledged. The aged and discreet here see with pleasure the promise of usefulness in the young, and fail not to reward with honorable testimonials every valuable effort of the rising generation. The questions agitated, though affecting only local concerns, and a moderate number of people, are still interesting, and often deeply. At times they furnish full scope for the genius, understanding, and eloquence, of any man; are ably discussed, and command profound attention. The sober, busy citizens of Connecticut are, however, very little inclined to commend, or even listen to, the eloquence which is intended merely for show. He, who would be heard with approbation, or mentioned with praise, must speak, only because there is occasion to speak; must speak with modesty, with brevity, to forward or improve the measures proposed, or those which he substitutes; and not to show that he can speak, however ingeniously.

. . . Virtues are here tried, and talents occupied, in a manner safe alike to the employer and the agent. On the one hand the capacity for business is enlarged; and on the other the best proof is given, which can be given, of the proper preparatory qualifications for business of a superior and more extensive nature. In the closet no man ever becomes acquainted with either the concerns or the character of men, or with the manner in which business ought to be conducted. The general principles of political science a scholar may understand, equally with those of other sciences. But of business, which is necessarily done in detail, if done to any purpose, the mere scholar literally knows nothing. He may be able to write a good political book: but he cannot do political business, because he never has done it. A plain man, educated in the business of a town, will easily show him, that in knowledge of this kind he is an infant; and that, whatever may be his genius or his acquisitions.

. . . No method hitherto adopted by mankind has been equally successful with this, in forming that opinion, and in fitting men to judge well concerning governmental measures. A large proportion of the citizens of this state have actually sustained one public office, and multitudes several, and have of course been personally concerned in transacting public business. Hence they have already known, by experience, the difficulties incident to public concerns; and are, in a degree superior to what is usually found elsewhere, prepared to form judicious opinions concerning the measures of the legislature. I have heard laws discussed by plain men with more good sense, than any mere scholar could have displayed on the same subjects. By these men they were canvassed as to their operation on the actual interests of themselves and others. By a scholar they would have been examined as to their accordance with preconceived general principles. The former were certain means of determining on the merits of a law; the latter, only probable, and very imperfect.

BOOK II, LETTER XIII

. . . In the formation of colonies, those, who are first inclined to emigrate, are usually such as have met with difficulties at home. These are commonly joined by persons, who, having large families and small farms, are induced, for the sake of settling their children comfortably, to seek for new and cheaper lands. To both are always added the discontented, the enterprising, the ambitious, and the covetous. Many of the first, and some of all these classes, are found in every new American country, within ten years after its settlement has commenced. From this period, kindred, friendship, and former neighborhood, prompt others to follow them. Others, still, are allured by the prospect of gain, presented in every new country to the sagacious, from the purchase and sale of lands; while not a small number are influenced by the brilliant stories, which everywhere are told concerning most tracts during the early progress of their settlement. A considerable part of all those, who *begin* the cultivation of the wilderness, may be denominated foresters, or pioneers. The business of these persons is no other than to cut down trees, build log-houses, lay open forested grounds to cultivation, and prepare the way for those who come after them. These men cannot live in regular society. They are too idle, too talkative, too passionate, too prodigal, and too shiftless, to acquire either property or character . . . and finding all their efforts vain, they become at length discouraged; and under the pressure of poverty, the fear of a jail, and the consciousness of public contempt, leave their native places, and betake themselves to the wilderness.

Here they are obliged either to work, or starve. They accordingly cut down some trees and girdle others; they furnish themselves with an ill-built log-house, and a worse barn; and reduce a part of the forest into fields, half-enclosed and half-cultivated. The forests furnish browse, and their fields yield a stinted herbage. On this scanty provision they feed a few cattle; and with these, and the penurious products of their labor, eked out by hunting and fishing, they keep their families alive.

A farm, thus far cleared, promises immediate subsistence to a better husbandman. A log-house, thus built, presents, when repaired with moderate exertions, a shelter for his family. Such a husbandman is therefore induced by these little advantages, where the soil and situation please him, to purchase such a farm, when he would not plant himself in an absolute wilderness. The proprietor is always ready to sell; for he loves this irregular, adventurous, half-working and half-lounging life; and hates the sober industry and prudent economy, by which his bush pasture might be changed into a farm, and himself raised to thrift and independence. The bargain is soon made. The forester, receiving more money for his improvements than he ever before possessed, and a price for the soil, somewhat enhanced by surrounding settlements, willingly quits his house, to build another like it, and his farm, to girdle trees, hunt, and saunter, in another place. . . .

The second proprietor is commonly a farmer; and with an industry and spirit, deserving no small commendation, changes the desert into a fruitful field. . . .

The class of men, who have been the principal subject of these remarks, have already straggled onward from New-England, as well as from other parts of the Union, to Louisiana. In a political view, their emigration is of very serious utility to the ancient settlements. All countries contain restless inhabitants; men impatient of labor; men, who will contract debts without intending to pay them; who had rather talk than work; whose vanity persuades them, that they are wise, and prevents them from knowing, that they are fools; . . . Under despotic governments they are awed into quiet; but in every free community they create, to a greater or less extent, continual turmoil; and have often overturned the peace, liberty, and happiness of their fellow-citizens. In the Roman commonwealth, as before in the republics of Greece, they were emptied out, as soldiers, upon the surrounding countries; and left the sober inhabitants in comparative quiet at home. It is true they often threw these states into confusion, and sometimes overturned the government. But if they had not been thus thrown off from the body politic, its life would have been of a momentary duration. As things actually were, they finally ruined all these states; for some of them had, as some of them always will have, sufficient talents to do mischief; at times, very extensive. The Gracchi, Clodius, Marius, and Mark Antony, were men of this character. Of this character is every demagogue, whatever may be his circumstances. Power and profit are the only ultimate objects, which every such man, with a direction as steady as that of the needle to the pole, pursues with a greediness unlimited and inextinguishable.

Formerly the energetic government established in New-England, together with the prevailing high sense of religion and morals, and the continually pressing danger from the French and the savages, compelled the inhabitants into habits of regularity and good order, not surpassed, perhaps, in the world. But since the American revolution our situation has become less favorable to the existence, as well as to the efficacy, of these great means of internal peace. The former exact and decisive energy of the government has been obviously weakened. From our ancient dangers we have been delivered, and the deliverance was a distinguished blessing; but the sense of danger regularly brings with it a strong conviction, that safety cannot be preserved without exact order, and a ready submission to lawful authority.

The institutions and the habits of New-England, more I suspect than those of any other country, have prevented or kept down this noxious disposition; but they cannot entirely prevent either its existence or its effects. In mercy, therefore, to the sober, industrious, and well-disposed inhabitants, Providence has opened in the vast western wilderness a retreat, sufficiently alluring to draw them away from the land of their nativity. We have many troubles even now; but we should have many more if this body of foresters had remained at home.

It is however to be observed, that a considerable number even of these people become sober, industrious citizens, merely by the acquisition of property. The love of property, to a certain degree, seems indispensable to the existence of sound morals. I have never had a servant, in whom I could confide, except such as were desirous to earn and preserve money. The conveniences and the character attendant on the possession of property fix even these restless men at times, when they find themselves really able to accumulate it, and persuade them to a course of regular industry. . . . The secure possession of property demands every moment the hedge of law, and reconciles a man, originally lawless, to the restraints of government. Thus situated, he sees that reputation also is within his reach. Ambition forces him to aim at it, and compels him to a life of sobriety and decency. That his children may obtain this benefit, he is obliged to send them to school, and to unite with those around him in supporting a schoolmaster. His neighbors are disposed to build a church, and settle a minister. A regard to his own character, to the character and feelings of his family, and very often to the solicitations of his wife, prompts him to contribute to both these objects; to attend, when they are compassed, upon the public worship of God, and perhaps to become in the end a religious man.

I am, Sir, &c.

BOOK III, LETTER IV

The whole body of these Indians are a poor, degraded, miserable race of beings. The former proud, heroic spirit of the Pequod, terrible even to other proud, heroic spirits around him, is shrunk into the tameness and torpor of reasoning brutism. All the vice of the original is left: all its energy has vanished. They are lazy in the extreme; and never labor, unless compelled by necessity. Nor are they less prodigal than lazy. The earnings of a year, hardly as they are acquired, they will spend in a day, without a thought of the morrow. Wherever they can obtain credit, they involve themselves in debt; and never dream of paying their debts, unless under the iron hand of law. Thieves they are of course, but have too little enterprise to steal any thing of importance. It is hardly necessary to observe, that they are liars. They have no such thing among them as marriage; but cohabit without ceremony or covenant, and desert each other at pleasure. . . . To strong drink their devotion is complete; and for ardent spirits, or cider, they will part with everything which they possess. Generally, they are healthy; but, when sick, seem in a great measure to be beyond the reach of medicine. Those, who live by themselves, are half-naked, and often half-starved.

The Indian, in a savage state, spent life chiefly in roving; but he roved in pursuit of the deer, the bear, the wolf, or his enemy. A high sense of glory, an ardent passion for achievement, a proud consciousness of independence, and a masculine spirit of exertion were the prominent features of his character. He had customarily an object before him; in his view great, useful, and honorable. He had, therefore, powerful motives to rouse his faculties into action. When he had not, he either spent his time in violent gambling, in which, like the polished adventurers of civilized society, he hazarded and lost his all; even his blanket and his gun; or, when he could not gamble, dozed away life in precisely the same paralytic inactivity, which is so remarkable in his tamed countrymen.

The Indian of the latter character lounges, saunters, gets drunk, eats when he can find food, and lies down to sleep under the nearest fence. Without any present or future object in view, without proposing any advantage to himself, or feeling any interest in what is proposed by others, he leads the life, not of a man, but of a snail; and is rather a moving vegetable than a rational being. . . .

If anything is necessary to complete the miserable and melancholy picture, it is this additional feature, that not one of the rising generation appears to aim, even remotely, at any higher character.

You have, here, an account of that very state of society, which is preferred and extolled by Godwin as the perfection of man. Here the human race, as nearly as possible, are without the restraint of law, morals, or religion. At the same time they are free in the fullest sense. . . . Why then are they not perfect and happy?

There are two great reasons to be assigned as an answer to this question, both of which have escaped this hoodwinked philosopher. The first is, that human depravity, or, in other words, sin, has no tendency to make a happy society; but among all intelligent beings, will always render the social state unhappy, in exact proportion to the degree in which it exists. The other is, that labor is the only source of those enjoyments, which make up what Godwin calls happiness, and that, without the dominion of law, which alone secures to man the benefit of his efforts, no human being will labor. Godwin and his associates feel as if themselves should be happier if they were freed from the restraints which I have mentioned; not mistrusting, that without them others, enjoying the same licentiousness of disposition, and the same impunity in indulging it, would plunder them of liberty, property, and life. Equally are they insensible, that without the protection of law none would labor, and no part of those enjoyments, on which they riot, be brought into existence. Without law, religion, and morals, they might indeed be fornicators and adulterers, thieves and assassins, but they would be beggars and vagabonds. . . .

The great calamity experienced by these Indians, and by all other people in the like circumstances, is this: within the horizon of their thought not a single motive arises, not a single inducement is visible, which might awaken their dozing energy, or prompt them to any useful effort. Man, without motives to exertion, is a beast or a log; with them, he can become an Alfred or a Paul. But the motives must be such as he is fitted to feel; and Indians, without greater exertions in their behalf than those which have hitherto been made, will never feel, nor even comprehend, such motives as influence civilized man. The great hindrance to their improvement does not lie, as some dreaming European philosophers have supposed, in the inferiority of their minds. . . . The real cause of all this degradation in the Indian is the want of such motives to exertion as he is prepared to feel within the view of his mind. The only cause of human distinction, also, is the existence of such motives. Where nothing prompts to action, nothing will be done; where sufficient inducements are presented, everything will be done which is within the grasp of human power. When motives cease to operate and excite, man will lounge away life; saunter from place to place without knowing why; dress himself in a blanket; seat himself upon a stone; smoke through the day at the door of a weekwam; or stretch himself to sleep under the nearest hedge. When motives arouse him to exertion, he will cross unknown oceans to discover new countries; coast the polar ice to attack the whale; ascend the Andes to measure the equatorial latitude; ransack the bowels of the earth to enlarge the science of mineralogy; imprison himself in a cell for seven years to obtain the palm of eloquence; face the fangs of the catamount or the tiger, to be called the best huntsman; toil through life to accumulate an inheritance for his children; or fight battles, or slaughter millions, to wreathe upon his brow the garland of triumph. With sufficient motives, also, he will resist temptation; subdue his lusts; expend his substance; and yield his life for the cause of Christianity, the salvation of men, and the glory of the Redeemer.   c. 1795, 1821–1822

VERSE

Ebenezer Cook

(c. 1670–c. 1732)

Born in London, Ebenezer Cook apparently journeyed to Maryland early in the 18th century and on his return to England wrote *The Sot-Weed Factor; or A Voyage to Maryland* (London, 1708). Two other works are "An Elegy on the Death of . . . Nicholas Lowe" (1728) and *Sot-Weed Redivivus; or the Planters' Looking Glass* (Annapolis, 1730). William Parks of Annapolis printed *The Maryland Muse* (1731), a verse account of Bacon's Rebellion with another edition of *The Sot-Weed Factor*.

BIBLIOGRAPHY: B. C. Steiner, *Early Maryland Poetry* (Baltimore, 1900). L. C. Wroth, ed. *The Maryland Muse* (1731), *Proc. of the Amer. Ant. Soc.*, XLIV (1934), 267–335.

From *The Sot-Weed Factor*

Condemn'd by Fate to way-ward Curse,
Of Friends unkind, and empty Purse;
Plagues worse than fill'd Pandora's Box,
I took my leave of Albion's Rocks:
With heavy Heart, concern'd that I   5
Was forc'd my Native Soil to fly,
And the Old World must bid good-by.
But Heav'n ordain'd it should be so,
And to repine is vain we know:
Freighted with Fools, from Plymouth sound,   10
To Mary-Land our Ship was bound,
Where we arriv'd in dreadful Pain,
Shock'd by the Terrors of the Main;
For full three Months, our wavering Boat,
Did thro' the surly Ocean float,   15
And furious Storms and threat'ning Blasts,
Both tore our Sails and sprung our Masts:
Wearied, yet pleas'd, we did escape

389

Such Ills, we anchor'd at the Cape;[1]
But weighing soon, we plough'd the Bay,   20
To Cove[2] it in Piscato-way,[3]
Intending there to open Store,
I put myself and Goods a-shore:
Where soon repair'd a numerous Crew,
In Shirts and Drawers of Scotch-cloth Blue.[4]   25
With neither Stockings, Hat, nor Shoe.
These Sot-weed Planters Crowd the Shore,
In Hue as tawny as a Moor:
Figures so strange, no God design'd,
To be a part of Human Kind: 30
But wanton Nature, void of Rest,
Moulded the brittle Clay in Jest.
At last a Fancy very odd
Took me, this was the Land of Nod;
Planted at first, when Vagrant Cain,   35
His Brother had unjustly slain:
Then conscious of the Crime he'd done,
From Vengeance dire, he hither run;
And in a Hut supinely dwelt,
The first in Furs and Sot-weed dealt.   40
And ever since his Time, the Place,
Has harbor'd a detested Race;
Who when they could not live at Home,
For Refuge to these Worlds did roam;
In hopes by Flight they might prevent,   45
The Devil and his fell intent;
Obtain from Triple Tree reprieve,
And Heav'n and Hell alike deceive. . . .

While riding near a Sandy Bay,
I met a Quaker, Yea and Nay;   50
A Pious Conscientious Rogue,
As e'er wore Bonnet or a Brogue,
Who neither Swore nor kept his Word,
But cheated in the Fear of God;
And when his Debts he would not pay,   55
By Light within he ran away.

---

[1] By the Cape, is meant the Capes of Virginia, the first Land on the Coast of Virginia and Mary-Land. [The notes in this selection are Cook's.]

[2] To Cove is to lie at Anchor safe in Harbor.

[3] The Bay of Piscato-way, the usual place where our Ships come to an Anchor in Mary-Land.

[4] The Planters generally wear Blue Linen.

With this sly Zealot soon I struck
A Bargain for my English Truck,
Agreeing for ten thousand weight,
Of Sot-weed good and fit for freight,   60
Broad Oronooko bright and sound,
The growth and product of his ground;
In Cask that should contain complete,
Five hundred of Tobacco neat.
The Contract thus betwixt us made,   65
Not well acquainted with the Trade,
My Goods I trusted to the Cheat,
Whose crop was then aboard the Fleet;
And going to receive my own,
I found the Bird was newly flown: 70
Cursing this execrable Slave,
This damn'd pretended Godly Knave;
On due Revenge and Justice bent,
I instantly to Counsel went,
Unto an ambidexter Quack,[5]   75
Who learnedly had got the knack
Of giving Glisters, making Pills,
Of filling Bonds, and forging Wills;
And with a stock of Impudence,
Supply'd his want of Wit and Sense;   80
With Looks demure, amazing People,
No wiser than a Daw in Steeple;
My Anger flushing in my Face,
I stated the preceding Case:
And of my Money was so lavish,   85
That he'd have poison'd half the Parish,
And hang'd his Father on a Tree,
For such another tempting Fee;
Smiling, said he, the Cause is clear,
I'll manage him you need not fear;   90
The Case is judg'd, good Sir, but look
In Galen, No—in my Lord Cook,
I vow to God I was mistook:
I'll take out a Provincial Writ,
And Trounce him for his Knavish Wit;   95
Upon my life we'll win the Cause,
With all the ease I cure the Yaws:[6]
Resolv'd to plague the holy Brother,
I set one Rogue to catch another;

[5] This Fellow was an Apothecary, and turn'd an Attorney at Law.
[6] The Yaws is the Pox.

To try the Cause then fully bent,   100
Up to Annapolis I went,[7]
A City Situate on a Plain,
Where scarce a House will keep out Rain;
The Buildings fram'd with Cyprus rare,
Resembles much our Southwark Fair: 105
But Stranger here will scarcely meet
With Market-place, Exchange, or Street;
And if the Truth I may report,
'Tis not so large as Tottenham Court.
St. Mary's once was in repute,   110
Now here the Judges try the Suit,
And Lawyers twice a Year dispute.
As oft the Bench most gravely meet,
Some to get Drunk, and some to eat
A swinging share of Country Treat.   115
But as for Justice right or wrong,
Not one amongst the numerous throng,
Knows what they mean, or has the Heart,
To give his Verdict on a Stranger's part:
Now Court being call'd by beat of Drum,   120
The Judges left their Punch and Rum,
When Pettifogger Doctor draws,
His Paper forth, and opens Cause:
And lest I should the better get,
Brib'd Quack supprest his Knavish Wit.   125
So Maid upon the downy Field,
Pretends a Force, and Fights to yield:
The Biased Court without delay,
Adjudg'd my Debt in Country Pay;
In Pipe staves, Corn, or Flesh of Boar,[8]   130
Rare Cargo for the English Shore:
Raging with Grief, full speed I ran,
To join the Fleet at Kicketan;[9]
Embark'd and waiting for a Wind,
I left this dreadful Curse behind.   135

May Cannibals transported o'er the Sea
Prey on these Slaves, as they have done on me;
May never Merchant's trading Sails explore
This Cruel, this Inhospitable Shore;

[7] The chief of Mary-Land containing about twenty-four Houses.
[8] There is a Law in this Country, the Plaintiff may pay his Debt in Country pay, which
consists in the produce of his Plantation.
[9] The homeward bound Fleet meets here.

But left abandon'd by the World to starve,   140
May they sustain the Fate they well deserve:
May they turn Savage, or as Indians Wild,
From Trade, Converse, and Happiness exil'd;
Recreant to Heaven, may they adore the Sun,
And into Pagan Superstitions run   145
For Vengeance ripe ———
May Wrath Divine then lay those Regions waste
Where no Man's Faithful, nor a Woman Chaste.[10]

                              1708

William Dawson
(1704-1752)

William Dawson of Virginia has been identified as the anonymous author of *Poems on Several Occasions,* "by a Gentleman of Virginia," published by William Parks at Williamsburg in 1736. Dawson, the second president of William and Mary College, described the poems in his preface as "the casual productions of youth."

BIBLIOGRAPHY: *Poems on Several Occasions* (1736), ed. Ralph L. Rusk (New York, 1930). Also edited by E. G. Swem (New York, 1920).

To Sylvia

ON APPROACH OF WINTER

Come, my Sylvia, come away;
Youth and Beauty will not stay;
   Let's enjoy the present now.
Hear, tempestuous Winter's Roar,
How it blusters at the Door,   5
   Charg'd with Frosts, and Storms, and Snow.

Seated near the crackling Fire,
Let's indulge our fond Desire,
   Careless of rough Borea's Blast:
Let us teach the blooming Youth,   10
What Joys attend on Love and Truth;
   How much they please, how long they last.

[10] The Author does not intend by this, any of the English Gentlemen resident there.

The am'rous Warblers of the Grove,
That in sweet Carols chant their Love,
    Can only sing, whilst Spring inspires;   15
But let us show, no Age, no Time,
No warring Seasons, frozen Clime,
    Can damp the Warmth of our Desires.
                                                    1736

Anacreontic

Old Poets sing the Dame, to Stone
Converted by Jove's radiant Son:
How Progne builds her clayey Cell
In Chimneys, where she once did dwell.
For me, (did Fate permit to use,   5
Whatever Form our Fancies choose)
I'd be my lovely Sylvia's Glass,
Still to reflect her beauteous Face;
I'd be the pure and limpid Wave,
In which my Fair delights to lave;   10
I'd be her Garment, still to hide
Her snowy Limbs, with decent Pride;
I'd be the Girdle, to embrace
The gradual Taper of her Waist;
I'd be her Tippet, still to press   15
The snowy Velvet of her Breast;
But if the rigid Fates denied
Such Ornaments of Grace and Pride,
I'd be her very Shoe, that she
With scornful Tread might Trample me.   20
                                                    1736

Charles Hansford
(c. 1685-1761)

Charles Hansford of Virginia worked as a blacksmith most of his life, but between 1749 and 1752, he wrote several poems—most of them either autobiographical or on religious subjects. None of his verse was pub- lished during his lifetime.

BIBLIOGRAPHY: J. A. Servies and C. R. Dolmetsch, eds. *The Poems of Charles Hansford* (Chapel Hill, N.C., 1961).

From *Of Body and of Soul*

How true is that by Holy David said,
Man wonderfully, fearfully is made!
A compound creature whose essential whole
Is made, compos'd of body and of soul.
But those two parts quite different are in worth: 5
The body matter taken from the earth;
Not so the soul, that claims a higher birth.
A ray from Heaven is her original.
Though much deprav'd and darken'd since the Fall,
She still remains an active, restless thing: 10
Always awake, forever on the wing,
Ready to act (or, rather, acting ever)
On subjects good or bad, suspending never
Her busy searches. When the body seems
As dead in sleep, the soul then acts in dreams.   15

c. 1749, 1961

From *Barzillai*

But yet of all the horrors Nature yields,
And frequent are in Neptune's wat'ry fields,
The voyages to Greenland seem to me
Most dreadful, hideous, shocking for to be.
Their canvas wings they spread, fly from the sun   5
To horrid frosts; mountains of ice they run;
Long and cold nights with very little day;
Shiv'ring upon the deck the sailors stay.
Their sails are frozen stiff, their cordage cast
With slippery ice; brandy they drink in haste   10
To cheer their hearts and give their blood a flow;
Long icicles unto their beards do grow.
Their clumsy fingers scarce can knit a knot;
Their peas soon freeze when from the kettle got.
Now rum and brandy with them bear great price,   15
For weaker liquors soon are turn'd to ice.
The North Star near their zenith they behold,
Whose rays, though bright, dart down a piercing cold.
If land they ken, vast rifts of snow appear;
At sea, mountains of ice their heads uprear.   20
Furr'd caps and mittens, double-sol'd shoes,
With jackets lin'd with foxes' skins, they use.

Now to their business ev'ry hand is set:
Their double-headed boats they ready get;
The harpooner whets up his bearded spear   25
Fine as his warp and drag; thus, all appear
In readiness, with hearts as hard as wood,
To hunt the whale amidst the liquid flood.
Him having found and view'd with fearless eyes,
They then consider how they may surprise   30
The unwieldy monster. Now the harpooner
Directs the crew how and which way to steer;
Revers'd they ply their oars, in silence move.
The harpooner stands ready for to shove
His prongy harpoon just above the fin   35
That's next the head; and, having fix'd it in,
The crew of rowers ready on the stretch.
Their safety is to get out of the reach
Of his most dangerous, destructive tail
Which, when he's wounded, he doth seldom fail   40
In frightful manner up aloft to show
And, at that instant, with it give a blow
Which, if it should upon a tower light
(Were it of stone), would be demolish'd quite.
If out of danger they do hap to get,   45
The harpooner, a-running, then doth set
His well-coiled warp. When that is all run out,
He throws his drag; the oarsmen turn about
And now the chase begins. The wounded whale
Lugs on the stopping drag 'til strength does fail,   50
And by the wake that by the drag is made
The boats pursue. The monster they invade;
With lances long and sharp they pierce the lubber
And, having kill'd him, of his fat make blubber.
The bone about his jaws they home do send,   55
The ladies' petticoats for to extend.
(A fond and foolish fashion now 'tis grown,
In former, modest times not us'd, not known.)

                                        c. 1749, 1961

Mather Byles

(1707-1788)

Mather Byles received his A.B. from Harvard in 1725 and his A.M. in 1728; in 1732 he was ordained pastor of the Hollis St. Congregational Church, Boston. An admirer of and correspondent with Pope, Watts, and Thomson, Byles earned a reputation as a forceful preacher, a scholar, a wit, and an incorrigible punster. His work was collected in *Poems on Sev-eral Occasions* (Boston, 1744).

BIBLIOGRAPHY: A. W. H. Eaton, *The Famous Mather Byles* (Boston, 1914). C. K. Shipton, *Sibley's Harvard Graduates*, VII (1946), 464–493. C. L. Carlson, ed. *Poems on Several Occasions* (New York, 1940), a facsimile of 1744 edition.

Hymn at Sea

Great God, thy works our wonder raise,
　To thee our swelling notes belong;
While skies, and winds, and rocks, and seas,
　Around shall echo to our song.

Thy power produced this mighty frame,　　　　5
　Aloud to thee the tempests roar,
Or softer breezes tune thy name
　Gently along the shelly shore.

Round thee the scaly nation roves,
　Thy opening hands their joys bestow,　　　　10
Through all the blushing coral groves,
　These silent, gay retreats below.

See the broad sun forsake the skies,
　Glow on the waves, and downward slide!
Anon, heaven opens all its eyes,　　　　15
　And star-beams tremble o'er the tide.

Each various scene, or day or night,
　Lord, points to thee our ravished soul;
Thy glories fix our whole delight;
　So the touch'd needle courts the pole.　　　　20

c. 1732, 1744

Elegy

ADDRESSED TO GOVERNOR BELCHER ON THE DEATH OF HIS LADY

Belcher, once more permit the muse you loved,
By honor, and by sacred friendship moved,
Waked by your woe, her numbers to prolong,
And pay her tribute in a funeral song.

From you, great heaven with undisputed voice,   5
Has snatch'd the partner of your youthful joys.
Her beauties, ere slow hectic fires consumed,
Her eyes shone cheerful, and her roses bloom'd:
Long lingering sickness broke the lovely form,
Shock after shock, and storm succeeding storm,   10
Till death, relentless, seized the wasting clay,
Stopp'd the faint voice, and catch'd the soul away.

No more in converse sprightly she appears,
With nice decorum, and obliging airs:
Ye poor, no more expecting round her stand,   15
Where soft compassion stretch'd her bounteous hand:
Her house her happy skill no more shall boast;
"Be all things plentiful, but nothing lost."
Cold to the tomb see the pale corpse convey'd,
Wrapt up in silence, and the dismal shade.   20

Ah! what avail the sable velvet spread,
And golden ornaments amidst the dead?
No beam smiles there, no eye can there discern
The vulgar coffin from the marble urn:
The costly honors, preaching, seem to say,   25
"Magnificence must mingle with the clay."

Learn here, ye fair, the frailty of your face,
Ravish'd by death, or nature's slow decays:
Ye great, must so resign your transient power,
Heroes of dust, and monarchs of an hour!   30
So must each pleasing air, each gentle fire,
And all that's soft, and all that's sweet expire.

But you, O Belcher, mourn the absent fair,
Feel the keen pang, and drop the tender tear:
The God approves that nature do her part,   35
A panting bosom, and a bleeding heart.

Ye baser arts of flattery, away!
The virtuous muse shall moralize her lay.
To you, O favorite man, the power supreme
Gives wealth, and titles, and extent of fame;   40
Joys from beneath, and blessings from above;
Thy monarch's plaudit; and thy people's love:
The same high power, unbounded, and alone,
Resumes his gifts, and puts your mourning on.
His edict issues, and his vassal, death,   45
Requires your consort's,—or your flying breath.
Still be your glory at his feet to bend,
Kiss thou the Son, and own his sovereign hand;
For his high honors all thy powers exert,
The gifts of nature, and the charms of art;   50
So over death the conquest shall be given,
Your name shall live on earth, your soul in heaven.

Meantime my name to thine allied shall stand,
Still our warm friendship, mutual flames extend;
The muse shall so survive from age to age,   55
And Belcher's name protect his Byles's page.

                                   1736

The God of Tempest

Thy dreadful power, Almighty God,
    Thy works to speak conspire;
This earth declares thy fame abroad,
    With water, air, and fire.

At thy command, in glaring streaks,   5
    The ruddy lightning flies;
Loud thunder the creation shakes,
    And rapid tempests rise.

Now gathering glooms obscure the day,
    And shed a solemn night;   10
And now the heavenly engines play,
    And shoot devouring light.

The attending sea thy will performs,
    Waves tumble to the shore,
And toss, and foam amidst the storms,   15
    And dash, and rage, and roar.

The earth, and all her trembling hills,
    Thy marching footsteps own;
A shuddering fear her entrails fills,
    Her hideous caverns groan.   20

My God, when terrors thickest throng
    Through all the mighty space,
And rattling thunders roar along,
    And bloody lightnings blaze:

When wild confusion wrecks the air,   25
    And tempests rend the skies,
Whilst blended ruin, clouds and fire
    In harsh disorder rise:

Amid the hurricane I'll stand,
    And strike a tuneful song;   30
My harp all trembling in my hand,
    And all inspired my tongue.

I'll shout aloud, "Ye thunders! roll,
    And shake the sullen sky;
Your sounding voice from pole to pole   35
    In angry murmurs try.

"Thou sun! retire, refuse thy light,
    And let thy beams decay;
Ye lightnings, flash along the night,
    And dart a dreadful day.   40

"Let the earth totter on her base,
    Clouds heaven's wide arch deform;
Blow, all ye winds, from every place,
    And breathe the final storm.

"O Jesus, haste the glorious day,   45
    When thou shalt come in flame,
And burn the earth, and waste the sea,
    And break all nature's frame.

"Come quickly, blessed hope, appear,
    Bid thy swift chariot fly: 50
Let angels warn thy coming near,
    And snatch me to the sky.

"Around thy wheels, in the glad throng,
   I'd bear a joyful part;
All Hallelujah on my tongue,   55
   All rapture in my heart."

1727

Benjamin Church
(1734-1776)

After graduating from Harvard in 1754, Benjamin Church studied medicine in London and later opened his practice in Boston. A British spy for General Thomas Gage during the Revolution, Church was found guilty and sentenced to prison. His best-known poems are *The Choice; A Poem After the Manner of Mr. Pomfret* (Boston, 1757) and *The Times; A Poem* (1765).

BIBLIOGRAPHY: *DAB*. Allen French *General Gage's Informers* (Ann Arbor, Mich., 1932), pp. 147–201.

From *The Times*

Witness, ye fathers! whose protracted time;
Fruitful of story, chronicles the clime;
These howling deserts, hospitably tame,
Erst snatch'd ye, martyrs, from the hungry flame;
'Twas heaven's own cause, beneath whose sheltering power,   5
Ye grew the wonder of the present hour;
With anxious ear we've drank your piteous tale,
Where woes unnumber'd long and loud prevail;
Here savage demons, sporting with your pains,
There boding mischief in a Stuart reigns;   10
Mark the glad era, when prevailing foes,
The state's fell harpies, doubling woes on woes,
Had wing'd destruction—vengeance slept no more,
But flung the tyrant from the British shore:
Learn hence, ye minions! reverence to the law,   15
Salvation died not with the great Nassau.
And shall such sons, from such distinguished sires,
Nurtured to hardships, heirs of all their sires,
Shall they, O pang of heart! thus tamely bear,
Who stalk erect, and toss their heads in air?   20

Let beasts of burden meanly woo the chain,
We talk of masters with a proud disdain.
"Prythee forbear, rash youth! conceal thy fears,
A modest silence best becomes thy years;
Submit, be prudent—in some future hour,   25
You'll feel the iron-gripe of ruthless power":
Truce, spawn of phlegm! thy frozen heart conceal,
Benumb'd, unerring, and unapt to feel;
No deed of glory can that soul entice,
Involved in adamantine walls of ice;   30
Within that bosom is a nook so warm,
That vice or virtue kindles to a storm?
Could nature ever lure thee into sin?
Or bursts of passion thaw the frost within?
Thou happy cynic! still thy senses lull,   35
Profoundly cautious, and supinely dull;
And should some hero start his rash career,
Eccentric to thy lazy, drowsy sphere;
Be wondrous wise, thy frigid temper bless,
That never wrought thee to a bold excess: 40
Call truth a libel, treason, honest zeal,
So strange is virtue, and so few can feel;
Call Churchill blockhead, Freedom, madness, rage,
Call injured Wilkes a monster of the age;
To make me blest, unite this lay with those,   45
And then, then kindly rate yourselves my foes.

　　Fop, witling, favorite, stampman, tyrant, tool,
Or all those mighty names in one, thou fool!
Let mean ambition, sordid lust of pride,
League thee, vile pander! to a tyrant's side.   50
Sport with thy country's groans, and be the first
To stab the bosom which a traitor nursed;
Rifle the womb, and on those bowels prey,
To plague mankind, that spawn'd thee into day;
Be eminent, thy little soul exert,   55
And call forth all the rancor of thy heart:
But should the eye of merit on thee lower,
(Though lowly crush'd beneath the wheel of power,)
Thou art my pity, monster! I forgive,
And beg one only curse, that thou mayst live.   60

　　Where lies our remedy, in humble prayer?
Our lordly butchers have forgot to hear;
'Tis rank rebellion, rashness to complain,

And all submission tighter tugs the chain:
Go ask your heart, your honest heart regard,   65
And manumission is your sure reward;
Would'st thou be blest, thy sovereign pride lay by,
To tyrant custom give the hardy lie;
Yon shag will warm thee, in thy country fleece
Sleeps independence lined with balmy peace;   70
Wouldst thou be blest? be diligent! be wise!
And make a chaste sufficiency suffice:
Ye lovely fair! whom heaven's blest charms array,
The proud Sultanas of some future day;
Sweet as ye are, complete in every grace,   75
That spreads angelic softness o'er the face;
Go ply the loom—there lies the happy art,
By new avenues to attack the heart;
With labors of your own, but deck those charms,
We'll rush with transport to your blissful arms.   80
Amid this wreck—from all aspersions clear,
Nay blush not, Peter, honest truths to hear;
Base adulation never stain'd my lay,
But modest merit must be brought to day;
What though thy great desert mounts far above   85
The mean expression of thy country's love;
In praise like thine the rustic muse will soar,
Then damn'd to endless silence sing no more.
"With great contempt of power, alone to stand,
Thy life, and spotless honors in thy hand;   90
To wage unequal wars—and dare the worst,
And if thy country perish, perish first;
With pious vigilance the state to guard,
And eminent in virtue, shun reward;
No force of avarice warps thy steady heart,   95
To meanness, falsehood, or dishonest art;
A tyrant's mandate, thy supreme disdain,
Our last, best bulwark in a Scottish reign."
These are the honors we to fame consign,
Nay blush not, Peter—these are surely thine.   100

    To close—dread sovereign at whose sacred seat,
Justice and mercy, spotless maidens meet;
George! parent! king! our guardian, glory, pride,
And thou, fair regent! blooming by his side!
Thy offspring pleads a parent's fostering care,   105
Reject not, frown not, but in mercy spare;
Besprent with dust, the lowly suppliant lies,

A helpless, guilty, injured sacrifice:
If e'er our infant efforts could delight,
Or growing worth found favor in thy sight,   110
If warm affection due returns may plead,
Or faith unshaken ever intercede;
With modest boldness we thy smiles demand,
Nor wish salvation from another hand;
Depress'd, not helpless, while a Brunswick reigns,   115
Whose righteous scepter, no injustice stains.

                                                    1765

Joseph Green
(1706-1780)

Graduated from Harvard in 1726, Joseph Green was a merchant and a member of the Boston social circle which included Mather Byles. *Entertainment for a Winter's Evening* (Boston, 1750), *A Mournful Lamentation for . . . Mr. Old Tenor* (1750?), and *The Grand Arcanum Detected* (Boston, 1755) are his most important works. A Loyalist, Green fled to England in 1775.

BIBLIOGRAPHY: Samuel Curwen, ed. *The Journal and Letters of Joseph Green* (Boston, 1864).

Lines on Byles's Voyage

In David's Psalms an oversight
    Byles found one morning at his tea,
Alas! that he should never write
    A proper psalm to sing at sea.

Thus ruminating on his seat,   5
    Ambitious thoughts at length prevail'd.
The bard determined to complete
    The part wherein the prophet fail'd.

He sat awhile and stroked his muse,[1]
    Then taking up his tuneful pen,   10
Wrote a few stanzas for the use
    Of his seafaring brethren.

[1] Byles's favorite cat, so named by his friends.

The task perform'd, the bard content,
    Well chosen was each flowing word;
On a short voyage himself he went,   15
    To hear it read and sung on board.

Most serious Christians do aver,
    (Their credit sure we may rely on,)
In former times that after prayer,
    They used to sing a song of Zion.   20

Our modern parson having pray'd,
    Unless loud fame our faith beguiles,
Sat down, took out his book and said,
    "Let's sing a psalm on Mather Byles."

At first, when he began to read,   25
    Their heads the assembly downward hung.
But he with boldness did proceed,
    And thus he read, and thus they sung.

THE PSALM

With vast amazement we survey
    The wonders of the deep,   30
Where mackerel swim, and porpoise play,
    And crabs and lobsters creep.

Fish of all kinds inhabit here,
    And throng the dark abode.
Here haddock, hake, and flounders are,   35
    And eels, and perch, and cod,

From raging winds and tempests free,
    So smoothly as we pass,
The shining surface seems to be
    A piece of Bristol glass.   40

But when the winds and tempests rise,
    And foaming billows swell,
The vessel mounts above the skies,
    And lower sinks than hell.

Our heads the tottering motion feel,   45
    And quickly we become
Giddy as new-dropp'd calves, and reel
    Like Indians drunk with rum.

What praises then are due that we
    Thus far have safely got,   50
Amarescoggin tribe to see,
    And tribe of Penobscot.

                                          1733

From *Entertainment for a Winter's Evening*

    The Masons by procession
Having already honor'd one,
(Thou, to perpetuate their glory,
Clio, didst then relate the story.)
To show the world they mean fair play,   5
And that each saint should have his day,
Now order store of belly-timber
'Gainst twenty-seventh of December.
For that's the day of Saint John's feast
Fix'd by the holy Roman priest.   10
They then in mood religious chose
Their brother of the roll and rose
The ceremony to commence:
He from the sacred eminence
Must first explain and then apply   15
The duties of Free Masonry. . . .

    The crowds attending gaze around,
And awful silence reigns profound.
Till from the seat which he'd sat arse on
Uprose and thus began the parson.   20

    "Right Worshipful, at whose command
Obedient I in Rostra stand;
It proper is and fit to show
Unto the crowds that gape below,
Who wonder much, and well they may,   25
What on the occasion I can say,
Why in the church are met together,
Especially in such cold weather,
Such folk as never did appear
So overfond of coming there.   30
Know then, my friends, without more pother,
That these are Masons, I'm a Brother.
'Masons' said I?—yes Masons Free;

Their deeds and title both agree.
While other sects fall out and fight   35
About a trifling mode or rite,
We firm by Love cemented stand,
'Tis Love unites us heart and hand.
Love to a party not confin'd,
A Love embracing all mankind,   40
Both catholic and protestant,
The Scots and eke New England saint. . . .

  "But hark, methinks I hear
One shrewdly whisp'ring in my ear;
'Pray, parson, don't affirm but prove;   45
Do they all meet and part in love?
Quarrels oft times don't they delight in,
And now and then a little fighting?
Did there not (for the Secret's out)
In the last Lodge arise a rout?   50
M—— with a first of brass
Laid T——s nose level with his face,
And scarcely had he let his hand go
When he receiv'd from T—— a d—d blow.
Now parson, when a nose is broken,   55
Pray, is it friendly sign or token?'

  " 'Tis true—but trifling is th' objection,
All general rules have an exception.
Oft from themselves the best men vary,
Humanum enim est errare.   60
But what I've said I'll say again,
And what I say I will maintain:
'Tis Love, pure Love cements the whole,
Love—of the Bottle and the Bowl.

  "But 'tis high time to let you go   65
Where you had rather be, I know:
And by proceeding I delay
The weightier business of the day;
For eating solid sense affords,
Whilst nonsense lurks in many words.   70
Doubting does oft arise from thinking,
But truth is only found in drinking."
This having said, the reverend vicar
Dismiss'd them to their food and liquor.

From church to Stone's they go to eat,   75
In order walking through the street,
But no Right Worshipful was there,
Pallas forbad him to appear,
For, well foreseeing that the job
Would from all parts collect the mob,   80
He wisely catch'd a cold and stay'd
At home, at least, if not in bed.
So when the Greeks 'gainst Trojans went,
Achilles tarry'd in his tent;
Asham'd he hides himself, nor draws   85
His conquering sword in harlot's cause.

                                        1750

Nathaniel Evans
(1742-1767)

Nathaniel Evans was ordained a minister in the English Church after completing his M.A. at the College of Philadelphia in 1765. He served at Haddonfield, N.J., as a missionary for the Society for the Propagation of the Gospel. Evans edited Thomas Godfrey's *Poems on Various Subjects* (Philadelphia, 1765); his own verse was collected and published by William Smith in *Poems on Several Occasions* (Philadelphia, 1772).

BIBLIOGRAPHY: E. L. Pennington, *Nathaniel Evans; A Poet of Colonial America* (Ocala, Fla., 1935). B. A. Milligan, "An Early American Imitator of Milton," *Amer. Lit.*, XI (1939), 200–206.

Ode to My Ingenious Friend

While you, dear Tom, are forced to roam,
In search of fortune, far from home,
    O'er bogs, o'er seas and mountains;
I too, debarr'd the soft retreat
Of shady groves, and murmur sweet   5
    Of silver prattling fountains,

Must mingle with the bustling throng,
And bear my load of cares along,
    Like any other sinner:
For, where's the ecstasy in this,   10

To loiter in poetic bliss,
    And go without a dinner?

Flaccus, we know, immortal bard!
With mighty kings and statesmen fared,
    And lived in cheerful plenty: 15
But now, in these degenerate days,
The slight reward of empty praise,
    Scarce one receives in twenty.

Well might the Roman swan, along
The pleasing Tiber pour his song,   20
    When bless'd with ease and quiet;
Oft did he grace Mæcenas' board,
Who would for him throw by the lord,
    And in Falernian riot.

But, dearest Tom! these days are past,   25
And we are in a climate cast
    Where few the muse can relish;
Where all the doctrine now that's told,
Is that a shining heap of gold
    Alone can man embellish.   30

Then since 'tis thus, my honest friend,
If you be wise, my strain attend,
    And counsel sage adhere to;
With me, henceforward, join the crowd,
And like the rest proclaim aloud,   35
    That money is all virtue!

Then may we both, in time, retreat
To some fair villa, sweetly neat,
    To entertain the muses;
And then life's noise and trouble leave—   40
Supremely blest, we'll never grieve
    At what the world refuses.

                              c. 1762, 1772

Hymn to May

Now had the beam of Titan gay
Usher'd in the blissful May,
Scattering from his pearly bed,

Fresh dew on every mountain's head;
Nature mild and debonair,   5
To thee, fair maid, yields up her care.
May, with gentle plastic hand,
Clothes in flowery robe the land;
O'er the vales the cowslips spreads,
And eglantine beneath the shades;   10
Violets blue befringe each fountain,
Woodbines lace each steepy mountain;
Hyacinths their sweets diffuse,
And the rose its blush renews;
With the rest of Flora's train,   15
Decking lowly dale or plain.

   Through creation's range, sweet May!
Nature's children own thy sway—
Whether in the crystal flood,
Amorous, sport the finny brood;   20
Or the feather'd tribes declare,
That they breathe thy genial air,
While they warble in each grove
Sweetest notes of artless love;
Or their wound the beasts proclaim,   25
Smitten with a fiercer flame;
Or the passions higher rise,
Sparing none beneath the skies,
But swaying soft the human mind
With feelings of ecstatic kind—   30
Through wide creation's range, sweet May!
All Nature's children own thy sway.

   Oft will I, (e'er Phosphor's light
Quits the glimmering skirts of night)
Meet thee in the clover field,   35
Where thy beauties thou shalt yield
To my fancy, quick and warm,
Listening to the dawn's alarm,
Sounded loud by Chanticleer,
In peals that sharply pierce the ear.   40
And, as Sol his flaming car
Urges up the vaulted air,
Shunning quick the scorching ray,
I will to some covert stray,
Coolly bowers or latent dells,   45
Where light-footed silence dwells,

And whispers to my heaven-born dream,
Fair Schuylkill, by thy winding stream!
There I'll devote full many an hour,
To the still-finger'd Morphean power,   50
And entertain my thirsty soul
With draughts from Fancy's fairy bowl;
Or mount her orb of varied hue,
And scenes of heaven and earth review.

Nor in milder Eve's decline,   55
As the sun forgets to shine,
And sloping down the ethereal plain,
Plunges in the western main,
Will I forbear due strain to pay
To the song-inspiring May;   60
But as Hesper 'gins to move
Round the radiant court of Jove,
(Leading through the azure sky
All the starry progeny,
Emitting prone their silver light,   65
To re-illume the shades of night)
Then, the dewy lawn along,
I'll carol forth my grateful song,
Viewing with transported eye
The blazing orbs that roll on high,   70
Beaming luster, bright and clear,
O'er the glowing hemisphere.
Thus from the early blushing morn,
Till the dappled eve's return,
Will I, in free unlabor'd lay,   75
Sweetly sing the charming May!

                                        c. 1762, 1772

Ode to the Memory of Mr. Thomas Godfrey

O Death! thou victor of the human frame!
The soul's poor fabric trembles at thy name!
How long shall man be urged to dread thy sway,
For those whom thou untimely tak'st away?
Life's blooming spring just opens to our eyes,   5
And strikes the senses with a sweet surprise,
When thy fierce arm uplifts the fatal blow
That hurls us breathless to the earth below.

Sudden, as darts the lightning through the sky,
Around the globe thy various weapons fly.   10
Here war's red engines heap the field with slain,
And pallid sickness there extends thy reign;
Here the soft virgin weeps her lover dead,
There maiden beauty sinks the graceful head;
Here infants grieve their parents are no more,   15
There reverend sires their children's deaths deplore;
Here the sad friend—O! save the sacred name,
Yields half his soul to thy relentless claim;
O pardon, pardon the descending tear!
Friendship commands, and not the muses, here.   20
O say, thou much loved dear departed shade,
To what celestial region hast thou stray'd?
Where is that vein of thought, that noble fire
Which fed thy soul, and bade the world admire?
That manly strife with fortune to be just,   25
That love of praise? an honorable thirst!
The Soul, alas! has fled to endless day,
And left its house a mouldering mass of clay.

There, where no fears invade, nor ills molest,
Thy soul shall dwell immortal with the blest;   30
In that bright realm, where dearest friends no more
Shall from each other's throbbing breasts be tore,
Where all those glorious spirits sit enshrined,
The just, the good, the virtuous of mankind.
There shall fair angels in a radiant ring,   35
And the great Son of heaven's eternal King,
Proclaim thee welcome to the blissful skies,
And wipe the tears forever from thine eyes.

How did we hope—alas! the hope how vain!
To hear thy future more enripen'd strain;   40
When fancy's fire with judgment had combined
To guide each effort of the enraptured mind.
Yet are those youthful glowing lays of thine
The emanations of a soul divine;
Who heard thee sing, but felt sweet music's dart   45
In thrilling transports pierce his captiv'd heart?
Whether soft melting airs attuned thy song,
Or pleased to pour the thundering verse along,
Still nobly great, true offspring of the Nine,
Alas! how blasted in thy glorious prime!   50
So when first ope the eyelids of the morn,

A radiant purple does the heavens adorn,
Fresh smiling glory streaks the skies around,
And gaily silvers each enamel'd mound,
Till some black storm o'erclouds the ether fair,   55
And all its beauties vanish into air.

    Stranger, whoe'er thou art, by fortune's hand
Toss'd on the baleful Carolinian strand,
Oh! if thou seest perchance the Poet's grave,
The sacred spot with tears of sorrow lave;   60
Oh! shade it, shade it with ne'er fading bays.
Hallow'd's the place where gentle Godfrey lays.
(So may no sudden dart from death's dread bow,
Far from the friends thou lov'st, e'er lay thee low,)
There may the weeping morn its tribute bring,   65
And angels shield it with their golden wing,
Till the last trump shall burst the womb of night,
And the purged atoms to their soul unite!

                 1763, 1765

Thomas Godfrey
(1736-1763)

Thomas Godfrey of Philadelphia moved to Wilmington, N.C., in 1758 to take a position as a factor. There he completed the poem *The Court of Fancy* (Philadelphia, 1762) and his blank verse drama, *The Prince of Parthia*, first staged in Philadelphia in 1767. Nathaniel Evans wrote a biographical sketch for and edited *Juvenile Poems on Various Subjects, With the Prince of Parthia, A Tragedy* (Philadelphia, 1765).

BIBLIOGRAPHY: A. F. Gegenheimer, *Thomas Godfrey: Protégé of William Smith* (Philadelphia, 1943). Edward A. Oldham, "Thomas Godfrey," *North Carolina Poetry Rev.*, III (1936).

From *The Court of Fancy*

'Twas sultry noon, impatient of the heat
I sought the covert of a close retreat;
Soft by a bubbling fountain was I laid,
And o'er my head the spreading branches play'd;
When gentle slumber stole upon my eyes,   5
And busy Fiction bid this vision rise.

Methought I pensive, unattended, stood,
Wrapp'd in the horrors of a desert wood;
Old Night and Silence spread their sway around,
And not a breeze disturb'd the dread profound.   10
To break the wild, and gain the neighboring plain
Oft I essay'd, and oft essay'd in vain;
Still in intricate mazes round I run;
And ever ended where I first begun.
While thus I laboring strove t' explore my way,   15
Bright on my sense broke unexpected day:
Retiring Night in haste withdrew her shade,
And sudden morn shone through the opening glade.
No more the scene a desert wild appear'd,
A smiling grove its vernal honors rear'd;   20
While sweetness on the balmy breezes hung,
And all around a joyful Matin rung.
Soft was the strain of Zephyr in the grove,
Or purling streams that through the meadows rove.
Now wild in air the varying strain is toss'd,   25
In distant echoes then the sound is lost;
Again revived, and lo! the willing trees
Rise to the powerful numbers by degrees.
Trees now no more, robb'd of their verdant bloom,
They shine supporters of a spacious dome,   30
The wood to bright transparent crystal changed,
High fluted columns rise, in order ranged. . . .

Now swiftly forward false Delusion came,
Wrapt in a fulvid cloud appear'd the Dame.
Thin was her form, in airy garments drest,   35
And grotesque figures flamed upon her vest;
In her right hand she held a magic glass,
From whence around reflected glories pass.
Blind by the subtle rays, the giddy Crowd
Rush'd wildly from the Dome and shouted loud.   40
The few remain'd whom Fancy did inspire,
Yet undeceived by vain Delusion's fire.

A Troop of shining forms the next came on,
Foremost bright Nature's awful Goddess shone.
Fair Truth she led, in spotless white array'd,   45
And pleasing Beauty, sweet celestial maid;
Where Truth and Nature aid the great design,
Beauty attends, and makes it all divine.

Sweet Poesy was seen their steps behind,
With golden tresses sporting in the wind;   50
In careless plaits did her bright garments flow,
And nodding laurels waved around her brow;
Sweetly she struck the string, and sweetly sung,
Th' attentive tribe on the soft accents hung.
'Tis hers to sing who great in arms excel,   55
Who bravely conquer'd or who glorious fell;
Heroes in verse still gain a deathless name,
And ceaseless ages their renown proclaim.
Oft to Philosophy she lends her aid,
And treads the Sage's solitary shade;   60
Her great first task is nobly to inspire
The immortal Soul with Virtue's sacred fire.

Then Painting forward moved in garlands drest,
The Rainbow's varied tints adorn'd her vest.
Great Nature's rival!—quick to her command   65
Beauty attends, and aids her powerful hand.
At her creative touch gay fictions glow,
Bright tulips bloom, and opening roses blow.
The canvas see, what pleasing prospects rise!
What varying Beauty strikes our wondering eyes!   70
Chill winter's wastes, or spring's delightful green,
Hot summer's pride, or autumn's yellow scene;
Here lawns are spread, there towering forests wave,
The heights we fear, or wish the cooling lave!

Her blooming Sister in her hand she led,   75
Joy in her eye, fair Sculpture, heaven-taught maid.
'Tis hers to stone a mimic life to give;
Heroes and sages at her call revive;
See flowery orators with out-stretched hand
Addressed to speak, in glowing marble stand!   80

Sudden I heard soft sounds, a pleasing strain!
Music advanced with all her heavenly train.
Sweetly enraptured then my pulse beat high,
And my breast glow'd fraught with unusual joy.
'Tis harmony can every passion move,   85
Give sorrow ease, or melt the soul to love;
Exulting Pleasure to her call attends,
E'en stormy Rage to powerful Music bends.

With turrets crown'd bright Architecture shone.
The lovely maid with easy steps came on;   90
Graceful her mien, her looks celestial shined,
Where majesty and softening beauty join'd.
At her command see lofty piles ascend,
Columns aspire, triumphal arches bend.

Astronomy, with proud aspiring eye,   95
Gazed on the glowing beauties of the sky.
Her vest with glittering stars was spangled o'er,
And in her hand a telescope she bore.
With this she marked the rolling planet's way,
Or where portentous comets dreadful stray.   100

Though last, not least, Philosophy was seen:
Slow was her step, and awful was her mien.
A volume open in her hand she held;
With Nature's law the ample page was fill'd.
'Tis hers great Nature's wondrous depths t' explore,   105
Or to the Gods in heavenly rapture soar.

With these bright Fancy's sons their hours employ,
Pursue their lore, and taste each rising joy.
                                         1762

Joseph Brown Ladd
(1764-1786)

Born and educated in Newport, R.I., Joseph Brown Ladd was licensed to practice medicine in 1783. Soon afterwards, he moved to Charleston, S.C., where he attained prominence as a physician and where *The Poems of Arouet* was published in 1786. Ladd was killed in a duel.

BIBLIOGRAPHY: Mrs. Elizabeth Haskins, ed. *The Literary Remains of Joseph Brown Ladd* (New York, 1832). Lewis Leary, "The Writings of Joseph Brown Ladd, 1764-1786," *Bul. of Bibl.*, XVIII (1945), 131-133.

What Is Happiness?

'Tis an empty fleeting shade,
By imagination made:
'Tis a bubble, straw, or worse;

'Tis a baby's hobby-horse:
'Tis a little living, clear;   5
'Tis ten thousand pounds a year:
'Tis a title, 'tis a name:
'Tis a puff of empty fame;
Fickle as the breezes blow:
'Tis a lady's YES or NO!   10
And when the description's crown'd,
'Tis just no where to be found.

                                                1786

Jonathan Odell

(1737-1818)

Following medical training at the College of New Jersey in 1759, Jonathan Odell served as a surgeon in the British Army in the West Indies and later in London, where he was ordained a minister in the English Church in 1767. A Loyalist during the Revolution, Odell wrote satirical verse lampooning the American cause. *The American Times; A Satire* was published in London in 1780.

BIBLIOGRAPHY: *DAB*. M. C. Tyler, *The Literary History of the American Revolution*, II (New York, 1897, 1957). Winthrop Sargent, ed. *The Loyalist Verse of the American Revolution* (Philadelphia, 1857). Winthrop Sargent, ed. *The Loyal Verse of Joseph Stansbury and Doctor Jonathan Odell* (Albany, N.Y., 1860).

Inscription

FOR A CURIOUS CHAMBER-STOVE . . .
INVENTED BY DR. FRANKLIN

Like a Newton sublimely he soar'd
    To a Summit before unattained;
New regions of Science explor'd,
    And the Palm of Philosophy gain'd.

With a Spark, that he caught from the Skies,   5
    He display'd an unparallel'd wonder:
And we saw, with delight and surprise,
    That his Rod could protect us from thunder.

O had he been wise to pursue
    The track for his talents design'd,   10

What a tribute of praise had been due
    To the teacher and friend of Mankind!

But to covet political fame
    Was, in him, a degrading ambition;
A Spark, that from Lucifer came,   15
    And kindled the blaze of Sedition.

Let Candor, then, write on his Urn—
    Here lies the renowned Inventor,
Whose flame to the Skies ought to burn,
    But, inverted, descends to the Center!   20

                                    1776

From *The American Times*

Bless me! what formidable figure's this
That interrupts my words with saucy hiss?
She seems at least a woman by her face,
With harlot smiles adorned and winning grace.
A glittering gorget on her breast she wears;   5
The shining silver two inscriptions bears:
"Servant of Servants," in a laurel wreath,
But "Lord of Lords," is written underneath.
A flowing robe, that reaches to her heels,
From sight the foulness of her shape conceals,   10
She holds with poisoned darts a quiver stored,
Circean potions, and a flaming sword.
This is Democracy—the case is plain;
She comes attended by a motley train:
Addresses to the people some unfold;   15
Rods, scourges, fetters, axes, others hold;
The sorceress waves her magic wand about,
And models at her will the rabble rout;
Here Violence puts on a close disguise
And Public Spirit's character belies.   20
The dress of Policy see Cunning steal,
And Persecution wear the coat of Zeal;
Hypocrisy Religion's garb assume,
Fraud Virtue strip, and figure in her room;
With other changes tedious to relate,   25
All emblematic of our present state.
She calls the nations—Lo! in crowds they sup
Intoxication from her golden cup.

Joy to my heart, and pleasure to my eye,
A chosen phalanx her attempts defy: 30
In rage she rises and her arrows throws;
O all ye saints and angels interpose!

                                        1780

Joseph Stansbury
(1742-1809)

In 1767, Joseph Stansbury moved from London to Philadelphia, where he opened a china shop. Imprisoned in 1776 and later exiled from the city for his part in Benedict Arnold's treason, Stansbury returned to Philadelphia after the war, but was asked to leave again in 1783. He returned again in 1786, but moved his family to New York in 1793. His verse, much of which he burned after the war, appeared in Tory papers or remained in manuscript.

BIBLIOGRAPHY: *DAB*. See items for Jonathan Odell.

Verses to the Tories

Come, ye brave, by Fortune wounded
More than by the vaunting Foe,
Cheer your hearts, ne'er be confounded;
Trials all must undergo.
Though without or Rhyme or Reason   5
Hurried back through Wilds unknown,
Virtue's smiles can make a Prison
Far more charming than a Throne.
Think not, though wretched, poor or naked,
Your breast alone the Load sustains: 10
Sympathizing Hearts partake it—
Britain's Monarch shares your Pains.
This Night of Pride and Folly over,
A dawn of Hope will soon appear.
In its light you shall discover   15
Your triumphant day is near.

                        c. 1774

The United States

Now this War at length is o'er;
Let us think of it no more.
Every Party Lie or Name,
Cancel as our mutual Shame.
Bid each wound of Faction close, 5
Blushing we were ever Foes.

Now restor'd to Peace again,
Active Commerce ploughs the Main;
All the arts of Civil Life
Swift succeed the Martial Strife; 10
Britain now allows their claim,
Rising Empire, Wealth, and Fame.

c. 1784

To Cordelia

Believe me, Love, this vagrant life
    O'er Nova Scotia's wilds to roam,
While far from children, friends, or wife,
    Or place that I can call a home
Delights not me;—another way 5
My treasures, pleasures, wishes lay.

In piercing, wet, and wintry skies,
    Where man would seem in vain to toil
I see, where'er I turn my eyes,
    Luxuriant pasture, trees and soil 10
Uncharmed I see:—another way
My fondest hopes and wishes lay.

Oh could I through the future see
    Enough to form a settled plan,
To feed my infant train and thee 15
    And fill the rank and style of man:
I'd cheerful be the livelong day;
Since all my wishes point that way.

But when I see a sordid shed
    Of birchen bark, procured with care, 20

Design'd to shield my aged head
  Which British mercy placed there—
'Tis too, too much: I cannot stay,
But turn with streaming eyes away.

Oh! how your heart would bleed to view   25
  Six pretty prattlers like your own,
Expos'd to every wind that blew;
  Condemn'd in such a hut to moan.
Could this be borne, Cordelia, say?
Contented in your cottage stay.   30

'Tis true, that in this climate rude,
  The mind resolv'd may happy be;
And may, with toil and solitude,
  Live independent and be free.
So the lone hermit yields to slow decay: 35
Unfriended lives—unheeded glides away.

If so far humbled that no pride remains,
  But moot indifference which way flows the stream;
Resign'd to penury, its cares and pains;
  And hope has left you like a painted dream;   40
Then here, Cordelia, bend your pensive way,
And close the evening of Life's wretched day.

                              c. 1783, 1805

Francis Hopkinson
(1737-1791)

Francis Hopkinson, a 1757 graduate of the College of Philadelphia, was a musician, composer, poet, lawyer, teacher, and essayist. "The Battle of the Kegs" first appeared in the *Pennsylvania Packett*, March 4, 1778; other verse includes *A Dialogue and Ode . . . to . . . George II* (Philadelphia, 1761), *Science; A Poem* (Philadelphia, 1762), *A Tory Medley* (Philadelphia, 1777), and *The Miscellaneous Essays and Occasional Writings of Francis Hopkinson*, 3 Vols. (Philadelphia, 1792).

Volume III of this collection contains Hopkinson's verse.

BIBLIOGRAPHY: O. G. T. Sonneck, *Francis Hopkinson, the First American Poet-Composer* (Washington, D.C., 1905). G. E. Hastings, *The Life and Works of Francis Hopkinson* (Chicago, 1926). Philip Marsh, "The Freneau-Hopkinson Quarrel," *Proc. of the N. J. Hist. Soc.*, LXXIV (1956), 304-314.

The Battle of the Kegs[1]

Gallants attend, and hear a friend,
    Trill forth harmonious ditty,
Strange things I'll tell which late befell
    In Philadelphia city.

'Twas early day, as poets say,   5
    Just when the sun was rising,
A soldier stood on a log of wood,
    And saw a thing surprising.

As in amaze he stood to gaze,
    The truth can't be denied, sir,   10
He spied a score of kegs or more
    Come floating down the tide, sir.

A sailor too, in jerkin blue,
    This strange appearance viewing,
First damn'd his eyes, in great surprise,   15
    Then said, "Some mischief's brewing.

"These kegs, I'm told, the rebels bold,
    Pack'd up like pickled herring;
And they're come down t' attack the town,
    In this new way of ferrying."   20

The soldier flew, the sailor too,
    And scared almost to death, sir,
Wore out their shoes, to spread the news,
    And ran till out of breath, sir.

Now up and down, throughout the town,   25
    Most frantic scenes were acted;
And some ran here, and others there,
    Like men almost distracted.

Some fire cried, which some denied,
    But said the earth had quaked;   30
And girls and boys, with hideous noise,
    Ran through the streets half naked.

[1] This ballad was occasioned by a real incident. Certain machines, in the form of kegs, charged with gunpowder, were sent down the river to annoy the British shipping then at Philadelphia. The danger of these machines being discovered, the British manned the wharves and shipping, and discharged their small arms and cannons at everything they saw floating in the river, during the ebb tide. [Hopkinson's Note.]

Sir William he, snug as a flea,
   Lay all this time a snoring,
Nor dream'd of harm, as he lay warm,
   In bed with Mrs. L——g.   35

Now in a fright he starts upright,
   Awaked by such a clatter;
He rubs both eyes, and boldly cries,
   "For God's sake, what's the matter?"   40

At his bedside he then espied
   Sir Erskine at command, sir,
Upon one foot he had one boot,
   And the other in his hand, sir.

"Arise, arise," Sir Erskine cries,   45
   "The rebels—more's the pity,
Without a boat are all afloat,
   And ranged before the city.

"The motley crew, in vessels new,
   With Satan for their guide, sir.   50
Pack'd up in bags, or wooden kegs,
   Come driving down the tide, sir.

"Therefore prepare for bloody war,
   These kegs must all be routed,
Or surely we despised shall be,   55
   And British courage doubted."

The royal band now ready stand,
   All ranged in dread array, sir,
With stomach stout to see it out,
   And make a bloody day, sir.   60

The cannons roar from shore to shore,
   The small arms make a rattle;
Since wars began I'm sure no man
   E'er saw so strange a battle.

The rebel dales, the rebel vales,   65
   With rebel trees surrounded;
The distant wood, the hills and floods,
   With rebel echoes sounded.

The fish below swam to and fro,
    Attack'd from every quarter;
Why sure, thought they, the devil's to pay,   70
    'Mongst folks above the water.

The kegs, 'tis said, though strongly made,
    Of rebel staves and hoops, sir,
Could not oppose their powerful foes,   75
    The conquering British troops, sir.

From morn to night these men of might
    Display'd amazing courage;
And when the sun was fairly down,
    Retired to sup their porridge.   80

An hundred men with each a pen,
    Or more, upon my word, sir.
It is most true, would be too few,
    Their valor, to record, sir.

Such feats did they perform that day,   85
    Against these wicked kegs, sir,
That years to come, if they get home,
    They'll make their boasts and brags, sir.

1778

Royall Tyler
(1757-1826)

Graduated from Harvard in 1776, Royall Tyler practiced law and wrote essays and verse for periodicals, notably Joseph Dennie's *Portfolio*. He and Dennie formed the literary partnership of "Colon and Spondee," with Tyler using the latter name. Tyler's *The Contrast*, the first American comedy, played successfully in New York in 1787; he also wrote a novel, *The Algerine Captive*, published in 1797. Tyler's later years were occupied primarily with law.

BIBLIOGRAPHY: Helen T. Brown and Frederick Tupper, eds. *Grandmother Tyler's Book* (New York, 1925). Tupper, "Royall Tyler: Man of Law and Man of Letters," *Vt. Hist. Soc. Proc.* (1926-1928), 65-101.

My Mistresses

Let Cowley soft in amorous verse
The rovings of his love rehearse,
    With passion most unruly,
Boast how he woo'd sweet Amoret,
The sobbing Jane, and sprightly Bet,   5
The lily fair and smart brunette,
    In sweet succession truly.

But list, ye lovers, and you'll swear,
I roved with him beyond compare,
    And was far more unlucky.   10
For never yet in Yankee coast
Were found such girls, who so could boast,
An honest lover's heart to roast,
    From Casco to Kentucky.

When first the girls nicknamed me beau,   15
And I was all for dress and show,
    I set me out a courting.
A romping miss, with heedless art,
First caught, then almost broke, my heart.
Miss Conduct named; we soon did part,   20
    I did not like such sporting.

The next coquette, who raised a flame,
Was far more grave, and somewhat lame,
    She in my heart did rankle.
She conquer'd, with a sudden glance: 25
The spiteful slut was call'd Miss Chance;
I took the gypsy out to dance;
    She almost broke my ankle.

A thoughtless girl, just in her teens,
Was the next fair, whom love it seems   30
    Had made me prize most highly.
I thought to court a lovely mate,
But, how it made my heart to ache;
It was that jade, the vile Miss Take;
    In troth, love did it slyly.   35

And last Miss Fortune, whimpering came,
Cured me of love's tormenting flame,
  And all my beau pretences.
In widow's weeds, the prude appears;
See now—she drowns me with her tears,   40
With bony fist, now slaps my ears,
  And brings me to my senses.

       col. 1801

Choice of a Wife

 Fluttering lovers, giddy boys,
Sighing soft for Hymen's joys,
Would you shun the tricking arts,
Beauty's traps for youthful hearts,
Would you treasure in a wife,   5
Riches, which shall last through life;
Would you in your choice be nice,
Hear Minerva's sage advice.
 Be not caught with shape, nor air,
Coral lips, nor flowing hair;   10
Shape and jaunty air may cheat,
Coral lips may speak deceit.
Girls unmask'd would you descry,
Fix your fancy on the eye;
Nature there has truth design'd,   15
'Tis the eye, that speaks the mind.
Shun the proud, disdainful eye,
Frowning fancied dignity,
Shun the eye with vacant glare;
Cold indifference winters there.   20
Shun the eager orb of fire,
Gloating with impure desire;
Shun the wily eye of prude,
Looking coy to be pursued.
From the jilting eye refrain,   25
Glancing love, and now disdain.
Fly the fierce, satiric eye,
Shooting keen severity;
For nature thus, her truth design'd
And made the eye proclaim the mind.   30

       col. 1801

The Bookworm

Who is that meager, studious wight,
 Who sports the habit of our days,
And, in the reigning mode's despite
 His antique coat and vest displays?

In whose gaunt form, from head to feet,   5
 The antiquarian's air we trace,
While Hebrew roots and ancient Greek
 Plot out the features of his face.

His critic eye is fixed with glee
 On a worm-eaten, smoke-dried page;   10
The time-worn paper seems to be
 The relic of some long-past age.

In sooth, it is the manuscript
 Of this poor, feeble verse of mine;
Which, in despite of taste and wit,   15
 Has straggled down to future time.

The bookworm's features scrawl a smile
 While gloating on the musty page;
As we admire some ruined pile
 Not for its worth, but for its age.   20

The sprawling letters, yellow text,
 The formal phrase, the bald, stiff style,
The spelling quaint, the line perplexed,
 Provoke his unaccustomed smile.

Like Kennicut he cites and quotes,   25
 On illustration clear intent,
And in the margin gravely notes
 A thousand meanings never meant.

                    1891

Phillis Wheatley
(c. 1753-1784)

At the age of seven or eight, African-born Phillis Wheatley was purchased as a slave by John Wheatley, a Boston tailor. Adept at language, she was writing occasional verse at the age of thirteen, and published *An Elegaic Poem on the Death of . . . George Whitefield* in Boston in 1770. *Poems on Various Subjects, Religious and Moral* appeared in London in 1773, and went through numerous editions.

BIBLIOGRAPHY: C. F. Heartman, *Poems and Letters* (New York, 1915). Julian Mason, ed. *The Poems of Phillis Wheatley* (Chapel Hill, N.C., 1966).

An Hymn to the Morning

Attend my lays, ye ever honour'd nine,
Assist my labours, and my strains refine;
In smoothest numbers pour the notes along,
For bright Aurora now demands my song.

Aurora hail, and all the thousand dyes,   5
Which deck thy progress through the vaulted skies:
The morn awakes, and wide extends her rays,
On ev'ry leaf the gentle zephyr plays;
Harmonious lays the feather'd race resume,
Dart the bright eye, and shake the painted plume.   10

Ye shady groves, your verdant gloom display
To shield your poet from the burning day:
Calliope awake the sacred lyre,
While thy fair sisters fan the pleasing fire:
The bow'rs, the gales, the variegated skies   15
In all their pleasures in my bosom rise.

See in the east th' illustrious king of day!
His rising radiance drives the shades away—
But Oh! I feel his fervid beams too strong,
And scarce begun, concludes th' abortive song.   20

1773

An Hymn to the Evening

Soon as the sun forsook the eastern main
The pealing thunder shook the heav'nly plain;
Majestic grandeur! From the zephyr's wing,
Exhales the incense of the blooming spring.
Soft purl the streams, the birds renew their notes,   5
And through the air their mingled music floats.

Through all the heav'ns what beauteous dyes are spread!
But the west glories in the deepest red:
So may our breasts with ev'ry virtue glow,
The living temples of our God below!   10

Fill'd with the praise of him who gives the light;
And draws the sable curtains of the night,
Let placid slumbers soothe each weary mind,
At morn to wake more heav'nly, more refin'd;
So shall the labours of the day begin   15
More pure, more guarded from the snares of sin.

Night's leaden sceptre seals my drowsy eyes,
Then cease, my song, till fair Aurora rise.

1773

Liberty and Peace

Lo, Freedom comes. Th' prescient Muse foretold,
All Eyes th' accomplish'd Prophecy behold;
Her Port describ'd, "She moves divinely fair,
Olive and Laurel bind her golden Hair."
She, the bright Progeny of Heaven, descends,   5
And every Grace her sovereign Step attends;
For now kind Heaven, indulgent to our Prayer,
In smiling Peace resolves the Din of War.
Fix'd in Columbia her illustrious Line,
And bids in thee her future Councils shine.   10
To every Realm her Portals open'd wide,
Receives from each the full commercial Tide.
Each Art and Science now with rising Charms,
Th' expanding Heart with Emulation warms.
E'en great Britannia sees with dread Surprise,   15
And from the dazzling Splendors turns her Eyes!
Britain, whose Navies swept th' Atlantic o'er,

And Thunder sent to every distant Shore:
E'en thou, in Manners cruel as thou art,
The Sword resign'd, resume the friendly Part!   20
For Galia's Power espous'd Columbia's Cause,
And new-born Rome shall give Britannia Laws,
Nor unremember'd in the grateful Strain,
Shall princely Louis' friendly Deeds remain;
The generous Prince th' impending Vengeance eyes,   25
Sees the fierce Wrong, and to the rescue flies.
Perish that Thirst of boundless Power, that drew
On Albion's Head the Curse to Tyrants due.
But thou appeas'd submit to Heaven's decree,
That bids this Realm of Freedom rival thee!   30
Now sheathe the Sword that bade the Brave atone
With guiltless Blood for Madness not their own.
Sent from th' Enjoyment of their native Shore
Ill-fated—never to behold her more!
From every Kingdom on Europa's Coast   35
Throng'd various Troops, their Glory, Strength and Boast.
With heart-felt pity fair Hibernia saw
Columbia menac'd by the Tyrant's Law:
On hostile Fields fraternal Arms engage,
And mutual Deaths, all dealt with mutual Rage;   40
The Muse's Ear hears mother Earth deplore
Her ample Surface smoke with kindred Gore:
The hostile Field destroys the social Ties,
And everlasting Slumber seals their Eyes.
Columbia mourns, the haughty Foes deride,   45
Her Treasures plunder'd, and her Towns destroy'd:
Witness how Charlestown's curling Smokes arise,
In sable columns to the clouded Skies!
The ample Dome, high-wrought with curious Toil,
In one sad Hour the savage Troops despoil.   50
Descending Peace the Power of War confounds;
From every Tongue celestial Peace resounds:
As from the East th' illustrious King of Day,
With rising Radiance drives the Shades away,
So Freedom comes array'd with Charms divine,   55
And in her Train Commerce and Plenty shine.
Britannia owns her Independent Reign,
Hibernia, Scotia, and the Realms of Spain;
And great Germania's ample Coast admires
The generous Spirit that Columbia fires.   60
Auspicious Heaven shall fill with fav'ring Gales,
Where e'er Columbia speads her swelling Sails:

To every Realm shall Peace her Charms display,
And Heavenly Freedom spread her golden Ray.

1784

THE CONNECTICUT WITS

The Connecticut or Hartford Wits dominated American poetry in the last two decades of the eighteenth century. Joel Barlow, Timothy Dwight, John Trumbull, and David Humphreys were the most important writers of this group; Theodore Dwight (1764–1846), Lemuel Hopkins (1750–1801), and Richard Alsop were peripheral figures. The common bonds of the group were considerable: all were New Englanders, were associated with Yale, were strongly influenced by Calvinistic doctrines, espoused Federalist political sympathies, and wrote poetry chiefly imitative of the English Augustans. Barlow, Humphreys, Trumbull, and Hopkins collaborated on a long poem entitled *The Anarchiad,* which appeared in the *New Haven Gazette* and the *Connecticut Magazine* in 1786–1787. Alsop and Theodore Dwight were largely responsible for *The Echo,* and they, with Hopkins, wrote *The Political Greenhouse for the Year of 1798* (Hartford, Conn., 1799).

BIBLIOGRAPHY: H. A. Beers, *The Connecticut Wits and Other Essays* (New Haven, 1920), pp. 7–29. V. L. Parrington, *The Connecticut Wits* (New York, 1926). Leon Howard, *The Connecticut Wits* (Chicago, 1943).

Joel Barlow
(1754-1812)

Poet, lawyer, and diplomat, Joel Barlow received his B.A. at Yale in 1778, was admitted to law practice in 1786, and after 1788, resided for seventeen years in Europe. As James Madison's Minister to France, Barlow met for trade discussions with Napoleon in Poland; he died and was buried at Welna. Most famous for *The Hasty Pudding* (New Haven, 1796—written in 1793), Barlow also wrote *A Vision of Columbus; A Poem in Nine Books* (Hartford, 1787), which he later expanded from 5000 lines to 7350 lines as *The Columbiad* (Philadelphia, 1807, 1809; London, 1809). Other verse includes *The Prospect of Peace* (New Haven, 1788) and *The Conspiracy of Kings* (London, 1792).

BIBLIOGRAPHY: T. A. Zunder, *The Early Days of Joel Barlow, a Connecticut Wit* (New Haven, 1934). M. C. Tyler, *Three Men of Letters* (New York, 1895). Charles B. Todd, *Life and Letters of Joel Barlow* (New York, 1886). James Woodress, *A Yankee's Odyssey: The Life of Joel Barlow* (Philadelphia, 1958).

The Hasty Pudding

[The Hasty Pudding. A Poem in Three Cantos. Written at Chambery in Savoy, January, 1793.—New Haven, 1796.]

Omne tulit punctum qui miscuit utile dulci.
He makes a good breakfast who mixes pudding with molasses.

To Mrs. Washington

Madam:—A simplicity in diet, whether it be considered with reference to the happiness of individuals or the prosperity of a nation, is of more consequence than we are apt to imagine. In recommending so great and necessary a virtue to the rational part of mankind, I wish it were in my power to do it in such a manner as would be likely to gain their attention. I am sensible that it is one of those subjects in which example has infinitely more power than the most convincing arguments, or the highest charms of poetry. Goldsmith's *Deserted Village,* though possessing these two advantages in a greater degree than any other work of the kind, has not prevented villages in England from being deserted. The apparent interest of the rich individuals, who form the taste as well as the laws in that country, has been against him; and with that interest it has been vain to contend.

The vicious habits which in this little piece I endeavor to combat, seem to me not so difficult to cure. No class of people has any interest in supporting them, unless it be the interest which certain families may feel in vying with each other in sumptuous entertainments. There may indeed be some instances of depraved appetites which no arguments will conquer; but these must be rare. There are very few persons but would always prefer a plain dish for themselves, and would prefer it likewise for their guests, if there were no risk of reputation in the case. This difficulty can only be removed by example; and the example should proceed from those whose situation enables them to take the lead in forming the manners of a nation. Persons of this description in America, I should hope, are neither above nor below the influence of truth and reason when conveyed in language suited to the subject.

Whether the manner I have chosen to address my arguments to them be such as to promise any success, is what I cannot decide. But I certainly had hopes of doing some good, or I should not have taken the pains of putting so many rhymes together; and much less should I have ventured to place your name at the head of these observations.

Your situation commands the respect and your character the affections of a numerous people. These circumstances impose a duty upon you, which I believe you discharge to your own satisfaction and that of others. The example of your domestic virtues has doubtless a great effect among your countrywomen. I only wish to rank simplicitly of diet among the virtues. In that case it will certainly be cherished by you, and I should hope more esteemed by others than it is at present.

THE AUTHOR

CANTO I

Ye Alps audacious, through the heavens that rise,
To cramp the day and hide me from the skies;
Ye Gallic flags, that o'er their heights unfurled,
Bear death to kings, and freedom to the world,
I sing not you. A softer theme I choose,   5
A virgin theme, unconscious of the Muse,
But fruitful, rich, well suited to inspire
The purest frenzy of poetic fire.
   Despise it not, ye bards to terror steel'd,
Who hurl your thunders round the epic field;   10
Nor ye who strain your midnight throats to sing
Joys that the vineyard and the still-house bring;
Or on some distant fair your notes employ,
And speak of raptures that you ne'er enjoy.
I sing the sweets I know, the charms I feel,   15
My morning incense, and my evening meal,
The sweets of Hasty Pudding. Come, dear bowl,
Glide o'er my palate, and inspire my soul.
The milk beside thee, smoking from the kine,
Its substance mingle, married in with thine,   20
Shall cool and temper thy superior heat,
And save the pains of blowing while I eat.
  Oh! could the smooth, the emblematic song
 Flow like thy genial juices o'er my tongue,
Could those mild morsels in my numbers chime,   25
And, as they roll in substance, roll in rhyme,
No more thy awkward unpoetic name
Should shun the muse, or prejudice thy fame;
But rising grateful to the accustom'd ear,
All bards should catch it, and all realms revere!   30
   Assist me first with pious toil to trace
Through wrecks of time, thy lineage and thy race;
Declare what lovely squaw, in days of yore,
(Ere great Columbus sought thy native shore)
First gave thee to the world; her works of fame   35
Have lived indeed, but lived without a name.
Some tawny Ceres, goddess of her days,
First learn'd with stones to crack the well dried maize,
Through the rough sieve to shake the golden shower,

In boiling water stir the yellow flour: 40
The yellow flour, bestrew'd and stirr'd with haste,
Swells in the flood and thickens to a paste,
Then puffs and wallops, rises to the brim,
Drinks the dry knobs that on the surface swim;
The knobs at last the busy ladle breaks,   45
And the whole mass its true consistence takes.
    Could but her sacred name, unknown so long,
Rise, like her labors, to the son of song,
To her, to them, I'd consecrate my lays,
And blow her pudding with the breath of praise.   50
If 'twas Oella whom I sang before
I here ascribe her one great virtue more.
Not through the rich Peruvian realms alone
The fame of Sol's sweet daughter should be known,
But o'er the world's wide clime should live secure,   55
Far as his rays extend, as long as they endure.
    Dear Hasty Pudding, what unpromised joy
Expands my heart, to meet thee in Savoy!
Doom'd o'er the world through devious paths to roam,
Each clime my country, and each house my home,   60
My soul is soothed, my cares have found an end,
I greet my long lost, unforgotten friend.
    For thee through Paris, that corrupted town,
How long in vain I wandered up and down,
Where shameless Bacchus, with his drenching hoard,   65
Cold from his cave usurps the morning board.
London is lost in smoke and steep'd in tea;
No Yankee there can lisp the name of thee;
The uncouth word, a libel on the town,
Would call a proclamation from the crown.   70
From climes oblique, that fear the sun's full rays,
Chill'd in their fogs, exclude the generous maize:
A grain, whose rich, luxuriant growth requires
Short gentle showers, and bright ethereal fires.
    But here, though distant from our native shore,   75
With mutual glee, we meet and laugh once more,
The same! I know thee by that yellow face,
That strong complexion of true Indian race,
Which time can never change, nor soil impair,
Nor Alpine snows, nor Turkey's morbid air;   80
For endless years, through every mild domain,
Where grows the maize, there thou art sure to reign.
    But man, more fickle, the bold license claims,

In different realms to give thee different names.
Thee the soft nations round the warm Levant   85
Polenta call, the French of course *Polente*.
E'en in thy native regions, how I blush
To hear the Pennsylvanians call thee *Mush!*
On Hudson's banks, while men of Belgic spawn
Insult and eat thee by the name *Suppawn*.   90
All spurious appellations, void of truth;
I've better known thee from my earliest youth,
Thy name is *Hasty Pudding!* thus my sire
Was wont to greet thee fuming from his fire;
And while he argued in thy just defense   95
With logic clear, he thus explain'd the sense:—
"In *haste* the boiling cauldron o'er the blaze,
Receives and cooks the ready powder'd maize;
In *haste* 'tis served, and then in equal *haste*,
With cooling milk, we make the sweet repast.   100
No carving to be done, no knife to grate
The tender ear, and wound the stony plate;
But the smooth spoon, just fitted to the lip,
And taught with art the yielding mass to dip,
By frequent journeys to the bowl well stored,   105
Performs the *hasty* honors of the board."
Such is thy name, significant and clear,
A name, a sound to every Yankee dear,
But most to me, whose heart and palate chaste
Preserve my pure hereditary taste.   110
     There are who strive to stamp with disrepute
The luscious food, because it feeds the brute;
In tropes of high-strain'd wit, while gaudy prigs
Compare thy nursling, man, to pamper'd pigs;
With sovereign scorn I treat the vulgar jest,   115
Nor fear to share thy bounties with the beast.
What though the generous cow gives me to quaff
The milk nutritious: am I then a calf?
Or can the genius of the noisy swine,
Though nursed on pudding, claim a kin to mine?   120
Sure the sweet song, I fashion to thy praise,
Runs more melodious than the notes they raise.
     My song resounding in its grateful glee,
No merit claims: I praise myself in thee.
My father loved thee through his length of days!   125
For thee his fields were shaded o'er with maize;
From thee what health, what vigor he possess'd,

Ten sturdy freemen from his loins attest;
Thy constellation ruled my natal morn,
And all my bones were made of Indian corn. 130
Delicious grain! whatever form it take,
To roast or boil, to smother or to bake,
In every dish 'tis welcome still to me,
But most, my Hasty Pudding, most in thee.
  Let the green succotash with thee contend, 135
Let beans and corn their sweetest juices blend,
Let butter drench them in its yellow tide,
And a long slice of bacon grace their side;
Not all the plate, how famed soe'er it be,
Can please my palate like a bowl of thee. 140
Some talk of Hoe-Cake, fair Virginia's pride,
Rich Johnny-Cake, this mouth has often tried;
Both please me well, their virtues much the same,
Alike their fabric, as allied their fame,
Except in dear New England, where the last 145
Receives a dash of pumpkin in the paste,
To give it sweetness and improve the taste.
But place them all before me, smoking hot,
The big, round dumpling, rolling from the pot,
The pudding of the bag, whose quivering breast, 150
With suet lined, leads on the Yankee feast,
The Charlotte brown, within whose crusty sides
A belly soft the pulpy apple hides;
The yellow bread whose face like amber glows,
And all of Indian that the bake-pan knows,— 155
You tempt me not—my fav'rite greets my eyes,
To that loved bowl my spoon by instinct flies.

CANTO II

  To mix the food by vicious rules of art,
To kill the stomach, and to sink the heart
To make mankind to social virtue sour, 160
Cram o'er each dish, and be what they devour;
For this the kitchen muse first fram'd her book,
Commanding sweats to stream from every cook;
Children no more their antic gambols tried,
And friends to physic wonder'd why they died. 165
  Not so the Yankee—his abundant feast,
With simples furnish'd and with plainness drest,
A numerous offspring gathers round the board,
And cheers alike the servant and the lord;
Whose well-bought hunger prompts the joyous taste 170

And health attends them from the short repast.
   While the full pail rewards the milkmaid's toil,
The mother sees the morning caldron boil;
To stir the pudding next demands their care;
To spread the table and the bowls prepare;   175
To feed the household as their portions cool
And send them all to labor or to school.
   Yet may the simplest dish some rules impart,
For nature scorns not all the aids of art.
E'en Hasty Pudding, purest of all food,   180
May still be bad, indifferent, or good,
As sage experience the short process guides,
Or want of skill, or want of care presides.
Whoe'er would form it on the surest plan,
To rear the child and long sustain the man;   185
To shield the morals while it mends the size,
And all the powers of every food supplies,
Attend the lesson that the muse shall bring,
Suspend your spoons, and listen while I sing.
   But since, O man! thy life and health demand   190
Not food alone but labor from thy hand,
First in the field, beneath the sun's strong rays,
Ask of thy mother earth the needful maize;
She loves the race that courts her yielding soil,
And gives her bounties to the sons of toil.   195
   When now the ox, obedient to thy call,
Repays the loan that fill'd the winter stall,
Pursue his traces o'er the furrow'd plain,
And plant in measur'd hills the golden grain.
But when the tender germ begins to shoot,   200
And the green spire declares the sprouting root,
Then guard your nursling from each greedy foe,
The insidious worm, the all-devouring crow.
A little ashes, sprinkled round the spire,
Soon steep'd in rain, will bid the worm retire;   205
The feather'd robber with his hungry maw
Swift flies the field before your man of straw,
A frightful image, such as school-boys bring,
When met to burn the pope or hang the king.
   Thrice in the season, through each verdant row   210
Wield the strong ploughshare and the faithful hoe:
The faithful hoe, a double task that takes,
To till the summer corn, and roast the winter cakes.
   Slow springs the blade, while check'd by chilling rains,
Ere yet the sun the seat of Cancer gains;   215

But when his fiercest fires emblaze the land,
Then start the juices, then the roots expand;
Then, like a column of Corinthian mould,
The stalk struts upward and the leaves unfold;
The busy branches all the ridges fill,   220
Entwine their arms, and kiss from hill to hill.
Here cease to vex them, all your cares are done:
Leave the last labors to the parent sun;
Beneath his genial smiles, the well-drest field,
When autumn calls, a plenteous crop shall yield.   225
    Now the strong foliage bears the standards high,
And shoots the tall top-gallants to the sky;
The suckling ears their silky fringes bend,
And pregnant grown, their swelling coats distend;
The loaded stalk, while still the burden grows,   230
O'erhangs the space that runs between the rows;
High as a hop-field waves the silent grove,
A safe retreat for little thefts of love,
When the pledged roasting-ears invite the maid,
To meet her swain beneath the new-form'd shade;   235
His generous hand unloads the cumbrous hill,
And the green spoils her ready basket fill;
Small compensation for the twofold bliss,
The promised wedding, and the present kiss.
    Slight depredations these; but now the moon   240
Calls from his hollow tree the sly raccoon;
And while by night he bears his prize away,
The bolder squirrel labors through the day.
Both thieves alike, but provident of time,
A virtue rare, that almost hides their crime.   245
Then let them steal the little stores they can,
And fill their gran'ries from the toils of man;
We've one advantage, where they take no part,—
With all their wiles they ne'er have found the art
To boil the Hasty Pudding; here we shine   250
Superior far to tenants of the pine;
This envied boon to man shall still belong,
Unshared by them, in substance or in song.
    At last the closing season browns the plain,
And ripe October gathers in the grain;   255
Deep loaded carts the spacious corn-house fill,
The sack distended marches to the mill;
The lab'ring mill beneath the burden groans
And showers the future pudding from the stones;
Till the glad housewife greets the powder'd gold,   260

And the new crop exterminates the old.
Ah, who can sing what every wight must feel,
The joy that enters with the bag of meal,
A general jubilee pervades the house,
Wakes every child and gladdens every mouse.   265

CANTO III

The days grow short; but though the falling sun
To the glad swain proclaims his day's work done,
Night's pleasing shades his various tasks prolong,
And yield new subjects to my various song.
For now, the corn-house fill'd, the harvest home,   270
The invited neighbors to the husking come;
A frolic scene, where work, and mirth, and play,
Unite their charms to chase the hours away.
Where the huge heap lies centered in the hall,
The lamp suspended from the cheerful wall,   275
Brown corn-fed nymphs, and strong hard-handed beaux,
Alternate ranged, extend in circling rows,
Assume their seats, the solid mass attack;
The dry husks rustle, and the corncobs crack;
The song, the laugh, alternate notes resound,   280
And the sweet cider trips in silence round.
The laws of husking every wight can tell;
And sure no laws he ever keeps so well:
For each red ear a general kiss he gains,
With each smut ear he smuts the luckless swains;   285
But when to some sweet maid a prize is cast,
Red as her lips, and taper as her waist,
She walks the round, and culls one favored beau,
Who leaps, the luscious tribute to bestow.
Various the sport, as are the wits and brains   290
Of well pleased lassies and contending swains;
Till the vast mound of corn is swept away,
And he that gets the last ear wins the day.
Meanwhile the housewife urges all her care,
The well-earn'd feast to hasten and prepare.   295
The sifted meal already waits her hand,
The milk is strain'd, the bowls in order stand,
The fire flames high; and, as a pool (that takes
The headlong stream that o'er the mill-dam breaks)
Foams, roars, and rages with incessant toils,   300
So the vex'd caldron rages, roars and boils.
First with clean salt, she seasons well the food,
Then strews the flour, and thickens all the flood.

Long o'er the simmering fire she lets it stand;
To stir it well demands a stronger hand; 305
The husband takes his turn: and round and round
The ladle flies; at last the toil is crown'd;
When to the board the thronging huskers pour,
And take their seats as at the corn before.
    I leave them to their feast. There still belong 310
More useful matters to my faithful song.
For rules there are, though ne'er unfolded yet,
Nice rules and wise, how pudding should be ate.
    Some with molasses grace the luscious treat,
And mix, like bards, the useful and the sweet, 315
A wholesome dish, and well deserving praise,
A great resource in those bleak wintry days,
When the chill'd earth lies buried deep in snow,
And raging Boreas dries the shivering cow.
    Blest cow! thy praise shall still my notes employ, 320
Great source of health, the only source of joy;
Mother of Egypt's god,—but sure, for me,
Were I to leave my God, I'd worship thee.
How oft thy teats these pious hands have press'd!
How oft thy bounties prove my only feast! 325
How oft I've fed thee with my favorite grain!
And roar'd, like thee, to see thy children slain!
    Ye swains who know her various worth to prize,
Ah! house her well from winter's angry skies.
Potatoes, pumpkins, should her sadness cheer, 330
Corn from your crib, and mashes from your beer;
When spring returns, she'll well acquit the loan,
And nurse at once your infants and her own.
    Milk then with pudding I should always choose;
To this in future I confine my muse, 335
Till she in haste some further hints unfold,
Good for the young, nor useless to the old.
First in your bowl the milk abundant take,
Then drop with care along the silver lake
Your flakes of pudding; these at first will hide 340
Their little bulk beneath the swelling tide;
But when their growing mass no more can sink,
When the soft island looms above the brink,
Then check your hand; you've got the portion due,
So taught my sire, and what he taught is true. 345
    There is a choice in spoons. Though small appear
The nice distinction, yet to me 'tis clear.
The deep bowl'd Gallic spoon, contrived to scoop

In ample draughts the thin diluted soup,
Performs not well in those substantial things,   350
Whose mass adhesive to the metal clings;
Where the strong labial muscles must embrace,
The gentle curve, and sweep the hollow space.
With ease to enter and discharge the freight,
A bowl less concave, but still more dilate,   355
Becomes the pudding best. The shape, the size,
A secret rests, unknown to vulgar eyes.
Experienced feeders can alone impart
A rule so much above the lore of art.
These tuneful lips that thousand spoons have tried,   360
With just precision could the point decide.
Though not in song; the muse but poorly shines
In cones, and cubes, and geometric lines;
Yet the true form, as near as she can tell,
Is that small section of a goose egg shell,   365
Which in two equal portions shall divide
The distance from the center to the side.
    Fear not to slaver; 'tis no deadly sin:—
Like the free Frenchman, from your joyous chin
Suspend the ready napkin; or like me,   370
Poise with one hand your bowl upon your knee;
Just in the zenith your wise head project,
Your full spoon, rising in a line direct,
Bold as a bucket, heed no drops that fall,
The wide mouth'd bowl will surely catch them all!   375

NOTE

    There are various ways of preparing and eating it; with molasses, butter, sugar, cream, and fried. Why so excellent a thing cannot be eaten alone? Nothing is perfect alone, even man who boasts of so much perfection is nothing without his fellow substance. In eating, beware of the lurking heat that lies deep in the mass; dip your spoon gently, take shallow dips and cool it by degrees. It is sometimes necessary to blow. This is indicated by certain signs which every experienced feeder knows. They should be taught to young beginners. I have known a child's tongue blistered for want of this attention, and then the school-dame would insist that the poor thing had told a lie. A mistake: the falsehood was in the faithless pudding. A prudent mother will cool it for her child with her own sweet breath. The husband, seeing this, pretends his own wants blowing too from the same lips. A sly deceit of love. She knows the cheat, but feigning ignorance, lends her pouting lips and gives a gentle blast, which warms the husband's heart more than it cools his pudding.

1793, 1796

Timothy Dwight
(1752-1817)

Timothy Dwight entered Yale at the age of thirteen, was graduated in 1769, and received his M.A. there in 1772. After studying law, he became interested in religion, and in 1777 resigned as a tutor at Yale to preach and to serve as chaplain at West Point. From 1779 to 1783, he preached at Northampton, Mass., his birthplace; in 1783 he accepted the pastorate of the Congregational Church at Greenfield Hill, Conn., a post which he held for twelve years. Dwight was president of Yale from 1795 until his death. His poetry includes *The Conquest of Canaan* (Hartford, 1785), *Greenfield Hill: A Poem in Seven Parts* (New York, 1794), and *The Triumph of Infidelity* (1788), a poem condemning democracy.

BIBLIOGRAPHY: Benjamin Sillman, *A Sketch of the Life and Character of President Timothy Dwight* (New Haven, 1817). M. C. Tyler, *Three Men of Letters* (New York, 1895). C. E. Cuningham, *Timothy Dwight: 1752-1817: A Biography* (New York, 1942).

From *Greenfield Hill*

PART II

THE FLOURISHING VILLAGE

Fair Verna! loveliest village of the west;
Of every joy, and every charm, possess'd;
How pleas'd amid thy varied walks I rove,
Sweet, cheerful walks of innocence, and love,
And o'er thy smiling prospects cast my eyes,　　　5
And see the seats of peace, and pleasure, rise,
And hear the voice of Industry resound,
And mark the smile of Competence, around!
Hail, happy village! O'er the cheerful lawns,
With earliest beauty, spring delighted dawns;　　　10
The northward sun begins his vernal smile;
The spring-bird carols o'er the cressy rill:
The shower, that patters in the ruffled stream,
The ploughboy's voice, that chides the lingering team,
The bee, industrious, with his busy song,　　　15
The woodman's axe, the distant groves among,
The wagon, rattling down the rugged steep,
The light wind, lulling every care to sleep,
All these, with mingled music, from below,
Deceive intruding sorrow, as I go.　　　20

How pleas'd, fond Recollection, with a smile,
Surveys the varied round of wintery toil!
How pleas'd, amid the flowers, that scent the plain,
Recalls the vanish'd frost, and sleeted rain;
The chilling damp, the ice-endangering street,   25
And treacherous earth that slump'd beneath the feet.

Yet even stern winter's glooms could joy inspire:
Then social circles grac'd the nutwood fire;
The axe resounded, at the sunny door;
The swain, industrious, trimm'd his flaxen store;   30
Or thresh'd, with vigorous flail, the bounding wheat,
His poultry round him pilfering for their meat;
Or slid his firewood on the creaking snow;
Or bore his produce to the main below;
Or o'er his rich returns exulting laugh'd;   35
Or pledg'd the healthful orchard's sparkling draught:
While, on his board, for friends and neighbors spread,
The turkey smok'd, his busy housewife fed;
And Hospitality look'd smiling round,
And Leisure told his tale, with gleeful sound.   40

Then too, the rough road hid beneath the sleigh,
The distant friend despis'd a length of way,
And join'd the warm embrace, and mingling smile,
And told of all his bliss, and all his toil;
And, many a month elaps'd, was pleas'd to view   45
How well the household far'd, the children grew;
While tales of sympathy deceiv'd the hour,
And Sleep, amus'd, resign'd his wonted power.

Yes! let the proud despise, the rich deride,
These humble joys, to Competence allied: 50
To me, they bloom, all fragrant to my heart,
Nor ask the pomp of wealth, nor gloss of art.
And as a bird, in prison long confin'd,
Springs from his open'd cage, and mounts the wind,
Thro' fields of flowers, and fragrance, gaily flies,   55
Or reassumes his birth-right, in the skies:
Unprison'd thus from artificial joys,
Where pomp fatigues, and fussful fashion cloys,
The soul, reviving, loves to wander free
Thro' native scenes of sweet simplicity;   60
Thro' Peace' low vale, where Pleasure lingers long,
And every songster tunes his sweetest song,

And Zephyr hastes, to breathe his first perfume,
And Autumn stays, to drop his latest bloom:
'Till grown mature, and gathering strength to roam,   65
She lifts her lengthen'd wings, and seeks her home.

But now the wintery glooms are vanish'd all;
The lingering drift behind the shady wall;
The dark-brown spots, that patch'd the snowy field;
The surly frost, that every bud conceal'd;   70
The russet veil, the way with slime o'erspread,
And all the saddening scenes of March are fled.

Sweet-smiling village! loveliest of the hills!
How green thy groves! How pure thy glassy rills!
With what new joy, I walk thy verdant streets!   75
How often pause, to breathe thy gale of sweets;
To mark thy well-built walls! thy budding fields!
And every charm, that rural nature yields;
And every joy, to Competence allied,
And every good, that Virtue gains from Pride!   80

No griping landlord here alarms the door,
To halve, for rent, the poor man's little store.
No haughty owner drives the humble swain
To some far refuge from his dread domain;
Nor wastes, upon his robe of useless pride,   85
The wealth, which shivering thousands want beside;
Nor in one palace sinks a hundred cots;
Nor in one manor drowns a thousand lots;
Nor, on one table, spread for death and pain,
Devours what would a village well sustain.   90

O Competence, thou bless'd by Heaven's decree,
How well exchang'd is empty pride for thee!
Oft to thy cot my feet delighted turn,
To meet thy cheerful smile, at peep of morn;
To join thy toils, that bid the earth look gay;   95
To mark thy sports, that hail the eve of May;
To see thy ruddy children, at thy board,
And share thy temperate meal, and frugal hoard;
And every joy, by winning prattlers giv'n,
And every earnest of a future Heaven.   100

There the poor wanderer finds a table spread,
The fireside welcome, and the peaceful bed.

The needy neighbor, oft by wealth denied,
There finds the little aids of life supplied;
The horse, that bears to mill the hard-earn'd grain;   105
The day's work given, to reap the ripen'd plain;
The useful team, to house the precious food,
And all the offices of real good.

    There too, divine Religion is a guest,
And all the Virtues join the daily feast.   110
Kind Hospitality attends the door,
To welcome in the stranger and the poor;
Sweet Chastity, still blushing as she goes;
And Patience smiling at her train of woes;
And meek-eyed Innocence, and Truth refin'd,   115
And Fortitude, of bold, but gentle mind.

    Thou pay'st the tax, the rich man will not pay;
Thou feed'st the poor, the rich man drives away.
Thy sons, for freedom, hazard limbs, and life,
While pride applauds, but shuns the manly strife: 120
Thou prop'st religion's cause, the world around,
And show'st thy faith in works, and not in sound.

    Say, child of passion! while, with idiot stare,
Thou seest proud grandeur wheel her sunny car;
While kings, and nobles, roll bespangled by,   125
And the tall palace lessens in the sky;
Say, while with pomp thy giddy brain runs round,
What joys, like these, in splendor can be found?
Ah, yonder turn thy wealth-enchanted eyes,
Where that poor, friendless wretch expiring lies!   130
Hear his sad partner shriek, beside his bed,
And call down curses on her landlord's head,
Who drove, from yon small cot, her household sweet,
To pine with want, and perish in the street.
See the pale tradesman toil, the livelong day,   135
To deck imperious lords, who never pay!
Who waste, at dice, their boundless breadth of soil,
But grudge the scanty meed of honest toil.
See hounds and horses riot on the store,
By Heaven created for the hapless poor!   140
See half a realm one tyrant scarce sustain,
While meager thousands round him glean the plain!
See, for his mistress' robe, a village sold,
Whose matrons shrink from nakedness and cold!

446 / Timothy Dwight

See too the Farmer prowl around the shed,   145
To rob the starving household of their bread;
And seize, with cruel fangs, the helpless swain,
While wives, and daughters, plead, and weep, in vain;
Or yield to infamy themselves, to save
Their sire from prison, famine, and the grave.   150

There too foul luxury taints the putrid mind,
And slavery there imbrutes the reasoning kind:
There humble worth, in damps of deep despair,
Is bound by poverty's eternal bar:
No motives bright the ethereal aim impart,   155
Nor one fair ray of hope allures the heart.

But, O sweet Competence! how chang'd the scene,
Where thy soft footsteps lightly print the green!
Where Freedom walks erect, with manly port,
And all the blessings to his side resort,   160
In every hamlet, Learning builds her schools,
And beggars, children gain her arts, and rules;
And mild Simplicity o'er manners reigns,
And blameless morals Purity sustains.

From thee the rich enjoyments round me spring,   165
Where every farmer reigns a little king;
Where all to comfort, none to danger, rise;
Where pride finds few, but nature all supplies;
Where peace and sweet civility are seen,
And meek good-neighborhood endears the green.   170
Here every class (if classes those we call,
Where one extended class embraces all,
All mingling, as the rainbow's beauty blends,
Unknown where every hue begins or ends)
Each following, each, with uninvidious strife,   175
Wears every feature of improving life.
Each gains from other comeliness of dress,
And learns, with gentle mein to win and bless,
With welcome mild the stranger to receive,
And with plain, pleasing decency to live.   180
Refinement hence even humblest life improves;
Not the loose fair, that form and frippery loves;
But she, whose mansion is the gentle mind,
In thought, and action, virtuously refin'd.
Hence, wives and husbands act a lovelier part,   185
More just the conduct, and more kind the heart;

Hence brother, sister, parent, child, and friend,
The harmony of life more sweetly blend;
Hence labor brightens every rural scene;
Hence cheerful plenty lives along the green;   190
Still Prudence eyes her hoard, with watchful care,
And robes of thrift and neatness, all things wear.

1794

David Humphreys
(1752-1818)

After entering Yale in 1771 and receiving his M.A. there in 1774, David Humphreys served with and was an admirer of George Washington. Following the Revolution, Humphreys held several diplomatic and elective offices. His verse includes *A Poem Addressed to the Armies of the United States of America* (New Haven, 1780), *A Poem on the Hap-* *piness of America* (London, 1780), *The Glory of America* (Philadelphia, 1788), *A Poem on Industry* (Philadelphia, 1794), and *The Miscellaneous Works of Colonel Humphreys* (New York, 1790, 1804).

BIBLIOGRAPHY: F. L. Humphreys, *The Life and Times of David Humphreys*, 2 Vols. (New York, 1917).

The Monkey Who Shaved Himself and His Friends

A FABLE

A man who own'd a barber shop
At York, and shaved full many a fop,
A monkey kept for their amusement;
He made no other kind of use on't—
This monkey took great observation,   5
Was wonderful at imitation,
And all he saw the barber do,
He mimic'd straight, and did it too.
    It chanced in shop, the dog and cat,
While friseur dined, demurely sat,   10
Jacko found nought to play the knave in,
So thought he'd try his hand at shaving.
Around the shop in haste he rushes,
And gets the razors, soap, and brushes;
Now puss he fix'd (no muscle misstirs)   15
And lather'd well her beard and whiskers,

Then gave a gash, as he began—
The cat cry'd "waugh!" and off she ran.
  Next Towser's beard he try'd his skill in,
Though Towser seem'd somewhat unwilling: 20
As badly here again succeeding,
The dog runs howling round and bleeding.
  Nor yet was tired our roguish elf,
He'd seen the barber shave himself;
So by the glass, upon the table,   25
He rubs with soap his visage sable,
Then with left hand holds smooth his jaw,—
The razor, in his dexter paw;
Around he flourishes and slashes,
Till all his face is seam'd with gashes.   30
His cheeks dispatch'd—his visage thin
He cock'd, to shave beneath his chin;
Drew razor swift as he could pull it,
And cut, from ear to ear, his gullet.[1]

MORAL

Who cannot write, yet handle pens,   35
Are apt to hurt themselves and friends.
Though others use them well, yet fools
Should never meddle with edge tools.

1788

On Life

Ere we can think of time, the moment's past,
And straight another since that thought began:
So swift each instant mingles with the last,
The flying *now* exists no more for man.

With consciousness suspended even by sleep,   5
To what this phantom, life, then likest seems?
Say, thou, whose doubtful being (lost in dreams)
Allows the 'wildered but to wake and weep,
So thoughtless hurried to the eternal deep!

[1] Humphreys had completed this fable with the exception of the last couplet, and made several attempts to give it that pointed finish which he desired, but could not succeed. He then went with it to the author of M'Fingal, and told him his difficulty. Trumbull took the piece and read it aloud; then looking upward with that keen glance for which his eye was remarkable, added without pausing—
"Drew razor swift as he could pull it,
And cut from ear to ear his gullet."

'Tis like a moonlight vision's airy shade,   10
A bubble driving down the deep beneath—
Then, ere the bubble burst, the vision fade,
Dissolved in air this evanescent breath!
Let man, not mortal, learn true life begins at death.

                                        c. 1788, 1804

From *A Poem on Industry*

Genius of Culture! thou, whose chaster taste
Can clothe with beauty ev'n the dreary waste:
Teach me to sing, what bright'ning charms unfold,
The bearded ears, that bend with more than gold;
How empire rises, and how morals spring,   5
From lowly labor, teach my lips to sing;
Exalt the numbers with thy gifts supreme,
Ennobler of the song, my guide and theme! . . .

    Should peace, like sorcery, with her spells control
Our innate springs and energies of soul;   10
To you, Columbian dames! my accents call,
Oh, save your country from the threaten'd fall!
Will ye, blest fair! adopt from every zone
Fantastic fashions, noxious in your own?
At wintry balls in gauzy garments drest,   15
Admit the dire destroyer in your breast?
Oft when nocturnal sports your visage flush,
As gay and heedless to the halls ye rush,
Then death your doom prepares: cough, fever, rheum,
And pale consumption nip your rosy bloom.   20
Hence many a flow'r in beauty's damask pride,
Wither'd, at morn, has droop'd its head and died.[2]
While youthful crimson hurries through your veins,
No cynic bard from licit joys restrains;
Or bids with nature hold unequal strife,   25
And still go sorrowing through the road of life.
Nor deem him hostile who of danger warns,
Who leaves the rose, but plucks away its thorns . . . .

    Ere ye begin to tread life's wider stage,
In manhood's prime, dear, interesting age!   30
Attend a time-taught bard, to toils inur'd,

[2] This, it is wished, may be received as a useful warning by young persons against exposing themselves, when too thinly clad, to the winter air. Many deaths have been occasioned by imprudencies of this nature. [Humphreys' Note.]

With those bold chiefs whose blood your rights secur'd:
Ye junior patriots, listen! learn, my friends!
How much your lot on industry depends:
For God, a God of order, ne'er design'd   35
Equal conditions for the human kind.
Equality of rights your bliss maintains,
While law protects what honest labor gains.
Your great exertions by restraint uncheck'd,
Your gen'rous heat undamp'd by cold neglect;   40
The wide career for freemen open lies,
Where wealth, and pow'r, and honor yield the prize.
Yet should dark discord's clouds your land o'ercast,
Lost is your freedom and your empire past.
Be union yours! To guard your union, heav'n   45
The general government, in *trust,* has giv'n:
Then, when ere long your fathers sleep in dust,
Preserve, like vestal fire, that *sacred* TRUST!

1794, rev. 1804

John Trumbull
(1750-1831)

John Trumbull passed his entrance examinations at Yale at the age of seven, but did not enter until he was thirteen. He was graduated in 1767, received his M.A. in 1770, returned as a tutor in 1772, and was admitted to law practice in 1773. Later in his life he held numerous political posts. Trumbull contributed to the *Boston Chronicle* in 1769, and between 1770 and 1773, wrote thirty-eight essays for the *Connecticut Journal* under the name of "The Correspondent." His verse includes *The Progress of Dulness* (Hartford, 1772-1773) in three parts; *An Elegy on the Times* (Boston, 1774); and *M'Fingal; A Modern Epic* (Philadelphia, 1775), which included what is now Cantos I and II of the poem. *M'Fingal: A Modern Epic Poem in Four Cantos* (Hartford, 1782), expanded from some 1700 lines to more than 3000 lines,

was reprinted thirty times between 1782 and 1840. *The Poetical Works of John Trumbull,* 2 Vols. (Hartford, 1820), includes an autobiographical sketch. Trumbull died in Detroit, Mich.

BIBLIOGRAPHY: B. J. Lossing, ed. *M'Fingal* (New York, 1864), with detailed notes. J. H. Trumbull, *The Origin of M'Fingal* (Morrisania, N.Y., 1868). Alexander Cowie, *John Trumbull: Connecticut Wit* (Chapel Hill, N.C., 1936). E. T. Bowden, ed. *The Satiric Poems of John Trumbull* (Austin, Tex., 1962). B. I. Granger, "John Trumbull and Religion," *Amer. Lit.,* XXIII (1951), 57-79. Cowie, "John Trumbull as a Critic of Poetry," *N. Eng. Quart.,* XI (1938), 773-793. Cowie, "John Trumbull Glances at Fiction," *Amer. Lit.,* XII (1940), 69-73.

From *M'Fingal*

CANTO I

The Town-Meeting, A.M.

When Yankees, skill'd in martial rule,
First put the British troops to school;[1]
Instructed them in warlike trade,
And new manœuvers of parade,
The true war-dance of Yankee reels,   5
And manual exercise of heels;
Made them give up, like saints complete,
The arm of flesh, and trust the feet,
And work, like Christians undissembling,
Salvation out, by fear and trembling;   10
Taught Percy fashionable races,
And modern modes of Chevy-Chases:
From Boston, in his best array,
Great 'Squire M'Fingal took his way,
And graced with ensigns of renown,   15
Steer'd homeward to his native town.
   His high descent our heralds trace
From Ossian's famed Fingalian race:[2]
For though their name some part may lack,
Old Fingal spelt it with a Mac;   20
Which great M'Pherson, with submission,
We hope will add the next edition.
   His fathers flourish'd in the Highlands
Of Scotia's fog-benighted islands;
Whence gain'd our 'Squire two gifts by right,   25
Rebellion, and the Second-sight.
Of these, the first, in ancient days,
Had gain'd the noblest palm of praise,
'Gainst kings stood forth and many a crown'd head
With terror of its might confounded;   30
Till rose a king with potent charm
His foes by meekness to disarm,
Whom every Scot and Jacobite

---

[1] At the battle of Lexington. The reader will easily recollect how often these salutary lessons have been since repeated—from the action at Bunker-hill to the battle of New-Orleans inclusive. [The notes in this selection are Trumbull's.]

[2] See Fingal, an ancient Epic Poem, published as the work of Ossian, a Caledonian Bard of the third century, by James M'Pherson. The complete name of Ossian, according to the Scottish nomenclature, will be Ossian M'Fingal.

Straight fell in love with at first sight;
Whose gracious speech with aid of pensions,   35
Hush'd down all murmurs of dissensions,
And with the sound of potent metal
Brought all their buzzing swarms to settle;
Who rain'd his ministerial manna,
Till loud Sedition sung hosanna;   40
The grave Lords-Bishops and the Kirk
United in the public work;
Rebellion, from the northern regions,
With Bute and Mansfield swore allegiance;
All hands combin'd to raze, as nuisance,   45
Of church and state the Constitutions,
Pull down the empire, on whose ruins
They meant to edify their new ones;
Enslave th' American wildernesses,
And rend the provinces in pieces.   50
With these our 'Squire, among the valiant'st,
Employ'd his time, and tools and talents,
And found this new rebellion pleasing
As his old king-destroying treason.
    Nor less avail'd his optic sleight,   55
And Scottish gift of second-sight.[3]
No ancient sybil, famed in rhyme,
Saw deeper in the womb of time;
No block in old Dodona's grove
Could ever more orac'lar prove.   60
Nor only saw he all that could be,
But much that never was, nor would be;
Whereby all prophets far outwent he,
Though former days produced a plenty:
For any man with half an eye   65
What stands before him can espy;
But optics sharp it needs, I ween,
To see what is not to be seen.
As in the days of ancient fame,
Prophets and poets were the same,   70
And all the praise that poets gain
Is for the tales they forge and feign:
So gain'd our 'Squire his fame by seeing
Such things, as never would have being;
Whence he for oracles was grown   75

---

[3] They, who wish to understand the nature, and *modus operandi,* of the Highland vision by second-sight, may consult the profound Johnson, in his Tour to the Hebrides.

The very tripod of his town.[4]
Gazettes no sooner rose a lie in,
But straight he fell to prophesying;
Made dreadful slaughter in his course,
O'erthrew provincials, foot and horse,   80
Brought armies o'er, by sudden pressings,
Of Hanoverians, Swiss and Hessians,
Feasted with blood his Scottish clan,
And hang'd all rebels to a man,
Divided their estates and pelf,   85
And took a goodly share himself.
All this with spirit energetic,
He did by second-sight prophetic.
    Thus stored with intellectual riches,
Skill'd was our 'Squire in making speeches;   90
Where strength of brains united centers
With strength of lungs surpassing Stentor's.[5]
But as some muskets so contrive it,
As oft to miss the mark they drive at,
And though well aim'd at duck or plover,   95
Bear wide, and kick their owners over:
So fared our 'Squire, whose reas'ning toil
Would often on himself recoil,
And so much injured more his side,
The stronger arguments he applied;   100
As old war-elephants, dismay'd,
Trod down the troops they came to aid,
And hurt their own side more in battle,
Than less and ordinary cattle.
Yet at Town-meetings every chief   105
Pinn'd faith on great M'Fingal's sleeve;
Which when he lifted, all by rote
Raised sympathetic hands to vote. . . .

CANTO III

The Liberty Pole

Now warm with ministerial ire,
Fierce sallied forth our loyal 'Squire,
And on his striding steps attends
His desperate clan of Tory friends.

[4] The tripod was a sacred three-legged stool, from which the ancient priests uttered their oracles.
[5] Stentor, the loud-voic'd herald in Homer.

When sudden met his wrathful eye 5
A pole ascending through the sky,
Which numerous throngs of whiggish race
Were raising in the market-place.
Not higher school-boy's kites aspire,
Or royal mast, or country spire; 10
Like spears at Brobdignagian tilting,
Or Satan's walking-staff in Milton.
And on its top, the flag unfurl'd
Waved trumph o'er the gazing world,
Inscribed with inconsistent types 15
Of *Liberty* and *thirteen stripes*.
Beneath, the crowd without delay
The dedication-rites essay,
And gladly pay, in ancient fashion,
The ceremonies of libation; 20
While briskly to each patriot lip
Walks eager round the inspiring flip:[6]
Delicious draught! whose powers inherit
The quintessence of public spirit;
Which whoso tastes, perceives his mind 25
To nobler politics refined;
Or roused to martial controversy,
As from transforming cups of Circe;
Or warm'd with Homer's nectar'd liquor,
That fill'd the veins of gods with ichor. 30
At hand for new supplies in store,
The tavern opes its friendly door,
Whence to and fro the waiters run,
Like bucket-men at fires in town.
Then with three shouts that tore the sky, 35
'Tis consecrate to Liberty.
To guard it from th' attacks of Tories,
A grand Committee cull'd of four is;
Who foremost on the patriot spot,
Had brought the flip, and paid the shot. 40
    By this, M'Fingal with his train
Advanced upon th' adjacent plain,
And full with loyalty possest,
Pour'd forth the zeal, that fired his breast.
    "What mad-brain'd rebel gave commission, 45
To raise this May-pole of sedition?
Like Babel, rear'd by bawling throngs,

[6] Flip, a liquor composed of beer, rum and sugar; the common treat at that time in the country towns of New-England.

With like confusion too of tongues,
To point at heaven and summon down
The thunders of the British crown?   50
Say, will this paltry Pole secure
Your forfeit heads from Gage's power?
Attack'd by heroes brave and crafty,
Is this to stand your ark of safety;
Or driven by Scottish laird and laddie,   55
Think ye to rest beneath its shadow?
When bombs, like fiery serpents, fly,
And balls rush hissing through the sky,
Will this vile Pole, devote to freedom,
Save like the Jewish pole in Edom;   60
Or like the brazen snake of Moses,
Cure your crackt skulls and batter'd noses?
    "Ye dupes to every factious rogue
And tavern-prating demagogue,
Whose tongue but rings, with sound more full,   65
On th' empty drumhead of his skull;
Behold you not what noisy fools
Use you, worse simpletons, for tools?
For Liberty, in your own by-sense,
Is but for crimes a patent license,   70
To break of law th' Egyptian yoke,
And throw the world in common stock;
Reduce all grievances and ills
To Magna Charta of your wills;
Establish cheats and frauds and nonsense,   75
Framed to the model of your conscience. . . .
And when by clamors and confusions,
Your freedom's grown a public nuisance,
Cry 'Liberty,' with powerful yearning,
As he does 'Fire!' whose house is burning;   80
Though he already has much more
Than he can find occasion for.
While every clown, that tills the plains,
Though bankrupt in estate and brains,
By this new light transform'd to traitor,   85
Forsakes his plough to turn dictator,
Starts an haranguing chief of Whigs,
And drags you by the ears, like pigs.
All bluster, arm'd with factious license,
New-born at once to politicians.   90
Each leather-apron'd dunce, grown wise,
Presents his forward face t' advise,

And tatter'd legislators meet,
From every workshop through the street.
His goose the tailor finds new use in,   95
To patch and turn the Constitution;
The blacksmith comes with sledge and grate
To iron-bind the wheels of state;
The quack forbears his patients' souse,
To purge the Council and the House;   100
The tinker quits his moulds and doxies,
To cast assembly-men and proxies.
From dunghills deep of blackest hue,
Your dirt-bred patriots spring to view,
To wealth and power and honors rise,   105
Like new-wing'd maggots changed to flies,
And fluttering round in high parade,
Strut in the robe, or gay cockade. . . .
What wild confusion hence must ensue?
Tho' common danger yet cements you: 110
So some wreck'd vessel, all in shatters,
Is held up by surrounding waters,
But stranded, when the pressure ceases,
Falls by its rottenness to pieces.
And fall it must! if wars were ended,   115
You'll ne'er have sense enough to mend it:
But creeping on, by low intrigues,
Like vermin of a thousand legs,[7]
'Twill find as short a life assign'd,
As all things else of reptile kind.   120
Your Commonwealth's a common harlot,
The property of every varlet;
Which now in taste, and full employ,
All sorts admire, as all enjoy:
But soon a batter'd strumpet grown,   125
You'll curse and drum her out of town.
Such is the government you chose;
For this you bade the world be foes;
For this, so mark'd for dissolution,
You scorn the British Constitution,   130
That constitution form'd by sages,
The wonder of all modern ages;
Which owns no failure in reality,
Except corruption and venality;
And merely proves the adage just,   135

[7] Millepedes.

That best things spoil'd corrupt to worst:
So man supreme in earthly station,
And mighty lord of this creation,
When once his corpse is dead as herring,
Becomes the most offensive carrion,   140
And sooner breeds the plague, 'tis found,
Than all beast rotting on the ground.
Yet with republics to dismay us,
You've call'd up Anarchy from chaos,
With all the followers of her school,   145
Uproar and Rage and wild Misrule:
For whom this rout of Whigs distracted,
And ravings dire of every crack'd head;
These new-cast legislative engines
Of County-meetings and Conventions;   150
Committees vile of correspondence,
And mobs, whose tricks have almost undone 's:
While reason fails to check your course,
And Loyalty's kick'd out of doors,
And Folly, like inviting landlord,   155
Hoists on your poles her royal standard;
While the king's friends, in doleful dumps,
Have worn their courage to the stumps,
And leaving George in sad disaster,
Most sinfully deny their master. . . .   160
Now rising in progression fatal,
Have you not ventured to give battle?
When Treason chased our heroes troubled,
With rusty gun, and leathern doublet;[8]
Turn'd all stone-walls and groves and bushes,   165
To batteries arm'd with blunderbusses;
And with deep wounds, that fate portend,
Gall'd many a Briton's latter end;
Drove them to Boston, as in jail,
Confined without mainprize or bail.   170
Were not these deeds enough betimes,
To heap the measure of your crimes:
But in this loyal town and dwelling,
You raise these ensigns of rebellion?
'Tis done! fair Mercy shuts her door;   175
And Vengeance now shall sleep no more.
Rise then, my friends, in terror rise,
And sweep this scandal from the skies.

[8] At the battle of Lexington.

You'll see their Dagon, though well jointed,
Will shrink before the Lord's anointed;[9]   180
And like old Jericho's proud wall,
Before our ram's horns prostrate fall."
   This said, our 'Squire, yet undismay'd,
Call'd forth the Constable to aid,
And bade him read, in nearer station,   185
The Riot-act and Proclamation.
He swift, advancing to the ring,
Began, "Our Sovereign Lord, the King"—
When thousand clam'rous tongues he hears,
And clubs and stones assail his ears.   190
To fly was vain; to fight was idle;
By foes encompass'd in the middle,
His hope, in stratagems, he found,
And fell right craftily to ground;
Then crept to seek an hiding place,   195
'Twas all he could, beneath a brace;
Where soon the conq'ring crew espied him,
And where he lurk'd, they caught and tied **him.**
   At once with resolution fatal,
Both Whigs and Tories rush'd to battle.   200
Instead of weapons, either band
Seized on such arms as came to hand.
And as famed Ovid paints th' adventures[10]
Of wrangling Lapithæ and Centaurs,
Who at their feast, by Bacchus led,   205
Threw bottles at each other's head;
And these arms failing in their scuffles,
Attack'd with andirons, tongs and shovels:
So clubs and billets, staves and stones
Met fierce, encountering every sconce,   210
And cover'd o'er with knobs and pains
Each void receptacle for brains;
Their clamours rend the skies around,
The hills rebellow to the sound;
And many a groan increas'd the din   215
From batter'd nose and broken shin.
M'Fingal, rising at the word,
Drew forth his old militia-sword;
Thrice cried "King George," as erst in distress,
Knights of romance invoked a mistress;   220

[9] The Tory clergy always styled the King, the Lord's Anointed. The language of Cromwell's and Charles' days was yet frequent in New-England.
[10] See Ovid's Metamorphoses, book 12th.

And brandishing the blade in air,
Struck terror through th' opposing war.
The Whigs, unsafe within the wind
Of such commotion, shrunk behind.
With whirling steel around address'd,   225
Fierce through their thickest throng he press'd,
(Who roll'd on either side in arch,
Like Red Sea waves in Israel's march)
And like a meteor rushing through,
Struck on their Pole a vengeful blow.   230
Around, the Whigs, of clubs and stones
Discharged whole volleys, in platoons,
That o'er in whistling fury fly;
But not a foe dares venture nigh.
And now perhaps with glory crown'd   235
Our 'Squire had fell'd the pole to ground,
Had not some Pow'r, a whig at heart,
Descended down and took their part;[11]
(Whether 'twere Pallas, Mars or Iris,
'Tis scarce worth while to make inquiries)   240
Who at the nick of time alarming,
Assumed the solemn form of Chairman,
Address'd a Whig, in every scene
The stoutest wrestler on the green,
And pointed where the spade was found,   245
Late used to set their pole in ground,
And urged, with equal arms and might,
To dare our 'Squire to single fight.
The Whig thus arm'd, untaught to yield,
Advanced tremendous to the field: 250
Nor did M'Fingal shun the foe,
But stood to brave the desp'rate blow;
While all the party gazed, suspended
To see the deadly combat ended;
And Jove in equal balance weigh'd[12]   255
The sword against the brandish'd spade,
He weigh'd; but lighter than a dream,
The sword flew up, and kick'd the beam.
Our 'Squire on tiptoe rising fair
Lifts high a noble stroke in air,   260

[11] The learned reader will readily observe the allusions in this scene, to the single combats of Paris and Menelaus in Homer, Æneas and the Turnus in Virgil, and Michael and Satan in Milton.
[12] Jupiter ipse duas æquato examine lances
Sustinent & fata imponit diversa duorum,
Quem damnet labor, &c.—*Æneid*, 12.

Which hung not, but like dreadful engines,
Descended on his foe in vengeance.
But ah! in danger, with dishonor
The sword perfidious fails its owner;
That sword, which oft had stood its ground,   265
By huge trainbands encircled round;
And on the bench, with blade right loyal,
Had won the day at many a trial,[13]
Of stones and clubs had braved th' alarms,
Shrunk from these new Vulcanian arms.[14]   270
The spade so temper'd from the sledge,
Nor keen nor solid harm'd its edge,
Now met it, from his arm of might,
Descending with steep force to smite;
The blade snapp'd short—and from his hand,   275
With rust embrown'd the glittering sand.
Swift turn'd M'Fingal at the view,
And call'd to aid th' attendant crew,
In vain; the Tories all had run,
When scarce the fight was well begun;   280
Their setting wigs he saw decreas'd
Far in th' horizon tow'rd the west.
Amazed he view'd the shameful sight,
And saw no refuge, but in flight:
But age unwieldy check'd his pace,   285
Though fear had wing'd his flying race;
For not a trifling prize at stake;
No less than great M'Fingal's back.[15]
With legs and arms he work'd his course,
Like rider that outgoes his horse,   290
And labor'd hard to get away, as
Old Satan struggling on through chaos;[16]
'Till looking back, he spied in rear
The spade-arm'd chief advanced too near:

[13] It was the fashion in New-England at that time, for judges to wear swords on the bench.

[14] ————Postquam arma Dei ad Vulcania ventum est,
Mortalis mucro, glacies ceu futilis, ictu
Dissiluit; fulva resplendent fragmina arena.—Virgil
————The sword
Was given him temper'd so, that neither keen
Nor solid might resist that edge; it met
The sword of Satan with steep force to smite
Descending and in half cut sheer.—Milton

[15] ————nec enim levia aut ludicra petuntur
Præmia, sed Turni de vita et sanguine certant.—Virgil

[16] In Milton.

Then stopp'd and seized a stone, that lay   295
An ancient landmark near the way;
Nor shall we as old bards have done,
Affirm it weigh'd an hundred ton;[17]
But such a stone, as at a shift
A modern might suffice to lift,   300
Since men, to credit their enigmas,
Are dwindled down to dwarfs and pigmies,
And giants exiled with their cronies
To Brobdignags and Patagonias.
But while our Hero turn'd him round,   305
And tugg'd to raise it from the ground,
The fatal spade discharged a blow
Tremendous on his rear below:
His bent knee fail'd, and void of strength[18]
Stretch'd on the ground his manly length.   310
Like ancient oak o'erturn'd, he lay,
Or tower to tempests fall'n a prey,
Or mountain sunk with all his pines,
Or flow'r the plow to dust consigns,
And more things else—but all men know 'em,   315
If slightly versed in epic poem.
At once the crew, at this dread crisis,
Fall on, and bind him, ere he rises;
And with loud shouts and joyful soul,
Conduct him prisoner to the pole.   320
When now the mob in lucky hour
Had got their en'mies in their power,
They first proceed, by grave command,
To take the Constable in hand.
Then from the pole's sublimest top   325
The active crew let down the rope,
At once its other end in haste bind,
And make it fast upon his waistband;
Till like the earth, as stretch'd on tenter,
He hung self-balanced on his center.[19]   330
Then upwards, all hands hoisting sail,
They swung him, like a keg of ale,
Till to the pinnacle in height
He vaulted, like balloon or kite.

---

[17] This thought is taken from Juvenal, Satire 15.
[18] Genua labant———incidit ictus,
Ingens ad terram duplicato poplite Turnus.—Virgil.
[19] And earth self-balanced on her center hung.—Milton.

As Socrates of old at first did[20]   335
To aid philosophy get hoisted,
And found his thoughts flow strangely clear,
Swung in a basket in mid air:
Our culprit thus, in purer sky,
With like advantage raised his eye,   340
And looking forth in prospect wide,
His Tory errors clearly spied,
And from his elevated station,
With bawling voice began addressing.
    "Good Gentlemen and friends and kin,   345
For heaven's sake hear, if not for mine!
I here renounce the Pope, the Turks,
The King, the Devil and all their works;
And will, set me but once at ease,
Turn Whig or Christian, what you please;   350
And always mind your rules so justly,
Should I live long as old Methus'lah,
I'll never join in British rage,
Nor help Lord North, nor Gen'ral Gage;
Nor lift my gun in future fights,   355
Nor take away your Charter-rights;
Nor overcome your new-raised levies,
Destroy your towns, nor burn your navies;
Nor cut your poles down while I've breath,
Though raised more thick than hatchel-teeth: 360
But leave King George and all his elves
To do their conq'ring work themselves."
    This said, they lower'd him down in state,
Spread at all points, like falling cat;
But took a vote first on the question,   365
That they'd accept this full confession,
And to their fellowship and favor,
Restore him on his good behavior.
    Not so our 'Squire submits to rule,
But stood, heroic as a mule.   370
"You'll find it all in vain, quoth he,
To play your rebel tricks on me.
All punishments, the world can render,
Serve only to provoke th' offender;
The will gains strength from treatment horrid,   375
As hides grow harder when they're curried.
No man e'er felt the halter draw,

[20] In Aristophanes' Comedy of the Clouds, Socrates is represented as hoisted in basket to aid contemplation.

With good opinion of the law;
Or held in method orthodox
His love of justice, in the stocks;   380
Or fail'd to lose by sheriff's shears
At once his loyalty and ears.
Have you made Murray look less big,
Or smoked old Williams to a Whig?[21]
Did our mobb'd Ol'ver quit his station,[22]   385
Or heed his vows of resignation?
Has Rivington, in dread of stripes,[23]
Ceased lying since you stole his types?
And can you think my faith will alter,
By tarring, whipping or the halter?   390
I'll stand the worst; for recompense
I trust King George and Providence.
And when with conquest gain'd I come,
Array'd in law and terror home,
Ye'll rue this inauspicious morn,   395
And curse the day, when ye were born,
In Job's high style of imprecations,
With all his plagues, without his patience."
     Meanwhile beside the pole, the guard
A Bench of Justice had prepared,[24]   400
Where sitting round in awful sort
The grand Committee hold their Court;
While all the crew, in silent awe,
Wait from their lips the lore of law.
Few moments with deliberation   405
They hold the solemn consultation;
When soon in judgment all agree,
And Clerk proclaims the dread decree;
"That 'Squire M'Fingal having grown
The vilest Tory in the town,   410
And now in full examination
Convicted by his own confession,
Finding no tokens of repentance,
This Court proceeds to render sentence:
That first the Mob a slip-knot single   415

[21] Members of the Mandamus Council in Massachusetts. The operation of smoking Tories was thus performed. The victim was confined in a close room before a large fire of green wood, and a cover applied to the top of the chimney.
[22] Thomas Oliver, Esq. Lieut. Governor of Massachusetts. He was surrounded at his seat in the country and intimidated by the mob into the signing of his resignation.
[23] Rivington was a tory Printer in New-York. Just before the commencement of the war, a party from New-Haven attacked his press, and carried off or destroyed the types.
[24] An imitation of legal forms was universally practised by the mobs in New-England, in the trial and condemnation of Tories. This marks a curious trait of national character.

Tie round the neck of said M'Fingal,
And in due form do tar him next,
And feather, as the law directs;
Then through the town attendant ride him
In cart with Constable beside him,   420
And having held him up to shame,
Bring to the pole, from whence he came."
    Forthwith the crowd proceed to deck
With halter'd noose M'Fingal's neck,
While he in peril of his soul   425
Stood tied half-hanging to the pole;
Then lifting high the ponderous jar,
Pour'd o'er his head the smoking tar.
With less profusion once was spread
Oil on the Jewish monarch's head,   430
That down his beard and vestments ran,
And cover'd all his outward man.
As when (so Claudian sings) the Gods[25]
And earth-born Giants fell at odds,
The stout Enceladus in malice   435
Tore mountains up to throw at Pallas;
And while he held them o'er his head,
The river, from their fountains fed,
Pour'd down his back its copious tide,
And wore its channels in his hide: 440
So from the high-raised urn the torrents
Spread down his side their various currents;
His flowing wig, as next the brim,
First met and drank the sable stream;
Adown his visage stern and grave   445
Roll'd and adhered the viscid wave;
With arms depending as he stood,
Each cuff capacious holds the flood;
From nose and chin's remotest end,
The tarry icicles descend;   450
Till all o'erspread, with colors gay,
He glitter'd to the western ray,
Like sleet-bound trees in wintry skies,
Or Lapland idol carved in ice.
And now the feather-bag display'd   455
Is waved in triumph o'er his head,
And clouds him o'er with feathers missive,
And down, upon the tar, adhesive:[26]

[25] Claudian's Gigantomachia.
[26] Mercury, described by the Poets with wings on his head and feet.

Not Maia's son, with wings for ears,
Such plumage round his visage wears;   460
Nor Milton's six-wing'd angel gathers[27]
Such superfluity of feathers.
Now all complete appears our 'Squire,
Like Gorgon or Chimæra dire;
Nor more could boast on Plato's plan[28]   465
To rank among the race of man,
Or prove his claim to human nature,
As a two-legg'd, unfeather'd creature.
    Then on the fatal cart, in state
They raised our grand Duumvirate.   470
And as at Rome a like committee,[29]
Who found an owl within their city,
With solemn rites and grave processions
At every shrine perform'd lustrations;
And lest infection might take place   475
From such grim fowl with feather'd face,
All Rome attends him through the street
In triumph to his country seat:
With like devotion all the choir
Paraded round our awful 'Squire;   480
In front the martial music comes
Of horns and fiddles, fifes and drums,
With jingling sound of carriage bells,
And treble creak of rusted wheels.
Behind, the crowd, in lengthen'd row   485
With proud procession, closed the show.
And at fit periods every throat
Combined in universal shout;
And hail'd great Liberty in chorus,
Or bawl'd "confusion to the Tories."   490
Not louder storm the welkin braves
From clamors of conflicting waves;
Less dire in Lybian wilds the noise
When rav'ning lions lift their voice;
Or triumphs at town-meetings made,   495
On passing votes to regulate trade.[30]
    Thus having borne them round the town,
Last at the pole they set them down;

---

[27] And angel wing'd—six wings he wore—Milton.
[28] Alluding to Plato's famous definition of Man, Animal bipes implume—a two-legged animal without feathers.
[29] Livy's History.
[30] Such votes were frequently passed at town-meetings, with the view to prevent the augmentation of prices, and stop the depreciation of the paper money.

And to the tavern take their way
To end in mirth the festal day.   500
    And now the Mob, dispersed and gone,
Left 'Squire and Constable alone.
The constable with rueful face
Lean'd sad and solemn o'er a brace;
And fast beside him, cheek by jowl,   505
Stuck 'Squire M'Fingal 'gainst the pole,
Glued by the tar t' his rear applied,
Like barnacle on vessel's side.
But though his body lack'd physician,
His spirit was in worse condition.   510
He found his fears of whips and ropes
By many a drachm outweigh'd his hopes.
As men in jail without mainprize
View every thing with other eyes,
And all goes wrong in church and state,   515
Seen through perspective of the grate:
So now M'Fingal's Second-sight
Beheld all things in gloomier light;
His visual nerve, well purged with tar,
Saw all the coming scenes of war.   520
As his prophetic soul grew stronger,
He found he could hold in no longer.
First from the pole, as fierce he shook,
His wig from pitchy durance broke,
His mouth unglued, his feathers flutter'd,   525
His tarr'd skirts crack'd, and thus he utter'd.
    "Ah, Mr. Constable, in vain
We strive 'gainst wind and tide and rain!
Behold my doom! this feathery omen
Portends what dismal times are coming.   530
Now future scenes, before my eyes,
And second-sighted forms arise.
I hear a voice, that calls away,[31]
And cries 'The Whigs will win the day.'
My beck'ning Genius gives command,   535
And bids me fly the fatal land;
Where changing name and constitution,
Rebellion turns to Revolution,
While Loyalty, oppress'd, in tears,
Stands trembling for its neck and ears.   540
    "Go, summon all our brethren, greeting,

[31] I hear a voice, you cannot hear,
That says, I must not stay—*Tickell's Ballad.*

To muster at our usual meeting;
There my prophetic voice shall warn 'em
Of all things future that concern 'em,
And scenes disclose on which, my friend,   545
Their conduct and their lives depend.
There I—but first 'tis more of use,[32]
From this vile pole to set me loose;
Then go with cautious steps and steady,
While I steer home and make all ready."   550

                                    1775, 1782

[32] Quos Ego—sed motos præstat componere fluctus.—Virgil.

WILLIAM BYRD, II

(1674-1744)

1736 Present building at Westover probably completed.

1744 Died August 26; buried at Westover.

1841 First publication of Byrd's work in *The Westover Manuscripts: Containing the History of the Dividing Line Betwixt Virginia and North Carolina; A Journey to the Land of Eden, A.D. 1733; and A Progress to the Mines,* ed. Edmund Ruffin (Petersburg, Va., 1841).

BIBLIOGRAPHY:

The Writings of Colonel William Byrd of Westover, ed. J. S. Bassett (New York, 1901). *William Byrd's Histories of the Dividing Line,* ed. W. K. Boyd (Raleigh, N.C., 1929), contains text of *The Secret History of the Line. A Journey to the Land of Eden and Other Papers,* ed. Mark Van Doren (New York, 1928). *The Secret Diary of William Byrd of Westover, 1709-1712,* ed. Louis B. Wright and Marion Tinling (Richmond, Va., 1941). *Another Secret Diary of William Byrd of Westover, 1739-1741,* ed. Maude H. Woodfin and Marion Tinling (Richmond, Va., 1942). *The London Diary (1717-1721) and Other Writings,* ed. Louis B. Wright and Marion Tinling (New York, 1958). Richmond C. Beatty, *William Byrd of Westover* (Boston, 1932).

From *The History of the Dividing Line*

The first Settlement of this fine Country was owing to that great Ornament of the British Nation, Sir Walter Raleigh, who obtained a Grant thereof from Queen Elizabeth of ever-glorious Memory, by Letters Patent, dated March the 25th, 1584.

But whether that Gentleman ever made a Voyage thither himself is uncertain; because those who have favor'd the Public with an Account of His Life mention nothing if it. However, thus much may be depended on, that Sir Walter invited sundry persons of Distinction to Share in his Charter, and join their Purses with his in the laudable project of fitting out a Colony to Virginia.

Accordingly, 2 Ships were Sent away that very Year, under the Command of his good Friends Amidas and Barlow, to take possession of the Country in the Name of his Royal Mistress, the Queen of England. . . .

These first Adventurers made a very profitable Voyage, raising at least a Thousand per cent upon their Cargo. Amongst other Indian Commodities, they brought over Some of that bewitching Vegetable, Tobacco. And this being the first that ever came to England, Sir Walter thought he could do no less than make a present of Some of the brightest of it to His Royal Mistress for her own Smoking.

The Queen graciously accepted of it, but finding her Stomach sicken after two or three Whiffs, it was presently whispered by the earl of Leicester's Faction, that Sir Walter had certainly Poison'd Her. But Her Majesty soon recovering her Disorder, obliged the Countess of Nottingham and all her Maids to Smoke a whole Pipe out amongst them.

As it happened some Ages before to be the fashion to Saunter to the Holy Land, and go upon other Quixote Adventures, so it was now grown the Humor to take a Trip to America. The Spaniards had lately discovered Rich Mines in their Part of the West Indies, which made their Maritime Neighbors eager to do so too. This Modish Frenzy being still more Inflam'd by the Charming Account given of Virginia, by the first Adventurers, made many fond of removing to such a Paradise.

Happy was he, and still happier She, that could get themselves transported, fondly expecting their Coarsest Utensils, in that happy place, would be of Massy Silver.

This made it easy for the Company to procure as many Volunteers as they wanted for their new Colony; but, like most other Undertakers who have no Assistance from the Public, they Starved the Design by too much Frugality; for, unwilling to Launch out at first into too much Expense, they Ship't off but few People at a Time, and Those but Scantily provided. The Adventurers were, besides, Idle and extravagant, and expected they might live without work in so plentiful a Country.

These Wretches were set Ashore not far from Roanoke Inlet, but by some fatal disagreement, or Laziness, were either Starved or cut to Pieces by the Indians.

Several repeated Misadventures of this kind did, for some time, allay the Itch of Sailing to this New World; but the Distemper broke out again about the Year 1606. Then it happened that the Earl of Southampton and several other Persons, eminent for their Quality and Estates, were invited into the Company, who apply'd themselves once more to People the then almost abandon'd Colony. For this purpose they embarkt about an Hundred men, most of them Reprobates of good Families, and related to some of the company, who were men of Quality and Fortune.

The Ships that carried them made a Shift to find a more direct way to Virginia, and ventured thro the Capes into the Bay of Chesapeake. The same Night they came to an Anchor at the Mouth of Powatan, the same as James River, where they built a Small Fort at a Place call'd Point Comfort.

This Settlement stood its ground from that time forward in spite of all the Blunders and Disagreement of the first Adventurers, and the many Calamities that befell the Colony afterwards.

The six gentlemen who were first named of the company by the crown, and who were empowered to choose an annual President from among themselves, were always engaged in Factions and Quarrels, while the rest detested Work more than Famine. At this rate the Colony must have come to nothing, had it not been for the vigilance and Bravery of Capt. Smith, who struck a Terror into all the Indians round about. This Gentleman took some pains to persuade the men to plant Indian corn, but they lookt upon all Labor as a Curse.

. . . From Kiquotan they extended themselves as far as James-Town, where like true Englishmen, they built a Church that cost no more than Fifty Pounds, and a Tavern that cost Five hundred.

They had now made peace with the Indians, but there was one thing wanting to make that peace lasting. The Natives could, by no means, persuade themselves that the English were heartily their Friends, so long as they disdained to intermarry with them. And, in earnest, had the English consulted their own Security and the good of the Colony—Had they intended either to Civilize or Convert these Gentiles, they would have brought their Stomachs to embrace this prudent Alliance.

The Indians are generally tall and well-proportion'd, which may make full Amends for the Darkness of their Complexions. Add to this, that they are healthy & Strong, with Constitutions untainted by Lewdness, and not enfeebled by Luxury. Besides, Morals and all considered, I can't think the Indians were much greater Heathens than the first Adventurers, who, had they been good Christians, would have had the Charity to take this only method of converting the Natives to Christianity. For, after all that can be said, a sprightly Lover is the most prevailing Missionary that can be sent amongst these, or any other Infidels.

Besides, the poor Indians would have had less reason to Complain that the English took away their Land, if they had received it by way of Portion with their Daughters. Had such Affinities been contracted in the Beginning, how much Bloodshed had been prevented, and how populous would the Country have been, and, consequently, how considerable? Nor would the Shade of the Skin have been any reproach at this day; for if a Moor may be washt white in 3 Generations, Surely an Indian might have been blancht in two. . . .

Both the French and the Spaniards had, in the Name of their Respective Monarchs, long ago taken Possession of that Part of the Northern Continent that now goes by the Name of Carolina; but finding it Produced neither Gold nor Silver, as they greedily expected, and meeting such returns from the Indians as their own Cruelty and Treachery deserved, they totally abandoned it. In this deserted Condition that country lay for the Space of 90 Years, till King Charles the 2nd, finding it a Derelict, granted it away to the Earl of Clarendon and others, by His Royal Charter, dated March the 24th, 1663. The boundary of that Grant towards Virginia was a due West Line from Luck-Island, (the same as Colleton Island,) lying in 36 degrees N. Latitude, quite to the South Sea.

But afterwards Sir William Berkeley, who was one of the Grantees and at that time Governor of Virginia, finding a Territory of 31 Miles in Breadth between the Inhabited Part of Virginia and the above-mentioned Boundary of Carolina, advised the Lord Clarendon of it. And His Lordship had Interest enough with the King to obtain a Second Patent to include it, dated June the 30th, 1665.

This last Grant describes the Bounds between Virginia and Carolina in these Words: "To run from the North End of Corotuck-Inlet, due West to Weyanoke Creek, lying within or about the Degree of Thirty-Six and Thirty Minutes of Northern Latitude, and from thence West, in a direct Line, as far as the South-Sea." Without question, this Boundary was well known at the time the Charter was Granted, but in a long Course of years Weynoke Creek lost its name, so that it became a Controversy where it lay. Some Ancient Persons in Virginia affirmed it was the same with Wicocon, and others again in Carolina were as Positive it was Nottoway River. . . .

This Consideration put that Government upon entering into Measures with North Carolina, to terminate the Dispute, and settle a Certain Boundary between the two colonies. . . .

[*March* 5.] The day being now come, on which we had agreed to meet the Commissioners of North Carolina, we embarked very early, which we could the easier do, having no Temptation to stay where we were. We Shapt our Course along the South End of Knot's Island, there being no Passage open on the North.

Farther Still to the Southward of us, we discovered two Smaller Islands, that go by the names of Bell's and Churche's Isles. We also saw a small New England Sloop riding in the Sound, a little to the South of our Course. She had come in at the New-Inlet, as all other Vessels have done since the opening of it. This Navigation is a little difficult, and fit only for Vessels that draw no more than ten feet Water.

The Trade hither is engrosst by the Saints of New England, who carry off a great deal of Tobacco, without troubling themselves with paying that Impertinent duty of a Penny a Pound.

It was just Noon before we arrived at Coratuck Inlet, which is now so shallow that the Breakers fly over it with a horrible Sound, and at the same time afford a very wild Prospect. On the North side of the Inlet, the High Land terminated in a Bluff Point, from which a Spit of Sand extended itself towards the South-East, full half a Mile. The Inlet lies between that Spit and another on the South of it, leaving an Opening of not quite a Mile, which at this day is not practicable for any Vessel whatsoever. And as shallow as it now is, it continues to fill up more and more, both the Wind and Waves rolling in the Sands from the Eastern Shoals.

About two o'clock in the Afternoon we were joined by two of the Carolina Commissioners, attended by Mr. S——n, their Surveyor. The other two were not quite so punctual, which was the more unlucky for us, because there could be no sport till they came. These Gentlemen, it seems, had the Carolina-Commission in their keeping, notwithstanding which they could not forbear paying too much regard to a Proverb—fashionable in their Country,—not to make more haste than good Speed.

However, that we who were punctual might not spend our precious time unprofitably, we took the Several bearings of the Coast. We also surveyed part of the Adjacent High Land, which had scarcely any Trees growing upon it, but Cedars. Among the Shrubs, we were showed here and there a Bush of Carolina-Tea called Japon, which is one Species of the Phylarrea. This is an Evergreen, the Leaves whereof have some resemblance to Tea, but differ very widely both in Taste and Flavor.

We also found some few Plants of the Spired Leaf Silk grass, which is likewise an Evergreen, bearing on a lofty Stem a large Cluster of Flowers of a Pale Yellow. Of the Leaves of this Plant the People thereabouts twist very strong Cordage.

A virtuoso might divert himself here very well, in picking up Shells of various Hue and Figure, and amongst the rest, that Species of Conch Shell which the Indian Peak is made of. The Extremities of these Shells are Blue and the rest white, so that Peak of both these Colors are drilled out of one and the same Shell, Serving the Natives both for Ornament and Money, and are esteemed by them far beyond Gold and Silver.

The Cedars were of Singular use to us in the Absence of our Tent, which we had left with the rest of the Baggage for fear of overloading the Periaugas. We made a Circular Hedge of the Branches of this Tree, Wrought so close together as to fence us against the Cold Winds. We then kindled a rousing fire in the Center of it, and lay round it, like so many Knights Templars. But, as comfortable as this Lodging was, the Surveyors turned out about 2 in the Morning to try the Variation by a Meridian taken from the North Star, and found it to be somewhat less than three degrees West.

The Commissioners of the Neighboring Colony came better provided for the Belly than the Business. They brought not above two men along with them that would put their Hands to anything but the Kettle and the Frying-Pan. These spent so much of their Industry that way, that they had as little Spirit as Inclination for Work. . . .

[*March 10.*] The Sabbath happen'd very opportunely to give some ease to our jaded People, who rested religiously from every work, but that of cooking the Kettle. We observed very few corn-fields in our Walks, and those very small, which seem'd the Stranger to us, because we could see no other Tokens of Husbandry or Improvement. But, upon further Inquiry, we were given to understand People only made Corn for themselves and not for their Stocks, which know very well how to get their own Living.

Both Cattle and Hogs ramble in the Neighboring Marshes and Swamps, where they maintain themselves the whole Winter long, and are not fetch'd home till the Spring. Thus these Indolent Wretches, during one half of the Year, lose the Advantage of the Milk of their cattle, as well as their Dung, and many of the poor Creatures perish in the Mire, into the Bargain, by this ill Management.

Some, who pique themselves more upon Industry than their Neighbors, will, now and then, in compliment to their Cattle, cut down a Tree whose Limbs are loaden with the Moss aforemention'd. The trouble would be too great to Climb the Tree in order to gather this Provender, but the Shortest way (which in this Country is always counted the best) is to fell it, just like the Lazy Indians, who do the same by such Trees as bear fruit, and so make one Harvest for all. By this bad Husbandry Milk is so Scarce, in the Winter Season, that were a Big-belly'd Woman to long for it, She would lose her Longing. And, in truth, I believe this is often the Case, and at the same time a very good reason why so many People in this Province are markt with a Custard Complexion.

The only Business here is raising of Hogs, which is manag'd with the least Trouble, and affords the diet they are most fond of. The Truth of it is, the Inhabitants of N Carolina devour so much Swine's flesh, that it fills them full of gross Humors. For want too of a constant Supply of Salt, they are commonly obliged to eat it Fresh, and that begets the highest taint of Scurvy. Thus, whenever a Severe Cold happens to Constitutions thus Vitiated, 'tis apt to improve into the Yaws, called there very justly the country-Distemper. This has all the Symptoms of the Pox, with this Aggravation, that no Preparation of Mercury will touch it. First it seizes the Throat, next the Palate, and lastly shows its spite to the poor Nose, of which 'tis apt in a small time treacherously to undermine the Foundation.

This Calamity is so common and familiar here, that it ceases to be a Scandal, and in the disputes that happen about Beauty, the Noses have in some Companies much ado to carry it. Nay, 'tis said that once, after three good Pork years, a Motion had like to have been made in the House of Burgesses, that a Man with a Nose should be incapable of holding any Place of Profit in the Province; which Extraordinary Motion could never have been intended without Some Hopes of a Majority.

Thus, considering the foul and pernicious Effects of Eating Swine's Flesh in a hot Country, it was wisely forbidden and made an Abomination to the Jews, who liv'd much in the same Latitude with Carolina. . . .

[*March 23.*] It was very reasonable that the Surveyors, and the men who had been Sharers in their Fatigue, should now have a little Rest. They were all, except one, in good Health and good heart, blessed be God! notwithstanding the dreadful Hardships they have gone through. It was really a Pleasure to see the Cheerfulness wherewith they receiv'd the Order to prepare to re-enter the Dismal on the Monday following, in order to continue the Line from the Place where they had left off measuring, that so we might have the Exact Breadth of that Dirty Place. There were no more than two of them that could be persuaded to be reliev'd on this Occasion, or Suffer the other men to Share the Credit of that bold Undertaking, Neither would these have Suffer'd it had not one of them been very lame, and the Other much Indispos'd.

By the Description the Surveyors gave of the Dismal, we were convinc'd that nothing but the Exceeding dry Season we had been bless'd with could have made the passing of it practicable. It is the Source of no less than five Several Rivers which discharge themselves Southward into

Albemarle Sound, and of two that run northerly into Virignia. From thence 'tis easy to imagine that the Soil must be thoroughly Soakt with Water, or else there must be plentiful Stores of it under Ground; to supply so many Rivers; especially since there is no Lake, or any considerable Body of that Element to be seen on the Surface. The Rivers that Head in it from Virginia are the South Branch of Nansimond, and the West Branch of Elizabeth; and those from Carolina are North-west River, North River, Pasquetank, Little River, and Pequimons.

There is one remarkable part of the Dismal, lying to the south of the Line, that has few or no Trees growing on it, but contains a large Tract of tall Reeds. These being green all the Year round, and waving with every Wind, have procur'd it the Name of the Green Sea.

We are not yet acquainted with the precise Extent of the Dismal, the whole having never been Survey'd; but it may be Computed at a Medium to be about 30 Miles long and 10 Miles broad, tho' where the Line crost it, 'twas completely 15 Miles wide. But it seems to grow Narrower towards the North, or at least does so in many Places. The Exhalations that continually rise from this vast Body of mire and Nastiness infect the Air for many Miles round, and render it very unwholesome for the Bordering Inhabitants. It makes them liable to Agues, Pleurisies, and many other Distempers, that kill abundance of People, and make the rest look no better than Ghosts. It would require a great Sum of Money to drain it, but the Public Treasure could not be better bestow'd, than to preserve the Lives of his Majesty's Liege People, and at the same time render so great a Tract of swamp very Profitable, besides the advantage of making a Channel to transport by water-carriage goods from Albemarle Sound into Nansimond and Elizabeth Rivers, in Virginia.

[*March 24.*] This being Sunday, we had a Numerous congregation, which flockt to our Quarters from all the adjacent Country. The News that our Surveyors were come out of the Dismal, increas'd the Number very much, because it would give them an Opportunity of guessing, at least, whereabouts the Line would cut, whereby they might form Some Judgment whether they belong'd to Virginia or Carolina. Those who had taken up Land within the Disputed Bounds were in great pain lest it should be found to lie in Virginia; because this being done contrary to an Express Order of that government, the Patentees had great reason to fear they should in that case have lost their land. But their Apprehensions were now at an end, when they understood that all the Territory which had been controverted was like to be left in Carolina.

In the afternoon, those who were to re-enter the Dismal were furnisht with the Necessary Provisions, and Order'd to repair the Over-Night to their Landlord, Peter Binkley's, that they might be ready to begin their Business early on Monday Morning. Mr. Irvin was excus'd from the Fatigue, in compliment to his Lungs; but Mr. Mayo and Mr. Swan were Robust enough to return upon that painful Service, and, to do them Justice, they went with great Alacrity. The Truth was, they now knew the worst of it; and could guess pretty near at the time when they might hope to return to Land again.

[*March* 25.] The Air was chill'd this Morning with a Smart North-west Wind, which favored the Dismalites in their Dirty March. They return'd by the Path they had made in coming out, and with great Industry arriv'd in the Evening at the Spot where the Line had been discontinued.

After so long and laborious a Journey, they were glad to repose themselves on their couches of Cypress-bark, where their sleep was as sweet as it would have been on a Bed of Finland Down.

In the meantime, we who stay'd behind had nothing to do, but to make the best observations we could upon that Part of the Country. The Soil of our Landlord's Plantation, tho' none of the best, seem'd more fertile than any thereabouts, where the Ground is near as Sandy as the Deserts of Africa, and consequently barren. The Road leading from thence to Edenton, being in distance about 27 Miles, lies upon a Ridge call'd Sandy-Ridge, which is so wretchedly Poor that it will not bring Potatoes.

The Pines in this Part of the country are of a different Species from those that grow in Virginia: their bearded Leaves are much longer and their Cones much larger. Each Cell contains a Seed of the Size and Figure of a black-ey'd Pea, which, Shedding in November, is very good Mast for Hogs, and fattens them in a Short time.

The Smallest of these Pines are full of Cones, which are 8 or 9 Inches long, and each affords commonly 60 or 70 Seeds. This Kind of Mast has the Advantage of all other, by being more constant, and less liable to be nippt by the Frost, or Eaten by the Caterpillars. The Trees also abound more with Turpentine, and consequently yield more Tar, than either the Yellow or the White Pine; And for the same reason make more durable Timber for building. The Inhabitants hereabouts pick up Knots of Lightwood in Abundance, which they burn into tar, and then carry it to Norfolk or Nansimond for a Market. The Tar made in this method is the less Valuable, because it is said to burn the Cordage, tho' it is full as good for all other uses, as that made in Sweden and Muscovy.

Surely there is no place in the World where the Inhabitants live with less Labor than in N Carolina. It approaches nearer to the Description of Lubberland than any other, by the great felicity of the Climate, the easiness of raising Provisions, and the Slothfulness of the People.

Indian Corn is of so great increase, that a little Pains will Subsist a very large Family with Bread, and then they may have meat without any pains at all, by the Help of the Low Grounds, and the great Variety of Mast that grows on the High-land. The Men, for their Parts, just like the Indians, impose all the Work upon the poor Women. They make their Wives rise out of their Beds early in the Morning, at the same time that they lie and Snore, till the Sun has run one third of his course, and disperst all the unwholesome Damps. Then, after Stretching and Yawning for half an Hour, they light their Pipes, and, under the Protection of a cloud of Smoke, venture out into the open Air; tho', if it happens to be never so little cold, they quickly return Shivering into the Chimney corner. When the weather is mild, they stand leaning with both their arms upon the corn-field fence, and gravely consider whether they had best go and take a Small Heat at the Hough: but generally find reasons to put it off till another time.

Thus they loiter away their Lives, like Solomon's Sluggard, with their Arms across, and at the Winding up of the Year Scarcely have Bread to Eat.

To speak the Truth, 'tis a thorough Aversion to Labor that makes People file off to N Carolina, where Plenty and a Warm Sun confirm them in their Disposition to Laziness for their whole Lives.

[*March* 26.] Since we were like to be confin'd to this place, till the People return'd out of the Dismal, 'twas agreed that our Chaplain might Safely take a turn to Edenton, to preach the Gospel to the Infidels there, and Christen their Children. He was accompany'd thither by Mr. Little, One of the Carolina Commissioners, who, to show his regard for the Church, offer'd to treat Him on the Road with a Fricassee of Rum. They fried half a Dozen Rashers of very fat Bacon in a Pint of Rum, both which being disht up together, serv'd the Company at once for meat and Drink.

Most of the Rum they get in this Country comes from New England, and is so bad and unwholesome, that it is not improperly call'd "Kill-Devil." It is distill'd there from foreign molasses, which, if Skilfully manag'd, yields near Gallon for Gallon. Their molasses comes from the same country, and has the name of "Long Sugar" in Carolina, I suppose from the Ropiness of it, and Serves all the purposes of Sugar, both in their Eating and Drinking.

When they entertain their Friends bountifully, they fail not to set before them a Capacious Bowl of Bombo, so call'd from the Admiral of that name. This is a Compound of Rum and Water in Equal Parts, made palatable with the said long Sugar. As good Humor begins to flow, and the Bowl to Ebb, they take care to replenish it with Shear Rum, of which there always is a Reserve under the Table. But such Generous doings happen only when that Balsam of life is plenty; for they have often such Melancholy times, that neither Land-graves nor Cassicks can procure one drop for their Wives, when they lie in, or are troubled with the Colic or Vapors. Very few in this Country have the Industry to plant Orchards, which, in a Dearth of Rum, might supply them with much better Liquor.

The Truth is, there is one Inconvenience that easily discourages lazy People from making This improvement: very often, in Autumn, when the Apples begin to ripen, they are visited with Numerous Flights of parrakeets, that bite all the Fruit to Pieces in a moment, for the sake of the Kernels. The Havoc they make is Sometimes so great, that whole Orchards are laid waste in Spite of all the Noises that can be made, or Mawkins that can be dresst up, to fright 'em away. These Ravenous Birds visit North Carolina only during the warm Season, and so soon as the Cold begins to come on, retire back towards the Sun. They rarely Venture so far North as Virginia, except in a very hot Summer, when they visit the most Southern Parts of it. They are very Beautiful; but like some other pretty Creatures, are apt to be loud and mischievous.

[*March 27.*] . . . Within 3 or 4 Miles of Edenton, the Soil appears to be a little more fertile, tho' it is much cut with Slashes, which seem all to have a tendency towards the Dismal.

This Town is Situate on the North side of Albemarle Sound, which is there about 5 miles over. A Dirty Slash runs all along the Back of it, which in the Summer is a foul annoyance, and furnishes abundance of that Carolina plague, mosquitoes. There may be 40 or 50 Houses, most of them Small, and built without Expense. A Citizen here is counted Extravagant, if he has Ambition enough to aspire to a Brick-chimney. Justice herself is but indifferently Lodged, the Court-House having much the Air of a Common Tobacco-House. I believe this is the only Metropolis in the Christian or Mahometan World, where there is neither Church, Chapel, Mosque, Synagogue, or any other Place of Public Worship of any Sect or Religion whatsoever.

What little Devotion there may happen to be is much more private than their vices. The People seem easy without a Minister, as long as they are exempted from paying Him. Sometimes the Society for propagating the Gospel has had the Charity to send over Missionaries to this Country; but unfortunately the Priest has been too Lewd for the people, or, which oftener happens, they too lewd for the Priest. For these Reasons these Reverend Gentlemen have always left their Flocks as arrant Heathen as they found them. Thus much however may be said for the Inhabitants of Edenton, that not a Soul has the least taint of Hypocrisy, or Superstition, acting very Frankly and above-board in all their Excesses.

Provisions here are extremely cheap, and extremely good, so that People may live plentifully at a trifling expense. Nothing is dear but Law, Physic, and Strong Drink, which are all bad in their Kind, and the last they get with so much Difficulty, that they are never guilty of the Sin of Suffering it to Sour upon their Hands. Their Vanity generally lies not so much in having a handsome Dining-Room, as a Handsome House of Office: in this Kind of Structure they are really extravagant.

They are rarely guilty of Flattering or making any Court to their governors, but treat them with all the Excesses of Freedom and Familiarity. They are of Opinion their rulers would be apt to grow insolent, if they grew Rich, and for that reason take care to keep them poorer, and more dependent, if possible, than the Saints in New England used to do their Governors. They have very little coin, so they are forced to carry on their Home-Traffic with Paper-Money. This is the only Cash that will tarry in the Country, and for that reason the Discount goes on increasing between that and real Money, and will do so to the End of the Chapter.

1728, 1841

From *The Secret History of the Dividing Line*

[*March 23.*] The Surveyors described the Dismal to us in the following Manner. That it was in many places overgrown with tall Reeds interwoven with large Briars in which the Men were frequently entangled. And that not only in the Skirts of it, but likewise towards the Middle. In other places it was full of Juniper Trees, commonly so call'd, tho' they seem rather to be white Cedars. Some of these are of a great Bigness: but the Soil being soft & boggy, there is little hold for the Roots, & consequently any high Wind blows many of them down. By this means they lie in heaps, horsing upon one another, and brittling out with Sharp Snaggs, so that Passage in many places is difficult and Dangerous. The Ground was generally very quaggy, & the Impressions of the Men's feet were immediately fill'd with Water. So if there was any hole made it was soon full of that Element, & by that Method it was that our People supply'd themselves with drink. Nay if they made a Fire, in less than half an Hour, when the crust of Leaves & Trash were burnt thro', it would sink down into a Hole, & be extinguish't. So replete is this Soil with Water, that it could never have been passable, but in a very dry Season. And indeed considering it is the Source of 6 or 7 Rivers, without any Visible Body of Water to supply them, there must be great Stores of it under Ground. Some part of this Swamp has few or no Trees growing in it, but contains a large Tract of Reeds, which being perpetually green, & waving in the Wind, it is call'd the Green Sea. Gall-Bushes grow very thick in many parts of it, which are ever green Shrubs, bearing a Berry which dies a Black Color like the Galls of the Oak, & from thence they receive their Name.

Abundance of Cypress Trees grow likewise in this Swamp, and some Pines upon the Borders towards the firm Land, but the Soil is so moist & miry, that like the Junipers a high wind mows many of them down. It is remarkable that towards the middle of the Dismal no Beast or Bird or even Reptile can live, not only because of the softness of the Ground, but likewise because it is so overgrown with Thickets, that the Genial Beams of the Sun can never penetrate them. Indeed on the Skirts of it Cattle & Hogs will venture for the Sake of the Reeds, & Roots, with which they will keep themselves fat all the winter. This is a great Advantage to the Bordering Inhabitants in that particular, tho' they pay dear for it by the Agues & other distemper occasion'd by the Noxious Vapors that rise perpetually from that vast Extent of Mire & Nastiness. And a vast Extent it is, being computed at a Medium 10 Miles Broad, & 30 Miles long, tho' where the Line passed it, 'twas completely 15 miles broad. However this dirty Dismal is in many parts of it very pleasant to the Eye, tho' disagreeable to the other Senses, because there is an everlasting Verdure, which makes every Season look like the Spring. The way the Men took to Secure their Bedding here from moisture, was, by laying Cypress Bark under their Blankets, etc. which made their Lodging hard, but much more wholesome.

It is easy to imagine the hardships the poor Men underwent in this intolerable place, who besides the Burdens on their Backs, were oblig'd to clear the way before the Surveyors, & to measure & mark after them. However they went thro' it all not only with Patience, but cheerfulness. Tho' Orion was as peevish as an old Maid all the way, & more so, because he could persuade Nobody to be out of Humor but himself. The merriment of the Men, & their Innocent Jokes with one another, gave him great offense, whereas if he had had a grain of good Nature, he should have rejoiced to find, that the greatest difficulties could not break their Spirits, or lessen their good Humor. Robin Hix took the Liberty to make him some short replies, that discompos'd him very much, particularly one hot day when the poor Fellow had a Load fit for a Horse upon his Back, Orion had the Conscience to desire him to carry his great Coat. But he roundly refus'd it, telling him frankly he has already as great a Burden as he could Stagger under. This Orion stomach't so much, that he complain'd privately of it to Firebrand as soon as he saw him, but said not one Syllable of it to me. However I was inform'd of it by Astrolabe, but resolved to take no Notice, unless the cause was brought before us in Form, that the Person accus'd might have the English Liberty of being heard in his turn. But Firebrand Said a Gentleman should be believ'd on his bare word without Evidence, and a poor Man condemned without Trial, which agreed not at all with my Notions of Justice. I understand all this at 2nd hand, but Meanwell was let into the Secret by the Parties themselves, with the hopes of perverting him into their Sentiments, but he was Stauch, & they were not able to make the least Impression upon him. This was a grievous Balk, because if they could have gain'd him over, they flatter'd themselves they might have been as unrighteous as they pleased by a majority. As it happens to Persons disappointed it broil'd upon our Gentlemen's Stomachs so much, that they were but indifferent Company; and I observ'd very plain, that Firebrand joked less a days & swore more a Nights ever after. After these Misfortunes, to be formally civil was as much as we could afford to be to one another. Neither of us could dissemble enough to put on a gay outside when it was cloudy within. However this inward uneasiness helpt to make the rest of our Sufferings the more intolerable. When People are join'd together in a troublesome Commission, they should endeavor to sweeten by Complacency & good Humor all the Hazards & Hardships they are bound to encounter, & not like marry'd People make their condition worse by everlasting discord. Tho' in this indeed we had the Advantage of marry'd People, that a few Weeks would part us.   1728, 1929

From *A Journey to the Land of Eden, A. D. 1733*

[*Sept. 20.*] Everything being ready for a March, we left Blue Stone Castle about ten. My Company consisted of 4 Gentlemen (Namely, Maj. Mayo, Maj. Mumford, Mr. Banister and Mr. Jones,) and 5 Woodsmen, Thomas Wilson, Henry Morris, Joseph Colson, Robert Bolling and Thomas Hooper, 4 Negroes and 3 Tuscaruda Indians. With this small Troop we proceeded up the River as far as Hogen's, above which, about a quarter of a Mile, we forded into the little Island, and from thence into the Fork of the River. The Water was risen so high, that it ran into the Top of my Boots, but without giving me any Cold, altho I rid in my wet Stockings. We Landed 3 Miles above the point of the Fork, and, after marching three Miles farther, reacht the Tenement of Peter Mitchell, the highest Inhabitant on Roanoke River. Two Miles above that we forded a Water, which we named Birch's Creek, not far from the Mouth, where it discharges itself into the Dan. From thence we rode thro charming Low-Grounds, for 6 Miles together, to a larger Stream, which we agreed to call Banister River. We were puzzled to find a Ford by reason the Water was very high, but at last got safe over, about 1½ Mile from the Banks of the Dan. In our way we kill'd 2 very large Rattle-Snakes, One of 15 and the other of 12 Rattles. They were both fat, but nobody would be persuaded to carry them to our Quarters, altho they would have added much to the Luxury of our Supper. We pitcht our Tents upon Banister River, where we feasted on a Young Buck which had the ill luck to cross our way. It rain'd great part of the Night, with very loud Thunder, which rumbled frightfully amongst the tall Trees that Surrounded us in that low Ground, but, thank God! without any Damage. Our Indians kill'd 3 deer, but were so lazy they brought them not to the Camp, pretending for their Excuse that they were too lean.

[*Sept. 21.*] The necessity of drying our Baggage prevented us from marching till 11 o'clock. Then we proceeded thro low-Grounds which were tolerably wide for 3 Miles together, as far as a Small Creek, named by us Morris's Creek. This Tract of Land I persuaded Mr. Banister to enter for, that he might not be a loser by the Expedition. The Low Grounds held good a Mile beyond the Creek, and then the Highland came quite to the River, and made our traveling more difficult. All the way we went we perceiv'd there had been tall Canes lately growing on the Bank of the River, but were universally kill'd; And inquiring into the reason of this destruction, we were told that the Nature of those Canes was, to shed their Seed but once in Seven Years, and the Succeeding

Winter to die, and make Room for Young ones to grow up in their Places. Thus much was certain, that 4 Years before we saw Canes grow and flourish in Several Places, where they now lay dead and dry upon the Ground. The whole distance we travel'd in this day by Computation was 15 Miles, and then the Appearance of a black Cloud, which threaten'd a Gust, oblig'd us to take up our Quarters. We had no sooner got our Tents over our Heads, but it began to rain and thunder furiously, and one Clap succeeded the Lightening the same Instant, and made all tremble before it. But, blessed be God! it spent its fury upon a tall Oak just by our Camp. Our Indians were so fearful of falling into the hands of the Cataubas, that they durst not lose Sight of us all day; so they kill'd nothing, and we were forc'd to make a temperate Supper upon Bread and Cheese. It was Strange we met with no Wild Turkeys, this being the Season in which great Numbers of them used to be seen towards the Mountains. They commonly perch on the high Trees near the Rivers and Creeks. But this Voyage, to our great Misfortune, there were none to be found. So that we could not commit that Abomination, in the Sight of all Indians, of mixing the Flesh of Deer & Turkey in our Broth.

[*Sept. 22.*] We were again oblig'd to dry our Baggage, which had thoroughly soakt with the heavy Rain that fell in the Night. While we stayed for that, our Hunters knockt down a Brace of Bucks, wherewith we made ourselves amends for our Scanty Supper the aforegoing Night. All these Matters being duly perform'd made it near Noon before we Sounded to Horse. We marcht about 2 Miles over fine low-Grounds to a most pleasant Stream, which we nam'd the Medway, and by the way discover'd a rich Neck of Highland that lay on the South Side of the Dan, and lookt very tempting. Two Miles beyond the Medway, we forded another Creek, which we called Maosty Creek. The whole distance between these 2 Streams lay exceeding rich Land, & the same continued 2 Miles higher. This body of Low-Ground tempted me to enter for it, to serve as a Stage between my Land at the Fork, and the Land of Eden. The Heavens lookt so menacing that we resolved to take up our Quarters 2 Miles above Maosty Creek, where we intrencht ourselves on a rising Ground. We had no sooner taken these Precautions, but it began to rain unmercifully, and to put out our Fire as fast as we could kindle it; nor was it only a hasty Shower, but continued with great impetuosity most part of the Night. We preferred a dry Fast to a Wet Feast, being unwilling to expose the People to the Weather, to gratify an unreasonable Appetite. However it was some comfort, in the Midst of our Abstinence, to dream of the delicious Breakfast we intended to make next Morning, upon a fat Doe and two-year-Old Bear our Hunters had kill'd the Evening before. Notwithstanding all the Care we could take, several of the Men were dripping wet, and among the rest, Harry Morris dabbled so long in the Rain, that he was seized with a Violent Fit of an Ague that Shook him almost out of all his Patience. . . .

[*Sept.* 25.] The Weather now befriending us, we despatcht our little Affairs in good time, and marcht in a Body to the Line. It was already grown very dim, by reason many of the markt Trees were burnt or blown down. However, we made Shift, after riding little more than half a Mile, to find it, and having once found it, stuck as close to it as we could. After a March of 2 Miles, we got upon Cane Creek, where we saw the same Havoc amongst the Old Canes that we had observ'd in other places, & a whole Forest of Young Ones Springing up in their Stead. We pursued our Journey over Hills and Dales till we arriv'd at the Second Ford of the Dan, which we past with no other Damage than Sopping a little of our Bread, and Shipping some Water at the Tops of our Boots. The late Rains having been a little immoderate, had rais'd the Water and made a current in the River. We drove on 4 Miles farther to a plentiful Run of very clear Water, and quarter'd on a rising Ground a Bow-Shot from it. We had no sooner pitcht the Tents, but one of our Woodsmen alarm'd us with the News that he had follow'd the Track of a great Body of Indians to the place where they had lately encampt. That there he had found no less than Ten Huts, the Poles whereof had Green Leaves still fresh upon them. That each of these Huts had Shelter'd at least Ten Indians, who, by some infallible Marks, must have been Northern Indians. That they must needs have taken their departure from thence no longer ago than the day before, having erected those Huts to protect themselves from the late Heavy Rains. These Tidings I could perceive were a little Shocking to some of the Company, and particularly the little Major, whose Tongue had never lain still, was taken Speechless for 16 Hours. I put as good a Countenance upon the Matter as I could, assuring my Fellow Travelers, that the Northern Indians were at Peace with us, and altho one or two of them may now and then commit a Robbery or a Murder, (as other Rogues do,) yet nationally and avowedly they would not venture to hurt us. And in Case they were Cataubas, the Danger would be as little from them, because they are too fond of our Trade to lose it for the pleasure of Shedding a little English Blood. But Supposing the worst, that they might break thro all the Rules of Self-Interest, and attack us, yet we ought to stand bravely on our defense, and sell our lives as dear as we could. That we should have no more fear on this Occasion, than just to make us more watchful and better provided to receive the Enemy, if they had the Spirit to venture upon us. This reasoning of mine, tho it could not remove the Panic, yet it abated something of the Palpitation, and made us double our Guard. However, I found it took off the Edge of most of our Appetites, for every thing but the Rum Bottle, which was more in favor than ever, because of its Cordial Quality. I Hurt my other Knee this afternoon, but not enough to spoil either my dancing or my Stomach.

[*Sept.* 26.] We liked the place so little that we were glad to leave it this Morning as soon as we could. For that reason we were all on Horseback before Nine, and after riding 4 Miles arriv'd at the Mouth of Sable Creek. On the Eastern Bank of that Creek, 6 Paces from the Mouth, and just at the Brink of the River Dan, stands a Sugar Tree, which is the beginning of my fine Tract of land in Carolina, call'd the Land of Eden. I caus'd the Initial Letters of my name to be cut on a large Poplar and Beech near my Corner, for the more easy finding it another time. We then made a beginning of my Survey, directing our Course due South from the Sugar Tree above-mention'd. In a little way we perceived the Creek forkt, and the Western Branch was wide enough to merit the name of a River. That to the East was much less, which we intersected with this Course. We ran Southerly a Mile, and found the Land good all the way, only towards the End of it we saw the Trees destroy'd in such a Manner that there were hardly any left to mark my Bounds. Having finisht this Course, we encampt in a charming Peninsula, form'd by the Western Branch of the Creek. It contain'd about 40 Acres of very Rich Land, gradually descending to the Creek, and is a delightful Situation for the Manor House. My Servant had fed so intemperately upon Bear, that it gave him a Scouring, and that was followed by the Piles, which made riding worse to him than Purgatory. But anointing with the Fat of the same Bear, he soon grew easy again.

[*Sept. 27.*] We were stirring early from this enchanting place, and ran 8 Miles of my back Line, which tended South 84½ Westerly. We found the Land uneven, but tolerably good, tho very thin of Trees, and those that were standing fit for little but fuel and Fence-Rails. Some Conflagration had effectually open'd the Country, and made room for the Air to circulate. We crost both the Branches of Low Land Creek, and Sundry other Rills of fine Water. From every Eminence we discovr'd the Mountains to the N. West of us, tho' they seem'd to be a long way off. Here the Air felt very refreshing and agreeable to the Lungs, having no Swamps or Marshes to taint it. Nor was this the only good Effect it had, but it likewise made us very hungry, so that we were forc'd to halt and pacify our Appetites with a frugal Repast out of our Pockets, which we washt down with Water from a Purling Stream just by. My knees pain'd me very much, tho' I broke not the Laws of Travelling by uttering the least Complaint. Measuring and marking spent so much of our Time, that we could advance no further than 8 Miles, and the Chain Carriers thought that a great way. In the Evening we took up our Quarters in the Low-Grounds of the River, which our Scouts inform'd us was but 200 Yards ahead of us. This was no Small surprise, because we had flatter'd ourselves that this Back Line would not have Intersected the Dan at all; but we found Ourselves mistaken, and plainly perceived that it ran more Southerly than we imagined, and in all likelihood pierces the Mountains where they form an Amphitheater. The Venison here was lean; and the misfortune was we met no Bear in so open a Country, to grease the way and make it Slip down. In the Night our Sentinel alarm'd us with an Idle Suspicion that he heard the Indian Whistle, (which amongst them is a Signal for attacking their Enemies.) This made every one Stand manfully to his Arms in a Moment, and I found nobody more undismayed in this Surprise than Mr. Banister; But after we had put ourselves in Battle Array, we discover'd this Whistle to be nothing but the Nocturnal Note of a little harmless Bird, that inhabits those Woods. We were glad to find the Mistake, and commending the Sentinel for his great Vigilance, compos'd our Noble Spirits again to rest till the Morning. However, some of the Company dream'd of nothing but Scalping all the rest of the Night.

1733, 1841

From *The Secret Diary*

[1709]

[*March 25.*] I rose at 6 o'clock and read two chapters in Hebrew and 200 verses in Homer's *Odyssey*. I said my prayers and ate milk for breakfast. I danced my dance. The Doctor went to Williamsburg. I wrote a letter to England. Parson Ware sent to me for a pint of canary, he being sick of the gripes with the New England rum, which I sent him, notwithstanding I have but a little, because I should be glad if I were in his condition to receive such a kindness from another. Mrs. J-f-r-y was sick again today. I ate nothing but hash of beef. In the afternoon I took a nap, contrary to custom. I settled my accounts. In the evening we walked about the plantation. I said my prayers. I had good thoughts, good health, and good humor all day, thanks to God Almighty. . . .

26. I rose at 6 o'clock and read three chapters in Hebrew and 200 verses in Homer's *Odyssey*. I said my prayers, and ate milk for breakfast. I danced my dance. I wrote a letter to England. My river sloop came about noon from Appomattox, with 25 hogsheads of tobacco. I ate tripe for dinner. Before we had dined Mr. Hardiman came to see me but would not eat. In the afternoon Peter Hamlin came also. We played at billiards. In the evening we took a walk about the plantation. I read Italian and some of my own work to the ladies. I had good health, good thoughts, and good humor all day, thanks be to God Almighty. The sloop brought two barrels of tar and 10 hides. . . .

[*April 23.*] I rose at 6 o'clock and read two books in Homer. I said my prayers, and ate milk for breakfast. I went to the President's, where I learned that the Tuscarora Indians would not deliver up the men we demanded and Colonel Harrison now wrote that now it was his opinion the trade should be open, contrary to what he thought before. I did a great deal of business and dined with the President because it was St. George his day. Then I went with Colonel Ludwell to Green Springs with Colonel Carter, where we danced and were very merry. I neglected to say my prayers. I had good thoughts, good humor, and good health, thanks be to God Almighty.

24. I rose at 6 o'clock and said my prayers very shortly. We breakfasted about 10 o'clock and I ate nothing but bread and butter and sack. We rode to Jamestown Church, where Mr. Commissary preached. When church was done I gave 10 shillings to the poor. Nothing could hinder me from sleeping at church, though I took a great deal of pains against it. We rode home to Colonel Ludwell's again where we dined and I ate fish and asparagus. In the afternoon we took a walk and saw the carcasses of 50 cows which had been burnt in a house belonging to Colonel Ludwell. Mr. W-l-s ran two races and beat John Custis and Mr. [Hawkins]. He likewise jumped over the fence which was a very great jump. Colonel Carter returned to town with Mr. Harrison and we stayed and ate syllabub for supper. I neglected to say my prayers. I had good thoughts, good humor, and good health, thanks be to God Almighty. . . .

26. I rose at 6 o'clock and read two books in Homer and two chapters in Hebrew. I said my prayers, and ate milk for breakfast. We went to the Council where it was agreed to open the Indian trade. I did a great deal of business. The sheriffs were appointed this day. They passed several accounts. About 4 o'clock we went to dinner and I ate nothing but beef. Then I took a walk and came to Mr. Bland's, from whence Mr. Will Randolph and I went to Colonel Bray's, where we found abundance of ladies and gentlemen dancing. We did not dance but got some kisses among them. About 11 o'clock we returned home. I recommended myself to the divine protection. I had good health, good thoughts, and good humor, thanks be to God Almighty.

27. I rose at 6 o'clock and read two books in Homer and a chapter in Hebrew. I said my prayers and ate milk for breakfast. I wrote a letter to my wife by Will Randolph. I did abundance of business. My sister Custis came to town on her way to Major Burwell's. I went to wait on her at Mr. Bland's, where came abundance of other ladies. I stayed with them two hours. My brother and sister Custis went away. I paid several of the Council their money. I agreed with Captain C–l to give him bills for money at five guineas per cent. I went to dinner where I ate nothing but mutton hash. After dinner we played at cricket and then went to whist and I lost 30 shillings. I went home about 11 o'clock. I had good health, good thoughts, and good humor all day, thanks be to God Almighty. . . .

[May 4.] I rose at 6 o'clock and read in Lucian, ate milk for breakfast, and walked out and said my prayers in the open. A ship arrived in York River about 9 o'clock. Captain Berkeley came to see us, who is a very good-humored man. We walked in the garden about an hour; then we went to dinner and I ate boiled beef. In the afternoon we danced a minuet and then took our leave and returned over the river again to Major Burwell's where we found Colonel Bassett and his lady who are very good people. In the evening we saw a great ship sail up the river. The Major sent on board for his letters which brought no news. We sat up talking till 10 o'clock. I had good health, good thoughts, and good humor, thanks be to God Almighty.

5. I rose at 6 o'clock and ate milk for breakfast, and neglected to say my prayers, for which God forgive me. I read in Lucian. About 11 o'clock I ate some bread and butter and sack, and then took leave of Major Burwell and rode to Williamsburg with Colonel Bassett. On the way we met Mr. Ingles with his wife and daughter who were going to see us. When we came to Williamsburg, I delivered to Mr. Bland £600 in money to pay for the use of the vessel to guard the country. I gave Colonel Bassett a bottle of wine and then took our leave of him and Mr. Bland and proceeded to Green Springs where we found Nat Harrison and his wife and Mr. Edwards. I ate mutton and salad for supper. About 11 o'clock we went to bed. I had good health, good thoughts, and good humor, thanks be to God Almighty.

6. I rose about 6 o'clock and Colonel Ludwell, Nat Harrison, Mr. Edwards and myself played at cricket, and I won a bit. Then we played at whist and I won. About 10 o'clock we went to breakfast and I ate some boiled rice. Then Colonel Ludwell went to Jamestown court and then we played at [l-n-s-n-t] and I lost £4, most of which Nat Harrison won. In the afternoon Colonel Ludwell returned and brought us the bad news that Captain Morgan had lost his ship in Margate Roads by a storm as likewise had several others. My loss was very great in this ship where I had seven hogsheads of skins and 60 hogsheads of heavy tobacco. The Lord gives and the Lord has taken away—blessed be the name of the Lord. In the evening Mr. Clayton and Mr. Robinson came and confirmed the same bad news. However I ate a good supper of mutton and asparagus. Then we went to dance away sorrow. I had good health, good thoughts, and good humor, notwithstanding my misfortune, thanks be to God Almighty. . . .

[June 10.] I rose at 5 o'clock this morning but could not read anything because of Captain Keeling, but I played at billiards with him and won a half a crown of him and the Doctor. George B-th brought home my boy Eugene. I ate milk for breakfast, but neglected to say my prayers, for which God forgive me. The Captain and I had some discourse about the philosopher's stone which he [is following with great diligence]. He stayed to dinner. I ate mutton for dinner. In the afternoon he went away. I read some Greek in Homer. In the evening I took a walk about the plantation. Eugene was whipped for running away and had the [bit] put on him. I said my prayers and had good health, good thoughts, and good humor, thanks be to God Almighty. . . .

12. I rose at 5 o'clock and read two chapters in Hebrew and some Greek in Josephus. I said my prayers and ate milk for breakfast. I re-

ceived a letter from my dear friend Admiral Wager from Jamaica which signified his health and the continuance of his friendship. We went to church and heard a sermon. Nobody came home with us but Mr. Gee. I ate mutton pie for dinner. Mr. Gee stayed here till the evening and according to his custom spoke against several people like any woman. I walked about the plantation. The weather was grown much cooler. I said my prayers and had good health, good thoughts, and good humor, thanks be to God Almighty.

13. I rose at 5 o'clock and read two chapters in Hebrew but no Greek by reason that Captain Collins came to see me, who came out of England about seven weeks ago and says the fleet came out 13 days before him and may be every day expected because they had been above nine weeks out of England. He brought me some letters from England. I had a great deal of discourse with him and drank chocolate for breakfast. I said my prayers. About 11 o'clock we rode to Drury Stith's where we met Mr. Anderson and his wife and Mr. Eppes. I ate pork and turnips for dinner. Then we played at nine-pins. In the evening Mr. Harrison and Colonel Eppes came to us, having been around the neighborhood of Chickahominy. We returned home and found all well, thanks be to God. I neglected to say my prayers. I had good health, good thoughts, and good humor, thanks to be God Almighty. . . .

[Nov. 1.] I rose at 8 o'clock because I could not leave my wife sooner. Then I ate milk for breakfast. I neglected to say my [prayers] nor could I read anything. About 11 o'clock I went to Williamsburg and about 12 took my place in court. I sat there till about 4 and could not go out of town because I had accounts to settle with several people. About 5 o'clock we went to dinner and I ate boiled beef. Then the President took us home to his house, where I played at cards and won 35 shillings. We were very merry and in that condition went to the coffee house and again disturbed Colonel Churchill. About 11 o'clock I went home and said a short prayer. I had good health, good thoughts, and good humor, thanks be to God Almighty.

2. I rose at 6 o'clock and read a chapter in Hebrew and some Greek in Lucian. I said my prayers and ate milk for breakfast, and settled some accounts, and then went to court where we made an end of the business. We went to dinner about 4 o'clock and I ate boiled beef again. In the evening I went to Dr. [Barret's] where my wife came this afternoon. Here I found Mrs. Chiswell, my sister Custis, and other ladies. We sat and talked till about 11 o'clock and then retired to our chambers. I played at [r-m] with Mrs. Chiswell and kissed her on the bed till she was angry and my wife also was uneasy about it, and cried as soon as the company was gone. I neglected to say my prayers, which I should not have done, because I ought to beg pardon for the lust I had for another man's wife. However I had good health, good thoughts, and good humor, thanks be to God Almighty. . . .

[1710]

[*Sept. 19.*] I rose at 6 o'clock and read a chapter in Hebrew and some Greek in Lucian. I said my prayers and ate boiled milk for breakfast. I danced my dance. The house and ground was made clean to receive the Governor. We gave the child the bark which put away her fit. Several of the negroes were sick. I ate roast beef for dinner. In the afternoon I caused all the rut to be cut away that lay at the woodpile and the pasture to be made clean. I caused a hogshead of punch to be made for the people when they should come to muster. Joe Wilkinson sent us some strawberries and peaches by little Peter who told me all the people were well and that Joe Wilkinson carried all the cider away. In the evening I took a walk. I neglected to say my prayers but had good health, good thoughts, and good humor, thank God Almighty.

20. I rose at 6 o'clock and read nothing because I prepared for the Governor's coming in the evening. I neglected to say my prayers but ate milk for breakfast. I settled several things in my library. All the wood was removed from the place where it used to lay to a better place. I sent John to kill some blue wing and he had good luck. I ate some boiled beef for dinner. In the afternoon all things were put into the best order because Captain Burbydge sent word that the Governor would be here at 4 o'clock but he did not come till 5. Captain Burbydge sent his boat for him and fired as he came up the river. I received at the landing with Mr. C—s and gave him three guns. Mr. Clayton and Mr. Robinson came with him. After he had drunk some wine he walked in the garden and into the library till it was dark. Then we went to supper and ate some blue wing. After supper we sat and talked till 9 o'clock. I neglected to say my prayers but had good health, good thoughts, and good humor, thank God Almighty.

21. I rose at 6 o'clock and read nothing but got ready to receive the company. About 8 o'clock the Governor came down. I offered him some of my fine water. Then we had milk, tea and bread and butter for breakfast. The Governor was pleased with everything and very complaisant. About 10 o'clock Captain Stith came and soon after him Colonel Hill, Mr. Anderson, and several others of the militia officers. The Governor was extremely courteous to them. About 12 o'clock Mr. Clayton went to Mrs. Harrison's and then orders were given to bring all the men into the pasture to muster. Just as we got on our horses it began to rain hard; however, this did not discourage the Governor but away we rode to the men. It rained half an hour and the Governor mustered them all the while and he presented me to the people to be their colonel and commander-in-chief. About 3 o'clock we returned to the house and as many of the officers as could sit at the table stayed to dine with the Governor, and the rest went to take part of the hogshead in the churchyard. We had a good dinner, well served, with which the Governor seemed to be well pleased. I ate venison for dinner. In the evening all the company

went away and we took a walk and found a comic freak of a man that was drunk that hung on the pales. Then we went home and played at piquet and I won the pool. About 9 the Governor went to bed. I had good health, good thoughts, and good humor, thank God, but neglected to say my prayers.

22. I rose at 6 o'clock but read nothing. About 8 the Governor appeared and we had nothing but milk tea for breakfast, and bread and butter. I neglected to say my prayers. About 10 o'clock we got on our horses and rode towards Henrico to see the militia. Colonel Randolph with a troop met us at Pleasant's mill and conducted us to his plantation, where all the men were drawn up in good order. The Governor was pleased with them and exercised them for two or three hours together. He presented me likewise to them to be their commander-in-chief [who] received me with an huzzah. About 3 o'clock we went to Colonel Randolph's house and had a dinner and several of the officers dined with us and my hogshead of punch entertained all the people and made them drunk and fighting all the evening, but without much mischief. Some of the French came to wait on the Governor and Mr. Salle made him a speech. We sat up till 10 o'clock. I neglected to say my prayers but had good health, good thoughts, and good humor, thank God Almighty.

23. I rose about 7 o'clock but read nothing. About 8 the Governor appeared and several of the French came to wait on the Governor. He recommended to them, and particularly to Mr. Salle and to the parson, to live in peace and to be reconciled to one another. The parson [seemed] more difficult to be reconciled than anybody, which the Governor resented and told them if they put him to the trouble of hearing their disagreement he would never forgive them that were in fault. This frightened them into an agreement and they promised that they would forgive what was past and for the future live with kindness to one another. Mr. Anderson made them a speech to that purpose. We had breakfast about 10 o'clock and I ate blue wing. Then the French company was exercised and performed very well and the Governor made out of them a troop of dragoons with orders that Mr. Salle should command them as well as the foot. About 3 o'clock we went from hence to Colonel Hill's where we supped and I ate roast beef. We sat up till 9 o'clock but I was sleepy before that. I neglected to say my prayers but had good health, good thoughts, and good humor, thank God Almighty. . . .

[1711]

[*Feb. 6.*] I rose about 9 o'clock but was so bad I thought I should not have been in condition to go to Williamsburg, and my wife was so kind to [say] she would stay with me, but rather than keep her from going I resolved to go if possible. I was shaved with a very dull razor, and ate some boiled milk for breakfast but neglected to say my prayers. About 10 o'clock I went to Williamsburg without the ladies. As soon as I got there it began to rain, which hindered about [sic] the company from coming. I went to the President's where I drank tea and went with him to the Governor's and found him at home. Several gentlemen were there and about 12 o'clock several ladies came. My wife and her sister came about 2. We had a short Council but more for form than for business. There was no other appointed in the room of Colonel Digges. My cold was a little better so that I ventured among the ladies, and Colonel Carter's wife and daughter were among them. It was night before we went to supper, which was very fine and in good order. It rained so that several did not come that were expected. About 7 o'clock the company went in coaches from the Governor's house to the capitol where the Governor opened the ball with a French dance with my wife. Then I danced with Mrs. Russell and then several others and among the rest Colonel Smith's son, who made a sad freak. Then we danced country dances for an hour and the company was carried into another room where was a very fine collation of sweetmeats. The Governor was very gallant to the ladies and very courteous to the gentlemen. About 2 o'clock the company returned in the coaches and because the drive was dirty the Governor carried the ladies into their coaches. My wife and I lay at my lodgings. Colonel Carter's family and Mr. Blair were stopped by the unruliness of the horses and Daniel Wilkinson was so gallant as to lead the horses himself through all the dirt and rain to Mr. Blair's house. My cold continued bad. I neglected to say my prayers and had good thoughts, good humor, but indifferent health, thank God Almighty. It rained all day and all night. The President had the worst clothes of anybody there.

7. I rose at 8 o'clock and found my cold continued. I said my prayers and ate boiled milk for breakfast. I went to see Mr. Clayton who lay sick of the gout. About 11 o'clock my wife and I went to wait on the Governor in the President's coach. We went there to take our leave but were forced to stay all day. The Governor had made a bargain with his servants that if they would forbear to drink upon the Queen's birthday, they might be drunk this day. They observed their contract and did their business very well and got very drunk today, in such a manner that Mrs. Russell's maid was forced to lay the cloth, but the cook in that condition made a shift to send in a pretty little dinner. I ate some mutton cutlets. In the afternoon I persuaded my wife to stay all night in town and so it was resolved to spend the evening in cards. My cold was very bad and I lost my money. About 10 o'clock the Governor's coach carried us home to our lodgings where my wife was out of humor and I out of order. I said a short prayer and had good thoughts and good humor, thank God Almighty. . . .

[*Sept. 23.*] I rose about 7 o'clock and found the weather grown very cold, the wind at northeast. I said my prayers and ate boiled milk for breakfast. All the rest of the company drank drams plentifully. Everybody showed me abundance of respect. About 10 o'clock the whole company went to breakfast and I among them and I ate some stewed fowl. About 11 we went to church with Will Kennon's troop to wait on me and there we found Captain Jefferson's, Captain Bolling's, Captain Eppes', and Captain Worsham's troops and companies which made a good appearance. Everybody respected me like a king. Mr. Robinson gave us a sermon and when church was done I reviewed the troops again and then with all the officers we went to Colonel Eppes' to dinner and I ate boiled beef. All the drink I used was cider. We were very merry all the evening only the Colonel had his ague moderately. I said my prayers and had good health, good thoughts, and good humor, thank God Almighty. . . .

[1712]

[*March* 9.] I rose about 6 o'clock and read two chapters in Hebrew and some Greek in Lucian. I said my prayers devoutly and ate boiled milk for breakfast. I danced my dance. The weather was pretty warm and clear, notwithstanding it had been a frost this night. I took a walk about the plantation and my wife with me and then read some English in Milton. The man returned who came from my brother Duke's and promised to come about 14 days hence to work for me, he being a bricklayer. His name is Cornelius H—l, a man of above 80 years old and yet he walked from Mr. Duke's over. I ate some fish for dinner. In the afternoon I read some English in Milton but was ready to fall asleep and therefore I took a walk about the plantation and saw several hogs of other people in my pasture. When I returned I found Mr. Mumford who told me all was well at Appomattox. In the evening the sloop came and brought me news that my negro C-c-r, the smith, was dead. I neglected to say my prayers but had good health, good thoughts, and good humor, thank God Almighty.

10. I . . . rose about 7 o'clock but read nothing because Mr. Mumford was here and because they set up a case for my clothes. I neglected to say my prayers but had boiled milk for breakfast. I caused the sloop to be unloaded and then sent her away with 25 hogsheads of tobacco on board the [. . .] "Pelican". Mr. Mumford and I took a walk with our bows and then played at billiards and he beat me. I ate some cod sounds for dinner. John G—r—l had a pain in his ear very violently. In the afternoon we played at billiards again and he beat me. Then we took a walk again about the plantation. The weather was warm and clear. At night I read some news but found myself exceedingly sleepy and took a nap in the chair for about an hour and Mr. Mumford took a nap also but the women sang and were merry. I said my prayers and had good health, good thoughts, and good humor, thank God Almighty.

11. I rose about 6 o'clock and read a little Greek but no Hebrew because I prepared for my journey to Major Harrison's. I said my prayers and ate boiled milk for breakfast. About 8 o'clock Mr. Mumford went away. John G-r-l was not well and I caused him to be bled and then he

found himself better. The weather was clear and cold; however I went over the river about 11 o'clock and then proceeded on my journey to Major Harrison's where I got about 3 o'clock and [found] him at home but he was indisposed in his breast, for which I persuaded him to enter into a milk diet. About 5 o'clock I ate some bacon and fowl for dinner. In the evening Peter Poythress came with 14 of the Tuscarora Indians whom he was going to conduct to the Governor. They told us the Carolina men had killed no more than about 20 old men and women of their people and had taken about 30 children prisoners when all the young men were not at home, that the Tuscaroras could [cut] them all off but that they saw some English among them which hindered them and their business with the Governor was to give the reason why they could not perform their articles and to inquire whether they might defend themselves in case they're attacked. We were merry till about 9 o'clock and then retired. I neglected to say my prayers but had good health, good thoughts, and good humor, thank God Almighty.

12. I rose about 7 o'clock and read a little Latin in Horace. I said my prayers and ate chocolate for breakfast. About 10 o'clock came Mr. Cargill the minister, who agreed to go with [us] on board the "Pelican," but Frank Lightfoot who had promised broke his word. We took a walk and I saw the Major's improvements about his [threshing] and his [c-l-g grass] and I saw him trim his vines. About 12 o'clock we went on board and were saluted with seven guns and a glass of canary. About 2 o'clock we went to dinner and I ate some of the beef that was preserved after the new manner and found it very juicy and not very salt. It is the best way of saving meat and will preserve it for several years free from taint and was found out by chance by a poor carpenter who keeps the secret to himself and gets abundance of money.   1941

Literary Exercises

A POEM UPON SOME LADIES AT TUNBRIDGE 1700

Lady C.D.

Upon the Walks Cornelia moves,
    With such a soft engaging Grace:
Her Air and easy manner proves
    Her high descent from Royal Race.

Lady S.

Plautina's wit divinely draws,
    Our adoration and surprise:
Her charms invite, her Conduct awes,
    And wounds like Parthians as she flies.

5

Mrs. W . . .

Cold Phebe's too neglectful air,
    The humble Crowd of Lovers mourn: 10
Obsequiously her Chains they wear,
    And much for Eyes & acres burn.

Mrs. E . . . k

Drusilla warms us with her fire,
    Which her too Icy breast denies:
At every smile, some swains expire,   15
    At every frown some Hero dies.

Lady Sm.

Foul Madget bursting at such sights,
    Confesst her malice and despair:
The Poplars on the walk she bites,
    And with these words she blasts the Air.   20

What have not I and Envy done?
    Bright looks thro me their bloom forsake:
Whole Families my Rancor own.
    And each gray hair that's left's a snake.

Ease o ye Powers a restless mind,   25
    Some vengeance on these nymphs decree:
Or make their curst Adorers blind,
    Or make their features loath'd like me.

The Naiad Phoce then appears,
    Which Goddess guards these healing springs: 30
Her head above the surface rears,
    And bubbling in these Accents sings.

Quick to the neighbouring Grove begone,
    A bleak & barren Rock you'll find:
Thence throw your crippl'd carcass down,   35
    And ease your self & all mankind.

                1700, 1942

INAMORATO L'OISEAUX

    Never did the sun shine upon a Swain who had more combustible matter in his constitution than the unfortunate Inamorato. Love broke out upon him before his Beard, and he could distinguish sexes long before he could the difference betwixt Good & Evil. 'Tis well he had not a Twin-sister as Osiris had, for without doubt like him he would have had an amourette with her in his mother's belly. Love was born in him so long before Reason, that it has ever since slighted its rebukes, as much as old Fops do the good sense of a young man. However this Frailty has never been without some check, For Diana threw such a Weight of Grace into the opposite scale, that the Balance has commonly been held very even. And if the Love-scale has happen'd to be carry'd down sometimes, the Counterpoise has not fail'd to mount it up again very suddenly. The struggle between the Senate and the Plebeians in the Roman Commonwealth, or betwixt the King and the Parliament in England, was never half so violent as the Civil war between this Hero's Principles and his Inclinations. Sometimes Grace would be uppermost and sometimes Love, neither would yield and neither could conquer. Like Caesar and Pompey one could not bear an Equal nor t'other a superior. It must be confesst indeed, His Principles have been sometimes happily supported by the misadventures of his Love, by which means its own cannon have been turn'd against itself. This Foible has been an unhappy Clog to all his Fortunes, and hinder'd him From reaching that Eminence in the World, which his Friends and his Abilities might possibly have advanct him to. Nature gave him all the Talents in the World for business except Industry, which of all others is the most necessary. This is the spring and life and spirit of all preferment, and makes a man bustle through all difficulty, and foil all opposition. Laziness mires a man in the degree in which he was born, and clogs the wheels of the finest qualifications. Fortune may make a Lazy Fellow great: but he will never make himself so. Diligence gives Wings to ambition by which it soars up to the highest pitch of advancement. These Wings Inamorato wanted, as he did constancy, which is another ingredient to raise a great Fortune. To What purpose is it for a man to be always upon the wing, if he only fly backward and forward. He must go right out or else he will never go far. He should fix one certain end in his own thoughts, and towards that all his designs, and all his motions should unalterably tend. But poor Inamorato had too much mercury to fix to one thing. His Brain was too hot to jog on eternally in the same dull road. He liv'd more by the lively movement of his Passions, than by the cold and unromantic dictates of Reason. This made him wavering in his Resolutions, and inconstant after he had taken them. He would follow a scent with great eagerness for a little while, but then a fresh scent would cross it and carry him as violently another way. One while the ease with which the Judges loll in their Coaches and doze upon the Bench, tempted him to study the Law: but he was soon taken off by the rapine and mercenariness of that Profession. Then the Gaiety of St. James's made him fancy to be a Courtier: but the falseness and treachery, the envy and corruption in fashion there quickly made him abandon that pursuit. When this fit was over he was charm'd with the Glory of serving in the army, and thought it a shame for a proper Fellow to live at home in ease, when the Liberties of Europe were in danger:

but before he had provided his Equipage, he was discourag'd by the confinement, dependence, & barbarity of that service. In some frolics no state appear'd so happy to him as matrimony, the convenience, the tenderness, the society of that condition, made him reslove upon his own ruin, and set up for a Wife. He fanci'd it too sullen, too splenatique to continue single, and too liable to the inconveniences that attend accidental and promiscuous gallantry. In this humor he'd work himself violently in love with some nymph of good sense, whose Understanding forsooth might keep under all the impertinent starts of a Woman's temper. And when he was in love no man ever made so disengaging a figure. Instead of that life and gaiety, that freedom and pushing confidence which hits the Ladies, he would look as dismal as if he appear'd before his Judge, and not his mistress. Venus and all the Graces would leave him in the lurch in the critical time when they should have assisted him most. When he ought to have had the most fire he had the most phlegm, and he was all form and constraint when he should have the most freedom and spirit. He would look like a fool, & talk like a Philosopher, when both his Eyes and his Tongue should have sparkled with wit and waggery. He would sigh as ruefully as if he sat over a dead friend, and not a live mistress. No wonder this awkward conduct was without success for what woman would venture upon a solemn swain that lookt more like her Confessor than her Gallant, and put her more in mind of a sullen Husband than a sprightly lover? The miscarriage of an honorable amour never disturb'd him so much, but that he would sleep and look much better in his dispair, than he did in the hottest of his Expectation. He was not in half the jeopardy of hanging himself when he lost a mistress, that he was while he was in danger of getting her. While there was hopes he would be assiduous to a fault, nor considering that a little neglect in love (like saltpeter in Gunpowder) serves to give force to the Passion. Whenever his bashfulness gave him leave to declare his mind something would rise in his throat and intercept the untimely Question. A Woman is with more ease deliver'd of a huge boy, than he was of the painful secret. His Eyeballs would roll with as much ghastliness as if he had been strangled. 'Twas melancholy to see how his heart panted, his spirits flutter'd, his hands trembled, his knees knockt against one another, and the whole machine was in a deplorable confusion. You may guess how engaging a Declaration must be that was attended with so many sorrowful symptoms. It moved the Nymph's pity at least, if it could not move her inclination. If she could not be kind to a man to whom she had created so much disturbance, yet she could not forbear being civil. Thus whenever Inamorato lost a mistress, he got a friend by way of equivalent, and so Providence made a good Bargain for him when he would have made a woeful one for himself. His Person was agreeable enough though he had a certain cast of pride in his look, which clouded some of the grace of it. Hardly anybody likt him that did not know him, and nobody hated him that did. He had almost as many friends as he had acquaintance and no-body ever fell out with him for any other reason: but because they thought he neglected them.

His conversation was easy, sensible and inoffensive, never bordering either upon profaneness, or indecency. He was always tender of the mod-esty of those that were present, and of the reputation of those that were absent. He was incapable of saving a shocking thing, or of acting an un-just one. He was the never failing friend of the unfortunate, and good nature was the constantest of all his virtues. He pay'd his Court more to obscure merit, than to corrupt Greatness. He never could flatter anybody, no not himself, which were two invincible bars to all preferment. He was much readier to tell people of their faults, than their fine qualities, be-cause they were already too sensible of these, whereas they were too ig-norant of the first. His soul is so tun'd to those things that are right, that he is too ready to be moved at those that are wrong. This makes him passionate, and sorely sensible of Injuries, but he punishes himself more by the resentment than he does the Party by revenge. If the sun go down upon his wrath 'twill be sure to rise upon his reconciliation. An Injury never festers or rankles upon his mind: but wastes itself in the First sally of indignation. He is frugal in all Expenses upon himself, that he may be generous to the Distressed. He takes more pleasure to supply the wants of others than his own Wantonness. His religion is more in sub-stance than in form, and he is more forward to practice virtue than pro-fess it. He is sincere to an indiscretion himself, and therefore abhors dis-simulation in other people. He can sooner be reconcil'd to a professed Enemy than to a pretended Friend. Of all cheats in the world he has least charity for the Holy Cheat, that makes Religion bawd for his Interest and serves the Devil in the Livery of Godliness. His memory is in noth-ing so punctual as in performing of Promises. He thinks himself as firmly bound by his Word as by his hand & seal, and would be as much asham'd to be put in mind of one, as to be sue'd for the other. He knows the World perfectly well, and thinks himself a citizen of it without the distinctions of kindred sect or Country. He has learning without ostenta-tion. By Reading he's acquainted with ages past, and with the present by voyaging & conversation, He knew how to keep company with Rakes without being infected with their Vices, and had the secret of giving Vir-tue so good a grace that Wit itself could not make it ridiculous. He could return from one of the Convents in Drury Lane with as much inno-cence, as any of the saints from a meeting. He Lov'd to undress wicked-ness of all its paint, and disguise, that he might loathe its deformity. His discretion never gave him an opportunity to try his courage for he would never provoke a sober man, nor be provokt by a man in drink. He never interlop't with another's wife or mistress, but dealt altogether where the Trade was open & free for all Adventurers. If he reflected upon anyone 'twas by Irony, which a wise man would take for a banter, and a fool for a compliment. His Tongue was so far from embroiling the rest of his Person that upon some occasions it has happily protected it. He abhors all excesses of strong drink because it wholly removes those Guards that can defend a man from doing & suffering Harm. He's a great friend to temperance, because 'tis the security of all the other virtues. It disarms Flesh & blood of those Tempests with which it puts out all the lights of Reason. By talking little he is quit of a World of Folly & repentance. His silence proceeds not from want of matter, but from plenty of discretion. He is so great a friend to exactness, that he sometimes allows too little to the frailty of mankind. He wishes everybody so perfect, that he overlooks the impossibility of reaching it in this World. He would have men Angels before their time, and would bring down that perfection upon Earth which is the peculiar privilege of Heaven. This makes him a little too severe upon Faults, which it would not be unjust to forgive. However he would not have Transgressors punisht to procure them pain, but reformation. It proceeds from his hatred of the fault, and not of the offender. He loves retirement, that while he is acquainted with the world, he may not be a stranger to himself. Too much company distracts his thoughts, and hinders him from digesting his observations into good sense. It makes a man superficial, penetrating no deeper than the surface of things. One notice crowds out another, having no time to sink into the mind. A constant hurry of visits & conversation gives a man a habit of inadvertency, which betrays him into faults without measure & without end. For this reason he commonly reserv'd the morning to himself, and bestow'd the rest upon his business and his friends. He often frequented the company of Women, not so much to improve his mind as to polish his behavior. There is something in female conversation, that softens the roughness, tames the wildness, & refines the indecency too common amongst the men. He laid it down as a maxim that without the Ladies, a scholar is a Pedant, a Philosopher, a Cynic, all morality is morose, & all behavior either too Formal or too licentious. He has an excellent talent at keeping a secret, which neither love nor resentment, Vanity nor lightness can ever draw from him. All the ingenious tortures of the Inquisition can't force him to betray either his Faith, or his Friend. He always thought Ingratitude the most monstrous of all the vices, because it makes a man unfit for society, which subsists by mutual returns of kindness. His good-nature is so universal as to extend to all Brute creatures. He cannot see them ill us'd without the tenderest sentiments of compassion. They are helpless and must submit to all sorts of tyranny while men have some way or other of righting themselves. They have no refuge, no friend, no laws to protect them from injury, but are liable to suffer by the neglect, the wantonness, and cruelty of men. This hard fate he bemoans with a very sensible concern, and the rather, because they have often more merit than their oppressors.   1723, 1942

JONATHAN EDWARDS

(1703-1758)

Two Dissertations . . . (Boston, 1765).

1757 Selected president of the College of New Jersey (Princeton).

1758 Died of smallpox March 22 in Princeton; *The Great Christian Doctrine of Original Sin Defended* (Boston).

BIBLIOGRAPHY:

Thomas H. Johnson, *The Printed Writing of Jonathan Edwards* (Princeton, 1940). *The Works of President Edwards*, 8 vols., eds. Edward Williams and Edward Parsons (Leeds, 1806-1811), reprinted in London, 1817, and again in 1847 with a two-volume Supplement ed. R. Ogle (Edinburgh). *The Works of President Edwards*, 8 vols., ed. Samuel Austin (Worcester, Mass., 1808-1809). *The Works of President Edwards, With A Memoir of His Life*, 10 vols., ed. Sereno E. Dwight (New York, 1829-1830). Vol. I is a biography by Dwight. *Jonathan Edwards: Representative Selections*, ed. Clarence H. Faust and Thomas H. Johnson (New York, 1935; re-issued with bibliography brought up to date New York, 1962). *The Works of Jonathan Edwards*, 2 vols., gen. ed. Perry Miller (New Haven, 1957-1959), in progress. *Puritan Sage: Collected Writings of Jonathan Edwards*, ed. Vergilius Ferm (New York, 1953). Ola E. Winslow, *Jonathan Edwards, 1702-1758: A Biography* (New York, 1940, 1961). Perry Miller, *Jonathan Edwards* (New York, 1949). *The Philosophy of Jonathan Edwards from His Private Notebooks*, ed. H. G. Townsend (Eugene, Ore., 1955). See Riley and Adams entries in Samuel Johnson headnote.

From *The Personal Narrative*

I had a variety of concerns and exercises about my soul from my childhood; but had two more remarkable seasons of awakening, before I met with that change by which I was brought to those new dispositions, and that new sense of things, that I have since had. The first time was when I was a boy, some years before I went to college, at a time of remarkable awakening in my father's congregation. I was then very much affected for many months, and concerned about the things of religion, and my soul's salvation; and was abundant in duties. I used to pray five times a day in secret, and to spend much time in religious talk with other boys; and used to meet with them to pray together. I experienced I know not what kind of delight in religion. My mind was much engaged in it, and had much self-righteous pleasure; and it was my delight to abound in religious duties. I with some of my school-mates joined together, and built a booth in a swamp, in a very retired spot, for a place of prayer.—And besides, I had particular secret places of my own in the woods, where I used to retire by myself; and was from time to time much affected. My affections seemed to be lively and easily moved, and I seemed to be in my element when engaged in religious duties. And I am ready to think, many are deceived with such affections, and such a kind of delight as I then had in religion, and mistake it for grace.

But in process of time, my convictions and affections wore off; and I entirely lost all those affections and delights, and left off secret prayer, at least as to any constant performance of it; and returned like a dog to his vomit, and went on in the ways of sin. Indeed I was at times very uneasy, especially towards the latter part of my time at college; when it pleased God, to seize me with a pleurisy; in which he brought me nigh to the grave, and shook me over the pit of hell. And yet, it was not long after my recovery, before I fell again into my old ways of sin. But God would not suffer me to go on with any quietness; I had great and violent inward struggles, till, after many conflicts with wicked inclinations, repeated resolutions, and bonds that I laid myself under by a kind of vows to God, I was brought wholly to break off all former wicked ways, and all ways of known outward sin; and to apply myself to seek salvation, and practice many religious duties; but without that kind of affection and delight which I had formerly experienced. My concern now wrought more by inward struggles and conflicts, and self-reflections. I made seeking my salvation the main business of my life. But yet, it seems to me, I sought after a miserable manner; which has made me sometimes since to question, whether ever it issued in that which was saving; being ready to doubt, whether such miserable seeking ever succeeded. I was indeed brought to seek salvation in a manner that I never was before; I felt a spirit to part with all things in the world, for an interest in Christ. My concern continued and prevailed, with many exercising thoughts and inward struggles; but yet it never seemed to be proper to express that concern by the name of terror.

From my childhood up, my mind had been full of objections against the doctrine of God's sovereignty, in choosing whom he would to eternal life, and rejecting whom he pleased; leaving them eternally to perish, and be everlastingly tormented in hell. It used to appear like a horrible doctrine to me. But I remember the time very well, when I seemed to be convinced, and fully satisfied, as to this sovereignty of God, and his justice in thus eternally disposing of men, according to his sovereign pleasure. But never could give an account, how, or by what means, I was thus convinced, not in the least imagining at the time, nor a long time after, that there was any extraordinary influence of God's Spirit in it; but only that now I saw further, and my reason apprehended the justice and reasonableness of it. However, my mind rested in it; and it put an end to all those cavils and objections. And there has been a wonderful alteration in my mind, with respect to the doctrine of God's sovereignty, from that day to this; so that I scarce ever have found so much as the rising of an objection against it, in the most absolute sense, in God showing mercy to whom he will show mercy, and hardening whom he will. God's absolute sovereignty and justice, with respect to salvation and damnation, is what my mind seems to rest assured of, as much as of anything that I see with my eyes; at least it is so at times. But I have often, since that first conviction, had quite another kind of sense of God's sovereignty than I had then. I have often since had not only a conviction, but a *delightful* conviction. The doctrine has very often appeared exceeding pleasant, bright,

and sweet. Absolute sovereignty is what I love to ascribe to God. But my
first conviction was not so.

The first instance that I remember of that sort of inward, sweet delight
in God and divine things that I have lived much in since, was on reading
those words, 1 Tim. i. 17. *Now unto the King eternal, immortal, invisible,
the only wise God, be honor and glory for ever and ever, Amen.* As I read
the words, there came into my soul, and was as it were diffused through
it, a sense of the glory of the Divine Being; a new sense, quite different
from anything I ever experienced before. Never any words of scripture
seemed to me as these words did. I thought with myself, how excellent a
Being that was, and how happy I should be, if I might enjoy that God,
and be rapt up to him in heaven, and be as it were swallowed up in him
forever! I kept saying, and as it were singing over these words of scripture to myself; and went to pray to God that I might enjoy him, and
prayed in a manner quite different from what I used to do; with a new
sort of affection. But it never came into my thought, that there was anything spiritual, or of a saving nature in this.

From about that time, I began to have a new kind of apprehensions
and ideas of Christ, and the work of redemption, and the glorious way of
salvation by him. An inward, sweet sense of these things, at times, came
into my heart; and my soul was led away in pleasant views and contemplations of them. And my mind was greatly engaged to spend my time in
reading and meditating on Christ, on the beauty and excellency of his
person, and the lovely way of salvation by free grace in him. I found no
books so delightful to me, as those that treated of these subjects. Those
words Cant. ii. 1. used to be abundantly with me, *I am the Rose of Shar-
on, and the Lily of the valleys.* The words seemed to me, sweetly to
represent the loveliness and beauty of Jesus Christ. The whole book of
Canticles used to be pleasant to me, and I used to be much in reading it,
about that time; and found, from time to time, an inward sweetness, that
would carry me away, in my contemplations. This I know not how to express otherwise, than by a calm, sweet abstraction of soul from all the
concerns of this world; and sometimes a kind of vision, or fixed ideas and
imaginations, of being alone in the mountains, or some solitary wilderness, far from all mankind, sweetly conversing with Christ, and wrapt
and swallowed up in God. The sense I had of divine things, would often
of a sudden kindle up, as it were, a sweet burning in my heart; an ardor
of soul, that I know not how to express.

Not long after I first began to experience these things, I gave an account to my father of some things that had passed in my mind. I was
pretty much affected by the discourse we had together; and when the
discourse was ended, I walked abroad alone, in a solitary place in my father's pasture, for contemplation. And as I was walking there, and looking up on the sky and clouds, there came into my mind so sweet a sense
of the glorious majesty and grace of God, that I know not how to ex-

press.—I seemed to see them both in a sweet conjunction; majesty and meekness joined together: it was a sweet, and gentle, and holy majesty; and also a majestic meekness; an awful sweetness; a high, and great, and holy gentleness.

After this my sense of divine things gradually increased, and became more and more lively, and had more of that inward sweetness. The appearance of everything was altered; there seemed to be, as it were, a calm, sweet cast, or appearance of divine glory, in almost everything. God's excellency, his wisdom, his purity and love, seemed to appear in everything; in the sun, moon, and stars; in the clouds, and blue sky; in the grass, flowers, trees; in the water, and all nature; which used greatly to fix my mind. I often used to sit and view the moon for continuance; and in the day, spent much time in viewing the clouds and sky, to behold the sweet glory of God in these things: in the meantime, singing forth, with a low voice, my contemplations of the Creator and Redeemer. And scarce anything, among all the works of nature, was so sweet to me as thunder and lightning; formerly, nothing had been so terrible to me. Before, I used to be uncommonly terrified with thunder, and to be struck with terror when I saw a thunder-storm rising; but now, on the contrary, it rejoiced me. I felt God, so to speak, at the first appearance of a thunder-storm; and used to take the opportunity, at such times, to fix myself in order to view the clouds, and see the lightnings play, and hear the majestic and awful voice of God's thunder, which oftentimes was exceedingly entertaining, leading me to sweet contemplations of my great and glorious God. While thus engaged, it always seemed natural to me to sing, or chant forth my meditations; or, to speak my thoughts in soliloquies with a singing voice.

I felt then great satisfaction, as to my good state; but that did not content me. I had vehement longings of soul after God and Christ, and after more holiness, wherewith my heart seemed to be full, and ready to break; which often brought to my mind the words of the Psalmist, Psal. cxix. 28. *My soul breaketh for the longing it hath.* I often felt a mourning and lamenting in my heart, that I had not turned to God sooner, that I might have had more time to grow in grace. My mind was greatly fixed on divine things; almost perpetually in the contemplation of them. I spent most of my time in thinking of divine things, year after year; often walking alone in the woods, and solitary places, for meditation, soliloquy, and prayer, and converse with God; and it was always my manner, at such times, to sing forth my contemplations. I was almost constantly in ejaculatory prayer, wherever I was. Prayer seemed to be natural to me, as the breath by which the inward burnings of my heart had vent. The delights which I now felt in the things of religion, were of an exceeding different kind from those before-mentioned, that I had when a boy; and what I then had no more notion of, than one born blind has of pleasant and beautiful colors. They were of a more inward, pure, soul-animating and refreshing nature. Those former delights never reached the heart; and did not arise from any sight of the divine excellency of the things of God; or any taste of the soul-satisfying and life-giving good there is in them.

My sense of divine things seemed gradually to increase, till I went to preach at New York, which was about a year and a half after they began; and while I was there, I felt them, very sensibly, in a much higher degree than I had done before. My longings after God and holiness, were much increased. Pure and humble, holy and heavenly Christianity, appeared exceeding amiable to me. I felt a burning desire to be in everything a complete Christian; and conformed to the blessed image of Christ; and that I might live, in all things, according to the pure, sweet and blessed rules of the gospel. I had an eager thirsting after progress in these things; which put me upon pursuing and pressing after them. It was my continual strife day and night, and constant inquiry, how I should *be* more holy, and *live* more holily, and more becoming a child of God, and a disciple of Christ. I now sought an increase of grace and holiness, and a holy life, with much more earnestness, than ever I sought grace before I had it. I used to be continually examining myself, and studying and contriving for likely ways and means, how I should live holily, with far greater diligence and earnestness, than ever I pursued anything in my life; but yet with too great a dependence on my own strength; which afterwards proved a great damage to me. My experience had not then taught me, as it has done since, my extreme feebleness and impotence, every manner of way; and the bottomless depths of secret corruption and deceit there was in my heart. However, I went on with my eager pursuit after more holiness, and conformity to Christ.

The heaven I desired was a heaven of holiness; to be with God, and to spend my eternity in divine love, and holy communion with Christ. My mind was very much taken up with contemplations on heaven, and the enjoyments there; and living there in perfect holiness, humility and love: and it used at that time to appear a great part of the happiness of heaven, that there the saints could express their love to Christ. It appeared to me a great clog and burden, that what I felt within, I could not express as I desired. The inward ardor of my soul, seemed to be hindered and pent up, and could not freely flame out as it would. I used often to think, how in heaven this principle should freely and fully vent and express itself. Heaven appeared exceedingly delightful, as a world of love; and that all happiness consisted in living in pure, humble, heavenly, divine love.

I remember the thoughts I used then to have of holiness; and said sometimes to myself, "I do certainly know that I love holiness, such as the gospel prescribes." It appeared to me, that there was nothing in it but what was ravishingly lovely; the highest beauty and amiableness—a *divine* beauty; far purer than anything here upon earth; and that everything else was like mire and defilement, in comparison of it.

Holiness, as I then wrote down some of my contemplations on it, appeared to me to be of a sweet, pleasant, charming, serene, calm nature; which brought an inexpressible purity, brightness, peacefulness and ravishment to the soul. In other words, that it made the soul like a field or garden of God, with all manner of pleasant flowers; all pleasant, delightful and undisturbed; enjoying a sweet calm, and the gently vivifying beams of the sun. The soul of a true Christian, as I then wrote my meditations, appeared like such a little white flower as we see in the spring of the year; low and humble on the ground, opening its bosom, to receive the pleasant beams of the sun's glory; rejoicing, as it were, in a calm rapture; diffusing around a sweet fragrancy; standing peacefully and lovingly, in the midst of other flowers round about; all in like manner opening their bosoms, to drink in the light of the sun. There was no part of creature-holiness, that I had so great a sense of its loveliness, as humility, brokenness of heart and poverty of spirit; and there was nothing that I so earnestly longed for. My heart panted after this,—to lie low before God, as in the dust; that I might be nothing, and that God might be ALL, that I might become as a little child. 1739, 1808

From *A Divine and Supernatural Light*

MATT. XVI. 17

And Jesus answered and said unto him, Blessed art thou, Simon Bar-jona: for flesh and blood hath not revealed it unto thee, but my Father which is in heaven.

DOCTRINE

That there is such a thing as a spiritual and divine light, immediately imparted to the soul by God, of a different nature from any that is obtained by natural means. And on this subject I would,

I. Show what this divine light is.
II. How it is given immediately by God, and not obtained by natural means.
III. Show the truth of the doctrine.
And then conclude with a brief improvement.

I. I would show what this spiritual and divine light is. And in order to it would show,
First, In a few things what it is not. And here,
1. Those convictions that natural men may have of their sin and misery, is not this spiritual and divine light. Men in a natural condition may

have convictions of the guilt that lies upon them, and of the anger of God, and their danger of divine vengeance. Such convictions are from the light of truth. That some sinners have a greater conviction of their guilt and misery than others, is because some have more light, or more of an apprehension of truth than others. And this light and conviction may be from the Spirit of God; the Spirit convinces men of sin: but yet nature is much more concerned in it than in the communication of that spiritual and divine light that is spoken of in the doctrine; it is from the Spirit of God only as assisting natural principles, and not as infusing any new principles. Common grace differs from special, in that it influences only by assisting of nature; and not by imparting grace, or bestowing anything above nature. The light that is obtained is wholly natural, or of no superior kind to what mere nature attains to, though more of that kind be obtained than would be obtained, if men were left wholly to themselves: or, in other words, common grace only assists the faculties of the soul to do that more fully which they do by nature, as natural conscience or reason will by mere nature make a man sensible of guilt, and will accuse and condemn him when he has done amiss. Conscience is a principle natural to men; and the work that it doth naturally, or of itself, is to give an apprehension of right and wrong, and to suggest to the mind the relation that there is between right and wrong and a retribution. The Spirit of God, in those convictions which unregenerate men sometimes have, assists conscience to do this work in a further degree than it would do if they were left to themselves. He helps it against those things that tend to stupify it, and obstruct its exercise. But in the renewing and sanctifying work of the Holy Ghost, those things are wrought in the soul that are above nature, and of which there is nothing of the like kind in the soul by nature; and they are caused to exist in the soul habitually, and according to such a stated constitution or law, that lays such a foundation for exercises in a continued course, as is called a principle of nature. Not only are remaining principles assisted to do their work more freely and fully, but those principles are restored that were utterly destroyed by the fall; and the mind thenceforward habitually exerts those acts that the dominion of sin had made it as wholly destitute of as a dead body is of vital acts.

The Spirit of God acts in a very different manner in the one case, from what he doth in the other. He may indeed act upon the mind of a natural man, but he acts in the mind of a saint as an indwelling vital principle. He acts upon the mind of an unregenerate person as an extrinsic occasional agent; for in acting upon them, he doth not unite himself to them: for notwithstanding all his influences that they may possess, they are still sensual, having not the Spirit. Jude 19. But he unites himself with the mind of a saint, takes him for his temple, actuates and influences him as a new supernatural principle of life and action. There is this difference, that the Spirit of God, in acting in the soul of a godly man, exerts and communicates himself there in his own proper nature. Holiness is the proper nature of the Spirit of God. The Holy Spirit operates in the minds of the godly, by uniting himself to them, and living in them, and exerting his own nature in the exercise of their faculties. The Spirit of God may act upon a creature, and yet not in acting communicate himself. The Spirit of God may act upon inanimate creatures; as, *the Spirit moved upon the face of the waters,* in the beginning of the creation; so the Spirit of God may act upon the minds of men many ways, and communicate himself no more than when he acts upon an inanimate creature. For instance, he may excite thoughts in them, may assist their natural reason and understanding, or may assist other natural principles, and this without any union with the soul, but may act, as it were, upon an external object. But as he acts in his holy influences and spiritual operations, he acts in a way of peculiar communication of himself; so that the subject is thence denominated spiritual.

2. This spiritual and divine light does not consist in any impression made upon the imagination. It is no impression upon the mind, as though one saw anything with the bodily eyes. It is no imagination or idea of an outward light or glory, or any beauty of form or countenance, or a visible luster or brightness of any object. The imagination may be strongly impressed with such things; but this is not spiritual light. Indeed when the mind has a lively discovery of spiritual things, and is greatly affected by the power of divine light, it may, and probably very commonly doth, much affect the imagination; so that impressions of an outward beauty or brightness may *accompany* those spiritual discoveries. But spiritual light is not that impression upon the imagination, but an exceedingly different thing. Natural men may have lively impressions on their imaginations; and we cannot determine but that the devil, who transforms himself into an angel of light, may cause imaginations of an outward beauty, or visible glory, and of sounds and speeches, and other such things; but these are things of a vastly inferior nature to spiritual light.

3. This spiritual light is not the suggesting of any new truths or propositions not contained in the word of God. This suggesting of new truths or doctrines to the mind, independent of any antecedent revelations of those propositions, either in word or writing, is inspiration; such as the prophets and apostles had, and such as some enthusiasts pretend to. But this spiritual light that I am speaking of, is quite a different thing from inspiration. It reveals no new doctrine, it suggests no new proposition to the mind, it teaches no new thing of God, or Christ, or another world, not taught in the Bible, but only gives a due apprehension of those things that are taught in the word of God.

4. It is not every affecting view that men have of religious things that is this spiritual and divine light. Men by mere principles of nature are capable of being affected with things that have a special relation to religion as well as other things. A person by mere nature, for instance, may

be liable to be affected with the story of Jesus Christ, and the sufferings he underwent, as well as by any other tragical story. He may be the more affected with it from the interest he conceives mankind to have in it. Yea, he may be affected with it without believing it; as well as a man may be affected with what he reads in a romance, or sees acted in a stage-play. He may be affected with a lively and eloquent description of many pleasant things that attend the state of the blessed in heaven, as well as his imagination be entertained by a romantic description of the pleasantness of fairy land, or the like. And a common belief of the truth of such things, from education or otherwise, may help forward their affection. We read in Scripture of many that were greatly affected with things of a religious nature, who yet are there represented as wholly graceless, and many of them very ill men. A person therefore may have affecting views of the things of religion, and yet be very destitute of spiritual light. Flesh and blood may be the author of this: One man may give another an affecting view of divine things with but common assistance; but God alone can give a spiritual discovery of them.—But I proceed to show,

Secondly, Positively what this spiritual and divine light is.

And it may be thus described: A true sense of the divine excellency of the things revealed in the word of God, and a conviction of the truth and reality of them thence arising. This spiritual light primarily consists in the former of these, viz. A real sense and apprehension of the divine excellency of things revealed in the word of God. A spiritual and saving conviction of the truth and reality of these things, arises from such a sight of their divine excellency and glory; so that this conviction of their truth is an effect and natural consequence of this sight of their divine glory. There is therefore in this spiritual light,

1. A true sense of the divine and superlative excellency of the things of religion; a real sense of the excellency of God and Jesus Christ, and of the work of redemption, and the ways and works of God revealed in the gospel. There is a divine and superlative glory in these things; an excellency that is of a vastly higher kind, and more sublime nature than in other things; a glory greatly distinguishing them from all that is earthly and temporal. He that is spiritually enlightened truly apprehends and sees it, or has a sense of it. He does not merely rationally believe that God is glorious, but he has a sense of the gloriousness of God in his heart. There is not only a rational belief that God is holy, and that holiness is a good thing, but there is a sense of the loveliness of God's holiness. There is not only a speculatively judging that God is gracious, but a sense how amiable God is on account of the beauty of this divine attribute.

There is a twofold knowledge of good of which God has made the mind of man capable. The first, that which is merely notional; as when a person only speculatively judges that anything is, which, by the agreement of mankind, is called good or excellent, viz. that which is most to general advantage, and between which and a reward there is a suitableness,—and the like. And the other is, that which consists in the sense of the heart; as when the heart is sensible of pleasure and delight in the presence of the idea of it. In the former is exercised merely the speculative faculty, or the understanding, in distinction from the will or disposition of the soul. In the latter, the will, or inclination, or heart, are mainly concerned.

Thus there is a difference between having an *opinion*, that God is holy and gracious, and having a *sense* of the loveliness and beauty of that holiness and grace. There is a difference between having a rational judgment that honey is sweet, and having a sense of its sweetness. A man may have the former, that knows not how honey tastes; but a man cannot have the latter unless he has an idea of the taste of honey in his mind. So there is a difference between believing that a person is beautiful, and having a sense of his beauty. The former may be obtained by hearsay, but the latter only by seeing the countenance. When the heart is sensible of the beauty and amiableness of a thing, it necessarily feels pleasure in the apprehension. It is implied in a person's being heartily sensible of the loveliness of a thing, that the idea of it is pleasant to his soul; which is a far different thing from having a rational opinion that it is excellent.

2. There arises from this sense of the divine excellency of things contained in the word of God, a conviction of the truth and reality of them; and that either indirectly or directly.

First, Indirectly, and that two ways:

1. As the prejudices of the heart, against the truth of divine things, are hereby removed; so that the mind becomes susceptive of the due force of rational arguments for their truth. The mind of man is naturally full of prejudices against divine truth. It is full of enmity against the doctrines of the gospel; which is a disadvantage to those arguments that prove their truth, and causes them to lose their force upon the mind. But when a person has discovered to him the divine excellency of Christian doctrines, this destroys the enmity, removes those prejudices, sanctifies the reason, and causes it to lie open to the force of arguments for their truth.

Hence was the different effect that Christ's miracles had to convince the disciples, from what they had to convince the Scribes and Pharisees. Not that they had a stronger reason, or had their reason more improved; but their reason was sanctified, and those blinding prejudices, that the Scribes and Pharisees were under, were removed by the sense they had of the excellency of Christ, and his doctrine.

It not only removes the hindrances of reason, but positively helps reason. It makes even the speculative notions more lively. It engages the attention of the mind, with more fixedness and intenseness to that kind of objects; which causes it to have a clearer view of them, and enables it more clearly to see their mutual relations, and occasions it to take more notice of them. The ideas themselves that otherwise are dim and obscure, are by this means impressed with the greater strength, and have a light cast upon them; so that the mind can better judge of them. As he that beholds objects on the face of the earth, when the light of the sun is cast upon them, is under greater advantage to discern them in their true forms and natural relations, than he that sees them in a dim twilight.

The mind being sensible of the excellency of divine objects, dwells upon them with delight; and the powers of the soul are more awakened and enlivened to employ themselves in the contemplation of them, and exert themselves more fully and much more to the purpose. The beauty of the objects draws on the faculties, and draws forth their exercises: So that reason itself is under far greater advantages for its proper and free exercises, and to attain its proper end, free of darkness and delusion.— But,

Secondly, A true sense of the divine excellency of the things of God's word doth more directly and immediately convince us of their truth; and that because the excellency of these things is so superlative. There is a beauty in them so divine and godlike, that it greatly and evidently distinguishes them from things merely human, or that of which men are the inventors and authors; a glory so high and great, that when clearly seen, commands assent to their divine reality. When there is an actual and lively discovery of this beauty and excellency, it will not allow of any such thought as that it is the fruit of men's invention. This is a kind of intuitive and immediate evidence. They believe the doctrines of God's word to be divine, because they see a divine, and transcendent, and most evidently distinguishing glory in them; such a glory as, if clearly seen, does not leave room to doubt of their being of God, and not of men.

Such a conviction of the truths of religion as this, arising from a sense of their divine excellency, is included in saving faith. And this original of it, is that by which it is most essentially distinguished from that common assent, of which unregenerate men are capable.

II. I proceed now to the second thing proposed, viz. To show how this light is immediately given by God, and not obtained by natural means. And here,

1. It is not intended that the natural faculties are not used in it. They are the subject of this light; and in such a manner, that they are not merely passive, but active in it. God, in letting in this light into the soul, deals with man according to his nature, and makes use of his rational faculties. But yet this light is not the less immediately from God for that; the faculties are made use of as the subject, and not as the cause. As the use we make of our eyes in beholding various objects, when the sun arises, is not the cause of the light that discovers those objects to us.

2. It is not intended that outward means have no concern in this affiair. It is not in this affair, as in inspiration, where new truths are sug-

gested: for, by this light is given only a due apprehension of the same truths that are revealed in the word of God; and therefore it is not given without the word. The gospel is employed in this affair. This light is the "light of the glorious gospel of Christ." 2 Cor. iv. 4. The gospel is as a glass, by which this light is conveyed to us. 1 Cor. xiii. 12. "Now we see through a glass."—But,

3. When it is said that this light is given immediately by God, and not obtained by natural means, hereby is intended, that it is given by God without making use of any means that operate by their own power or natural force. God makes use of means; but it is not as mediate causes to produce this effect. There are not truly any second causes of it; but it is produced by God immediately. The word of God is no proper cause of this effect; but is made use of only to convey to the mind the subject-matter of this saving instruction: And this indeed it doth convey to us by natural force or influence. It conveys to our minds these doctrines; it is the cause of a notion of them in our heads, but not of the sense of their divine excellency in our hearts. Indeed a person cannot have spiritual light without the word. But that does not argue, that the word properly causes that light. The mind cannot see the excellency of any doctrine, unless that doctrine be first in the mind; but seeing the excellency of the doctrine may be immediately from the Spirit of God; though the conveying of the doctrine or proposition itself may be by the word. So that the notions which are the subject-matter of this light, are conveyed to the mind by the word of God; but that due sense of the heart, wherein this light formally consists, is immediately by the Spirit of God. As for instance, the notion that there is a Christ, and that Christ is holy and gracious, is conveyed to the mind by the word of God: But the sense of the excellency of Christ by reason of that holiness and grace, is nevertheless immediately the work of the Holy Spirit.   1734

From *A Faithful Narrative of the Surprising Work of God*

SECTION I

A General Introductory Statement

The people of the country, in general, I suppose, are as sober, orderly, and good sort of people, as in any part of New England; and I believe they have been preserved the freest by far of any part of the country, from error, and variety of sects and opinions. Our being so far within the land, at a distance from sea-ports, and in a corner of the country, has doubtless been one reason why we have not been so much corrupted with vice, as most other parts. But without question, the religion and good order of the county, and purity in doctrine, has, under God, been very much owing to the great abilities, and eminent piety, of my venerable and honored grandfather Stoddard. I suppose we have been the freest of any part of the land from unhappy divisions and quarrels in our ecclesiastical and religious affairs, till the late lamentable Springfield contention.

Being much separated from other parts of the province, and having comparatively but little intercourse with them, we have always managed our ecclesiastical affairs within ourselves. It is the way in which the country, from its infancy, has gone on, by the practical agreement of all; and the way in which our peace and good order has hitherto been maintained.

. . . Just after my grandfather's death, it seemed to be a time of extraordinary dullness in religion. Licentiousness for some years greatly prevailed among the youth of the town; they were many of them very much addicted to night-walking, and frequenting the tavern, and lewd practices, wherein some, by their example, exceedingly corrupted others. It was their manner very frequently to get together, in conventions of both sexes, for mirth and jollity, which they called frolics; and they would often spend the greater part of the night in them, without regard to any order in the families they belonged to: and indeed family government did too much fail in the town. It was become very customary with many of our young people to be indecent in their carriage at meeting, which doubtless would not have prevailed in such a degree, had it not been that my grandfather through his great age, (though he retained his powers surprisingly to the last) was not so able to observe them. There had also long prevailed in the town a spirit of contention between two parties, into which they had for many years been divided; by which they maintained a jealousy one of the other, and were prepared to oppose one another in all public affairs. . . .

At the latter end of the year 1733, there appeared a very unusual flexibleness, and yielding to advice, in our young people. It had been too long their manner to make the evening after the sabbath, and after our public lecture, to be especially the times of their mirth, and company-keeping. But a sermon was now preached on the sabbath before the lecture, to show the evil tendency of the practice, and to persuade them to reform it; and it was urged on heads of families that it should be a thing agreed upon among them, to govern their families, and keep their children at home, at these times. It was also more privately moved, that they should meet together the next day, in their several neighborhoods, to know each other's minds; which was accordingly done, and the motion complied with throughout the town. But parents found little or no occasion for the exercise of government in the case. The young people declared themselves convinced by what they had heard from the pulpit, and were willing of themselves to comply with the counsel that had been given: and it was immediately, and, I suppose, almost universally complied with; and there was a thorough reformation of these disorders thenceforward, which has continued ever since. . . .

In the fall of the year I proposed it to the young people, that they should agree among themselves to spend the evenings after lectures in social religion, and to that end divide themselves into several companies to meet in various parts of the town; which was accordingly done, and those meetings have been since continued, and the example imitated by elder people. This was followed with the death of an elderly person, which was attended with many unusual circumstances, by which many were much moved and affected. . . .

Particularly, I was surprised with the relation of a young woman, who had been one of the greatest company-keepers in the whole town. When she came to me, I had never heard that she was become in any wise serious, but by the conversation I then had with her, it appeared to me, that what she gave an account of, was a glorious work of God's infinite power and sovereign grace; and that God had given her a new heart, truly broken and sanctified. I could not then doubt of it, and have seen much in my acquaintance with her since to confirm it.

Though the work was glorious, yet I was filled with concern about the effect it might have upon others. I was ready to conclude, (though too rashly) that some would be hardened by it, in carelessness and looseness of life; and would take occasion from it to open their mouths in reproaches of religion. But the event was the reverse, to a wonderful degree. God made it, I suppose, the greatest occasion of awakening to others, of anything that ever came to pass in the town. I have had abundant opportunity to know the effect it had, by my private conversation with many. The news of it seemed to be almost like a flash of lightning, upon the hearts of young people, all over the town, and upon many others. Those persons amongst us, who used to be farthest from seriousness, and that I most feared would make an ill improvement of it, seemed greatly to be awakened with it. Many went to talk with her, concerning what she had met with; and what appeared in her seemed to be to the satisfaction of all that did so.

Presently upon this, a great and earnest concern about the great things of religion, and the eternal world, became universal in all parts of the town, and among persons of all degrees, and all ages. The noise amongst the dry bones waxed louder and louder; all other talk but about spiritual and eternal things, was soon thrown by; all the conversation, in all companies and upon all occasions, was upon these things only, unless so much as was necessary for people carrying on their ordinary secular business. Other discourse than of the things of religion, would scarcely be tolerated in any company. The minds of people were wonderfully taken off from the world, it was treated amongst us as a thing of very little consequence. They seemed to follow their worldly business, more as a part of their duty, than from any disposition they had to it; the temptation now seemed to lie on that hand, to neglect worldly affairs too much, and to spend too much time in the immediate exercise of religion. This was exceedingly misrepresented by reports that were spread in distant parts of the land, as though the people here had wholly thrown by all worldly business, and betook themselves entirely to reading and praying, and such like religious exercises.

But although people did not ordinarily neglect their worldly business; yet Religion was with all sorts the great concern, and the world was a thing only by the bye. The only thing in their view was to get the kingdom of heaven, and everyone appeared pressing into it. The engagedness of their hearts in this great concern could not be hid, it appeared in their very countenances. It then was a dreadful thing amongst us to lie out of Christ, in danger every day of dropping into hell; and what persons' minds were intent upon was to escape for their lives, and to fly from the wrath to come. All would eargerly lay hold of opportunities for their souls; and were wont very often to meet together in private houses, for religious purposes: and such meetings when appointed were greatly thronged.

There was scarcely a single person in the town, old or young, left unconcerned about the great things of the eternal world. Those who were wont to be the vainest, and loosest; and those who had been most disposed to think, and speak slightly of vital and experimental religion, were now generally subject to great awakenings. And the work of conversion was carried on in a most astonishing manner, and increased more and more; souls did as it were come by flocks to Jesus Christ. From day to day, for many months together, might be seen evident instances of sinners brought out of darkness into marvellous light, and delivered out of an horrible pit, and from the miry clay, and set upon a rock with a new song of praise to God in their mouths. . . .

When this work first appeared, and was so extraordinarily carried on amongst us in the winter, others round about us seemed not to know what to make of it. Many scoffed at and ridiculed it; and some compared what we called conversion, to certain distempers. But it was very observable of many, who occasionally came amongst us from abroad with disregardful hearts, that what they saw here cured them of such a temper of mind. Strangers were generally surprised to find things so much beyond what they had heard, and were wont to tell others that the state of the town could not be conceived of by those who had not seen it. The notice that was taken of it by the people who came to town on occasion of the court that sat here in the beginning of March, was very observable. And those who came from the neighborhood to our public lectures, were for the most part remarkably affected. Many who came to town, on one occasion or other, had their consciences smitten, and awakened; and went home with wounded hearts, and with those impressions that never wore off till they had hopefully a saving issue; and those who before had serious thoughts, had their awakenings and convictions greatly increased.

There were many instances of persons who came from abroad on visits, or on business, who had not been long here before, to all appearance, they were savingly wrought upon; and partook of that shower of divine blessing which God rained down here, and went home rejoicing; till at length the same work began evidently to appear and prevail in several other towns in the county. . . .

As what other towns heard of and found in this, was a great means of awakening them; so our hearing of such a swift, and extraordinary propagation, and extent of this work, did doubtless for a time serve to uphold the work amongst us. The continual news kept alive the talk of religion, and did greatly quicken and rejoice the hearts of God's people, and much awakened those who looked on themselves as still left behind, and made them the more earnest that they also might share in the great blessings that others had obtained. . . .

This seems to have been a very extraordinary dispensation of providence; God has in many respects gone out of, and much beyond his usual, and ordinary way. The work in this town, and some others about us, has been extraordinary on account of the universality of it, affecting all sorts, sober and vicious, high and low, rich and poor, wise and unwise. It reached the most considerable families and persons, to all appearance, as much as others. In former stirrings of this nature, the bulk of the young people have been greatly affected; but old men and little children have been so now. Many of the last have, of their own accord, formed themselves into religious societies, in different parts of the town. A loose careless person could scarcely be found in the whole neighborhood; and if there was anyone that seemed to remain senseless or unconcerned, it would be spoken of as a strange thing. . . .

This work seemed to be at its greatest height in this town, in the former part of the spring, in March and April. At that time, God's work in the conversion of souls was carried on amongst us in so wonderful a manner, that, so far as I can judge, it appears to have been at the rate, at least, of four persons in a day; or near thirty in a week, take one with another, for five or six weeks together. When God in so remarkable a manner took the work into his own hands, there was as much done in a day or two as at ordinary times, with all endeavors that men can use, and with such a blessing as we commonly have, is done in a year.

I am very sensible how apt many would be, if they should see the account I have here given, presently to think with themselves that I am very fond of making a great many converts, and of magnifying the matter; and to think that, for want of judgment, I take every religious pang, and enthusiastic conceit, for saving conversion. I do not much wonder, if they should be apt to think so; and, for this reason, I have forborne to publish an account of this great work of God, though I have often been solicited. But having now a special call to give an account of it, upon mature consideration I thought it might not be beside my duty to declare this amazing work, as it appeared to me to be indeed divine, and to conceal no part of the glory of it; leaving it with God to take care of the credit of his own work, and running the venture of any censorious thoughts, which might be entertained of me to my disadvantage. That distant persons may be under as great advantage as may be, to judge for themselves of this matter, I would be a little more large and particular.

1737

From *A Treatise Concerning Religious Affections*

PART II

Showing what are no certain signs that religious affections are truly gracious, or that they are not.

If anyone, on reading what has been just now said, is ready to acquit himself, and say,"I am not one of those who have no religious affections; I am often greatly moved with the consideration of the great things of religion"; let him not content himself with this: for, as we ought not to reject and condemn all affections, as though true religion did not at all consist in them; so, on the other hand, we ought not to approve of all, as though everyone that was religiously affected had true grace, and was therein the subject of the saving influences of the Spirit of God. Therefore, the right way is to distinguish, among religious affections, between one sort and another. Let us now endeavor to do this, by noticing, in the first place, some things, which are no signs that affections are gracious, or that they are not.

SECTION I

It is no sign, one way or other, that religious affections are very great, or raised very high.

Some are ready to condemn all high affection: if persons appear to have their religious affections raised to an extraordinary pitch, they are prejudiced against them, and determine that they are delusions, without further inquiry. But if, as before proved, true religion lies very much in religious affections, then it follows, that if there be a great deal of true religion, there will be great religious affections; if true religion in the hearts of men be raised to a great height, divine and holy affections will be raised to a great height.

Love is an affection; but will any Christian say, men ought not to love God and Jesus Christ in a high degree? and will any say, we ought not to have a very great hatred of sin, and a very deep sorrow for it? or that we ought not to exercise a high degree of gratitude to God, for the mercies we receive of him, and the great things he has done for the salvation of fallen men? or that we should not have very great and strong desires after God and holiness? . . .

It is no sign that affections have the nature of true religion, or that they have not, that they have great effects on the body.

All affections whatsoever have in some respect or degree, an effect on the body. As was observed before, such is our nature, and such are the laws of union of soul and body, that the mind can have no lively or vigorous exercise, without some effect upon the body. So subject is the body to the mind, and so much do its fluids, especially the animal spirits, attend the motions and exercises of the mind, that there cannot be so much as an intense thought, without an effect upon them. Yea it is questionable, whether an embodied soul ever so much as thinks one thought, or has any exercise at all, but that there is some corresponding motion or alteration of the fluids, in some part of the body. But universal experience shows, that the exercise of the affections have, in a special manner, a tendency to some sensible effect upon the body. And if all affections have some effect on the body, we may then well suppose, the greater those affections, and the more vigorous their exercises are, (other circumstances being equal), the greater will be the effect on the body. Hence it is not to be wondered at, that very great and strong exercises of the affections should have great effects on the body. And therefore, seeing there are very great affections, both common and spiritual; hence it is not to be wondered at, that great effects on the body should arise from both these kinds of affections. And consequently these effects are no signs, that the affections they arise from, are of one kind or the other. . . .

PART III

Showing what are distinguishing signs of truly gracious and holy affections.

Affections that are truly spiritual and gracious, arise from those influences and operations on the heart, which are spiritual, supernatural, and divine.

I will explain what I mean by these terms, whence will appear their use to distinguish between those affections which are spiritual, and those which are not so.—We find that true saints, or those persons who are sanctified by the Spirit of God, are in the New Testament called spiritual persons. And their being spiritual is spoken of as their peculiar character, and that wherein they are distinguished from those who are not sanctified. This is evident, because those who are spiritual are set in opposition to natural men, and carnal men. . . .

From these things it is evident, that those gracious influences of the saints, and the effects of God's Spirit which they experience, are entirely above nature, and altogether of a different kind from anything that men find in themselves by the exercise of natural principles. No improvement of those principles that are natural, no advancing or exalting of them to higher degrees, and no kind of composition will ever bring men to them; because they not only differ from what is natural, and from everything that natural men experience, in degree and circumstances, but also in kind; and are of a nature vastly more excellent. And this is what I mean by supernatural, when I say, that gracious affections are from those influences that are supernatural.

From hence it follows, that in those gracious exercises and affections which are wrought in the saints, through the saving influences of the Spirit of God, there is a new inward perception or sensation of their minds, entirely different in its nature and kind, from anything that ever their minds were the subjects of before they were sanctified. For, if God by his mighty power produces something that is new, not only in degree and circumstances, but in its whole nature—and that which could be produced by no exalting, varying, or compounding of what was there before, or by adding anything of the like kind—then, doubtless, something entirely new is felt, or perceived. There is what some metaphysicians call a new simple idea. If grace be, in the sense above described, an entirely new kind of principle; then the exercises of it are also new. And if there be in the soul a new sort of conscious exercises, which the soul knew nothing of before, and which no improvement, composition, or management of what it was before could produce; then it follows that the mind has an entirely new kind of perception or sensation. Here is, as it were, a new spiritual sense, or a principle of new kind of perception or spiritual sensation, which is in its whole nature different from any former kinds of sensation of the mind, as tasting is diverse from any of the other senses. And something is perceived by a true saint, in the exercise of this new sense of mind, in spiritual and divine things, as entirely diverse from anything that is perceived in them, by natural men, as the sweet taste of honey is diverse from the ideas men get of honey by only looking on and feeling it. So that the spiritual perceptions which a sanctified and spiritual person has, are not only diverse from all that natural men have as the perceptions of the same sense may differ one from another, but rather as the ideas and sensations of different senses differ. . . .

This new spiritual sense, and the new dispositions that attend it, are no new faculties, but new principles of nature, I use the word principles, for want of a word of a more determinate signification. By a principle of nature in this place, I mean that foundation which is laid in nature, either old or new, for any particular manner or kind of exercise of the faculties of the soul; or a natural habit, or foundation for action, giving a person ability and disposition to exert the faculties in exercises of such a certain kind; so that to exert the faculties in that kind of exercises, may be said to be his nature. So this new spiritual sense is not a new faculty of understanding, but it is a new foundation laid in the nature of the soul, for a new kind of exercises of the same faculty of understanding. So that new holy disposition of heart that attends this new sense, is not a new faculty of will, but a foundation laid in the nature of the soul, for a new kind of exercises of the same faculty of will. . . .

From what has been said it follows, that all spiritual and gracious affections are attended with, and arise from some apprehension, idea, or sensation of mind, which is in its whole nature different, yea exceeding different from all that is or can be in the mind of a natural man. The natural man discerns nothing of it (1 Cor. ii. 14.) any more than a man without the sense of tasting can conceive of the sweet taste of honey; or a man without the sense of hearing can conceive of the melody of a tune; or a man born blind can have a notion of the beauty of the rainbow.

But here two things must be observed, in order to the right understanding of this.

1. On the one hand it must be observed, that not everything which appertains to spiritual affections, is new and entirely different from what natural men experience; some things are common to gracious affections with other affections; many circumstances, appendages, and effects are common. Thus a saint's love to God has a great many things appertaining to it, which are common with a man's natural love to a near relation. Love to God makes a man seek the honor of God, and desire to please him; so does a natural man's love to his friend make him desire his honor, and to please him. Love to God causes a man to delight in the thoughts of him, in his presence; to desire conformity to God, and the enjoyment of him; and so it is with a man's love to his friend. Many other things might be mentioned which are common to both. But yet, that idea which the saint has of the loveliness of God, and the kind of delight he has in that view, which is as it were the marrow and quintessence of his love, is peculiar, and entirely diverse from anything that a natural man has, or can have any notion of. And even in those things that seem to be common, there is something peculiar. Both spiritual love and natural, cause desires after the object beloved; but they are not the same sort of desires; there is a sensation of soul in the spiritual desires of one that loves God, which is entirely different from all natural desires. Both spiritual and natural love are attended with delight in the object beloved; but the sensations of delight are not the same, but entirely and exceedingly diverse. Natural men may have conceptions of many things about spiritual affections; but there is something in them which is as it were the nucleus, or kernel, of which they have no more conceptions, than one born blind has of colors. . . .

I have insisted the more largely on this matter, because this view of the subject is evidently of great importance and use, in order to discover the delusions of Satan, in many kinds of false religious affections, by which multitudes are deluded, and probably have been in all ages of the

Christian church; also in order to settle and determine many articles of doctrine, concerning the operations of the Spirit of God, and the nature of true grace.—Let us now, therefore, apply these things to the purpose of this discourse.

From hence it appears, that impressions which some have on their imagination—their imaginary ideas of God, or Christ, or heaven, or anything appertaining to religion—have nothing in them that is spiritual, or of the nature of true grace. Though such things may attend what is spiritual, and be mixed with it, yet in themselves they are not any part of gracious experience.

Here, for the sake of the less informed, I will explain what is intended by impressions on the imagination, and imaginary ideas. The imagination is that power of the mind, whereby it can have a conception, or idea, of external things, or objects of the outward senses, when those things are not present, and therefore not perceived by the senses. It is called *imagination,* from the word *image;* because thereby a person can have an image of some external thing in his mind, when that thing is not present in reality, nor anything like it. What we perceive by our five senses, seeing, hearing, smelling, tasting, and feeling, are external things: and when a person has an image of these things in his mind, but does not really see, hear, smell, taste, nor feel them; that is to have an imagination of them, and these ideas are imaginary ideas. When such ideas are strongly impressed upon the mind, and the image is very lively, almost as if one saw, or heard them, &c. that is called an impression on the imagination. Thus colors and shapes, are outward things, objects of the outward sense of seeing: therefore, when any person has in his mind a lively idea of any shape, or color, or form of countenance; of light or darkness, such as he perceives by the sense of seeing; of any marks made on paper, suppose letters and words written in a book: that is to have an imagination, or an external and imaginary idea of such things as we sometimes perceive by our bodily eyes. And when we have the ideas of sounds, voices, or words spoken; this is only to have ideas of outward things, perceived by the external sense of hearing, and so that also is imagination. When these ideas are impressed with liveliness, almost as if they were really heard with the ears, this is to have an impression on the imagination. And so I might instance in the ideas of things appertaining to the other three senses of smelling, tasting, and feeling.

Many who have had such things, have ignorantly supposed them to be of the nature of spiritual discoveries. . . .

But it is exceedingly apparent that such ideas have nothing in them which is spiritual and divine, in the sense wherein it has been demonstrated that all gracious experiences are spiritual and divine. These external ideas are in no wise entirely, and in their whole nature, diverse from all that men have by nature: so far from this, they are of the same sort which we have by the external senses, among the inferior powers of human nature. They are merely ideas of external objects, of the outward sensitive kind; the same sort of sensations of mind (differing not in degree, but only in circumstances) that we have by those natural principles which are common to us with the beasts. This is a low, miserable notion of spiritual sense, to suppose that it is only a conceiving or imagining that sort of ideas which we have by our animal senses, which senses the beasts have in as great perfection as we. Is this anything better than, as it were, a turning of Christ, or the divine nature in the soul, into a mere animal? Is there anything wanting in the soul, as it is by nature, to render it capable of being the subject of all these external ideas, without any new principles? A natural man is capable of having an idea, and a lively idea of shapes, and colors, and sounds, when they are absent, even as capable as a regenerate man is: so there is nothing supernatural in them. And it is known by abundant experience, that it is not the advancing or perfecting of human nature, which makes persons more capable of having such lively and strong imaginary ideas; but on the contrary, the weakness of body and mind, makes persons abundantly more susceptive of such impressions.[1]

As to a truly spiritual sensation, not only is the manner of its coming into the mind extraordinary, but the sensation itself is totally diverse from all that men have, or can have, in a state of nature, as has been shown. But as to these external ideas, though the way of their coming into the mind is sometimes unusual, yet the ideas in themselves are not the better for that; they are still of no different sort from what men have by their senses; they are of no higher kind, nor a whit better. . . .

And if Satan, or any created being, has power to impress the mind with outward representations, then no particular sort of outward representations can be any evidence of a divine power. Is almighty power any more requisite to represent the shape of man to the imagination, than the shape of anything else? Is there any higher kind of power necessary to form in the brain one bodily shape or color than another? Does it need a power any more glorious to represent the form of the body of man, than the form of a chip or block; though it be of a very beautiful human body, with a sweet smile in his countenance, or arms open, or blood running from hands, feet, and side? May not that sort of power which can represent blackness or darkness to the imagination, also represent white and shining brightness? May not the power and skill which can well and exactly paint a straw, or a stick, on a piece of paper or canvass, only perhaps further improved, be sufficient to paint the body of a man, with

---

[1] "Conceits and whimsies abound most in men of weak reason; children, and such as are cracked in their understanding, have most of them; strength of reason banishes them, as the sun does mists and vapors. But now the more rational any gracious person is, by so much more is he fixed and settled, and satisfied in the grounds of religion: yea, there is the highest and purest reason in religion; and when this change is wrought upon men, it is carried on in a rational way, Is. 1. 18. John xix. 9."—Flavel's *Preparation for Sufferings*, Chap. vi. [Edwards' Note.]

great beauty and in royal majesty, or a magnificent city, paved with gold, full of brightness, and a glorious throne? So it is no more than the same sort of power, that is requisite to paint one as the other of these on the brain. The same sort of power that can put ink upon paper, can put on leaf-gold. So that it is evident to a demonstration, if we suppose it to be in the devil's power to make any sort of external representation at all on the fancy—and never anyone questioned it who believed there was a devil, that had any agency with mankind—that a created power may extend to all kinds of external appearances and ideas in the mind.

From hence it again clearly appears, that no such things have anything in them that is spiritual, supernatural, and divine, in the sense in which it has been proved that all truly gracious experiences have. And though external ideas, through man's make and frame, ordinarily in some degree attend spiritual experiences; yet these ideas are no part of their spiritual experience, any more than the motion of the blood, and beating of the pulse. And though, undoubtedly, through men's infirmity in the present state, and especially through the weak constitution of some persons, gracious affections which are very strong, do excite lively ideas in the imagination; yet it is also undoubted, that when affections are founded on imaginations, which is often the case, those affections are merely natural and common, because they are built on a foundation that is not spiritual; and so are entirely different from gracious affections, which, as has been proved, do evermore arise from those operations that are spiritual and divine.   1743, 1746

From *The Nature of True Virtue*

CHAPTER I

Showing wherein the Essence of true Virtue consists.

Whatever controversies and variety of opinions there are about the nature of virtue, yet all excepting some sceptics, who deny any real difference between virtue and vice, mean by it something beautiful, or rather some kind of beauty, or excellency. It is not all beauty that is called virtue; for instance, not the beauty of a building, of a flower, or of the rainbow; but some beauty belonging to beings that have perception and will. It is not all beauty of mankind that is called virtue; for instance, not the external beauty of the countenance, or shape, gracefulness of motion, or harmony of voice: but it is a beauty that has its original seat in the mind. But yet perhaps not everything that may be called a beauty of mind, is properly called virtue. There is a beauty of understanding and speculation; there is something in the ideas and conceptions of great philosophers and statesmen, that may be called beautiful; which is a different thing from what is most commonly meant by virtue.

But virtue is the beauty of those qualities and acts of the mind, that are of a moral nature, i.e. such as are attended with desert or worthiness of praise or blame. Things of this sort, it is generally agreed, so far as I know, do not belong merely to speculation; but to the disposition and will, or (to use a general word, I suppose commonly well understood) to the heart. Therefore, I suppose, I shall not depart from the common opinion, when I say, that virtue is the beauty of the qualities and exercises of the heart, or those actions which proceed from them. So that when it is inquired, what is the nature of true virtue? This is the same as to inquire, what that is, which renders any habit, disposition, or exercise of the heart truly beautiful?

I use the phrase true virtue, and speak of things truly beautiful, because I suppose it will generally be allowed, that there is a distinction to be made between some things which are truly virtuous, and others which only seem to be so, through a partial and imperfect view of things: that some actions and dispositions appear beautiful, if considered partially and superficially, or with regard to some things belonging to them, and in some of their circumstances and tendencies, which would appear otherwise in a more extensive and comprehensive view, wherein they are seen clearly in their whole nature, and the extent of their connections in the universality of things.

There is a general and particular beauty. By a particular beauty, I mean that by which a thing appears beautiful when considered only with regard to its connection with, and tendency to, some particular things within a limited, and as it were a private sphere. And a general beauty is that by which a thing appears beautiful when viewed most perfectly, comprehensively and universally, with regard to all its tendencies, and its connections with everything to which it stands related. The former may be without and against the latter. As a few notes in a tune, taken only by themselves, and in their relation to one another, may be harmonious; which, when considered with respect to all the notes in the tune, or the entire series of sounds they are connected with, may be very discordant, and disagreeable. That only, therefore, is what I mean by true virtue, which, belonging to the heart of an intelligent being, is beautiful by a general beauty, or beautiful in a comprehensive view, as it is in itself, and, as related to everything with which it stands connected. And therefore, when we are inquiring concerning the nature of true virtue—wherein this true and general beauty of the heart does most essentially consist —this is my answer to the inquiry:—

True virtue most essentially consists in Benevolence to Being in General. Or perhaps, to speak more accurately, it is that consent, propensity and union of heart to being in general, which is immediately exercised in a general good will.

The things before observed respecting the nature of true virtue, naturally lead us to such a notion of it. If it has its seat in the heart, and is the general goodness and beauty of the disposition and its exercise, in the most comprehensive view, considered with regard to its universal tendency, and as related to everything with which it stands connected; what can it consist in, but a consent and good will to being in general? Beauty does not consist in discord and dissent, but in consent and agreement. And if every intelligent being is some way related to being in general, and is a part of the universal system of existence; and so stands in connection with the whole; what can its general and true beauty be, but its union and consent with the great whole?

If any such thing can be supposed as an union of heart to some particular being, or number of beings, disposing it to benevolence to a private circle or system of beings, which are but a small part of the whole; not implying a tendency to an union with the great system, and not at all inconsistent with enmity towards being in general; this I suppose not to be of the nature of true virtue; although it may in some respects be good, and may appear beautiful in a confined and contracted view of things.— But of this more afterwards.

It is abundantly plain by the holy scriptures, and generally allowed, not only by Christian divines, but by the more considerable Deists, that virtue most essentially consists in love. And I suppose, it is owned by the most considerable writers, to consist in general love of benevolence, or kind affection: though it seems to me the meaning of some in this affair is not sufficiently explained; which perhaps occasions some error or confusion in discourses on this subject.

When I say, true virtue consists in love to being in general, I shall not be likely to be understood, that no one act of the mind or exercise of love is of the nature of true virtue, but what has being in general, or the great system of universal existence, for its direct and immediate object: so that no exercise of love, or kind affection to any one particular being, that is but a small part of this whole, has anything of the nature of true virtue. But, that the nature of true virtue consists in a disposition to benevolence towards being in general; though from such a disposition may arise exercises of love to particular beings, as objects are presented, and occasions arise. No wonder, that he who is of a generally benevolent disposition, should be more disposed than another to have his heart moved with benevolent affection to particular persons, with whom he is acquainted and conversant, and from whom arise the greatest and most frequent occasions for exciting his benevolent temper. But my meaning is, that no affections towards particular persons or beings are of the nature of true virtue, but such as arise from a generally benevolent temper, or from that habit or frame of mind, wherein consists a disposition to love being in general.

And perhaps it is needless for me to give notice to my readers, that when I speak of an intelligent being having a heart united and benevolently disposed to being in general I thereby mean intelligent being in general. Not inanimate things, or beings that have no perception or will; which are not properly capable objects of benevolence.

Love is commonly distinguished into love of benevolence, and love of complacence. Love of benevolence is that affection or propensity of the heart to any being, which causes it to incline to its well-being, or disposes it to desire and take pleasure in its happiness. And if I mistake not, it is agreeable to the common opinion, that beauty in the object is not always the ground of this propensity; but that there may be a disposition to the welfare of those that are not considered as beautiful, unless mere existence be accounted a beauty. And benevolence or goodness in the divine Being is generally supposed, not only to be prior to the beauty of many of its objects, but to their existence; so as to be the ground both of their existence and their beauty, rather than the foundation of God's benevolence; as it is supposed that it is God's goodness which moved him to give them both being and beauty. So that if all virtue primarily consists in that affection of heart to being, which is exercised in benevolence, or an inclination to its good, then God's virtue is so extended as to include a propensity not only to being actually existing, and actually beautiful, but to possible being, so as to incline him to give a being beauty and happiness.

What is commonly called love of complacence, presupposes beauty. For it is no other than delight in beauty; or complacence in the person or being beloved for his beauty. If virtue be the beauty of an intelligent being, and virtue consists in love, then it is a plain inconsistence, to suppose that virtue primarily consists in any love to its object for its beauty; either in a love of complacence, which is delight in a being for his beauty, or in a love of benevolence, that has the beauty of its object for its foundation. For that would be to suppose, that the beauty of intelligent beings primarily consists in love to beauty; or that their virtue first of all consists in their love to virtue. Which is an inconsistence, and going in a circle. Because it makes virtue, or beauty of mind, the foundation or first motive of that love wherein virtue originally consists, or wherein the very first virtue consists; or, it supposes the first virtue to be the consequence and effect of virtue. Which makes the first virtue, both the ground and the consequence, both cause and effect of itself. Doubtless virtue primarily consists in something else besides any effect or consequence of virtue. If virtue consists primarily in love to virtue, then virtue, the thing loved, is the love of virtue: so that virtue must consist in the love of the love of virtue—and so on in infinitum. For there is no end of going back in a circle. We never come to any beginning or foundation; it is without beginning, and hangs on nothing.—Therefore, if the essence of virtue, or beauty of mind, lies in love, or a disposition to love, it must primarily consist in something different both from complacence, which is a delight in beauty, and also from any benevolence that has the beauty of its object for its foundation. Because it is absurd to say, that virtue is primarily and first of all the consequence of itself; which makes virtue primarily prior to itself.

Nor can virtue primarily consist in gratitude; or one being's benevolence to another for his benevolence to him. Because this implies the same inconsistence. For it supposes a benevolence prior to gratitude, which is the cause of gratitude. The first benevolence cannot be gratitude. Therefore there is room left for no other conclusion, than that the primary object of virtuous love is being, simply considered; or that true virtue primarily consists, not in love to any particular beings, because of their virtue or beauty, nor in gratitude, because they love us; but in a propensity and union of heart to being simply considered; exciting absolute benevolence, if I may so call it, to being in general. I say, true virtue primarily consists in this. For I am far from asserting, that there is no true virtue in any other love than this absolute benevolence. But I would express what appears to me to be the truth, on this subject, in the following particulars.

The first object of a virtuous benevolence is being, simply considered: and if being, simply considered, be its object, then being in general is its object; and what it has an ultimate propensity to, is the highest good of being in general. And it will seek the good of every individual being unless it be conceived as not consistent with the highest good of being in general. In which case the good of a particular being, or some beings, may be given up for the sake of the highest good of being in general. And particularly, if there be any being statedly and irreclaimably opposite, and an enemy to being in general, then consent and adherence to being in general will induce the truly virtuous heart to forsake that enemy, and to oppose it.

Further, if Being, simply considered, be the first object of a truly virtuous benevolence, then that object who has most of being, or has the greatest share of existence, other things being equal, so far as such a being is exhibited to our faculties, will have the greatest share of the propensity and benevolent affection of the heart. I say, "other things being equal," especially because there is a secondary object of virtuous benevolence, that I shall take notice of presently, which must be considered as the ground or motive to a purely virtuous benevolence. Pure benevolence in its first exercise is nothing else but being's uniting consent, or propensity to being; and inclining to the general highest good, and to each being, whose welfare is consistent with the highest general good, in proportion to the degree of existence,[2] understand, "other things being equal."

---

[2] I say, "in proportion to the degree of existence" because one being may have more existence than another, as he may be greater than another. That which is great, has more existence, and is further from nothing, than that which is little. One being may have everything positive belonging to it, or everything which goes to its positive existence (in opposition to defect) in an higher degree than another; or a greater capacity and

The second object of a virtuous propensity of heart is benevolent being. A secondary ground of pure benevolence is virtuous benevolence itself in its object. When anyone under the influence of general benevolence, sees another being possessed of the like general benevolence, this attaches his heart to him, and draws forth greater love to him, than merely his having existence: because so far as the being beloved has love to being in general, so far his own being is, as it were, enlarged; extends to, and in some sort comprehends being in general: and therefore, he that is governed by love to being in general, must of necessity have complacence in him, and the greater degree of benevolence to him, as it were out of gratitude to him for his love to general existence, that his own heart is extended and united to, and so looks on its interest as its own. It is because his heart is thus united to being in general, that he looks on a benevolent propensity to being in general, wherever he sees it, as the beauty of the being in whom it is; an excellency that renders him worthy of esteem, complacence, and the greater good will.—But several things may be noted more particularly concerning this secondary ground of a truly virtuous love.

1. That loving a being on this ground necessarily arises from pure benevolence to being in general, and comes to the same thing. For he that has a simple and pure good will to general existence, must love that temper in others, that agrees and conspires with itself. A spirit of consent to being must agree with consent to being. That which truly and sincerely seeks the good of others, must approve of, and love that which joins with him in seeking the good of others.

2. This secondary ground of virtuous love, is the thing wherein true moral or spiritual beauty primarily consists. Yea, spiritual beauty consists wholly in this, and in the various qualities and exercises of mind which proceed from it, and the external actions which proceed from these internal qualities and exercises. And in these things consists all true virtue, viz. in this love of being, and the qualities and acts which arise from it.

3. As all spiritual beauty lies in these virtuous principles and acts, so it is primarily on this account they are beautiful, viz. that they imply consent and union with being in general. This is the primary and most essential beauty of everything that can justly be called by the name of virtue, or is any moral excellency in the eye of one that has a perfect view of things. I say, "the primary and most essential beauty," because there is a secondary and inferior sort of beauty; which I shall take notice of afterwards.

4. This spiritual beauty, which is but a secondary ground of virtuous benevolence, is the ground, not only of benevolence, but complacence, and is the primary ground of the latter; that is, when the complacence is

---

power, greater understanding, every faculty and every positive quality in an higher degree. An Archangel must be supposed to have more existence, and to be every way further removed from nonentity, than a worm. [Edwards' Note.]

truly virtuous. Love to us in particular, and kindness received, may be a secondary ground; but this is the primary objective foundation of it.

5. It must be noted, that the degree of the amiableness of true virtue, primarily consisting in consent, and a benevolent propensity of heart to being in general, is not in the simple proportion of the degree of benevolent affection seen, but in a proportion compounded of the greatness of the benevolent being, or the degree of being and the degree of benevolence. One that loves being in general, will necessarily value good will to being in general, wherever he sees it. But if he sees the same benevolence in two beings, he will value it more in two, than in one only. Because it is a greater thing, more favorable to being in general, to have two beings to favor it, than only one of them. For there is more being that favors being: both together having more being than one alone. So, if one being be as great as two, has as much existence as both together, and has the same degree of general benevolence, it is more favorable to being in general, than if there were general benevolence in a being that had but half that share of existence. As a large quantity of gold, with the same quality, is more valuable than a small quantity of the same metal.

6. It is impossible that any one should truly relish this beauty, consisting in general benevolence, who has not that temper himself. I have observed, that if any being is possessed of such a temper, he will unavoidably be pleased with the same temper in another. And it may in like manner be demonstrated, that it is such a spirit, and nothing else, which will relish such a spirit. For if a being, destitute of benevolence, should love benevolence to being in general, it would prize and seek that for which it had no value. For how should one love and value a disposition to a thing, or a tendency to promote it, and for that very reason, when the thing itself is what he is regardless of, and has no value for, nor desires to have promoted.   1755, 1765

BENJAMIN FRANKLIN

(1706-1790)

French; invented lightning rod; kite experiment; helped found first fire insurance company.

1753 Deputy Postmaster-General of North America; awarded Copley medal by Royal Society.

1754 Proposed Albany Plan for union of colonies in defense against French-Indians.

1756 Member of British Royal Society and London Society of Arts; *Plan for Settling Two Western Colonies* (Philadelphia).

1757-62 To England as agent for Pennsylvania.

1758 *The Way to Wealth* in *Poor Richard's Almanac.*

1759 Doctor of Laws from University of St. Andrews; member of Philosophical Society, Edinburgh.

1760 *The Interest of Great Britain Considered with Regard to Her Colonies* (London).

1761 Toured Holland and Belguim.

1762 Doctor of Civil Laws from Oxford; returned to America in October.

1764-75 Agent for Pennsylvania (and other colonies) in England.

1766 Appeared before Commons on repeal of Stamp Act; member of Royal Society of Sciences, University of Gottingen.

1767 Visited France and met French Physiocrats.

1769 Second trip to France; first president of American Philosophical Society.

1771 Began work on *Autobiography;* member of Learned Society of Sciences, Rotterdam.

1772 Member of Royal Academy of Sciences, Paris.

1773 *Rules by Which a Great Empire May be Reduced to a Small One* (London); *An Edict by the King of Prussia* (London); French edition of Franklin's *Works.*

1774 Deborah Franklin died, December 19.

1775 Returned to America in May; member of Committee of Secret Correspondence; first postmaster under Articles of Confederation; delegate to Second Continental Congress.

1776 Member of committee to write Declaration of Independence; one of three commissioners to French Court; arrived in Paris, December 21.

1777-85 Residence in France.

1777 Member of Loge des Neuf Soeurs and of Royal Medical Society, Paris.

1778 "The Ephemera" written; U. S. Minister to France, 1778-1784.

1779 "The Whistle" written; Benjamin Vaughn edited Franklin's *Political, Miscellaneous, and Philosophical Pieces* (London).

1780 *Dialogue between Franklin and the Gout.*

1781 Appointed one of commissioners to negotiate peace treaty between England and United States.

1783 Signed Treaty of Paris; Honorary Fellow of Royal Society, Edinburgh.

1784 Resumed work on *Autobiography* at Passy; member Royal Academy of Madrid; *Remarks Concerning the Savages of North America* (Passy); *Advice to Such as Would Remove to America* (Passy).

1785 Resigned as minister to French Court; returned to Philadelphia.

1787 Pennsylvania delegate to Constitutional Convention.

1788 Worked on *Autobiography* at Philadelphia.

1790 Died April 17 in Philadelphia.

BIBLIOGRAPHY:
Paul L. Ford, *Franklin Bibliography* (Brooklyn, 1889). *The Writings of Benjamin Franklin,* 10 vols., ed. Albert H. Smyth (New York, 1905-1907), vol. X is a biography. *The Papers of Benjamin Franklin,* in progress, gen. eds. Leonard W. Labaree and Whitfield J. Bell, Jr., 8 vols.

(New Haven, 1959-1965). *Benjamin Franklin: Representative Selections,* eds. Frank L. Mott and Chester E. Jorgenson (New York, 1936). *A Benjamin Franklin Reader,* ed. Nathan G. Goodman (New York, 1945). Among numerous reprints of *The Autobiography* is *The Autobiography of Benjamin Franklin,* ed. Leonard W. Labaree, *et al.* (New Haven, 1964).

Carl Van Doren, *Benjamin Franklin* (New York, 1938). James Parton, *Life and Times of Benjamin Franklin,* 2 vols. (New York, 1864). Bernard Fay, *Franklin: The Apostle of Modern Times* (Boston, 1929). Carl L. Becker, *Benjamin Franklin* (Ithaca, N.Y., 1946). Richard E. Amacher, *Benjamin Franklin* (New York, 1962).

From *The Autobiography*

Twyford, at the Bishop of St. Asaph's, 1771.

Dear Son: I have ever had pleasure in obtaining any little anecdotes of my ancestors. You may remember the inquiries I made among the remains of my relations when you were with me in England, and the journey I undertook for that purpose. Imagining it may be equally agreeable to you to know the circumstances of my life, many of which you are yet unacquainted with, and expecting the enjoyment of a week's uninterrupted leisure in my present country retirement, I sit down to write them for you. To which I have besides some other inducements. Having emerged from the poverty and obscurity in which I was born and bred, to a state of affluence and some degree of reputation in the world, and having gone so far through life with a considerable share of felicity, the conducing means I made use of, which with the blessing of God so well succeeded, my posterity may like to know, as they may find some of them suitable to their own situations, and therefore fit to be imitated.

That felicity, when I reflected on it, has induced me sometimes to say, that were it offered to my choice, I should have no objection to a repetition of the same life from its beginning, only asking the advantages authors have in a second edition to correct some faults of the first. So I might, besides correcting the faults, change some sinister accidents and events of it for others more favorable. But though this were denied, I should still accept the offer. Since such a repetition is not to be expected, the next thing most like living one's life over again seems to be a recollection of that life, and to make that recollection as durable as possible by putting it down in writing.

Hereby, too, I shall indulge the inclination so natural in old men, to be talking of themselves and their own past actions; and I shall indulge it without being tiresome to others, who, through respect to age, might conceive themselves obliged to give me a hearing, since this may be read or not as any one pleases. And, lastly (I may as well confess it, since my denial of it will be believed by nobody), perhaps I shall a good deal gratify my own vanity. Indeed, I scarce ever heard or saw the introductory words, "Without vanity I may say," etc., but some vain thing immediately followed. Most people dislike vanity in others, whatever share they have of it themselves; but I give it fair quarter wherever I meet with it, being persuaded that it is often productive of good to the possessor, and to others that are within his sphere of action; and therefore, in many cases, it would not be altogether absurd if a man were to thank God for his vanity among the other comforts of life.

And now I speak of thanking God, I desire with all humility to acknowledge that I owe the mentioned happiness of my past life to His kind providence, which lead me to the means I used and gave them success. My belief of this induces me to hope, though I must not presume, that the same goodness will still be exercised toward me, in continuing that happiness, or enabling me to bear a fatal reverse, which I may experience as others have done; the complexion of my future fortune being known to Him only in whose power it is to bless to us even our afflictions. . . .

Josiah, my father, married young, and carried his wife with three children into New England, about 1682. The conventicles having been forbidden by law, and frequently disturbed, induced some considerable men of his acquaintance to remove to that country, and he was prevailed with to accompany them thither, where they expected to enjoy their mode of religion with freedom. By the same wife he had four children more born there, and by a second wife ten more, in all seventeen; of which I remember thirteen sitting at one time at his table, who all grew up to be men and women, and married; I was the youngest son, and the youngest child but two, and was born in Boston, New England. My mother, the second wife, was Abiah Folger, daughter of Peter Folger, one of the first settlers of New England, of whom honorable mention is made by Cotton Mather, in his church history of that country, entitled *Magnalia Christi Americana,* as "a godly, learned Englishman," if I remember the words rightly. . . .

My elder brothers were all put apprentices to different trades. I was put to the grammar school at eight years of age, my father intending to devote me, as the tithe of his sons, to the service of the Church. My early readiness in learning to read (which must have been very early, as I do not remember when I could not read), and the opinion of all his friends, that I should certainly make a good scholar, encouraged him in this purpose of his. My uncle Benjamin, too, approved of it, and proposed to give me all his short-hand volumes of sermons, I suppose as a stock to set up with, if I would learn his character. I continued, however, at the grammar school not quite one year, though in that time I had risen gradually from the middle of the class of that year to be the head of it, and farther was removed into the next class above it, in order to go with that into the third at the end of the year. But my father, in the meantime, from a view of the expense of a college education, which having so large a family he could not well afford, and the mean living many so educated were afterwards able to obtain—reasons that he gave to his friends in my hearing—altered his first intention, took me from the grammar-school, and sent me to a school for writing and arithmetic, kept by a then famous man, Mr. George Brownell, very successful in his profession generally, and that by mild, encouraging methods. Under him I acquired fair writing pretty soon, but I failed in the arithmetic, and made no progress in it. At ten years old I was taken home to assist my father in his business, which was that of a tallow-chandler and soap-boiler; a business he was not bred to, but had assumed on his arrival in New England, and on finding his dying trade would not maintain his family, being in little request. Accordingly, I was employed in cutting wick for the candles, filling the dipping mold and the molds for cast candles, attending the shop, going of errands, etc.

I disliked the trade, and had a strong inclination for the sea, but my father declared against it; however, living near the water, I was much in and about it, learnt early to swim well, and to manage boats; and when in a boat or canoe with other boys, I was commonly allowed to govern, especially in any case of difficulty; and upon other occasions I was generally a leader among the boys, and sometimes led them into scrapes, of which I will mention one instance, as it shows an early projecting public spirit, tho' not then justly conducted.

There was a salt-marsh that bounded part of the mill-pond, on the edge of which, at high water, we used to stand to fish for minnows. By much trampling, we had made it a mere quagmire. My proposal was to build a wharf there fit for us to stand upon, and I showed my comrades a large heap of stones, which were intended for a new house near the marsh, and which would very well suit our purpose. Accordingly, in the evening, when the workmen were gone, I assembled a number of my play-fellows, and working with them diligently like so many emmets, sometimes two or three to a stone, we brought them all away and built our little wharf. The next morning the workmen were surprised at missing the stones, which were found in our wharf. Inquiry was made after the removers; we were discovered and complained of; several of us were corrected by our fathers; and, though I pleaded the usefulness of the work, mine convinced me that nothing was useful which was not honest. . . .

From a child I was fond of reading, and all the little money that came into my hands was ever laid out in books. Pleased with the *Pilgrim's Progress*, my first collection was of John Bunyan's works in separate little volumes. I afterward sold them to enable me to buy R. Burton's *Historical Collections;* they were small chapmen's books, and cheap, 40 or 50 in all. My father's little library consisted chiefly of books in polemic divinity, most of which I read, and have since often regretted that, at a time when

I had such a thirst for knowledge, more proper books had not fallen in my way, since it was now resolved I should not be a clergyman. Plutarch's *Lives* there was in which I read abundantly, and I still think that time spent to great advantage. There was also a book of De Foe's, called *An Essay on Projects*, and another of Dr. Mather's, called *Essays to Do Good*, which perhaps gave me a turn of thinking that had an influence on some of the principal future events of my life.

This bookish inclination at length determined my father to make me a printer, though he had already one son (James) of that profession. In 1717 my brother James returned from England with a press and letters to set up his business in Boston. I liked it much better than that of my father, but still had a hankering for the sea. To prevent the apprehended effect of such an inclination, my father was impatient to have me bound to my brother. I stood out some time, but at last was persuaded, and signed the indentures when I was yet but twelve years old. I was to serve as an apprentice till I was twenty-one years of age, only I was to be allowed journeyman's wages during the last year. In a little time I made great proficiency in the business, and became a useful hand to my brother. I now had access to better books. An acquaintance with the apprentices of booksellers enabled me sometimes to borrow a small one, which I was careful to return soon and clean. Often I sat up in my room reading the greatest part of the night, when the book was borrowed in the evening and to be returned early in the morning, lest it should be missed or wanted.

And after some time an ingenious tradesman, Mr. Matthew Adams, who had a pretty collection of books, and who frequented our printing-house, took notice of me, invited me to his library, and very kindly lent me such books as I chose to read. I now took a fancy to poetry, and made some little pieces; my brother, thinking it might turn to account, encouraged me and put me on composing occasional ballads. One was called *The Lighthouse Tragedy*, and contained an account of the drowning of Captain Worthilake, with his two daughters: the other was a sailor's song, on the taking of Teach (or Blackbeard) the pirate. They were wretched stuff, in the Grub-street-ballad style; and when they were printed he sent me about the town to sell them. The first sold wonderfully, the event being recent, having made a great noise. This flattered my vanity; but my father discouraged me by ridiculing my performances, and telling me verse-makers were generally beggars. So I escaped being a poet, most probably a very bad one; but as prose writing has been of great use to me in the course of my life, and was a principal means of my advancement, I shall tell you how, in such a situation, I acquired what little ability I have in that way. . . .

About this time I met with an odd volume of the *Spectator*. It was the third. I had never before seen any of them. I bought it, read it over and over, and was much delighted with it. I thought the writing excellent, and wished, if possible, to imitate it. With this view I took some of the papers, and, making short hints of the sentiment in each sentence, laid them by a few days, and then, without looking at the book, try'd to complete the papers again, by expressing each hinted sentiment at length, and as fully as it had been expressed before, in any suitable words that should come to hand. Then I compared my *Spectator* with the original, discovered some of my faults, and corrected them. But I found I wanted a stock of words, or a readiness in recollecting and using them, which I thought I should have acquired before that time if I had gone on making verses; since the continual occasion for words of the same import, but of different length, to suit the measure, or of different sound for the rhyme, would have laid me under a constant necessity of searching for variety, and also have tended to fix that variety in my mind, and make me master of it. Therefore I took some of the tales and turned them into verse; and, after a time, when I had pretty well forgotten the prose, turned them back again. I also sometimes jumbled my collections of hints into confusion, and after some weeks endeavored to reduce them into the best order, before I began to form the full sentences and complete the paper. This was to teach me method in the arrangement of thoughts. By comparing my work afterwards with the original, I discovered many faults and amended them; but I sometimes had the pleasure of fancying that, in certain particulars of small import, I had been lucky enough to improve the method or the language, and this encouraged me to think I might possibly in time come to be a tolerable English writer, of which I was extremely ambitious. My time for these exercises and for reading was at night, after work or before it began in the morning, or on Sundays, when I contrived to be in the printing-house alone, evading as much as I could the common attendance on public worship which my father used to exact of me when I was under his care, and which indeed I still thought a duty, though I could not, as it seemed to me, afford time to practice it. . . .

And now it was that, being on some occasion made asham'd of my ignorance in figures, which I had twice failed in learning when at school, I took Cocker's book of Arithmetic, and went through the whole by myself with great ease. I also read Seller's and Shermy's books of Navigation, and became acquainted with the little geometry they contain; but never proceeded far in that science. And I read about this time Locke *On Human Understanding*, and the *Art of Thinking*, by Messrs. du Port Royal.

While I was intent on improving my language, I met with an English grammar (I think it was Greenwood's), at the end of which there were two little sketches of the arts of rhetoric and logic, the latter finishing with a specimen of a dispute in the Socratic method; and soon after I procur'd Xenophon's *Memorable Things of Socrates*, wherein there are many instances of the same method. I was charm'd with it, adopted it, dropt my abrupt contradiction and positive argumentation, and put on the humble inquirer and doubter. And being then, from reading Shaftesbury and Collins, become a real doubter in many points of our religious doctrine, I found this method safest for myself and very embarrassing to those against whom I used it; therefore I took a delight in it, practis'd it continually, and grew very artful and expert in drawing people, even of superior knowledge, into concessions, the consequences of which they did not foresee, entangling them in difficulties out of which they could not extricate themselves, and so obtaining victories that neither myself nor my cause always deserved. I continu'd this method some few years, but gradually left it, retaining only the habit of expressing myself in terms of modest diffidence; never using, when I advanced anything that may possibly be disputed, the words *certainly*, *undoubtedly*, or any others that give the air of positiveness to an opinion; but rather say, I conceive or apprehend a thing to be so and so; it appears to me, or I should think it so or so, for such and such reasons; or I imagine it to be so; or it is so, if I am not mistaken. This habit, I believe, has been of great advantage to me when I have had occasion to inculcate my opinions, and persuade men into measures that I have been from time to time engag'd in promoting; and, as the chief ends of conversation are to inform or to be informed, to please or to persuade, I wish well-meaning, sensible men would not lessen their power of doing good by a positive, assuming manner, that seldom fails to disgust, tends to create opposition, and to defeat everyone of those purposes for which speech was given to us, to wit, giving or receiving information or pleasure. For, if you would inform, a positive and dogmatical manner in advancing your sentiments may provoke contradiction and prevent a candid attention. If you wish information and improvement from the knowledge of others, and yet at the same time express yourself as firmly fix'd in your present opinions, modest, sensible men, who do not love disputation, will probably leave you undisturbed in the possession of your error. And by such a manner, you can seldom hope to recommend yourself in pleasing your hearers, or to persuade those whose concurrence you desire. . . .

My brother had, in 1720 or 1721, begun to print a newspaper. It was the second that appeared in America, and was called the *New England Courant*. The only one before it was the *Boston News-Letter*. I remember his being dissuaded by some of his friends from the undertaking, as not likely to succeed, one newspaper being, in their judgment, enough for America. At this time (1771) there are not less than five-and-twenty. He went on, however, with the undertaking, and after having worked in composing the types and printing off the sheets, I was employed to carry the papers thro' the streets to the customers.

He had some ingenious men among his friends, who amus'd themselves by writing little pieces for this paper, which gain'd it credit and made it more in demand, and these gentlemen often visited us. Hearing their conversations, and their accounts of the approbation their papers were received with, I was excited to try my hand among them; but, being still a boy, and suspecting that my brother would object to printing anything of mine in his paper if he knew it to be mine, I contrived to disguise my hand, and, writing an anonymous paper, I put it in at night under the door of the printing-house. It was found in the morning, and communicated to his writing friends when they call'd in as usual. They read it, commented on it in my hearing, and I had the exquisite pleasure of finding it met with their approbation, and that, in their different guesses at the author, none were named but men of some character among us for learning and ingenuity. I suppose now that I was rather lucky in my judges, and that perhaps they were not really so very good ones as I then esteem'd them.

Encourag'd, however, by this, I wrote and convey'd in the same way to the press several more papers which were equally approv'd; and I kept my secret till my small fund of sense for such performances was pretty well exhausted, and then I discovered it, when I began to be considered a little more by my brother's acquaintance, and in a manner that did not quite please him, as he thought, probably with reason, that it tended to make me too vain. And, perhaps, this might be one occasion of the differences that we began to have about this time. Though a brother, he considered himself as my master, and me as his apprentice, and, accordingly, expected the same services from me as he would from another, while I thought he demean'd me too much in some he requir'd of me, who from a brother expected more indulgence. Our disputes were often brought before our father, and I fancy I was either generally in the right, or else a better pleader, because the judgment was generally in my favor. But my brother was passionate, and had often beaten me, which I took extremely amiss; and, thinking my apprenticeship very tedious, I was continually wishing for some opportunity of shortening it, which at length offered in a manner unexpected.

One of the pieces in our newspaper on some political point, which I have now forgotten, gave offense to the Assembly. He was taken up, censur'd, and imprison'd for a month, by the speaker's warrant, I suppose, because he would not discover his author. I too was taken up and examin'd before the council; but, tho' I did not give them any satisfaction, they content'd themselves with admonishing me, and dismissed me, considering me, perhaps, as an apprentice, who was bound to keep his master's secrets.

During my brother's confinement, which I resented a good deal, notwithstanding our private differences, I had the management of the paper; and I made bold to give our rulers some rubs in it, which my brother took very kindly, while others began to consider me in an unfavorable light, as a young genius that had a turn for libeling and satire. My brother's discharge was accompany'd with an order of the House (a very odd one), that "James Franklin should no longer print the paper called the *New England Courant.*"

There was a consultation held in our printing-house among his friends, what he should do in this case. Some proposed to evade the order by changing the name of the paper; but my brother, seeing inconveniences in that, it was finally concluded on as a better way, to let it be printed for the future under the name of Benjamin Franklin; and to avoid the censure of the Assembly, that might fall on him as still printing it by his apprentice, the contrivance was that my old indenture should be return'd to me, with a full discharge on the back of it, to be shown on occasion, but to secure to him the benefit of my service, I was to sign new indentures for the remainder of the term, which were to be kept private. A very flimsy scheme it was; however, it was immediately executed, and the paper went on accordingly, under my name for several months.

At length, a fresh difference arising between my brother and me, I took upon me to assert my freedom, presuming that he would not venture to produce the new indentures. It was not fair in me to take this advantage, and this I therefore reckon one of the first errata of my life; but the unfairness of it weighed little with me, when under the impressions of resentment for the blows his passion too often urged him to bestow upon me, though he was otherwise not an ill-natur'd man: perhaps I was too saucy and provoking.

When he found I would leave him, he took care to prevent my getting employment in any other printing-house of the town, by going round and speaking to every master, who accordingly refus'd to give me work. I then thought of going to New York, as the nearest place where there was a printer; and I was rather inclin'd to leave Boston when I reflected that I had already made myself a little obnoxious to the governing party, and, from the arbitrary proceedings of the Assembly in my brother's case, it was likely I might, if I stay'd, soon bring myself into scrapes; and farther, that my indiscrete disputations about religion began to make me pointed at with horror by good people as an infidel or atheist. I determin'd on the point, but my father now siding with my brother, I was sensible that, if I attempted to go openly, means would be used to prevent me. My friend Collins, therefore, undertook to manage a little for me. He agreed with the captain of a New York sloop for my passage, under the notion of my being a young acquaintance of his, that had got a naughty girl with child, whose friends would compel me to marry her, and therefore I could not appear or come away publicly. So I sold some of my books to raise a little money, was taken on board privately, and as we had a fair wind, in three days I found myself in New York, near 300 miles from home, a boy of but 17, without the least recommendation to, or knowledge of any person in the place, and with very little money in my pocket.

. . . I now began to think of getting a little money beforehand, and, expecting better work, I left Palmer's to work at Watts's, near Lincoln's Inn Fields, a still greater printing-house. Here I continued all the rest of my stay in London.

At my first admission into this printing-house I took to working at press, imagining I felt a want of the bodily exercise I had been us'd to in America, where presswork is mix'd with composing. I drank only water; the other workmen, near fifty in number, were great guzzlers of beer. On occasion, I carried up and down stairs a large form of types in each hand, when others carried but one in both hands. They wondered to see, from this and several instances, that the Water-American, as they called me, was stronger than themselves, who drank strong beer! We had an alehouse boy who attended always in the house to supply the workmen. My companion at the press drank every day a pint before breakfast, a pint at breakfast with his bread and cheese, a pint between breakfast and dinner, a pint at dinner, a pint in the afternoon about six o'clock, and another when he had done his day's work. I thought it a detestable custom; but it was necessary, he suppos'd, to drink strong beer, that he might be strong to labor. I endeavored to convince him that the bodily strength afforded by beer could only be in proportion to the grain or flour of the barley dissolved in the water of which it was made; that there was more flour in a pennyworth of bread; and therefore, if he would eat that with a pint of water, it would give him more strength than a quart of beer. He drank on, however, and had four or five shillings to pay out of his wages every Saturday night for that muddling liquor; an expense I was free from. And thus these poor devils keep themselves always under.

Watts, after some weeks, desiring to have me in the composing-room, I left the pressmen; a new bien venu or sum for drink, being five shillings, was demanded of me by the compositors. I thought it an imposition, as I had paid below; the master thought so too, and forbad my paying it. I stood out two or three weeks, was accordingly considered as an excommunicate, and had so many little pieces of private mischief done me, by mixing my sorts, transposing my pages, breaking my matter, etc., etc., if I were ever so little out of the room, and all ascribed to the chapel ghost, which they said ever haunted those not regularly admitted, that, notwithstanding the master's protection, I found myself oblig'd to comply and to pay the money, convinc'd of the folly of being on ill terms with those one is to live with continually. . . .

At Watts's printing-house I contracted an acquaintance with an ingenious young man, one Wygate, who, having wealthy relations, had been better educated than most printers; was a tolerable Latinist, spoke French, and lov'd reading. I taught him and a friend of his to swim at twice going into the river, and they soon became good swimmers. They introduc'd me to some gentlemen from the country, who went to Chelsea by water to see the College and Don Saltero's curiosities. In our return, at the request of the company, whose curiosity Wygate had excited, I stripped and leaped into the river, and swam from near Chelsea to Black-friar's, performing on the way many feats of activity, both upon and under water, that surpris'd and pleas'd those to whom they were novelties.

I had from a child been ever delighted with this exercise, had studied and practis'd all Thevenot's motions and positions, added some of my own, aiming at the graceful and easy as well as the useful. All these I took this occasion of exhibiting to the company, and was much flatter'd by their admiration; and Wygate, who was desirous of becoming a master, grew more and more attach'd to me on that account, as well as from the similarity of our studies. He at length proposed to me traveling all over Europe together, supporting ourselves everywhere by working at our business. I was once inclined to it; but, mentioning it to my good friend Mr. Denham, with whom I often spent an hour when I had leisure, he dissuaded me from it, advising me to think only of returning to Pennsylvania, which he was now about to do. . . .

Thus I spent about eighteen months in London; most part of the time I work'd hard at my business, and spent but little upon myself except in seeing plays and in books. My friend Ralph had kept me poor; he owed me about twenty-seven pounds, which I was now never likely to receive; a great sum out of my small earnings! I lov'd him, notwithstanding, for he had many amiable qualities. I had by no means improv'd my fortune; but I had picked up some very ingenious acquaintance, whose conversation was of great advantage to me; and I had read considerably. . . .

Before I enter upon my public appearance in business, it may be well to let you know the then state of my mind with regard to my principles and morals, that you may see how far those influenc'd the future events of my life. My parents had early given me religious impressions, and brought me through my childhood piously in the Dissenting way. But I was scarce fifteen, when, after doubting by turns of several points, as I found them disputed in the different books I read, I began to doubt of Revelation itself. Some books against Deism fell into my hands; they were said to be the substance of sermons preached at Boyle's Lectures. It happened that they wrought an effect on me quite contrary to what was intended by them; for the arguments of the Deists, which were quoted to be refuted, appeared to me much stronger than the refutations; in short, I soon became a thorough Deist. My arguments perverted some others, particularly Collins and Ralph; but, each of them having afterwards wrong'd me greatly without the least compunction, and recollecting Keith's conduct towards me (who was another freethinker), and my own towards Vernon and Miss Read, which at times gave me great trouble, I began to suspect that this doctrine, tho' it might be true, was not very useful. My London pamphlet, which had for its motto these lines of Dryden:

"Whatever is, is right. Though purblind man
Sees but a part o' the chain, the nearest link:
His eyes not carrying to the equal beam,
That poises all above;"

and from the attributes of God, his infinite wisdom, goodness and power, concluded that nothing could possibly be wrong in the world, and that vice and virtue were empty distinctions, no such things existing, appear'd now not so clever a performance as I once thought it; and I doubted whether some error had not insinuated itself unperceiv'd into my argument, so as to infect all that follow'd, as is common in metaphysical reasonings.

I grew convinc'd that truth, sincerity and integrity in dealings between man and man were of the utmost importance to the felicity of life; and I form'd written resolutions, which still remain in my journal book, to practice them ever while I lived. Revelation had indeed no weight with me, as such; but I entertain'd an opinion that, though certain actions might not be bad because they were forbidden by it, or good because it commanded them, yet probably these actions might be forbidden because they were bad for us, or commanded because they were beneficial to us, in their own natures, all the circumstances of things considered. And this persuasion, with the kind hand of Providence, or some guardian angel, or accidental favorable circumstances and situations, or all together, preserved me, thro' this dangerous time of youth, and the hazardous situations I was sometimes in among strangers, remote from the eye and advice of my father, without any willful gross immorality or injustice, that might have been expected from my want of religion. I say willful, because the instances I have mentioned had something of necessity in them, from my youth, inexperience, and the knavery of others. I had therefore a tolerable character to begin the world with; I valued it properly, and determin'd to preserve it. . . .

I had been religiously educated as a Presbyterian; and tho' some of the dogmas of that persuasion, such as the eternal decrees of God, election, reprobation, etc., appeared to me unintelligible, others doubtful, and I early absented myself from the public assemblies of the sect, Sunday being my studying day, I never was without some religious principles. I never doubted, for instance, the existence of the Deity; that he made the world, and govern'd it by his Providence; that the most acceptable service of God was the doing good to man; that our souls are immortal; and that all crime will be punished, and virtue rewarded, either here or hereafter. These I esteem'd the essentials of every religion; and, being to be found in all the religions we had in our country, I respected them all, tho' with different degrees of respect, as I found them more or less mix'd with other articles, which, without any tendency to inspire, promote, or confirm morality, serv'd principally to divide us, and make us unfriendly to one another. This respect to all, with an opinion that the worst had some good effects, induc'd me to avoid all discourse that might tend to lessen the good opinion another might have of his own religion; and as our province increas'd in people, and new places of worship were continually wanted, and generally erected by voluntary contribution, my mite for such purpose, whatever might be the sect, was never refused.

Tho' I seldom attended any public worship, I had still an opinion of its propriety, and of its utility when rightly conducted, and I regularly paid my annual subscription for the support of the only Presbyterian minister or meeting we had in Philadelphia. He us'd to visit me sometimes as a friend, and admonish me to attend his administrations, and I was now and then prevail'd on to do so, once for five Sundays successively. Had he been in my opinion a good preacher, perhaps I might have continued, notwithstanding the occasion I had for the Sunday's leisure in my course of study. . . .

It was about this time I conceiv'd the bold and arduous project of arriving at moral perfection. I wish'd to live without committing any fault at any time; I would conquer all that either natural inclination, custom, or company might lead me into. As I knew, or thought I knew, what was right and wrong, I did not see why I might not always do the one and avoid the other. But I soon found I had undertaken a task of more difficulty than I had imagined. While my care was employ'd in guarding against one fault, I was often surprised by another; habit took the advantage of inattention; inclination was sometimes too strong for reason. I concluded, at length, that the mere speculative conviction that it was our interest to be completely virtuous, was not sufficient to prevent our slipping; and that the contrary habits must be broken, and good ones acquired and established, before we can have any dependence on a steady, uniform rectitude of conduct. For this purpose I therefore contrived the following method.

In the various enumerations of the moral virtues I had met within my reading, I found the catalogue more or less numerous, as different writers included more or fewer ideas under the same name. Temperance, for example, was by some confined to eating and drinking, while by others it was extended to mean the moderating every other pleasure, appetite, inclination, or passion, bodily or mental, even to our avarice and ambition. I propos'd to myself, for the sake of clearness, to use rather more names, with fewer ideas annex'd to each, than a few names with more ideas; and I included under thirteen names of virtues all that at that time occurr'd to me as necessary or desirable, and annexed to each a short precept, which fully express'd the extent I gave to its meaning.

These names of virtues, with their precepts, were:

1. TEMPERANCE.

Eat not to dullness; drink not to elevation.

2. SILENCE.

Speak not but what may benefit others or yourself; avoid trifling conversation.

3. ORDER.

Let all your things have their places; let each part of your business have its time.

4. RESOLUTION.

Resolve to perform what you ought; perform without fail what you resolve.

5. FRUGALITY.

Make no expense but to do good to others or yourself; i.e., waste nothing.

6. INDUSTRY.

Lose no time; be always employ'd in something useful; cut off all unnecessary actions.

7. SINCERITY.

Use no hurtful deceit; think innocently and justly, and, if you speak, speak accordingly.

8. JUSTICE.

Wrong none by doing injuries, or omitting the benefits that are your duty.

9. MODERATION.

Avoid extremes; forbear resenting injuries so much as you think they deserve.

10. CLEANLINESS.

Tolerate no uncleanliness in body, clothes, or habitation.

11. TRANQUILLITY.

Be not disturbed at trifles, or at accidents common or unavoidable.

12. CHASTITY.

Rarely use venery but for health or offspring, never to dullness, weakness, or the injury of your own or another's peace or reputation.

13. HUMILITY.

Imitate Jesus and Socrates.

My intention being to acquire the habitude of all these virtues, I judg'd it would be well not to distract my attention by attempting the whole at once, but to fix it on one of them at a time; and, when I should be master of that, then to proceed to another, and so on, till I should have gone thro' the thirteen; and, as the previous acquisition of some might facilitate the acquisition of certain others, I arrang'd them with that view, as they stand above. Temperance first, as it tends to procure that coolness and clearness of head, which is so necessary where constant vigilance was to be kept up, and guard maintained against the unremitting attraction of ancient habits, and the force of perpetual temptations. This being acquir'd and establish'd, Silence would be more easy; and my desire being to gain knowledge at the same time that I improv'd in virtue, and considering that in conversation it was obtain'd rather by the use of the ears than of the tongue, and therefore wishing to break a habit I was getting into of prattling, punning, and joking, which only made me acceptable to trifling company, I gave Silence the second place. This and the next, Order, I expected would allow me more time for attending to my project and my studies. Resolution, once become habitual, would keep me firm in my endeavors to obtain all the subsequent virtues; Frugality and Industry freeing me from my remaining debt, and producing affluence and independence, would make more easy the practice of Sincerity and Justice, etc., etc. Conceiving then, that, agreeably to the advice of Pythagoras in his Golden Verses, daily examination would be necessary, I contrived the following method for conducting that examination. . . .

The precept of Order requiring that every part of my business should have its allotted time, one page in my little book contain'd the following scheme of employment for the twenty-four hours of a natural day.

THE MORNING. *Question.* What good shall I do this day?	5 6 7	Rise, wash, and address *Powerful Goodness!* Contrive day's business, and take the resolution of the day; prosecute the present study, and breakfast.
	8 9 10 11	Work.
NOON.	12 1	Read, or overlook my accounts, and dine.
	2 3 4 5	Work.

EVENING.
Question. What good have I done today?

	6	Put things in their places. Supper. Music or diversion, or conversation. Examination of the day.
	7	
	8	
	9	

NIGHT.

	10	
	11	
	12	
	1	Sleep.
	2	
	3	
	4	

I enter'd upon the execution of this plan for self-examination, and continu'd it with occasional intermissions for some time. I was surpris'd to find myself so much fuller of faults than I had imagined; but I had the satisfaction of seeing them diminish. To avoid the trouble of renewing now and then my little book, which, by scraping out the marks on the paper of old faults to make room for new ones in a new course, became full of holes, I transferr'd my tables and precepts to the ivory leaves of a memorandum book, on which the lines were drawn with red ink, that made a durable stain, and on those lines I mark'd my faults with a black-lead pencil, which marks I could easily wipe out with a wet sponge. After a while I went thro' one course only in a year, and afterward only one in several years, till at length I omitted them entirely, being employ'd in voyages and business abroad, with a multiplicity of affairs that interfered; but I always carried my little book with me.

My scheme of Order gave me the most trouble; and I found that, tho' it might be practicable where a man's business was such as to leave him the disposition of his time, that of a journeyman printer, for instance, it was not possible to be exactly observed by a master, who must mix with the world, and often receive people of business at their own hours. Order, too, with regard to places for things, papers, etc., I found extremely difficult to acquire. I had not been early accustomed to it, and, having an exceeding good memory, I was not so sensible of the inconvenience attending want of method. This article, therefore, cost me so much painful attention, and my faults in it vexed me so much, and I made so little progress in amendment, and had such frequent relapses, that I was almost ready to give up the attempt, and content myself with a faulty character in that respect, like the man who, in buying an ax of a smith, my neighbor, desired to have the whole of its surface as bright as the edge. The smith consented to grind it bright for him if he would turn the wheel; he turn'd, while the smith press'd the broad face of the ax hard and heavily on the stone, which made the turning of it very fatiguing. The man came every now and then from the wheel to see how the work went on, and at length would take his ax as it was, without farther grinding. "No," said the smith, "turn on, turn on; we shall have it bright by-and-by; as yet, it is only speckled." "Yes," says the man, "but I think I like a speckled ax best." And I believe this may have been the case with many, who, having, for want of some such means as I employ'd, found the difficulty of obtaining good and breaking bad habits in other points of vice and virtue, have given up the struggle, and concluded that "a speckled ax was best"; for something, that pretended to be reason, was every now and then suggesting to me that such extreme nicety as I exacted of myself might be a kind of foppery in morals, which, if it were known, would make me ridiculous; that a perfect character might be attended with the inconvenience of being envied and hated; and that a benevolent man should allow a few faults in himself, to keep his friends in countenance.

In truth, I found myself incorrigible with respect to Order; and now I am grown old, and my memory bad, I feel very sensibly the want of it. But, on the whole, tho' I never arrived at the perfection I had been so ambitious of obtaining, but fell far short of it, yet I was, by the endeavor, a better and a happier man than I otherwise should have been if I had not attempted it; as those who aim at perfect writing by imitating the engraved copies, tho' they never reach the wish'd-for excellence of those copies, their hand is mended by the endeavor, and is tolerable while it continues fair and legible.

It may be well my posterity should be informed that to this little artifice, with the blessing of God, their ancestor ow'd the constant felicity of his life, down to his 79th year in which this is written. What reverses may attend the remainder is in the hand of Providence; but, if they arrive, the reflection on past happiness enjoy'd ought to help his bearing them with more resignation. To Temperance he ascribes his long-continued health, and what is still left to him of a good constitution; to Industry and Frugality, the early easiness of his circumstances and acquisition of his fortune, with all that knowledge that enabled him to be a useful citizen, and obtained for him some degree of reputation among the learned; to Sincerity and Justice, the confidence of his country, and the honorable employs it conferred upon him; and to the joint influence of the whole mass of the virtues, even in the imperfect state he was able to acquire them, all that evenness of temper, and that cheerfulness in conversation, which makes his company still sought for, and agreeable even to his younger acquaintance. I hope, therefore, that some of my descendants may follow the example and reap the benefit.

1791-1868

From *The Dogood Papers*

[*The New-England Courant*, Monday March 26 to Monday April 2, 1722]

To the Author of the *New-England Courant*.

Sir,

It may not be improper in the first Place to inform your Readers, that I intend once a Fortnight to present them, by the Help of this Paper, with a short Epistle, which I presume will add somewhat to their Entertainment.

And since it is observed, that the Generality of People, nowadays, are unwilling either to commend or dispraise what they read, until they are in some measure informed who or what the Author of it is, whether he be poor or rich, old or young, a Scholar or a Leather Apron Man, &c. and give their Opinion of the Performance, according to the Knowledge which they have of the Author's Circumstances, it may not be amiss to begin with a short Account of my past Life and present Condition, that the Reader may not be at a Loss to judge whether or no my Lucubrations are worth his reading.

At the time of my Birth, my Parents were on Shipboard in their Way from London to N. England. My Entrance into this troublesome World was attended with the Death of my Father, a Misfortune, which tho' I was not then capable of knowing, I shall never be able to forget; for as he, poor Man, stood upon the Deck rejoicing at my Birth, a merciless Wave entered the Ship, and in one Moment carry'd him beyond Reprieve. Thus was the first Day which I saw, the last that was seen by my Father; and thus was my disconsolate Mother at once made both a Parent and a Widow.

When we arrived at Boston (which was not long after) I was put to Nurse in a Country Place, at a small Distance from the Town, where I went to School, and past my Infancy and Childhood in Vanity and Idleness, until I was bound out Apprentice, that I might no longer be a Charge to my Indigent Mother, who was put to hard Shifts for a Living.

My Master was a Country Minister, a pious good-natur'd young Man, & a Bachelor: He labor'd with all his Might to instill virtuous and godly Principles into my tender Soul, well knowing that it was the most suitable Time to make deep and lasting Impressions on the Mind, while it was yet untainted with Vice, free and unbias'd. He endeavor'd that I might be instructed in all that Knowledge and Learning which is necessary for our Sex, and deny'd me no Accomplishment that could possibly be attained in a Country Place, such as all Sorts of Needle-Work, Writing, Arithmetic, &c. and observing that I took a more than ordinary Delight in reading ingenious Books, he gave me the free Use of his Library, which tho' it was but small, yet it was well chose, to inform the Understanding rightly and enable the Mind to frame great and noble Ideas.

Before I had liv'd quite two Years with this Reverend Gentleman, my indulgent Mother departed this Life, leaving me as it were by my self, having no Relation on Earth within my Knowledge.

I will not abuse your Patience with a tedious Recital of all the frivolous Accidents of my Life, that happened from this Time until I arrived to Years of Discretion, only inform you that I liv'd a cheerful Country Life, spending my leisure Time either in some innocent Diversion with the neighboring Females, or in some shady Retirement, with the best of Company, Books. Thus I past away the Time with a Mixture of Profit and Pleasure, having no Affliction but what was imaginary, and created in my own Fancy; as nothing is more common with us Women, than to be grieving for nothing, when we have nothing else to grieve for.

As I would not engross too much of your Paper at once, I will defer the Remainder of my Story until my next Letter; in the meantime desiring your Readers to exercise their Patience, and bear with my Humors now and then, because I shall trouble them but seldom. I am not insensible of the Impossibility of pleasing all, but I would not willingly displease any; and for those who will take Offense where none is intended, they are beneath the Notice of

Your Humble Servant,
SILENCE DOGOOD

[*The New-England Courant,* Monday September 17 to Monday September 24, 1722]

To the Author of the *New-England Courant.*

Sir,

In Persons of a contemplative Disposition, the most indifferent Things provoke the Exercise of the Imagination; and the Satisfactions which often arise to them thereby, are a certain Relief to the Labor of the Mind (when it has been intensely fix'd on more substantial Subjects) as well as to that of the Body.

In one of the late pleasant Moon-light Evenings, I so far indulg'd in myself the Humor of the Town in walking abroad, as to continue from my Lodgings two or three Hours later than usual, & was pleas'd beyond Expectation before my Return. Here I found various Company to observe, and various Discourse to attend to. I met indeed with the common Fate of Listeners, who hear no good of themselves, but from a Consciousness of my Innocence, receiv'd it with a Satisfaction beyond what the Love of Flattery and the Daubings of a Parasite could produce. The Company who rally'd me were about Twenty in Number, of both Sexes; and tho' the Confusion of Tongues (like that of Babel) which always happens among so many impetuous Talkers, render'd their Discourse not so intelligible as I could wish, I learnt thus much, That one of the Females pretended to know me, from some Discourse she had heard at a certain House before the Publication of one of my Letters; adding, That I was a Person of an ill Character, and kept a criminal Correspondence with a Gentleman who assisted me in Writing. One of the Gallants clear'd me of this random Charge, by saying, That tho' I wrote in the Character of a Woman, he knew me to be a Man; But, continu'd he, he has more need of endeavoring a Reformation in himself, then spending his Wit in satirizing others.

I had no sooner left this Set of Ramblers, but I met a Crowd of Tarpaulins and their Doxies, link'd to each other by the Arms, who ran (by their own Account) after the Rate of Six Knots an Hour, and bent their Course towards the Common. Their eager and amorous Emotions of Body, occasion'd by taking their Mistresses in Tow, they call'd wild Steerage: And as a Pair of them happen'd to trip and come to the Ground, the Company were call'd upon to bring to, for that Jack and Betty were founder'd. But this Fleet were not less comical or irregular in their Progress than a Company of Females I soon after came up with, who, by throwing their Heads to the Right and Left, at everyone who pass'd by them, I concluded came out with no other Design than to revive the Spirit of Love in Disappointed Bachelors, and expose themselves to Sale to the first Bidder.

But it would take up too much Room in your Paper to mention all the Occasions of Diversion I met with in this Night's Ramble. As it grew later, I observed, that many pensive Youths with down looks and a slow Pace, would be ever now and then crying out on the Cruelty of their Mistresses; others with a more rapid Pace and cheerful Air, would be swinging their Canes, and clapping their Cheeks, and whispering at certain Intervals, *I'm certain I shall have her! This is more than I expected! How charmingly she talks!* &c.

Upon the whole I conclude, That our Night-Walkers are a Set of People, who contribute very much to the Health and Satisfaction of those who have been fatigu'd with Business or Study, and occasionally observe their pretty Gestures and Impertinencies. But among Men of Business, the Shoemakers, and other Dealers in Leather, are doubly oblig'd to them, inasmuch as they exceedingly promote the Consumption of their Ware: And I have heard of a Shoemaker, who being ask'd by a noted Rambler, Whether he could tell how long her Shoes would last; very prettily answer'd, That he knew how many Days she might wear them, but not how many Nights; because they were then put to a more violent and irregular Service than when she employ'd herself in the common Affairs of the House.

I am, Sir,
Your Humble Servant,
SILENCE DOGOOD

From Prefaces to *Poor Richard*

Courteous Reader,

I might in this place attempt to gain thy Favor, by declaring that I write Almanacs with no other View than that of the public Good; but in this I should not be sincere; and Men are nowadays too wise to be deceiv'd by Pretenses how specious soever. The plain Truth of the Matter is, I am excessive poor, and my Wife, good Woman, is, I tell her, excessive proud; she cannot bear, she says to sit spinning in her Shift of Tow while I do nothing but gaze at the Stars; and has threatened more than once to burn all my Books and Rattling-Traps (as she calls my Instruments) if I do not make some profitable Use of them for the Good of my Family. The Printer has offer'd me some considerable share of the Profits, and I have thus begun to comply with my Dame's Desire.

Indeed this Motive would have had Force enough to have made me publish an Almanac many Years since, had it not been overpowered by my Regard for my good Friend and Fellow Student Mr. Titan Leeds, whose Interest I was extremely unwilling to hurt: But this Obstacle (I am far from speaking it with Pleasure) is soon to be removed, since inexorable Death, who was never known to respect Merit, has already prepared the mortal Dart, the fatal Sister has already extended her destroying Shears, and that ingenious Man must soon be taken from us. He dies, by my Calculation made at his Request, on Oct. 17. 1733. 3 h. 29 m. P. M. at the very instant of the ♂ of ☉ and ☿ : By his own Calculation he will survive till the 26th of the same Month. This small Difference between us we have disputed whenever we have met these 9 Years past; but at length he is inclinable to agree with my Judgment: Which of us is most exact, a little Time will now determine. As therefore these Provinces may not longer expect to see any of his Performances after this Year, I think myself free to take up the Task, and request a share of the public Encouragement; which I am the more apt to hope for on this Account, that the Buyer of my Almanac may consider himself, not only as purchasing an useful Utensil, but as performing an Act of Charity, to his poor Friend and Servant

R. SAUNDERS

Dear Readers,

My good Man set out last week for Potowmack, to visit an old Stargazer of his Acquaintance, and see about a little Place for us to settle and end our Days on. He left the Copy of his Almanac seal'd up, and bid me send it to the Press. I suspected something, and therefore as soon as he was gone, I open'd it, to see if he had not been flinging some of his old Skits at me. Just as I thought, so it was. And truly, (for want of some-what else to say, I suppose) he had put into his Preface, that his Wife Bridget . . . was this, and that, and t'other. . . . What a peasecods! cannot I have a little Fault or two, but all the Country must see it in print! They have already been told, at one time that I am proud, another that I am loud, and that I have got a new Petticoat, and abundance of such kind of stuff; and now, forsooth! all the World must know, that Poor Dick's Wife has lately taken a fancy to drink a little Tea now and then. A mighty matter, truly, to make a Song of! 'Tis true; I had a little Tea of a Present from the Printer last Year; and what, must a body throw it away? In short, I thought the Preface was not worth a printing, and so I fairly scratch'd it all out, and I believe you'll like our Almanac never the worse for it.

Upon looking over the Months, I see he has put in abundance of foul Weather this Year; and therefore I have scatter'd here and there, where I could find room, some fair, pleasant, sunshiny, &c. for the Good-Women to dry their Clothes in. If it does not come to pass according to my De-sire, I have shown my Good-will, however; and I hope they'll take it in good part.

I had a Design to make some other Corrections; and particularly to change some of the Verses that I don't very well like; but I have just now unluckily broke my Spectacles; which obliges me to give it you as it is, and conclude

Your loving Friend,
BRIDGET SAUNDERS

POOR RICHARD, 1758

The Way to Wealth

Father Abraham's Speech introduced by Poor Richard, viz.

Courteous Reader,

I have heard that Nothing gives an Author so great Pleasure, as to find his Works respectfully quoted by other learned Authors. This Pleasure I have seldom enjoyed; for though I have been, if I may say it without Vanity, an eminent Author of Almanacs annually now a full Quarter of a Century, my Brother-Authors in the same Way, for what Reason I know not, have ever been very sparing in their Applauses; and no other Author has taken the least Notice of me, so that did not my Writings produce me some solid Pudding, the great Deficiency of Praise would have quite discouraged me.

I concluded at length, that the People were the best Judges of my Merit; for they buy my Works; and besides, in my Rambles, where I am not personally known, I have frequently heard one or other of my Adages repeated, with *as Poor Richard says,* at the End on't. This gave me some Satisfaction, as it showed not only that my Instructions were regarded, but discovered likewise some Respect for my Authority; and I own that, to encourage the Practice of remembering and repeating those wise Sentences, I have sometimes quoted myself with great Gravity.

Judge then how much I must have been gratified by an Incident I am going to relate to you. I stopt my Horse lately where a great Number of People were collected at a Vendue of Merchant Goods. The Hour of Sale not being come, they were conversing on the Badness of the Times, and one of the Company call'd to a plain clean old Man, with white Locks, Pray, Father Abraham, what think you of the Times? Won't these heavy Taxes quite ruin the Country? How shall we be ever able to pay them? What would you advise us to?—Father Abraham stood up and reply'd, If you'd have my Advice, I'll give it you in short, for A Word to the Wise is enough, and Many Words won't fill a Bushel, as Poor Richard says. They joined in desiring him to speak his Mind, and gathering round him, he proceeded as follows.

Friends, says he, and Neighbors, the Taxes are indeed very heavy, and if those laid on by the Government were the only Ones we had to pay, we might more easily discharge them; but we have many others, and much more grievous to some of us. We are taxed twice as much by our Idleness, three times as much by our Pride, and four times as much by our Folly, and from these Taxes the Commissioners cannot ease or deliver us by allowing an Abatement. However, let us hearken to good Advice, and something may be done for us. God helps them that help themselves, as Poor Richard says, in his Almanac of 1733.

It would be thought a hard Government that should tax its People one tenth Part of their Time, to be employed in its Service. But Idleness taxes many of us much more, if we reckon all that is spent in absolute Sloth, or doing of Nothing, with that which is spent in idle Employments or Amusements, that amount to Nothing. Sloth, by bringing on Diseases, absolutely shortens Life. Sloth, like Rust, consumes faster than Labor wears, while the used Key is always bright, as Poor Richard says. But Dost thou love Life? then do not squander Time, for that's the Stuff Life is made of, as Poor Richard says.—How much more than is necessary do we spend in Sleep! forgetting that The sleeping Fox catches no Poultry, and There will be sleeping enough in the Grave, as Poor Richard says. If Time be of all Things the most precious, then wasting Time must be, as Poor Richard says, the greatest Prodigality, since, as he elsewhere tells us, Lost Time is never found again; and what we call Time enough, always proves little enough. Let us then up and be doing, and doing to

The Way to Wealth / 553

the Purpose; so by Diligence shall we do more with less Perplexity. Sloth makes all Things difficult, but Industry all easy, as Poor Richard says; and He that riseth late, must trot all Day, and shall scarce overtake his Business at Night. While Laziness travels so slowly, that Poverty soon overtakes him, as we read in Poor Richard; who adds Drive thy Business, let not that drive thee; and Early to Bed, and early to rise, makes a Man healthy, wealthy and wise.

So what signifies wishing and hoping for better Times. We may make these Times better if we bestir ourselves. Industry need not wish, as Poor Richard says, and He that lives upon Hope will die fasting. There are no Gains without Pains; then Help Hands, for I have no Lands, or if I have, they are smartly taxed. And, as Poor Richard likewise observes, He that hath a Trade hath an Estate, and He that hath a Calling hath an Office of Profit and Honor; but then the Trade must be worked at, and the Calling well followed, or neither the Estate, nor the Office, will enable us to pay our Taxes.—If we are industrious we shall never starve; for, as Poor Richard says, At the working Man's House Hunger looks in, but dares not enter. Nor will the Bailiff or the Constable enter, for Industry pays Debts, while Despair increaseth them, says Poor Richard.—What though you have found no Treasure, nor has any rich Relation left you a Legacy, Diligence is the Mother of Good-luck, as Poor Richard says, and God gives all Things to Industry. Then Plough deep, while Sluggards sleep, and you shall have Corn to sell and to keep, says Poor Dick. Work while it is called Today, for you know not how much you may be hindered Tomorrow, which makes Poor Richard say One Today is worth two Tomorrows; and farther, Have you somewhat to do Tomorrow? do it Today. If you were a Servant, would you not be ashamed that a good Master should catch you idle? Are you then your own Master, be ashamed to catch yourself idle, as Poor Dick says. When there is so much to be done for yourself, your Family, your Country, and your gracious King, be up by Peep of Day: Let not the Sun look down and say, Inglorious here he lies. Handle your Tools without Mittens; remember that The Cat in Gloves catches no Mice, as Poor Richard says. 'Tis true there is much to be done, and perhaps you are weak handed, but stick to it steadily, and you will see great Effects, for Constant Dropping wears away Stones, and By Diligence and Patience the Mouse ate in two the Cable; and Little Strokes fell great Oaks, as Poor Richard says in his Almanac, the Year I cannot just now remember.

Methinks I hear some of you say, Must a Man afford himself no Leisure? I will tell thee, my Friend, what Poor Richard says, Employ thy Time well if thou meanest to gain Leisure; and, Since thou are not sure of a Minute, throw not away an Hour. Leisure, is Time for doing something useful; this Leisure the diligent Man will obtain, but the lazy Man never; so that, as Poor Richard says, A Life of Leisure and a Life of Laziness are two Things. Do you imagine that Sloth will afford you more

Comfort than Labor? No, for as Poor Richard says, Trouble springs from Idleness, and grievous Toil from needless Ease. Many without Labor would live by their Wits only, but they break for want of Stock. Whereas Industry gives Comfort, and Plenty, and Respect. Fly from Pleasures and they'll follow you. The diligent Spinner has a large Shift; and Now I have a Sheep and a Cow, everybody bids me Good-Morrow; all which is well said by Poor Richard.

But with our Industry, we must likewise be steady, settled and careful, and oversee our own Affairs with our own Eyes, and not trust too much to others; for, as Poor Richard says,

> I never saw an oft removed Tree,
> Nor yet an oft removed Family,
> That throve so well as those that settled be.

And again, Three Removes is as bad as a Fire; and again, Keep thy Shop, and thy Shop will keep thee; and again, If you would have your Business done, go; if not, send. And again,

> He that by the Plough would thrive,
> Himself must either hold or drive.

And again, The Eye of a Master will do more Work than both his Hands; and again, Want of Care does us more Damage than want of Knowledge; and again, Not to oversee Workmen is to leave them your Purse open. Trusting too much to others' Care is the Ruin of many; for, as the Almanac says, In the Affairs of this World, Men are saved, not by Faith, but by the Want of it; but a Man's own Care is profitable; for, saith Poor Dick, Learning is to the Studious, and Riches to the Careful, as well as Power to the Bold, and Heaven to the Virtuous. And farther, If you would have a faithful Servant, and one that you like,—serve yourself. And again, he adviseth to Circumspection and Care, even in the smallest Matters, because sometimes A little Neglect may breed great Mischief; adding, For want of a Nail the Shoe was lost; for want of a Shoe the Horse was lost; and for want of a Horse the Rider was lost, being overtaken and slain by the Enemy, all for want of Care about a Horse-shoe Nail.

So much for Industry, my Friends, and Attention to one's own Business; but to these we must add Frugality, if we would make our Industry more certainly successful. A Man may, if he knows not how to save as he gets, keep his Nose all his Life to the Grindstone, and die not worth a Groat at last. A fat Kitchen makes a lean Will, as Poor Richard says; and,

> Many Estates are spent in the Getting,
> Since Women for Tea forsook Spinning & Knitting,
> And Men for Punch forsook Hewing & Splitting.

If you would be wealthy, says he, in another Almanac, think of Saving, as well as of Getting: The Indies have not made Spain rich, because her Outgoes are greater than her Incomes. Away then with your expensive Follies, and you will not have so much Cause to complain of hard Times, heavy Taxes, and chargeable Families; for, as Poor Dick says,

> Women and Wine, Game and Deceit,
> Make the Wealth small, and the Wants great.

And farther, What maintains one Vice, would bring up two Children. You may think perhaps, that a little Tea, or a little Punch now and then, Diet a little more costly, Clothes a little finer, and a little Entertainment now and then, can be no great Matter; but remember what Poor Richards says, Many a Little makes a Mickle; and farther Beware of little Expenses; a small Leak will sink a great Ship; and again, Who Dainties love, shall Beggars prove; and moreover, Fools make Feasts, and wise Men eat them.

Here you are all got together at this Vendue of Fineries and Knick-nacks. You call them Goods, but if you do not take Care, they will prove Evils to some of you. You expect they will be sold cheap, and perhaps they may for less than they cost; but if you have no Occasion for them, they must be dear to you. Remember what Poor Richard says, Buy what thou hast no Need of, and ere long thou shalt sell thy Necessaries. And again, At a great Pennyworth Pause a While: He means, that perhaps the Cheapness is apparent only, and not real; or the Bargain, by straitening thee in thy Business, may do thee more Harm than Good. For in another Place he says, Many have been ruined by buying good Pennyworths. Again, Poor Richard says, 'Tis foolish to lay out Money in a Purchase of Repentance; and yet this Folly is practiced every Day at Vendues, for want of minding the Almanac. Wise Men, as Poor Dick says, learn by others' Harms, Fools scarcely by their own; but *Felix quem faciunt aliena Pericula cautum.* Many a One, for the Sake of Finery on the Back, have gone with a hungry Belly, and half starved their Families. Silks and Satins, Scarlet and Velvets, have put out the Kitchen Fire. These are not the Necessaries of Life, they can scarcely be called the Conveniencies; and yet, only because they look pretty, how many want to have them. The artificial Wants of Mankind thus become more numerous than the natural; and, as Poor Dick says, For one poor Person, there are an hundred indigent. By these, and other Extravancies, the Genteel are reduced to Poverty, and forced to borrow of those whom they formerly despised, but who, through Industry and Frugality, have maintained their Standing; in which Case it appears plainly, that A Ploughman on his Legs is higher than a Gentleman on his Knees, as Poor Richard says. Perhaps they have had a small Estate left them, which they knew not the Getting of; they think 'tis Day and will never be Night; that a little to be spent out of so much, is not worth minding; (A Child and a Fool, as Poor Richard says, imagine Twenty Shillings and Twenty Years can never be spent) but, Always taking out of the Meal-Tub and never putting in, soon comes to the Bottom; then, as Poor Dick says, When the Well's dry they know the Worth of Water. But this they might have known before, if they had taken his Advice. If you would know the Value of Money, go and try to borrow some; for, He that goes a borrowing goes a sorrowing; and indeed so does he that lends to such People, when he goes to get it in again.—Poor Dick farther advises and says,

> Fond Pride of Dress, is sure a very Curse.
> E'er Fancy you consult, consult your Purse.

And again, Pride is as loud a Beggar as Want, and a great deal more saucy. When you have bought one fine Thing you must buy ten more, that your Appearance may be all of a Piece; but Poor Dick says, 'Tis easier to suppress the first Desire, than to satisfy all that follow it. And 'tis as truly Folly for the Poor to ape the Rich, as for the Frog to swell in order to equal the Ox.

> Great Estates may venture more,
> But little Boats should keep near Shore.

'Tis however a Folly soon punished; for Pride that dines on Vanity sups on Contempt, as Poor Richard says. And in another Place, Pride breakfasted with Plenty, dined with Poverty, and supped with Infamy. And after all, of what Use is this Pride of Appearance,[1] for which so much is risked, so much is suffered? It cannot promote Health, or ease Pain; it makes no Increase of Merit in the Person; it creates Envy, it hastens Misfortune.

> What is a Butterfly? At best
> He's but a Caterpillar drest.
> The gaudy Fop's his Picture just;

as Poor Richard says.

But what Madness must it be to run in Debt for these Superfluities! We are offered, by the Terms of this Vendue, Six Months' Credit; and that perhaps has induced some of us to attend it, because we cannot spare the ready Money, and hope now to be fine without it. But, ah, think what you do when you run in Debt: You give to another Power over your Liberty. If you cannot pay at the Time, you will be ashamed to see your Creditor; you will be in Fear when you speak to him; you

---

[1] "The first and capital Article of Town-Effeminacy is that of dress: which, in all its Variety of modern Excess and Ridicule, is too low for serious Animadversion. Yet in thus must every Man, of every Rank and Age, employ his Mornings, who pretends to keep good Company. The wisest, the most virtuous, the most polite, if defective in these exterior and unmanly Delicacies, are avoided as low People, who Nobody knows, and with whom One is ashamed to be seen"—[See a modern Pamphlet, entitled, *An Estimate of the Manners and Principles of the Times*, by the Reverend John Brown, D.D. reprinted and sold by Messrs. Green & Russel, Page 22.] [Franklin's Notes.]

will make poor–pitiful–sneaking Excuses, and by Degrees come to lose your Veracity, and sink into base downright Lying; for, as Poor Richard says, The second Vice is Lying, the first is running in Debt. And again, to the same Purpose, Lying rides upon Debt's Back. Whereas a free-born Englishman ought not to be ashamed or afraid to see or speak to any Man living. But Poverty often deprives a Man of all Spirit and Virtue. 'Tis hard for an empty Bag to stand upright, if it does 'tis a stout one, as Poor Richard truly says. What would you think of that Prince, or that Government, who should issue an Edict forbidding you to dress like a Gentleman or a Gentlewoman, on Pain of Imprisonment or Servitude? Would you not say that you are free, have a Right to dress as you please, and that such an Edict would be a Breach of your Privileges, and such a Government tyrannical? And yet you are about to put yourself under that Tyranny, when you run in Debt for such Dress! Your Creditor has Authority, at his Pleasure, to deprive you of your Liberty, by confining you in Jail for Life, or to Sell You for a Servant, if you should not be able to pay him! When you have got your Bargain, you may, perhaps, think little of Payment; but Creditors (Poor Richard tells us) have better Memories than Debtors; and in another Place says, Creditors are a superstitious Sect,–great Observers of set Days and Times. The Day comes round before you are aware, and the Demand is made before you are prepared to satisfy it. Or if you bear your Debt in Mind, the Term which at first seemed so long, will, as it lessens, appear extremely short. Time will seem to have added Wings to his Heels as well as Shoulders. Those have a short Lent (saith Poor Richard) who owe Money to be paid at Easter. Then since, as he says, The Borrower is a Slave to the Lender, and the Debtor to the Creditor, disdain the Chain, preserve your Freedom, and maintain your Independency. Be industrious and free: Be frugal and free. At present, perhaps, you may think yourself in thriving Circumstances, and that you can bear a little Extravagance without Injury; but

> For Age and Want save while you may,
> No Morning-Sun lasts a whole Day;

as Poor Richard says.–Gain may be temporary and uncertain, but ever while you live, Expense is constant and certain; and 'Tis easier to build two Chimneys, than to keep one in Fuel, as Poor Richard says. So, Rather go to Bed supperless than rise in Debt.

> Get what you can, and what you get hold:
> 'Tis the Thing that will turn all your Lead into Gold.

as Poor Richard says.

And when you have got the Philosopher's Stone, sure you will no longer complain of bad Times, or the Difficulty of paying Taxes.

This Doctrine, my Friends, is Reason and Wisdom; but, after all, do not depend too much upon your own Industry, and Frugality, and Prudence, though excellent Things, for they may all be blasted without the Blessing of Heaven; and therefore ask that Blessing humbly, and be not uncharitable to those that at present seem to want it, but comfort and help them. Remember Job suffered, and was afterwards prosperous.

And now to conclude, Experience keeps a dear School, but Fools will learn in no other, and scarce in that; for it is true, We may give Advice, but we cannot give Conduct, as Poor Richard says: However, remember this, They that won't be counseled can't be helped, as Poor Richard says: And farther, that If you will not hear and obey Reason, she'll surely rap your Knuckles.

Thus the old Gentleman ended his Harangue. The People heard it, and approved the Doctrine, and—

Immediately practised the Contrary,[2]

just as if it had been a common Sermon; for the Vendue opened, and they began to buy extravagantly, notwithstanding all his Cautions, and their own Fear of Taxes.—I found the good Man had thoroughly studied my Almanacs, and digested all I had dropt on those Topics during the Course of five-and-twenty Years. The frequent Mention he made of me, must have tired anyone else, but by Vanity was wonderfully delighted with it, tho I was conscious that not a tenth Part of the Wisdom was my own which he ascribed to me, but rather the Gleanings I had made of the Sense of all Ages and Nations. However, I resolved to be the better for the Echo of it; and though I had at first determined to buy Stuff for a new Coat, I went away resolved to wear my old one a little longer. Reader, if thou wilt do the same, thy Profit will be as great as mine.

I am, as ever,
Thine to serve thee,

July 7, 1757.   RICHARD SAUNDERS

[2] Mr. Brown, in his Estimate (Page 35) says, "We not only suffer our ruling Vices and Follies to be ridiculed, but we cordially join in the Laugh. We Laugh at the Picture of our own Defects; [as represented on the Stage at the Play Houses] we go home, and without a Blush repeat them. We can see and own our Vices and Follies without being touched with Shame."—Poor Richard says, that Shame and the Dry-Belly-Ache were Diseases of the last Age; this seems to be cured of them.

From *Proposals Relating to the Education of the Youth of Pennsylvania*

PROPOSALS

The good Education of Youth has been esteemed by wise Men in all Ages, as the surest Foundation of the Happiness both of private Families and of Commonwealths. Almost all Governments have therefore made it a principal Object of their Attention, to establish and endow with proper Revenues, such Seminaries of Learning, as might supply the succeeding Age with Men qualified to serve the Public with Honor to themselves, and to their Country.

Many of the first Settlers of these Provinces were Men who had received a good Education in Europe, and to their Wisdom and good Management we owe much of our present Prosperity. But their Hands were full, and they could not do all Things. The present Race are not thought to be generally of equal Ability: For though the American Youth are allow'd not to want Capacity; yet the best Capacities require Cultivation, it being truly with them, as with the best Ground, which unless well tilled and sowed with profitable Seed, produces only ranker Weeds.

That we may obtain the Advantages arising from an Increase of Knowledge, and prevent as much as may be the mischievous Consequences that would attend a general Ignorance among us, the following Hints are offered towards forming a Plan for the Education of the Youth of Pennsylvania, viz.

It is propos'd,

That some Persons of Leisure and public Spirit apply for a Charter, by which they may be incorporated, with the Power to erect an Academy for the Education of Youth, to govern the same, provide Masters, and make Rules, receive Donations, purchase Lands, etc., and to add to their Number, from Time to Time such other Persons as they shall judge suitable.

That the Members of the Corporation make it their Pleasure, and in some Degree their Business, to visit the Academy often, encourage and countenance Youth, countenance and assist the Masters, and by all Means in their Power advance the Usefulness and Reputation of the Design; that they look on the Students as in some Sort their Children, treat them with Familiarity and Affection, and, when they have behav'd well, and gone through their Studies, and are to enter the World, zealously unite, and make all the Interest that can be made to establish them, whether in Business, Offices, Marriages, or any other Thing for their Advantage, preferably to all other Persons whatsoever even of equal Merit. . . .

As to their Studies, it would be well if they could be taught everything that is useful, and everything that is ornamental: But Art is long, and their Time is short. It is therefore propos'd that they learn those Things that are likely to be most useful and most ornamental. Regard being had to the several Professions for which they are intended.

All should be taught to write a fair Hand, and swift, as that is useful to All. And with it may be learnt something of Drawing, by Imitation of Prints, and some of the first Principles of Perspective.

Arithmetic, Accounts, and some of the first Principles of Geometry and Astronomy.

The English Language might be taught by Grammar; in which some of our best Writers, as Tillotson, Addison, Pope, Algernon Sidney, Cato's *Letters*, &c., should be Classics: the Styles principally to be cultivated, being the clear and the concise. Reading should also be taught, and pronouncing, properly, distinctly, emphatically; not with an even Tone, which underdoes, nor a theatrical, which overdoes Nature.

To form their Style they should be put on Writing Letters to each other, making Abstracts of what they read; or writing the same Things in their own Words; telling or writing Stories lately read, in their own Expressions. All to be revis'd and corrected by the Tutor, who should give his Reasons, and explain the Force and Import of Words, &c.

To form their Pronunciation, they may be put on making Declamations, repeating Speeches, delivering Orations, &c.; The Tutor assisting at the Rehearsals, teaching, advising, correcting their Accent, &c.

But if History be made a constant Part of their Reading, such as the Translations of the Greek and Roman Historians, and the modern Histories of ancient Greece and Rome, &c. may not almost all Kinds of useful Knowledge be that Way introduc'd to Advantage, and with Pleasure to the Student? As

Geography, by reading with Maps, and being required to point out the Places where the greatest Actions were done, to give their old and new Names, with the Bounds, Situations, Extent of the Countries concern'd, &c.

Chronology, by the Help of Helvicus or some other Writer of the Kind, who will enable them to tell when those Events happened; what Princes were Contemporaries, what States or famous Men flourish'd about that Time, &c. The several principal Epochs to be first well fix'd in their Memories.

Ancient Customs, religious and civil, being frequently mentioned in History, will give Occasion for explaining them; in which the Prints of Medals, Basso-Relievos, and ancient Monuments will greatly assist.

Morality, by descanting and making continual Observations on the Causes of the Rise or Fall of any Man's Character, Fortune, Power &c. mention'd in History; the Advantages of Temperance, Order, Frugality, Industry, Perseverance &c. &c. Indeed the general natural Tendency of Reading good History must be, to fix in the Minds of Youth deep Impressions of the Beauty and Usefulness of Virtue of all Kinds, Public Spirit, Fortitude, &c.

History will show the wonderful Effects of Oratory, in governing, turning and leading great Bodies of Mankind, Armies, Cities, Nations. When the Minds of Youth are struck with Admiration at this, then is the Time to give them the Principles of that Art, which they will study with Taste and Application. Then they may be made acquainted with the best Models among the ancients, their Beauties being particularly pointed out to them. Modern Political Oratory being chiefly performed by the Pen and Press, its Advantages over the Ancient in some Respects are to be shown; as that its Effects are more extensive, more lasting, &c.

History will also afford frequent Opportunities of showing the Necessity of a Public Religion, from its Usefulness to the Public; the Advantage of a Religious Character among private Persons; the Mischief of Superstitions, &c. and the Excellence of the Christian Religion above all others ancient or modern.

History will also give Occasion to expatiate on the Advantage of Civil Orders and Constitutions; how Men and their Properties are protected by joining in Societies and establishing Government; their Industry encouraged and rewarded, Arts invented, and Life made more comfortable: The Advantages of Liberty, Mischiefs of Licentiousness, Benefits arising from good Laws and a due Execution of Justice, &c. Thus may the first Principles of sound Politics be fix'd in the Minds of Youth.

On Historical Occasions, Questions of Right and Wrong, Justice and Injustice, will naturally arise, and may be put to Youth, which they may debate in Conversation and in Writing. When they ardently desire Victory, for the Sake of the Praise attending it, they will begin to feel the Want, and be sensible of the Use of Logic, or the Art of Reasoning to discover Truth, and of Arguing to defend it, and convince Adversaries. This would be the Time to acquaint them with the Principles of that Art. Grotius, Puffendorff, and some other Writers of the same Kind, may be used on these Occasions to decide their Disputes. Public Disputes warm the Imagination, whet the Industry, and strengthen the natural Abilities.

When Youth are told, that the Great Men whose Lives and Actions they read in History, spoke two of the best Languages that ever were, the most expressive, copious, beautiful; and that the finest Writings, the most correct Compositions, the most perfect Productions of human Wit and Wisdom, are in those Languages, which have endured Ages, and will endure while there are Men; that no Translation can do them Justice, or give the Pleasure found in Reading the Originals; that those Languages contain all Science; that one of them is become almost universal, being the Language of Learned Men in all Countries; that to understand them is a distinguishing Ornament, &c. they may be thereby made desirous of learning those Languages, and their Industry sharpen'd in the Acquisition of them. All intended for Divinity, should be taught the Latin and Greek; for Physic, the Latin, Greek, and French; for Law, the Latin and French; Merchants, the French, German, and Spanish: And though all should not be compell'd to learn Latin, Greek, or the modern foreign Languages; yet none that have an ardent Desire to learn them should be refused; their English, Arithmetic and other Studies absolutely necessary, being at the same Time not neglected.

If the new Universal History were also read, it would give a connected Idea of human Affairs, so far as it goes, which should be follow'd by the best modern Histories, particularly of our Mother Country; then of these Colonies; which should be accompanied with Observations on their Rise, Increase, Use to Great Britain, Encouragements, Discouragements, etc. the Means to make them flourish, secure their Liberties, &c.

With the History of Men, Times, and Nations, should be read at proper Hours or Days, some of the best Histories of Nature, which would not only be delightful to Youth, and furnish them with Matter for their Letters, &c. as well as other History; but afterwards of great Use to them, whether they are Merchants, Handicrafts, or Divines; enabling the first the better to understand Commodities, Drugs, &c.; the second to improve his Trade and Handicraft by new Mixtures, Materials, &c., and the last to adorn his Discourses by beautiful Comparisons, and strengthen them by new Proofs of Divine Providence. The Conversation of all will be improved by it, as Occasions frequently occur of making Natural Observations, which are instructive, agreeable, and entertaining in almost all Companies. Natural History will also afford Opportunities of introducing many Observations, relating to the Preservation of Health, which may be afterwards of great Use. Arbuthnot on Air and Aliment, Sanctorius on Perspiration, Lemery on Foods, and some others, may now be read, and a very little Explanation will make them sufficiently intelligible to Youth.

While they are reading Natural History, might not a little Gardening, Planting, Grafting, Inoculating, etc., be taught and practiced; and now and then Excursions made to the neighboring Plantations of the best Farmers, their Methods observ'd and reason'd upon for the Information of Youth? The Improvement of Agriculture being useful to all, and Skill in it not Disparagement to any.

The History of Commerce, of the Invention of Arts, Rise of Manufactures, Progress of Trade, Change of its Seats, with the Reasons, Causes, &c., may also be made entertaining to Youth, and will be useful to all. And this, with the Accounts in other History of the prodigious Force and Effect of Engines and Machines used in War, will naturally introduce a Desire to be instructed in Mechanics, and to be inform'd of the Principles of that Art by which weak Men perform such Wonders, Labor is sav'd, Manufactures expedited, &c. This will be the Time to show them Prints of ancient and modern Machines, to explain them, and to let them be copied, and to give Lectures in Mechanical Philosophy.

With the whole should be constantly inculcated and cultivated, that Benignity of Mind, which shows itself in searching for and seizing every Opportunity to serve and to oblige; and is the Foundation of what is called Good Breeding; highly useful to the Possessor, and most agreeable to all.

The Idea of what is true Merit should also be often presented to Youth, explain'd and impress'd on their Minds, as consisting in an Inclination join'd with an Ability to serve Mankind, one's Country, Friends and Family; which Ability is (with the Blessing of God) to be acquir'd or greatly increas'd by true Learning; and should indeed be the great Aim and End of all Learning.   1749

The Craven-Street Gazette

Saturday, September 22, 1770

This morning Queen Margaret, accompanied by her first maid of honor, Miss Franklin, set out for Rochester. Immediately on their departure, the whole street was in tears—from a heavy shower of rain. It is whispered, that the new family administration, which took place on her Majesty's departure, promises, like all other new administrations, to govern much better than the old one.

We hear, that the great person (so called from his enormous size), of a certain family in a certain street, is grievously affected at the late changes, and could hardly be comforted this morning, though the new ministry promised him a roasted shoulder of mutton and potatoes for his dinner.

It is said, that the same great person intended to pay his respects to another great personage this day, at St. James's, it being coronation-day; hoping thereby a little to amuse his grief; but was prevented by an accident, Queen Margaret, or her maid of honor, having carried off the key of the drawers, so that the lady of the bed-chamber could not come at a laced shirt for his Highness. Great clamors were made on this occasion against her Majesty.

Other accounts say, that the shirts were afterwards found, though too late, in another place. And some suspect, that the wanting a shirt from those drawers was only a ministerial pretence to excuse picking the locks, that the new administration might have everything at command.

We hear that the lady chamberlain of the household went to market this morning by her own self, gave the butcher whatever he asked for the mutton, and had no dispute with the potato-woman, to their great amazement at the change of times.

It is confidently asserted, that this afternoon, the weather being wet, the great person a little chilly and nobody at home to find fault with the expense of fuel, he was indulged with a fire in his chamber. It seems the design is, to make him contented by degrees with the absence of the Queen.

A project has been under consideration of government, to take the opportunity of her Majesty's absence for doing a thing she was always averse to, namely, fixing a new lock on the street door, or getting a key made to the old one; it being found extremely inconvenient, that one or other of the great officers of state should, whenever the maid goes out for a ha'penny worth of sand, or a pint of porter, be obliged to attend the door to let her in again. But opinions being divided, which of the two expedients to adopt, the project is, for the present, laid aside.

We have good authority to assure our readers, that a Cabinet Council was held this afternoon at tea; the subject of which was a proposal for the reformation of manners, and a more strict observation of the Lord's day. The result was a unanimous resolution, that no meat should be dressed tomorrow; whereby the cook and the first minister will both be at liberty to go to church, the one having nothing to do, and the other no roast to rule. It seems the cold shoulder of mutton, and the apple-pie, were thought sufficient for Sunday's dinner. All pious people applaud this measure, and it is thought the new ministry will soon become popular.

We hear that Mr. Wilkes was at a certain house in Craven Street this day, and inquired after the absent Queen. His good lady and the children are well.

The report, that Mr. Wilkes, the patriot, made the above visit, is without foundation, it being his brother, the courtier.

Sunday, September 23

It is now found by sad experience, that good resolutions are easier made than executed. Notwithstanding yesterday's solemn order of Council, nobody went to church today. It seems the great person's broad-built bulk lay so long abed, that the breakfast was not over till it was too late to dress. At least this is the excuse. In fine, it seems a vain thing to hope reformation from the example of our great folks.

The cook and the minister, however, both took advantage of the order so far, as to save themselves all trouble, and the clause of cold dinner was enforced, though the going to church was dispensed with; just as common working folks observe the commandments. *The seventh day thou shalt rest,* they think a sacred injunction; but the other *six days thou shalt labor* is deemed a mere piece of advice, which they may practice when they want bread and are out of credit at the alehouse, and may neglect whenever they have money in their pockets.

It must, nevertheless, be said, in justice to our court, that, whatever inclination they had to gaming, no cards were brought out today. Lord and Lady Hewson walked after dinner to Kensington, to pay their duty to the Dowager, and Dr. Fatsides made four hundred and sixty-nine turns in his dining-room, as the exact distance of a visit to the lovely Lady Barwell, whom he did not find at home; so there was no struggle for and against a kiss, and he sat down to dream in the easy-chair, that he had it without any trouble.

Monday, September 24

We are credibly informed, that the great person dined this day with the Club at the Cat and Bagpipes in the City, on cold round of boiled beef. This, it seems, he was under some necessity of doing (though he rather dislikes beef), because truly the ministers were to be all abroad somewhere to dine on hot roast venison. It is thought, that, if the Queen had been at home, he would not have been so slighted. And though he shows outwardly no marks of dissatisfaction, it is suspected, that he begins to wish for her Majesty's return.

It is currently reported, that poor Nanny had nothing for dinner in the kitchen, for herself and puss, but the scrapings of the bones of Saturday's mutton.

This evening there was high play at Craven Street House. The great person lost money. It is supposed the ministers, as is usually supposed of all ministers, shared the emoluments among them.

Tuesday, Sept. 25

This Morning my good Lord Hutton call'd at Craven-Street House, and inquir'd very respectfully & affectionately concerning the Welfare of the Queen. He then imparted to the big Man a Piece of Intelligence important to them both, and but just communicated by Lady Hawkesworth, viz. that the amiable and delectable Companion, Miss Dorothea Blount, had made a Vow to marry absolutely him of the two whose Wife should first depart this Life. It is impossible to express the various Agitations of Mind appearing in both their Faces on this Occasion. Vanity at the Preference given them over the rest of Mankind; Affection to their present Wives, Fear of losing them, Hope, if they must lose them, to obtain the proposed Comfort; Jealousy of each other in case both Wives should die together, &c. &c. &c.,—all working at the same time jumbled their Features into inexplicable Confusion. They parted at length with Professions & outward Appearances indeed of ever-during Friendship, but it was shrewdly suspected that each of them sincerely wished Health & long Life to the other's Wife; & that however long either of these Friends might like to live himself, the other would be very well pleas'd to survive him.

It is remark'd, that the Skies have wept every Day in Craven Street, the Absence of the Queen.

The Public may be assured that this Morning a certain great Personage was asked very complaisantly by the Mistress of the Household, if he would choose to have the Blade-Bone of Saturday's Mutton that had been kept for his Dinner today, broil'd or cold. He answer'd gravely, *If there is any Flesh on it, it may be broil'd; if not, it may as well be cold.* Orders were accordingly given for Broiling it. But when it came to Table, there was indeed so very little Flesh, or rather none, (Puss having din'd on it yesterday after Nanny) that if our new Administration had been as good Economists as they would be thought, the Expense of Broiling might well have been saved to the Public, and carried to the Sinking Fund. It is assured the great Person bears all with infinite Patience. But the Nation is astonish'd at the insolent Presumption, that dares treat so much Mildness in so cruel a manner!

A terrible Accident had like to have happened this Afternoon at Tea. The Boiler was set too near the End of the little square Table. The first Ministress was sitting at one End of the Table to administer the Tea; the great Person was about to sit down at the other End where the Boiler stood. By a sudden Motion the Lady gave the Table a Tilt. Had it gone over, the G. P. must have been scalded, perhaps to Death. Various are the Surmises and Observations on this Occasion. The Godly say it would have been a just Judgment on him, for preventing, by his Laziness, the Family's going to Church last Sunday. The Opposition do not stick to insinuate that there was a Design to scald him, prevented only by his quick Catching the Table. The Friends of the Ministry give it out, that he carelessly jogg'd the Table himself, & would have been inevitably scalded, had not the Ministress sav'd him. It is hard for the Public to come at the Truth in these Cases.

At six o'Clock this Afternoon, News came by the Post, that her Majesty arrived safely at Rochester on Saturday Night. The Bells immediately rang,—for Candles to illuminate the Parlor, the Court went into Cribbage, and the Evening concluded with every other Demonstration of Joy.

It is reported that all the principal Officers of the State have received an Invitation from the Duchess Dowager of Rochester to go down thither on Saturday next. But it is not yet known whether the great Affairs they have on their Hands will permit them to make this Excursion.

We hear that from the Time of her Majesty's leaving Craven-Street House to this Day, no Care is taken to file the Newspapers; but they lie about in every Room in every Window, and on every Chair, just where the Great Person lays them when he reads them. It is impossible Government can long go on in such Hands.

To the Publisher of the Craven-Street Gazette.

Sir,

I make no doubt of the Truth of what the Papers tell us, that a certain great Person is half-starved on the Blade-Bone of a Sheep (I cannot call it of Mutton, there being none on it) by a Set of the most careless, worthless, thoughtless, inconsiderate, corrupt, ignorant, blundering, foolish, crafty, & knavish Ministers, that ever got into a House and pretended to govern a Family and provide a Dinner. Alas for the poor old England of Craven Street! If they continue in Power another Week, the Nation will be ruined. Undone, totally undone, if I and my Friends are not appointed to succeed them. I am a great Admirer of your useful and impartial Paper; and therefore request you will insert this without fail, from

Your humble Servant,
INDIGNATION

To the Publisher of the Craven-Street Gazette.

Sir,

Your Correspondent, *Indignation*, has made a fine Story in your Paper against our Craven Street Ministry, as if they meant to starve his Highness, giving him only a bare Blade-Bone for his Dinner, while they riot upon roast Venison. The Wickedness of Writers in this Age is truly amazing. I believe that if even the Angel Gabriel would condescend to be our Minister, and provide our Dinners, he could scarcely escape Newspaper Defamation from a Gang of hungry, ever-restless, discontented, and malicious Scribblers.

It is, Sir, a Piece of Justice you owe our righteous Administration to undeceive the Public on this Occasion, by assuring them of the Fact, which is, that there was provided, and actually smoking on the Table under his Royal Nose at the same Instant, as fine a Piece of Ribs of Beef roasted as ever Knife was put into, with Potatoes, Horseradish, Pickled Walnuts, &c. which his Highness might have eaten of if so he had pleased to do; and which he forbore to do merely from a whimsical Opinion (with Respect be it spoken) that Beef doth not with him perspire well, but makes his Back itch, to his no small Vexation, now that he has lost the little Chinese ivory Hand at the End of a Stick, commonly called a Scratch back, presented to him by her Majesty. This is the Truth, and if your boasted Impartiality is real, you will not hesitate a Moment to insert this Letter in your next Paper.

I am, tho' a little angry at present,
Yours as you behave,
A HATER OF SCANDAL

Junius and Cinna came to hand too late for this Paper, but shall be inserted in our next.

MARRIAGES, none since our last;—but Puss begins to go a Courting.

DEATHS. In the back Closet and elsewhere, many poor Mice.

STOCKS. Biscuit—very low. Buckwheat & Indian Meal—both sour. Tea, lowering daily—in the Canister. Wine, shut.

Wednesday, September 26th. Postscript.—Those in the Secret of Affairs do not scruple to assert roundly, that our present First Ministress is very notable, having this Day been at Market, bought Mutton-Chops, and Apples 4 a Penny, made an excellent Applepie with her own Hands, and mended two Pair of Breeches.

1770, 1907

An Edict by the King of Prussia

Danzig, Sept. 5, [1773]

We have long wondered here at the supineness of the English nation, under the Prussian impositions upon its trade entering our port. We did not, till lately, know the claims, ancient and modern, that hang over that nation; and therefore could not suspect that it might submit to those impositions from a sense of duty or from principles of equity. The following Edict, just made public, may, if serious, throw some light upon this matter.

"Frederic, by the grace of God, King of Prussia, &c. &c. &c., to all present and to come, (à tous présens et à venir,) Health. The peace now enjoyed throughout our dominions, having afforded us leisure to apply ourselves to the regulation of commerce, the improvement of our finances, and at the same time the easing our domestic subjects in their taxes: For these causes, and other good considerations us thereunto moving, we hereby make known, that, after having deliberated these affairs in our council, present our dear brothers, and other great officers of the state, members of the same, we, of our certain knowledge, full power, and authority royal have made and issued this present Edict, viz.

"Whereas it is well known to all the world, that the first German settlements made in the Island of Britain, were by colonies of people, subject to our renowned ducal ancestors, and drawn from their dominions, under the conduct of Hengist, Horsa, Hella, Uff, Cerdicus, Ida, and others; and that the said colonies have flourished under the protection of our august house for ages past; have never been emancipated therefrom; and yet have hitherto yielded little profit to the same: And whereas we ourself have in the last war fought for and defended the said colonies, against the power of France, and thereby enabled them to make conquests from the said power in America, for which we have not yet received adequate compensation: And whereas it is just and expedient that a revenue should be raised from the said colonies in Britain, towards our indemnification; and that those who are descendants of our ancient subjects, and thence still owe us due obedience, should contribute to the replenishing of our royal coffers as they must have done, had their ancestors remained in the territories now to us appertaining: We do therefore hereby ordain and command, that, from and after the date of these presents, there shall be levied and paid to our officers of the customs, on all goods, wares, and merchandises, and on all grain and other produce of the earth, exported from the said Island of Britain, and on all goods of whatever kind imported into the same, a duty of four and a half per cent *ad valorem*, for the use of us and our successors. And that the said duty may more effectually be collected, we do hereby ordain, that all ships or vessels bound from Great Britain to any other part of the world, or from any other part of the world to Great Britain, shall in their respective voyages touch at our port of Koningsberg, there to be unladen, searched, and charged with the said duties.

"And whereas there hath been from time to time discovered in the said island of Great Britain, by our colonists there, many mines or beds of iron-stone; and sundry subjects, of our ancient dominion, skillful in converting the said stone into metal, have in time past transported themselves thither, carrying with them and communicating that art; and the inhabitants of the said island, presuming that they had a natural right to make the best use they could of the natural productions of their country for their own benefit, have not only built furnaces for smelting the said stone into iron, but have erected plating-forges, slitting-mills, and steel-furnaces, for the more convenient manufacturing of the same; thereby endangering a diminution of the said manufacture in our ancient dominion;—we do therefore hereby farther ordain, that, from and after the date hereof, no mill or other engine for slitting or rolling of iron, or any plating-forge to work with a tilt-hammer, or any furnace for making steel, shall be erected or continued in the said island of Great Britain: And the Lord Lieutenant of every county in the said island is hereby commanded, on information of any such erection within his county, to order and by force to cause the same to be abated and destroyed; as he shall answer the neglect thereof to us at his peril. But we are nevertheless graciously pleased to permit the inhabitants of the said island to transport their iron into Prussia, there to be manufactured, and to them returned; they paying our Prussian subjects for the workmanship, with all the costs of commission, freight, and risk, coming and returning; any thing herein contained to the contrary notwithstanding.

"We do not, however, think fit to extend this our indulgence to the article of wool; but, meaning to encourage, not only the manufacturing of woolen cloth, but also the raising of wool, in our ancient dominions, and to prevent both, as much as may be, in our said island, we do hereby absolutely forbid the transportation of wool from thence, even to the mother country, Prussia; and that those islanders may be farther and more effectually restrained in making any advantage of their own wool in the way of manufacture, we command that none shall be carried out of one county into another; nor shall any worsted, bay, or woolen yarn, cloth, says, bays, kerseys, serges, frizes, druggets, cloth-serges, shalloons, or any other drapery stuffs, or woolen manufactures whatsoever, made up or mixed with wool in any of the said counties, be carried into any other county, or be water-borne even across the smallest river or creek, on penalty of forfeiture of the same, together with the boats, carriages, horses, &c., that shall be employed in removing them. Nevertheless, our loving subjects there are hereby permitted (if they think proper) to use all their wool as manure for the improvement of their lands.

"And whereas the art and mystery of making hats hath arrived at great perfection in Prussia, and the making of hats by our remoter subjects ought to be as much as possible restrained: And forasmuch as the islanders before mentioned, being in possession of wool, beaver and other furs, have presumptuously conceived they had a right to make some advantage thereof, by manufacturing the same into hats, to the prejudice of our domestic manufacture: We do therefore hereby strictly command and ordain, that no hats or felts whatsoever, dyed or undyed, finished or unfinished, shall be loaded or put into or upon any vessel, cart, carriage, or horse, to be transported or conveyed out of one county in the said island into another county, or to any other place whatsoever, by any person or persons whatsoever; on pain of forfeiting the same, with a penalty of five hundred pounds sterling for every offense. Nor shall any hatmaker, in any of the said counties, employ more than two apprentices, on penalty of five pounds sterling per month; we intending hereby, that such hatmakers, being so restrained, both in the production and sale of their commodity, may find no advantage in continuing their business. But, lest the said islanders should suffer inconveniency by the want of hats, we are farther graciously pleased to permit them to send their beaver furs to Prussia; and we also permit hats made thereof to be exported from Prussia to Britain; the people thus favored to pay all costs and charges of manufacturing, interest, commission to our merchants, insurance and freight going and returning, as in the case of iron.

"And, lastly, being willing farther to favor our said colonies in Britain, we do hereby also ordain and command, that all the thieves, highway and street robbers, house-breakers, forgerers, murderers, s—d—tes, and villains of every denomination, who have forfeited their lives to the law in Prussia; but whom we, in our great clemency, do not think fit here to hang, shall be emptied out of our jails into the said island of Great Britain, for the better peopling of that country.

"We flatter ourselves, that these our royal regulations and commands will be thought just and reasonable by our much-favored colonists in England; the said regulations being copied from their statutes of 10 and 11 William III. c. 10, 5 Geo. II. c. 22, 23, Geo. II. c. 29, 4 Geo. I c. 11, and from other equitable laws made by their parliaments; or from instructions given by their Princes; or from resolutions of both Houses, entered into for the good government of their own colonies in Ireland and America.

"And all persons in the said island are hereby cautioned not to oppose in any wise the execution of this our Edict, or any part thereof, such opposition being high treason; of which all who are suspected shall be transported in fetters from Britain to Prussia, there to be tried and executed according to the Prussian law.

"Such is our pleasure.

"Given at Potsdam, this twenty-fifth day of the month of August, one thousand seven hundred and seventy-three, and in the thirty-third year of our reign.
"By the King, in his Council.

"RECHTMAESSIG, Sec."

Some take this Edict to be merely one of the King's *Jeux d'Esprit:* others suppose it serious, and that he means a quarrel with England; but all here think the assertion it concludes with, "that these regulations are copied from acts of the English parliament respecting their colonies," a very injurious one; it being impossible to believe, that a people distinguished for their love of liberty, a nation so wise, so liberal in its sentiments, so just and equitable towards its neighbors, should, from mean and injudicious views of petty immediate profit, treat its own children in a manner so arbitrary and tyrannical!

1773

The Whistle

To Madame Brillon

Passy, November 10, 1779

I received my dear friend's two letters, one for Wednesday and one for Saturday. This is again Wednesday, I do not deserve one for today, because I have not answered the former. But, indolent as I am, and averse to writing, the fear of having no more of your pleasing epistles, if I do not contribute to the correspondence, obliges me to take up my pen; and as Mr. B. has kindly sent me word, that he sets out tomorrow to see you, instead of spending this Wednesday evening as I have done its namesakes, in your delightful company, I sit down to spend it in thinking of you, in writing to you, and in reading over and over again your letters.

I am charmed with your description of Paradise, and with your plan of living there; and I approve much of your conclusion, that, in the meantime, we should draw all the good we can from this world. In my opinion, we might all draw more good from it than we do, and suffer less evil, if we would take care not to give too much for whistles. For to me it seems, that most of the unhappy people we meet with, are become so by neglect of that caution.

You ask what I mean? You love stories, and will excuse my telling one of myself.

When I was a child of seven years old, my friends, on a holiday, filled my pocket with coppers. I went directly to a shop where they sold toys for children; and, being charmed with the sound of a whistle, that I met by the way in the hands of another boy, I voluntarily offered and gave all my money for one. I then came home, and went whistling all over the house, much pleased with my whistle, but disturbing all the family. My brothers, and sisters, and cousins, understanding the bargain I had made, told me I had given four times as much for it as it was worth; put me in mind what good things I might have bought with the rest of the money; and laughed at me so much for my folly, that I cried with vexation; and the reflection gave me more chagrin than the whistle gave me pleasure.

This however was afterwards of use to me, the impression continuing on my mind; so that often, when I was tempted to buy some unnecessary thing, I said to myself, Don't give too much for the whistle; and I saved my money.

As I grew up, came into the world, and observed the actions of men, I thought I met with many, very many, who gave too much for the whistle.

When I saw one too ambitious of court favor, sacrificing his time in attendance on levees, his repose, his liberty, his virtue, and perhaps his friends, to attain it, I have said to myself, This man gives too much for his whistle.

When I saw another fond of popularity, constantly employing himself in political bustles, neglecting his own affairs, and ruining them by that neglect, He pays, indeed, said I, too much for his whistle.

If I knew a miser, who gave up every kind of comfortable living, all the pleasure of doing good to others, all the esteem of his fellow-citizens, and the joys of benevolent friendship, for the sake of accumulating wealth, Poor man, said I, you pay too much for your whistle.

When I met with a man of pleasure, sacrificing every laudable improvement of the mind, or of his fortune, to mere corporeal sensations, and ruining his health in their pursuit, Mistaken man, said I, you are providing pain for yourself, instead of pleasure; you give too much for your whistle.

If I see one fond of appearance, or fine clothes, fine houses, fine furniture, fine equipages, all above his fortune, for which he contracts debts, and ends his career in a prison, Alas! say I, he has paid dear, very dear for his whistle.

When I see a beautiful, sweet-tempered girl married to an ill-natured brute of a husband, What a pity, say I, that she should pay so much for a whistle!

In short, I conceive that great part of the miseries of mankind are brought upon them by the false estimates they have made of the value of things, and by their giving too much for their whistles.

Yet I ought to have charity for these unhappy people, when I consider, that, with all this wisdom of which I am boasting, there are certain things in the world so tempting, for example, the apples of King John, which happily are not to be bought; for if they were put to sale by auction, I might very easily be led to ruin myself in the purchase, and find that I had once more given too much for the whistle.

Adieu, my dear friend, and believe me ever yours very sincerely and with unalterable affection,

B. FRANKLIN
1779, 1818

The Federal Period

INTRODUCTION

The adoption of the Constitution in 1789 had a greater impact on the American attitude than the successful conclusion of the Revolutionary War; the latter left a confederation of independent and sometimes jealous states, the former proclaimed a more perfect union and a nation. The instrument itself was both affirmation and challenge; it defined the political nature of the new government, but left the national character undetermined. In consequence, the three or four decades following saw an intense and self-conscious effort to create a national identity. The dominant notions were that the national character should be as unique as the governmental system was thought to be, should be independent of the European cultural past, and should serve as a model for the rest of the world. The extraordinary presumptuousness of such an undertaking seems to have been sensed by few Americans, though the presence of some doubt is suggested by the hyper-sensitivity to foreign criticism. The task before the new Americans was to evolve a social structure, a philosophic and religious attitude, an economic system, and an art and a literature commensurate with the republican political system created in the Constitution. Though the effort failed to produce the consistent American image desired, it did create a national patriotism that for a time disguised the real social and sectional differences existing in the nation.

The political issues of the times grew out of the effort to adjust property rights and human rights, to expand American commerce throughout the globe, and to develop the potential of the vast area west of the Appalachian mountains. The federal Constitution established a government close to the citizens but not immediately responsive to popular whim. A built-in system of delays was designed to maintain equilibrium during change and to prevent sudden reversals. The election procedures were designed to elevate to office men of merit rather than men of position or popularity. On the nature of the government and its officers there was no real disagreement between Federalists (Hamiltonians) and Republicans (Jeffersonians); disagreement arose over the question of what the government should do. The Hamiltonians saw the future greatness of America dependent upon the expansion of trade and industry, and on an ordered society stablized by property rights. The Jeffersonians saw the future dependent on the development of an agrarian economy with the attendant guarantees of human rights, which were thought to include not only the promotion of those stated in the "Bill of Rights" amendments to the Constitution, but also the governmental obligation to educate and to assist the individual citizen in his pursuit of those rights. The contest was won by neither side, circumstances forcing concession and compromise. For trade and industry, the nation adopted many internal measures, notably the National Bank, and fought the Tripolitan wars and the War of 1812; for agrarian development, it acquired the Louisiana Territory and developed roads, canals, and river transportation to the trans-Alleghanian area. In the Whiskey Insurrection, the grandiloquent schemes of Aaron Burr, and the Hartford convention, it survived abortive separatist movements. By the Monroe Doctrine and the Russian Treaty the nation sought to exclude foreign powers from participation in the development of America and, in its efforts towards self-development, added eleven states to the original thirteen—nine of them across the Appalachians and two west of the Mississippi River. How rapid this expansion was is readily demonstrated; in 1830, Ohio had a larger population than all but three of the original thirteen states and nearly a third of the nation's people lived west of the Appalachians. The political impact of this population shift is symbolized by the election of Andrew Jackson, a citizen of Tennessee, to the presidency in 1828. A new sectional interest had emerged in the nation—the West. Out of the political debates of these four decades, two national policies were formed: first, that the best interests of the United States would be served by remaining at peace with the nations of the world, a peace secured by a determined neutrality in all foreign controversies, and second, that the business of the federal government was to serve the interests of the democratic mass, not those of a section or class.

The concept of the West was a compound of geographic reality and a state of mind. There lay a vast area of immeasurable potentials, encumbered only by the natural hazards of frontier life and the hostile Indians, but offering such independence and wealth as individual sagacity, endeavor, and persistence could attain. There, too, the New Zions could be built, and the New Harmonies achieved. And there, too, the destinies of the new nation could be fulfilled. If the West attracted the sober, serious, and self-reliant, it also attracted the opportunist, the parasite, the scalawag, and the lawless. It acquired an almost magical attractiveness for many on the Atlantic seaboard, but created an intense distrust in others.

The preoccupation with the economic and geographic expansion of the nation pushed the earlier religious concerns into the background. The Deistic inclinations of the previous period contributed to the development of Unitarianism, an ecclesiastical embodiment of many Deistic principles and a movement prominent along the northeastern seaboard. The religious enthusiasm of the earlier period moved to the back country regions and became the prevailing religious practice of the West, where the circuit rider, the river baptism, and the revival became notable aspects of the sectional scene.

Public education, having both a practical and political import, underwent considerable expansion, and some of the arts began to flourish.
Private "academies" sprang up by the dozens in both old and new
states, and some thirty-seven modern colleges and universities had their
origins in the period, fifteen of them in the newly admitted states. If the
Federalist period produced few superior authors, it did produce a literate
public. In the arts, the period produced such notable painters as Gilbert
Stuart, John Trumbull, and the Hudson River school of landscapists,
professional architects like Charles Bulfinch, Samuel McIntyre, and John
McComb, and furniture designers like Duncan Phyfe. These men contributed to the national character by preserving likenesses of the national
heroes, by depicting great moments in the nation's history, by presenting
panoramic views of the native land, by applying the stately elegance of
the Greek Revival to public and private buildings, and by refining furniture and furnishings.

Socially, the period is marked by the emergence of a new class of
"leading citizens" based on wealth and political power, and by the continued urbanization of the population. War losses, the flight of the Tories,
currency inflation, and restrictions on shipping had removed many of the
older families from prominence, while shrewd investment, manufacturing,
land speculation, and trade in the West established newcomers in positions of power and influence. For the first time in the United States appeared men of fabulous fortune like Stephen Girard and John Jacob
Astor. Elegant living and conspicuous spending increased in frequency until it was in evidence in all of the major cities, and even in Cincinnati,
Louisville, and St. Louis. Cities and towns grew in population at a rate
faster than the total population, the great port cities of New York and
Philadelphia grew to metropolitan size, and a relative newcomer, Baltimore, challenged in size the older Boston and Charleston. Theaters existed in all the major and some of the lesser cities, and theatrical productions, concerts, and exhibitions provided regular entertainment for the
citizenry. The clubs and literary coteries expanded in numbers, and public and private balls and celebrations were numerous. If manners were
gross and bumptious in the mass, there was considerable sophistication
among the well-to-do. If there were canings, fisticuffs, and duels, there
were also Cooper's "Lunch" and similar gatherings given to good food
and good conversation; if there were verbal abuse and extreme
vilification in the newspapers, there were also the more witty and equally influential *Salmagundi* and *Croaker* papers. While Andrew Johnson
came to the presidency from a log house, the Blennerhassetts lived in an
English manor set in formal gardens and parks on an Ohio river island.
The republican code of conduct was in fact what any individual chose to
make it.

Printers and printing establishments were even more numerous than in
the previous period, and the production of newspapers and magazines

was greatly increased. In the early years of the period Philadelphia, the capital and "the Athens of America" according to John Neal, was the leading publishing center and the home of such authors as William Bartram, Alexander Wilson, Benjamin Rush, David Rittenhouse, Charles Brockden Brown, Joseph Dennie, Hugh Henry Brackenridge, Mathew Carey, and Philip Freneau. By the end of the period New York had surpassed Philadelphia as a publishing center; it too was the home of prominent authors—Daniel Webster, William Dunlap, Washington Irving, James K. Paulding, James Fenimore Cooper, William C. Bryant, George P. Morris, Fitz-Greene Halleck, Joseph R. Drake, and Samuel Woodworth. Boston lagged behind Philadelphia and New York as a publishing center, despite the availability of the Harvard faculty and such authors as Richard H. Dana, Sr., Robert Treat Paine, John Pierpont, Charles Sprague, Mrs. Susanna Rowson, and Mrs. Mercy Warren. The boom city Baltimore—with J. P. Kennedy, Edward C. Pinkney, Francis Scott Key, T. S. Arthur, John Latrobe, Jared Sparks for a time, and John Neal for ten years—threatened briefly to challenge Boston as a publishing center.

The ever-present newspaper was a marvel to foreign visitors, unaccustomed to such ubiquity. Literally thousands of newspapers were begun in the first forty years of our national life, and in 1830 some 1200 were publishing. Daily in the principal cities, semi-weekly or weekly in the smaller towns, these papers printed feature articles, history, poetry, and political essays as well as news. Many of them were scarcely distinguishable from the literary weeklies. Some, like Joseph Dennie's and Thomas Green Fessenden's *Farmer's Weekly Museum,* achieved wide reputation for their literary content. As political parties developed, so did such party papers as the Federalist Fenno's *Gazette of the United States* (1789), the Republican Freneau's *National Gazette* (1791), and Benjamin Bache's *Republican Aurora* (1790), whose scurrilous attacks led to a public brawl with Fenno, the first of a series of such fisticuffs by rival editors. The later *National Intelligencer* was the quasi-official paper of the Madison and Monroe administrations, and the *United States Telegraph* spoke for the Jacksonians. The political quarrels produced a yellow journalism unequaled in any period since; assaults, duels, and libel suits became commonplaces in newspaper publishing. But the partisan press brought other and more significant developments: the professional editor, new techniques in gathering the news, and the maintenance of correspondents at important sources of news—by 1794 newsmen were admitted to both houses of Congress. The period also saw the publication of Isaiah Thomas' *History of Printing in America,* an invaluable record first published in 1810.

Magazine publication also increased in the period. Although most of the magazines were short-lived, and none were financially successful, some five or six hundred periodicals were undertaken in the first quarter of the century. These were quarterlies, monthlies, semi-monthlies, and weeklies, and many changed periodicity during the life of the magazine. Besides the general magazines, many appealed to specialized interests; there were religious magazines, medical and scientific journals, legal periodicals, agricultural journals, women's and children's magazines, and comic magazines. The most successful of them was the *Portfolio*, started by Joseph Dennie in 1801 and continued by others until 1825, the longest run of any magazine in the period. Among its contributors were Joseph Hopkinson, Richard Rush, John Quincy Adams, Charles B. Brown, John Blair Linn, and Alexander Wilson. Other notable magazines were *The Columbian Magazine* (1786-1792), which had been founded by Mathew Carey and, after him, was continued by others; Carey's *American Museum* (1787-1792), containing significant short fiction; Isaiah Thomas' *Massachusetts Magazine* (1789-1796), publishing fictional "fragments" and "characters"; Swords' *New York Magazine* (1790-1797), with contributions from the Friendly Club; C. B. Brown's *Monthly Magazine* (1799-1800), with valuable critical summaries; *The North American Review* (1815-1940), numbering among its editors Jared Sparks, Edward Tyrrell Channing, and Edward Everett; *The Christian Examiner*, begun as *The Christian Disciple* in 1813, having among its editors Noah Webster, and publishing many valuable reviews; the *New York Mirror*, begun in 1823 and one of the leading magazines of the succeeding period; the *Lady's Book* (1830-1898), to become later the well-known *Godey's Lady's Book;* the *Saturday Evening Post* (1821-   ), still being published; and Hezekiah Niles' *Niles Weekly Register* (1811-1849), a periodical which contains a great deal of valuable information about the period. Circulation was never large; the *Portfolio* in its best years had only 2000 subscribers, editors received small salaries or none at all, and contributors in the early years got only the satisfaction of being published. In many instances the magazine was the product of a local literary coterie—the Tuesday Club in Philadelphia, the Anthology Society in Boston, the Friendly Club in New York, and lesser groups in these and other cities. When in the last decade of the period editors received more than nominal salaries and contributors were paid, the professional magazinist, prominent in the succeeding period, began to appear.

The essay and article predominated as the staples in the magazine while poetry, biography, and travel sketches were next in importance; but short fiction and criticism became increasingly frequent in the later years. The topics were manners and fashions, politics and public events (the National Bank), education and reforms (the mania for founding colleges, the emerging slavery debate), style and language (particularly after the publication of Webster's *Dictionary*), the theater, and, later, books. At the turn of the century Charles Brockden Brown, in the *Monthly Magazine,* attributed the paucity of good American writing to (1) the national preoccupation with business, (2) defective education in college, (3) lack of competition in scholarship, (4) lack of reward, and (5) the scarcity of good models. Subsequent editors said much the same thing, adding the dominance of politics and the absence of an American language, tradition, and antiquity. If these editors are to be believed, magazines failed because there were not enough capable authors to fill them. The more probable reason was cost and bad management. Printing and postage costs were high, subscriptions were difficult to collect, amateur contributors were unreliable, the projects were undertaken with inadequate financial backing, and the editors were often uninterested or inept. When Irving was offered the editorship of *The Analectic Magazine,* he accepted because he thought it would be an "amusing occupation" for his "idle hours." The position of editor acquired dignity, however; Freneau, Brown, Bryant, and Irving all were editors at one time or another. Indeed it is possible that Bryant made a greater impact on American life as editor of the *New York Evening Post,* a position he held for half a century, than as poet.

Sympathetic to the demand for a literature indigenous in theme, form, and language, the writers in the period struggled to produce one. Native themes were all around them in the facts of American life and in the patriotic articles in periodicals: the beauty and potential of the land, the struggles and triumphs of the local past, the opportunities and oddities of republican society, and the glorious destiny of the new nation. The land offered scenic wonders enough for all, and from either the agrarian or romantic view it was a setting for the new Eden, though the literary treatment of it seldom went beyond the rhapsodic and picturesque. Rarely was the growing industrial urbanization of the nation a part of this scene, except to be deplored. Attached to the land was the Indian, who provided matter obviously unique and who was both an impediment to the advances of civilized republicanism and a noble example of a vanishing race to be viewed with sympathy and sentiment. The examination of the local past supplied the nation with its mythic heroes and heroic events. From Colonial times came Columbus and Pocahontas; from the Revolution came George Washington, John Paul Jones, Francis Marion, Mad Anthony Wayne and others; from the naval wars, Edward Preble, Stephen Decatur, and Oliver Hazard Perry; from the West, Dan'l Boone and Davy Crockett. Distilled from the idealizations of these heroes, rather than from fact, came the ideal republican common man, homespun or inconspicuous in dress, rough but considerate in manners, open and sometimes eloquent in speech, independent and virtuous in character, untutored but sage in thought. Embodied in him were all the middle-class virtues cast by the shadow of Poor Richard. Equality, opportunity, and recognized merit were proclaimed to be the marks of a republican society, and its agents were church, school, courts, and property. Judged on these principles, the sins of American society—imprudence or greed, pretense or pride, falseness or duplicity—were not only unpatriotic but somehow foreign in derivation. Most villains were aliens or, if native born, outcasts, traitors, or Tories. On the destiny of America all were agreed; she was to be the model for the world.

What constituted a native style was more difficult to determine. Critical thinking and rhetorical notions were dominated by the Scots "common sense" school, particularly by Hugh Blair's *Lectures on Rhetoric and Belles Lettres,* which had many American editions in the period, was used as a school text, and was excerpted in many periodicals. Two "styles" predominated—the native vernacular and the proper literary style. The vernacular was vigorous and picturesque, but it was also considered vulgar; it could be used only for comic effect. The proper style was simple, clear, dignified, and embroidered with appropriate imagery so long as the imagery did not obscure the thought. Such a style was not to be derived from the purified language of common men but from the clarified language of books. Here the writer was confronted with a dilemma; if he followed Blair he could be neither national nor republican, if he endeavored to be native he was almost certain to be condemned as barbarous. And what the American language was or should be no one knew with certainty, not even Noah Webster, whose first *Dictionary* was condemned by many. In this situation, the writers' conception of themselves as literary artists prevailed and they followed Blair.

The adaptation of older literary forms to the new themes was difficult only in certain genres. Biography, history, essay, and tract were easily put to patriotic or republican purposes, though they acquired a difference in tone because of the shift in intended audience from peer or posterity to the average reader. To acquaint the citizen with the lesser-known areas of his land, travel accounts were useful, and many appeared. The enthusiasm of these travelers and their awe and wonder at the marvels of the American scene contributed to the development of the nature essay, which began to take form in the writing of Audubon and Wilson. Though the poetry of the period differs from the earlier verse, that difference is in mood and content rather than in form. Odes, elegies, verse satires, and meditative verse were still written, but there was a noticeable increase in the composition of short lyrics, which became more fanciful, more personal, and more varied in mood. There was an increasing use of blank verse and the simpler stanzaic patterns, but these were not American innovations.

The adaptation of older fictional forms, short and long, gave the native writer most difficulty. Fiction was late in developing in American writing, partially because of the moral objection to the genre, which was thought vicious at worst and useless at best, partially because it was of recent development abroad, and partially because at the time of its development there, the American colonies had, instead, been deeply preoccupied with their growing independence from England. The appearance of fiction in America in this period is not thus to be attributed to a sudden discovery of the genre but rather to a shift in attitudes and conditions that now permitted its development. The growth in periodical publications nurtured the development of the short tale as the growth of printing supported the longer story. Of the older forms of the short tale, the fable and allegory had been used for propaganda purposes during the Revolution and were similarly used now, but their purposes were restricted by custom to moral or political themes and their novelty was gone. The character was useful in presenting both idealized American and local or social types and was so used, but it was a static form. With the addition to the character sketch of dramatic action, local setting, and idiosyncratic characters, something new emerged, a *Rip Van Winkle*, for example, the action supplied in this instance by old legend. Of the newer forms, the oriental fantasy, though attempted, had obviously little pertinence to the American scene. When national attention was directed to the Mediterranean by our wars with the Barbary pirates and Tripoli, the fiction that grew out of them took on some of the coloring of the oriental tale. The Gothic tale was generally thought unadaptable largely because the nation had no medieval ruins for settings and no appropriate characters with which to people it. By finding substitute horrors in the forest maze, in predatory animals, and in Indians, the Gothic tale was domesticated but with a difference that made it seem native. When coupled with the older Indian captivity narratives a new form emerged. The sentimental tale, so long as it confined itself to the treatment of sensibilities, could be domesticated by being given local atmospheres and settings, though seduction was not so lightly regarded here as it appeared to be abroad. When caste distinctions were attempted, however, difficulties arose; a republican society was classless, or should be, and privilege could not be allowed to individuals without doing violence to national ideals. Popular though the type was, many efforts to domesticate it were failures, although on occasion a tale like "The Stout Gentleman" was successful. The writers of the times were not fully aware of these adaptive processes; rather they effected them as a consequence of the national demand for a native literature.

The novel had an equally sudden upsurge in this period. Over two hundred were written in the forty year period by native writers, over a hundred in the last ten years before 1830. Few of the authors are read today, and the most popular novel, Susanna Rowson's *Charlotte Temple* (1794), which had over fifty printings before 1830, is largely indulged as a curiosity. The more noted of the authors were Hugh Henry Brackenridge, Charles Brockden Brown, James Kirke Paulding, and James Fenimore Cooper. The problems of adaptation faced by the novelists were the same as those faced by the tale writers; the available forms were not entirely suited to the American scene, real or ideal. In their efforts to domesticate the forms they did produce some effective novels and some new types. Brackenridge manipulated the picaresque form to provide a commentary on all aspects of American life from the city (Philadelphia, the capital), to the farm (rural Pennsylvania), to the trans-Allegheny settlement (Pittsburgh), to the frontier (Ohio), including in the survey most of the institutions—social, intellectual, religious, judicial, and political—then existent, many of the dialects then spoken, and many of the ethnic groups then present. The result was not successful, but the conception had an element of greatness in it. Brown put the Godwinian villain in the Gothic novel, substituted the horrors and terrors of the American scene for European conventions, focused on the psychological responses of his characters, and produced an American Gothicism. Paulding, writing in the tradition of Fielding, applied its methods to the life of the Hudson River valley, where the patroon was the nearest native equivalent of the English squire. Cooper, who used Fielding and Scott and who was endowed with greater versatility and a keener sense than any of his contemporaries for what were the essential native concerns, established two new forms—the forest romance and the deep-sea story—and in the Littlepage trilogy approached the novel of social purpose. Although the most popular with readers, the sentimental novel was less successfully domesticated than any of the available genres. It failed for the same reasons the sentimental tale failed. In contrast, the historic romance was rapidly transplanted; the simple substitution of events in American history, particularly Revolutionary history, supplied the conflicting loyalties and the dramatic incident, and the assumed nobility of the American cause made the result patriotically satisfying, although fictional skill was often lacking.

As in fiction, there was a burst of activity in the drama. Over three hundred dramatic pieces of all sorts, from interludes to heroic tragedies, were written by native authors in the forty years of the period. Much of the dramatic writing was highly imitative, much of it was translation or adaptation of European dramas, and little was truly indigenous. The principal native dramatists were William Dunlap, who chiefly engaged in translating, adapting, or reconstructing French and German drama for the American stage; George Nelson Barker, who consciously set out to develop a natural drama on national themes exhibiting "our national peculiarities"; and John Howard Payne, who was conventional and imitative in most respects though republican in attitudes. Almost all the great moments in American history from the adventures of Captain John Smith to the War of 1812 were dramatized and all the American heroes including Jackson appeared. American manners, sentiments, and politics were represented, and the stage Yankee, the stage Negro, the frontiersman, and the noble Red Man were established. The dramatization of *Rip Van Winkle* became the most popular theatrical piece of the nineteenth century. Yet despite the employment of native themes and native material, the only indigenous form to develop in the period was the minstrel show.

Though the effort to produce genuinely native literary forms failed in the main, the period made positive contributions to the development of a native literature. The search of the American past encouraged the national pride, provided a common bond for all sections of the country, and embodied the American Dream in usable symbolic figures. The examination of the contemporary scene clarified the essential issues of the republican society, exposed its faults and affirmed its virtues, and projected many of the later themes: the epic expansion westward, the confidence in the capacities of the common man, the integrity of individuality, the delights of local idiosyncracy. The depiction of the natural scene encouraged the conception of nature as ameliorator, if not mentor. The writers of the period were more successful in their effort than they knew; much that is native in American literature had its origins in them.

BIOGRAPHY

Mason Locke Weems
(1759-1825)

Born in Anne Arundel County, Maryland, Mason Locke Weems was an Episcopal clergyman, a bookseller, and a biographer. Following a trip to England, Weems served as a clergyman in Maryland from 1784 to 1792; he began reprinting a series of conduct books in 1791, and after 1794, was an agent on the eastern seaboard for Mathew Carey's publishing house. Weems' own conduct books include *God's Revenge Against Murder* (1807), *Against Gambling* (c. 1810), *Against Adultery* (1815), and *Against Duelling* (1820). He wrote biographies of Francis Marion and Franklin, but is best remembered for *A History of the Life and Death, Virtues and Exploits, of General George Washington* (Philadelphia, 1800), which went through more than seventy editions. To the fifth edition (1806), Weems added the famous cherry-tree story.

BIBLIOGRAPHY: L. C. Wroth, *Parson Weems* (Baltimore, 1911), P. L. Ford and Emily E. F. Skeel, *Mason Locke Weems*, 3 vols. (New York, 1928–1929). *A History of the Life and Death . . . of . . . Washington*, ed. Mark Van Doren (n.p., 1927).

From *The Life of George Washington*
CHAPTER I

. . . Since then it is the private virtues that lay the foundation of all human excellence—since it was these that exalted Washington to be "Columbia's first and greatest Son," be it our first care to present these, in all their luster, before the admiring eyes of our children. To them his private character is everything; his public, hardly anything.—For how glorious soever it may have been in Washington to have undertaken the emancipation of his country; to have stemmed the long tide of adversity; to have baffled every effort of a wealthy and warlike nation; to have obtained for his countrymen the completest victory, and for himself the most unbounded power; and then to have returned that power, accompanied with all the weight of his own great character and advice to establish a government that should immortalize the blessings of liberty—however glorious, I say, all this may have been to himself, or instructive to future generals and presidents, yet does it but little concern our children. For who among us can hope that his son shall ever be called, like Washington, to direct the storm of war, or to ravish the ears of deeply listening Senates? To be constantly placing him then, before our children, in this high character, what is it but like springing in the clouds a golden Phoenix, which no mortal caliber can ever hope to reach? Or like setting pictures of the Mammoth before the mice, whom "not all the manna of Heaven" can ever raise to equality? Oh no! give us his private virtues! In these, every youth is interested, because in these every youth may become a Washington—a Washington in piety and patriotism,—in industry and honor—and consequently a Washington, in what alone deserves the name, self esteem and universal respect.

CHAPTER II

Birth and Education

. . . Never did the wise Ulysses take more pains with his beloved Telemachus, than did Mr. Washington with George, to inspire him with an early love of truth. "Truth, George," said he, "is the loveliest quality of youth. I would ride fifty miles, my son, to see the little boy whose heart is so honest, and his lips so pure, that we may depend on every word he says. O how lovely does such a child appear in the eyes of everybody! his parents dote on him. His relations glory in him. They are constantly praising him to their children, whom they beg to imitate him. They are often sending for him to visit them; and receive him, when he comes, with as much joy as if he were a little angel, come to set pretty examples to their children.

"But, Oh! how different, George, is the case with the boy who is so given to lying, that nobody can believe a word he says! He is looked at with aversion wherever he goes, and parents dread to see him come among their children. Oh, George! my son! rather than see you come to this pass, dear as you are to my heart, gladly would I assist to nail you up in your little coffin, and follow you to your grave. Hard, indeed, would it be to me to give up my son, whose little feet are always so ready to run about with me, and whose fondly looking eyes, and sweet prattle make so large a part of my happiness. But still I would give him up, rather than see him a common liar."

"Pa," said George very seriously, "do I ever tell lies?"

"No, George, I thank God you do not, my son; and I rejoice in the hope you never will. At least, you shall never, from me, have cause to be guilty of so shameful a thing. Many parents, indeed, even compel their children to this vile practice, by barbarously beating them for every little fault: hence, on the next offense, the little terrified creature slips out a lie! just to escape the rod. But as to yourself George, you know I have always told you, and now tell you again, that, whenever by accident, you do anything wrong, which must often be the case, as you are but a poor little boy yet, without experience or knowledge, you must never tell a falsehood to conceal it; but come bravely up, my son, like a little man, and tell me of it: and, instead of beating you, George, I will but the more honor and love you for it, my dear."

This, you'll say, was sowing good seed!—Yes, it was: and the crop, thank God, was, as I believe it ever will be, where a man acts the true parent, that is, the Guardian Angel, by his child.

The following anecdote is a case in point. It is too valuable to be lost, and too true to be doubted; for it was communicated to me by the same excellent lady to whom I am indebted for the last.

"When George," said she, "was about six years old, he was made the wealthy master of a hatchet! of which, like most little boys, he was immoderately fond, and was constantly going about chopping every thing that came in his way. One day, in the garden, where he often amused himself hacking his mother's pea-sticks, he unluckily tried the edge of his hatchet on the body of a beautiful young English cherry tree, which he barked so terribly, that I don't believe the tree ever got the better of it. The next morning the old gentleman, finding out what had befallen his tree, which, by the by, was a great favorite, came into the house; and with much warmth asked for the mischievous author, declaring at the same time, that he would not have taken five guineas for his tree. Nobody could tell him anything about it. Presently George and his hatchet made their appearance. "George," said his father, "do you know who killed that beautiful little cherry tree yonder in the garden?" This was a tough question; and George staggered under it for a moment; but quickly recovered himself: and looking at his father, with the sweet face of youth brightened with the inexpressible charm of all-conquering truth, he bravely cried out, "I can't tell a lie, Pa; you know I can't tell a lie. I did cut it with my hatchet."—"Run to my arms, you dearest boy," cried his father in transports, "run to my arms; glad am I, George, that you killed my tree; for you have paid me for it a thousandfold. Such an act of heoism in my son is more worth than a thousand trees, though blossomed with silver, and their fruits of purest gold."

It was in this way by interesting at once both his heart and head, that Mr. Washington conducted George with great ease and pleasure along the happy paths of virtue.   1806

NATURE ESSAYS

William Bartram

(1739-1823)

William Bartram, the son of naturalist John Bartram, was born and educated at Philadelphia. After several ventures into business, Bartram resumed his earlier interest in nature. He accompanied his father on an exploration of the St. John's River in 1765–1766 and at the expense of Dr. John Fothergill, an Englishman, explored the southeastern states from 1773 to 1777. Bartram recorded his discoveries in *Travels Through North and South Carolina, Georgia, East and West Florida* (Philadelphia, 1791). His *Travels* was printed in London (1792) and translated into German (1793), Dutch (1797), and French (1799). In 1789, Bartram wrote *Observations on the Creek and Cherokee Indians,* unpublished until 1853.

BIBLIOGRAPHY: *Travels,* ed. Francis Harper (New Haven, 1958) and by Mark Van Doren (New York, 1928, 1947). Ernest Earnest, *John and William Bartram, Botanists and Explorers* (Philadelphia, 1940). Nathan B. Fagin, *William Bartram, Interpreter of the American Landscape* (Baltimore, 1933).

From *Travels Through North and South Carolina, Georgia, East and West Florida*

PART I, CHAPTER III

. . . It may be proper to observe, that I had now passed the utmost frontier of the white settlements on that border. It was drawing on towards the close of day, the skies serene and calm, the air temperately cool, and gentle zephyrs breathing through the fragrant pines; the prospect around enchantingly varied and beautiful; endless green savannas, checkered with coppices of fragrant shrubs, filled the air with the richest perfume. The gaily attired plants which enameled the green had begun to imbibe the pearly dew of evening; nature seemed silent, and nothing appeared to ruffle the happy moments of evening contemplation: when, on a sudden, an Indian appeared crossing the path, at a considerable distance before me. On perceiving that he was armed with a rifle, the first sight of him startled me, and I endeavored to elude his sight by stopping my pace, and keeping large trees between us; but he espied me, and turning short about, sat spurs to his horse, and came up on full gallop. I never before this was afraid at the sight of an Indian, but at this time, I must own that my spirits were very much agitated: I saw at once, that being unarmed, I was in his power, and having now but a few moments to prepare, I resigned myself entirely to the will of the Almighty, trusting to his mercies for my preservation; my mind then became tranquil, and I resolved to meet the dreaded foe with resolution and cheerful confidence. The intrepid Seminole stopped suddenly, three or four yards before me, and silently viewed me, his countenance angry and fierce, shifting his rifle from shoulder to shoulder, and looking about instantly on all sides. I advanced towards him, and with an air of confidence offered him my hand, hailing him, brother; at this he hastily jerked back his arm, with a look of malice, rage and disdain, seeming everyway disconcerted; when again looking at me more attentively, he instantly spurred up to me, and, with dignity in his look and action, gave me his hand. Possibly the silent language of his soul, during the moment of suspense (for I believe his design was to kill me when he first came up) was after this manner: "White man, thou art my enemy, and thou and thy brethren may have killed mine; yet it may not be so, and even were that the case, thou art now alone, and in my power. Live; the Great Spirit forbids me to touch thy life; go to thy brethren, tell them thou sawest an Indian in the forests, who knew how to be humane and compassionate." In fine, we shook hands, and parted in a friendly manner, in the midst of a dreary wilderness; and he informed me of the course and distance to the trading house, where I found he had been extremely ill-treated the day before.

I now sat forward again, and after eight or ten miles' riding, arrived at the banks of St. Mary's, opposite the stores, and got safe over before dark. The river is here about one hundred yards across, has ten feet water, and, following its course, about sixty miles to the sea, though but about twenty miles by land. The trading company here received and treated me with great civility. On relating my adventures on the road, particularly the last with the Indian, the chief replied, with a countenance that at once bespoke surprise and pleasure, "My friend, consider yourself a fortunate man: that fellow," said he, "is one of the greatest villains on earth, a noted murderer, and outlawed by his countrymen. Last evening he was here, we took his gun from him, broke it in pieces, and gave him a severe drubbing: he, however, made his escape, carrying off a new rifle gun, with which, he said, going off, he would kill the first white man he met."

On seriously contemplating the behavior of this Indian towards me, so soon after his ill treatment, the following train of sentiments insensibly crowded in upon my mind.

Can it be denied, but that the moral principle, which directs the savages to virtuous and praiseworthy actions, is natural or innate? It is certain they have not the assistance of letters, or those means of education in the schools of philosophy, where the virtuous sentiments and actions of the most illustrious characters are recorded, and carefully laid before the youth of civilized nations: therefore this moral principle must be innate, or they must be under the immediate influence and guidance of a more divine and powerful preceptor, who, on these occasions, instantly inspires them, and as with a ray of divine light, points out to them at once the dignity, propriety, and beauty of virtue. . . .

PART I, CHAPTER V

. . . My barque being securely moored, and having reconnoitered the surrounding groves, and collected firewood, I spread my skins and blanket by my cheerful fire, under the protecting shade of the hospitable Live oak, and reclined my head on my hard but healthy couch. I listened, undisturbed, to the divine hymns of the feathered songsters of the groves, whilst the softly whispering breezes faintly died away.

The sun now below the western horizon, the moon majestically rising in the east; again the tuneful birds become inspired; how melodious is the social mockbird! the groves resound the unceasing cries of the whippoor-will; the moon about an hour above the horizon; lo! a dark esclipse[1] of her glorious brightness comes slowly on; at length, a silver thread alone encircles her temples: at this boding change, an universal silence prevails.

Nature now weary, I resigned myself to rest; the night passed over; the cool dews of the morning awake me; my fire burnt low; the blue smoke scarce rises above the moistened embers; all is gloomy: the late starry skies, now overcast by thick clouds, I am warned to rise and be going. The livid purple clouds thicken on the frowning brows of the morning; the tumultuous winds from the east now exert their power. O peaceful Alatamaha! gentle by nature! how thou art ruffled! thy wavy surface disfigures every object, presenting them obscurely to the sight, and they at length totally disappear, whilst the furious winds and sweeping rains bend the lofty groves, and prostrate the quaking grass, driving the affrighted creatures to their dens and caverns.

The tempest now relaxes, its impetus is spent, and a calm serenity gradually takes place; by noon they break away, the blue sky appears, the fulgid sunbeams spread abroad their animating light, and the steady western wind resumes his peaceful reign. The waters are purified, the waves subside, and the beautiful river regains its native calmness: so it is with the varied and mutable scenes of human events on the stream of

---

[1] The air at this time being serene, and not a cloud to be seen, I saw this annual almost total autumnal eclipse, in its highest degree of perfection. [All notes in this selection are Bartram's.]

life. The higher powers and affections of the soul are so blended and connected with the inferior passions, that the most painful feelings are excited in the mind when the latter are crossed: thus in the moral system, which we have planned for our conduct, as a ladder whereby to mount to the summit of terrestrial glory and happiness, and from whence we perhaps meditated our flight to heaven itself, at the very moment when we vainly imagine ourselves to have attained its point, some unforeseen accident intervenes, and surprises us; the chain is violently shaken, we quit our hold and fall: the well contrived system at once becomes a chaos; every idea of happiness recedes; the splendor of glory darkens, and at length totally disappears: every pleasing object is defaced, all is deranged, and the flattering scene passes quite away, a gloomy cloud pervades the understanding, and when we see our progress retarded, and our best intentions frustrated, we are apt to deviate from the admonitions and convictions of virtue, to shut our eyes upon our guide and protector, doubt of his power, and despair of his assistance. But let us wait and rely on our God, who in due time will shine forth in brightness, dissipate the envious cloud, and reveal to us how finite and circumscribed is human power, when assuming to itself independent wisdom.

But, before I leave the river Alatamaha, we will proceed to give a further and more particular account of it. It has its source in the Cherokee mountains, near the head of Tugilo, the great west branch of Savanna, and, before it leaves the mountains, is joined and augmented by innumerable rivulets; thence it descends through the hilly country, with all its collateral branches, and winds rapidly amongst the hills two hundred and fifty miles, and then enters the flat plain country, by the name of the Oakmulge; thence meandering an hundred and fifty miles, it is joined on the east side by the Ocone, which likewise heads in the lower ridges of the mountains. After this confluence, having now gained a vast acquisition of waters, it assumes the name of Alatamaha, when it becomes a large majestic river, flowing with gentle windings through a vast plain forest, near an hundred miles, and enters the Atlantic by several mouths. The north channel, or entrance, glides by the heights of Darien, on the east bank, about ten miles above the bar, and, running from thence with several turnings, enters the ocean between Sapello and Wolf islands. The south channel, which is esteemed the largest and deepest, after its separation from the north, descends gently, winding by M'Intosh's and Broughton islands; and lastly, by the west coast of St. Simon's island, enters the ocean, through St. Simon's Sound, between the south end of the island of that name and the north end of Jekyl island. On the west banks of the south channel, ten or twelve miles above its mouth, and nearly apposite Darien, are to be seen, the remains of an ancient fort, or fortification; it is now a regular tetragon terrace, about four feet high, with bastions at each angle; the area may contain about an acre of ground, but the fosse which surrounded it is nearly filled up. There are large Live Oaks, Pines, and other trees, growing upon it, and in the old fields adjoining. It is supposed to have been the work of the French or Spaniards. A large swamp lies betwixt it and the river, and a considerable creek runs close by the works, and enters the river through the swamp, a small distance above Broughton Island. About seventy or eighty miles above the confluence of the Oakmulge and Ocone, the trading path, from Augusta to the Creek nation, crosses these fine rivers, which are there forty miles apart. On the east banks of the Oakmulge, this trading road runs nearly two miles through ancient Indian fields, which are called the Oakmulge fields: they are the rich low lands of the river. On the heights of these low grounds are yet visible monuments, or traces, of an ancient town, such as artificial mounts or terraces, squares and banks, encircling considerable areas. Their old fields and planting land extend up and down the river, fifteen or twenty miles from this site.

And, if we are to give credit to the account the Creeks give of themselves, this place is remarkable for being the first town or settlement, when they sat down (as they term it) or established themselves, after their emigration from the west, beyond the Mississippi, their original native country. On this long journey they suffered great and innumerable difficulties, encountering and vanquishing numerous and valiant tribes of Indians, who opposed and retarded their march. Having crossed the river, still pushing eastward, they were obliged to make a stand, and fortify themselves in this place, as their only remaining hope, being to the last degree persecuted and weakened by their surrounding foes. Having formed for themselves this retreat, and driven off the inhabitants by degrees, they recovered their spirits, and again faced their enemies, when they came off victorious in a memorable and decisive battle. They afterwards gradually subdued their surrounding enemies, strengthening themselves by taking into confederacy the vanquished tribes.

PART II, CHAPTER III

. . . At the cool eve's approach, the sweet enchanting melody of the feathered songsters gradually ceases, and they betake themselves to their leafy coverts for security and repose.

Solemnly and slowly move onward, to the river's shore, the rustling clouds of the Ephemera. How awful the procession! innumerable millions of winged beings, voluntarily verging on to destruction, to the brink of the grave, where they behold bands of their enemies with wide open jaws, ready to receive them. But as if insensible of their danger, gay and tranquil each meets his beloved mate, in the still air, inimitably bedecked in their new nuptial robes. What eye can trace them, in their varied wanton amorous chases, bounding and fluttering on the odoriferous air? with what peace, love and joy, do they end the last moments of their existence?

I think we may assert, without any fear of exaggeration, that there are annually of these beautiful winged beings, which rise into existence, and for a few moments take a transient view of the glory of the Creator's works, a number greater than the whole race of mankind that have ever existed since the creation; and that only, from the shores of this river. How many then must have been produced since the creation, when we consider the number of large rivers in America, in comparison with which, this river is but a brook or rivulet.

The importance of the existence of these beautiful and delicately formed little creatures, in the creation, whose frame and organization is equally wonderful, more delicate, and perhaps as complicated as that of the most perfect human being, is well worth a few moments' contemplation; I mean particularly when they appear in the fly state. And if we consider the very short period, of that stage of existence, which we may reasonably suppose, to be the only space of their life that admits of pleasure and enjoyment, what a lesson doth it not afford us of the vanity of our own pursuits.

Their whole existence in this world, is but one complete year, and at least three hundred and sixty days of that time, they are in the form of an ugly grub, buried in mud, eighteen inches under water, and in this condition scarcely locomotive, as each Larva or grub, has but its own narrow solitary cell, from which it never travels, or moves, but in a perpendicular progression, of a few inches, up and down, from the bottom to the surface of the mud, in order to intercept the passing atoms for its food, and get a momentary respiration of fresh air; and even here it must be perpetually on its guard, in order to escape the troops of fish and shrimps, watching to catch it, and from whom it has no escape, but by instantly retreating back into its cell. One would be apt almost to imagine them created merely for the food of fish and other animals.

PART II, CHAPTER IV

. . . The evening drawing on, and there being no convenient landing place, for several miles higher up the river, we concluded to remain here all night. Whilst my fellow travelers were employing themselves in collecting firewood, and fixing our camp, I improved the opportunity, in reconnoitering our ground; and taking my fusee with me, I penetrated the grove, and afterwards entered some almost unlimited savannas and plains, which were absolutely enchanting; they had been lately burnt by the Indian hunters, and had just now recovered their vernal verdure and gaiety.

How happily situated is this retired spot of earth! What an elysium it is! where the wandering Seminole, the naked red warrior, roams at large, and after the vigorous chase retires from the scorching heat of the meridian sun. Here he reclines, and reposes under the odoriferous shades of

Zanthoxilon, his verdant couch guarded by the Deity; Liberty, and the Muses, inspiring him with wisdom and valor, whilst the balmy zephyrs fan him to sleep.

Seduced by these sublime enchanting scenes of primitive nature, and these visions of terrestrial happiness, I had roved far away from Cedar Point, but awakening to my cares, I turned about, and in the evening regained our camp.

On my return, I found some of my companions fishing for trout, round about the edges of the floating nymphaea, and not unsuccessfully, having then caught more than sufficient for us all. As the method of taking these fish is curious and singular, I shall just mention it.

They are taken with a hook and line, but without any bait. Two people are in a little canoe, one sitting in the stern to steer, and the other near the bow, having a rod ten or twelve feet in length, to one end of which is tied a strong line, about twenty inches in length, to which is fastened three large hooks, back to back. These are fixed very securely, and covered with the white hair of a deer's tail, shreds of a red garter, and some particolored feathers, all which form a tuft, or tassel, nearly as large as one's fist, and entirely cover and conceal the hooks: this is called a bob. The steersman paddles softly, and proceeds slowly along shore, keeping the boat parallel to it, at a distance just sufficient to admit the fisherman to reach the edge of the floating weeds along shore: he now ingeniously swings the bob backwards and forwards, just above the surface, and sometimes tips the water with it; when the unfortunate cheated trout instantly springs from under the weeds, and seizes the supposed prey. Thus he is caught without a possibility of escape, unless he break the hooks, line, or rod, which he, however, sometimes does by dint of strength; but, to prevent this, the fisherman used to the sport is careful not to raise the reed suddenly up, but jerks it instantly backwards, then steadily drags the sturdy reluctant fish to the side of the canoe, and with a sudden upright jerk brings him into it.

The head of this fish makes about one third of his length, and consequently the mouth is very large: birds, fish, frogs, and even serpents, are frequently found in its stomach.

The trout is of lead color, inclining to a deep blue, and marked with transverse waved lists, of a deep slate color, and when fully grown, has a cast of red, or brick color. The fins, with the tail, which is large, and beautifully formed, are of a light reddish purple, or flesh color, the whole body is covered with large scales. But what is most singular, this fish is remarkably ravenous; nothing living, that he can seize upon, escapes his jaws, and the opening and extending of the branchiostega, at the moment he rises to the surface to seize his prey, discovering his bright red gills, through the transparent waters, give him a very terrible appearance. Indeed it may be observed, that all fish of prey have this opening and covering of the gills very large, in order to discharge the great quantity of water, which they take in at their mouth, when they strike at their prey. This fish is nearly cuneiform, the body tapering gradually from the breast to the tail, and lightly compressed on each side. They frequently weigh fifteen, twenty and thirty pounds, and are delicious food.

My companion, the trader, being desirous of crossing the river to the opposite shore, in hopes of getting a turkey, I chose to accompany him, as it offered a good opportunity to observe the natural productions of those rich swamps and islands of the river. Having crossed the river, which is here five or six hundred yards wide, we entered a narrow channel, which after a serpentine course, for some miles, rejoins the main river again, above; forming a large fertile island, of rich low land. We landed on this island, and soon saw a fine roebuck,[2] at some distance from us, who appeared leader of a company of deer, that were feeding near him, on the verge of a green meadow. My companion parting from me, in pursuit of the deer, one way, and I, observing a flock of turkeys at some distance, on the other, directed my steps towards them, and with great caution, got near them; when singling out a large cock, and being just on the point of firing, I observed that several young cocks were affrighted, and in their language, warned the rest to be on their guard, against an enemy, whom I plainly perceived was industriously making his subtle approaches towards them, behind the fallen trunk of a tree, about twenty yards from me. This cunning fellow hunter, was a large fat wild cat (lynx); he saw me, and at times seemed to watch my motions, as if determined to seize the delicious prey before me. Upon which I changed my object, and leveled my piece at him. At that instant, my companion, at a distance, also discharged his piece at the deer, the report of which alarmed the flock of turkeys, and my fellow hunter, the cat, sprang over the log and trotted off. The trader also missed his deer: thus we foiled each other. By this time it being near night, we returned to camp, where having a delicious meal, ready prepared for our hungry stomachs, we sat down in a circle round our wholesome repast.

How supremely blessed were our hours at this time! plenty of delicious and healthful food, our stomachs keen, with contented minds; under no control, but what reason and ordinate passions dictated, far removed from the seats of strife.

Our situation was like that of the primitive state of man, peaceable, contented, and sociable. The simple and necessary calls of nature, being satisfied. We were altogether as brethren of one family, strangers to envy, malice and rapine.

The night being over we arose, and pursued our course up the river, and in the evening reached the trading house, Spalding's upper store, where I took up my quarters for several weeks.

[2] Cervus sylvaticus. The American deer.

PART II, CHAPTER V

. . . I now directed my steps towards my encampment, in a different direction. I seated myself upon a swelling green knoll, at the head of the crystal basin. Near me, on the left, was a point or projection of an entire grove of the aromatic Illisium Floridanum; on my right and all around behind me, was a fruitful Orange grove, with Palms and Magnolias interspersed; in front, just under my feet was the enchanting and amazing crystal fountain, which incessantly threw up, from dark, rocky caverns below, tons of water every minute, forming a basin, capacious enough for large shallops to ride in, and a creek of four or five feet depth of water, and near twenty yards over, which meanders six miles through green meadows, pouring its limpid waters into the great Lake George, where they seem to remain pure and unmixed. About twenty yards from the upper edge of the basin, and directly opposite to the mouth or outlet to the creek, is a continual and amazing ebullition, where the waters are thrown up in such abundance and amazing force, as to jet and swell up two or three feet above the common surface: white sand and small particles of shells are thrown up with the waters, near to the top, when they diverge from the center, subside with the expanding flood, and gently sink again, forming a large rim or funnel round about the aperture or mouth of the fountain, which is a vast perforation through a bed of rocks, the ragged points of which are projected out on every side. Thus far I know to be matter of real fact, and I have related it as near as I could conceive or express myself. But there are yet remaining scenes inexpressibly admirable and pleasing.

Behold, for instance, a vast circular expanse before you, the waters of which are so extremely clear as to be absolutely diaphanous or transparent as the ether; the margin of the basin ornamented with a great variety of fruitful and floriferous trees, shrubs and plants, the pendant golden Orange dancing on the surface of the pellucid waters, the balmy air vibrates the melody of the merry birds, tenants of the encircling aromatic grove.

At the same instant innumerable bands of fish are seen, some clothed in the most brilliant colors; the voracious crocodile stretched along at full length, as the great trunk of a tree in size, the devouring garfish, inimical trout, and all the varieties of gilded painted bream, the barbed catfish, dreaded stingray, skate and flounder, spotted bass, sheepshead and ominous drum; all in their separate bands and communities, with free and unsuspicious intercourse performing their evolutions: there are no signs of enmity, no attempt to devour each other; the different bands seem peaceably and complaisantly to move a little aside, as it were to make room for others to pass by.

But behold yet something far more admirable, see whole armies descending into an abyss, into the mouth of the bubbling fountain, they disappear! are they gone forever? is it real? I raise my eyes with terror and astonishment,—I look down again to the fountain with anxiety, when behold them as it were emerging from the blue ether of another world, apparently at a vast distance, at their first appearance, no bigger than flies or minnows, now gradually enlarging, their brilliant colors begin to paint the fluid.

Now they come forward rapidly, and instantly emerge, with the elastic expanding column of crystaline waters, into the circular basin or funnel, see now how gently they rise, some upright, others obliquely, or seem to lay as it were on their sides, suffering themselves to be gently lifted or borne up, by the expanding fluid towards the surface, sailing or floating like butterflies in the cerulean ether: then again they as gently descend, diverge and move off; when they rally, form again and rejoin their kindred tribes.

This amazing and delightful scene, though real, appears at first but as a piece of excellent painting; there seems no medium, you imagine the picture to be within a few inches of your eyes, and that you may without the least difficulty touch any one of the fish, or put your finger upon the crocodile's eye, when it really is twenty or thirty feet under water.

And although this paradise of fish, may seem to exhibit a just representation of the peaceable and happy state of nature which existed before the fall, yet in reality it is a mere representation; for the nature of the fish is the same as if they were in Lake George or the river; but here the water or element in which they live and move, is so perfectly clear and transparent, it places them all on an equality with regard to their ability to injure or escape from one another; (as all river fish of prey, or such as feed upon each other, as well as the unwieldy crocodile, take their prey by surprise; secreting themselves under covert or in ambush, until an opportunity offers, when they rush suddenly upon them:) but here is no covert, no ambush, here the trout freely passes by the very nose of the alligator and laughs in his face, and the bream by the trout.

But what is really surprising, that the consciousness of each other's safety or some other latent cause, should so absolutely alter their conduct, for here is not the least attempt made to injure or disturb one another.

The sun passing below the horizon, and night approaching, I arose from my seat, and proceeding on arrived at my camp, kindled my fire, supped and reposed peaceably. . . .   1791

John James Audubon
(1785-1851)

Born at Las Cayes, Santo Domingo, and educated in France, John James Audubon arrived at Philadelphia in 1804 and began his bird studies shortly thereafter. From 1807 to 1819, Audubon lived in Kentucky, where he kept a general store and continued his ornithological investigations. After 1820, he spent most of his energies studying birds and publishing his observations. Unable to find an American publisher, Audubon went to England in 1826; there he published his *Birds of America*, 4 vols. (London, 1827–1838), and *Ornithological Biography*, 5 vols. After further travels in Texas, Florida, and Labrador (1831–1834) and trips to England to supervise publication of his books, Audubon settled in New York City in 1842. Other works include *The Viviparous Quadrupeds of North America*, 2 vols. (New York, 1845–1846), and *Quadrupeds of North America*, 3 vols. (New York, 1854), both with John Bachman. The "Episodes," also called "Delineations of American Scenery and Character," were originally printed in the first three volumes of *Ornithological Biography*.

BIBLIOGRAPHY: *Audubon and His Journals*, ed. Maria R. Audubon, 2 vols. (London, 1897, New York, 1960), with notes by Elliott Coues. Francis H. Herrick, *Audubon the Naturalist*, 2 vols. (New York, 1917). Constance Rourke, *Audubon* (New York, 1936). *Delineations of American Scenery and Character*, ed. Herrick (New York, 1926). *The Birds of America*, 7 vols. (New York and Philadelphia, 1840–1844).

From *Ornithological Biography*

THE PRAIRIE

On my return from the Upper Mississippi I found myself obliged to cross one of the wide prairies which, in that portion of the United States, vary the appearance of the country. The weather was fine; all around me was as fresh and blooming as if it had just issued from the bosom of Nature. My knapsack, my gun, and my dog were all I had for baggage and company. But, although well moccasined, I moved slowly along, attracted by the brilliancy of the flowers, and the gambols of the fawns around their dams, to all appearance as thoughtless of danger as I felt myself.

My march was of long duration; I saw the sun sinking below the horizon long before I could perceive any appearance of woodland, and nothing in the shape of man had I met with that day. The track which I followed was only an old Indian trace, and as darkness overshadowed the prairie I felt some desire to reach at least a copse, in which I might lie down to rest. The Night Hawks were skimming over and around me, attracted by the buzzing wings of the beetles which form their food, and the distant howling of wolves gave me some hope that I should soon arrive at the skirts of some woodlands.

I did so, and almost at the same instant, a firelight attracting my eye, I moved towards it, full of confidence that it proceeded from the camp of some wandering Indians. I was mistaken: I discovered by its glare that it was from the hearth of a small log cabin, and that a tall figure passed and repassed between it and me, as if busily engaged in household arrangements.

I reached the spot, and presenting myself at the door, asked the tall figure, which proved to be a woman, if I might take shelter under her roof for the night. Her voice was gruff, and her attire negligently thrown about her. She answered in the affirmative. I walked in, took a wooden stool, and quietly seated myself by the fire. The next object that attracted my notice was a finely formed young Indian, resting his head between his hands, with his elbows on his knees. A long bow rested against the log wall near him, while a quantity of arrows and two or three Raccoon skins lay at his feet. He moved not; he apparently breathed not. Accustomed to the habits of Indians, and knowing that they pay little attention to the approach of civilized strangers (a circumstance which in some countries is considered as evincing the apathy of their character), I addressed him in French, a language not infrequently partially known to the people in that neighborhood. He raised his head, pointed to one of his eyes with his finger, and gave me a significant glance with the other. His face was covered with blood. The fact was that an hour before this, as he was in the act of discharging an arrow at a Raccoon in the top of a tree, the arrow had split upon the cord, and sprung back with such violence into his right eye as to destroy it forever.

Feeling hungry, I inquired what sort of fare I might expect. Such a thing as a bed was not to be seen, but many large untanned Bear and Buffalo hides lay piled in a corner. I drew a fine time-piece from my breast, and told the woman that it was late, and that I was fatigued. She had espied my watch, the richness of which seemed to operate upon her feelings with electric quickness. She told me there was plenty of venison and jerked buffalo meat, and that on removing the ashes I should find a cake. But my watch had struck her fancy, and her curiosity had to be gratified by an immediate sight of it. I took off the gold chain that secured it, from around my neck, and presented it to her; she was all ecstasy, spoke of its beauty, asked me its value, and put the chain round her brawny neck, saying how happy the possession of such a watch would make her. Thoughtless, and as I fancied myself in so retired a spot secure, I paid little attention to her talk or her movements. I helped my dog to a good supper of venison, and was not long in satisfying the demands of my own appetite.

The Indian rose from his seat, as if in extreme suffering. He passed and repassed me several times, and once pinched me on the side so violently that the pain nearly brought forth an exclamation of anger. I looked at him. His eye met mine, but his look was so forbidding that it struck a chill into the more nervous part of my system. He again seated himself, drew his butcher-knife from its greasy scabbard, examined its edge, as I would do that of a razor suspected dull, replaced it, and again taking his tomahawk from his back, filled the pipe of it with tobacco, and sent me expressive glances, whenever our hostess chanced to have her back towards us.

Never until that moment had my senses been awakened to the danger which I now suspected to be about me. I returned glance for glance to my companion, and rested well assured that, whatever enemies I might have, he was not of their number.

I asked the woman for my watch, wound it up, and under pretence of wishing to see how the weather might probably be on the morrow, took up my gun, and walked out of the cabin. I slipped a ball into each barrel, scraped the edges of my flints, renewed the primings, and returning to the hut gave a favorable report of my observations. I took a few Bear skins, made a pallet of them, and calling my faithful dog to my side, lay down, with my gun close to my body, and in a few minutes was, to all appearance, fast asleep.

A short time had elapsed when some voices were heard, and from the corner of my eye I saw two athletic youths making their entrance, bearing a dead stag on a pole. They disposed of their burden, and asking for whiskey, helped themselves freely to it. Observing me and the wounded Indian, they asked who I was, and why the devil that rascal (meaning the Indian, who, they knew, understood not a word of English) was in the house. The mother—for so she proved to be—bade them speak less loudly, made mention of my watch, and took them to a corner, where a conversation took place, the purport of which it required little shrewdness in me to guess. I tapped my dog gently. He moved his tail, and with indescribable pleasure I saw his fine eyes alternately fixed on me, and raised towards the trio in the corner. I felt that he perceived danger in my situation. The Indian exchanged a last glance with me.

The lads had eaten and drunk themselves into such a condition that I already looked upon them as *hors de combat;* and the frequent visits of the whiskey bottle to the ugly mouth of their dam, I hoped would soon reduce her to a like state. Judge of my astonishment, reader, when I saw this incarnate fiend take a large carving-knife, and go to the grindstone to whet its edge; I saw her pour the water on the turning machine, and watched her working away with the dangerous instrument, until the cold sweat covered every part of my body, in despite of my determination to defend myself to the last. Her task finished, she walked to her reeling sons, and said: "There, that'll soon settle him! Boys, kill yon —— ——, and then for the watch."

I turned, cocked my gun-locks silently, touched my faithful companion, and lay ready to start up and shoot the first who might attempt my life. The moment was fast approaching, and that night might have been my last in this world, had not Providence made preparations for my rescue. All was ready. The infernal hag was advancing slowly, probably contemplating the best way of despatching me, whilst her sons should be engaged with the Indian. I was several times on the eve of rising and shooting her on the spot; but she was not to be punished thus. The door was suddenly opened, and there entered two stout travelers, each with a long rifle on his shoulder. I bounced up on my feet, and making them most heartily welcome, told them how well it was for me that they should have arrived at that moment. The tale was told in a minute. The drunken sons were secured, and the woman, in spite of her defense and vociferations, shared the same fate. The Indian fairly danced with joy, and gave us to understand that, as he could not sleep for pain, he would watch over us. You may suppose we slept much less than we talked. The two strangers gave me an account of their once having been themselves in a somewhat similar situation. Day came, fair and rosy, and with it the punishment of our captives.

They were now quite sobered. Their feet were unbound, but their arms were still securely tied. We marched them into the woods off the road, and having used them as Regulators were wont to use such delinquents, we set fire to the cabin, gave all the skins and implements to the young Indian warrior, and proceeded, well pleased, towards the settlements.

During upwards of twenty-five years, when my wanderings extended to all parts of our country, this was the only time at which my life was in danger from my fellow creatures. Indeed, so little risk do travelers run in the United States that no one born there ever dreams of any to be encountered on the road; and I can only account for this occurrence by supposing that the inhabitants of the cabin were not Americans.

Will you believe, good-natured reader, that not many miles from the place where this adventure happened, and where fifteen years ago, no habitation belonging to civilized man was expected, and very few ever seen, large roads are now laid out, cultivation has converted the woods into fertile fields, taverns have been erected, and much of what we Americans call comfort is to be met with? So fast does improvement proceed in our abundant and free country.   1831

NIAGARA

After wandering on some of our great lakes for many months, I bent my course towards the celebrated Falls of Niagara, being desirous of taking a sketch of them. This was not my first visit to them, and I hoped it should not be the last.

Artists (I know not if I can be called one) too often imagine that what they produce must be excellent, and with that foolish idea go on spoiling much paper and canvas, when their time might have been better employed in a different manner. But, digressions aside, I directed my steps towards the Falls of Niagara, with the view of representing them on paper, for the amusement of my family.

Returning as I then was from a tedious journey, and possessing little more than some drawings of rare birds and plants, I reached the tavern at Niagara Falls in such plight as might have deterred many an individual from obtruding himself upon a circle of well-clad and perhaps well-bred society. Months had passed since the last of my linen had been taken from my body, and used to clean that useful companion, my gun. I was in fact covered just like one of the poorer class of Indians, and was rendered even more disagreeable to the eye of civilized man by not having, like them, plucked my beard, or trimmed my hair in any way. Had Hogarth been living, and there when I arrived, he could not have found a fitter subject for a Robinson Crusoe. My beard covered my neck in front, my hair fell much lower at my back, the leather dress which I wore had for months stood in need of repair, a large knife hung at my side, a rusty tin-box containing my drawings and colors, and wrapped up in a worn-out blanket that had served me for a bed, was buckled to my shoulders. To everyone I must have seemed immersed in the depths of poverty, perhaps of despair. Nevertheless, as I cared little about my appearance during those happy rambles, I pushed into the sitting-room, unstrapped my little burden, and asked how soon breakfast would be ready.

In America, no person is ever refused entrance to the inns, at least far from cities. We know too well how many poor creatures are forced to make their way from other countries in search of employment or to seek uncultivated land, and we are ever ready to let them have what they may call for. No one knew who I was, and the landlord, looking at me with an eye of close scrutiny, answered that breakfast would be on the table as soon as the company should come down from their rooms. I approached this important personage, told him of my avocations, and convinced him that he might feel safe as to remuneration. From this moment I was, with him at least, on equal footing with every other person in his house. He talked a good deal of the many artists who had visited the Falls that season, from different parts, and offered to assist me by giving such accommodations as I might require to finish the drawings I had in contemplation. He left me, and as I looked about the room I saw several views of the Falls, by which I was so disgusted that I suddenly came to my better senses. "What!" thought I, "have I come here to mimic nature in her grandest enterprise, and add *my* caricature of one of the wonders of the world to those which I here see? No; I give up the vain attempt. I shall look on these mighty cataracts and imprint them, where alone they can be represented—on my mind!"

Had I taken a view, I might as well have given you what might be termed a regular account of the form, the height, the tremendous roar of

these Falls; might have spoken of people periling their lives by going between the rock and the sheet of water, calculated the density of the atmosphere in that strange position, related wondrous tales of Indians and
their canoes having been precipitated the whole depth—might have told
of the narrow, rapid, and rockbound river that leads the waters of the
Erie into those of Ontario, remarking *en passant* the Devil's Hole and
sundry other places or objects. But, supposing you had been there, my
description would prove useless, and quite as puny as my intended view
would have been for my family; and should you not have seen them, and
are fond of contemplating the more magnificent of the Creator's works,
go to Niagara, reader; for all the pictures you may see, all the descriptions
you may read, of these mighty Falls, can only produce in your mind the
faint glimmer of a glowworm compared with the overpowering glory of
the meridian sun.

I breakfasted amid a crowd of strangers, who gazed and laughed at
me, paid my bill, rambled about and admired the Falls for a while, saw
several young gentlemen sketching on cards the mighty mass of foaming
waters, and walked to Buffalo, where I purchased new apparel and
sheared my beard. I then enjoyed civilized life as much as, a month before, I had enjoyed the wildest solitudes and the darkest recesses of
mountain and forest.   1831

SCIPIO AND THE BEAR

The Black Bear (*Ursus americanus*), however clumsy in appearance, is
active, vigilant, and persevering; possesses great strength, courage, and
address; and undergoes with little injury the greatest fatigues and hardships in avoiding the pursuit of the hunter. Like the Deer, it changes its
haunts with the seasons, and for the same reason, namely, the desire of
obtaining suitable food, or of retiring to the more inaccessible parts,
where it can pass the time in security, unobserved by man, the most dangerous of its enemies. During the spring months, it searches for food in
the low rich alluvial lands that border the rivers, or by the margins of
such inland lakes as, on account of their small size, are called by us
ponds. There it procures abundance of succulent roots, and of the tender
juicy stems of plants, upon which it chiefly feeds at that season. During
the summer heat, it enters the gloomy swamps, passes much of its time in
wallowing in the mud, like a hog, and contents itself with crayfish, roots,
and nettles, now and then, when hard pressed by hunger, seizing on a
young pig, or perhaps a sow, or even a calf. As soon as the different
kinds of berries which grow on the mountains begin to ripen, the Bears
betake themselves to the high grounds, followed by their cubs. In such
retired parts of the country where there are no hilly grounds, it pays visits to the maize fields, which it ravages for a while. After this, the various
species of nuts, acorns, grapes, and other forest fruits, that form what in
the western country is called *mast*, attract its attention. The Bear is then

seen rambling singly through the woods to gather this harvest, not forgetting meanwhile to rob every Bee tree it meets with, Bears being, as you
well know, expert at this operation. You also know that they are good
climbers, and may have been told, or at least may now be told, that the
Black Bear now and then houses itself in the hollow trunks of the larger
trees for weeks together, when it is said to suck its paws. You are probably not aware of a habit in which it indulges, and which, being curious,
must be interesting to you.

At one season, the Black Bear may be seen examining the lower part
of the trunk of a tree for several minutes with much attention, at the
same time looking around, and snuffing the air, to assure itself that no
enemy is near. It then raises itself on its hind legs, approaches the trunk,
embraces it with its forelegs, and scratches the bark with its teeth and
claws for several minutes in continuance. Its jaws clash against each
other, until a mass of foam runs down on both sides of the mouth. After
this it continues its rambles.

In various portions of our country, many of our woodsmen and hunters
who have seen the Bear performing the singular operation just described,
imagine that it does so for the purpose of leaving behind it an indication
of its size and power. They measure the height at which the scratches are
made, and in this manner can, in fact, form an estimate of the magnitude
of the individual. My own opinion, however, is different. It seems to me
that the Bear scratches the trees, not for the purpose of showing its size
or its strength, but merely for that of sharpening its teeth and claws, to
enable it better to encounter a rival of its own species during the amatory
season. The Wild Boar of Europe clashes its tusks and scrapes the earth
with its feet, and the Deer rubs its antlers against the lower part of the
stems of young trees or bushes, for the same purpose.

Being one night sleeping in the house of a friend, I was wakened by a
negro servant bearing a light, who gave me a note, which he said his
master had just received. I ran my eye over the paper, and found it to be
a communication from a neighbor, requesting my friend and myself to
join him as soon as possible, and assist in killing some Bears at that moment engaged in destroying his corn. I was not long in dressing, you may
be assured, and, on entering the parlor, found my friend equipped and
only waiting for some bullets, which a negro was employed in casting.
The overseer's horn was heard calling up the negroes from their different
cabins. Some were already engaged in saddling our horses, whilst others
were gathering all the cur-dogs of the plantation. All was bustle. Before
half an hour had elapsed, four stout negro men, armed with axes and
knives, and mounted on strong nags of their own (for you must know,
kind reader, that many of our slaves rear horses, cattle, pigs, and poultry,
which are exclusively their own property), were following us at a round
gallop through the woods, as we made directly for the neighbor's plantation, a little more than five miles off.

The night was none of the most favorable, a drizzling rain rendering the atmosphere thick and rather sultry; but as we were well acquainted with the course, we soon reached the house, where the owner was waiting our arrival. There were now three of us armed with guns, half a dozen servants, and a good pack of dogs of all kinds. We jogged on towards the detached field in which the Bears were at work. The owner told us that for some days several of these animals had visited his corn, and that a negro who was sent every afternoon to see at what part of the enclosure they entered, had assured him there were at least five in the field that night. A plan of attack was formed: the bars at the usual gap of the fence were to be put down without noise; the men and dogs were to divide, and afterwards proceed so as to surround the Bears, when, at the sounding of our horns, everyone was to charge towards the center of the field, and shout as loudly as possible, which it was judged would so intimidate the animals as to induce them to seek refuge upon the dead trees with which the field was still partially covered.

The plan succeeded. The horns sounded, the horses galloped forward, the men shouted, the dogs barked and howled. The shrieks of the negroes were enough to frighten a legion of Bears, and those in the field took to flight, so that by the time we reached the center they were heard hurrying towards the tops of the trees. Fires were immediately lighted by the negroes. The drizzling rain had ceased, the sky cleared, and the glare of the crackling fires proved of great assistance to us. The Bears had been so terrified that we now saw several of them crouched at the junction of the larger boughs with the trunks. Two were immediately shot down. They were cubs of no great size, and being already half dead, we left them to the dogs, which quickly despatched them.

We were anxious to procure as much sport as possible, and having observed one of the Bears, which from its size we conjectured to be the mother, ordered the negroes to cut down the tree on which it was perched, when it was intended the dogs should have a tug with it, while we should support them, and assist in preventing the Bear from escaping by wounding it in one of the hind-legs. The surrounding woods now echoed to the blows of the axemen. The tree was large and tough, having been girded more than two years, and the operation of felling it seemed extremely tedious. However, it began to vibrate at each stroke; a few inches alone now supported it; and in a short time it came crashing to the ground, in so awful a manner that Bruin must doubtless have felt the shock as severe as we should feel a shake of the globe produced by the sudden collision of a comet.

The dogs rushed to the charge, and harassed the Bear on all sides. We had remounted, and now surrounded the poor animal. As its life depended upon its courage and strength, it exercised both in the most energetic manner. Now and then it seized a dog, and killed him by a single stroke. At another time, a well administered blow of one of its forelegs sent an assailant off yelping so piteously that he might be looked upon as *hors de combat*. A cur had daringly ventured to seize the Bear by the snout, and was seen hanging to it, covered with blood, whilst a dozen or more scrambled over its back. Now and then the infuriated animal was seen to cast a revengeful glance at some of the party, and we had already determined to despatch it, when, to our astonishment, it suddenly shook off all the dogs, and, before we could fire, charged upon one of the negroes, who was mounted on a pied horse. The Bear seized the steed with teeth and claws, and clung to its breast. The terrified horse snorted and plunged. The rider, an athletic young man, and a capital horseman, kept his seat, although only saddled on a sheep's-skin tightly girthed, and requested his master not to fire at the Bear. Notwithstanding his coolness and courage, our anxiety for his safety was raised to the highest pitch, especially when in a moment we saw rider and horse come to the ground together; but we were instantly relieved on witnessing the masterly manner in which Scipio despatched his adversary, by laying open his skull with a single well-directed blow of his axe, when a deep growl announced the death of the Bear, and the valorous negro sprung to his feet unhurt.

Day dawned, and we renewed our search. Two of the remaining Bears were soon discovered, lodged in a tree about a hundred yards from the spot where the last one had been overpowered. On approaching them in a circle, we found that they manifested no desire to come down, and we resolved to try smoking. We surrounded the tree with a pile of brush-wood and large branches. The flames ascended and caught hold of the dry bark. At length the tree assumed the appearance of a pillar of flame. The Bears mounted to the top branches. When they had reached the uppermost, they were seen to totter, and soon after, the branch cracking and snapping across, they came to the ground, bringing with them a mass of broken twigs. They were cubs, and the dogs soon worried them to death.

The party returned to the house in triumph. Scipio's horse, being severely wounded, was let loose in the field, to repair his strength by eating the corn. A cart was afterwards sent for the game. But before we had left the field, the horses, dogs, and Bears, together with the fires, had destroyed more corn within a few hours than the poor Bear and her cubs had during the whole of their visits.   1835

Alexander Wilson

(1766-1813)

Alexander Wilson was born in Scotland and was apprenticed at the age of thirteen to a weaver. An aspiring poet, Wilson was disappointed in the reception of his *Poems* (Paisley, Scotland, 1790), which failed to bring him the recognition he sought. In 1794, he migrated to Philadelphia. He taught school for about ten years in Pennsylvania and New Jersey, but after meeting William Bartram in 1802, he turned his attention to the study of nature. His paintings and findings were published in *American Ornithology; or, The Natural History of Birds of the United States,* 9 vols. (Philadelphia, 1808–1814). Wilson's friend George Ord supervised printing of the last volume. Other works are *Poems, Chiefly in the Scottish Dialect* (London, 1816) and *The Foresters: A Poem* (Newtown, Pa., 1818).

BIBLIOGRAPHY: *The Poems and Literary Prose of Alexander Wilson,* ed. Alexander B. Grosart, 2 vols. (Paisley, Scotland, 1876). Robert Cantwell, *Alexander Wilson, Naturalist and Pioneer* (Philadelphia, 1961).

From *American Ornithology*

HUMMINGBIRD

Trochilus Colubris

Nature in every department of her works seems to delight in variety; and the present subject of our history is almost as singular for its minuteness, beauty, want of song and manner of feeding, as the preceding is for unrivaled excellence of notes, and plainness of plumage. Tho' this interesting and beautiful genus of birds comprehends upwards of seventy species, all of which, with a very few exceptions, are natives of America and its adjacent islands, it is yet singular, that the species now before us should be the only one of its tribe that ever visits the territory of the United States.

According to the observations of my friend Mr. Abbot, of Savannah, in Georgia, who has been engaged these thirty years in collecting and drawing subjects of natural history in that part of the country, the Hummingbird makes its first appearance there, from the south, about the twenty-third of March; two weeks earlier than it does in the county of Burke, sixty miles higher up the country towards the interior; and at least five weeks sooner than it reaches this part of Pennsylvania. As it passes on to the northward as far as the interior of Canada, where it is seen in great numbers,[1] the wonder is excited how so feebly constructed and delicate a little creature can make its way over such extensive regions of lakes and forests, among so many enemies, all its superiors in strength and magnitude. But its very minuteness, the rapidity of its flight, which almost eludes the eye, and that admirable instinct, reason, or whatever else it may be called, and daring courage which heaven has implanted in its bosom, are its guides and protectors. In these we may also perceive the reason, why an all-wise Providence has made this little hero an exception to a rule which prevails almost universally thro nature, viz. that the smallest species of a tribe are the most prolific. The Eagle lays one, sometimes two, eggs; the Crow five; the Titmouse seven or eight; the small European Wren fifteen; the Hummingbird two: and yet this latter is abundantly more numerous in America than the Wren is in Europe.

About the twenty-fifth of April the Hummingbird usually arrives in Pennsylvania; and about the tenth of May begins to build its nest. This is generally fixed on the upper side of a horizontal branch, not among the twigs, but on the body of the branch itself. Yet I have known instances where it was attached by the side to an old moss-grown trunk; and others where it was fastened on a strong rank stalk, or weed, in the garden; but these cases are rare. In the woods it very often chooses a white oak sapling to build on; and in the orchard, or garden, selects a pear tree for that purpose. The branch is seldom more than ten feet from the ground. The nest is about an inch in diameter, and as much in depth. A very complete one is now lying before me, and the materials of which it is composed are as follows:—The outward coat is formed of small pieces of a species of bluish grey lichen that vegetates on old trees and fences, thickly glued on with the saliva of the bird, giving firmness and consistency to the whole, as well as keeping out moisture. Within this are thick matted layers of the fine wings of certain flying seeds, closely laid together; and, lastly, the downy substance from the great mullein, and from the stalks of the common fern, lines the whole. The base of the nest is continued round the stem of the branch, to which it closely adheres; and, when viewed from below, appears a mere mossy knot or accidental protuberance. The eggs are two, pure white, and of equal thickness at both ends. The nest and eggs in the plate were copied with great precision, and by actual measurement, from one just taken in from the woods. On a person's approaching their nest, the little proprietors dart around with a humming sound, passing frequently within a few inches of one's head; and should the young be newly hatched, the female will resume her place on the nest even while you stand within a yard or two of the spot. The precise period of incubation I am unable to give; but the young are in the habit, a short time before they leave the nest, of thrusting their

[1] Mr. M'Kenzie speaks of seeing a "beautiful Hummingbird" near the head of the Unjigah or Peace river, in lat. 54°; but has not particularized the species. [Wilson's Notes.]

bills into the mouths of their parents, and sucking what they have brought them. I never could perceive that they carried them any animal food; tho, from circumstances that will presently be mentioned, I think it highly probable they do. As I have found their nests with eggs so late as the twelfth of July, I do not doubt but that they frequently, and perhaps usually, raise two broods in the same season.

The Hummingbird is extremely fond of tubular flowers, and I have often stopt, with pleasure, to observe his maneuvers among the blossoms of the trumpet flower. When arrived before a thicket of these that are full blown, he poises, or suspends himself on wing, for the space of two or three seconds, so steadily, that his wings become invisible, or only like a mist; and you can plainly distinguish the pupil of his eye looking round with great quickness and circumspection; the glossy golden green of his back, and the fire of his throat, dazzling in the sun, form altogether a most interesting appearance. The position into which his body is usually thrown while in the act of thrusting his slender tubular tongue into the flower, to extract its sweets, is exhibited in the figure on the plate. [Not included here.] When he alights, which is frequently, he always prefers the small dead twigs of a tree, or bush, where he dresses and arranges his plumage with great dexterity. His only note is a single chirp, not louder than that of a small cricket or grasshopper, generally uttered while passing from flower to flower, or when engaged in fight with his fellows; for when two males meet at the same bush, or flower, a battle instantly takes place; and the combatants ascend in the air, chirping, darting and circling around each other, till the eye is no longer able to follow them. The conqueror, however, generally returns to the place, to reap the fruits of his victory. I have seen him attack, and for a few moments tease the Kingbird; and have also seen him, in his turn, assaulted by a humble-bee, which he soon put to flight. He is one of those few birds that are universally beloved; and amidst the sweet dewy serenity of a summer's morning, his appearance among the arbors of honeysuckles, and beds of flowers, is truly interesting.

> When morning dawns, and the blest sun, again
> Lifts his red glories from the Eastern main,
> Then thro our woodbines, wet with glittering dews,
> The flower-fed Hummingbird his round pursues;
> Sips with inserted tube, the honeyed blooms,
> And chirps his gratitude as round he roams;
> While richest roses, tho in crimson drest,
> Shrink from the splendor of his gorgeous breast;
> What heav'nly tints in mingling radiance fly!
> Each rapid movement gives a different dye;
> Like scales of burnish'd gold they dazzling show,
> Now sink to shade . . . now like a furnace glow!

The singularity of this little bird has induced many persons to attempt to raise them from the nest, and accustom them to the cage. Mr. Coffer, of Fairfax county, Virginia, a gentleman who has paid great attention to the manners and peculiarities of our native birds, told me, that he raised and kept two, for some months, in a cage; supplying them with honey dissolved in water, on which they readily fed. As the sweetness of the liquid frequently brought small flies and gnats about the cage, and cup, the birds amused themselves by snapping at them on wing, and swallowing them with eagerness, so that these insects formed no inconsiderable part of their food. Mr. Charles Wilson Peale, proprietor of the Museum, tells me, that he had two young Hummingbirds which he raised from the nest. They used to fly about the room; and would frequently perch on Mrs. Peale's shoulder to be fed. When the sun shone strongly into the chamber, he has observed them darting after the motes that floated in the light, as Flycatchers would after flies. In the summer of 1803 a nest of young Hummingbirds was brought me, that were nearly fit to fly. One of them actually flew out by the window the same evening, and falling against a wall, was killed. The other refused food, and the next morning I could but just perceive that it had life. A lady in the house undertook to be its nurse, placed it in her bosom, and as it began to revive, dissolved a little sugar in her mouth, into which she thrust its bill, and it sucked with great avidity. In this manner it was brought up until fit for the cage. I kept it upwards of three months, supplied it with loaf sugar dissolved in water, which it preferred to honey and water, gave it fresh flowers every morning sprinkled with the liquid, and surrounded the space in which I kept it with gauze, that it might not injure itself. It appeared gay, active and full of spirit, hovering from flower to flower as if in its native wilds, and always expressed by its motions and chirping, great pleasure at seeing fresh flowers introduced to its cage. Numbers of people visited it from motives of curiosity, and I took every precaution to preserve it, if possible, thro the winter. Unfortunately, however, by some means it got at large, and, flying about the room, so injured itself that it soon after died.

This little bird is extremely susceptible of cold, and if long deprived of the animating influence of the sunbeams, droops and soon dies. A very beautiful male was brought me this season, which I put into a wire cage, and placed in a retired shaded part of the room. After fluttering about for some time, the weather being uncommonly cool, it clung by the wires, and hung in a seemingly torpid state for a whole forenoon. No motion whatever of the lungs could be perceived, on the closest inspection; tho at other times this is remarkably observable; the eyes were shut; and when touched by the finger it gave no signs of life or motion. I carried it out to the open air, and placed it directly in the rays of the sun, in a sheltered situation. In a few seconds respiration became very apparent; the bird breathed faster and faster, opened its eyes, and began to look about, with as much seeming vivacity as ever. After it had completely recovered, I restored it to liberty; and it flew off to the withered top of a pear tree, where it sat for some time dressing its disordered plumage, and then shot off like a meteor.

The flight of the Hummingbird from flower to flower, greatly resembles that of a bee; but is so much more rapid, that the latter appears a mere loiterer to him. He poises himself on wing, while he thrusts his long slender tubular tongue into the flowers in search of food. He sometimes enters a room by the window, examines the bouquets of flowers, and passes out by the opposite door or window. He has been known to take refuge in a hothouse during the cool nights of autumn; to go regularly out in the morning, and to return as regularly in the evening, for several days together.

The Hummingbird has, hitherto, been supposed to subsist altogether on the honey, or liquid sweets, which it extracts from flowers. One or two curious observers have indeed remarked, that they have found evident fragments of insects in the stomach of this species; but these have been generally believed to have been taken in by accident. The few opportunities which Europeans have to determine this point by observations made on the living bird, or by dissection of the newly-killed one, have rendered this mistaken opinion almost general in Europe. For myself I can speak decisively on this subject. I have seen the Hummingbird for half an hour at a time darting at those little groups of insects that dance in the air in a fine summer evening, retiring to an adjoining twig to rest, and renewing the attack with a dexterity that sets all our other Flycatchers at defiance. I have opened from time to time great numbers of these birds; have examined the contents of the stomach with suitable glasses, and in three cases out of four, have found these to consist of broken fragments of insects. In many subjects entire insects of the coleopterous class, but very small, were found unbroken. The observations of Mr. Coffer as detailed above, and the remarks of my worthy friend Mr. Peale, are corroborative of these facts. It is well known that the Hummingbird is particularly fond of tubular flowers where numerous small insects of this kind resort to feed on the farina, &c. and there is every reason for believing that he is as often in search of these insects as of honey; and that the former compose at least as great a portion of his usual sustenance as the latter. If this food be so necessary for the parents there is no doubt but the young also occasionally partake of it.

To enumerate all the flowers of which this little bird is fond, would be to repeat the names of half our American Flora. From the blossoms of the towering poplar, or tulip tree, thro a thousand intermediate flowers to those of the humble larkspur, he ranges at will, and almost incessantly. Every period of the season produces a fresh multitude of new favorites. Towards the month of September there is a yellow flower which grows in great luxuriance along the sides of creeks and rivers, and in low moist situations; it grows to the height of two or three feet, and the flower, which is about the size of a thimble, hangs in the shape of a cap of liberty above a luxuriant growth of green leaves. It is the *Balsamina noli me tangere* of botanists, and is the greatest favorite with the Hummingbird of all our other flowers. In some places where these plants abound you may see at one time ten or twelve Hummingbirds darting about, and fighting with and pursuing each other. About the twentieth of September they generally retire to the south. I have, indeed, sometimes seen a solitary individual on the twenty-eighth and thirtieth of that month, and sometimes even in October; but these cases are rare. About the beginning of November they pass the southern boundary of the United States into Florida.

The Hummingbird is three inches and a half in length, and four and a quarter in extent; the whole back, upper part of the neck, sides under the wings, tail coverts, and two middle feathers of the tail, are of a rich golden green; the tail is forked, and, as well as the wings, of a deep brownish purple; the bill and eyes are black; the legs and feet, both of which are extremely small, are also black; the bill is straight, very slender, a little inflated at the tip, and very incompetent to the exploit of penetrating the tough sinewy side of a crow, and precipitating it from the clouds to the earth, as Charlevoix would persuade his readers to believe. The nostrils are two small oblong slits, situated at the base of the upper mandible, scarcely perceivable when the bird is dead, tho very distinguishable and prominent when living; the sides of the belly and belly itself dusky white, mixed with green; but what constitutes the chief ornament of this little bird, is the splendor of the feathers of his throat, which, when placed in a proper position, glow with all the brilliancy of the ruby. These feathers are of singular strength and texture, lying close together like scales, and vary when moved before the eye from a deep black to a fiery crimson and burning orange. The female is destitute of this ornament; but differs little in other appearance from the male; her tail is tipt with white, and the whole lower parts are of the same tint. The young birds of the first season, both male and female, have the tail tipt with white, and the whole lower parts nearly white; in the month of September the ornamental feathers on the throat of the young males begin to appear.

On dissection the heart was found to be remarkably large, nearly as big as the cranium, and the stomach, tho distended with food, uncommonly small, not exceeding the globe of the eye, and scarcely more than one-sixth part as large as the heart; the fibers of the last were also exceedingly strong. The brain was in large quantity, and very thin; the tongue, from the tip to an extent equal with the length of the bill, was perforated, forming two closely attached parallel and cylindrical tubes; the other extremities of the tongue corresponded exactly to those of the Woodpecker, passing up the hind head, and reaching to the base of the upper mandible. These observations were verified in five different subjects, all of whose stomachs contained fragments of insects, and some of them whole ones.   1810

CATBIRD

Turdus Lividus

We have here before us a very common and very numerous species, in this part of the United States; and one as well known to all classes of people, as his favorite briars, or blackberry bushes. In spring or summer, on approaching thickets of brambles, the first salutation you receive is from the Catbird; and a stranger, unacquainted with its note, would instantly conclude that some vagrant orphan kitten had got bewildered among the briars, and wanted assistance; so exactly does the call of the bird resemble the voice of that animal. Unsuspicious, and extremely familiar, he seems less apprehensive of man than almost any other of our summer visitants; for whether in the woods, or in the garden, where he frequently builds his nest, he seldom allows you to pass without approaching to pay his respects, in his usual way. This humble familiarity and deference, from a stranger too, who comes to rear his young, and spend the summer with us, ought to entitle him to a full share of our hospitality. Sorry I am, however, to say, that this, in too many instances, is cruelly the reverse. Of this I will speak more particularly in the sequel.

About the twenty-eighth of February the Catbird first arrives in the lower parts of Georgia from the south, consequently winters not far distant, probably in Florida. On the second week in April he usually reaches this part of Pennsylvania; and about the beginning of May has already succeeded in building his nest. The place chosen for this purpose is generally a thicket of briars or brambles, a thorn bush, thick vine, or the fork of a small sapling; no great solicitude is shown for concealment; tho few birds appear more interested for the safety of their nest and young. The materials are dry leaves and weeds, small twigs and fine dry grass, the inside is lined with the fine black fibrous roots of some plant. The female lays four, sometimes five eggs, of a uniform greenish blue color, without any spots. They generally raise two, and sometimes three brood in a season.

In passing thro the woods in summer I have sometimes amused myself with imitating the violent chirping or squeaking of young birds, in order to observe what different species were around me, for such sounds, at such a season in the woods, are no less alarming to the feathered tenants of the bushes than the cry of fire or murder in the streets, is to the inhabitants of a large and populous city. On such occasions of alarm and consternation, the Catbird is the first to make his appearance, not singly, but sometimes half a dozen at a time, flying from different quarters to the spot. At this time those who are disposed to play with his feelings may almost throw him into fits, his emotion and agitation are so great, at the distressful cries of what he supposes to be his suffering young. Other birds are variously affected; but none show symptoms of such extreme suffering. He hurries backwards and forwards, with hanging wings and open mouth, calling out louder and faster, and actually screaming with distress, till he appears hoarse with his exertions. He attempts no offensive means; but he bewails, he implores, in the most pathetic terms with which nature has supplied him, and with an agony of feeling which is truly affecting. Every feathered neighbor within hearing hastens to the place, to learn the cause of the alarm, peeping about with looks of consternation and sympathy. But their own powerful parental duties and domestic concerns soon oblige each to withdraw. At any other season, the most perfect imitations have no effect whatever on him.

The Catbird will not easily desert its nest. I took two eggs from one which was sitting, and in their place put two of the Brown Thrush, or Thrasher; and took my stand at a convenient distance to see how she would behave. In a minute or two the male made his approaches, stooped down and looked earnestly at the strange eggs; then flew off to his mate, who was not far distant, with whom he seemed to have some conversation, and instantly returning, with the greatest gentleness took out both the Thrasher's eggs, first one and then the other, carried them singly about thirty yards, and dropt them among the bushes. I then returned the two eggs I had taken, and soon after the female resumed her place on the nest as before.

From the nest of another Catbird I took two half fledged young, and placed them in that of another which was sitting on five eggs. She soon turned them both out. The place where the nest was not being far from the ground, they were little injured, and the male observing their helpless situation, began to feed them with great assiduity and tenderness.

I removed the nest of a Catbird, which contained four eggs, nearly hatched, from a fox grape vine, and fixed it firmly and carefully in a thicket of briars close by, without injuring its contents. In less than half an hour I returned, and found it again occupied by the female.

The Catbird is one of our earliest morning songsters, beginning generally before break of day, and hovering from bush to bush, with great sprightliness, when there is scarce light sufficient to distinguish him. His notes are more remarkable for singularity than for melody. They consist of short imitations of other birds, and other sounds; but his pipe being rather deficient in clearness and strength of tone, his imitations fail where these are requisite. Yet he is not easily discouraged, but seems to study certain passages with great perseverance; uttering them at first low, and as he succeeds, higher and more free; no ways embarrassed by the presence of a spectator even within a few yards of him. On attentively listening for some time to him one can perceive considerable variety in his performance, in which he seems to introduce all the odd sounds and quaint passages he has been able to collect. Upon the whole, tho we cannot arrange him with the grand leaders of our vernal choristers, he well merits a place among the most agreeable general performers.

This bird, as has been before observed, is very numerous in summer, in the middle states. Scarcely a thicket in the country is without its Catbirds; and were they to fly in flocks, like many other birds, they would darken the air with their numbers. But their migrations are seldom observed, owing to their gradual progress and recession, in spring and autumn, to and from their breeding places. They enter Georgia late in February; and reach New England about the beginning of May. In their migrations they keep pace with the progress of agriculture; and the first settlers in many parts of the Gennesee country have told me, that it was several years after they removed there before the Catbird made his appearance among them. With all these amiable qualities to recommend him few people in the country respect the Catbird. On the contrary, it is generally the object of dislike; and the boys of the United States entertain the same prejudice and contempt for this bird, its nest and young, as those of Britain do for the Yellowhammer and its nest, eggs and young. I am at a loss to account for this cruel prejudice. Even those by whom it is entertained, can scarcely tell you why; only they "hate Catbirds"; as some persons tell you they hate Frenchmen, they hate Dutchmen, &c. expressions that bespeak their own narrowness of understanding, and want of liberality. Yet, after ruminating over in my own mind all the probable causes, I think I have at last hit on some of them; the principal of which seems to me to be a certain similarity of taste, and clashing of interest, between the Catbird and the farmer. The Catbird is fond of large ripe garden strawberries; so is the farmer, for the good price they bring in market. The Catbird loves the best and richest early cherries; so does the farmer, for they are sometimes the most profitable of his early fruit. The Catbird has a particular partiality for the finest ripe mellow pears; and these are also particular favorites with the farmer. But the Catbird has frequently the advantage of the farmer by snatching off the first-fruits of these delicious productions; and the farmer takes revenge by shooting him down with his gun, as he finds old hats, windmills and scarecrows are no impediments in his way to these forbidden fruits; and nothing but this resource, the ultimatum of farmers as well as kings, can restrain his visits. The boys are now set to watch the cherry trees with the gun; and thus commences a train of prejudices and antipathies that commonly continue thro life. Perhaps too, the common note of the Catbird, so like the mewing of the animal whose name it bears, and who itself sustains no small share of prejudice, the homeliness of his plumage, and even his familiarity, so proverbially known to beget contempt, may also contribute to this mean, illiberal and persecuting prejudice; but with the generous and the good, the lovers of nature and of rural charms, the confidence which this familiar bird places in man by building in his garden, under his eye, the music of his song, and the interesting playfulness of his manners, will always be more than a recompense for all the little stolen morsels he snatches.

The Catbird measures nine inches in length; at a small distance he appears nearly black; but on a closer examination is of a deep slate color above, lightest on the edges of the primaries, and of a considerably lighter slate color below, except the under tail coverts, which are very dark red; the tail, which is rounded, and upper part of the head, as well as the legs and bill, are black. The female differs little in color from the male. Latham takes notice of a bird exactly resembling this, being found at Kamtschatka; only it wanted the red under the tail: probably it might have been a young bird, in which the red is scarcely observable.

This bird has been very improperly classed among the Flycatchers. As he never seizes his prey on wing, has none of their manners, feeds principally on fruit, and seems to differ so little from the Thrushes, I think he more properly belongs to the latter tribe than to any other genus we have. His bill, legs and feet, place and mode of building, the color of the eggs, his imitative notes, food and general manners, all jusitfy me in removing him to this genus.

The Catbird is one of those unfortunate victims, and indeed the principal, against which credulity and ignorance have so often directed the fascinating quality of the black-snake. A multitude of marvellous stories have been told me by people who have themselves seen the poor Catbirds drawn, or sucked; as they sometimes express it, from the tops of the trees (which by the bye the Catbird rarely visits) one by one, into the yawning mouth of the immoveable snake. It has so happened with me that in all the adventures of this kind that I have personally witnessed, the Catbird was actually the assailant, and always the successful one. These rencontres never take place but during the breeding time of birds; for whose eggs and young the snake has a particular partiality. It is no wonder that those species whose nests are usually built near the ground, should be the greatest sufferers, and the most solicitous for their safety; hence the cause why the Catbird makes such a distinguished figure in most of these marvellous narrations. That a poisonous snake will strike a bird or mouse, and allow it to remain till nearly expiring before he begins to devour it, our observations on the living rattlesnake at present kept by Mr. Peale, satisfy us is a fact; but that the same snake, with eyes, breath, or any other known quality he possesses, should be capable of drawing a bird, reluctantly, from the tree tops to its mouth, is an absurdity too great for *me* to swallow.   1810

PROSE

Noah Webster
(1758-1843)

Lexicographer and essayist, Noah Webster was born at West Hartford, Connecticut, and was graduated from Yale in 1778. Webster began his lexical studies shortly after leaving Yale; he taught at Goshen, N. Y., in 1782, and during that time prepared *A Grammatical Institute of the English Language* (Hartford, 1783), the famous elementary speller, to which he added a grammar (1784) and a reader (1785). By 1890, Webster's speller had sold more than 60 million copies. Between 1787 and 1803, Webster held several editorial positions, among them the editorship of the *American Minerva* at New York. After 1803, he devoted the remainder of his life to compiling *An American Dictionary of the English Language*, 2 vols. (New York, 1828), a project completed in 1825. *Dissertations on the English Language* (Boston, 1789) was originally a series of lectures Webster prepared in Baltimore in 1785.

BIBLIOGRAPHY: *Letters*, ed. Harry R. Warfel (New York, 1953). Emily E. F. Ford, *Notes on the Life of Noah Webster*, 2 vols., (New York, 1912). Warfel, *Noah Webster: Schoolmaster to America* (New York, 1936). Warfel has edited facsimile editions of *Dissertations on the English Language* (Gainesville, Fla., 1951) and *Sketches of American Policy* (New York, 1937).

From *Dissertations on the English Language*
DISSERTATION I
INTRODUCTION

A regular study of language has, in all civilized countries, formed a part of a liberal education. The Greeks, Romans, Italians and French successively improved their native tongues, taught them in Academies at home, and rendered them entertaining and useful to the foreign student.

The English tongue, tho later in its progress towards perfection, has attained to a considerable degree of purity, strength and elegance, and been employed, by an active and scientific nation, to record almost all the events and discoveries of ancient and modern times.

This language is the inheritance which the Americans have received from their British parents. To cultivate and adorn it, is a task reserved for men who shall understand the connection between language and logic, and form an adequate idea of the influence which a uniformity of speech may have on national attachments.

It will be readily admitted that the pleasures of reading and conversing, the advantage of accuracy in business, the necessity of clearness and precision in communicating ideas, require us to be able to speak and write our own tongue with ease and correctness. But there are more important reasons, why the language of this country should be reduced to such fixed principles, as may give its pronunciation and construction all the certainty and uniformity which any living tongue is capable of receiving.

The United States were settled by emigrants from different parts of Europe. But their descendants mostly speak the same tongue; and the intercourse among the learned of the different States, which the revolution has begun, and an American Court will perpetuate, must gradually destroy the differences of dialect which our ancestors brought from their native countries. This approximation of dialects will be certain; but without the operation of other causes than an intercourse at Court, it will be slow and partial. The body of the people, governed by habit, will still retain their respective peculiarities of speaking; and for want of schools and proper books, fall into many inaccuracies, which, incorporating with the language of the state where they live, may imperceptibly corrupt the national language. Nothing but the establishment of schools and some uniformity in the use of books, can annihilate differences in speaking and preserve the purity of the American tongue. A sameness of pronunciation is of considerable consequence in a political view; for provincial accents are disagreeable to strangers and sometimes have an unhappy effect upon the social affections. All men have local attachments, which lead them to believe their own practice to be the least exceptionable. Pride and prejudice incline men to treat the practice of their neighbors with some degree of contempt. Thus small differences in pronunciation at first excite ridicule—a habit of laughing at the singularities of strangers is followed by disrespect—and without respect friendship is a name, and social intercourse a mere ceremony.

These remarks hold equally true, with respect to individuals, to small societies and to large communities. Small causes, such as a nickname, or a vulgar tone in speaking, have actually created a dissocial spirit between the inhabitants of the different states, which is often discoverable in private business and public deliberations. Our political harmony is therefore concerned in a uniformity of language.

As an independent nation, our honor requires us to have a system of our own, in language as well as government. Great Britain, whose children we are, and whose language we speak, should no longer be our standard; for the taste of her writers is already corrupted, and her language on the decline. But if it were not so, she is at too great a distance to be our model, and to instruct us in the principles of our own tongue.

It must be considered further, that the English is the common root or stock from which our national language will be derived. All others will gradually waste away—and within a century and a half, North America will be peopled with a hundred millions of men, all speaking the same language. Place this idea in comparison with the present and possible future bounds of the language in Europe—consider the Eastern Continent as inhabited by nations, whose knowledge and intercourse are embarrassed by differences of language; then anticipate the period when the people of one quarter of the world, will be able to associate and converse together like children of the same family.[1] Compare this prospect, which is not visionary, with the state of the English language in Europe, almost confined to an Island and to a few millions of people; then let reason and reputation decide, how far America should be dependent on a transatlantic nation, for her standard and improvements in language.

Let me add, that whatever predilection the Americans may have for their native European tongues, and particularly the British descendants for the English, yet several circumstances render a future separation of the American tongue from the English, necessary and unavoidable. The vicinity of the European nations, with the uninterrupted communication in peace, and the changes of dominion in war, are gradually assimilating their respective languages. The English with others is suffering continual alterations. America, placed at a distance from those nations, will feel, in a much less degree, the influence of the assimilating causes; at the same time, numerous local causes, such as a new country, new associations of people, new combinations of ideas in arts and science, and some intercourse with tribes wholly unknown in Europe, will introduce new words into the American tongue. These causes will produce, in a course of time, a language in North America, as different from the future language of England, as the modern Dutch, Danish and Swedish are from the German, or from one another: Like remote branches of a tree springing from the same stock; or rays of light, shot from the same center, and diverging from each other, in proportion to their distance from the point of separation.

Whether the inhabitants of America can be brought to a perfect uniformity in the pronunciation of words, it is not easy to predict; but it is certain that no attempt of the kind has been made, and an experiment, begun and pursued on the right principles, is the only way to decide the question. Schools in Great Britain have gone far towards demolishing local dialects—commerce has also had its influence—and in America these causes, operating more generally, must have a proportional effect.

---

[1] Even supposing that a number of republics, kingdoms or empires, should within a century arise and divide this vast territory; still the subjects of all will speak the same language, and the consequence of this uniformity will be an intimacy of social intercourse hitherto unknown, and a boundless diffusion of knowledge. [All notes are Webster's.]

In many parts of America, people at present attempt to copy the English phrases and pronunciation—an attempt that is favored by their habits, their prepossessions and the intercourse between the two countries. This attempt has, within the period of a few years, produced a multitude of changes in these particulars, especially among the leading classes of people. These changes make a difference between the language of the higher and common ranks; and indeed between the same ranks in different states; as the rage for copying the English, does not prevail equally in every part of North America.

But besides the reasons already assigned to prove this imitation absurd, there is a difficulty attending it, which will defeat the end proposed by its advocates; which is, that the English themselves have no standard of pronunciation, nor can they ever have one on the plan they propose. The Authors, who have attempted to give us a standard, make the practice of the court and stage in London the sole criterion of propriety in speaking. An attempt to establish a standard on this foundation is both unjust and idle. It is unjust, because it is abridging the nation of its rights: The general practice of a nation is the rule of propriety, and this practice should at least be consulted in so important a matter, as that of making laws for speaking. While all men are upon a footing and no singularities are accounted vulgar or ridiculous, every man enjoys perfect liberty. But when a particular set of men, in exalted stations, undertake to say, "we are the standards of propriety and elegance, and if all men do not conform to our practice, they shall be accounted vulgar and ignorant," they take a very great liberty with the rules of the language and the rights of civility.

But an attempt to fix a standard on the practice of any particular class of people is highly absurd: As a friend of mine once observed, it is like fixing a lighthouse on a floating island. It is an attempt to fix that which is in itself variable; at least it must be variable so long as it is supposed that a local practice has no standard but a local practice; that is, no standard but itself. While this doctrine is believed, it will be impossible for a nation to follow as fast as the standard changes—for if the gentlemen at court constitute a standard, they are above it themselves, and their practice must shift with their passions and their whims.

But this is not all. If the practice of a few men in the capital is to be the standard, a knowledge of this must be communicated to the whole nation. Who shall do this? An able compiler perhaps attempts to give this practice in a dictionary; but it is probable that the pronunciation, even at court, or on the stage, is not uniform. The compiler therefore must follow his particular friends and patrons; in which case he is sure to be opposed and the authority of his standard called in question; or he must give two pronunciations as the standard, which leaves the student in the same uncertainty as it found him. Both these events have actually taken place in

England, with respect to the most approved standards; and of course no one is universally followed.

Besides, if language must vary, like fashions, at the caprice of a court, we must have our standard dictionaries republished, with the fashionable pronunciation, at least once in five years; otherwise a gentleman in the country will become intolerably vulgar, by not being in a situation to adopt the fashion of the day. The new editions of them will supersede the old, and we shall have our pronunciation to re-learn, with the polite alterations, which are generally corruptions.

Such are the consequences of attempting to make a local practice the standard of language in a nation. The attempt must keep the language in perpetual fluctuation, and the learner in uncertainty.

If a standard therefore cannot be fixed on local and variable custom, on what shall it be fixed? If the most eminent speakers are not to direct our practice, where shall we look for a guide? The answer is extremely easy; the rules of the language itself, and the general practice of the nation, constitute propriety in speaking. If we examine the structure of any language, we shall find a certain principle of analogy running through the whole. We shall find in English that similar combinations of letters have usually the same pronunciation; and that words, having the same terminating syllable, generally have the accent at the same distance from that termination. These principles of analogy were not the result of design—they must have been the effect of accident, or that tendency which all men feel towards uniformity.[2] But the principles, when established, are productive of great convenience, and become an authority superior to the arbitrary decisions of any man or class of men. There is one exception only to this remark: When a deviation from analogy has become the universal practice of a nation, it then takes place of all rules and becomes the standard of propriety.

The two points therefore, which I conceive to be the basis of a standard in speaking, are these; universal undisputed practice, and the principle of analogy. Universal practice is generally, perhaps always, a rule of propriety; and in disputed points, where people differ in opinion and practice, analogy should always decide the controversy.

These are authorities to which all men will submit—they are superior to

[2] This disposition is taken notice of by Dr. Blair, Lect. 8. Where he observes, "that tho the formation of abstract or general conceptions is supposed to be a difficult operation of the mind, yet such conceptions must have entered into the first formation of languages" —"this invention of abstract terms requires no great exertion of metaphysical capacity"— "Men are *naturally* inclined to call all those objects which resemeble each other by one common name—We may daily observe this practiced by children, in their first attempts towards acquiring language."

I cannot, with this great critic, call the process by which similar objects acquire the same name, an act of abstraction, or the name an abstract term. Logical distinctions may lead us astray. There is in the mind an instinctive disposition, or principle of association, which will account for all common names and the analogies in language.

the opinions and caprices of the great, and to the negligence and ignorance of the multitude. The authority of individuals is always liable to be
called in question—but the unanimous consent of a nation, and a fixed
principle interwoven with the very construction of a language, coeval and
coextensive with it, are like the common laws of a land, or the immutable
rules of morality, the propriety of which every man, however refractory,
is forced to acknowledge, and to which most men will readily submit.
Fashion is usually the child of caprice and the being of a day; principles
of propriety are founded in the very nature of things, and remain unmoved and unchanged, amidst all the fluctuations of human affairs and
the revolutions of time.

It must be confessed that languages are changing, from age to age, in
proportion to improvements in science. Words, as Horace observes, are
like leaves of trees; the old ones are dropping off and new ones growing.
These changes are the necessary consequence of changes in customs, the
introduction of new arts, and new ideas in the sciences. Still the body of
a language and its general rules remain for ages the same, and the new
words usually conform to these rules; otherwise they stand as exceptions,
which are not to overthrow the principle of analogy already established.

But when a language has arrived at a certain stage of improvement, it
must be stationary or become retrograde; for improvements in science
either cease, or become slow and too inconsiderable to affect materially
the tone of a language. This stage of improvement is the period when a
nation abounds with writers of the first class, both for abilities and taste.
This period in England commenced with the age of Queen Elizabeth and
ended with the reign of George II. It would have been fortunate for the
language, had the style of writing and the pronunciation of words been
fixed, as they stood in the reign of Queen Anne and her successor. Few
improvements have been made since that time; but innumerable corruptions in pronunciation have been introduced by Garrick, and in style, by
Johnson, Gibbon and their imitators.[3]

[3] The progress of corruption in language is described with precision, and philosophical
reasons assigned with great judgement, by that celebrated French writer, Condillac, in his
Origin of Human Knowledge. Part 2.

"It is nearly the same here as in physics, where motion, the source of life, becomes
the principle of destruction. When a language abounds with original writers in every
kind, the more a person is endowed with abilities, the more difficult he thinks it will be
to surpass them. A mere equality would not satisfy his ambition; like them he wants
the pre-eminence. He therefore tries a new road. But as every style analogous to the
character of the language and to his own, has been already used by preceding writers, he
has nothing left but to deviate from analogy. Thus in order to be an original, he is
obliged to contribute to the ruin of a language, which, a century sooner, he would have
helped to improve.

"Tho such writers may be criticized, their superior abilities must still command success. The ease there is in copying their defects, soon persuades men of indifferent capacities, that they shall acquire the same degree of reputation. Then begins the reign of
strained and subtle conceits, of affected antitheses, of specious paradoxes, of frivolous and
far-fetched expressions, of new-fangled words, and in short, of the jargon of persons,
whose understandings have been debauched by bad metaphysics. The public applauds;

The great Sidney wrote in a pure style; yet the best models of purity and elegance, are the works of Sir William Temple, Dr. Middleton, Lord Bolingbroke, Mr. Addison and Dean Swift. But a little inferior to these, are the writings of Mr. Pope, Sir Richard Steele, Dr. Arbuthnot, with some of their contemporaries. Sir William Blackstone has given the law style all the elegance and precision of which it is capable. Dr. Price and Dr. Priestley write with purity, and Sir William Jones seems to have copied the ease, simplicity and elegance of Middleton and Addison.

But how few of the modern writers have pursued the same manner of writing? Johnson's style is a mixture of Latin and English; an intolerable composition of Latinity, affected smoothness, scholastic accuracy and roundness of periods. The benefits derived from his morality and his erudition, will hardly counterbalance the mischief done by his manner of writing. The names of a Robertson, a Hume, a Home and a Blair, almost silence criticism; but I must repeat what a very learned Scotch gentleman once acknowledged to me, "that the Scotch writers are not models of the pure English style." Their style is generally stiff, sometimes very awkward, and not always correct.[4] Robertson labors his style and sometimes introduces a word merely for the sake of rounding a period. Hume has borrowed French idioms without number; in other respects he has given an excellent model of historical style. Lord Kames' manner is stiff; and Dr. Blair, whose style is less exceptionable in these particulars, has however introduced, into his writings, several foreign idioms and ungrammatical phrases. The Scotch writers now stand almost the first for erudition; but perhaps no man can write a foreign language with genuine purity.

Gibbon's harmony of prose is calculated to delight our ears; but it is difficult to comprehend his meaning and the chain of his ideas, as fast as we naturally read; and almost impossible to recollect them, at any subsequent period. Perspicuity, the first requisite in style, is sometimes sacrificed to melody; the mind of a reader is constantly dazzled by a

---

foolish and ridiculous writings, the beings of a day, are surprisingly multiplied; a vicious taste infects the arts and sciences, which is followed by a visible decrease of men of abilities."

One would think that Condillac had designed here to give a description of the present taste of the English writers, and a state of their literature.

The foregoing sentiments seem to have been borrowed from Velleius Paterculus. Hist. Rom. L. 1, Cap. 17.

The same passage is copied by Sig. Carlo Denina, Professor of Eloquence and Belles Lettres in the University of Turin, in his "Revolutions of Literature," page 47; and if I mistake not, the sentiments are adopted by Lord Kames, in his Sketches of the History of Man.

Similar reasons may be assigned for the prevalence of an affected and vicious pronunciation.

[4] Dr. Witherspoon is an exception. His style is easy, simple and elegant. I consider Dr. Franklin and Dr. Witherspoon as the two best writers in America. The words they use, and their arrangement, appear to flow spontaneously from their manner of thinking. The vast superiority of their styles over those of Gibbon and Gillies, is owing to this circumstance, that the two American writers have bestowed their labor upon ideas, and the English historians upon words.

glare of ornament, or charmed from the subject by the music of the language. As he is one of the first, it is hoped he may be the last, to attempt the gratification of our ears, at the expense of our understanding.

Such however is the taste of the age; simplicity of style is neglected for ornament; and sense is sacrificed to sound.[5]

Altho style, or the choice of words and manner of arranging them, may be necessarily liable to change, yet it does not follow that pronunciation and orthography cannot be rendered in a great measure permanent. An orthography, in which there would be a perfect correspondence between the spelling and pronunciation, would go very far towards effecting this desirable object. The Greek language suffered little or no change in these particulars, for about a thousand years; and the Roman was in a great degree fixed for several centuries.

Rapid changes of language proceed from violent causes; but these causes cannot be supposed to exist in North America. It is contrary to all rational calculation, that the United States will ever be conquered by any one nation, speaking a different language from that of the country. Removed from the danger of corruption by conquest, our language can change only with the slow operation of the causes before-mentioned and the progress of arts and sciences, unless the folly of imitating our parent country should continue to govern us, and lead us into endless innovation. This folly however will lose its influence gradually, as our particular habits of respect for that country shall wear away, and our *amor partriæ* acquire strength and inspire us with a suitable respect for our own national character.

We have therefore the fairest opportunity of establishing a national language, and of giving it uniformity and perspecuity, in North America, that ever presented itself to mankind. Now is the time to begin the plan. The minds of the Americans are roused by the events of a revolution; the necessity of organizing the political body and of forming constitutions of government that shall secure freedom and property, has called all the faculties of the mind into exertion; and the danger of losing the benefits of independence, has disposed every man to embrace any scheme that shall tend, in its future operation, to reconcile the people of America to each other, and weaken the prejudices which oppose a cordial union.

[5] The same taste prevailed in Rome, under the Emperors, when genius was prostituted to the mean purposes of flattery. "It must be acknowledged indeed, that after the dissolution of the Roman republic, this art began to be perverted by being too much admired. Men grew excessively fond of the numerous style, and readily sacrificed the strength and energy of their discourse to the harmony of their language. Pliny the younger often complains of this contemptible affection: And Quintilian speaks of certain prose writers in his time, who boasted that their compositions were so strictly numerous, that their hearers might even beat time to their measures. And it should seem that even in Tully's time, this matter was carried to excess; since even then the orators dealt so much in numbers, that it was made a question, wherein they differed from the Poets."—Mason's Essay on the Power and Harmony of Prosaic Numbers. Introduction, page 4.

This was an abuse of the art. Melody should be studied; but not principally.

My design, in these dissertations, is critically to investigate the rules of pronunciation in our language; to examine the past and present practice of the English, both in the pronunciation of words and construction of sentences; to exhibit the principal differences between the practice in England and America, and the differences in the several parts of America, with a view to reconcile them on the principles of universal practice and analogy. I have no system of my own to offer; my sole design is to explain what I suppose to be authorities, superior to all private opinions, and to examine local dialects by those authorities.

Most writers upon this subject have split upon one rock: They lay down certain rules, arbitrary perhaps or drawn from the principles of other languages, and then condemn all English phrases which do not coincide with those rules. They seem not to consider that grammar is formed on language, and not language on grammar. Instead of examining to find what the English language is, they endeavor to show what it ought to be according to their rules. It is for this reason that some of the criticisms of the most celebrated philologers are so far from being just, that they tend to overthrow the rules, and corrupt the true idiom, of the English tongue. Several examples of this will appear in the course of these Dissertations.

To learn the English language in its purity, it is necessary to examine and compare the best authors from Chaucer to the present time. In executing the following work, the most approved compilations have been consulted, and the opinions of the learned authors considered as respectable, not as decisive, authorities. The language itself has been examined with great industry, with a view to discover and defend its principles on the best grounds, analogies in structure, and immemorial usage. I have had recourse to the works of authors who wrote prior to Chaucer, and have even borrowed some light upon this subject, from the early ages of Gothic ignorance. Believing, with the author of "Diversions of Purley," that the peculiar structure of our language is Saxon, and that its principles can be discovered only in its Teutonic original, it has been my business, as far as the materials in my possession would permit, to compare the English with the other branches of the same stock, particularly the German and the Danish. These researches have thrown light upon the meaning and construction of particular phrases, and enabled me to vindicate some expressions in the language which are often used, but generally condemned by grammarians.

My knowledge of the practice of speaking in different parts of America, is derived from personal observation. My knowledge of the past and present state of the language in England, is taken from the writers who have treated expressly of the subject.[6] The authorities necessary to prove particular points will be quoted, as occasion shall require.

---

[6] Wallis, Johnson, Kenrick, Sheridan, with a multitude of inferior compilers.

The task of examining words cannot be agreeable to a writer, nor can his criticisms be very entertaining to the reader. Yet this task I have imposed upon myself; for I believe it the only method to correct common mistakes. A general rule may be sufficient for a classical scholar, who makes it his business to apply the rule to all cases: But most readers must have their particular errors laid before their eyes, or they will not discover them.

To offer to correct the mistakes of others, is also a hazardous task, and commonly exposes a man to abuse and ill will. To avoid this I can only say, that my motives for the undertaking were not local nor personal; my inquiries are for truth, and my criticisms, it is hoped, will be marked with candor.   1789

Joseph Dennie
(1768-1812)

Following his graduation from Harvard in 1790, Joseph Dennie was admitted to law practice in 1794; however, he spent most of his life as a contributor to and editor of periodicals. He edited *The Tablet* (1795) at Boston, *The Farmer's Weekly Museum* (1795–1799) at Walpole, New Hampshire, and *The Gazette of the United States* (1799–1800) at Philadelphia. Dennie then founded *The Port-Folio* at Philadelphia on Jan. 3, 1801, and edited this magazine until his death. Of the 118 "Lay Preacher" essays, written between 1795 and 1801, ninety were originally pub-

lished in *The Farmer's Museum* and eleven in *The Port-Folio*. Collections were published as *The Lay Preacher; or Short Sermons for Idle Readers* (Walpole, N.H., 1796) and as *The Lay Preacher,* ed. John E. Hall (Philadelphia, 1817).

BIBLIOGRAPHY: *The Lay Preacher,* ed. Milton Ellis (New York, 1943). *The Letters of Joseph Dennie, 1768–1812,* ed. Laura G. Pedder in *Univ. of Maine Studies,* 2nd series, No. 36, XXXVIII (1936). Milton Ellis, *Joseph Dennie and His Circle* (Austin, Tex., 1915).

From *The Lay Preacher*
ADVERTISEMENT

Most of the following pages originally appeared in the *Farmer's Weekly Museum,* a rural paper of New Hampshire. Surrounded by plain husbandmen, rather than by polished scholars, the Author, both in the selection of his subjects, and their vehicle, has been more studious of the useful, than the brilliant. To instruct the villager, was his primary object. Hence, an easy and obvious style was indispensable. To rise to the gorgeous phrase of Bolingbroke would have been absurd, to sink to the vulgarity of L'Estrange would have been ignominous. The familiarity of Franklin's manner, and the simplicity of Sterne's proved most auxiliary to his design. He, therefore, adventured their union. Diffident of success, and prepared for censure, he will not be surprised at a harsh sentence from the critical tribunal. The vanity of authorship has already caused him to prove the negligence of his natal town; the same passion now urges him to try the suffrages of the country. Should this, like former attempts, slide rapidly down the slope of oblivion, it will add the last item to the catalogue of literary disappointments, and cure

THE AUTHOR

NO. V

"Favor is Deceitful."

Undoubtedly, though Lavater, a Swiss clergyman, whose faith, it seems could remove mountains, has, in a book, which treats of faces, asserted that the nose is no cheat, and that he can see every man's character, sitting astride on his nose.

This is a whimsical age; who would believe that a man could be found, sufficiently bold, and readers, sufficiently credulous, to suppose that Favor is not deceitful.

More than forty years since, when my grandmother suffered my elder brother to lead me by the hand into company, I was pleased with all faces. You, charming maid, says I to a smiling lass, have a benevolent countenance, you must lend a favorable ear to my vows—a sudden coquettish wave of her fan, and a scorning nose proved that Favor was deceitful.

A buyer goes into a country store, and, leaning over the counter, asks the shopkeeper for changeable silk. He holds up a piece in a favorable point of view, and smiling plausibly, declaims an hour upon its cheapness and durability. The silk is bought; when daughter Dolly had worn it two Sundays, it was still changeable; spotted with bilge water, and torn by a pin; even one eye might read on the hem that Favor is deceitful?

I recollect that, during my nonage, I rested many hopes upon the plausibility of a simpering courtier: He had been educated by the Jesuits, noted for giant promise, and pigmy performance. This man had a sweet smile and a silver tongue. His smile and tongue were worth a Prince's ransom to him. He had a wonderful knack of being agreeable; as to being useful, that was of no consequence. He set up a school for smiling, and his pupils might there learn to nod and smirk cash away from the purse. Nothing obstructed this man; every road was a river road to him; his neighbors called him the smoothing plane, he removed all asperities. But all was "false and hollow." He planed away the rough planks of life it is true, but he kept the shavings himself. The man was selfish and his Favor was deceitful.

I saw lately a morose wretch with a book in his hand. His urchin form reminded me of a gnarly crab apple, at once misshapen and sour; the leaves he turned over were Sterne's and his cheeks were moistened by the death of Le Fevre. How, whispered I, can this man boast sensibility? I know him well, a grinder of poverty's face—who understands distress and sale, better than a deputy sheriff; this is he, who drives away the cottager's cow, and plucks from under her the widow's bed.—I paused; and reflection convinced me, that his was a mechanical and crocodile grief, that though he wept, he could wound, and that his Favor was deceitful.

Thomas Paine, that infidel in religion, and that visionary in politics, seduces many of you, my countrymen. You read his "Age of Reason," and think the Bible a last year's Almanac: You read his "Rights of Man," and think government slavery, and Washington an imposter. But the man who labors to destroy the pious hope, or to raise the ferment of faction, is an enemy to your peace. Be your devotions and your government equally undisturbed: Attendance at church, at least, preserves your neatness and sociability. Obedience to government causes you to sit in peace under the fig tree. Trust me, he who jeers received truths, or who tells you that there is no distinction among men, and that *all* are equally qualified to govern, is an imposter more pernicious than Mahomet and his Favor is deceitful. 1796

NO. XII
"Remove Sorrow Far From Thee: For Sorrow Hath Killed Many, and There Is No Profit Therein."

Dry up your eyes, then, ye mourners, for grief will not restore the friends you have lost, nor abate the edge of misfortune, but as oil and the whetstone to the razor, it will sharpen that which is already too acute, and the bleeding heart will show a still deeper wound. Why will you strive to add one drop to this "vale of tears," which, trust me, is already too full, why court the acquaintance of grief, that sorry companion, who, sobbing and silent as he journeys with you through the wilderness of this world, multiplies every brake, and adds tenfold horror to the gloom. You have various and real ills to encounter in your sore travail; the climate is vaporous, and you must be sick, men are treacherous, and you will be deceived, poverty will sometimes start up "like an armed man" before you, and your careful days be like those of an hireling. But be of good cheer, and repeat not in the day of adversity, with erring Solomon, that laughter is mad, nor impertinently inquire of Mirth what doeth she, but believe with my predecessor Sterne, that comfortable assertion, worth a million of cold homilies, that every time we smile, and still more every time we laugh, it adds something to the fragment of life.

No profit therein: No verily; the man of sorrow, who, with sullen Ahab, refuses to eat bread, and changes his time for tears, is engaged in one of the most barren and least lucrative employments, you can conceive. Sighs I have always considered as the very canker of the heart, and sobs the grand epitomizers of existence. Child of melancholy! If sorrow hath killed many, and there is no profit therein, banish it from thy shades, for why, in the pathetic language of Ecclesiastes, shouldst thou die before thy time?

But who are those fair forms, the one with folded arms, and the other with bounding step, ministering, O kindly handmaids, at the bedside of the Philosopher. I see his pallid cheek already flush, I hear his voice utter a bolder tone, wrinkles are no more seen on his brow, and not a solitary tear traces a lonely way down his cheek, for Patience and Mirth are before him. At their salutary approach, the troop of cares, the family of pain fly disconsolate, and free the vacant heart, from their torturing sway. Gentle and benignant spirits, meekest Patience, and chirping Mirth, whether my cottage is unroofed by the storm, or my couch thorned by disease, whether friends grow lukewarm, or lovers be put far away, let your gay forms appear and the load of life will no more be irksome. For well I know your pleasing arts, I well remember your numerous topics of consolation, your music, your song, your carelessness, Mirth, and Patience, your philosophy and resignation. Sorrow, as the wise son of Sirach tells us, may kill many, but ye can make alive: Come then to the unfortunate, and let the adverse hour be your favorite hour of visitation.

1796

NO. XXI
"The Fashion of This World Passeth Away."

As I am only a Lay Preacher, it must not be expected that I should always exhibit that accuracy of sermonizing, which characterizes the settled Pastor. But having observed in the course of a long and regular attendance of public worship, that Divines are in the habit of dividing their matter, and of adjourning, sometimes, the morning exhortation till after dinner, I thought it expedient, when I selected the fruitful theme of last week's meditation, to reserve part of its topics till now. For, during the process of critically examining my subject in all lights, I found that fashion regulated speculation no less than practice, and that opinions, as well as dresses had their times and seasons. As we are told by a profound reasoner, that as there is but one sun in the natural, so there can be but one truth in the intellectual world, an abstract metaphysician, in his cell, would suppose that, by this time, that one truth was discovered, and hence necessarily induced uniformity of thinking. But this is a mere reverie of a novice in the history of man. In theology, in the healing art, in politics, in the fine arts, and in polite literature, in whatever interests, in whatever amuses our species, perpetual vicissitudes occur, and what is supposed to be settled by one party at one time, is unhinged by different theories at another.

In the infancy of the colony at Plymouth, and at the erection of the Saybrook platform, our emigrant forefathers, rejected, with loathing, the fat luxury of Luther, and starved themselves on the mean fare of Calvin. They were doubtful even of scriptural truth, if it had issued from the Clarendon Press, and would not read the sermon on the mount to edification, unless imprinted in a Bible at Geneva. Willard's body of divinity was their law and testimony, and reprobate was that sinner, who would adventure to read and practice a more gentle and generous system. But such heavy and clanking fetters of the mind, were too irksome to be long worn patiently by fretful sceptics, and infant Catholicism in its cradle at length ventured innovation. Good works were sometimes associated with implicit faith, and the piety of our primitive Christians was not always horror struck at the union. In process of time the reign of rigor declined, and now it may be said the high prerogative of superstition has become as nugatory as kingly power in France. For, a new dictator in divinity who knew not Calvin arose, and Chauncy considering brimstone as a Scottish, or an old wive's fable, proclaimed salvation to all men, and insisted that a profligate should not be eternally singed for his sins. Hume and Bolingbroke, with elegance and elaboration, but with the darkest sophistry, and Boulanger, an audacious Frenchman, in his "Christianity unveiled," have presumptuously attempted to sap the Christian's fortress, and now, to represent the son of Mary as a mere man, and now as an imposter. These writings have induced flimsy opinions, called, from their nature, Deistical, to predominate, and their professors, far from consulting the editions, either of England or Geneva, will inspect no Bible. Perhaps the accurate reader will pronounce my enumeration incomplete, unless I notice that second edition of Tom Thumb's folio, called "The Age of Reason." But as this, in mechanic's phrase, is but a bungling vamp of obsolete infidelity, written by a drunken author, rarely quoted, except by the lowest vulgar, and then in the lisping accents of intoxication, I will not condescend to an analysis, but terminate this head of my discourse with the warmest wishes, that, in spite of jarring opinions, gospel charity and benevolence, may be everlastingly fashionable, and that men will not expect a more excellent mode from the new fangled looms of Paine and of Paris.

Physic has experienced more revolutions than Poland, or even France, since the Capets are no more. Boerhaave has prescribed at Leyden, what Brown would reject at Edinburgh. Gout must be pampered according to one Physician, and starved by another. The small pox, like Sancho Panza, is sometimes blanketed into submission, and sometimes every wintry wind, must be invoked to blow the infection away. Dr. Cheyne insists that his patients shall quaff a perpetual bowl of milk, while a more jolly physician directs as perpetual and much ruddier draughts. Le Sage's Sangrado drained every vein, and now every vein must be inflated like a bladder. Cullen departed from Boerhaave, Brown has exposed and abjured the heresy of Cullen, and probably by this time some European projector has started a new theory to the utter destruction of the old.

A Logician, considering the two subjects as equally variable, would infallibly class weathercocks and politics together. We behold vast empires sometimes governed by a solitary woman—and petty states headed by a mob of rulers. Kings, once ranked with Gods, are suddenly and capriciously degraded among felons. Government, as a nervous writer expresses it, is sometimes scandalously relaxed, and then violently stretched beyond its tone. The Corinthian capital of society, laboriously erected by aristocratical artists, is prostrated by popular fury in an hour. In our own Country, political modes are perpetually fluctuating. Prior to the formation of French friendship, that people, their religion, and their politics were equally detested. The Pope was Antichrist, the French King his high Steward, the government of France was the archtype of Turkish despotism, and the nation viewed as a motley collection of coxcombs and slaves. Mark the instant operation of a single defeat, on the whole political sense of America! A captured Burgoyne could metamorphose an arbitrary Louis into the friend, the patron of republicans. But the love towards Louis soon waxed cold, and Marat had his proselytes here as well as at Paris.

Very suddenly have most of our political fashions past away. Britain has been called a mother, a hag, a sister or a friend. Our rulers are perpetually wrangling concerning the garb of government. Some, from Geneva or Virginia, affect the broad mantle of republicanism, which covers a multitude of sins. Others prefer French manufacture of the Paris cut. A few, perhaps, wish to import materials from England, but there is a good warm well made, easy garment, made to fit anyone, called Federalism, which the Lay Preacher actually prefers to his canonicals, and prays may be constantly worn, and an unchangeable mode.

1796

John Neal
(1793-1876)

Born at Falmouth (now Portsmouth), Maine, John Neal had little formal education, but worked as a clerk and an itinerate teacher in his youth. After working in Baltimore as a newspaper and periodical writer, Neal went to England in 1823; there he wrote, posing as an Englishman, five essays entitled "American Writers" for *Blackwood's Magazine* (September 1824-February 1825). Neal's essays included comments on numerous American writers, and a long essay on his own works. In 1827, he returned to the United States and shortly thereafter settled in Portland,

Me., where he lived the rest of his life. Neal practiced law, and after 1840, turned his attention to real estate and civic interests. Among Neal's novels are *Seventy-Six* (Baltimore, 1823), an historical novel, and *Rachel Dyer; A North American Story* (Portland, Me., 1828). *Wandering Recollections of a Somewhat Busy Life* (Boston, 1869) is Neal's autobiography.

BIBLIOGRAPHY: *DAB*. *American Writers, A Series of Papers Contributed to 'Blackwood's Magazine'* (*1824–1825*), ed. Fred L. Pattee (Durham, N. C., 1937). *Rachel Dyer* (*1828*), ed. John D. Seelye (Gainesville, Fla., 1964), facsimile edition.

From *American Writers*

NO. I

Sept., 1824

One is continually hearing, more or less, about American literature, of late, as if there were any such thing in the world as American literature; or any such thing in the United States of North America, as a body of native literature—the production of native writers—bearing any sort of national character, either of wisdom or beauty—heavy or light—or having any established authority, even among the people of the United States. And go where one will, since the apparition of one American writer among us, (of whom a word or two more by and by,) some half-a-dozen stories and storybooks; a little good poetry (with some very bad poems;) four or five respectable, and as many more trumpery novels—with a book or two about theology—one is pretty sure to hear the most ridiculous and exaggerated misrepresentations, one way or the other, for or against American authorship, as if American authorship (so far as it goes) were anything different from English, or Scotch, or Irish authorship; as if there were any decided nationality in the style or manner of a book-maker in America—who writes English, or endeavors to write English—to set him apart, or distinguish him from a book-maker in the United Kingdom, who is engaged in the same business.

With two exceptions, or at the most three, there is no American writer who would not pass just as readily for an English writer, as for an American, whatever were the subject upon which he was writing; and these three are Paulding, Neal, and Charles Brockden Brown, of whom we shall speak separately in due time.

We have hitherto underrated, or, more properly speaking, overlooked the American writers. But we are now running into a contrary extreme; abundantly overrating some, and in a fair way, if a decided stand be not taken against the popular infatuation, of neglecting our own for the encouragement of American talent.

Give the Americans fair play—that we owe to ourselves. Deal justly with all who venture upon the perilous life of authorship—a life that ends oftener than any other in a broken heart, or a disordered mind—that we owe to humanity.

But if we would not over-cuddle the young American writers; kill them with kindness; turn their heads with our trumpeting, or produce a fatal revulsion in the popular mind, let us never make a prodigious fuss about any American book, which, if it were English, would produce little or no sensation. It is the sure way to defeat our own plans in the long run, however profound our calculations may be. Honesty is the best policy after all,—even for booksellers.

It is only insulting the Americans, whom we desire to conciliate by our gentlemanly candor, if we so cry up any tolerable book of theirs, as if it were a wonder to meet with anything tolerable from an American writer.

These noisy rushes of popularity never do any good. They are alike affronting to our countrymen and to the Americans; injurious to our literary men, and ruinous to theirs. They discourage ours, and spoil theirs; or, what is quite sure to be fatal, they provoke a calm, severe investigation of the grounds upon which judgment has been rendered.

The truth is, that there are more American writers in every branch of literature, and they are more respectable, ten times over, than our countrymen would readily believe; but then, there is no one of them whose works would abide a temperate, firm, unsparing examination, as a standard in its way, much less a conspiracy to write it down. We happen to know something of the matter, and without any professions of impartiality, (leaving our behavior to speak for us on that score,) shall proceed in arranging it systematically, after a few observations. . . .

Some of these American writers have been very popular of late, and all are aiming to become so—as who, indeed, is not, even among our own countrymen! But let them be wary. Nothing is more short-lived than violent popularity. It is the tempestuous brightness of a moment—a single moment only—the sound of passing music—the brief blossoming of summer flowers.

Let them remember, that there is one law of nature which governs alike through all creation. It is one to which all things, animate and inanimate, are subject; and which, if it were thought of, would make men tremble at sudden popularity. It is this—That which is a given time in coming to maturity, shall abide a like time without beginning to decay; and be a like time again in returning to the earth.

It is a law alike of the animal, the vegetable, and the mineral kingdom, applicable alike to the productions of nature and of art.

The longest-lived animals are the longest in coming to maturity. Diamonds, it is thought, since the discoveries of Professor Silliman, may require ages to consummate their virtues; other crystals are formed instantaneously. But the diamond is indestructible, and the latter dissolve in your breath. . . .

Let no man be in a hurry about getting a reputation. That reputation is not worth having, which can be had easily, or in a little time.

Why is it that we are astonished at the first efforts of the unknown? It is for that very reason—it is because they *are* unknown. They have grown up in "brave neglect," in wind and storm; disclosed their powers unexpectedly, without being intimidated or abashed by observation, or worried and fretted with public guardianship. It were better for the very giants to be unknown; and better for all, who would have their progeny either grand or beautiful, to bring forth all their young in the solitude, or the mountain. The world, and the temptations of the world, only enfeeble and enervate them. A sickly offspring is produced with more hardship in the crowded atmosphere of a city, than young lions in the wilderness. . . .

Why is it, that we are continually amazed at the first efforts—and with only the first efforts—of a thousand wonderful young men? It is because they were not popular. It is because we expected nothing from them, and they knew it. After their first essay, no matter in what department of art or science, they were known—and of course popular. Our expectations became unreasonable; we worked them beyond all decency,—all humanity. We called upon them to produce, in a few years, or perhaps a few months, amid the bustle, strangeness, and confusion of a great city, that which would be more wonderful than their first effort, though *that* had been the production of many years, in the spring-time of their heart's valor—in solitude—and had appeared even to ourselves miraculous.

So with all mankind. They never permit the same person to astonish them a second time, if they know it. To be astonished, indeed!—what is it but an imputation upon their breeding, foresight, wisdom, and experience? So they set their faces against it.—They seek, as it were, to avenge themselves for having been surprised into anything so ungenteel as a stare, (of astonishment, I mean,) by resolving never to be caught again—by him—whatever he may do.

Let him do better a second time, and he will appear to do worse. Do what he will, they are, and always will be, disappointed. But it is a thousand to one that he does worse. He becomes, on a second appearance, neither one thing nor another. One minute he will repeat himself; the next he will imitate himself, with variations, in those passages, attitudes, and peculiarities, which have taken well; then he will be caught with a sudden whim, (like an only child,) trusting to the partiality of his friends, or to his reputation for genius or eccentricity—coquetting timidly with popular favor, in awkward imitation of established favorites, who do what they please, and are liked the better for it; then, without any sort of notice or preparation, he will be seized with a sudden paroxysm of originality. He springs into the saddle—up goes the whip, and he precipitates himself, head foremost, at some object, which other people dare not venture upon. But, just at the critical moment, just when nothing but desperation can carry him through, his heart fails him, he pulls up, (like the inexperienced rider, who gives whip and spur over the field, and check at a five-bar gate;) and finishes the adventure either by shutting his eyes and breaking his neck, or by turning aside with a laugh that is anything but natural or hearty, or with some unprofitable appeal to the indulgence of a jaded and disappointed public, as if any public ever cared a farthing for one of their pets, after a tumble or a balk.

The unknown do well at first, because they are unknown; because nothing was expected of them; because they had everything to gain, and nothing to lose. That made them fearless of heart. And they do badly in a second effort, because their whole situation is reversed; because they are known—because too much is expected of them; and because, in one word, they have everything to lose, and nothing to gain.

That very reputation, in the pursuit of which they have accomplished incredible things—when overtaken, is a crushing load—a destroying power, upon all their finer and more sensible faculties. Hence it is, that some distinguished men (like Scott and Byron) so often adventure anonymously, or under fictitious names, into the field, whenever they begin to distrust the partiality of the public, or to suspect the mischievous influence of that partiality, upon themselves, or their weapons. There is no other way to reassure their own hearts, when they begin to doubt a diminution of edge or power—they must on with their ponderous armor once more—away from the banqueting place—and scour the world anew, under a blank pennon, or a blank shield: and hence is it, that the course of others (like Moore and Southey) is one eternal zig-zag—through every kind of prose, and every kind of poetry—on every subject—now on one side of the question—now on the other.

All are striving by these expedients to avoid the inevitable catastrophe of popular favor: to prolong their dominion; to keep off the evil day; when, whatever may have been their merit, their thrones will be demolished; their crowns trampled on, and their sceptres quenched, by that very multitude who have built pyramids, and burnt incense to them.

The world are unreasonable; and always unmerciful to the second essay of every man—(that is, to his next effort after that which has made him known) but they always appear to the candidate himself, of course, far more unreasonable and unmerciful than they are. And hence is it, that, ninety-nine times out of one hundred, nothing more is ever heard of him. He generally perishes in obscurity, sore and sick at heart, or dies cursing the caprice of the world.—Indeed—indeed—that reputation is not worth having which can be easily obtained.

The truth is, that we dread this kind of popularity, not only for others, but, strange as it may seem, for ourselves; and we would seriously admonish all young writers to be on their guard against it—never to relax— never to lie upon their oars. Beside, there is a kind of reputation that rises about one, like the sea, while, to the common observer who looks only at the surface, it may appear to be receding: and there is another, which goes on slowly, accumulating against the barriers and obstacles which oppose it, until they give way on every side at last, and only serve to augment the power and impetus of that which has overborne them.

But, while we put those who are popular upon their guard against popularity; and apprise others, who are slowly and silently making their way into popular favor, of how much they have to be thankful for, in the neglect of the public—we may as well add a word or two of encouragement for all, by assuring them that the multitude are never long insensible to extraordinary power; that sooner or later, opportunity will arrive to the watchful and brave; that those who deserve to succeed, will, one day or other, succeed; and that good sense, enthusiasm, perseverance, and originality, combined, are never unsuccessful, or out of fashion for a long time together.

Now, then, for the American Writers.

. . . . .

Bryant—William Cullen.—This gentleman's poetry has found its way, piecemeal, into England, and having met with a little of our newspaper praise, which has been repeated with great emphasis in America, is now set up among his associates for a poet of extraordinary promise, on the ground of having produced, within the course of several years, about fifty duodecimo pages of poetry, such as we shall give a specimen of. Mr B. is not, and never will be, a great poet. He wants fire—he wants the very rashness of a poet—the prodigality and fervor of those, who are overflowing with inspiration. Mr B., in fact, is a sensible young man, of a thrifty disposition, who knows how to manage a few plain ideas in a very handsome way. It is a bad thing for a poet, or for one whom his friends believe to be a poet, ever to spend a long time about the manufacture of musical prose, in imitation of anybody,—as Mr Bryant and Mr Percival both do of Milman, who has quite set the fashion in America for blank verse. Some lines, (about fifteen or twenty,) to a "Water-Fowl," which are very beautiful, to be sure, but with no more poetry in them than there is in the Sermon on the Mount, are supposed, by his countrymen, "to be well known in Europe."

NO. II

Oct., 1824

Brown—Charles Brockden.—This was a good fellow; a sound, hearty specimen of Trans-Atlantic stuff. Brown was an American to the back-bone—without knowing it. He was a novelist; an imitator of Godwin, whose *Caleb Williams* made him. He had no poetry; no pathos; no wit; no humor; no pleasantry; no playfulness; no passion; little or no eloquence; no imagination—and, except where panthers were concerned, a most penurious and bony invention—meager as death,—and yet—lacking all these natural powers—and working away, in a style with nothing remarkable in it—except a sort of absolute sincerity, like that of a man, who is altogether in earnest, and believes every word of his own story—he was able to secure the attention of extraordinary men, as other people (who write better) would that of children;—to impress his pictures upon the human heart, with such unexampled vivacity, that no time can obliterate them: and, withal, to fasten himself, with such tremendous power, upon a common incident, as to hold the spectator breathless. . . .

Brown was one of the only three or four professional authors, that America has ever produced. He was the first. He began, as all do, by writing for the newspapers—where that splendor of diction, for which the Southern Americans are so famous—is always in blast: He was thought little or nothing of, by his countrymen; rose, gradually, from the newspapers to the magazines, and circulating libraries; lived miserably poor; died, as he lived, miserably poor; and went into his grave with a broken heart. . . .

Arthur Mervyn is remarkably well managed, on many accounts; and miserably in others. It was the first, the germ of all his future productions. Walbeck was himself—he never equalled him, afterwards—though he did play him off, with a new name and a new dress, in every new piece. Explanations were designed—half-given, but never finished: machinery, half disclosed—and then forgotten, or abandoned.—Brown intended, at some future day, to explain the schoolmaster, that seduced the sister of Mervyn, into Walbeck:—Incidents are introduced, with great emphasis, which lead nowhere—to nothing; and, yet, are repeated in successive works.—Thus—(we speak only from recollection and have not seen one of the books for many a year)—in *Arthur Mervyn, Edgar Huntly,* and, perhaps, in *Jane Talbot,* a sum of money comes into the possession of "another person"—who converts it, under strong temptation, to his own use.—Let us pass on.

Edgar Huntly was the second essay—*Ormond,* the last. About *Wieland* we are not very certain. These three are unfinished, irregular, surprising affairs. All are remarkable for vividness, circumstantiality, and startling disclosures, here and there: yet all are full of perplexity—incoherence—and contradiction. Sometimes, you are ready to believe that Brown had made up the whole stories, in his own mind, before he had put his pen to the paper; at others, you would swear that he had either never seen, or forgotten, the beginning, before he came to the end, of his own story. You never know, for example, in *Edgar Huntly,* whether——an Irishman, whose name we forget—a principal character, is, or is not, a murderer. Brown, himself, seems never to have made up his own mind on that point. So—in *Wieland*—you never know whether Brown is, or is not, in earnest—whether Wieland was, or was not, supernaturally made away with. So—in *Ormond*—who *was* the secret witness?—to what purpose?—What a miserable catastrophe it is—Quite enough to make anybody sick of puling explanations.—Now, all this mystery is well enough, when you understand the author's intention. Byron leaves a broken chain—for us to guess by—when his Corsair is gone. We see that he scorns to explain. Byron is mysterious—Brown only perplexing. Why?—Because Brown undertakes to explain; and fails. Brown might have refused as Byron did. We should have liked him, if he had, all the better for it; as we do Byron. But we shall never forgive him, or any other man; dead or alive, who skulks out of any undertaking, with an air—as if not he, but other people are to be pitied.——We have our eye on a case, in point; but—no matter now.

Brown wanted material. What little he found, though it had all the tenuity of pure gold, he drew out, by one contrivance and another, till it disappeared in his own hands. So long as it would bear its own weight, he would never let go of it; and, when it broke—he would leave off spinning, for a time, as if his heart had broken with it. He would seem to have always taken up a new piece before he had thrown off the old one (we do not mean that Old One, whom it is rather difficult for any author to throw off, after he has once given himself up to, the harlotry of the imagination)—to have clung, always, to one or two favorite ideas—the Ventriloquist—and the yellow fever——as if they were his nest-eggs: one might have written, with as much propriety, at the end of any story that he ever wrote, as in almost any part of it—after the fashion of Magazines —"to be continued." This grew, of course, out of a system which prevailed, then—and is now taking a new shape in the twopenny publication of costly works, by the number. He was a story-teller by profession. . . . If you nibbled, you were in, for the whole—like a woman in love—hook, trap, and all. Money-lenders; gamblers; and subscribers to a story—which is "to be continued," nobody knows how long, are all in the same pickle. . . . He never let go of more than one end of a story, at a time—even when he had sold out. It is amusing to see how entirely he would forget where his own traps lay—while he was forging bait; his own hooks, while he was counterfeiting the flies. The curious box—broken to pieces, at night, so mysteriously (in the *Sleep Walker*) is in point. We could cite fifty more cases. The *Secret Witness* is hardly anything else, but a similar box— knocked apart, in a mysterious manner—the Lord knows wherefore. So with *Wieland:* In every case, you leave off, in a tease—a sort of uncomfortable, fidgetting, angry perplexity—ashamed of the concern, that you have shown—and quite in a huff with him—very much as if you had been running yourself to death—in a hot wind—after a catastrophe—with the tail soaped.

Yet, our conclusion respecting Charles Brockden Brown, is this. He was the Godwin of America. Had he lived here or anywhere, but in America—he would have been one of the most capital story-tellers—in a serious way, that ever lived. As it is, there is no one story of his, which will be remembered or read, after his countrymen shall have done justice to the genius that is really among them. They have enough of it—and of the right sort—if they will only give it fair play. Let them remember that no man will be great, unless he work hard; that no man will work hard, unless he is obliged—and that those who do so work, cannot afford to work for nothing, and find themselves. It would be well for his country-men to profit by—not imitate—we despise imitation even of what is excellent—it would be well for them to profit by his example. We want once more, before we die, to look upon the face of a real North American. God send that we may! . . .

Cooper—Novelist: formerly a midshipman in the United States navy: wrote *Precaution; The Spy; The Pioneers;* and *The Pilot.*—Style without peculiarity—brilliancy, or force—very much improved of late: considerable dramatic power; very fine talents in filling up a picture:—imitates the great Scotch Novelist—not so much, in any one thing—as altogether: has done his best.—*Precaution* is mere newspaper stuff.—There is hardly a fine passage in it with which our memory is afflicted. *The Spy*—the most popular novel ever produced in that country, by a native, is very good—as a whole: but rather too full of stage-tricks and clap-traps. Thus, the Spy himself—(who is a failure, by the way—a dead hum—anything might have been made of him, after the allusion to his father—nothing is)—appears whenever he is *not* expected—it is a pretty rule in the drama—bad in a novel: and swallows, among other matters, a protection, given to save his life—just when the time arrives, for which it was given; and where nothing else can save him:—the disguises; the pathos; the love-parts; the heroics—are all contemptible. In other matters, it is a capital novel. *Pioneers*—(observe the order in which these works have appeared—it looks well, for a young author, who grows bold with success)—a heavy piece of repetition in all the best characters: some noble scenes: and a pretty considerable share of lead. *Leather-stocking* is true—we have known such a fellow.—*Pilot*—have never read it properly: style greatly improved—some passages quite beyond Cooper—beyond our hopes of him, we mean. Mr C. is a man of sober talent—nothing more. There are no fine individualities about him. Nobody would know a work of his, by the work, itself. Talk as you please about mannerism. Extraordinary power cannot conceal itself. The stature of a giant cannot be hidden.

NO. IV

Jan., 1825

Irving—Washington— . . . Come we now, to the author.—Irving has been foolishly praised; cruelly, wickedly abused. He went up too high; he has fallen too low. They made an idol of him; they could see no fault or blemish in him; they crowned him; set him above other men; offered up his fellows to him—in spite of his continual, sincere expostulation. He was no Cromwell; no Caesar—and he knew it: He did not refuse the honor, that it might be put upon him, by force. Well—they did this—it was very foolish of them; very profane. But he was innocent; he should not have suffered. . . .

What we say, therefore, now, of Washington Irving, we say, with a full knowledge, that a time will come, when it shall appear against us. We shall put our opinion here, as upon record—believing, in our hearts—for we have no temporary purpose to gratify—that, after many years he will find consolation, support in it; others—that, in the time of these changes, there was one, at least—who had courage, power, and patience, to tell the truth of him—utterly careless of what other men thought, or said. . . .

Knickerbocker: A droll, humorous history of New York, while the Dutch, who settled it, were in power: conceived, matured, and brought forth, in a bold, original temper—unaided—and alone—by Irving: more entirely the natural thought, language, humor, and feeling of the man himself—without imitation or plagiarism—far more—than either of his late works: It was written, too, in the fervor and flush of his popularity, at home—after he had got a name, such as no other man had, among his countrymen; after *Salamagundi* had been read, with pleasure, all over North America: In it, however, there is a world of rich allusion—a vein of sober caricature—the merit of which is little understood here: Take an example—"Von Poffenburg" is a portrait—outrageously distorted, on some accounts, but nevertheless a portrait, of General Wilkinson—a "bellipotent" officer, who sent in a bill, to Congress, for sugar plums, or segars, or both, after "throwing up"—in disgust we dare say, as "he could not stomach it," his military command upon the Florida frontier: So too—in the three Dutch governors, we could point out a multitude of laughable secret allusions to three of the American chief magistrates (Adams, Jefferson, Madison)—which have not always been well understood, anywhere—by anybody—save those who are familiar with American history.

By nine readers out of ten, perhaps, *Knickerbocker* is read, as a piece of generous drollery—nothing more. Be it so. It will wear the better—The design of Irving himself is not always clear: nor was he always undeviating, in his course. Truth or fable, fact or falsehood—it was all the same to him, if a bit of material came in his way.

In a word, we look upon this volume of *Knickerbocker;* though it is tiresome, though there *are* some wretched failures in it; a little overdoing of the humorous—and a little confusion of purpose, throughout—as a work, honorable to English literature—manly—bold—and so altogether original, without being extravagant, as to stand alone, among the labors of men. . . .

Sketch-Book. Irving had now come to be regarded as a professional author: to think of his pen for a livelihood. His mercantile speculations were disastrous. We are glad of it. It is all the better for him—his country

—our literature—us. But for that lucky misfortune, he would never have been half what he now is: But for his present humiliation, he would never be half what he will now be, if we rightly understand his character. . . .

The *Sketch-Book*—is a timid, beautiful work; with some childish pathos in it; some rich, pure, bold poetry: a little squeamish, puling, ladylike sentimentality: some courageous writing—some wit—and a world of humor, so happy, so natural—so altogether unlike that of any other man— dead or alive, that we would rather have been the writer of it, fifty times over, than of everything else, that he has ever written.—

The touches of poetry are everywhere; but never where one would look for them. Irving has no passion: he fails utterly, in true pathos—cannot speak, as if he were carried away, by anything. He is always thoughtful; and, save when he tries to be fine, or sentimental, always at home, always natural.—The "dusty splendor" of Westminster Abbey—the "ship staggering" over the precipices of the ocean—the shark "darting, like a spectre, through the blue waters."—All these things are poetry— such poetry as never was—never will be surpassed.—We could mention fifty more passages—epithets—words of power, which no mere prose writer would have dared, under any circumstances, to use. They are like the "invincible locks" of Milton—revealing the God, in spite of every disguise. —They remind us of Leigh Hunt, who, to do him justice—notwithstanding all his "tricksey" prettinesses, does talk more genuine poetry, in his epithets, than any other man that ever lived. We know well what we say— we except nobody.—We hate his affectation; despise—pity his daintiness, trick and foppery, but cannot refuse to say, that in his delicate, fine, exquisite adaptation of descriptive words, to the things described, in his poetry he has no equal.—The "loosened silver" of the fountain; the "golden ferment" of the sunshine, upon the wet grass; the large raindrops, that fall upon the dry leaves, like "twanging pearl"—all these, with a thousand others, are in proof.

The epithets of Hunt are pictures—portraits—likenesses: those of Geoffrey, shadows. Those of the former frequently take off your attention from the principal object: outshine, overtop, that, of which they should be only the auxiliaries: Those of the latter never do this—they only help the chief thought. The associations of Hunt startle us, like Moore's "unexpected light"; in the cool grass—the trodden velvet of his poetry: those of Irving never startle us; never thrill us; never "go a-rippling to our fingerends"; but are always agreeable—affecting us, like the sweet quiet luster of the stars, or moon. When we come upon the epithets of Hunt, we feel as if we had caught something—a butterfly, or a bug, perhaps, while running with our mouth open: or detected some hidden relationship of things: But when we come upon the epithets of Geoffrey, we feel as if we had found, accidentally, after we had given up all hope—some part or parcel, which had always been missing (as everybody could see, though nobody knew where to look for it), of the very thoughts or words, with which he has now coupled it forever. . . .

"Rip Van Winkle" is well done; but we have no patience with such a man as Washington Irving.—We cannot keep our temper, when we catch him pilfering the materials of other men; working up old stories. We had as lief see him before the public, for some Bow-street offence.

"The Wife" is ridiculous, with some beautiful description; but Irving, as we said before, has no idea of true passion—suffering—or deep, desolating fervor. . . .

Bracebridge-Hall. "Stout Gentleman"— very good; and a pretty fair account of a real occurrence; "Student of Salamanca"; beneath contempt: Irving has no idea of genuine romance; or love—or anything else, we believe, that ever seriously troubles the blood of men:—"Rookery"—struck off in a few hours; contrary to what has been said: Irving does not labor as people suppose—he is too indolent—given, too much, we know, to reverie: "Dolph Heyliger"; "The Haunted House"; "Storm Ship"—all in the fashion of his early time: perhaps—we are greatly inclined so to believe— perhaps the remains of what was meant for *Salamagundi*, or *Knicker-bocker*:—the rest of the two volumes quite unworthy of Irving's reputation.

Hugh Henry Brackenridge
(1748-1816)

Hugh Henry Brackenridge moved with his parents from his birthplace near Campbeltown, Scotland, to York County, Pennsylvania, in 1753. He received his B.A. at Princeton in 1771, his M.A. in 1774, and wrote with Philip Freneau a commencement poem, *The Rising Glory of America* (Philadelphia, 1772). After editing the *United States Magazine* (January-December, 1779) at Philadelphia, Brackenridge was admitted to law practice in 1780. The following year he moved to Pittsburgh, then a frontier village, where he helped establish the *Pittsburgh Gazette* (in 1781) and frequently contributed to it. Brackenridge served in the state legislature from 1786–1787, and was appointed a justice of the State Supreme Court

in 1791. In 1801, he moved to Carlisle, where he lived until his death. Between 1792 and 1815, Brackenridge wrote his most important work, *Modern Chivalry;* publication of the various volumes is as follows: Vols. I and II (Philadelphia, 1792); Vol. III (Pittsburgh, 1793); Vol. IV (Philadelphia, 1797); Part II, Vol. I (Carlisle, Pa., dated 1804, published 1805); Part II, Vol. II (Carlisle, Pa., 1805). *Modern Chivalry,* 4 vols. (Philadelphia, 1815) includes some added material.

BIBLIOGRAPHY: C. M. Newlin, *The Life and Writings of Hugh Henry Brackenridge* (Princeton, 1932). *Modern Chivalry,* ed. C. M. Newlin (New York, 1937).

From *Modern Chivalry*

BOOK III, CHAPTER XXVI

It may be asked, of what use, is a great part of the preceding book? Some things may have a moral and carry instruction to the mind. But a great part can have no meaning or effect; farther than to raise a laugh, or to make a person smile for a moment. That itself is something; and may conciliate the reader to what is more solid. An ingredient, not in itself savory, may give a relish to substantial good. Asafoetida gives a flavor to a beef-steak.

Let me get a man to laugh, and I put him in a good humor. The whole book from beginning to end, has a moral, which, if anyone has not found out, let him read again.

It may argue a light airy mind in the writer; and yet these things are sometimes the offspring, as in the present case, of a mind, far from being at ease; on the contrary, it is to get ease, and allay pain, that it is written. —Pain of mind is relieved by an abstraction of solid thought. The early paroxysm of deep grief, may be incompatible with a playful fancy; but gradually and insensibly, the heart-ache may be cheated of its sensations. What else effect has conversation or music? Neither of these can assuage great pain; or torture; but will be felt to alleviate, in a lesser degree of body or mind. The mind is drawn off, and kept from reflecting. We use laudanum to allay acute bodily pains; and it gives a pleasing delirium, and insensibility for a time. But in the case of mental suffering, it is much safer to attack the imagination by an intellectual paregoric. There is less danger that the use will grow to excess, and induce habit.

Scarron wrote his comical Romance under great bodily pain. But ease to the mind has been more frequently sought by the amusement of writing. It is a fortunate thing for the writers, that it keeps off hunger: for many of them in the garrets of cities, if we may believe themselves, while they lived, or their friends after they were dead, are reduced to short commons. Certain it is, that the occupation of the mind saves food. Literary men, are in general but small eaters. The spirits are exhausted in the thought of the brain, and are less active, in the juices of the stomach. So that from a man's eating I can give a pretty good guess, whether he thinks, or speaks most.

But it may be said, this book might have been written, from the motive suggested; but why let it go to the press? Because there is a pleasure in seeing what you have written appear in a book; and the correcting the proof sheets as you go along, pleases. It is on the same principle that the child is delighted with its baby-house; the grown person with the gratification of his fancy in architecture or gardening. All the objects of men, are in great part to please the imagination. Utility is but one half. I admit at the same time, that he who comprises both, hits the nail on the head, and carries all votes. But it is even something to attain one of these.—This much it may suffice to say, as an apology for the publication.

But it may be said, why not cast the salt of your pleasantry upon some substantial food to the mind of a young person, and not upon vapor, which constitutes little nourishment? You would seem to be a moralist; and to have some knowledge of practical philosophy. Hence we should expect in your page, observations conducive to regulate life, and to form manners. If for instance you had taken a youth from his early age, and conducted him to manhood, insinuating by example, or precept, the best lessons, it might have been a school book. I answer, there has been a great deal in this way already; and my mind led me more to give lessons to grown people. Was I to set myself about such a work as is suggested; I do not know that I could mend the matter.—I believe, I would change a little the system of education; in one particular; but it might not be for the better. As already hinted by some things put into the mouth of the Captain, I could make it a principal matter to form the heart to a republican government. And in order to this; keep out of view all that nourishes ambition, the poison of public virtue. "In honor preferring one another," is an apostolic, and Christian injunction. But it is as wise in philosophy, as it is true in religion. Honor is the principle of monarchy, distinction of rank, titles, dignities. In the American republics, we retain yet a great deal of the spirit of monarchy. The people are not aware of the phraseology itself, in some instances. When an individual solicits a vote, his language is that he will serve the people. They take him at his word, and when he is sent to a public body, he is called their servant. He goes farther himself, and will talk of the majesty of the people.

No disgrace is supposed to attach itself to the soliciting votes, any more than petitioning the monarch for a place. This is not in the spirit of a republic. It is contrary to the nature of it; it is subversive of it. But I would begin at the foundation, by inculcating the folly of coveting a public appointment. The private interest of a man is better cultivated by staying at home. The first lesson I would give to a son of mine would be to have nothing to do with public business, but as a duty to his country. To consider service in civil life, no more to be desired than service in the military. In this last, there is danger of rheumatism, and ague; or of a wound, or of death in battle; but in civil trusts, there is danger of obloquy and disrespect.

But an individual that accepts a trust is no servant.—He is an agent, a delegate, a commissioner. Nor is a house of representatives the people. Nor can majesty be predicated of them. It is a monarchical phrase, and I would not apply it, even to the people themselves.

But take away the spring of ambition; that is, distinction, and preference; and you relax industry; you increase indolence. I grant it. But it saves the heart.—There may be less eminence; but there will be more goodness. It is on this principle that I condemn the distribution of honors in academies. It is beginning by corrupting the affections. It is planting the poison weed of ambition; the upas-tree that taints the breeze, and kills the visitant. I shall have accomplished something by this book, if it shall keep some honest man from lessening his respectability by pushing himself into public trusts for which he is not qualified; or when pushed forward into a public station, if it shall contribute to keep him honest by teaching him the folly of ambition, and farther advancement; when in fact, the shade is more to be coveted, and the mind, on reflection, will be better satisfied with itself for having chosen it. This is in great part, the moral of this book; if it should be at all necessary to give a hint of it. Will not an honest man feel compunction, when after some experience, he comes to look back, and see the mischief he has done in a public station; sapped, perhaps the foundations of the constitution; misled by the ambitious; when at the same time, he thought he was establishing the republic? Understanding is therefore requisite; not common sense merely; but knowledge of the subject. But what is knowledge without integrity? And how can there be integrity, where there is ambition? Is there not the ambition of doing good? I do not call that ambition. The praise of doing good? I do not even like the word, praise. I would say the pleasure of doing good. For it is the greatest possible pleasure to a mind rightly informed; properly cultivated, to have done good. A consciousness of this, consoles under public obloquy, and ingratitude.

In looking over what is written, it strikes me that by introducing Teague to the levee, I may be thought to mean a burlesque on the president. It is not so; I meant a burlesque on Teague. As to levee holding, I do not know whether it is right or wrong; nor do I care. Because be it as it may, I believe it can do little harm, and is one of those insipidities in the affairs of men which are of no account. Universal prudence is a characteristic of the president, with a capacity of attending to substantial business, and being able at the same time to accommodate himself to forms and ceremonies. As all mankind are not philosophers, perhaps it is well to possess this talent, in order to please them.

Observing several errors of the press, I had thoughts of giving a table of them. But I recollect that in other books, a table of this kind has appeared to me unnecessary. Because the intelligent reader could in general himself see what were errors, and as to the unintelligent it made no great odds whether he did or not.

I have only farther to say at present, that I wish I could get this work to make a little more noise. Will nobody attack it and prove that it is insipid, libellous, treasonable, immoral, or irreligious? If they will not do this, let them do something else; praise it, call it excellent, say it contains wit, erudition, genius, and the Lord knows what! Will nobody speak? What? Ho! are ye all asleep in the hold there? Will none of you abuse, praise, reprobate, or commend this performance? It is ill usage, that is all I can say, and all that is necessary for the present.   1793

BOOK IV, CHAPTER XIV

. . . There is a natural alliance between liberty and letters. Men of letters are seldom men of wealth, and these naturally ally themselves with the democratic interest in a commonwealth. These form a balance with the bulk of the people, against power, springing from family interest, and large estates. It is not good policy in republicans to declare war against letters; or even to frown upon them, for in literary men is their best support. They are as necessary to them as light to the steps. They are a safe auxiliary: for all they want is, to have the praise of giving information. The study of political law, and municipal jurisprudence qualifies to inform, and hence at the commencement of the American revolution, lawyers were the first to give the alarm and assert the rights of the people. Shall we forget the recent services of lawyers in framing the federal, and state constitutions? The name of lawyer ought not to be hunted down, because there are characters, unworthy of the profession, with whom the love of money is inordinate, and insatiable.

There is ground, for the regret, that literary institutions are not favored; that it has become a popular thing to call out against learning, as not necessary to make republicans. The knowledge of our rights, and capacity to prosecute, and defend them, does not spring from the ground; but from education and study. Under a federal government, we are peculiarly situated. We stand in need of law, learning, and legal abilities to support ourselves in a contest with the claims of the general government, which, as it bounds the state jurisdiction, must, in the nature of things, encroach upon it. It is of great moment, with a view to this very object, that our judiciary be composed of able men that under the concurrent jurisdiction of the courts, it may be able to hold its own: or more especially, that from a want of confidence in the abilities of the state judges, recurrence may not be had to the tribunals of the United States, by legitimate election, or by those collusions against which it is difficult to guard.

CHAPTER XV

. . . It has been asked, why, in writing this memoir, have I taken my clown, from the Irish nation? The character of the English clown, I did not well understand; nor could I imitate the manner of speaking. That of the Scotch I have tried, as may be seen, in the character of Duncan. But I found it, in my hands, rather insipid. The character of the Irish clown, to use the language of Rousseau, "has more stuff in it." He will attempt anything.

The American has in fact, yet, no character; neither the clown, nor the gentleman; so that I could not take one from our own country; which I would much rather have done, as the scene lay here. But the midland states of America, and the western parts in general, being half Ireland, the character of the Irish clown, will not be wholly misunderstood. It is true the clown is taken from the aboriginal Irish; a character not so well known in the North of that country; nevertheless, it is still so much known, even there, and amongst the emigrants here, or their decendants, that it will not be wholly thrown away.

On the Irish stages, it is a standing character; and on the theater in Britain, it is also introduced. I have not been able to do it justice, being but half an Irishman, myself, and not so well acquainted with the reversions, and idiom, of the genuine Thady, as I could wish. However, the imitation at a distance from the original, will better pass than if it had been written, and read, nearer home. Foreigners will not so readily distinguish the incongruities; or, as it is the best we can produce for the present, will more indulgently consider them.

I think it the duty of every man who possesses a faculty, and perhaps a facility of drawing such images, as will amuse his neighbor, to lend a hand, and do something. Have those authors done nothing for the world, whose works would seem to have had no other object but to amuse? In low health; after the fatigue of great mental exertion on solid disquisition; in pain of mind, from disappointed passions; or broken with the sensibilities of sympathy, and affection; it is a relief to try not to think, and this is attainable, in some degree, by light reading. Under sensations of this kind, I have had recourse more than once to *Don Quixote;* which doubtless contains a great deal of excellent moral sentiment. But, at the same time, has much that can serve only to amuse. Even in health, and with a flow of spirits, from prosperous affairs, it diversifies enjoyments, and adds to the happiness of which the mind is capable. I trust, therefore, that the gravest persons, will not be of opinion that I ought to be put out of church, for any appearance of levity, which this work may seem to carry with it.

I know there have been instances amongst the puritans, of clergymen, degraded for singing a Scotch pastoral. But music is a carnal thing compared with putting thoughts upon paper. It requires an opening of the mouth, and a rolling of the tongue, whereas thought is wholly spiritual, and depends, not on any modification of the corporeal organs. Music, however, even by the strictest sects, is admissible in sacred harmony, which is an acknowledgement, that even sound, has its uses to soothe the mind or to fit it for contemplation.

I would ask, which is the most entertaining work, Smollett's *History of England;* or his *Humphrey Clinker?* For, as to the utility, so far as that depends upon truth, they are both alike. History has been well said to be the Romance of the human mind; and Romance the history of the heart. When the son of Robert Walpole asked his father, whether he should read to him out of a book of history; he said, "he was not fond of Romance." This minister had been long engaged in affairs; and from what he had seen of accounts of things within his own knowledge he had little confidence in the relation of things which he had not seen. Except memoirs of person's own times; biographical sketches by contemporary writers; Voyages, and Travels, that have geographical exactness, there is little of the historical kind, in point of truth, before *Roderick Random;* or *Gil Blas.*

The Eastern nations in their tales pretend to nothing but fiction. Nor is the story with them the less amusing because it is not true. Nor is the moral of it less impressive, because the actors never had existence.

1797

PART II

BOOK I, CHAPTER II

Observations

Among the Romans, there was a kind creature, of the name of Apollo, who stood by people, and when they were doing wrong, would give them a twitch of the ear, to bid them stop.

Aurum velluit.—

I cannot say, that I felt just such a twitch while I was writing the last chapter; unless figuratively; meaning some little twitch of the mind, re-collecting, and reflecting, that it might possibly give offence to public bodies and societies, especially the St. Tammany, and Cincinnati; though none was intended. But it is impossible to anticipate in all cases, the sensations of others.—Things will give offence, that were meant to inform, and assist: or to please and divert. In the case of public bodies especially, no man knows, what may make an unfavorable impression. It is necessary, or, unavoidable as it might be translated, "that offences come, but woe to him by whom they come." One would think that in a free country, there might be some little more moderation with regard to what is done and said. It is a maxim in law, that words are to be construed, "mitior sensu"; or in the milder sense. It is a scriptural definition of charity, "that it is not easily provoked."—Whereas, on the contrary, an uncharitable disposition is ready to misconstrue, & convert to an offence. A town, a society, a public body, of any kind might be presumed to bear more than an individual, because, the offence being divided amongst a greater number; it can be but a little, that will be at the expense of any one person. If therefore, any son of St. Tammany, or St. Cincinnatus, should feel himself hurt by our lucubration, let him consider that it is better to laugh than be angry; and he will save himself, if he begins to laugh first. Though, after all, some will say, there is nothing to laugh at; and in this, they will be right. For at the most, it can only be a smile. It is a characteristic of the comedy of Terence; that he never forces your laugh; but to smile only. That I take to be the criterion of a delicate and refined wit; and which was becoming the lepos, or humor of such men, as Lelius and Scipio, who are thought to have formed his taste, and assisted him in his dramatic compositions. Yet I must confess, if I could reach it, I would like the broad laugh; but it is difficult to effect this, and not, at the same time, fall into buffoonery, and low humor. Laughing is certainly favorable to the lungs; and happy the man, whose imagination leads him to risable sensations, rather than to melancholy.

All work, and no play, makes Jack a dull boy. But I have no idea of laughing, any more than of playing, without having performed the necessary task of duty, or labor. An idle laughing fool, is contemptible and odious; and laughing too much is an extreme which the wise will avoid. Take care not to laugh, when there is nothing to laugh at. I can always know a man's sense, by his song, his story, or his laugh. I will not say his temper, or principles; but certainly his share of understanding. The truth is, this composition has more for its object than merely to amuse, though that is an object. But I doubt whether we shall receive credit for our good intentions. For truth lies in a well; and unless there is someone to draw the bucket, there is no getting it up.

We have been often asked for a key to this work. Every man of sense has the key in his own pocket.—His own feelings; his own experience is the key. It is astonishing, with what avidity, we look for the application of satire which is general, and never had a prototype. But the fact is, that, in this work, the picture is taken from human nature, generally, and has no individual in view. It was never meant as a satire upon men; but upon things. An easy way, to slur sentiments, under the guise of allegory; which could not otherwise make their way to the ears of the curious. Can any man suppose, upon reflection, that if ridicule was intended upon real persons, it would be conveyed in so bungling a manner that people would be at a loss to know who was meant? That is not the way we fix our fool caps.

Let any man put it to himself, and say, would he wish to be of those that give pain by personal allusion, & abuse? Self-love, for a moment, may relish the stricture; but could never endure to be thought the author. In attacking reputation, there are two things to be considered, the manner, and the object. When the object is praise-worthy, there is an openness, a frankness, and manliness of manner, which commands respect. But even where the object is a public good, the manner may excite contempt. Let our editors of newspapers look to this, of them who wish to be considered gentlemen; such as have no character to lose, and never wish to have any, may take all liberties and occupy their own grade.

But as we were saying, public bodies and societies of men, ought not to take offense easily; nor resent violently. "As they are strong, be merciful." A single person is not on a footing with a great number. He cannot withstand the whole, if they should take offense without reason; and he may be conscientiously scrupulous of fighting; or may be afraid to fight; which will answer the end just as well; or he may have the good sense and fortitude, to declare off; which by the bye requires more courage, than the bulk of men possess. It requires a courage above all false opinion; and the custom will never be put out of countenance, until some brave men set the example.—There is nothing that a wise man need fear, but dishonor, founded on the charge of a want of virtue; on that which all men, of all places, and of all times, will acknowledge to be disreputable. Under this head, will not be found the refusal of a challenge. Nothing can be great, the contempt of which is great. Is it not great to despise prejudice, and false opinion? "He that ruleth his spirit, is greater than he that taketh a city:" but, he that is above the false sentiments of others, presents to me the image of a superior power, that ascends through the vapors of the atmosphere and dissipates the fog. The world is indebted to the man that refuses a challenge; but who can owe anything to him that accepts it? for he sanctions an unjust law.—Doubtless, the accepting of a challenge, is pardonable as a weakness; but still it is a weakness. The man is a hero, who can withstand unjust opinion. It requires more courage, than to fight duels.—To sustain life, under certain circumstances, calls for more resolution than to commit suicide. Yet suicide is not reputable. Brutus in the schools condemned it; but at Philippi, adopted it: Because his courage failed him.

But cudgelling, follows the refusal of a challenge. Not if there is instant notice given to a peace officer. But posting follows. Notice of that may be given also, and a court and jury brought to criticize upon the libel.

Why is it, that a public body is more apt to take offence than an individual? Because, everyone becomes of consequence in proportion as he is careful of the honor of the whole. It is oftentimes a mere matter of accident, whether the thing is well or ill taken. If one should happen to call out, that it is an insult, another is unwilling to question it, lest he should be suspected of incivicism, and lose his standing in society in general: or in that to which he more particularly belongs. The misconception of one forces itself upon another; and misconstruction prevails. That which was the strongest proof of confidence in the integrity and justice of the body, is viewed as distrust; and a concern for their honor, considered a reproach. The most respectful language termed insolence. Implicit submission attributed to disrespect. Self-denial overlooked, and wantonness of insult substituted in its place. This, all the offspring of mistake; which it is the duty of the individual to remove. But how can he speak if his head is off, before he knows that the offence is taken? Protesting therefore that I mean no offence to either of these societies, or the individual members, in anything I have said; I request them to take it in good part; or, if there should seem to be ground of affront, they will give me a hearing, and an opportunity to explain.

There is no anticipating absolutely, and to all extent, what a person might say for himself if he was heard. That presumption which had existed might be removed. His motives might appear laudable; or at the worst, originating in a pardonable weakness. Whether or not the credit of the tribunal with the world, might render it expedient to observe these appearances; they did it in France under the revolutionary government;

and even the emperor seems to consider it as indispensible. If therefore anything in these chapters should unfortunately give umbrage to the sons of St. Tammany, or to the Cincinnati members, I pray a citation, and demand a hearing. I trust I shall be able to convince them that I am not deficient in respect for them individually, or as public bodies.

1805

Samuel Knapp
(1783-1838)

Lawyer, journalist, and biographer, Samuel Knapp was born at Newburyport, Massachusetts, and was graduated from Dartmouth in 1804. He opened a law office in Newburyport in 1809, and from 1812 to 1816 was a representative in the General Court of Massachusetts. After 1816, Knapp edited and contributed to periodicals in Boston, New York, and Washington. Among his biographies, frequently inaccurate, are studies of Lafayette (1824), DeWitt Clinton (1828), Daniel Webster (1831), and Aaron Burr (1835). Other works include *Advice in the Pursuits of Literature* (New York, 1832) and *Lectures on American Literature* (New York, 1829), Knapp's history of American letters.

BIBLIOGRAPHY: *DAB. Lectures on American Literature*, eds. Richard B. Davis and Ben H. McClary (Gainesville, Fla., 1961), facsimile of 1829 edition. *Letters of Shahcoolen,* ed. Ben H. McClary (Gainesville, Fla., 1962), facsimile of 1802 edition.

From *Lectures on American Literature*

PREFACE

Every book that is ushered into the world, is a mental experiment of the writer, to ascertain the taste, and to obtain the judgement of the community; and the author can only be certain of one thing, and that is, of his intentions in his publication. Of my intentions, I can only say, as, perhaps, I have a dozen times said in the course of my work, they were to exhibit to the rising generation something of the history of the thoughts and intellectual labors of our forefathers, as well as of their deeds. There is, however, an intimate connection between thinking and acting, particularly among a free and an energetic people. My plan, when I commenced my researches, was an extensive one, and I gathered copious materials to carry it into effect. For several years past, I have had access to libraries rich in American literature; but when I sat down to work up the mass I had collected, the thought suggested itself to my mind, that no adequate compensation could ever be reasonably expected for my pains; and then the consciousness that I was in some measure trespassing upon my professional pursuits, went far to quench my zeal, and to chase away my visions of literary reputation. Still, I could not be persuaded to relinquish altogether my design, and I therefore set about abridging my outlines, dispensing with many of my remarks, and giving up numerous elaborate finishings I had promised myself to make in the course of my work. And another thought struck me most forcibly, that a heavy publication would not be readily within the reach of all classes of youth in our country, but that a single volume of common size, in a cheap edition, might find its way into some of our schools, and be of service in giving our children a wish to pursue the subject of our literary history, as they advanced in years and in knowledge. The instructors of our youth, when true to their trust, form a class in the community that I hold in respect and esteem, and they will pardon me for making a few remarks to them. Your calling is high, I had almost said holy. To your intelligence, patience, good temper, purity of life, and soundness of principles, parents look for the forming of healthy, vigorous minds, in their children. If you cannot create talents, you can do something better; you can guide the fiery, and wake up the dull; correct the mischievous, and encourage the timid. The temple of knowledge is committed to your care; the priesthood is a sacred one. Every inscription on the walls should be kept bright, that the dimmest eye may see, and the slowest comprehension may read and be taught to understand. Your task is great, and every member of the community, who is able to give you any assistance, should come to your aid in the great business of instruction. In this way much has been done;—much, however, remains to be done. The elements of learning have been simplified, and thousands of children have been beguiled along the pathway of knowledge, who never could have been driven onward. Geography has been made easy and fascinating, and the elements of natural philosophy very pleasant; and what was once difficult and harsh to young minds in many studies, has become attractive. History, both sacred and profane, has assumed new charms as it has been prepared for the schoolroom; I speak of the history of other countries, not of our own. We have very good histories—narrative, political, military, and constitutional; but I know none, as yet, that can be called literary—meaning by the term, a history of our literature, and of our literary men; and probably it will be a long time before we shall have such an one as we ought to have. Our Sismondis, D'Israelis, are yet to arise. You will struggle in vain to make American history well understood by your pupils, unless biographical sketches, anecdotes, and literary selections, are mingled with the mass of general facts. The heart must be affected, and the imagination seized, to make lasting impressions upon the memory.

One word to your pride:—you are aware that it has been said by foreigners, and often repeated, that there was no such thing as American literature; that it would be in vain for anyone to seek for proofs of taste, mind, or information, worth possessing, in our early records; and some of our citizens, who have never examined these matters, have rested so quietly after these declarations, or so faintly denied them, that the bold asserters of these libels have gained confidence in tauntingly repeating them. The great epoch in our history—the revolution of 1775—seemed sufficient, alone, to many of the present generation, to give us, as a people, all the celebrity and rank, among the nations of the earth, we ought to aspire to, without taking the trouble to go back to the previous ages of heroic virtue and gigantic labors. Many of the present generation are willing to think that our ancestors were a pious and persevering race of men, who really did possess some strength of character, but, without further reflection, they are ready to allow that a few pages are "ample room and verge enough" to trace their character and their history together. I have ventured to think differently, and also to flatter myself, that, at the present day, it would not be a thankless task to attempt to delineate some of the prominent features of our ancestors in justification of my opinion. This error can only be eradicated by your assistance, and that by instilling into the minds of our children, in your every-day lessons, correct information upon these subjects;—and while you lead your pupils through the paths of miscellaneous and classical literature—and, at the present day, even the humblest education partakes of much that is of a classical nature—be it your duty, also, to make them acquainted with the minutest portions of their country's history. No people, who do not love themselves better than all others, can ever be prosperous and great. A sort of inferiority always hangs about him who unduly reverences another. If "know thyself," be a sound maxim for individual consideration, "think well of thyself," should be a national one. Patriotism and greatness begin at the maternal bosom, are seen in the nursery and primary school, and quicken into life in every advancing stage of knowledge. Guardians of a nation's morals, framers of intellectual greatness, show to your charge, in proper lights, the varied talent of your country, in every age of her history; and inscribe her glories of mind, and heart, and deed, as with a sunbeam, upon their memories.

New-York, Nov. 1829

LECTURE VII

. . . The literature of theology in this country suffered, as well as the literature and science of other professions, during the revolution. The pulpit rang with patriotism and politics, and harangues upon the good and sound Christian duty of fighting for freedom; all very excellent lessons for the times, and which certainly had their uses. After the warning appeals to the brave defenders of the country, it was dull to go back to detailing the enormities of papal power, or speaking of the great beast of seven heads and ten horns; therefore his holiness was left quite alone, except now and then in some good man's form of prayer, from which the epithets of abhorrence for Babylon never had been expunged. Dissertations on Antinomians, Pelagians, and all the host of sectarians, had begun to grow stale, and the doctrines of eternal decrees and predestination were not so attractive to the new generations as they had been to their fathers. From all appearances, the timid began to fear that the pulpit had lost its legitimate, primitive influences. Under this impression, many were turned from the study of this profession, who were intended for it by their parents, and engaged in medicine or law. At this weak moment, if the defenders of the faith will allow that there ever were such moments, infidelity reared its monstrous head, and stalked through our part of Christendom with gigantic strides; but, as it has often happened, that which threatened destruction to the altar and the priest, was the cause of giving new and lasting honor to both. Infidelity had for years been disseminated by the philosophers into inquisitive minds, but had never come upon us in the form of popular eloquence, and had not reached common minds engaged in ordinary pursuits, until about the time of the French revolution; it now came under the potential form of superior wisdom, free from the thraldom of error. It dealt out a strong denial of the great truths of the gospel, and made impudence, with now and then a flash of witty scurrility, pass for common sense and true reasoning upon the revelations of God to man, through nature and her laws, and by the inspirations of holy writ. At first, great shipwreck was made of the faith of thousands; the weak were bewildered, and the unlearned entangled. The truly pious still believed that the church was built upon a rock, and that the gates of hell should not, finally, prevail against it, yet they were discouraged at the progress of infidelity, and were cut to the heart at hearing the authenticity of the scriptures doubted, and the ministers of our holy religion ridiculed in every possible form of contempt; called by opprobrious epithets; charged with ignorance and hypocrisy; and their downfall prophesied with confidence and joy. For a while there was some confusion in the church, but the purest men soon roused themselves from idleness, or rather from idle disputes about trifles, or non-essentials, and many of them plunged into the depths of learning, to answer the falsehoods and sneers of the scoffers, who laid pretensions to have penetrated into the recesses of oriental literature, and having detected the errors of Christianity. The contest was animated, and the ministers of light struggled hard with the ministers of darkness. Great minds entered the contest, and, after a while, the dreams of Condorcet and the scurrilities of Paine, were swept away together, and infidelity was first scouted by learning, piety, and taste, and, at length, proscribed by the irresistible power of fashion. The works of Watson and Tytler, and, towards the close of the struggle, of many others, were found, not only in the hands of the polemic, or in the library of the speculative, but on the toilets of the fair, with the last work of the imagination from Southey or Campbell;

for the ecclesiastical writers had added to the science of theology the most sublime of all contemplations, the charms of literature and taste. The reading and thinking part of the community were delighted to witness the commencement of a new era in the rhetoric, eloquence, and logic of the pulpit; useless divisions and subdivisions, and their scholastic divinity, with loose and spongy declamation, gave place to fair inductions, correct illustrations, and philanthropic views. The ways of God to man were satisfactorily justified to the understandings of the mighty in intellect, and to the humble and lowly seekers of the truth. Religion wore the smile of innocence and the robe of purity, as she was destined to do from the beginning. The charms of a delicate and finished literature now came from the pulpit, and the temple of God became, as it ought ever to be, a place of instruction for the mind and for the affections, as well as for learning the great doctrines of salvation.

LECTURE VIII

. . . Until lately, periodical journals were not so successful as newspapers among the good people of this country. The first published in the provinces, was in the year 1741, by Benjamin Franklin, then of Philadelphia, just ten years after Edward Cave, of London, commenced the *Gentleman's Magazine*. The English publication has continued until this time; but the American was soon discontinued. Franklin knew that such a work was wanted in the country, and he thought that he would try it, at that early date; but it was in advance of the age.

After the peace of 1783, there were several magazines started in different sections of the country, in New York, Boston, and Philadelphia, and flourished for some time with considerable success. Some of them are read with great pleasure at the present day. Mathew Carey, and his associates, published the *Museum*, a repository of literature, which flourished until the whole amounted to several large volumes. This was commenced in 1787, and contained the productions of Trumbull, Humphrey, and Dr. Ladd, with many other solutions of prose and verse. This work did not expire for want of patronage, but ceased because the publishers found better business. New York and Boston have supported a review in some shape or other ever since 1790. There were many well written pieces in these works; but the business of reviewing had not then assumed its shape, and form, and power, which it has since. The writers touched with a faltering hand upon the errors of others; but their general course was to pass in silence those they did not like in sentiment or manner. A bolder hand was soon tried, and the public supported freedom and vivacity in discussing the merits of authors; but this privilege has, since that period, often degenerated into dogmatism and censoriousness.

About the year 1801, the *Port Folio* was commenced by Joseph Dennie, in the city of Philadelphia. He had been known as the editor of a piquant and tasteful paper in the interior of New England, on the banks of the Connecticut river. He was then in a circle of wits, who threw their productions on the winds with careless profusion. Royall Tyler, long known as the Bonnel Thornton of America, who wrote that which the muses sometimes inspired in the shades of the evening, and blushed to acknowledge at the light of the morning sun, was one of the number. Dennie was free, easy, and readily excited to a stretch of thought, and latitude of expression, pardonable only, if ever, at the *"noctes cænæque Deum;"* but his feelings were naturally pure and sincere; and if, for a moment, his mind, like the cloth made of the asbestos, received a stain by contiguity with impurity, the blaze of his genius, like the operation of fire upon the imperishable texture of the web, burnt it all pure again at its first kindling up. If Dennie had not that intellectual vigor which crushes to obtain an essence, or dissolves to develop a principle; he had judgement and taste to arrange a sentence and to polish a period. His imagination was rich and excursive; it knew no thraldom, and spurned at all narrow bounds. He had that which the country wanted more than anything else, a refined taste. The *Port Folio* was then in full circulation; and this, more than any other work in the country, had an influence on the style of writing in our seminaries of learning. The young aspirants for fame saw how much the writings of Dennie were read, and they imitated him in their productions. This was fortunate. It is better for youths to emulate the flexible motions of the dancing master, to give grace and ease to their movements, than to practice the measured steps and stately demeanor of the knight in armor, before they have bone and muscle for the fight. Modern education, it may be said, has found a happy mean, or rather, has taught us how to unite both. Dennie did not live many years to continue his work. Since that period the *Port Folio* has fallen into other hands; and although it has frequently exhibited talent, yet it has lost its relative standing in the republic of letters. In 1802, the *Anthology* was established at Boston. It had a very considerable character from its commencement. It was often interesting, and sometimes learned; at times it assumed a consequential air and manner; but it cannot be said that it had as much weight as a leading journal ought to have had in the country at that time. It took another shape, and a milder character, in the *North American Review,* and has since been a well conducted journal; many times rivaling the first works of European fame; and if an imitation, in some degree, of the *Edinburgh,* it has no servility of thought or tone. The *Edinburgh* was the first of this class of works which are now so popular; and without which the literary world would be at a loss to fix on a course of reading to keep up with the literature of the day. The *Edinburgh Review* began its course as Hercules did his labors, not exactly when he was most wanted, but when his prowess could be most distinctly seen, and noted. The Edinburgh Reviewers course every field of literature, ancient or modern, often-times merely to show their speed and bottom. They come upon the literati as their conquerors and protectors; and if they deny the divine rights of kings in political governments, they assume the office of perpetual dictators in the community of letters. When they commenced their labors, the literary world was indeed overrun with monsters; and they laid aside the sword and the spear, and pursued their prey with club and blunderbuss, from jungle to crag, regardless of trespassing on rice-ground or cane-patch; but it must be acknowledged that they did more good than mischief in their sport. The *Quarterly* followed with as much ferocity, but not with more power, and our country became the object of their direst vengeance. They saw us rising rapidly in the scale of nations, and thought it wise, prudent, and, probably, fair in politics, to check our growth. They had no control over the progress of population, none over the increase of wealth, which was greater than they could imagine, or understand. Nothing was left but to attack our institutions, or manners and habits; and this was done with rancor and profligacy, and without regard to truth. They seized upon worthless tales of travellers, who wrote solely for the purpose of furnishing food for the cormorant appetites of these haters of America; the writers knowing that by such means they would be favorably noticed by the Reviewers, and of course their trash would find a ready market. Part of the people of England were with them from ancient prejudices, a part opposed to them from information and principle; but a still greater part were ignorant of the true state of facts. This evil was only for a season; and instead of disgracing our country, as the Reviewers intended, they raised up a host of able vindicators of American mind and literature, which they little expected. Dwight, sensitive upon this subject, came out in our defence with spirit and effect. And Walsh, a name identified with our literature, appealed to the common sense of the nations who knew us, and manfully repelled the coarse and wicked assaults which had been made upon us. Others, too, were engaged to repel these vile slanders. Much was felt, much was said and written upon the subject at home, and a reaction took place abroad; and in no place was this reaction greater than in England. Our novels, which had not gone farther than a second edition here, there passed through several editions with great éclat. Brown, whose grave could hardly be traced by us, was there ranked among the finest writers of fiction that any age or nation had produced. There are still a few traces of this malignity left, as may be seen in the miserable libel of De Roos, and a slight disposition to keep it alive, as seen in the patronage given him by the British admiralty; but no matter for that, this prejudice is, we pronounce, nearly over and gone. The literature of our country is increasing with a most astonishing rapidity; and knowledge is pouring upon us in its lesser and greater streams from all parts of the land; besides weekly and monthly magazines, which are profusely scattered throughout all our territories, we have several journals in medicine and law; and six established quarterly reviews, extensively read, and well supported. The editors of these quarterly works are pursuing a wise course, in repelling the attacks which have been made upon our literature, rather by exhibiting fine specimens of thought and taste in composition, than by retort and vituperation.

LECTURE XII

. . No country on earth has ever labored harder to make orators than our own. In addition to the fifty-three colleges, where classical educations are given, there are hundreds of minor institutions in which every rule of rhetoric is committed to memory; and every student can give you all the maxims, from Blair, Campbell, and others, necessary to make an orator; can tell you when to extend the arm, balance the body, raise the eyes, quicken the utterance, elevate the voice, and all the other golden rules to build up a Demosthenes or a Chatham. We have had most of the great dramatic actors from Europe to teach us; to those of our mother tongue we have paid great attention, from Hodgkinson to Macready. Fennel came to teach us to read, Ogilvie to speak; and teachers have swarmed upon our shores, and we have followed them, and paid them extravagant sums for years, for instruction; but our eloquence is not much benefited by all this. Our canons of criticism, no doubt, have been multiplied; and our taste grown more fastidious by all their precepts and examples; but for all this, our great orators have not increased in proportion to the number of public speakers. It may be asked, "do you mean to infer that all these rules and criticisms are of no advantage to the youthful aspirant in elocution?" We do not say this; but we do say, that all the rules in the world will not alone make an orator. The seeds of eloquence are sown while on the maternal bosom, and are developed with the first powers of utterance. It is taught in the nursery, in the primary, secondary, as well as in the high schools. It consists in the education of the human voice, together with the human mind. . . .

We have said something of the eloquence of those who reasoned the mass of the people into the opposition to the mother country; but it was said in so general a manner, that we, perhaps, may be indulged in selecting a few of the individuals who were distinguished in those days, and since; not that these we may select are the "twentieth of a tithe" of those who took a part in the debates upon the countless questions of right, and duty, and policy of our proceedings during the time we were growing into a nation; but a few may be brought forward to show the style and manner of the most conspicuous of them. Some of them have lived to the days of the lecturer, and their manner is fresh in his recollection. Of those he never heard, he forms his opinions upon the concurrent testimony of good judges, who have often heard them speak, and the reports of their speeches that have come down to us.

Patrick Henry, of Virginia, was a natural orator, as some gifted speakers are called, whose eloquence seems spontaneous, and is impassioned and free from the trammels of rules. It is said that he was a self-educated man, whose manner was his own, and was blessed with the power of utterance beyond most of those who had been taught in the groves of the academy. He felt deeply and made others feel. His flashes of eloquence gave an electric shock to the audience; and these were managed with great skill, and repeated at his will; or by some sudden transition, he let down his hearers to a common tone of feeling, by the most felicitous illustrations or playful similes. He was, however, more powerful in raising apprehensions than in allaying them. His eloquence was supported by his patriotism, and what in the warmth of debate he said he would do, he followed up in the coolness of reflection; and if not as powerful, was as fearless with his sword as with his tongue. His eloquence was not elaborate, nor his speeches long. His audience easily understood him, and his speech was ended before any part of them were tired of hearing him. His patriotism and his eloquence have had ample justice done them by his learned biographer.   1829

Timothy Flint

(1780-1840)

Born at North Reading, Massachusetts, and graduated from Harvard in 1800, Timothy Flint entered the ministry and preached at Lunenburg, Massachusetts, from 1802 to 1814. From 1815 to 1826, Flint did missionary work in the Ohio and Mississippi Valleys; in 1827 he settled at Cincinnati where he edited the *Western Monthly Magazine* (1827–1830) and wrote several novels, a biography of Daniel Boone (Cincinnati, 1833), and *A History and Geography of the Mississippi Valley*, 2 vols. (Cincinnati, 1832). After 1834, Flint fell ill and spent the rest of his life travelling in the effort to regain his health.

Recollections of the Last Ten Years (Boston, 1826) is a series of twenty-seven letters which recount his adventures in the West. The best known of his novels is *Francis Berrian; or the Mexican Patriot*, 2 vols. (Boston, 1826), one of the early novels of the trans-Mississippi West.

BIBLIOGRAPHY: John E. Kirkpatrick, *Timothy Flint, Pioneer, Missionary, Author, Editor, 1780–1840* (Cleveland). James K. Folsom, *Timothy Flint* (New York, 1965). *Recollections of the Last Ten Years*, ed. C. Hartley Grattan (New York, 1932).

From *Recollections of the Last Ten Years*

LETTER XIII.—ST. LOUIS

I am now near the central point of the great valley of the Mississippi; the largest valley or basin drained by one river, on the earth. From the Allegany ridges eastward, to the dividing ridge of the Chepywan or

Rocky Mountains, from whose eastern declivities flow the waters of the Missouri, on the west, is supposed to be twenty-five hundred miles in a right line, and double that distance, by the courses of the Ohio and Missouri. From the eminences that divide the waters of Red River of the north, Saskashawin and Slave Lake from those of the upper Mississippi, to the gulf of Mexico on the south, is more than three thousand miles. In its width, in its narrowest dimensions, where it converges toward the gulf, from the sources of the Tennessee, to those of Red River of the south, can scarcely be less than two thousand two hundred miles. A keel-boat of forty tons burden can take in its family and its load in the state of New York, and by the Allegany, the Ohio, the Mississippi, and Missouri, land them at the foot of the Stony Mountains; having made, in a continued course, a voyage of greater length than the crossing the Atlantic. It is stated that boats can ascend the "Roche Jaune," or Yellowstone of the Missouri, more than a thousand miles. Boats ascend the Arkansas and Red River, nearly two thousand miles. Boats come with very short portages from Montreal to the upper Mississippi, and I have seen a Mackinaw skiff, carrying five tons, which came from the lakes into the Chicago of Michigan, and from that over a morass, from one end of which run the waters of the Chicago, and from the other those of the Illinois, into the Missouri, without any portage at all. The waters of the morass were found sufficiently deep for her to make her way from the river of the lake, to that of the Mississippi. Boats pass New Madrid, some of which come down the Wabash many hundred miles, before it reaches the Ohio; and others in an opposite direction, down the Tennessee, much farther than the course of the Wabash.

In the spring, one hundred boats have been numbered, that landed in one day at the mouth of the Bayan, at New Madrid. I have strolled to the point on a spring evening, and seen them arriving in fleets. The boisterous gaiety of the hands, the congratulations, the moving picture of life on board the boats, in the numerous animals, large and small, which they carry, their different loads, the evidence of the increasing agriculture of the country above, and more than all, the immense distances which they have already come, and those which they have still to go, afforded to me copious sources of meditation. You can name no point from the numerous rivers of the Ohio and the Mississippi, from which some of these boats have not come. In one place there are boats loaded with planks, from the pine forests of the southwest of New York. In another quarter there are the Yankee notions of Ohio. From Kentucky, pork, flour, whiskey, hemp, tobacco, bagging, and bale-rope. From Tennessee there are the same articles, together with great quantities of cotton. From Missouri and Illinois, cattle and horses, the same articles generally as from Ohio, together with peltry and lead from Missouri. Some boats are loaded with corn in the ear and in bulk; others with barrels of apples and potatoes. Some have loads of cider, and what they call "cider royal," or cider that has been strengthened by boiling or freezing. There are dried fruits, every kind of spirits manufactured in these regions, and in short, the products of the ingenuity and agriculture of the whole upper country of the west. They have come from regions, thousands of miles apart. They have float-ed to a common point of union. The surfaces of the boats cover some acres. Dunghill fowls are fluttering over the roofs, as an invariable ap-pendage. The chanticleer raises his piercing note. The swine utter their cries. The cattle low. The horses trample, as in their stables. There are boats fitted on purpose, and loaded entirely with turkeys, that, having little else to do, gobble most furiously. The hands travel about from boat to boat, make inquiries, and acquaintances, and form alliances to yield mutual assistance to each other, on their descent from this to New Or-leans. After an hour or two passed in this way, they spring on shore to raise the wind in town. It is well for the people of the village, if they do not become riotous in the course of the evening; in which case I have often seen the most summary and strong measures taken. About midnight the uproar is all hushed. The fleet unites once more at Natchez, or New Orleans, and, although they live on the same river, they may, perhaps, never meet each other again on the earth.

Next morning at the first dawn, the bugles sound. Everything in and about the boats, that has life, is in motion. The boats, in half an hour, are all under way. In a little while they have all disappeared, and nothing is seen, as before they came, but the regular current of the river. In passing down the Mississippi, we often see a number of boats lashed and floating together. I was once on board a fleet of eight, that were in this way mov-ing on together. It was a considerable walk, to travel over the roofs of this floating town. On board of one boat they were killing swine. In an-other they had apples, cider, nuts, and dried fruit. One of the boats was a retail or dram shop. It seems that the object in lashing so many boats, had been to barter, and obtain supplies. These confederacies often com-mence in a frolic, and end in a quarrel, in which case the aggrieved party dissolves the partnership by unlashing, and managing his own boat in his own way. While this fleet of boats is floating separately, but each carried by the same current, nearly at the same rate, visits take place from boat to boat in skiffs.

While I was at New Madrid, a large tinner's establishment floated there in a boat. In it all the different articles of tin-ware were manufac-tured and sold by wholesale and retail. There were three large apart-ments, where the different branches of the art were carried on in this floating manufactory. When they had mended all the tin, and vended all that they could sell in one place, they floated on to another. A still more extraordinary manufactory, we were told, was floating down the Ohio, and shortly expected at New Madrid. Aboard this were manufactured axes, scythes, and all other iron tools of this description, and in it horses were shod. In short it was a complete blacksmith's shop of a higher order, and it is said that they jestingly talked of having a trip-hammer worked by a horse power on board. I have frequently seen in this region a dry goods shop in a boat, with its articles very handsomely arranged on shelves. Nor would the delicate hands of the vendor have disgraced the spruce clerk behind our city counters. It is now common to see flat-boats worked by a bucket wheel, and a horse power, after the fashion of steamboat movement. Indeed, every spring brings forth new contrivances of this sort, the result of the farmer's meditations over his winter's fire.

St. Louis is a kind of central point, in this immense valley. From this point, outfits are constantly making to the military posts, and to the remotest regions by the hunters for furs. Boats are also constantly ascending to the lead-mine districts, on the upper Mississippi. From our boat, as we lay in the habor of St. Louis, we could see "The Mandan," as the name of a boat bound far up the Missouri. Another was up for "Prairie du Chien," and the Falls of St. Anthony; another for the highest points of the Illinois; another for the Arkansas; and "The Gumbo," for Natchez and New Orleans.

Consider that the lakes are wedded to the ocean by the New York canal. The Illinois will shortly be with Chicago and Michigan; for it is, for a little while in the spring, partially so by nature. The union of the Ohio with the lakes, on the one hand, and with the tide waters of Virginia, on the other, is not only contemplated, but the labor to effect it is commenced. When these contemplated canals are completed, certainly no country in the world can equal ours in the number, convenience, and extent of its internal water communications.

The advantage of steam-boats, great as it is every where, can no where be appreciated as in this country. The distant points of the Ohio and Mississippi used to be separated from New Orleans by an internal obstruction, far more formidable in the passing, than the Atlantic. If I may use a hard word, they are now brought into *juxtaposition*. To feel what an invention this is for these regions, one must have seen and felt, as I have seen and felt, the difficulty and danger of forcing a boat against the current of these mighty rivers, on which a progress of ten miles in a day, is a good one. Indeed those huge and unwieldy boats, the barges in which a great proportion of the articles from New Orleans used to be transported to the upper country, required twenty or thirty hands to work them. I have seen them day after day, on the lower portions of the Mississippi, where there was no other way of working them up, than carrying out a cable half a mile in length, in advance of the barge, and fastening it to a tree. The hands on board then draw it up to the tree. While this is transacting, another yawl, still in advance of that, has ascended to a higher tree, and made another cable fast to it, to be ready to be drawn upon, as soon as the first is coiled. This is the most dangerous and fatiguing way of all, and six miles advance in a day, is good progress.

It is now refreshing, and imparts a feeling of energy and power to the beholder, to see the large and beautiful steam-boats scudding up the eddies, as though on the wing; and when they have run out the eddy, strike the current. The foam bursts in a sheet quite over the deck. She quivers for a moment with the concussion; and then, as though she had collected her energy, and vanquished her enemy, she resumes her stately march, and mounts against the current, five or six miles an hour. I have traveled in this way for days together, more than a hundred miles in a day, against the current of the Mississippi. The difficulty of ascending, used to be the only circumstance of a voyage that was dreaded in the anticipation. This difficulty now disappears. A family in Pittsburgh wishes to make a social visit to a kindred family on Red River. The trip is but two thousand miles. They all go together; servants, baggage or "plunder," as the phrase is, to any amount. In twelve days they reach the point proposed. Even the return is but a short voyage. Surely the people of this country will have to resist strong temptations, if they do not become a social people. You are invited to a breakfast, at seventy miles' distance. You go on board the passing steam-boat and awake in the morning in season for your appointment. The day will probably come, when the inhabitants of the warm and sickly regions of the lower points of the Mississippi, will take their periodical migrations to the north, with the geese and swans of the gulf, and with them return in the winter.

A sea voyage, after all that can be said in its favor, is a very different thing from all this. The barren and boundless expanse of waters, soon tires upon every eye but a seaman's. I say nothing of fastening tables, and holding fast to beds, or inability to write or to cook. I leave out of sight sea-sickness, and the danger of descending to those sea-green caves of which poetry has so much to say. Here you are always near the shore, always see the green earth, can always eat, write, and sleep undisturbed. You can always obtain cream, fowls, vegetables, fruit, wild game; and in my mind there is no kind of comparison between the comforts and discomforts of a sea and river voyage.

A stranger to this mode of traveling, would find it difficult to describe his impressions upon first descending the Mississippi in one of the better steam-boats. He contemplates the prodigious establishment, with all its fitting of deck common, and ladies' cabin apartments. Over head, about him and below him, all is life and movement. He sees its splendid cabin, richly carpeted, its finishings of mahogany, its mirrors and fine furniture, its bar-room, and sliding-tables, to which eighty passengers can sit down with comfort. The fare is sumptuous, and everything in a style of splendor, order, quiet, and regularity, far exceeding that of taverns in general. You read, you converse, you walk, you sleep, as you choose; for custom has prescribed that everything shall be "sans cérémonie." The varied and verdant scenery shifts around you. The trees, the green islands, have an appearance, as by enchantment, of moving by you. The river-fowl, with their white and extended lines, are wheeling their flight above you.

The sky is bright. The river is dotted with boats above you, beside, and below you. You hear the echo of their bugles reverberating from the woods. Behind the wooded point, you see the ascending column of smoke, rising above the trees, which announces that another steam-boat is approaching you. This moving pageant glides through a narrow passage between an island, thick set with young cottonwoods, so even, so regular, and beautiful that they seem to have been planted for a pleasure ground, and the main shore. As you shoot out again into the broad stream, you come in view of a plantation, with all its busy and cheerful accompaniments. At other times you are sweeping along for many leagues together, where either shore is a boundless and pathless wilderness. And the contrast, which is thus so strongly forced upon the mind, of the highest improvement and the latest invention of art, with the most lonely aspect of a grand but desolate nature,—the most striking and complete assemblage of splendor and comfort, the cheerfulness of a floating hotel, which carries, perhaps, two hundred guests, with a wild and uninhabited forest, one hundred miles in width, the abode only of owls, bears, and noxious animals,—this strong contrast produces, to me at least, something of the same pleasant sensation that is produced by lying down to sleep with the rain pouring on the roof, immediately over head.

LETTER XXVII

. . . I passed two weeks here [Natchitoches], receiving daily invitations to entertainments by the hospitable citizens of this place. The luxury of the table is understood and practiced in great perfection. I was charmed with the singing and playing of two young ladies in this place, the one Spanish, the other American. While here, I witnessed a sad spectacle, which left a deep impression, and which I will take leave to relate. A French Surgeon, of the name of Prevot, who was said to have received a regular education to his profession in France, came here at the age, probably, of thirty-six. He was arrested, treated with gross and unwarrantable indignity, and brought to this town for commitment to jail. He was liberated on a writ of habeas corpus, and conceived a deep purpose of revenge towards the district attorney, who made out the instrument of his commitment. On a certain evening he supped with this gentleman, and after supper walked with him apart, challenged him, as he said, and offered him his choice of weapons. Mr. Mills refused to fight him, and, as he avers, added the epithet *menteur*, which he said, no Frenchman could ever forgive. He drew his dirk, and plunged it into the bosom of Mr. Mills, giving him a wound, of which in a few minutes he expired. Prevot walked deliberately away to the bridge that leads over the river, and was there arrested. He was tried, and condemned sometime in autumn, and had been lying in prison under sentence of death until my arrival. Three days before his execution, I called upon him in prison, and offered him my services as a minister. He enquired if I were a Catholic priest, informing me, that if I came, as he phrased it, with any of the mummery of confession, mass, &c. he wished to have nothing to say to me. I answered, that I was a Protestant. He eagerly rejoined, "vous avez raison donc," adding that he should be glad to see me. He explained that he had been brought up in the school of Voltaire and Delambert, and amidst the storms of the revolution; "a bad kind of discipline," he rejoined, "to make a good Christian." He averred, that he did not repent of his murder, and that under similar circumstances he should repeat the act. I visited him repeatedly, and still found him in the same frame of mind. He requested me to attend him to the gallows. He was executed half a mile from the prison, in the pine woods. A cart with a coffin was brought to the prison, and in the midst of a vast concourse, the poor wretch, after a long confinement in a dark prison, was brought forth to die. He had a fine countenance, was pale and emaciated, and was supposed to be still under the influence of arsenic, by which he had attempted to poison himself the night before. The view of a brilliant sun seemed to have a bewildering effect upon him. I persuaded him to walk rather than ride. He took my arm, and we were a most melancholy pair, the one as pale and feeble from disease as the other was from long confinement and the scene before him. As we ascended the bluffs to the pine woods, he bowed gracefully, and with true French ease, to all that he recognized among the assembled multitudes.

Arrived at the summit of the bluff, from which the pleasant village and a vast extent of delightful scenery were visible, he gave a long and fixed look at the outstretched prospect before him. He then looked up to the sky and the sun. He waved his head, with a kind of convulsive shudder, as he seemed to be taking his final leave of nature. "Ah!" said he, "je suis las du cœur; mais c'est pour la dernière fois." "I am oppressed at heart, but it is for the last time!" When we arrived at the gallows, he remarked, that it was a spectacle terrible to poor, feeble human nature. "But I must finish," said he, and we helped him mount the cart. He then held out his hand and said, "Adieu, ministre!" I requested leave to pray, and prayed, according to his wish, in English, which he did not understand. But he seemed to understand the heart-felt tone of the prayer. When it was finished, he seemed softened, and begged me to say to the people, that he asked the mercy of God, and died in charity with all the world. He then added, with emphatic earnestness, "Adieu, ministre! je vous remercie." He then desired the sheriff to proceed, and remonstrated against longer delay. The moment before the cart was driven from under him, he took out his snuffbox, took in each nostril a large and deliberate pinch of snuff, was returning his snuffbox to his waistcoat pocket, but recollecting that he would have no further use for it, he laid it down on the coffin, intimated that he was ready, and was launched into eternity.

1826

William Ellery Channing
(1780-1842)

William Ellery Channing was born at Newport, Rhode Island, and was graduated from Harvard in 1798. In 1803, he was ordained minister of the Federal Street Church at Boston, a pastorate he held until his death. Channing became involved in the so-called "Unitarian controversy" in 1815, and for the next few years wrote and preached sermons defining the position of Unitarianism. Among his works are *The Moral Argument Against Calvinism* (Boston, 1820), *Sermons and Tracts, including the Analysis of the Character of Napoleon,* and *Remarks on the Life and Writings of John Milton* (Boston, 1828), and several tracts on war and slavery. "Remarks on National Literature," first published as "The Importance and Means of a National Literature," was printed in *The Christian Examiner* (Jan., 1830).

BIBLIOGRAPHY: *The Works of William Ellery Channing* (Boston, 1888). *Correspondence of William Ellery Channing,* ed. Ann L. Le Breton (Boston, 1874). *Memoir of William Ellery Channing,* 3 vols., ed. William H. Channing (Boston, 1848). David P. Edgell, *William Ellery Channing: An Intellectual Portrait* (Boston, 1955). Arthur W. Brown, *William Ellery Channing* (New York, 1962).

From Remarks on National Literature

[Review of a Discourse concerning the Influence of America on the Mind; being the Annual Oration delivered before the American Philosophical Society, at the University in Philadelphia, October 18, 1823. By C. J. Ingersoll.]

. . . We begin with stating what we mean by national literature. We mean the expression of a nation's mind in writing. We mean the production among a people of important works in philosophy, and in the departments of imagination and taste. We mean the contributions of new truths to the stock of human knowledge. We mean the thoughts of profound and original minds, elaborated by the toil of composition, and fixed and made immortal in books. We mean the manifestation of a nation's intellect in the only forms by which it can multiply itself at home, and send itself abroad. We mean that a nation shall take a place, by its authors, among the lights of the world. It will be seen that we include under literature all the writings of superior minds, be the subjects what they may. We are aware that the term is often confined to compositions which relate to human nature and human life; that it is not generally extended to physical science; that mind, not matter, is regarded as its main subject and sphere. But the worlds of matter and mind are too intimately connected to admit of exact partition. All the objects of human thought flow into one another. Moral and physical truths have many bonds and analogies, and, whilst the former are the chosen and noblest themes of literature, we are not anxious to divorce them from the latter, or to shut them up in a separate department. The expression of superior mind in writing we regard, then, as a nation's literature. We regard its gifted men, whether devoted to the exact sciences, to mental and ethical philosophy, to history and legislation, or to fiction and poetry, as forming a noble intellectual brotherhood; and it is for the purpose of quickening all to join their labors for the public good that we offer the present plea in behalf of a national literature. . . .

If we have succeeded in conveying the impressions which we have aimed to make, our readers are now prepared to inquire with interest into the condition and prospects of literature among ourselves. Do we possess, indeed, what may be called a national literature? Have we produced eminent writers in the various departments of intellectual effort? Are our chief resources of instruction and literary enjoyment furnished from ourselves? We regret that the reply to these questions is so obvious. The few standard works which we have produced, and which promise to live, can hardly, by any courtesy, be denominated a national literature. On this point, if marks and proofs of our real condition were needed, we should find them in the current apologies for our deficiencies. Our writers are accustomed to plead in our excuse our youth, the necessities of a newly settled country, and the direction of our best talents to practical life. Be the pleas sufficient or not, one thing they prove, and that is, our consciousness of having failed to make important contributions to the interests of the intellect. We have few names to place by the side of the great names in science and literature on the other side of the ocean. We want those lights which make a country conspicuous at a distance. . . .

We have spoken of the condition of our literature. We now proceed to the consideration of the causes which obstruct its advancement; and we are immediately struck by one so prevalent as to deserve distinct notice. We refer to the common doctrine that we need, in this country, useful knowledge, rather than profound, extensive, and elegant literature, and that this last, if we covet it, may be imported from abroad in such variety and abundance as to save us the necessity of producing it among ourselves. How far are these opinions just? This question we purpose to answer.

That useful knowledge should receive our first and chief care we mean not to dispute. But in our views of utility we may differ from some who take this position. These are those who confine this term to the necessaries and comforts of life, and to the means of producing them. And is it true that we need no knowledge but that which clothes and feeds us? Is it true that all studies may be dispensed with but such as teach us to act on matter, and to turn it to our use? Happily, human nature is too stubborn to yield to this narrow utility. It is interesting to observe how the very mechanical arts, which are especially designed to minister to the necessities and comforts of life, are perpetually passing these limits,—how they disdain to stop at mere convenience. A large and increasing proportion of mechanical labor is given to the gratification of an elegant taste. How simple would be the art of building, if it limited itself to the construction of a comfortable shelter! How many ships should we dismantle, and how many busy trades put to rest, were dress and furniture reduced to the standard of convenience! This "utility" would work a great change in town and country, would level to the dust the wonders of architecture, would annihilate the fine arts, and blot our innumerable beauties which the hand of taste has spread over the face of the earth. Happily, human nature is too strong for the ultilitarian. It cannot satisfy itself with the convenient.

. . . It will be seen from these remarks that utility, with us, has a broad meaning. In truth, we are slow to condemn as useless any researches or discoveries of original and strong minds, even when we discern in them no bearing on any interests of mankind; for all truth is of a prolific nature, and has connections not immediately perceived; and it may be that what we call vain speculations may, at no distant period, link themselves with some new facts or theories, and guide a profound thinker to the most important results. . . .

Let us not be misunderstood. We have no desire to rear in our country a race of pedants, of solemn triflers, of laborious commentators on the mysteries of a Greek accent or a rusty coin. We would have men explore antiquity, not to bury themselves in its dust, but to learn its spirit, and so to commune with its superior minds as to accumulate on the present age the influences of whatever was great and wise in former times. What we want is, that those among us whom God has gifted to comprehend whatever is now known, and to rise to new truths, may find aids and institutions to fit them for their high calling, and may become at once springs of a higher intellectual life to their own country, and joint workers with the great of all nations and times in carrying forward their race. . . .

We next observe—and we think the observation important—that the facility with which we receive the literature of foreign countries, instead of being a reason for neglecting our own, is a strong motive for its cultivation. We mean not to be paradoxical, but we believe that it would be better to admit no books from abroad than to make them substitutes for our own intellectual activity. The more we receive from other countries, the greater the need of an original literature. A people into whose minds the thoughts of foreigners are poured perpetually, needs an energy within itself to resist, to modify this mighty influence, and, without it, will inevitably sink under the worst bondage, will become intellectually tame and enslaved. We have certainly no desire to complete our restrictive system by adding to it a literary nonintercourse law. We rejoice in the increasing intellectual connection between this country and the Old World;

but sooner would we rupture it than see our country sitting passively at the feet of foreign teachers. It were better to have no literature than form ourselves unresistingly on a foreign one. The true sovereigns of a country are those who determine its mind, its modes of thinking, its tastes, its principles; and we cannot consent to lodge this sovereignty in the hands of strangers. A country, like an individual, has dignity and power only in proportion as it is self-formed. There is a great stir to secure to ourselves the manufacturing of our own clothing. We say, let others spin and weave for us, but let them not think for us. A people whose government and laws are nothing but the embodying of public opinion, should jealously guard this opinion against foreign dictation. We need a literature to counteract, and to use wisely the literature which we import. We need an inward power proportionate to that which is exerted on us, as the means of self-subsistence. It is particularly true of a people whose institutions demand for their support a free and bold spirit, that they should be able to subject to a manly and independent criticism whatever comes from abroad. These views seem to us to deserve serious attention. . . .

We now proceed to an argument in favor of native literature, which, if less obvious, is, we believe, not less sound than those now already adduced. We have hitherto spoken of literature as the expression, the communication, of the higher minds in a community. We now add that it does much more than is commonly supposed to form such minds, so that, without it, a people wants one of the chief means of educating or perfecting talent and genius. One of the great laws of our nature, and a law singularly important to social beings, is, that the intellect enlarges and strenthens itself by expressing worthily its best views. In this, as in other respects, it is more blessed to give than to receive. Superior minds are formed, not merely by solitary thought, but almost as much by communication. Great thoughts are never fully possessed till he who has conceived them has given them fit utterance. One of the noblest and most invigorating labors of genius is to clothe its conceptions in clear and glorious forms, to give them existence in other souls. Thus literature creates, as well as manifests, intellectual power, and, without it, the highest minds will never be summoned to the most invigorating action. . . .

We come now to our last—and what we deem a weighty—argument in favor of a native literature. We desire and would cherish it, because we hope from it important aids to the cause of truth and human nature. We believe that a literature, springing up in this new soil, would bear new fruits, and, in some respects, more precious fruits, than are elsewhere produced. We know that our hopes may be set down to the account of that national vanity which, with too much reason, is placed by foreigners among our besetting sins. But we speak from calm and deliberate conviction. We are inclined to believe that, as a people, we occupy a position from which the great subjects of literature may be viewed more justly than from those which most other nations hold. Undoubtedly we labor under disadvantages. We want the literary apparatus of Europe,—her libraries, her universities, her learned institutions, her race of professed scholars, her spots consecrated by the memory of sages, and a thousand stirring associations which hover over ancient nurseries of learning. But the mind is not a local power. Its spring is within itself, and, under the inspiration of liberal and high feeling, it may attain and worthily express nobler truth than outward helps could reveal.

The great distinction of our country is, that we enjoy some peculiar advantages for understanding our own nature. Man is the great subject of literature, and juster and profounder views of man may be expected here than elsewhere. In Europe, political and artificial distinctions have, more or less, triumphed over and obscured our common nature. In Europe, we meet kings, nobles, priests, peasants. How much rarer is it to meet *men;* by which we mean human beings conscious of their own nature, and conscious of the utter worthlessness of all outward distinctions compared with what is treasured up in their own souls. Man does not value himself as man. It is for his blood, his rank, or some artificial distinction, and not for the attributes of humanity, that he holds himself in respect. The institutions of the Old World all tend to throw obscurity over what we most need to know, and that is, the worth and claims of a human being. We know that great improvements in this respect are going on abroad. Still the many are too often postponed to the few. The mass of men are regarded as instruments to work with, as materials to be shaped for the use of their superiors. That consciousness of our own nature which contains, as a germ, all nobler thoughts, which teaches us at once self-respect and respect for others, and which binds us to God by filial sentiment and hope,—this has been repressed, kept down by establishments founded in force; and literature, in all its departments, bears, we think, the traces of this inward degradation. We conceive that our position favors a juster and profounder estimate of human nature. We mean not to boast, but there are fewer obstructions to that moral consciousness, that consciousness of humanity, of which we have spoken. Man is not hidden from us by so many disguises as in the Old World. The essential equality of all human beings, founded on the possession of a spiritual, progressive, immortal nature, is, we hope, better understood; and nothing more than this single conviction is needed to work the mightiest changes in every province of human life and of human thought.

We have stated what seems to us our most important distinction. But our position has other advantages. The mere circumstance of its being a new one gives reason to hope for some new intellectual activity, some fresher views of nature and life. We are not borne down by the weight of antiquated institutions, time-hallowed abuses, and the remnants of feudal barbarism. The absence of a religious establishment is an immense gain, as far as originality of mind is in question; for an establishment, however advantageous in other respects, is, by its nature, hostile to discovery and progress. To keep the mind where it is, to fasten the notions of one age on all future time, is its aim and proper business; and if it happened, as has generally been the case, to grow up in an age of strife and passion, when, as history demonstrates, the church was overrun with error, it cannot but perpetuate darkness and mental bondage. Among us, intellect, though far from being free, has broken some of the chains of other countries, and is more likely, we conceive, to propose to itself its legitimate object, truth,—everlasting and universal truth.

We have no thought of speaking contemptuously of the literature of the Old World. It is our daily nutriment. We feel our debt to be immense to the glorious company of pure and wise minds which in foreign lands have bequeathed us in writing their choicest thoughts and holiest feelings. Still, we feel that all existing literature has been produced under influences which have necessarily mixed with it much error and corruption; and that the whole of it ought to pass, and must pass, under rigorous review. For example, we think that the history of the human race is to be rewritten. Men imbued with the prejudices which thrive under aristocracies and state religions cannot understand it. Past ages, with their great events and great men, are to undergo, we think, a new trial, and to yield new results. It is plain that history is already viewed under new aspects, and we believe that the true principles for studying and writing it are to be unfolded here, at least as rapidly as in other countries. It seems to us that in literature an immense work is yet to be done. The most interesting questions to mankind are yet in debate. Great principles are yet to be settled in criticism, in morals, in politics; and, above all, the true character of religion is to be rescued from the disguises and corruptions of ages. We want a reformation. We want a literature, in which genius will pay supreme if not undivided homage to truth and virtue; in which the childish admiration of what has been called greatness will give place to a wise moral judgment; which will breathe reverence for the mind, and elevating thoughts of God. The part which this country is to bear in this great intellectual reform we presume not to predict. We feel, however, that, if true to itself, it will have the glory and happiness of giving new impulses to the human mind. This is our cherished hope. We should have no heart to encourage native literature, did we not hope that it would become instinct with a new spirit. We cannot admit the thought that this country is to be only a repetition of the Old World. We delight to believe that God, in the fulness of time, has brought a new continent to light, in order that the human mind should move here with a new freedom, should frame new social institutions, should explore new paths, and reap new harvests. We are accustomed to estimate nations by their creative energies; and we shall blush for our country if, in circumstances so peculiar, original, and creative, it shall satisfy itself with a passive reception and mechanical reiteration of the thoughts of strangers.

We have now completed our remarks on the importance of a native literature. The next great topic is, the means of producing it. And here our limits forbid us to enlarge; yet we cannot pass it over in silence. A primary and essential means of the improvement of our literature is, that, as a people, we should feel its value, should desire it, should demand it, should encourage it, and should give it a hearty welcome. It will come if called for; and, under this conviction, we have now labored to create a want for it in the community. We say that we must call for it; by which we mean not merely that we must invite it by good wishes and kind words, but must make liberal provision for intellectual education. We must enlarge our literary institutions, secure more extensive and profound teaching, and furnish helps and resources to men of superior talent for continued laborious research. As yet, intellectual labor, devoted to a thorough investigation and a full development of great subjects, is almost unknown among us; and, without it, we shall certainly rear few lasting monuments of thought. We boast of our primary schools. We want universities worthy of the name, where a man of genius and literary zeal may possess himself of all that is yet known, and may strengthen himself by intercourse with kindred minds. We know it will be said that we cannot afford these. But it is not so. We are rich enough for ostentation, for intemperance, for luxury. We can lavish millions on fashion, on furniture, on dress, on our palaces, on our pleasures; but we have nothing to spend for the mind. Where lies our poverty? In the purse, or in the soul?

We have spoken of improved institutions as essential to an improved literature. We beg, however, not to be misunderstood, as if these were invested with a creating power, or would necessarily yield the results which we desire. They are the means, not causes, of advancement. Literature depends on individual genius, and this, though fostered, cannot be created by outward helps. No human mechanism can produce original thought. After all the attempts to explain by education the varieties of intellect, we are compelled to believe that minds, like all the other products of nature, have original and indestructible differences; that they are not exempted from that great and beautiful law which joins with strong resemblances as strong diversities; and, of consequence, we believe that the men who are to be the lights of the world bring with them their commission and power from God. Still, whilst institutions cannot create, they may and do unfold genius; and, for want of them, great minds often slumber or run to waste, whilst a still larger class, who want genius, but possess admirable powers, fail of that culture through which they might enjoy and approach their more gifted brethren.

A people, as we have said, are to give aid to literature by founding wise and enlarged institutions. They may do much more. They may exert a nobler patronage. By cherishing in their own breasts the love of truth, virtue, and freedom, they may do much to nurse and kindle genius in its favored possessors. There is a constant reaction between a community and the great minds which spring up within it, and they form one an-

other. In truth, great minds are developed more by the spirit and character of the people to which they belong than by all other causes. Thus, a
free spirit, a thirst for new and higher knowledge in a community, does
infinitely more for literature than the most splendid benefactions under
despotism. A nation under any powerful excitement becomes fruitful of
talent. Among a people called to discuss great questions, to contend for
great interests, to make great sacrifices for the public weal, we always
find new and unsuspected energies of thought brought out. A mercenary,
selfish, luxurious sensual people, toiling only to secure the pleasures of
sloth, will often communicate their own softness and baseness to the superior minds which dwell among them. In this impure atmosphere the
celestial spark burns dim; and well will it be if God's great gift of genius
be not impiously prostituted to lust and crime. . . .

From these remarks it will be seen that our chief hopes of an improved
literature rest on our hopes of an improved religion. From the prevalent
theology which has come down to us from the dark ages, we hope nothing. It has done its best. All that can grow up under its sad shade has already been brought forth. It wraps the divine nature and human nature
in impenetrable gloom. It overlays Christianity with technical, arbitrary
dogmas. True faith is of another lineage. It comes from the same source
with reason, conscience, and our best affections, and is in harmony with
them all. True faith is essentially a moral conviction; a confidence in the
reality and immutableness of moral distinctions; a confidence in disinterested virtue or in spiritual excellence as the supreme good; a confidence
in God as its fountain and Almighty Friend, and in Jesus Christ as
having lived and died to breathe it into the soul; a confidence in its
power, triumphs, and immortality; a confidence, through which outward
changes, obstructions, disasters, sufferings, are overcome, or rather made
instruments of perfection. Such a faith, unfolded freely and powerfully,
must "work mightily" on the intellect as well as on practice. By revealing
to us the supreme purpose of the Creator, it places us, as it were, in the
center of the universe, from which the harmonies, true relations, and
brightest aspect of things are discerned. It unites calmness and enthusiasm,
and the concord of these seemingly hostile elements is essential to the full
and healthy action of the creative powers of the soul. It opens the eye to
beauty and the heart to love. Literature, under this influence, will become more ingenuous and single-hearted; will penetrate farther into the
soul; will find new interpretations of nature and life; will breathe a martyr's love of truth, tempered with a never-failing charity; and, whilst
sympathizing with all human suffering, will still be pervaded by a healthful cheerfulness, and will often break forth in tones of irrepressible joy,
responsive to that happiness which fills God's universe.

1830

VERSE

Thomas Odiorne
(1769-1851)

Thomas Odiorne, a bookseller in Exeter, New Hampshire, following his graduation from Dartmouth in 1791, was a Boston businessman from 1800 to 1811, and later an iron manufacturer in Malden, Massachusetts. *The Progress of Refinement, A Poem in Three Books* (Boston, 1792) and *Moral Evil No Accident* (Boston, 1821) both included other miscellaneous verse.

BIBLIOGRAPHY: Leon Howard, "Thomas Odiorne: An American Predecessor of Wordsworth," *Amer. Lit.,* X (1939), 417–436.

From *The Progress of Refinement*

BOOK I

INFLUENCE OF NATURE

. . . The scenes of nature, whether regular
Or wild, or gay or gloomy; whether robed
In wintry mourning, or in vernal green;
In leaves of vegetable life deprived,
By frost discolored; or in foliage   5
All languishing in summer heat; when viewed
Descriptive, as the year revolves, have power,
In turn, to move, have efficacious power,
To heighten pleasure by the touch of sense.
   On every mind the effects of images   10
Are similar; but happier as the taste
Refines; and different as the different scenes.
The prospects various, nature shows, appear
Peculiarly contrived, and fitly ranged
In contrast, as to suit the intellect   15
Of man, and move him with surprising power.

The daring precipice, the rapid stream,
The sudden lapse of waters, headlong prone,
And the sublimity of objects, seize
At once the soul, arrest it from itself,   20
And far more violent sensations prompt,
Than the slow-rising eminence, the rill
Symphonious tinkling, or less striking scenes.
Dissimilar emotions they produce,
Which, singly viewed, touch all mankind alike;   25
Yet do not equally move all; but strike
With double force the mind, of taste improved. . . .

BOOK II

INFLUENCE OF THE FINE ARTS

. . . The thoughts and exercises, prevalent
In man, form the complexion of his powers,
And give to character its general traits.
The mind, that most the beautiful admires
In prospect; that delights in gentler scenes,   5
Where, in sweet graces, delicacy shines;
That at the softer strains of melody,
Feels finer charms, is genuinely formed
For friendship's clime, and for the sympathies,
The tender sympathies of nuptial life.   10
    Beauty, thou paragon of nature! all
Thy features, singularly fair, display
Attractions, which enkindle flames divine.
A cherished fondness for thy pleasing train,
Sweetness, simplicity, and gaiety,   15
Thy favorite graces, with a love to scan,
Minutely, thy perfections, and admire,
In every shape, thy image, indicates
A mind, complexioned with refinement nice,
Of delicate sensations, and a heart   20
Trained to the gentler feelings. Where thy charms
And lineaments are seen, they operate
To instill their magic through the partial breast.
Whoever cherishes thy influence sweet,
Retains thy fine impressions, and becomes   25
Engaging, pleasing, delicate like thee.
Engaging in demeanor, delicate
In sentiment, and pleasing in the traits,
Humane, of genius, character, and heart.

But the sublime, with magnitude august   30
Endowed, of wondrous power to captivate,
Darting sometimes chill terror through the soul,
Different effects produces. It inspires
With dignity and nobler turn the thought.
The mind, conversant with its scenes, expands   35
To vast designs, with enterprising acts,
Seeks daring ends, and, rather than the abodes,
Endearing of connubial life, prefers
Heroic virtue, scorns the frowns of war,
Danger provokes, encounters hardy toils,   40
And all to gain the palm, or find a grave,
That fame deems glorious. Magnanimity
To acquire, and to maintain a temper calm,
In the vicissitudes of changeful fate,
Prosperous or sad, converse with the sublime.   45
Cherish its inspirations in thy breast,
And it will stamp its nobler image there.
    Still, other prospects, scenes of novelty,
To sweet sensations wake the mind of man,
And stimulate in search of knowledge, new   50
And wondrous. Geniuses inquisitive
The strange and marvelous admire, and take
Delight peculiar, to investigate
The secret springs of ingenuity,
In human nature, actions, and effects.   55
    Thus, by the different prospects we behold,
Emotions different, in the breast, are raised;
And an attachment to peculiar sights
Distinguishes the genius and the heart.
To impressions of external images   60
Exposed, man feels their energetic power,
And, with partiality for favorite scenes,
Cherished in early youth, imbibes their stamp,
And genial tincture. His identic turn
Of mind, of manners, and affections, bears   65
A likeness to the livery they assume.
    But other movements in the human breast,
Are roused to exercise, beside those caused
By prospect. The dissocial passions there,
And social, are predominant in turn,   70
As moral causes vex or please the mind.
With rational sense endowed, from falsehood man
Distinguishes the truth, and actions right
From wrong; propriety in inference

Discerns; and his esteem of social worth,   75
Of actions virtuous; and dislike to vice,
Sanctions with passion. When the suppliant hand
Of injured innocence bespeaks its wrong,
And insolence and cruelty appear,
Can anger slumber in the feeling breast?   80
Where is the generous but would lend relief?
Or when benevolence and virtue kind
Confer their favors, liberal, on mankind,
Cherish and bless, what bosom is not warmed?
The mind of moral excellence possessed,   85
Of loveliness, humanity, and truth,
The social passions claim of kindred souls.
But the deformities of vice, disgust
Excite in every amiable mind.
All moral actions cause dislike or love.   90
    Emotion is the effect of things impressed,
The pleasures of perception: and the sweets
Of scenery, the vast magnificence
Of objects striking, and the novelty
Of curious unfamiliar images,   95
United with the liveliness of view,
Determine its degree of pleasantry.
But passion is desire. The cordial glow
Of approbation, followed by a wish
Of goodness; or aversion's vengeful flame,   100
Mark its complexion. By its vicious cause
Or virtuous, is its kind and nature known.
'Tis moral evil prompts to exercise
The passions, turbulent, in human minds:
Which, when let loose, unduly bridled, cause   105
Confusions dreadful in the mental world,
Like those, by warring elements produced,
Wide-spreading desolation o'er the globe.
But social passions of a gentler mould,
Resemble summer with its genial warmth   110
Prolific, brilliancy, and tranquil skies.
    As man more fondly cherishes a love
Of scenes, which sweetly ravish and exalt,
More perfect grows the standard of fine arts.
Genius' warm efforts skillfully succeed,   115
And give them happier influence o'er the mind.
As taste improves, susceptibility
Of beauty, elegance, and harmony
Increases, and the emotions are possessed

Of livelier mood to please: and while, with them,   120
The socal feelings in refinement vie;
Dissocial passions lose their rougher sway,
And grow more mild, pacific, and humane.
    Reared by ingenious man whose taste improved
Conducts to pomp of thought, to pleasures fine,   125
And elegance of life, the liberal arts
Thus beam their lavish honors. They diffuse
Their charmful influence o'er the mental powers,
Sweet as the spicy gales, all hovering round
With recent coolness, and allure the mind,   130
Auspicious, from its rustic mood. They quell
Its stern ferocity; and, by their charms,
They soften and refine. 'Tis not for thought
Uncultured, nor for unharmonious sounds,
To harmonize the passions, or beguile,   135
Into the maze of musical delight,
The finer ear. But when the mind expands,
And fairer genius blossoms, human works
Receive the touch of beauty, elegance,
And power, like nature's scenes, to move; to inspire   140
Emotions delicate, sublime, or rare.
Then thought refined can sweetly harmonize
The passions, and well modulated voice,
Into the maze of musical delight,
The finer ear beguile. Man then, elate,   145
Prides in refinement; and *society*
Is *high, polite,* and *happy.* Far emerged
From rudeness, with benevolence' brightening ray
His heart distends; the social passions rule
The breast; and virtue, generous virtue reigns.   150

                                    1792

Robert Treat Paine, Jr.
(1773-1811)

Robert Treat Paine, Jr., a graduate of Harvard in 1792, was an editor, writer of occasional verse, and Master of Ceremonies at the Boston Theater. From 1802 to 1809, Paine practiced law in Boston. Most of his work was occasional verse.

BIBLIOGRAPHY: Charles Prentiss, *The Works in Verse and Prose of the Late Robert Treat Paine, Jr.* (Boston, 1812), with biographical sketch. Michael L. Lasser, "Thomas Paine and Robert Treat Paine: A Case of Mistaken Identity," *Jour. of Rutgers U. Lib.,* XXV (1962), 24–27.

Ode: Adams and Liberty

*Written for, and sung at the fourth Anniversary of the Massachusetts
Charitable Fire Society, 1798.*

Ye sons of Columbia, who bravely have fought,
  For those rights, which unstained from your Sires had descended,
May you long taste the blessings your valor has bought,
  And your sons reap the soil which their fathers defended.
      'Mid the reign of mild Peace,   5
      May your nation increase,
With the glory of Rome, and the wisdom of Greece;
  And ne'er shall the sons of Columbia be slaves,
  While the earth bears a plant, or the sea rolls its waves.

In a clime, whose rich vales feed the marts of the world,   10
  Whose shores are unshaken by Europe's commotion,
The trident of Commerce should never be hurled,
  To incense the legitimate powers of the ocean.
      But should pirates invade,
      Though in thunder arrayed,   15
Let your cannon declare the free charter of trade.
      For ne'er shall the sons, &c.

The fame of our arms, of our laws the mild sway,
  Had justly ennobled our nation in story,
'Till the dark clouds of faction obscured our young day,   20
  And enveloped the sun of American glory.
      But let traitors be told,
      Who their country have sold,
And bartered their God for his image in gold,
      That ne'er will the sons, &c.   25

While France her huge limbs bathes recumbent in blood,
  And Society's base threats with wide dissolution;
May Peace like the dove, who returned from the flood,
  Find an ark of abode in our mild constitution.
      But though Peace is our aim,
      Yet the boon we disclaim,   30
If bought by our Sov'reignty, Justice or Fame.
      For ne'er shall the sons, &c.

'Tis the fire of the flint, each American warms;
  Let Rome's haughty victors beware of collision,   35
Let them bring all the vassals of Europe in arms,

We're a world by ourselves, and disdain a division.
    While with patriot pride,
    To our laws we're allied,
No foe can subdue us, no faction divide.   40
    For ne'er shall the sons, &c.

Our mountains are crowned with imperial oak;
    Whose roots, like our liberties, ages have nourished;
But long e'er our nation submits to the yoke,
    Not a tree shall be left on the field where it flourished.   45
    Should invasion impend,
    Every grove would descend,
From the hill-tops, they shaded, our shores to defend.
    For ne'er shall the sons, &c.

Let our patriots destroy Anarch's pestilent worm;   50
    Lest our Liberty's growth should be checked by corrosion;
Then let clouds thicken round us; we heed not the storm;
    Our realm fears no shock, but the earth's own explosion.
    Foes assail us in vain,
    Though their fleets bridge the main,   55
For our altars and laws with our lives we'll maintain.
    For ne'er shall the sons, &c.

Should the Tempest of War overshadow our land,
    Its bolts could ne'er rend Freedom's temple asunder;
For, unmoved, at its portal, would Washington stand,   60
    And repulse, with his Breast, the assaults of the thunder!
    His sword, from the sleep
    Of its scabbard would leap,
And conduct, with its point, ev'ry flash to the deep!
    For ne'er shall the sons, &c.   65

Let Fame to the world sound America's voice;
    No intrigues can her sons from their government sever;
Her pride is her Adams; her laws are his choice,
    And shall flourish, till Liberty slumbers forever.
    Then unite heart and hand,   70
    Like Leonidas' band,
And swear to the God of the ocean and land;
    That ne'er shall the sons of Columbia be slaves,
    While the earth bears a plant, or the sea rolls its waves.

1798

Richard Henry Wilde

(1789-1847)

Irish-born Richard Henry Wilde was a lawyer, an Attorney General of Georgia, and served five terms in the United States Congress. "My Life Is Like a Summer Rose" appeared in the *Analectic Magazine* (1819), and "To the Mocking-Bird" in *Hesperia: A Poem,* published posthumously in 1867.

BIBLIOGRAPHY: Edd W. Parks, "Richard Henry Wilde on the Making of Poetry," *Tenn. Studies in Lit.,* III (1958), 73–81. Nathalia Wright, "The Italian Son of Richard Henry Wilde," *Ga. Hist. Quart.,* XLIII (1959), 419–427. *DAB.*

Stanzas

My life is like the summer rose,
    That opens to the morning sky,
But, ere the shades of evening close,
    Is scattered on the ground—to die!
Yet on the rose's humble bed   5
The sweetest dews of night are shed,
As if she wept the waste to see—
But none shall weep a tear for me!

My life is like the autumn leaf
    That trembles in the moon's pale ray: 10
Its hold is frail—its date is brief,
    Restless—and soon to pass away!
Yet, ere that leaf shall fall and fade,
The parent tree will mourn its shade,
The winds bewail the leafless tree—   15
But none shall breathe a sigh for me!

My life is like the prints, which feet
    Have left on Tampa's desert strand;
Soon as the rising tide shall beat,
    All trace will vanish from the sand;   20
Yet, as if grieving to efface
All vestige of the human race,
On that lone shore loud moans the sea—
But none, alas! shall mourn for me![1]   1819

[1] Final line of *Analectic Magazine* text reads: "But none shall e'er lament for me."

John Pierpont
(1785-1866)

John Pierpont, an 1804 Yale graduate, abandoned law to study for the ministry; in 1819 he was ordained pastor of the Hollis Street Church, Boston. His work includes *The Portrait* (Boston, 1812), *Airs of Palestine* (Baltimore, 1816), *Airs of Palestine and Other Poems* (Boston, 1840), and *The Anti-Slavery Poems of*

John Pierpont (Boston, 1843).

BIBLIOGRAPHY: A. A. Ford, *John Pierpont, a Biographical Sketch* (Boston, 1909). Abe Ravitz, "John Pierpont and the Federalist Muse in Essex County," *Essex County Hist. Col.*, XCVI (1960), 140–148.

Warren's Address to the American Soldiers

Stand! the ground's your own, my braves!
Will ye give it up to slaves?
Will ye look for greener graves?
   Hope ye mercy still?
What's the mercy despots feel?   5
Hear it in that battle-peal!
Read it on yon bristling steel!
   Ask it,—ye who will.

Fear ye foes who kill for hire!
Will ye to your homes retire?   10
Look behind you! they're afire!
   And, before you, see
Who have done it!—From the vale
On they come!—And will ye quail?—
Leaden rain and iron hail   15
   Let their welcome be!

In the God of battles trust!
Die we may,—and die we must;—
But, O, where can dust to dust
   Be consign'd so well,   20
As where Heaven its dews shall shed
On the martyr'd patriot's bed,
And the rocks shall raise their head,
   Of his deeds to tell!

1840

James Gates Percival

(1795-1856)

A physician, geologist, and journalist, James Gates Percival received his B.A. from Yale in 1815, and his M.D. there in 1820. Failing at medicine, Percival edited the *Connecticut Herald* and taught chemistry at West Point. Among his works are *Poems* (New Haven, 1821), *Clio I and II* (Charleston and New Haven, 1822), *Poems* (N.Y., 1823), *Clio III* (N.Y., 1827), and *The Dream of a Day, and Other Poems* (New Haven, 1843).

BIBLIOGRAPHY: L. W. Fitch, ed. *The Poetical Works of James Gates Percival* (Boston, 1859), with biographical sketch. J. H. Ward, *The Life and Letters of James Gates Percival* (1866). James R. Lowell, *My Study Window* (Boston, 1913), pp. 178–192. Harry R. Warfel, ed. *Uncollected Letters of James Gates Percival* (Gainesville, Fla., 1959).

Spring

Again the infant flowers of Spring
Call thee to sport on thy rainbow wing—
Spirit of Beauty! the air is bright
With the boundless flow of thy mellow light;
The woods are ready to bud and bloom,   5
And are weaving for Summer their quiet gloom;
The turfed brook reflects, as it flows,
The tips of the half-unopen'd rose,
And the early bird, as he carols free,
Sings to his little love, and thee.   10

See how the clouds, as they fleetly pass,
Throw their shadowy veil on the darkening grass;
And the pattering showers and stealing dews,
With their starry gems and skyey hues,
From the oozy meadow, that drinks the tide,   15
To the shelter'd vale on the mountain side,
Wake to a new and fresher birth
The tenderest tribes of teeming earth,
And scatter with light and dallying play
Their earliest flowers on the Zephyr's way.   20

He comes from the mountain's piny steep,
For the long boughs bend with a silent sweep;

And his rapid steps have hurried o'er
The grassy hills to the pebbly shore;
And now, on the breast of the lonely lake,   25
The waves in silvery glances break;
Like a short and quickly rolling sea,
When the gale first feels its liberty,
And the flakes of foam, like coursers, run,
Rejoicing beneath the vertical sun.   30

He has cross'd the lake, and the forest heaves,
To the sway of his wings, its billowy leaves,
And the downy tufts of the meadow fly
In snowy clouds, as he passes by,
And softly beneath his noiseless tread   35
The odorous spring-grass bends its head;
And now he reaches the woven bower,
Where he meets his own beloved flower,
And gladly his wearied limbs repose
In the shade of the newly-opening rose.   40

                                                    1827

The Coral Grove

Deep in the wave is a coral grove,
Where the purple mullet, and gold-fish rove,
Where the sea-flower spreads its leaves of blue,
That never are wet with falling dew,
But in bright and changeful beauty shine,   5
Far down in the green and glassy brine.
The floor is of sand, like the mountain drift,
And the pearl shells spangle the flinty snow;
From coral rocks the sea plants lift
Their boughs, where the tides and billows flow;   10
The water is calm and still below,
For the winds and waves are absent there,
And the sands are bright as the stars that glow
In the motionless fields of upper air:
There with its waving blade of green,   15
The sea-flag streams through the silent water,
And the crimson leaf of the dulse is seen
To blush, like a banner bathed in slaughter:
There with a light and easy motion,
The fan-coral sweeps through the clear deep sea;   20

And the yellow and scarlet tufts of ocean
Are bending like corn on the upland lea:
And life, in rare and beautiful forms,
Is sporting amid those bowers of stone,
And is safe, when the wrathful spirit of storms,   25
Has made the top of the waves his own:
And when the ship from his fury flies,
Where the myriad voices of ocean roar,
When the wind-god frowns in the murky skies,
And demons are waiting the wreck on shore;   30
Then far below in the peaceful sea,
The purple mullet, and gold-fish rove,
Where the waters murmur tranquilly,
Through the bending twigs of the coral grove.

                         1822

Edward Coote Pinkney
(1802–1828)

A midshipman in the United States Navy from 1815 to 1822, Edward Coote Pinkney resigned his commission to study law in Baltimore. Unsuccessful as a lawyer, he edited briefly *The Marylander. Rodolph, A Fragment* (Baltimore, 1823) and *Poems* (Baltimore, 1825) were both admired by Poe.

BIBLIOGRAPHY: T. O. Mabbott and F. L. Pleadwell, *The Life and Works of Edward Coote Pinkney* (New York, 1926).

A Health

I fill this cup to one made up of loveliness alone,
A woman, of her gentle sex the seeming paragon;
To whom the better elements and kindly stars have given,
A form so fair, that, like the air, 't is less of earth than heaven.

Her every tone is music's own, like those of morning birds,   5
And something more than melody dwells ever in her words;
The coinage of her heart are they, and from her lips each flows
As one may see the burthen'd bee forth issue from the rose.

Affections are as thoughts to her, the measure of her hours;
Her feelings have the fragrancy, the freshness, of young flowers;   10
And lovely passions, changing oft, so fill her, she appears
The image of themselves by turns,—the idol of past years!

Of her bright face one glance will trace a picture on the brain,
And of her voice in echoing hearts a sound must long remain,
But memory such as mine of her so very much endears,   15
When death is nigh my latest sigh will not be life's but hers.

I fill this cup to one made up of loveliness alone,
A woman, of her gentle sex the seeming paragon—
Her health! and would on earth there stood some more of such a frame,
That life might be all poetry, and weariness a name.   20

                                                       1825

Song

    We break the glass, whose sacred wine
        To some beloved health we drain,
    Lest future pledges, less divine,
        Should e'er the hallow'd toy profane;
    And thus I broke a heart that poured   5
        Its tide of feeling out for thee,
    In draughts, by after-times deplored,
        Yet dear to memory.

    But still the old impassion'd ways
        And habits of my mind remain,   10
    And still unhappy light displays
        Thine image chamber'd in my brain.
    And still it looks as when the hours
        Went by like flights of singing birds,
    On that soft chain of spoken flowers,   15
        And airy gems, thy words.

                                      1825

Thomas Green Fessenden

(1771-1837)

Poet, politician, editor, and lawyer, Thomas Green Fessenden graduated from Dartmouth in 1796. "The Country Lovers; or Jonathan's Courtship" appeared as a broadside in 1795; other works include *Terrible Tractoration* (London, 1803), *Original Poems* (London, 1804; Philadelphia, 1806), *Democracy Unveiled* (Boston, 1805), and *The Ladies Monitor* (Brattleboro, Vt., 1818). From 1822 until his death, he edited the *New England Farmer* (Boston).

BIBLIOGRAPHY: Porter Gale Perrin, *The Life and Works of Thomas Green Fessenden, 1771–1837*, in *Maine University Studies*, Sec. Ser., No. 4 (Orono, Me., 1925).

The Country Lovers

or, Mr. Jonathan Jolthead's Courtship with Miss Sally Snapper: an excellent New Song, said to be written by its author; And really founded on fact. Tune—"Yankee Doodle."

A merry tale I will rehearse,
    As ever you did hear, sir,
How Jonathan set out, so fierce,
    To see his dearest dear, sir.

> Yankee doodle, keep it up,   5
>   Yankee doodle dandy,
> Mind the music—mind the step,
>   And with the girls be handy.[1]

His father gave him bran new suit,
    And money, sir, in plenty,   10
Besides a prancing nag to boot,
    When he was one-and-twenty.

Moreover, sir, I'd have you know,
    That he had got some knowledge,
Enough for common use, I trow,   15
    But had not been at college.

---

[1] Yankee doodle, a ludicrous musical air, which I believe was first invented by the English, in derision of the Americans, whom they styled "Yankees." The Americans frequently wrote ludicrous songs to this tune. This chorus is quoted from a song, written, I believe, in Boston. [All notes in this selection are Fessenden's.]

A hundred he could count, 'tis said,
    And in the bible read, sir,
And by good Christian parents bred,
    Could even say the creed, sir.   20

He'd been to school to Master Drawl,
    To spell a-bom-in-a-ble,
And when he miss'd, he had to crawl,
    Straight under master's table.

One day his mother said to him,   25
    "My darling son, come here,
Come fix you up, so neat and trim,
    And go a courting, dear."

"Why, what the deuce does mother want?
    I snigs—I *daresn't* go;   30
I shall get funn'd—and then—plague on't
    Folks will laugh at me so!"

"Pho! pho! fix up, a courting go,
    To see the deacon's Sarah,
Who'll have a hundred pound, you know,   35
    As soon as she does marry."

Then Jonathan, in best array,
    Mounted his dappled nag, sir;
But trembled, sadly, all the way,
    Lest he should get the bag, sir.   40

He mutter'd as he rode along,
    Our Jotham overheard, sir,
And if 'twill jingle in my song,
    I'll tell you every word, sir.

"I wonder mother 'll make me go,   45
    Since girls I am afraid of;
I never know'd, nor want to know,
    What sort of stuff they're made of.

"A wife would make good housen stuff,[2]
    If she were downright clever,
And Sal would suit me well enough,   50
    If she would let me have her.

---

[2] *Housen* is a corruption for household.

"But then, I shan't know what to say,[3]
    When we are left together,
I'd rather lie in stack of hay,   55
    In coldest winter weather."

He reach'd the house, as people say,
    Not far from eight o'clock, sir;
And Joel hollow'd "in, I say,"
    As soon as he did knock, sir.   60

He made of bows, 'twixt two and three,
    Just as his mother taught him,
All which were droll enough to see:
    You'd think the cramp had caught him.

At length came in the deacon's Sal   65
    From milking at the barn, sir;
And faith she is as good a gal[4]
    As ever twisted yarn, sir.

For she knows all about affairs,
    Can wash, and bake, and brew, sir,[5]   70
Sing "Now I lay me," say her prayers,
    And make a pudding too, sir.

To Boston market she has been
    On horse, and in a wagon,
And many pretty things has seen,   75
    Which every one can't brag on.

She's courted been, by many a lad,
    And knows how sparking's done, sir,
With Jonathan she was right glad,
    To have a little fun, sir.   80

The ladies all, as I should guess,
    And many a lady's man, sir,
Would wish to know about her dress;
    I'll tell them all I can, sir.

---

[3] "A courting I went to my love,
      Who is fairer than roses in May;
    And when I got to her, by Jove,
      The devil a word could I say."
                See *An Old English Comedy*.
[4] *Gal* is, in New England, the vulgar, pronunciation of the word *Girl*.
[5] Most of the householders in New England have their washing, baking, and brewing
done within their own precincts. A young lady who does not understand these branches
of business is considered as not qualified for matrimony.

Her wrapper, grey, was not so bad, 85
   Her apron check'd with blue, sir,
One stocking on one foot she had,
   On t'other foot a shoe, sir.

Now, should a Boston lady read,
   Of Sally's shoe and stocking, 90
She'd say a "monstrous slut, indeed,
   Oh la!—she is quite shocking!"

You fine Miss Boston lady, gay,
   For this your speech, I thank ye,
Call on me, when you come this way, 95
   And take a drachm of Yankee.[6]

Now Jonathan did scratch his head,
   When first he saw his dearest;
Got up—sat down—and nothing said,
   But felt about the queerest, 100

Then talk'd with Sally's Brother Joe
   'Bout sheep, and cows, and oxen,
How wicked folks to church did go,
   With dirty woollen frocks on.

And how a witch, in shape of owl, 105
   Did steal her neighbor's geese, sir,
And turkeys too, and other fowl,
   When people did not please her.

And how a man, one dismal night,
   Shot her with silver bullet,[7] 110
And then she flew straight out of sight,
   As fast as she could pull it.

How Widow Wunks was sick next day.
   The parson went to view her,
And saw the very place, they say, 115
   Where foresaid ball went through her!

And now the people went to bed:
   They guess'd for what he'd come, sir;

[6] A glass of whiskey, mixed with molasses, is so called in New England, and is a common beverage with the peasantry.
[7] There is a tale among the ghost-hunters in New England, that silver bullets will be fatal to witches when those of lead would not avail.

But Jonathan was much afraid,
    And wish'd himself at home, sir.   120

At length, says Sal, "They're gone, you see,
    And we are left together;"
Says Jonathan, "Indeed—they be—
    'Tis mighty pleasant weather!"

Sal cast a sheep's eye at the dunce,   125
    Then turn'd towards the fire;
He muster'd courage, all at once,
    And hitch'd a little nigher.

Ye young men all, and lads so smart,
    Who chance to head these vasses,[8]   130
His next address pray learn by heart,
    To whisper to the lasses.

"Miss Sal, I's going to say, as how,
    We'll spark it here to-night,
I kind of love you, Sal, I vow,   135
    And mother said I might."

Then Jonathan, as we are told,
    Did even think to smack her;
Sal cock'd her chin, and look'd so bold,
    He did not dare attack her!   140

"Well done, my man, you've broke the ice,
    And that with little pother,
Now, Jonathan, take my advice,
    And always mind your mother!

"This courting is a kind of job   145
    I always did admire, sir,
And these two brands, with one dry *cob*,
    Will make a courting fire, sir."

"Miss Sal, you are the very she,
    If you will love me now,   150
That I will marry—then you see,
    You'll have our brindled cow.

[8] Verses are thus pronounced by the rustics in New England.

"Then we will live, both I and you,
 In father's t'other room,
For that will sartain hold us two,   155
 When we've mov'd out the loom.

"Next Sabbath-day we will be cried,
 And have a 'taring' wedding,
And lads and lasses take a ride,
 If it should be good sledding.   160

"My father has a nice bull calf,
 Which shall be your's, my sweet one;
'Twill weigh two hundred and a half,"
 Says Sal, "Well, that's a neat one."

"Your father's full of fun, d'ye see,   165
 And faith, I likes his sporting,
To send his favorite calf to me,
 His nice bull calf a courting."

"Are you the lad who went to town,
 Put on your streaked trowses,[9]   170
Then vow'd you could not see the town,
 There were so many houses?"

Our lover hung his under lip,
 He thought she meant to joke him;
Like heartless hen that has the pip,   175
 His courage all forsook him.

For he to Boston town had been,
 As matters here are stated;
Came home and told what he had seen,
 As Sally has related.   180

And now he wish'd he could retreat,
 But dar'd not make a racket;
It seem'd as if his heart would beat
 The buttons off his jacket!

Sal ask'd him "if his heart was whole?"   185
 His chin began to quiver;
He said, he felt so deuced droll,
 He guess'd he'd lost his liver!

[9] Vulgar pronunciation of the word trousers.

Now Sal was scar'd out of her wits,
    To see his trepidation,   190
She bawl'd "He's going into fits,"
    And scamper'd like the nation!

A pail of water she did throw,
    All on her trembling lover,
Which wet the lad from top to toe,   195
    Like drowned rat all over.

Then Jonathan straight hied him home,
    And since I've heard him brag, sir,
That though the jade did wet him some,
    He didn't get the bag, sir!   200

            1804

Joseph Rodman Drake
(1795-1820)

A physician and poet, Joseph Rodman Drake and Fitz-Greene Halleck wrote *The Croaker Papers,* published in the *New York Evening Post* (March 10–July 24, 1819); Halleck contributed the last quatrain of "The American Flag" (*Evening Post,* May 29, 1819). Written in 1816, "The Culprit Fay" was first printed in *The Culprit Fay and Other Poems* (New York, 1835).

BIBLIOGRAPHY: Frank L. Pleadwell, *The Life and Works of Joseph Rodman Drake, 1795–1820* (Boston, 1935). See Halleck headnote.

The American Flag

I

When Freedom from her mountain height
    Unfurled her standard to the air,
She tore the azure robe of night,
    And set the stars of glory there.
She mingled with its gorgeous dyes   5
The milky baldric of the skies,
And striped its pure celestial white
With streakings of the morning light;
Then from his mansion in the sun
She called her eagle bearer down,   10
And gave into his mighty hand
    The symbol of her chosen land.

696 / Joseph Rodman Drake

II

Majestic monarch of the cloud,
  Who rear'st aloft thy regal form,
To hear the tempest trumpings loud   15
  And see the lightning lances driven,
When strike the warriors of the storm,
  And rolls the thunder-drum of heaven,
Child of the sun! to thee 'tis given
  To guard the banner of the free,   20
To hover in the sulphur smoke,
To ward away the battle stroke,
And bid its blendings shine afar,
Like rainbows on the cloud of war,
  The harbingers of victory!   25

III

Flag of the brave! thy folds shall fly,
  The sign of hope and triumph high,
When speaks the signal trumpet tone,
  And the long line comes gleaming on.
Ere yet the life-blood, warm and wet,   30
  Has dimmed the glistening bayonet,
Each soldier eye shall brightly turn
  To where thy sky-born glories burn;
And as his springing steps advance,
  Catch war and vengeance from the glance.   35
And when the cannon-mouthings loud
  Heave in wild wreaths the battle shroud,
And gory sabres rise and fall
Like shoots of flame on midnight's pall;
  Then shall thy meteor glances glow,   40
And cowering foes shall shrink beneath
  Each gallant arm that strikes below
That lovely messenger of death.

IV

Flag of the seas! on ocean wave
  Thy stars shall glitter o'er the brave;   45
When death, careering on the gale,
  Sweeps darkly round the bellied sail,
And frighted waves rush wildly back
  Before the broadside's reeling rack,
Each dying wanderer of the sea   50
  Shall look at once to heaven and thee,
And smile to see thy splendors fly
  In triumph o'er his closing eye.

v

Flag of the free heart's hope and home!
 By angel hands to valor given;   55
Thy stars have lit the welkin dome,
 And all thy hues were born in heaven.
Forever float that standard sheet!
 Where breathes the foe but falls before us,
With Freedom's soil beneath our feet,   60
 And Freedom's banner streaming o'er us?

          1819

From The Culprit Fay

"My visual orbs are purged from film, and lo!
 Instead of Anster's turnip-bearing vales
I see old fairy land's miraculous show!
 Her trees of tinsel kissed by freakish gales,
Her Ouphs that, cloaked in leaf-gold, skim the breeze,
 And fairies, swarming . . . ."

      TENNANT, *Anster Fair.*

I

'Tis the middle watch of a summer's night—
The earth is dark, but the heavens are bright;
Naught is seen in the vault on high
But the moon, and the stars, and the cloudless sky,
And the flood which rolls its milky hue,   5
A river of light on the welkin blue.
The moon looks down on old Croenest;
She mellows the shades on his shaggy breast,
And seems his huge gray form to throw
In a silver cone on the wave below;   10
His sides are broken by spots of shade,
By the walnut bough and the cedar made,
And through their clustering branches dark
Glimmers and dies the fire-fly's spark—
Like starry twinkles that momently break   15
Through the rifts of the gathering tempest's rack.

II

The stars are on the moving stream,
 And fling, as its ripples gently flow,
A burnished length of wavy beam
 In an eel-like, spiral line below;   20

The winds are whist, and the owl is still,
  The bat in the shelvy rock is hid,
And naught is heard on the lonely hill
But the cricket's chirp, and the answer shrill
  Of the gauze-winged katy-did;   25
And the plaint of the wailing whip-poor-will,
  Who mourns unseen, and ceaseless sings,
Ever a note of wail and woe,
  Till morning spreads her rosy wings,
And earth and sky in her glances glow.   30

III

'Tis the hour of fairy ban and spell:
The wood-tick has kept the minutes well;
He has counted them all with click and stroke,
Deep in the heart of the mountain oak,
And he has awakened the sentry elve   35
  Who sleeps with him in the haunted tree,
To bid him ring the hour of twelve,
  And call the fays to their revelry;
Twelve small strokes on his tinkling bell—
('Twas made of the white snail's pearly shell:—)   40
"Midnight comes, and all is well!
Hither, hither, wing your way!
'Tis the dawn of the fairy day."

IV

They come from beds of lichen green,
They creep from the mullen's velvet screen;   45
  Some on the backs of beetles fly
From the silver tops of moon-touched trees,
  Where they swung in their cobweb hammocks high,
And rocked about in the evening breeze;
  Some from the hum-bird's downy nest—   50
They had driven him out by elfin power,
  And, pillowed on plumes of his rainbow breast,
Had slumbered there till the charmed hour;
  Some had lain in the scoop of the rock,
With glittering ising-stars inlaid;   55
  And some had opened the four-o'clock,
And stole within its purple shade.
  And now they throng the moonlight glade,
Above—below—on every side,
  Their little minim forms arrayed   60
In the tricksy pomp of fairy pride!

V

They come not now to print the lea,
In freak and dance around the tree,
Or at the mushroom board to sup,
And drink the dew from the buttercup;—   65
A scene of sorrow waits them now,
For an Ouphe has broken his vestal vow;
He has loved an earthly maid,
And left for her his woodland shade;
He has lain upon her lip of dew,   70
And sunned him in her eye of blue,
Fanned her cheek with his wing of air,
Played with the ringlets of her hair,
And, nestlng on her snowy breast,
Forgot the lily-king's behest.   75
For this the shadowy tribes of air
    To the elfin court must haste away:—
And now they stand expectant there,
    To hear the doom of the Culprit Fay.

VI

The throne was reared upon the grass   80
Of spice-wood and of sassafras;
On pillars of mottled tortoise-shell
    Hung the burnished canopy—
And o'er it gorgeous curtains fell
    Of the tulip's crimson drapery.   85
The monarch sat on his judgment-seat,
    On his brow the crown imperial shone,
The prisoner Fay was at his feet,
    And his peers were ranged around the throne.
He waved his sceptre in the air,   90
    He looked around and calmly spoke;
His brow was grave and his eye severe,
    But his voice in a softened accent broke:

VII

"Fairy! Fairy! list and mark,
    Thou has broke thine elfin chain,   95
Thy flame-wood lamp is quenched and dark,
    And thy wings are dyed with a deadly stain—
Thou hast sullied thine elfin purity
    In the glance of a mortal maiden's eye,
Thou hast scorned our dread decree,   100
And thou shouldst pay the forfeit high,

But well I know her sinless mind
Is pure as the angel forms above,
Gentle and meek, and chaste and kind,
Such as a spirit well might love;   105
Fairy! had she spot or taint,
Bitter had been thy punishment.
Tied to the hornet's shardy wings;
Tossed on the pricks of nettle's stings;
Or seven long ages doomed to dwell   110
With the lazy worm in the walnut-shell;
Or every night to writhe and bleed
Beneath the tread of the centipede;
Or bound in a cobweb dungeon dim,
Your jailer a spider huge and grim,   115
Amid the carrion bodies to lie,
Of the worm, and the bug, and the murdered fly;
These it had been your lot to bear,
Had a stain been found on the earthly fair.
Now list, and mark our mild decree—   120
Fairy, this your doom must be:

VIII

"Thou shalt seek the beach of sand
Where the water bounds the elfin land,
Thou shalt watch the oozy brine
Till the sturgeon leaps in the bright moonshine,   125
Then dart the glistening arch below,
And catch a drop from his silver bow.
The water-sprites will wield their arms
    And dash around, with roar and rave,
And vain are the woodland spirits' charms,   130
    They are the imps that rule the wave.
Yet trust thee in thy single might,
If thy heart be pure and thy spirit right,
Thou shalt win the warlock fight.

IX

"If the spray-bead gem be won,   135
    The stain of thy wing is washed away,
But another errand must be done
    Ere thy crime be lost for aye;
Thy flame-wood lamp is quenched and dark,
Thou must re-illume its spark.   140
Mount thy steed and spur him high
To the heaven's blue canopy;

And when thou seest a shooting star,
Follow it fast, and follow it far—
The last faint spark of its burning train   145
Shall light the elfin lamp again.
Thou hast heard our sentence, Fay;
Hence! to the water-side, away!"

x

The goblin marked his monarch well;
   He spake not, but he bowed him low,   150
Then plucked a crimson colen-bell,
   And turned him round in act to go. . . .

XXIX

Up to the cope careering swift
   In breathless motion fast,
Fleet as the swallow cuts the drift,   155
   Or the sea-roc rides the blast,
The sapphire sheet of eve is shot,
   The sphered moon is past,
The earth but seems a tiny blot
   On a sheet of azure cast.   160
O! it was sweet in the clear moonlight,
   To tread the starry plain of even,
To meet the thousand eyes of night,
   And feel the cooling breath of heaven!
But the Elfin made no stop or stay   165
Till he came to the bank of the milky-way,
Then he checked his courser's foot
And watched for the glimpse of the planet-shoot.

XXX

Sudden along the snowy tide
   That swelled to meet their footsteps' fall,   170
The sylphs of heaven were seen to glide,
   Attired in sunset's crimson pall;
Around the Fay they weave the dance,
   They skip before him on the plain,
And one has taken his wasp-sting lance,   175
   And one upholds his bridle rein;
With warblings wild they lead him on
   To where through clouds of amber seen,
Studded with stars, resplendent shone
   The palace of the sylphid queen.   180

Its spiral columns gleaming bright
Were streamers of the northern light;
Its curtain's light and lovely flush
Was of the morning's rosy blush,
And the ceiling fair that rose aboon   185
The white and feathery fleece of noon.

XXXI

But oh! how fair the shape that lay
   Beneath a rainbow bending bright;
She seemed to the entranced Fay
   The loveliest of the forms of light;   190
Her mantle was the purple rolled
   At twilight in the west afar;
'Twas tied with threads of dawning gold,
   And buttoned with a sparkling star.
Her face was like the lily roon   195
   That veils the vestal planet's hue;
Her eyes, two beamlets from the moon,
   Set floating in the welkin blue.
Her hair is like the sunny beam,
And the diamond gems which round it gleam   200
Are the pure drops of dewy even
That ne'er have left their native heaven.

XXXII

She raised her eyes to the wondering sprite,
   And they leapt with smiles, for well I ween
Never before in the bowers of light   205
   Had the form of an earthly Fay been seen.
Long she looked in his tiny face;
   Long with his butterfly cloak she played;
She smoothed his wings of azure lace,
   And handled the tassel of his blade;   210
And as he told in accents low
The story of his love and woe,
She felt new pain in her bosom rise,
   And the tear-drop started in her eyes.
And "O sweet spirit of earth," she cried,   215
   "Return no more to your woodland height,
But ever here with me abide
   In the land of everlasting light!
Within the fleecy drift we'll lie,
   We'll hang upon the rainbow's rim;   220
And all the jewels of the sky

Around thy brow shall brightly beam!
And thou shalt bathe thee in the stream
   That rolls its whitening foam aboon,
And ride upon the lightning's gleam,   225
   And dance upon the orbed moon!
We'll sit within the Pleiad ring,
   We'll rest on Orion's starry belt,
And I will bid my sylphs to sing
   The song that makes the dew-mist melt;   230
Their harps are of the umber shade,
   That hides the blush of waking day,
And every gleamy string is made
   Of silvery moonshine's lengthened ray;
And thou shalt pillow on my breast,   235
   While heavenly breathings float around,
And, with the sylphs of ether blest,
   Forget the joys of fairy ground."

XXXIII

She was lovely and fair to see
And the elfin's heart beat fitfully;   240
But lovelier far, and still more fair,
The earthly form imprinted there;
Naught he saw in the heavens above
Was half so dear as his mortal love,
For he thought upon her looks so meek,   245
And he thought of the light flush on her cheek;
Never again might he bask and lie
On that sweet cheek and moonlight eye,
But in his dreams her form to see,
To clasp her in his reverie,   250
To think upon his virgin bride,
Was worth all heaven and earth beside.

XXXIV

"Lady," he cried, "I have sworn to-night,
On the word of a fairy knight,
To do my sentence-task aright;   255
My honor scarce is free from stain,
I may not soil its snows again;
Betide me weal, betide me woe,
Its mandate must be answered now."
Her bosom heaved with many a sigh,   260
The tear was in her drooping eye;
   But she led him to the palace gate,

And called the sylphs who hovered there,
    And bade them fly and bring him straight
Of clouds condensed a sable car.   265
With charm and spell she blessed it there,
From all the fiends of upper air;
Then round him cast the shadowy shroud,
And tied his steed behind the cloud;
And pressed his hand as she bade him fly   270
Far to the verge of the northern sky,
For by its wane and wavering light
There was a star would fall to-night.

XXXV

Borne afar on the wings of the blast,
Northward away, he speeds him fast,   275
And his courser follows the cloudy wain
Till the hoof-strokes fall like pattering rain.
The clouds roll backward as he flies,
Each flickering star behind him lies,
And he has reached the northern plain,   280
And backed his fire-fly steed again,
Ready to follow in its flight
The streaming of the rocket-light.

XXXVI

The star is yet in the vault of heaven,
    But it rocks in the summer gale;   285
And now 'tis fitful and uneven,
    And now 'tis deadly pale;
And now 'tis wrapped in sulphur smoke,
    And quenched is its rayless beam,
And now with a rattling thunder-stroke   290
    It bursts in flash and flame.
As swift as the glance of the arrowy lance
    That the storm-spirit flings from high,
The star-shot flew o'er the welkin blue,
    As it fell from the sheeted sky.   295
As swift as the wind in its trail behind
    The elfin gallops along,
The fiends of the clouds are bellowing loud,
    But the sylphid charm is strong;
He gallops unhurt in the shower of fire,   300
    While the cloud-fiends fly from the blaze;
He watches each flake till its sparks expire,
    And rides in the light of its rays.

But he drove his steed to the lightning's speed,
  And caught a glimmering spark;   305
Then wheeled around to the fairy ground,
  And sped through the midnight dark.

        *   *   *

Ouphe and goblin! imp and sprite!
  Elf of eve! and starry Fay!
Ye that love the moon's soft light,   310
  Hither—hither wend your way;
Twine ye in a jocund ring,
  Sing and trip it merrily,
Hand to hand, and wing to wing,
  Round the wild witch-hazel tree.   315

Hail the wanderer again,
  With dance and song, and lute and lyre,
Pure his wing and strong his chain,
  And doubly bright his fairy fire.
Twine ye in an airy round,   320
  Brush the dew and print the lea;
Skip and gambol, hop and bound,
  Round the wild witch-hazel tree.

The beetle guards our holy ground,
  He flies about the haunted place,   325
And if mortal there be found,
  He hums in his ears and flaps his face;
The leaf-harp sounds our roundelay,
  The owlet's eyes our lanterns be;
Thus we sing, and dance, and play,   330
  Round the wild witch-hazel tree.

But hark! from tower on tree-top high,
  The sentry elf his call has made,
A streak is in the eastern sky,
  Shapes of moonlight! flit and fade!   335
The hill-tops gleam in morning's spring,
The sky-lark shakes his dappled wing,
The day-glimpse glimmers on the lawn,
The cock has crowed and the Fays are gone.

                1835

Fitz-Greene Halleck

(1790-1867)

In 1811, Fitz-Greene Halleck of Guilford, Connecticut, arrived in New York City, where he worked for eighteen years in a banking house and for John Jacob Astor from 1832–1849. In 1813, he met Joseph Rodman Drake, his literary collaborator in *The Croaker Papers* (1819). Other works include *Fanny* (New York, 1819, rev, 1821), "Marco Bozzaris" (1825), *Alnwick Castle, with Other Poems* (New York, 1827), and his *Poetical Works*, published in 1847, 1852, 1858, and 1859.

BIBLIOGRAPHY: *The Croakers,* (New York, 1860), Bradford Club Series. James G. Wilson, *The Life and Letters of Fitz-Greene Halleck, with Extracts from those of Joseph Rodman Drake* (New York, 1869). Nelson F. Adkins, *Fitz-Greene Halleck: An Early Knickerbocker Wit and Poet* (New Haven, 1930).

Marco Bozzaris

At midnight, in his guarded tent,
The Turk was dreaming of the hour
When Greece, her knee in suppliance bent,
    Should tremble at his power:
In dreams, through camp and court, he bore   5
The trophies of a conqueror;
    In dreams his song of triumph heard;
Then wore his monarch's signet ring:
Then pressed that monarch's throne—a king;
As wild his thoughts, and gay of wing,   10
    As Eden's garden bird.

At midnight, in the forest shades,
    Bozzaris ranged his Suliote band,
True as the steel of their tried blades,
    Heroes in heart and hand.
There had the Persian's thousands stood,   15
There had the glad earth drunk their blood
    On old Platæa's day;
And now there breathed that haunted air
The sons of sires who conquered there,   20
With arm to strike and soul to dare,
    As quick, as far as they.

An hour passed on—the Turk awoke;
   That bright dream was his last;
He woke—to hear his sentries shriek,   25
"To arms! they come! the Greek! the Greek!"
He woke—to die midst flame, and smoke,
And shout, and groan, and sabre-stroke,
   And death-shots falling thick and fast
As lightnings from the mountain-cloud;   30
And heard, with voice as trumpet loud,
   Bozzaris cheer his band:
"Strike—till the last armed foe expires;
Strike—for your altars and your fires;
Strike—for the green graves of your sires;   35
   God—and your native land!"

They fought—like brave men, long and well;
   They piled that ground with Moslem slain,
They conquered—but Bozzaris fell,
   Bleeding at every vein.   40
His few surviving comrades saw
His smile when rang their proud hurrah,
   And the red field was won;
Then saw in death his eyelids close
Calmly, as to a night's repose,   45
   Like flowers at set of sun.

Come to the bridal-chamber, Death!
   Come to the mother's, when she feels,
For the first time, her first-born's breath;
   Come when the blessed seals   50
That close the pestilence are broke,
And crowded cities wail its stroke;
Come in consumption's ghastly form,
The earthquake shock, the ocean storm;
Come when the heart beats high and warm,   55
   With banquet-song, and dance and wine;
And thou are terrible—the tear,
The groan, the knell, the pall, the bier;
And all we know, or dream, or fear
   Of agony, are thine.   60

But to the hero, when his sword
   Has won the battle for the free,
Thy voice sounds like a prophet's word;
And in its hollow tones are heard
   The thanks of millions yet to be.   65

Come, when his task of fame is wrought—
Come, with her laurel-leaf, blood-bought—
    Come in her crowning hour—and then
Thy sunken eye's unearthly light
To him is welcome as the sight   70
    Of sky and stars to prisoned men:
Thy grasp is welcome as the hand
Of brother in a foreign land;
Thy summons welcome as the cry
That told the Indian isles were nigh   75
    To the world-seeking Genoese,
When the land wind, from woods of palm,
And orange-groves, and fields of balm,
    Blew o'er the Haitian seas.

Bozzaris! with the storied brave   80
    Greece nurtured in her glory's time,
Rest thee—there is no prouder grave,
    Even in her own proud clime.
She wore no funeral-weeds for thee,
    Nor bade the dark hearse wave its plume   85
Like torn branch from death's leafless tree
In sorrow's pomp and pageantry,
    The heartless luxury of the tomb:
But she remembers thee as one
Long loved and for a season gone;   90
For thee her poet's lyre is wreathed,
Her marble wrought, her music breathed;
For thee she rings the birthday bells;
Of thee her babes' first lisping tells;
For thine her evening prayer is said   95
At palace-couch and cottage-bed;
Her soldier, closing with the foe,
Gives for thy sake a deadlier blow;
His plighted maiden, when she fears
For him the joy of her young years,   100
Thinks of thy fate, and checks her tears:
    And she, the mother of thy boys,
Though in her eye and faded cheek
Is read the grief she will not speak,
    The memory of her buried joys,   105
And even she who gave thee birth,
Will, by their pilgrim-circled hearth,

Talk of thy doom without a sigh:
For thou are Freedom's now, and Fame's;
One of the few, the immortal names,   110
    That were not born to die.

                                        1825

On the Death of Joseph Rodman Drake

"The good die first,
And they, whose hearts are dry as summer dust,
Burn to the sockets."—WORDSWORTH

Green be the turf above thee,
    Friend of my better days!
None knew thee but to love thee,
    Nor named thee but to praise.

Tears fell when thou wert dying,   5
    From eyes unused to weep,
And long, where thou art lying,
    Will tears the cold turf steep.

When hearts, whose truth was proven,
    Like thine, are laid in earth,   10
There should a wreath be woven
    To tell the world their worth;

And I who woke each morrow
    To clasp thy hand in mine,
Who shared thy joy and sorrow,   15
    Whose weal and woe were thine:

It should be mine to braid it
    Around thy faded brow,
But I've in vain essayed it,
    And feel I cannot now.   20

While memory bids me weep thee,
    Nor thoughts nor words are free,
The grief is fixed too deeply
    That mourns a man like thee.

                                        1821

From *Fanny*

I

Fanny was younger once than she is now,
    And prettier of course; I do not mean
To say that there are wrinkles on her brow;
    Yet, to be candid, she is past eighteen—
Perhaps past twenty—but the girl is shy   5
About her age, and Heaven forbid that I

II

Should get myself in trouble by revealing
    A secret of this sort; I have too long
Loved pretty women with a poet's feeling,
    And when a boy, in day-dream and in song,   10
Have knelt me down and worshipped them: alas!
They never thanked me for't—but let that pass.

III

I've felt full many a heartache in my day,
    At the mere rustling of a muslin gown,
And caught some dreadful colds, I blush to say,   15
    While shivering in the shade of beauty's frown.
They say her smiles are sunbeams—it may be—
But never a sunbeam would she throw on me.

IV

But Fanny's is an eye that you may gaze on
    For half an hour, without the slightest harm;   20
E'en when she wore her smiling summer face on
    There was but little danger, and the charm
That youth and wealth once gave, has bade farewell:
Hers is a sad, sad tale—'tis mine its woes to tell.

V

Her father kept, some fifteen years ago,   25
    A retail dry-goods shop in Chatham Street,
And nursed his little earnings, sure though slow,
    Till, having mustered wherewithal to meet
The gaze of the great world, he breathed the air
Of Pearl Street—and "set up" in Hanover Square.   30

VI

Money is power, 'tis said—I never tried;
 I'm but a poet—and bank-notes to me
Are curiosities, as closely eyed,
 Whene'er I get them, as a stone would be,
Tossed from the moon on Doctor Mitchill's table,   35
Or classic brickbat from the tower of Babel.

VII

But he I sing of well has known and felt
 That money hath a power and a dominion;
For when in Chatham Street the good man dwelt,
 No one would give a *sous* for his opinion.   40
And though his neighbors were extremely civil,
Yet, on the whole, they thought him—a poor devil.

VIII

A decent kind of person; one whose head
 Was not of brains particularly full;
It was not known that he had ever said   45
 Any thing worth repeating—'twas a dull,
Good, honest man—what Paulding's muse would call
A "cabbage-head"—but he excelled them all

IX

In that most noble of the sciences,
 The art of making money; and he found   50
The zeal for quizzing him grew less and less,
 As he grew richer; till upon the ground
Of Pearl Street, treading proudly in the might
And majesty of wealth, a sudden light

X

Flashed like the midnight lightning on the eyes   55
 Of all who knew him: brilliant traits of mind,
And genius, clear, and countless as the dyes
 Upon the peacock's plumage; taste refined,
Wisdom and wit, were his—perhaps much more—
'Twas strange they had not found it out before.   60

. . . . .

CIV

But where is Fanny? She has long been thrown
   Where cheeks and roses wither—in the shade.
The age of chivalry, you know, is gone;
   And although, as I once before have said,
I love a pretty face to adoration,   65
Yet, still, I must preserve my reputation,

CV

As a true dandy of the modern schools.
   One hates to be old-fashioned; it would be
A violation of the latest rules,
   To treat the sex with too much courtesy.   70
'Tis not to worship beauty, as she glows
In all her diamond lustre, that the beaux

CVI

Of these enlightened days at evening crowd,
   Where Fashion welcomes in her rooms of light
That "dignified obedience; that proud   75
   Submission," which, in times of yore, the knight
Gave to his "ladye-love," is now a scandal,
And practised only by your Goth and Vandal.

CVII

To lounge in graceful attitudes—be stared
   Upon, the while, by every fair one's eye,   80
And stare one's self, in turn: to be prepared
   To dart upon the trays, as swiftly by
The dexterous Simon bears them, and to take
One's share at least of coffee, cream, and cake,

CVIII

Is now to be "the ton." The pouting lip,   85
   And sad, upbraiding eye of the poor girl,
Who hardly of joy's cup one drop can sip,
   Ere in the wild confusion, and the whirl,
And tumult of the hour, its bubbles vanish,
Must now be disregarded. One must banish   90

CIX

Those antiquated feelings, that belong
   To feudal manners and a barbarous age.

Time was—when woman "poured her soul" in song,
   That all was hushed around. 'Tis now "the rage"
To deem a song, like bugle-tones in battle,   95
   A signal-note, that bids each tongue's artillery rattle.

CX

And, therefore, I have made Miss Fanny wait
   My leisure. She had changed, as you will see, as
Much as her worthy sire, and made as great
   Proficiency in taste and high ideas.   100
The careless smile of other days was gone,
And every gesture spoke *"qu'en dira-t-on?"*

CXI

She long had known that in her father's coffers,
   And also to his credit in the banks,
There was some cash; and therefore all the offers   105
   Made her, by gentlemen of the middle ranks,
Of heart and hand, had spurned, as far beneath
One whose high destiny, it was to breathe,

CXII

Ere long, the air of Broadway or Park Place,
   And reign a fairy queen in fairy land;   110
Display in the gay dance her form of grace,
   Or touch with rounded arm and gloveless hand,
Harp or piano.—Madame Catilani
Forgot awhile, and every eye on Fanny.

CXIII

And in anticipation of that hour,   115
   Her star of hope, her paradise of thought,
She'd had as many masters as the power
   Of riches could bestow; and had been taught
The thousand nameless graces that adorn
The daughters of the wealthy and high-born.   120

CXIV

She had been noticed at some public places
   (The Battery, and the balls of Mr. Whale),
For hers was one of those attractive faces,
   That when you gaze upon them, never fail
To bid you look again; there was a beam,   125
A lustre in her eye, that oft would seem

CXV

A little like effrontery; and yet
   The lady meant no harm; her only aim
Was but to be admired by all she met,
   And the free homage of the heart to claim;   130
And if she showed too plainly this intention,
Others have done the same—'twas not of her invention.

CXVI

She shone at every concert; where are bought
   Tickets by all who wish them, for a dollar;
She patronized the Theatre, and thought   135
   That Wallack looked extremely well in Rolla;
She fell in love, as all the ladies do,
With Mr. Simpson—talked as loudly, too,

CXVII

As any beauty of the highest grade
   To the gay circle in the box beside her;   140
And when the pit—half vexed and half afraid,
   With looks of smothered indignation eyed her,
She calmly met their gaze, and stood before 'em,
Smiling at vulgar taste and mock decorum.

CXVIII

And though by no means a *bas bleu,* she had   145
   For literature a most becoming passion;
Had skimmed the latest novels, good and bad,
   And read the Croakers, when they were in fashion;
And Dr. Chalmers' sermons of a Sunday;
And Woodworth's Cabinet, and the new Salmagundi.   150

CXIX

She was among the first and warmest patrons
   Of Griscom's *conversaziones,* where
In rainbow groups, our bright-eyed maids and matrons,
   On science bent, assemble; to prepare
Themselves for acting well, in life, their part   155
As wives and mothers. There she learned by heart

CXX

Words, to the witches in Macbeth unknown.
   Hydraulics, hydrostatics, and *pneumatics,*
Dioptics, optics, katoptrics, carbon,
   Chlorine and *iodine,* and *aërostatics;*   160

Also,—why frogs, for want of air, expire;
And how to set the Tappan Sea on fire!

CXXI

In all the modern languages she was
    Exceedingly well-versed; and had devoted,
To their attainment, far more time than has,   165
    By the best teachers, lately been allotted;
For she had taken lessons, twice a week,
For a full month in each; and she could speak

CXXII

French and Italian, equally as well
    As Chinese, Portuguese, or German; and,   170
What is still more surprising, she could spell
    Most of our longest English words off-hand;
Was quite familiar in Low Dutch and Spanish,
And thought of studying modern Greek and Danish.

CXXIII

She sang divinely; and in "Love's young dream"   175
    And "Fanny dearest," and "The soldier's bride;"
And every song, whose dear delightful theme,
    Is "Love, still love," had oft till midnight tried
Her finest, loftiest "pigeon-wings" of sound,
Waking the very watchmen far around.   180

CXXIV

For her pure taste in dress, I can appeal to
    Madame Bouquet, and Monsieur Pardessus;
She was, in short, a woman you might kneel to,
    If kneeling were in fashion; or if you
Were wearied of your duns and single life,   185
And wanted a few thousands and a wife. . . .

1819

John Howard Payne

(1791-1852)

John Howard Payne, anonymous editor of the *Thespian Mirror* (New York, 1805–1806) at the age of fourteen, was an actor and playwright in New York, London, and Paris. "Home, Sweet Home!" was a lyric from his drama *Clari, or, The Maid of Milan*, produced at Covent Garden on May 8, 1823. Other poetry includes *Juvenile Poems* (Baltimore, 1813) reprinted as *Lispings of the Muse* (London, 1815).

BIBLIOGRAPHY: Gabriel Harrison, *John Howard Payne* (Philadelphia, 1885). W. T. Hanson, Jr., *The Early Life of John Howard Payne* (Boston, 1913). Charles H. Brainard, *John Howard Payne* (Washington, D.C., 1885). Rosa P. Chiles, *John Howard Payne* (Washington, D.C., 1930).

Home, Sweet Home!

'Mid pleasures and palaces though we may roam,
Be it ever so humble, there's no place like Home!
A charm from the skies seems to hallow us there,
　　(Like the love of a mother,
　　Surpassing all other),　　　　　　　　　　　　5
Which, seek through the world, is ne'er met with elsewhere.
　　　There's a spell in the shade
　　　Where our infancy play'd,
Even stronger than Time, and more deep than despair!

An exile from Home, splendor dazzles in vain!　　　　10
Oh, give me my lowly, thatch'd cottage again!
The birds and the lambkins that came at my call,—
　　　Those who nam'd me with pride,—
　　　Those who play'd by my side,—
Give me them! with the innocence dearer than all!　　15
　　The joys of the palaces through which I roam
Only swell my heart's anguish—There's no place like Home!

To *us,* in despite of the absence of years,
How sweet the remembrance of *home* still appears;
From allurements abroad, which but flatter the eye,　　20
The unsatisfied heart turns, and says, with a sigh,
　　　"Home, home, sweet, sweet home!
　　　There's no place like home!"
　　　There's no place like home!

Your exile is blest with all fate can bestow;   25
But *mine* has been checkered with many a woe!
Yet, tho' different our fortunes, our thoughts are the same,
And both, as we think of Columbia, exclaim,
      "Home, home, sweet, sweet home!
          There's no place like home!   30
          There's no place like home!"

                              1823

Samuel Woodworth

(1784-1842)

A printer, playwright, and editor of numerous periodicals, Samuel Woodworth wrote social satires under the pseudonym of "Selim." Among his poems are *Beasts at Law* (New York, 1811), *The Complete Coiffeur* (New York, 1817), and *Poems, Odes, Songs,* *and Other Metrical Effusions* (New York, 1818, 1821).

BIBLIOGRAPHY: F. A. Woodworth, ed. *The Poetical Works of Samuel Woodworth*, 2 Vols. (New York, 1861), with biographical note by G. P. Morris.

The Bucket

How dear to this heart are the scenes of my childhood!
    When fond recollection presents them to view;
The orchard, the meadow, the deep tangled wild wood,
    And every loved spot which my infancy knew;
The wide spreading pond, and the mill which stood by it,   5
    The bridge, and the rock where the cataract fell;
The cot of my father, the dairy house nigh it,
    And e'en the rude bucket which hung in the well.
The old oaken bucket, the iron-bound bucket,
The moss-cover'd bucket which hung in the well.   10

That moss-cover'd vessel I hail as a treasure,
    For often at noon, when return'd from the field,
I found it the source of an exquisite pleasure,

The purest and sweetest that nature can yield.
How ardent I seized it with hands that were glowing,   15
    And quick to the white pebbled bottom it fell,
Then soon with the emblem of truth overflowing,
    And dripping with coolness, it rose from the well.
The old oaken bucket, the iron-bound bucket,
The moss-cover'd bucket arose from the well.   20

How sweet from the green mossy brim to receive it,
    As poised on the curb it inclined to my lips!
Not a full blushing goblet could tempt me to leave it,
    Though fill'd with the nectar that Jupiter sips.
And now far removed from the loved situation,   25
    The tear of regret will intrusively swell,
As fancy reverts to my father's plantation,
    And sighs for the bucket which hangs in the well.
The old oaken bucket, the iron-bound bucket,
The moss-cover'd bucket which hangs in his well.   30
                     1818

The Pride of the Valley

The pride of the valley is lovely young Ellen,
    Who dwells in a cottage enshrined by a thicket,
Sweet peace and content are the wealth of her dwelling,
    And Truth is the porter that waits at the wicket.
The zephyr that lingers on violet-down pinion,   5
    With Spring's blushing honors delighted to dally,
Ne'er breathed on a blossom in Flora's dominion,
    So lovely as Ellen, the pride of the valley.

She's true to her Willie, and kind to her mother,
    Nor riches nor honors can tempt her from duty;   10
Content with her station, she sighs for no other,
    Though fortunes and titles have knelt to her beauty.
To me her affections and promise are plighted,
    Our ages are equal, our tempers will tally;
O moment of rapture, that sees me united   15
    To lovely young Ellen, the pride of the valley.

The Hunters of Kentucky

Ye gentlemen and ladies fair,
  Who grace this famous city,
Just listen, if ye've time to spare,
  While I rehearse a ditty;
And for the opportunity,   5
  Conceive yourselves quite lucky,
For 'tis not often that you see,
  A hunter from Kentucky.
Oh! Kentucky, the hunters of Kentucky,
  The hunters of Kentucky.   10

We are a hardy free-born race,
  Each man to fear a stranger,
Whate'er the game, we join in chase,
  Despising toil and danger;
And if a daring foe annoys,   15
  Whate'er his strength and forces,
We'll show him that Kentucky boys
  Are "alligator horses."
Oh! Kentucky, the hunters of Kentucky,
  The hunters of Kentucky.   20

I s'pose you've read it in the prints,
  How Packenham attempted
To make Old Hickory Jackson wince,
  But soon his scheme repented;
For we with rifles ready cock'd,   25
  Thought such occasion lucky,
And soon around the General flock'd
  The hunters of Kentucky.
         Oh! Kentucky, &c.

You've heard, I s'pose, how New Orleans   30
  Is famed for wealth and beauty—
There's girls of every hue, it seems,
  From snowy white to sooty;
So Packenham he made his brags,
  If he in fight was lucky,   35
He'd have their girls and cotton bags,
  In spite of Old Kentucky.
         Oh! Kentucky, &c.

But Jackson, he was wide awake,
   And wasn't scared at trifles;   40
For well he knew what aim we take,
   With our Kentucky rifles;
So he led us down to Cypress swamp,
   The ground was low and mucky;
There stood John Bull, in martial pomp,   45
   And here was Old Kentucky.
              Oh! Kentucky, &c.

A bank was raised to hide our breast,
   Not that we thought of dying,
But then we always like to rest,   50
   Unless the game is flying;
Behind it stood our little force—
   None wished it to be greater,
For every man was half a horse,
   And half an alligator.   55
              Oh! Kentucky, &c.

They did not let our patience tire,
   Before they showed their faces—
We did not choose to waste our fire,
   So snugly kept our places;   60
But when so near we saw them wink,
   We thought it time to stop them;
And 'twould have done you good, I think,
   To see Kentucky pop them.
              Oh! Kentucky, &c.   65

They found at last 'twas vain to fight
   Where lead was all their booty,
And so they wisely took to flight,
   And left us all the beauty.
And now, if danger e'er annoys,   70
   Remember what our trade is,
Just send for us Kentucky boys,
   And we'll protect you, Ladies.
              Oh! Kentucky, &c.

1821

Thy Ruby Lips Must Kiss the Brim

Thy ruby lips must kiss the brim
Before I drain the cup,
Its lustre else will be too dim
To light my spirits up.
Nay, taste, my love—its purple hue   5
Will brighter paint thy lip;
Thine eye will gain new lustre too,
Thy soul new ardor—sip!

If rosy wine have power to cheer
The regents of the sky,   10
It sure will chase away the tear
That dims an angel's eye.
Then taste, my love—its purple hue
Will brighter dye thy lip;
Thine eye will gain new lustre too,   15
Thy soul new ardor—sip!

1827

George Pope Morris
(1802-1864)

Author of "Woodman Spare That Tree," George Pope Morris was a founder and editor of the *New-York Mirror and Ladies Literary Gazette* (1823–1842). His poetry includes *The Deserted Bride and Other Poems* (New York, 1838), *The Songs and Ballads of George P. Morris* (New York, 1844), and *Poems by George P. Morris* (New York, 1853, 1860). The 1860 edition includes a biographical sketch by Horace B. Wallace.

BIBLIOGRAPHY: *DAB.*

What Can It Mean?

I'm much too young to marry,
For I am only seventeen;
Why think I then of Harry?—
What can it mean—what can it mean?

Whenever Harry meets me,   5
Beside the brook, or on the green,
How tenderly he greets me!
What can it mean—what can it mean?

Whene'er my name he utters,
   A blush upon my cheek is seen,   10
And then my heart so flutters—
   What can it mean—what can it mean?

And when he mentions Cupid,
   Or, smiling, calls me "fairy queen,"
I sigh and look so stupid!—   15
   What can it mean—what can it mean?

Oh mercy! what can ail me?
   I'm growing pale and very lean;
My spirits often fail me!
   What can it mean—what can it mean?   20

I'm not in love!—oh smother
   Such a thought at seventeen:
I'll go and ask my mother
   What it can mean—what it can mean.

James Kirke Paulding
(1778-1860)

James Kirke Paulding achieved literary fame for his periodical pieces, particularly for *Salmagundi* (1807–1808), written with Washington Irving. His poetry includes *The Lay of the Scottish Fiddle* (Philadelphia, 1813), a parody of Walter Scott's verse, and *The Backwoodsman* (Philadelphia, 1818). In addition, Paulding attained some stature as a novelist and playwright. For years, he served the Navy Department in Washington, D.C., and New York City; from 1838–1840, he was Secretary of the Navy in the Cabinet of President Van Buren.

BIBLIOGRAPHY: William I. Paulding, *The Literary Life of James K. Paulding* (New York, 1867). Amos L. Herold, *James Kirke Paulding, Versatile American* (New York, 1926). V. L. Parington, *Main Currents in American Thought* (New York, 1927), II, 212–221. Ralph M. Aderman, ed. *The Letters of James Kirke Paulding* (Madison, Wis., 1962). See Headnote to Paulding's short fiction.

From *The Backwoodsman*

BOOK III

. . . Thus Basil—when he left his rural home,
In search of better fortune far to roam,
His fancy pictur'd years of solitude,
Far from the haunts of men in regions rude;

That shut from all the sweets of social life,   5
Himself, his growing boys, and faithful wife,
With howling beasts would congregate the while,
And never see another being smile,
Or hear a human voice, save Indian yell,
Shaking the forest with its echoing swell.   10
But happy Chance, that like the Summer breeze,
Can bring or rain or sunshine as she please,
And oft with her good-natur'd gambols cheers
The present sorrow, or the future fears,
Ordain'd that here a little band he found,   15
With him upon the self same errand bound,
Who hail'd with welcome our wayfaring man,
And joy'd in such associates in their plan.
Now blither was the hope that led the way,
And Basil's heart wax'd lighter every day,   20
Till all the little preparations o'er,
Our vent'rous band sought fair Ohio's shore,
Loosen'd their boats, and grasp'd the offer'd hand
Of many a stranger that around did stand;
For now about to leave, a long, long while,   25
The gentle world of courtesy and smile,
And reft of all its hallow'd sweets, sojourn
In lonely lands, whence they might ne'er return;
Around their lingering eyes full oft they cast,
And gaz'd, as people do, who look their last,   30
While every soul of all the stranger train
Seem'd a dear friend they ne'er should meet again.
A simple scene! yet if we view it well,
'Twill soon to grander outlines happly swell,
For here we see, as on a chart unfurl'd,   35
The destinies of this great Western world.
So came our ancestors, stern volunteers!
Who knew the dangers, yet despis'd the fears;
Thus did they sever many a heart-knit tie
Freedom and competence to win, or die;   40
And thus their hardy offspring dare to roam,
Far in the West, to seek a happier home,
To push the red-man from his solitude,
And plant refinement in the forest rude,
Thus daringly their glorious race to run,   45
Ev'n to the regions of yon setting sun.

    Now, fare thee well—dear haunts of social men!
Long may it be, ere we shall meet again!

Farewell the village church, and tolling bell,
Sounding to prayers, or rustic fun'ral knell;   50
The lively fields, where men and herds are seen
Sporting, and lab'ring morn and eve between;
The smoke of rural hamlet curling high
Above the trees, in peaceful Summer sky;
The ploughman's whistle, and the lambkin's bleat,   55
The tinkling music of the herd, so sweet—
All, all farewell! far other scenes of life,
Rude forest labors, and wild savage strife,
My vent'rous song, perchance, will soon rehearse,
And rougher scenes demand a loftier verse. . . .   60

   As down Ohio's ever ebbing tide,
Oarless and sailless silently they glide,
How still the scene, how lifeless, yet how fair,
Was the lone land that met the strangers there!
No smiling villages, or curling smoke,   65
The busy haunts of busy men bespoke,
No solitary hut, the banks along,
Sent forth blithe Labor's homely rustic song,
No urchin gambol'd on the smooth white sand,
Or hurl'd the skipping-stone with playful hand,   70
While playmate dog plung'd in the clear blue wave,
And swam, in vain, the sinking prize to save.
Where now are seen along the river side,
Young busy towns, in buxom painted pride,
And fleets of gliding boats with riches crown'd,   75
To distant Orleans or St. Louis bound,
Nothing appear'd, but Nature unsubdu'd,
One endless, noiseless, woodland solitude,
Or boundless prairie, that aye seem'd to be
As level, and as lifeless as the sea;   80
They seem'd to breathe in this wide world alone,
Heirs of the Earth—the land was all their own!

                                         1818

Gulian Crommelin Verplanck
(1786-1870)

A graduate of Columbia in 1801, Gulian Crommelin Verplanck was a lawyer, teacher, journalist, and politician. *The Bucktail Bards* (New York, 1819), first printed serially in the *New York American*, was satirical verse directed at Gov. DeWitt Clinton.

Verplanck also edited *Shakespeare's Plays: with His Life*, 3 vols. (New York, 1845).

BIBLIOGRAPHY: Sara King Harvey, *Gulian Crommelin Verplanck* (Chicago, 1936).

From *The Bucktail Bards*

From The Second Epistle to the Author of Dick Shift,
From Brevet Major Pindar Puff,
Poet Laureate to His Excellency the Governor

I told thee, friend, when first thy rhyming fit
Urg'd thee to try in verse thy desperate wit,
That Pindar Puff, by bold ambition fir'd,
To rise to fame by dint of rhyme aspir'd:
I told thee, too, that whilst you roughly rail'd,   5
And quacks and sharpers, knaves and fools assail'd,
My prudent verse, no sour, malignant bile,
Should with sarcastic censure e'er defile;
That sweetest flattery o'er my page should glide,
And mild eulogiums pour their honied tide;   10
That I would C—ld—n puff, and Sp—nc—r laud,
And all that Clinton e'er has done applaud,
Till to such notes of praise my voice should swell,
That my loud puffs would drown the puffs of Pell.
This have I done, and rich rewards have found,   15
With honors, office, fame, and titles crown'd;
No more obscure, a starv'd attorney's scribe,
Behold me member of each learned tribe:
Saddled on G—lb—rt, half his fees I get,
And Mister, now no more, am Major, by Brevet.   20
Nor is the labor great, or service hard,
By which I earn so ample a reward.
Thou know'st how erst at Rome, in Leo's days,
Fat Querno earn'd, and wore the laureate's bays,
(For I remember, once thou lov'dst that lore,   25
Which still sheds glory on fall'n Latium's shore—

Latium, no more by arms or empire grac'd,
Yet still belov'd of science, wit, and taste.)
Me, as its Querno, pleas'd Albania hails,
And, in his barge when our great chieftain sails,   30
I to his praises duteous tune my lyre,
His bard, his butt, his flatterer, and his squire.
Safely on me he tries his clumsy wit,
Still at his festive board I joyous sit,
Laugh at each filthy tale, each half-form'd pun,   35
And all his awkward arts of vulgar fun.
Then to my chief, his praises I rehearse
In pompous, Pell-like prose, or high heroic verse;
Charm'd with the theme, the chief attentive hears,
And drinks my flattery in, with eager ears;   40
Or, as the vapor mounts, and fires his brain,
Craves yet another, still more fulsome strain.
To me an easy task—for long has fled
From my bronz'd cheek, its blushing, boyish red:
Boldly I laud his science, genius, grace,   45
And call him Newton, Mansfield—to his face.

1819

SHORT FICTION

Theological Magazine

The *Theological Magazine*, published at New York between July–August, 1795, and February, 1799, printed few prose narratives. Among those few narratives, however, is "Of the Unpardonable Sin," written by an anonymous "N" for the September–October, 1796 issue.

Of The Unpardonable Sin

Vermont, August, 1796

Mr. Editor,

If you judge the following Narrative merits a Place in your Magazine, please to insert it.

But a few years since, in my travels, I was invited to preach a lecture in a town, where the work of God, in awakening, convincing, and changing the hearts of sinners, prevailed. After the lecture I conversed with a number of persons about the great concerns of their souls. Directly one of the assembly came to me, and informed me of a certain young man, who said he had committed the unpardonable sin, and desired me to converse with him. He was accordingly brought forward. After asking him a few questions, to ascertain, in some measure, his feelings, I endeavored to convince him, that he was under peculiar temptation, and had no reason to despair of mercy: for at that time I did not suppose his apprehensions respecting himself were well founded. "It is in vain," said he, "to labor with me in this manner, for I know I have committed that sin against the Holy Ghost, which is unpardonable, and never, never can mercy be exercised towards me."

These words were spoken with such an emphasis, and his countenance at the same time discovered something so very uncommon, that they made a strong impression on my mind, and produced in me a desire to be more particular in my inquiries. I asked him, if he knew when he

727

committed that sin, and what made him believe it was the unpardonable sin? He then gave this account. He had been, he said, under religious impressions for some time, till, at last, he was beset with a strong temptation to do a certain thing, which he knew was expressly prohibited in the word of God. What it was he was tempted to do he would not tell. He resisted, he said, the temptation for some time—reflected upon the subject frequently, whether he could entertain any hope of salvation, if he should commit that sin. At last, he said, within himself, "I will do the thing if I am damned forever the next hour," and accordingly did it. "Immediately," said he, "I had feelings which I never experienced in such a sensible degree before"—his heart became hard as an adamant—his enmity against God increased to a great degree. Since that time he had not felt one desire to ask or receive mercy, or the least favor of God. He never reflected on the divine character, but his heart rose in the most violent opposition. "Whenever," said he, "I reflect that God is Almighty, just, and holy—that I am dependent on him—that he can and will do with me as he pleases, my heart burns with rage and fury, and had I power, I would execute vengeance on the Almighty."

He then addressed himself to a number under religious impressions who stood around. "I have heard you relate the feelings of your hearts, and you appear to have some sense of your wickedness; but if enmity of heart against God is wickedness, (and that it is, I am fully convinced, though I wish to believe to the contrary) your present sense is nothing compared with the fountain of iniquity within. I know, if all men's hearts are naturally alike, you would dethrone the Almighty if you had power. Had I an omnipotent arm, heaven would soon be stormed, and God be cast headlong from his throne." In expressions like these, he uttered himself for some time, to appearance actuated with the highest rage. "I have no peace," said he, "day nor night, my torment is as great, seemingly, as I can endure. God is constantly in my view, and my heart is constantly burning with rage and fury." His eyes, his countenance and air, expressed the same feelings with his words; such a sight I never saw since nor before. Nothing I could say availed anything, unless to increase his rage and enmity. He had, as it appeared to me, the most clear and lively sense of the wickedness of the human heart—of the divine character—the creature's dependence, and the nature of future torments of any person with whom I was ever acquainted.

Some of his friends told me, that his distress was sometimes so great, that he would lie down and roll on the floor from one side of the room to the other, and groan like a man exercised with excruciating pain, and cry, "Oh! that I could banish all thoughts of God from my mind forever and ever." At one time he traveled barefoot in the night, twelve miles, in a deep snow, without making one stop. He was followed by the track he made, and when inquired of, why he conducted thus, he replied, that bodily pain was the only mean by which he could divert his mind from those objects, which gave him greater distress than what he experienced in his travel. He, therefore, did it to mitigate his distress. This person exhibited to my view a lively picture of hell, where the anguish and distress of all impenitent sinners will exceed all expression, when they have a lively sense of divine and eternal realities.

N.

Philadelphia Minerva

The *Philadelphia Minerva*, a weekly literary magazine published by W. T. Palmer, was issued at Philadelphia from Feb. 7, 1795 to July 7, 1798. Its columns included short fiction, poetry, essays, and some criticism. "Caroline: Or, The Seduced American," an anonymously contributed tale, appeared in two installments in the January 14 and January 21, 1797, numbers.

Caroline

Or, The Seduced American

When an Italian Countess, in the court of Mary de Medicis, was tried for having bewitched her royal mistress, she told her judges and accusers, that she never had employed any supernatural means to govern the mind of the Queen; nor had possessed any other ascendant over it, than that which a strong mind must naturally have over a weak one. This sort of witchcraft Henry practiced in such a degree, that there were few of his intimate companions who were ever hardy enough to maintain an opinion opposed to his own; but they not only did not maintain a contradictory opinion, they insensibly changed their own, their sentiments, and their wishes: seeming emulous to be, as nearly as possible, what he was: whose understanding was of the first order, whose heart was pure, and who was, notwithstanding, so far from being puritanical, that his taste lent grace to fashion, and was aided by a passion of expense, which could only be corrected by his still stronger passion for independence.

Such was he who now entered the unconfined unwholesome chamber of an old man approaching fast to dissolution. The curtains of the bed were open, and disclosed the venerable object, supported by his nurse. His sand was running low: the pallid hue of death had already taken possession of his cheek, and the luster of the eye began to be dimmed by the deep shade of its approaching night. His faculties, however, seemed yet awake, and the voice of his benefactor called a faint flush, which struggled a moment in his pale face, and then subsided forever.

"Ah, Sir!" he said, "you, whose soul is so full of benevolence! you, to whom the tear which steals from your eye in pity, is dearer than that which gushes there from rapture—to you this moment will not be unwelcome! I speak not of myself; for the hour is arrived, in which I shall cease to mourn; in which this wearied heart will render up its last sigh to him who gave the agonizing nerve. Another child of sorrow is at hand! This long, sad night, in which my soul has been struggling to meet its God, the inhabitant of the next melancholy chamber has had the power to arrest its flight—her voice has penetrated through the darkness of the night; chained down my spirit, and kept my languid pulse still beating."

The person to whom this was addressed turned towards the nurse for information: all he could learn was, that, by the patient's order, she had been several times in the adjacent room to offer consolation and assistance to a person who seemed resolved to accept of neither. "But you, perhaps, Sir," added she, "may be able to speak comfort to the poor young thing."

A voice now issued from the apartment; for the partition was so thin, and its apertures so frequent, that every word was distinctly heard. "Whoever you are," said the voice, "come and receive my sad tale whilst I have breath to utter it, in a few moments my lips will close forever." This was articulated in a tone so faint, that there could be no doubt that the person who uttered it was indeed expiring; and the two friends, in awful silence, entered her apartment. A curtain prevented the fair mourner's seeing them, which Henry gently touched, to inform her that they were present, and it was immediately opened. But Frederick, who thought he had had quite enough of dying faces for one morning, turned from the bed, and endeavored to find more agreeable ones in the street, into which the solitary window looked.

The young woman found herself addressed in the softest accents: argument of consolation was poured forth before her. "Alas," said she, "it is all, all too late; and the only comfort I now taste, is the certainty that I cannot live to profit by your goodness.—But burden your memory with my woes; that if, in your journey through life, you should meet with the author of them, he may know the fate of her who once reigned the mistress of his.

"I am by birth an American; the child of parents far advanced in life; consequently I was the blessing of their existence. My father was a planter respected for his riches, and beloved for his goodness! How unworthy have I been of such a parent!—My youth was passed beneath his eye, in which period I was instructed in all the accomplishments which are supposed to give force to beauty. Of beauty, too, I had my share; and was an object of envy to some of my own sex, whose charms I could not help thinking were superior to my own.

"At the age of seventeen, my father gave me in marriage to a young gentleman of amiable manners, who loved me to distraction. I, alas! was not sensible of passion in the degree in which my husband felt it; but I loved no other, and my innocence made me believe I felt for him all the tenderness my heart was capable of feeling—Oh, why was I ever awakened from the happy error!

"My father and my husband were both of the Loyalist party, and consequently the British officers were treated in their houses with particular attention and favor. A few months after our marriage, towards the close of the war, a young soldier, who was said to be of fashion and of great fortune in England, found admittance to our table. His manners were so engaging, that, after a few visits, my husband requested him to reside with us entirely. The invitation was gracefully accepted, and he became one of our family. Oh, how did the hours glide in his society! Without our walls, all was anarchy, distress, and war; but within all was elegance, and taste, and pleasure. My husband was never wearied of praising his guest; and my heart, unconscious of its error, fluttered with delight at hearing those praises.

"Alas, Sir, how shall I add the rest? By degrees my heart became sensible of its situation, and knew it loved—knew that it madly loved! My husband was often absent; at those periods, our guest never. It cannot be, that I should now go through all the scenes of seduction and guilt—for seduction and guilt did indeed follow; and I became abandoned to my lover!"

Here tears and groans interrupted the dying penitent; who, at length, with many interruptions, continued—"Think not that I became at once dead to honor, and to every consideration of duty! Slow, though sure, was my progress in the road of iniquity. Many were self-upbraidings, numberless my resolutions; but at last the voice of duty was dead in my heart, and love reigned there a ruining conqueror! I had retired one afternoon to a summer house in the farthest part of the garden. My lover unexpectedly appeared there—I say, unexpectedly. The suddenness of his approach, and the joy which accompanied my surprise, made me neglectful of everything but him. I abandoned myself to the ardor of his caresses; and, whilst I was reclining on his bosom, and encircled by his arms, my much injured husband entered the apartment.

"A cry of horror was the first intimation we received of his presence. He viewed us without speaking, whilst we remained absolutely motionless on the spot where he first beheld us. His first action was towards his sword; but pausing, and viewing us awhile with mingled rage and grief, he uttered another cry, and fled through the garden with incredible quickness. This was the last moment in which I ever saw my husband!

"We remained long in the fatal summer-house, not knowing what steps to pursue. The sense of my guilt overpowered me, and I felt that happiness was fled from me forever. At length I ventured to return to the house; I asked the servants, with my eyes, what was become of their master? but with my lips I dared not articulate his name. The servants did not seem to be conscious that any extraordinary event had happened, and all things appeared in their usual state of composure. Thus the night passed, three succeeding days and nights, in all which time I heard neither of my husband, nor of the man who had usurped his rights. This frightful calm was at length broken in upon—and by a tempest!

"On the fourth morning my father, my dear father! entered my apartment, with a countenance which expressed unusual sorrow. He took my hand, however, with the utmost tenderness; and, by the softness of his tones, removed the terror which had seized me on his appearance. He told me he had a deep affliction to prepare me for; and endeavored to fortify my mind with every argument of religion and submission, before he revealed it. In this dreadful suspense I uttered not a word; my mind was stretched with horrid expectation!

"At length the millstone crushed me. He informed me, that three days before, my husband had joined the American army; that an engagement had taken place, and that he was amongst the first victims of the battle. The effect this intelligence had on me was scarcely short of madness—I did not weep, but I grew furious; I called myself my husband's murderer, demanded justice on myself, and talked of circumstances which, though true, passed on those about me as the effect of a sudden frenzy. Those violent perturbations ended in a fever, from which it was my punishment to recover. With shame I acknowledge, that as my health returned, my passion revived. I now considered myself at liberty, and had no doubt but my tender passionate lover, panted for the hour in which he could throw himself at my feet, and recompense all my suffering by uniting himself to me forever. The days and weeks wore on, and he appeared not. At first I considered him as sacrificing to decorum; but at the end of two months I could no longer resist enquiring of a lady, who visited in my chamber, when she had seen the object of all my thought. She answered with great unconcern, that he had hardly been seen at all for the last month; for that he was so devoted to Mrs. Hiss, whose husband was in England, that he never spent an hour out of her house; that he boasted everywhere of his passion and of his happiness; and had told his friends he doted on her to such distraction, that, for her sake, he had half resolved to give up his country and his profession, and become an American planter.

"How long my friend might have continued in this interesting detail I know not, had not my suddenly falling senseless at her feet shocked her into silence. She had discernment, and perhaps guessed, in some measure, the cause of so strong an emotion. Urged, therefore, either by her prudence or her curiosity, she called no assistance, but endeavored to recall me to the recollection of my miseries by the common methods. On awaking from the fainting, I found my head reposed on her bosom, and her tears bedewed my face. The tenderness unlocked my whole soul—my woes were too poignant to admit of concealment, and they were all poured out before her.

"My failing spirit," said the sad narrator, "will not permit me to continue in a thread—I must pass over many events to tell you that this friend prevailed on me to accompany her to England. Her husband was a Loyalist; mine had been so, and the Americans made this a pretext to rob me of all my possessions—too light a punishment for crimes so deep! I left America without daring to mention such a design to my father.—I could not bear to stab him with the intelligence; and I could bear still less to remain on a spot where every object kept dishonor and wretchedness alive: yet I wrote to him from the first port, and confessed all my criminality; with a view to make his mind yield to the propriety of my absence, and to lessen his regrets for the loss of a child whom he could no longer think worthy of his love.

"On our arrival in England, my friends carried me to a Northern country, where I resided with them almost two years in tolerable tranquility. My tears were frequently poured before the Almighty for my past offenses; but they were tears which always left me more peaceable and serene. This quiet state was at length interrupted by the passion of the man in whose protection I lived. My friend had unwisely informed her husband of my former guilt, and he received the intelligence with malicious pleasure—he considered now, that I had no *right* to defend myself from his addresses on principles of honor, having once outraged them, and had the cruelty to inform me so. On my expressing horror at such a declaration, he had the brutality to add, that my affected niceness was an ill return to his benevolence in having so long supported me; and that, if I chose to cherish such ungrateful sentiments, it must be under some other roof.

"*His* roof I instantly quitted, though a stranger in the kingdom, and known to no human being in it, out of the little village in which we resided: but to remain *there* would have been as though I did not wish to fly from the enemy who pursued me; and I surely owed it to his wife, to leave a situation in which I was every hour exposed to the danger of his visits.

"A stage, which passed at the instant of these cogitations offered me relief: it was in winter, and there was not a creature in it; which gloomy circumstance was to me a desirable one, for it gave me the leisure of 200 miles to ponder over my sorrows, and to consider of my future fate. The bitterness of these reflections so overpowered me, that when the coach arrived in London, I was so ill as to seem to the people of the inn in a dying state—I bless Heaven they were right! The coachman recommended me to this house, kept by his relation as he informed me. I delivered my purse to the mistress of it, who for a fortnight gave me some attendance; but since that period she had kindly left me a prey to my disorder, which will presently——"

"D——! unfeeling wretch!" exclaimed Frederick, who had till now seemed attentive only to what passed in the street, though the restlessness of his motions and now and then a heavy sigh, gave his friends room to suspect him of more tenderness and compassion than was thought to belong to his character. The sudden force of this execration had a visible effect on the dying lady; but neither she, nor the gentlemen who had been listening to her melancholy tale, had time to notice it; for the door instantaneously opened, and divulged the venerable patient whom they had first visited. The nurse tottered beneath his weight, whilst with ghastly eyes he surveyed the lovely creature, already on the threshold of death. He stretched his arms towards her, uttered a deep cry, and falling on the bed, expired!

"My father, my father!" exclaimed the lady, clasping her hands with a wild air, and bending over the corpse; "but I shall join thee—my woes are at an end!"

"Yes, *thy* woes are over," said the youth, who now turned from the window:"*thy* woes are over; but oh! Caroline, where will end the anguish which now seizes my soul! Behold the author of all thy afflictions! thy husband's murderer, thy murderer, and the murderer of thy father!"

The lady started from her father's corpse; she fixed her eyes on him for a moment with the most dreadful expression, and essayed to speak—but death had already rendered rigid the organs of speech—his chill hand was on her heart—she struggled a moment; and then, without uttering a groan, sunk dead on the pillow!

Pause here, behold the two friends! Both young, both equally the favorites of health and of fortune. They had arisen in the morning fresh as the sun, when through the portals of the east he first glances his golden beams! The day was before them—their actions were to be chosen. One of them passed its opening hours in indolence, in folly, and expense—the hour of noon beholds him a conscious murderer; an accumulator of crimes; wretch bowed down with a sense of his iniquities. The other begun his day like a favorite son of Heaven; his heart was filled with benevolence; wherever he trod, his steps, like the steps of spring, gave hope, and joy, and consolation. Having feasted his mind with its own beneficence, he retires from the woes he had contributed to lessen; he is prepared to taste the pleasures which lay before him, to refine them, and to possess them with a zest of which the palsied libertine can form no idea. He is, indeed, an epicure—a voluptuary of the first order!—Ye sons of pleasure, copy the portrait!   1797

Massachusetts Magazine

The *Massachusetts Magazine,* founded by Isaiah Thomas, was one of the important periodicals of its day. It was published monthly at Boston from January, 1789, to December, 1796, and included much literary material—poetry, essays, plays, novels, and short fiction. Anonymously written tales like "The Bear: An Anecdote," published in the April, 1794, number, appeared frequently in the magazine. "The Child of Snow" is from the December, 1792, number.

The Bear: An Anecdote

Not long after the settlement of this country, a saw-mill was erected in the southern part of Norton. The audacity and singular fate of a bear at this place, on a certain time, perhaps a century ago, merit a place in the cabinet of the virtuoso.

The sawyer had just fixed a log on the carriages, and was sitting on it busily engaged in eating some bread and cheese. A bear at that instant came in without hesitancy, sat down very independently on the log between the man and the saw, and partook with the greatest freedom in the repast. The sawyer could not conveniently encounter him without hazard. Besides, he was well satisfied in his own mind, from his knowledge of the innate revengeful disposition incident to this species of animals, how his fate would soon turn. The event showed the rationality of his inference. They continued mutually to participate in the portion, till the log, by its gradual movement, had carried the bear to the teeth of the saw. A full stroke on his posteriors wrought his ire to the highest pitch. He instantly turned about, *grasped the rending saw with all his might, and hugged it till sawn in pieces!*

Q.

1794

The Child of Snow

An active and industrious merchant, had occasion often to be abroad for a considerable time together, in the pursuit of his traffic. During one of his voyages, which lasted for more than two years, it happened that his wife became enamored of a young neighbor. Love, which is restrained with difficulty, soon brought them together; but they managed their affairs in so bungling a manner, that at the expiraton of about nine months, the merchant's wife found herself for the first time a mother.

The husband, on his return, was greatly surprised to find this acquisition to his family, and asked his wife to what accident they were indebted for it.—"Sir," said she, "I happened one day to be reclined above stairs at the window, giving vent to my grief for your absence. It was in the winter season, and there was at the time a heavy fall of snow. As I cast up my streaming eyes to heaven, and heaved a sigh on thinking of you, a flake of snow accidentally made its way into my mouth, and I immediately found that I had conceived this child whom you now see."

The merchant on hearing this story, did not betray the least symptoms of discontent or ill humor. "Thanks be to God," said he; "I have wished for an heir, and he has sent me one: I am satisfied and thankful for his bounty." He, indeed thereafterward, affected the most entire satisfaction, never offered the least reproach to his wife, but lived in the same good understanding with her as before. Nevertheless this was all dissimulation —he had formed inwardly a resolution to be one day or another amply revenged.

The child, however, grew up, and had attained the age of fifteen, when the merchant, who was still occupied with his project of revenge, thought seriously of putting it into execution.—"Wife," said he one day, "you must not be afflicted, if I once more take my leave of you for a time. I am going upon a long journey tomorrow; and I desire you will get ready my baggage, and that of my son: For I mean to take him with me, that he may acquire some knowledge of trading while he is young." "Alas!" replied the mother, "I am much grieved to hear that you are going to take him abroad so soon; but since it is for your satisfaction and his advantage, I submit. God be with you both, and bring you back in safety." Matters being thus arranged, the merchant set off early next morning; and took the Child of Snow along with him.

It is needless to give the particulars of the journey, or an account of the countries through which he passed. It is enough to mention, that on his arrival at Genoa, he found a Saracen merchant bound for Alexandria, to whom he sold the boy as a slave. Afterwards having settled his own affairs at leisure, he returned home.

The imagination of an hundred poets combined would not give you an adequate description of the distraction of the mother, when she saw the merchant return without her son. She tore her hair, and fell into a fit of frenzy. At length having recovered herself, she conjured her husband to tell her without reserve what had happened to the youth. The husband expected all this uproar; and therefore was not puzzled for an answer. "Wife," said he, "one cannot arrive to my age, without having had experience enough in the world, to know the necessity of reconciling one's self to whatever may happen. For what do we gain by giving way to our affliction? Listen with fortitude to the misfortune that happened to us in the country whence I come. Your son and myself were, on a sultry day, climbing up a steep and lofty mountain. It was about noon, the sun was vertical over our heads and burned like fire. When, behold, on a sudden, your son began to dissolve, and melted before my eyes! I would have offered him assistance, but knew that it would be vain; for I recollected that you told me he sprang out of a flake of snow."

The wife knew perfectly well the merchant's meaning. She durst not, however, break out, but was obliged to swallow the liquor which she had brewed.   1792

James Kirke Paulding

(1778-1860)

Salmagundi: Second Series, entirely the work of James Kirke Paulding, was published in New York in 1819–1820. Like *Salmagundi: First Series* (1807–1808), which Paulding wrote in collaboration with William and Washington Irving, the *Second Series* included letters, essays, social commentaries, and some short narratives. "Vrouwen Dagh" first appeared in the October 2, 1819, paper. "The Yankee Roué," really a novelette, was published in a collection of narratives entitled *Tales of the Good Woman* (New York, 1829).

BIBLIOGRAPHY: *Paulding's Works,* 14 vols. (New York, 1835–1837) and a 4 vol. collection, ed. William Paulding (New York, 1867–1868). See headnote to *The Backwoodsman.*

Vrouwen Dagh

WOMAN'S DAY

In rummaging the other day among some of the old archives of the Hall, treating concerning the early history of this fair and excellent city, I came unexpectedly upon a singular custom, which prevailed about a century and a half ago, among our worthy ancestors. It is recorded that on Valentine's day, every young damsel was furnished with a piece of rope about a yard in length, with which they lurked behind the corners of the streets, waiting the appearance of the young fellows, whom they were privileged to beat, until they got out of the way by running. This day of license was called, in the classical language of our early times, VROUWEN DAGH; and it was held a disgrace for any young fellow to return these blows with anything but a kiss, during the period of license. It is recorded that a smart blow was considered a peculiar proof of regard, especially if it left a memento on the skin, which was held equivalent to those marks by which country people designate sheep and cattle as their own.

This custom continued to prevail until about the beginning of the seventeenth century, when, as the historian relates, the married women, doubtless in consequence of the unseemly liberty allowed them when single, became so grievously addicted to arrant scolding, and lectured their husbands in such a way, that a law was passed empowering the sheriff to erect a ducking-stool, directly in front of the old City Hall, for the purpose of restraining this liberty of speech. It was, however, taken down some years afterward, being found unnecessary in consequence of the wonderful reformation of the sex about that time, which, I am happy to say, has continued ever since.

Reflecting the other evening on these and other matters connected with our patriarchal age, I insensibly yielded to the influence of the dog-days, and fell asleep. The human mind may be likened to a well-broken steed, whose sprightly gambols are restrained by a habit of submission to his rider, but who, the moment he slips his rein, bounds over the fences, and riots in forbidden pastures. So with our reason; while waking, it only indulges in a few occasional curvettings; but when sleep comes, and steals away the bridle, placing it in the hands of nimble fancy, we disdain the limits of possibility, and triumph for a while over time and space.

I fancied myself all at once standing close by the ducking-stool, erected by the before-named sheriff, in front of the old City Hall, at the moment the worshipful magistrate was adjudging a number of cases in which the liberty of speech had been grossly abused, by certain married ladies, as was alleged. The first offender, I remember, was a goodly-sized dame, of some fifty years old. She wore a little cap, partly inclining to one ear, and carried her arms a-kimbo, as if in defiance both of the husband and magistrate. She was arraigned on the complaint of a stout, brawny, weather-beaten gentleman, wearing a little cocked hat, ornamented with broad copper lace. A short pipe was stuck in the buttonhole of his waistcoat, that bore some vestiges of lace also, and it was remarked that the circumstance of the pipe indicated great wrath in the owner, as this was the first time he had ever been seen without carrying it in his mouth. He announced himself as the renowned Mynheer Adrian Block, the first navigator that ever sailed through Hell Gate, an adventure which he considered as nothing, compared to weathering a matrimonial gale at home. The sheriff having found out, by cross-questioning the parties, that the scolding arose entirely from the provoking silence of the skipper, who obstinately refused to quarrel with his wife, decreed that this was some little excuse, and dismissed her with a caution. Before she got fairly out of hearing, however, she attacked Mynheer Block so vigorously, that the magistrate ordered her back, and sentenced her to a ducking.

The next culprit was a brisk, snub-nosed, skinny little dame, with peculiarly sharp black eyes, that boded no good. Her husband, one Wyngaard, stated that he kept the sign of Santa Claas near the corner of the Cherry Garden, and that he was doing pretty well, till his wife drove away all his customers, by scolding from morning to night. The little woman urged, as an offset, that her husband did nothing but tipple with every person that came into the house. She would not have minded this so much had he drunk out of his customer's cup; but the gentleman, forsooth, must treat in his turn, by means of which he was bringing them to poverty, and the only method she could think of to prevent his beggaring herself and children, was to drive people away as soon as possible. The sheriff hereupon decreed Mynheer Wyngaard a sound ducking at the hands of his wife, which was administered to the great content of Mrs. Block, who stood shaking her feathers like an old hen in a corner.

A man now came up, leading a fashionable lady with red clocks to her stockings, and little square silver buckles to her shoes, the heels whereof, to the best of my recollection, were nearly six inches high. From these indications I judged her to be a person of consequence, especially as the sheriff nodded his head to the husband as he came up to make his complaint. The lady appeared with such an air of modesty, that I confess I felt interested in her favor; but it being satisfactorily proved that she waked her husband several nights in succession, only to lecture him for snoring, the whole assembly murmured her condemnation, and the poor lady underwent the penalty of thus interfering with the unalienable birthright of a genuine Dutchman.

The next offender was brought by a person carrying a broken pipe in his hand. He announced himself as the keeper of the old Ferry-house in Broad-street, to which highly important situation he had been appointed, as his worship well knew, for his unrivaled skill in blowing the horn. Though his wife was reckoned the greatest shrew in the whole street, he had managed to get the better of her by blowing his horn stoutly whenever she talked too loud, until that very morning, when, on taking up his instrument to argue with her, she actually knocked his pipe out of his mouth, an offense not to be tolerated in a Christian community. The good woman denied the charge with unparalleled volubility, but the broken pipe was considered conclusive. The offense being enormous, she was sentenced to two duckings.

The severity of this infliction created a solemn pause, and seemed to have a great effect on the bystanders. During the dead silence, a middle-aged citizen, of a quiet, inoffensive physiognomy, came forward and lodged a grievous complaint against his wife. It seems she was an heiress, having brought him, as a marriage portion, a cow, a feather-bed, and a black silk gown. On the strength of this dowry she ran into every kind of extravagance, buying two gowns a year, and changing the fashion of her dress every four or five years, to the great scandal of the neighborhood, as well as the ruin of his fortune. Whenever he refused her money to supply these enormous caprices, she always threw the cow, the featherbed, and the silk gown in his teeth, so that, though her fortune was gone long ago, he was likely never to hear the last of it while he lived. The popular feeling seemed very strong against this offender, and everyone pronounced her worthy a ducking, which was, however, remitted on the score of her being a great heiress and brought up like a lady. The magistrate decided that she should be shut up a couple of days with the lady of the broken pipe, who appeared so discontented with the alleged partiality of the sheriff, that it was shrewdly suspected there would be some smart sparring between them.

The next case was a very curious one. The person complained of had, it seems, lost her speech several years before, by some accident I don't recollect, but the complainant alleged that, notwithstanding this, she had a most emphatic way of making herself understood by a box on the ear, or some equally expressive gesture. The sheriff having neither law-books or lawyers to decide the question, whether a dumb lady could possibly come under the act, seemed inclined to dismiss the complaint, when a person who had just drove up in an old chair, and who, I understood, was a famous physician, begged to propose a plan of settling this difficult question. As the poor woman could not enter upon her own defense, it seemed rather hard to duck her on the charge of being a shrew; he therefore suggested her being ducked by way of experiment, as he had known instances of persons recovering their speech by the sudden shock from cold water. Everybody seeming to think this a capital plan, except the husband, who appeared rather alarmed concerning the event of the experiment, it was accordingly put in execution with the most complete success. The moment the shock had passed, the patient announced her recovery by a volley which caused the husband to retreat with great precipitation. Being apparently determined to make herself amends for lost time, she next attacked the sheriff with such vigor, that the worthy magistrate was fain to break up the court, and dismiss the bystanders rather unceremoniously. At this moment, methought she cast her eye on me with such a peculiar expression of hostility, that I considered my time as having actually come. The very idea of the approaching storm caused such a trepidation, that I suddenly awoke, and mistook Mrs. Cockloft for the dumb lady, so fully was I impressed with my dream.

1819

From The Yankee Roué

Stafford Sheffield, the poor nephew of the wealthy Calvin Sopus, is the "hero" of "The Yankee Roué." Taken in by his uncle, young Sheffield inherits the Sopus wealth upon the conditions that he change his name to Sopus and that he go to Europe for his schooling. Young Sopus loses his inheritance in his dissipations in Europe

and has returned to America looking for "a single lady with plenty
of money for a wife; a married one with plenty of beauty for a
friend." Hartwell, an acquaintance of young Sopus, "had been
abroad too, but he brought home something besides vices and
follies." [Editors' note.]

CHAPTER VI

Rouéism and the Fine Arts

Our hero had brought home with him a thorough contempt for his
own country. Ignorant himself of literature, and the first rudiments of the
fine arts, still he fancied that, having been abroad, he must of necessity
be highly accomplished both in one and the other. He had never read
anything but the lowest periodicals in foreign literature, and from these
had learned all the self-sufficient arrogance for which they are so peculiarly distinguished. Without knowing what his countrymen had done, or
being able to judge of what they were capable of doing, he adopted the
slang of those who knew as little as himself. He pronounced them destitute of genius, devoid of taste, and ignorant of all the refinements of civilization. It is a common foible with my countrymen abroad, basely to surrender their country to the scoffs of witlings, and to imagine they exempt
themselves from the general condemnation, by joining in the sneer or the
laugh.

Our country affords but few resources for idle men. They are not yet
sufficiently numerous and rich to form a separate caste, and afford themselves the means of a perpetual succession of amusements. Sopus was
soon at a loss what to do with himself, for he could not be always playing the fiddle, or devoting himself to the married ladies. He sometimes
found them actually busy; sometimes not fit to be seen; and sometimes,
though of course very rarely, he found them out. What, however, most
annoyed him, was their condign ignorance of fashionable life abroad, in
supposing that his visits were either to their husbands or their daughters.
One of them, in particular, came nigh to causing his utter annihilation.
He had paid her most obsequious homage at all places where he happened to meet her, and from the smiles and simperings with which it was
received, had already begun to cherish hopes that his person and accomplishments would prove irresistible.

One delicious morning in the month of June, when the purity of the air
and the luxurious blandness of the weather reminded him of Italy, he
called upon the lady, at an hour when he knew the husband was absent.
He found her in the graceful undress of a matron, sitting on a rich ottoman of pale yellow silk. The curtains of the windows were of a pink
color, and as the sun shone upon them, threw a rich tint and delicious
glow upon the face, the arms, and the neck of the beautiful wife. Sopus
mistook it for a blush, and at that moment determined to make his dec-

laration. The lady had been buying silk stockings. He took one up, and it afforded him a theme for some very pretty little sly hints and innuendoes, which a truly modest woman never understands. Our hero's experience had made him estimate all women by the same standard. I must speak plainer, thought he, and allow her at least the honor of a summons before she surrenders.

He dropped on his knee, and exclaimed—

"Madam, I am the most miserable of men!"

"I am sorry for it, Mr. Sopus," replied the lady.

"You pity me then, angel of a woman!"

"If you are miserable, I certainly do."

"And pity is akin to love."

"So they say," replied the lady, quietly.

"But will you not permit me to love—to hope—to be happy?"

"Ask my daughter."

Zounds! thought Sopus, what a barbarous country, where the mothers ask the consent of the daughters, instead of the daughters the mothers.

"Your daughter, madam?"

"Yes; I never mean to give my daughter away without her own consent. I'll send her to you," and the good matron took the silk stockings, and quietly walked out of the room.

Friend Sopus was in a dilemma. The daughter was a fine, intelligent, wellbred girl, much admired by Heartwell; but her father was a hale, hearty, middle-aged man, and, though rich, might not die in half a century. "These fellows," quoth our hero, "nine times in ten outlive their heirs—but mum." The young lady entered, curtsied, I mean bowed, and sat down on the sofa, with as little emotion as if the room had been empty. These American women have no more sensibility and warmth than a cucumber, quoth our hero. At length the young lady broke silence.

"My mother mentioned you had something particular to communicate, Mr. Sopus," said she, while a little shade of a smile passed over her face, and settled in the corner of her eye, as she pronounced his name. Ah! that cursed name, thought he, I shall never prosper under it; and now the fortune is gone, I wish the name were gone with it.

"Madam," said he, and though he had finished his education abroad, he actually felt a little awkward, "do you mean to go to the fancy ball tonight?"

The young lady laughed. "I believe I shall."

"Well then—hem—ha—may I have the superlative pleasure of dancing the first cotillion with you,"

"Certainly, Mr. Sopus," and again that wicked laugh lurked in the corner of her eye.

Sopus made a profound bow, and so did the lady, not being able to curtsy, on account of the Cantelos, and thus they parted.

What a barbarous country! thought our hero, where a married woman don't know whether you are making love to herself or her daughter.

"Well, Julia," said the mother, "are you engaged?"

"To dance the first cotillion," said Julia; and she threw herself on the sofa, and laughed till she got a great pain in her side.

Coming out of the house, he encountered Heartwell, who was passing up the street.

"So," said he, "you've been paying your morning devoirs to Miss Wingate—a fine girl."

"Delightful," answered the other, and fell to praising her to the skies.

Heartwell paused, and looked a little serious; but, suddenly resuming his wonted free and spirited manner, he proposed to take Sopus to the Academy of Arts, to see a collection of original paintings, by the most celebrated masters of the Italian and Flemish schools, exhibiting there.

"An Academy of Arts!" quoth Sopus. "Pooh, what can you have worth seeing there? But come, anything to kill time."

"Ah!" cried he, as they entered the exhibition-room, and saw the very worst collection ever imposed upon the good people of the city, labelled with the names of Michael Angelo, Raphael, Domenichino, Salvator, and the Carracci. "Ah! really now, this is something like; I declare this really does honor to the country. It reminds me of the gallery at Florence. Why, the names are the very same." Whereupon, he out with his glass, after the manner of traveled men, and, fixing himself opposite to an immeasurable daub, full of green lions and brown trees, labelled Sal. Rosa, began to be quite enthusiastic. "What expression in the trees! What grace in the very rocks! What dignity in the lions! Anybody could tell they were the kings of the beasts! There is nobody, after all, equal to Sally Rosa for persuasive grace of attitude, softness of expression, and felicity of groping," as he was pleased to call it—"I knew her in Florence. She was a most elegant woman."

Heartwell stuffed the whole catalogue into his mouth, and walked away at a quick step. He however returned in a few moments.

"You are right," said he; "Miss Sally was particularly remarkable for all these characteristics. I see you are a connoisseur."

"A piece of a one," answered he, pulling up his stock, and adjusting his striped gingham collar. "But, my dear Heartwell, never again call a foreign lady Miss or Mistress. It is Madame or Signora Sally Rosa."

"I shall bear it in mind," said the other.

After spending some time in pointing out the various excellences of this rare collection of originals by the great Italian and Flemish masters, in which Sopus displayed equal taste and accuracy, he was carried into the apartment where the statuary and busts are deposited.

"What, in the name of all that is monstrous and vulgar, have we got here?" cried he, stopping opposite the Laocoon.

"'Tis the famous Laocoon," said Heartwell.

"La—La—ocoon," said Sopus, "who is it by?"

"The name of the artist is somewhat doubtful. It is supposed to be a work of great antiquity."

"Yes, anybody can see it must have been done in the infancy of the arts. The artist did well to keep his name secret. But who is this tall, long-spliced, sprawling fellow, standing on one leg?"

"That is the Apollo Belvidere; you must have seen it before."

"O, ay—I think I do recollect something of a wooden statue stuck up at the Belvidere House, where my uncle's club used to meet. I suppose they call it the Apollo Belvidere on that account. Can you tell me who carved it?"

"No, I regret to say that I have forgot it," replied Heartwell, again having recourse to the system of gagging.

"No matter," said the other, "it is not worth remembering. Let us go back; I want to take another look at the Sally—or, as these vulgarians call her, Sal."

Coming out of the Academy through the park, Heartwell said something about the City Hall, which set Sopus retailing the cant he had learned from the foreign periodicals.

"I've seen a handsomer stable than that in England," said he. "Do you remember Lord Darlington's stables?"

"No," said Heartwell, "I confess I did not pay any particular attention to stables."

"No!" said the other, in astonishment. "Were you never at Tattersall's?"

"Never."

"Why, what the d——l did you travel for?"

"To see the world," replied Heartwell.

"And where could you see it better than at Tattersall's?"

"Why, as far as grooms, jockeys, blacklegs, and sporting heroes go to the formation of a world, I don't know a better place. But I had no ambition to figure in such society."

"No!" answered the other, with a look of wonder. "But did you ever see Carlton House?"

"I did, and thought it a disgrace to the nation and its king."

"What, when it was lighted up with gas lamps?"

"Even when it was lighted up with gas lamps."

"But what think you of Windsor Castle? Is not that a palace worthy of a king?"

"Certainly; but that is a building of another age, and even the bad taste of the present has not been able to spoil it altogether. Indeed, I may say of England, and of all Europe in fact, that, so far as my experience goes, there is no building, erected within the last two hundred years, that can claim the rank of a model. All the most perfect specimens of architecture are of a date anterior to the settlement of this country; and our people are no more to be reproached for a bad taste in architecture, than those nations which have not, any more than ourselves, produced masterpieces within that period. The cathedrals, which comprise all the treasures of architecture in England, and nearly all of later origin in Europe, are, without exception, comparatively ancient. They belong to other times; they are the proper boast of our ancestors; and as we are equally the descendants of the different nations of Europe with the present race of Europeans, we have as fair a right to plume ourselves upon the triumphs of former ages. It is so with painting, sculpture, and poetry. The highest honors in all these belong to ages anterior to our existence as a separate nation. The modern Greeks might as well boast of their Homer, as the modern English of their Shakspeare and Milton."

Heartwell, who all this time had been looking at the City Hall, turned to see what effect his harangue had produced upon the roué, and found him busily employed in jerking pebbles at a tree a little way off. "I'll bet you ten I hit it three times out of five," quoth he.

CHAPTER XIII

The Dishing of A Roué

Both Heartwell and Sopus court the wealthy Julia Wingate. Heart-well, of course, marries Julia. Chapter XII closes with Sopus commenting upon Heartwell's good fortune: "There is but one more misery I wish him," quoth Sopus; "may old Wingate live a hundred years, and his wife fifty." [Editors' note.]

The summer now came on, bringing in its train a thousand blessings: relieving the poor from the pinching cold of winter, and exchanging chilling frosts and howling blasts for two of the best gifts of heaven, sunshine and sweet south winds. The town thinned apace, and everything in the shape of a human being, I mean the fashionable brokers, speculators, and people that make money genteelly, were either gone or going to the Springs, the mountains, the shore, or the grand tour. Our hero had a run of luck, that is, he had been well paid of late for finishing the education of certain young gentlemen of fashion. He determined on a trip to the Springs, for he had heard it was an excellent place for flirting and getting an appetite. But he had a secret and a stronger motive.

For some time past he had been in the habit of dining with an acquaintance at a fashionable Broadway house, frequented by travelers coming from the south to spend the summer. Here he met with a Mr. and Mrs. Sarsfield, who had come, I believe, from the western part of Virginia, and stopped a few weeks in the city on their way to Saratoga. Mr. Sarsfield was a tall, upright figure, rather of a brown complexion, although his hair and eyes were of a light color. He wore a white hat with a broad brim; a blue frock, not of the first cut, or finest materials; and his hair was tied behind with a black riband. He had no more whiskers than the palm of my hand, and was otherwise exceedingly defective in fashionable indispensables. Yet with all this, a better taste and a keener eye than that of our hero, would have distinctly recognized the air, the manner, and, above all, the look of a well-bred, well-educated gentleman. There are none who make such fatal blunders as those who judge a man by the standard of his dress. Sopus determined to give the tall gentleman with the long queue a touch of his foreign education. "I've caught a quiz," thought he. It turned out he had caught a Tartar.

The tall gentleman with the long queue and no whiskers had a charming wife, much younger than himself, and, to say the truth, much handsomer. Her complexion, though she was born under a southern sun, was extremely fair; her eyes of a most equivocal color, whether black, hazel, or gray, I could never make out to my satisfaction; teeth white and even; lips, cheeks, &c. of nature's best handiwork; and a figure "too short for a long praise, and too tall for a short one;" it was the very thing. Her hair was brown and dazzling, and though I hardly expect to be credited by my fashionable readers, it curled naturally, a thousand times more gracefully than either Monsieur Manuel or Monsieur Sebastian could make it, with all their matchless "gramary." She was as lively as a singing-bird in its native forest; as unsuspecting as Eve, when she first met the first man; and as innocent as when she first listened to the song of the serpent. "A prize!" thought our roué; and forthwith he laid out upon the beautiful matron all the stock of his foreign importations.

The lady had never met with a creature of his species before. She laughed at him and with him; she danced with him at several parties; she walked with him on the Battery by moonlight, and took his arm with as innocent a frankness as she would that of her grandfather. The tall gentleman with the long queue had seen a little more of the world than his wife. He had actually seen Chargé at a foreign court, and spent a winter in Paris. But he never spoke of it except it was necessary. He had his eye upon our hero, having seen enough of the world to fathom his intentions; but he knew his wife, and the only feeling he had on the subject was of insulted honor rather than suspicion or jealousy. The very idea that there is a being breathing on the face of the earth who dares to dream of, much more to meditate, seducing the wife of our bosom, is intolerable to a man of spirit and honor.

Our hero took passage in the steamboat with the beautiful Virginia wife and her tall husband. He played the roué in the very first style; handed the lady upstairs and downstairs; was at her elbow from morning till night; and took up so much of her attention that two or three times she actually forgot her husband. "Is that pretty lady your wife?" asked an old lady, very significantly. "Heaven forbid!" quoth Sopus. In this way he traveled with them to the Springs, kindly taking upon himself all the trouble of entertaining and waiting upon the fair matron. All this while Mr. Sarsfield said nothing; for there is no task from which a proud man more shrinks than that of indicating, either in word or act, that he disapproves another man's attentions to his wife. He knows that, if matters are going wrong, it will only make them worse; and he scorns to become the Argus of what a woman ought herself to guard. Besides, he saw as clearly that his wife was innocent as that the roué was intent on making her otherwise. He held his tongue; but it was the silence of the brewing tempest.

At the Springs, one of the principal occupations of people is to watch one another, and the principal amusement to detail the result. Sopus continued his attentions without the inexperienced wife being in the remotest degree the wiser for his significant looks and speaking sighs. But other people saw clearer. There was an old lady in spectacles, who had spent a month or six weeks at the Springs every summer since the discovery of America. Of course she knew a little of the world. One day she said to Mrs. Sarsfield, "What does that young man want, that he is always following you about?"—"I don't know," replied the other.—"I do," said the old lady. Soon after, Sopus met Mrs. Sarsfield alone in the music-room, and kissed her hand, in full view of the husband, who was standing unseen. Mr. Sarsfield felt an almost irresistible impulse to kick Mr. Sopus on the spot. But, checking himself, he sent his wife upstairs to get ready for a ride, and shutting the door of the music-room, addressed our hero as follows, in a mild, firm voice.

"Mr. Sopus, your attentions to my wife are becoming disagreeable to me."

"So long as they are not disagreeable to the lady, I presume there is no harm done," replied our hero, with a laugh, for he thought he had to do with a clodhopper of the first pretensions.

Sarsfield's eyes flashed fire, but he restrained himself.

"Mr. Sopus, you must be aware that this is not a place where anything like particular and constant attention can be paid to a married woman, without giving occasion to ill-natured remarks and suspicions, real or pretended. Mrs. Sarsfield is not aware of this; I therefore speak to you rather than her. I again take the freedom to observe, that your attentions to Mrs. Sarsfield are disagreeable to me."

"And I," said Sopus, pertly, "again observe, that so long as they are not disagreeable to the lady, I shall continue my attentions."

Heaven and earth! what a shower of blows was just on the point of wetting the shoulders of our hero. But Mr. Sarsfield, as I observed before, was a man of the world, and knew that, were he to take any measure of this kind, it would set ten thousand tongues running like millclappers. He accordingly restrained himself once more; and that very afternoon went with Mrs. Sarsfield over to Ballston. The very next morning Mr. Sopus was at Ballston renewing his devoirs. Sarsfield was out of all patience, and swore he would have satisfaction for this insolent perseverance. He took occasion, upon pretense of some little impertinence of our hero, which had no reference to the more weighty cause of complaint, to pass upon him a direct and palpable insult, such as no man, pretending to the character of a gentleman, could overlook without being dishonored. There are some men who possess that amiable philosophy which putteth up with insult, not in the spirit of forgiveness, but from a natural insensibility to such trifles. Our hero was of this sect of philosophers, and accordingly suffered the insult of Mr. Sarsfield to pass unnoticed. The company, instead of admiring this singular magnanimity, hereupon began to look askance, and to shun the society of the accomplished Mr. Sopus, who soon saw himself in the enviable situation of a man alone in a crowd. One day at dinner, he asked a gentleman to take wine with him. The gentleman politely answered, "I never drink wine," and a moment after drank a glass with Mr. Sarsfield.

Our hero saw that he must either call out the tall man with the long queue, and peril his life, or die to the fashionable world. He neither had an office nor a commission in the militia, and could, therefore, plead no privilege. Accordingly he resolved on challenging Mr. Sarsfield, being pretty confident that a man without whiskers, and who wore a long queue tied with a black riband, could never be a man of courage. Under this consoling conviction he sent Mr. Sarsfield a challenge, which, greatly to his surprise and mortification, was promptly accepted. They went over into Vermont, that being the nearest "debatable land."

"You don't mean to harm this calf?" asked Mr. Sarsfield's second.

"Not much; I shall only give him a lesson he will be the better for all his life."

The distance was paced, the preliminaries settled, and the word about being given, when, just at the critical moment, the pistol of the gallant roué went off—it was a hair trigger—and inflicted a sore wound in the lower part of his leg. He fell; and his antagonist, learning that our hero was satisfied, fired his pistol in the air, at the same time politely expressing his regrets at the accident. "I shall be at your service at any time," said he, and thus ended this affair of honor.

Sopus was carried to a neighboring village, and deposited in a hotel, where he remained nearly three months, and became not only very tired, but ran up a bill which he had not the means of paying. He had plenty of leisure to moralize, and accordingly came to the conclusion that the American husbands were a set of vulgar semi-barbarians. He tried to seduce the landlord into a little gambling, both as a means of passing his time and providing for the payment of his bill. But mine host was a man of nice scruples. He speculated in lottery tickets, but he was principled against all sorts of gambling.

His long stay at this place, and his long bill, fairly emptied his pockets, and left him in debt besides. He quitted the hotel a lame duck in both senses—he was lame of a leg, and out at the elbows. When he got to the city he forgot to send the scrupulous landlord his money, as he had pledged himself to do. Mine host, impatient at the delay, had him arrested and put in prison, to the horror of good society, and the consternation of divers fashionable young roués, who felt a sort of instinctive dislike to such vulgar places as jails. Poor Sopus, not being in business, had not the enviable privilege of taking the benefit of the bankrupt law three or four times, without being at all the worse for it, either in reputation or estate.

An old uncle, a grocer in Pump-street, whose acquaintance our hero had cut from the moment he was transplanted to the Square, hearing of his situation, came to see him; and such was the wonderful virtue of the specific administered by the hand of honest adversity, that Sopus actually forgave the old man for being a grocer and living in Pump-street.

"You shall go home and live with me," said the good man.

"On one condition," replied our hero.

"What is that?"

"That you get the name of the street changed, and promise not to degrade me into your shop boy."

The old grocer promised, and subsequently made such pathetic representations to the corporation of that day, that they changed the name of Pump to that of Cistern-street, which it bears even at the present time. Sopus was in hopes that this gentle appellation would tempt all the beau monde of Broadway to let their houses for taverns and ordinaries, and come and live in Cistern-street. And so it will probably be in good time.

Our hero was now lame of a leg, like the great Tamerlane, and lived with a retail grocer up in the Bowery. Had it only been a wholesale grocery, he might have been permitted to subscribe to the City Assembly. But the retail business was the bar sinister; and our hero fell from the height of fashionable renown, to be trodden underfoot like the worms that hang from the elm trees in Broadway, now vaulting to and fro in gallant trim, and anon groveling in the dust ingloriously. At present, instead of aspiring to instruct fashionable matrons in the cabalistics of foreign manners, and the young gentlemen in the canons of European perfectibility, he contents himself with talking a little equivocally to the ladies who preside over the apple stalls and cookey shops in Cheapside and Chatham Square, where he is still venerated as a roué razeed.

I met him the other day, hobbling along, with little remains of his ancient glories except his whiskers, and inquired how he came to be in such a condition.

"I am a sufferer in the cause of 'Public Improvement' and 'Domestic Policy.' "

"What! you could not civilize us after all?"

"No; I would as soon attempt to civilize the Indians," replied THE ROUÉ.   1829

James Hall
(1793-1868)

Born and educated at Philadelphia, James Hall served in the army (1812–1817), entered law practice (1818), and headed west to Illinois in 1820. At Shawneetown, he was a lawyer, a prosecuting attorney, and editor of the *Illinois Gazette*, a newspaper. In 1828, he moved to Vandalia, Ill., where he edited a newspaper, the *Illinois Intelligencer* (1829–1832), and the *Illinois Monthly Magazine* (October, 1830–September, 1832), one of the early western periodicals. Hall moved to Cincinnati in 1833; there he edited the *Western Monthly Magazine* (1833–1836) and continued to write. He spent his later years as a banker and businessman. Hall's short fiction, much of which originally appeared in his magazines, includes *Legends of the West* (Philadelphia, 1832), *Tales of the Border* (Philadelphia, 1835) and *The Wilderness and the Warpath* (New York, 1846). He wrote one novel, *The Harpe's Head; a Legend of Kentucky* (Philadelphia, 1833), and several studies of the West, among them *Sketches of History, Life, and Manners in the West*, 2 Vols. (Philadelphia, 1834-1835). "The Divining Rod" appeared in *Legends of the West*.

BIBLIOGRAPHY: John T. Flanagan, *James Hall, Literary Pioneer of the Ohio Valley* (Minneapolis, Minn., 1941). Randolph C. Randall, *James Hall, Spokesman of the New West* (Columbus, Ohio, 1964).

From *Legends of the West*

The Divining Rod

On a pleasant evening in the autumn of the year 18——, two travelers were slowly winding their way along a narrow road which led among the hills that overhang the Cumberland river, in Tennessee. One of these was a farmer of the neighborhood—a large, robust, sunburnt man, mounted on a sleek plough horse. He was one of the early settlers, who had fought and hunted in his youth, among the same valleys that now teemed with abundant harvests; a rough plain man clad in substantial homespun, he had about him an air of plenty and independence, which is never deceptive, and which belongs almost exculsively to our free and fertile country. His companion was of a different cast—a small, thin, grey haired man, who seemed worn down by bodily and mental fatigue to almost a shadow. He was a preacher, but one who would have deemed it an insult to be called a clergyman; for he belonged to a sect who condemn all human learning as vanity, and who consider a trained minister as little better than an imposter. The person before us was a champion of the sect. He boasted that he had nearly grown to manhood before he knew one letter from another; that he had learned to read for the sole purpose of gaining access to the Scriptures, and, with the exception of the hymns used in his church, had never read a page in any other book. With considerable natural sagacity, and an abundance of zeal, he had a gift of words, which enabled him at times to support his favorite tenets with a plausibility and force, amounting to something very nearly akin to eloquence, and which, while it gave him unbounded sway among his own followers, was sometimes not a little troublesome to his learned opponents. His sermons presented a curious mixture of the sententious and the declamatory, an unconnected mass of argument and assertion, through which there ran a vein of dry original humor, which, though it often provoked a smile, never failed to rivet the attention of the audience. But these flashes were like sparks of fire, struck from a rock; they communicated a life and warmth to˙ the hearts of others, which seemed to have no existence in that from which they sprung, for that humor never flashed in his own eye, nor relaxed a muscle of his melancholy, cadaverous countenance. Yet that eye was not destitute of expression; there were times when it beamed with intelligence, moments when it softened into tenderness; but its usual character was that of a visionary, fanatic enthusiasm. His ideas were not numerous, and the general theme of his declamation consisted of metaphysical distinctions between what he called "head religion," and "heart religion," the one being a direct inspiration, and the other a spurious substitute learned from vain books. He wrote a tract to show it was the thirst after human knowledge, which drove our first parents from paradise, that through the whole course of succeeding time *school larning* had been the most prolific source of human misery and mental degradation, and that bible societies, free masonry, the holy alliance, and the inquisition, were so many engines devised by king-craft, priest-craft and school-craft, to subjugate the world to the power of Satan. He spoke of the millennium as a time when "there should be no king, nor printer, nor sunday school, nor outlandish tongue, nor vain doctrine—when men would plough, and women milk the cows, and talk plain English to each other, and worship God out of the fullness of their hearts, and not after vain forms written by men." In short, this worthy man was entirely opposed to the spread of religious knowledge; "when a man has head religion," he would say, "he is in a bad fix to die—cut off his head, and away goes his soul and body to the devil." The remainder of his character may be briefly sketched. Honest, humane, and harmless in private life, impetuous in his feelings, fearless and independent by nature, and reared in a country where speech is as free as thought, he pursued his vocation without intolerance, but with a zeal which sometimes bordered on insanity. He spoke of his opponents more in sorrow than in anger, and bewailed the increase of knowledge as a mother mourns over her first born. He was of course ignorant and illiterate; and with a mind naturally vigorous, and capable of high attainments, his visionary theories, and perhaps a slight estrangement of intellect, had left the soil open to superstition, so that while at one time he discovered and exposed a popular error with wonderful acuteness, at another he blindly adopted the grossest fallacy. Such was Mr. Zedekiah Bangs. His innocent and patriarchal manners insured him universal esteem, and rendered him famous, far and wide, under the title of Uncle Zeddy; while his acknowledged zeal and sanctity gained for him in his own church, and among the religious generally, the more reverend appellation of Father Bangs.

Our worthy preacher, having no regular stipend—for he would have scorned to preach for the lucre of gain, cultivated a small farm, or as the phrase is, raised a crop, in the summer, for the subsistence of his family. During this season he ministered diligently among his neighbors; but in the autumn and winter his labors were more extensive. Then it was that he mounted his nag, and rode forth to spread his doctrines, and to carry light and encouragement to the numerous churches of his sect. Then it was that he traveled thousands of miles, encountering every extreme of fatigue and privation, and every vicissitude of climate, seldom sleeping twice in the same bed, or eating two meals at the same place, and counting every day lost in which he did not preach a sermon. Gentlemen who pursue the same avocation with praiseworthy assiduity in other countries, have little notion of the hardships which are endured by the class of men of whom I am writing. Living on the frontier, where the settlements are separated from each other by immense tracts of wilderness, they brave toil and hunger with the patience of the hunter. They traverse pathless wilds, swim rivers, encamp in the open air, and learn the arts, while they acquire the hardihood of backwoodsmen. Such were the labors of our worthy preacher; yet he would accept no pay; requiring only his food and lodging, which are always cheerfully accorded, at every dwelling in the west, to the traveling minister.

Among his converts was Johnson, the farmer in whose company we found him at the commencement of this history. Tom Johnson, as he was familiarly called, had been a daring warrior and hunter, in the first settlement of this country. When times became peaceable he married and settled down, and, as is not unusual, by the mere rise in value of his land, and the natural increase of his stock, became in a few years comparatively wealthy, with but little labor. A state of ease and affluence was not without its dangers to a man of his temperament and desultory habits; and Tom was beginning to become what in this country is called a "Rowdy," that is to say a gentleman of pleasure, without the high finish which adorns that character in more polished societies. He "swapped" horses, bred fine colts, and attended at the race paths; he frequented all public meetings, talked big at elections, and was courted by candidates for office; he played loo, drank deep, and on proper occasions "took a small chunk of a fight."

Tom "got religion" at a camp meeting, and for a while was quite a reformed man. Then he relapsed a little, and finally settled down into a doubtful state, which the church could not approve, yet could not conveniently punish. He neither drank nor swore: he wore the plain dress, kept the Sabbath, attended meetings, and gave a cordial welcome to the clergy at his house. But he had not sold his colts; he went sometimes to the race ground; he could count the run of the cards and the chances of candidates; and it was even reported that he had betted on the high trump. From this state he was awakened by Father Bangs, who boldly arraigned him as a backslider. "You've got head religion," said the preacher, "you're a Sunday Christian—on the Sabbath you put on a straight coat and your long face, and serve your Master—the rest of the week you serve Satan; now it doesn't take a Philadelphia lawyer to tell, that the man who serves the master one day, and the enemy six, has just six chances out of seven to go to the devil; you are *barking up the wrong tree*, Johnson,—take a fresh start, and try to get on the right trail." Tom was convinced by this argument, became a changed man, and felt that he owed a heavy debt of gratitude to the venerable instrument of his reformation, whom he always insisted on entertaining at his house when he visited the neighborhood. On this occasion, the good man, having preached in the vicinity, was going to spend the night with his friend Johnson.

As the travelers passed along, I am not aware that either of them cast a thought upon the romantic and picturesque beauties by which they were surrounded. The banks of the Cumberland, at this point, are rocky and precipitous; sometimes presenting a parapet of several hundred feet in height, and sometimes shooting up into cliffs, which overhang the stream. The river itself, rushing through the deep abyss, appears as a small rivulet to the beholder; the steamboats, struggling with mighty power against the rapid current, are diminished to the eye, while the roaring of the steam and the rattling of wheels come exaggerated by a hundred echoes.

The travelers halted to gaze at one of these vessels, which was about to ascend a difficult pass, where the river, confined on either side by jutting rocks, rushed through the narrow channel with increased velocity. The prow of the boat plunged into the swift current, dashing the foam over the deck. Then it paused and trembled; a powerful conflict succeeded, and for a time the vessel neither advanced nor receded. Her struggles resembled those of an animated creature. Her huge hull seemed to writhe upon the water. The rapid motion of the wheels, the increased noise of the engine, the bursting of the escape-steam from the valve, showed that the impelling power had been raised to the highest point. It was a moment of thrilling suspense. A slight addition of power would enable the boat to advance,—the least failure, the slightest accident, would expose her to the fury of the torrent and dash her on the rocks. Thus she remained for several minutes; then resuming her way, crept heavily over the ripple, reached the smooth water above, and darted swiftly forward.

"Them sort of craft didn't use to crawl about on the rivers, when we first knew the country, brother Johnson," said the preacher.

"No indeed," returned the other.

"And more's the pity," continued the preacher; "does not the apostle caution us against the inventions of men? We had vain and idle devices enough to lead our minds off from our true good, without these smoking furnaces of Satan, these floating towers of Babel, that belch forth huge volumes of brimstone, and seduce honest men and women from home, to go visiting around the land in large companies, and talk to each other in strange tongues."

"I am told," said Johnson, "that some of them carry tracts and good books, for the edification of the passengers."

"Worse and worse!" replied the preacher; "tracts! what are they but printed snares for the soul? There was no printing office in Eden—oh no! and when all the creatures of the earth were gathered into the ark, there was no missionary, male or female. But go thy way," he exclaimed, raising his voice, "thou floating synagogue of Satan! soon shall the time arrive when there shall be neither steam boat, nor Sunday school, nor other devices of vain philosophy!"

"Others of these boats," said the farmer, "have cards and music and wine, with every sort of amusement, on board."

"These are bad things," returned the preacher; "men and women should not drink rum, nor swear, nor gamble, nor make uncouth noises with outlandish instruments; but all these are not so bad as tracts—for these former are open enemies, while the latter catch a man's soul asleep under a tree, and kidnap him when he is camped out afar from home."

"In our day, father, the merchants were well enough satisfied to tote their plunder upon mules and pack horses. And that puts me in mind of a story that happened near about where we are riding."

"What is that, brother Johnson?"

"In an early time, some traders were crossing the country, and aimed to make the river at the ford just below this. They had a great deal of money, all in silver, packed upon mules, for in them days we hadn't any of this nasty paper money."

"No—nor much of any sort," said the preacher slyly.

"If we hadn't," replied the former sturdily, "we had what answered the purpose as well. I mind the time when tobacco was a legal tender, and 'coon-skins passed currenter than bank notes does now. In them days, if a man got into a chunk of a fight with his neighbor, a lawyer would clear him for half a dozen muskrat skins, and the justice and constable would have scorned to take a fee, more than just a treat or so. But you know all that—so I'll tell my tale out, though I reckon you've heard it before?"

"I think I have," said the other, "but I'd like to hear it again—it sort o' stirs one up, to hear about old times."

"Well, the traders had got here safe, with their plunder, when the news came that Indians were about. There was no chance to escape with their loaded mules; so they unloaded them, and buried the money somewhere among these rocks; and then being light, made their escape. So far, the old settlers all agree; but then some say that the Indians pursued on after them, a great way into Kentucky, and killed them all; others say that they finally escaped, the fact is, that the people never came back after the money, and it is supposed that it lies hid somewhere about here to this day."

"Has not that money often been searched after?"

"Oh, bless you, yes; a heap of times. Many a chap has sweated among these rocks by the hour. Only a few years ago, a great gang of folks came out of Kentucky, and dug all around here, as if they were going to make a crop; but to no purpose."

"And what, think you, became of the money?"

"People say it is there yet."

"But your own opinion?"

"Why, to tell you my opinion sentimentally," replied Tom, winking and lowering his voice, "I don't believe in that story."

"How?" exclaimed the other incredulously.

"It's just a tale—a mere *noration*," said Tom, "there's no two ways about it."

"Indeed! how can you think so?"

"Why, look here, father Zedekiah,—I know, very well, that every man, woman, and child within fifty miles, thinks there is certainly a vast treasure buried in these rocks; but when I almost as good as know to the contrary, I am not bound to give up my opinion."

"Very right, that's just my way; but let us have your reasons."

"I have fought the Indians myself," said the farmer, "and I know all their ways. They never come out boldly into the open field, and take a fair fight, fist and skull, as Christians do; but are always sneaking about in the bushes, studying out some devilment. The traders and hunters understand them perfectly well; the Indians and they are continually practicing devices on each other. Many a trick I've played on them, and they have played me as many. Now it seems to me to be *nateral*—just as plain as if I was on the ground and saw it, that them traders should have made a sham of burying money, and run off while the Indians were looking for it."

"That's not a good argument, brother Johnson."

"I have great respect for your opinion," replied the farmer, "but on this subject I have made up my mind—"

"So have I," interrupted the preacher, and reining his horse, he fell in the rear of his companion, as if determined to hear no more.

Johnson, in broaching this subject, had not been aware of the interest it possessed in the mind of his friend. The fact was, that Bangs in his visit to this country had frequently heard the report alluded to, and it was precisely suited to operate upon his credulous and enthusiastic mind. At first he pondered on it as a matter of curiosity, until it fastened itself upon his imagination. In his long and lonesome journeys, when he rode for whole days without seeing a human face, or habitation, he amused himself in calculating the probable amount of the buried treasure. The first step was to fix in his own mind the number of mules, and as the tradition varied from one to thirty, he prudently adopted the medium between these extremes. He found some difficulty in determining the burden of a single mule, but to fix the number of dollars which would be required to make up that burden, was impossible, because the worthy divine was so little acquainted with money, as not to know the weight of a single coin. For the first time in his life he lacked arithmetic, and found himself in a strait, in which he conceived that it might be prudent to take the counsel of a friend.

Near the residence of the reverend man dwelt an industrious pedagogue. He was a tall, sallow, unhealthy looking youth, with a fine clear blue eye, and a melancholy countenance, which at times assumed a sly sarcastic expression that few could interpret. In the winter, when the farmers' children had a season of respite from labor, he diligently pursued his vocation. In the summer he strolled listlessly about the country, sometimes roaming the forest with his rifle, sometimes eagerly devouring any book that might chance to fall into his hands. Between him and the preacher there was little community of sentiment; yet they were often together: the scholar found a source of inexhuastible amusement in the odd, quaint, original arguments of the divine, and the latter was well pleased to measure weapons with so respectable an opponent. They never met without disputation, yet they always parted in kindness. The preacher, instead of wondering, with the rest of the neighbors, how "one small head could carry all he knew," derided the acquirements of his friend as worse than vanity; and the latter respectfully, but stoutly, maintained the dignity of his profession.

It was not without many qualms of pride that the worthy father now sought the school-master, with the intention of gaining information which he knew not how to get from any other source. Having once made up his mind, he acted with his usual promptness, and unused to intrigue or circumlocution, proceeded directly to his point.

"Charles," said he, "can you tell me how many dollars a stout mule might conveniently carry?"

"Indeed I cannot."

"Do none of your trumpery books treat of these things?"

"They do not, Uncle Zeddy; but they lay down the principles upon which such results may be ascertained."

"Very well; let us see you resolve this question by your arithmetic."

"You must first give me the data: what is the burden of a mule?"

"Can't tell; never backed one in my life."

"Well, let us see:—we will say that a stout animal of this class might easily carry you and me, with all our books, money, and learning; now we cannot rate our two selves at more than two hundred and fifty pounds, and for our luggage, tangible and intellectual, we may set down ciphers; a dollar weighs an ounce, and there is the question stated; if one dollar weighs one ounce, how many dollars will it take to make two hundred and fifty pounds? Work it by the rule of three and there is the answer."

The preacher's eyes glistened as he saw the figures; a long deep groan, such as he was in the habit of heaving upon all occasions, whether of joy or sorrow, burst involuntarily from him.

"Charles, my son," said he, gasping for breath, and lowering his voice to a whisper, while his eyes, riveted upon the sum total, seemed ready to start from their sockets, "suppose there were fifteen such mules?"

"In that case," replied the pedagogue carelessly, as he multiplied his former product by the sum named, "in that case the result would be so much."

"Read the figures to me," said the preacher, groaning again, "I am not certain that I can make them out."

"It is only about forty-five thousand dollars."

"Only! oh the blasphemy of learning! Young man, the wealth of Solomon was nothing to this—yea, the treasures of Nebuchadnezzar were as dust in the balance compared with this hoard!" and he walked slowly away, muttering "it is too much! it is too much!"

It was indeed a vast sum! more than honest Zedekiah had even thought or dreamt of; and to a mind like his, confined heretofore to a single subject, it developed a new and immense field of speculation. He seemed to have opened his eyes upon a new world. He conjured up in his mind all the harm that a bad man might do with so much money; and trembled to think that any one individual might, by possibility, become master of a treasure so great, as to be fraught with destruction to its possessor, and danger to the whole community in which he lived. He thought of the luxury, the dissipation, the corruption, that it might lead to; and rising gradually to a climax, he adverted to the ruinous and dreadful consequences, if this wealth should fall into the hands of some weak minded, zealous man, who was misled by false doctrines: how many Sunday schools it would establish, how many preachers it would educate, how many missionaries it would send forth, to disseminate a spurious head religion throughout the world!

Turning from this picture, he reflected on the benefits which a good man might with all this money confer on his fellows. Ah! Zedekiah, now it was that the tempter who had been all along sounding thee at a distance, began to lay a regular siege to thy integrity! Now it was that he sought to creep into the breast, yea, into the very heart's core, of worthy Zedekiah. He had always been poor and contented. But age was now approaching, and he could fancy a train of wants attendant upon helpless decrepitude. He glanced at the tattered sleeve of his coat, and straightway the vision of a new suit of snuff-colored broadcloth rose upon his mind. He thought of his old wife who sat spinning in the chimney corner at home; she was lame, and almost blind, poor woman! and he promised to carry her a pound of tea, and a bottle of good brandy. In short, the Reverend Mr. Bangs set his heart upon having the money.

Such was the state of matters, when the conversation occurred which I have just related. It was again renewed at Johnson's house, that night, after a substantial supper, and ended as such conversations usually do, in confirming each party in his own opinion. Indeed the old man had that day got, as he thought, a clue, which might lead to the wished for discovery. He had heard of an ancient dame, who many years before had dropped mysterious hints, which induced a belief that she knew more of this subject than she chose to tell.

On the following morning, the preacher rose early, saddled his nag and rode forth in search of the old woman's dwelling, without apprising anyone of his intention. He soon found the spot, and the object of his search. She was a poor, decrepid, superannuated virago, who dwelt in a hovel as crazy, as weatherbeaten, and as frail, as herself. She was crouched over the fire smoking a short pipe, and barely turned her head, as the reverend man seated himself on the bench beside her.

"It's a raw morning," said the preacher.

"I've seen colder," was the reply.

"So have I," returned Zedekiah, and there the *tete a tete* flagged. The old man warmed his hands, stirred the fire with his stick, and being a bold man, advanced again to the charge.

"Pray, madam, are you the widow Anderson?"

"That's my name; I'm not ashamed to own it," replied the woman sullenly.

"You're the person then that I was directed to; I wished to get some information on a particular subject."

"Aye; you're after the money too, I suppose—the devil's in all the men!"

"The devil never had a worse enemy than I am," said the old man archly.

"I don't know who you are," replied the woman, "but you may travel back as wise as you came."

The preacher mentioned his name, his vocation, and the object of his visit. The virago, in spite of her ill-nature, was evidently soothed when she learned that her visitor was no less a person than the Reverend Mr. Bangs. "Who'd have thought that the like of you would come on such an errand?" said she; "well, well, it's little I know, but you are welcome to that."

Now came the secret. The husband of Mrs. Anderson had been a water-witch, a finder of living fountains. These he discovered by the use of the divining rod, which is well known to possess a virtue in the hands of a favored few, of which it is destitute when used by others. Anderson wielded the hazel twig with wonderful success, and became so celebrated that he was sent for far and near to find water. Inflated with success, he became ambitious of higher distinction and greater gain. He imagined that the same art by which he discovered subterranean fountains, would enable him to find mineral treasurers in the bowels of the earth. He fancied his fortune already made by the discovery of mines of precious metals; the hidden silver on the shores of the Cumberland would of itself repay his labors. He put all his ingenuity in requisition, and busied himself for years in endeavoring to find a wand that would "work" in the vicinity of minerals, as the ordinary divining rod operates in the neighborhood of water. In the latter process, much depends on the kind of wood of which the rod is composed; the hazel, the peach, the mulberry, and a few others, all of rapid growth, are the most approved. Proceeding upon the same principle, he endeavored to find a tree or shrub which should possess an attractive sympathy for metals. Success at length crowned his operations; he found a tree whose branches had the desired virtue. He discovered veins of iron ore in the surrounding hills, and had announced to his wife that he was on the point of finding the buried money, when death, who respects a water-witch no more than a beggar or a king, arrested his career.

But when she came to speak of the manner of his death, her voice faltered. She had often warned Anderson that it was dangerous to meddle with hidden treasures. They were generally protected by supernatural beings, who would not allow them to be removed with impunity; and several persons who had been engaged in the same search before Anderson, had been alarmed by appearances which caused them to desist. One day he came home to his dinner in high glee, and throwing aside his rod, for which he declared he had now no farther use, he swore he would have the money before he slept. It was deposited, he said, in a certain cliff, which was very difficult of access, and which he was determined to visit that afternoon. It was midnight before he returned. He crawled into his cabin and sunk with a groan on the floor. His wife struck a light, and hastened to his assistance, but he was speechless, and soon expired. His body was covered with bruises, and the general opinion was that he had been precipitated from the rocks by some invisible hand.

The rod remained in the possession of his wife, but its existence was a secret to all others. Fear had prevented her from ever trying its efficacy, and inasmuch as it was useless to herself, she took the wise and spirited resolution, that no other person should profit by its virtues, and uniformly turned a deaf ear to the applications frequently made by those who, knowing the habits of her husband and his researches in relation to the matter, applied to her for information. She now presented to the preacher the long treasured wand, the bark of which having been peeled off, it was impossible to discover from what tree it had been taken.

For several days after this event, the reverend man continued to traverse the neighborhood, carefully concealing himself from observation, and exploring with the metallic rod every spot where it was probable the treasure might be hidden, and particularly the cliffs near to Anderson's cabin. One day he returned to the house of Johnson with a look of triumph, and desiring a private interview with his host, informed him that he had found the spot! It was so situated that he could not reach it without assistance, and having described the place accurately to his friend, he concluded by offering him a liberal share, if he would accompany and aid him. To his surprise Johnson briefly and peremptorily refused.

Offended at the obstinacy of the farmer, Father Bangs left his house. On the road he met a stranger travelling on foot, with whom he entered into conversation, and finding him prompt and intelligent in his replies, he engaged him as an assistant, and appointed a spot at which they were to meet to the following morning.

At the hour appointed Uncle Zeddy proceeded to the rendezvous, where the stranger soon appeared, bearing on his shoulder an immense coil of rope. They proceeded to a tall cliff, which, springing from the margin of the river, towered into the air to the height of two hundred feet. The summit on which they stood presented a table surface of a rock, to which they had ascended by a gentle acclivity. Few ventured to the edge of that precipice, for its verge, projecting over the river, overhung it at such a fearful distance that the boldest trembled as they looked into the abyss. The face of the precipice as viewed from the opposite shore seemed to be nearly perpendicular, the slight curve by which the summit projected over the water, being not observable from that direction; and about one-third of the way down, might be seen the mouth of a cave, which was deemed inaccessible to all but the birds of the air. The preacher, after due consideration, had arrived at the conclusion, that the money was in this cave; and having fastened the cable about his own waist, he required his assistant to lower him into the gulf.

It would have been edifying to have seen the courage with which that old man passed over the verge, and the steady eye with which he looked down upon the deep abyss, the jutting rocks, and the foaming torrent below; while his companion, having passed the end of the rope round a tree, advanced to the edge of the rock, and gazed after him with wonder. Uncle Zeddy found no difficulty in descending: but on getting opposite to the mouth of the cave, it was no small exploit to achieve an entrance, for as the cable hung perpendicularly from the projecting peak, he found himself swinging in the air, several feet in advance of the face of the rock. The only chance for it, was to swing in by an horizontal movement, and to do this it was necessary first to give the rope a motion like that of a pendulum. It was not easy to produce this effect, for as the preacher hung suspended by the middle, like the golden fleece, it was difficult to throw his weight in the desired direction. This, however, was at last accomplished; and, after swinging to and fro for half an hour, Uncle Zeddy succeeded in grasping the rock at the opening, and drew himself into the cave.

The cavern was small and our worthy adventurer soon satisfied himself that it did not contain the object of his search. The sides were all of solid rock, without a crevice or other place of concealment. Being ready to return, he gave the signal agreed upon, by jerking the rope; he waited a few minutes and jerked again—and again—and again, but without success. Was it possible that his assistant could be so depraved as to abandon him? He crept to the mouth of the aperture, and looked out. Under different circumstances he could have enjoyed the rushing of the water, and the pleasant fanning of the breeze as it swept along the valley. But now the wind seemed to murmur dolefully, the waves looked angry, and the cragged rocks had a fearful aspect of danger. He shuddered at the thought of being forsaken to die of hunger. He shouted and his voice echoed from rock to rock. An hour, and another hour, passed. A steam boat came paddling along, and he screamed for help. The crew looked up; they saw the cable, and a man's head peeping out of the cavern at a dizzy height above them, and shouted loud in admiration of his daring exploit. He waved his neckcloth in the air, and uttered piteous cries, but they understood him not, and only shouted and laughed the louder as they beheld what they supposed to be the antic bravadoes of some daring hunter. The boat passed on. Night came, and he gave himself up for lost. The sun rose and he was still a prisoner. The morning wore away wearily; loss of sleep, hunger, and terror, had nearly worn the old man out—when he felt the rope move! A thrill of joy passed through his chilled frame. He sprung to his feet, and jerked it violently. The signal was successful; he felt that a strong and steady arm was drawing him, as it were from the grave, into the regions of the living. In a few minutes he passed over the verge, and found himself in the arms of Johnson. The latter, alarmed at the unusual length of his friend's absence, had set out in search of him, and knowing his plan of visiting the cave, had hastened to this spot, where, finding the cable attached to a tree, he was so fortunate as to save the life of his friend in the manner described. The assistant had absconded with the preacher's horse.

When Father Bangs was a little recovered from his terror, he said, "I have not found what I went for, but I have discovered something that convinces me I am not far from the spot. It was here that Anderson met his fate."

"How did you find that out? there was a heavy fall of rain, the night of his death, and we could afterwards find no marks to satisfy us where he fell."

"As I passed over the edge of the cliff I found this watch lying in a crevice of the rock. It seems to have been a long time exposed to the weather, and must have been in Anderson's pocket, when the demon, or whatever it was, cast him over?"

"You still believe in this story, then?"

"I have seen nothing to shake my belief; but I begin to feel sort o' dubious that if there be money buried here, it is not altogether lawful for any but the right heirs to search after it. Anderson was punished for making the attempt, and you see what a fix I am in. This thought came over me while I lay confined, and I trembled for the young man whom I left on the rock, lest he should have been spirited away, or brought to an untimely end."

"He has been spirited away by that good horse of yours, and if ever he comes to a violent death it will be under the gallows."

"Well, be it so; but my own confinement and suffering, I cannot but think, was meant as a punishment."

"Have your own way," said the farmer, "if you do but quit money hunting, I am satisfied, but I must say, when I hear you talk of spirits and such like, that I am sorry to find you are still *barking up the wrong tree*."

1832

PHILIP FRENEAU

(1752-1832)

delphia to New York (Philadelphia).

1815 *A Collection of Poems,* 2 Vols. (New York).

1832 Died December 18 in snowstorm near his home.

1899 *Some Account of the Capture of the Ship 'Aurora'* (New York).

BIBLIOGRAPHY:

Owen P. Thomas, "Philip Freneau: A Bibliography," *Proc. of N.J. Hist. Soc.,* LXXV (1957), 197–205. Fred L. Pattee, *Poems of Philip Freneau, Poet of the American Revolution,* 3 Vols. (Princeton, 1902–1907), reissued in 1963. H. H. Clark, ed. *Poems of Freneau* (New York, 1929, 1960). Lewis Leary, ed. *The Last Poems of Philip Freneau* (New Brunswick, N.J., 1945). H. H. Clark, ed. *Letters on Various Interesting and Important Subjects* (New York, 1943). Philip Marsh, ed. *The Prose of Philip Freneau* (New Brunswick, N.J., 1955). Marsh, ed. *A Freneau Sampler* (New York, 1963). Mary S. Austin, *Philip Freneau, the Poet of the Revolution* (New York, 1901). Lewis Leary, *That Rascal Freneau: A Study in Literary Failure* (New Brunswick, N.J., 1941, 1964). N. F. Adkins, *Philip Freneau and the Cosmic Enigma* (New York, 1949).

From *The British Prison Ship*

CANTO III

THE HOSPITAL PRISON SHIP

. . . Now tow'rd the *Hunter's* gloomy sides we came,
A slaughter-house, yet hospital in name;
For none came there (to pass through all degrees)
'Till half consum'd, and dying with disease;—
But when too near with laboring oars we ply'd,   5
The Mate with curses drove us from the side;
That wretch who, banish'd from the navy crew,
Grown old in blood, did here his trade renew;
His serpent's tongue, when on his charge let loose,
Utter'd reproaches, scandal, and abuse,   10
Gave all to hell who dar'd his king disown,
And swore mankind were made for George alone:
Ten thousand times, to irritate our woe,
He wish'd us founder'd in the gulf below;
Ten thousand times he brandish'd high his stick,   15
And swore as often that we were not sick—
And yet so pale!—that we were thought by some
A freight of ghosts from Death's dominions come—
But calm'd at length—for who can always rage,
Or the fierce war of endless passion wage,   20
He pointed to the stairs that led below
To damps, disease, and varied shapes of woe—
Down to the gloom I took my pensive way,
Along the decks the dying captives lay;

Some struck with madness, some with scurvy pain'd,   25
But still of putrid fevers most complain'd!
On the hard floors these wasted objects laid,
There toss'd and tumbled in the dismal shade,
There no soft voice their bitter fate bemoan'd,
And Death strode stately, while the victims groan'd;   30
Of leaky decks I heard them long complain,
Drown'd as they were in deluges of rain,
Deny'd the comforts of a dying bed,
And not a pillow to support the head—
How could they else put pine, and grieve, and sigh,   35
Detest a wretched life—and wish to die?
   Scarce had I mingled with this dismal band
When a thin spectre seiz'd me by the hand—
"And art thou come, (death heavy on his eyes)
And art thou come to these abodes," he cries;   40
"Why didst thou leave the *Scorpion's* dark retreat,
And hither haste a surer death to meet?
Why didst thou leave thy damp infected cell?
If that was purgatory, this is hell—
We, too, grown weary of that horrid shade,   45
Petitioned early for the doctor's aid;
His aid denied, more deadly symptoms came,
Weak, and yet weaker, glow'd the vital flame;
And when disease had worn us down so low
That few could tell if we were ghosts or no,   50
And all asserted, death would be our fate—
Then to the doctor we were sent—too late." . . .
   From Brookland groves a Hessian doctor came,
Not great his skill, nor greater much his fame;
Fair Science never call'd the wretch her son,   55
And Art disdain'd the stupid man to own;—
Can you admire that Science was so coy,
Or Art refus'd his genius to employ!—
Do men with brutes an equal dullness share,
Or cuts yon' groveling mole the midway air?   60
In polar worlds can Eden's blossoms blow?
Do trees of God in barren deserts grow?
Are loaded vines to Etna's summit known,
Or swells the peach beneath the torrid zone?—
Yet still he doom'd his genius to the rack,   65
And, as you may suppose, was own'd a quack.
   He on his charge the healing work begun
With antimonial mixtures, by the ton,
Ten minutes was the time he deign'd to stay,

The time of grace allotted once a day— 70
He drencht us well with bitter draughts, 'tis true,
Nostrums from hell, and cortex from Peru—
Some with his pills he sent to Pluto's reign,
And some he blister'd with his flies of Spain;
His cream of Tartar walk'd its deadly round, 75
Till the lean patient at the potion frown'd,
And swore that hemlock, death, or what you will,
Were nonsense to the drugs that stuff'd his bill.—
On those refusing he bestow'd a kick,
Or menac'd vengeance with his walking stick; 80
Here uncontroll'd he exercis'd his trade,
And grew experienced by the deaths he made;
By frequent blows we from his cane endur'd
He kill'd at least as many as he cur'd;
On our lost comrades built his future fame, 85
And scatter'd fate, where'er his footsteps came.
    Some did not seem obedient to his will,
And swore he mingled poison with his pill,
But I acquit him by a fair confession,
He was no Englishman—he was a Hessian— 90
Although a dunce, he had some sense of sin,
Or else the Lord knows where we now had been;
Perhaps in that far country sent to range
Where never prisoner meets with an exchange—
Then had we all been banish'd out of time 95
Nor I return'd to plague the world with rhyme.
    Fool though he was, yet candor must confess
Not chief Physician was this dog of Hesse—
One master o'er the murdering tribe was plac'd,
By him the rest were honor'd or disgrac'd;— 100
Once, and but once, by some strange fortune led
He came to see the dying and the dead—
He came—but anger so deform'd his eye,
And such a falchion glitter'd on his thigh,
And such a gloom his visage darken'd o'er, 105
And two such pistols in his hands he bore!
That, by the gods!—with such a load of steel
He came, we thought, to murder, not to heal—
Hell in his heart, and mischief in his head,
He gloom'd destruction, and had smote us dead, 110
Had he so dar'd—but fate withheld his hand—
He came—blasphem'd—and turn'd again to land.
    From this poor vessel, and her sickly crew
An English ruffian all his titles drew,

Captain, esquire, commander, too, in chief,   115
And hence he gain'd his bread, and hence his beef,
But, sir, you might have search'd creation round
Ere such another miscreant could be found—
Though unprovok'd, an angry face he bore,
We stood astonish'd at the oaths he swore;   120
He swore, till every prisoner stood aghast,
And thought him Satan in a brimstone blast;
He wish'd us banish'd from the public light,
He wish'd us shrouded in perpetual night! . . .
    Such food they sent, to make complete our woes,   125
It look'd like carrion torn from hungry crows,
Such vermin vile on every joint were seen,
So black, corrupted, mortified, and lean
That once we try'd to move our flinty chief,
And thus address'd him, holding up the beef: 130
    "See, captain, see! what rotten bones we pick,
What kills the healthy cannot cure the sick:
Not dogs on such by Christian men are fed,
And see, good master, see, what lousy bread!"
    "Your meat or bread (this man of flint replied)   135
Is not my care to manage or provide—
But this, damn'd rebel dogs, I'd have you know,
That better than you merit we bestow;
Out of my sight!"—nor more he deign'd to say,
But whisk'd about, and frowning, strode away.   140
    Each day, at least three carcasses we bore,
And scratch'd them graves along the sandy shore;
By feeble hands the shallow graves were made,
No stone memorial o'er the corpses laid;
In barren sands, and far from home, they lie,   145
No friend to shed a tear, when passing by;
O'er the mean tombs insulting Britons tread,
Spurn at the sand, and curse the rebel dead.
    When to your arms these fatal islands fall,
(For first or last they must be conquer'd all)   150
Americans! to rites sepulchral just,
With gentlest footstep press this kindred dust,
And o'er the tombs, if tombs can then be found,
Place the green turf, and plant the myrtle round.
    Americans! a just resentment show,   155
And glut revenge on this detested foe;
While the warm blood exults the glowing vein
Still shall resentment in your bosoms reign,
Can you forget the greedy Briton's ire,

Your fields in ruin, and your domes on fire,   160
No age, no sex from lust and murder free,
And, black as night, the hell born refugee!
Must York forever your best blood entomb,
And these gorg'd monsters triumph in their doom,
Who leave no art of cruelty untry'd;   165
Such heavy vengeance, and such hellish pride!
Death has no charms—his realms dejected lie
In the dull climate of a clouded sky:
Death has no charms, except in British eyes,
See, arm'd for death, the infernal miscreants rise;   170
See how they pant to stain the world with gore,
And millions murder'd, still would murder more;
This selfish race, from all the world disjoin'd,
Perpetual discord spread throughout mankind,
Aim to extend their empire o'er the ball,   175
Subject, destroy, absorb, and conquer all,
As if the power that form'd us did condemn
All other nations to be slaves to them—
Rouse from your sleep, and crush the thievish band,
Defeat, destroy, and sweep them from the land,   180
Ally'd like you, what madness to despair,
Attack the ruffians while they linger there;
There Tryon sits, a monster all complete,
See Clinton there with vile Knyphausen meet,
And every wretch whom honor should detest   185
There finds a home—and Arnold with the rest.
Ah! traitors, lost to every sense of shame,
Unjust supporters of a tyrant's claim;
Foes to the rights of freedom and of men,
Flush'd with the blood of thousands you have slain,   190
To the just doom the righteous skies decree
We leave you, toiling still in cruelty,
Or on dark plans in future herds to meet,
Plans form'd in hell, and projects half complete:
The years approach that shall to ruin bring   195
Your lords, your chiefs, your miscreant of a king,
Whose murderous acts shall stamp his name accurs'd,
And his last triumphs more than damn the first.

1781

On the Memorable Victory

Obtained by the gallant Captain Paul Jones, of the Good Man Richard, over the Seraphis, etc., under the command of Captain Pearson.

1

O'er the rough main with flowing sheet
The guardian of a numerous fleet,
    Seraphis from the Baltic came;
A ship of less tremendous force
Sail'd by her side the self-same course,   5
    Countess of Scarb'ro' was her name.

2

And now their native coasts appear,
Britannia's hills their summits rear
    Above the German main;
Fond to suppose their dangers o'er,   10
They southward coast along the shore,
    Thy waters, gentle Thames, to gain.

3

Full forty guns *Seraphis* bore,
And *Scarb'ro's Countess* twenty-four,
    Mann'd with Old England's boldest tars—   15
What flag that rides the Gallic seas
Shall dare attack such piles as these,
    Design'd for tumults and for wars!

4

Now from the top-mast's giddy height
A seaman cry'd—"Four sail in sight   20
    Approach with favoring gales;"
Pearson, resolved to save the fleet,
Stood off to sea these ships to meet,
    And closely brac'd his shivering sails.

5

With him advanc'd the *Countess* bold,   25
Like a black tar in wars grown old:
    And now these floating piles drew nigh;
But, muse, unfold what chief of fame
In th' other warlike squadron came,
    Whose standards at his masthead fly.   30

6

'Twas Jones, brave Jones, to battle led
As bold a crew as ever bled
    Upon the sky surrounded main;
The standards of the Western World
Were to the willing winds unfurl'd,   35
    Denying Britain's tyrant reign.

7

The *Good Man Richard* led the line;
The *Alliance* next: with these combine
    The Gallic ship they *Pallas* call:
The *Vengeance,* arm'd with sword and flame,   40
These to attack the Britains came—
    But two accomplish'd all.

8

Now Phœbus sought his pearly bed:
But who can tell the scenes of dread,
    The horrors of that fatal night!   45
Close up these floating castles came;
The *Good Man Richard* bursts in flame;
    Seraphis trembled at the sight.

9

She felt the fury of her ball,
Down, prostrate down, the Britains fall;   50
    The decks were strew'd with slain:
Jones to the foe his vessel lash'd;
And, while the black artillery flash'd,
    Loud thunders shook the main.

10

Alas! that mortals should employ   55
Such murdering engines, to destroy
    That frame by heav'n so nicely join'd;
Alas! That e'er the god decreed
That brother should by brother bleed,
    And pour'd such madness in the mind.   60

11

But thou, brave Jones, no blame shalt bear;
The rights of men demand thy care:

For these you dare the greedy waves—
No tyrant on destruction bent
Has planned thy conquests—thou art sent   65
    To humble tryants and their slaves.

12

See!—dread *Seraphis* flames again—
And art thou, Jones, among the slain,
    And sunk to Neptune's caves below—
He lives—though crowds around him fall,   70
Still he, unhurt, survives them all;
    Almost alone he fights the foe.

13

And can thy ship these strokes sustain?
Behold thy brave companions slain,
    All clasp'd in ocean's dark embrace.   75
"Strike, or be sunk!"—the Britain cries—
"Sink, if you can!"—the chief replies,
    Fierce lightnings blazing in his face.

14

Then to the side three guns he drew,
(Almost deserted by his crew)   80
    And charg'd them deep with woe:
By Pearson's flash he aim'd the balls;
His main-mast totters—down it falls—
    Tremendous was the blow.

15

Pearson as yet disdain'd to yield,   85
But scarce his secret fears conceal'd,
    And thus was heard to cry—
"With hell, not mortals, I contend;
What art thou—human, or a fiend,
    That dost my force defy?   90

16

"Return, my lads, the fight renew!"
So call'd bold Pearson to his crew;
    But call'd, alas! in vain;
Some on the decks lay maim'd and dead;
Some to their deep recesses fled,   95
    And more were bury'd in the main.

17

Distress'd, forsaken, and alone,
He haul'd his tatter'd standard down,
   And yielded to his gallant foe;
Bold *Pallas* soon the *Countess* took,   100
Thus both their haughty colors struck,
   Confessing what the brave can do.

18

But, Jones, too dearly didst thou buy
These ships possess so gloriously,
   Too many deaths disgrac'd the fray: 105
Thy barque that bore the conquering flame,
That the proud Briton overcame,
   Even she forsook thee on thy way;

19

For when the morn began to shine,
Fatal to her, the ocean brine   110
   Pour'd through each spacious wound;
Quick in the deep she disappear'd,
But Jones to friendly Belgia steer'd,
   With conquest and with glory crown'd.

20

Go on, great man, to daunt the foe,   115
And bid the haughty Britons know
   They to our Thirteen Stars shall bend;
The Stars that veil'd in dark attire,
Long glimmer'd with a feeble fire,
   But radiant now ascend;   120

21

Bend to the Stars that flaming rise
In western, not in eastern, skies,
   Fair Freedom's reign restor'd.
So when the Magi, come from far,
Beheld the God-attending Star,   125
   They trembled and ador'd.

                    1781

To Sir Toby

A Sugar Planter in the interior parts of Jamaica, near the City of San Jago de la Vega, (Spanish Town) 1784

*"The motions of his spirit are black as night,
And his affections dark as Erebus."*—SHAKESPEARE.

If there exists a hell—the case is clear—
Sir Toby's slaves enjoy that portion here:
Here are no blazing brimstone lakes—'tis true;
But kindled Rum too often burns as blue;
In which some fiend, whom nature must detest,   5
Steeps Toby's brand, and marks poor Cudjoe's breast.[1]
Here whips on whips excite perpetual fears,
And mingled howlings vibrate on my ears:
Here nature's plagues abound, to fret and tease,
Snakes, scorpions, despots, lizards, centipees—   10
No art, no care escapes the busy lash;
All have their dues—and all are paid in cash—
The eternal driver keeps a steady eye
On a black herd, who would his vengeance fly,
But chained, imprisoned, on a burning soil,   15
For the mean avarice of a tryant, toil!
The lengthy cart-whip guards this monster's reign—
And cracks, like pistols, from the fields of cane.
Ye powers! who formed these wretched tribes, relate,
What had they done, to merit such a fate!   20
Why were they brought from Eboe's sultry waste,[2]
To see that plenty which they must not taste—
Food, which they cannot buy, and dare not steal;
Yams and potatoes—many a scanty meal!—
One, with a gibbet wakes his negro's fears,   25
One to the windmill nails him by the ears;
One keeps his slave in darkened dens, unfed,
One puts the wretch in pickle ere he's dead:
This, from a tree suspends him by the thumbs,
That, from his table grudges even the crumbs!   30
O'er yond' rough hills a tribe of females go,
Each with her gourd, her infant, and her hoe;

[1] This passage has a reference to the West India custom (sanctioned by law) of branding a newly imported slave on the breast, with a red hot iron, as an evidence of the purchaser's property. [The notes in this selection are Freneau's.]
[2] A small negro kingdom near the river Senegal.

774 / Philip Freneau

Scorched by a sun that has no mercy here,
Driven by a devil, whom men call overseer—
In chains, twelve wretches to their labors haste;   35
Twice twelve I saw, with iron collars graced!—
    Are such the fruits that spring from vast domains?
Is wealth, thus got, Sir Toby, worth your pains!—
Who would your wealth on terms, like these, possess,
Where all we see is pregnant with distress—   40
Angola's natives scourged by ruffian hands,
And toil's hard product shipp'd to foreign lands.
    Talk not of blossoms, and your endless spring;
What joy, what smile, can scenes of misery bring?—
Though Nature, here, has every blessing spread,   45
Poor is the laborer—and how meanly fed!
    Here Stygian paintings light and shade renew,
Pictures of hell, that Virgil's pencil drew:[3]
Here, surly Charons make their annual trip,
And ghosts arrive in every Guinea ship,   50
To find what beasts these western isles afford,
Plutonian scourges, and despotic lords:—
    Here, they, of stuff determined to be free,
Must climb the rude cliffs of the Liguanee;[4]
Beyond the clouds, in skulking haste repair,   55
And hardly safe from brother traitors there.—[5]

                                                        1792

To Shylock Ap-Shenkin

Since the day I attempted to print a gazette,
This Shylock Ap-Shenkin does nothing but fret:
Now preaching and screeching, then nibbling and scribbling,
Remarking and barking, and whining and pining, and still in a pet,
From morning 'till night, with my humble gazette.   5

Instead of whole columns our page to abuse,
Your readers would rather be treated with News:
While wars are a-brewing, and kingdoms undoing,
While monarchs are falling, and princesses squalling,
While France is reforming, and Irishmen storming—   10
In a glare of such splendor, what folly to fret
At so humble a thing as a poet's Gazette!

[3] See Aeneid, Book 6th.—and Fenelon's Telamachus, Book 18.
[4] The mountains northward of Kingston.
[5] Alluding to the Independent negroes in the blue mountains, who for a stipulated reward, deliver up every fugitive that falls into their hands, to the English Government.

No favors I ask'd from your friends in the East:
On your wretched soup-meagre I left them to feast;
So many base lies you have sent them in print,   15
That scarcely a man at our paper will squint:—
And now you begin (with a grunt and a grin,
With the bray of an ass, and a visage of brass,
With a quill in your hand and a Lie in your mouth)
To play the same trick on the men of the South!   20

One Printer for Congress (some think) is enough,
To flatter, and lie, to palaver, and puff,
To preach up in favor of monarchs and titles,
And garters, and ribands, to prey on our vitals:

Who knows but Pomposo will give it in fee,   25
Or make mister Shenkin the Grand Patentee!!!
Then take to your scrapers, ye Republican Papers,
No rogue shall go snacks—and the News-Paper Tax
Shall be puff'd to the skies, as a measure most wise—
So, a spaniel, when master is angry, and kicks it,   30
Sneaks up to his shoe, and submissively licks it.

                                        1792

Ode

God save the Rights of Man!
Give us a heart to scan
Blessings so dear:
Let them be spread around
Wherever man is found,   5
And with the welcome sound
Ravish his ear.

Let us with France agree,
And bid the world be free,
While tyrants fall!   10
Let the rude savage host
Of their vast numbers boast—
Freedom's almighty trust
Laughs at them all!

Though hosts of slaves conspire   15
To quench fair Gallia's fire,

Still shall they fail:
Though traitors round her rise,
Leagu'd with her enemies,
To war each patriot flies,   20
And will prevail.

No more is valor's flame
Devoted to a name,
Taught to adore—
Soldiers of Liberty   25
Disdain to bow the knee,
But teach Equality
To every shore.

The world at last will join
To aid thy grand design,   30
Dear Liberty!
To Russia's frozen lands
The generous flame expands:
On Afric's burning sands
Shall man be free!   35

In this our western world
Be Freedom's flag unfurl'd
Through all its shores!
May no destructive blast
Our heaven of joy o'ercast,   40
May Freedom's fabric last
While time endures.

If e'er her cause require!—
Should tyrants e'er aspire
To aim their stroke,   45
May no proud despot daunt—
Should he his standard plant,
Freedom will never want
Her hearts of oak!

                                        1795

From The House of Night

A VISION

ADVERTISEMENT—This Poem is founded upon the authority of Scripture, inasmuch as these sacred books assert, that *the last enemy that shall be conquered is Death.* For the purposes of poetry he is here personified, and represented as on his dying bed. The scene is laid at a solitary palace, (the time midnight) which, tho' before beautiful and joyous, is now become sad and gloomy, as being the abode and receptacle of Death. Its owner, an amiable, majestic youth, who had lately lost a beloved consort, nevertheless with a noble philosophical fortitude and humanity, entertains him in a friendly manner, and by employing Physicians, endeavors to restore him to health, altho' an enemy; convinced of the excellence and propriety of that divine precept, *If thine enemy hunger, feed him; if he thirst, give him drink.* He nevertheless, as if by a spirit of prophecy, informs this (fictitiously) wicked being of the certainty of his doom, and represents to him in a pathetic manner the vanity of his expectations, either of a reception into the abodes of the just, or continuing longer to make havoc of mankind upon earth. The patient finding his end approaching, composes his epitaph, and orders it to be engraved on his tombstone, hinting to us thereby, that even Death and Distress have vanity; and would be remembered with honor after he is no more, altho' his whole life has been spent in deeds of devastation and murder. He dies at last in the utmost agonies of despair, after agreeing with an avaricious Undertaker to intomb his bones. This reflects upon the inhumanity of those men, who, not to mention an enemy, would scarcely cover a departed friend with a little dust, without certainty of reward for so doing. The circumstances of his funeral are then recited, and the visionary and fabulous part of the poem disappears. It concludes with a few reflexions on the impropriety of a too great attachment to the present life, and incentives to such moral virtue as may assist in conducting us to a better. [Freneau's Note]

[Death, himself about to die, commands the narrator of the vision to "go three miles o'er the plain" to a cemetery where he will find an eight-foot tombstone. Death then instructs the narrator to engrave on the tombstone the following epitaph.—Editors' Note]

98

"*Death in this tomb his weary bones hath laid,*
Sick of dominion o'er the human kind—
Behold what devastations he hath made,
Survey the millions by his arm confin'd.

99

"Six thousand years has sovereign sway been mine,   5
None, but myself, can real glory claim;
Great Regent of the world I reign'd alone,
And princes trembled when my mandate came.

100

"Vast and unmatch'd throughout the world, my fame
Takes place of gods, and asks no mortal date—   ·   10
No; by myself, and by the heavens, I swear,
Not Alexander's name is half so great.

101

"Nor swords nor darts my prowess could withstand,
All quit their arms, and bowed to my decree,
Even mighty Julius died beneath my hand,   15
For slaves and Cæsars were the same to me!

102

"Traveler, wouldst thou his noblest trophies seek,
Search in no narrow spot obscure for those;
The sea profound, the surface of all land
Is moulded with the myriads of his foes."   20

103

Scare had he spoke, when on the lofty dome
Rush'd from the clouds a hoarse resounding blast—
Round the four eaves so loud and sad it play'd
As though all music were to breathe its last.

104

Warm was the gale, and such as travelers say   25
Sport with the winds on Zaara's barren waste;
Black was the sky, a mourning carpet spread,
Its azure blotted, and its stars o'ercast!

105

Lights in the air like burning stars were hurl'd,
Dogs howl'd, heaven mutter'd, and the tempest blew,   30
The red half-moon peeped from behind a cloud
As if in dread the amazing scene to view.

106

The mournful trees that in the garden stood
Bent to the tempest as it rush'd along,

The elm, the myrtle, and the cypress sad   35
More melancholy tun'd its bellowing song.

107

No more that elm its noble branches spread,
The yew, the cypress, or the myrtle tree,
Rent from the roots the tempest tore them down,
And all the grove in wild confusion lay.   40

108

Yet, mindful of his dread command, I part
Glad from the magic dome—nor found relief;
Damps from the dead hung heavier round my heart,
While sad remembrance rous'd her stores of grief.

109

O'er dark field I held my dubious way   45
Where Jack-a-lanthorn walk'd his lonely round,
Beneath my feet substantial darkness lay,
And screams were heard from the distemper'd ground.

110

Nor look'd I back, till to a far off wood,
Trembling with fear, my weary feet had sped—   50
Dark was the night, but at the enchanted dome
I saw the infernal windows flaming red.

111

And from within the howls of Death I heard,
Cursing the dismal night that gave him birth,
Damning his ancient sire, and mother sin,   55
Who at the gates of hell, accursed, brought him forth.

112

For fancy gave to my enraptur'd soul
An eagle's eye, with keenest glance to see,
And bade those distant sounds distinctly roll,
Which, waking, never had affected me.   60

113

Oft his pale breast with cruel hand he smote,
And tearing from his limbs a winding sheet,
Roar'd to the black skies, while the woods around,
As wicked as himself, his words repeat.

114

Thrice tow'rd skies his meagre arms he rear'd,   65
Invok'd all hell, and thunders on his head,
Bid light'nings fly, earth yawn, and tempests roar,
And the sea wrap him in its oozy bed.

[After Death dies saying "All hell demands me hence," the narrator meets Death's ghastly funeral train, which returns to the House of Night. Both the funeral train and the House of Night disappear, leaving "no trace behind." Morning comes and the narrator reflects:]

132

What is this Death, ye deep read sophists, say?–
Death is no more than one unceasing change;   70
New forms arise, while other forms decay,
Yet all is Life throughout creation's range.

133

The towering Alps, the haughty Apennine,
The Andes, wrapt in everlasting snow,
The Appalachian and the Ararat   75
Sooner or later must to ruin go.

134

Hills sink to plains, and man returns to dust,
That dust supports a reptile or a flower;
Each changeful atom by some other nurs'd
Takes some new form, to perish in an hour.   80

135

Too nearly join'd to sickness, toils, and pains,
(Perhaps for former crimes imprison'd here)
True to itself the immortal soul remains,
And seeks new mansions in the starry sphere.

136

When Nature bids thee from the world retire,   85
With joy thy lodging leave, a fated guest;
In Paradise, the land of thy desire,
Existing always, always to be blest.

1779

The Dying Indian

TOMO-CHEQUI

"On yonder lake I spread the sail no more!
Vigor, and youth, and active days are past—
Relentless demons urge me to that shore
On whose black forests all the dead are cast:—
Ye solemn train, prepare the funeral song,   5
For I must go to shades below,
Where all is strange and all is new;
Companion to the airy throng!—
    What solitary streams,
      In dull and dreary dreams,   10
All melancholy, must I rove along!

To what strange lands must Chequi take his way!
Groves of the dead departed mortals trace:
No deer along those gloomy forests stray,
No huntsmen there take pleasure in the chase,   15
But all are empty unsubstantial shades,
That ramble through those visionary glades;
No spongy fruits from verdant trees depend,
    But sickly orchards there
      Do fruits as sickly bear,   20
And apples a consumptive visage shew,
And withered hangs the hurtle-berry blue.

Ah me! what mischiefs on the dead attend!
Wandering a stranger to the shores below,
Where shall I brook or real fountain find?   25
Lazy and sad deluding waters flow—
Such is the picture in my boding mind!
    Fine tales, indeed, they tell
      Of shades and purling rills,
      Where our dead fathers dwell   30
      Beyond the western hills,
But when did ghost return his state to shew;
Or who can promise half the tale is true?

I too must be a fleeting ghost!—no more—
None, none but shadows to those mansions go;   35
I leave my woods, I leave the Huron shore,
For emptier groves below!

Ye charming solitudes,
Ye tall ascending woods,
Ye glassy lakes and prattling streams,   40
 Whose aspect still was sweet,
 Whether the sun did greet,
Or the pale moon embraced you with her beams—
 Adieu to all!
To all, that charmed me where I strayed,   45
The winding stream, the dark sequested shade;
  Adieu all triumphs here!
 Adieu the mountain's lofty swell,
 Adieu, thou little verdant hill,
 And seas, and stars, and skies—farewell,   50
  For some remoter sphere!

Perplexed with doubts and tortured with despair,
Why so dejected at this hopeless sleep?
Nature at last these ruins may repair,
When fate's long dream is o'er, and she forgets to weep   55
Some real world once more may be assigned,
Some new born mansion for the immortal mind!
Farewell, sweet lake; farewell surrounding woods,
To other groves, through midnight glooms, I stray,
Beyond the mountains and beyond the floods,   60
 Beyond the Huron bay!
Prepare the hollow tomb, and place me low,
My trusty bow and arrows by my side,
The cheerful bottle and the venison store;
For long the journey is that I must go,   65
Without a partner, and without a guide."
 He spoke, and bid the attending mourners weep,
Then closed his eyes, and sunk to endless sleep!

          1784

The Deserted Farm-House

This antique dome the insatiate tooth of time
 Now level with the dust has almost laid;—
Yet ere 'tis gone, I seize my humble theme
 From these low ruins, that his years have made.

Behold the unsocial hearth!—where once the fires   5
 Blazed high, and soothed the storm-stay'd traveler's woes;
See! the weak roof, that abler props requires,
 Admits the winds, and swift descending snows.

Here, to forget the labors of the day,
　　No more the swains at evening hours repair,　　　　10
But wandering flocks assume the well known way
　　To shun the rigors of the midnight air.

In yonder chamber, half to ruin gone,
　　Once stood the ancient housewife's curtained bed—
Timely the prudent matron has withdrawn,　　　　15
　　And each domestic comfort with her fled.

The trees, the flowers that her own hands had reared,
　　The plants, the vines, that were so verdant seen,—
The trees, the flowers the vines have disappear'd,
　　And every plant has vanish'd from the green.　　　　20

So sits in tears on wide Campania's plain
　　Rome, once the mistress of a world enslaved;
That triumph'd o'er the land; subdued the main,
　　And Time himself, in her wild transports, braved.

So sits in tears on Palestina's shore　　　　25
　　The Hebrew town, of splendor once divine—
Her kings, her lords, her triumphs are no more;
　　Slain are her priests, and ruin'd every shrine.

Once, in the bounds of this deserted room,
　　Perhaps some swain nocturnal courtship made,　　　　30
Perhaps some Sherlock mused amidst the gloom;
　　Since Love and Death forever seek the shade.

Perhaps some miser, doom'd to discontent,
　　Here counted o'er the heaps acquired with pain;
He to the dust—his gold, on traffic sent,　　　　35
　　Shall ne'er disgrace these mouldering walls again.

Nor shall the glow-worm fopling, sunshine bred,
　　Seek, at the evening hour this wonted dome—
Time has reduced the fabric to a shed,
　　Scarce fit to be the wandering beggar's home.　　　　40

And none but I its dismal case lament—
　　None, none but I o'er its cold relics mourn,
Sent by the muse—(the time perhaps misspent)—
　　To write dull stanzas on this dome forlorn.

　　　　　　　　　1785

The Wild Honey Suckle

Fair flower, that dost so comely grow,
Hid in this silent, dull retreat,
Untouched thy honied blossoms blow,
Unseen thy little branches greet:
    No roving foot shall crush thee here,   5
    No busy hand provoke a tear.

By Nature's self in white arrayed,
She bade thee shun the vulgar eye,
And planted here the guardian shade,
And sent soft waters murmuring by;   10
    Thus quietly thy summer goes,
    Thy days declining to repose.

Smit with those charms, that must decay,
I grieve to see your future doom;
They died—nor were those flowers more gay,   15
The flowers that did in Eden bloom;
    Unpitying frosts, and Autumn's power
    Shall leave no vestige of this flower.

From morning suns and evening dews
At first thy little being came: 20
If nothing once, you nothing lose,
For when you die you are the same;
    The space between, is but an hour,
    The frail duration of a flower.

                    1786

To an Author

Your leaves bound up compact and fair,
In neat array at length prepare,
To pass their hour on learning's stage,
To meet the surly critic's rage;
The statesman's slight, the smatterer's sneer—   5
Were these, indeed, your only fear,
You might be tranquil and resigned:
What most should touch your fluttering mind;
Is that, few critics will be found
To sift your works, and deal the wound.   10

Thus, when one fleeting year is past
On some bye-shelf your book is cast—
Another comes, with something new,
And drives you fairly out of view:
With some to praise, but more to blame,   15
The mind returns to—whence it came;
And some alive, who scarce could read
Will publish satires on the dead.

Thrice happy Dryden, who could meet
Some rival bard in every street!   20
When all were bent on writing well
It was some credit to excel:—

Thrice happy Dryden, who could find
A Milbourne for his sport designed—
And Pope, who saw the harmless rage   25
Of Dennis bursting o'er his page
Might justly spurn the critic's aim,
Who only helped to swell his fame.

On these bleak climes by Fortune thrown,
Where rigid Reason reigns alone,   30
Where lovely Fancy has no sway,
Nor magic forms about us play—
Nor nature takes her summer hue
Tell me, what has the muse to do?—

An age employed in edging steel   35
Can no poetic raptures feel;
No solitude's attracting power,
No leisure of the noon day hour,
No shaded stream, no quiet grove
Can this fantastic century move;   40

The muse of love in no request—
Go—try your fortune with the rest,
One of the nine you should engage,
To meet the follies of the age:—

On one, we fear, your choice must fall—   45
The least engaging of them all—
Her visage stern—an angry style—
A clouded brow—malicious smile—
A mind on murdered victims placed—
She, only she, can please the taste!   50

1788

On the Religion of Nature

The power, that gives with liberal hand
  The blessings man enjoys, while here,
And scatters through a smiling land
  The abundant products of the year;
    That power of nature, ever bless'd,   5
    Bestow'd religion with the rest.

Born with ourselves, her early sway
  Inclines the tender mind to take
The path of right, fair virtue's way
  Its own felicity to make.   10
    This universally extends
    And leads to no mysterious ends.

Religion, such as nature taught,
  With all divine perfection suits;
Had all mankind this system sought   15
    Sophists would cease their vain disputes,
      And from this source would nations know
      All that can make their heaven below.

This deals not curses to mankind,
  Or dooms them to perpetual grief,   20
If from its aid no joys they find,
  It damns them not for unbelief;
    Upon a more exalted plan
    Creatress nature dealt with man—

Joy to the day, when all agree   25
  On such grand systems to proceed,
From fraud, design, and error free,
  And which to truth and goodness lead:
    Then persecution will retreat
    And man's religion be complete.   30

                                        1815

On a Honey Bee

Drinking from a Glass of Wine and Drowned Therein

(By Hezekiah Salem.)

Thou, born to sip the lake or spring,
Or quaff the waters of the stream,
Why hither come on vagrant wing?—
Does Bacchus tempting seem—
Did he, for you, this glass prepare?—   5
Will I admit you to a share?

Did storms harass or foes perplex,
Did wasps or king-birds bring dismay—
Did wars distress, or labors vex,
Or did you miss your way?—   10
A better seat you could not take
Than on the margin of this lake.

Welcome!—I hail you to my glass:
All welcome, here, you find;
Here, let the cloud of trouble pass,   15
Here, be all care resigned.—
This fluid never fails to please,
And drown the griefs of men or bees.

What forced you here, we cannot know,
And you will scarcely tell—   20
But cheery we would have you go
And bid a glad farewell:
On lighter wings we bid you fly,
Your dart will now all foes defy.

Yet take not, oh! too deep a drink,   25
And in this ocean die;
Here bigger bees than you might sink,
Even bees full six feet high.
Like Pharoah, then, you would be said
To perish in a sea of red.   30

Do as you please, your will is mine;
Enjoy it without fear—
And your grave will be this glass of wine,
Your epitaph—a tear—
Go, take your seat in Charon's boat,   35
We'll tell the hive, you died afloat.

1809

To a Caty-Did[6]

In a branch of willow hid
Sings the evening Caty-did:
From the lofty locust bough
Feeding on a drop of dew,
In her suit of green array'd   5
Hear her singing in the shade
   Caty-did, Caty-did, Caty-did!

While upon a leaf you tread,
Or repose your little head,
On your sheet of shadows laid,   10
All the day you nothing said:
Half the night your cheery tongue
Revel'd out its little song,
   Nothing else but Caty-did.

From your lodgings on the leaf   15
Did you utter joy or grief—?
Did you only mean to say,
I have had my summer's day,
And am passing, soon, away
To the grave of Caty-did:—   20
   Poor, unhappy Caty-did!

But you would have utter'd more
Had you known of nature's power—
From the world when you retreat,
And a leaf's your winding sheet,   25
Long before your spirit fled,
Who can tell but nature said,
Live again, my Caty-did!
   Live, and chatter Caty-did.

Tell me, what did Caty do?   30
Did she mean to trouble you?—
Why was Caty not forbid
To trouble little Caty-did?—

A well-known insect, when full grown, about two inches in length, and of the exact
color of a green leaf. It is of the genus cicada, or grasshopper kind, inhabiting the green
foliage of trees and singing such a song as Caty-did in the evening, towards autumn.
[Freneau's Note.]

Wrong, indeed at you to fling,
Hurting no one while you sing   35
  Caty-did! Caty-did! Caty-did!

  Why continue to complain?
Caty tells me, she again
Will not give you plague or pain:—
Caty says you may be hid   40
Caty will not go to bed
While you sing us Caty-did.
  Caty-did! Caty-did! Caty-did!

  But, while singing, you forgot
To tell us what did Caty not: 45
Caty-did not think of cold,
Flocks retiring to the fold,
Winter, with his wrinkles old,
Winter, that yourself foretold
  When you gave us Caty-did.   50

  Stay securely in your nest;
Caty now, will do her best,
All she can, to make you blest;
But, you want no human aid—
Nature, when she form'd you, said,   55
"Independent you are made,
My dear little Caty-did:
Soon yourself must disappear
With the verdure of the year,"—
And to go, we know not where,   60
  With your song of Caty-did.

1815

From *Letters on Various Interesting and Important Subjects*

PREFACE

Fellow Citizens,

    After having debated the matter with myself at least twenty times, at last I determined to publish all my letters, agreeably to the request of my friends, with several others which I have prepared, and some trifles, that may at least amuse the ignorant, whose brains, like my own, are not able to bear deep reasoning, because they have never learned Latin.

Having come to this conclusion, in I stepped to my neighbor the Latinist, and told him the scheme, with as few round-about digressions as I could: he heard me to the end of my tale with great patience, and then, emphatically shaking his head, exclaimed, Ah! Robert, I much fear you'll find the truth of the old Latin proverb, *Sutor ne ultra crepidam,*—let the cobbler stick to his last. 'Tis a mad thing of you to commence author; for, first, you know you are not rich: you don't boast of great connections, but stand, as you yourself have said, a timorous little fellow, undistinguished among the swinish herd. Secondly, you cannot come before the public with a flourish, thus—By Robert Slender, A.M. or D.M. or LL.D. or F.R.S. And in the last place, you have no great man to whom you can dedicate your performance: and let me tell you, that a number of the poets and historians, of both modern and ancient times, would never have obtained the celebrity they enjoy, if they had not been patronized by some great men—Odds my heart, cried I, for I could hold no longer, I thought you would have applauded my resolution, and offered me your assistance; but instead of that, you come forward with your doubts and difficulties. To be sure I am not rich, but what says that to my letters; the public say they like them, and why should I deny them that gratification?—Indeed, I grant that I cannot write myself, with truth, A.M. or D.M. or LL.D. or F.R.S.; but I can write myself, O.S.M. and that will do quite as well. In the name of common sense, said my friend, what do you mean by O.S.M. I'm sure I never heard of it before? Why, answered I, I believe it has very seldom been chosen by any of your great men and great scholars; but it suits me exactly—its meaning, is, *One of the Swinish Multitude:* and for dedicating, continued I, I'll dedicate to the President of the United States. Nay, replied my friend, that could not otherwise be construed than daring presumption—Well then, to Timothy Pickering—That would be deemed an insult—I'll dedicate, answered I, much agitated, to our own governor Thomas M'Kean, for whom I have more real respect than I have for them both—Why Robert, that would argue too great familiarity—It don't signify, said I, leaping to my feet, I'll dedicate to all their masters—To the Freemen of the United States; and I'll bet you a pair of boots, that my plain stories, shall be by them as well received, with my plain name, and O.S.M. as some of the productions of these flashy fellows, with a string of titles, which are of no other use to American freemen, than to lull them to sleep. Robert, replied my friend, I'll not bet with you; I have gotten more boots, shoes and hats, by the election, than I'll wear these three years; but I doubt you will make a poor job of it—dedications are of all others, the most difficult—Have you studied the art of flattery? Can you new vamp a character as easily as you would a pair of old boots; and make it appear fair and unsullied, though many years have passed since a single virtuous trait was found in it? Can you collect as many mouthfuls of moonshine as the pallet of vanity can easily admit? Or with a good grace and pious countenance, offer incense to a mortal, who is only clothed with a little brief authority?—If you can do these things, go, dedicate to any great man you please, he'll be your patron; and though your pages be as dull and as stupid as ever disgraced the republic of letters, yet the great man's nod of approbation will place sterling value on the performance; but if you dedicate to the freemen of the United States, you—I'll have none of your buts, said I, out of all patience—I'll never flatter vice as long as I live; nay, first, as your book says, I'll "sow nether socks, foot them and mend them too;" and placing my hands in my sides, and looking as big as if I was worth a 1000 a year, Do you think sir, said I, I'd gather moonshine for any man? No sir, if the sides of vanity never stand prominent till they are puffed out by the breath of Robert Slender's flattery, they will be as lean as a lath to the day of judgment—I say, I will dedicate my works to the Freemen, the Lovers of Liberty, the Asserters, Maintainers and Supporters of Independence throughout the United States—And not my works only, added I, but my life also, and all I have, and God knows that's not much, shall be ever at their service, to defend and preserve that invaluable Constitution and glorious Independence, which is their indescribable honor, and the richest patrimony that true republicans can hand down untarnished to posterity—And if my plain told stories, continued I, can have the effect of calling up the republican spirits to a more ardent love of their country's rights—to more watchfulness, and stricter inquiry, I shall abundantly receive that which I expect—For the good of his country, must undoubtedly be the good of Robert Slender—

And, said my friend, seeing I had talked myself out of breath, What will you do now?—Why, answered I, go home and write my dedication.— Why, answered he, you have done it already. Out of a frolic, when I saw you so earnest, I took down your last reply—here it is—I pronounce it a complete dedication, and anything you could say after this, would be as fulsome as the flatteries of Dryden—Odds my heart, said I, I did not intend to have been cheated into a dedication neither, I would have—Hold, hold, says he, placing his hand before my mouth, not another word, or all's ruined. Well, well, said I, so be it, if it must be so—only with your consent, I would add, that with the sincerest wishes for your real happiness,

I am,
Fellow Citizens,
Yours very humble servant,
Robert Slender

1799

LETTER II

Mr. Editor,

Until of late your paper never came into the neighborhood where I live: we all with one consent pronounced it a French paper; and yet, when I begin to think why we did so, I cannot, for my life, find a reason; for none of us ever read a word of it. However, it came into my hands in the following manner: A few weeks ago a man came to be my next door neighbor, who we soon found took the *Aurora;* and, indeed when we found *that,* we determined to keep ourselves to ourselves, and not to be defiled by democrats; but this resolution we somehow or other have entirely broken through; for he is a sober, quiet, religious sort of a man, and the whole family are the most obliging you ever knew. As we grew intimate I thought it could do me no hurt to read a paragraph of his paper, just for sake of curiosity, as I had no paper of my own, for I gave up the English paper six months ago; not that I disliked his politics, but because he taught the children to curse, and speak bawdy. Well, to be sure since that time I have every now and then, when tired of working, read a little; and it has produced on me strange effects: my neighbors say I am bewitched, and point their fingers at me, and call me a turn-coat; and then I wish your paper had never been seen,—but the next day the paper comes, and I cannot for the soul of me keep from reading it. It makes everything appear so fair, open, and so like a history, that I believe my neighbors may hoot on, for I am determined to read a little longer.

Indeed, Mr. Editor you publish some strange things; I am often very much surprised: the other day, for instance, I was almost thunderstruck with the account of the liberties allowed to kings and princes, in that piece signed a Monarchist—Lord bless me, said I to my neighbor, can this be true? True, says he, aye, and this is only a very small and imperfect sketch of their character. Saying this, he took down a large Chronology book (I think he called it) and read to me about fifty instances of kings and princes swearing to do one thing, and doing immediately the contrary: of their treachery, malice, unforgiving temper, cruelty; of their secret murdering, covetousness, and usury; until my hair nearly stood on end. But God be thanked, says I, these were all heathens, I am sure Christians could not be guilty of such crimes. My neighbor smiled, and said, I am sorry my friend to inform you, that the infamy of kings *professing* Christianity, has been more notorious than that of the Heathen or Pagan monarchs: well says I, if this be so, how can they ever say the Lord's prayer? Can they ever think of being Christians, without following Christ's rule, of doing as they would be done by? Do they ever think on death? Do you suppose that they can be Christians, and yet strive to cheat and defraud? Kiss like Judas, and stab like Joab; make fair promises and base performances; wink at wickedness, and suffer every species of fraud to pass unpunished; reward people for acting as spies; honor the adulterer, and laugh at the crime!—Lord keep me from unbelief, said I; these men are great men, high in learning and in fame—Do they think religion a cheat, or a bug-bear only to frighten children? I believe, says my neighbor, they think nothing at all about it! The scripture says, the god of this world hath blinded their eyes—and I verily believe it; but, surely said I, if the rulers of this world would act so, the clergy would excommunicate them, and would not suffer them thus to wear the Christian name, without its power. I cannot, said I, believe it; it cannot be. Do you know, said my neighbor, any wicked men who are very rich? Yes, says I, there is X. Y. and Z., they are very rich, and everybody knows they are great rascals. Well, says my neighbor, are they excommunicated? No—I protest said I, now when I think of it, the Rev. Mr. W. dined with X. on——, and with Y. on——, and six or seven clergymen dined with Z. a few days ago. God preserve us, said I, where shall we look for help; in the great depravity is permitted, some kinds of wickedness counted laudable, and every species winked at. It is our great comfort, said my friend, that although here some things are wrong, I must confess, among the rich and great, yet the great, the honorable and very worthy, our American Farmers Are Virtuous, not in name but in Reality. Vice has not been able to entice them from the standard of Virtue, Independence, and Freedom. To *them* we look—they are our bulwark, the guardians of our rights, the supporters of our dignity, and the pillars of our Constitution. The mist of darkness, ignorance and error, begins to dissipate; party-spirit will soon, like a fretful child, cry itself to rest; the seeds of reform that are sown in our constitution, will bring forth fruit; the storm indeed may awfully growl and grumble at a distance: but said my friend (leaping to his feet, whilst I shrunk into a corner) the sun will arise with ten-fold glory; the demons of war, discord, and desolation shall be disappointed— true religion shall banish pretence and hypocrisy, and America Shall Still Be Free.

1799

Advice to Authors

BY THE LATE MR. ROBERT SLENDER[7]

There are few writers of books in this new world, and amongst these very few that deal in works of imagination, and, I am sorry to say, fewer still that have any success attending their lucubrations. Perhaps, however, the world thinks justly on this subject. The productions of the most

[7] Many people, no doubt, will be anxious to know something of the history and character of the above named *Robert Slender;* and the Editor is really sorry it is not in his power to afford them the most ample information. Of two things, however, the reader may be assured, that he was a Pennsylvanian by birth, and a stocking and tape weaver by trade, and has now been dead something more than a year and half; having been buried with very little ceremony by a few of his most intimate friends and neighbours. —Notwithstanding he was an author as well as a weaver of stockings and tape (both of which articles he manufactured on a curious loom of his own invention) we cannot say he ever possessed the least faculty or turn of mind for amassing the treasures of this world; so that when his executors came to examine his strong-box, little or nothing was discovered therein more than a bundle of manuscripts, penned in a very antiquated, obscure and perplexing hand; from which, however, we shall now and then present such extracts to the public in the course of this work, as shall appear to be best deserving of

brilliant imagination are at best but mere beautiful flowers, that may amuse us in a walk through a garden in a fine afternoon, but can by no means be expected to engage much of that time which God and nature designed to be spent in very different employments. In a country, which two hundred years ago was peopled only by savages, and where the government has ever, in effect, since the first establishment of the white men in these parts, been no other than republican, it is really wonderful there should be any polite original authors at all in any line, especially when it is considered, that according to the common course of things, any particular nation or people must have arrived to, or rather passed, their meridian of opulence and refinement, before they consider the professors of the fine arts in any other light than a nuisance to the community. This is evidently the case at present in our age and country; all you have to do then, my good friends, is to graft your authorship upon some other calling, or support drooping genius by the assistance of some mechanical employment, in the same manner as the helpless ivy takes hold of the vigorous oak, and cleaves to it for support—I mean to say, in plain language, that you may make something by weaving garters, or mending old sails, when an Epic poem would be your utter destruction.

But I see no reason that, because we are all striving to live by the same idle trade, we should suffer ourselves to be embittered against each other, like a fraternity of rival mechanics in the same street. Authors (such I mean as are not possessed of fortunes) are at present considered as the dregs of the community: their situation and prospects are truly humiliating, and any other set of men in a similar state of calamitous ad-

their notice: Indeed, had our old friend stuck closer to his loom for any length of time than he was wont to do, it is highly probable his box would have been stored with riches of a very different nature; but such as they are, gentle reader, they are wholly and sincerely at thy service.—Robert Slender was in his person, a tall spare man with a meagre aspect, of a sociable disposition; fond of traveling from place to place, and was known to have made frequent visits to the several capitals of the American continent and islands, while his brother weavers were more profitably employed at home at their looms. Writing and weaving seem to have been rather his amusements than his serious occupations; and one proof of his having been a man of sense is, his not having depended upon authorship alone for a subsistence. In his temper he was extremely irascible; but I have often remarked that when he saw his writings treated with malevolence, contempt or neglect, he never became angry or outrageous; whereas, when his stockings or tape were calumniated, he was instantly changed into a monster of passion and revenge, breathing out nothing but menaces and curses against the enemies of his loom. He was extremely fond of sunning himself in clear winter mornings, and has been known to sit three hours together on the south side of a hill in December or January, enjoying the salutary beams of the great and splendid luminary.—Reader, if these few particulars will at all gratify thee, our purpose is answered. In this miscellaneous collection of original papers we shall now and then present thee with an essay, a paragraph, a sentiment, or a poem of the late facetious *Robert Slender;* all of which, it is hoped, will be treated by the critics with more indulgence than the rest, since these effusions are to be considered as the works of a deceased author, who, it does not appear, ever intended his lucubrations, at least the greater part of them, for the eye of the public. The first piece of his with which we shall present thee is the above, containing his *Advice to Authors,* which, from several circumstances, we conclude was written in the latter part of his life. [Freneau's Note.]

versity would unite together for their mutual defence, instead of worrying and lampooning each other for the amusement of the illiberal vulgar. —And I cannot do otherwise than freely declare, that where the whole profits of a company amount to little or nothing at all, there ought not, in the nature of things, to be any quarreling about shares and dividends.

As to those authors who have lately exported themselves from Britain and Ireland, and boast that they have introduced the Muses among us since the conclusion of the late war, I really believe them to be a very good natured set of gentlemen, notwithstanding they, in the course of the last winter, called me *poetaster* and *scribbler*, and some other names still more unsavory. They are, however, excuseable in treating the American authors as inferiors; a political and a literary independence of their nation being two very different things—the first was accomplished in about seven years, the latter will not be completely effected, perhaps, in as many centuries. It is my opinion, nevertheless, that a duty ought to be laid upon all imported authors, the net proceeds of which should be appropriated to the benefit of real American writers, when become old and helpless, and no longer able to wield the pen to advantage.

If a coach or a chariot constructed in Britain, pays an impost of twenty pounds at the custom-house, why should not at least twice that sum be laid upon all imported authors who are able to do twice as much mischief with their rumbling, pindaric odes, and gorgeous apparatus of strophes, antistrophes and recitativos?—I, for my own part, am clearly of opinion, that these gentlemen should be taxed; not that I would wish to nip their buds of beauty with the untimely frost of excise, but merely to teach them that our own natural manufactures ought to be primarily attended to and encouraged.

I will now, gentlemen, with your leave, lay down a few simple rules, to which, in my opinion, every genuine author will make no difficulty to conform.

1. When you write a book for the public, have nothing to do with *Epistles dedicatory*. They were first invented by slaves, and have been continued by fools and sycophants. I would not give a farthing more for a book on account of its being patronized by all the noblemen or crowned heads in Christendom. If it does not possess intrinsic merit enough to protect itself, and force its way through the world, their supposed protection will be of no avail: besides, by this ridiculous practice you degrade the *dignity authorial*, the honor of authorship, which ought evermore to be uppermost in your thoughts. The silly unthinking author addresses a great man in the style of a servile dependent, whereas a real author, and a man of true genius, has upon all occasions a bold, disinterested and daring confidence in himself, and considers the common cant of adulation to the sons of fortune as the basest and most abominable of all prostitution.

2. Be particularly careful to avoid all connection with doctors of law

and divinity, masters of arts, professors of colleges, and in general all those that wear square black caps. A mere scholar and an original author are two animals as different from each other as a fresh and salt water sailor. There has been an old rooted enmity between them from the earliest ages, and which it is likely will forever continue. The scholar is not unlike that piddling orator, who, cold and inanimate, not roused into action by the impelling flame of inspiration, can only pronounce the oration he has learned by rote; the real author, on the contrary, is the nervous Demosthenes, who stored with an immensity of ideas, awakened within him he knows not how, has them at command upon every occasion; and must therefore be disregarded as a madman or an enthusiast by the narrow and limited capacity, as well as the natural self-sufficiency of the other.

3. It is risking a great deal to propose a subscription for an original work. The world will be ready enough to anticipate your best endeavors; and that which has been long and anxiously expected, rarely or never comes up to their expectations at last.

4. If you are so poor that you are compelled to live in some miserable garret or cottage; do not repine, but give thanks to heaven that you are not forced to pass your life in a tub, as was the fate of Diogenes of old. Few authors in any country are rich, because a man must first be reduced to a state of penury before he will commence author. Being poor therefore in externals, take care, gentlemen, that you say or do nothing that may argue a poverty of spirit. Riches, we have often heard, are by no means the standard of the value of a man. This maxim the world allows to be true, and yet contradicts it every hour and minute in the year. Fortune most commonly bestows wealth and abundance upon fools and idiots; and men of the dullest natural parts are, notwithstanding, generally best calculated to acquire large estates, and hoard up immense sums from small beginnings.

5. Never borrow money of any man, for if you should once be mean enough to fall into such a habit you will find yourselves unwelcome guests everywhere. If upon actual trial you are at length convinced you possess no abilities that will command the esteem, veneration or gratitude of mankind, apply yourselves without loss of time to some of the lower arts, since it is far more honorable to be a good bricklayer or a skillful weaver than an indifferent poet.—If you cannot at all exist without now and then gratifying your itch for scribbling, follow my example who can both weave stockings and write poems.—But, if you really possess that sprightliness of fancy and elevation of soul which alone constitute an author, do not on that account be troublesome to your friends. A little reflection will point out other means to extract money from the hands and pockets of your fellow citizens than by poorly borrowing what, perhaps, you will never be able to repay.

6. Never engage in any business as an inferior or understrapper. I can-

not endure to see an author debase his profession so far as to submit to be second or third in any office or employment whatever. If fortune, or the ill taste of the public compels you even to turn shallopman on the Delaware, let it be your first care to have the command of the boat. Beggary itself, with all its hideous apparatus of rags and misery, becomes at once respectable whenever it exhibits the least token of independence of spirit and a single spark of laudable ambition.

7. If you are in low circumstances, do not forget that there is such a thing in the world as a decent pride. They are only cowards and miscreants that poverty can render servile in their behavior. Your haughtiness should always rise in proportion to the wretchedness and desperation of your circumstances. If you have only a single guinea in the world be complaisant and obliging to everyone: if you are absolutely destitute of a shilling, immediately assume the air of a despot, pull off your hat to no one, let your discourse, in every company, turn upon the vanity of riches, the insignificancy of the great men of the earth, the revolution of empires, and the final consummation of all things.—By such means you will at least conceal a secret of some importance to yourself—that you have not a shilling in the world to pay for your last night's lodging.

8. Should you ever be prevailed upon to dedicate your book to any great man or woman, consider first, whether the tenor and subject of it be such as may in some measure coincide with the age, temper, education, business and general conversation of the person whose patronage is requested. A friend of mine once committed a great error on this score. He wrote a bawdy poem, and dedicated it to the principal in the department of finance.

9. Never make a present of your works to great men. If they do not think them worth purchasing, trust me, they will never think them worth reading.

10. If fortune seems absolutely determined to starve you, and you can by no means whatever make your works sell; to keep up as much as in you lies, the expiring dignity of authorship, do not take to drinking, gambling or bridge-building as some have done, thereby bringing the trade of authorship into disrepute; but retire to some uninhabited island or desert, and there, at your leisure, end your life with decency.

The above is all that has yet been found written by Robert Slender relative to authors and authorship—and further the copyist at this time sayeth not.   1788

WILLIAM CULLEN BRYANT

(1794-1878)

BIBLIOGRAPHY:

Parke Godwin, ed. *The Poetical
Works of William Cullen Bryant*, 2
vols. (New York, 1883). Godwin, ed.
*A Biography of William Cullen Bryant,
with Extracts from His Private Cor-*

respondence, 2 vols. (New York, 1883). Godwin, ed. *The Prose Writings of William Cullen Bryant,* 2 vols. (New York, 1884). H. C. Sturges, *Chronologies of the Life and Writings of William Cullen Bryant* (New York, 1903). James G. Wilson, *Bryant and His Friends* (New York, 1886). John Bigelow, *William Cullen Bryant* (Boston, 1890). William A. Bradley, *William Cullen Bryant* (Boston, 1905).

Tremaine McDowell, ed. *William Cullen Bryant: Representative Selections* (New York, 1935). Harry H. Peckham, *Gotham Yankee: A Biography of William Cullen Bryant* (New York, 1950). Curtis S. Johnson, *Politics and a Belly-Full; the Journalistic Career of William Cullen Bryant* (New York, 1962). Albert F. McLean, Jr., *William Cullen Bryant* (New York, 1964).

Thanatopsis

To him who in the love of Nature holds
Communion with her visible forms, she speaks
A various language; for his gayer hours
She has a voice of gladness, and a smile
And eloquence of beauty, and she glides   5
Into his darker musings, with a mild
And healing sympathy, that steals away
Their sharpness, ere he is aware. When thoughts
Of the last bitter hour come like a blight
Over thy spirit, and sad images   10
Of the stern agony, and shroud, and pall,
And breathless darkness, and the narrow house,
Make thee to shudder and grow sick at heart;—
Go forth, under the open sky, and list
To Nature's teachings, while from all around—   15
Earth and her waters, and the depths of air—
Comes a still voice—Yet a few days, and thee
The all-beholding sun shall see no more
In all his course; nor yet in the cold ground,
Where thy pale form was laid, with many tears,   20
Nor in the embrace of ocean, shall exist
Thy image. Earth, that nourished thee, shall claim
Thy growth, to be resolved to earth again,
And, lost each human trace, surrendering up
Thine individual being, shalt thou go   25
To mix forever with the elements,
To be a brother to the insensible rock
And to the sluggish clod, which the rude swain
Turns with his share, and treads upon. The oak
Shall send his roots abroad, and pierce thy mould.   30

Yet not to thine eternal resting-place
Shalt thou retire alone, nor couldst thou wish
Couch more magnificent. Thou shalt lie down
With patriarchs of the infant world—with kings,
The powerful of the earth—the wise, the good,   35
Fair forms, and hoary seers of ages past,
All in one mighty sepulchre. The hills
Rock-ribbed and ancient as the sun,—the vales
Stretching in pensive quietness between;
The venerable woods—rivers that move   40
In majesty, and the complaining brooks
That make the meadows green; and, poured round all,
Old Ocean's gray and melancholy waste,—
Are but the solemn decorations all
Of the great tomb of man. The golden sun,   45
The planets, all the infinte host of heaven,
Are shining on the sad abodes of death,
Through the still lapse of ages. All that tread
The globe are but a handful to the tribes
That slumber in its bosom.—Take the wings   50
Of morning, pierce the Barcan wilderness,
Or lose thyself in the continuous woods
Where rolls the Oregon, and hears no sound,
Save his own dashings—yet the dead are there:
And millions in those solitudes, since first   55
The flight of years began, have laid them down
In their last sleep—the dead reign there alone.
So shalt thou rest, and what if thou withdraw
In silence from the living, and no friend
Take note of thy departure? All that breathe   60
Will share thy destiny. The gay will laugh
When thou are gone, the solemn brood of care
Plod on, and each one as before will chase
His favorite phantom; yet all these shall leave
Their mirth and their employments, and shall come   65
And make their bed with thee. As the long train
Of ages glide away, the sons of men,
The youth in life's green spring, and he who goes
In the full strength of years, matron and maid,
The speechless babe, and the gray-headed man—   70
Shall one by one be gathered to thy side,
By those, who in their turn shall follow them.

So live, that when thy summons comes to join
The innumerable caravan, which moves
To that mysterious realm, where each shall take   75
His chamber in the silent halls of death,
Thou go not, like the quarry-slave at night,
Scourged to his dungeon, but, sustained and soothed
By an unfaltering trust, approach thy grave,
Like one who wraps the drapery of his couch   80
About him, and lies down to pleasant dreams.

                                        1817

Inscription for the Entrance to a Wood

Stranger, if thou hast learned a truth which needs
No school of long experience, that the world
Is full of guilt and misery, and hast seen
Enough of all its sorrows, crimes, and cares,
To tire thee of it, enter this wild wood   5
And view the haunts of Nature. The calm shade
Shall bring a kindred calm, and the sweet breeze
That makes the green leaves dance, shall waft a balm
To thy sick heart. Thou wilt find nothing here
Of all that pained thee in the haunts of men,   10
And made thee loathe thy life. The primal curse
Fell, it is true, upon the unsinning earth,
But not in vengeance. God hath yoked to guilt
Her pale tormentor, misery. Hence, these shades
Are still the abodes of gladness; the thick roof   15
Of green and stirring branches is alive
And musical with birds, that sing and sport
In wantonness of spirit; while below
The squirrel, with raised paws and form erect,
Chirps merrily. Throngs of insects in the shade   20
Try their thin wings and dance in the warm beam
That waked them into life. Even the green trees
Partake the deep contentment; as they bend
To the soft winds, the sun from the blue sky
Looks in and sheds a blessing on the scene.   25
Scarce less the cleft-born wild-flower seems to enjoy
Existence, than the winged plunderer
That sucks its sweets. The mossy rocks themselves,

And the old and ponderous trunks of prostrate trees
That lead from knoll to knoll a causey rude   30
Or bridge the sunken brook, and their dark roots,
With all their earth upon them, twisting high,
Breathe fixed tranquillity. The rivulet
Sends forth glad sounds, and tripping o'er its bed
Of pebbly sands, or leaping down the rocks,   35
Seems, with continuous laughter, to rejoice
In its own being. Softly tread the marge,
Lest from her midway perch thou scare the wren
That dips her bill in water. The cool wind,
That stirs the stream in play, shall come to thee,   40
Like one that loves thee nor will let thee pass
Ungreeted, and shall give its light embrace.

                                            1817

To a Waterfowl

    Whither, midst falling dew,
While glow the heavens with the last steps of day,
Far, through their rosy depths, dost thou pursue
    Thy solitary way?

    Vainly the fowler's eye   5
Might mark thy distant flight to do thee wrong,
As, darkly seen against the crimson sky,
    Thy figure floats along.

    Seek'st thou the plashy brink
Of weedy lake, or marge of river wide,   10
Or where the rocking billows rise and sink
    On the chafed ocean-side?

    There is a Power whose care
Teaches thy way along that pathless coast—
The desert and illimitable air—   15
    Lone wandering, but not lost.

    All day thy wings have fanned,
At that far height, the cold, thin atmosphere,
Yet stoop not, weary, to the welcome land,
    Though the dark night is near.   20

And soon that toil shall end;
Soon shalt thou find a summer home, and rest,
And scream among thy fellows; reeds shall bend,
    Soon, o'er thy sheltered nest.

    Thou'rt gone, the abyss of heaven   25
Hath swallowed up thy form; yet, on my heart
Deeply hath sunk the lesson thou hast given,
    And shall not soon depart.

    He who, from zone to zone,
Guides through the boundless sky thy certain flight,   30
In the long way that I must tread alone,
    Will lead my steps aright.

                            1818

Green River

When breezes are soft and skies are fair,
I steal an hour from study and care,
And hie me away to the woodland scene,
Where wanders the stream with waters of green,
As if the bright fringe of herbs on its brink   5
Had given their stain to the wave they drink;
And they, whose meadows it murmurs through,
Have named the stream from its own fair hue.

Yet pure its waters—its shallows are bright
With colored pebbles and sparkles of light,   10
And clear the depths where its eddies play,
And dimples deepen and whirl away,
And the plane-tree's speckled arms o'ershoot
The swifter current that mines its root,
Through whose shifting leaves, as you walk the hill,   15
The quivering glimmer of sun and rill
With a sudden flash on the eye is thrown,
Like the ray that streams from the diamond-stone.
Oh, loveliest there the spring days come,
With blossoms, and birds, and wild-bees' hum;   20
The flowers of summer are fairest there,
And freshest the breath of the summer air;
And sweetest the golden autumn day
In silence and sunshine glides away.

Yet fair as thou art, thou shunnest to glide,   25
Beautiful stream! by the village side;
But windest away from haunts of men,
To quiet valley and shaded glen;
And forest, and meadow, and slope of hill,
Around thee, are lonely, lovely, and still,   30
Lonely—save when, by thy rippling tides,
From thicket to thicket the angler glides;
Or the simpler comes, with basket and book
For herbs of power on thy banks to look;
Or haply, some idle dreamer, like me,   35
To wander, and muse, and gaze on thee,
Still—save the chirp of birds that feed
On the river cherry and seedy reed.
And thy own wild music gushing out
With mellow murmur of fairy shout,   40
From dawn to the blush of another day,
Like traveler singing along his way.

That fairy music I never hear,
Nor gaze on those waters so green and clear,
And mark them winding away from sight,   45
Darkened with shade or flashing with light,
While o'er them the vine to its thicket clings,
And the zephyr stoops to freshen his wings,
But I wish that fate had left me free
To wander these quiet haunts with thee,   50
Till the eating cares of earth should depart,
And the peace of the scene pass into my heart;
And I envy thy stream, as it glides along
Through its beautiful banks in a trance of song.

Though forced to drudge for the dregs of men,   55
And scrawl strange words with the barbarous pen,
And mingle among the jostling crowd,
Where the sons of strife are subtle and loud—
I often come to this quiet place,
To breathe the airs that ruffle thy face,   60
And gaze upon thee in silent dream,
For in thy lonely and lovely stream
An image of that calm life appears
That won my heart in my greener years.

                                                    1821

A Winter Piece

The time has been that these wild solitudes,
Yet beautiful as wild, were trod by me
Oftener than now; and when the ills of life
Had chafed my spirit—when the unsteady pulse
Beat with strange flutterings—I would wander forth   5
And seek the woods. The sunshine on my path
Was to me as a friend. The swelling hills,
The quiet dells retiring far between,
With gentle invitation to explore
Their windings, were a calm society   10
That talked with me and soothed me. Then the chant
Of birds, and chime of brooks, and soft caress
Of the fresh sylvan air, made me forget
The thoughts that broke my peace, and I began
To gather simples by the fountain's brink,   15
And lose myself in day-dreams. While I stood
In Nature's loneliness, I was with one
With whom I early grew familiar, one
Who never had a frown for me, whose voice
Never rebuked me for the hours I stole   20
From cares I loved not, but of which the world
Deems highest, to converse with her. When shrieked
The bleak November winds, and smote the woods,
And the brown fields were herbless, and the shades,
That met above the merry rivulet,   25
Were spoiled, I sought, I loved them still; they seemed
Like old companions in adversity.
Still there was beauty in my walks; the brook,
Bordered with sparkling frost-work, was as gay
As with its fringe of summer flowers. Afar,   30
The village with its spires, the path of streams
And dim receding valleys, hid before
By interposing trees, lay visible
Through the bare grove, and my familiar haunts
Seemed new to me. Nor was I slow to come   35
Among them, when the clouds, from their still skirts,
Had shaken down on earth the feathery snow,
And all was white. The pure keen air abroad,
Albeit it breathed no scent of herb, nor heard
Love-call of bird nor merry hum of bee,   40
Was not the air of death. Bright mosses crept
Over the spotted trunks, and the close buds,

That lay along the boughs, instinct with life,
Patient, and waiting the soft breath of Spring,
Feared not the piercing spirit of the North.   45
The snow-bird twittered on the beechen bough,
And 'neath the hemlock, whose thick branches bent
Beneath its bright cold burden, and kept dry
A circle, on the earth, of withered leaves,
The partridge found a shelter. Through the snow   50
The rabbit sprang away. The lighter track
Of fox, and the raccoon's broad path, were there,
Crossing each other. From his hollow tree
The squirrel was abroad, gathering the nuts
Just fallen, that asked the winter cold and sway   55
Of winter blast, to shake them from their hold.

But Winter has yet brighter scenes—he boasts
Splendors beyond what gorgeous Summer knows;
Or Autumn with his many fruits, and woods
All flushed with many hues. Come when the rains   60
Have glazed the snow and clothed the trees with ice,
While the slant sun of February pours
Into the bowers a flood of light. Approach!
The incrusted surface shall upbear thy steps,
And the broad arching portals of the grove   65
Welcome thy entering. Look! the massy trunks
Are cased in the pure crystal; each light spray,
Nodding and tinkling in the breath of heaven,
Is studded with its trembling water-drops,
That glimmer with an amethystine light.   70
But round the parent-stem the long low boughs
Bend, in a glittering ring, and arbors hide
The glassy floor. Oh! you might deem the spot
The spacious cavern of some virgin mine,
Deep in the womb of earth—where the gems grow,   75
And diamonds put forth radiant rods and bud
With amethyst and topaz—and the place
Lit up, most royally, with the pure beam
That dwells in them. Or haply the vast hall
Of fairy palace, that outlasts the night,   80
And fades not in the glory of the sun;—
Where crystal columns send forth slender shafts
And crossing arches; and fantastic aisles
Wind from the sight in brightness, and are lost
Among the crowded pillars. Raise thine eye;   85
Thou seest no cavern roof, no palace vault;

There the blue sky and the white drifting cloud
Look in. Again the wildered fancy dreams
Of spouting fountains, frozen as they rose,
And fixed, with all their branching jets, in air,   90
And all their sluices sealed. All, all is light;
Light without shade. But all shall pass away
With the next sun. From numberless vast trunks
Loosened, the crashing ice shall make a sound
Like the far roar of rivers, and the eve   95
Shall close o'er the brown woods as it was wont.

And it is pleasant, when the noisy streams
Are just set free, and milder suns melt off
The plashy snow, save only the firm drift
In the deep glen or the close shade of pines—   100
'Tis pleasant to behold the wreaths of smoke
Roll up among the maples of the hill,
Where the shrill sound of youthful voices wakes
The shriller echo, as the clear pure lymph,
That from the wounded trees, in twinkling drops,   105
Falls, mid the golden brightness of the morn,
Is gathered in with brimming pails, and oft,
Wielded by sturdy hands, the stroke of axe
Makes the woods ring. Along the quiet air,
Come and float calmly off the soft light clouds,   110
Such as you see in summer, and the winds
Scarce stir the branches. Lodged in sunny cleft,
Where the cold breezes come not, blooms alone
The little wind-flower, whose just opened eye
Is blue as the spring heaven it gazes at—   115
Startling the loiterer in the naked groves
With unexpected beauty, for the time
Of blossoms and green leaves is yet afar.
And ere it comes, the encountering winds shall oft
Muster their wrath again, and rapid clouds   120
Shade heaven, and bounding on the frozen earth
Shall fall their volleyed stores, rounded like hail
And white like snow, and the loud North again
Shall buffet the vexed forest in his rage.

      1821

The Yellow Violet

When beechen buds begin to swell,
   And woods the blue-bird's warble know,
The yellow violet's modest bell
   Peeps from the last year's leaves below.

Ere russet fields their green resume,   5
   Sweet flower, I love, in forest bare,
To meet thee, when thy faint perfume
   Alone is in the virgin air.

Of all her train, the hands of Spring
   First plant thee in the watery mould,   10
And I have seen thee blossoming
   Beside the snow-bank's edges cold.

Thy parent sun, who bade thee view
   Pale skies, and chilling moisture sip,
Has bathed thee in his own bright hue,   15
   And streaked with jet thy glowing lip.

Yet slight thy form, and low thy seat,
   And earthward bent thy gentle eye,
Unapt the passing view to meet
   When loftier flowers are flaunting nigh.   20

Oft, in the sunless April day,
   Thy early smile has stayed my walk;
But midst the gorgeous blooms of May,
   I passed thee on thy humble stalk.

So they, who climb to wealth, forget   25
   The friends in darker fortunes tried.
I copied them—but I regret
   That I should ape the ways of pride.

And when again the genial hour
   Awakes the painted tribes of light,   30
I'll not o'erlook the modest flower
   That made the woods of April bright.

1821

Monument Mountain

Thou who wouldst see the lovely and the wild
Mingled in harmony on Nature's face,
Ascend our rocky mountains. Let thy foot
Fail not with weariness, for on their tops
The beauty and the majesty of earth,   5
Spread wide beneath, shall make thee to forget
The steep and toilsome way. There, as thou stand'st,
The haunts of men below thee, and around
The mountain-summits, thy expanding heart
Shall feel a kindred with that loftier world   10
To which thou art translated, and partake
The enlargement of thy vision. Thou shalt look
Upon the green and rolling forest-tops,
And down into the secrets of the glens,
And streams that with their bordering thickets strive   15
To hide their windings. Thou shalt gaze, at once,
Here on white villages, and tilth, and herds,
And swarming roads, and there on solitudes
That only hear the torrent, and the wind,
And eagle's shriek. There is a precipice   20
That seems a fragment of some mighty wall,
Built by the hand that fashioned the old world,
To separate its nations, and thrown down
When the flood drowned them. To the north, a path
Conducts you up the narrow battlement.   25
Steep is the western side, shaggy and wild
With mossy trees, and pinnacles of flint,
And many a hanging crag. But, to the east,
Sheer to the vale go down the bare old cliffs—
Huge pillars, that in middle heaven upbear   30
Their weather-beaten capitals, here dark
With moss, the growth of centuries, and there
Of chalky whiteness where the thunderbolt
Has splintered them. It is a fearful thing
To stand upon the beetling verge, and see   35
Where storm and lightning, from that huge gray wall,
Have tumbled down vast blocks, and at the base
Dashed them in fragments, and to lay thine ear
Over the dizzy depth, and hear the sound
Of winds, that struggle with the woods below,   40
Come up like ocean-murmurs. But the scene
Is lovely round; a beautiful river there

Wanders amid the fresh and fertile meads,
The paradise he made unto himself,
Mining the soil for ages. On each side   45
The fields swell upward to the hills; beyond,
Above the hills, in the blue distance, rise
The mountain-columns with which earth props heaven.

There is a tale about these reverend rocks,
A sad tradition of unhappy love,   50
And sorrows borne and ended, long ago,
When over these fair vales the savage sought
His game in the thick woods. There was a maid
The fairest of the Indian maids, bright-eyed,
With wealth of raven tresses, a light form,   55
And a gay heart. About her cabin-door
The wide old woods resounded with her song
And fairy laughter all the summer day.
She loved her cousin; such a love was deemed,
By the morality of those stern tribes,   60
Incestuous, and she struggled hard and long
Against her love, and reasoned with her heart,
As simple Indian maiden might. In vain.
Then her eye lost its lustre, and her step
Its lightness, and the gray-haired men that passed   65
Her dwelling, wondered that they heard no more
The accustomed song and laugh of her, whose looks
Were like the cheerful smile of Spring, they said,
Upon the Winter of their age. She went
To weep where no eye saw, and was not found   70
When all the merry girls were met to dance,
And all the hunters of the tribe were out;
Nor when they gathered from the rustling husk
The shining ear; nor when, by the river's side,
They pulled the grape and startled the wild shades   75
With sounds of mirth. The keen-eyed Indian dames
Would whisper to each other, as they saw
Her wasting form, and say, *The girl will die.*

One day into the bosom of a friend,
A playmate of her young and innocent years,   80
She poured her griefs. "Thou know'st, and thou alone,"
She said, "for I have told thee, all my love,
And guilt, and sorrow. I am sick of life.
All night I weep in darkness, and the morn
Glares on me, as upon a thing accursed,   85

That has no business on the earth. I hate
The pastimes and the pleasant toils that once
I loved; the cheerful voices of my friends
Sound in my ear like mockings, and, at night,
In dreams, my mother, from the land of souls,   90
Calls me and chides me. All that look on me
Do seem to know my shame; I cannot bear
Their eyes; I cannot from my heart root out
The love that wrings it so, and I must die."

    It was a summer morning, and they went   95
To this old precipice. About the cliffs
Lay garlands, ears of maize, and shaggy skins
Of wolf and bear, the offerings of the tribe
Here made to the Great Spirit, for they deemed,
Like worshippers of the elder time, that God   100
Doth walk on the high places and affect
The earth-o'erlooking mountains. She had on
The ornaments with which her father loved
To deck the beauty of his bright-eyed girl,
And bade her wear when stranger warriors came   105
To be his guests. Here the friends sat them down,
And sang, all day, old songs of love and death,
And decked the poor wan victim's hair with flowers,
And prayed that safe and swift might be her way
To the calm world of sunshine, where no grief   110
Makes the heart heavy and the eyelids red.
Beautiful lay the region of her tribe
Below her—waters resting in the embrace
Of the wide forest, and maize-planted glades
Opening amid the leafy wilderness.   115
She gazed upon it long, and at the sight
Of her own village peeping through the trees,
And her own dwelling, and the cabin-roof
Of him she loved with an unlawful love,
And came to die for, a warm gush of tears   120
Ran from her eyes. But when the sun grew low
And the hill-shadows long, she threw herself
From the steep rock and perished. There was scooped,
Upon the mountain's southern slope, a grave;
And there they laid her, in the very garb   125
With which the maiden decked herself for death,
With the same withering wild-flowers in her hair.
And o'er the mould that covered her, the tribe
Built up a simple monument, a cone

Of small loose stones. Thenceforward all who passed,   130
Hunter, and dame, and virgin, laid a stone
In silence on the pile. It stands there yet.
And Indians from the distant West, who come
To visit where their fathers' bones are laid,
Yet tell the sorrowful tale, and to this day   135
The mountain where the hapless maiden died
Is called the Mountain of the Monument.

                        1824

A Forest Hymn

The groves were God's first temples. Ere man learned
To hew the shaft, and lay the architrave,
And spread the roof above them—ere he framed
The lofty vault, to gather and roll back
The sound of anthems; in the darkling wood.   5
Amid the cool and silence, he knelt down,
And offered to the Mightiest solemn thanks
And supplication. For his simple heart
Might not resist the sacred influences
Which, from the stilly twilight of the place,   10
And from the gray old trunks that high in heaven
Mingled their mossy boughs, and from the sound
Of the invisible breath that swayed at once
All their green tops, stole over him, and bowed
His spirit with the thought of boundless power   15
And inaccessible majesty. Ah, why
Should we, in the world's riper years, neglect
God's ancient sanctuaries, and adore
Only among the crowd, and under roofs
That our frail hands have raised? Let me, at least,   20
Here, in the shadow of this aged wood,
Offer one hymn—thrice happy, if it find
Acceptance in His ear.

                    Father, thy hand
Hath reared these venerable columns, thou   25
Didst weave this verdant roof. Thou didst look down
Upon the naked earth, and, forthwith, rose
All these fair ranks of trees. They, in thy sun,
Budded, and shook their green leaves in thy breeze,
And shot toward heaven. The century-living crow   30
Whose birth was in their tops, grew old and died
Among their branches, till, at last, they stood,

As now they stand, massy, and tall and dark,
Fit shrine for humble worshipper to hold
Communion with his Maker. These dim vaults, 35
These winding aisles, of human pomp or pride
Report not. No fantastic carvings show
The boast of our vain race to change the form
Of thy fair works. But thou art here—thou fill'st
The solitude. Thou art in the soft winds 40
That run along the summit of these trees
In music; thou art in the cooler breath
That from the inmost darkness of the place
Comes, scarcely felt; the barky trunks, the ground,
The fresh moist ground, are all instinct with thee. 45
Here is continual worship;—Nature, here,
In the tranquillity that thou dost love,
Enjoys thy presence. Noiselessly, around,
From perch to perch, the solitary bird
Passes; and yon clear spring, that, midst its herbs, 50
Wells softly forth and wandering steeps the roots
Of half the mighty forest, tells no tale
Of all the good it does. Thou hast not left
Thyself without a witness, in these shades,
Of thy perfections. Grandeur, strength, and grace, 55
Are here to speak of thee. This mighty oak—
By whose immovable stem I stand and seem
Almost annihilated—not a prince,
In all that proud old world beyond the deep,
E'er wore his crown as loftily as he 60
Wears the green coronal of leaves with which
Thy hand has graced him. Nestled at his root
Is beauty, such as blooms not in the glare
Of the broad sun. That delicate forest flower,
With scented breath and look so like a smile, 65
Seems, as it issues from the shapeless mould,
An emanation of the indwelling Life,
A visible token of the upholding Love,
That are the soul of this great universe.

My heart is awed within me when I think 70
Of the great miracle that still goes on,
In silence, round me—the perpetual work
Of thy creation, finished, yet renewed
Forever. Written on thy works I read
The lesson of thy own eternity. 75
Lo! all grow old and die—but see again,

How on the faltering footsteps of decay
Youth presses—ever-gay and beautiful youth
In all its beautiful forms. These lofty trees
Wave not less proudly that their ancestors   80
Moulder beneath them. Oh, there is not lost
One of earth's charms: upon her bosom yet,
After the flight of untold centuries,
The freshness of her far beginning lies
And yet shall lie. Life mocks the idle hate   85
Of his arch-enemy Death—yea, seats himself
Upon the tyrant's throne—the sepulchre,
And of the triumphs of his ghastly foe
Makes his own nourishment. For he came forth
From thine own bosom, and shall have no end.   90

There have been holy men who hid themselves
Deep in the woody wilderness, and gave
Their lives to thought and prayer, till they outlived
The generation born with them, nor seemed
Less aged than the hoary trees and rocks   95
Around them;—and there have been holy men
Who deemed it were not well to pass life thus.
But let me often to these solitudes
Retire, and in thy presence reassure
My feeble virtue. Here its enemies,   100
The passions, at thy plainer footsteps shrink
And tremble and are still. O God! when thou
Dost scare the world with tempests, set on fire
The heavens with falling thunderbolts, or fill,
With all the waters of the firmament,   105
The swift dark whirlwind that uproots the woods
And drowns the villages; when, at thy call,
Uprises the great deep and throws himself
Upon the continent, and overwhelms
Its cities—who forgets not, at the sight   110
Of these tremendous tokens of thy power,
His pride, and lays his strifes and follies by?
Oh, from these sterner aspects of thy face
Spare me and mine, nor let us need the wrath
Of the mad, unchained elements to teach   115
Who rules them. Be it ours to meditate,
In these calm shades, thy milder majesty,
And to the beautiful order of thy works
Learn to conform the order of our lives.

                                        1825

June

I gazed upon the glorious sky
    And the green mountains round,
And thought that when I came to lie
    At rest within the ground,
'Twere pleasant, that in flowery June,   5
When brooks send up a cheerful tune,
    And groves a joyous sound,
The sexton's hand, my grave to make,
The rich, green mountain-turf should break.

A cell within the frozen mould,   10
    A coffin borne through sleet,
And icy clods above it rolled,
    While fierce the tempests beat—
Away!—I will not think of these—
Blue be the sky and soft the breeze,   15
    Earth green beneath the feet,
And be the damp mould gently pressed
Into my narrow place of rest.

There through the long, long summer hours,
    The golden light should lie,   20
And thick young herbs and groups of flowers
    Stand in their beauty by.
The oriole should build and tell
His love-tale close beside my cell;
    The idle butterfly   25
Should rest him there, and there be heard
The housewife bee and humming-bird.

And what if cheerful shouts at noon
    Come, from the village sent,
Or song of maids, beneath the moon   30
    With fairy laughter blent?
And what if, in the evening light,
Betrothed lovers walk in sight
    Of my low monument?
I would the lovely scene around   35
Might know no sadder sight nor sound.

I know that I no more should see
    The season's glorious show,
Nor would its brightness shine for me,
    Nor its wild music flow;   40
But if, around my place of sleep,
The friends I love should come to weep,
    They might not haste to go.
Soft airs, and song, and light, and bloom
Should keep them lingering by my tomb.   45

These to their softened hearts should bear
    The thought of what has been,
And speak of one who cannot share
    The gladness of the scene;
Whose part, in all the pomp that fills   50
The circuit of the summer hills,
    Is that his grave is green;
And deeply would their hearts rejoice
To hear again his living voice.

                1826

"I Cannot Forget with What Fervid Devotion"

I cannot forget with what fervid devotion
    I worshipped the visions of verse and of fame;
Each gaze at the glories of earth, sky, and ocean,
    To my kindled emotions, was wind over flame.

And deep were my musings in life's early blossom,   5
    'Mid the twilight of mountain-groves wandering long;
How thrilled my young veins, and how throbbed my full bosom,
    When o'er me descended the spirit of song!

'Mong the deep-cloven fells that for ages had listened
    To the rush of the pebble-paved river between,   10
Where the kingfisher screamed and gray precipice glistened,
    All breathless with awe have I gazed on the scene;

Till I felt the dark power o'er my reveries stealing,
    From the gloom of the thickets that over me hung,
And the thoughts that awoke, in that rapture of feeling,   15
    Were formed into verse as they rose to my tongue.

Bright visions! I mixed with the world, and ye faded,
   No longer your pure rural worshipper now;
In the haunts your continual presence pervaded,
   Ye shrink from the signet of care on my brow.   20

In the old mossy groves on the breast of the mountain,
   In deep lonely glens where the waters complain,
By the shade of the rock, by the gush of the fountain,
   I seek your loved footsteps, but seek them in vain.

Oh, leave not forlorn and forever forsaken,   25
   Your pupil and victim to life and its tears!
But sometimes return, and in mercy awaken
   The glories ye showed to his earlier years.

1826

Song of Marion's Men

   Our band is few but true and tried,
      Our leader frank and bold;
   The British soldier trembles
      When Marion's name is told.
   Our fortress is the good greenwood,   5
      Our tent the cypress-tree;
   We know the forest round us,
      As seamen know the sea.
   We know its walls of thorny vines,
      Its glades of reedy grass,   10
   Its safe and silent islands
      Within the dark morass.

   Woe to the English soldiery
      That little dread us near!
   On them shall light at midnight   15
      A strange and sudden fear:
   When, waking to their tents on fire,
      They grasp their arms in vain,
   And they who stand to face us
      Are beat to earth again;   20
   And they who fly in terror deem
      A mighty host behind,
   And hear the tramp of thousands
      Upon the hollow wind.

Then sweet the hour that brings release 25
  From danger and from toil:
We talk the battle over,
  And share the battle's spoil.
The woodland rings with laugh and shout,
  As if a hunt were up, 30
And woodland flowers are gathered
  To crown the soldier's cup.
With merry songs we mock the wind
  That in the pine-top grieves,
And slumber long and sweetly 35
  On beds of oaken leaves.

Well knows the fair and friendly moon
  The band that Marion leads—
The glitter of their rifles,
  The scampering of their steeds. 40
'Tis life to guide the fiery barb
  Across the moonlit plain;
'Tis life to feel the night-wind
  That lifts his tossing mane.
A moment in the British camp— 45
  A moment—and away
Back to the pathless forest,
  Before the peep of day.

Grave men there are by broad Santee,
  Grave men with hoary hairs; 50
Their hearts are all with Marion,
  For Marion are their prayers.
And lovely ladies greet our band
  With kindliest welcoming,
With smiles like those of summer, 55
  And tears like those of spring.
For them we wear these trusty arms,
  And lay them down no more
Till we have driven the Briton,
  Forever, from our shore. 60

                        1831

"Oh, Fairest of the Rural Maids"

Oh, fairest of the rural maids!
Thy birth was in the forest shades;
Green boughs, and glimpses of the sky,
Were all that met thine infant eye.

Thy sports, thy wanderings, when a child,   5
Were ever in the sylvan wild;
And all the beauty of the place
Is in thy heart and on thy face.

The twilight of the trees and rocks
Is in the light shade of thy locks;   10
Thy step is as the wind, that weaves
Its playful way among the leaves.

Thine eyes are springs, in whose serene
And silent waters heaven is seen;
Their lashes are the herbs that look   15
On their young figures in the brook.

The forest depths, by foot unpressed,
Are not more sinless than thy breast;
The holy peace, that fills the air
Of those calm solitudes, is there.   20

                                    1832

To the Fringed Gentian

Thou blossom bright with autumn dew
And colored with the heaven's own blue,
That openest when the quiet light
Succeeds the keen and frosty night—

Thou comest not when violets lean   5
O'er wandering brooks and springs unseen,
Or columbines, in purple dressed,
Nod o'er the ground-bird's hidden nest.

Thou waitest late and com'st alone
When woods are bare and birds are flown,   10
And frosts and shortening days portend
The aged year is near his end.

Then doth thy sweet and quiet eye
Look through its fringes to the sky,
Blue—blue—as if that sky let fall   15
A flower from its cerulean wall.

I would that thus, when I shall see
The hour of death draw near to me,
Hope, blossoming within my heart,
May look to heaven as I depart.   20

1832

The Prairies

These are the gardens of the Desert, these
The unshorn fields, boundless and beautiful,
For which the speech of England has no name—
The Prairies. I behold them for the first,
And my heart swells, while the dilated sight   5
Takes in the encircling vastness. Lo! they stretch
In airy undulations, far away,
As if the Ocean, in his gentlest swell,
Stood still, with all his rounded billows fixed,
And motionless forever. Motionless?—   10
No—they are all unchained again. The clouds
Sweep over with their shadows, and, beneath,
The surface rolls and fluctuates to the eye;
Dark hollows seem to glide along and chase
The sunny ridges. Breezes of the South!   15
Who toss the golden and the flame-like flowers,
And pass the prairie-hawk that, poised on high,
Flaps his broad wings, yet moves not—ye have played
Among the palms of Mexico and vines
Of Texas, and have crisped the limpid brooks   20
That from the fountains of Sonora glide
Into the calm Pacific—have ye fanned
A nobler or a lovlier scene than this?
Man hath no part in all this glorious work:
The hand that built the firmament hath heaved   25
And smoothed these verdant swells, and sown their slopes

With herbage, planted them with island-groves,
And hedged them round with forests. Fitting floor
For this magnificent temple of the sky—
With flowers whose glory and whose multitude   30
Rival the constellations! The great heavens
Seem to stoop down upon the scene in love,—
A nearer vault, and of a tenderer blue,
Than that which bends above our Eastern hills.

As o'er the verdant waste I guide my steed,   35
Among the high rank grass that sweeps his sides
The hollow beating of his footstep seems
A sacrilegious sound. I think of those
Upon whose rest he tramples. Are they here—
The dead of other days?—and did the dust   40
Of these fair solitudes once stir with life
And burn with passion? Let the mighty mounds
That overlook the rivers, or that rise
In the dim forest crowded with old oaks,
Answer. A race, that long has passed away,   45
Built them; a disciplined and populous race
Heaped, with long toil, the earth, while yet the Greek
Was hewing the Pentelicus to forms
Of symmetry, and rearing on its rock
The glittering Parthenon. These ample fields   50
Nourished their harvests, here their herds were fed,
When haply by their stalls the bison lowed,
And bowed his maned shoulder to the yoke.
All day this desert murmured with their toils,
Till twilight blushed, and lovers walked, and wooed   55
In a forgotten language, and old tunes,
From instruments of unremembered form,
Gave the soft winds a voice. The red-man came—
The roaming hunter-tribes, warlike and fierce,
And the mound-builders vanished from the earth.   60
The solitude of centuries untold
Has settled where they dwelt. The prairie-wolf
Hunts in their meadows, and his fresh-dug den
Yawns by my path. The gopher mines the ground
Where stood their swarming cities. All is gone;   65
All—save the piles of earth that hold their bones,
The platforms where they worshipped unknown gods,
The barriers which they builded from the soil
To keep the foe at bay—till o'er the walls
The wild beleaguerers broke, and, one by one,   70

The strongholds of the plain were forced, and heaped
With corpses. The brown vultures of the wood
Flocked to those vast uncovered sepulchres,
And sat, unscared and silent, at their feast.
Haply some solitary fugitive,   75
Lurking in marsh and forest, till the sense
Of desolation and of fear became
Bitterer than death, yielded himself to die.
Man's better nature triumphed then. Kind words
Welcomed and soothed him; the rude conquerors   80
Seated the captive with their chiefs; he chose
A bride among their maidens, and at length
Seemed to forget—yet ne'er forgot—the wife
Of his first love, and her sweet little ones,
Butchered, amid their shrieks, with all his race.   85

    Thus change the forms of being. Thus arise
Races of living things glorious in strength,
And perish, as the quickening breath of God
Fills them, or is withdrawn. The red-man, too,
Has left the blooming wilds he ranged so long,   90
And, nearer to the Rocky Mountains, sought
A wilder hunting-ground. The beaver builds
No longer by these streams, but far away,
On waters whose blue surface ne'er gave back
The white man's face—among Missouri's springs,   95
And pools whose issues swell the Oregon—
He rears his little Venice. In these plains
The bison feeds no more. Twice twenty leagues
Beyond remotest smoke of hunter's camp,
Roams the majestic brute, in herds that shake   100
The earth with thundering steps—yet here I meet
His ancient footprints stamped beside the pool.

    Still this great solitude is quick with life.
Myriads of insects, gaudy as the flowers
They flutter over, gentle quadrupeds,   105
And birds, that scarce have learned the fear of man,
Are here, and sliding reptiles of the ground,
Startlingly beautiful. The graceful deer
Bounds to the wood at my approach. The bee,
A more adventurous colonist than man,   110
With whom he came across the eastern deep,
Fills the savannas with his murmurings,
And hides his sweets, as in the golden age,

Within the hollow oak. I listen long
To his domestic hum, and think I hear   115
The sound of that advancing multitude
Which soon shall fill these deserts. From the ground
Comes up the laugh of children, the soft voice
Of maidens, and the sweet and solemn hymn
Of Sabbath worshippers. The low of herds   120
Blends with the rustling of the heavy grain
Over the dark-brown furrows. All at once
A fresher wind sweeps by, and breaks my dream,
And I am in the wilderness alone.

                                                    1833

"Oh Mother of a Mighty Race"

Oh mother of a mighty race,
Yet lovely in thy youthful grace!
The elder dames, thy haughty peers,
Admire and hate thy blooming years.
   With words of shame   5
And taunts of scorn they join thy name.

For on thy cheeks the glow is spread
That tints thy morning hills with red;
Thy step—the wild-deer's rustling feet,
Within thy woods are not more fleet;   10
   Thy hopeful eye
Is bright as thine own sunny sky.

Ay, let them rail—those haughty ones,
While safe thou dwellest with thy sons.
They do not know how loved thou art,   15
How many a fond and fearless heart
   Would rise to throw
Its life between thee and the foe.

They know not, in their hate and pride,
What virtues with thy children bide;   20
How true, how good, thy graceful maids
Make bright, like flowers, the valley-shades;
   What generous men
Spring, like thine oaks, by hill and glen.

What cordial welcomes greet the guest   25
By thy lone rivers of the West;
How faith is kept, and truth revered,
And man is loved, and God is feared,
  In woodland homes,
And where the ocean-border foams.   30

There's freedom at thy gates and rest
For Earth's down-trodden and opprest,
A shelter for the hunted head,
For the starved laborer toil and bread.
  Power, at thy bounds,   35
Stops and calls back his baffled hounds.

Oh, fair young mother! on thy brow
Shall sit a nobler grace than now.
Deep in the brightness of thy skies
The thronging years in glory rise,   40
  And, as they fleet,
Drop strength and riches at thy feet.

Thine eye, with every coming hour,
Shall brighten, and thy form shall tower;
And when thy sisters, elder born,   45
Would brand thy name with words of scorn,
  Before thine eye,
Upon their lips the taunt shall die.

       1847

The Death of Lincoln

Oh, slow to smite and swift to spare,
 Gentle and merciful and just!
Who, in the fear of God, didst bear
 The sword of power, a nation's trust!

In sorrow by thy bier we stand,   5
 Amid the awe that hushes all,
And speak the anguish of a land
 That shook with horror at thy fall.

Thy task is done; the bond are free:
    We bear thee to an honored grave,   10
Whose proudest monument shall be
    The broken fetters of the slave.

Pure was thy life; its bloody close
    Hath placed thee with the sons of light,
Among the noble host of those   15
    Who perished in the cause of Right.

                                        1865

From An Essay on American Poetry

Of the poetry of the United States different opinions have been entertained, and prejudice on the one side and partiality on the other have
equally prevented a just and rational estimate of its merits. Abroad our
literature has fallen under unmerited contumely, from those who were
but slenderly acquainted with the subject on which they professed to decide, and at home it must be confessed that the swaggering and pompous
pretensions of many have done not a little to provoke and excuse the ridicule of foreigners. Either of these extremes exerts an injurious influence
on the cause of letters in our country. To encourage exertion and embol-
den merit to come forward, it is necessary that they should be acknowledged and rewarded. Few men have the confidence to solicit what is
wantonly withheld, or the courage to tread a path which presents no
prospect but the melancholy wrecks of those who have gone before them.
National gratitude, national pride—every high and generous feeling that
attaches us to the land of our birth, or that exalts our characters as individuals—ask of us that we should foster the infant literature of our country, and that genius and industry, employing their efforts to hasten its
perfection, should receive from our hands that celebrity which reflects as
much honor on the nation which confers it as on those to whom it is extended.

On the other hand, it is not necessary for these purposes—it is even
detrimental—to bestow on mediocrity the praise due to excellence, and
still more so is the attempt to persuade ourselves and others into an admiration of the faults of favorite writers. We make but a contemptible
figure in the eyes of the world, and set ourselves up as objects of pity to
our posterity, when we affect to rank the poets of our own country with
those mighty masters of song who have flourished in Greece, Italy, and
Britain. Such extravagant admiration may spring from a praiseworthy and
patriotic motive, but it seems to us that it defeats its own object of encouraging our literature, by seducing those who would aspire to the favor

of the public into an imitation of imperfect models, and leading them to rely too much on the partiality of their countrymen to overlook their deficiencies. Were our rewards bestowed only on what is intrinsically meritorious, merit alone would have any apology for appearing before the public. The poetical adventurer should be taught that it is only the productions of genius, taste, and diligence that can find favor at the bar of criticism; that his writings are not to be applauded merely because they are written by an American, and are not decidedly bad; and that he must produce some more satisfactory evidence of his claim to celebrity than an extract from the parish register. To show him what we expect of him, it is as necessary to point out the faults of his predecessors as to commend their excellences. He must be taught as well what to avoid as what to imitate. This is the only way of diffusing and preserving a pure taste, both among those who read and those who write, and, in our opinion, the only way of affording merit a proper and effectual encouragement. . . .

For the first century after the settlement of this country, the few quaint and unskillful specimens of poetry which yet remain to us are looked upon merely as objects of curiosity, are preserved only in the cabinet of the antiquary, and give little pleasure if read without reference to the age and people which produced them. After this period a purer taste began to prevail. The poems of the Rev. John Adams, written in the early part of the eighteenth century, which have been considered as no bad specimen of the poetry of his time, are tolerably free from the faults of the generation that preceded him, and show the dawnings of an ambition of correctness and elegance. The poetical writings of Joseph Green, also, who wrote about the middle of the same century, have been admired for their humor and the playful ease of their composition. But previous to the contest which terminated in the independence of the United States we can hardly be said to have had any national poetry at all. Literary ambition was not yet awakened among us; there was little motive for it, and few rewards. We were contented to consider ourselves as participating in the literary fame of that nation of which we were a part, and of which many of us were natives, and therefore aspired to no separate distinction. And, indeed, we might well lay an equal claim, with those who remained on the British soil, to whatever glory the genius and learning, as well as the virtue and bravery, of other times reflected on the British name. . . .

Yet here was no theatre for the display of literary talent. The worshippers of fame could find no altars erected to that divinity in America, and he who would live by his pen must seek patronage in the parent country. Some men of taste and learning among us might occasionally amuse their leisure with poetical trifles, but a country struggling with the difficulties of colonization, and possessing no superfluous wealth, wanted any other class of men rather than poets. Accordingly, we find the specimens of

American poetry before this period mostly desultory and occasional—rare and delicate exotics, cultivated only by the curious.

When we became an independent empire, a different spirit began to manifest itself, and the general ambition to distinguish ourselves as a nation was not without its effect on our literature. It seems to us that it is from this time only that we can be said to have poets of our own, and from this period it is that we must date the origin of American poetry. About this time flourished Francis Hopkinson, whose humorous ballad, entitled "The Battle of the Kegs," is in most of our memories, and whose other attempts, though deficient in vigor, are not inelegant. The keen and forcible invectives of Dr. Church, which are still recollected by his contemporaries, received an additional edge and sharpness from the exasperated feelings of the times. A writer in verse of inferior note was Philip Freneau, whose pen seems to have been chiefly employed on political subjects, and whose occasional productions, distinguished by a coarse strength of sarcasm, and abounding with allusions to passing events, which are perhaps their greatest merit, attracted in their time considerable notice, and, in the year 1786, were collected into a volume.

But the influence of that principle which awoke and animated the exertions of all who participated in the political enthusiasm of that time was still more strongly exemplified in the Connecticut poets—Trumbull, Dwight, Barlow, Humphreys, and Hopkins. In all the productions of these authors, there is a pervading spirit of nationality and patriotism, a desire to reflect credit on the country to which they belonged, which seems, as much as individual ambition, to have prompted their efforts, and which at times gives a certain glow and interest to their manner. "McFingal," the most popular of the writings of the former of these poets, first appeared in the year 1782. This pleasant satire on the adherents of Britain in those times may be pronounced a tolerably successful imitation of the great work of Butler, though, like every other imitation of that author, it wants that varied and inexhaustible fertility of allusion which made all subjects of thought, the lightest and most abstruse parts of learning—everything in the physical and moral world, in art and nature, the playthings of his wit. The work of Trumbull cannot be much praised for the purity of its diction. Yet, perhaps, great scrupulousness in this particular was not consistent with the plan of the author, and, to give the scenes of this poem their full effect, it might have been thought necessary to adopt the familiar dialect of the country and the times. We think his "Progress of Dullness" a more pleasing poem, more finished and more perfect in its kind, and, though written in the same manner, more free from the constraint and servility of imitation. The graver poems of Trumbull contain some vigorous and animated declamation.

Of Dr. Dwight we would speak with all the respect due to talents, to learning, to piety, and a long life of virtuous usefulness; but we must be excused from feeling any high admiration of his poetry. It seems to us modeled upon a manner altogether too artificial and mechanical. There is something strained, violent, and out of nature in all his attempts. His "Conquest of Canaan" will not secure immortality to its author. In this work he has been considered by some critics as by no means happy in the choice of his fable. However this may be, he has certainly failed to avail himself of the advantages it offered him; his epic wants the creations and colorings of an inventive and poetical fancy—the charm which, in the hands of a genius, communicates an interest to the simplest incidents, and something of the illusion of reality to the most improbable fictions. The versification is remarkable for its unbroken monotony. Yet it contains splendid passages, which, separated from the body of the work, might be admired, but a few pages pall both on the ear and the imagination. It has been urged in its favor that the writer was young. The poetry of his maturer years does not, however, seem to possess greater beauties or fewer faults. . . . In the other poems of Dr. Dwight, which are generally liable to the same criticisms, he sometimes endeavors to descend to a more familiar style, and entertains his reader with laborious attempts at wit; and here he is still unsuccessful. His "Greenfield Hill," and that most unfortunate of his productions, the "Triumph of Infidelity," will confirm the truth of our remarks.

Barlow, when he began to write, was a poet of no inconsiderable promise. His "Hasty Pudding," one of his earliest productions, is a good specimen of mock-heroic verse, and his "Vision of Columbus," at the time of its first appearance, attracted much attention, and was hailed as an earnest of better things. . . . In his maturer years Barlow became ambitious of distinguishing himself and doing honor to his country by some more splendid and important exertions of his talents, and, for this purpose, projected a national epic, in which was sung the "Discovery of America," the successful struggle of the States in the defence of their liberties, and the exalted prospects which were opening before them. It is to be regretted that a design, so honorable and so generously conceived, should have failed. In 1807 appeared the "Columbiad," which was his poem of the "Vision of Columbus," much enlarged, and with such variations as the feelings and reflections of his riper age and judgment led him to make. The "Columbiad" is not, in our opinion, so pleasing a poem in its present form as in that in which it was originally written. The plan of the work is utterly destitute of interest, and that, which was at first sufficiently wearisome, has become doubly so by being drawn out to its present length. Nor are the additions of much value, on account of the taste in which they are composed. Barlow, in his later poetry, attempted to invigorate his style, but, instead of drawing strength and salubrity from the pure wells of ancient English, he corrupted and debased it with foreign infusions. . . . But, notwithstanding the bad taste in which his principal work is composed, notwithstanding he cannot be said to write with much pathos or many of the native felicities of fancy, there is yet enough in the poetry of Mr. Barlow to prove that, had he fixed his eye on purer models, he might have excelled, not indeed in epic or narrative poetry nor in the delineation of passion and feeling, but in that calm, lofty, sustained style which suits best with topics of morality and philosophy, and for which the vigor and spirit of his natural manner, whenever he permits it to appear, show him to have been well qualified.

Humphreys was a poet of humbler pretensions. His writings, which were first collected in 1790, are composed in a better taste than those of the two last, and, if he has less genius, he has likewise fewer faults. Some of his lighter pieces are sufficiently pretty. He is most happy when he aims at nothing beyond an elegant mediocrity, and, to do him justice, this is generally the extent of his ambition. On the whole, he may be considered as sustaining a respectable rank among the poets of our country. . . .

One material error of taste pervades the graver productions of these authors, into which it would seem they were led by copying certain of the poets of England, who flourished near the period in which they began to write. It was their highest ambition to attain a certain lofty, measured, declamatory manner—an artificial elevation of style, from which it is impossible to rise or descend without abruptness and violence, and which allows just as much play and freedom to the faculties of the writer as a pair of stilts allows the body. The imagination is confined to one trodden circle, doomed to the chains of a perpetual mannerism, and condemned to tinkle the same eternal time with its fetters. Their versification, though not equally exceptionable in all, is formed upon the same stately model of balanced and wearisome regularity. Another fault, which arises naturally enough out of the peculiar style which we have imputed to these poets, is the want of pathos and feeling in their writings; the heart is rarely addressed, and never with much power or success. Amid this coldness of manner, sameness of imagery, and monotony of versification, the reader lays down his book, dazzled and fatigued.

In 1800 appeared the poems of William Clifton, who fell, at the age of twenty-seven a victim to that scourge of our climate which ceases not to waste when other diseases are sated—the pulmonary consumption. There is none of our American poetry on which we dwell with more pleasure, mingled, indeed, with regret at the untimely fate of the writer, than these charming remains. Amid many of the immature effusions of his greener years, and unfinished productions which were never meant to meet the eye of the world, there are to be found specimens of poetry, not only more delicate, classical, and polished, but more varied in imagery, and possessing more of that flexibility of style, of the want of which in others we have complained, and more faithful to nature and the feelings, than it has often been our lot to meet with in the works of our native poets. In his later and more finished productions, his diction is refined to an unusual degree of purity, and through this lucid medium the creations of his elegant fancy appear, with nothing to obscure their loveliness.

The posthumous works of St. John Honeywood, Esq., were published in the year 1801. These modest remains, the imperfect but vigorous productions of no common mind, have not been noticed as they deserved. They contain many polished and nervous lines.

We should not expect to be easily pardoned were we to pass by the writings of a poet who enjoyed, during his lifetime, so extensive a popularity as the late Mr. Robert Treat Paine. The first glow of admiration, which the splendid errors of his manner excited in the public, is now over, and we can calmly estimate his merits and defects. He must be allowed to have possessed an active and fertile fancy. Even in the misty obscurity which often shrouds his conceptions, not only from the understanding of the reader, but, it would seem, from that of the writer himself, there sometimes break out glimpses of greatness and majesty. Yet, with a force and exuberance of imagination which, if soberly directed, might have gained him the praise of magnificence, he is perpetually wandering in search of conceits and extravagances. He is ambitious of the epigrammatic style, and often bewilders himself with attempts to express pointedly what he does not conceive clearly. More instances of the false sublime might, perhaps, be selected from the writings of this poet than from those of any other of equal talents who lived in the same period. The brilliancy of Paine's poetry is like the brilliancy of frost-work—cold and fantastic. Who can point out the passage in his works in which he speaks to the heart in its own language? He was a fine but misguided genius. . . .

With respect to the style of poetry prevailing at the present day in our country, we apprehend that it will be found, in too many instances, tinged with a sickly and affected imitation of the peculiar manner of some of the late popular poets of England. We speak not of a disposition to emulate whatever is beautiful and excellent in their writings, still less would we be understood as intending to censure that sort of imitation which, exploring all the treasures of English poetry, culls from all a diction that shall form a natural and becoming dress for the conceptions of the writer—this is a course of preparation which everyone ought to go through before he appears before the public—but we desire to set a mark on that servile habit of copying which adopts the vocabulary of some favorite author, and apes the fashion of his sentences, and cramps and forces the ideas into a shape which they would not naturally have taken, and of which the only recommendation is, not that it is most elegant or most striking, but that it bears some resemblance to the manner of him who is proposed as a model. This way of writing has an air of poverty and meanness; it seems to indicate a paucity of reading as well as a perversion of taste; it might almost lead us to suspect that the writer had but one or two examples of poetical composition in his hands, and was afraid of expressing himself, except according to some formula which they might contain; and it ever has been, and ever will be, the resort of those who are sensible that their works need some factitious recommendation to give them even a temporary popularity.

On the whole, there seems to be more good taste among those who read than those who write poetry in our country. With respect to the poets whom we have enumerated, and whose merits we have discussed, we think the judgment pronounced on their works by the public will be found, generally speaking, just. They hold that station in our literature to which they are entitled, and could hardly be admired more than they are without danger to the taste of the nation. We know of no instance in which great poetical merit has come forward, and, finding its claims unallowed, been obliged to retire to the shade from which it emerged. Whenever splendid talents of this description shall appear, we believe that there will be found a disposition to encourage and reward them. . . .

1819.

From *Lectures on Poetry*

LECTURE FIRST

ON THE NATURE OF POETRY

. . . Of the nature of poetry different ideas have been entertained. The ancient critics seemed to suppose that they did something toward giving a tolerable notion of it by calling it a mimetic or imitative art, and classing it with sculpture and painting. Of its affinity with these arts there can be no doubt; but that affinity seems to me to consist almost wholly in the principles by which they all produce their effect, and not in the manner in which those principles are reduced to practice. There is no propriety in applying to poetry the term *imitative* in a literal and philosophical sense, as there is in applying it to painting and sculpture. The latter speak to the senses; poetry speaks directly to the mind. They reproduce sensible objects, and, by means of these, suggest the feeling or sentiment connected with them; poetry, by the symbols of words, suggests both the sensible object and the association. I should be glad to learn how a poem descriptive of a scene or an event is any more an imitation of that scene or that event than a prose description would be. A prose composition giving an account of the proportions and dimensions of a building, and the materials of which it is constructed, is certainly, so far as mere exactness is concerned, a better imitation of it than the finest poem that could be written about it. Yet who, after all, ever thought of giving such a composition the name of an imitation? The truth is, painting and sculpture are, literally, imitative arts, while poetry is only metaphorically so. The epithet as applied to poetry may be well enough, perhaps, as a figure of speech, but to make a metaphor the foundation of a philosophical classification is putting it to a service in which it is sure to confuse what it professes to make clear.

I would rather call poetry a suggestive art. Its power of affecting the mind by pure suggestion, and employing, instead of a visible or tangible imitation, arbitrary symbols, as unlike as possible to the things with which it deals, is what distinguishes this from its two sister arts. It is owing to its operation by means of suggestion that it affects different minds with such different degrees of force. In a picture or a statue the colors and forms employed by the artist impress the senses with the greatest distinctness. In painting, there is little—in sculpture, there is less —for the imagination to supply. It is true that different minds, according to their several degrees of cultivation, will receive different degrees of pleasure from the productions of these arts, and that the moral associations they suggest will be variously felt, and in some instances variously interpreted. Still, the impression made on the senses is in all cases the same; the same figures, the same lights and shades, are seen by all beholders alike. But the creations of Poetry have in themselves nothing of this precision and fixedness of form, and depend greatly for their vividness and clearness of impression upon the mind to which they are presented. Language, the great machine with which her miracles are wrought, is contrived to have an application to all possible things; and wonderful as this contrivance is, and numerous and varied as are its combinations, it is still limited and imperfect, and, in point of comprehensiveness, distinctness, and variety, falls infinitely short of the mighty and diversified world of matter and mind of which it professes to be the representative. It is, however, to the very limitation of this power of language, as it seems to me, that Poetry owes her magic. The most detailed of her descriptions, which, by the way, are not always the most striking, are composed of a few touches; they are glimpses of things thrown into the mind; here and there a trace of the outline; here a gleam of light, and there a dash of shade. But these very touches act like a spell upon the imagination and awaken it to greater activity, and fill it, perhaps, with greater delight than the best defined objects could do. The imagination is the most active and the least susceptible of fatigue of all the faculties of the human mind; its more intense exercise is tremendous, and sometimes unsettles the reason; its repose is only a gentle sort of activity; nor am I certain that it is ever quite unemployed, for even in our sleep it is still awake and busy, and amuses itself with fabricating our dreams. To this restless faculty—which is unsatisfied when the whole of its work is done to its hands, and which is ever wandering from the combination of ideas directly presented to it to other combinations of its own—it is the office of poetry to furnish the exercise in which it delights. Poetry is that art which selects and arranges the symbols of thought in such a manner as to excite it the most powerfully and delightfully. The imagination of the reader is guided, it is true, by the poet, and it is his business to guide it skillfully and agreeably; but the imagination in the meantime is by no means passive. It pursues the path which the poet only points out, and shapes its visions from the scenes and allusions which he gives. It fills up his sketches of beauty with what suits its own highest conceptions of the beautiful, and completes his outline of grandeur with the noblest images its own stores can furnish. It is obvious that the degree of perfection with which this is done must depend greatly upon the strength and cultivation of that faculty. For example, in the following passage, in which Milton describes the general mother passing to her daily task among the flowers:

"With goddess-like demeanor forth she went
Not unattended, for on her as queen
A pomp of winning graces waited still."

The coldest imagination, on reading it, will figure to itself, in the person of Eve, the finest forms, attitudes, and movements of female loveliness and dignity, which, after all, are not described, but only hinted at by the poet. A warmer fancy, kindling at the delicate allusions in these lines, will not only bestow these attractions on the principal figure, but will fill the air around her with beauty, and people it with the airy forms of the graces; it will see the delicate proportions of their limbs, the lustre of their flowing hair, and the soft light of their eyes. . . .

There is no question that one principal office of poetry is to excite the imagination, but this is not its sole, nor perhaps its chief, province; another of its ends is to touch the heart, and, as I expect to show in this lecture, it has something to do with the understanding. I know that some critics have made poetry to consist solely in the exercise of the imagination. They distinguish poetry from pathos. They talk of pure poetry, and by this phrase they mean passages of mere imagery, with the least possible infusion of human emotion. I do not know by what authority these gentlemen take the term poetry from the people, and thus limit its meaning.

In its ordinary acceptation, it has, in all ages and all countries, included something more. When we speak of a poem, we do not mean merely a tissue of striking images. The most beautiful poetry is that which takes the strongest hold of the feelings, and, if it is really the most beautiful, then it is poetry in the highest sense. Poetry is constantly resorting to the language of the passions to heighten the effect of her pictures; and, if this be not enough to entitle that language to the appellation of poetical, I am not aware of the meaning of the term. . . . The truth is, that poetry which does not find its way to the heart is scarcely deserving of the name; it may be brilliant and ingenious, but it soon wearies the attention. The feelings and the imagination, when skillfully touched, act reciprocally on each other. For example, when the poet introduces Ophelia, young, beautiful, and unfortunate, the wildness of frenzy in her eye, dressed with fantastic garlands of wild flowers, and singing snatches of old tunes, there is a picture for the imagination, but it is one which affects the heart. But when, in the midst of her incoherent talk, she utters some simple allusion to her own sorrows, as when she says,

"We know what we are, but know not what we may be,"

this touching sentence, addressed merely to our sympathy, strongly excites the imagination. . . .

Those poems, however, as I have already hinted, which are apparently the most affluent of imagery, are not always those which most kindle the reader's imagination. It is because the ornaments with which they abound are not naturally suggested by the subject, not poured forth from a mind warmed and occupied by it; but a forced fruit of the fancy, produced by labor, without spontaneity or excitement.

The language of passion is naturally figurative, but its figures are only employed to heighten the intensity of the expression; they are never introduced for their own sake. Important, therefore, as may be the office of the imagination in poetry, the great spring of poetry is emotion. It is this power that holds the key of the storehouse where the mind has laid up its images, and that alone can open it without violence. All the forms of fancy stand ever in its sight, ready to execute its bidding. Indeed, I doubt not that most of the offenses against good taste in this kind of composition are to be traced to the absence of emotion. A desire to treat agreeably or impressively a subject by which the writer is himself little moved, leads him into great mistakes about the means of effecting his purpose. This is the origin of cold conceits, of prosing reflections, of the minute painting of uninteresting circumstances, and of the opposite extremes of tameness and extravagance. On the other hand, strong feeling is always a sure guide. It rarely offends against good taste, because it instinctively chooses the most effectual means of communicating itself to others. It gives a variety to the composition it inspires, with which the severest taste is delighted. It may sometimes transgress arbitrary rules, or offend against local associations, but it speaks a language which reaches the heart in all countries and all times. Everywhere are the sentiments of fortitude and magnanimity uttered in strains that brace our own nerves, and the dead mourned in accents that draw our tears.

But poetry not only addresses the passions and the imagination; it appeals to the understanding also. So far as this position relates to the principles of taste which lie at the foundation of all poetry, and by which its merits are tried, I believe its truth will not be doubted. These principles have their origin in the reason of things, and are investigated and applied by the judgment. True it is that they may be observed by one who has never speculated about them, but it is no less true that their observance always gratifies the understanding with the fitness, the symmetry, and the congruity it produces. To write fine poetry requires intellectual faculties of the highest order, and among these, not the least important, is the faculty of reason. Poetry is the worst mask in the world behind which folly and stupidity could attempt to hide their features. Fitter, safer, and more congenial to them is the solemn discussion of unprofitable questions. Any obtuseness of apprehension or incapacity for drawing conclusions, which shows a deficiency or want of cultivation of the reasoning power, is sure to expose the unfortunate poet to contempt and ridicule.

But there is another point of view in which poetry may be said to address the understanding—I mean in the direct lessons of wisdom that it delivers. Remember that it does not concern itself with abstract reasonings, nor with any course of investigation that fatigues the mind. Nor is it merely didactic; but this does not prevent it from teaching truths which the mind instinctively acknowledges. The elements of moral truth are few and simple, but their combinations with human actions are as innumerable and diversified as the combinations of language. Thousands of inductions resulting from the application of great principles to human life and conduct lie, as it were, latent in our minds, which we have never drawn for ourselves, but which we admit the moment they are hinted at, and which, though not abstruse, are yet new. Nor are these of less value because they require no laborious research to discover them. The best riches of the earth are produced on its surface, and we need no reasoning to teach us the folly of a people who should leave its harvests ungathered to dig for its ores. The truths of which I have spoken, when possessing any peculiar force or beauty, are properly within the province of the art of which I am treating; and, when recommended by harmony of numbers, become poetry of the highest kind. Accordingly, they abound in the works of the most celebrated poets. When Shakespeare says of mercy,

> "it is twice blessed—
> It blesses him that gives and him that takes,"

does he not utter beautiful poetry as well as unquestionable truth? There are passages also in Milton of the same kind, which sink into the heart like the words of an oracle. For instance:

> "Evil into the mind of God or man
> May come and go so unapproved, and leave
> No spot or blame behind."

Take, also, the following example from Cowper, in which he bears witness against the guilt and folly of princes:

> "War is a game which, were their subjects wise,
> Kings should not play at. Nations would do well
> To extort their truncheons from the puny hands
> Of heroes whose infirm and baby minds
> Are gratified with mischief, and who spoil,
> Because men suffer it, their toy—the world."

I call these passages poetry, because the mind instantly acknowledges their truth and feels their force, and is moved and filled and elevated by them. Nor does poetry refuse to carry on a sort of process of reasoning by deducing one truth from another. Her demonstrations differ, however, from ordinary ones by requiring that each step should be in itself beautiful or striking, and that they all should carry the mind to the final conclusion without the consciousness of labor.

All the ways by which poetry affects the mind are open also to the prose-writer. All that kindles the imagination, all that excites emotion, all those moral truths that find an echo in our bosoms, are his property as well as that of the poet. It is true that in the ornaments of style the poet is allowed a greater license, but there are many excellent poems which are not distinguished by any liberal use of the figures of speech from prose writings composed with the same degree of excitement. What, then, is the ground of the distinction between prose and poetry? This is a question about which there has been much debate, but one which seems to me of easy solution to those who are not too ambitious of distinguishing themselves by profound researches into things already sufficiently clear. I suppose that poetry differs from prose, in the first place, by the employment of metrical harmony. It differs from it, in the next place, by excluding all that disgusts, all that tasks and fatigues the understanding, and all matters which are too trivial and common to excite any emotion whatever. Some of these, verse cannot raise into dignity; to others, verse is an encumbrance: they are, therefore, all unfit for poetry; put them into verse, and they are prose still.

A distinction has been attempted to be made between poetry and eloquence, and I acknowledge that there is one; but it seems to me that it consists solely in metrical arrangement. Eloquence is the poetry of prose; poetry is the eloquence of verse. The maxim that the poet is born and the orator made is a pretty antithesis, but a moment's reflection will convince us that one can become neither without natural gifts improved by cultivation. By eloquence I do not mean mere persuasiveness: there are many processes of argument that are not susceptible of eloquence, because they require close and painful attention. But by eloquence I understand those appeals to our moral perceptions that produce emotion as soon as they are uttered. It is in these that the orator is himself affected with the feelings he would communicate, that his eyes glisten, and his frame seems to dilate, and his voice acquires an unwonted melody, and his sentences arrange themselves into a sort of measure and harmony, and the listener is chained in involuntary and breathless attention. This is the very enthusiasm that is the parent of poetry. Let the same man go to his closet and clothe in numbers conceptions full of the same fire and spirit, and they will be poetry.   1826

LECTURE THIRD

ON POETRY IN ITS RELATION TO OUR AGE AND COUNTRY

An opinion prevails, which neither wants the support of respectable names nor of plausible reasonings, that the art of poetry, in common with its sister arts, painting and sculpture, cannot in the present age be cultivated with the same degree of success as formerly. It has been supposed that the progress of reason, of science, and of the useful arts has a tendency to narrow the sphere of the imagination, and to repress the enthusiasm of the affections. Poetry, it is alleged, whose office it was to nurse the infancy of the human race, and to give it its first lessons of wisdom, having fulfilled the part to which she was appointed, now resigns her charge to severer instructors. Others, again, refining upon this idea, maintain that not only the age in which we live must fail to produce anything to rival the productions of the ancient masters of song, but that our own country, of all parts of the globe, is likely to remain the most distant from such a distinction.

Our citizens are held to possess, in a remarkable degree, the heedful, calculating, prosaic spirit of the age, while our country is decried as peculiarly barren of the materials of poetry. The scenery of our land these reasoners admit to be beautiful, but they urge that it is the beauty of a face without expression; that it wants the associations of tradition which are the soul and interest of scenery; that it wants the national superstitions which linger yet in every district in Europe, and the legends of distant and dark ages and of wild and unsettled times of which the old world reminds you at every step. Nor can our country, they say, ever be more fruitful of these materials than at present. For this is not an age to give birth to new superstitions, but to explode and root out old, however harmless and agreeable they may be, while half the world is already wondering how little the other half will finally believe. Is it likely, then, that a multitude of interesting traditions will spring up in our land to ally themselves with every mountain, every hill, every forest, every river, and every tributary brook. There may be some passages of our early history which associate themselves with particular places, but the argument is that the number of these will never be greatly augmented. The genius of our nation is quiet and commercial. Our people are too much in love with peace and gain, the state of society is too settled, and the laws too well enforced and respected, to allow of wild and strange adventures. There is no romance either in our character, our history, or our condition of society; and, therefore, it is neither likely to encourage poetry, nor capable of supplying it with those materials—materials drawn from domestic traditions and manners—which render it popular.

If these views of the tendency of the present age, and the state of things in our own country, are to be received as true, it must be acknowledged that they are not only exceedingly discouraging to those who make national literature a matter of pride, but, what is worse, that they go far toward causing that very inferiority on which they so strongly insist. . . .

But, if it be a fact that poetry in the present age is unable to attain the same degree of excellence as formerly, it cannot certainly be ascribed to any change in the original and natural faculties and dispositions of mind by which it is produced and by which it is enjoyed. The theory that men have degenerated in their mental powers and moral temperament is even more absurd than the notion of a decline in their physical strength, and is too fanciful to be combated by grave reasoning. . . . Degeneracy, if it has taken place, must be owing to one of two things—either to the absence of those circumstances which, in former times, developed and cherished the poetical faculty to an extraordinary degree, or to the existence of other intellectual interests which, in the present age, tend to repress its natural exercise.

What, then, were the circumstances which fostered the art of poetry in ancient times? They have been defined to be the mystery impressed on all the operations of nature as yet not investigated and traced to their laws—the beautiful systems of ancient mythology, and, after their extinction, the superstitions that linger like ghosts in the twilight of a later age. Let us examine separately each of these alleged advantages. That there is something in whatever is unknown and inscrutable which strongly excites the imagination and awes the heart, particularly when connected with things of unusual vastness and grandeur, is not to be denied. But I deny that much of this mystery is apparent to an ignorant age, and I maintain that no small degree of inquiry and illumination is necessary to enable the mind to perceive it. He who takes all things to be as they appear, who supposes the earth to be a great plain, the sun a moving ball of fire, the heavens a vault of sapphire, and the stars a multitude of little flames lighted up in its arches—what does he think of mysteries, or care for them? But enlighten him a little further. Teach him that the earth is an immense sphere; that the wide land whose bounds he knows so imperfectly is an isle in the great oceans that flow all over it; talk to him of the boundlessness of the skies, and the army of worlds that move through them—and, by means of the knowledge that you communicate, you have opened to him a vast field of the unknown and the wonderful. Thus it ever was and ever will be with the human mind; everything which it knows introduces to its observation a greater multitude of things which it does not know; the clearing up of one mystery conducts it to another; all its discoveries are bounded by a circle of doubt and ignorance which is wide in proportion to the knowledge it enfolds. It is a pledge of the immortal destinies of the human intellect that it is forever drawn by a strong attraction to the darker edge of this circle, and forever attempting to penetrate the obscurities beyond. The old world, then, is welcome to its mysteries; we need not envy it on that account: for, in addition to our superior knowledge and as a consequence of it, we have even more of them than it, and they are loftier, deeper, and more spiritual. . . .

It is especially the privilege of an age which has no engrossing superstitions of its own, to make use in its poetry of those of past ages; to levy contributions from the credulity of all time, and thus to diversify indefinitely the situations in which its human agents are placed. If these materials are managed with sufficient skill to win the temporary assent of the reader to the probability of the supernatural circumstances related, the purpose of the poet is answered. This is precisely the condition of the present age; it has the advantage over all ages that have preceded it in the abundance of those collected materials, and its poets have not been slow to avail themselves of their aid.

In regard to the circumstances which are thought in the present age to repress and limit the exercise of the poetical faculty, the principal if not the only one is supposed to be the prevalence of studies and pursuits unfavorable to the cultivation of the imagination and to enthusiasm of feeling. True it is that there are studies and pursuits which principally call into exercise other faculties of the mind, and that they are competitors with Poetry for the favor of the public. But it is not certain that the patronage bestowed on them would be extended to her, even if they should cease to exist. Nay, there is strong reason to suppose that they have done something to extend her influence, for they have certainly multiplied the number of readers, and everybody who reads at all sometimes reads poetry, and generally professes to admire what the best judges pronounce excellent, and, perhaps, in time come to enjoy it. Various inclinations continue, as heretofore, to impel one individual to one pursuit, and another to another—one to chemistry and another to poetry—yet I cannot see that their different labors interfere with each other, or that, because the chemist prosecutes his science successfully, therefore the poet should lose his inspiration. Take the example of Great Britain. In no country are the sciences studied with greater success, yet in no country is poetry pursued with more ardor. Spring and autumn reign hand in hand in her literature; it is loaded at once with blossoms and fruits. Does the poetry of that island at the present day—the poetry of Wordsworth, Scott, Coleridge, Byron, Southey, Shelley, and others—smack of the chilling tendencies of the physical sciences? Or, rather, is it not bold, varied, impassioned, irregular, and impatient of precise laws, beyond that of any former age? Indeed, has it not the freshness, the vigor, and perhaps also the disorder, of a new literature?

The amount of knowledge necessary to be possessed by all who would keep pace with the age, as much greater as it is than formerly, is not, I apprehend, in danger of oppressing and smothering poetical talent. Knowledge is the material with which Genius builds her fabrics. The greater its abundance, the more power is required to dispose it into order and beauty, but the more vast and magnificent will be the structure. All great poets have been men of great knowledge. Some have gathered it from books, as Spenser and Milton; others from keen observation of men and things, as Homer and Shakespeare. On the other hand, the poetry of Ossian, whether genuine or not, is an instance of no inconsiderable poetical talent struggling with the disadvantages of a want of knowledge. It is this want which renders it so singularly monotonous. The poverty of the poet's ideas confined his mind to a narrow circle, and his poems are a series of changes rung upon a few thoughts and a few images. Single passages are beautiful and affecting, but each poem, as a whole, is tiresome and uninteresting.

I come, in the last place, to consider the question of our own expectations in literature, and the probability of our producing in the new world anything to rival the immortal poems of the old. Many of the remarks already made on the literary spirit of the present age will apply also to this part of the subject. Indeed, in this point of view, we should do ill to despair of our country, at least until the lapse of many years shall seem to have settled the question against us. Where the fountains of knowledge are by the roadside, and where the volumes from which poetic enthusiasms are caught and fed are in everybody's hands, it would be singularly strange if, amid the multitude of pursuits which occupy our citizens, nobody should think of taking verse as a path to fame. Yet, if it shall be chosen and pursued with the characteristic ardor of our countrymen, what can prevent its being brought to the same degree of perfection here as in other countries? Not the want of encouragement surely, for the literary man needs but little to stimulate his exertions, and with that little his exertions are undoubtedly greater. Who would think of fattening a race-horse? Complaints of the poverty of poets are as old as their art, but I never heard that they wrote the worse verses for it. It is enough, probably, to call forth their most vigorous efforts, that poetry is admired and honored by their countrymen. With respect to the paucity of national traditions, it will be time to complain of it when all those of which we are possessed are exhausted. Besides, as I have already shown, it is the privilege of poets, when they suppose themselves in need of materials, to seek them in other countries. The best English poets have done this. The events of Spenser's celebrated poem take place within the shadowy limits of fairy-land. Shakespeare has laid the scene of many of his finest tragedies in foreign countries. Milton went out of the world for the subject of his two epics. Byron has taken the incidents of all his poems from outside of England. Southey's best work is a poem of Spain—of chivalry, and of the Roman Church. For the story of one of his narrative poems, Moore went to Persia; for that of another, to the antediluvian world. Wordsworth and Crabbe, each in a different way, and each with great power, abjuring all heroic traditions and recollections, and all aid from the supernatural and the marvelous, have drawn their subjects from modern manners and the simple occurrences of common life. Are they read, for that reason, with any the less avidity by the multitudes who resort to their pages for pastime, for edification, for solace, for noble joy, and for the ecstacies of pure delight?

It has been urged by some, as an obstacle to the growth of elegant literature among us, that our language is a transplanted one, framed for a country and for institutions different from ours, and, therefore, not likely to be wielded by us with such force, effect, and grace, as it would have been if it had grown up with our nation, and received its forms and its accessions from the exigencies of our experience. It seems to me that this is one of the most unsubstantial of all the brood of phantoms which have been conjured up to alarm us. Let those who press this opinion descend to particulars. Let them point out the peculiar defects of our language in its application to our natural and political situation. Let them show in what respects it refuses to accommodate itself easily and gracefully to all the wants of expression that are felt among us. Till they do this, let us be satisfied that the copious and flexible dialect we speak is as equally proper to be used at the equator as at the poles, and at any intermediate latitude; and alike in monarchies or republics. It has grown up, as every forcible and beautiful language has done, among a simple and unlettered people; it has accommodated itself, in the first place, to the things of nature, and, as civilization advanced, to the things of art; and thus it has become a language full of picturesque forms of expression, yet fitted for the purposes of science. . . .

I infer, then, that all the materials of poetry exist in our own country, with all the ordinary encouragements and opportunities for making a successful use of them. The elements of beauty and grandeur, intellectual greatness and moral truth, the stormy and the gentle passions, the casualties and the changes of life, and the light shed upon man's nature by the story of past times and the knowledge of foreign manners, have not made their sole abode in the old world beyond the waters. If under these circumstances our poetry should finally fail of rivaling that of Europe, it will be because Genius sits idle in the midst of its treasures.

1826

WASHINGTON IRVING

(1783-1859)

(Philadelphia, London, Paris).

1832 Returned to New York; *The Alhambra* (Philadelphia, London); tour of the West and South.

1835 *The Crayon Miscellany* (Philadelphia, London, Paris), included "A Tour on the Prairies," "Abbotsford and Newstead Abbey," and "Legends of the Conquest of Spain."

1836 Moved to Sunnyside, Tarrytown, New York; *Astoria* (Philadelphia, London, Paris).

1837 *The Adventures of Captain Bonneville* (Philadelphia, London).

1838 Declined nomination for Mayor of New York City.

1840 *The Life of Oliver Goldsmith.*

1841 *The Biography of Margaret Davidson* (Philadelphia); appointed Minister to Spain.

1845 Resigned as Minister to Spain.

1846 Returned to New York.

1848 Arranged for publication of revised edition of his works.

1849 *The Life of Oliver Goldsmith,* revised and expanded (New York, London).

1850 *Mahomet and His Successors* (New York, London).

1855 *Wolfert's Roost* (New York, London); began publication of *The Life of George Washington* (New York, London): I (1855), II and III (1856), IV (1857), V (1859).

1859 Died November 28.

BIBLIOGRAPHY:

A *Bibliography of the Writings of Washington Irving,* comp. Stanley T. William and Mary E. Edge (New York, 1936). *The Works of Washington Irving,* 21 vols. (New York, 1860–1861) and *Works . . . ,* 12 vols. (New York, 1881) are standard editions. Pierre Irving, *The Life and Letters of Washington Irving,* 4 vols. (New York, 1862–1864). Journals and Notebooks have been edited by William P. Trent and George S. Hellman, 3 vols. (Boston, 1919); Trent, 3 vols. (New York, 1921); Clara L. Penny (New York, 1926); Stanley T. Williams, 5 vols. (New Haven, 1927; Cambridge, 1931; New York, 1934, 1937); and John F. McDermott (Norman, Okla., 1944). Stanley T. Williams, *The Life of Washington Irving,* 2 vols. (New York, 1935). Henry A. Pochmann, *Washington Irving: Representative Selections* (New York, 1934).

From *Salmagundi*

NO. I SATURDAY, JANUARY 24, 1807

As everybody knows, or ought to know, what a Salmagund is, we shall spare ourselves the trouble of an explanation; besides, we despise trouble as we do everything low and mean, and hold the man who would incur it unnecessarily as an object worthy our highest pity and contempt. Neither will we puzzle our heads to give an account of ourselves, for two reasons; first, because it is nobody's business; secondly, because if it were, we do not hold ourselves bound to attend to anybody's business but our own; and even *that* we take the liberty of neglecting when it suits our inclination. To these we might add a third, that very few men can give a tolerable account of themselves, let them try ever so hard; but this reason we candidly avow, would not hold good with ourselves.

There are, however, two or three pieces of information which we bestow gratis on the public, chiefly because it suits our own pleasure and convenience that they should be known, and partly because we do not wish that there should be any ill will between us at the commencement of our acquaintance.

Our intention is simply to instruct the young, reform the old, correct the town, and castigate the age; this is an arduous task, and therefore we undertake it with confidence. We intend for this purpose to present a striking picture of the town; and as everybody is anxious to see his own phiz on canvas, however stupid or ugly it may be, we have no doubt but the whole town will flock to our exhibition. Our picture will necessarily include a vast variety of figures; and should any gentleman or lady be displeased with the inveterate truth of their likenesses, they may ease their spleen by laughing at those of their neighbors—this being what we understand by poetical justice.

Like all true and able editors, we consider ourselves infallible; and therefore, with the customary diffidence of our brethren of the quill, we shall take the liberty of interfering in all matters either of a public or a private nature. We are critics, amateurs, dilettanti, and cognoscenti; and as we know "by the pricking of our thumbs," that every opinion which we may advance in either of those characters will be correct, we are determined, though it may be questioned, contradicted, or even controverted, yet it shall never be revoked.

We beg the public particularly to understand that we solicit no patronage. We are determined, on the contrary, that the patronage shall be entirely on our side. We have nothing to do with the pecuniary concerns of the paper; its success will yield us neither pride nor profit—nor will its failure occasion to us either loss or mortification. We advise the public, therefore, to purchase our numbers merely for their own sakes; if they do not, let them settle the affair with their consciences and posterity.

To conclude, we invite all editors of newspapers and literary journals to praise us heartily in advance, as we assure them that we intend to deserve their praises. To our next-door neighbor, "Town," we hold out a hand of amity, declaring to him that, after ours, his paper will stand the best chance for immortality. We proffer an exchange of civilities: he shall furnish us with notices of epic poems and tobacco; and we in return will enrich him with original speculations on all manner of subjects, together with "the rummaging of my grandfather's mahogany chest of drawers," "the life and amours of mine Uncle John," "anecdotes of the Cockloft Family," and learned quotations from that unheard of writer of folios, *Linkum Fidelius.*

From *A History of New York*

BOOK IV

*Containing the Chronicles of the Reign of William
the Testy*

CHAPTER I

*Showing the Nature of History in General; Containing Farthermore
the Universal Acquirements of William the Testy, and How a Man
May Learn so Much as to Render Himself Good for Nothing.*

When the lofty Thucydides is about to enter upon his description of
the plague that desolated Athens, one of his modern commentators assures the reader, that the history is now going to be exceeding solemn,
serious, and pathetic, and hints, with that air of chuckling gratulation
with which a good dame draws forth a choice morsel from a cupboard to
regale a favorite, that this plague will give his history a most agreeable
variety.

In like manner did my heart leap within me, when I came to the dolo-
rous dilemma of Fort Goed Hoop, which I at once perceived to be the
forerunner of a series of great events and entertaining disasters. Such are
the true subjects for the historic pen. For what is history, in fact, but a
kind of Newgate calendar, a register of the crimes and miseries that man
has inflicted on his fellow-man? It is a huge libel on human nature, to
which we industriously add page after page, volume after volume, as if
we were building up a monument to the honor, rather than the infamy of
our species. If we turn over the pages of these chronicles that man has
written of himself, what are the characters dignified by the appellation of
great, and held up to the admiration of posterity? Tyrants, robbers, conquerors, renowned only for the magnitude of their misdeeds, and the stu-
pendous wrongs and miseries they have inflicted on mankind,—warriors,
who have hired themselves to the trade of blood, not from motives of virtuous patriotism, or to protect the injured and defenseless, but merely to
gain the vaunted glory of being adroit and successful in massacring their
fellow-beings! What are the great events that constitute a glorious era?—
The fall of empires; the desolation of happy countries; splendid cities
smoking in their ruins; the proudest works of art tumbled in the dust; the
shrieks and groans of whole nations ascending unto heaven!

It is thus the historian may be said to thrive on the miseries of mankind, like birds of prey which hover over the field of battle to fatten on
the mighty dead. It was observed by a great projector of inland lock-nav-
igation, that rivers, lakes, and oceans were only formed to feed canals. In
like manner I am tempted to believe that plots, conspiracies, wars, victories, and massacres are ordained by Providence only as food for the historian.

It is a source of great delight to the philosopher, in studying the wonderful economy of nature, to trace the mutual dependencies of things, how they are created reciprocally for each other, and how the most noxious and apparently unnecessary animal has its uses. Thus those swarms of flies, which are so often execrated as useless vermin, are created for the sustenance of spiders; and spiders, on the other hand, are evidently made to devour flies. So those heroes, who have been such scourges to the world, were bounteously provided as themes for the poet and historian, while the poet and the historian were destined to record the achievements of heroes!

These, and many similar reflections, naturally arose in my mind as I took up my pen to commence the reign of William Kieft: for now the stream of our history, which hitherto has rolled in a tranquil current, is about to depart forever from its peaceful haunts, and brawl through many a turbulent and rugged scene.

As some sleek ox, sunk in the rich repose of a clover-field, dozing and chewing the cud, will bear repeated blows before it raises itself, so the province of Nieuw Nederlandts, having waxed fat under the drowsy reign of the Doubter, needed cuffs and kicks to rouse it into action. The reader will now witness the manner in which a peaceful community advances towards a state of war; which is apt to be like the approach of a horse to a drum, with much prancing and little progress, and too often with the wrong end foremost.

Wilhelmus Kieft, who in 1634 ascended the gubernatorial chair, (to borrow a favorite though clumsy appellation of modern phraseologists,) was of a lofty descent, his father being inspector of wind-mills in the ancient town of Saardam; and our hero, we are told, when a boy, made very curious investigations into the nature and operation of these machines, which was one reason why he afterwards came to be so ingenious a governor. His name, according to the most authentic etymologists, was a corruption of Kyver, that is to say, a *wrangler* or *scolder*, and expressed the characteristic of his family, which, for nearly two centuries, had kept the windy town of Saardam in hot water, and produced more tartars and brimstones than any ten families in the place; and so truly did he inherit this family peculiarity, that he had not been a year in the government of the province, before he was universally denominated William the Testy. His appearance answered to his name. He was a brisk, wiry, waspish little old gentleman; such a one as may now and then be seen stumping about our city in a broad-skirted coat with huge buttons, a cocked hat stuck on the back of his head, and a cane as high as his chin. His face was broad, but his features were sharp; his cheeks were scorched into a dusky red by two fiery little gray eyes; his nose turned up, and the corners of his mouth turned down, pretty much like the muzzle of an irritable pug-dog.

I have heard it observed by a profound adept in human physiology, that if a woman waxes fat with the progress of years, her tenure of life is somewhat precarious, but if happily she withers as she grows old, she lives forever. Such promised to be the case with William the Testy, who grew tough in proportion as he dried. He had withered, in fact, not through the process of years, but through the tropical fervor of his soul, which burnt like a vehement rush-light in his bosom, inciting him to incessant broils and bickerings. Ancient traditions speak much of his learning, and of the gallant inroads he had made into the dead languages, in which he had made captive a host of Greek nouns and Latin verbs, and brought off rich booty in ancient saws and apothegms, which he was wont to parade in his public harangues, as a triumphant general of yore his *spolia opima*. Of metaphysics he knew enough to confound all hearers and himself into the bargain. In logic, he knew the whole family of syllogisms and dilemmas, and was so proud of his skill that he never suffered even a self-evident fact to pass unargued. It was observed, however, that he seldom got into an argument without getting into a perplexity, and then into a passion with his adversary for not being convinced gratis.

He had, moreover, skirmished smartly on the frontiers of several of the sciences, was fond of experimental philosophy, and prided himself upon inventions of all kinds. His abode, which he had fixed at a Bowerie or country-seat at a short distance from the city, just at what is now called Dutch Street, soon abounded with proofs of his ingenuity: patent smoke-jacks that required a horse to work them; Dutch ovens that roasted meat without fire; carts that went before the horses; weather-cocks that turned against the wind; and other wrong-headed contrivances that astonished and confounded all beholders. The house, too, was beset with paralytic cats and dogs, the subjects of his experimental philosophy; and the yelling and yelping of the latter unhappy victims of science, while aiding in the pursuit of knowledge, soon gained for the place the name of "Dog's Misery," by which it continues to be known even at the present day.

It is in knowledge as in swimming: he who flounders and splashes on the surface makes more noise, and attracts more attention, than the pearl-diver who quietly dives in quest of treasures to the bottom. The vast acquirements of the new governor were the theme of marvel among the simple burghers of New Amsterdam; he figured about the place as learned a man as a Bonze at Pekin, who has mastered one half of the Chinese alphabet, and was unanimously pronounced a "universal genius!"

I have known in my time many a genius of this stamp; but, to speak my mind freely, I never knew one who, for the ordinary purposes of life, was worth his weight in straw. In this respect, a little sound judgment and plain common sense is worth all the sparkling genius that ever wrote poetry or invented theories. Let us see how the universal acquirements of William the Testy aided him in the affairs of government.

CHAPTER III

In Which Are Recorded The Sage Projects of a Ruler of Universal Genius—The Art of Fighting by Proclamation—and How That the Valiant Jacobus Van Curlet Came to be Foully Dishonored at Fort Goed Hoop.

Never was a more comprehensive, a more expeditious, or, what is still better, a more economical measure devised, than this of defeating the Yankees by proclamation,—an expedient, likewise, so gentle and humane, there were ten chances to one in favor of its succeeding; but then there was one chance to ten that it would not succeed,—as the ill-natured fates would have it, that single chance carried the day! The proclamation was perfect in all its parts, well constructed, well written, well sealed, and well published; all that was wanting to insure its effect was, that the Yankees should stand in awe of it; but, provoking to relate, they treated it with the most absolute contempt, applied it to an unseemly purpose; and thus did the first warlike proclamation come to a shameful end,—a fate which I am credibly informed has befallen but too many of its successors.

So far from abandoning the country, those varlets continued their encroachments, squatting along the green banks of the Varsche river, and founding Hartford, Stamford, New Haven, and other border-towns. I have already shown how the onion patches of Pyquag were an eye-sore to Jacobus Van Curlet and his garrison; but now these moss-troopers increased in their atrocities, kidnappping hogs, impounding horses, and sometimes grievously rib-roasting their owners. Our worthy forefathers could scarcely stir abroad without danger of being out-jockeyed in horseflesh, or taken in in bargaining; while, in their absence, some daring Yankee peddler would penetrate to their household, and nearly ruin the good housewives with tin ware and wooden bowls.[1]

I am well aware of the perils which environ me in this part of my history. While raking, with curious hand but pious heart, among the mouldering remains of former days, anxious to draw therefrom the honey of wis-

[1] The following cases in point appear in Hazard's Collection of State Papers.

"In the meantime, they of Hartford have not only usurped and taken in the lands of Connecticut, although unrighteously and against the laws of the nations but have hindered our nation in sowing their own purchased broken up lands, but have also sowed them with corn in the night, which the Nederlanders had broken up and intended to sow: and have beaten the servants of the high and mighty the honored company, which were laboring upon their master's lands, from their lands, with sticks and plow staves in hostile manner laming, and among the rest, struck Ever Duckings [Evert Duyckink] a hole in his head, with a stick, so that the blood ran down very strongly down upon his body."

"Those of Hartford sold a hog, that belonged to the honored company, under pretence that it had eaten of their ground grass, when they not any foot of inheritance. They proffered the hog for 5s. if the commissioners would have given 5s. for damage; which the commissioners denied, because no man's own hog (as men used to say) can trespass upon his own master's grounds." [This and the following note are Irving's.]

dom, I may fare somewhat like that valiant worthy, Samson, who, in meddling with the carcass of a dead lion, drew a swarm of bees about his ears. Thus, while narrating the many misdeeds of the Yanokie or Yankee race, it is ten chances to one but I offend the morbid sensibilities of certain of their unreasonable descendants, who may fly out and raise such a buzzing about this unlucky head of mine, that I shall need the tough hide of an Achilles, or an Orlando Furioso, to protect me from their stings.

Should such be the case, I should deeply and sincerely lament,—not my misfortune in giving offense, but the wrong-headed perverseness of an ill-natured generation, in taking offense at anything I say. That their ancestors did use my ancestors ill is true, and I am very sorry for it. I would, with all my heart, the fact were otherwise; but as I am recording the sacred events of history, I'd not bate one nail's breadth of the honest truth, though I were sure the whole edition of my work would be brought up and burnt by the common hangman of Connecticut. And in sooth, now that these testy gentlemen have drawn me out, I will make bold to go farther, and observe that this is one of the grand purposes for which we impartial historians are sent into the world,—to redress wrongs and render justice on the heads of the guilty. So that, though a powerful nation may wrong its neighbors with temporary impunity, yet sooner or later an historian springs up, who wreaks ample chastisement on it in return.

Thus these moss-troopers of the east little thought, I'll warrant it, while they were harassing the inoffensive province of Nieuw Nederlandts, and driving its unhappy governor to his wit's end, that an historian would ever arise, and give them their own, with interest. Since, then, I am but performing my bounden duty as an historian, in avenging the wrongs of our revered ancestors, I shall make no further apology; and, indeed, when it is considered that I have all these ancient borderers of the east in my power, and at the mercy of my pen, I trust that it will be admitted I conduct myself with great humanity and moderation.

It was long before William the Testy could be persuaded that his much-vaunted war-measure was ineffectual; on the contrary, he flew in a passion whenever it was doubted, swearing that, though slow in operating, yet when it once began to work, it would soon purge the land of these invaders. When convinced, at length, of the truth, like a shrewd physician he attributed the failure to the quantity, not the quality of the medicine, and resolved to double the dose. He fulminated, therefore, a second proclamation, more vehement than the first, forbidding all intercourse with these Yankee intruders, ordering the Dutch burghers on the frontiers to buy none of their pacing horses, measly pork, apple-sweetmeats, Weathersfield onions, or wooden bowls, and to furnish them with no supplies of gin, gingerbread, or sauerkraut.

Another interval elapsed, during which the last proclamation was as little regarded as the first; and the non-intercourse was especially set at naught by the young folks of both sexes, if we may judge by the active bundling which took place along the borders.

At length, one day the inhabitants of New Amsterdam were aroused by a furious barking of dogs, great and small, and beheld, to their surprise, the whole garrison of Fort Goed Hoop straggling into town all tattered and wayworn, with Jacobus Van Curlet at their head, bringing the melancholy intelligence of the capture of Fort Goed Hoop by the Yankees.

The fate of this important fortress is an impressive warning to all military commanders. It was neither carried by storm nor famine; nor was it undermined; nor bombarded; nor set on fire by red-hot shot; but was taken by a stratagem no less singular than effectual, and which can never fail of success, whenever an opportunity occurs of putting it in practice.

It seems that the Yankees had received intelligence that the garrison of Jacobus Van Curlet had been reduced nearly one eighth by the death of two of his most corpulent soldiers, who had overeaten themselves on fat salmon caught in the Varsche river. A secret expedition was immediately set on foot to surprise the fortress. The crafty enemy, knowing the habits of the garrison to sleep soundly after they had eaten their dinners and smoked their pipes, stole upon them at the noontide of a sultry summer's day, and surprised them in the midst of their slumbers.

In an instant the flag of their High Mightinesses was lowered, and the Yankee standard elevated in its stead, being a dried codfish, by way of a spread eagle. A strong garrison was appointed, of long-sided, hard-fisted Yankees, with Weathersfield onions for cockades and feathers. As to Jacobus Van Curlet and his men, they were seized by the nape of the neck, conducted to the gate, and one by one dismissed with a kick in the crupper, as Charles XII dismissed the heavy-bottomed Russians at the battle of Narva; Jacobus Van Curlet receiving two kicks in consideration of his official dignity.

CHAPTER IV

Containing the Fearful Wrath of William the Testy, and the Alarm of New Amsterdam—How the Governor Did Strongly Fortify the City—Of the Rise of Antony the Trumpeter, and the Windy Addition to the Armorial Bearings of New Amsterdam.

Language cannot express the awful ire of William the Testy on hearing of the catastrophe at Fort Goed Hoop. For three good hours his rage was too great for words, or rather the words were too great for him, (being a very small man,) and he was nearly choked by the misshappen, nine-cornered Dutch oaths and epithets which crowded at once into his gullet. At length his words found vent, and for three days he kept up a constant discharge, anathematizing the Yankees, man, woman, and child, for a set of dieven, schobbejacken, deugenieten, twistzoekeren, blaes-kaken, loosen-schalken, kakken-bedden, and a thousand other names, of which, un-fortunately for posterity, history does not make mention. Finally, he swore that he would have nothing more to do with such a squatting, bundling, guessing, questioning, swapping, pumpkin-eating, molasses-daubing, shingle-splitting, cider-watering, horse-jockeying, notion-ped-dling crew; that they might stay at Fort Goed Hoop and rot, before he would dirty his hands by attempting to drive them away: in proof of which he ordered the new-raised troops to be marched forthwith into winter-quarters, although it was not as yet quite midsummer. Great des-pondency now fell upon the city of New Amsterdam. It was feared that the conquerors of Fort Goed Hoop, flushed with victory and apple-bran-dy, might march on to the capital, take it by storm, and annex the whole province to Connecticut. The name of Yankee became as terrible among the Nieuw Nederlanders as was that of Gaul among the ancient Romans; insomuch that the good wives of the Manhattoes used it as a bugbear wherewith to frighten their unruly children.

Everybody clamored around the governor, imploring him to put the city in a complete posture of defense; and he listened to their clamors. Nobody could accuse William the Testy of being idle in time of danger, or at any other time. He was never idle, but then he was often busy to very little purpose. When a youngling, he had been impressed with the words of Solomon, "Go to the ant, thou sluggard, observe her ways and be wise;" in conformity to which he had ever been of a restless, ant-like turn, hurrying hither and thither, nobody knew why or wherefore, busy-ing himself about small matters with an air of great importance and anxi-ety, and toiling at a grain of mustard-seed in the full conviction that he was moving a mountain. In the present instance, he called in all his in-ventive powers to his aid, and was continually pondering over plans, making diagrams, and worrying about with a troop of workmen and pro-jectors at his heels. At length, after a world of consultation and contri-vance, his plans of defense ended in rearing a great flag-staff in the center of the fort, and perching a wind-mill on each bastion.

These warlike preparations in some measure allayed the public alarm, especially after an additional means of securing the safety of the city had been suggested by the governor's lady. It has already been hinted in this most authentic history, that in the domestic establishment of William the Testy "the gray mare was the better horse"; in other words, that his wife "ruled the roast," and in governing the governor, governed the province, which might thus be said to be under petticoat government.

Now it came to pass, that about this time there lived in the Manhat-toes a jolly, robustious trumpeter, named Antony Van Corlear, famous for his long wind; and who, as the story goes, could twang so potently upon his instrument, that the effect upon all within hearing was like that as-cribed to the Scotch bagpipe when it sings right lustily in the nose.

This sounder of brass was moreover a lusty bachelor, with a pleasant, burly visage, a long nose, and huge whiskers. He had his little bowerie, or retreat, in the country, where he led a roistering life, giving dances to the wives and daughters of the burghers of the Manhattoes, insomuch that he became a prodigious favorite with all the women, young and old. He is said to have been the first to collect that famous toll levied on the fair sex at Kissing Bridge, on the highway to Hellgate.[2]

To this sturdy bachelor the eyes of all the women were turned in this time of darkness and peril, as the very man to second and carry out the plans of defense of the governor. A kind of petticoat council was forthwith held at the government house, at which the governor's lady presided; and this lady, as has been hinted, being all potent with the governor, the result of these councils was the elevation of Antony the Trumpeter to the post of commandant of wind-mills and champion of New Amsterdam.

The city being thus fortified and garrisoned, it would have done one's heart good to see the governor snapping his fingers and fidgeting with delight, as the trumpeter strutted up and down the ramparts, twanging defiance to the whole Yankee race, as does a modern editor to all the principalities and powers on the other side of the Atlantic. In the hands of Antony Van Corlear this windy instrument appeared to him as potent as the horn of the paladin Astolpho, or even the more classic horn of Alecto; nay, he had almost the temerity to compare it with the rams' horns celebrated in holy writ, at the very sound of which the walls of Jericho fell down.

Be all this as it may, the apprehensions of hostilities from the east gradually died away. The Yankees made no further invasion; nay, they declared they had only taken possession of Fort Goed Hoop as being erected within their territories. So far from manifesting hostility, they continued to throng to New Amsterdam with the most innocent countenances imaginable, filling the market with their notions, being as ready to trade with the Nederlanders as ever, and not a whit more prone to get to the windward of them in a bargain.

The old wives of the Manhattoes, who took tea with the governor's lady, attributed all this affected moderation to the awe inspired by the military preparations of the governor, and the windy prowess of Antony the Trumpeter.

There were not wanting illiberal minds, however, who sneered at the governor for thinking to defend his city as he governed it, by mere wind; but William Kieft was not to be jeered out of his wind-mills: he had seen them perched upon the ramparts of his native city of Saardam, and was persuaded they were connected with the great science of defense; nay, so much piqued was he by having them made a matter of ridicule, that he introduced them into the arms of the city, where they remain to this day,

---

[2] The bridge here mentioned by Mr. Knickerbocker still exists; but it is said that the toll is seldom collected nowadays, excepting on sleighing-parties, by the descendants of the patriarchs, who still preserve the traditions of the city.

quartered with the ancient beaver of the Manhattoes, an emblem and memento of his policy.

I must not omit to mention that certain wise old burghers of the Manhattoes, skillful in expounding signs and mysteries, after events have come to pass, consider this early intrusion of the wind-mill into the escutcheon of our city, which before had been wholly occupied by the beaver, as portentous of its after fortune, when the quiet Dutchman would be elbowed aside by the enterprising Yankee, and patient industry overtopped by windy speculation.

CHAPTER VIII

Of the Edict of William the Testy Against Tobacco—Of the Pipe-Plot, and the Rise of Feuds and Parties.

Wilhelmus Kieft, as has already been observed, was a great legislator on a small scale, and had a microscopic eye in public affairs. He had been greatly annoyed by the factious meeting of the good people of New Amsterdam, but, observing that on these occasions the pipe was ever in their mouth, he began to think that the pipe was at the bottom of the affair, and that there was some mysterious affinity between politics and tobacco-smoke. Determined to strike at the root of the evil, he began forthwith to rail at tobacco, as a noxious, nauseous weed, filthy in all its uses; and as to smoking, he denounced it as a heavy tax upon the public pocket,—a vast consumer of time, a great encourager of idleness, and a deadly bane to the prosperity and morals of the people. Finally he issued an edict, prohibiting the smoking of tobacco throughout the New Netherlands. Ill-fated Kieft! Had he lived in the present age and attempted to check the unbounded license of the press, he could not have struck more sorely upon the sensibilities of the million. The pipe, in fact, was the great organ of reflection and deliberation of the New Netherlander. It was his constant companion and solace: was he gay, he smoked; was he sad, he smoked; his pipe was never our of his mouth; it was a part of his physiognomy; without it his best friends would not know him. Take away his pipe? You might as well take away his nose!

The immediate effect of the edict of William the Testy was a popular commotion. A vast multitude, armed with pipes and tobacco-boxes, and an immense supply of ammunition, sat themselves down before the governor's house, and fell to smoking with tremendous violence. The testy William issued forth like a wrathful spider, demanding the reason of this lawless fumigation. The sturdy rioters replied by lolling back in their seats, and puffing away with redoubled fury, raising such a murky cloud that the governor was fain to take refuge in the interior of his castle.

A long negotiation ensued through the medium of Antony the Trumpeter. The governor was at first wrathful and unyielding, but was gradu-

ally smoked into terms. He concluded by permitting the smoking of tobacco, but he abolished the fair long pipes used in the days of Wouter
Van Twiller, denoting ease, tranquility, and sobriety of deportment; these
he condemned as incompatible with the dispatch of business, in place
whereof he substituted little captious short pipes, two inches in length,
which, he observed, could be stuck in one corner of the mouth, or twisted
in the hat-band, and would never be in the way. Thus ended this alarming insurrection, which was long known by the name of The Pipe-Plot,
and which, it has been somewhat quaintly observed, did end, like most
plots and seditions, in mere smoke.

But mark, oh, reader! the deplorable evils which did afterwards result.
The smoke of these villainous little pipes, continually ascending in a cloud
about the nose, penetrated into and befogged the cerebellum, dried up
all the kindly moisture of the brain, and rendered the people who use
them as vaporish and testy as the governor himself. Nay, what is worse,
from being goodly, burly, sleek-conditioned men, they became, like our
Dutch yeomanry who smoke short pipes, a lantern-jawed, smoke-dried,
leathern-hided race.

Nor was this all. From this fatal schism in tobacco-pipes we may date
the rise of parties in the Nieuw Nederlands. The rich and self-important
burghers who had made their fortunes, and could afford to be lazy, adhered to the ancient fashion, and formed a kind of aristocracy known as
the Long Pipes; while the lower order, adopting the reform of William
Kieft as more convenient in their handicraft employments, were branded
with the plebeian name of Short Pipes.

A third party sprang up, headed by the descendants of Robert Chewit,
the companion of the great Hudson. These discarded pipes altogether
and took to chewing tobacco; hence, they were called Quids,—an appellation since given to those political mongrels, which sometimes spring up between two great parties, as a mule is produced between a horse and an ass.

And here I would note the great benefit of party distinctions in saving
the people at large the trouble of thinking. Hesiod divides mankind into
three classes,—those who think for themselves, those who think as others
think, and those who do not think at all. The second class comprises the
great mass of society; for most people require a set creed and a file-lead-
er. Hence the origin of party: which means a large body of people, some
few of whom think, and all the rest talk. The former take the lead and
discipline the latter; prescribing what they must say, what they must approve, what they must hoot at, whom they must support, but, above all,
whom they must hate; for no one can be a right good partisan, who is
not a thorough-going hater.

The enlightened inhabitants of the Manhattoes, therefore, being divided into parties, were enabled to hate each other with great accuracy.
And now the great business of politics went bravely on, the long pipes
and short pipes assembling in separate beer-houses, and smoking at each

other with implacable vehemence, to the great support of the State and profit of the tavern-keepers. Some, indeed, went so far as to bespatter their adversaries with those odoriferous little words which smell so strong in the Dutch language, believing, like true politicians, that they served their party, and glorified themselves in proportion as they bewrayed their neighbors. But, however they might differ among themselves, all parties agreed in abusing the governor, seeing that he was not a governor of their choice, but appointed by others to rule over them.

Unhapppy William Kieft! exclaims the sage writer of the Stuyvesant manuscript, doomed to contend with enemies too knowing to be entrapped, and to reign over a people too wise to be governed. All his foreign expeditions were baffled and set at naught by the all-pervading Yankees; all his home measures were canvassed and condemned by "numerous and respectable meetings" of pot-house politicians.

In the multitude of counsellors, we are told, there is safety; but the multitude of counsellors was a continual source of perplexity to William Kieft. With a temperament as hot as an old radish, and a mind subject to perpetual whirlwinds and tornadoes, he never failed to get into a passion with everyone who undertook to advise him. I have observed, however, that your passionate little men, like small boats with large sails, are easily upset or blown out of their course; so was it with William the Testy, who was prone to be carried away by the last piece of advice blown into his ear. The consequence was, that, though a projector of the first class, yet by continually changing his projects he gave none a fair trial; and by endeavoring to do everything, he in sober truth did nothing.

In the meantime, the sovereign people got into the saddle, showed themselves, as usual, unmerciful riders; spurring on the little governor with harangues and petitions, and thwarting him with memorials and reproaches, in much the same way as holiday apprentices manage an unlucky devil of a hack-horse,—so that Wilhelmus Kieft was kept at a worry or a gallop throughout the whole of his administration.

1809

From *The Sketch-Book*

The Author's Account of Himself

"I am of this mind with Homer, that as the snail that crept out of her shell was turned eftsoons into a toad, and thereby was forced to make a stool to sit on; so the traveller that straggleth from his own country is in a short time transformed into so monstrous a shape, that he is fain to alter his mansion with his manners, and to live where he can, not where he would."

LYLY's *Euphues*

I was always fond of visiting new scenes, and observing strange characters and manners. Even when a mere child I began my travels, and made many tours of discovery into foreign parts and unknown regions of my native city, to the frequent alarm of my parents, and the emolument of the town-crier. As I grew into boyhood, I extended the range of my observations. My holiday afternoons were spent in rambles about the surrounding country. I made myself familiar with all its places famous in history or fable. I knew every spot where a murder or robbery had been committed, or a ghost seen. I visited the neighboring villages, and added greatly to my stock of knowledge, by noting their habits and customs, and conversing with their sages and great men. I even journeyed one long summer's day to the summit of the most distant hill, whence I stretched my eye over many a mile of terra incognita, and was astonished to find how vast a globe I inhabited.

This rambling propensity strengthened with my years. Books of voyages and travels became my passion, and in devouring their contents, I neglected the regular exercises of the school. How wistfully would I wander about the pier-heads in fine weather, and watch the parting ships, bound to distant climes—with what longing eyes would I gaze after their lessening sails, and waft myself in imagination to the ends of the earth!

Further reading and thinking, though they brought this vague inclination into more reasonable bounds, only served to make it more decided. I visited various parts of my own country; and had I been merely a lover of fine scenery, I should have felt little desire to seek elsewhere its gratification, for on no country have the charms of nature been more prodigally lavished. Her mighty lakes, like oceans of liquid silver; her mountains, with their bright aerial tints; her valleys, teeming with wild fertility; her tremendous cataracts, thundering in their solitudes; her boundless plains, waving with spontaneous verdure; her broad deep rivers, rolling in solemn silence to the ocean; her trackless forests, where vegetation puts forth all its magnificence; her skies, kindling with the magic of summer clouds and glorious sunshine;—no, never need an American look beyond his own country for the sublime and beautiful of natural scenery.

But Europe held forth the charms of storied and poetical association. There were to be seen the masterpieces of art, the refinements of highly-cultivated society, the quaint peculiarities of ancient and local custom. My native country was full of youthful promise: Europe was rich in the accumulated treasures of age. Her very ruins told the history of times gone by, and every mouldering stone was a chronicle. I longed to wander over the scenes of renowned achievement—to tread, as it were, in the footsteps of antiquity—to loiter about the ruined castle—to meditate on the falling tower—to escape, in short, from the commonplace realities of the present, and lose myself among the shadowy grandeurs of the past.

I had, beside all this, an earnest desire to see the great men of the earth. We have, it is true, our great men in America: not a city but has an ample share of them. I have mingled among them in my time, and been almost withered by the shade into which they cast me; for there is nothing so baleful to a small man as the shade of a great one, particularly the great man of a city. But I was anxious to see the great men of Europe; for I had read in the works of various philosophers, that all animals degenerated in America, and man among the number. A great man of Europe, thought I, must therefore be as superior to a great man of America, as a peak of the Alps to a highland of the Hudson; and in this idea I was confirmed, by observing the comparative importance and swelling magnitude of many English travelers among us, who, I was assured, were very little people in their own country. I will visit this land of wonders, thought I, and see the gigantic race from which I am degenerated.

It has been either my good or evil lot to have my roving passion gratified. I have wandered through different countries, and witnessed many of the shifting scenes of life. I cannot say that I have studied them with the eye of a philosopher; but rather with the sauntering gaze with which humble lovers of the picturesque stroll from the window of one print-shop to another; caught sometimes by the delineations of beauty, sometimes by the distortions of caricature, and sometimes by the loveliness of landscape. As it is the fashion for modern tourists to travel pencil in hand, and bring home their port-folios filled with sketches, I am disposed to get up a few for the entertainment of my friends. When, however, I look over the hints and memorandums I have taken down for the purpose, my heart almost fails me at finding how my idle humor has led me aside from the great objects studied by every regular traveler who would make a book. I fear I shall give equal disappointment with an unlucky landscape painter, who had traveled on the continent, but, following the bent of his vagrant inclination, had sketched in nooks, and corners, and by-places. His sketch-book was accordingly crowded with cottages, and landscapes, and obscure ruins; but he had neglected to paint St. Peter's, or the Coliseum; the cascade of Terni, or the bay of Naples, and had not a single glacier or volcano in his whole collection.

1819-1820

Rip Van Winkle

A POSTHUMOUS WRITING OF DIEDRICH KNICKERBOCKER

By Woden, God of Saxons,
From whence comes Wensday, that is Wodensday,
Truth is a thing that ever I will keep
Unto thylke day in which I creep into
My sepulchre——

CARTWRIGHT

[The following Tale was found among the papers of the late Diedrich Knickerbocker, an old gentleman of New York, who was very curious in the Dutch history of the province, and the manners of the descendants from its primitive settlers. His historical researches, however, did not lie so much among books as among men; for the former are lamentably scanty on his favorite topics; whereas he found the old burghers, and still more their wives, rich in that legendary lore, so invaluable to true history. Whenever, therefore, he happened upon a genuine Dutch family, snugly shut up in its low-roofed farmhouse, under a spreading sycamore, he looked upon it as a little clasped volume of black-letter, and studied it with the zeal of a book-worm.

The result of all these researches was a history of the province during the reign of the Dutch governors, which he published some years since. There have been various opinions as to the literary character of his work, and, to tell the truth, it is not a whit better than it should be. Its chief merit is its scrupulous accuracy, which indeed was a little questioned on its first appearance, but has since been completely established; and it is now admitted into all historical collections, as a book of unquestionable authority.

The old gentleman died shortly after the publication of his work, and now that he is dead and gone, it cannot do much harm to his memory to say that his time might have been much better employed in weightier labors. He, however, was apt to ride his hobby his own way; and though it did now and then kick up the dust a little in the eyes of his neighbors, and grieve the spirit of some friends, for whom he felt the truest deference and affection; yet his errors and follies are remembered "more in sorrow than in anger," and it begins to be suspected, that he never intended to injure or offend. But however his memory may be appreciated by critics, it is still held dear by many folks, whose good opinion is well worth having; particularly by certain biscuit-bakers, who have gone so far as to imprint his likeness on their new-year cakes; and have thus given him a chance for immortality, almost equal to the being stamped on a Waterloo Medal, or a Queen Anne's Farthing.]

Whoever has made a voyage up the Hudson must remember the Kaatskill mountains. They are a dismembered branch of the great Appalachian family, and are seen away to the west of the river, swelling up to a noble height, and lording it over the surrounding country. Every change of season, every change of weather, indeed, every hour of the day, produces some change in the magical hues and shapes of these mountains, and they are regarded by all the good wives, far and near, as perfect barometers. When the weather is fair and settled, they are clothed in blue and purple, and print their bold outlines on the clear evening sky; but, sometimes, when the rest of the landscape is cloudless, they will gather a hood of gray vapors about their summits, which, in the last rays of the setting sun, will glow and light up like a crown of glory.

At the foot of these fairy mountains, the voyager may have descried the light smoke curling up from a village, whose shingle-roofs gleam among the trees, just where the blue tints of the upland melt away into the fresh green of the nearer landscape. It is a little village of great antiquity, having been founded by some of the Dutch colonists, in the early times of the province, just about the beginning of the government of the good Peter Stuyvesant, (may he rest in peace!) and there were some of the houses of the original settlers standing within a few years, built of small yellow bricks brought from Holland, having latticed windows and gable fronts, surmounted with weather-cocks.

In that same village, and in one of these very houses (which, to tell the precise truth, was sadly time-worn and weather-beaten), there lived many years since, while the country was yet a province of Great Britain, a simple good-natured fellow of the name of Rip Van Winkle. He was a descendant of the Van Winkles who figured so gallantly in the chivalrous days of Peter Stuyvesant, and accompanied him to the siege of Fort Christina. He inherited, however, but little of the martial character of his ancestors. I have observed that he was a simple good-natured man; he was, moreover, a kind neighbor, and an obedient hen-pecked husband. Indeed, to the latter circumstance might be owing that meekness of spirit which gained him such universal popularity; for those men are most apt to be obsequious and conciliating abroad, who are under the discipline of shrews at home. Their tempers, doubtless, are rendered pliant and malleable in the fiery furnace of domestic tribulation; and a curtain lecture is worth all the sermons in the world for teaching the virtues of patience and long-suffering. A termagant wife may, therefore, in some respects, be considered a tolerable blessing; and if so, Rip Van Winkle was thrice blessed.

Certain it is, that he was a great favorite among all the good wives of the village, who, as usual, with the amiable sex, took his part in all family squabbles; and never failed, whenever they talked those matters over in their evening gossipings, to lay all the blame on Dame Van Winkle. The children of the village, too, would shout with joy whenever he approached. He assisted at their sports, made their playthings, taught them to fly kites and shoot marbles, and told them long stories of ghosts, witches, and Indians. Whenever he went dodging about the village, he was surrounded by a troop of them, hanging on his skirts, clambering on his back, and playing a thousand tricks on him with impunity; and not a dog would bark at him throughout the neighborhood.

The great error in Rip's composition was an insuperable aversion to all kinds of profitable labor. It could not be from the want of assiduity or perserverance; for he would sit on a wet rock, with a rod as long and heavy as a Tartar's lance, and fish all day without a murmur, even though he should not be encouraged by a single nibble. He would carry a fowling-piece on his shoulder for hours together, trudging through woods and swamps, and up hill and down dale, to shoot a few squirrels or wild pigeons. He would never refuse to assist a neighbor even in the roughest toil, and was a foremost man at all country frolics for husking

Indian corn, or building stone-fences; the women of the village, too, used to employ him to run their errands, and to do such little odd jobs as their less obliging husbands would not do for them. In a word Rip was ready to attend to anybody's business but his own; but as to doing family duty, and keeping his farm in order, he found it impossible.

In fact, he declared it was of no use to work on his farm; it was the most pestilent little piece of ground in the whole country; everything about it went wrong, and would go wrong, in spite of him. His fences were continually falling to pieces; his cow would either go astray, or get among the cabbages; weeds were sure to grow quicker in his fields than anywhere else; the rain always made a point of setting in just as he had some outdoor work to do; so that though his patrimonial estate had dwindled away under his management, acre by acre, until there was little more left than a mere patch of Indian corn and potatoes, yet it was the worst conditioned farm in the neighborhood.

His children, too, were as ragged and wild as if they belonged to nobody. His son Rip, an urchin begotten in his own likeness, promised to inherit the habits, with the old clothes of his father. He was generally seen trooping like a colt at his mother's heels, equipped in a pair of his father's cast-off galligaskins, which he had much ado to hold up with one hand, as a fine lady does her train in bad weather.

Rip Van Winkle, however, was one of those happy mortals, of foolish, well-oiled dispositions, who take the world easy, eat white bread or brown, whichever can be got with least thought or trouble, and would rather starve on a penny than work for a pound. If left to himself, he would have whistled life away in perfect contentment; but his wife kept continually dinning in his ears about his idleness, his carelessness, and the ruin he was bringing on his family. Morning, noon, and night, her tongue was incessantly going, and everything he said or did was sure to produce a torrent of household eloquence. Rip had but one way of replying to all lectures of the kind, and that, by frequent use, had grown into a habit. He shrugged his shoulders, shook his head, cast up his eyes, but said nothing. This, however, always provoked a fresh volley from his wife; so that he was fain to draw off his forces, and take to the outside of the house—the only side which, in truth, belongs to a hen-pecked husband.

Rip's sole domestic adherent was his dog Wolf, who was as much hen-pecked as his master; for Dame Van Winkle regarded them as companions in idleness, and even looked upon Wolf with an evil eye, as the cause of his master's going so often astray. True it is, in all points of spirit befitting an honorable dog, he was a courageous an animal as ever scoured the woods—but what courage can withstand the ever-during and all-besetting terrors of a woman's tongue? The moment Wolf entered the house his crest fell, his tail drooped to the ground, or curled between his legs, he sneaked about with a gallows air, casting many a sidelong glance at Dame Van Winkle, and at the least flourish of a broomstick or ladle, he would fly to the door with yelping precipitation.

Times grew worse and worse with Rip Van Winkle as years of matrimony rolled on; a tart temper never mellows with age, and a sharp tongue is the only edged tool that grows keener with constant use. For a long while he used to console himself, when driven from home, by frequenting a kind of perpetual club of the sages, philosophers, and other idle personages of the village; which held its sessions on a bench before a small inn, designated by a rubicund portrait of His Majesty George the Third. Here they used to sit in the shade through a long lazy summer's day, talking listlessly over village gossip, or telling endless sleepy stories about nothing. But it would have been worth any statesman's money to have heard the profound discussions that sometimes took place, when by chance an old newspaper fell into their hands from some passing traveler. How solemnly they would listen to the contents, as drawled out by Derrick Van Bummel, the schoolmaster, a dapper learned little man, who was not to be daunted by the most gigantic word in the dictionary; and how sagely they would deliberate upon public events some months after they had taken place.

The opinions of this junto were completely controlled by Nicholas Vedder, a patriarch of the village, and landlord of the inn, at the door of which he took his seat from morning till night, just moving sufficiently to avoid the sun and keep in the shade of a large tree; so that the neighbors could tell the hour by his movements as accurately as by a sun-dial. It is true he was rarely heard to speak, but smoked his pipe incessantly. His adherents, however (for every great man has his adherents), perfectly understood him, and knew how to gather his opinions. When anything that was read or related displeased him, he was observed to smoke his pipe vehemently, and to send forth short, frequent and angry puffs; but when pleased, he would inhale the smoke slowly and tranquilly, and emit it in light and placid clouds; and sometimes, taking the pipe from his mouth, and letting the fragrant vapor curl about his nose, would gravely nod his head in token of perfect approbation.

From even this stronghold the unlucky Rip was at length routed by his termagant wife, who would suddenly break in upon the tranquility of the assemblage and call the members all to naught; nor was that august personage, Nicholas Vedder himself, sacred from the daring tongue of this terrible virago, who charged him outright with encouraging her husband in habits of idleness.

Poor Rip was at last reduced almost to despair; and his only alternative, to escape from the labor of the farm and clamor of his wife, was to take gun in hand and stroll away into the woods. Here he would sometimes seat himself at the foot of a tree, and share the contents of his wallet with Wolf, with whom he sympathized as a fellow-sufferer in persecution. "Poor Wolf," he would say, "thy mistress leads thee a dog's life of it; but never mind, my lad, whilst I live thou shalt never want a friend to stand by thee!" Wolf would wag his tail, look wistfully in his master's face, and if dogs can feel pity I verily believe he reciprocated the sentiment with all his heart.

In a long ramble of the kind on a fine autumnal day, Rip had unconsciously scrambled to one of the highest parts of the Kaatskill mountains. He was after his favorite sport of squirrel shooting, and the still solitudes had echoed and re-echoed with the reports of his gun. Panting and fatigued, he threw himself, late in the afternoon, on a green knoll, covered with mountain herbage, that crowned the brow of a precipice. From an opening between the trees he could overlook all the lower country for many a mile of rich woodland. He saw at a distance the lordly Hudson, far, far below him, moving on its silent but majestic course, with the reflection of a purple cloud, or the sail of a lagging bark, here and there sleeping on its glassy bosom, and at last losing itself in the blue highlands.

On the other side he looked down into a deep mountain glen, wild, lonely, and shagged, the bottom filled with fragments from the impending cliffs, and scarcely lighted by the reflected rays of the setting sun. For some time Rip lay musing on this scene; evening was gradually advancing; the mountains began to throw their long blue shadows over the valleys; he saw that it would be dark long before he could reach the village, and he heaved a heavy sigh when he thought of encountering the terrors of Dame Van Winkle.

As he was about to descend, he heard a voice from a distance, hallooing, "Rip Van Winkle! Rip Van Winkle!" He looked round, but could see nothing but a crow winging its solitary flight across the mountain. He thought his fancy must have deceived him, and turned again to descend, when he heard the same cry ring through the still evening air; "Rip Van Winkle! Rip Van Winkle!"—at the same time Wolf bristled up his back, and giving a low growl, skulked to his master's side, looking fearfully down into the glen. Rip now felt a vague apprehension stealing over him; he looked anxiously in the same direction, and perceived a strange figure slowly toiling up the rocks, and bending under the weight of something he carried on his back. He was surprised to see any human being in this lonely and unfrequented place, but supposing it to be someone of the neighborhood in need of his assistance, he hastened down to yield it.

On nearer approach he was still more surprised at the singularity of the stranger's appearance. He was a short square-built old fellow, with thick bushy hair, and a grizzled beard. His dress was of the antique Dutch fashion—a cloth jerkin strapped round the waist—several pair of breeches, the outer one of ample volume, decorated with rows of buttons down the sides, and bunches at the knees. He bore on his shoulder a stout keg, that seemed full of liquor, and made signs for Rip to approach and assist him with the load. Though rather shy and distrustful of this new acquaintance, Rip complied with his usual alacrity; and mutually relieving one another, they clambered up a narrow gully, apparently the dry bed of a mountain torrent. As they ascended, Rip every now and then heard long rolling peals, like distant thunder, that seemed to issue out of a deep ravine, or rather cleft, between lofty rocks, toward which their rugged path conducted. He paused for an instant, but supposing it to be the muttering of one of those transient thunder-showers which often take place in mountain heights, he proceeded. Passing through the ravine, they came to a hollow, like a small amphitheater, surrounded by perpendicular precipices, over the brinks of which impending trees shot their branches, so that you only caught glimpses of the azure sky and the bright evening cloud. During the whole time Rip and his companion had labored on in silence; for though the former marveled greatly what could be the object of carrying a keg of liquor up this wild mountain, yet there was something strange and incomprehensible about the unknown, that inspired awe and checked familiarity.

On entering the amphitheater, new objects of wonder presented themselves. On a level spot in the center was a company of odd-looking personages playing at nine-pins. They were dressed in a quaint outlandish fashion; some wore short doublets, others jerkins, with long knives in their belts, and most of them had enormous breeches, of similar style with that of the guide's. Their visages, too, were peculiar: one had a large beard, broad face, and small piggish eyes: the face of another seemed to consist entirely of nose, and was surmounted by a white sugar-loaf hat set off with a little red cock's tail. They all had beards, of various shapes and colors. There was one who seemed to be the commander. He was a stout old gentleman, with a weather-beaten countenance; he wore a laced doublet, broad belt and hanger, high-crowned hat and feather, red stockings, and high-heeled shoes, with roses in them. The whole group reminded Rip of the figures in an old Flemish painting, in the parlor of Dominie Van Shaick, the village parson, and which had been brought over from Holland at the time of the settlement.

What seemed particularly odd to Rip was, that though these folks were evidently amusing themselves, yet they maintained the gravest faces, the most mysterious silence, and were, withal, the most melancholy party of pleasure he had ever witnessed. Nothing interrupted the stillness of the scene but the noise of the balls, which, whenever they were rolled, echoed along the mountains like rumbling peals of thunder.

As Rip and his companion approached them, they suddenly desisted from their play, and stared at him with such fixed statue-like gaze, and such strange, uncouth, lack-lustre countenances, that his heart turned within him, and his knees smote together. His companion now emptied the contents of the keg into large flagons, and made signs to him to wait upon the company. He obeyed with fear and trembling; they quaffed the liquor in profound silence, and then returned to their game.

By degrees Rip's awe and apprehension subsided. He even ventured, when no eye was fixed upon him, to taste the beverage, which he found had much of the flavor of excellent Hollands. He was naturally a thirsty soul, and was soon tempted to repeat the draught. One taste provoked another; and he reiterated his visits to the flagon so often that at length his senses were overpowered, his eyes swam in his head, his head gradually declined, and he fell into a deep sleep.

On waking, he found himself on the green knoll whence he had first seen the old man of the glen. He rubbed his eyes—it was a bright sunny morning. The birds were hopping and twittering among the bushes, and the eagle was wheeling aloft, and breasting the pure mountain breeze. "Surely," thought Rip, "I have not slept here all night." He recalled the occurrences before he fell asleep. The strange man with a keg of liquor—the mountain ravine—the wild retreat among the rocks—the woe-begone party at nine-pins—the flagon. "Oh! that flagon! that wicked flagon!" thought Rip—"what excuse shall I make to Dame Van Winkle!"

He looked round for his gun, but in place of the clean well-oiled fowling-piece, he found an old firelock lying by him, the barrel encrusted with rust, the lock falling off, and the stock worm-eaten. He now suspected that the grave roisters of the mountain had put a trick upon him, and, having dosed him with liquor, had robbed him of his gun. Wolf, too, had disappeared, but he might have strayed away after a squirrel or partridge. He whistled after him and shouted his name, but all in vain; the echoes repeated his whistle and shout, but no dog was to be seen.

He determined to revisit the scene of the last evening's gambol, and if he met with any of the party, to demand his dog and gun. As he rose to walk, he found himself stiff in the joints, and wanting in his usual activity. "These mountain beds do not agree with me," thought Rip, "and if this frolic should lay me up with a fit of the rheumatism, I shall have a blessed time with Dame Van Winkle." With some difficulty he got down into the glen: he found the gully up which he and his companion had ascended the preceding evening; but to his astonishment a mountain stream was now foaming down it, leaping from rock to rock, and filling the glen with babbling murmurs. He, however, made shift to scramble up its sides, working his toilsome way through thickets of birch, sassafras, and witch-hazel, and sometimes tripped up or entangled by the wild grapevines that twisted their coils or tendrils from tree to tree, and spread a kind of network in his path.

At length he reached to where the ravine had opened through the cliffs to the amphitheater; but no traces of such opening remained. The rocks presented a high impenetrable wall over which the torrent came tumbling in a sheet of feathery foam, and fell into a broad deep basin, black from the shadows of the surrounding forest. Here, then, poor Rip was brought to a stand. He again called and whistled after his dog; he was only answered by the cawing of a flock of idle crows, sporting high in air about a dry tree that overhung a sunny precipice; and who, secure in their elevation, seemed to look down and scoff at the poor man's perplexities. What was to be done? the morning was passing away, and Rip felt famished for want of his breakfast. He grieved to give up his dog and gun; he dreaded to meet his wife; but it would not do to starve among the mountains. He shook his head, shouldered the rusty firelock, and, with a heart full of trouble and anxiety, turned his steps homeward.

As he approached the village he met a number of people, but none whom he knew, which somewhat surprised him, for he had thought himself acquainted with everyone in the country round. Their dress, too, was of a different fashion from that to which he was accustomed. They all stared at him with equal marks of surprise, and whenever they cast their eyes upon him, invariably stroked their chins. The constant recurrence of this gesture induced Rip, involuntarily, to do the same, when, to his astonishment, he found his beard had grown a foot long!

He had now entered the skirts of the village. A troop of strange children ran at his heels, hooting after him, and pointing at his gray beard. The dogs, too, not one of which he recognized for an old acquaintance, barked at him as he passed. The very village was altered; it was larger and more populous. There were rows of houses which he had never seen before, and those which had been his familiar haunts had disappeared. Strange names were over the doors—strange faces at the windows—everything was strange. His mind now misgave him; he began to doubt whether both he and the world around him were not bewitched. Surely this was his native village, which he had left but the day before. There stood the Kaatskill mountains—there ran the silver Hudson at a distance—there was every hill and dale precisely as it had always been—Rip was sorely perplexed—"That flagon last night," thought he, "has addled my poor head sadly!"

It was with some difficulty that he found the way to his own house, which he approached with silent awe, expecting every moment to hear the shrill voice of Dame Van Winkle. He found the house gone to decay—the roof fallen in, the windows shattered, and the doors off the hinges. A half-starved dog that looked like Wolf was skulking about it. Rip called him by name, but the cur snarled, showed his teeth, and passed on. This was an unkind cut indeed—"My very dog," sighed poor Rip, "has forgotten me!"

He entered the house, which, to tell the truth, Dame Van Winkle had always kept in neat order. It was empty, forlorn, and apparently abandoned. This desolateness overcame all his connubial fears—he called loudly for his wife and children—the lonely chambers rang for a moment with his voice, and then all again was silence.

He now hurried forth, and hastened to his old resort, the village inn—but it too was gone. A large rickety wooden building stood in its place, with great gaping windows, some of them broken and mended with old hats and petticoats, and over the door was painted, "the Union Hotel, by Jonathan Doolittle." Instead of the great tree that used to shelter the quiet little Dutch inn of yore, there now was reared a tall naked pole, with something on the top that looked like a red night-cap, and from it was fluttering a flag, on which was a singular assemblage of stars and stripes—all this was strange and incomprehensible. He recognized on the sign, however, the ruby face of King George, under which he had smoked so many a peaceful pipe; but even this was singularly metamorphosed. The red coat was changed for one of blue and buff, a sword was held in the hand instead of a scepter, the head was decorated with a cocked hat, and underneath was painted in large characters, GENERAL WASHINGTON.

There was, as usual, a crowd of folk about the door, but none that Rip recollected. The very character of the people seemed changed. There was a busy, bustling, disputatious tone about it, instead of the accustomed phlegm and drowsy tranquility. He looked in vain for the sage Nicholas Vedder, with his broad face, double chin, and fair long pipe, uttering clouds of tobacco-smoke instead of idle speeches; or Van Bummel, the schoolmaster, doling forth the contents of an ancient newspaper. In place of these, a lean, bilious-looking fellow, with his pockets full of handbills, was haranguing vehemently about rights of citizens—elections—members of congress—liberty—Bunker's Hill—heroes of seventy-six—and other words, which were a perfect Babylonish jargon to the bewildered Van Winkle.

The appearance of Rip, with his long grizzled beard, his rusty fowling-piece, his uncouth dress, and an army of women and children at his heels, soon attracted the attention of the tavern politicians. They crowded round him, eyeing him from head to foot with great curiosity. The orator bustled up to him, and, drawing him partly aside, inquired "on which side he voted?" Rip stared in vacant stupidity. Another short but busy little fellow pulled him by the arm, and, rising on tiptoe, inquired in his ear, "Whether he was Federal or Democrat?" Rip was equally at a loss to comprehend the question; when a knowing, self-important old gentleman, in a sharp cocked hat, made his way through the crowd, putting them to the right and left with his elbows as he passed, and planting himself before Van Winkle, with one arm akimbo, the other resting on his cane, his keen eyes and sharp hat penetrating, as it were, into his very soul, demanded in an austere tone, "what brought him to the election with a gun on his shoulder, and a mob at his heels, and whether he meant to breed a riot in the village?"—"Alas! gentlemen," cried Rip, somewhat dismayed, "I am a poor quiet man, a native of the place, and a loyal subject of the king, God bless him!"

Here a general shout burst from the by-standers—"A tory! a tory! a spy! a refugee! hustle him! away with him!" It was with great difficulty that the self-important man in the cocked hat restored order; and, having assumed a tenfold austerity of brow, demanded again of the unknown culprit, what he came there for, and whom he was seeking? The poor man humbly assured him that he meant no harm, but merely came there in search of some of his neighbors, who used to keep about the tavern.

"Well—who are they?—name them."

Rip bethought himself a moment, and inquired, "Where's Nicholas Vedder?"

There was a silence for a little while, when an old man replied, in a thin piping voice, "Nicholas Vedder! why, he is dead and gone these eighteen years! There was a wooden tombstone in the church-yard that used to tell all about him, but that's rotten and gone too."

"Where's Brom Dutcher?"

"Oh, he went off to the army in the beginning of the war; some say he was killed at the storming of Stony Point—others say he was drowned in a squall at the foot of Antony's Nose. I don't know—he never came back again."

"Where's Van Bummel, the schoolmaster?"

"He went off to the wars too, was a great militia general, and is now in congress."

Rip's heart died away at hearing of these sad changes in his home and friends, and finding himself thus alone in the world. Every answer puzzled him too, by treating of such enormous lapses of time, and of matters which he could not understand: war—congress—Stony Point;—he had no courage to ask after any more friends, but cried out in despair, "Does nobody here know Rip Van Winkle?"

"Oh, Rip Van Winkle!" exclaimed two or three, "Oh, to be sure! that's Rip Van Winkle yonder, leaning against the tree."

Rip looked, and beheld a precise counterpart of himself, as he went up the mountain: apparently as lazy, and certainly as ragged. The poor fellow was now completely confounded. He doubted his own identity, and whether he was himself or another man. In the midst of his bewilderment, the man in the cocked hat demanded who he was, and what was his name?

"God knows," exclaimed he, at his wit's end; "I'm not myself—I'm somebody else—that's me yonder—no—that's somebody else got into my shoes—I was myself last night, but I fell asleep on the mountain, and they've changed my gun, and everything's changed, and I'm changed, and I can't tell what's my name, or who I am!"

The by-standers began now to look at each other, nod, wink significantly, and tap their fingers against their foreheads. There was a whisper, also, about securing the gun, and keeping the old fellow from doing mischief, at the very suggestion of which the self-important man in the cocked hat retired with some precipitation. At this critical moment a fresh comely woman pressed through the throng to get a peep at the gray-bearded man. She had a chubby child in her arms, which, frightened at his looks, began to cry. "Hush, Rip," cried she, "hush, you little fool; the old man won't hurt you." The name of the child, the air of the mother, the tone of her voice, all awakened a train of recollections in his mind. "What is your name, my good woman?" asked he.

"Judith Gardenier."

"And your father's name?"

"Ah, poor man, Rip Van Winkle was his name, but it's twenty years since he went away from home with his gun, and never has been heard of since—his dog came home without him; but whether he shot himself, or was carried away by the Indians, nobody can tell. I was then but a little girl."

Rip had but one question more to ask; but he put it with a faltering voice:

"Where's your mother?"

"Oh, she too had died but a short time since; she broke a blood-vessel in a fit of passion at a New England peddler."

There was a drop of comfort, at least, in this intelligence. The honest man could contain himself no longer. He caught his daughter and her child in his arms. "I am your father!" cried he—"Young Rip Van Winkle once—old Rip Van Winkle now!—Does anybody know poor Rip Van Winkle?"

All stood amazed, until an old woman, tottering out from among the crowd, put her hand to her brow, and peering under it in his face for a moment, exclaimed, "Sure enough! it is Rip Van Winkle—it is himself! Welcome home again, old neighbor—Why, where have you been these twenty long years?"

Rip's story was soon told, for the whole twenty years had been to him but as one night. The neighbors stared when they heard it; some were seen to wink at each other, and put their tongues in their cheeks: and the self-important man in the cocked hat, who, when the alarm was over, had returned to the field, screwed down the corners of his mouth, and shook his head—upon which there was a general shaking of the head throughout the assemblage.

It was determined, however, to take the opinion of old Peter Vanderdonk, who was seen slowly advancing up the road. He was a descendant of the historian of that name, who wrote one of the earliest accounts of the province. Peter was the most ancient inhabitant of the village, and well versed in all the wonderful events and traditions of the neighborhood. He recollected Rip at once, and corroborated his story in the most satisfactory manner. He assured the company that it was a fact, handed down from his ancestor the historian, that the Kaatskill mountains had always been haunted by strange beings. That it was affirmed that the great Hendrick Hudson, the first discoverer of the river and country, kept a kind of vigil there every twenty years, with his crew of the Half-moon; being permitted in this way to revisit the scenes of his enterprise, and keep a guardian eye upon the river, and the great city called by his name. That his father had once seen them in their old Dutch dresses playing at nine-pins in a hollow of the mountain; and that he himself had heard, one summer afternoon, the sound of their balls, like distant peals of thunder.

To make a long story short, the company broke up, and returned to the more important concerns of the election. Rip's daughter took him home to live with her; she had a snug, well-furnished house, and a stout cheery farmer for a husband, whom Rip recollected for one of the urchins that used to climb upon his back. As to Rip's son and heir, who was the ditto of himself, seen leaning against the tree, he was employed to work on the farm; but evinced an hereditary disposition to attend to any thing else but his business.

Rip now resumed his old walks and habits; he soon found many of his former cronies, though all rather the worse for the wear and tear of time; and preferred making friends among the rising generation, with whom he soon grew into great favor.

Having nothing to do at home, and being arrived at that happy age when a man can be idle with impunity, he took his place once more on the bench at the inn door, and was reverenced as one of the patriarchs of the village, and a chronicle of the old times "before the war." It was some time before he could get into the regular track of gossip, or could be made to comprehend the strange events that had taken place during his torpor. How that there had been a revolutionary war—that the country had thrown off the yoke of old England—and that, instead of being a subject of his Majesty George the Third, he was now a free citizen of the United States. Rip, in fact, was no politician; the changes of states and empires made but little impression on him; but there was one species of despotism under which he had long groaned, and that was—petticoat government. Happily that was at an end; he had got his neck out of the yoke of matrimony, and could go in and out whenever he pleased, without dreading the tyranny of Dame Van Winkle. Whenever her name was mentioned, however, he shook his head, shrugged his shoulders, and cast up his eyes; which might pass either for an expression of resignation to his fate, or joy at his deliverance.

He used to tell his story to every stranger that arrived at Mr. Doolittle's hotel. He was observed, at first, to vary on some points every time he told it, which was, doubtless, owing to his having so recently awaked. It at last settled down precisely to the tale I have related, and not a man, woman, or child in the neighborhood, but knew it by heart. Some always pretended to doubt the reality of it, and insisted that Rip had been out of his head, and that this was one point on which he always remained flighty. The old Dutch inhabitants, however, almost universally gave it full credit. Even to this day they never hear a thunderstorm of a summer afternoon about the Kaatskill, but they say Hendrick Hudson and his crew are at their game of nine-pins; and it is a common wish of all hen-pecked husbands in the neighborhood, when life hangs heavy on their hands, that they might have a quieting draught out of Rip Van Winkle's flagon.

NOTE

The foregoing Tale, one would suspect, had been suggested to Mr. Knickerbocker by a little German superstition about the Emperor Fred-erick *der Rothbart,* and the Kypphaüser mountain: the subjoined note, however, which he had appended to the tale, shows that it is an absolute fact, narrated with his usual fidelity:

"The story of Rip Van Winkle may seem incredible to many, but nevertheless I give it my full belief, for I know the vicinity of our old Dutch settlements to have been very subject to marvelous events and appearances. Indeed, I have heard many stranger stories than this, in the villages along the Hudson; all of which were too well authenticated to admit of a doubt. I have even talked with Rip Van Winkle myself, who, when last I saw him, was a very venerable old man, and so per-fectly rational and consistent on every other point, that I think no con-scientious person could refuse to take this into the bargain; nay, I have seen a certificate on the subject taken before a country justice and signed with a cross, in the justice's own handwriting. The story, there-fore, is beyond the possibility of doubt.

D.K."

POSTSCRIPT

The following are traveling notes from a memorandum-book of Mr. Knickerbocker:

The Kaatsberg, or Catskill mountains, have always been a region full of fable. The Indians considered them the abode of spirits, who influ-enced the weather, spreading sunshine or clouds over the landscape, and sending good or bad hunting seasons. They were ruled by an old squaw spirit, said to be their mother. She dwelt on the highest peak of the Catskills, and had charge of the doors of day and night to open and shut them at the proper hour. She hung up the new moons in the skies, and cut up the old ones into stars. In times of drought, if properly propi-tiated, she would spin light summer clouds out of cobwebs and morning dew, and send them off from the crest of the mountain, flake after flake, like flakes of carded cotton, to float in the air; until, dissolved by the heat of the sun, they would fall in gentle showers, causing the grass to spring, the fruits to ripen, and the corn to grow an inch an hour. If displeased, however, she would brew up clouds black as ink, sitting in the midst of them like a bottle-bellied spider in the midst of its web; and when these clouds broke, woe betide the valleys!

In old times, say the Indian traditions, there was a kind of Manitou or Spirit, who kept about the wildest recesses of the Catskill Mountains, and took a mischievous pleasure in wreaking all kinds of evils and vexations upon the red men. Sometimes he would assume the form of a bear, a panther, or a deer, lead the bewildered hunter a weary chase through tangled forests and among ragged rocks; and then spring off with a loud ho! ho! leaving him aghast on the brink of a beetling precipice or raging torrent.

The favorite abode of this Manitou is still shown. It is a great rock or cliff on the loneliest part of the mountains, and, from the flowering vines which clamber about it, and the wild flowers which abound in its neighborhood, is known by the name of the Garden Rock. Near the foot of it is a small lake, the haunt of the solitary bittern, with water-snakes basking in the sun on the leaves of the pond-lilies which lie on the surface. This place was held in great awe by the Indians, insomuch that the boldest hunter would not pursue his game within its precincts. Once upon a time, however, a hunter who had lost his way, penetrated to the garden rock, where he beheld a number of gourds placed in the crotches of trees. One of these he seized and made off with it, but in the hurry of his retreat he let it fall among the rocks, when a great stream gushed forth, which washed him away and swept him down precipices, where he was dashed to pieces, and the stream made its way to the Hudson, and continues to flow to the present day; being the identical stream known by the name of the Kaaters-kill.

1819-1820

From *Bracebridge Hall*

The Stout Gentleman

A STAGE-COACH ROMANCE

I'll cross it, though it blast me!

HAMLET

It was a rainy Sunday in the gloomy month of November. I had been detained, in the course of a journey, by a slight indisposition, from which I was recovering; but was still feverish, and obliged to keep within doors all day, in an inn of the small town of Derby. A wet Sunday in a country inn!—whoever has had the luck to experience one can alone judge of my situation. The rain pattered against the casements; the bells tolled for church with a melancholy sound. I went to the windows in quest of something to amuse the eye; but it seemed as if I had been placed completely out of the reach of all amusement. The windows of my bedroom looked out among tiled roofs and stacks of chimneys, while those of my sitting-room commanded a full view of the stable-yard. I know of nothing more calculated to make a man sick of this world than a stable-yard on a rainy day. The place was littered with wet straw that had been kicked about by travelers and stable boys. In one corner was a stagnant pool of water, surrounding an island of muck; there were several half-drowned fowls crowded together under a cart, among which was a miserable, crest-fallen cock, drenched out of all life and spirit; his drooping tail matted, as it were, into a single feather, along which the water trickled from his back; near the cart was a half-dozing cow, chewing the cud, and standing patiently to be rained on, with wreaths of vapor rising from her reeking hide; a wall-eyed horse, tired of the loneliness of the stable, was poking his spectral head out of a window, with the rain dripping on it from the eaves; an unhappy cur, chained to a doghouse hard by, uttered something, every now and then, between a bark and a yelp; a drab of a kitchen-wench tramped backwards and forwards through the yard in patterns, looking as sulky as the weather itself; everything, in short, was comfortless and forlorn, excepting a crew of hardened ducks, assembled like boon companions round a puddle, and making a riotous noise over their liquor.

I was lonely and listless, and wanted amusement. My room soon became insupportable. I abandoned it, and sought what is technically called the travelers'-room. This is a public room set apart at most inns for the accommodation of a class of wayfarers called travelers, or riders: a kind of commercial knights-errant, who are incessantly scouring the kingdom in gigs, on horseback, or by coach. They are the only successors that I know of at the present day to the knights-errant of yore. They lead the same kind of roving, adventurous life, only changing the lance for a driving-whip, the buckler for a pattern-card, and the coat of mail for an upper Benjamin. Instead of vindicating the charms of peerless beauty, they rove about, spreading the fame and standing of some substantial tradesman, or manufacturer, and are ready at any time to bargain in his name; it being the fashion nowadays to trade, instead of fight, with one another. As the room of the hostel, in the good old fighting-times, would be hung round at night with the armor of way-worn warriors, such as coats of mail, falchions, and yawning helmets, so the travelers'-room is garnished with the harnessing of their successors, with box-coats, whips of all kinds, spurs, gaiters, and oil-cloth covered hats.

I was in hopes of finding some of these worthies to talk with, but was disappointed. There were, indeed, two or three in the room; but I could make nothing of them. One was just finishing his breakfast, quarreling with his bread and butter, and huffing the waiter; another buttoned on a pair of gaiters, with many execrations at Boots for not having cleaned his shoes well; a third sat drumming on the table with his fingers and looking at the rain as it streamed down the window-glass; they all appeared infected by the weather, and disapppeared, one after the other, without exchanging a word.

I sauntered to the window, and stood gazing at the people, picking their way to church, with petticoats hoisted midleg high, and dripping umbrellas. The bell ceased to toll, and the streets became silent. I then amused myself with watching the daughters of a tradesman opposite; who, being confined to the house for fear of wetting their Sunday finery, played off their charms at the front windows, to fascinate the chance tenants of the inn. They at length were summoned away by a vigilant vinegar-faced mother, and I had nothing further from without to amuse me.

What was I to do to pass away the long-lived day? I was sadly nervous and lonely; and everything about an inn seems calculated to make a dull day ten times duller. Old newspapers, smelling of beer and tobacco-smoke, and which I had already read half a dozen times. Good-for-nothing books, that were worse than rainy weather. I bored myself to death with an old volume of the Lady's Magazine. I read all the commonplace names of ambitious travelers scrawled on the panes of glass; the eternal families of the Smiths, and the Browns, and the Jacksons, and the Johnsons, and all the other sons; and I deciphered several scraps of fatiguing inn-window poetry which I have met with in all parts of the world.

The day continued lowering and gloomy; the slovenly, ragged, spongy cloud drifted heavily along; there was no variety even in the rain: it was one dull, continued, monotonous patter—patter—patter, excepting that now and then I was enlivened by the idea of a brisk shower, from the rattling of the drops upon a passing umbrella.

It was quite refreshing (if I may be allowed a hackneyed phrase of the day) when, in the course of the morning, a horn blew, and a stage-coach whirled through the street, with outside passengers stuck all over it, cowering under cotton umbrellas, and seethed together, and reeking with the steams of wet box-coats and upper Benjamins.

The sound brought out from their lurking-places a crew of vagabond boys, and vagabond dogs, and the carroty-headed hostler, and that nondescript animal ycleped Boots, and all the other vagabond race that infest the purlieus of an inn; but the bustle was transient; the coach again whirled on its way; and boy and dog, and hostler and Boots, all slunk back again to their holes; the street again became silent, and the rain continued to rain on. In fact, there was no hope of its clearing up; the barometer pointed to rainy weather; mine hostess's tortoise-shell cat sat by the fire washing her face, and rubbing her paws over her ears; and, on referring to the Almanac, I found a direful prediction stretching from the top of the page to the bottom through the whole month, "expect —much—rain—about—this—time!"

I was dreadfully hipped. The hours seemed as if they would never creep by. The very ticking of the clock became irksome. At length the stillness of the house was interrupted by the ringing of a bell. Shortly after I heard the voice of a waiter at the bar: "The stout gentleman in No. 13 wants his breakfast. Tea and bread and butter, with ham and eggs; the eggs not to be too much done."

In such a situation as mine, every incident is of importance. Here was a subject of speculation presented to my mind, and ample exercise for my imagination. I am prone to paint pictures to myself, and on this occasion I had some materials to work upon. Had the guest upstairs been mentioned as Mr. Smith, or Mr. Brown, or Mr. Jackson, or Mr. Johnson, or merely as "the gentleman in No. 13," it would have been a perfect blank to me. I should have thought nothing of it; but "The stout gentleman!"—the very name had something in it of the picturesque. It at once gave the size; it embodied the personage to my mind's eye, and my fancy did the rest.

He was stout, or, as some term it, lusty; in all probability, therefore, he was advanced in life, some people expanding as they grow old. By his breakfasting rather late, and in his own room, he must be a man accustomed to live at his ease, and above the necessity of early rising; no doubt a round, rosy, lusty old gentleman.

There was another violent ringing. The stout gentleman was impatient for his breakfast. He was evidently a man of importance; "well to do in the world;" accustomed to be promptly waited upon; of a keen appetite, and a little cross when hungry; "perhaps," thought I, "he may be some London Alderman; or who knows but he may be a Member of Parliament?"

The breakfast was sent up, and there was a short interval of silence; he was doubtless, making the tea. Presently there was a violent ringing; and before it could be answered, another ringing still more violent. "Bless me! what a choleric old gentleman!" The waiter came down in a huff. The butter was rancid, the eggs were overdone, the ham was too salty;—the stout gentleman was evidently nice in his eating; one of those who eat and growl, and keep the waiter on the trot, and live in a state militant with the household.

The hostess got into a fume. I should observe that she was a brisk, coquettish woman; a little of a shrew, and something of a slammerkin, but very pretty withal; with a nincompoop for a husband, as shrews are apt to have. She rated the servants roundly for their negligence in sending up so bad a breakfast, but said not a word against the stout gentleman; by which I clearly perceived that he must be a man of consequence, entitled to make a noise and to give trouble at a country inn. Other eggs, and ham, and bread and butter were sent up. They appeared to be more graciously received; at least there was no further complaint.

I had not made many turns about the travelers'-room, when there was another ringing. Shortly afterwards there was a stir and an inquest about the house. The stout gentleman wanted the Times or the Chronicle newspaper. I set him down, therefore, for a Whig; or rather, from his being so absolute and lordly where he had a chance, I suspected him of being a Radical. Hunt, I had heard, was a large man; "who knows," thought I, "but it is Hunt himself!"

My curiosity began to be awakened. I inquired of the waiter who was this stout gentleman that was making all this stir; but I could get no information: nobody seemed to know his name. The landlords of bustling inns seldom trouble their heads about the names or occupations of their transient guests. The color of a coat, the shape or size of the person, is enough to suggest a traveling name. It is either the tall gentleman, or the short gentleman, or the gentleman in black, or the gentleman in snuff-color; or, as in the present instance, the stout gentleman. A designation of the kind once hit on, answers every purpose, and saves all further inquiry.

Rain—rain—rain! pitiless, ceaseless rain! No such thing as putting a foot out of doors, and no occupation nor amusement within. By and by I heard someone walking overhead. It was in the stout gentleman's room. He evidently was a large man by the heaviness of his tread; and an old man from his wearing such creaking soles. "He is doubtless," thought I, "some rich old square-toes of regular habits, and is now taking exercise after breakfast."

I now read all the advertisements of coaches and hotels that were stuck about the mantlepiece. The Lady's Magazine had become an abomination to me; it was as tedious as the day itself. I wandered out, not knowing what to do, and ascended again to my room. I had not been there long, when there was a squall from a neighboring bedroom. A door opened and slammed violently; a chamber-maid, that I had remarked for having a ruddy, good-humored face, went downstairs in a violent flurry. The stout gentleman had been rude to her!

This sent a whole host of my deductions to the deuce in a moment. This unknown personage could not be an old gentleman; for old gentlemen are not apt to be so obstreperous to chamber-maids. He could not be a young gentleman; for young gentlemen are not apt to inspire such indignation. He must be a middle-aged man, and confounded ugly into the bargain, or the girl would not have taken the matter in such terrible dudgeon. I confess I was sorely puzzled.

In a few minutes I heard the voice of my landlady. I caught a glance of her as she came tramping upstairs,—her face glowing, her cap flaring, her tongue wagging the whole way. "She'd have no such doings in her house, she'd warrant. If gentlemen did spend money freely, it was no rule. She'd have no servant-maids of hers treated in that way, when they were about their work, that's what she wouldn't."

As I hate squabbles, particularly with women, and above all with pretty women, I slunk back into my room, and partly closed the door; but my curiosity was too much excited not to listen. The landlady marched intrepidly to the enemy's citadel, and entered it with a storm: the door closed after her. I heard her voice in high windy clamor for a moment or two. Then it gradually subsided, like a gust of wind in a garret; then there was a laugh; then I heard nothing more.

After a little while my landlady came out with an odd smile on her face, adjusting her cap, which was a little on one side. As she went down-stairs, I heard the landlord ask her what was the matter; she said, "Noth-ing at all, only the girl's a fool."—I was more than ever perplexed what to make of this unaccountable personage, who could put a good-natured chamber-maid in a passion, and send away a termagant landlady in smiles. He could not be so old, nor cross, nor ugly either.

I had to go to work at his picture again, and to paint him entirely different. I now set him down for one of those stout gentlemen that are frequently met with swaggering about the doors of country inns. Moist, merry fellows, in Belcher handkerchiefs, whose bulk is a little assisted by malt-liquors. Men who have seen the world, and been sworn at High-gate; who are used to tavern-life; up to all the tricks of tapsters, and knowing in the ways of sinful publicans. Free-livers on a small scale; who are prodigal within the compass of a guinea; who call all the waiters by name, tousle the maids, gossip with the landlady at the bar, and prose over a pint of port, or a glass of negus, after dinner.

The morning wore away in forming these and similar surmises. As fast as I wove one system of belief, some movement of the unknown would completely overturn it, and throw all my thoughts again into confusion. Such are the solitary operations of a feverish mind. I was, as I have said, extremely nervous; and the continual meditation on the concerns of this invisible personage began to have its effect:—I was getting a fit of the fidgets.

Dinner-time came. I hoped the stout gentleman might dine in the tra-velers'-room, and that I might at length get a view of his person; but no —he had dinner served in his own room. What could be the meaning of this solitude and mystery? He could not be a radical; there was some-thing too aristocratical in thus keeping himself apart from the rest of the world, and condemning himself to his own dull company throughout a rainy day. And then, too, he lived too well for a discontented politician. He seemed to expatiate on a variety of dishes, and to sit over his wine like a jolly friend of good living. Indeed, my doubts on this head were soon at an end; for he could not have finished his first bottle before I could faintly hear him humming a tune; and on listening I found it to be "God save the King." 'Twas plain, then, he was no radical, but a faithful subject; one who grew loyal over his bottle, and was ready to stand by king and constitution, when he could stand by nothing else. But who could he be? My conjectures began to run wild. Was he not some person-age of distinction traveling incog.? "God knows!" said I, at my wit's end; "it may be one of the royal family for aught I know, for they are all stout gentlemen!"

The weather continued rainy. The mysterious unknown kept his room, and, as far as I could judge, his chair, for I did not hear him move. In the meantime, as the day advanced, the travelers'-room began to be fre-quented. Some, who had just arrived, came in buttoned up in box-coats;

others came home who had been dispersed about the town; some took their dinners, and some their tea. Had I been in a different mood, I should have found entertainment in studying this peculiar class of men. There were two especially, who were regular wags of the road, and up to all the standing jokes of travelers. They had a thousand sly things to say to the waiting-maid, whom they called Louisa, and Ethelinda, and a dozen other fine names, changing the name every time, and chuckling amazingly at their own waggery. My mind, however, had been completely engrossed by the stout gentleman. He had kept my fancy in chase during a long day, and it was not now to be diverted from the scent.

The evening gradually wore away. The travelers read the papers two or three times over. Some drew round the fire and told long stories about their horses, about their adventures, their overturns, and breakings-down. They discussed the credit of different merchants and different inns; and the two wags told several choice anecdotes of pretty chamber-maids and kind landladies. All this passed as they were quietly taking what they called their night-caps, that is to say, strong glasses of brandy and water and sugar, or some other mixture of the kind; after which they one after another rang for "Boots" and the chamber-maid, and walked off to bed in old shoes cut down into marvelously uncomfortable slippers.

There was now only one man left: a short-legged, long-bodied, plethoric fellow, with a very large, sandy head. He sat by himself, with a glass of port-wine negus, and a spoon; sipping and stirring, and meditating and sipping, until nothing was left but the spoon. He gradually fell asleep bolt upright in his chair, with the empty glass standing before him; and the candle seemed to fall asleep too, for the wick grew long, and black, and cabbaged at the end, and dimmed the little light that remained in the chamber. The gloom that now prevailed was contagious. Around hung the shapeless, and almost spectral, box-coats of departed travelers, long since buried in deep sleep. I only heard the ticking of the clock, with the deep-drawn breathings of the sleeping topers, and the drippings of the rain, drop—drop—drop, from the eaves of the house. The church-bells chimed midnight. All at once the stout gentleman began to walk overhead, pacing slowly backwards and forwards. There was something extremely awful in all this, especially to one in my state of nerves. These ghastly great-coats, these guttural breathings, and the creaking footsteps of this mysterious being. His steps grew fainter and fainter, and at length died away. I could bear it no longer. I was wound up to the desperation of a hero of romance. "Be he who or what he may," said I to myself, "I'll have a sight of him!" I seized a chamber-candle, and hurried up to No. 13. The door stood ajar. I hesitated—I entered: the room was deserted. There stood a large, broad-bottomed elbow-chair at a table, on which as an empty tumbler, and a "Times," newspaper, and the room smelt powerfully of Stilton cheese.

The mysterious stranger had evidently but just retired. I turned off, sorely disappointed, to my room, which had been changed to the front of the house. As I went along the corridor, I saw a large pair of boots, with dirty, waxed tops, standing at the door of a bedchamber. They doubtless belonged to the unknown; but it would not do to disturb so redoubtable a personage in his den: he might discharge a pistol, or something worse, at my head. I went to bed, therefore, and lay awake half the night in a terribly nervous state; and even when I fell asleep, I was still haunted in my dreams by the idea of the stout gentleman and his wax-topped boots.

I slept rather late the next morning, and was awakened by some stir and bustle in the house, which I could not at first comprehend; until getting more awake, I found there was a mail coach starting from the door. Suddenly there was a cry from below, "The gentleman has forgot his umbrella! Look for the gentleman's umbrella in No. 13!" I heard an immediate scampering of a chamber-maid along the passage, and a shrill reply as she ran, "Here it is! here's the gentleman's umbrella!"

The mysterious stranger then was on the point of setting off. This was the only chance I should ever have of knowing him. I sprang out of bed, scrambled to the window, snatched aside the curtains, and just caught a glimpse of the rear of a person getting in at the coach-door. The skirts of a brown coat parted behind, and gave me a full view of the broad disk of a pair of drab breeches. The door closed—"all right!" was the word—the coach whirled off;—and that was all I ever saw of the stout gentleman!

1822

From *Tales of a Traveller*

Adventure of the German Student

On a stormy night, in the tempestuous times of the French revolution, a young German was returning to his lodgings, at a late hour, across the old part of Paris. The lightning gleamed, and the loud claps of thunder rattled through the lofty narrow streets—but I should first tell you something about this young German.

Gottfried Wolfgang was a young man of good family. He had studied for some time at Göttingen, but being of a visionary and enthusiastic character, he had wandered into those wild and speculative doctrines which have so often bewildered German students. His secluded life, his intense application, and the singular nature of his studies, had an effect on both mind and body. His health was impaired; his imagination diseased. He had been indulging in fanciful speculations on spiritual essences, until, like Swedenborg, he had an ideal world of his own around him. He took up a notion, I do not know from what cause, that there was an evil influence hanging over him; an evil genius or spirit seeking to ensnare him and ensure his perdition. Such an idea working on his melancholy temperament, produced the most gloomy effects. He became haggard and desponding. His friends discovered the mental malady preying upon him, and determined that the best cure was a change of scene; he was sent, therefore, to finish his studies amidst the splendors and gayeties of Paris.

Wolfgang arrived at Paris at the breaking out of the revolution. The popular delirium at first caught his enthusiastic mind, and he was captivated by the political and philosophical theories of the day: but the scenes of blood which followed shocked his sensitive nature, disgusted him with society and the world, and made him more than ever a recluse. He shut himself up in a solitary apartment in the *Pays Latin*, the quarter of students. There, in a gloomy street not far from the monastic walls of the Sorbonne, he pursued his favorite speculations. Sometimes he spent hours together in the great libraries of Paris, those catacombs of departed authors, rummaging among their hoards of dusty and obsolete works in quest of food for his unhealthy appetite. He was, in a manner, a literary ghoul, feeding in the charnel-house of decayed literature.

Wolfgang, though solitary and recluse, was of an ardent temperament, but for a time it operated merely upon his imagination. He was too shy and ignorant of the world to make any advances to the fair, but he was a passionate admirer of female beauty, and in his lonely chamber would often lose himself in reveries on forms and faces which he had seen, and his fancy would deck out images of loveliness far surpassing the reality.

While his mind was in this excited and sublimated state, a dream produced an extraordinary effect upon him. It was of a female face of transcendent beauty. So strong was the impression made, that he dreamt of it again and again. It haunted his thoughts by day, his slumbers by night; in fine, he became passionately enamored of this shadow of a dream. This lasted so long that it became one of those fixed ideas which haunt the minds of melancholy men, and are at times mistaken for madness.

Such was Gottfried Wolfgang, and such his situation at the time I mentioned. He was returning home late one stormy night, through some of the old and gloomy streets of the *Marais*, the ancient part of Paris. The loud claps of thunder rattled among the high houses of the narrow streets. He came to the Place de Grève, the square where public executions are performed. The lightning quivered about the pinnacles of the ancient Hôtel de Ville, and shed flickering gleams over the open space in front. As Wolfgang was crossing the square, he shrank back with horror at finding himself close by the guillotine. It was the height of the reign of terror, when this dreadful instrument of death stood ever ready, and its scaffold was continually running with the blood of the virtuous and the brave. It had that very day been actively employed in the work of carnage, and there it stood in grim array, amidst a silent and sleeping city, waiting for fresh victims.

Wolfgang's heart sickened within him, and he was turning shuddering from the horrible engine, when he beheld a shadowy form, cowering as it were at the foot of the steps which led up to the scaffold. A succession of vivid flashes of lightning revealed it more distinctly. It was a female figure, dressed in black. She was seated on one of the lower steps of the scaffold, leaning forward, her face hid in her lap; and her long disheveled tresses hanging to the ground, streaming with the rain which fell in torrents. Wolfgang paused. There was something awful in this solitary monument of woe. The female had the appearance of being above the common order. He knew the times to be full of vicissitude, and that many a fair head, which had once been pillowed on down, now wandered houseless. Perhaps this was some poor mourner whom the dreadful axe had rendered desolate, and who sat here heart-broken on the strand of existence, from which all that was dear to her had been launched into eternity.

He approached, and addressed her in the accents of sympathy. She raised her head and gazed wildly at him. What was his astonishment at beholding, by the bright glare of the lightning, the very face which had haunted him in his dreams. It was pale and disconsolate, but ravishingly beautiful.

Trembling with violent and conflicting emotions, Wolfgang again accosted her. He spoke something of her being exposed at such an hour of the night, and to the fury of such a storm, and offered to conduct her to her friends. She pointed to the guillotine with a gesture of dreadful signification.

"I have no friend on earth!" said she.

"But you have a home," said Wolfgang.

"Yes—in the grave!"

The heart of the student melted at the words.

"If a stranger dare make an offer," said he, "without danger of being misunderstood, I would offer my humble dwelling as a shelter; myself as a devoted friend. I am friendless myself in Paris, and a stranger in the land; but if my life could be of service, it is at your disposal, and should be sacrificed before harm or indignity should come to you."

There was an honest earnestness in the young man's manner that had its effect. His foreign accent, too, was in his favor; it showed him not to be a hackneyed inhabitant of Paris. Indeed, there is an eloquence in true enthusiasm that is not to be doubted. The homeless stranger confided herself implicity to the protection of the student.

He supported her faltering steps across the Pont Neuf, and by the place where the statue of Henry the Fourth had been overthrown by the populace. The storm had abated, and the thunder rumbled at a distance. All Paris was quiet; that great volcano of human passion slumbered for a while, to gather fresh strength for the next day's eruption. The student conducted his charge through the ancient streets of the *Pays Latin,* and by the dusky walls of the Sorbonne, to the great dingy hotel which he inhabited. The old portress who admitted them stared with surprise at the unusual sight of the melancholy Wolfgang with a female companion. On entering his apartment, the student, for the first time, blushed at the scantiness and indifference of his dwelling. He had but one chamber —an old-fashioned saloon—heavily carved, and fantastically furnished with the remains of former magnificence, for it was one of those hotels in the quarter of the Luxembourg palace, which had once belonged to nobility. It was lumbered with books and papers, and all the usual apparatus of a student, and his bed stood in a recess at one end.

When lights were brought, and Wolfgang had a better opportunity of contemplating the stranger, he was more than ever intoxicated by her beauty. Her face was pale, but of a dazzling fairness, set off by a profusion of raven hair that hung clustering about it. Her eyes were large and brilliant, with a singular expression approaching almost to wildness. As far as her black dress permitted her shape to be seen, it was of perfect symmetry. Her whole appearance was highly striking, though she was dressed in the simplest style. The only thing approaching to an ornament which she wore, was a broad black band round her neck, clasped by diamonds.

The perplexity now commenced with the student how to dispose of the helpless being thus thrown upon his protection. He thought of abandoning his chamber to her, and seeking shelter for himself elsewhere. Still he was so fascinated by her charms, there seemed to be such a spell upon his thoughts and senses, that he could not tear himself from her presence. Her manner, too, was singular and unaccountable. She spoke no more of the guillotine. Her grief had abated. The attentions of the student had first won her confidence, and then, apparently, her heart. She was evidently an enthusiast like himself, and enthusiasts soon understand each other.

In the infatuation of the moment, Wolfgang avowed his passion for her. He told her the story of his mysterious dream, and how she had possessed his heart before he had even seen her. She was strangely affected by his recital, and acknowledged to have felt an impulse towards him equally unaccountable. It was the time for wild theory and wild actions. Old prejudices and superstitions were done away; everything was under the sway of the "Goddess of Reason." Among other rubbish of the old times, the forms and ceremonies of marriage began to be considered superfluous bonds for honorable minds. Social compacts were the vogue. Wolfgang was too much of a theorist not to be tainted by the liberal doctrines of the day.

"Why should we separate?" said he: "our hearts are united; in the eye of reason and honor we are as one. What need is there of sordid forms to bind high souls together?"

The stranger listened with emotion: she had evidently received illumination at the same school.

"You have no home nor family," continued he; "let me be everything to you, or rather let us be everything to one another. If form is necessary, form shall be observed—there is my hand. I pledge myself to you forever."

"Forever?" said the stranger, solemnly.

"Forever!" repeated Wolfgang.

The stranger clasped the hand extended to her: "Then I am yours," murmured she, and sank upon his bosom.

The next morning the student left his bride sleeping, and sallied forth at an early hour to seek more spacious apartments suitable to the change in his situation. When he returned, he found the stranger lying with her head hanging over the bed, and one arm thrown over it. He spoke to her, but received no reply. He advanced to awaken her from her uneasy posture. On taking her hand, it was cold—there was no pulsation—her face was pallid and ghastly. In a word, she was a corpse.

Horrified and frantic, he alarmed the house. A scene of confusion ensued. The police was summoned. As the officer of police entered the room, he started back on beholding the corpse.

"Great heaven!" cried he, "how did this woman come here?"

"Do you know anything about her?" said Wolfgang eagerly.

"Do I?" exclaimed the officer: "she was guillotined yesterday."

He stepped forward; undid the black collar round the neck of the corpse, and the head rolled on the floor!

The student burst into a frenzy. "The fiend! the fiend has gained possession of me!" shrieked he: "I am lost forever."

They tried to soothe him, but in vain. He was possessed with the frightful belief that an evil spirit had reanimated the dead body to ensnare him. He went distracted, and died in a mad-house.

Here the old gentleman with the haunted head finished his narrative.

"And is this really a fact?" said the inquisitive gentleman.

"A fact not to be doubted," replied the other. "I had it from the best authority. The student told it me himself. I saw him in a mad-house in Paris."

1824

From *The Alhambra*

Legend of the Rose of the Alhambra

For some time after the surrender of Granada by the Moors, that delightful city was a frequent and favorite residence of the Spanish sovereigns, until they were frightened away by successive shocks of earthquakes, which toppled down various houses, and made the old Moslem towers rock to their foundation.

Many, many years then rolled away, during which Granada was rarely honored by a royal guest. The palaces of the nobility remained silent and shut up; and the Alhambra, like a slighted beauty, sat in mournful desolation among her neglected gardens. The tower of the Infantas, once the residence of the three beautiful Moorish princesses, partook of the general desolation; the spider spun her web athwart the gilded vault, and bats and owls nestled in those chambers that had been graced by the presence of Zayda, Zorayda, and Zorahayda. The neglect of this tower may have been partly owing to some superstitious notions of the neighbors. It was rumored that the spirit of the youthful Zorahayda, who had perished in that tower, was often seen by moonlight seated beside the fountain in the hall, or moaning about the battlements, and that the notes of her silver lute would be heard at midnight by wayfarers passing along the glen.

At length the city of Granada was once more welcomed by the royal presence. All the world knows that Philip V was the first Bourbon that swayed the Spanish scepter. All the world knows that he married, in second nuptials, Elizabetta or Isabella (for they are the same), the beautiful princess of Parma; and all the world knows that by this chain of contingencies a French prince and an Italian princess were seated together on the Spanish throne. For a visit of this illustrious pair, the Alhambra was repaired and fitted up with all possible expedition. The arrival of the court changed the whole aspect of the lately deserted palace. The clangor of drum and trumpet, the tramp of steed about the avenues and outer court, the glitter of arms and display of banners about barbican and battlement, recalled the ancient and warlike glories of the fortress. A softer spirit, however, reigned within the royal palace. There was the rustling of robes and the cautious tread and murmuring voice of reverential courtiers about the antechambers; a loitering of pages and maids of honor about the gardens, and the sound of music stealing from open casements.

Among those who attended in the train of the monarchs was a favorite page of the queen, named Ruyz de Alarcon. To say that he was a favorite page of the queen was at once to speak his eulogium, for everyone in the suite of the stately Elizabetta was chosen for grace, and beauty, and accomplishments. He was just turned of eighteen, light and lithe of form, and graceful as a young Antinous. To the queen he was all deference and respect, yet he was at heart a roguish stripling, petted and spoiled by the ladies about the court, and experienced in the ways of women far beyond his years.

This loitering page was one morning rambling about the groves of the Generalife, which overlook the grounds of the Alhambra. He had taken with him for his amusement a favorite ger-falcon of the queen. In the course of his rambles, seeing a bird rising from a thicket, he unhooded the hawk and let him fly. The falcon towered high in the air, made a swoop at his quarry, but missing it, soared away, regardless of the calls of the page. The latter followed the truant bird with his eye, in its capricious flight, until he saw it alight upon the battlements of a remote and lonely tower, in the outer wall of the Alhambra, built on the edge of a ravine that separated the royal fortress from the grounds of the General-ife. It was in fact the "Tower of the Princesses."

The page descended into the ravine and approached the tower, but it had no entrance from the glen, and its lofty height rendered any attempt to scale it fruitless. Seeking one of the gates of the fortress, therefore, he made a wide circuit to that side of the tower facing within the walls.

A small garden, enclosed by a trellis-work of reeds overhung with myrtle, lay before the tower. Opening a wicket, the page passed between beds of flowers and thickets of roses to the door. It was closed and bolted. A crevice in the door gave him a peep into the interior. There was a small Moorish hall with fretted walls, light marble columns, and an alabaster fountain surrounded with flowers. In the center hung a gilt cage containing a singing-bird; beneath it, on a chair, lay a tortoise-shell cat among reels of silk and other articles of female labor, and a guitar decorated with ribbons leaned against the fountain.

Ruyz de Alarcon was struck with these traces of female taste and elegance in a lonely, and, as he had supposed, deserted tower. They reminded him of the tales of enchanted halls current in the Alhambra; and the tortoise-shell cat might be some spellbound princess.

He knocked gently at the door. A beautiful face peeped out from a little window above, but was instantly withdrawn. He waited, expecting that the door would be opened, but he waited in vain; no footstep was to be heard within—all was silent. Had his senses deceived him, or was this beautiful apparition the fairy of the tower? He knocked again, and more loudly. After a little while the beaming face once more peeped forth; it was that of a blooming damsel of fifteen.

The page immediately doffed his plumed bonnet, and entreated in the most courteous accents to be permitted to ascend the tower in pursuit of his falcon.

"I dare not open the door, Señor," replied the little damsel, blushing, "my aunt has forbidden it."

"I do beseech you, fair maid—it is the favorite falcon of the queen: I dare not return to the palace without it."

"Are you then one of the cavaliers of the court?"

"I am, fair maid; but I shall lose the queen's favor and my place, if I lose this hawk."

"Santa Maria! It is against you cavaliers of the court my aunt has charged me especially to bar the door."

"Against wicked cavaliers doubtless, but I am none of these, but a simple, harmless page, who will be ruined and undone if you deny me this small request."

The heart of the little damsel was touched by the distress of the page. It was a thousand pities he should be ruined for the want of so trifling a boon. Surely too he could not be one of those dangerous beings whom her aunt had described as a species of cannibal, ever on the prowl to make prey of thoughtless damsels; he was gentle and modest, and stood so entreatingly with cap in hand, and looked so charming.

The sly page saw that the garrison began to waver, and redoubled his entreaties in such moving terms that it was not in the nature of mortal maiden to deny him; so the blushing little warden of the tower descended, and opened the door with a trembling hand, and if the page had been charmed by a mere glimpse of her countenance from the window, he was ravished by the full-length portrait now revealed to him.

Her Andalusian bodice and trim basquiña set off the round but delicate symmetry of her form, which was as yet scarce verging into womanhood. Her glossy hair was parted on her forehead with scrupulous exactness, and decorated with a fresh plucked rose, according to the universal custom of the country. It is true her complexion was tinged by the ardor of a southern sun, but it served to give richness to the mantling bloom of her cheek, and to heighten the lustre of her melting eyes.

Ruyz de Alarcon beheld all this with a single glance, for it became him not to tarry; he merely murmured his acknowledgments, and then bounded lightly up the spiral staircase in quest of his falcon.

He soon returned with the truant bird upon his fist. The damsel, in the meantime, had seated herself by the fountain in the hall, and was winding silk; but in her agitation she let fall the reel upon the pavement. The page sprang and picked it up, then dropping gracefully on one knee, presented it to her; but, seizing the hand extended to receive it, imprinted on it a kiss more fervent and devout than he had ever imprinted on the fair hand of his sovereign.

"Ave Maria, Señor!" exclaimed the damsel, blushing still deeper with confusion and surprise, for never before had she received such a salutation.

The modest page made a thousand apologies, assuring her it was the way at court of expressing the most profound homage and respect.

Her anger, if anger she felt, was easily pacified, but her agitation and embarrassment continued, and she sat blushing deeper and deeper, with her eyes cast down upon her work, entangling the silk which she attempted to wind.

The cunning page saw the confusion in the opposite camp, and would fain have profited by it, but the fine speeches he would have uttered died upon his lips; his attempts at gallantry were awkward and ineffectual; and to his surprise, the adroit page, who had figured with such grace and effrontery among the most knowing and experienced ladies of the court, found himself awed and abashed in the presence of a simple damsel of fifteen.

In fact, the artless maiden, in her own modesty and innocence, had guardians more effectual than the bolts and bars prescribed by her vigilant aunt. Still, where is the female bosom proof against the first whisperings of love? The little damsel, with all her artlessness, instinctively comprehended all that the faltering tongue of the page failed to express, and her heart was fluttered at beholding, for the first time, a lover at her feet—and such a lover!

The diffidence of the page, though genuine, was short-lived, and he was recovering his usual ease and confidence, when a shrill voice was heard at a distance.

"My aunt is returning from mass!" cried the damsel in affright: "I pray you, Señor, depart."

"Not until you grant me that rose from your hair as a remembrance."

She hastily untwisted the rose from her raven locks. "Take it," cried she, agitated and blushing, "but pray begone."

The page took the rose, and at the same time covered with kisses the fair hand that gave it. Then, placing the flower in his bonnet, and taking the falcon upon his fist, he bounded off through the garden, bearing away with him the heart of the gentle Jacinta.

When the vigilant aunt arrived at the tower, she remarked the agitation of her niece, and an air of confusion in the hall; but a word of explanation sufficed. "A ger-falcon had pursued his prey into the hall."

"Mercy on us! to think of a falcon flying into the tower. Did ever one hear of so saucy a hawk? Why, the very bird in the cage is not safe!"

The vigilant Fredegonda was one of the most wary of ancient spinsters. She had a becoming terror and distrust of what she denominated "the opposite sex," which had gradually increased through a long life of celibacy. Not that the good lady had ever suffered from their wiles, nature having set up a safeguard in her face that forbade all trespass upon her premises; but ladies who have least cause to fear for themselves are most ready to keep a watch over their more tempting neighbors.

The niece was the orphan of an officer who had fallen in the wars. She had been educated in a convent, and had recently been transferred from her sacred asylum to the immediate guardianship of her aunt, under whose overshadowing care she vegetated in obscurity, like an opening rose blooming beneath a brier. Nor indeed is this comparison entirely accidental; for, to tell the truth, her fresh and dawning beauty had caught the public eye, even in her seclusion, and, with that poetical turn common to the people of Andalusia, the peasantry of the neighborhood had given her the appellation of "the Rose of the Alhambra."

The wary aunt continued to keep a faithful watch over her tempting little niece as long as the court continued at Granada, and flattered herself that her vigilance had been successful. It is true the good lady was now and then discomposed by the tinkling of guitars and chanting of love-ditties from the moonlit groves beneath the tower; but she would exhort her niece to shut her ears against such idle minstrelsy, assuring her that it was one of the arts of the opposite sex, by which simple maids were often lured to their undoing. Alas! what chance with a simple maid has a dry lecture against a moonlight serenade?

At length King Philip cut short his sojourn at Granada, and suddenly departed with all his train. The vigilant Fredegonda watched the royal pageant as it issued forth from the Gate of Justice, and descended the great avenue leading to the city. When the last banner disappeared from her sight, she returned exulting to her tower, for all her cares were over. To her surprise, a light Arabian steed pawed the ground at the wicket-gate of the garden;—to her horror she saw through the thickets of roses a youth in gayly embroidered dress, at the feet of her niece. At the sound of her footsteps he gave a tender adieu, bounded lightly over the barrier of reeds and myrtles, sprang upon his horse, and was out of sight in an instant.

The tender Jacinta, in the agony of her grief, lost all thought of her aunt's displeasure. Throwing herself into her arms, she broke forth into sobs and tears.

"Ay de mi!" cried she; "he's gone!—he's gone!—he's gone! and I shall never see him more!"

"Gone!—who is gone?—what youth is that I saw at your feet?"

"A queen's page, aunt, who came to bid me farewell."

"A queen's page, child!" echoed the vigilant Fredegonda, faintly, "and when did you become acquainted with the queen's page?"

"The morning that the ger-falcon came into the tower. It was the queen's ger-falcon, and he came in pursuit of it."

"Ah silly, silly girl! know that there are no ger-falcons half so dangerous as these young prankling pages, and it is precisely such simple birds as thee that they pounce upon."

The aunt was at first indignant at learning that in despite of her boasted vigilance, a tender intercourse had been carried on by the youthful lovers, almost beneath her eye; but when she found that her simple-hearted niece, though thus exposed, without the protection of bolt or bar, to all the machinations of the opposite sex, had come forth unsinged from the fiery ordeal, she consoled herself with the persuasion that it was owing to the chaste and cautious maxims in which she had, as it were, steeped her to the very lips.

While the aunt laid this soothing unction to her pride, the niece treasured up the oft-repeated vows of fidelity of the page. But what is the love of restless, roving man? A vagrant stream that dallies for a time with each flower upon its bank, then passes on, and leaves them all in tears.

Days, weeks, months elapsed, and nothing more was heard of the page. The pomegranate ripened, the vine yielded up its fruit, the autumnal rains descended in torrents from the mountains; the Sierra Nevada became covered with a snowy mantle, and wintry blasts howled through the halls of the Alhambra—still he came not. The winter passed away.

Again the genial spring burst forth with song and blossom and balmy zephyr; the snows melted from the mountains, until none remained but on the lofty summit of Nevada, glistening through the sultry summer air. Still nothing was heard of the forgetful page.

In the meantime the poor little Jacinta grew pale and thoughtful. Her former occupations and amusements were abandoned, her silk lay entangled, her guitar unstrung, her flowers were neglected, the notes of her bird unheeded, and her eyes, once so bright, were dimmed with secret weeping. If any solitude could be devised to foster the passion of a lovelorn damsel, it would be such a place as the Alhambra, where everything seems disposed to produce tender and romantic reveries. It is a very paradise for lovers: how hard then to be alone in such a paradise—and not merely alone, but forsaken!

"Alas, silly child!" would the staid and immaculate Fredegonda say, when she found her niece in one of her desponding moods—"did I not warn thee against the wiles and deceptions of these men? What couldst thou expect, too, from one of a haughty and aspiring family—thou an orphan, the descendant of a fallen and impoverished line? Be assured, if the youth were true, his father, who is one of the proudest nobles about the court, would prohibit his union with one so humble and portionless as thou. Pluck up thy resolution, therefore, and drive these idle notions from thy mind."

The words of the immaculate Fredegonda only served to increase the melancholy of her niece, but she sought to indulge it in private. At a late hour one midsummer night, after her aunt had retired to rest, she remained alone in the hall of the tower, seated beside the alabaster fountain. It was here that the faithless page had first knelt and kissed her hand; it was here that he had often vowed eternal fidelity. The poor little damsel's heart was overladen with sad and tender recollections, her tears began to flow, and slowly fell drop by drop into the fountain. By degrees the crystal water became agitated, and—bubble—bubble—bubble—boiled up and was tossed about, until a female figure, richly clad in Moorish robes, slowly rose to view.

Jacinta was so frightened that she fled from the hall, and did not venture to return. The next morning she related what she had seen to her aunt, but the good lady treated it as a fantasy of her troubled mind, or supposed she had fallen asleep and dreamt beside the fountain. "Thou hast been thinking of the story of the three Moorish princesses that once inhabited this tower," continued she, "and it has entered into thy dreams."

"What story, aunt? I know nothing of it."

"Thou hast certainly heard of the three princesses, Zayda, Zorayda, and Zorahayda, who were confined in this tower by the king their father, and agreed to fly with three Christian cavaliers. The two first accomplished their escape, but the third failed in her resolution, and, it is said, died in this tower."

"I now recollect to have heard of it," said Jacinta, "and to have wept over the fate of the gentle Zorahayda."

"Thou mayest well weep over her fate," continued the aunt, "for the lover of Zorahayda was thy ancestor. He long bemoaned his Moorish love; but time cured him of his grief, and he married a Spanish lady, from whom thou art descended."

Jacinta ruminated upon these words. "That what I have seen is no fantasy of the brain," said she to herself, "I am confident. If indeed it be the spirit of the gentle Zorahayda, which I have heard lingers about this tower, of what should I be afraid? I'll watch by the fountain tonight— perhaps the visit will be repeated."

Towards midnight, when everything was quiet, she again took her seat in the hall. As the bell in the distant watch-tower of the Alhambra struck the midnight hour, the fountain was again agitated; and bubble—bubble —bubble—it tossed about the waters until the Moorish female again rose to view. She was young and beautiful; her dress was rich with jewels, and in her hand she held a silver lute. Jacinta trembled and was faint, but was reassured by the soft and plaintive voice of the apparition, and the sweet expression of her pale, melancholy countenance.

"Daughter of mortality," said she, "what aileth thee? Why do thy tears trouble my fountain, and thy sighs and plaints disturb the quiet watches of the night?"

"I weep because of the faithlessness of man, and I bemoan my solitary and forsaken state."

"Take comfort; thy sorrows may yet have an end. Thou beholdest a Moorish princess, who, like thee, was unhappy in her love. A Christian knight, thy ancestor, won my heart, and would have borne me to his native land and to the bosom of his church. I was a convert in my heart, but I lacked courage equal to my faith, and lingered till too late. For this the evil genii are permitted to have power over me, and I remain enchanted in this tower until some pure Christian will deign to break the magic spell. Wilt thou undertake the task?"

"I will," replied the damsel, trembling.

"Come hither then, and fear not; dip thy hand in the fountain, sprinkle the water over me, and baptize me after the manner of thy faith; so shall the enchantment be dispelled, and my troubled spirit have repose."

The damsel advanced with faltering steps, dipped her hand in the fountain, collected water in the palm, and sprinkled it over the pale face of the phantom.

The latter smiled with ineffable benignity. She dropped her silver lute at the feet of Jacinta, crossed her white arms upon her bosom, and melted from sight, so that it seemed merely as if a shower of dew-drops had fallen into the fountain.

Jacinta retired from the hall filled with awe and wonder. She scarcely closed her eyes that night; but when she awoke at daybreak out of a troubled slumber, the whole appeared to her like a distempered dream. On descending into the hall, however, the truth of the vision was established, for beside the fountain she beheld the silver lute glittering in the morning sunshine.

She hastened to her aunt, to relate all that had befallen her, and called her to behold the lute as a testimonial of the reality of her story. If the good lady had any lingering doubts, they were removed when Jacinta touched the instrument, for she drew forth such ravishing tones as to thaw even the frigid bosom of the immaculate Fredegonda, that region of eternal winter, into a genial flow. Nothing but supernatural melody could have produced such an effect.

The extraordinary power of the lute became every day more and more apparent. The wayfarer passing by the tower was detained, and, as it were, spell-bound, in breathless ecstasy. The very birds gathered in the neighboring trees, and hushing their own strains, listened in charmed silence.

Rumor soon spread the news abroad. The inhabitants of Granada thronged to the Alhambra to catch a few notes of the transcendent music that floated about the tower of Las Infantas.

The lovely little minstrel was at length drawn forth from her retreat. The rich and powerful of the land contended who should entertain and do honor to her; or rather, who should secure the charms of her lute to draw fashionable throngs to their saloons. Wherever she went her vigilant aunt kept a dragon watch at her elbow, awing the throngs of impassioned admirers who hung in raptures on her strains. The report of her wonderful powers spread from city to city. Malaga, Seville, Cordova, all became successively mad on the theme; nothing was talked of throughout Andalusia but the beautiful minstrel of the Alhambra. How could it be otherwise among a people so musical and gallant as the Andalusians, when the lute was magical in its powers, and the minstrel inspired by love!

While all Andalusia was thus music mad, a different mood prevailed at the court of Spain. Philip V, as is well known, was a miserable hypochondriac, and subject to all kinds of fancies. Sometimes he would keep to his bed for weeks together, groaning under imaginary complaints. At other times he would insist upon abdicating his throne, to the great annoyance of his royal spouse, who had a strong relish for the splendors of a court and the glories of a crown, and guided the scepter of her imbecile lord with an expert and steady hand.

Nothing was found to be so efficacious in dispelling the royal megrims as the power of music; the queen took care, therefore, to have the best performers, both vocal and instrumental, at hand, and retained the famous Italian singer Farinelli about the court as a kind of royal physician.

At the moment we treat of, however, a freak had come over the mind of this sapient and illustrious Bourbon that surpassed all former vagaries.

After a long spell of imaginary illness, which set all the strains of Farinelli and the consultations of a whole orchestra of court-fiddlers at defiance, the monarch fairly, in idea, gave up the ghost, and considered himself absolutely dead.

This would have been harmless enough, and even convenient both to his queen and courtiers, had he been content to remain in the quietude befitting a dead man; but to their annoyance he insisted upon having the funeral ceremonies performed over him, and, to their inexpressible perplexity, began to grow impatient, and to revile bitterly at them for negligence and disrespect, in leaving him unburied. What was to be done? To disobey the king's positive commands was monstrous in the eyes of the obsequious courtiers of a punctilious court—but to obey him, and bury him alive would be downright regicide!

In the midst of this fearful dilemma a rumor reached the court of the female minstrel who was turning the brains of all Andalusia. The queen dispatched missions in all haste to summon her to St. Ildefonso, where the court at that time resided.

Within a few days, as the queen with her maids of honor was walking in those stately gardens, intended, with their avenues and terraces and fountains, to eclipse the glories of Versailles, the far famed minstrel was conducted into her presence. The imperial Elizabetta gazed with surprise at the youthful and unpretending appearance of the little being that had set the world madding. She was in her picturesque Andalusian dress, her silver lute in hand, and stood with modest and downcast eyes, but with a simplicity and freshness of beauty that still bespoke her "the Rose of the Alhambra."

As usual she was accompanied by the ever-vigilant Fredegonda, who gave the whole history of her parentage and descent to the inquiring queen. If the stately Elizabetta had been interested by the appearance of Jacinta, she was still more pleased when she learnt that she was of a meritorious though impoverished line, and that her father had bravely fallen in the service of the crown. "If thy powers equal their renown," said she, "and thou canst cast forth this evil spirit that possesses thy sovereign, thy fortunes shall henceforth be my care, and honors and wealth attend thee."

Impatient to make trial of her skill, she led the way at once to the apartment of the moody monarch.

Jacinta followed with downcast eyes through files of guards and crowds of courtiers. They arrived at length at a great chamber hung with black. The windows were closed to exclude the light of day: a number of yellow wax tapers in silver sconces diffused a lugubrious light, and dimly revealed the figures of mutes in mourning dresses, and courtiers who glided about with noiseless step and woe-begone visage. In the midst of a funeral bed or bier, his hands folded on his breast, and the tip of his nose just visible, lay extended this would-be-buried monarch.

The queen entered the chamber in silence, and pointing to a footstool in an obscure corner, beckoned to Jacinta to sit down and commence.

At first she touched her lute with a faltering hand, but gathering confidence and animation as she proceeded, drew forth such soft aërial harmony, that all present could scarce believe it mortal. As to the monarch, who had already considered himself in the world of spirits, he set it down for some angelic melody or the music of the spheres. By degrees the theme was varied, and the voice of the minstrel accompanied the instrument. She poured forth one of the legendary ballads treating of the ancient glories of the Alhambra and the achievements of the Moors. Her whole soul entered into the theme, for with the recollections of the Alhambra was associated the story of her love. The funeral-chamber resounded with the animating strain. It entered into the gloomy heart of the monarch. He raised his head and gazed around: he sat up on his couch, his eye began to kindle—at length, leaping upon the floor, he called for sword and buckler.

The triumph of music, or rather of the enchanted lute, was complete; the demon of melancholy was cast forth; and, as it were, a dead man brought to life. The windows of the apartment were thrown open; the glorious effulgence of Spanish sunshine burst into the late lugubrious chamber; all eyes sought the lovely enchantress, but the lute had fallen from her hand, she had sunk upon the earth, and the next moment was clasped to the bosom of Ruyz de Alarcon.

The nuptials of the happy couple were celebrated soon afterwards with great splendor, and the Rose of the Alhambra became the ornament and delight of the court. "But hold—not so fast"—I hear the reader exclaim; "this is jumping to the end of a story at a furious rate! First let us know how Ruyz de Alarcon managed to account to Jacinta for his long neglect?" Nothing more easy; the venerable, time-honored excuse, the opposition to his wishes by a proud, pragmatical old father: besides, young people who really like one another soon come to an amicable understanding, and bury all past grievances when once they meet.

But how was the proud, pragmatical old father reconciled to the match?

Oh! as to that, his scruples were easily overcome by a word or two from the queen; especially as dignities and rewards were showered upon the blooming favorite of royalty. Besides, the lute of Jacinta, you know, possessed a magic power, and could control the most stubborn head and hardest breast.

And what came of the enchanted lute?

Oh, that is the most curious matter of all, and plainly proves the truth of the whole story. That lute remained for some time in the family, but was purloined and carried off, as was supposed, by the great singer Farinelli, in pure jealousy. At his death it passed into other hands in Italy, who were ignorant of its mystic powers, and melting down the silver, transferred the strings to an old Cremona fiddle. The strings still retain something of their magic virtues. A word in the reader's ear, but let it go no further: that fiddle is now bewitching the whole world,—it is the fiddle of Paganini!   1832

From *The Crayon Miscellany*

From A Tour on the Prairies

CHAPTER XX

THE CAMP OF THE WILD HORSE

Hunters' Stories.—Habits of the Wild Horse.—The Half-Breed and His Prize.—A Horse Chase.—A Wild Spirit Tamed.

We had encamped in a good neighborhood for game, as the reports of rifles in various directions speedily gave notice. One of our hunters soon returned with the meat of a doe, tied up in the skin, and slung across his shoulders. Another brought a fat buck across his horse. Two other deer were brought in, and a number of turkeys. All the game was thrown down in front of the Captain's fire, to be portioned out among the various messes. The spits and camp-kettles were soon in full employ, and throughout the evening there was a scene of hunters' feasting and profusion.

We had been disappointed this day in our hopes of meeting with buffalo, but the sight of the wild horse had been a great novelty, and gave a turn to the conversation of the camp for the evening. There were several anecdotes told of a famous gray horse, which has ranged the prairies of this neighborhood for six or seven years, setting at naught every attempt of the hunters to capture him. They say he can pace and rack (or amble) faster than the fleetest horses can run. Equally marvelous accounts were given of a black horse on the Brassos, who grazed the prairies on that river's banks in the Texas. For years he outstripped all pursuit. His fame spread far and wide; offers were made for him to the amount of a thousand dollars; the boldest and most hard-riding hunters tried incessantly to make prize of him, but in vain. At length he fell a victim to his gallantry, being decoyed under a tree by a tame mare, and a noose dropped over his head by a boy perched among the branches.

The capture of the wild horse is one of the most favorite achievements of the prairie tribes; and, indeed, it is from this source that the Indian hunters chiefly supply themselves. The wild horses which range those vast grassy plains, extending from the Arkansas to the Spanish settlements, are of various forms and colors, betraying their various descents. Some resemble the common English stock, and are probably descended from horses which have escaped from our border settlements. Others are of a low but strong make, and are supposed to be of the Andalusian breed, brought out by the Spanish discoverers.

Some fanciful speculatists have seen in them descendants of the Arab stock, brought into Spain from Africa, and thence transferred to this country; and have pleased themselves with the idea that their sires may have been of the pure coursers of the desert, that once bore Mahomet and his warlike disciples across the sandy plains of Arabia.

The habits of the Arab seem to have come with the steed. The introduction of the horse on the boundless prairies of the Far West changed the whole mode of living of their inhabitants. It gave them that facility of rapid motion, and of sudden and distant change of place, so dear to the roving propensities of man. Instead of lurking in the depths of gloomy forests, and patiently threading the mazes of a tangled wilderness on foot, like his brethren of the north, the Indian of the West is a rover of the plain; he leads a brighter and more sunshiny life; almost always on horseback, on vast flowery prairies and under cloudless skies.

I was lying by the Captain's fire, late in the evening, listening to stories about those coursers of the prairies, and weaving speculations of my own, when there was a clamor of voices and a loud cheering at the other end of the camp; and word was passed that Beatte, the half-breed, had brought in a wild horse.

In an instant every fire was deserted; the whole camp crowded to see the Indian and his prize. It was a colt about two years old, well grown, finely limbed, with bright prominent eyes, and a spirited yet gentle demeanor. He gazed about him with an air of mingled stupefaction and surprise, at the men, the horses, and the camp-fires; while the Indian stood before him with folded arms, having hold of the other end of the cord which noosed his captive, and gazing on him with a most imperturbable aspect. Beatte, as I have before observed, has a greenish olive complexion, with a strongly marked countenance, not unlike the bronze casts of Napoleon; and as he stood before his captive horse, with folded arms and fixed aspect, he looked more like a statue than a man.

If the horse, however, manifested the least restiveness, Beatte would immediately worry him with the lariat, jerking him first on one side, then on the other, so as almost to throw him on the ground; when he had thus rendered him passive, he would resume his statue-like attitude, and gaze at him in silence.

The whole scene was singularly wild: the tall grove, partially illumined by the flashing fires of the camp, the horses tethered here and there among the trees, the carcasses of deer hanging around, and, in the midst of all, the wild huntsman and his wild horse, with an admiring throng of rangers almost as wild.

In the eagerness of their excitement, several of the young rangers sought to get the horse by purchase or barter, and even offered extravagant terms; but Beatte declined all their offers. "You give great price now," said he; "tomorrow you be sorry, and take back, and say d—d Indian!"

The young men importuned him with questions about the mode in which he took the horse, but his answers were dry and laconic; he evidently retained some pique at having been undervalued and sneered at by them; and at the same time looked down upon them with contempt as greenhorns little versed in the noble science of woodcraft.

Afterwards, however, when he was seated by our fire, I readily drew from him an account of his exploit; for, though taciturn among strangers, and little prone to boast of his actions, yet his taciturnity, like that of all Indians, had its times of relaxation.

He informed me, that on leaving the camp he had returned to the place where we had lost sight of the wild horse. Soon getting upon its track, he followed it to the banks of the river. Here, the prints being more distinct in the sand, he perceived that one of the hoofs was broken and defective, so he gave up the pursuit.

As he was returning to the camp, he came upon a gang of six horses, which immediately made for the river. He pursued them across the stream, left his rifle on the river-bank, and putting his horse to full speed, soon came up with the fugitives. He attempted to noose one of them, but the lariat hitched on one of his ears, and he shook it off. The horses dashed up a hill, he followed hard at their heels, when, of a sudden, he saw their tails whisking in the air, and they plunging down a precipice. It was too late to stop. He shut his eyes, held in his breath, and went over with them—neck or nothing. The descent was between twenty and thirty feet, but they all came down safe upon a sandy bottom.

He now succeeded in throwing his noose round a fine young horse. As he galloped alongside of him, the two horses passed each side of a sapling, and the end of the lariat was jerked out of his hand. He regained it, but an intervening tree obliged him again to let it go. Having once more caught it, and coming to a more open country, he was enabled to play the young horse with the line until he gradually checked and subdued him, so as to lead him to the place where he had left his rifle.

He had another formidable difficulty in getting him across the river, where both horses stuck for a time in the mire, and Beatte was nearly unseated from his saddle by the force of the current and the struggles of his captive. After much toil and trouble, however, he got across the stream, and brought his prize safe into camp.

For the remainder of the evening the camp remained in a high state of excitement; nothing was talked of but the capture of wild horses; every youngster of the troop was for this harum-scarum kind of chase; everyone promised himself to return from the campaign in triumph, bestriding one of these wild coursers of the prairies. Beatte had suddenly risen to great importance; he was the prime hunter, the hero of the day. Offers were made him by the best-mounted rangers, to let him ride their horses in the chase, provided he would give them a share of the spoil. Beatte bore his honors in silence, and closed with none of the offers. Our stammering, chattering, gasconading little Frenchman, however, made up for his taciturnity by vaunting as much upon the subject as if it were he that had caught the horse. Indeed he held forth so learnedly in the matter, and boasted so much of the many horses he had taken, that he began to be considered an oracle; and some of the youngsters were inclined to doubt whether he were not superior even to the taciturn Beatte.

The excitement kept the camp awake later than usual. The hum of voices, interrupted by occasional peals of laughter, was heard from the groups around the various fires, and the night was considerably advanced before all had sunk to sleep.

With the morning dawn the excitement revived, and Beatte and his wild horse were again the gaze and talk of the camp. The captive had been tied all night to a tree among the other horses. He was again led forth by Beatte, by a long halter or lariat, and, on his manifesting the least restiveness, was, as before, jerked and worried into passive submission. He appeared to be gentle and docile by nature, and had a beautifully mild expression of the eye. In his strange and forlorn situation, the poor animal seemed to seek protection and companionship in the very horse which had aided to capture him.

Seeing him thus gentle and tractable, Beatte, just as we were about to march, strapped a light pack upon his back, by way of giving him the first lesson in servitude. The native pride and independence of the animal took fire at this indignity. He reared, and plunged, and kicked, and tried in every way to get rid of the degrading burden. The Indian was too potent for him. At every paroxysm he renewed the discipline of the halter, until the poor animal, driven to despair, threw himself prostrate on the ground, and lay motionless, as if acknowledging himself vanquished. A stage hero, representing the despair of a captive prince, could not have played his part more dramatically. There was absolutely a moral grandeur in it.

The imperturbable Beatte folded his arms, and stood for a time, looking down in silence upon his captive; until seeing him perfectly subdued, he nodded his head slowly, screwed his mouth into a sardonic smile of triumph, and, with a jerk of the halter, ordered him to rise. He obeyed, and from that time forward offered no resistance. During that day he bore his pack patiently, and was led by the halter; but in two days he followed voluntarily at large among the supernumerary horses of the troop.

I could not but look with compassion upon this fine young animal, whose whole course of existence had been so suddenly reversed. From being a denizen of these vast pastures, ranging at will from plain to plain and mead to mead, cropping of every herb and flower, and drinking of every stream, he was suddenly reduced to perpetual and painful servitude, to pass his life under the harness and the curb, amid, perhaps, the din and dust and drudgery of cities. The transition in his lot was such as sometimes takes place in human affairs, and in the fortunes of towering individuals:—one day, a prince of the prairies—the next day, a pack-horse!

1835

JAMES FENIMORE COOPER

(1789-1851)

1838 *Gleanings in Europe: Italy* (London, Philadelphia); *The American Democrat* (Cooperstown, N.Y.); *The Chronicles of Cooperstown* (Cooperstown, N.Y.); *Homeward Bound* (London, Philadelphia); *Home as Found* (Philadelphia, London).

1839 *The History of the Navy of the United States of America* (Philadelphia, London).

1840 *The Pathfinder* (London, Philadelphia); *Mercedes of Castile* (Philadelphia, London).

1841 *The Deerslayer* (Philadelphia, London).

1842 *The Two Admirals* (London, Philadelphia); *The Wing-and-Wing* (London, Philadelphia).

1843 *The Battle of Lake Erie* (Cooperstown, N.Y.); *Wyandotte* (London, Philadelphia); *Ned Myers* (London, Philadelphia).

1844 *Afloat and Ashore* (Philadelphia, New York).

1845 *Satanstoe* (London, New York); *The Chainbearer* (London, New York).

1846 *Lives of Distinguished American Naval Officers* (Philadelphia) collected; *The Redskins* (London, New York). Beginning of serial publication of *Jack Tier* in *Graham's Magazine* and *Bentley's Miscellany.*

1847 *The Crater* (London, New York); first trip west, to Detroit.

1848 *Jack Tier* (London, New York) published as a book. *The Oak*

Openings (London, New York).

1849 *The Sea Lions* (London, New York).

1850 *The Ways of the Hour* (London, New York); a comedy, *Upside Down, or Philosophy in Petticoats* produced in New York City, but never published; supervised Putnam edition of his novels.

1851 Became communicant in the Episcopal church in July; died September 15 at Cooperstown.

BIBLIOGRAPHY:

A *Descriptive Bibliography of the Writings of James Fenimore Cooper*, comp. Robert E. Spiller and Philip G. Blackburn (New York, 1934). *The Works of James Fenimore Cooper*, 12 vols. (New York, 1849–1851), and *Works*, 32 vols. (New York, 1859–1861), illustrated by F. O. C. Darley are standard editions. *Correspondence of James Fenimore Cooper*, ed. James F. Cooper, 2 vols. (New Haven, 1922). *The Letters and Journals of James Fenimore Cooper*, ed. James F. Beard, 4 vols. (Cambridge, 1960–64). Thomas R. Lounsbury, *James Fenimore Cooper* (Boston, 1882). Robert E. Spiller, *James Fenimore Cooper, Critic of His Times* (New York, 1931, 1963). Spiller, *James Fenimore Cooper: Representative Selections* (New York, 1936). Donald A. Ringe, *James Fenimore Cooper* (New York, 1962). *James Fenimore Cooper: A Re-appraisal*, special issue of *New York History*, XXXV (1954).

From *Notions of the Americans*

LETTER XXIII

Learning and Literature

To the Abbate Giromachi, &c. &c. Florence.

Washington,——

You ask me to write freely on the subject of the literature and the arts of the United States. The subjects are so meager as to render it a task that would require no small portion of the talents necessary to figure in either, in order to render them of interest. Still, as the request has come in so urgent a form, I shall endeavor to oblige you.

The Americans have been placed, as respects moral and intellectual advancement, different from all other infant nations. They have never been without the wants of civilization, nor have they ever been entirely without the means of a supply. Thus pictures, and books, and statuary, and everything else which appertains to elegant life, have always been known to them in an abundance, and of a quality exactly proportioned to their cost. Books, being the cheapest, and the nation having great leisure and prodigious zest for information, are not only the most common, as you will readily suppose, but they are probably more common than among any other people. I scarcely remember ever to have entered an American dwelling, however humble, without finding fewer or more books. As they form the most essential division of the subject, not only on account of their greater frequency, but on account of their far greater importance, I shall give them the first notice in this letter.

Unlike the progress of the two professions in the countries of our hemisphere, in America the printer came into existence before the author. Reprints of English works gave the first employment to the press. Then came almanacs, psalm-books, religious tracts, sermons, journals, political essays, and even rude attempts at poetry. All these preceded the revolution. The first journal was established in Boston at the commencement of the last century. There are several original polemical works of great originality and power that belong to the same period. I do not know that more learning and talents existed at that early day in the states of New England than in Virginia, Maryland and the Carolinas, but there was certainly a stronger desire to exhibit them.

. . . This country possesses neither the population nor the endowments to maintain a large class of learned idlers, in order that one man in a hundred may contribute a mite to the growing stock of general knowledge. There is a luxury in this expenditure of animal force, to which the Americans have not yet attained. The good is far too problematical and remote, and the expense of man too certain, to be prematurely sought. I have heard, I will confess, an American legislator quote Horace and Cicero; but it is far from being the humor of the country. I thought the taste of the orator questionable. A learned quotation is rarely of any use in an argument, since few men are fools enough not to see that the application of any maxim to politics is liable to a thousand practical objections, and, nine times in ten, they are evidences of the want of a direct, natural, and vigorous train of thought. They are the affectations, but rarely the ebullitions of true talent. When a man feels strongly, or thinks strongly, or speaks strongly, he is just as apt to do it in his native tongue as he is to laugh when he is tickled, or to weep when in sorrow. The Americans are strong speakers and acute thinkers, but no great quoters of the morals and axioms of a heathen age, because they happen to be recorded in Latin. . . .

But the effects of the literary institutions of the United States are somewhat peculiar. Few men devote their lives to scholarship. The knowledge that is actually acquired, is perhaps quite sufficient for the more practical and useful pursuits. Thousands of young men, who have read the more familiar classics, who have gone through enough of mathematics to obtain a sense of their own tastes, and of the value of precision, who have cultivated *belles lettres* to a reasonable extent, and who have been moderately instructed in the arts of composition, and in the rules of taste, are given forth to the country to mingle in its active employments. I am inclined to believe that a class of American graduates carries away with it quite as much general and diversified knowledge, as a class from one of our own universities. The excellence in particular branches is commonly wanting; but the deficiency is more than supplied by variety of information. The youth who has passed four years within the walls of a college, goes into the office of a lawyer for a few more. The profession of the law is not subdivided in America. The same man is counsellor, attorney, and conveyancer. Here the student gets a general insight into the principles, and a familiarity with the practice of the law, rather than an acquaintance with the study as a science. With this instruction he enters the world as a practitioner. Instead of existing in a state of dreaming retrospection, lost in a maze of theories, he is at once turned loose into the jostlings of the world. If perchance he encounters an antagonist a little more erudite than himself, he seizes the natural truth for his sheet anchor, and leaves precedent and quaint follies to him who has made them his study and delight. No doubt he often blunders, and is frequently, of necessity, defeated. But in the course of this irreverent treatment, usages and opinions, which are bottomed in no better foundation than antiquity, and which are as inapplicable to the present state of the world, as the present state of the world is, or ought to be, unfavorable to all feudal absurdities, come to receive their death warrants. In the meantime, by dint of sheer experience, and by the collision of intellects, the practitioner gets a stock of learning, that is acquired in the best possible school; and, what is of far more importance, the laws themselves get a dress which brings them within the fashions of the day. This same man becomes a legislator perhaps, and, if particularly clever, he is made to take an active part in the framing of laws that are not to harmonize with the other parts of an elaborate theory, but which are intended to make men comfortable and happy. Now, taken with more or less qualification, this is the history of thousands in this country, and it is also an important part of the history of the country itself. . . .

As respects authorship, there is not much to be said. Compared to the books that are printed and read, those of native origin are few indeed.

The principal reason of this poverty of original writers, is owing to the circumstance that men are not yet driven to their wits for bread. The United States are the first nation that possessed institutions, and, of course, distinctive opinions of its own, that was ever dependent on a foreign people for its literature. Speaking the same language as the English, and long in the habit of importing their books from the mother country, the revolution effected no immediate change in the nature of their studies, or mental amusements. The works were reprinted, it is true, for the purposes of economy, but they still continued English. Had the latter nation used this powerful engine with tolerable address, I think they would have secured such an ally in this country as would have rendered their own decline not only more secure, but as illustrious as had been their rise. There are many theories entertained as to the effect produced in this country by the falsehoods and jealous calumnies which have been undeniably uttered in the mother country, by means of the press, concerning her republican descendant. It is my own opinion that, like all other ridiculous absurdities, they have defeated themselves, and that they are now more laughed at and derided, even here, than resented. By all that I can learn, twenty years ago, the Americans were, perhaps, far too much disposed to receive the opinions and to adopt the prejudices of their relatives; whereas, I think it is very apparent that they are now beginning to receive them with singular distrust. It is not worth our while to enter further into this subject, except as it has had, or is likely to have, an influence on the national literature.[1]

It is quite obvious, that, so far as taste and forms alone are concerned, the literature of England and that of America must be fashioned after the same models. The authors, previously to the revolution, are common property, and it is quite idle to say that the American has not just as good a right to claim Milton, and Shakespeare, and all the old masters of the language, for his countrymen, as an Englishman. The Americans having continued to cultivate, and to cultivate extensively, an acquaintance with the writers of the mother country, since the separation, it is evident they must have kept pace with the trifling changes of the day. The only peculiarity that can, or ought to be expected in their literature, is that which is connected with the promulgation of their distinctive political opinions. They have not been remiss in this duty, as anyone may see, who chooses to examine their books. But we will devote a few minutes to a more minute account of the actual condition of American literature.

The first, and the most important, though certainly the most familiar branch of this subject, is connected with the public journals. It is not

---

[1] The writer might give, in proof of this opinion, one fact. He is led to believe that, so lately as within ten years, several English periodical works were re-printed, and much read in the United States, and that now they patronize their own, while the former are far less sought, though the demand, by means of the increased population, should have been nearly doubled. Some of the works are no longer even re-printed. [Cooper's Note.]

easy to say how many newspapers are printed in the United States. The estimated number varies from six hundred to a thousand. In the State of New York there are more than fifty counties. Now, it is rare that a county, in a state as old as that of New York (especially in the more northern parts of the country), does not possess one paper at least. The cities have many. The smaller towns sometimes have three or four, and very many of the counties four or five. . . .

As might be expected, there is nearly every degree of merit to be found in these journals. No one of them has the benefit of that collected talent which is so often enlisted in the support of the more important journals of Europe. There is not often more than one editor to the best; but he is usually some man who has seen, in his own person, enough of men and things to enable him to speak with tolerable discretion on passing events. The usefulness of the American journals, however, does not consist in their giving the tone to the public mind, in politics and morals, but in imparting facts. It is certain that, could the journals agree, they might, by their united efforts, give a powerful inclination to the common will. But, in point of fact, they do not agree on any one subject or set of subjects, except, perhaps, on those which directly affect their own interests. They, consequently, counteract, instead of aiding each other, on all points of disputed policy; and it is in the bold and sturdy discussions that follow, that men arrive at the truth. The occasional union in their own favor, is a thing too easily seen through to do either good or harm. So far, then, from the journals succeeding in leading the public opinion astray, they are invariably obliged to submit to it. They serve to keep it alive, by furnishing the means for its expression, but they rarely do more. Of course, the influence of each particular press is in proportion to the constancy and the ability with which it is found to support what is thought to be sound principles; but those principles must be in accordance with the private opinions of men, or most of their labor is lost.

The public press in America is rather more decent than that of England, and less decorous than that of France. The tone of the nation, and the respect for private feelings, which are, perhaps, in some measure, the consequence of a less artificial state of society, produce the former; and the liberty, which is a necessary attendant of fearless discussion, is, I think, the cause of the latter. The affairs of an individual are rarely touched upon in the journals of this country; never, unless it is thought they have a direct connection with the public interests, or from a wish to do him good. Still there is a habit, getting into use in America, no less than in France, that is borrowed from the English, which proves that the more unworthy feelings of our nature are common to men under all systems, and only need opportunity to find encouragement. I allude to the practice of repeating the proceedings of the courts of justice, in order to cater to a vicious appetite for amusement in the public. . . .

Nothing can be more free than the press of this country, on all subjects connected with politics. Treason cannot be written, unless by communicating with an open enemy. There is no other protection to a public man than that which is given by an independent jury, which punishes, of course, in proportion to the dignity and importance of the injured party. But the utmost lenity is always used in construing the right of the press to canvass the public acts of public men. Mere commonplace charges defeat themselves, and get into discredit so soon as to be lost, while graver accusations are met by grave replies. There is no doubt that the complacency of individuals is sometimes disturbed by these liberties; but they serve to keep the officers of the government to their work, while they rarely do any lasting, or even temporary injury. Serious and criminal accusations against a public man, if groundless, are, by the law of reason, a crime against the community, and, as such, they are punished. The general principle observed in these matters is very simple. If A. accuse B. of an act that is an offense against law, he may be called on for his proof, and if he fail he must take the consequences. But an editor of a paper, or anyone else, who should bring a criminal charge, no matter how grave, against the president, and who could prove it, is just as certain of doing it with impunity, as if he held the whole power in his own hands. He would be protected by the invincible shield of public opinion, which is not only in consonance with the law, but which, in this country, makes law.

Actions for injuries done by the press, considering the number of journals, are astonishingly rare in America. When one remembers the usual difficulty of obtaining legal proof, which is a constant temptation, even to the guilty, to appeal to the courts; and, on the other hand, the great freedom of the press, which is a constant temptation to abuse the trust, this fact, in itself, furnishes irresistible evidence of the general tone of decency which predominates in this nation. The truth is, that public opinion, among its other laws, has imperiously prescribed that, amidst the utmost latitude of discussion, certain limits shall not be passed; and public opinion, which is so completely the offspring of a free press, must be obeyed in this, as well as in other matters. . . .

The literature of the United States has, indeed, too powerful obstacles to conquer before (to use a mercantile expression) it can ever enter the markets of its own country on terms of perfect equality with that of England. Solitary and individual works of genius may, indeed, be occasionally brought to light, under the impulses of the high feeling which has conceived them; but, I fear, a good, wholesome, profitable, and continued pecuniary support is the applause that talent most craves. The fact, that an American publisher can get an English work without money, must, for a few years longer (unless legislative protection shall be extended to their own authors), have a tendency to repress a national literature. No man will pay a writer for an epic, a tragedy, a sonnet, a history, or a romance, when he can get a work of equal merit for nothing. I have conversed with those who are conversant on the subject, and, I confess, I have been astonished at the information they imparted.

A capital American publisher has assured me that there are not a dozen writers in this country, whose works he should feel confidence in publishing at all, while he reprints hundreds of English books without the least hesitation. This preference is by no means so much owing to any difference in merit, as to the fact that, when the price of the original author is to be added to the uniform hazard which accompanies all literary speculations, the risk becomes too great. . . .

When I say that books are not rejected here, from any want of talent in the writers, perhaps I ought to explain. I wish to express something a little different. Talent is sure of too many avenues to wealth and honors, in America, to seek, unnecessarily, an unknown and hazardous path. It is better paid in the ordinary pursuits of life, than it would be likely to be paid by an adventure in which an extraordinary and skillful, because practiced, foreign competition is certain. Perhaps high talent does not often make the trial with the American bookseller; but it is precisely for the reason I have named.

The second obstacle against which American literature has to contend is in the poverty of materials. There is scarcely an ore which contributes to the wealth of the author, that is found, here, in veins as rich as in Europe. There are no annals for the historian; no follies (beyond the most vulgar and commonplace) for the satirist; no manners for the dramatist; no obscure fictions for the writer of romance; no gross and hardy offenses against decorum for the moralist; nor any of the rich artificial auxiliaries of poetry. The weakest hand can extract a spark from the flint, but it would baffle the strength of a giant to attempt kindling a flame with a pudding stone. I very well know there are theorists who assume that the society and institutions of this country are, or ought to be, particularly favorable to novelties and variety. But the experience of one month, in these states, is sufficient to show any observant man the falsity of their position. The effect of a promiscuous assemblage anywhere, is to create a standard of deportment; and great liberty permits everyone to aim at its attainment. I have never seen a nation so much alike in my life, as the people of the United States, and what is more, they are not only like each other, but they are remarkably like that which common sense tells them they ought to resemble. No doubt, traits of character that are a little peculiar, without, however, being either very poetical, or very rich, are to be found in remote districts; but they are rare, and not always happy exceptions. In short, it is not possible to conceive a state of society in which more of the attributes of plain good sense, or fewer of the artificial absurdities of life, are to be found, than here. There is no costume for the peasant, (there is scarcely a peasant at all,) no wig for the judge, no baton for the general, no diadem for the chief magistrate. The darkest ages of their history are illuminated by the light of truth; the utmost efforts of their chivalry are limited by the laws of God; and even the deeds of their sages and heroes are to be sung in a language that would differ but little from a version of the ten commandments. However useful and respectable all this may be in actual life, it indicates but one direction to the man of genius.

It is very true there are a few young poets now living in this country, who have known how to extract sweets from even these wholesome, but scentless native plants. They have, however, been compelled to seek their inspiration in the universal laws of nature, and they have succeeded, precisely in proportion as they have been most general in their application. . . .

The next, though certainly an inferior branch of imaginative writing, is fictitious composition. From the facts just named, you cannot expect that the novelists, or romance writers of the United States, should be very successful. The same reason will be likely, for a long time to come, to repress the ardor of dramatic genius. Still, tales and plays are no novelties in the literature of this country. Of the former, there are many as old as soon after the revolution; and a vast number have been published within the last five years. One of their authors of romance, who curbed his talents by as few allusions as possible to actual society, is distinguished for power and comprehensiveness of thought. I remember to have read one of his books (Wieland) when a boy, and I take it to be a never-failing evidence of genius, that, amid a thousand similar pictures which have succeeded, the images it has left still stand distinct and prominent in my recollection. This author (Mr. Brockden Brown) enjoys a high reputation among his countrymen, whose opinions are sufficiently impartial, since he flattered no particular prejudice of the nation in any of his works.

The reputation of Irving is well known to you. He is an author distinguished for a quality (humor) that has been denied his countrymen; and his merit is the more rare, that it has been shown in a state of society so cold and so restrained. Besides these writers, there are many others of a similar character, who enjoy a greater or less degree of favor in their own country. The works of two or three have even been translated (into French) in Europe, and a great many are reprinted in England. Though every writer of fiction in America has to contend against the difficulties I have named, there is a certain interest in the novelty of the subject, which is not without its charm. I think, however, it will be found that they have all been successful, or the reverse, just as they have drawn warily, or freely, on the distinctive habits of their own country. I now speak of their success purely as writers of romance. It certainly would be possible for an American to give a description of the manners of his own country, in a book that he might choose to call a romance, which should be read, because the world is curious on the subject, but which would certainly never be read for that nearly indefinable poetical interest which attaches itself to a description of manners less bald and uniform. All the attempts to blend history with romance in America, have been comparative failures, (and perhaps fortunately,) since the subjects are too familiar to be treated with the freedom that the imagination absolutely requires. Some of the descriptions of the progress of society on the borders, have had a rather better success, since there is a positive, though no very poetical, novelty in the subject; but, on the whole, the books which have been best received, are those in which the authors have trusted most to their own conceptions of character, and to qualities that are common to the rest of the world and to human nature. This fact, if its truth be admitted, will serve to prove that the American writer must seek his renown in the exhibition of qualities that are general, while he is confessedly compelled to limit his observations to a state of society that has a wonderful tendency not only to repress passion, but to equalize humors.

The Americans have always been prolific writers on polemics and politics. Their sermons and fourth of July orations are numberless. Their historians, without being very classical or very profound, are remarkable for truth and good sense. There is not, perhaps, in the language a closer reasoner in metaphysics than Edwards; and their theological writers find great favor among the sectarians of their respective schools.

The stage of the United States is decidedly English. Both plays and players, with few exceptions, are imported. Theaters are numerous, and they are to be found in places where a traveler would little expect to meet them. . . .

The Americans pay well for dramatic talent. Cooke, the greatest English tragedian of our age, died on this side of the Atlantic; and there are few players of eminence in the mother country who are not tempted, at some time or other, to cross the ocean. Shakespeare, is of course, the great author of America, as he is of England, and I think he is quite as well relished here as there. In point of taste, if all the rest of the world be anything against England, that of America is the best, since it unquestionably approaches nearest to that of the continent of Europe. Nearly one half of the theatrical taste of the English is condemned by their own judgments, since the stage is not much supported by those who have had an opportunity of seeing any other. You will be apt to ask me how it happens, then, that the American taste is better? Because the people, being less exaggerated in their habits, are less disposed to tolerate caricatures, and because the theaters are not yet sufficiently numerous (though that hour is near) to admit of a representation that shall not be subject to the control of a certain degree of intelligence. I have heard an English player complain that he never saw such a dull audience as the one before which he had just been exhibiting; and I heard the same audience complain that they never listened to such dull jokes. Now, there was talent enough in both parties; but the one had formed his taste in a coarse school, and the others had formed theirs under the dominion of common sense. Independently of this peculiarity, there is a vast deal of acquired, traveled taste in this country. English tragedy, and high English comedy, both of which, you know, are excellent, never fail here, if well played; that is, they never fail under the usual limits of all amusement. One will cloy of sweets. But the fact of the taste and judgment of these people, in theatrical exhibitions, is proved by the number of their good theaters, compared to their population.

Of dramatic writers there are none, or next to none. The remarks I have made in respect to novels apply with double force to this species of composition. A witty and successful American comedy could only proceed from extraordinary talent. There would be less difficulty, certainly, with a tragedy; but still, there is rather too much foreign competition, and too much domestic employment in other pursuits, to invite genius to so doubtful an enterprise. The very baldness of ordinary American life is in deadly hostility to scenic representation. The character must be supported solely by its intrinsic power. The judge, the footman, the clown, the lawyer, the belle, or the beau, can receive no great assistance from dress. Melodramas, except the scene should be laid in the woods, are out of the question. It would be necessary to seek the great clock, which is to strike the portentous twelve blows, in the nearest church; a vaulted passage would degenerate into a cellar; and, as for ghosts, the country was discovered, since their visitations have ceased. The smallest departure from the incidents of ordinary life would do violence to every man's experience; and, as already mentioned, the passions which belong to human nature must be delineated, in America, subject to the influence of that despot—common sense.

Notwithstanding the overwhelming influence of British publications, and all the difficulties I have named, original books are getting to be numerous in the United States. The impulses of talent and intelligence are bearing down a thousand obstacles. I think the new works will increase rapidly, and that they are destined to produce a powerful influence on the world. We will pursue this subject another time.—Adieu.

1828

From *The American Democrat*

ON DISTINCTIVE AMERICAN PRINCIPLES

Distinctive American principles as properly refer to the institutions of the states as to those of the Union. A correct notion of the first cannot be formed without keeping the latter constantly in view.

The leading distinctive principle of this country, is connected with the fact that all political power is strictly a trust, granted by the constituent to the representative. These representatives possess different duties, and as the greatest check that is imposed on them, while in the exercise of their offices, exists in the manner in which the functions are balanced by each other, it is of the last importance that neither class trespass on the trusts that are not especially committed to its keeping.

The machinery of the state being the same in appearance, in this country and in that from which we are derived, inconsiderate commentators are apt to confound their principles. In England, the institutions have been the result of those circumstances to which time has accidentally given birth. The power of the king was derived from violence, the monarch, before the act of succession, in the reign of Queen Anne, claiming the throne in virtue of the conquest by William, in 1060. In America, the institutions are the result of deliberate consultation, mutual concessions, and design. In England, the people may have gained by diminishing the power of the king, who first obtained it by force; but, in America, to assail the rightful authority of the executive, is attacking a system framed by the constituencies of the states, who are virtually the people, for their own benefit. No assault can be made on any branch of this government, while in the exercise of its constitutional duties, without assaulting the right of the body of the nation, which is the foundation of the whole polity.

In countries, in which executive power is hereditary, and clothed with high prerogatives, it may be struggling for liberty to strive to diminish its influence; but, in this republic, in which the executive is elective, has no absolute authority in framing the laws, serves for a short period, is responsible, and has been created by the people, through the states, for their own purposes, it is assailing the rights of that people, to attempt in any manner to impede its legal and just action.

It is a general law in politics, that the power most to be distrusted, is that which, possessing the greatest force, is the least responsible. . . .

In this country, there is far more to apprehend from congress, than from the executive, as is seen in the following reasons:—Congress is composed of many, while the executive is one, bodies of men notoriously acting with less personal responsibilities than individuals; congress has power to enact laws, which it becomes the duty of the executive to see enforced, and the really legislative authority of a country is always its greatest authority; from the decisions and constructions of the executive, the citizen can always appeal to the courts for protection, but no appeal can lie from the acts of congress, except on the ground of unconstitutionality; the executive has direct personal responsibilities under the laws of the land, for any abuses of his authority, but the member of congress, unless guilty of open corruption, is almost beyond personal liabilities.

It follows that the legislature of this country, by the intention of the constitution, wields the highest authority under the least responsibility, and that it is the power most to be distrusted. Still, all who possess trusts, are to be diligently watched, for there is no protection against abuses without responsibility, nor any real responsibility, without vigilance.

Political partisans, who are too apt to mistake the impulses of their own hostilities and friendships for truths, have laid down many false principles on the subject of the duties of the executive. When a law is passed, it goes to the executive for execution, through the executive agents, and, at need, to the courts for interpretation. It would seem that there is no discretion vested in the executive concerning the constitutionality of a law. If he distrust the constitutionality of any law, he can set forth his objections by resorting to the veto; but it is clearly the intention of the system that the whole legislative power, in the last resort, shall abide in congress, while it is necessary to the regular action of the government, that none of its agents, but those who are especially appointed for that purpose, shall pretend to interpret the constitution, in practice. The citizen is differently situated. If he conceive himself oppressed by an unconstitutional law, it is his inalienable privilege to raise the question before the courts, where a final interpretation can be had. By this interpretation the executive and all his agents are equally bound to abide. This obligation arises from the necessity of things, as well as from the nature of the institutions. There must be somewhere a power to decide on the constitutionality of laws, and this power is vested in the supreme court of the United States, on final appeal. . . .

Although the court can render a law null, its power does not extend beyond the law already passed. Congress may reenact it, as often as it please, and the court will still exercise its reason in rejecting it. This is the balance of the constitution, which invites inquiry, the constituencies of the states holding a legal authority to render that constitutional which the courts have declared to be unconstitutional, or vice versa, by amendments to the instrument itself; the supremacy of the court being merely temporary, conditional, and growing out of expediency and necessity.

It has been said that it is a vital principle of this government, that each of its branches should confine itself to the particular duties assigned it by the constitution, and in no manner exceed them. Many grave abuses have already arisen from loosing sight of this truth, and there is danger that the whole system will be perverted from its intention, if not destroyed, unless they are seasonably corrected. Of these, the most prevalent, the one most injurious to the public service, that which has been introduced the most on foreign and the least on American principles, is the practice of using the time and influence of the legislatures, for the purpose of acting on the public mind, with a view to affect the elections. The usage has already gained so much footing, as seriously to impede the course of legislation. . . .

Political systems ought to be, and usually are, framed on certain great and governing principles. These principles cannot be perverted, or lost sight of, without perverting, or rendering nugatory the system itself; and, under a popular government, in an age like this, far more is to be apprehended from indirect attacks on the institutions, than from those which are direct. It is usual to excuse these departures from the right on the plea of human propensities, but human institutions are framed expressly to curb such propensities, and no truth is more salutary than that which is contained in the homely saying, that "law makers should not be law breakers."

It is the duty of the citizen to judge of all political acts on the great principles of the government, and not according to his own political partialities, or prejudices. His own particular representative is no more a representative of the people, than the representative of any other man, and one branch of the government is no more representative than another. All are to keep within their respective spheres, and it may be laid down as a governing maxim of the institutions, *that the representative who exceeds his trusts, trespasses on the rights of the people.* . . .

In estimating the powers of congress, there is a rule that may be safely confided in, and which has been already hinted at. The powers of congress are express and limited. That body therefore, can have no right *to pass resolutions* other than those which affect their own police, or, in a moral sense, even to make speeches, except on subjects on which *they have a right to pass laws.* The instant they exceed these limits, they exceed the bounds of their delegated authority. By applying this simple test to their proceedings, any citizen may, in ordinary cases, ascertain how far the representatives of the nation abuse their trusts.

Liberty is not a matter of words, but a positive and important condition of society. Its great safeguards, after placing its foundations on a popular base, is in the checks and balances imposed on the public servants, and all its real friends ought to know that the most insidious attacks, are made on it by those who are the largest trustees of authority, in their efforts to increase their power. . . .

ON EQUALITY

Equality, in a social sense, may be divided into that of condition, and that of rights. Equality of condition is incompatible with civilization, and is found only to exist in those communities that are but slightly removed from the savage state. In practice, it can only mean a common misery.

Equality of rights is a peculiar feature of democracies. These rights are properly divided into civil and political, though even these definitions are not to be taken as absolute, or as literally exact.

Under the monarchies of the old world, there exist privileged classes, possessed of exclusive rights. For a long period the nobles were exempted from taxes, and many other charges, advantages that are still enjoyed by them, in certain countries. In England, even, the nobles are entitled to hereditary advantages that are denied to those who are of inferior birth. All these distinctions are done away with in principle, in countries where there exists a professed equality of rights, though there is probably no community that does not make some distinctions between the political privileges of men. If this be true, there is strictly no equality of political rights, anywhere, although there may be, and is, a nearer approach to an equality of civil rights.

By political rights we understand, the suffrage, eligibility to office, and a condition of things that admits of no distinction between men, unless on principles that are common to all. Thus, though a man is not qualified to vote until he has reached the age of twenty-one, the regulation does not effect political equality, since all are equally subjected to the rule, and all become electors on attaining the same age.

With an equality of civil rights, all men are equal before the law; all classes of the community being liable equally to taxation, military service, jury duties, and to the other impositions attendant on civilization, and no one being exempted from its control, except on general rules, which are dependent on the good of all, instead of the exemption's belonging to the immunities of individuals, estates, or families. An equality of civil rights may be briefly defined to be an absence of privileges.

The distinction between the equality of civil and of political rights is material, one implying mere equality before the administration of the law, the other, equality in the power to frame it.

An equality of civil rights is never absolute, but we are to understand by the term, such an equality only, as is compatible with general justice and the relations between the different members of families. Thus, women nowhere possess precisely the same rights as men, or men the same rights as women. The wife, usually, can neither sue nor be sued, while the husband, except in particular cases, is made liable to all legal claims on account of the wife. Minors are deprived of many of their civil rights, or, it would be better to say, do not attain them, until they reach a period of life that has been arbitrarily fixed, and which varies in different countries, according to their several policies.

Neither is equality of political rights ever absolute. In those countries where the suffrage is said to be universal, exceptions exist, that arise from the necessity of things, or from that controlling policy which can never be safely lost sight of in the management of human affairs. The interests of women being thought to be so identified with those of their male relatives as to become, in a great degree, inseparable, females are, almost generally, excluded from the possession of political rights. There can be no doubt that society is greatly the gainer, by thus excluding one half its members, and the half that is best adapted to give a tone to its domestic happiness, from the strife of parties, and the fierce struggles of political controversies. Men are also excluded from political rights previously to having attained the age prescribed by law. Paupers, those who have no fixed abodes, and aliens in law, though their lives may have been principally passed in the country, are also excluded from the enjoyment of political rights, everywhere. Thus birthright is almost universally made a source of advantage. These exceptions, however, do not very materially affect the principle of political equality, since the rules are general and have been made solely with a reference to the good of society, or to render the laws less liable to abuses in practice.

It follows, that equality, whether considered in connection with our civil or political rights, must not be taken as a general and absolute condition of society, but as such an equality as depends on principles that are equitable, and which are suited to the actual wants of men.

ON LIBERTY

Liberty, like equality, is a word more used than understood. Perfect and absolute liberty is as incompatible with the existence of society, as equality of condition. It is impracticable in a state of nature even, since, without the protection of the law, the strong would oppress and enslave the weak. We are then to understand by liberty, merely such a state of the social compact as permits the members of a community to lay no more restraints on themselves, than are required by their real necessities, and obvious interests. To this definition may be added, that it is a requisite of liberty, that the body of a nation should retain the power to modify its institutions, as circumstances shall require.

The natural disposition of all men being to enjoy a perfect freedom of action, it is a common error to suppose that the nation which possesses the mildest laws, or laws that impose the least personal restraints, is the freest. This opinion is untenable, since the power that concedes this freedom of action, can recall it. Unless it is lodged in the body of the community itself, there is, therefore, no pledge for the continuance of such a liberty. . . .

This is an all important distinction in the consideration of political liberty, since the circumstances of no two countries are precisely the same, and all municipal regulations ought to have direct reference to the actual condition of a community. It follows, that no country can properly be deemed free, unless the body of the nation possess, in the last resort, the legal power to frame its laws according to its wants. This power must also abide in the nation, or it becomes merely an historical fact, for he that was once free is not necessarily free always, any more than he that was once happy, is to consider himself happy in perpetuity.

This definition of liberty is new to the world, for a government founded on such principles is a novelty. Hitherto, a nation has been deemed free, whose people were possessed of a certain amount of franchises, without any reference to the general repository of power. Such a nation may not be absolutely enslaved, but it can scarcely be considered in possession of an affirmative political liberty, since it is not the master of its own fortunes.

Having settled what is the foundation of liberty, it remains to be seen by what process a people can exercise this authority over themselves. The usual course is to refer all matters of choice to the decision of majorities. The common axiom of democracies, however, which says that "the majority must rule," is to be received with many limitations. Were the majority of a country to rule without restraint, it is probable as much injustice and oppression would follow, as are found under the dominion of one. It belongs to the nature of men to arrange themselves in parties, to lose sight of truth and justice in partisanship and prejudice, to mistake their own impulses for that which is proper, and to do wrong because they are indisposed to seek the right. Were it wise to trust power, unreservedly, to majorities, all fundamental and controlling laws would be unnecessary, since they might, as occasion required, emanate from the will of numbers. Constitutions would be useless.

The majority rules in prescribed cases, and in no other. It elects to office, it enacts ordinary laws, subject however to the restrictions of the constitution, and it decides most of the questions that arise in the primitive meetings of the people; questions that do not usually effect any of the principal interests of life.

The majority does not rule in settling fundamental laws, under the constitution; or when it does rule in such cases, it is with particular checks produced by time and new combinations; it does not pass judgment in trials at law, or under impeachment, and it is impotent in many matters touching vested rights. . . .

Though majorities often decide wrong, it is believed that they are less liable to do so than minorities. There can be no question that the educated and affluent classes of a country, are more capable of coming to wise and intelligent decisions in affairs of state, than the mass of a population. Their wealth and leisure afford them opportunities for observation and comparison, while their general information and greater knowledge of character, enable them to judge more accurately of men and measures. That these opportunities are not properly used, is owing to the unceasing desire of men to turn their advantages to their own particular benefit, and to their passions. All history proves, when power is the sole possession of a few, that it is perverted to their sole advantage, the public suffering in order that their rulers may prosper. The same nature which imposes the necessity of governments at all, seems to point out the expediency of confiding its control, in the last resort, to the body of the nation, as the only lasting protection against gross abuses.

We do not adopt the popular polity because it is perfect, but because it is less imperfect than any other. As man, by his nature, is liable to err, it is vain to expect an infallible whole that is composed of fallible parts. The government that emanates from a single will, supposing that will to be pure, enlightened, impartial, just and consistent, would be the best in the world, were it attainable for men. Such is the government of the universe, the result of which is perfect harmony. As no man is without spot in his justice, as no man has infinite wisdom, or infinite mercy, we are driven to take refuge in the opposite extreme, or in a government of many.

It is common for the advocates of monarchy and aristocracy to deride the opinions of the mass, as no more than the impulses of ignorance and prejudices. While experience unhappily shows that this charge has too much truth, it also shows that the educated and few form no exemption to the common rule of humanity. The most intelligent men of every country in which there is liberty of thought and action, yielding to their interests or their passions, are always found taking the opposite extremes of contested questions, thus triumphantly refuting an arrogant proposition, that of the exclusive fitness of the few to govern, by an unanswerable fact. The minority of a country is never known to agree, except in its efforts to reduce and oppress the majority. Were this not so, parties would be unknown in all countries but democracies, whereas the factions of aristocracies have been among the fiercest and least governable of any recorded in history.

Although real political liberty can have but one character, that of a popular base, the world contains many modifications of governments that are, more or less, worthy to be termed free. In most of these states, however, the liberties of the mass, are of the negative character of franchises, which franchises are not power of themselves, but merely an exemption from the abuses of power. Perhaps no state exists, in which the people, either by usage, or by direct concessions from the source of authority, do not possess some of these franchises; for, if there is no such thing, in practice, as perfect and absolute liberty, neither is there any such thing, in practice, as total and unmitigated slavery. In the one case, nature has rendered man incapable of enjoying freedom without restraint, and in the other, incapable of submitting, entirely without resistance, to oppression. The harshest despots are compelled to acknowledge the immutable principles of eternal justice, affecting necessity and the love of right, for their most ruthless deeds.

England is a country in which the franchises of the subject are more than usually numerous. Among the most conspicuous of these are the right of trial by jury, and that of the *habeas corpus*. . . .

By comparing the privileges of the *Habeas Corpus*, where it exists alone, and as a franchise, with those of the citizen who enjoys it merely as a provision of his own, against the abuses of ordinances that he had a voice in framing, we learn the essential difference between real liberty and franchises. The Englishman can appeal to a tribunal, against the abuse of an existing law, but if the law be not with him, he has no power to evade it, however unjust, or oppressive. The American has the same appeal against the abuse of a law, with the additional power to vote for its repeal, should the law itself be vicious. The one profits by a franchise to liberate his person only, submitting to his imprisonment however, if legality has been respected; while the other, in addition to this privilege, has a voice in getting rid of the obnoxious law, itself, and in preventing a recurrence of the wrong. . . .

It is usual to maintain, that in democracies the tyranny of majorities is a greater evil than the oppression of minorities in narrow systems. Although this evil is exaggerated, since the laws being equal in their action it is not easy to oppress the few without oppressing all, it undeniably is the weak side of a popular government. To guard against this, we have framed constitutions, which point out the cases in which the majority shall decide, limiting their power, and bringing that they do possess within the circle of certain general and just principles. . . .

Although it is true, that no genuine liberty can exist without being based on popular authority in the last resort, it is equally true that it cannot exist when thus based, without many restraints on the power of the mass. These restraints are necessarily various and numerous. . . .

Liberty therefore may be defined to be a controlling authority that resides in the body of a nation, but so restrained as only to be exercised on certain general principles that shall do as little violence to natural justice, as is compatible with the peace and security of society.

ON STATION

Station may be divided into that which is political, or public, and that which is social, or private. In monarchies and aristocracies the two are found united, since the higher classes, as a matter of course, monopolize all the offices of consideration; but, in democracies, there is not, nor is it proper that there should be, any intimate connection between them.

Political, or public station, is that which is derived from office, and, in a democracy, must embrace men of very different degrees of leisure, refinement, habits and knowledge. This is characteristic of the institutions, which, under a popular government, confer on political station more power than rank, since the latter is expressly avoided in this system.

Social station is that which one possesses in the ordinary associations, and is dependent on birth, education, personal qualities, property, tastes, habits, and, in some instances, on caprice, or fashion. Although the latter undeniably is sometimes admitted to control social station, it generally depends, however, on the other considerations named.

Social station, in the main, is a consequence of property. So long as there is civilization there must be the rights of property, and so long as there are the rights of property, their obvious consequences must follow. All that democracies legitimately attempt is to prevent the advantages which accompany social station from accumulating rights that do not properly belong to the condition, which is effected by pronouncing that it shall have no factitious political aids.

They who have reasoned ignorantly, or who have aimed at effecting their personal ends by flattering the popular feeling, have boldly affirmed that "one man is as good as another;" a maxim that is true in neither nature, revealed morals, nor political theory.

That one man is not as good as another in natural qualities, is proved on the testimony of our senses. One man is stronger than another; he is handsomer, taller, swifter, wiser, or braver, than all his fellows. In short, the physical and moral qualities are unequally distributed, and, as a necessary consequence, in none of them, can one man be justly said to be as good as another. Perhaps no two human beings can be found so precisely equal in everything, that one shall not be pronounced the superior of the other; which, of course, establishes the fact that there is no natural equality.

The advocates of exclusive political privileges reason on this circumstance by assuming, that as nature has made differences between men, those institutions which create political orders, are no more than carrying out the great designs of providence. The error of their argument is in supposing it a confirmation of the designs of nature to attempt to supplant her, for, while the latter has rendered men unequal, it is not from male to male, according to the order of primogeniture, as is usually established by human ordinances. In order not to interfere with the inequality of nature, her laws must be left to their own operations, which is just what is done in democracies, after a proper attention has been paid to the peace of society, by protecting the weak against the strong.

That one man is not deemed as good as another in the grand moral system of providence, is revealed to us in Holy Writ, by the scheme of future rewards and punishments, as well as by the whole history of those whom God has favored in this world, for their piety, or punished for their rebellion. As compared with perfect holiness, all men are frail; but, as compared with each other, we are throughout the whole of sacred history made to see, that, in a moral sense, one man is not as good as another. The evil doer is punished, while they who are distinguished for their qualities and acts, are intended to be preferred.

The absolute moral and physical equality that are inferred by the maxim, that "one man is as good as another," would at once do away with the elections, since a lottery would be both simpler, easier and cheaper than the present mode of selecting representatives. Men, in such a case, would draw lots for office, as they are now drawn for juries. Choice supposes a preference, and preference inequality of merit, or of fitness.

We are then to discard all visionary theories on this head, and look at things as they are. All that the most popular institutions attempt, is to prohibit that one *race* of men shall be made better than another by law, from father to son, which would be defeating the intentions of providence, creating a superiority that exists in neither physical nor moral nature, and substituting a political scheme for the will of God and the force of things.

As a principle, one man is as good as another in rights. Such is the extent of the most liberal institutions of this country, and this provision is not general. The slave is not as good as his owner, even in rights. But in those states where slavery does not exist, all men have essentially the same rights, an equality, which, so far from establishing that "one man is as good as another," in a social sense, is the very means of producing the inequality of condition that actually exists. By possessing the same rights to exercise their respective faculties, the active and frugal become more wealthy than the idle and dissolute; the wise and gifted more trusted than the silly and ignorant; the polished and refined more respected and sought, than the rude and vulgar.

In most countries, birth is a principal source of social distinction, society being divided into castes, the noble having an hereditary claim to be the superior of the plebeian. This is an unwise and an arbitrary distinction that has led to most of the social diseases of the old world, and from which America is happily exempt. But great care must be had in construing the principles which have led to this great change, for America is the first important country of modern times, in which such positive distinctions have been destroyed.

Still some legal differences, and more social advantages, are produced by birth, even in America. The child inherits the property, and a portion of the consideration of the parent. Without the first of these privileges, men would not exert themselves to acquire more property than would suffice for their own personal necessities, parental affection being one of the most powerful incentives to industry. Without such an inducement, then, it would follow that civilization would become stationary, or, it would recede; the incentives of individuality and of the affections, being absolutely necessary to impel men to endure the labor and privations that alone can advance it. . . .

It is as vain to think of altogether setting aside sentiment and the affections, in regulating human affairs, as to imagine it possible to raise a nature, known to be erring and weak, to the level of perfection.

The Deity, in that terrible warning delivered from the mount, where he declares that he "will visit the sins of the fathers upon the children, unto the third and fourth generation," does no more than utter one of those sublime moral truths, which, in conformity with his divine providence, pervade nature. It is merely an announcement of a principle that cannot safely be separated from justice, and one that is closely connected with all the purest motives and highest aspirations of man. . . .

It is a natural consequence of the rights of property and of the sentiment named, that birth should produce some advantages, in a social sense, even in the most democratical of the American communities. The son imbibes a portion of the intelligence, refinement and habits of the father, and he shares in his associations. These must be enumerated as the legitimate advantages of birth, and without invading the private arrangements of families and individuals, and establishing a perfect community of education, they are unavoidable. Men of the same habits, the same degree of cultivation and refinement, the same opinions, naturally associate together, in every class of life. The day laborer will not mingle with the slave; the skillful mechanic feels his superiority over the mere laborer, claims higher wages and has a pride in his craft; the man in trade justly fancies that his habits elevate him above the mechanic, so far as social position is concerned, and the man of refinement, with his education, tastes and sentiments, is superior to all. Idle declamation on these points, does not impair the force of things, and life is a series of facts. These inequalities of condition, of manners, of mental cultivation must exist, unless it be intended to reduce all to a common level of ignorance and vulgarity, which would be virtually to return to a condition of barbarism.

The result of these undeniable facts, is the inequalities of social station, in America, as elsewhere, though it is an inequality that exists without any more arbitrary distinctions than are indispensably connected with the maintenance of civilization. In a social sense, there are orders here, as in all other countries, but the classes run into each other more easily, the lines of separation are less strongly drawn, and their shadows are more intimately blended.

This social inequality of America is an unavoidable result of the institutions, though nowhere proclaimed in them, the different constitutions maintaining a profound silence on the subject, they who framed them probably knowing that it is as much a consequence of civilized society, as breathing is a vital function of animal life.

AN ARISTOCRAT AND A DEMOCRAT

We live in an age, when the words aristocrat and democrat are much used, without regard to the real significations. An aristocrat is one of a few, who possess the political power of a country; a democrat, one of the many. The words are also properly applied to those who entertain notions favorable to aristocratical, or democratical forms of government. Such persons are not, necessarily, either aristocrats, or democrats in fact, but merely so in opinion. Thus a member of a democratical government may have an aristocratical bias, and vice versa.

To call a man who has the habits and opinions of a gentleman, an aristocrat, from that fact alone, is an abuse of terms, and betrays ignorance of the true principles of government, as well as of the world. It must be an equivocal freedom, under which everyone is not the master of his own innocent acts and associations, and he is a sneaking democrat, indeed, who will submit to be dictated to, in those habits over which neither law nor morality assumes a right of control.

Some men fancy that a democrat can only be one who seeks the level, social, mental and moral, of the majority, a rule that would at once exclude all men of refinement, education and taste from the class. These persons are enemies of democracy, as they at once render it impracticable. They are usually great sticklers for their own associations and habits, too, though unable to comprehend any of a nature that are superior. They are, in truth, aristocrats in principle, though assuming a contrary pretension; the ground work of all their feelings and arguments being self. Such is not the intention of liberty, whose aim is to leave every man to be the master of his own acts; denying hereditary honors, it is true, as unjust and unnecessary, but not denying the inevitable consequences of civilization.

The law of God is the only rule of conduct, in this, as in other matters. Each man should do as he would be done by. Were the question put to the greatest advocate of indiscriminate association, whether he would submit to have his company and habits dictated to him, he would be one of the first to resist the tyranny; for they, who are the most rigid in maintaining their own claims, in such matters, are usually the loudest in decrying those whom they fancy to be better off than themselves. Indeed, it may be taken as a rule in social intercourse, that he who is the most apt to question the pretensions of others, is the most conscious of the doubtful position he himself occupies; thus establishing the very claims he affects to deny, by letting his jealousy of it be seen. Manners, education and refinement, are positive things, and they bring with them innocent tastes which are productive of high enjoyments; and it is as unjust to deny their possessors their indulgence, as it would be to insist on the less fortunate's passing the time they would rather devote to athletic amusements, in listening to operas for which they have no relish, sung in a language they do not understand.

All that democracy means, is as equal a participation in rights as is practicable; and to pretend that social equality is a condition of popular institutions, is to assume that the latter are destructive of civilization, for, as nothing is more self-evident than the impossibility of raising all men to the highest standard of tastes and refinement, the alternative would be to reduce the entire community to the lowest. The whole embarrassment on this point exists in the difficulty of making men comprehend qualities they do not themselves possess. We can all perceive the difference between ourselves and our inferiors, but when it comes to a question of the difference between us and our superiors, we fail to appreciate merits of which we have no proper conceptions. In face of this obvious difficulty, there is the safe and just governing rule, already mentioned, or that of permitting everyone to be the undisturbed judge of his own habits and associations, so long as they are innocent, and do not impair the rights of others to be equally judges for themselves. It follows, that social intercourse must regulate itself, independently of institutions, with the exception that the latter, while they withhold no natural, bestow no factitious advantages beyond those which are inseparable from the rights of property, and general civilization.

In a democracy, men are just as free to aim at the highest attainable places in society, as to obtain the largest fortunes; and it would be clearly unworthy of all noble sentiment to say, that the groveling competition for money shall alone be free, while that which enlists all the liberal acquirements and elevated sentiments of the race, is denied the democrat. Such an avowal would be at once, a declaration of the inferiority of the system, since nothing but ignorance and vulgarity could be its fruits.

The democratic gentleman must differ in many essential particulars, from the aristocratical gentleman, though in their ordinary habits and tastes they are virtually identical. Their principles vary; and, to a slight degree, their deportment accordingly. The democrat, recognizing the right of all to participate in power, will be more liberal in his general sentiments, a quality of superiority in itself; but, in conceding this much to his fellowman, he will proudly maintain his own independence of vulgar domination, as indispensable to his personal habits. The same principles and manliness that would induce him to depose a royal despot, would induce him to resist a vulgar tyrant.

There is no more capital, though more common error, than to suppose him an aristocrat who maintains his independence of habits; for democracy asserts the control of the majority, only, in matters of law, and not in matters of custom. The very object of the institution is the utmost practicable personal liberty, and to affirm the contrary, would be sacrificing the end to the means.

An aristocrat, therefore, is merely one who fortifies his exclusive privileges by positive institutions, and a democrat, one who is willing to admit of a free competition, in all things. To say, however, that the last supposes this competition will lead to nothing, is an assumption that means are employed without any reference to an end. He is the purest democrat who best maintains his rights, and no rights can be dearer to a man of cultivation, than exemptions from unseasonable invasions on his time, by the coarse-minded and ignorant.

ON THE PRESS

It would seem that providence, for some of its own great ends, has denied to man any particular blessing, which his own waywardness is not destined to lessen, if not entirely to neutralize. In nothing connected with human happiness, is this grave truth more apparent than in the history of the press.

In despotisms, where the weakness of the bodies of nations, is derived from an ignorance of their force, and from the want of means to act in concert, the press is the lever by which the thrones of tyrants and prejudices are the most easily overturned, and, under such circumstances, men often contend for privileges in its behalf, that become dangerous to the peace of society, when civil and political rights are obtained.

In a popular government, so far from according an entire immunity from penalties to the press, its abuses are those which society is required, by its very safety, to visit with its heaviest punishments. In a democracy, misleading the public mind, as regards facts, characters, or principles, is corrupting all that is dear to society at its source, opinion being the fountain whence justice, honors, and the laws, equally flow.

It is a misfortune that necessity has induced men to accord greater license to this formidable engine, in order to obtain liberty, than can be borne with less important objects in view; for the press, like fire, is an excellent servant, but a terrible master.

It may be taken as rules, that without the liberty of the press, there can be no popular liberty in a nation, and with its licentiousness, neither public honesty, justice, nor a proper regard for character. Of the two, perhaps, that people is the happiest which is deprived altogether of a free press, since private honesty, and a healthful tone of the public mind are not incompatible with narrow institutions though neither can well exist under the constant corrupting action of a licentious press.

The governing principle connected with this interest, would seem to depend on a general law, which, under abuses, converts the most beneficial moral agents to be the greatest enemies of the race. The press is equally capable of being made the instrument of elevating man to the highest point of which his faculties admit, or of depressing him to the lowest.

In struggling for liberty and emancipation from errors and prejudices, men have not always paused to reflect on the influence of the agents they have employed, when those agents, from contending with a powerful enemy, shall have become conquerors, and have begun to look about them for the fruits of victory. The press, so efficient as the opponent of tyrants, may become despotic itself; it may substitute new errors for those it has eradicated, and, like an individual spoiled by success, may generally abuse its advantages.

Many false notions have been introduced into society, in the desire to vindicate the rights of so powerful an agent. Of these, one of the worst is the admission of a claim in the press to interfere, in any manner, with private character. The good of such an interference, is at the best but doubtful, and the oppression, in those cases in which injustice is done, is of the most intolerable and irreparable kind.

It would be a proper and a just, though an insufficient atonement, in cases of established libel, to vest a power in the courts to compel the libeler to publish, for a series of weeks, or months, or even years, his own condemnation in his own columns, that the antidote might accompany the poison; though it is to be feared, that the possession of popular rights is still too recent, to permit the majority of men to entertain correct notions concerning an instrument that, they rightly fancy, has been so serviceable in the conflict they have just escaped.

It ought never to be forgotten, that the press, contending for natural but forbidden rights, is no more like the press when these rights are obtained, than the man struggling with adversity, and chastened by misfortune, is like the man flushed with success and corrupted by prosperity.

The history of the press is everywhere the same. In its infancy it is timid, distrustful, and dependent on truth for success. As it acquires confidence with force, it propagates just opinions with energy; scattering errors and repelling falsehood, until it prevails; when abuses rush in, confounding principles, truths, and all else that is estimable, until it becomes a serious matter of doubt, whether a community derives most good or evil, from the institution.

ON PROPERTY

As property is the base of all civilization, its existence and security are indispensable to social improvement. Were it possible to have a community of property, it would soon be found that no one would toil, but that men would be disposed to be satisfied with barely enough for the supply of their physical wants, since none would exert themselves to obtain advantages solely for the use of others. The failure of all attempts to form communities, even on a small scale, with a common interest, goes to prove this. Where there is a rigid equality of condition, as well as of rights, that condition must necessarily be one of a low scale of mediocrity, since it is impossible to elevate those who do not possess the requisite qualities any higher. Thus we see that the societies, or religious sects, in which a community of property prevails, are content with merely supplying the wants of life, knowing little or nothing of its elegancies, refinements, or mental pleasures. These communities, moreover, possess an outlet for their idle and dissolute, by resorting to expulsion, a remedy that society itself cannot apply.

The principle of individuality, or to use a less winning term, of selfishness, lies at the root of all voluntary human exertion. We toil for food, for clothes, for houses, lands, and for property, in general. This is done, because we know that the fruits of our labor will belong to ourselves, or to those who are most dear to us. It follows, that all which society enjoys beyond the mere supply of its first necessities, is dependent on the rights of property.

It is not known that man exists anywhere without establishing rules for the protection of property. Even insects, reptiles, beasts and birds, have their several possessions, in their nests, dens and supplies. So completely is animal exertion, in general, whether in man or beast, dependent on the enjoyment of this right, under limitations which mark their several conditions, that we may infer that the rights of property, to a certain extent, are founded in nature. The food obtained by his toil, cannot be taken from the mouth of man, or beast, without doing violence to one of the first of our natural rights. We apply the term of robber, or despoiler, to the reptile or bird, that preys on the aliment of another animal, as well as to the human thief. So long as natural justice is admitted to exist, the party assailed, in such cases, has a right to defend his own.

The rights of property become artificial and extended, as society becomes civilized. In the savage state the land is without owners, property consisting in the hut, the food, and the arms used in war and in the chase. In pastoral, or semi-barbarous states, use gives claims, not to individuals, but to tribes, and flocks are pastured on grounds that belong to one entire community, but to that one only. Private property is composed of cattle, sheep, tents, horses, camels, with the common claims to share in the common fields.

Civilization has established various, and in some cases, arbitrary and unjust distinctions, as pertaining to the rights of property. These are abuses, the tendency of man being to convert into curses things that Providence designed to prove benefits. Still, most of the ordinances of civilized society, that are connected with this interest, are founded in reason, and ought to be rigidly maintained.

The first great principle connected with the rights of property, is its inviolability in all cases in which the laws leave it in possession of the proprietor. Every child should be taught to respect the sanctity of his neighbor's house, garden, fields and all that is his. On those parts of another's possessions, where it is permitted to go, he should go with care not to abuse the privilege, and from those parts which he is forbidden to use, he should religiously abstain. The child that is properly impressed in infancy, with the rights of property, is in little danger of committing theft in after life, or, in any other manner of invading that which is the just possession of another.

The doctrine that anyone "may do what he please with his own," however, is false. One may do with his own, whatever the laws and institutions of his country allow, and no more. One may even respect the letter, and yet violate the spirit of those laws and institutions, committing a moral, if not a legal offense, in so doing. Thus, he, who would bring his money to bear upon the elections of a country like this, abuses his situation, unless his efforts are confined to fair and manly discussions before the body of the people.

In nations where the mass have no political rights, means have been found to accumulate power by the aid of wealth. The pretense has been that none but the rich have a stake in society. Every man who has wants, feelings, affections and character, has a stake in society. Of the two, perhaps, the necessities of men are a greater corrective of political abuses, than their surplus means. Both may lead to evil, beyond a doubt, but, as laws which are framed by all, must be tolerably impartial and general in their operation, less danger arises from the rule of the former, than from the rule of the latter. When property rules, it rules alone; but when the poor are admitted to have a voice in government, the rich are never excluded. Such is the nature of man, that all exclusive power is uniformly directed to exclusive purposes. Property always carries with it a portion of indirect political influence, and it is unwise, and even dangerous, to strengthen this influence by adding to it constitutional privileges; the result always being to make the strong stronger, and the weak weaker.

On the other hand, all who love equal justice, and, indeed, the safety of free institutions, should understand that property has its rights, and the necessity of rigidly respecting them. It is the right of the possessor of property to be placed on an equal footing with all his fellow citizens, in every respect. If he is not to be exalted on account of his wealth, neither is he to be denounced. In this country, it is the intention of the institutions, that money should neither increase nor lessen political influence.

There are habits that belong to every condition of life. The man of hereditary wealth, is usually a man of leisure, and he little understands the true spirit of democracy, who supposes that such a man is not to enjoy the tastes and inclinations, which are the fruits of leisure and cultivation, without let or hindrance. Democracy leaves every man the master of his acts and time, his tastes and habits, so long as he discharges his duty to the public, and respects the laws. He who declaims against another for holding himself aloof from general association, arrogates to himself a power of censure that he does not rightly possess, and betrays his own consciousness of inferiority. Men of really high social station never make this complaint, for they are above jealousy; and they who do, only discover a feeling that is every way removed from the manliness and spirit of true independence.

One may certainly be purse-proud, and of all the sources of human pride, mere wealth is the basest and most vulgar minded. Real gentlemen are almost invariably above this low feeling, and they who attribute habits, that have their rise in sentiment, tastes, knowledge and refinement, to such a cause, usually make the mistake of letting their own ignorance of the existence of motives so elevated, be known. In a word, if the man of property has no more personal legal immunities, than the man who has none, neither has he fewer. He is privileged to use his own means, under the general regulations of society, in the pursuit of his own happiness, and they who would interfere with him, so far from appreciating liberty, are ignorant of its vital principles.

If left to itself, unsupported by factitious political aid, but sufficiently protected against the designs and rapacity of the dishonest, property is an instrument of working most of the good that society enjoys. It elevates a national character, by affording the means of cultivating knowledge and the tastes; it introduces all above barbarism into society; and it encourages and sustains laudable and useful efforts in individuals. Like every other great good, its abuses are in proportion to its benefits.

The possessor of property is not, half the time, as much the object of envy as the needy imagine, for its corrupting influence endangers eternal peace. Great estates are generally of more benefit to the community than to their owners. They bring with them anxiety, cares, demands, and, usually, exaggerated notions, on the part of the public, of the duties of the rich. So far from being objects of envy, their possessors are oftener the subjects of commiseration; he who has enough for his rational wants, agreeably to his habits and education, always proving the happier man.

The possessions of new families are commonly exaggerated in the public mind, while those of long established families are as commonly diminished.

A people that deems the possession of riches its highest source of distinction, admits one of the most degrading of all influences to preside over its opinions. At no time, should money be ever ranked as more than a means, and he who lives as if the acquisition of property were the sole end of his existence, betrays the dominion of the most sordid, base, and groveling motive, that life offers.

Property is desirable as the groundwork of moral independence, as a means of improving the faculties, and of doing good to others, and as the agent in all that distinguishes the civilized man from the savage.

Property has been made the test of political rights, in two distinct forms. It has been *represented,* and it has been established as a *qualification.* The representation of property is effected in two modes; first, by giving the proprietor more votes than one, according to the number and situation of his freeholds; and, secondly, by raising the test of qualification so high, as to exclude all but the affluent from the franchise. The first was the English system, previously to the recent changes; the last, is the actual system of France.

A government founded on the representation of property, however direct or indirect, is radically vicious, since it is a union of two of the most corrupting influences to which man is subject. It is the proper business of government to resist the corruptions of money, and not to depend on them.

To a qualification of property, if placed so low as to embrace the great majority of the people, there is no very serious objection, though better tests might, perhaps, be devised. Residence, character, information, and fixed relations with society, ought to be added to this qualification; and it might be better, even, could they be made entirely to supersede it. In local governments, or those of towns and villages, which do little more than control property, a low property qualification is the true test of the franchise, though even in these cases, it might be well to add information and character.   1838

From Introduction to *The Pioneers*

As this work professes, in its title page, to be a descriptive tale, they who will take the trouble to read it may be glad to know how much of its contents is literal fact, and how much is intended to represent a general picture. The Author is very sensible that, had he confined himself to the latter, always the most effective, as it is the most valuable, mode of conveying knowledge of this nature, he would have made a far better book. But in commencing to describe scenes, and perhaps he may add characters, that were so familiar to his own youth, there was a constant temptation to delineate that which he had known, rather than that which he might have imagined. This rigid adhesion to truth, an indispensable requisite in history and travels, destroys the charm of fiction; for all that is necessary to be conveyed to the mind by the latter had better be done by delineations of principles, and of characters in their classes, than by a too fastidious attention to originals.

New York having but one county of Otsego, and the Susquehanna but one proper source, there can be no mistake as to the site of the tale. . . . The face of the country, the climate as it was found by the whites, and the manners of the settlers, are described with a minuteness for which the Author has no other apology than the force of his own recollections. . . .

In 1785, the Author's father, who had an interest in extensive tracts of land in this wilderness, arrived with a party of surveyors. The manner in which the scene met his eye is described by Judge Temple. At the commencement of the following year the settlement began; and from that time to this the country has continued to flourish. It is a singular feature in American life, that, at the beginning of this century, when the proprietor of the estate had occasion for settlers on a new settlement, and in a remote county, he was enabled to draw them from among the increase of the former colony. . . .

Otsego has now become one of the most populous districts of New York. It sends forth its emigrants like any other old region; and it is pregnant with industry and enterprise. Its manufactures are prosperous; and it is worthy of remark, that one of the most ingenious machines known in European art is derived from the keen ingenuity which is exercised in this remote region.

In order to prevent mistake, it may be well to say that the incidents of this tale are purely a fiction. The literal facts are chiefly connected with the natural and artificial objects, and the customs of the inhabitants. Thus the academy, and courthouse, and jail, and inn, and most similar things, are tolerably exact. They have all, long since, given place to other buildings of a more pretending character. There is also some liberty taken with the truth in the description of the principal dwelling: the real building had no "firstly" and "lastly." It was of bricks, and not of stone; and its roof exhibited none of the peculiar beauties of the "composite order." It was erected in an age too primitive for that ambitious school of architecture. But the Author indulged his recollections freely when he had fairly entered the door. Here all is literal, even to the severed arm of Wolfe, and the urn which held the ashes of Queen Dido.[2]

The Author has elsewhere said that the character of Leather-Stocking is a creation, rendered probable by such auxiliaries as were necessary to produce that effect. Had he drawn still more upon fancy, the lovers of fiction would not have so much cause for their objections to his work. Still the picture would not have been in the least true, without some substitutes for most of the other personages. The great proprietor resident on his lands, and giving his name to, instead of receiving it from his estates, as in Europe, is common over the whole of New York. The physician, with his theory, rather obtained than corrected by experiments on the human constitution; the pious, self-denying, laborious, and ill-paid missionary; the half-educated, litigious, envious, and disreputable lawyer, with his counterpoise, a brother of the profession, of better origin and of better character; the shiftless, bargaining, discontented seller of his "betterments;" the plausible carpenter, and most of the others, are more familiar to all who have ever dwelt in a new country.

It may be well to say here, a little more explicitly, that there was no intention to describe with particular accuracy any real characters in this book. . . .

From circumstances which, after this introduction, will be obvious to all, the Author has had more pleasure in writing *The Pioneers* than the book will, probably, ever give any of its readers. He is quite aware of its numerous faults, some of which he has endeavored to repair in this edition; but as he has—in intention, at least—done his full share in amusing the world, he trusts to its good nature for overlooking this attempt to please himself.   1850

From Preface to *The Pilot*

It is probable a true history of human events would show that a far larger proportion of our acts are the results of sudden impulses and accident, than of that reason of which we so much boast. However true, or

---

[2] Though forests still crown the mountains of Otsego, the bear, the wolf, and the panther are nearly strangers to them. Even the innocent deer is rarely seen bounding beneath their arches; for the rifle, and the activity of the settlers, have driven them to other haunts. To this change (which, in some particulars, is melancholy to one who knew the country in its infancy) it may be added, that the Otsego is beginning to be a niggard of its treasures. [Cooper's Note.]

false, this opinion may be in more important matters, it is certainly and strictly correct as relates to the conception and execution of this book.

The Pilot was published in 1823. This was not long after the appearance of *The Pirate*, a work which it is hardly necessary to remind the reader, has a direct connection with the sea. In a conversation with a friend, a man of polished taste and extensive reading, the authorship of the Scottish novels came under discussion. The claims of Sir Walter were a little distrusted, on account of the peculiar and minute information that the romances were then very generally thought to display. *The Pirate* was cited as a very marked instance of this universal knowledge, and it was wondered where a man of Scott's habits and associations could have become so familiar with the sea. The writer had frequently observed that there was much looseness in this universal knowledge, and that the secret of its success was to be traced to the power of creating that *vraisemblance*, which is so remarkably exhibited in those world-renowned fictions, rather than to any very accurate information on the part of their author. It would have been hypercritical to object to *The Pirate*, that it was not strictly nautical, or true in its details; but, when the reverse was urged as a proof of what, considering the character of other portions of the work, would have been most extraordinary attainments, it was a sort of provocation to dispute the seamanship of *The Pirate*, a quality to which the book has certainly very little just pretension. The result of this conversation was a sudden determination to produce a work which, if it had no other merit, might present truer pictures of the ocean and ships than any that are to be found in *The Pirate*. To this unpremeditated decision, purely an impulse, is not only *The Pilot* due, but a tolerably numerous school of nautical romances that have succeeded it.

The author had many misgivings concerning the success of the undertaking, after he had made some progress in the work; the opinions of his different friends being anything but encouraging. One would declare that the sea could not be made interesting; that it was tame, monotonous, and without any other movement than unpleasant storms, and that, for his part, the less he got of it the better. The women very generally protested that such a book would have the odor of bilge water, and that it would give them the *maladie de mer*. Not a single individual among all those who discussed the merits of the project, within the range of the author's knowledge, either spoke, or looked, encouragingly. It is probable that all these persons anticipated a signal failure.

So very discouraging did these ominous opinions get to be, that the writer was, once or twice, tempted to throw his manuscript aside, and turn to something new. A favorable opinion, however, coming from a very unexpected quarter, put a new face on the matter, and raised new hopes. . . .

Thus encouraged, one more experiment was made, a seaman being selected for the critic. A kinsman, a namesake, and an old messmate of the author, one now in command on a foreign station, was chosen, and a considerable portion of the first volume was read to him. There is no wish to conceal the satisfaction with which the effect on this listener was observed. He treated the whole matter as fact, and his criticisms were strictly professional, and perfectly just. But the interest he betrayed could not be mistaken. It gave a perfect and most gratifying assurance that the work would be more likely to find favor with nautical men, than with any other class of readers.

The Pilot could scarcely be a favorite with females. The story has little interest for them, nor was it much heeded by the author of the book, in the progress of his labors. His aim was to illustrate vessels and the ocean, rather than to draw any pictures of sentiment and love. In this last respect, the book has small claims on the reader's attention, though it is hoped that the story has sufficient interest to relieve the more strictly nautical features of the work.

It would be affectation to deny that *The Pilot* met with a most unlooked-for success. The novelty of the design probably contributed a large share of this result. Sea tales came into vogue, as a consequence; and, as every practical part of knowledge has its uses, something has been gained by letting the landsman into the secrets of the seaman's manner of life. Perhaps, in some small degree, an interest has been awakened in behalf of a very numerous, and what has hitherto been a sort of proscribed class of men, that may directly tend to a melioration of their condition.

1831

Preface to *The Bravo*

It is to be regretted the world does not discriminate more justly in its use of political terms. Governments are usually called either monarchies or republics. The former class embraces equally those institutions in which the sovereign is worshipped as a god, and those in which he performs the humble office of a manikin. In the latter we find aristocracies and democracies blended in the same generic appellation. The consequence of a generalization so wide is an utter confusion on the subject of the polity of states.

The author has endeavored to give his countrymen, in this book, a picture of the social system of one of the *soi-disant* republics of the other hemisphere. There has been no attempt to portray historical characters, only too fictitious in their graver dress, but simply to set forth the familiar operations of Venetian policy. For the justification of his likeness, after allowing for the defects of execution, he refers to the well-known work of M. Daru.

A history of the progress of political liberty, written purely in the interests of humanity, is still a desideratum in literature. In nations which have made a false commencement, it would be found that the citizen, or rather the subject, has extorted immunity after immunity, as his growing intelligence and importance have both instructed and required him to defend those particular rights which were necessary to his well-being. A certain accumulation of these immunities constitutes, with a solitary and recent exception in Switzerland, the essence of European liberty, even at this hour. It is scarcely necessary to tell the reader, that this freedom, be it more or less, depends on a principle entirely different from our own. Here the immunities do not proceed from, but they are granted to, the government, being, in other words, concessions of natural rights made by the people to the state, for the benefits of social protection. So long as this vital difference exists between ourselves and other nations, it will be vain to think of finding analogies in their institutions. It is true that, in an age like this, public opinion is itself a charter, and that the most despotic government which exists within the pale of Christendom, must, in some degree, respect its influence. The mildest and justest governments in Europe are, at this moment, theoretically despotisms. The characters of both prince and people enter largely into the consideration of so extraordinary results; and it should never be forgotten that, though the character of the latter be sufficiently secure, that of the former is liable to change. But, admitting every benefit which possibly can flow from a just administration, with wise and humane princes, a government which is not properly based on the people, possesses an unavoidable and oppressive evil of the first magnitude, in the necessity of supporting itself by physical force and onerous impositions, against the natural action of the majority.

Were we to characterize a republic, we should say it was a state in which power, both theoretically and practically, is derived from the nation, with a constant responsibility of the agents of the public to the people—a responsibility that is neither to be evaded nor denied. That such a system is better on a large than on a small scale, though contrary to brilliant theories which have been written to uphold different institutions, must be evident on the smallest reflection, since the danger of all popular governments is from popular mistakes; and a people of diversified interests and extended territorial possessions, are much less likely to be the subjects of sinister passions than the inhabitants of a single town or county. If to this definition we should add, as an infallible test of the genus, that a true republic is a government of which all others are jealous and vituperative, on the instinct of self-preservation, we believe there would be no mistaking the class. How far Venice would have been obnoxious to this proof, the reader is left to judge for himself.   1831

Preface to *Home as Found*

Those who have done us the favor to read *Homeward Bound* will at once perceive that the incidents of this book commence at the point where those of the work just mentioned ceased. We are fully aware of the disadvantage of dividing the interest of a tale in this manner; but in the present instance, the separation has been produced by circumstances over which the writer had very little control. As anyone who may happen to take up this volume will very soon discover that there is other matter which it is necessary to know, it may be as well to tell all such persons, in commencement, therefore, that their reading will be bootless, unless they have leisure to turn to the pages of *Homeward Bound* for their cue.

We remember the despair with which that admirable observer of men, Mr. Mathews the comedian, confessed the hopelessness of success, in his endeavors to obtain a sufficiency of prominent and distinctive features to compose an entertainment founded on American character. The whole nation struck him as being destitute of salient points, and as characterized by a respectable mediocrity, that, however useful it might be in its way, was utterly without poetry, humor, or interest to the observer. For one who dealt principally with the more conspicuous absurdities of his fellow creatures, Mr. Mathews was certainly right; we also believe him to have been right in the main, in the general tenor of his opinion; for this country, in its ordinary aspects, probably presents as barren a field to the writer of fiction, and to the dramatist, as any other on earth; we are not certain that we might not say the most barren. We believe that no attempt to delineate ordinary American life, either on the stage or in the pages of a novel, has been rewarded with success. Even those works in which the desire to illustrate a principle has been the aim, when the picture has been brought within this homely frame, have had to contend with disadvantages that have been commonly found insurmountable. The latter being the intention of this book, the task has been undertaken with a perfect consciousness of all its difficulties, and with scarcely a hope of success. It would be indeed a desperate undertaking, to think of making anything interesting in the way of a *Roman de Société* in this country; still useful glances may possibly be made even in that direction, and we trust that the fidelity of one or two of our portraits will be recognized by the looker-on, although they will very likely be denied by the sitters themselves.

There seems to be a pervading principle in things, which gives an accumulating energy to any active property that may happen to be in the ascendant, at the time being—money produces money; knowledge is the parent of knowledge; and ignorance fortifies ignorance. In a word, like begets like. The governing social evil of America is provincialism; a misfortune that is perhaps inseparable from her situation. Without a social capital, with twenty or more communities divided by distance and political barriers, her people, who are really more homogeneous than any other of the same numbers in the world perhaps, possess no standard for opinion, manners, social maxims, or even language. Every man, as a matter of course, refers to his own particular experience, and praises or condemns agreeably to notions contracted in the circle of his own habits, however narrow, provincial, or erroneous they may happen to be. As a consequence, no useful stage can exist; for the dramatist who should endeavor to delineate the faults of society, would find a formidable party arrayed against him, in a moment, with no party to defend. As another consequence, we see individuals constantly assailed with a wolf-like ferocity, while society is everywhere permitted to pass unscathed.

That the American nation is a great nation, in some particulars the greatest the world ever saw, we hold to be true, and are as ready to maintain as any one can be; but we are also equally ready to concede, that it is very far behind most polished nations in various essentials, and chiefly, that it is lamentably in arrears to its own avowed principles. Perhaps this truth will be found to be the predominant thought, throughout the pages of *Home As Found*.   1838

Preface to "The Leather-Stocking Tales" from *The Deerslayer*

This series of Stories, which has obtained the name of "The Leather-Stocking Tales," has been written in a very desultory and inartificial manner. The order in which the several books appeared was essentially different from that in which they would have been presented to the world, had the regular course of their incidents been consulted. In *The Pioneers*, the first of the series written, the Leather-Stocking is represented as already old, and driven from his early haunts in the forest, by the sound of the axe, and the smoke of the settler. *The Last of the Mohicans*, the next book in the order of publication, carried the readers back to a much earlier period in the history of our hero, representing him as middle-aged, and in the fullest vigor of manhood. In *The Prairie*, his career terminates, and he is laid in his grave. There, it was originally the intention to leave him, in the expectation that, as in the case of the human mass, he would soon be forgotten. But a latent regard for this character induced the author to resuscitate him in *The Pathfinder*, a book that was not long after succeeded by *The Deerslayer*, thus completing the series as it now exists.

While the five books that have been written were originally published in the order just mentioned, that of the incidents, insomuch as they are connected with the career of their principal character, is, as has been stated, very different. Taking the life of the Leather-Stocking as a guide,

The Deerslayer should have been the opening book, for in that work he is seen just emerging into manhood; to be succeeded by *The Last of the Mohicans, The Pathfinder, The Pioneers,* and *The Prairie.* This arrangement embraces the order of events, though far from being that in which the books at first appeared. *The Pioneers* was published in 1822; *The Deerslayer* in 1841; making the interval between them nineteen years. Whether these progressive years have had a tendency to lessen the value of the last-named book, by lessening the native fire of its author, or of adding somewhat in the way of improved taste and a more matured judgment, is for others to decide.

If anything from the pen of the writer of these romances is at all to outlive himself, it is, unquestionably, the series of "The Leather-Stocking Tales." To say this, is not to predict a very lasting reputation for the series itself, but simply to express the belief it will outlast any, or all, of the works from the same hand.

It is undeniable that the desultory manner in which "The Leather-Stocking Tales" were written, has, in a measure, impaired their harmony, and otherwise lessened their interest. This is proved by the fate of the two books last published, though probably the two most worthy an enlightened and cultivated reader's notice. If the facts could be ascertained, it is probable the result would show that of all those (in America, in particular) who have read the three first books of the series, not one in ten has a knowledge of the existence even of the two last. Several causes have tended to produce this result. The long interval of time between the appearance of *The Prairie* and that of *The Pathfinder,* was itself a reason why the later books of the series should be overlooked. There was no longer novelty to attract attention, and the interest was materially impaired by the manner in which events were necessarily anticipated, in laying the last of the series first before the world. With the generation that is now coming on the stage this fault will be partially removed by the edition contained in the present work, in which the several tales will be arranged solely in reference to their connection with each other.

The author has often been asked if he had any original in his mind, for the character of Leather-Stocking. In a physical sense, different individuals known to the writer in early life, certainly presented themselves as models, through his recollections; but in a moral sense this man of the forest is purely a creation. The idea of delineating a character that possessed little of civilization but its highest principles as they are exhibited in the uneducated, and all of savage life that is not incompatible with these great rules of conduct, is perhaps natural to the situation in which Natty was placed. He is too proud of his origin to sink into the condition of the wild Indian, and too much a man of the woods not to imbibe as much as was at all desirable, from his friends and companions. In a moral point of view it was the intention to illustrate the effect of seed scattered by the wayside. To use his own language, his "gifts" were "white gifts," and he was not disposed to bring on them discredit. On the other hand, removed from nearly all the temptations of civilized life, placed in the best associations of that which is deemed savage, and favorably disposed by nature to improve such advantages, it appeared to the writer that his hero was a fit subject to represent the better qualities of both conditions, without pushing either to extremes.

There was no violent stretch of the imagination, perhaps, in supposing one of civilized associations in childhood, retaining many of his earliest lessons amid the scenes of the forest. Had these early impressions, however, not been sustained by continued, though casual connection with men of his own color, if not of his own caste, all our information goes to show he would soon have lost every trace of his origin. It is believed that sufficient attention was paid to the particular circumstances in which this individual was placed, to justify the picture of his qualities that has been drawn. The Delawares early attracted the attention of the missionaries, and were a tribe unusually influenced by their precepts and example. In many instances they became Christians, and cases occurred in which their subsequent lives gave proof of the efficacy of the great moral changes that had taken place within them.

A leading character in a work of fiction has a fair right to the aid which can be obtained from a poetical view of the subject. It is in this view, rather than in one more strictly circumstantial, that Leather-Stocking has been drawn. The imagination has no great task in portraying to itself a being removed from the everyday inducements to err, which abound in civilized life, while he retains the best and simplest of his early impressions; who sees God in the forest; hears him in the winds; bows to him in the firmament that o'ercanopies all; submits to his sway in a humble belief of his justice and mercy; in a word, a being who finds the impress of the Deity in all the works of nature, without any of the blots produced by the expedients, and passion, and mistakes of man. This is the most that has been attempted in the character of Leather-Stocking. Had this been done without any of the drawbacks of humanity, the picture would have been, in all probability, more pleasing than just. In order to preserve the *vraisemblable*, therefore, traits derived from the prejudices, tastes, and even the weaknesses of his youth, have been mixed up with these higher qualities and longings, in a way, it is hoped, to represent a reasonable picture of human nature, without offering to the spectator a "monster of goodness."

It has been objected to these books that they give a more favorable picture of the red man than he deserves. The writer apprehends that much of this objection arises from the habits of those who have made it. One of his critics, on the appearance of the first work in which Indian character was portrayed, objected that its "characters were Indians of the school of Heckewelder, rather than of the school of nature. These words quite probably contain the substance of the true answer to the objection.

Heckewelder was an ardent, benevolent missionary, bent on the good of the red man, and seeing in him one who had the soul, reason, and characteristics of a fellow-being. The critic is understood to have been a very distinguished agent of the government, one very familiar with Indians, as they are seen at the councils to treat for the sale of their lands, where little or none of their domestic qualities come in play, and where, indeed, their evil passions are known to have the fullest scope. As just would it be to draw conclusions of the general state of American society from the scenes of the capital, as to suppose that the negotiating of one of these treaties is a fair picture of Indian life.

It is the privilege of all writers of fiction, more particularly when their works aspire to the elevation of romances, to present the *beau-idéal* of their characters to the reader. This it is which constitutes poetry, and to suppose that the red man is to be represented only in the squalid misery or in the degraded moral state that certainly more or less belongs to his condition, is, we apprehend, taking a very narrow view of an author's privileges. Such criticism would have deprived the world of even Homer.

1850

From Preface to *Afloat and Ashore*

The writer has published so much truth which the world has insisted was fiction, and so much fiction which has been received as truth, that, in the present instance, he is resolved to say nothing on the subject. Each of his readers is at liberty to believe just as much, or as little, of the matter here laid before him, or her, as may suit his or her notions, prejudices, knowledge of the world, or ignorance. . . .

It is possible that certain captious persons may be disposed to inquire into the *cui bono?* of such a book. The answer is this. Everything which can convey to the human mind distinct and accurate impressions of events, social facts, professional peculiarities, or past history, whether of the higher or more familiar character, is of use. All that is necessary is, that the pictures should be true to nature, if not absolutely drawn from living sitters. The knowledge we gain by our looser reading often becomes serviceable in modes and manners little anticipated in the moments when it is acquired.

Perhaps the greater portion of all our peculiar opinions have their foundation in prejudices. These prejudices are produced in consequence of its being out of the power of any one man to see, or know, everything. The most favored mortal must receive far more than half of all that he learns on his faith in others; and it may aid those who can never be placed in positions to judge for themselves of certain phases of men and things, to get pictures of the same, drawn in a way to give them nearer views than they might otherwise obtain. This is the greatest benefit of all light literature in general, it being possible to render that which is purely fictitious even more useful than that which is strictly true, by avoiding extravagances, by portraying with fidelity, and, as our friend Marble might say, by "generalizing" with discretion.

This country has undergone many important changes since the commencement of the present century. Some of these changes have been for the better; others, we think out of all question, for the worse. The last is a fact that can be known to the generation which is coming into life by report only, and these pages may possibly throw some little light on both points, in representing things as they were. . . . Although an increase of numbers does not necessarily infer an increase of high civilization, it reasonably leads to the expectation of great melioration in the commoner comforts. Such has been the result, and to those familiar with facts as they now exist, the difference will probably be apparent in these pages.

Although the moral changes in American society have not kept pace with those that are purely physical, many that are essential have nevertheless occurred. Of all the British possessions on this continent, New York, after its conquest from the Dutch, received most of the social organization of the mother country. Under the Dutch, even, it had some of these characteristic peculiarities in its patroons; the lords of the manor of the New Netherlands. Some of the southern colonies, it is true, had their caciques and other semi-feudal and semi-savage noblesse, but the system was of short continuance; the peculiarities of that section of the country arising principally from the existence of domestic slavery on an extended scale. With New York it was different. A conquered colony, the mother country left the impression of its own institutions more deeply engraved than on any of the settlements that were commenced by grants to proprietors, or under charters from the crown. It was strictly a royal colony, and so continued to be, down to the hour of separation. The social consequences of this state of things were to be traced in her habits until the current of immigration became so strong as to bring with it those that were conflicting, if not absolutely antagonist. The influence of these two sources of thought is still obvious to the reflecting, giving rise to a double set of social opinions; one of which bears all the characteristics of its New England and puritanical origin, while the other may be said to come of the usages and notions of the middle states, proper. . . .

The author—perhaps editor would be the better word—does not feel himself responsible for all the notions advanced by the hero of this tale, and it may be as well to say as much. That one born in the Revolution should think differently from the men of the present day, in a hundred things, is to be expected. It is in just this difference of opinion that the lessons of the book are to be found.   1844

Preface to *Satanstoe*

Every chronicle of manners has a certain value. When customs are connected with principles, in their origin, development, or end, such records have a double importance; and it is because we think we see such a connection between the facts and incidents of the Littlepage Manuscripts, and certain important theories of our own time, that we give the former to the world.

It is perhaps a fault of your professed historian, to refer too much to philosophical agencies, and too little to those that are humbler. The foundations of great events are often remotely laid in very capricious and uncalculated passions, motives, or impulses. Chance has usually as much to do with the fortunes of states, as with those of individuals; or, if there be calculations connected with them at all, they are the calculations of a power superior to any that exists in man.

We had been led to lay these manuscripts before the world, partly by considerations of the above nature, and partly on account of the manner in which the two works we have named, *Satanstoe* and the *Chainbearer*, relate directly to the great New York question of the day, Anti-Rentism; which question will be found to be pretty fully laid bare, in the third and last book of the series. These three works, which contain all the Littlepage Manuscripts, do not form sequels to each other, in the sense of personal histories, or as narratives; while they do in that of principles. The reader will see that the early career, the attachment, the marriage, etc., of Mr. Cornelius Littlepage are completely related in the present book, for instance; while those of his son, Mr. Mordaunt Littlepage, will be just as fully given in the *Chainbearer*, its successor. It is hoped that the connection, which certainly does exist between these three works, will have more tendency to increase the value of each, than to produce the ordinary effect of what are properly called sequels, which are known to lessen the interest a narrative might otherwise have with the reader. Each of these three books has its own hero, its own heroine, and its own picture of manners, complete; though the latter may be, and is, more or less thrown into relief by its pendants.

We conceive no apology is necessary for treating the subject of anti-rentism with the utmost frankness. Agreeably to our views of the matter, the existence of true liberty among us, the perpetuity of the institutions, and the safety of public morals, are all dependent on putting down, wholly, absolutely, and unqualifiedly, the false and dishonest theories and statements that have been boldly advanced in connection with this subject. In our view, New York is, at this moment, much the most disgraced state in the Union, notwithstanding she has never failed to pay the interest on her public debt; and her disgrace arises from the fact that her laws are trampled underfoot, without any efforts, at all commensurate with the object, being made to enforce them. If words and professions can save the character of a community, all may yet be well; but if states, like individuals, are to be judged by their actions, and the "tree is to be known by its fruit," God help us!

For ourselves, we conceive that true patriotism consists in laying bare everything like public vice, and in calling such things by their right names. The great enemy of the race has made a deep inroad upon us, within the last ten or a dozen years, under cover of a spurious delicacy on the subject of exposing national ills; and it is time that they who have not been afraid to praise, when praise was merited, should not shrink from the office of censuring, when the want of timely warnings may be one cause of the most fatal evils. The great practical defect of institutions like ours, is the circumstance that "what is everybody's business, is nobody's business;" a neglect that gives to the activity of the rogue a very dangerous ascendency over the more dilatory correctives of the honest man.

1845

INDEX

AUTHORS, TITLES, AND
FIRST LINES OF POEMS